Routledge Revivals

CLEMENT OF ALEXANDRIA MISCELLANIES BOOK VII

CLEMENT OF ALEXANDRIA MISCELLANIES BOOK VII

THE GREEK TEXT

WITH INTRODUCTION, TRANSLATION, NOTES, DISSERTATIONS AND INDICES

BY THE LATE

FENTON JOHN ANTHONY HORT

AND

JOSEPH B. MAYOR

First published in 1902 by Macmillan and Co. Limited

This edition first published in 2018 by Routledge
2 Park Square, Milton Park, Abingdon, Oxon, OX14 4RN
and by Routledge
52 Vanderbilt Avenue, New York, NY 10017, USA

Routledge is an imprint of the Taylor & Francis Group, an informa business

© 1902 by Taylor and Francis

All rights reserved. No part of this book may be reprinted or reproduced or utilised in any form or by any electronic, mechanical, or other means, now known or hereafter invented, including photocopying and recording, or in any information storage or retrieval system, without permission in writing from the publishers.

Publisher's Note
The publisher has gone to great lengths to ensure the quality of this reprint but points out that some imperfections in the original copies may be apparent.

Disclaimer
The publisher has made every effort to trace copyright holders and welcomes correspondence from those they have been unable to contact.
A Library of Congress record exists under ISBN:

ISBN 13: 978-0-367-17827-7 (hbk)
ISBN 13: 978-0-367-17829-1 (pbk)
ISBN 13: 978-0-429-05790-8 (ebk)

1,000,000 Books

are available to read at

www.ForgottenBooks.com

Read online
Download PDF
Purchase in print

ISBN 978-0-259-51845-7
PIBN 10821189

This book is a reproduction of an important historical work. Forgotten Books uses state-of-the-art technology to digitally reconstruct the work, preserving the original format whilst repairing imperfections present in the aged copy. In rare cases, an imperfection in the original, such as a blemish or missing page, may be replicated in our edition. We do, however, repair the vast majority of imperfections successfully; any imperfections that remain are intentionally left to preserve the state of such historical works.

Forgotten Books is a registered trademark of FB &c Ltd.
Copyright © 2018 FB &c Ltd.
FB &c Ltd, Dalton House, 60 Windsor Avenue, London, SW19 2RR.
Company number 08720141. Registered in England and Wales.

For support please visit www.forgottenbooks.com

1 MONTH OF FREE READING

at

www.ForgottenBooks.com

By purchasing this book you are eligible for one month membership to ForgottenBooks.com, giving you unlimited access to our entire collection of over 1,000,000 titles via our web site and mobile apps.

To claim your free month visit:

www.forgottenbooks.com/free821189

* Offer is valid for 45 days from date of purchase. Terms and conditions apply.

English
Français
Deutsche
Italiano
Español
Português

www.forgottenbooks.com

Mythology Photography **Fiction** Fishing Christianity **Art** Cooking Essays Buddhism Freemasonry Medicine **Biology** Music **Ancient Egypt** Evolution Carpentry Physics Dance Geology **Mathematics** Fitness Shakespeare **Folklore** Yoga Marketing **Confidence** Immortality Biographies Poetry **Psychology** Witchcraft Electronics Chemistry History **Law** Accounting **Philosophy** Anthropology Alchemy Drama Quantum Mechanics Atheism Sexual Health **Ancient History Entrepreneurship** Languages Sport Paleontology Needlework Islam **Metaphysics** Investment Archaeology Parenting Statistics Criminology **Motivational**

CLEMENT OF ALEXANDRIA
MISCELLANIES BOOK VII

THE GREEK TEXT

WITH INTRODUCTION, TRANSLATION, NOTES,
DISSERTATIONS AND INDICES

BY THE LATE

FENTON JOHN ANTHONY HORT, D.D., D.C.L., LL.D.

SOMETIME HULSEAN PROFESSOR
AND LADY MARGARET'S READER IN DIVINITY
IN THE UNIVERSITY OF CAMBRIDGE

AND

JOSEPH B. MAYOR, M.A.

EMERITUS PROFESSOR OF KING'S COLLEGE, LONDON
HONORARY FELLOW OF ST JOHN'S COLLEGE, CAMBRIDGE
HON. LITT.D., DUBLIN.

London
MACMILLAN AND CO., Limited
NEW YORK: THE MACMILLAN COMPANY
1902

PREFACE.

NOT Cambridge only but the Church at large is under deep obligations to the wise and public-spirited action of the Master, the Rev. Dr Phear, and the Fellows of Emmanuel College, when, in the year 1872, they persuaded the former Fellow of Trinity to leave the loved and fruitful seclusion of St Ippolyt's and become a resident member of their own society. During the six years which intervened before Dr Hort was elected to a Divinity Professorship, he lectured in College on Origen *contra Celsum*, the Epistle to the Ephesians, Irenaeus Book III, the First Epistle of St Peter, the First Epistle to the Corinthians, the Epistle of St James, the Seventh Book of the *Stromateis* and chapters 1—3 of the Apocalypse.

I felt it to be a high privilege and honour, when I was intrusted with the task of editing the notes on Clement, which had been left behind by my old friend and schoolfellow. The notes, which are written partly in pencil and partly in ink on an interleaved copy of Dindorf's text, were not continued beyond § 69. At the end of § 66 occurs the date March 15, 1875, denoting probably the conclusion of a course of lectures.

As is natural, I found the notes to vary much in value and importance, some appearing to have been hastily jotted down for future consideration, while others contained the results of long research and deep meditation. I was equally unwilling to print anything which Dr Hort would himself have been likely to reject if he had been preparing a commentary for publication, and to omit anything which he would have retained. In this difficulty I was fortunate in being able to appeal to his eldest son and biographer, Sir Arthur Hort of Harrow, and to his old college friend Dr Henry Jackson, who went most carefully through the notes, and without whose sanction no omission has been made. Many of the notes have been incorporated in the Translation, which I have added as a necessary help in dealing with so difficult and puzzling an author.

As Dr Hort's marginalia on the first 69 sections make no pretension to completeness, I have supplemented his work on these sections by considerable additions of my own; while for the notes which follow § 69, as well as for the Introduction, Appendices and Indices, I am alone responsible.

To prevent any confusion Dr Hort's notes are all marked with H. Notes marked with the initials H. J. and B. are by Dr Jackson and the Rev. P. Mordaunt Barnard, who have most kindly read and criticized my proofs. The names of both are well known to students of Clement, the former by notes and articles in the *Journal of Philology*, the latter by his excellent edition of the *Quis Dives Salvetur*. My thanks are also due to

Dr E. A. Abbott and Dr Gifford for useful suggestions, and to Dr Otto Stählin, who is now occupied with a complete edition of the works of Clement, for allowing me to use his collation of the Clementine Anthologies, as well as of the Laurentian MS for this book, the accuracy of which I have been able to test by my own examination of the MS.

Other obligations are acknowledged in particular sections of the work, but I feel bound to express my thanks here for the great help I have received from the reader of the Cambridge press, especially in revising the Index of Greek words.

Perhaps it may be well to add that, in the years which have passed since I undertook this work, my views have sometimes undergone modification. The readings in the text are not always those which have commended themselves to me, when I was engaged on the notes. Such differences are noted in the Addenda. Again, as to the Translation, I have sometimes given the meaning of an emendation, suggested in the critical notes, though I might not feel so sure of its correctness as to alter the text.

J. B. M.

July 1902.

TABLE OF CONTENTS.

INTRODUCTION.

CHAPTER I.
On the Title Stromateis.

Meaning of the term στρωματεύς. Its use to denote a particular kind of composition. The Stromateis of Clement in their relation to his earlier writings. Why he made use of this form of composition. He had to clear away the prejudices of his hearers and prepare them to receive his more advanced teaching. pp. xi—xxi.

CHAPTER II.
Influence of Greek Philosophy on the Theology and Ethics of Clement.

Views of Harnack, Hatch and Deissmann as to the secularization of Christianity in the second and third centuries. Good and bad secularization. The former pervades the Bible from one end to the other. Spread of Hellenism among the Jews. Hellenism in the N.T. Beneficial effect of Greek philosophy as brought to bear on the Judaizing morality of the Didache. Ambrose's adaptation of Cicero's De Officiis becomes the text-book of Christian ethics. Clement a representative of Hellenic culture. Harnack's judgment of him. Introduces Greek method into Theology. Instances of definition and of syllogistic reasoning. The criterion of truth to be found in the general voice of Scripture as interpreted by the tradition of the Church and by our sense of what is in harmony with the character of God. Principle of allegorical interpretation borrowed from the Stoics. Typical instances of right and wrong borrowing from philosophy on the part of Clement, (1) as regards the idea of God, (2) the identity of virtue in man and God, (3) the nature of punishment, (4) the introduction of a double standard by means of distinction between the gnostic and the ordinary believer. List of philosophical terms used in *Strom.* VII. pp. xxii—xlix.

CHAPTER III.

Clement and the Mysteries.

Nature and influence of the Eleusinian Mysteries. Use of figurative language derived from the Mysteries by Plato and Philo, by the Sacred Writers, and by Clement, both in reference to rites and to doctrine. The *Disciplina Arcani*. Resemblance between the rites of Mithras and the Christian Sacraments. How far was Christianity influenced by the Mysteries, and what was the nature of that influence? pp. 1—lx.

CHAPTER IV.

Estimates of Clement.

Position of Clement in the Church up to the middle of the eighteenth century. Held in high esteem by recent Roman Catholic writers as well as by Protestants. pp. lxi—lxiv.

CHAPTER V.

The Text of the Stromateis.

Description of the Laurentian MS. Analysis and exemplification of corruptions. Remarks of Dr Kenyon on these corruptions. Various Readings found in quotations from Clement by Eusebius, Theodoret, Photius, Damascenus. Various readings in the Florilegia, and in Clementine Anthologies. Stählin's Collation of the Laurentian MS, supplementing Dindorf's Critical Notes. pp. lxv—xci.

CHAPTER VI.

Analysis of Strom. VII. pp. xcii—ci.

	PAGES
BIBLIOGRAPHICAL NOTE	cii, ciii
ADDENDA	civ—cxi
GREEK TEXT WITH ENGLISH TRANSLATION	1—197
EXPLANATORY NOTES	199—360
Appendix A. *Unrecorded uses of* αὐτίκα	361—364
Appendix B. *On Clement's use of* ἄν	365—373
Appendix C. *On the relation of the Agape to the Eucharist in Clement*	374—384
INDEX OF QUOTATIONS	385, 386
INDEX OF GREEK WORDS	387—446
ENGLISH INDEX	447—455

INTRODUCTION.

CHAPTER I.

ON THE TITLE *STROMATEIS*.

It is unnecessary to repeat here what may be found in Bp Westcott's excellent article on Clement in the *Dict. of Chr. Biog.* published in 1877. I shall confine my remarks to the fuller treatment of some of the points on which he has only slightly touched. And, first, what did Clement mean by giving to his third treatise the title Στρωματεῖς, or, more fully, as at the end of Books I., III., V., οἱ τῶν κατὰ τὴν ἀληθῆ φιλοσοφίαν γνωστικῶν ὑπομνημάτων Στρωματεῖς? As to the literal sense of the word, Moeris in his *Lex. Att.* tells us στρωματόδεσμος, Ἀττικῶς· στρωματεύς, Ἑλληνικῶς. Pollux speaks to the same effect (VII. 19, x. 31) and Phrynichus p. 401[1]. Accordingly we read (Theophr. *H. Pl.* IV. 2) of the use of the cocoanut to make rings for the striped bags in which the bed-clothes were tied up (ἐξ οὗ τοὺς κρίκους τορνεύουσι τοὺς εἰς τοὺς στρωματεῖς τοὺς διαποικίλους), and in the Ἀντευεργετῶν of Apollodorus Carystius we find the phrase τοὺς στρωματεῖς ἔλυον. Hence the name was applied to a striped fish found in the Red Sea, see Artem. II. 14, and Athen. VII. p. 322, ὁ καλούμενος στρωματεὺς ῥάβδους ἔχων δι' ὅλου τοῦ σώματος τεταμένας χρυσιζούσας. Casaubon in his n. on Ath. I. 5 says that both the coverlets (στρώματα) and the στρωματόδεσμος or στρωματεύς,

---

[1] The passages quoted under στρωματεύς in L. and S., as examples of the meaning 'coverlet,' seem to me to be more naturally explained in the sense of στρωματόδεσμος.

which contained them, were of variegated colour; but the στρώματα seem to have been usually purple and the στρωματεῖς striped. He understands στρωματόδεσμος, in the phrase παρεῖναι δείπνῳ, ὥσπερ συμβολὰς κομίζοντας τὰ ἀπὸ τῶν στρωματοδέσμων γράμματα, in a metaphorical sense, like στρωματεῖς, of collections of good sayings. Is the simple word στρῶμα ever used in the same way? It would appear so from the lexicons; but the only instances seem to be found in Jerome, *De Viris Ill.* 38, where, after mentioning 'στρωματεῖς libri octo' in his catalogue of Clement's works, he afterwards says 'meminit autem in *stromatibus* suis Tatiani' (translated ἐν τοῖς ἰδίοις στρώμασι by Sophronius). So in his transl. of the Chronicle of Euseb. Ol. 47 and Ol. 64, 'Clem. in primo stromate,' also *Comm. in Gal. Prol.* where he refers to 'decimum librum stromatum' of Origen. He probably used this form to avoid the awkwardness of the oblique cases of 'stromateus.' The word στρωματεύς was also used as an epithet of Cl. himself by later writers.

Let us now see what Cl. himself has to say of the word. In *Str.* IV. § 4 he tells us that his ὑπομνήματα are intentionally scattered in various ways (reading ποικίλως), as the name (στρωματεύς) implies, passing rapidly from one point to another, and signifying one thing to the careless reader, according to the straightforward connexion of the words, while suggesting something different to the more thoughtful; so that what is said requires sifting. *Str.* I. § 18 'The Stromateis will contain the truth, mixed up with, or hidden in the teaching of the philosophers, as the kernel is in the husk.' Clement is aware that there are many who are suspicious of philosophy, holding that faith is all-sufficient, and that all besides is superfluous. § 55 He fears to cast his pearls before swine. § 56 ἔστι τῷ ὄντι ἡ τῶν ὑπομνημάτων ὑποτύπωσις ὅσα δὴ σποράδην καὶ διερριμμένως ἐγκατεσπαρμένην ἔχουσι τὴν ἀλήθειαν. *Str.* VI. § 2 'In meadows and parks the various kinds of flowers and trees are not separated from one another. And so such titles, as Meadow or Helicon or Honeycomb or Robe (of Athena), have been used for their learned collections by the writers of anthologies; and the form of my own Miscellanies has the variegated appearance of a meadow, from the haphazard way in which things came into my mind, not clarified either by arrangement or style, but mingled together in a studied disorder' (ἐν μὲν οὖν τῷ λειμῶνι τὰ ἄνθη ποικίλως ἀνθοῦντα, κἀν τῷ παραδείσῳ ἡ τῶν ἀκροδρύων φυτεία, οὐ κατὰ εἶδος ἕκαστον κεχώρισται τῶν ἀλλογενῶν· ἢ (MS. εἰ) καὶ λειμῶνάς τινες καὶ Ἑλικῶνας καὶ κηρία καὶ πέπλους, συναγωγὰς φιλομαθεῖς ποικίλως ἐξανθισάμενοι, συνεγράψαντο· τοῖς δ' ὡς ἔτυχεν ἐπὶ μνήμην ἐλθοῦσι, καὶ μήτε τῇ τάξει μήτε τῇ φράσει διακεκαθαρμένοις, διεσπαρμένοις δὲ ἐπίτηδες ἀναμίξ, ἡ τῶν στρωματέων ἡμῖν ὑποτύπωσις λειμῶνος δίκην πεποίκιλται). Compare to the same effect *Str.* VII. 110. In *Str.* I. 11 he tells us that he intends to record, for his own use and that of others, the teaching of the elders, received by them through tradition from Peter and James and John and Paul. § 14 'This will not be understood by all, but only by those who are prepared for it. I am not able to give their teaching perfectly. Part has slipped my memory: part I omit intentionally; not from jealousy, God forbid, but for fear that it might be misunderstood and do mischief.' § 15 ἔστι δ' ἃ αἰνίξεταί μοι <ἡ> γραφή...πειράσεται δὲ καὶ λανθάνουσα εἰπεῖν καὶ ἐπικρυπτομένη ἐκφῆναι: 'it will contain all that is necessary as an introduction to the knowledge based on mystic contemplation, which will guide us as we advance onwards from the creation of the world in accordance with the venerable rule of tradition; furnishing[1] the necessary equipment for the study of natural philosophy, and removing the obstacles which might interfere with the methodical treatment of the subject...for the preliminaries of the mysteries are themselves mysteries' (ἡ κατὰ τὴν ἐποπτικὴν θεωρίαν γνῶσις, ἣ προβήσεται κατὰ τὸν σεμνὸν τῆς παραδόσεως κανόνα ἀπὸ τῆς τοῦ κόσμου γενέσεως προϊοῦσιν, <τὰ> ἀναγκαίως ἔχοντα προδιαληφθῆναι τῆς φυσικῆς θεωρίας προπαρατιθεμένη, καὶ τὰ ἐμποδὼν ἱστάμενα τῇ ἀκολουθίᾳ προαπολυομένη...ἀγὼν γὰρ καὶ ὁ προαγὼν καὶ μυστήρια τὰ πρὸ μυστηρίων).

From the above passages we gather that Clement chose this form of composition mainly with the view of discriminating between his readers, giving sufficient light to enable the more earnest and intelligent to penetrate to his inner meaning, without arousing unnecessary prejudice in the minds of the

---

[1] I take the preceding γραφή to be the subject of προπαρατιθεμένη.

less enlightened. The result is that readers of the present day are often puzzled to know what he is driving at. It is his nature to fly off at a tangent, and in the *Stromateis* he indulges his natural bent without restraint, though he is quite aware that it is incompatible with a clear logical statement of the points at issue. In the chase to which he invites us we often lose the scent, and only come upon it again, as it were, accidentally. He drops *aperçus* and leaves it to his readers to follow them out at their own discretion. Clement also warns us that the mysteries of which a foretaste is given in the *Stromateis* are merely preliminary to the greater mysteries which he reserves for another treatise.

Eusebius tells us that the same title was used by Plutarch, (*Pr. Ev* I. c. 7 *fin.*) τῶν παρ' Ἕλλησι φιλοσόφων…τὰς περὶ ἀρχῶν δόξας…ἀπὸ τῶν Πλουτάρχου στρωματέων ἐκθήσομαι: as to which Diels says (*Doxographi* p. 156) 'nobilissimi scriptoris nomen sine dubio ementitur.' He adds on p. 157 that the title was used by Caesellius Vindex under Trajan (cf. Priscian *Inst.* VI. 18 'Caesellius in Stromateo,' Teuffel *Rom. Lit.* § 338); but that it was unknown to Pliny the Elder, who in his preface speaks of the ingenuity shown by the Greeks in their choice of names. 'Κηρίον inscripsere, quod volebant intellegi favum; alii Κέρας Ἀμαλθείας…ἰωνιά, Μοῦσαι, πανδέκται, ἐγχειρίδιον, λειμών, πινακίδιον, inscriptiones propter quas vadimonium deseri possit. At cum intraveris, di deaeque! quam nihil in medio invenies.' On the other hand it is mentioned by Gellius, an elder contemporary of Clemens, whose preface may be compared with the words we have quoted from Cl. above: 'perinde ut librum quemque in manus ceperam…vel quid memoratu dignum audieram, ita, quae libitum erat, cuius generis cumque erant, indistincte atque promisce annotabam; eaque mihi ad subsidium memoriae, quasi quoddam litterarum penus, recondebam …inscripsimus *Noctium Atticarum*, nihil imitati festivitates inscriptionum, quas plerique alii utriusque linguae scriptores in id genus libris fecerunt. Nam quia variam et miscellam et quasi confusaneam doctrinam conquisiverant, eo titulos quoque ad eam sententiam exquisitissimos indiderunt…Namque alii *Musarum* inscripserunt, alii *Silvarum*, ille Πέπλον, hic Ἀμαλθείας Κέρας, alius Κηρία, partim Λειμῶνας,…atque alius

Ἀνθηρῶν, et item alius Εὑρημάτων. Sunt etiam qui Λύχνους inscripserunt; sunt item qui Στρωματεῖς etc.' He mentions as his aim to select from his reading 'ea sola quae aut ingenia prompta expeditaque ad honestae eruditionis cupidinem utiliumque artium contemplationem celeri facilique compendio ducerent, aut &c.'; but warns off the frivolous and the idle. It was the fashion of the time to publish such miscellanies; compare the works of Aelian, some of Plutarch, and the *Deipnosophistae* of Athenaeus. Origen published ten books of Στρωματεῖς in which he is said to have aimed, like Clement, at showing the agreement between Greek philosophy and the Christian religion. (Jerome *Ep.* 70. 4 'Origenes decem scripsit *stromateas*'; just before he had said 'Clemens octo scripsit *stromatum* libros.')

What do we learn from Clem. as to the relation of the *Stromateis* to the earlier writings? The *Protrepticus* was written as an independent work; but the *Paedagogus* looks back to it and forward to the *Stromateis*, or rather to the Διδάσκαλος, which is the name he commonly assigns to the final teaching of the Logos: cf. *Paed.* I. 1 τριῶν γέ τοι τούτων περὶ τὸν ἄνθρωπον ὄντων, ἠθῶν, πράξεων, παθῶν, ὁ προτρεπτικὸς εἴληχεν τὰ ἤθη αὐτοῦ...ὁ τροπιδίου δίκην ὑποκείμενος λόγος εἰς οἰκοδομὴν πίστεως...ὁ γοῦν οὐράνιος ἡγεμὼν ὁ λόγος, ὁπηνίκα μὲν ἐπὶ σωτηρίαν παρεκάλει, προτρεπτικὸς ὄνομα αὐτῷ ἦν...νυνὶ δὲ θεραπευτικός τε ὢν καὶ ὑποθετικὸς παραινεῖ τὸ προγεγραμμένον κεφάλαιον, τῶν ἐν ἡμῖν παθῶν ὑπισχνούμενος τὴν ἴασιν. κεκλήσθω δὲ ἡμῖν...παιδαγωγός, πρακτικός οὐ μεθοδικὸς ὤν, ᾗ καὶ τὸ τέλος αὐτοῦ βελτιῶσαι τὴν ψυχὴν ἐστιν, οὐ διδάξαι. § 2 καίτοι καὶ διδασκαλικὸς ὁ αὐτός ἐστι λόγος, ἀλλ' οὐ νῦν. ὁ μὲν γὰρ ἐν τοῖς δογματικοῖς δηλωτικὸς καὶ ἀποκαλυπτικός, ὁ διδασκαλικός, πρακτικὸς δὲ ὢν ὁ παιδαγωγὸς πρότερον μὲν εἰς διάθεσιν ἠθοποιΐας προυτρέψατο, ἤδη δὲ εἰς τὴν τῶν δεόντων ἐνέργειαν παρακαλεῖ. § 3 καθάπερ οὖν τοῖς νοσοῦσι τὸ σῶμα ἰατροῦ χρῄζει, ταύτῃ καὶ τοῖς ἀσθενοῦσι τὴν ψυχὴν παιδαγωγοῦ δεῖ, ἵν' ἡμῶν ἰάσηται τὰ πάθη, εἶτα δὲ καὶ διδασκάλου ὃς καθηγήσεται πρὸς καθαρὰν γνώσεως ἐπιτηδειότητα. He sums up by saying that ὁ πάντα φιλάνθρωπος λόγος seeks our perfection, προτρέπων ἄνωθεν, ἔπειτα παιδαγωγῶν, ἐπὶ πᾶσιν ἐκδιδάσκων. Towards the end of the third book (§ 97) he distinguishes between the teaching of the Paedagogus and that of the Teacher 'whose aid we need εἰς τὴν ἐξήγησιν τῶν ἁγίων λόγων...καὶ δὴ ὥρα γε ἐμοὶ μὲν πεπαῦσθαι τῆς παιδαγωγίας, ὑμᾶς δὲ ἀκροᾶσθαι διδασκάλου. παραλαβὼν δὲ οὗτος ὑμᾶς, ὑπὸ καλῇ τεθραμμένους ἀγωγῇ, ἐκδιδάξεται τὰ λόγια.' The same distinction is found in § 87 ὅσα μὲν οἴκοι παραφυλακτέον, καὶ ὡς τὸν βίον ἐπανορθωτέον ὁ παιδαγωγὸς ἡμῖν ἄδην διείλεκται, ἄχρις ἂν ἀγάγῃ πρὸς τὸν διδάσκαλον, and in *Paed.* II. 76, where after giving a mystical interpretation of the appearance in the Burning Bush, he breaks off ἀλλ' ἐξέβην γὰρ τοῦ παιδαγωγικοῦ τόπου τὸ διδασκαλικὸν εἶδος παρεισάγων. Again towards the end of the *Paedagogus* (III. 97) ἀλλ' οὐκ ἐμόν, φησὶν ὁ παιδαγωγός, διδάσκειν ἔτι ταῦτα (the instructions to be found in the Bible for bishops, priests and deacons &c.), διδασκάλου δὲ εἰς τὴν ἐξήγησιν τῶν ἁγίων ἐκείνων λόγων χρῄζομεν, πρὸς ὃν ἡμῖν βαδιστέον.

De Faye argues with force, as it seems to me, that when Cl. wrote these words, he intended to give the name Διδάσκαλος to the third part of his great work, which was to treat of the Christian mysteries. Other writers on Clement have assumed that the Στρωματεῖς are merely the Διδάσκαλος under a different name. But is this so? De Faye calls attention to the fact that there is no appearance of finality in the *Miscellanies*. They, like the *Paedagogus*, are paving the way for a more advanced treatise. Thus in *Str.* IV. § 1, after laying out the subjects which remain to be discussed in the later books, he continues § 2 ἐπὶ τούτοις ὕστερον, πληρωθείσης ὡς ἔνι μάλιστα τῆς κατὰ τὰ προκείμενα ἡμῖν ὑποτυπώσεως, τὰ περὶ ἀρχῶν φυσιολογηθέντα τοῖς τε Ἕλλησι τοῖς τε ἄλλοις βαρβάροις, ὅσων (MS. ὅσον) ἧκον εἰς ἡμᾶς αἱ δόξαι, ἐξιστορητέον, καὶ πρὸς τὰ κυριώτατα τῶν τοῖς φιλοσόφοις ἐπινενοημένων ἐγχειρητέον[1], οἷς ἑπόμενον ἂν εἴη μετὰ τὴν ἐπιδρομὴν τῆς θεολογίας τὰ περὶ τῆς προφητείας παραδεδομένα διαλαβεῖν, and to confute the heresies from the Scripture. § 3 τελειωθείσης τοίνυν τῆς προθέσεως ἡμῖν ἁπάσης...τότε δὴ τὴν τῷ ὄντι γνωστικὴν φυσιολογίαν μέτιμεν, τὰ μικρὰ πρὸ τῶν μεγάλων μυηθέντες μυστηρίων ...ἀλλὰ γὰρ τὸ μὲν γεγράψεται, ἢν θεός γε ἐθέλῃ καὶ ὅπως ἂν ἐμπνέῃ, νυνὶ δὲ ἐπὶ τὸ προκείμενον μετιτέον καὶ τὸν ἠθικὸν ἀπο-

[1] Cf. *Str.* II. 184, where the discussion of theories of happiness is deferred.

πληρωτέον λόγον. References to this more advanced treatise are also to be found in *Str.* VII., where he promises to give a view of gnostic teaching (τὴν τῶν δογμάτων θεωρίαν) on some future occasion (§ 59); *Str.* v. 68 'the allegorical meaning of the anthropomorphic descriptions of God will be explained further on.' In IV. 162 having strayed into the region of the higher philosophy he recalls himself to his proper province (μετιτέον δὲ ἀπὸ τῶν φυσικωτέρων ἐπὶ τὰ προφανέστερα ἠθικά), cf. VI. 4 'I postpone the elucidation of the Greek mysteries, until we have examined their philosophy of first principles, on which it will be shown that their mysteries depend.' Similarly in *Str.* II. 37 the treatment of the First Cause is postponed. *Str.* VI. 168 *fin.* 'I have shown the *character* of the gnostic; what he is κατὰ τὴν θεωρίαν will be shown hereafter ἐν τοῖς φυσικοῖς, ἐπὰν περὶ γενέσεως κόσμου διαλαμβάνειν ἀρξώμεθα.' The same is said with regard to the interpretation of prophecy in VII. 1; and the refutation of the heretical depreciation of prayer in VII. 41. The questions of metempsychosis and of the nature of the devil are reserved for a future occasion in IV. 85; so for providential discipline in IV. 89 *init.*; for the Basilidean view of the creation in IV. 91 *init.*; for the Divine attributes in *Str.* V. 71 κατὰ τὸν οἰκεῖον ἐπιδειχθήσεται τόπον, and for the Monad in reference to the Church VII. 108 *init.*

Besides these somewhat vague references to the future developments of his work, Cl. names particular topics, on which he means to write—what most interpreters have understood to be—distinct treatises. Such are (1) the περὶ προφητείας referred to in *Str.* I. 158 ὅπως μὲν οὖν ὁ Μωυσῆς ἦν προφητικὸς μετὰ ταῦτα λεχθήσεται, ὁπηνίκα ἂν περὶ προφητείας διαλαμβάνωμεν: cf. *Str.* IV. 2 already cited, and § 93 πρὸς οὓς (τοὺς Φρύγας) ἐν τοῖς περὶ προφητείας διαλεξόμεθα, *Str.* V. 88 ὅπως δὲ ἡ διανομὴ αὕτη (τοῦ πνεύματος) καὶ ὅ τί ποτέ ἐστι τὸ ἅγιον πνεῦμα ἐν τοῖς περὶ προφητείας κἂν τοῖς περὶ ψυχῆς ἐπιδειχθήσεται ἡμῖν. (2) The περὶ ψυχῆς mentioned here is also referred to in *Str.* III. 13, where the question of metempsychosis (see IV. 85 referred to above) is reserved for another opportunity, ὁπηνίκα ἂν περὶ ψυχῆς διαλαμβάνωμεν. Also *Str.* II. 113 πρὸς τὸ δόγμα τοῦτο (the Basilidean doctrine of the passions) διαλεξόμεθα ὕστερον, ὁπηνίκα περὶ ψυχῆς διαλαμβάνομεν.

the ideal Church to the *corpus permixtum* was due to the fact that 'the attention of the majority of Christians was turned to the intellectual as distinguished from the moral element in Christian life' (p. 164). This however belongs to Greek speculation, not to Greek ethics. He then draws attention to the secession of the Puritan party, and the doubling of the Christian ideal, which divided off the clergy and the ascetics from the general body of the Church, to the great detriment of the latter. Here, at last, we come to a *vera causa*, which does really touch both Clement and the philosophers. I shall return to it shortly. But that which constitutes 'the victory of Greek ethics' (p. 169) is that Cicero's *De Officiis* should have been selected by Ambrose as the basis of his text-book of morality, and should have remained the chief authority during the Middle Ages. 'The Pauline ethics vanished from the Christian world.' 'Instead of the code of morals, which was "briefly comprehended in this saying, namely, Thou shalt love thy neighbour as thyself," there was the old enumeration of duties.' But so it was, we have seen, in that compendium of duty for which Dr Hatch has such a paradoxical admiration. If we are asked which discipline was better adapted for the training of the rude nations of the north, that robust and manly teaching which was handed down from Plato and Aristotle and Zeno and Panaetius and Cicero, or the fanatical asceticism which prevailed among the Montanists and other early Puritans, surely there can be no doubt as to our answer. Aristotle is not even yet superseded as an ethical teacher. He has his defects no doubt, but to him and to the other ancient moralists we are indebted for an indispensable supplement to the Bible, in so far as they make explicit what in it is still implicit.

I proceed now to consider in what way the development of Christian doctrine was affected by Greek logic and rhetoric. Dr Hatch says (pp. 116—137) that the logical habit of mind was injurious to theology in two ways. (1) Clearness of thought and logical consistency were regarded as guaranteeing the objective truth of the conclusions arrived at in reference to ethics and metaphysics, as much as in regard to geometrical abstractions. (2) The theological conclusions thus arrived at were held to be as necessary to salvation as trust in God and

the *Hypotyposes* and the *Q. D. S.* preceded the *Miscellanies*. The former, and possibly the latter, may be referred to in the promised discussion περὶ προφητείας. Granting that it was at one time Clement's intention to bring out a complete treatise on Christian Gnosis under the name Διδάσκαλος, I do not see why the same reasons which led him to prepare the way for this by the *Stromateis* should not also have suggested to him to bring out his great work in portions.

We have still to answer the question, what were the reasons which induced Clement to follow up the *Paedagogus* by a work, of which the real character was disguised by its apparent disorder? Perhaps the following quotation from De Faye's preface may help to clear the ground.

'Ce qui rend le siècle de Clément d'Alexandrie si intéressant, c'est qu'il est, comme le nôtre, une époque de transition où fermentent les germes féconds de l'avenir. C'est une heure indécise et trouble, où se préparent les croyances et les institutions des siècles suivants. Clément lui-même et son œuvre ne sauraient nous laisser indifférents. Il a été essentiellement un homme de transition. Avant lui, le Christianisme a encore quelque chose de primitif; à bien des égards la foi nouvelle n'avait pas dépassé l'état embryonnaire. Après lui, c'est une religion constituée. Il se fait, vers la fin du IIe siècle, une prodigieuse transformation au sein de l'Eglise. Clément en fut l'un des plus puissants ouvriers. Il est le véritable créateur de la théologie ecclésiastique. Quel chemin parcouru par la pensée chrétienne depuis les Pères apostoliques jusqu'à Origène! C'est Clément qui est l'auteur responsable de cette étonnante évolution. C'est pour cela qu'il occupe dans l'histoire des idées chrétiennes une place de premier ordre.'

The early Christians for the most part looked upon the Greco-Roman literature as a part of the hostile world against which they were warned. It was necessity which compelled the Apologists, such as Quadratus and Aristides, to enter this new domain in the reign of Hadrian. Though they professed a distaste for the rules of composition and rhetoric, which were current in the world, they were forced to adopt them to a certain extent in order to gain a hearing, and thus prepared the way for a Christian literature. The conflict with heresy carried further the process begun by the conflict with the heathen and the Jew. But while it widened the range of thought and developed the reasoning powers of the few, it had a tendency to drive back the mass of Christians upon an unreasoning dependence on tradition and authority. And this tendency found a voice in Tertullian's vehement denunciation of philosophy as the source of all heresy, and in his fierce denial of the right of inquiry and private judgment[1].

In contrast to the Roman lawyer we have the Greek professor. In the catechetical school of Alexandria Clement was accustomed to lecture both to believers and to unbelievers, opening the eyes of both alike to the divine revelation around and within them, a revelation to be found in its purest form in the Christian Scriptures, but which was also reflected in Greek poetry and philosophy, especially in 'the inspired writings of Plato.' Philosophy was for the Greeks what the law was for the Jews. Nor had its use ceased even for Christians. It is the appointed means of education: it serves to protect the believer from the sophistries of a pseudo-gnosticism: it throws light on the meaning of Scripture: it helps to the attainment of divine truth. Hence Clement begins his *Stromateis* with the defence of philosophy. He is aware that the general opinion is opposed to him, ὡς ἔοικεν, οἱ πλεῖστοι τῶν τὸ ὄνομα ἐπιγραφομένων, καθάπερ οἱ τοῦ Ὀδυσσέως ἑταῖροι, ἀγροίκως μετίασι τὸν λόγον, …ἀμαθίᾳ βύσαντες τὰ ὦτα, ἐπείπερ ἴσασιν οὐ δυνησόμενοι, ἅπαξ ὑποσχόντες τὰς ἀκοὰς Ἑλληνικοῖς μαθήμασι, μετὰ ταῦτα τοῦ νόστου τυχεῖν. 'He who remembers that the earth is the Lord's and the fulness thereof, will not shun philosophy.' Similarly in VII. 1 Clement assumes that his language will be suspected by many as unfamiliar, though it is really founded on Scripture and breathes the spirit of the Gospel. These 'Orthodoxastae,' as he calls them in *Str.* I. 45, even go so far as to condemn writing altogether. Clement has seriously to argue that, if it

[1] He even forbids discussion on the meaning of Scripture as dangerous or superfluous for the orthodox, (*Praescr.* 19) 'Ergo non ad Scripturas provocandum est: nec in his constituendum certamen, in quibus aut nulla aut incerta victoria est, aut par incertae...Ubi enim apparuerit esse veritatem et disciplinae et fidei Christianae, illic erit veritas Scripturarum et expositionum et omnium traditionum christianarum'; on which Pamelius naturally observes 'Locus insignis pro Catholicis.'

be right to teach by hearing, it cannot be wrong to teach by sight (*Str.* I. 1 foll.). Hence it was impossible, as De Faye says (p. 133), for Clement to lay before the public 'sans explication et sans préambule la partie de son grand ouvrage qui, dans sa pensée, devait exposer tout un système de dogmes conçus et formulés selon les méthodes de la philosophie. Il aurait soulevé une réprobation générale; il aurait perdu toute autorité sur ses coreligionnaires; il aurait été traité de gnostique, tout en combattant le gnosticisme. Voilà pourquoi il lui fallait écrire un traité qui préparerait l'ouvrage doctrinal et lui aplanirait les voies. Il y a plus...Clément a eu l'heureuse idée de choisir pour son livre un genre littéraire qui lui laissait une liberté particulièrement favorable à son dessein. Dans ses *Stromates*, il lui était parfaitement loisible de présenter ses vues au moment et de la manière qui lui convenaient.'

We may find examples of the vari-coloured texture of the *Stromateis* in the admixture of topics which would be more agreeable to the ordinary taste than the systematic exposition of his views on theology. The praise of philosophy is mixed with polemic against the heretics and with the attempt to prove that all that is best in philosophy is ultimately derived from Scripture. Faith is the subject of high panegyric, and the use of the motive of fear is urged against the gnostic teachers. The third book has a long dissertation on marriage, which scarcely belongs to the context. Then we have interesting discussions on martyrdom and on symbolism; the absurdity of pagan superstition is shown in a number of amusing examples; in fine the whole work teems with quotations and anecdotes; and it is partly under cover of these things that Clement suggests the doctrines on which he lays the greatest stress.

Another art which Clement employs to avoid giving offence is his profession to be merely a reporter of the sayings of the elders, and of a secret tradition handed down from the Apostles. It is quite possible that he is indebted to Pantaenus for the germ of some of his opinions, and his allegorical interpretations of Scripture often agree with what we find in Philo or Barnabas or Irenaeus, cf. VII. 109 foll.; but it can hardly be doubted that many of his ideas are original or, in any case, largely developed by himself.

CHAPTER II.

INFLUENCE OF GREEK PHILOSOPHY ON THE THEOLOGY AND ETHICS OF CLEMENT.

If I am not mistaken, there has been of late years a tendency to exaggerate the difference between the teaching of the Bible and that of Clement in regard both to ethics and theology. A reader of Harnack and of Hatch would, I think, gather that genuine apostolic Christianity was an unreasoning, enthusiastic revivalism, fed on visions and miracles, and looking forward to the immediate coming of the Lord and the reign of the Saints for a thousand years on earth; that the second and third centuries witnessed an illegitimate development of the teaching of Christ and His Apostles in the hellenizing and secularizing of Christian doctrine, by which the new wine of the Day of Pentecost, the ardours of the first faith and love, were changed into correctness of creed and of conduct[1]; and that in this transformation Clement was the leading agent.

---

[1] Perhaps the most startling assertion made on this subject is that which traces the commencement of secularism to the existence of the N.T. Thus Deissmann (*Bible Studies* p. 59) says 'The beginnings of Christian literature are really the beginnings of the secularization of Christianity: the Church becomes a book-religion.' 'The Church required literature, and hence it made literature, and made books out of letters: hence also, at length, the N.T. came into existence.' If the existence of sacred books naturally leads to the secularisation of religion, then all who held that the Law and Prophets of the O.T. were inspired, whether under the old or the new dispensation, including the Apostles themselves, must have been subject to this baneful influence. To much the same effect Hatch says (*Influence of Greek Ideas on the Christian Church* pp. 106, 107) 'prophesying died when the Catholic Church was formed,' 'the prophet preached because he could not help it, because there was a divine breath breathing within him, which must needs find utterance,' 'they did not practise beforehand how or what they should say, for the "Holy Ghost taught them in that very hour what they should say".' [This quotation is wrongly applied; it is a promise to Christians generally, to keep them from over-anxiety if they should be called before magistrates to answer for their religion: it gives no

If by 'hellenism' and 'secularism' it is simply meant that

encouragement to preaching without preparation.] As evidence how far the Church had fallen away from this ideal by the end of the 2nd century, Dr Hatch states (p. 109) that Origen's addresses, 'like those of the best professors, were carefully prepared: he was sixty years of age, we are told, before he preached an extempore sermon.' It may be well to put side by side of this depreciation of the work of reason and reflexion, as contrasted with the outpourings of emotion, the judgment of contemporaries who were familiar with prophets and prophesyings. The Epistles to the Romans and to the Hebrews are the outcome of long-continued thought, and make the utmost demand on the thoughtful intelligence of the reader. St Paul in one place seems to speak of prophecy as especially useful for the unbeliever or unlearned, probably because it rouses the sluggish or indifferent by the impressive utterance of simple truths: but he has to find fault with the prophets for their disorderly behaviour; even in his day διακρίσεις πνευμάτων were needed, and he speaks ironically of some who think themselves prophets. While he places the gift of prophecy above that of tongues, he does not seem to make any broad distinction between the work of the prophet, and that of the evangelist, the pastor and the teacher. The word of wisdom and the word of knowledge are gifts of the Spirit, just as much as prophecy. Again, St John speaks of many false prophets, and his warning is repeated in the *Didache* xi. 8 f. where the marks of a false prophet are given. It is really astonishing to find the superstitious belief of the vulgar in the virtue of extemporaneousness entertained by learned writers. Doubtless it would have been interesting to have acted as St Paul's amanuensis and watched his kindling eye, as he poured forth his inspired hymn on Christian charity, but the sacred flame has been caught from the glowing page by hundreds of thousands in later times, who never heard his voice or saw his face.

Harnack, while avoiding the extravagances of Deissmann and of Hatch, still specifies as the main factors in the development of Christianity in the 2nd and 3rd centuries, (1) 'the Fixing and gradual Secularizing (Verweltlichung) of Christianity as a Church, (2) 'the Fixing and gradual Hellenizing (Hellenisirung) of Christianity as a system of doctrine' (*Hist. of Dogma* vol. II. pp. 18—168, 169—230); and states that it was 'between the years 190 and 220 (just the period of Clement and Origen) that the secularization of the Church made the greatest strides' (*ib.* p. 100). What he means by this secularization is explained in p. 125: 'What made the Christian a Christian, was no longer the possession of charisms, but obedience to ecclesiastical authority, share in the gifts of the Church, and the performance of penance and good works....The dispensations of grace, that is, Absolution and the Lord's Supper, abolished the charismatic gifts. The Holy Scriptures, the apostolic episcopate, the priests, the sacraments, average morality...were mutually conditioned....And yet, alongside of a code of morals, to which anyone in case of need could adapt himself, the Church began to legitimize a morality of self-chosen, refined sanctity, which really required no Redeemer.' I must say I entertain the gravest doubts as to the correctness of this diagnosis of the Church of Clement and of Origen. If St Paul's eye had travelled over the whole course of subsequent Christianity I believe it would have rested upon none with more sympathy and complacency than on these two. See further my note on p. xxxiii below.

when the Church overstept the limits of the Hebrew race and language, and became more fully conscious of its mission to preach the Gospel to every creature, it became also to the Greeks as Greek, to the Romans as Roman, and claimed as its own those seeds or fragments of divine teaching which it found embodied in the thoughts or institutions of other races;—if so, then, though one might object to the use of the ambiguous term 'secularism,' I think none who had paid attention to the subject, would question the truth of the assertion. But such secularization as this is no illegitimate development of Christianity: it is only carrying out the principle which pervades the whole history of revelation, and which is taught and exemplified by the Apostles and Evangelists themselves in such words as ἦν τὸ φῶς τὸ ἀληθινόν, ὃ φωτίζει πάντα ἄνθρωπον ἐρχόμενον εἰς τὸν κόσμον, and τὸ γνωστὸν τοῦ θεοῦ φανερόν ἐστιν ἐν αὐτοῖς, ὁ γὰρ θεὸς αὐτοῖς ἐφανέρωσε, and οὐκ ἀμάρτυρον ἑαυτὸν ἀφῆκεν, and ἐν αὐτῷ γὰρ ζῶμεν καὶ κινούμεθα καὶ ἐσμέν· ὡς καί τινες τῶν καθ᾽ ὑμᾶς ποιητῶν εἰρήκασι· Τοῦ γὰρ καὶ γένος ἐσμέν, above all perhaps τὸ πνεῦμα ὅπου θέλει πνεῖ, and ἔτι πολλὰ ἔχω λέγειν ὑμῖν, ἀλλ᾽ οὐ δύνασθε βαστάζειν ἄρτι and (a text often quoted by Clement) τοῦ γὰρ κυρίου ἡ γῆ καὶ τὸ πλήρωμα αὐτῆς.

From the beginning of the Bible to the end of it, we have evidence of the working of the Divine Spirit, even in the form of direct inspiration, outside of the race or the class which may have been chosen as its appointed organ. Modern research has shown that the story of the Creation and the Fall is older than Moses; Abraham is blessed by one, and rebuked by another, who did not belong to the chosen seed: Moses, we are told, was learned in all the wisdom of the Egyptians: the words which God spoke through Balaam, enemy and seducer of Israel as he was, are quoted by the prophet Micah as showing 'the righteousness of the Lord.' The priests and the judges vainly resist the calling of the prophets and kings. Amos, the herdsman, is bidden to prophesy, though he was no prophet nor prophet's son. Dramas, stories, love-poems, and prudential maxims are admitted into the 'Divine Library.' Heathen kings and heathen nations come under the discipline, and receive the forgiveness and blessing of God. Even the beliefs of the chosen people are modified by what they were taught in Babylon and Persia: and the apocryphal writings, especially the book of Wisdom and the Fourth book of Maccabees, exhibit the influence of Greek philosophy, which is also perceptible throughout the Septuagint translation. The New Testament is addressed to Greek readers: many of the terms employed bear the stamp of the Academy or the Porch. St John's use of the word Logos, while it reminds us of the phrase used by the prophets 'the Word of the Lord came to me,' yet betrays a consciousness of the later philosophic application of the term; and St Paul's language continually bears witness to his studies in the university of Tarsus. See Lightfoot's notes on πολίτευμα Phil. iii. 20, αὐτάρκης Phil. iv. 11, ἀπέχω Phil. iv. 18, μορφή *ib.* p. 127, on συνέστηκεν Col. i. 17, μυστήριον *ib.* i. 26, and the essay on St Paul and Seneca in *Gal.* pp. 270—328, esp. 307, see also Harnack, *Dogmeng.* I.³ pp. 41, 56, 208. In my introduction to the Epistle of St James, I have endeavoured to show that there is evidence of a similar acquaintance with Greek philosophy in what I hold to be the earliest of the N.T. documents. One of St Paul's most trusted followers, who is described as an ἀνὴρ λόγιος of Alexandria, has been supposed by some to be the author of the Epistle to the Hebrews, which certainly shows an acquaintance with the teaching of Philo. The reference in St John's Gospel to the Greeks who desired to see Jesus, and the remark which their request elicited from Him, ἐὰν μὴ ὁ κόκκος τοῦ σίτου πεσὼν εἰς τὴν γῆν ἀποθάνῃ, αὐτὸς μόνος μένει· ἐὰν δὲ ἀποθάνῃ, πολὺν καρπὸν φέρει, suggest that the Lord Himself looked to Greece as the soil in which the seed of the Gospel was to take root and flourish.

There is then something of Hellenism in primitive Christianity, as there is a great deal of it in the contemporary Judaism of the Diaspora. On the other side there is a remarkable approach to Christianity in Greek philosophy from the time of the Christian era. If it can be said with any truth that there was a secularization of Christianity going on in the 2nd century, it is at least as true to say, there was a de-secularization of philosophy. I need not go into detail on this point, for it is admitted by all. It may suffice to repeat words in which I have elsewhere summed up the work of Greek Philosophy as preparing the way for Christianity. 'Just as deeper thoughts about the nature of knowledge forced on men the conviction of their own ignorance, so deeper thoughts about virtue made men conscious of their own deficiency in virtue, and produced in them the new conviction of sin. The one conviction taught them their need of a revelation, the other conviction taught them their need of a purifying and sanctifying power[1].' Even in that school, which is usually regarded as the very embodiment of 'proud philosophy,' we find examples of the enthusiasm and unction, which Dr Hatch seems to regard as the exclusive possession of the Christian prophets. Never has the human spirit uttered its longings and its aspirations with a more pathetic earnestness than in the Lectures of Epictetus and the Diary of M. Aurelius. If a Christian preacher of the 2nd century might be tempted (as Hatch suggests, pp. 105 foll.) to adorn his sermon with the rhetorical charms of a Dio Chrysostom, he might be shamed out of it by the stern simplicity of these typical Stoics.

To consider first the ethical side of the question. Is it true that Hellenism is responsible for degrading the aspiration after holiness, the fruits of the Spirit, and the self-sacrifice of love, into a dull morality, changing the ethics of the Sermon on the Mount into the ethics of Roman Law? So Dr Hatch seems to think (pp. 164—170); but, if I am not mistaken, there is the same exaggeration here as in the rest of his book, interesting and valuable as it is. Perhaps exaggeration is unavoidable in pioneer work, such as he claims his to be (p. 353), but at any rate it is the duty of those who come after him to be on their guard against over-statements on one side or the other.

No one can complain that Dr Hatch is unfair in his description of the ethical teaching of Epictetus. 'Moral conduct,' he says, is made by him a 'sublime religion.' The difficulty is to understand the steps by which he passes from this appreciation to his conclusion, that the morality of Christians was lowered owing to the influence of Hellenism. He begins by taking the Didache as exhibiting the primitive form of Christian

---

[1] See also Harnack, *Dogmeng.* i.² 111—123.

morality, and notes that in it 'the moral law is regarded as a positive enactment of God' (p. 159), while in Stoicism morality appears as a 'law revealed in the nature of the universe and of man.' He points out that, in the Way of Life embodied in the Didache, doctrine has no place (p. 160). I quite agree: but if this is a true account of the Didache, is it possible to conceive a more entire departure from the teaching of St Paul, when, in the Romans, he speaks of the Gentiles showing 'the work of the law written in their hearts,' and when he reminds the Galatians that 'by the works of the law shall no flesh be justified,' but that 'God sent forth his Son to redeem them that were under the law, that we might receive the adoption of sons'? What we have in the Didache is the very moralism decried by Harnack in the words, 'Die Kräftigkeit und Unmittelbarkeit des religiösen Gefühls stumpfte sich zu einem Moralismus ab.' We find in it, says Dr Bigg (p. 84) 'a law which differs from the Mosaic mainly in being more searching and elaborate'; and that too combined with a pettiness and a superstition, which testify alike to the simplicity and the defective intelligence of those for whom it was intended. Thus we read 'If you are able to bear the whole yoke of the Lord, you will be perfect: if you are not able, do what you can. As to meat, bear what you are able, and abstain altogether from what is offered to idols. Before baptism let both minister and catechumen fast. Do not fast like the hypocrites on the 2nd and 5th day, but on the 4th and 6th. If a prophet remains in one place more than two days, it shows he is a false prophet,' and so on. And it is for a community of this kind that Dr Hatch deprecates the admission of the free air of Greece.

The next point noted is Church discipline. 'To be a member of the community was to be in reality a child of God and heir of everlasting salvation: to be excluded from the community was to pass again into the outer darkness.' A close community of this sort has undoubtedly both its good and its bad sides. Our Lord in His parables of the Tares and the Fishes pronounces His judgment against it. I do not see that Hellenism was necessarily opposed to it, any more than to the withdrawal from the world into schools of philosophy, or to the initiation into the mysteries. Dr Hatch thinks that the change from the ideal Church to the *corpus permixtum* was due to the fact that 'the attention of the majority of Christians was turned to the intellectual as distinguished from the moral element in Christian life' (p. 164). This however belongs to Greek speculation, not to Greek ethics. He then draws attention to the secession of the Puritan party, and the doubling of the Christian ideal, which divided off the clergy and the ascetics from the general body of the Church, to the great detriment of the latter. Here, at last, we come to a *vera causa*, which does really touch both Clement and the philosophers. I shall return to it shortly. But that which constitutes 'the victory of Greek ethics' (p. 169) is that Cicero's *De Officiis* should have been selected by Ambrose as the basis of his text-book of morality, and should have remained the chief authority during the Middle Ages. 'The Pauline ethics vanished from the Christian world.' 'Instead of the code of morals, which was "briefly comprehended in this saying, namely, Thou shalt love thy neighbour as thyself," there was the old enumeration of duties.' But so it was, we have seen, in that compendium of duty for which Dr Hatch has such a paradoxical admiration. If we are asked which discipline was better adapted for the training of the rude nations of the north, that robust and manly teaching which was handed down from Plato and Aristotle and Zeno and Panaetius and Cicero, or the fanatical asceticism which prevailed among the Montanists and other early Puritans, surely there can be no doubt as to our answer. Aristotle is not even yet superseded as an ethical teacher. He has his defects no doubt, but to him and to the other ancient moralists we are indebted for an indispensable supplement to the Bible, in so far as they make explicit what in it is still implicit.

I proceed now to consider in what way the development of Christian doctrine was affected by Greek logic and rhetoric. Dr Hatch says (pp. 116—137) that the logical habit of mind was injurious to theology in two ways. (1) Clearness of thought and logical consistency were regarded as guaranteeing the objective truth of the conclusions arrived at in reference to ethics and metaphysics, as much as in regard to geometrical abstractions. (2) The theological conclusions thus arrived at were held to be as necessary to salvation as trust in God and the effort to lead a holy life. This is illustrated by an instructive anecdote, quoted with approval by Eusebius (*H. E.* v. 13), of a controversy which took place in the latter part of the second century between the orthodox Rhodon and Apelles, who was in some respects in sympathy with Marcion. "Apelles was often refuted for his errors, which indeed made him say that we ought not to inquire too closely into doctrine; but that, as every one had believed, so he should remain. For he declared that those who set their hopes on the Crucified One would be saved, if only they were found in good works....He held no doubt that there is One Principle, just as we hold too; but when I said to him 'Tell me how do you demonstrate that, or on what grounds are you able to assert that there is One Principle'...he said that he did not know, but that this was his conviction. When I thereupon adjured him to tell me the truth, he swore that...he did not know how there is one unbegotten God, but that nevertheless so he believed. Then I laughed at him and denounced him for that, giving himself out as a teacher, he did not know how to prove what he taught" (Hatch p. 135 f.). So far, I think, we shall agree. There *is* a danger of confounding the subjective and the objective: there is a danger of denying the legitimacy of conviction, which is not capable of being expressed in logical forms. But was this danger confined to Greek philosophy and the habits of thought engendered by it? What of the Palestinian philosophy which 'reflected, as in a mirror, the difficulties, the contradictions, the unsolved enigmas of the world of fact'[1]? Yet here too the rabbis 'taught for doctrines the commandments of men,' and 'made the word of God of none effect by their tradition.' There are many errors which arise from haziness of mind, from mistaking resemblance for identity, from being unable to see the subject as a whole: there are the *idola fori* and *idola specus*. From such errors and from the sophistical use of logical processes, the methods of Plato and Aristotle are a preservative: and, as a consequence, they were able to throw a flood of light on what was dark before in regard to the nature of man and of God. It would greatly have increased the value of Clement's writings

---

[1] Hatch p. 125.

if he had been more penetrated by the logical spirit; if he had thought more clearly and more consecutively. To what extent he used logical methods and how far he was misled by them will be discussed further on. If he has sometimes been tempted to make assumptions in matters which transcend man's understanding, he has never, so far as I remember, fallen into the second error specified by Dr Hatch, and demanded assent to his conclusions on pain of anathema.

Dr Hatch is no less severe on Greek rhetoric. It 'killed philosophy' he says, and 'has arrested the progress of Christianity, because many of its preachers live in an unreal world' and 'cultivate style for the style's sake' (pp. 113, 114). Here too we must allow that there is a real danger[1]. And yet there is a place for rhetoric, as for logic, in the right training of the Christian philosopher. As logic is needed to teach clear thought and consecutive reasoning, so rhetoric is needed for clear and appropriate expression; and as in the one case, so in the other, the remedy for possible abuses is to be sought from the science itself.

The charges against rhetoric have been answered once for all by Aristotle. If it is abused, as all powers may be, the fault lies in the motive ($\pi\rho o a i\rho \epsilon \sigma \iota s$) of the speaker, not in the command of the resources of speech supplied by the art. It is unfair to expose unarmed justice to the attack of injustice armed with rhetoric (*Rhet.* I. 2). As to mere rhetorical ornaments, nothing can be more contemptuous than the language in which they are spoken of by Clement in *Strom.* I. 22.

But what, after all, is the good of all these protests against Hellenism? Granting that it had its weak side, like all things human, can we really suppose that it would have been better for the Church and for the World, if thought and learning had been permanently excluded from the Christian community;

---

[1] Cf. Gardner (*Expl. Ev.* p. 856), 'Rhetoric, which one may fairly call the evil genius of Greece, had a constant tendency to drag doctrine away from the base of experience, and to make it depend rather on words than on facts.' If we are speaking of Christian rhetoric, I should be inclined to say it is more conspicuous in Latin than in Greek writers, in Minucius, in Tertullian, in Arnobius, rather than in Justin, or Clement; the latter of whom would indeed be very much more intelligible if he had had a better rhetorical training, say, under such a teacher as Quintilian or Longinus.

if there had been no Paul, no Clement, no Origen, no Tertullian, no Augustine; if our theological and religious formularies had been framed by men of the calibre of Hermas and the compilers of the Didache, nay, even by martyrs and saints such as Ignatius or Polycarp, or Perpetua herself, that fairest flower in the garden of post-Apostolic Christendom? Yet the language of Deissmann and of Hatch, if literally interpreted, would seem to go even further than this, and imply that formularies altogether are a mistake; that nothing should be done to check the spontaneous overflow of religious emotions; that the exercise of Church authority was always mischievous; that each generation should act as if it stood alone in the world, regardless alike of the experience of the past, and of its responsibility for the future. Of course an absolute absurdity and impossibility: and yet, I think, the necessary consequence of their premisses[1].

To return, Hellenism, as we have seen, is not contrary to the Christianity of the N.T.: it is involved in the teaching of Christ and His Apostles, and is its pre-ordained, its natural

[1] A far truer account of the transition from the creative to the regulative stage in the development of religious thought is to be found in Gardner's *Exploratio Evangelica* pp. 322—324. 'The development of a scheme of doctrine is seldom the work of one of those great religious leaders who make epochs in human history. But after such leaders have broken the way and prepared the ground, doctrines arise among their successors....There are periods of enthusiasm; but enthusiasm cannot last for ever in any community. While the enthusiasm lasts, men despise all worldly considerations and act only for the glory of God. And at the same time they are ready to make light of the needs of the intellect, to make religious zeal all in all, and to despise mere knowledge. But these powerful movements sooner or later lose their first energy....Then comes the necessity of clear definitions, of exact statements, of a scheme of the universe framed from the new point of view, and capable of being defended against the philosophic assaults of those who maintain the old order of things. It may be that the new movement had not sufficient intellectual force and rational basis to develop a new system of thought. In that case it is doomed at once to pass away....If however the new movement has enough vital force to frame a satisfactory scheme of the world, it may grow and flourish. It was thus with Christianity....But, unless Christianity had presented to the thinking part of mankind a system of the world and of human life which they felt to be higher and truer than others, it must have failed to make its way. For if the emotions are the sails of life, the intellect is the rudder....Religion is more closely connected with emotion and action than with thought, yet if we love religion we must think about it. And if we think about it at all, it is of the utmost consequence to think about it rightly.'

and necessary development. The emotional and physical accompaniments of the first reception of the Gospel were mere passing phenomena, perhaps unavoidable, like the excitement attending the preaching of Wesley or Whitfield; anyhow not to be encouraged. Indeed we have frequent warnings against them, as in St Paul's depreciation of the charismata as compared with charity; in his insistence on order and self-control, on worship with the understanding as well as with the spirit (1 Cor. xiv.); in his exhortation to the Thessalonians (2 ep. iii. 6—13) to go on quietly with their own business, undisturbed by the thought of the Day of the Lord at hand.

We may say then that Clement is entirely justified in his assumption that the working of the Divine Spirit was to be traced in the history of Greece and Rome as well as in that of Judaea; that philosophy had been to the Greeks what the law was to Jews, a covenant with God[1], a παιδαγωγός to bring them to Christ; that a Socrates or Plato, a Pythagoras or Cleanthes, who acted up to the light which he had received from heaven, was as truly a sharer of the heavenly citizenship as any devout Jew under the Old Dispensation[2]. More generally we may say that it is only a partial aspect of God which is revealed to any individual, to any race, or to any age, and that the Jewish conception of God and of man needed to be supplemented by the Greek conception, just as in later ages the ecclesiastical conception of God is continually widened and modified by the scientific conception. The Church which is not always learning, which is merely traditional, is doomed to sterility, if it is not already dead. It does not of course follow that the Greek conception was on the whole as adequate as the Jewish conception. Clement allows that it is altogether defective as compared with the teaching of Christ[3]; yet still it is of use as a handmaid for the highest wisdom, just as the ordinary course of instruction is for philosophy[4]; it prepares the soul to receive the faith[5], though even in a Greek it is not absolutely indispensable[6]. Clement would no doubt have maintained that

---

[1] *Str.* vi. 42, 67.   [2] *Protr.* § 68 foll., *Str.* i. 28, vi. 156.
[3] *Str.* i. 28, 98, vi. 68.   [4] *Str.* i. 80.   [5] *Str.* vii. 70.
[6] *Str.* vii. 11.

all the books in the world taken together cannot compare with the value of the revelation contained in the Scriptures: are we to censure him if he finds more of divine truth in the writings of Plato than in the books, say, of Chronicles and Esther, in other words, if he holds that the portion of the Διαθήκη which is contained in the latter is of less importance than that which is contained in the former?

I am far from asserting that Clement was never mistaken in accepting the Greek ideas. Whether he was or was not mistaken, is a matter for investigation; but we need not embarrass ourselves beforehand by the use of question-begging terms, and condemn his proceeding off-hand as a 'de-potentiation' and 'secularization' of the Christian religion[1].

---

[1] These terms occur in Harnack's *Hist. of Dogma*. See vol. II. p. 4, 'Catholicism preserved Christianity from being hellenized to the most extreme extent; but, as time went on, it was forced to admit into this religion an ever greater measure of secularisation.' 'It permitted the genesis of a Church which was no longer a communion of faith, hope and discipline, but a political commonwealth, in which the Gospel merely had a place beside other things': *ib.* p. 6 'The depotentiation (depotenzirung) to which Christianity was here (in its ecclesiastical organisation) subjected, appears most plainly in the fact that the secularising of the Christian life was tolerated or even legitimised': p. 11 'In the case of the Alexandrines, heathen syncretism in the entire breadth of its development was united with the doctrine of the Church': p. 14 'The union of the Christian religion with a definite historical phase of human knowledge and culture may be lamented in the interest of the Christian religion, which was thereby secularised, and in the interest of the development of culture, which was thereby retarded': in p. 22 he praises the wisdom with which 'the bishops carried out the great revolution which so depotentiated the Church as to make her capable of becoming a prop of civil society and of the state, without forcing any great changes upon them': p. 105 'The ultimate motive (of the Montanists) was the effort to stop the continuous secularising of the Christian life': the same thing is said of the Encratites and Marcionites in p. 123, and of Novatian in p. 118: the followers of the last 'neither transformed the gifts of salvation into means of education, nor confused the reality with the possibility of Redemption; and they did not completely lower the requirement for a holy life' (p. 120): 'In this conception (that the Church alone saves from damnation, which is otherwise certain) the nature of the Church is depotentiated, but her powers are widened' (p. 113): 'To them (Clement and Origen) the ethical and religious ideal is the state without sorrow, the state of insensibility to all evils, of order and peace—but peace in God. Reconciled to the course of the world, trusting in the divine Logos, rich in disinterested love to God and the brethren, reproducing the divine thoughts, looking up with longing to heaven its native city, the created spirit attains its likeness to God and eternal bliss' (p. 337): it is apparently of this that we read just before 'No

M. C.

What then is the extent of Clement's borrowing from philosophy? How far does he discriminate between one school and another? He tells us that tares have been sown in Greek as in Hebrew philosophy (*Str.* VI. P. 774) and compares the teaching of Epicurus to the heresies which vex the Church. In *Str.* I P 338 he defines more exactly what is the philosophy which he follows: φιλοσοφίαν οὐ τὴν Στωικὴν λέγω οὐδὲ τὴν Πλατωνικὴν ἢ τὴν Ἐπικούρειόν τε καὶ Ἀριστοτελικήν, ἀλλ' ὅσα εἴρηται παρ' ἑκάστῃ τῶν αἱρέσεων τούτων καλῶς, δικαιο-

one can deny that this sort of flight from the world and possession of God involves a specific secularisation of Christianity': p. 141 'Systematic theology always starts, as Clement and Origen also did, with the conscious or unconscious thought of emancipating itself from the outward revelation and community of worship, which are the outward marks of positive religion. The place of these is taken by the results of speculative cosmogony.'

I have stated before (note on p. xxiii) that this diagnosis of the Church of Clement and of Origen appears to me mistaken. It would be more applicable two hundred years later to the Church as we know it from the writings of Jerome and Chrysostom, though even then the cancer of worldliness was, I think, due less to intellectual, than to social and political causes. I will not however dwell further on this, but proceed to quote from Harnack what seems to me a perfectly accurate appreciation of Clement's great work (vol. II. p. 324): this, which 'has been rightly called the boldest literary undertaking in the history of the Church, is the first attempt to use Holy Scripture and the Church tradition, together with the assumption that Christ, as the Reason of the world, is the source of all truth, as the basis of a presentation of Christianity, which at once addresses itself to the cultured by satisfying the scientific demand for a philosophical ethic and theory of the world, and at the same time reveals to the believer the rich content of his faith. Here then is found, in form and content, the scientific Christian doctrine of religion which, while not contradicting the faith, does not merely support or explain it in a few places, but raises it to another and higher intellectual sphere, namely, out of the province of authority and obedience into that of clear knowledge and inward intellectual assent emanating from love to God.' And again, 'Through Clement theology became the crowning stage of piety; the highest philosophy of the Greeks was placed under the protection and guarantee of the Church, and the whole Hellenic civilisation was at the same time legitimised within Christianity. The Logos is Christ, but the Logos is at the same time the moral and rational in all stages of development. The Logos is the teacher, not only in cases where an intelligent self-restraint, as understood by the ancients, bridles the passions and instincts, and wards off excesses of all sorts; but also, and here of course the revelation is of a higher kind, wherever love to God determines the whole life and exalts man above everything sensuous and finite. What Gnostic moralists merely regarded as contrasts, Clement, the Christian and Greek, was able to view as stages. He was thus led to include the history of pre-Christian humanity in the system he regarded as a unity, and to form a theory of univeral history

σύνην μετὰ εὐσεβοῦς ἐπιστήμης ἐκδιδάσκοντα, τοῦτο σύμπαν τὸ ἐκλεκτικὸν φιλοσοφίαν λέγω. ὅσα δὲ ἀνθρωπίνων λόγων ἀποτεμόμενοι παρεχάραξαν, ταῦτα οὐκ ἄν ποτε θεῖα εἴποιμ' ἄν. That is, he accepts as Divine teaching whatever sayings of philosophers seem to him to promote religion and virtue. As regards religion and the theory of the universe he finds this teaching chiefly in Plato, as regards ethics in the Stoics, but

satisfactory to his mind. If we compare this theory with the rudimentary ideas of a similar kind in Irenaeus, we see clearly the meagreness and want of freedom, the uncertainty and narrowness in the case of the latter.'...'Clement was the first to grasp the task of future theology' (p. 328 f.). Yet just below we read 'But does the Christianity of Clement correspond to the Gospel? We can only give a qualified affirmation to this question. For the danger of secularisation is evident, since apostasy from the Gospel would be completely accomplished as soon as the ideal of the self-sufficient Greek sage came to supplant the feeling that man lives by the grace of God. But the danger of secularisation lies in the cramped conception of Irenaeus, who sets up authorities which have nothing to do with the Gospel, and creates facts of salvation (Heilsthatsachen aufrichtet) which have a no less deadening effect, though in a different way.' 'What would be left of Christianity, if the practical aim given by Clement to this religious philosophy were lost? A depotentiated system which could absolutely no longer be called Christian. On the other hand there were many valuable features in the ecclesiastical *regula* literally interpreted: and the attempts of Irenaeus to extract an authoritative religious meaning from the literal sense of Church tradition and of New Testament passages, must be regarded as conservative efforts of the highest kind' (p. 331).

I yield to no one in my admiration of the qualities shown in the *Dogmen-geschichte*. It is a stupendous monument of learning, combined with great power of generalization, transparent honesty, and many-sided sympathy. And the result is perhaps the most interesting and stimulating book that has ever been written on what would commonly be regarded as a dry subject. I wish it could be made a text-book in all our schools of theology. What appear to me the defects of the book spring partly from its excellences. The perpetual activity of thought leads to over-hasty generalization; and hence the original generalization has continually to be modified by others, given sometimes in a note or in the next sentence, which are quite at variance with it, so that it is very hard to get a total impression. At least that is my experience. I do not know that there is anything in my text for which Harnack's authority might not be cited, but then it may equally be cited for quite the opposite view. It reminds me of the wavering of the needle, after the compass has been shaken, before it finds its way back to the north. Perhaps, however, nothing could be better than this for rousing independent thought on the part of the reader. Only it behoves the latter to be constantly on his guard against the assumptions which he will meet with in every page; and to keep in mind that a student is guilty of treason to the cause of truth if, either from too great regard for authority or from delight in novel and brilliant combinations, he neglects to prove all things to the very best of his power.

for both he leans much on the authority of Philo, the great leader in the work of reconciling Hebraic and Hellenic thought.

My space does not allow me to give a full account of Clement's obligations to philosophy thus understood; I will therefore confine my attention mainly to the book which is the subject of this volume, the Seventh Miscellany.

The first and most general modification in the form of religious teaching introduced by Clement is the adoption of the philosophic method. This is alluded to in *Str.* VII. 1 ἐναργεστέροις δ', οἶμαι, πρὸς τοὺς φιλοσόφους χρῆσθαι προσήκει τοῖς λόγοις, ὡς ἐπαΐειν ἐκ τῆς παρ' αὐτοῖς παιδείας ἤδη γεγυμνασμένους δύνασθαι, and shortly below it is stated that the modification is in form only, not in the substance of the teaching. This method is fully explained in *Strom.* VIII. It is the dialectic of Plato, commencing with the thirst for knowledge which is caused by the consciousness of ignorance, and proceeding by way of question and answer to define the subject treated of, and so to advance step by step from what is admitted to what is still matter of dispute. The first principle in reasoning is necessarily indemonstrable; ἐπὶ τὴν ἀναπόδεικτον ἄρα πίστιν ἡ πᾶσα ἀπόδειξις ἀνάγεται (§ 7). Reference is made to this in *Str.* VII. 95 πίστει περιλαβόντες ἀναπόδεικτον τὴν ἀρχήν, § 98 ἡ πίστις οὐσία ἀποδείξεως, § 95 τῇ τοῦ κυρίου φωνῇ πιστούμεθα τὸ ζητούμενον, ἣ πασῶν ἀποδείξεων ἐχεγγυωτέρα, μᾶλλον δὲ ἡ μόνη ἀπόδειξις οὖσα τυγχάνει. See Index *s.v.* ἀρχή and ἀπόδειξις. Definition and division are treated of in VIII. 9—21. We have examples of both in Bk VII. 3 where θεραπεία is defined and divided into species; θεοπρέπεια is defined in the same §, and ἄθεος and δεισιδαίμων in § 4. Specimens of Disjunctive Syllogism are found in § 6: 'either God cares not for man, which might arise from want of will, or want of power, or want of knowledge (but all these are shown to be impossible); or He cares for all, ὅπερ καθήκει τῷ κυρίῳ πάντων γενομένῳ.' In § 17 we have the Stoic definition of ἐπιστήμη, in § 18 the philosophic division of ἀνδρεία. In § 20 rhetorical arguments are said to be too superficial to establish the truth. In §§ 28 foll. we have a sceptical argument probably taken from some Academic source, to show that the supposed necessity of material enshrinement proves the non-existence of the enshrined God. Again in § 37 we have a most unnecessary and unsatisfactory argument to prove that God can hear and see without having a human body. In § 55 we have definitions, very unsatisfactory ones, I allow, of γνῶσις and σοφία, and again of γνῶσις and πίστις in § 57, of σοφία in § 70, of γνῶσις in § 71. It is a fault in Clement, perhaps from an amiable syncretism, or a wish to see his subject from all sides, that he often tries to combine various definitions instead of adhering to one. In § 68 we have a definition of ὁμόνοια, in § 80 the Stoic definition of ὁσιότης. In § 93, speaking of the criteria of truth, he distinguishes between the senses, which are common to all, and the logical criteria, in the use of which we have to be trained. No attention is to be paid to arbitrary assertion: we must submit to the dictates of reason: inconsistency is a sign of error (§§ 94, 95, 97, 100, 103). The heretics refuse to listen to argument, though they do not formally deny the possibility of proof. They refuse to meet us because they are afraid of being confuted, and meanwhile they impose on their fellows by sophisms (§ 91). The heretics profess to find their doctrines in Scripture, but they reject some of the sacred writings, and they lay stress on isolated passages, without regard to the context or the natural sense of words; whereas the true way to get at the meaning of Scripture, and so to learn what is the teaching of the Holy Spirit, is to compare one part with another, the Prophets with the Gospel and Epistles; and to consider that no interpretation can be true, which is inconsistent with the character of God, and with the tradition handed down in the Church from the Apostles (§§ 38, 96, 97, 99, 104).

Dr Bigg says (p. 51) that 'the great Platonic maxim' of the Alexandrines, 'that nothing is to be believed which is unworthy of God,' 'makes reason a judge of revelation.' It is balanced, as we have seen, by another maxim, viz. the respect due to Church or Apostolic tradition. But it is of great importance in reference to the employment of the system of allegorical interpretation. Marcion and others had laid stress on the fact of the difference between the idea of God in the O.T. and in the N.T., and explained this by the supposition of an inferior and superior Deity. Clement, following the example of Philo, adopted the Stoic method of explaining away the immoralities of the Greek mythology by the method of allegory; not that this method was peculiar to the Stoics,—it was known to the Greeks in the time of Plato[1] and to the Jews long before Philo[2]—but it was brought to perfection by the Stoics.

Clement again was not the first Christian to apply this method to the O.T.: it had been used by St Paul, by the writer of the Epistle of Barnabas and by Irenaeus. It was thus a recognized principle of interpretation, and Clement makes use of it partly as a cover under which to introduce ideas which might be otherwise suspected. Examples from the Seventh Book of the Miscellanies will be found *s.v.* 'Allegory' in the English Index, one of them taken from the New Testament.

We will now consider some typical examples of cases in which Clement seems to me (1) to have been right in borrowing from philosophy, (2) to have been wrong in borrowing, (3) to have been wrong in refusing to borrow, (4) to have been both right and wrong in the use he has made of philosophy. I leave it to my readers to apply these categories for themselves in the instances which follow. Take first the conception of God. The Stoics believed in the *immanence* of a material Deity: the Platonists in the *transcendence* of the Idea of Good. Philo carried the Platonic view to a higher abstraction. The mind of the universe is κρείττων ἡ ἀρετὴ καὶ κρείττων ἡ ἐπιστήμη καὶ κρεῖττον ἢ αὐτὸ τὸ ἀγαθὸν καὶ αὐτὸ τὸ καλόν[3]. Clement even goes further. By the method of elimination (ἀνάλυσις) he strips from concrete existence all physical attributes, and then, by removing the three dimensions of space, arrives at the conception of a point having position. Remove position and you have the pure Monad[4]. But even this is not enough: in *Paed.* I. P. 140 we read ἓν δὲ ὁ θεὸς καὶ ἐπέκεινα τοῦ ἑνὸς καὶ ὑπὲρ αὐτὴν μονάδα. Similarly in *Str.* V. 81 πῶς γὰρ ἂν εἴη ῥητὸν ὃ μήτε γένος ἐστὶ μήτε διαφορὰ

---

[1] *Phaedr.* 229.
[2] See Funk's *Jewish Encyclopaedia* under 'Allegory.'
[3] *De Opif.* 2M, quoted by De Faye, p. 218.
[4] Cf. *Str.* v. 71 quoted by De Faye and Bigg, p. 63.

μήτε εἶδος μήτε ἄτομον μήτε ἀριθμός, ἀλλὰ μήτε συμβεβηκός τι μήτε ᾧ συμβέβηκέν τι...κἂν ὀνομάζωμεν αὐτό ποτε οὐ κυρίως, καλοῦντες ἤτοι ἓν ἢ τἀγαθὸν ἢ νοῦν ἢ αὐτὸ τὸ ὂν ἢ πατέρα ἢ θεὸν ἢ δημιουργὸν ἢ κύριον, οὐχ ὡς ὄνομα αὐτοῦ προφερόμενοι λέγομεν, ὑπὸ δὲ ἀπορίας ὀνόμασι καλοῖς προσχρώμεθα. Is there any real distinction between this deification of zero, and a speculative atheism? In point of fact, however, it is with Clement only an exaggerated way of saying that man can know nothing of God except through God's revelation of Himself in the Word, as he himself confesses (*Str.* v. 82) λείπεται δὴ θείᾳ χάριτι καὶ μόνῳ τῷ παρ' αὐτοῦ λόγῳ τὸ ἄγνωστον νοεῖν. Nor does it appear that this abstract speculation had any influence on Clement's positive view of the Divine Nature, except in one respect which I shall presently notice. God is the First Cause (*Str.* VII. 2), Omnipotent (*ib.* §§ 5, 12), Omniscient (§ 36), Omnipresent (§§ 35, 51), Creator and Governor of the world (§§ 69, 20), the Lover of all that He has made (§ 69), the Cause of eternal Salvation (§ 48), the Guardian of our faith and love (§ 56), the Benefactor of all, not of necessity, but of His own free-will (§ 42), His goodness is shown in His justice (§ 73, *Paed.* I. 88 ἀγαθὸς μὲν ὁ θεὸς δι' ἑαυτόν, δίκαιος δὲ ἤδη δι' ἡμᾶς, καὶ τοῦτο ὅτι ἀγαθός). The one point in which Clement was led astray by his theological abstractions, is his condemnation of the Stoic doctrine of the identity of divine and human virtue (§ 88), following, in this, Aristotle and the later Academy. It would seem that such a negation must have led straight to the denial of the Incarnation; but here too his theory is not allowed to influence his practical belief. 'Man may be assimilated to God by knowing God, by the indwelling of the Word, by knowledge, by piety, by justice, by purity, by placability, by exemption from passion[1].' Compare also *Protr.* I. 8 ὁ λόγος τοῦ θεοῦ ἄνθρωπος γενόμενος, ἵνα δὴ καὶ σὺ παρὰ ἀνθρώπου μάθῃς πῇ ποτε ἄρα ἄνθρωπος γένηται θεός.

My next example shall be the nature and use of punishment. Here Clement's view is mainly based on Plato. The object of punishment (κόλασις) is the reformation of the offender; pain inflicted with a different object is vengeance (τιμωρία). God κολάζει, for ἡ κόλασις is ἐπ' ἀγαθῷ καὶ ἐπ'

[1] See references in Kaye, p. 136.

ὠφελείᾳ τοῦ κολαζομένου: but he does not take vengeance, for τιμωρία is ἀνταπόδοσις κακοῦ ἐπὶ τὸ τιμωροῦντος συμφέρον ἀναπεμπομένη (*Paed.* I. 140, cf. *Str.* VII. 102). It is a means of education employed in the case of those who will not yield to gentler influences (*Str.* VII. 6, 7). It is not confined to this life, see § 12, 'Those who are more hardened are constrained to repent by necessary chastisements, inflicted through various preliminary judgments or through the final judgment by the goodness of the great Judge'; § 78 'The gnostic pities those who undergo discipline after death and are brought to repentance against their will by means of punishment'; *Str.* IV. 37 *fin.* 'There are two forms of repentance, the more common the fear which follows wrong-doing, the rarer the inward shame arising from conscience, whether it be in this world or another, since no region is without God's goodness.' In one passage Clement, like Plato, speaks of the ἀνίατοι, *Str.* I. 171 *fin.* ὅταν δέ τινα οὕτως ἔχοντα κατίδῃ ὡς ἀνίατον δοκεῖν, εἰς ἔσχατον ἀδικίας ἐλαύνοντα, τότε ἤδη τῶν ἄλλων κηδόμενος...ὥσπερ μέρος τι τοῦ παντὸς σώματος ἀποτεμών, οὕτω που τὸν τοιοῦτον ὑγιέστατα ἀποκτίννυσι, and again in § 173 τελεώτατον ἀγαθὸν ὅταν τινὰ ἐκ τοῦ κακῶς πράττειν εἰς ἀρετήν...μετάγειν δύνηταί τις, ὅπερ ὁ νόμος ἐργάζεται. ὥστε καὶ ὅταν ἀνηκέστῳ τινὶ κακῷ περιπέσῃ τις, ὑπό τε ἀδικίας καὶ πλεονεξίας καταληφθείς, εὐεργετοῖτ' ἂν ὁ ἀποκτιννύμενος· εὐεργέτης γὰρ ὁ νόμος τοὺς μὲν δικαίους ἐξ ἀδίκων ποιεῖν δυνάμενος, ἢν μόνον ἐπαΐειν ἐθελήσωσιν αὐτοῦ, τοὺς δὲ ἀπαλλάττων τῶν παρόντων κακῶν. Here annihilation seems to be regarded as the destiny of the ἀνίατοι, but in *Ecl. Proph.* § 26 he interprets the words πῦρ ἦλθον βαλεῖν ἐπὶ τὴν γῆν as implying δύναμιν τῶν μὲν ἁγίων καθαρτικήν, τῶν δὲ ὑλικῶν, ὡς μὲν ἐκεῖνοί φασιν, ἀφανιστικήν, ὡς δὲ ἡμεῖς ἂν φαίημεν, παιδευτικήν, see my note on *Str.* VII. § 34 *fin.* τὸ νοερὸν πῦρ.

I do not remember that Clement ever attempts to deal with the passages of Scripture which seem to imply endless punishment. And the only ones of an opposite tendency which he quotes seem to be 1 Pet. iii. 19 'the spirits in prison' (*Str.* VI. 44), Job xxviii. 22 (*ib.*), Isa. iv. 4 'when the Lord shall have purged the blood of Jerusalem by the spirit of judgment and the spirit of burning' (*Paed.* III. 48), 1 Cor. iii. 10 (*Str.* V. 26),

Ezek. xvi. 53 (on the restoration of Sodom), apparently alluded to in *Adumbr.* P. 1008. He twice refers to a remarkable passage in Hermas (*Sim.* 9. 16) founded on 1 Pet. iii. 19 f. See *Str.* II. 43 f. 'The Shepherd, speaking plainly of those who had fallen asleep...says that the Apostles and teachers, who had preached the name of the Son of God and fallen asleep, preached to those who had fallen asleep before them, and bestowed upon them the seal of their preaching. Accordingly they descended with them into the water and again ascended. They descended alive and ascended alive. But the others descended dead, but ascended alive': also *Str.* VI. 44 *fin.* 'Wherefore the Lord preached the Gospel to those in Hades, according to what is written "Hades says to Destruction, we have heard his voice"...The Lord preached the Gospel to those who perished in the Flood, or rather to those who were fettered and kept in watch and ward...we have also read that the Apostles did the same: ἐχρῆν γάρ, οἶμαι, ὥσπερ κἀνταῦθα, οὕτως δὲ κἀκεῖσε τοὺς ἀρίστους τῶν μαθητῶν μιμητὰς γίνεσθαι τοῦ διδασκάλου, in order that they might call to repentance those who had lived in the righteousness of the law and of philosophy, but had ended their life οὐ τελείως ἀλλ' ἁμαρτητικῶς... If then the Lord descended to Hades for no other end but to preach the Gospel, it was either to preach the Gospel to all, or to the Hebrews only. If to all, then all who believe shall be saved, on making their confession even in that other world, ἐπεὶ σωτήριοι καὶ παιδευτικαὶ αἱ κολάσεις τοῦ θεοῦ εἰς ἐπιστροφὴν ἄγουσαι καὶ τὴν μετάνοιαν τοῦ ἁμαρτωλοῦ μᾶλλον ἢ τὸν θάνατον αἱρούμεναι...Thus is shown the goodness of God and the power of the Lord to save with equal justice all that turn to Him, whether here or elsewhere. For the active[1] power of God is not confined to this world, but is at work everywhere and at all times.' In the same strain he continues to the end of § 52.

What is Dr Hatch's attitude in regard to such teaching as this? He professes to object to the hellenizing of Christianity and to speculation about matters of faith; and there can be no doubt that Clement's view of punishment is distinctly hellenistic, and involves much free speculation on a matter which the

---

[1] Perhaps we should read here εὐεργετική for ἐνεργητική.

majority of contemporary Christians would have regarded as beyond the region of debate. And yet when I read such words as the following 'The Spirit of God has not ceased to speak to men: it is important for us to know not only what He told the men of other days, but also what He tells us now' (p. 84), I am at a loss to understand why free thought on religion should be right for us now, and wrong for Clement in the 2nd century. Still more when I read in p. 237 the eloquent panegyric on 'Origen's sublime conception of an infinite stairway of worlds with its perpetual ascent and descent of souls, ending at last in the union of all souls with God' —a conception which differs from Clement's only in one point, viz. that there is no 'descent of souls,' no falling away from God and from blessedness in another world,—I begin to doubt whether Dr Hatch has really made clear to his own mind what it is he dislikes; whether it is not rather the setting the stamp of Church authority on speculation, than the freedom of speculation in itself. I cannot but think that, if the question had been fairly put to him, he would have acknowledged that the great need of our time, as of every age of the Church, is the multiplication of men like Clement, equally gifted on the side of religious thought and on the side of religious emotion, utterly fearless in the pursuit of truth of every kind, because they have an absolute faith in the God of truth and know Him to be the God of love.

I proceed now to the broad distinction made between the 'gnostic' and the ordinary believer, a distinction which Clement held to be founded on St Paul's distinction between the grown men, who have put away childish things and passed out of the rudimentary discipline of ordinances, and the children, who must still be fed with milk (see Lightfoot's n. on Phil. iii. 15). To this we have an allusion in *Str.* VII. 67 παῖδες ἐν πίστει, οὐδέπω ἄνδρες ἐν ἀγάπῃ, καθάπερ ὁ γνωστικός. The distinction was also to be found in philosophy, as in Plato's ideal State, where the Guardians do right on principle and insight, as opposed to the Auxiliaries who do right from habit and training; and, more broadly and offensively, in the Wise Man and the Fool of the Stoics; and the πνευματικός and ψυχικός of the pseudo-Gnostics. Clement's interest in the subject is partly controversial: he is altogether opposed to the Gnostic view that there is a difference of nature and of kind between these two classes. In his view the difference is one of degree; all are alike saved by faith, and by the God-given power of free choice, working through the ability which divine grace supplies. There are different stages in the heaven-ward progress, faith, knowledge, love, all culminating in the κληρονομία (§ 55). The difference between the lower and the higher stages is shown in various ways: he who is merely πιστός is actuated by fear, or hope of reward; the gnostic by the motive of love (§ 67); the perfection of the former consists in abstaining from evil, that of the latter in doing good (§ 79); the former prays at a fixed time and place for seeming good, the latter everywhere and at all times for that which is really good (§§ 35, 38, 40, 43); in the latter virtue has become a second nature (§ 46), in the former it is a struggle against inveterate habit; the latter has trained himself to apathy, the former is still labouring to acquire self-control (§§ 13, 67, 74, 84); the latter is sinless (§§ 14, 80), equal to the angels (§§ 57, 78), is already holy and divine, bearing God within him and being borne of God (§ 82), ἐν σαρκὶ περιπολῶν θεός (§ 101).

There is certainly much room for criticism in this view of the two stages of Christianity. Clement has evidently been too much attracted by the Stoic ideal. We should all agree that he is wrong in regarding apathy as a part of Christian perfection, and speaking of Him who wept over Jerusalem and over the grave of Lazarus as ἀπαθὴς ἀνάρχως γενόμενος[1]. It is extraordinary that he was not struck with the contradiction between such a view and the exalted place he has himself assigned to love,—between love which is life, sensitiveness carried to its highest point, and apathy which is death. The

[1] See § 7, and *Str.* vi. 71 where it is even denied that Christ suffered hunger or thirst, or was accessible to any movement whether of pleasure or pain. So the Apostles after the Resurrection were not liable to emotion of any sort, not even to zeal or joy or desire [and yet Clement had read the 2nd epistle to the Corinthians]. Shortly afterwards he endeavours to show that love is not a πάθος (§ 73): πῶς ἀπαθὴς μένει, φησίν, ὁ τῶν καλῶν ὀρεγόμενος; ἀλλ' οὐκ ἴσασιν, ὡς ἔοικεν, οὗτοι τὸ θεῖον τῆς ἀγάπης· οὐ γάρ ἐστιν ἔτι ὄρεξις τοῦ ἀγαπῶντος ἡ ἀγάπη, στερκτικὴ δὲ οἰκείωσις εἰς τὴν ἑνότητα τῆς πίστεως ἀποκαθεστηκυῖα τὸν γνωστικόν, χρόνου καὶ τόπου μὴ προσδεόμενον.

hyperbolical language used to express man's participation in the divine nature (2 Pet. i. 4) is supported by quotations from Scripture, Ps. lxxxii. 6, Joh. x. 35 (*Paed.* I. 26, *Str.* II. 125), and from Greek philosophers (see the note below on § 3 ἐσομένῳ θεῷ): it was also facilitated by the very free use of the word θεός at that time[1]; but, joined with other terms employed to express the superiority of the gnostic, it certainly leaves an impression very unlike that which we should gather from the Gospel. Compare our Lord's words in Luke xvii. 10 'we are unprofitable servants' with the language of the Olympian victor which Clement holds up for the imitation of the gnostic, ἀπόδος φέρων δικαίως τὴν νίκην ἐμοί (*Str.* VII. 48); and the words put in the mouth of the 'gnostic souls' in § 72, ἀκολούθως οἷς ἐνετείλω ἐζήσαμεν μηδὲν τῶν παρηγγελμένων παραβεβηκυῖαι· διὸ καὶ τὰς ὑποσχέσεις ἀπαιτοῦμεν; or compare § 6 'it is not the way of the Lord to compel τὸν ἐξ αὐτοῦ τὴν σωτηρίαν λαβεῖν διὰ τοῦ ἑλέσθαι καὶ πάντα ὑποπληρῶσαι τὰ παρ' αὐτοῦ πρὸς τὸ λαβέσθαι τῆς ἐλπίδος δυνάμενον, also §§ 48 and 81, with Joh. xv. on the Vine and the branches. I think also that on coming to this book of the *Stromateis* from, say, the Epistle to the Romans, we are struck with the comparatively small part assigned by Clement to the sense of sin, the need of Grace and the virtue of humility. We must not indeed forget what is the object of this particular book. It is not a missionary address, or a book of confessions, or a penitential hymn. And again it is not the writing of a Paul or an Augustine, whose consciences could never forget the contrast between their past and their present. Its object is to present the gnostic Christian in the most favourable aspect to Greek philosophers.

Nor again is the other side entirely neglected by Clement. In *Paed.* I. 4, III. 93, *Str.* IV. 130 we read that Christ alone of men is without sin, in *Str.* VII. 88 that no human perfection is for a moment to be compared to the perfection of God: in *Str.* II. 74 Clement protests against the heretical notion that man is a portion of God, 'I know not how one who knows God can bear to hear this, when he looks to our life, and sees in what evils we are involved.' 'No, God in consequence of His

[1] On this see Harn. *Hist. of D.* I. p. 119, Inge *App. C on Mysticism.*

own goodness cares for us, who are by nature wholly estranged.' In *Str.* VII. 87 we read 'Ye were justified by the name of the Lord, ye were made by Him to be just as He is just, and ye were joined in closest union with the Holy Spirit': in § 76 he speaks of the Resurrection power of the Lord exhibited in the gnostic; in § 9, of the blessed hierarchy linked together by the magnetic attraction of the Spirit, in which all the members are saved by and through the One great High Priest; in § 35 'the gnostic, being always in the uninterrupted presence of God, is raised above himself in action, word and temper'; § 12 'God made all things to be helpful for virtue, in so far as might be without interfering with the freedom of man's choice, in order that He who is indeed the One alone Almighty might, even to those who can only see darkly, be revealed as a good God, a Saviour from age to age (ἐξ αἰῶνος εἰς αἰῶνα) through the instrumentality of His Son.' On humility we may compare what is said of the gnostic in § 75 συστελλόμενος ἐφ' οἷς ἐπεγκυλίεται τῇ τοῦ βίου ἀνάγκῃ, μηδέπω καταξιούμενος τῆς ὧν ἔγνω ἐνεργούσης μεταλήψεως.

Dr Hatch has much to say on the introduction of the double standard into the Christian Church (p. 162 foll.). After dwelling on the ideal purity of the earlier Christian communities, he speaks of the 'enormous change' which passed over them in the latter half of the second and the earlier half of the third century mainly owing to theory superseding practice, doctrine being exalted above morality. The lowering of the general tone led to an outward and an inward secession. The Puritans, *i.e.* the Montanists, 'endeavoured to live on a higher plane than their fellows,' and followed 'such counsels of perfection as abstinence from marriage and from animal food.' This was known by the name of ἄσκησις. After the banishing of the Montanists, the same tendency showed itself in the Monks within the Church. The consequence was that less and less strictness was expected of the ordinary layman.

I will not stop to inquire how far this description is in accordance with facts. My object is to consider how far it can be truly alleged that Clement's teaching tended to produce such a result. It certainly cannot be said that he lowers the standard for laymen. He expects ἄσκησις of all: he vindicates for all, man, woman, child, slave, the right to philosophize (*Str.* IV. 58 f.). He does not insist on abstaining from animal food, though he allows that it may sometimes be useful (*Paed.* II. 10 f., *Str.* VII. 32); on the other hand he defends marriage as superior to celibacy (§ 70). He insists continually on the duty of the gnostic towards other men (§§ 3, 4, 16, 18, 19, 21 &c.); lays small stress on the distinction between clergy and laity; thus in *Str.* VI. 106, after speaking of the appointment of Matthias in place of Judas, he says that even now those who have exercised themselves in the Lord's commandments and lived perfectly according to the Gospel may be enrolled εἰς τὴν ἐκλογὴν τῶν ἀποστόλων· οὗτος πρεσβύτερός ἐστι τῷ ὄντι τῆς ἐκκλησίας καὶ διάκονος ἀληθὴς τῆς τοῦ θεοῦ βουλήσεως, ἐὰν ποιῇ καὶ διδάσκῃ τὰ τοῦ κυρίου, οὐχ ὑπ' ἀνθρώπων χειροτονούμενος οὐδ', ὅτι πρεσβύτερος, δίκαιος νομιζόμενος, ἀλλ', ὅτι δίκαιος, ἐν πρεσβυτερίῳ καταλεγόμενος, κἂν ἐνταῦθα ἐπὶ γῆς πρωτοκαθεδρίᾳ μὴ τιμηθῇ κ.τ.λ., cf. *Str.* VII. 77. Again, there is no broad line of demarcation between the gnostic and the man of faith. All 'must start with faith and, having waxed strong in it by the grace of God, must thus attain to insight concerning Him, as far as is possible' (VII. 55). The gnostic desires that his brother's sins may be imputed to him (VII. 80). Clement classes himself amongst those for whom the gnostic prays 'that we may be comforted about our sins and converted to knowledge' (§ 79). In all his good actions the gnostic shuns ostentation (§§ 77, 81).

Lastly, is it true that Clement lays more stress on orthodox doctrine than on a good life? Those who called themselves ὀρθοδοξασταί were the men who repudiated all aid from reason and professed to follow faith alone. Clement held it to be his bounden duty to seek for truth in every way. Faith was worthless if it were faith only in the sound of words, without understanding their meaning: ἐμοὶ πρόκειται βιοῦν μὲν κατὰ τὸν λόγον καὶ νοεῖν τὰ σημαινόμενα...σωθῆναι γὰρ εὖ οἶδ' ὅτι καὶ συνάρασθαι τοῖς σώζεσθαι γλιχομένοις βέλτιστόν ἐστιν (*Str.* I. 43—48). So far from his pressing the claims of doctrine apart from practice, I think it may be safely asserted that he never lays stress on doctrine except with a practical aim in view. His ideal Christian is characterized at least as much by prayer[1] and love as by knowledge and thought. To know what is right, to do what is right, and to help others to do the same, are the ἀποτελέσματα of the gnostic[2]. It may perhaps be objected that these characteristics are not always to be found together; that there may be much love where there is not much knowledge, and *vice versa*; but at any rate the fact that they are joined together by him as components of the Christian ideal is sufficient to show how little he is liable to the charge of turning Christianity into an abstract system of doctrine[3].

I will end with a list of philosophical terms used by Clement in *Strom.* VII.[4]

ἀγροικία, Arist., see n. on p. 116. 20.
ἀγωγός, Plato, p. 18. 5.
ἀθλητής, Stoic, p. 22. 10, 116. 12, cf. for the same metaphor ἀλείφω p. 116. 11, παγκράτιον p. 32. 15.
αἱρεῖ ὁ λόγος, Platonic, see Index *s.v.*
αἰσθητά)(νοητά, Plato, p. 4. 15.
ἀκολουθίαν σώζειν, perhaps Peripatetic; the phrase occurs in Alex. Aphrod. quoted under σώζω in Stephanus, p. 104. 2.
κατὰ τὸ ἀκόλουθον)(κατὰ τὸ προηγούμενον and similar phrases, Stoic, p. 152. 25, and n. p. 122. 6.
ἀλλότρια)(οἰκεῖα, so τὰ ἐκτός)(τὰ ἴδια and τὰ ἐφ' ἡμῖν, Stoic, p. 106. 29, p. 136. 1.
ἄλογον μέρος ψυχῆς, Platonic, p. 54. 27.
ἀμετάπτωτος, Arist., see below, Index of Greek words *s.v.*
ἀναθυμίασις, Arist., p. 24. 4.
ἀνάκρασις, Stoic, p. 138. 7.
ἀνεπιστρεψία, Epict., p. 34. 19.
ἀνορέκτως, Arist., p. 52. 15.

[1] All his life is a festival of prayer and praise, an uninterrupted converse with God. See *s.v.* 'Prayer' in the Index.
[2] See *Str.* II. 46, VII. 4.
[3] I may notice here an expression used by Dr Hatch (p. 165) where he says that the tendency to asceticism was increased by 'the strain and despair of an age of decadence.' This is true enough of the pagans, but not, I think, of any large body of Christians during the first four centuries. Of Clement it is the very opposite of truth. He makes joy (χαρά) the mark of the Church and gladness (εὐφροσύνη) of the gnostic (*Str.* VII. 101). Harnack describes him as a bold and joyous thinker (vol. II. 328), Bigg (p. 72) says 'No later writer has so serene and hopeful a view of human nature,' 'His idea of the Saviour is larger and nobler than that of any other doctor of the Church.'
[4] One of the greatest desiderata for the study of Patristic Literature is a complete glossary of post-Aristotelian philosophy to the death of Proclus.

ἀπάθεια and ἀπαθής, Stoic, see Index s.v. Apathy, and cf. ἀπροσπαθής and ἐμπαθής.
ἀπερίσπαστος, περισπάω, Stoic, see Index s.v.
ἀπόδειξις, cf. ἀρχὴ ἀναπόδεικτος, Arist., see Index.
ἀποκατάστασις, Stoic, p. 98. 17.
ἀπροσπαθής, προσπαθής, Stoic, p. 110. 7.
ἄσκησις, συνάσκησις, Plato, see Gr. Index and 'Virtue' in Eng. Index.
γνῶθι σεαυτόν, p. 32. 27.
διάθεσις)(ἕξις, Arist., p. 112. 11.
διακριτικὴ νόησις, Plato, p. 64. 16, see *Addenda*.
διαλεκτικός, Arist., p. 178. 8.
διήκω, Stoic, p. 28. 4.
διοίκησις, Stoic, p. 14. 28.
ἐγκρατής, ἐγκρατεύομαι, ἀκρατής, Arist., see Gr. Index and 'Virtue' in Eng. Index.
ἐγκύκλιος παιδεία, Arist., Philo, p. 32. 2.
ἐγχειρέω, ἐπιχείρημα, παρεγχείρησις, Arist., Philo, see Index.
εἰκών, ἐξομοιόω, ἐξομοίωσις, Plato, see Index.
ἐμπαθής)(ἀπαθής, Stoic, see Index.
ἐναποκείμενος, Plato, p. 72. 10.
ἔναυλος, Plato, p. 128. 30.
ἐνδιάθετος)(προφορικός, Stoic, p. 68. 21.
ἐνέργεια)(ἕξις, Arist., p. 114. 2.
ἔνστασις, Stoic, p. 102. 23.
ἐξομοιόω, see εἰκών.
κατ' ἐπακολούθημα, Stoic, p. 122. 6, see above on ἀκόλουθος.
τὸ ἐπέκεινα αἴτιον, Plato, p. 4. 19.
ἐπιγεννηματικός, Stoic, p. 84. 7.
ἐπίστασις, Arist., p. 98. 7.
ἐπιτυγχάνω)(περιπίπτω, Stoic, cf. Epict. *Ench.* 2 ὀρέξεως ἐπαγγελία ἐπιτυχία οὗ ὀρέγῃ, ἐκκλίσεως ἐπαγγελία τὸ μὴ περιπεσεῖν ἐκείνῳ ὃ ἐκκλίνεται, see Index.
ἐραστής (ἀληθείας), ἐραστός, Plato, p. 18. 5.
ἐριστικός, Arist., p. 178. 7.
εὐάρεστος, εὐαρεστέω, εὐαρέστησις, Stoic, p. 34. 2 and Index.
εὐεμπτωσία, Stoic, p. 180. 18.
εὐλογιστία, Stoic, p. 82. 3.
εὐπαθής, Stoic, p. 64. 20.
εὐτονία, τόνος, ἀτονία, Stoic, p. 80. 23, 166. 6.
ζώπυρον, Plato, p. 194. 9.
ἠθικὸς τύπος, ὁ, Arist., p. 194. 7.
θαρραλέα, τά, Plato, p. 112. 7.
θαυμάζω, see Plato and Arist. in n. on p. 104. 6.
θεσμός, a Stoic name for God, p. 26. 16.
θεωρία, Plato, p. 18. 7.
θυμοειδής, Plato, p. 102. 14.

καθῆκον, τό, Stoic, p. 90. 5.
κατάληψις, καταληπτικός, καταληπτός, Stoic, see Index.
κατορθόω, κατόρθωμα, κατόρθωσις, κατορθωτικός, Stoic, see Index.
κόλασις)(τιμωρία, Plato, Arist., see Index, and n. on p. 180. 14.
κριτήριον, Stoic, p. 162. 29.
μέσα, τά = ἀδιάφορα, Stoic, p. 28. 11.
μετουσίᾳ θερμότητος θερμόν, Plato's μέθεξις, p. 138. 9.
μονάς, Pythag., p. 190. 9.
οἰακίζω, Heracl., p. 8. 21.
οἴησις, Stoic, p. 164. 4.
ὁμόνοια ἡ, ἡ περὶ ταὐτὸ συγκατάθεσίς ἐστι, Stoic, p. 118. 8.
παράστασις, παραστατικός, Stoic (?), p. 88. 20, 22.
περιέχω, Stoic, p. 28. 4.
περίστασις, περιστατικός, Stoic, p. 28. 16, and Index.
περιτροπαί, Stoic, p. 16. 30.
περιωπή, Plato, p. 8. 24.
πνεῦμα, Stoic, p. 16. 12.
προαίρεσις, προαιρετικῶς, Arist., see Index.
προηγούμενος, -νως, Stoic, p. 152. 26, 122. 18.
προκοπή, προκόπτω, Stoic, p. 16. 28 and Index.
πρόνοια, esp. Stoic, see Index.
προσβολή, Plato, p. 76. 27.
πρωτουργός, Plato, p. 14. 21.
πτερόω, Plato, p. 68. 28.
πῦρ νοερόν or φρόνιμον)(π. παμφάγον, Stoic, p. 60. 11.
σπερματικῶς, Stoic, p. 146. 15.
συγκατάθεσις, Stoic, see p. 28. 1 and Index.
συμπεριφέρομαι, -φορά, Stoic, see Index.
ὕλη κακῶν αἰτία, Plato, p. 26. 2.
ὑπομονητικός, ὑπομενετέος, Arist., p. 140. 7, 112. 20.
φαντασία πρόχειρος, καταληπτική, Stoic, p. 176. 7, 160. 8.
φίλαυτος, φιλαυτία, Arist., Index.
φιλοθεάμων, Plato, Index.
ψοφοδεής, Plato, Index.

CHAPTER III.

CLEMENT AND THE MYSTERIES[1].

NEXT to philosophy the most powerful spiritual influence in the Hellenic world of the second century was that exercised by the Mysteries; the former appealing to the reason and judgment, the latter to feeling and imagination. As long ago as the time of Pindar, the Eleusinian Mysteries were famed as ennobling men's ideas of life and of death[2]. In the great revival of religious feeling which took place about the time of the Christian era, partly owing to the loss of national independence, and the consequent decay of higher secular interests; partly to the recognition that philosophy, while it awoke the sense of individual responsibility, had yet failed to explain the deeper riddles of life; men turned more and more

---

[1] On the subject of this chapter see Purser's articles on 'Eleusinia,' 'Mysteria,' 'Orphica' in the new edition of Smith's *D. of Ant.*; Ramsay on 'Mysteries' in *Enc. Brit.*; Lenormant in *Cont. Rev.* for May, July, Sept. 1880; Döllinger *Gentile and Jew*, vol. I. Book III.; Hatch *Influence of Greek Ideas*, 1890, pp. 283—309; Gardner *Exploratio Evangelica*, 1899, pp. 325—345, 456 f.; Inge *Christian Mysticism*, App. B, 1899; Anrich *Das antike Mysterienwesen in seinem Einfluss auf das Christenthum*, 1894; Wobbermin *Beeinflussung des Urchristenthums durch das antike Mysterienwesen*, 1896.

[2] Clement (*Str.* III. 518) quotes Pindar speaking of these mysteries ὄλβιος ὅστις ἰδὼν κεῖν' εἶσ' ὑπὸ χθόν'· οἶδε μὲν βίου τελευτάν οἶδεν δὲ διόσδοτον ἀρχάν; cf. the Homeric Hymn to Demeter 476—482, and Cicero (*Legg.* II. 36). Plato gives an uncertain sound: on the one hand, in the *Phaedo*, p. 69 c, we read κινδυνεύουσιν οἱ τὰς τελετὰς ἡμῖν καταστήσαντες οὐ φαῦλοί τινες εἶναι, ἀλλὰ τῷ ὄντι πάλαι αἰνίττεσθαι ὅτι ὃς ἂν ἀμύητος καὶ ἀτέλεστος εἰς Ἅιδου ἀφίκηται ἐν βορβόρῳ κείσεται, ὁ δὲ κεκαθαρμένος τε καὶ τετελεσμένος ἐκεῖσε ἀφικόμενος μετὰ θεῶν οἰκήσει: on the other hand he speaks (*Rep.* II. 364 *fin.* and 366) of the evil effect of the Orphic teaching in persuading men that the wrath of heaven against sin may be averted by καθαρμοί and τελεταί of the λύσιοι θεοί.

to those mystic rites which professed to provide healing and rest for the sick and weary soul, to enable it to enter into communion with God and look forward with hope to a blissful immortality[1]. The influence of the Mysteries is reflected in Christian writers from opposite points of view. In the first place there is an attempt to lessen the prestige of the Pagan mysteries by calling attention to the frivolities and obscenities connected with them (Clement *Protr.* 12—24). In the next place there is an attempt to show that the Christians also have their own far worthier mysteries, secret rites and secret doctrines, which were imparted only to the initiated. I shall presently point out the allusions to the latter effect which may be found in Clement: but before doing so it may be well to give a very brief account of the nature and character of the Eleusinian Mysteries so far as may serve to explain the allusions which follow, and then to illustrate from earlier writers, Pagan as well as Jewish and Christian, the use of figurative language borrowed from the Mysteries.

The disappearance and seeming death of the seed in the ground and its springing up into the living plant, with its suggestion of man's resurrection from the dead, are symbolized in the story of Demeter and Persephone, who were honoured in Attica by the Lesser Mysteries held in spring

---

[1] Ramsay in the *Encycl. Brit.* speaks of the Mysteries as 'an attempt of the Hellenic genius to take into its service the spirit of Oriental religion.' Wobbermin distinguishes the following elements in the influence of the Mysteries (1) the *soteriological motive* ('moment'), which he finds in the epithet σωτήρ frequently appended to Chthonian deities, compare Clem. *Protr.* II. 26 τὸν γὰρ εὐεργετοῦντα μὴ συνιέντες θεὸν ἀνέπλασάν τινας σωτῆρας Διοσκούρους καί...᾿Ασκλήπιον ἰατρόν, Plut. *Mor.* 1119 ε τὰς συνεζευγμένας τοῖς θεοῖς προσηγορίας ἀποσπῶντες, συναναιρεῖτε θυσίας, μυστήρια, πομπάς, ἑορτάς. τίνι γάρ...σωτήρια θύσομεν...μὴ ἀπολιπόντες σωτῆρας; (2) the *henotheistic motive*, or religious syncretism, by which separate deities were confounded together as being different names for the same Being; (3) the *dualistic motive*, combining terror and love in such names as Erinyes—Eumenides, Ἅιδης—Εὐβουλεύς; (4) the *ethical motive*, shown in the demand for purity of heart and life, in purification and asceticism; (5) the *eschatological motive* shown in the constant reference to the rewards and punishments of another life. Inge gives a more useful analysis in p. 354, where he specifies as the main features of the Mysteries which passed into Catholicism 'the notions of secrecy, of symbolism, of mystical brotherhood, of sacramental grace, and, above all, of the three stages in the spiritual life, ascetic purification, illumination, and ἐποπτεία as the crown.'

on the banks of the Ilissus, and by the Greater Mysteries held in autumn at Eleusis. The former were a necessary preliminary to the latter[1]. Two years at least were as a rule required before the μύστης of the former could become an ἐπόπτης of the latter, thus completing his initiation into the Greater Mysteries. The first step to be taken by a candidate for admission to the latter was to apply to one who was already ἐπόπτης, and satisfy him that he was ἁγνὸς ἀπὸ παντὸς μύσους, and then to receive instruction from him as to the necessary purifications. If the instructor (μυσταγωγός) was in doubt on any point, he might appeal to the ἐξηγητής, who was a special adviser on questions of casuistry. The candidate had then to abstain from certain viands, especially fish, for nine days, during which occurred the immersion in the sea, following the proclamation ἅλαδε μύσται, and the great torch-bearing procession in which the image of Iacchus was carried along the Sacred Way from Athens to Eleusis[2]. At Eleusis there followed two παννυχίδες in which the initiated represented Demeter seeking for her daughter. After this they partook of the κυκεών, the Eleusinian sacrament of mint, meal and water, and were finally admitted by the δᾳδοῦχος from the outer darkness into the brilliantly lighted temple, where the holy drama was enacted before their eyes, and the sacred relics were exhibited by the ἱεροφάντης. Death was the punishment for divulging the mysteries[3].

[1] Plato *Gorg.* 497 c, εὐδαίμων εἶ, ὦ Καλλίκλεις, ὅτι τὰ μεγάλα μεμύησαι πρὶν τὰ σμικρά· ἐγὼ δ' οὐκ ᾤμην θεμιτὸν εἶναι.

[2] The worship of Iacchus is said to have been joined to that of the goddesses by Epimenides at the end of the seventh century B.C.

[3] The quotations which follow will illustrate some of the above statements: Hor. *C.* III. 2. 26 vetabo qui Cereris sacrum volgarit arcanae sub isdem sit trabibus, Strabo X. 717 ἡ κρύψις ἡ μυστικὴ τῶν ἱερῶν σεμνοποιεῖ τὸ θεῖον, μιμουμένη τὴν φύσιν αὐτοῦ ἐκφεύγουσαν τὴν αἴσθησιν, Synesius *Dion* 47 *fin.* Ἀριστοτέλης ἀξιοῖ τοὺς τελουμένους οὐ μαθεῖν τι δεῖν, ἀλλὰ παθεῖν καὶ διατεθῆναι, γινομένους δηλονότι ἐπιτηδείους, Arist. *Ranae* 143 foll. μετὰ τοῦτ' ὄφεις καὶ θηρί' ὄψει μυρία...εἶτα βόρβορον πολύν...ἐν δὲ τούτῳ κειμένους, εἴ που ξένον τις ἠδίκησε πώποτε...ἐντεῦθεν αὐλῶν τίς σε περίεισιν πνοή, ὄψει τε φῶς κάλλιστον...καὶ θιάσους εὐδαίμονας...Οὗτοι δὲ δὴ τίνες εἰσίν; Οἱ μεμυημένοι, *ib.* 326 Ἴακχ', ὦ Ἴακχε ἐλθὲ τόνδ' ἀνὰ λειμῶνα χορεύσων ὁσίους ἐς θιασώτας...ἀγνὰν ὁσίοις μετὰ μύσταισι χορείαν...ἔγειρε φλογέας λαμπάδας ἐν χερσὶ τινάσσων, *ib.* 354 εὐφημεῖν χρὴ κἀξίστασθαι τοῖς ἡμετέροισι χοροῖσιν, ὅστις ἄπειρος τοιῶνδε λόγων ἢ γνώμῃ μὴ καθαρεύει, *ib.* 454 μόνοις γὰρ ἡμῖν ἥλιος καὶ φέγγος ἱλαρόν ἐστιν, ὅσοι μεμυήμεθ' εὐσεβῆ τε διήγομεν τρόπον, Clem. *Str.*

The Mysteries of Eleusis were the most famous, but they did not stand alone. The Phrygian Cybele and Sabazius, the Persian Mithras, the Egyptian Isis and Osiris and Serapis, the Syrian Adonis, the Samothracian Cabeiri, the Cretan Zagreus, all had their mystic thiasus, and their secret rites, which by their common meal and other ceremonials were supposed to establish an intimate communion between the deity and the worshipper. In all the common object was the attainment of σωτηρία in this life and the next.

I proceed now to give examples of the use of figurative language borrowed from the Mysteries. One of the most striking is found in Plato's allegory of pre-natal existence (*Phaedrus* 250): 'Beauty not only shone brightly on our view at the time when in the heavenly choir we followed in the band of Zeus...and were initiated in that which I fear not to pronounce the most blessed of all mysteries, εὐδαίμονα φάσματα μυούμενοι τε καὶ ἐποπτεύοντες ἐν αὐγῇ καθαρᾷ καθαροὶ ὄντες.' Philo I. p. 146 *fin.* (introducing an allegorical interpretation) τελετὰς ἀναδιδάσκομεν θείας τοὺς τελετῶν ἀξίους τῶν ἱερωτάτων μύστας...ἐκείνοις δὲ οὐχ ἱεροφαντήσομεν κατεσχημένοις ἀνιάτῳ κακῷ...ταῦτα, ὦ μύσται κεκαθαρμένοι τὰ ὦτα, ὡς ἱερὰ ὄντως μυστήρια ψυχαῖς ταῖς ἑαυτῶν παραδέχεσθε καὶ μηδενὶ τῶν ἀμυήτων ἐκλαλήσατε, II. p. 447 ὥσπερ ἐν ταῖς τελεταῖς ἱεροφαντηθέντες, ὅταν ὀργίων γεμισθῶσιν, πολλὰ τῆς πρόσθεν ὀλιγωρίας ἑαυτοὺς κακίζουσιν ὡς...βίον τρίψαντες ἀβίωτον ἐν ᾧ φρονήσεως ἐχήρευσαν. Elsewhere Philo strongly condemns the mysteries as betokening a jealous and exclusive spirit (II. 260). Epictetus III. 21. 13 foll. contrasts the teaching of a glib reporter of philosophical phrases with that of a true philosopher in the following terms: τί ἄλλο ποιεῖς ἢ τὰ μυστήρια ἐξορχῇ καὶ λέγεις 'οἴκημά ἐστι καὶ ἐν Ἐλευσῖνι, ἰδοὺ καὶ ἐνθάδε. ἐκεῖ ἱεροφάντης· καὶ ἐγὼ ποιήσω ἱεροφάντην.

---

v. 689 init. οὐκ ἀπεικότως καὶ τῶν μυστηρίων τῶν παρ' Ἕλλησιν ἄρχει μὲν τὰ καθάρσια, καθάπερ καὶ ἐν τοῖς βαρβάροις τὸ λουτρόν· μετὰ ταῦτα δὲ ἐστὶ τὰ μικρὰ μυστήρια διδασκαλίας ὑπόθεσιν ἔχοντα καὶ προπαρασκευῆς τῶν μελλόντων· τὰ δὲ μεγάλα περὶ τῶν συμπάντων οὐ μανθάνειν ἔτι ὑπολείπεται, ἐποπτεύειν δὲ καὶ περινοεῖν τήν τε φύσιν καὶ τὰ πράγματα, Protr. 12 Δηὼ καὶ Κόρη δρᾶμα ἐγενέσθην μυστικόν, καὶ τὴν πλάνην καὶ τὴν ἁρπαγὴν καὶ τὸ πένθος αὐταῖν Ἐλευσὶς δᾳδουχεῖ, Str. VII. 27 πρὸ τῆς τῶν μυστηρίων παραδόσεως καθαρμούς τινας προσάγειν τοῖς μυεῖσθαι μέλλουσιν ἀξιοῦσιν, ib. 88 οὐκ ἐκκυκλεῖν δεῖ τὸ μυστήριον.

ἐκεῖ κῆρυξ· κἀγὼ κήρυκα καταστήσω. ἐκεῖ δᾳδοῦχος· κἀγὼ δᾳδοῦχον. ἐκεῖ δᾷδες· καὶ ἐνθάδε᾽...ἄλλον τρόπον δεῖ ἐπὶ ταῦτα ἐλθεῖν· μέγα ἐστὶ τὸ πρᾶγμα, μυστικόν ἐστιν, οὐχ ὡς ἔτυχεν, οὐδὲ τῷ τυχόντι δεδομένον.

We find references to the Mysteries in the LXX, *e.g.* Dan. ii. 29 ὁ ἀποκαλύπτων μυστήρια ἐγνώρισέ σοι ἃ δεῖ γενέσθαι, Wisdom xiv. 23 ἢ γὰρ τεκνοφόνους τελετὰς ἢ κρύφια μυστήρια ...ἄγοντες, οὔτε βίους οὔτε γάμους καθαροὺς ἔτι φυλάσσουσιν, *ib.* xii. 5 ἐκ μέσου μύστας θιάσου, *ib.* viii. 4 (σοφία) μύστις ἐστὶ τῆς τοῦ θεοῦ ἐπιστήμης, and N.T. *e.g.* Matt. xiii. 11 ὑμῖν δέδοται γνῶναι τὰ μυστήρια τοῦ θεοῦ. The word is frequently used by St Paul in reference to the Gospel revealed in Christ: see Col. i. 26, where Lightfoot says 'this is not the only term borrowed from the ancient mysteries, which St Paul employs to describe the teaching of the Gospel. The word τέλειος just below (ver. 28) seems to be an extension of the same metaphor. In Phil. iv. 12 we have the word μεμύημαι, and in Eph. i. 14 σφραγίζεσθαι is perhaps an image derived from the same source. So the Ephesians are addressed as Παύλου συμμύσται in Ign. *Eph.* 12. The Christian teacher is thus regarded as a ἱεροφάντης (see Epict. III. 21. 13) who initiates his disciples into the rites. There is this difference however; that, whereas the heathen mysteries were strictly confined to a narrow circle, the Christian mysteries are freely communicated to all. There is therefore an intentional paradox in the use of the image by St Paul.' Cf. also Rom. xvi. 25, 26, Eph. v. 32 (of the mystical meaning of the marriage union), and Eph. iii. 3—5 cited by Clement *Str.* v. P. 682. Besides the direct reference to the Mysteries, we find the word ἐπόπτης used in 2 Pet. i. 16 ἐπόπται γενηθέντες τῆς ἐκείνου μεγαλειότητος, and there are two technical terms connected with the Mysteries, which are employed by writers of the N.T. when speaking of Baptism: these are φωτίζω and σφραγίζω. For the former compare Heb. vi. 4 ἀδύνατον τοὺς ἅπαξ φωτισθέντας...καὶ μετόχους γενηθέντας πνεύματος ἁγίου ...καὶ παραπεσόντας πάλιν ἀνακαινίζειν εἰς μετάνοιαν, *ib.* x. 32 ἀναμιμνήσκεσθε τὰς πρότερον ἡμέρας, ἐν αἷς φωτισθέντες πολλὴν ἄθλησιν ὑπεμείνατε παθημάτων; for the latter, Rev. vii. 3 μὴ ἀδικήσητε τὴν γῆν...ἄχρι σφραγίσωμεν τοὺς δούλους τοῦ θεοῦ ἡμῶν ἐπὶ τῶν προσώπων αὐτῶν, Eph. i. 13 ἐν ᾧ (τῷ

Χριστῷ) ἀκούσαντες τὸν λόγον τῆς ἀληθείας, τὸ εὐαγγέλιον τῆς σωτηρίας ὑμῶν...πιστεύσαντες ἐσφραγίσθητε τῷ πνεύματι τῆς ἐπαγγελίας τῷ ἁγίῳ, ib. iv. 30, 2 Cor. i. 22[1].

I turn now to Clement's use of mystical terms, and will deal first with his references to rites, and then with the references to doctrine. *Paed.* I. 26 βαπτιζόμενοι φωτιζόμεθα[2], φωτιζόμενοι υἱοποιούμεθα, υἱοποιούμενοι τελειούμεθα, τελειούμενοι ἀπαθανατιζόμεθα...καλεῖται δὲ πολλαχῶς τὸ ἔργον τοῦτο χάρισμα καὶ φώτισμα καὶ λουτρόν...φώτισμα δι' οὗ τὸ ἅγιον ἐκεῖνο φῶς τὸ σωτήριον ἐποπτεύεται, τουτέστιν δι' οὗ τὸ θεῖον ὀξυωποῦμεν, § 27 ὁ μόνον ἀναγεννηθεὶς...φωτισθεὶς ἀπήλλακται μὲν παράχρημα τοῦ σκότους, ἀπείληφεν αὐτόθεν τὸ φῶς, § 28 οἱ βαπτιζόμενοι τὰς ἐπισκοτούσας ἁμαρτίας τῷ θείῳ πνεύματι...ἀποτριψάμενοι...φωτεινὸν ὄμμα τοῦ πνεύματος ἴσχομεν, ᾧ δὴ μόνῳ τὸ θεῖον ἐποπτεύομεν, § 30 μία χάρις αὕτη τοῦ φωτίσματος τὸ μὴ τὸν αὐτὸν εἶναι τῷ πρὶν ἢ λούσασθαι τὸν τρόπον: *Protr.* § 120 ὦ τῶν ἁγίων ὡς ἀληθῶς μυστηρίων, ὦ φωτὸς ἀκηράτου. δᾳδουχοῦμαι τοὺς οὐρανούς, καὶ τὸν θεὸν ἐποπτεύσας ἅγιος γίνομαι μυούμενος, ἱεροφαντεῖ δὲ ὁ κύριος καὶ τὸν μύστην σφραγίζεται φωταγωγῶν: *Q. D. S.* 42 ὁ δὲ πρεσβύτερος ἀναλαβὼν οἴκαδε τὸν παραδοθέντα νεανίσκον...ἐφώτισε καὶ μετὰ τοῦτο ὑφῆκε τῆς πλείονος ἐπιμελείας...ὡς τέλεον αὐτῷ φυλακτήριον ἐπιστήσας τὴν σφραγῖδα τοῦ κυρίου. Clement's language about the Eucharist, as is natural from the less prominent position assigned to it by him, is less tinged with reminiscences of the Mysteries; still we meet with such phrases as the following: *Paed.* II. 29 μυστικὸν σύμβολον[3] ἡ γραφὴ αἵματος ἁγίου οἶνον ὠνόμασεν, ib. I. 43 ὦ τοῦ παραδόξου μυστηρίου· ἀποδύσασθαι ἡμῖν τὴν παλαιὰν ἐγκελεύεται φθορὰν ...καινῆς δὲ ἄλλης τῆς Χριστοῦ διαίτης μεταλαμβάνοντας...τὸν σωτῆρα ἐνστερνίσασθαι, ib. II. 20 ἧς (εὐχαριστίας) οἱ κατὰ πίστιν μεταλαμβάνοντες ἁγιάζονται καὶ σῶμα καὶ ψυχήν, τὸ θεῖον

---

[1] The evidence for the use of these terms in the Mysteries is given by Wobbermin in his book *On the Influence of the Mysteries upon Early Christianity*, pp. 144—172.

[2] The technical terms are distinguished by thick type.

[3] For the mystical use of this word compare Wobbermin pp. 174—183, where he refers to *Protr.* 15 τὰ σύμβολα τῆς μυήσεως ταύτης, ib. 16 Σαβαζίων μυστηρίων σύμβολον, ib. 22 τῆς Θέμιδος τὰ ἀπόρρητα σύμβολα, ib. 18, Orig. *c. Cels.* III. 51 where the catechumens are described as οἱ οὐδέπω τὸ σύμβολον τοῦ ἀποκεκαθάρθαι ἀνειληφότες.

κρᾶμα, τὸν ἄνθρωπον, τοῦ πατρικοῦ βουλήματος πνεύματι καὶ λόγῳ συγκρίναντος μυστικῶς.

It is chiefly however in reference to doctrine that Clement employs these figures, as in *Str.* I. 13 μεταδιδόναι τῶν θείων μυστηρίων καὶ τοῦ φωτὸς ἐκείνου τοῦ ἁγίου τοῖς χωρεῖν δυναμένοις συγκεχώρηκε...τὰ ἀπόρρητα λόγῳ πιστεύεται οὐ γράμματι, *ib.* τὰ μυστήρια μυστικῶς παραδίδοται, § 14 ἐκλέγων ἐπιστημόνως...δεδιὼς μὴ...παιδὶ μάχαιραν...ὀρέγοντες εὑρεθῶμεν, *ib.* V. 66 γάλα ἡ κατήχησις...βρῶμα δὲ ἡ ἐποπτικὴ θεωρία, *ib.* II. 47 θεωρία μεγίστη ἡ ἐποπτική, *ib.* IV. 3 τελειωθείσης τῆς προθέσεως ἡμῖν...τότε δὴ τὴν τῷ ὄντι γνωστικὴν φυσιολογίαν μέτιμεν, τὰ μικρὰ πρὸ τῶν μεγάλων μυηθέντες μυστηρίων ὡς μηδὲν ἐμποδὼν τῇ θείᾳ ὄντως ἱεροφαντίᾳ γίνεσθαι, IV. 162 ἡμᾶς ὁ σωτὴρ μυσταγωγεῖ, V. 56 ἐξηγητοῦ τινος καὶ καθηγητοῦ χρείαν ἔχειν ἡμᾶς βούλονται, § 57 οὐ γὰρ θέμις ὀρέγειν τοῖς ἀπαντῶσι τὰ μετὰ τοσούτων ἀγώνων πορισθέντα, οὐδὲ μὴν βεβήλοις τὰ τοῦ λόγου μυστήρια διηγεῖσθαι, § 63 οὐ γὰρ φθονῶν παρήγγειλεν ὁ κύριος ἔν τινι εὐαγγελίῳ 'μυστήριον ἐμὸν ἐμοὶ καὶ τοῖς υἱοῖς τοῦ οἴκου μου,' § 79 τὸ ἄρρητον τοῦ θεοῦ...ὑπὲρ οὐρανὸν τὸν τρίτον ἄρχεται λαλεῖσθαι ὡς θέμις τοῖς ἐκεῖ μυσταγωγεῖν τὰς ἐξειλεγμένας ψυχάς[1], VII. 4 τὰ θεῖα μυστήρια παρὰ τοῦ μονογενοῦς[2] παιδὸς ἐκμαθών, *ib.* 6 ὁ παιδεύων μυστηρίοις τὸν γνωστικόν, *ib.* 45 χορὸς μυστικὸς τῆς ἀληθείας, *ib.* 97 the heretics μὴ μαθόντες τὰ τῆς γνώσεως τῆς ἐκκλησιαστικῆς μυστήρια, *ib.* 106 μυσταγωγοὶ τῆς τῶν ἀσεβῶν ψυχῆς καθίστανται[3].

For the reasons and the subjects of this reticence, I may give in condensed form portions of the article on 'Disciplina Arcani' in the *D. of Chr. Ant.* It arose 'out of the principles (1) of imparting knowledge by degrees in methods suited to the capacity of the recipients, and (2) of cutting off occasions of profaneness by not proclaiming the mysteries of the faith indiscriminately to unbelievers.' These principles find support in the distinction between 'milk' and 'strong meat,' and in the warning against 'casting what is holy to dogs.' Thus arose a distinction between the degrees of knowledge permissible to

---

[1] Cf. 2 Cor. xii. 2 foll.
[2] On the use of this word in the Mysteries see Wobbermin pp. 113 foll. and the Orphic quotation in Clem. *Str.* v. 124.
[3] See also *Protr.* 12, *Str.* v. 689, VII. 27, 88 quoted above.

catechumens and to believers, and a spirit of reticence on the more mysterious doctrines of the faith, whether in speech or writing, when it might be accessible to the heathen. Again, in Alexandria especially, doctrines and facts of Scripture were expounded esoterically to the initiated (γνωστικοί), while their deeper meaning was disguised from others by an 'œconomy.' Origen (c. Cels. I. 7), enumerating the doctrines which were not hidden, mentions the birth, crucifixion and resurrection of the Lord, the resurrection of the dead, and the last judgment, but omits the doctrine of the Holy Trinity and of the Atonement.

So far I have confined my attention to the Eleusinian Mysteries, but 'it is not easy to draw a definite line between these and the forms of worship which went on side by side with them. Not only are they sometimes spoken of in common as mysteries, but there is a remarkable syncretist painting in a non-Christian catacomb at Rome, in which the elements of the Greek mysteries of Demeter are blended with those of Sabazius and Mithras in a way which shows that the worship was blended also[1].' Clement joins the Sabazian with the Eleusinian Mysteries, but does not, I think, mention Mithras, though the similarity of his rites to the Christian sacraments is admitted both by Pagan and Christian writers, each side retorting the charge of plagiarism on the other, just as was done in regard to the resemblances between Greek philosophy and the Scriptures[2]. In both cases we may allow that there was a

[1] Hatch p. 290 f.
[2] Cf. Justin Apol. I. 66 (the institution of bread and wine was imitated in the Mithraic Mysteries by the demons) ὅτι γὰρ ἄρτος καὶ ποτήριον τίθεται ἐν ταῖς τοῦ μυουμένου τελεταῖς μετ' ἐπιλόγων τινῶν ἐπίστασθε, Tert. Praescr. 40 (diabolus) ipsas quoque res sacramentorum divinorum idolorum mysteriis aemulatur. Tingit et ipse quosdam utique credentes et fideles suos; expositionem delictorum de lavacro repromittit...Mithra signat illic in frontibus milites suos; celebrat et panis oblationem et imaginem resurrectionis inducit, Orig. c. Cels. VI. 22, cited by Hatch l.c. For the Mysteries of Isis compare the account given by Apuleius of his own initiation (Met. XI. 21 foll.). The priest is speaking, 'inferum claustra et salutis tutelam in deae manu posita, ipsamque traditionem ad instar voluntariae mortis et precariae salutis celebrari; quippe cum transactis vitae temporibus iam in ipso finitae lucis limine constitutos, quibus tamen tuto possint magna religionis committi silentia, numen deae soleat elicere et sua providentia quodam modo renatos ad novae reponere rursus salutis curricula.'

reciprocal influence. The Christian Fathers were of course mistaken in regarding all that was good in philosophy as a theft from Christianity; but it is a mistake on the other hand to suppose that the Jewish Dispersion, which had such an extraordinary influence on Greek thought in Alexandria, could have been entirely without influence elsewhere, especially when we remember how many of the Stoics were of Eastern origin[1]. And so with the Mysteries. There can be no more doubt that these were modified in their later stages, to compete with the rival forces of Christianity, than that the romance of Apollonius and the reforms of Julian were suggested by the story of the Gospels and the ascetic training and philanthropic activity of the Church. On the other hand, there were original elements in these Mysteries (as we have seen in regard to the Eleusinia), which were akin to Christianity and helped to prepare the way for it; and there were other elements which, whether for good or evil, could easily be absorbed in it. How far was this actually the case? Dr Hatch traces the influence of the Mysteries down to the Middle Ages, and thinks that it was wide spreading and on the whole injurious. Mysteries take the place of the simple rites and open teaching of the early Church. Baptism no longer follows immediately on conversion, but is sometimes deferred to the end of life, and is always preceded by a long course of instruction. It is administered, as a rule, only once a year with ceremonies closely resembling those of Eleusis. A more recent writer carries back this influence to the New Testament itself. 'The great difference between the teaching of the Synoptic Jesus on the one hand, and the teaching of Paul, of the Fourth Evangelist, and of the author of the *Hebrews* on the other, is just that the latter is permeated, as the former is not, by the ideas of spiritual communion, of salvation, of justification and mediation: ideas which had found an utterance, however imperfect, in the teaching of the thiasi...Christians are, like the Pagan Mystae, called upon to be ὅσιοι and ἅγιοι. And in the second Corinthian Epistle Paul speaks of the Eucharist in a manner which shows that already, in the churches which he had founded, it had taken

---

[1] See Lightfoot, *Phil.* p. 273 foll.

the mystic and sacramental position which it has never since lost. It would be misleading to speak of this change...as due to the direct influence of the Pagan thiasi. My contention is quite different. I maintain that the language of the Pauline and Johannine writings shows the translation of Christianity on to a new level by the reception and the baptism into Christ of a set of ideas which at the time, coming from a divine source, were making their way into the various religions of the human race. These ideas...passing into ordinary Christianity... more fully adapted it for human reception.' Dr Percy Gardner, from whom I have taken this quotation, expresses a regret that 'the nobler doctrines of cults like those of Apollo and Athena' had less influence than the mysteries on the development of early Christianity. 'The divine nobleness of moderation and order, the charm of the *mens sana in corpore sano*, the beauty of a perfectly proportioned character, of manliness and a noble ambition, perfect freedom in thought and aspiration, in fact the whole range of higher Hellenic religious ideas were omitted in the web of Christianity[1].' This complaint is much the same as that made by J. S. Mill, where he deplores that the feminine virtues of Christianity were not combined with the manly virtues of Stoicism[2]; and no doubt there has been much to justify such complaint at particular times and in particular portions of the Church; but if we look to the Ideal held before us in the New Testament itself, I do not think we can better the saying of the old dramatist, that in it we have depicted before our eyes

'The first true gentleman that ever breathed.'

If there is less talk about ἀνδρεία and μεγαλοψυχία and ἐπιείκεια and τὸ καλόν than in Plato or Aristotle, there is more of the substance of these in St Peter's words 'whether it be right in the sight of God to hearken unto you more than unto God, judge ye' (that worthy pendant to the magnificent 'But if not' of Daniel); and again in St Paul's description of ἀγάπη and of the 'armour of God,' and his list

---

[1] *Expl. Evang.* pp. 840 foll.
[2] *Liberty*, pp. 89 f., 112.

of the things which should occupy a Christian's thoughts (Phil. iv. 8), and in St James' description of the wisdom from above. My chief reason however for touching on the subject here is to point the contrast between Dr Hatch and Dr Gardner on the introduction of Hellenic ethics into Christianity. The latter deplores that Christian morality was not hellenized: the former, as we saw in the last chapter, considers that it was hellenized by Ambrose's adaptation of Cicero's *Offices*, and regards this as a mark of the degeneration of Christianity.

CHAPTER IV.

ESTIMATES OF CLEMENT[1].

THE piety and learning of Clement, his power as a teacher and philosopher, are spoken of in the highest terms by succeeding Fathers[2].

The 4th of December was known in the middle ages as St Clement's Day. In the sixteenth century Pope Clement VIII. omitted his name from the martyrology at the instance of Baronius, and his judgment was confirmed by Boniface XIV. in 1748, when the matter was again brought before him by the admirers of the Alexandrian doctor; the grounds of the decision being the uncertainty as to the details of his life, the absence of proof as to his cultus, and the doubts raised as to his orthodoxy, though on this last point the Pope refused to pronounce. The original author of the doubts as to Clement's orthodoxy is Photius, a learned writer of the ninth century, who said that his treatise entitled *Hypotyposes* contained Gnostic errors, whether belonging to Clement himself or interpolated by heretics. We have fragments of this book, which certainly are opposed to orthodox doctrine, and also to what is said elsewhere by Clement himself; and there is every reason to believe that they are merely quotations from Gnostic writers with a view to commenting upon them. However, it must be allowed that he is sometimes incautious in his expressions. In one passage of the *Miscellanies* he seems

---

[1] The greater part of this chapter is a reprint from an Article which appeared in the *Expositor* for July, 1902.

[2] See *Testimonia Veterum* in Dindorf's ed., vol. I. pp. lv to lxiv.

to hold a kind of docetic view of the Person of our Lord, implying that His humanity was apparent only, *e.g.* that food was not really needed by Him; but this is not supported by anything else in his writings.

In the discussion between Fénelon and Bossuet on the disinterested love of God, Clement is quoted by both sides as an authority. In our own day his teaching and his method are being recalled by eminent French Catholics as giving an example of what is needed in order to meet the difficulties of a period of transition. The Abbé Cognat (1859) quotes with approval the words of Bossuet that in Clement's works we have 'une parfaite apologie de la religion chrétienne,' and contrasts his methods with those of the traditionalists, who deny the rights of reason, and declare an internecine strife between science and theology. Monseigneur Freppel, in his lectures delivered in 1865, says that Clement's boldness and largeness of view are enough of themselves to give him a high position in the history of theology. No defender of the faith ever studied so deeply the relations between science and faith, between the natural and the supernatural order. He has given a sketch of Christian science extending from the philosophy of history to the heights of mystical theology, which in its main lines is of permanent value. Eugène de Faye in his book, published in 1898, on the *Relation of Christianity to Greek Philosophy*, compares our age with that of Clement as a period of transition, in which the germs of the future are fermenting. 'We cannot be indifferent to him and his work. He is the true creator of ecclesiastical theology. In him the rational and mystical elements are equally mixed. He has a beautiful trust and a noble serenity which mark the depth of his Christianity. He feels himself possessed of a divine virtue which ensures to him the victory. He fears no one. He dares to measure himself against the philosophy and the spirit of his age, because he feels himself able to dominate them, *i.e.* to appropriate all that they offer of good. He feels in himself that the Truth has made him free. He is at once the firmest of believers and the most inquisitive and independent spirit that has perhaps ever appeared in the Church. Unhappily the legalistic spirit of Tertullian and

Cyprian prevailed over the free spirit of Clement and of Origen. It remains for Christians of to-day to revert to the wider theology[1].'

Of English writers who have held Clement in esteem, perhaps the most deserving of mention are the following. Maurice (in his *Ecclesiastical History*, p. 233) says: 'Clement's writings, though they are often censured as being learned and philosophical and mystical, were, I am convinced, written with a more distinctly practical purpose, and produced a more practical effect, than any which we have received from this or from almost any century'; (p. 239) 'I do not know where we shall look for a purer or a truer man than this Clement of Alexandria. I should like to be able to tell you more of his countenance and manner, as well as to give more particulars of his history.... But we must be content to make his acquaintance through the words which he has spoken. Judging from these he seems to me *that* one of the old Fathers whom we should all have reverenced most as a teacher and loved most as a friend.'

Bishop Westcott, speaking of the writings of Clement, says his three books 'correspond in a remarkable degree, as has frequently been remarked (Potter *ad Protr.* I.), with the stages of the Neo-Platonic course, the *Purification* ($\dot{a}\pi o\kappa\acute{a}\theta a\rho\sigma\iota\varsigma$), the *Initiation* ($\mu\acute{u}\eta\sigma\iota\varsigma$) and the *Vision* ($\dot{\epsilon}\pi o\pi\tau\epsilon\acute{\iota}a$)....If Clement had done no more than conceive such a plan, his service to the Gospel of the kingdom would not have been unfruitful. As it is, the execution of his work, if it falls short of the design, is still full of precious lessons. And when it is frankly admitted that his style is generally deficient in terseness and elegance; that his method is desultory, and his learning undigested; we can still thankfully admire his richness of information, his breadth of reading, his largeness of sympathy, his lofty aspirations, his noble conception of the office and capacities of the Faith.' 'The *Stromateis* is an endeavour to claim for the Gospel the power of fulfilling all the desires of men and of raising to a supreme unity all the objects of knowledge, in the soul of the true gnostic.' 'Towards this great unity of all science and all life Clement himself strove; and by the

---
[1] The quotation is condensed.

influence of his writings he has kept alive in others the sense of the magnificent promises included in the teaching of St Paul and St John, which by their very grandeur are apt to escape apprehension. He affirmed once for all, upon the threshold of the new age, that Christianity is the heir of all past time, and the interpreter of the future. Sixteen centuries have confirmed the truth of his principle, and left its application still fruitful.' (*D. of Chr. Biog.* I. pp. 561, 562, 566.)

I will conclude with a quotation from Hort's *Ante-Nicene Fathers* (p. 93): 'In Clement, Christian Theology in some important respects reaches its highest point. With all his manifest defects there was no one whose vision of what the faith of Jesus Christ was intended to do for mankind was so full or so true'; (p. 90) 'What he humbly and bravely attempted under great disadvantages...will have to be attempted afresh, with the added experience of more than seventeen centuries, if the Christian faith is still to hold its ground among men; and when the attempt is made, not a few of his thoughts and words will probably shine out with new force, full of light for dealing with new problems[1].'

---

[1] For estimates by Harnack and Bigg see above Ch. II. p. xxxiii n. and p. xlvii n.

CHAPTER V.

THE TEXT OF THE *STROMATEIS*.

THE *Stromateis* have been preserved to us in a single MS. (L) of the 11th century belonging to the Laurentian Library at Florence (Laur. v. 3). This was used for the Ed. Pr. (V), brought out by Victorius at Florence in 1550. A copy of L, made in the 15th century, is now in the Paris Library. This was used by Potter for his edition (Oxf. 1715). The latest edition, by G. Dindorf (Oxf. 1869), was based upon a collation of L made by J. Müller. A far more careful collation has since been made by Dr Otto Stählin with a view to his new edition of Clement. Dr Stählin has most kindly supplied me with a copy of his collation of *Strom.* VII, which has been tested by independent collations made by the Rev. P. Mordaunt Barnard and by myself.

As regards the condition of the text of the MS. from which L is derived, Prof. Bywater has the following remarks (*J. of Philology* IV. 204). 'The main difficulties connected with the critical study of Clement arise from three sources: (1) besides the recognized palaeographical causes of corruption, the text seems to have suffered from the transposition and repetition of words occurring in lines immediately above or below that on which the copyist was engaged; (2) words, and sometimes whole lines, have dropped out; (3) the Codex Laurentianus, which is our sole authority for the *Stromateis*, must be the descendant of a MS. which frequently exhibited words in a mutilated form through contraction and possibly also through injury similar to that sustained by the Bodleian Plato, where the ends of the lines are frequently illegible through damp.'

Prof. Bywater's remarks are illustrated and confirmed by the corruptions noted in the present book, which may be classified under the following heads. The classified statement may also serve to justify suggested emendations.

M. C.

ANALYSIS OF CORRUPTIONS.

A. *Vowel Changes.*
   (a) *Short and long interchanged.*
       $\epsilon = \eta$ or η.
       $o = \omega$ or φ.
   (b) *Itacism.*
       $\iota = \eta$.
       $\iota = \epsilon\iota$.
       $\eta = \epsilon\iota$.
   (c) *Other vowel changes.*
       $\alpha\iota = \epsilon$.
       $\alpha\iota = \eta$.
       $\alpha = \epsilon$.
       $\alpha = \epsilon\iota$.
       $\alpha\iota = \epsilon\iota$.
       $\alpha = \omega$.
       $\alpha = o\iota$.
       $\epsilon = o$.
       $\epsilon\iota = o$.
       $o = o\upsilon$.
       $o\upsilon = \omega$.
       $\omega = o\iota$.
       Omission or insertion of ι subs.

B. *Consonant Changes.*
   $\pi = \tau$.
   $\tau = \delta$.
   $\delta = \theta$.
   $\tau = \gamma$.
   $\delta = \gamma$.
   $\lambda = \delta$.
   $\mu = \nu$.
   $\sigma = $ *final* ι ⎫
   $\nu = $ *final* ι ⎬ See $H(b)$ on *Confusion of Terminations.*
   $\nu = $ *final* s ⎪
   $\nu = $ *final* υ ⎭
   $\theta = o$.
   $\delta = a$.

C. *Breathings and Accents.*

D. *Loss of Letters or Syllables.*
   Omission at beginning.
           in termination.
   Internal omission.

CH. V.   THE TEXT OF THE STROMATEIS.   lxvii

   Omission of repeated syllable.
     of article.
     of negatives.
     of ἄν and other particles.
     of preposition.
     of longer words or clauses.

E. *Additions.*

   Addition by immediate repetition.
     by repetition from context.
   Addition of initial letters or syllables.
   Terminational addition.
   Insertion of article.
     of ἄν and other particles.

F. *Wrong division of syllables.*

G. *Insertion from margin.*
 (a) *Remarks of reader.*
 (b) *Words accidentally omitted and afterwards wrongly inserted in Text.*

H. *Confusion of Inflexions and Words.*
 (a) *Abbreviations misunderstood.*
 (b) *Terminations confused.*
  (1) *Cases.*
  (2) *Gender and Number.*
  (3) *Voices, Moods and Tenses.*
  (4) *Other terminations.*
 (c) *Interchange of Words.*
  (1) *Interchange of prepositions and other short words.*
  (2) *Interchange of longer words resembling one another in sound, appearance or significance.*

I. *Misplacement of Sentences.*

K. *Loss of Sentences.*

EXEMPLIFICATION OF THE ABOVE CORRUPTIONS[1].

(A) Vowel Changes.

(a) *Short for long and vice versa*[2].

(1) ε = η and η. § 3 μὲν L, μὴν J; §§ 5, 6, 35 δὴ L, δὲ M; § 13 δὴ L, δὲ S, al.; § 41 ἐπιγινώσκεται L, ἐπιγινώσκηται H; § 69 λέγεται L, λέγηται P; § 102 ἀβελτηρίας L, ἀβελτερίας D; § 101 ἐὰν L, ᾖ ἂν S.

(2) ο = ω and ῳ. § 8 οὗτος L, οὕτως H; §§ 23, 51, 86 τὸ L, τῷ SD; § 34 ἀνειμένος L, ἀνειμένως Grot.; § 41 δίδοται L, διδῶται D; § 53 αὐτὸ L, αὐτῷ M; § 2 τῶν L, τὸν D; § 5 δι' ὧν L, δι' ὃν H; § 30 τῷ κατειπεῖν L, τὸ κ. Herm.; § 44 οὕτως L, οὗτος Barn.; § 50 θεῶν L, θεὸν S; § 81 τῷ L, τὸ M; § 109 καταπαύσωμεν L, -σομεν M; § 103 ὀριγνόμεναι...βιάζονται L, -γνώμεναι...-ζωνται edd.

(b) *Itacism.*

(1) ι = η. § 5 παντὶ L, πάντῃ S; § 17 κτίσιν L, κτῆσιν S; § 25 κατειλιμμένον L, κατειλημένον S; § 26 κιφῆνα L, κηφῆνα S; § 36 χρίσεως L, χρήσεως S.

(2) ι = ει. § 39 ἐκτείνειν L, ἐκτίνειν S; § 20 πιστικοὶ L, πειστικοὶ M; § 29 οἰκείας L, οἰκίας edd.; § 34 εὔπιστος L, εὔπειστος S; § 27 συνιδὼν L, συνειδὼς Bentley; § 47 ἐπὶ L, ἐπεὶ H.

(3) η = ει. § 3 η δ' L² (ᾖ δ' SD), εἰ δ' M after L¹; § 24 ἦ L, εἰ S; § 104 ἥτις L, εἴ τις Herv.; § 34 συγγενεῖ L, συγγενῇ SH; § 51 δὴ L, δεῖ S; § 101 Ἀριστοτέλη L, -λει S; § 100 ληπτέον L, λειπτέον edd.

(c) *Other vowel changes.*

(1) αι = ε. § 30 ἀποκρίνεται L, ἀποκρίνετε S; §§ 62 *bis*, 70, 78 ἔρῃ L, αἱρῇ S, cf. § 94; § 101 ἔρεσις L, αἵρεσις S; § 88 γίνεσθε L, γίνεσθαι S; § 111 μηλαίαις L, μηλέαις S.

(2) αι = η. § 85 κρίνῃ L, κρίναι D.

(3) α = ε. § 9 ἐφορώντων L, ἀφορώντων H; § 29 ἀνίδρυτον L, ἐνίδρυτον Lowth; § 71 ἐπείγων L, ἀπάγων S.

(4) α = ει. § 71 ἐπείγων L, ἀπάγων S.

---

[1] Among the emendations which follow are some which I have not admitted into the text, but which seem to me quite allowable.

[2] Explanation of symbols.

A. Arcerius in Sylburg's ed.
Barn. P. M. Barnard.
Byw. Bywater in *J. of Phil.*
Canterus, in Sylburg.
D. Dindorf, ed. 1869.
Grot. Hugo Grotius.
Heins. Heinsius, ed. 1614.
Herv. Simon Hervetus, ed. 1590.
Hoesch. Hoeschel in Sylburg.

H. Hort.
J. H. Jackson.
Kl. Klotz, ed. 1831.
L. The Laurentian ms.
Lowth, in Potter's ed.
M. Mayor.
P. Potter, ed. 1715.
S. Sylburg, ed. 1592.
V. Victorius, ed. pr. 1550.

CH. V.   THE TEXT OF THE STROMATEIS.   lxix

(5)   αι = ει.   § 106 αὐλαίαν L, αὐλείαν M, see (3).
(6)   α = ω.   § 30 θυσίαν L, θυσιῶν H ; § 104 ὡς L, ὣς Lowth.
(7)   α = οι.   § 28 πολυφλάσβοιοι L, πολυφλοίσβοιο S ; § 96 μαχόμενοι L, -να M.
(8)   ε = ο.   § 48 ὄντων L, ἐν τῶν H ; § 69 ὁρᾷ L, ἐρᾷ S ; § 72 συμφέρῳ L, συμφόρῳ S ; § 30 οὐ L, εὖ J ; § 105 ὑποσυρέντων L, -ρόντων Herv.
(9)   ο = ει.   § 17 ἀλλὰ πείθεσθαι L, ἀλλ' ἀποθέσθαι M.
(10)   ο = ου.   § 51 τὸ ψεύδεσθαι, τὸ ψευδορκεῖν L, τοῦ ψ. bis M ; § 56 διὰ τοῦ L, διὰ τὸ H ; § 82 τοῦ ἁμαρτῆσαι L, τὸ ἁμ. M ; § 97 περὶ τὸ L, περὶ τοῦ M ; § 98 τὸ πῶς L, τοῦ πῶς M.
(11)   ω = ου.   § 8 τοῦ δυναμένου L, τῷ -νῳ S ; § 38 κατ' ἀλλήλους L, καταλλήλως Heins.; § 42 τεταγμένους L, τεταγμένως P ; § 46 τοῦδε L, τῷδε M ; § 55 ἀνθρώπῳ L, ἀνθρώπου P.
(12)   ω = οι.   § 97 προχείρως L, προχείροις M ; see (13).
(13)   *Omission or insertion of ι subscript.*   § 3 παρεχομένη L, -μένῃ Kl.; § 4 ᾗ L, ῇ S ; § 30 τῷ μηρῷ L, τὼ μηρὼ S ; § 63 αὐτῇ L, αὐτῃ Eus.

(B) CONSONANT CHANGES.

(1)   π = τ.   § 13 ἐπί L, ἔτι P ; § 3 ὅτῳ L, ὅπως H ; § 26 πόσα L, τόσα Grot.; § 31 ἱπμὸν L, ἱπνὸν S ; § 98 οὕτω L, οὔπω Herv.   π = τι.   § 86 δῆλον ὁποῖοι L, δηλονότι οἷοι J.
(2)   τ = δ.   τε and δέ confused in §§ 6, 7, 17, 26, 35, 44, 51, 66 al.
(3)   δ = θ.   § 7 οὔδ' L, οὔδ' Kl.; § 37 τοῦδ' L, τοῦδ' S.
(4)   τ = γ.   § 23 αὐτή L, Αὔγη Grot.; § 29 ἀγύρτου L, Τυρίου J ; § 46 γωνία L, ἀτονία M.
(5)   δ = γ.   § 47 δ' οὖν L, γοῦν M ; § 48 τε L, γε J ; § 52 τῆς L, γῆς S.
(6)   λ = δ (Λ = Δ).   § 27 φιλιάζειν L, Φειδία ζητεῖν Grot.
(7)   μ = ν.   § 38 fin. μαθήματα L, ἀναθήματα H ; § 48 διαμονὴ L, διανομὴ M ; ib. τιμώμενος L, τιμῶν ἦν ὃς J.
(8)[1]   σ = final ς.   § 3 ὅτῳ L, ὅπως H ; § 28 παιδιᾶς L, παιδιᾷ Barn. (παιδιαῖς H) ; § 32 τῆς θυσίας L, τῇ θυσίᾳ H ; § 43 αὐτῆς L, αὐτῇ M ; § 45 ἀμεταστάτῳ L, ἀμεταστάτως S ; § 70 fin. τῇ τῆς ἀληθείας προνοίᾳ L, τῆς τῇ ἀληθείᾳ προνοίας M ; § 84 τῆς L, τῇ S.
(9)   ν = final ι.   § 13 τῇ λειτουργίᾳ…τῇ διδασκαλίᾳ…τῇ εὐποιίᾳ L, τὴν λειτουργίαν κ.τ.λ. S ; § 44 χρωμένηι L, χρωμένην S ; § 45 ἐνδεικνυμένων L, ἐνδεικνυμένῳ H ; § 69 αὐτῷ L, αὐτὸν H.
(10)   ν = final ς.   § 4 καταδεδουλωμένον L, -μένος S ; § 27 συνιδὼν L, συνειδὼς Bentley ; § 35 ὁμοίων L, ὁμοίως S ; § 44 ἀξιολόγως L, ἀξιολόγων H ; § 48 τὴν σωτηρίαν L, τῆς -ρίας M ; § 53 ψιλῆς L, ψιλὴν M ; § 76 γενόμενος L, γενόμενον S.
(11)   ν = final υ.   § 28 ἐλεφαντίνου L, -τινον S ; § 48 παρ' ἑαυτόν L, παρ' ἑαυτοῦ S ; § 67 καιροῦ L, καιρὸν M ; § 77 ἑαυτὸν L, ἑαυτοῦ J ; § 95 ἕτερον L, ἑτέρου Heins.; § 95 ἀνθρώπων L, ἀνθρώπου M.

---

[1] Compare with 8—11 the examples of *Confusion in terminations* below H (b).

(12) θ = ο. § 30 οὐ λήμασι L, θυλήμασι Grot.; § 63 μεμνήσθω αὐτῇ L, μέμνησο ὢ αὔτη Euseb.

(13) δ = α (Δ = Α). § 47 ἀποβληθῆναι δι' L (= ἀποβληθην<δι> δι'), ἀποβληθὲν δι' H.

(C) BREATHINGS AND ACCENTS.

These are constantly wrong in the MS. Thus μονή has the accent on the penultimate in § 55 (corrected by J), and αὐτοῦ is regularly written αὑτοῦ (see Index *s.v.*).

(D) LOSS OF LETTERS OR SYLLABLES.

(*a*) *Omission at beginning.* § 38 μαθήματα L, ἀναθήματα H; § 46 γωνία L, ἀτονία M; § 57 ἰδίως L, ἀϊδίως P; § 69 μισοπόνηροι L, ἀμνησιπόνηροι Lowth; § 76 ὁρατά L, ἀόρατα Lowth; § 25 θεῖν L, ἐσθίειν M; § 47 ἐνδεὲς L, ἀνενδεές M; § 56 κρεμασθῇ L, ἐκκρεμασθῇ M; § 99 οὖν L, γοῦν M (cf. §§ 44, 17); § 111 τύχοιεν L, ἐντύχοιεν S; § 107 ἥν L, τὴν S; § 90 κίβδηλον L, ἀκ. Resch.

(*b*) *Omission in terminations.* § 8 βελτίω L, βελτίων S; § 16 ὑπεράνω L, ὑπεράνω ὢν H; § 21 ἀμοιβῇ L, ἀμοιβὴν S; § 40 καταλέλοιπεν L, καταλελοιπέναι J; § 57 ὑποτεταγμένη L, -νην H; § 69 ἐπιδῷ L, ἐπιδῴη M; § 12 ἀμείνω L, ἀμείνους D.

(*c*) *Internal omission.* § 13 καταληπτὴ L, καταληπτικὴ P; § 21 οἴκους L, οἰκίσκους M; § 27 περιθέτωσαν L, περιθεωσάτωσαν Bentley; § 29 δεδαλμένον L, δεδαιδαλμένον S; *ib.* ἐνιδρυμένον L, ἐνιδρυόμενον H; § 83 γενέσθαι L, γενήσεσθαι M; § 36 συγκάττυσις L, συγκατάρτυσις J; § 51 εὑρεῖν L, εὐορκεῖν Heins.

(*d*) *Omission of repeated syllable.* § 65 μὴ κατὰ δὲ L, μὴ κα<κα> τὰ δὲ S; § 98 πρὸς τοῖς L, πρὸς <τὸ> τοῖς M; § 103 καίουσαν L, <καὶ> καίουσαν M; § 31 τὰ ἄβρωτα L, τὰ ἄβρωτα <ἃ> M; § 4 ἀποτελέσματα L, ἀπ. πρῶτον (= α') D.

(*e*) *Omission of article.* § 7 σοφία L, ἡ σ. H; § 15 ἄλλοι L, οἱ ἄλλοι M; § 65 μὴ L, τὰ μὴ Barn.; § 51 πρὸς ἑαυτὸν L, π. τοὺς ἑαυτοῦ M; § 94 πρὸς τοῖς L, πρὸς τὸ τοῖς M.

(*f*) *Omission of negative.* § 50 ὡς ἀδικῶν L, οὐχ ὡς ἀδικῶν M; § 83 γινομένων L, γινομένων οὐδὲν M; § 96 βιαζόμενοι L, μὴ β. M.

(*g*) *Omission of ἄν and other particles.* § 29 πῶς...ποιοίη L, πῶς ἄν... π. M; § 37 ἀναμεῖναι L, ἀναμεῖναι ἄν D; § 41 δοίη δὲ L, δοίη δὲ ἄν Barn.; § 48 ἀφέλοιτο L, ἀφ. ἄν D; § 90 προφασίσαιτο L, πρ. ἄν D; § 82 φήσαιμεν L, φ. ἄν D.

δέ, καί, τε, μέν, γάρ, οὖν, ὡς. § 5 μετὰ L, μετὰ δὲ M; § 31 τούτου L, τούτου δὲ H; § 47 ἄρα L, δ' ἄρα M; § 58 κατὰ L, καὶ κατὰ M; § 69 παρορμήσεσι L, καὶ π. M; § 2 ἄχρονον L, ἄχρονον καὶ P; § 30 ὤν L, ὤν γὰρ Abbott; *ib.* μὴ καρδίαν L, μὴ γὰρ κ. M; § 71 τῷ L, τῷ γὰρ M; § 51 ταύτῃ L, ταύτῃ μὲν M; § 19 μαθεῖν L, μαθὼν ὡς H; § 81 ἑαυτὸν L, ὡς ἑαυτὸν M; § 109 μήτε L, μήτ' οὖν M; § 27 κενὸν L, κενὸν οὖν M.

(*h*) *Omission of preposition.* § 83 τὰ πάντα ἑνὸς τοῦ παντοκράτορος θεοῦ ἵσταται L, ἐφ' ἑνὸς M.

(ι) *Omission of longer words or clauses*, (1) *sometimes owing to recurrence of the same sound or letters*, as in § 5 init. εἰδέναι <ἐνεργεῖ> M; § 17 <τὰ συνέχοντα> τὰ μὲν M; § 18 <πάντα> πράσσων H; § 21 ὀπῆς <πάσης> M; § 32 οὐδὲν <ἀνοῦ> (=ἀνθρώπου) M; § 35 <οἷδεν> οὐδὲ M; § 37 τινα, <τίνα> M; § 47 δι' εὐλαβείας <καὶ εὐλογιστίας> M; § 72 ὃν αὐτὸς <τοῖς ἑαυτοῦ> ᾔτησεν M; § 86 δοκᾷν <δεῖν> M; § 80 ἀσφαλὴς δὲ ἐν τῇ συμπεριφορᾷ L, ἀσφαλὴς δὲ <ἔστω> ἐν τ. σ. M. (2) *Sometimes apparently owing to the effacement of the word in the archetype*, as in § 17 ὀργῆς <κρατεῖν> P; § 41 δοίη δὲ <ἂν καὶ μὴ αἰτήσασιν> Barn.; § 80 καὶ τοῦ L, καταμεγαλοφρονεῖν τοῦ M; § 93 ἐπιγνῷ L, ἐκέγνω <μετὰ χαρᾶς λαβὼν> M; § 101 περὶ L, <τούτους> περὶ Heins.; ib. κριθεῖσιν <ἀκολουθεῖν> S; § 102 τοὺς δὲ <ἤδη αἱρετικοὺς> M; § 111 οὐχ L, οὐχ <ἡδυσμένην> M.

E. ADDITIONS.

(a) *By immediate repetition (dittography)*. § 11 ἐντολὰς ἃς L, ἐντολὰς H; § 22 βάρβαροι οἱ L, βάρβαροι H; ib. ἀδεισιδαίμων ὦν L, ἀδ. H; § 25 ὄφιν ἐν L, ὄφιν H; § 29 εἶναι ἐνιδρύσει L, ἐνιδρύσει M; § 37 τοῦδ' ἕνεκα καὶ ἵνα L, om. καὶ M; § 47 ἀποβληθῆναι δι' L, ἀποβληθὲν δι' H; § 82 υἱοθεσίαν ἀνακόλουθα L, υἱοθεσίαν ἀκόλουθα Barn.; § 96 fin. οὕτως repeated; § 100 ἣν ἐν L, ἣν M bis; ib. τῶν repeated L; § 55 διδάσκεται [ται] L; § 88 ἀποστάσει ἃ L, ἀποστάσει M.

(b) *Repeated from context.* § 30 κομιδῇ μέχρι L (repeated from κομιδῇ ψιλὴν below), μέχρι Herm.; § 36 διὰ τῆς δωρεᾶς L, om. διὰ as taken from following διὰ λόγου H; § 98 δι' ἣν ἐκείνην τὴν συμποτικὴν διὰ τῆς ψευδωνύμου ἀγάπης πρωτοκλισίαν ἀσπάζονται L, om. second διὰ M (cf. § 43 where διὰ is inserted before χάριν by L¹ from previous line and corrected by L²); § 54 ὁσίως προτρεπόμενος L, ὁσ. προστρεπόμενος Morell, om. ὁσίως as it occurs just before M; § 84 ἀλλ' οὐδὲ μὴν L, om. ἀλλ' as inserted from preceding ἀλλ' οὐ M.

(c) *Addition at beginning.* § 29 ἀγύρτου L, τυρίου J.

(d) *Addition at end.* § 2 ἐκμανθάνειν L, ἐκμανθάνει M; § 17 ἔχειν L, ἔχει S; § 92 ἐν μόνῃ τῇ ἀληθείᾳ καὶ τῇ ἀρχαίᾳ ἐκκλησίᾳ L, ἀληθεῖ M.

(e) *Insertion of article.* § 56 τῶν θεῶν L, θεὸν S; § 78 ὁ γνωστικὸς L, γνωστικὸς M; § 69 τοὺς διεχθρεύοντας L, om. τοὺς M; § 99 τοὺς κενοὺς L, κενοὺς Hoeschl; § 100 τοὺς τὰς L, τὰς Herv.

(f) *Insertion of ἂν or other particles.* § 28 ἂν ἦν L, ἦν J; § 4 φιλόθεός [τε] S; § 14 κελεύων [καὶ] M; § 18 [καὶ] δι' ἣν H; § 54 βασιλέα [καὶ] M; § 57 ἐπιστήμης [καὶ] S; § 62 καὶ λόγῳ [καὶ] D; § 69 πρὸς [τε] τοὺς M; § 78 [καὶ] τὴν μὲν M; § 80 δίκαια καὶ τὴν L, δικαίαν τὴν M; ib. λάθῃ ἡ ἤ L, λάθῃ ἢ M; § 108 [καὶ] ἂν M; § 43 μόνον [δ'] ἔνδοθεν Heins.; § 39 τοῖς [δ'] D; § 105 δήπου [γὰρ] M; § 81 οὐκ αὐτὸς αἰτήσεται ὁ γνωστικὸς [οὐ] χρημάτων περιουσίαν εἰς μετάδοσιν M.

(F) WRONG DIVISION OF SYLLABLES. § 11 αὐτοὺς L, αὖ τοὺς S; § 15 οὐκ ἀθεοράκασι L, οὐ καθ. S; § 17 ἀλλὰ πείθεσθαι L, ἀλλ' ἀποθέσθαι M; § 18 ἅλματι L, ἅμα τι Arc.; § 26 ἐν τοῖσδε δασμίας L, ἐπὶ τοῖσδε δᾳδὶ μιᾷ S; ib. ἴστα L, ἰὰ τὰ M; § 27 τούτους σε δεῖ L, τούτου σ' ἔδει Grot.; § 22 ὁμοιούσιν καὶ τοῖς αὐτοῖς L, ὁμοίας ἕκαστοι ἑαυτοῖς H; § 32 ῥυμουλκεῖ L, ῥυθμῷ ἕλκει M; § 38 κατ' ἀλλήλους L, καταλλήλως Heins.; § 43 ἅπαν τι πρόσωπον L, ἀπαντιπρόσωπα H, ἀπ' ἀντιπροσώπου J; § 46 οὔθοτ' οὖν L, εὐθετούντων H (εὐθετεῖν J, εὐθετῶν M); § 48 τιμώμενος L, τιμῶν ἦν ὃς J; § 49 διὰ τὸν δύσοιστον κοινὸν βίον διώκουσιν L, διὰ τὸ ἡδὺ τοῖς τὸν κ. β. δ. H; § 59 ἀνάλογον L, ἀνὰ λόγον M; § 63 μεμνήσθω L, μέμνησο ὦ Eus.; § 67 ἐπὶ τὸ μή L, ἐπιτομή S; § 76 ἀποκάθαρσιν L, αὐτοῦ κάθαρσιν J; § 80 καλῶς L, καὶ ἄλλους M; § 106 Θεοδάδι ἀκηκοέναι L, Θεοδᾶ διακηκοέναι Bentley.

(G) INSERTION FROM MARGIN.

(a) *Remark of reader.* § 81 ἀπαιτεῖ παρὰ κυρίου [οὐχὶ δὲ καὶ αἰτεῖ;], om. words in brackets M; § 37 καθάπερ ἤρεσεν τοῖς Στωικοῖς L. Anthropomorphism being the doctrine of the Epicureans and absolutely contrary to the Stoic view, Cl. must have written Ἐπικουρείοις, which may have been changed to Στωικοῖς from a marginal note (κ. ἤρ. τ. Στ.) on τὸ εὐπαθὲς τοῦ ἀέρος just below.

(b) *Words accidentally omitted in text and afterwards inserted in the wrong place.*

§ 33 (Aesop said) τοὺς ὗς κεκραγέναι μέγιστον· συνειδέναι γὰρ αὐτοῖς εἰς οὐδὲν ἄλλο χρησίμοις [ὅταν ἕλκωνται] πλὴν εἰς τὴν θυσίαν L; the words in brackets are placed after μέγιστον by Rittershus. Probably they were omitted, from illegibility or accident, in the text of the MS. from which L is derived, afterwards inserted in the margin and wrongly transferred to the text.

§ 37 ἀλλὰ [καὶ τὸ εὐπαθὲς τοῦ ἀέρος] καὶ ἡ ὀξυτάτη συναίσθησις τῶν ἀγγέλων...καὶ ἄνευ τῆς αἰσθητῆς ἀκοῆς ἅμα νοήματι πάντα γινώσκει. It seems impossible that Cl. should speak of the air as perceiving, apart from the sense of hearing. But the Stoics, in explaining the process of hearing and vision, dwelt much on the agency of the air, and the words κατὰ—ἀέρος would be quite in place two lines before, after ὄψεως. If they were accidentally omitted, and afterwards supplied in the margin, they may have been wrongly inserted as we find them in L.

§ 41 ἵν' ἐν τοῖς σωζομένοις διὰ τῆς σωτηρίας [κατ' ἐπίγνωσιν] ὁ θεὸς... δοξάζηται L: it seems necessary to read διὰ τῆς κατ' ἐπίγνωσιν σωτηρίας, the misplacement in L being probably due to the accidental omission of κατ' ἐπίγνωσιν and their subsequent insertion from the margin.

Ib. ἵνα...ὁ θεὸς [δοξάζηται καὶ] ὁ μόνος ἀγαθὸς καὶ ὁ μόνος σωτὴρ δι' υἱοῦ ἐξ αἰῶνος εἰς αἰῶνα ἐπιγινώσκηται L. This reads far more naturally if we suppose that δοξάζηται καὶ originally followed υἱοῦ and was wrongly transferred from the margin.

§ 47 πεπεισμένος [καὶ] ὡς ἔστιν ἕκαστον τῶν μελλόντων κέκτηται τοῦτο L. Probably καὶ originally preceded κέκτηται, was lost by dittography (και κε), then supplied in margin and wrongly reinserted.

§ 52 [τὰς] βεβαίας ἐπὶ τούτων (sc. τῶν ἀγαλμάτων) τιθέμενοι συνθήκας L. The sense seems to require that βεβαίας should be predicative and the article prefixed to συνθήκας.

§ 53 ἀδούλωτος οὗτος ἐν φόβῳ, [ἀληθὴς ἐν λόγῳ,] καρτερικὸς ἐν πόνῳ, μηδὲ ἐν τῷ προφορικῷ λόγῳ ψεύσασθαι θέλων L. The clause in brackets naturally follows after πόνῳ, being explained by the subsequent clause.

§ 59 ἐπί τι χρήσιμον τῶν ἐπὶ ἀρετὴν [καὶ ἀπὸ ἀρετῆς] καταστρεφόντων τὴν πρᾶξιν κατεύθυνει L. The words in brackets appear to have come from a marginal correction (ἐπὶ ἀρετῆς for ἐπὶ ἀρετήν), which was then added to the text, with a following καὶ and the change of ἐπὶ to ἀπὸ, to give an appearance of sense.

§ 63 (ἡ γνῶσις) πεῖσμα βεβαιότατον ἐνεγέννησεν τῆς τῶν μελλόντων [ἐλπίδων (ἐλπίδος L¹)] ἀπολήψεως L. Here D simply omits ἐλπίδων. It seems more probable that ἐλπίδος originally preceded ἐνεγέννησεν and that βεβαιότερον was read instead of the superlative. The pl. ἐλπίδων may have been introduced after the comparative had given place to the superlative.

§ 72 παρθένοι...ὡς κακῶν ἀπεσχημέναι, προσδεχόμεναι δέ...τὸν κύριον, καὶ τὸ οἰκεῖον ἀνάπτουσαι φῶς εἰς τὴν τῶν πραγμάτων θεωρίαν [φρόνιμαι ψυχαί]. The words in brackets probably preceded τὸ οἰκεῖον in the archetype and were added at the end from the margin in a later MS.

§ 82 μήτε μὴ γνοὺς τὸν θεόν, μᾶλλον δὲ γνωσθείς τε πρὸς αὐτοῦ, ἐπὶ τέλει...ἐνδεικνύμενος L. Here D brackets μήτε, and Herv. inserts a καὶ after τέλει. The only change required seems to be the removal of τε from γνωσθείς (where it is quite out of place) to follow τέλει, where it will correspond to μήτε.

§ 85 διὰ τί οὐχὶ μᾶλλον ἀδικεῖσθε; φησί, διὰ τί οὐχὶ μᾶλλον ἀποστερεῖσθε; ἀλλὰ ὑμεῖς ἀδικεῖτε [καὶ ἀποστερεῖτε] (εὐχόμενοι κατὰ τούτων δηλονότι τῶν κατ' ἄγνοιαν πλημμελούντων) καὶ ἀποστερεῖσθε τῆς τοῦ θεοῦ φιλανθρωπίας...τοὺς ἀδελφούς L. The words in square brackets are probably a marginal correction (adopted by P and succeeding edd.) of the second καὶ ἀποστερεῖσθε, which makes no sense.

§ 88 ὁ ταύτῃ κολλώμενος τῇ πόρνῃ τῇ παρὰ τὴν διαθήκην ἐνεργείᾳ [ἄλλο σῶμα γίνεται οὐχ ἅγιον] εἰς σάρκα μίαν καὶ βίον ἐθνικὸν καὶ ἄλλην ἐλπίδα L. The words in brackets should come after ἐλπίδα. At present they break the construction κολλώμενος εἰς.

Ib. ὁ δὲ κολλώμενος τῷ κυρίῳ ἐν πνεύματι πνευματικὸν σῶμα [τὸ διάφορον τῆς συνόδου γένος] L. The words in brackets have no construction as they stand. They come in naturally after κυρίῳ, as a cognate accusative to κολλώμενος.

§ 93 ἀλλ' [ὡς ἔοικεν] τοῖς πολλοῖς καὶ μέχρι νῦν δοκεῖ ἡ Μαριὰμ λεχὼ εἶναι...οὐκ οὖσα λεχώ...τοιαῦται δ' ἡμῖν αἱ κυριακαὶ γραφαί L. The general purport of the passage is to show that the Scriptures are the standard of truth. The reference to the Virgin is merely incidental and illustrative. This would be plain with the reading ὡς τοῖς πολλοῖς ὡς ἔοικεν. Probably the scribe's eye passed from the 1st to the 2nd ὡς and τοῖς πολλοῖς was afterwards added in the margin and the text.

§ 98 πάντα μᾶλλον ὑπομένουσι...ἤπερ μετατίθενται [ὑπὸ φιλοτιμίας] τῆς αἱρέσεως L. The words in brackets should be placed before ὑπομένουσι.

Doubtless they were omitted owing to the repeated ὑπό, and restored from the margin in the wrong place.

§ 101 καίτοι μεμαθήκαμεν ἄλλο μέντοι εἶναι ἡδονήν L, καὶ μέντοι μεμαθήκαμεν ἄλλο εἶναι ἡδονήν M (καίτοι having been accidentally written for καὶ μέντοι, we may suppose μέντοι to have been added in the margin and wrongly inserted in the text).

§ 106 (The teaching of the Lord) ἀπὸ Αὐγούστου [καὶ Τιβερίου] Καίσαρος ἀρξαμένη, μεσούντων τῶν Αὐγούστου χρόνων τελειοῦται L. The word Τιβερίου is evidently a marginal correction of the 2nd Αὐγούστου, inserted in the wrong place with a καὶ to introduce it.

§ 109 (Some light may be derived) ἐκ τοῦ κατὰ τὰς θυσίας νόμου περί τε Ἰουδαίων τῶν χυδαίων περί τε τῶν αἱρέσεων μυστικῶς διακρινομένων, ὡς ἀκαθάρτων, ἀπὸ τῆς [περὶ καθαρῶν καὶ ἀκαθάρτων ζῴων] θείας ἐκκλησίας L. The removal of the words in brackets from their present position shows the construction of θείας ἐκκλησίας: their insertion after νόμου by Lowth explains the reference to the law; while the repeated περὶ makes it easy to understand why they should have been lost from their true position.

(H) Confusion of Words or Inflexions.

(a) *Abbreviations misunderstood.* § 58 πνεύματος L, πατρὸς H; § 61 πρᾶγμα L, πνεῦμα M; § 17 γνωστικὸν L, γνῶσιν M; § 37 τῇ ἀρρήτῳ L, τινὶ ἀρρ. H; § 65 κατὰ τὸν αὐτὸν L, κατὰ ταὐτὸν M; § 79 φοβούμενος L, φόβος S. I have noticed two examples of the termination -κος being mistaken for κύριος, Str. III. § 89, P. 475 τῷ ἐρῶντι κυρίῳ τῆς αἰχμαλώτου γεγονότι οὐκ ἐπιτρέπει χαρίζεσθαι τῇ ἡδονῇ, where we should read ἐρωτικῷ, and Str. IV. § 165, P. 639 αἱ ἀγαθαὶ πράξεις ὡς ἀμείνους τῷ κρείττονι τῷ πνεύματι κυρίῳ προσάπτονται, αἱ δὲ φιλήδονοι καὶ ἁμαρτητικαὶ τῷ ἥττονι τῷ ἁμαρτητικῷ περιτίθενται, where we should read πνευματικῷ corresponding to the following ἁμαρτητικῷ.

(b) *Terminations confused.*

(1)[1] *Cases.* (Nom. and acc.) § 4 καταδεδουλωμένον (to suit previous acc.) L, -νος S; § 5 φῶς πατρῷος (to suit following ὅλος) L, πατρῷον S; § 16 fin. ἀναστρεφόμενον (to suit previous acc.) L, ἀναστρεφόμενοι H; § 57 ὑποτεταγμένη (to agree with subject of preceding ἔστιν) L, ὑποτεταγμένην (agreeing with subject of γίνεσθαι) H; § 76 γενόμενος L, γενόμενον S; § 81 δι' αὐτὸ τὸ εἶναι γνωστικὸν αὐτὸς ἐργάζεται L, read γνωστικὸς, as the subject of the inf. is the same as the subject of the sentence.

(Nom. and gen.) § 8 πρωτουργὸς κινήσεως δύναμις L, πρωτουργοῦ κ. δ. (as in Plato) H; § 10 καθ' ἑκάστην ἑκάστης (to agree with preceding μεταβολῆς) L, ἑκάστη H (in apposition to περιτροπαί); § 19 ἐκ τῆς τῶν συμβάντων καὶ ἐπιγινομένης συνηθείας L, ἐκ τῆς τῶν συμβιούντων ἐπιγινομένη συνηθείας (to agree with the following ἀρετή) M.

(Nom. and dat.) § 9 συγκινεῖται μικροτάτη σιδήρου μοῖρα τῷ τῆς Ἡρακλείας λίθου πνεύματι διὰ πολλῶν...ἐκτεινομένη δακτυλίων L, ...ἐκτεινομένῳ (agreeing

---

[1] Compare above on Vowel and Consonant changes.

with πνεύματι) Lowth; § 40 ὅσα μὴ χρησιμεύει **γενόμενος** ἐκεῖ L, γενομένῳ Η; § 41 ᾧ μόνῳ ἡ αἴτησις κατὰ τὴν τοῦ θεοῦ βούλησιν **ἀπονενεμημένῳ** γίνεται L, ἀπονενεμημένη Heins.

(Acc. and gen.) § 11 ἐπαίοντας **τὰς βαρβάρους** φιλοσοφίας L, ἐπ. τῆς β. φ. Η; § 13 (ψυχὰς) ταυτότητι τῆς ὑπεροχῆς **ἁπάσης** τετιμημένας διαμένειν L, ἁπάσας Η; § 48 τὸ πᾶν **συναιρεῖται** (συναίρεται H) πρὸς τὴν τελειότητα τὴν **σωτηρίαν** L, τῆς σωτηρίας Μ; § 53 μέχρι τῆς συμπεριφορᾶς διὰ τὴν τῶν πέλας σωτηρίαν συγκαταβαίνων **ψιλῆς** L, ψιλὴν Μ; § 80 (Job) προσαπέθετο πάντα διὰ **τῆς** πρὸς τὸν κύριον **ἀγάπης** L, διὰ τὴν...ἀγάπην Heins.; § 99 (τοὺς αἱρετικοὺς κενοὺς εἶναί φαμεν) **πικρίζοντας** ὡς ἀληθῶς κατὰ τὴν ἀγρίαν ἀμυγδάλην ἐξάρχοντας δογμάτων L, πικριζόντων Μ.

(Acc. and dat.) § 34 (τὰ πτηνὰ τρέφεται) **συγγενεῖ** τῷ ἀέρι τὴν ψυχὴν κεκτημένα L, συγγενῆ S; § 55 **τοὺς** ἀξίους σφᾶς αὐτοὺς τῆς διδασκαλίας **παρεχομένους** οἷον παρακαταθήκη ἐγχειρίζεται L, τοῖς ἀξίους...παρεχομένοις Herv.; § 86 αὐτοῖς L, αὐτοὺς Μ.

(Gen. and dat.) § 8 **τοῦ δυναμένου** (to suit preceding gen.)...ἀποδεδόσθαι τὴν ἐκείνου διοίκησιν L, τῷ δυναμένῳ S; § 10 παντὸς τοῦ ὅλον ἑαυτὸν **τοῦ τῆς γνώσεως ἀγάπῃ** ἐπιβεβληκότος τῇ θεωρίᾳ L, τῇ τῆς γνώσεως ἀγάπῃ edd.; § 32 ἐκκαλυπτομένης ἅμα **τῆς θυσίας** καὶ τῆς διανοίας ἁπάσης τῷ θεῷ L, τῇ θυσίᾳ Η; § 55 ἔστιν ἡ γνῶσις τελείωσίς τις ἀνθρώπου ὡς **ἀνθρώπῳ** L, ὡς ἀνθρώπου P; § 64 ψυχὴ τελείᾳ ἀρετῇ κεκοσμημένη ἐκ...φύσεως ἀσκήσεως λόγου **συνηυξημένου** L, συνηυξημένη Lowth, συνηυξημένῃ Μ.

(2) *Gender and Number.* (M. and f.) § 29 τὴν ἐκκλησίαν ἱερὸν ἂν **εἴποιμεν** θεοῦ, τὸ πολλοῦ ἄξιον...βουλεύσει δὲ τοῦ θεοῦ εἰς νεὼν **πεποιημένην** L, πεποιημένον Μ; § 72 ταῖς ἡγιασμένοις παρθένοις L, ἡγιασμέναις edd.; § 95 ὁ μὲν πιστὸς τῇ κυριακῇ φωνῇ ἀξιόπιστος, εἰκότως ἂν...πρὸς τὴν ἀνθρώπων εὐεργεσίαν **ἐνεργουμένη** L, ἐνεργουμένη P, ἐνεργούμενος Μ; § 100 (as a soldier must not leave his post) οὕτως οὐδὲ ὃν ἔδωκεν ὁ λόγος ἄρχοντα εἰλήφαμεν γνώσεώς τε καὶ βίου **ληπτέον** τάξιν L, ...ἣν ἔδωκεν ὁ λόγος, ὃν ἄρχοντα εἰλήφαμεν, **λειπτέον** τάξιν Herv. (when the ὃν before ἄρχοντα was lost, the ἣν before ἔδωκεν was naturally changed to ὄν).

(M. and n.) § 5 κράτιστον ἐν οὐρανῷ ἄγγελος τὸ πλησιαίτερον κατὰ τόπον καὶ ἤδη καθαρώτερον τῆς...ζωῆς μεταλαγχάνων L (mistaking the adverbial use of πλησιαίτερον), ὁ πλησιαίτερον Μ; § 22 (ὁ γνωστικὸς θεοσεβὴς) σεμνόν, **μεγαλοπρεπές**, εὐποιητικόν, ...ἁπάντων ἀρχηγὸν ἀγαθῶν...εἶναι τὸν μόνον θεὸν **πεπεισμένος** L (taking the m. σεμνὸν as n.), μεγαλοπρεπῆ J; § 80 τὸ δὲ **ὅσιον** τὰ πρὸς τὸν θεὸν **δίκαια καὶ** τὴν πᾶσαν οἰκονομίαν μηνύει L, Barnard reads ὅσιος, i.e. 'the word ὅσιος,' referring to the quotation just before: δίκαια seems to have been altered from δικαίαν to suit τὰ, and καὶ to have been inserted for a construction. § 96 φθάσαντες δὲ ἐξενεγκεῖν...δόγματα **ψευδῆ** σχεδὸν ἁπάσαις ταῖς γραφαῖς **μαχόμενοι** καὶ ἀεὶ...ἐλεγχόμενοι...ὑπομένουσι L, μαχόμενα Μ.

(S. and pl. of nouns) § 12 μεταβάλλει πᾶν τὸ ἐνάρετον εἰς **ἀμείνω** οἰκήσεις L (expecting the s. οἴκησιν after τὸ), ἀμείνους D; § 13 (τὰς ψυχὰς) ὑπερβαινούσας ἑκάστης ἁγίας τάξεως τὴν πολιτείαν, καθ' **ἃς** αἱ μακάριαι...οἰκήσεις...διακεκλήρωνται L (taking ἑκάστης τάξεως as antecedent to ἅς); it seems better to read ἦν referring to πολιτείαν M. § 34 συναγόμενα L, συναγόμενον S; § 58 ἕνα δὲ εἶναι τὸν θεὸν διὰ τῶν "ζητούντων τὸ πρόσωπον τοῦ θεοῦ Ἰακὼβ" μεμήνυται L; this is a parallel case to § 80 τὸ ὅσιος, and H has restored τοῦ, referring to the use of the word ζητούντων in Ps. xxiv. quoted a little before. § 84 ἄμεινον οἶμαι ὑπερθέσθαι τὴν τοιαύτην φιλοτιμίαν...τοῖς πονεῖν ἐθέλουσι καὶ προσεκπονεῖν τὰ δόγματα...ἐπιτρέψαντες L, ἐπιτρέψαντας S (to agree with the subject of ὑπερθέσθαι), ἐπιτρέψας M. § 95 εἴ τις ἐξ ἀνθρώπων θηρίον γένοιτο L, ἐξ ἀνθρώπου (as shortly afterwards) M. § 108 τῶν δ' αἱρέσεων αἱ μὲν ἀπὸ ὀνόματος προσαγορεύονται, ὡς ἡ ἀπὸ Οὐαλεντίνου καὶ Μαρκίωνος καὶ Βασιλείδου L; as these were distinct sects, we should probably read αἱ.

(S. and pl. verbs) § 23 ἤ φησι L, ᾗ φασι Herv.; § 28 αὐτοὶ φησὶν L, αὐτοί φασιν S. § 31 ἀλλ' οὐκ ἂν οὐδαμῶς φησί...τρέφεσθαι τὸν θεόν L, φασὶ S. § 104 ναί, φησίν, ἡ γνῶσις εἴρηται φυσιοῦν L, φασίν Arcer. § 69 ἔστι μὲν οὖν ἅ...πρός τινων κατορθοῦνται L, κατορθοῦται edd. § 74 ὁ γνωστικὸς οὗτος πειράζεται ὑπ' οὐδενὸς πλὴν...διὰ τὴν τῶν συνόντων ὠφέλειαν. ἐπιρρώννυται γοῦν...διὰ τῆς ἀνδρικῆς παρακαλούμενος ὑπομονῆς L. The subject is here οἱ συνόντες, not γνωστικὸς, and the pl. must be restored.

(3) *Voices, Moods and Tenses*. (Act. and pass.) § 67 αὐτίκα μάλα καταγνύουσι τὸ ἀκαμπὲς τῆς ἐγκρατείας εἰς τὰς ἡδονάς L, κατάγνυνται M. § 105 μεγαλοπρέπειαν τῆς σοφίας τῆς κατὰ τὴν μάθησιν ἐμφυτευούσης διδάσκει L, ἐμφυτευθείσης Lowth (but see Stählin in *Addenda*).

(Ind. and Inf.) § 17 (τῇ ἀνδρείᾳ κατακέχρηται ἐν τῷ ὀργῆς κρατεῖν) καὶ καθόλου πρὸς πᾶν τὸ...ψυχαγωγοῦν ἡμᾶς ἀντιτάσσεται L, ἀντιτάσσεσθαι P. § 25 (iambic line) τὰ πράγματα, ὡς πέφυκεν, οὕτως γίγνεσθαι L, πράγμαθ'... γίγνεται Theod. § 27 καθαρμούς τινας προσάγειν τοῖς μυεῖσθαι μέλλουσιν ἀξιοῦσθαι L (under the influence of preceding inf.); ἀξιοῦσιν S. § 38 τὸ δὲ εὔχεσθαι καὶ ὀρέγεσθαι καταλλήλως γίνεσθαι L (owing to preceding inf.), γίνεται P. § 105 (γνώσομαι τὴν δύναμιν τῶν πεφυσιωμένων) εἰ μεγαλοφρόνως, ὅπερ ἐστὶν ἀληθῶς,...τὰς γραφὰς συνιέναι L (making συνιέναι subject of ἐστίν), συνίετε S.

(Ind. and Part.) § 66 οἱ μὲν ἀφορμὰς παρέχοντες σφίσιν αὐτοῖς, ἐπιρριπτοῦντες ἑαυτούς L, παρέχουσιν H. § 76 τὸν κύριον ὁρᾶν νομίζει τὰς ὄψεις... χειραγωγῶν· κἂν βλέπειν δοκῇ, ἃ μὴ βλέπειν ἐθέλῃ, κολάζων τὸ ὁρατικόν, ὅταν...συναίσθηται L, κολάζει M. § 109 τὴν βάσιν δι' υἱοῦ πρὸς τὸν πατέρα παραπέμπουσαν οὐκ ἔχουσαν L (to suit preceding participle), ἔχουσιν edd.

(Inf. and Part.) § 5 πίστις...τὸ κατὰ μηδένα τρόπον ἄδικα δρᾶν, τοῦτ' εἶναι πρέπον ἡγεῖσθαι τῇ ἐπιγνώσει τοῦ θεοῦ L, ἡγούμενον M. § 19 μαθεῖν ἄρα δεῖ πιστὸν εἶναι L, μαθὼν <ὡς> ἄρα κ.τ.λ. H. § 79 σπεύδων ἐπὶ τὸ εὐχαριστῆσαι κἀκεῖ σὺν Χριστῷ γενόμενος ἄξιον ἑαυτὸν παρασχών...ἔχειν τὴν δύναμιν τοῦ θεοῦ L, παρασχεῖν Barn. § 83 οὐδὲ αἰσχύνεται ἀποθανὼν εὐσυνείδητος ὢν ταῖς ἐξουσίαις ὀφθῆναι L, ἀποθανὼν (making αἰσχύνεται govern ὀφθῆναι) Lowth.

(Ind. and Subj.) ἐν ᾗ ὥρᾳ ἐπιγνῷ L, ἐπέγνω M.

(Part. and Subj.) § 29 ὅταν μακαρία μὲν αὕτη τυγχάνῃ ἅτε προκεκαθαρμένη μακάρια δὲ διαπραττομένη ἔργα L; here the subjunctive διαπράττηται, contrasted by μὲν...δὲ with τυγχάνῃ, seems to have been altered to suit the preceding participle. § 80 ἀσφαλὴς δὲ ἐν συμπεριφορᾷ ὁ γνωστικὸς μὴ λάθῃ ἢ ἡ συμπεριφορὰ διάθεσις γένηται L, ἀσφαλὴς δὲ <ἔστιν> ἐν...μὴ λάθῃ ἡ συμπεριφορὰ...γενομένη M. § 87 (καταργήσει τοὺς οὕτω βιοῦντας) ὡς διὰ τὸ ἐσθίειν γενομένους, μὴ οὐχὶ δὲ ἐσθίοντας ἵνα ζῶσι μὲν κατὰ τὸ ἀκόλουθον, κατὰ δὲ τὸ προηγούμενον τῇ γνώσει προσανέχοντας L, προσανέχωσιν M.

(Ind. and Opt.) § 7 καταλείπει ποτ' ἂν L, καταλείποι ποτ' ἂν D. ib. πῶς δ' ἄν ἐστι L, πῶς δ' ἂν εἴη D. § 95 προσέχοιμεν L, προσέχομεν or προσέχοιμεν ἂν D.

(Opt. and Subj.) § 8 κἂν εἰς ἀρχὴν κατασταίη L, καταστῇ M. § 69 ὅτῳ ἂν τις μάλιστα ἐπιδῷ L, ἐπιδάῃ M. § 85 πῶς δ' ἄν τις καὶ ἀγγέλους κρίνῃ L, κρίναι D.

(Pres. and Perf.) § 28 ἱδρύεται L, ἴδρυται bis M. § 29 ἐνιδρυμένον L, ἐνιδρυόμενον H. § 103 παραδιδόμενα L, παραδεδομένα M.

(Pres. and Aor.) § 14 γενομένους L, γινομένους H. § 20 περιγινόμενος L, περιγενόμενος H. § 105 ὑποσυρέντων L, ὑποσυρόντων Herv.

(Pres. and Impf.) § 30 ἐνέμεσθ' L, νέμεθ' Kl.

(Fut. and Aor.) § 7 ἐξομολογήσεσθαι L, ἐξομολογήσασθαι S. § 83 γενέσθαι L, γενήσεσθαι M. § 92 ὁμολογήσειν L, ὁμολογῆσαι D.

(4) *Other terminations.* § 35 νύκτα L, νύκτωρ M. § 86 ἄνευ L, ἄνω S.

(c) *Interchange of words.*

(1) *Prepositions, whether simple or in composition, and other short words.* § 26 ἐν τοῖσδε L, ἐπὶ τοῖσδε D; § 8 εὐπάθειαν L, ἐμπάθειαν H; § 61 ἐναγωνίσασθαι L, ἐπαγωνίσασθαι H; § 29 ἀνίδρυτον L, ἐνίδρυτον Lowth; § 104 ἀναπεμπόμενος L, παραπεμπόμενος M; § 9 ἐφορώντων L, ἀφορώντων H; § 16 ἀπογράφοντες L, ὑπογράφοντες H; § 29 ἐφ' ἑαυτοῦ L, ὑφ' ἑαυτοῦ Heins.; § 71 ἐπείγων L, ἀπάγων S; § 77 ἀποβάλλων L, καταβάλλων M; § 78 περισπώμενος L, ἐπισπώμενος M; § 102 πρὸ τῆς προνοίας κολαζόμεθα L, πρὸς τ. π. κ. edd.; § 9 προσήκουσα L, προήκουσα S; § 54 προτρεπόμενος L, προστρεπόμενος Morell; § 61 πρόσεισιν L, πρόεισιν Herv.; § 96 προΐεσθαι L, προσίεσθαι Heins.; § 101 προκριτέον L, προσκριτέον M; § 107 ὑπήκουσεν L, ἐπήκουσεν Dodw.; § 1 συμπεριλαμβάνοντες L, συμπαραλαμβάνοντες S; § 35 κἂν καθ' ἑαυτὸν μόνος ὢν τυγχάνῃ καὶ ὅπου L, κἂν ὅπου M; § 61 κἂν νόσος ἐπίῃ καί τι L, κἂν τι M; § 17 καὶ τῷ L, κἂν τῷ D; § 37 καὶ τὸ εὐπαθὲς L, κατὰ τὸ εὐπ. M; § 89 ἤτοι φιλοσοφεῖν καὶ Ἰουδαΐζειν L, ἢ M; § 101 καὶ περὶ L, ἢ <τούτους> περὶ Heins.; § 109 ἑδραιότης τῶν L, ἑδρ. καὶ M; § 16 καὶ ὕλης L, τὴν ὕλης M; § 37 δυνάμει τῇ ἀρρήτῳ L, δ. τινὶ ἀρρ. H; § 31 δοξάζοντες ἃ μεμαθήκαμεν L, δ. ὃν μ. H; § 107 ἣν ἀρχαίαν L, τὴν ἀρχ. S; § 21 καθάπερ ἂν L, κ. γὰρ Herv., κ. οὖν M; § 1 οἷός τε L, οἷός τις H.

(2) *Interchange of longer words of similar sound, appearance or significance.* § 3 τὰς διακονίας L, τ. θεραπείας M. Ib. τὴν βελτιωτικὴν ἐνδεικνύμενος θεραπίαν L, perhaps θεραπείαν (as in § 68 θεραπείαν pr. m. corr. ex θεωρίαν L) M.

§ 8 ἐνεστάλθαι L, ἐνεστάχθαι S.   § 9 συγκινεῖται καὶ μικροτάτη σιδήρου μοῖρα L, μακροτάτη M.   § 11 ἐπιτομήν L, ἐπίτομον M.   § 15 καλεῖται L, κηλεῖται Lowth.   § 17 καλὰ L, κακὰ S.   § 33 καλῶς L, κακῶς edd.   § 19 συμβάντων L, συμβιούντων M.   § 20 ἐλεεῖται L, ἐλεῖται Byw.   § 21 ἄριστα L, ἀρεστὰ S.   § 24 λυκήθιον L, ληκύθιον S, θύλακον Porson.   § 25 περιειλημμένον L, περιειλημένον S (cf. for similar interchange *Paed.* II. § 81 ἐνειλημένον, where the MS. has ἐνειλημμένων, and *Str.* IV. § 72 ἐνειλημμένος αὐτούς, where D reads αὐτοῖς after Grabe, but I should prefer ἐνειλημένος with a middle sense).   § 29 παθῶν L, πάντων M. *Ib.* ἀγύρτου L, Τυρίου J.   § 33 ἄθεος L, ἄθετος S.   § 34 δεῖγμα L, ἔρεισμα M.   *Ib.* ἅπαντα L, ἅπαντας Cyril, ἀπαρχαῖς Porson.   § 35 αὐτὸν L, υἱὸν M.   *Ib.* ἐντέχνως L, ἐνθέως H.   § 47 οὐδὲ ἀφαιρομένου τινὸς οὐδὲ ἐνδεοῦς γινομένου L, ἀφαιρουμένου edd. Cf. § 48 τὸ πᾶν συναιρεῖται πρὸς τὴν τελειότητα L and § 103 τὸ...ταῖς ἡδοναῖς συναιρούμενον ἐκλεγόμενοι L, where H reads συναίρεται and συναιρόμενον.   § 48 τιμήσας ἐπισκοπῇ L, τηρήσας ἐπ. M.   *Ib.* διαμονὴ L, διανομὴ M.   § 49 συνεύξεται τοῖς καινότερον πεπιστευκόσι L, κοινότερον M.   § 50 ἐν τῷ πάθει κεῖται τοῦ διακονουμένου L, διαπονουμένου M.   *Ib.* οἴεται L, ὁμεῖται H.   § 55 τοῦτο L, ταύτῃ S.   § 59 βαναύσους L, βασάνους P.   § 66 κακία L, κακὴ M.   § 69 εὕροιμεν L, εἴποιμεν J.   § 74 τῶν αὐτῶν L, τοιούτων Heins.   § 77 ποιεῖν L, ποθεῖν Lowth.   § 84 δοκεῖν L, δεικνύει M.   § 85 κτῆσιν L, κρίσιν M.   *Ib.* τοὺς L, τοῦτο M.   § 86 ἀντιδικῶν L, ἀνταδικῶν M.   § 93 ἐθίζουσι L, ἐθνίζουσι M.   § 95 τὸν ἑαυτοῦ βίον ἐπιστρέψας τῇ ἀληθείᾳ L, ἐπιτρέψας Herv. *Ib.* περιβαλόντες L, περιλαβόντες M.   § 98 ἐκποριζόμενοι L, ἐκπονούμενοι M. *Ib.* κάλον L, κάλων edd.   § 101 ἄνοια L, ἄγνοια Herv.   § 99 ἐνέργειαν L, ἐνάργειαν Hoesch.   § 102 ἐνεργὴς L, ἐναργὴς S.   § 105 ἡ σοφία ἐνεφυσίωσεν τὰ ἑαυτῆς τέκνα.   οὐ δήπου τῦφον ἐνεποίησεν ὁ κύριος ταῖς μερικαῖς κατὰ τὴν διδασκαλίαν L, Stählin suggests τοῖς μειρακίοις.   § 107 Μαρκίων L, Μάρκος Gieseler.   § 108 ὑποθέσεων L, ὑποστάσεων M.   § 110 τρόπου L, τόπου Herv. *Ib.* ὑπόσχεσιν L, ὑπόθεσιν M.   § 111 στοιχείῳ L, στοίχῳ S.

(I) MISPLACEMENT OF SENTENCES.

In some cases it is possible to find a natural collocation for the intrusive sentence, as in § 18, p. 30. 12—14 δικαιοσύνης—οὐρανῷ, which, as it stands, breaks the connexion between the thought of the gnostic being in want of nothing himself (πλουτῶν μὲν—τἀγαθοῦ) and the thought of his generosity towards others (ταύτῃ καὶ μεταδοτικός). If, on the other hand, we place it before πλουτῶν, the words συνεῖναι τούτοις ἔν τε γῇ καὶ οὐρανῷ follow naturally on the sentence σώζων τε—πλημμελῶν, in which the gnostic is said to be a citizen, not of this world only, but of a higher order. In § 38, p. 66. 18—22, the sentence διόπερ οὐδεὶς ἐπιθυμεῖ πόματος—πολιτεύεσθαι, has nothing to do with what immediately precedes or follows, as to the true object of prayer; but it carries on the thought of the last sentence in § 38 ὡς μηκέτι ἔχειν τὰ ἀγαθά...εἶναι δὲ ἀγαθόν, except that the particle διόπερ seems out of place. It is more difficult to find a place for the sentence οὐ γὰρ εἰ δι' ἀφροσύνην—ἀπὸ κακίας φερόμενα in § 66, p. 112. 29— 114. 6. This is a very obscure statement on the relation of action to habit, which comes in the middle of a straightforward passage, proving that there can be no true courage apart from reason and knowledge; and I must confess I have not been able to find any suitable place for it.

(K) LOSS OF SENTENCE.

In § 47, p. 82. 15 it seems to me that something has been lost between πεπεισμένος ὡς ἔστιν ἕκαστον τῶν μελλόντων καὶ κέκτηται τοῦτο, and τὸ γὰρ ἀνενδεὴς (MS. ἐνδεὴς) καὶ ἐπιδεὴς πρὸς τὸ ἐπιβάλλον μετρεῖται. The connecting link would, I think, be something of this sort: ἀνθρώπῳ δὲ ὄντι ἀγαπητὸν τὸ οὕτως κεκτῆσθαι. So in § 72, p. 126. 7, I think something has been lost after ἀπέκτεινεν. The preceding sentence tells us that 'he who refuses to eradicate the passions of his soul causes his own death.' Then follows ἀλλ' ὡς ἔοικεν ἀτροφία μὲν ἡ ἄγνοια τῆς ψυχῆς, τροφὴ δὲ ἡ γνῶσις. It would seem that we want some such connecting link as οὐ γὰρ ὁ θεὸς ἀπέκτεινεν, which might be easily lost owing to the recurrence of ἀπέκτεινεν.

Dr Kenyon of the British Museum was kind enough to read the foregoing paper, and allows me to print his remarks upon it.

'The corruptions are so many and various that no single cause will account for them all. Some of them (ε for η, ο for ω, ι for η or ει, η for ει, αι for ε) are common vowel changes, due no doubt to modifications in pronunciation. Others are easy errors of transcription, owing to similarity of letters, such as ω=ει, π=τ, τ=γ, λ=γ, δ=α, and in some hands ε=ο, μ=ν, θ=ο. Others, namely the confusion of terminations, seem to point strongly to an ancestor in which contractions were used, and probably one in which the terminations were simply omitted (as often in papyri, the last written letter being raised above the line as a sign of contraction, e.g. γινεσθ = γίνεσθαι) rather than one in which the terminations were represented by constant symbols, like the later mediaeval minuscules. Others, and a great many, are simple blunders, of which no palaeographical explanation can be given, and which, if they only occur in moderate numbers, need only be ascribed to the human frailty of the copyist; but when they are very frequent they rather suggest a transcript from a damaged ancestor. Everything seems to point to that being the case here; but there is the further question whether we can determine what sort of a manuscript this damaged ancestor was. The *Stromateis* MS. itself being of the 11th cent., it must have been transcribed from an uncial copy, or else from an early minuscule, which would probably be as clear as an uncial. It is difficult, however, to imagine these corruptions as arising from an uncial MS. (especially those which appear to be due to transpositions and misplacings of words), the lines in an uncial MS. being large and clearly distinct; moreover it is highly improbable that contracted terminations would be largely used in an uncial or 10th century minuscule. The phenomena presented by the text of the *Stromateis* seem rather to suggest a papyrus archetype, written with a considerable number of contracted terminations, and having suffered

Quotations in the Florilegia[1].

Among the writings of Maximus Confessor (d. 655) is a Florilegium, entitled Κεφάλαια Θεολογικά (Migne *Patrologia* vol. 91 pp. 719—1018) consisting of extracts from authors both sacred and profane. From this the Melissa Antonii was compiled at a much later date. A similar work, the Ἱερὰ Παράλληλα (Migne *Patr.* vol. 95 pp. 1042—1587, vol. 96 pp. 1—466), is attributed to Johannes Damascenus (d. about 760). The Melissa Monacensis is taken partly from Maximus and partly from Damascenus. Quotations from Clement are found in all of these. Of the Parallela three main recensions are known: (*a*) one in Vat. Gr. 1236, printed by Lequien in his edition of Damascenus, Paris 1712, vol. II. pp. 279—790, and a nearly identical text in an Escurial MS. (Ω III. 9) collated by Mr Barnard, to whom I am indebted for the readings. He cites them by Lequien's paging as 'Parall. Vat. et Scor.' (*b*) The 2nd in the Codex Rupefucaldinus (now Berol. Phill. 1450). The Clementine fragments are printed by Harnack (*Gesch. d. altchr. Litteratur* I. pp. 317 ff.) and Zahn (*F.* III. 17—41) as Par. Rup. (*c*) The 3rd recension is found in Paris reg. 923. This has not been printed. The quotations from *Str.* VII. are as follows:

§ 4, P. 830 *fin.* (p. 6. 27—p. 8. 3) καί μοι καταφαίνεται—ἐπικεκρυμμένα. p. 8. 1 ὅ,τι—ὑπαγορεύῃ L, om. Vat. Scor. 399, ὑπαγορεύσῃ Rup. 130 (Harn. p. 324, Zahn III. 27), l. 2 καὶ τρίτον L, τρίτον Rup. Vat. [Both readings of Rup. seem to be improvements on L.]

§ 33, P. 850 (p. 56. 26) μητρόπολις κακίας ἡδονή L, μ. τῶν κακῶν ἡ ἡδονή Vat. Scor. 648, μ. κακῶν ἡδονή Rup. 244[b] (Harn. p. 327, Zahn 27). [Rup. may be right.]

§ 41, P. 855 (p. 70. 27—29) ὥσπερ γὰρ πᾶν ὃ βούλεται δύναται ὁ θεός, οὕτως πᾶν ὃ ἂν αἰτήσῃ ὁ γνωστικὸς λαμβάνει. Vat. Scor. 399, Rup. 130[b] (Harn. 324, Zahn 27). *Om.* γὰρ omnes, οὕτω omnes, ὃ ἐὰν Scor. λαμβάνει] τυγχάνει Scor.

§ 57, P. 865 *fin.* (p. 100. 3—11) ἡ μὲν—περαιουμένη. Cited in Rup. 233[b] (Harn. 320 f.), Melissa Ant. 5 (Zahn 27). l. 3 *om.* οὖν Rup. l. 5 βεβαία Ant. Mel. l. 7 καταληπτὸν L, ληπτὸν Rup. (καταληπτικὸν D). l. 9 ὡς προεῖπον *om.* Rup. l. 10 ἡ δὲ L, ἤδη Rup.

§ 59, P. 867 (p. 102. 21—23) πᾶσα οὖν ἡ διὰ τοῦ ἐπιστήμονος πρᾶξις εὐπραγία, ἡ δὲ διὰ τοῦ ἀνεπιστήμονος κακοπραγία. Cited in Vat. Scor. 649, Rup. 245[a] and 263[a] (Harn. pp. 321 and 327, Zahn 27). l. 22 ἡ *om.* Rup. 245[a]. διὰ *om.* omnes. πρᾶξις L aud Rup. 263[a], καὶ ἐμπείρου πρᾶξις Vat. Scor. Rup. 245[a]. διὰ (sec.) *om.* omnes.

§ 62, P. 868 (p. 107. 22—25) οὐ μνησικακεῖ—τὴν ἄγνοιαν αὐτοῦ. Cited in Vat. Scor. 399, Vat. 356 (*hiat* Scor.), Rup. 130[b] (Harn. 324, Zahn 27),

---

[1] See Barnard's ed. of the *Quis Dives Salvetur* pp. xxiv and xxix, Loofs *Studien über die dem J. von Damaskus zugeschriebenen Parallelen* 1892, Holl's *Sacra Parallela* 1896 (*Texte u. Unters.* vol. xvi. 1), Zahn *Forschungen* vol. III., Harnack *Gesch. d. altchr. Litteratur* I. pp. 317 ff.

Melissa Mon. 97ª (Zahn l.c.). l. 22 μνησικακεῖ ποτέ L, μνησικακήσει ὁ γνωστικὸς ποτέ omnes. l. 23 ἄξια omnes. l. 24 κοινωνικὸν Vat. 399, not Scor. l. 25 om. αὐτοῦ after ἄγνοιαν Vat. 356, not 399.

§ 73, P. 876 (p. 128. 8—11) ὅταν οὖν—ὁδεύει γένος. Cited in Rup. 210ª (Harn. p. 320). l. 8 om. οὖν Rup. l. 9 ἀλλά Rup.

§ 80, P. 881 (p. 140. 15—18) χρὴ γὰρ—παραπέμποντα. Cited in Scor. Vat. 506, Rup. 5ᵇ (Harn. 326 fin.). l. 15 χρὴ γὰρ μήτε, ἐὰν ἀγαθά ᾖ, προστετηκέναι τούτοις ἀνθρωπίνοις οὖσι L, om. γὰρ Scor. Vat. Rup. μήτε ἀγαθά τινα προστετηκέναι τούτοις ἀνθρώποις οὖσι Scor. Vat. Rup. except that Scor. has προστετικέναι, Vat. προστεθεικέναι.

§ 82, P. 882 (p. 144. 18) ἕπεται γὰρ τὰ ἔργα τῇ γνώσει ὡς τῷ σώματι ἡ σκιά. Cited in Vat. Scor. 399, Rup. 130ᵇ, Maximus 584, Melissa Ant. 56, Melissa Mon. 105ᵇ (Harn. 324, Zahn 27). om. γὰρ omnes. τῇ γνώσει τὰ ἔργα omnes.

§ 99, P. 893 (p. 174. 8—12) ὡς γὰρ ὀφθαλμὸς—ἀποτυφλουμέναις. Cited in Vat. Scor. 339, Rup. 237ª (Harn. 321). ll. 8—11 ὡς γὰρ—παρορᾷ Rup. 109ᵇ (Harn. 318, Zahn 27), Melissa Ant. 5 (Zahn l. c.). l. 8 ὡς γὰρ L, ὥσπερ Vat. Scor. Rup. 237ª, ὥσπερ ὁ Rup. 109ᵇ. οὕτω Vat. Scor. om. ἡ Scor. l. 10 δυδέναι Vat. Scor.

§ 100, P. 894 (p. 176. 16—18) ὡς ἔοικεν—σεμνή. Cited in Rup. 72ª (Harn. p. 317). l. 16 ἔοικε Rup. ἤπερ L, ἡ Rup. l. 17 ἀλήθειαν· αὐστηρὰ γὰρ L, ἀλήθειαν κἂν αὐστηρὰ Rup.

Clementine Anthologies.

Besides the extracts from Cl. included in these Florilegia, Dindorf (vol. I. xvii. f.) refers to collections of Clementine extracts contained in certain MSS. One of these is the Codex Ottobonianus 94 collated for Potter's edition by Montfaucon, another a MS. at Augsburg collated by Hoeschel for Sylburg's edition. Dindorf mentions a third in the Library of Naples (π. AA. 14), which is described as a paper codex of the 15th century, containing the three books of the *Paedagogus* (ff. 1—101) and a compendium of the seven books of the *Stromateis* (ff. 106—166). A fuller account is given in Dr Otto Staehlin's *Obs. Crit. in Clem. Al.* 1890 Erlangen. He found Hoeschel's own copy of Clement with various marginal readings in the Augsburg Library, of which Hoeschel was librarian for many years. Since then Staehlin[1] has discovered the actual MS. (Monac. 479) which was collated by Hoeschel, and has most kindly sent me his own collation, printed below. In p. 12 of the *Beiträge* he also describes another MS. (Ottob. 98) closely resembling the above, and thus summarizes his conclusions (p. 15). The parent of the four MSS. contained extracts from the *Paedagogus* and *Stromateis*. The extracts were imperfect, and the order was so confused that we find extracts from *Paed.* in the middle of *Strom.* V. and extracts from *Strom.* VI. at the beginning of the MSS. In a letter dated Jan. 7, 1902 he gives little hope of any light being thrown on the text of

[1] See his *Beiträge z. Kenntniss d. Handschriften d. Cl. Alex.* 1895 Nürnberg.

Clement from these excerpts: 'Es wird mir immer wahrscheinlicher dass der Archetypus der vier Excerpthandschriften doch aus L stammt. Die Varianten lassen sich fast durchweg leicht als Abschreibfehler erklären. Uebrigens werde ich in diesem Frühjahr noch einmal nach Italien reisen und dann auch die drei übrigen Excerpthandschriften genauer prüfen."

Excerpta e Clementis Alex. in Cod. Monac. gr. 479.

D. III. 252. 25 θεραπεία θεοῦ—253. 2 διάκονοι.
 30 ἐκ] καὶ.
253. 9 ὥσπερ—253. 26 ἐπικεκρυμμένα.
 14 γινομένων. 15 ἡ δ' ἡ. 16 πρέπον τὸ *in marg. man. sec.*
 17 εἰδώς. 23 om. πρῶτον. τὸ corr. ex. τὸν. 25 ἐπικεκρ.] κεκρ.
257. 5 ἔστιν—257. 10 τελειούμενοι.
 5 ἔστι. 6 ὥς supra lin. ab Hoeschelio additum.
 7 πάντα] πάντων (sic etiam Ott. 94 *ap.* Pott.).
267. 7 ὄνπερ—267. 12 ἐπιβλέπει.
 8 κόσμον ὅλον. 11 πάντι.
268. 5 ὀλίγα—268. 7 ἀπεικάζοντας.
268. 10 καθάπερ—268. 11 ἐκπικραίνονται.
 11 ἐκπικρένονται.
269. 12 τοιοῦτον—270. 8 φάγῃ.
 15 ἐμβάδος *in marg. ab Hoesch., in textu* ἑβδομάδος.
270. 1 σμικρόλογος.
270. 4 θεασάμενος corr. man. sec. 6 ὅτι] τούτῳ. ἔφαγε.
278. 2 ἔστι—278. 15 ἀέρα.
 8 περὶ τοῦ θεοῦ; πότερον om. 10 ἄνυδρα (*in marg. ab Hoesch.* ἔνυδρα)
 12 ἀλλ'—13 θέον om.
278. 17 ἤ—278. 18 κυρίως.
279. 3 εἰ—279. 5 χρῆται.
 17 ὁ—280. 4 κρέα.
 17 καὶ ὁ κωμικός. 18 φησι. 280. 3 ἔχει.
280. 5 διὰ—280. 10 λέγουσι.
 5 τινὲς διὰ τὸ. 6 ἐσθίουσι. 10 λέγουσα.
280. 16 οἶνος—280. 18 νωχαλεστέραν.
 18 νωχαλεστέραν corr. pr. man.
283. 12—283. 13 θεοῦ.
283. 15 οὐδαμῇ—283. 18 προσίεται.
 17 τὰ δὲ λεγόμενα.
283. 19 οὔτε—283. 24 ψυχήν.
 20 οἷον] ἤ. τὴν om. 23 εὐώδης.
284. 1 ἐπεὶ—284. 17 ψυχήν.
 7 ἤρεσε. 12 αἰσθητικῆς. 14 λέγει.
284. 24 ὅλος—284. 26 θεός.
     β a
 25 χρήσηται τούτοις (a et β *suprascr.* a man. pr.).

293. 21 ἀθλητής—293. 26 ἐμοί.
    21 ἀγενής.   23 ὀλυμπι' (ι corr. ex ει).
339. 27 τριῶν—340. 3 αἱρέσεις.
    27 διαθέσεων corr. man. pr. ex διαθέσεως.
340. 14 ὡς—340. 22 διδασκάλου.
    16 κροζύλῳ.   19 ἀριστοτέλει.   22 τελείως.
341. 17 εἰ—341. 21 μετανοήσωσιν.
    18 ἐπαίοιμεν.   20 καταισχυνθέντες (αις in litura pro εγ ?).
342. 9 καὶ—342. 17 ψυχῆς.
    13 μισήσειε.
343. 12 ὁ—343. 13 παραδόσει.
344. 16 γνωστὸς—344. 18 ἑρμηνεύεται.
    18 ἑρμηνεύεται] λέγεται.
344. 22 οὐ—344. 25 ἀπάτη.
    22 καθάπερ καὶ οἱ (sed καὶ a man. sec. del.).   24 κάνοννα.
345. 2 ὅσοι—345. 4 ἐπιτίμια.
          φα
    3 ἔγγρα (φα super lin. a man. sec.).
348. 19 ὑμεῖς—348. 21 ἀριθμῷ
    21 δυο δέκατοι.   } hoc ordine!
348. 17 ἀκάθαρτοι—348. 18 μηρυκισμόν.

Collation by Dr Otto Stählin of Dindorf's Text of Strom. VII. with the Laurentian MS. v. 3, supplementing Dindorf's Critical Notes.

pr. stands for 1st hand.

Dind. Vol. III. p. 251. 21. ὅτι] ὅ is added at the end of a line apparently by prima.

252. 2. ἐπεξἀργασια corrected by pr.
       4. κομιδῆι.
       8. το before μόνον erased by pr.
      10. φ erased by pr. after τό.
      18. αἴτιον τῶν πρᾱ τῶν ὅλων.
      19. οὐκ ἔτι.
      29. γονεῦσι.
253. 4. διακρονούμενος corrected by pr.
      10. συγκομιζόνται (i.e. -ζονται) corrected by pr.
      11. παρεχομένη.
      14. ταυτη.
      15. ῇ] εἰ corrected by the writer of the marginal scholia, who also inserts a comma before ἕξις in l. 16.

24. ὑπαγορεύῃ.
254. 20. μηδαμῆι.
  24. ἀναδεδειγμένωι corrected by pr.
255. 4. δέ] τέ.
  11. αυτου without breathing.
  20. ῥᾴθυμος without accent; breathing added by schol.
  29. τοῖς corrected from τοὺς by pr.
256. 5. ἐστὶν.
  7. οὐ̇κ corrected by pr. (with χ above)
  20. κατ' ἀλλήλου.
257. 1. βελτίω.
258. 2. σιδήρων.
  4. δὲ ἄλλοι.
  7. ἑλιχθέντες.
  13. ἡισθέντα.
  15. ἐπίδωσιν (ω corr. fr. ο), i.e. ἐπίδοσιν changed to ἐπίγνωσιν by pr. (with ΓΝ above)
  25. ἑαυτὸν τοῦ τῆς γνώσεως.
259. 3. τὰς βαρβάρους corr. fr. ταῖς β. by pr.
  15. ἀμηγέπηι.
260. 7. μακαρίαι (thus accented).
  13. ἐστιωμένας.
261. 13. ἀποκτειννῦντας.
  15. τοῦθ' ἦν.
262. 3. τισὶ.
  6. οὐ καθεοράκασι] οὐκ ἀθεοράκασι.
  9. ἴσοι.
  25. ὑπὲρ ἄνω.
263. 1. ἀπίστων corr. by pr. (with ρ above)
  6. γενήτωρ corr. by pr. (with υ above)
264. 8. τῶ.
  16. ἀνδρείας (ει changed to ι by pr.).
  22. ὑπὲρ ἄνω.
265. 6. πάσης] ἁπάσης.
  13. ἔθ'] ἔτ'.
  15. ἡ ἀρετή] ἡ erased by later hand.
  28. καλῶ.
266. 10. ἴσα.
  15. εἰ ἀπὸ corr. by pr.
267. 6. καθοσιωμένους.
  18. θράκες τε πυροὺς.
268. 7. ἀνθρώπων] ἀπῶν, ν erased by pr.
  11. ἢ φησι.

	17. σκύλα.
	18. ἐρείπια] ἐρίπεια.
269.	1. 'τεκον] τέκον.
	8. διορύξηι plainly (not διορίζῃ as in V.).
270.	2. πριᾶσθαι.
	12. περιειλημμένον (η in erasure by pr., probably taking the place of ι).
	16. δὴ] δι' (ι corr. fr. η).
	20. κωμωδεῖ ὅτ' ἂν.
271.	4. τῇ.
	16. χόνδρους] χρόνδους.
	17. δᾴδας.
	21. γ' οὖν ἐστι.
	24. κωμωδεῖ.
	25. πατέρ'] π̄ρα.
272.	1. ἐν τοῖσδε δασμίας.
	3. τ'] τε.
	3. πολυφλοίσβοιοι.
273.	3. ἁγνεία (D. ἀγνεία).
	5. καθαρὸς η̣ι̣ εἰ corr. by pr.
	22. παιδιὰς (thus accented).
274.	2. ἐλεφαντίνου (without breathing).
	6. ἐκτελέσῃς.
	13. ὄντος] ὄντως.
	14. Stop before ὄντος ὄν.
	19. ἱδρύσθαι (without breathing).
	23. οἰκείας.
	24. ομοσχημονες corr. by pr. (ιο above)
275.	24. χαριέντως αὐτοῖς.
	25. καταμεμφομενος (without accent).
	τοῖς ἀ̄νοις corr. fr. τοὺς ἀ̄νους by pr.
276.	4. κομιδῇ.
	5. ἐνεμεσθ'.
	15. οὐκ ἐσθίω κλυκείαν.
277.	3. κνίσσα.
	4. κνίσα (σ appears to have been written above the ι and erased.
	9. διαλαβεῖν.
	18. αὔξει.
278.	10. περιπνεῖται ν corr. from ρ by pr.
	22. τεθρυλήκασι.
279.	20. ὑῶν corr. fr. υἱῶν.
	23. Αἴσωπος] ἴσσωπος.
	κακῶς] καλῶς.
280.	1. αὐτοῖς.
	2. χρησίμοις ὅτ' ἂν ἕλκωνται· πλὴν (ἢ above the ι by pr.).

14. οὐκ ἔτι.
20. ἁγνείαις.
282. 23. πάντηι, as in 283. 1, 284. 22.
283. 15. οὐδαμῆι.
21. γοητεύουσα.
284. 6. τοῦδ'] τοῦθ' (thus accented).
23. ῇ] ἡ.
285. 15. μηκέτι.
19. εἰδόσι] εἰδόσι τε.
προσ| φον. Line ends with προσ, letters ορ written above by Schol.
20. τίνα (before τὰ) in margin by pr.
24. οντως (i.e. οντος) corr. by pr.
286. 4. ψηθυρίζοντες.
14. βιαζώμεθα.
20. ἐνάτην (not as D).
287. 10. ἂν ὁ.
22. ἐπιγινώσκεται.
26. οὐδὲ μίαν.
288. 26. λάβῃ.
29. διὰ χάριν, διὰ erased by pr.
δέδοται, ε corr. fr. ι by pr.
289. 12. ἀνετειλ̆ (sic) = ἀνέτειλεν.
21. εἰ'οξν' γ' above the ι by pr.
290. 20. χρωμένηι.
30. interpunction: αὐστηρὸς· οὗτος ἡμῖν αὐστηρὸς.
291. 5. ῇ] ἦι.
10. γενομενω corr. by pr.
17. οὐδ' ὁτιοῦν] οὐθότ' οὖν.
292. 18. ἆρα ὁ γνωστικὸς.
28. ἀφαιρομένου.
293. 6. χρῆσιν corr. fr. κτῆσιν by pr. (not as D.).
16. ὑγείαν bis.
23. ὀλυμπι'.
294. 21. No stop before οὐ.
295. 6. ὀμόσαι ὄρκος.
296. 2 and 3. ὀμνῦται
7. ὅρκου.
8. δεῖ Sylb. δὴ L.
16. πάντηι, and so in p. 301. 15.
298. 5. ποιοίηι.
299. 13. ἢ μὲν—ἢ δέ.
19. διδάσκεται | ται (ται bis at the end of one line and the beginning of the next).

300. 7. κατὰ τῶν θεῶν.
  15. κέκληται corr. by pr.
302. 26. σωίζῃ.
304. 3. ταύτῃ and so in 306. 12, 308. 25.
  5. αυτὸν.
  16. ἐπίῃ.
  20. μεταρυθμιζομένους.
  23 and 24. ἴρεῖ (with two accents).
306. 3. ἐλπίδων corr. fr. ἐλπίδος by pr.
307. 14. δει̇ corr. by pr.
308. 4. μόνος ὁ θαρραλέος corr. by pr.
  15. οὐδὲ τὰ] οὔτε τὰ (not αὖτε as D).
  18. ἀγνοία.
  22. κατοτεχνοῦνται.
  26. ἢ corr. by schol. into ᾗ.
309. 8. ὑπομένοντες, the 2nd o in rasura by pr.
  13. ἆθλα.
  20. αυτὴν.
310. 18. θεραπείαν corr. fr. θεωρίαν by pr.
311. 1. τῇ, as in 313. 5.
  14. ποιοίη.
  16. πόσω.
312. 9. ὡς οὕτως corr. by pr.
  18. μίμησιν corr. in marg. fr. μνήμην by pr.
314. 11. καθάπερ καὶ ἡ χήρα.
  21. ἡγιασμένοις.
  30. συμφέρῳ.
315. 5. εὐχὴ γὰρ αὐτῷ.
316. 2. ἐπιτρέψῃ.
  6. εἰς μὰρ πεῖραν καὶ μ. corr. by pr.
  28. ταύτῃ as in p. 318. 7, 319. 20.
317. 1. ἐπιφιμίζονται.
318. 12. δεικνύη.
  24. ῥᾶον.
319. 9. τῇδε.
  25. διπλή.
322. 13. γενόμενον in marg. by pr.
323. 9. ἐμβλέψῃις.
  14. ἀβραάμ.
  20. ἱέμενος.
324. 5. ἀποκεκαθαρμένους.
  28. ἰστέον.
325. 12. τολμᾶ.
326. 2. ἀπειθεῖς. a above ει by schol.

12. καθῶλην.
22. τίς.
327. 11. θεοῦ οὐ.
14. τινὲς.
25. τῷ] τὸ.
328. 17. οὐδ' ὅπως τι οὖν (not τις as D.).
28. μονήν.
329. 14. γίνεσθαι] γίγνεσθαι.
15. ἦν] ἦν.
330. 12. παραβαίηι.
29. ὑγιάναι.
331. 15. γλυκεία.
332. 6. τἀληθὲς, corr. by pr. (with οὐτ above)
17. μόνη...ἀρχαία.
333. 14. καὶ τὸ corr. by pr.
19. ἐπιγνῶ.
23. ἀμηγέπη.
334. 3. βασιλεία.
335. 26. προσωτέρω.
336. 1. τεχνῖται.
5. ἀποδεικνῦντες.
337. 5. πάσας ἐστιν.
9. δόγματός ἐστι.
11. πρὸς ἔτι.
23. ἀποραθυμήσαντες.
25. ἐπηιρμένοι μερίζοντες.
29. αὐτοῖς.
338. 2. κάλον.
4. πολυθρυλήτου.
23. Before ἑαυτῶν an erasure of three letters.
29. ἀμυγδαλαι (not as D. on 339. 4).
339. 10. ληπτέον.
20. τῶν bis, at the end and beginning of lines.
340. 4. ἐστι.
12. τῇ.
14. πρόσχηι, a late hand interpolates ι before σ.
21. τῇ δοθείσῃ.
341. 3. δύνατ'.
19. πατρώας.
27. πρὸς] πρὸ.
342. 17. ὑπεχέτω.
18. ῥαθυμεῖν.
19. ὀριγνόμενοι...βιάζονται.
343. 10. ἐπιζητήσῃ.
23. ἡμῶν.

344.	4.	τύφον.
	7.	παραδιδομένη.
	13.	τῆς γραφῆς] τὰς γραφὰς, in margin a by pr.
	18.	ἑρμηνεύεται in marg. by pr.
	22.	ὡς ἑαυτὸν. σ above the line by pr.
345.	13.	εἴσειμεν.
	23.	οἱ.
	24.	μέχρι τῆς. γε above the l. by pr.
346.	24.	ἴσον.
347.	4.	ἐγκρατητῶν.
	15.	ζώων.
	17.	ἱερείων. ει corr. fr. ι by pr.
348.	4.	ἔχουσαν.
	27.	τῷ in marg. ι.
349.	8.	ὅρια (sic) i.e. ὅρια corr. fr. ὅρια by pr.

CHAPTER VI.

ANALYSIS OF BOOK VII.

A. Defence of the gnostic Christian from the charges of atheism and irreverence. What is the nature of his worship of God, what his idea of the Son. Man's nature is perfected by his free choice of good under the Divine guidance (§§ 1—13).

B. More particular description of the worship (§§ 14, 15), *the knowledge* (§ 17), *and the virtue of the gnostic* (§§ 18—21).

C. Heathen superstition is really atheism (§§ 22—28).

D. What constitutes true worship in regard to place, time, symbolism, sacrifice, incense, fasting, festivals (§§ 29—37), *prayer, praise, study, instruction, self-discipline* (§§ 38—49).

E. The gnostic has no need of oaths (§§ 50, 51): *his word is always in accordance with his thoughts and with his life, unless reserve is needed medicinally, for the good of others* (§ 53). *As a teacher, his aim is to mould his scholars after the image of Christ* (§ 52).

F. (§§ 55—88). *Fuller description of the gnostic. Gnosis is built on faith, grows into love, and is consummated in the Beatific Vision. The gnostic not only does right actions, but does them on right principles. Starting with admiration, he has his eye always fixed on heaven, and so rises above temptations of sense, and acquires the habit of virtue. Difference of the particular virtues (courage, justice, temperance) as seen in the gnostic and in others. His whole life is a communion with God: he loves righteousness not for its results but for its own sake. His sufferings, his meekness, his self-mortification, his sympathy with others, his readiness to forgive, his readiness to die. The perfection of the gnostic exhibited in 1 Cor. vi.*

G. (§§ 89—110). *The existence of sects and heresies is no ground for denying the truth of Christianity, any more than for denying the use of philosophy and medicine. Heresy proceeds from self-conceit, rashness and haste, but is over-ruled for good, as it calls out more patient study and more earnest effort on the part of the true gnostic. The word of God is the criterion of truth. Heretics misapply Scripture, not caring to search out its true sense, and being ashamed to own themselves in the wrong. True knowledge does not puff up, but elevates and enlightens. Mystical meaning of the Jewish law respecting unclean animals.*

§ 1. The true gnostic is the truly religious man: he is wrongly accused of atheism by philosophers; in addressing whom ratiocination should be employed, rather than scriptural proof, for which place will be found in a later treatise. To superficial judgment our Miscellanies may differ from Scripture; but they are based upon it, and differ in language only, not in meaning.

§ 2. The gnostic alone worships God rightly. True worship leads to loving God and being loved by Him (cf. below, p. 6. 21 foll.). The reverence of the gnostic is proportioned to the worthiness of its object. In the world of sense he honours rulers; in teaching, the most ancient philosophy and prophecy (below, p. 162. 5 f., § 107); in the spiritual world, the Son, the beginning of all things. The Father, the ultimate cause, is made known through the Son to those elected for knowledge; is to be worshipped in silence (Ps. 4. 4; Eccl. 5. 2; below, p. 72. 9, 10, § 43).

§ 3. Service of God consists in self-discipline and love which fosters the divine in a man's self (below, § 13). Service of man is double, meliorative (as medicine and philosophy), ministrative (as that paid by children and subjects). In the Church the service of presbyters is meliorative, that of deacons ministrative. Both are performed by angels (below, p. 8. 15, 10. 21, 16. 9) and by the gnostic. True devotion is shewn in doing good to man for God's sake and living as one who will hereafter become God (pp. 5 and 7).

§ 4. Three marks of the gnostic: to know, to do, to teach (below, § 52). He is far removed from atheism, and from the superstition by which the real man is brought into bondage. The Son teaches us the Divine Mysteries (p. 10. 10).

§ 5. Faith in its first stage (i.e. the O.T.) imparts the knowledge of God; in its second (after the teaching of the Saviour) the conviction that absolute sinlessness is involved in the knowledge of God (cf. 1 Joh. 3. 4—10). Devotion is the best thing on earth. The angel who is nearest to the Throne is best in heaven. But far beyond all, is the Son, who steers the universe according to the Father's will, never moving, never divided; filling all space and all time, Himself all reason and all light. To Him are subject the host of angels and gods, and all men, either as slaves, or as faithful servants, or as friends.

§ 6. The Word is the teacher, training all in suitable ways, the gnostic by mysteries (above, p. 8. 3), the believer by hope, the hard of heart by punishment (below, p. 12. 29, § 12). That the Son is a Saviour, is asserted by prophecy. He does not compel, but persuades, because man is able to obtain salvation by free choice (below, p. 14. 8, 18). He gave to the Greeks philosophy by the hand of angels assigned to different nations, but the Lord Himself presides over believers. Proof that Christ is able and willing to save all.

§ 7. Envy belongs to the devil, not to Christ, who is free from all passion, being the Power and Wisdom of God, the Saviour and Lord of men, even of the disobedient, who will at last confess their sins and receive grace from Him (above, p. 10. 12, 13).

§ 8. That Christ is not a foe to man is shewn by His taking man's flesh, and so extending salvation to all that choose (above, p. 10. 18). It is the province of the superior to rule; and the highest rule is that of the Word, who by the Father's will is the invisible author of all movement.

§ 9. Nothing is neglected by His administration. All the members of the great organism have their attention fixed on Him. As the magnet holds a long chain of rings by its attractive force, so the Son by His Holy Spirit draws all creatures to Himself, constituting together one great hierarchy, with first and second and third orders, and then the angels (pp. 6. 6, 8. 15, § 9) on the margin of the visible world. The virtuous among men are raised to the highest mansion, but the weak being carried away by lusts fall to the ground. For it is the primal law that virtue must be won by choice (p. 10. 18).

§ 10. Hence the commandments, Mosaic and pre-Mosaic, appointed life for him who chose it, and permitted him who rejoiced in evil to consort with what he chose; while every improvement leads to a corresponding rise in the universal order (§ 12) ending in the transcendent orbit which lies nearest to the Lord, ever occupied in the contemplation of His loveliness.

§ 11. The Lord is the source both of the Mosaic and pre-Mosaic law: He also provided Greek philosophy for those who were ignorant of the Jewish philosophy, and thus limited unbelief to the period of His own Presence on earth. Some however of the Greeks have omitted the intermediate step of philosophy and passed on at once to salvation by faith.

§ 12. He made all things conduce to virtue, so far as might be without destroying man's free will (§§ 9, 10), exhibiting the goodness of God in ordering each particular with a view to the perfection of the whole; and thus each individual is treated according to the possibilities of his character, the good being advanced continually to higher abodes (§ 10), the more hardened chastened by angels or by judgments, preliminary or final (§§ 6, 7), compelling them to repent (§ 7).

§ 13. Aposiopesis. Constant progress of the blessed, advanced to higher and higher mansions (§§ 10, 12) till they arrive at the unchanging Beatific Vision (contemplation). During his life here the gnostic approaches ever more nearly to the Divine likeness by his service of God through serving man (§ 3), thus freeing himself from the yoke of passion and becoming truly ἀπαθής.

§ 14. It is thus that the gnostic offers to God the only true sacrifice (§ 1) by putting to death the old man. We consecrate ourselves to Him who consecrated Himself for us. On the other hand the smoke of material sacrifice is an offering to demons.

§ 15. God needs no material offering. He is eternally the same and cannot be propitiated by gifts and sacrifices, as some men believe, making Him an accomplice in the wickedness of man; while others ascribe to Him all the evil which flows from the abuse of man's free-will.

§ 16. The cause of these evils is ignorant impulsiveness, to be combated by reason, and by receiving into our hearts the stamp of the Divine image.

§ 17. The function of gnostic science is the contemplation of the Father and the Son, of the laws and constitution of the universe, and of the moral nature of man.

§ 18. Manhood is shewn in resistance and endurance. Its various forms. Raises the gnostic above the opinion of the world. His temperance is shewn in his submission to a higher order than that of this world: his justice in his communion with all that are like-minded in earth and heaven. Being filled with the fulness of God, he wants nothing, but is endowed with all riches, and distributes freely to all.

§ 19. His virtue does not come from nature or from training, but from knowledge, built upon the foundation of faith, for which building philosophy is useful as clearing the ground (§ 1).

§ 20. The good fight of the Christian in the amphitheatre of the world, where angels are spectators and God is the president, and whoever chooses wins the prize (Apoc. 22. 17).

§ 21. God accepts what is done for the good of man as done to Himself. This is our best return for all His goodness to us.

§ 22. The heathen make their gods human in feelings as in shape, assimilating them to their own nature. Hence the wicked make to themselves a wicked god, while the gnostic worships absolute goodness in God.

§§ 23—27. The heathen are really atheists when they liken God to the worst of men. Superstition naturally arises from the supposition of the irritability and injustice of the gods. Purity is not outward, but inward. The mind must be cleansed from impious opinions, before it is fit to receive our mysteries.

§ 28. The infinite God cannot be circumscribed in a given locality. The heathen think that they make God by the process of enshrinement. Absurdity of this shewn by the Academic reasoning.

§ 29. The true temple of God is the assembly of the elect, and His true image the righteous soul, wherein He is continually enshrined.

§§ 30—32. God needs no sacrifice or incense to support Him, as the heathen believe. The only sacrifice He demands is the prayers and praises of His people, the only altar the righteous soul, the only incense the prayer of holiness.

§ 33. On abstinence from certain kinds of food.

§ 34. The composite incense demanded by the Law is the joint worship of many hearts and many nations. The sacrificial fire sanctifies, not flesh, but sinful souls.

§ 35. The gnostic honours the Father and the Son, not in a special place or at a special time or by special rites, but everywhere, in every way and at all times, rising above himself into the actual presence of God.

§ 36. He takes no part in public spectacles (§ 74), or in festivals; but enjoys all things soberly, thanking God for all that he receives, and assured that God's eye is ever upon him, and that God's ear is open to every thought of his heart.

§ 37. Hence there is no need for anthropomorphism (§ 22). [Confused and inconclusive argument, probably Academic.]

§ 38. In the gnostic, desire takes the form of prayer; and his desire is only for real good, i.e. for goodness.

§ 39. To pray rightly requires knowledge of what good is, and what God is. It is the extreme of folly to pray for what is inexpedient, or to pray to any but God. True prayer, spoken or unspoken, is communion with God. The declaration of God's threats to the wicked is a form of prayer; but this must always be with the view of recalling them to righteousness. [For an instance see below, § 102.]

§ 40. In prayer the soul rises upwards scorning the impediments of the body. The gnostic does not confine himself to the three fixed hours of prayer (§ 35), though these are associated in his mind with the triad of the celestial mansions.

§ 41. The pseudo-gnostics deny the use of prayer. My answer to them is reserved for another place. Here I am only concerned to prove that the true gnostic knows how to pray, and that he always obtains his petitions (§ 73), aye, and even receives good without petition made. Besides petitions for himself, his communion with God includes thanksgiving and prayer for others. Faith too is a kind of silent prayer (p. 4. 21).

§ 42. The holiness of the gnostic is the result of free choice on the side both of God and of man.

§ 43. Wherever there is readiness, there God is worshipped, independently of place and time. If we turn to the East in prayer, it is only because the light comes from thence.

§ 44. To the bad man prayer is hurtful, as he knows not what is true good: to the good it gives command over his passions, and union with the Divine nature through contemplation.

§ 45. Such a man becomes impervious to temptation and perfectly resigned to God's will.

§ 46. Beginning with faith he goes on to knowledge and love and contemplation, and thus virtue becomes his second nature.

§ 47. While rejoicing in present good, he already possesses in thought the higher promised good (p. 130. 15), which will be gradually realized in accordance with the Divine decree.

§ 48. He who cooperates with the Divine working finds the whole world contributing to his perfection. Cf. § 12.

§ 49. Gnostic worship. His sacrifices are prayers and praises and study of the Scriptures, and the free imparting of instruction and money to others. This worship is continuous. His prayer goes up to heaven whatever he does. In all his acts he aims at the honourable and the expedient as distinguished from what is pleasant.

§§ 50, 51. On perjury and falsehood. A good man's life should be sufficient security without an oath. He is bound to truth by his duty to God, to his neighbour and to himself.

§ 52. The highest office of the gnostic is the teaching of the Word (§ 4), while he forms his scholars after the image of Christ.

§ 53. His word always corresponds with his thought and with his life, unless reserve is required medicinally for the good of the weak brother.

§ 54. Conclusion. The gnostic is the very opposite of atheist or impious.

§ 55. Gnosis is the perfecting of man's nature (§ 46), built on the foundation of faith, and itself naturally grows into love. Distinction between $\gamma\nu\hat{\omega}\sigma\iota\varsigma$ and $\sigma o\phi i a$.

§§ 56, 57. We are thus enabled to look forward to that supreme abode of rest where the soul ever enjoys the Beatific Vision. Faith believes it, gnosis has a fixed conviction of it. Distinction between the Sabbath and the Ogdoad.

§ 58. Description of the gnostic in the 24th Psalm.

§ 59. The actions of the gnostic are not merely good in themselves: they alone are done on right principles and in the right way.

§ 60. The gnostic starts with admiration for the Creation, and is thus prepared to accept the truth with regard to God and His Providence, and to understand the commandments in their higher spiritual sense.

§§ 61, 62. Having his eye always fixed upon the Lord, and feeling that every thought is open to Him, he is enabled to resist the temptations of sense, and to accept sorrow and pain as a healing medicine for the diseases of the soul.

§ 63. Having thus trained himself to a habit of virtue (§ 46), he despises both the persecutions and the flatteries of the world.

§ 64. Difficulty only serves to bring out his hidden strength, while his soul is built up into a Temple of the Holy Spirit by the combined action of nature, discipline, and reason.

§§ 65—68. The gnostic's courage and temperance distinguished from the qualities commonly so called. They have their root in the love of God (cf. § 73).

§ 69. Justice and liberality of the gnostic.

§ 70. Continence of the gnostic, shewn in marriage rather than in a celibate life.

§§ 71, 72. It is impossible for him whose aim is to please God, to be a slave to pleasure. God alone is originally free from desire. It is the gnostic's aim to eradicate his passions by discipline. He is like the wise virgins who waited for their Lord.

§ 73. The whole life of the gnostic is prayer and communion with God, and he receives whatever he asks for (§ 41). He loves righteousness for itself, not for its results. Herein he differs from the philosophers whose virtue flows from fear or from desire of applause (§ 67).

§§ 74—76. The gnostic is a labourer in the Lord's vineyard, and as such receives a double reward, though he may be tried, like the Apostles, for the instruction and encouragement of the brethren. He does not call down vengeance on his persecutors, but prays for their conversion. The spectacles, in which the punishment of criminals is turned into a public entertainment, have no warning and no attraction for him (§ 36). His life is no mere outward worship of prayer and fast, but a constant struggle against worldly desires, and mortification of the love of money and of pleasure. He fulfils the O.T. by fasting from wrong acts, the N.T. by fasting from wrong thoughts. He holds that to be a Lord's day on which he experiences the power of the Resurrection in himself. When his eyes are opened to a new truth he believes that it is a manifestation of the Lord.

§§ 77, 78. The gnostic is ashamed if he finds himself taking pleasure in anything which is attractive to the flesh. He is united with his brethren in a fellowship of holy and beautiful thoughts. Though in the world, he is unaffected by its spirit, passing through it as a stranger and pilgrim. He is a true successor of the Apostles, resembling them in knowledge and in charity : he looks for praise from God only : feels the sorrows of others as if they were his own, and pities those whose repentance only begins under stress of punishment after death : is ever listening for the call of God, having no will but God's will, and being always ready to be united with saints and angels in prayer.

§ 79. Righteousness proceeds both from fear and from love, the one prompting to abstain from evil, the other to do good. The latter is the case of the gnostic, whose prayer consists in thanksgiving for mercies, past, present, and future, in petitions for his own continuance in well-doing, and for the conversion of others. Being joined to Christ in his thanksgiving he receives the power of God by inward union, hating the lusts of the flesh and bringing into control the lower nature.

§ 80. He is eager to impart all goods to his brethren and even to take on himself the burden of their sins; though he is ever on his guard lest, in accommodating himself to their weakness, he should imbibe anything of their spirit. Like Job, he is patient under all affliction; nay, his life is filled with joy, being occupied with prayers and praises and good words and works.

§ 81. He bears a grudge against none, knowing that all are God's handiwork. Thus he is entitled to use the petition 'Forgive, as we forgive.' His help to others, even in his prayers, is in the most unostentatious form.

§ 82. In the *Traditions of Matthias*, it is written that 'if the neighbour of an elect person sins, it is the fault of the elect.' The gnostic is the living temple of God, carrying God within him and being carried by God; thus he is transported beyond the bounds of sense into the highest heaven.

§ 83. Having a good conscience, he does not shrink from appearing before the unseen Powers after death. In his use of the things of this lower world, he has trained himself in the habit of thankfulness and admiration, ever gathering new material for pious contemplation from every new advance in knowledge.

§§ 84—88. The teaching of Scripture as to the perfection of the gnostic shown in an examination of 1 Cor. vi.

§§ 89, 90. Answer to the attack made against Christianity on the ground of the variety of sects and heresies. (1) *ad hom.* The same charge may be alleged against the Jews and the philosophers. (2) The existence of such heresies was prophesied by Christ, and is in accordance with the law that the beautiful is always shadowed by its caricature. (3) In other cases we do not allow the existence of diversity to prevent us from coming to a decision. There are different schools of medicine, but this does not prevent us from calling in a physician. So neither should one who is diseased in soul refuse to be converted to God because of the diversity of preachers. This diversity was intended to be the means of training 'skilled money-changers.'

§ 91. Heresies spring from the vanity of teachers, who are too impatient to give the profound study needed for the discovery of the truth. Their effect should be to stimulate inquiry, not to stop it; just as the ready growth of weeds should increase the care and industry of the gardener. There are sure marks by which we may distinguish the true from the false.

§§ 92—94. If it is admitted that there is such a thing as demonstration, it is the duty of those who are capable of thought and have learnt to distinguish between true and false reasoning to try the doctrines of the various sects by the words of Scripture: and the indispensable preliminary is to get rid of self-conceit and keep an open mind. The Scriptures are pregnant to the gnostic, but barren to the heretic, who wrests them from their true meaning to suit his own desires. He who is indeed a lover of truth needs energy of soul.

§ 95. The Lord is the great teacher, communicating the truth in divers ways and divers portions, through the Prophets and the Gospel and the Apostles. His word is our criterion and needs no other proof. This is our first principle, which we apprehend by faith; and from it we obtain our proofs, being thus trained for the knowledge of the truth. Mere assertion is valueless. As compared with ordinary believers, the gnostic is like the expert in his judgment of truth.

§§ 96—100. The heretics misuse Scripture by picking out isolated expressions, not interpreting them according to the context or in accordance with the general teaching of the Bible, or even with the natural force of the words: whereas the true interpretation is that which is confirmed by parallel passages and by our knowledge of what befits the Divine nature. They are ashamed to confess themselves in the wrong, and unwilling to give up their lucrative positions and the presidency in their love-feasts. When confuted by us they deny the authority of our sacred books, or say that contradictory statements are both true, and that their mysteries are beyond our comprehension. Their self-conceit leads to constant quarrelling. They live at hap-hazard without any regular guidance, at one time carried away by a sudden impression (which ought to be resisted by reasonable impressions stored up in advance), at another time mastered by the tyranny of habit.

§§ 101, 102. Ignorance and voluptuousness are the mark of the heathen, knowledge and joy of the Church, opinion and strife of the heretic. The Lord trains His disciples to be partakers of the Divine nature, just as other teachers train their disciples to imitate them. Ignorance and weakness are the causes of heresy, as of every error. These causes are to be neutralized by instruction and discipline. If any fail to make use of these, our prayer should be that they may undergo the Divine chastisement which is sent not for vengeance, but for our good, and so be led to turn from their evil ways.

§ 103. Let those who are still curable be wise in time and submit themselves to the knife and cautery of the truth. Let them cease from the slothfulness and the delight in novelty, which now deter them from the patient study of the Word: and let them measure the value of a Marcion or a Prodicus by the standard of the Apostles.

§§ 104, 105. A further setting forth of the excellence of knowledge. We may be told however that 'knowledge puffs up.' But this does not apply to true, but only to seeming knowledge. Indeed, it is probable that the word is wrongly translated 'puffs up': it means rather 'elevates,' implying that knowledge makes a man disdain solicitations to evil. Such a man will cling to the truth himself, and declare the truth fearlessly and honestly to others.

§§ 106—108. On the other hand the heretics misinterpret the Scriptures, neither entering into the kingdom of God themselves, nor permitting others to enter. The founders of their sects did not arise till the time of Hadrian, long after the preaching of our Lord and His apostles (cf. § 2). The Unity of the Apostolic Church is broken up into fragments by their innovations and divisions. The heresies are named, some from their founder, some from their place or nation, and others from other causes.

§§ 109, 110. The Jewish law about clean and unclean animals is typical of the division between Jews and heretics and the true Church. The division of the hoof denotes the faith in the Father and the Son: the chewing of the cud denotes the careful study of the Word. Those who fail in either are deficient; those who fail in both are like the chaff scattered by the wind.

§ 111. The nature and use of the writings known as Στρωματεῖς.

BIBLIOGRAPHICAL NOTE.

The following publications may be added to the list given in Westcott's article on Clement:

Von Arnim, *De Octavo Stromateorum libro*, 1894.

Barnard, *Quis Dives Salvetur*, Gr. Text, with Introduction, Notes and Indices (greatly improved text), 1897.

Barnard, *Quis Dives Salvetur*, English Translation, S.P.C.K., 1901.

Barnard, *Clement's Biblical Text* (Gospels and Acts), 1899.

Bigg, *Christian Platonists of Alexandria*, 1886.

Bywater (Emendations), *Journal of Philology*, vol. IV. pp. 204 foll.

Chase, *Clement* (in *Lectures on Ecclesiastical History*), 1896.

Clement, Eng. tr. (in Ante-Nicene Lib.), 1867.

Diels, *Doxographi Graeci*, 1879 (points out, pp. 129 foll., resemblance between the list of philosophers given in Cic. *N. D.* I. and that in *Protr.* §§ 64 foll.).

Faye, E. de, *Clement d'Alexandrie*, 1898.

Harnack, *Hist. of Dogma*, vol. II. pp. 319—380.[*]

Hatch, *Influence of Greek Ideas and Usages upon the Christian Church*, 1890.

Hiller, *Zur Quellenkritik des Clem. Al.* in *Hermes*, vol. XXI. pp. 126—133.

Hitchcock, *Clement*, in the S.P.C.K. series of *Fathers for English Readers*, 1899.

Hort, *Six Lectures on the Ante-Nicene Fathers*, 1895.

Inge, *Christian Mysticism*, 1899.

Jackson, H. (Emendations), *J. of Phil.*, vol. XXIV. 263—271, vol. XXVII. 136—144, vol. XXVIII. 131—135.

---

[*] My references are sometimes to the 3rd German edition (*Dogmengeschichte*).

Koster, *Quis Dives Salvetur*, 1893.

Kutter, *Cl. Alex. und das Neue Testament*, 1897.

Maass, *De Biographis Graecis quaestiones selectae*, in *Philol. Unters.*, Berl., 1880 (on Clement's indebtedness to Favorinus).

Mayor, J. B. (Emendations on *Strom.* I.—VII.), *Class. Rev.* vol. VIII. pp. 233—238, 281—288, 385—391, vol. IX. pp. 97—105, 202—206, 297—302, 337—342. (On *Protr.*) *Philologus*, 1898.

Merk, *Clem. Al. in seiner Abhängigkeit von d. gr. Philosophie*, 1879.

Nicklin, *Alexandrian Evidence for Chronology of Gospels*, *J. of Phil.*, vol. XXVII. 232—252.

Overbeck, *Ueber die Anfänge des Patristischen Literatur* (*Hist. Zeitschrift*, vol. XLVIII. p. 417 foll., 1882).

Pascal, *La Foi et la Raison dans Cl. Alex.*, 1901.

Ruben, *Clementis Alexandri Excerpta ex Theodoto*, 1892.

Stählin, *Observationes Criticae*, Erlangen, 1890; *Beiträge z. Kenntniss der Handschriften des Clem. Al.*, Nürnberg, 1895; *Untersuchungen über die Scholien zu Clem. Al.*, Nürnberg, 1897; *Clem. Al. und die Septuaginta*, Nürnberg, 1901; *Zur handschriftlichen Ueberlieferung des Clem. Al.*, Leipzig, 1900.

Wendland, *Quaestiones Musonianeae*, 1886.

Winter, F. J., *Die Ethik des Clem. von Alex.*, Leipzig, 1882.

Zahn, *Forschungen*, vol. III. (*Supplementum Clementinum*), 1884.

Ziegert, *Zwei Abhandlungen über Clem. Al.*, Heidelberg, 1894.

ADDENDA.

p. 15. l. 9 up. Om. comma after 'nature.'

p. 21. l. 2. Om. 'even,' and insert 'also' in l. 8 after 'things.'

p. 23 bottom. Add Ezek. xviii. 4 after 'Deut. xiii.'

p. 24. In crit. note on l. 18 add 'καὶ om. Barn.'

p. 40. 11. crit. note ἐθέασω] τεθέασο Theod.

p. 48. 7. For ἀγγέλου read Τυρίου. In crit. note om. 'ἀγγέλου M.'

p. 49. 7. For 'may, not—hand' read 'no, nor embellished by Tyrian workmanship.'

p. 50. 9. For ὀσφῦν read ὀσφύν.

p. 52. 23. Comma after ἀναπέμπομεν, 24 dele comma after λόγῳ.

p. 53. 22. For 'to the most righteous Word' read 'most rightly.'

p. 55. 7 up. For 'personal' read 'Christian.'

p. 57. 9. For 'are' read 'have been.' l. 13. For 'well' read 'good.'

p. 60. 20. ἐντολήν in ordinary type.

p. 61. 7. For 'flesh' read 'the flesh of sacrifice.'

p. 64. not. crit. 24 add 'τῷ ἀρρ. Barn.'

p. 71. 25. For 'whether oral or mental' read 'spoken or unspoken.'

p. 80. 4. For εὐθετούντων read εὐθετῶν and in not. crit. insert (after 4) εὐθετῶν M.

p. 81. 3, 4. For 'after any of the necessary conveniences' read 'anything further when he is once supplied with the necessaries.'

p. 84. 5, not. crit. 5. τοῖς] τοὺς Jackson in J. of Phil. vol. 28. 184.

p. 87. 17, n. on 'sacrifice' Heb. 13. 16.

p. 100, not. crit. For 6 read 7, for 10 read 11, for 17 read 18, for 20 read 21, for 29 read 30. Insert 23 ἢ L, καὶ LXX. 25 οὐδὲ L, καὶ οὐκ LXX. 28 τὸν κύριον L, αὐτὸν LXX.

p. 103. 31. For 'religion' read 'piety.'

p. 105. 3 up. For '. Hence' read ', wherefore.' In n. 3 for 'XCIII' read 'XCIV.'

p. 110. 1. not. crit. insert after 1, ἀγομένην L, ἀπαγομένην Eus. 21 not. crit. read εὐθαρσής S for εὐθ. L, and transfer bef. εὐθαρσῶς.

p. 116. 4 and 6. Put dashes instead of brackets after γεγονότες and παίδων.

ADDENDA.

p. 119. 4 up. For 'despise' read 'neglect.'

p. 123. n. 1, add Ps. cxi. 10, Prov. i. 7.

p. 125. 15. For 'as a natural consequence' read 'incidentally.' l. 19. For 'also of any movement of thought or' read 'and of any mental excitement and.'

p. 130. 26. For *ol* read *al*.

p. 135. 6. For 'knowledge' read 'judgment.' In n. 2 add 'Mt. xvii. 20, xxi. 21, Lk. xvii. 6.'

p. 136. 1. *not. crit.* add μονῶν Stählin (*Obs. Crit.* 42).

p. 137. 8. For 'ocean' read 'end of the ocean.'

p. 141. n. 2, read Isa. vi.

p. 152. 3. For δῆλον ὁποῖα read δηλονότι οἷα and, in *not. crit.* insert '3. δηλονότι οἷα Jackson, δῆλον ὁποῖα L.' l. 81. Insert <τὸ> before πνευματικόν and add in *not. crit.* '31. τοῦτο τὸ M, τοῦτο L.'

p. 162. There seems to be no reason for changing the MS. readings εὑρηκέναι and ἐξευρημέναs in ll. 10 and 22.

p. 166. l. 81, put the figure '322 S' on the inner margin.

p. 182. 12. *not. crit.* add 'παραδιδόμενα ἑκόντες εἶναι L, παραδεδομένα ἑκόντες εἰδέναι Bywater (*J. of Phil.* iv. 216).'

p. 184. 19. For ταῖς μερικαῖς read τοῖς μειρακίοις, and insert in *not. crit.* 19 'τοῖς μειρακίοις Stählin, ταῖς μερικαῖς L.' 24 *not. crit.* ἐμφυτευσάσης L, add 'Stählin.' After διδάσκει] add 'διδάξει (dat. of δίδαξις) Stählin.'

p. 191. 5, 6. In italics 'God foreordained...before the foundation of the world' and give reference to Eph. i. 4, 5.

p. 199. *Note* on 7—9. insert after 'P. 341 *fin.*' P. 656. On 11 add after 'Christ,' cf. *Str.* vi. 128, Justin *Apol.* i. 80 (Prophecy) μεγίστη καὶ ἀληθεστάτη ἀπόδειξις, 2 Pet. i. 19 ἔχομεν βεβαιότερον τὸν προφητικὸν λόγον, Theophilus i. 14, Orig. *in Joann.* ii. 28 and xxxii. 9 *fin.*, *Cels.* vi. 10, viii. 48 (cited by Bigg, p. 264), *D. of Chr. B.* iii. 583 b, 'Prophecy is to Justin the main form of Christian evidence, and this for Gentile as much as for Jew.' On 13 add *Str.* iv. 1, where Cl. looks forward to giving ἡ κατ' ἐπιτομὴν τῶν γραφῶν ἔκθεσις. Cf. the exposition of 1 Cor. vi. contained in §§ 85 foll. below, of 1 Cor. x. below § 105, of unclean meats in §§ 109 foll.

p. 200. n. on παριστᾶν (p. 4. l. 2). 'For ἰστᾶν in Plato *Crat.* read ἰστάν with Cobet. H. J.' On τῷ θεοπρεπεῖ (l. 11) cf. below § 38 οὐδεμίαν σώζει θεοσέβειαν ἡ μὴ πρέπουσα περὶ τοῦ θεοῦ ὑπόληψις.

p. 202. n. on πρεσβύτεροι. For the comparison between angels and the orders of the ministry see Heb. i. 14 οὐχὶ πάντες εἰσὶν λειτουργικὰ πνεύματα εἰς διακονίαν ἀποστελλόμενα with Welstein's n. For the Egyptian episcopate cf. *J. of Theol. Stud.* Jan. 1900, p. 256 f., July 1901, p. 612 f., Bigg, p. 39 f., Harnack, *H. of D.* ii. p. 71 n.

p. 204. n. on ἐσομένῳ θεῷ. Cf. Inge, *Bampton Lect.*, App. C.

p. 205. On Faith see *Str.* ii. chapters 2—6.

p. 206. l. 1. Cf. Orig. *Cels.* iv. 5 where he answers the objection of Celsus that 'if God comes down to men, he must abandon his throne.' οὐ μεριζόμενος, cf. Bigg, p. 177. n. on 10. 2, 'see below p. 138. 10.'

p. 207. Insert n. on l. 10 'παιδεύων μυστηρίοις, see above p. 8. 5.'

p. 208. tr. § 7 before l. 5. n. on 13; 'cf. Wisdom ii. 24 φθόνῳ διαβόλου θάνατος εἰσῆλθεν.'

p. 210. n. on 4, 'cf. *Str.* iv. P. 636 on the seven planetary spheres and the

ADDENDA.

eighth sphere of the fixed stars.' *Dele* reference below to an Appendix on Angelology.

p. 212. Add n. on l. 10 ἐξ ἑνὸς καὶ δι' ἑνός. 'Cf. Rom. xi. 36.'

p. 213. n. on l. 22 δικαίῳ νόμος οὐ κεῖται. Add Arist. *Pol.* III. 13. p. 1284 a 3 (where one citizen far excels others in virtue, so that he seems like a God in comparison with them) τῶν τοιούτων οὐκ ἔστι νόμος, αὐτοὶ γάρ εἰσι νόμος.

p. 215. on l. 11 βαρβάρου φιλοσοφίας. Cf. Tatian c. 26, Porph. *de Abst.* II. 26 (the Jews) ἅτε φιλόσοφοι τὸ γένος ὄντες, Celsus *ap.* Orig. I. 2 'The Greeks perfect the doctrines received from barbarians.'

p. 216. on l. 27. Transpose the two notes.

p. 217. add n. on l. 3. τοῦ κρείττονος, i.e. the whole, previously mentioned. ἀναλόγως is explained by the variety of training and discipline described in what follows.

p. 217. n. on l. 7 παιδεύσεις. Add Orig. *Princ.* I. 6. 8 Tam in his temporalibus saeculis, quam in illis quae aeterna sunt, omnes isti pro ordine, pro ratione... dispensantur, ut alii in primis, alii in secundis, nonnulli etiam in ultimis temporibus et per maiora ac graviora supplicia...asperioribus emendationibus reparati...ad superiora provecti, usque ad ea quae sunt invisibilia et aeterna perveniant; *ib.* III. 18 Deus dispensat animos non ad istum solum vitae nostrae breve tempus...sed ad perpetuum et aeternum tempus, tanquam aeternus ipse et immortalis...et ideo non excluditur brevitate temporis huius vitae nostrae a curis et remediis divinis anima, quae immortalis est.

p. 218. l. 14, n. on ὑπερβαινούσας. See above 18. 17, below p. 112. 11. Cf. Lightfoot on Clem. Rom. 7, n. on σκάμματι.

Add n. on l. 19 f. Cf. *Str.* VI. 75 τελειωθέντα δι' ἀγάπης καὶ τὴν ἀπλήρωτον τῆς θεωρίας εὐφροσύνην διδίως καὶ ἀκορέστως ἑστιώμενον.

p. 219. n. on τὴν λειτουργίαν. Cf. Deissmann, *Bibl. Stud.* p. 140 'The papyri show that λειτουργέω and cognate words were commonly used in Egypt in the ceremonial sense,' of which he gives exx.

p. 220. n. on ὁλοκάρπωμα. Deissmann (p. 137) says that in the LXX the word καρπόω is used in the sense of 'burn' both in a ceremonial and non-ceremonial sense. He cites Lev. ii. 11, Deut. xxvi. 14, Sir. xlv. 14 θυσίαι αὐτῷ ὁλοκαρπωθήσονται, 4 Macc. xviii. 11, *Sibyll. Or.* III. 565.

ib. n. on ἕνωσις ll. 13, 14. Harnack (*H. of D.* II. 74) says the phrase ἕνωσις ἐκκλησίας is first found in Hegesippus *ap.* Eus. *H. E.* IV. 22. 5.

p. 222. n. on l. 19 ἀβουλήτοις. For κἂν read κἂν in 3rd line.

p. 224. n. on τὸ δεύτερον αἴτιον. See above, p. 4. 19.

p. 225. n. on l. 5. For the logical use cf. Eus. *H. E.* V. 28 κἂν προτείνῃ τις ῥητὸν γραφῆς θεικῆς, ἐξετάζουσι πότερον συνημμένον ἢ διεζευγμένον δύναται ποιῆσαι σχῆμα συλλογισμοῦ.

p. 226. n. on l. 15. Add *Paed.* P. 287 κεχρήσθω δὲ ἡ γυνὴ τῇ λιτῇ στολῇ.

p. 228. n. on ὑπερκόσμιος. Add Eus. *H. E.* X. 4 *fin.* ἡ ὑπερκόσμιος πόλις τοῦ ζῶντος θεοῦ.

p. 229. on ἐγκύκλιος παιδεία. Cf. *Str.* P. 429, Philo I. 520 ἀρετῆς πρόκειται τὰ ἐγκύκλια· ταῦτα γὰρ ὁδός ἐστιν ἐπ' ἐκείνην φέρουσα, Greg. Th. in Orig. L. vol. XXV. p. 339.

p. 230. on l. 8. Read ἑαυτοὺς for ἑαυτοῖς, for 'Col. III.' read 'Col. II.'

p. 233. on l. 9. Add 'But in *Str.* II. 74 this συγγένεια is denied, ὁ θεὸς οὐδεμίαν ἔχει πρὸς ἡμᾶς φυσικὴν σχέσιν, ὡς οἱ τῶν αἱρέσεων κτίσται θέλουσιν, and in

ADDENDA. cvii

v. 88 οἱ ἀμφὶ τὸν Πυθαγόραν θείᾳ μοίρᾳ τὸν νοῦν εἰς ἀνθρώπους ἥκειν φασί...ἀλλ' ἡμεῖς μὲν τῷ πεπιστευκότι προσεπιπνεῖσθαι τὸ ἅγιον πνεῦμά φαμεν, οἱ δὲ ἀμφὶ τὸν Πλάτωνα νοῦν μὲν ἐν ψυχῇ θείας μοίρας ἀπόρροιαν ὑπάρχοντα κ.τ.λ.

p. 235. add n. on ἀλεκτρυών l. 14. Cf. Plin. *H. N.* x. 21 habent ostenta et praeposteri gallorum vespertinique cautus.

p. 237. Add to n. on περικαθαρθέντων, Didache III. 4 μὴ γίνου ἐπαοιδὸς μηδὲ μαθηματικὸς μηδὲ περικαθαίρων.

p. 238. n. on l. 9 σύνεσις, cf. Tobit iii. 8 οὐ συνιεῖς ἀποπνίγουσα τοὺς ἄνδρας; ib. l. 17, for 'Appendix' read 'Introduction.' ib. βαναύσου (l. 23), cf. Luc. *Somn.* § 9.

p. 246. n. on l. 14 ἐκκαλυπτομένης. Cf. Prayer of Serapion in *J. of Theol. Studies,* I. p. 98 ἐκτείνομεν τὰς χεῖρας καὶ τὰς διανοίας ἀναπετάννυμεν πρός σε κύριε. ib. l. 20, cf. Robertson Smith, *Rel. of Sem.* p. 280 (quoted by Keating, p. 22) 'In old Israel all slaughter was sacrifice, and a man could never eat beef or mutton except as a religious act.'

p. 247. On ll. 9—11, add 'cf. *Paed.* II. 14 εἰ γὰρ τὰ μάλιστα ἕνεκεν τῶν ἀνθρώπων ἐγένετο τὰ πάντα, ἀλλ' οὐ πᾶσι χρῆσθαι καλόν, ἀλλ' οὐδὲ δεῖ.'

p. 248. n. on μητρόπολις. Read 'Philo' for 'Phil.' in l. 2, and add *Paed.* II. 88 πλοῦτος ἀκρόπολις κακίας.

p. 249. end of n. on συγγενῆ. Cf. Porph. *Abst.* I. 19 εἴ γε ὁμοούσιοι αἱ τῶν ζῴων ψυχαὶ ταῖς ἡμετέραις.

p. 250. end of 1st n. (l. 6). After 'Col.' insert 'I. 18 συνέστηκεν.'

p. 252. On l. 13 add 'γεωργοῦμεν αἰνοῦντες,' cf. Epict. *Diss.* I. 16. 15 foll. οὐκ ἔδει καὶ σκάπτοντας καὶ ἀροῦντας καὶ ἐσθίοντας ᾄδειν τὸν ὕμνον τὸν εἰς τὸν θεόν; κ.τ.λ.

p. 254. On l. 3, add Justin *Apol.* I. 9 θυσίαις καὶ πλοκαῖς ἀνθῶν τιμᾶν.

ib. On l. 16, add 'τῆς διακριτικῆς, cf. Plato, *Crat.* 388 B ὄνομα διδασκαλικόν τί ἐστιν ὄργανον καὶ διακριτικὸν τῆς οὐσίας.

p. 257. n. on ll. 7, 8, τῆς διηνέμεως. The expression φῶς is found in the LXX, λύχνος in the other versions. ib. Add on l. 13 ἡ μὴ πρέπουσα ὑπόληψις, see above p. 6. 20 ἡ θεοπρέπεια ἕξις ἐστὶ τὸ πρέπον τῷ θεῷ σῴζουσα, and below p. 170. 7 (truth is discovered) ἐν τῷ διασκέψασθαι τί τῷ κυρίῳ...πρέπον, Str. VI. 124 ψεῦσται τῷ ὄντι...οἱ μὴ κατ' ἀξίαν τοῦ θεοῦ καὶ τοῦ κυρίου τὰς γραφὰς λέγοντές τε καὶ παραδιδόντες. It was the principle on which Plato rejected the stories told about the gods by Homer and Hesiod (*Rep.* II. 377—383).

p. 259. n. on μηκέτι ἔχειν. Cf. Str. IV. 40 ὅταν τοίνυν ἐνδιατρίψῃ τῇ θεωρίᾳ, τῷ θείῳ καθαρῶς ὁμιλῶν, ὁ γνωστικῶς μετέχων τῆς ἁγίας ποιότητος, προσεχέστερον ἐν ἕξει γίνεται ταυτότητος ἀπαθοῦς, ὡς μηκέτι ἐπιστήμην ἔχειν καὶ γνῶσιν κεκτῆσθαι, ἐπιστήμην δὲ εἶναι καὶ γνῶσιν.

p. 260. n. on 19. Add 'see below n. on p. 70. 27.' Dele '24' before τοὺς πόδας.

p. 262. Add in top line 'cf. Stengel, *Gr. Kultusaltertümer,* p. 168 n.'

p. 264. Add in 1st n. after παλινδρομοῦσα (l. 3), 'cf. Str. II. 25 ὥσπερ οὖν τὸ σφαιρίζειν οὐκ ἐκ τοῦ κατὰ τέχνην πέμποντος τὴν σφαῖραν ἤρτηται μόνον, ἀλλὰ καὶ τοῦ εὐρύθμως ἀποδεχομένου προσδεῖ αὐτῷ, ἵνα δὴ κατὰ νόμους τοὺς σφαιριστικοὺς τὸ γυμνάσιον ἐκτελῆται, οὕτω καὶ τὴν διδασκαλίαν ἀξιόπιστον εἶναι συμβέβηκεν, ὅταν ἡ πίστις τῶν ἀκροωμένων, τέχνη τις ὡς εἰπεῖν ὑπάρχουσα φυσική, πρὸς μάθησιν συλλαμβάνῃ (MS. -νει).'

ib. Add n. on l. 19 ὃν τρόπον τὸ πῦρ θερμαντικόν, 'cf. below p. 80. 26, and

Plut. *Mor.* 1102 E (θεὸς) ἀγαθός ἐστιν, ἀγαθῷ δὲ περὶ οὐδὲν ἐγγίνεται φθόνος...οὔτε γὰρ θερμοῦ τὸ ψύχειν ἀλλὰ τὸ θερμαίνειν, which Bigg (p. 79 n.) thinks Cl. may have had in his mind here.'

p. 269. Add n. on l. 19 εἰς τὸ ἀπείραστον, 'cf. below p. 122. 29.' *ib.* Add at the end of n. on εὐθετούντων, 'cf. 1 Tim. vi. 8 ἔχοντες δὲ διατροφὰς καὶ σκεπάσματα τούτοις ἀρκεσθησόμεθα,' *Str.* VI. 75 οὐκέτι συγχρῆται τῷ σώματι, μόνον δὲ αὐτῷ ἐπιτρέπει χρῆσθαι τοῖς ἀναγκαίοις, ἵνα μὴ τὴν αἰτίαν τῆς διαλύσεως παράσχῃ.

p. 272. Add to n. on 14, 'cf. *Paed.* I. 26 *fin.* τὸ γὰρ μέλλον τοῦ χρόνου τῇ δυνάμει τοῦ θελήματος προλαμβάνεται.'

p. 274. Add at the bottom after αὐτῷ, '*ib.* VIII. 84. 4 πιστὸς μετὰ κατηχουμένου μηδὲ κατ᾽ οἶκον προσευχέσθω· οὐ γὰρ δίκαιον τὸν μεμυημένον μετὰ τοῦ ἀμυήτου συμμολύνεσθαι.'

p. 278. Add n. l. 21 ἔξαρνος. 'Tortures cannot make him deny his faith.'

p. 279. n. on 21. Add 'for ἐν μέρει cf. Lightfoot on Col. ii. 16 ἐν μέρει ἑορτῆς.'

p. 280. n. on 11. Add 'see below n. on 96. 15, and *Str.* P. 646 there quoted.'

p. 282. Add to n. on 15 προφορικοῦ λόγου, 'Cl. (P. 685) quotes 1 Cor. ii. 6 σοφίαν λαλοῦμεν ἐν τοῖς τελείοις...θεοῦ σοφίαν ἐν μυστηρίῳ τὴν ἀποκεκρυμμένην with a reference to Plato *Epist.* II. p. 312 μεγίστη φυλακὴ τὸ μὴ γράφειν ἀλλ᾽ ἐκμανθάνειν.'

p. 284. Add on l. 17 τῇ θεωρίᾳ, 'cf. *Exc. Theod.* 68 ἡ μὲν οὖν τῶν πνευματικῶν ἀνάπαυσις [ἐν κυριακῇ] ἐν ὀγδοάδι ἡ κυριακὴ ὀνομάζεται.'

p. 288. Add on 9, 'cf. P. 801 ζητεῖν τὴν γνῶσιν εἰς εὕρεσιν, also *Str.* IV. 1, where ζήτησις is mentioned as a subject for future discussion, and v. 11, 12. It is more fully treated in *Str.* VIII. 1 f.'

p. 289. n. on l. 2 σώζοντες τὴν ἀκολουθίαν. The phrase is used by Alex. Aphr. quoted in Steph. *Thes.* p. 1700 c.

p. 291. n. on 25. Add 'see Lightfoot on the repetition of ὑμᾶς in Phil. i. 7.' *ib.* n. on φάρμακον, add *Paed.* I. 100 ἀντίδοτος σωτηρίας, Serapion in *J. of Theol. Stud.* I. 106. 15 φ. ζωῆς.

p. 292. In n. on l. 29 read 'below p. 136. 1' for 'below 134. 31.'

p. 299. n. on ἀλείφουσα. The custom of anointing at baptism had grown up before the end of the 2nd century, see *D. of Chr. Ant.* under 'Chrism' and 'Unction.' Tertullian (*De Bapt.* 7) regards it as a sign of the universal priesthood of Christians. For the figure in the text, cf. Chrys. *ad Col.* XI. 342 (quoted by Hatch, p. 848) ἀλείφεται ὥσπερ οἱ ἀθληταὶ εἰς στάδιον ἐμβησόμενοι.

p. 300. Add on l. 8, 'for the word συγκατάθεσις see Cic. *Acad.* II. 37 and the definition of πίστις in *Str.* II. 9 ἀφανοῦς πράγματος ἐνωτικὴ συγκατάθεσις.'

p. 301. n. on l. 14. For 'p. 220' (in the third line) read 'p. 228.'

p. 305. Add n. on 11 foll. παρθένοι. Cf. *Str.* V. 655 ταύτῃ καὶ αἱ τῶν φρονίμων παρθένων λαμπάδες, αἱ νύκτωρ ἀνημμέναι ἐν πολλῷ τῷ τῆς ἀγνοίας σκότει...φρόνιμοι ψυχαὶ καθαραὶ ὡς παρθένοι, συνεῖσαι σφᾶς αὐτὰς ἐν ἀγνοίᾳ καθεστώσας κοσμικῇ, τὸ φῶς ἀνάπτουσι καὶ τὸν νοῦν ἐγείρουσιν.

p. 310. Add to n. on 6. Cf. *Str.* II. 117 οὐδὲν μέγα τὸ ἀπέχεσθαι ἡδονῆς μὴ πεπειραμένον.

ib. Add to n. on 8, 9, 'cf. Orig. *Cels.* VIII. 22 ὁ μὲν τέλειος, ἀεὶ ἐν τοῖς λόγοις ὢν καὶ τοῖς ἔργοις καὶ τοῖς διανοήμασι τοῦ τῇ φύσει κυρίου λόγου θεοῦ, ἀεὶ ἐστιν αὐτοῦ ἐν ταῖς ἡμέραις καὶ ἀεὶ ἄγει κυριακὰς ἡμέρας, Apoc. i. 10 with Alford's n. Deissmann (p. 218) compares the use of ἡ Σεβαστή for the 1st day of the month.

ADDENDA.

p. 311. Add n. on p. 134. ὁ τὴν ἀποστολικὴν ἀπουσίαν ἀναπληροῖ, cf. Str. VI. 106 quoted in *Intr.* ch. III. p. xlvi.

p. 312. n. on 14. Read in the 5th l. ἐκοινώνησε for ἐκοίνησε.

p. 313. n. on p. 136. 1 (last line but two). After μονῶν insert '(so Stählin, *Obs. Crit.* p. 42).'

p. 315. n. on. 9. Cf. Orig. *Cels.* VI. 64 ὁ σωτὴρ ἡμῶν οὐ μετέχει μὲν δικαιοσύνης, δικαιοσύνη δὲ ὢν μετέχεται ὑπὸ τῶν δικαίων.

p. 317. n. on 28. Add 1 Joh. iii. 9 πᾶς ὁ γεγεννημένος ἐκ τοῦ θεοῦ ἁμαρτίαν οὐ ποιεῖ ὅτι σπέρμα αὐτοῦ ἐν αὐτῷ μένει. *ib.* on 29, 30. Add Str. VI. 102 τὰ μὲν πρῶτα ἄφεσιν ἁμαρτιῶν αἰτήσεται, μετὰ δὲ τὸ μηκέτι ἁμαρτάνειν, ἔπειτα εὖ ποιεῖν δύνασθαι and 1 Joh. iii. 9 just cited.

p. 318. n. on l. 26 τέλειον. Cf. *Paed.* I. 52 ἐμοὶ δὲ καὶ θαυμάζειν ἔπεισιν ὅπως σφᾶς τελείους τινὲς τολμῶσι καλεῖν, ὑπὲρ τὸν ἀπόστολον φρονοῦντες (who) τέλειον μὲν ἑαυτὸν ἡγεῖται ὅτι ἀπήλλακται τοῦ προτέρου βίου, ἔχεται δὲ τοῦ κρείττονος, οὐχ ὡς ἐν γνώσει τέλειος, ἀλλ᾽ ὡς τοῦ τελείου ἐφιέμενος κ.τ.λ. *ib.* on l. 2 ἀκούσατε, substitute for present note 'In *Protr.* § 88 init. we have the LXX reading, ἀκούσατέ μου, φόβον κυρίου διδάξω ὑμᾶς.'

p. 319. n. on l. 28. Add (after P. 552), Str. IV. P. 568 fin. ταῖς ἁμαρτίαις πεπραμένους τοὺς φιληδόνους καὶ φιλοσωμάτους οἶδεν ἡ γραφή.

p. 320. In 1st note (3rd line) insert 'Rom. vii. 14.'

p. 321. n. on l. 10 (last sentence but two). For 'This would agree with' read 'This agrees with p. 180. 14 περὶ δὲ ὧν ἐγὼ τῶν μελλόντων καὶ ἀοράτων πεπεισμένος, and also with.'

ib. n. on ll. 21, 22. Add in second line (after 138. 3) 'Str. IV. 616 σύμβολον ἅγιον τὸν χαρακτῆρα τῆς δικαιοσύνης τὸν φωτεινὸν ἐπιδεικνύμενος τοῖς ἐφεστῶσιν τῇ ἀνόδῳ ἀγγέλοις, τὸ χρῖσμα τῆς εὐαρεστήσεως λέγω...τοὺς μὲν ἐπαγομένους τινὰ τῶν κοσμικῶν κατέχουσιν οἱ τὸ τέλος ἀπαιτοῦντες τοῖς σφετέροις βαρουμένους πάθεσι, τὸν δὲ γυμνὸν μὲν τῶν ὑποπιπτόντων τῷ τέλει, πλήρη δὲ γνώσεως καὶ τῆς ἐξ ἔργων δικαιοσύνης, συνευχόμενοι παραπέμπουσι τὸν ἄνδρα, σὺν καὶ τῷ ἔργῳ μακαρίσαντες, where see Potter.'

ib. same note (8th line). Insert, after ἀποκρίνεσθαι, Iren. I. 21. 5.

p. 323. in 1st note (3rd line). After πίστιν insert 'Orig. ap. Eus. *H. E.* VI. 36. 4 περὶ τῆς κατ᾽ αὐτὸν ὀρθοδοξίας.' *ib.* on l. 16. Add Str. IV. 614 μήτε ἀδικοῦσα μήτε ἀνταδικοῦσά ποτε, ἀγαθοποιοῦσα δέ.

p. 326. n. on ll. 24, 25 (middle). Insert after *Paed.* I. 'P. 120, *ib.*' and line below (before *Q. D. S.*) '*Paed.* II. P. 195 οὐχ οἷόν τέ ἐστι γελοίους προέσθαι λόγους, μὴ οὐχὶ ἀπὸ γελοίου ἤθους φερομένους.

p. 328. n. on ll. 26, 27. Insert (before 'Str. VI.') Str. II. P. 471 οὐδὲ ἐγκρατὲς κυρίως (τὸ θεῖον), οὐ γὰρ ὑποπίπτει πάθει ἵνα καὶ κρατήσῃ τοῦδε.

p. 329. add n. on l. 9 Ἰουδαίων. We find a reference to controversy with the Jews in Str. IV. 1 ἥ τε πρὸς τοὺς Ἕλληνας καὶ ἡ πρὸς Ἰουδαίους κατ᾽ ἐπιτομὴν τῶν γραφῶν ἔκθεσις παραδοθήσεται.

p. 330. n. on l. 8. Add 'See Harnack, *Hist. of D.* II. p. 36 n.' *ib.* on l. 20. Add 'See Harn. II. 35 n.'

p. 333. n. on 29. Add 'Str. II. 12 ἀμεταπτώτῳ κριτηρίῳ τῇ πίστει ἐπαναπαυώμεθα.'

ib. Add n. on 164. l. 2 τὰ διὰ νοῦ τεχνικά. Cf. Aristotle's distinction of ἔντεχνοι and ἄτεχνοι πίστεις in *Rhet.* I. 9 with Cope's n.

p. 334. add at end of first n. Plato, *Symp.* 204 A, τίνες οἱ φιλοσοφοῦντες εἰ μήτε οἱ σοφοὶ μήτε οἱ ἀμαθεῖς; οἱ μεταξὺ τούτων ἀμφοτέρων.

p. 336. n. on 26. Add *Paed.* I. P. 123 μία μόνη γίνεται μήτηρ παρθένος· ἐκκλησίαν ἐμοὶ φίλον αὐτὴν καλεῖν· γάλα οὐκ ἔσχεν ἡ μήτηρ αὕτη μόνη, ὅτι μόνη μὴ γέγονεν γυνή.

p. 337. n. on ll. 27, 28. Add 'cf. *Str.* II. 18 εἰ δέ τις λέγοι τὴν ἐπιστήμην ἀποδεικτικὴν εἶναι μετὰ λόγου, ἀκουσάτω ὅτι καὶ αἱ ἀρχαὶ ἀναπόδεικτοι, and for the term ἀρχή used of Christ, *Str.* V. 38, VI. 58.'

p. 339. end of first note. Add '*Mart. Petri et Pauli* 4 τῶν ἑαυτοῦ πράξεων τὸ ὕψος ἀπήγγειλεν.'

p. 346. n. on. p. 180, ll. 4, 5. Add (after ἐπᾳδόντων) 'quoted literally in P. 83 except that φωνῆς is read for φωνήν.'

p. 350. end of first note. After γράφει add '*Str.* II. 454 P. ἡ μὲν τῶν οἰησισόφων... γνῶσις φυσιοῖ.'

p. 353. n. on ll. 3, 4. Add 'Cf. Iren. III. 11. 8 τέσσαρες ἐδόθησαν καθολικαὶ διαθῆκαι τῇ ἀνθρωπότητι κ.τ.λ.'

p. 354. n. on ll. 14, 15 μία ἡ πάντων τῶν ἀποστόλων παράδοσις, cf. Harn. *Dogmeng.* I.³ p. 154 n.

ib. n. on 18. Add (after *Proph.* 999) 'with whom he joins Cassianus in P. 552 f.'

p. 359. n. on. ll. 11, 12. Add 'also Harn. *H. of D.* II. p. 35 n.'

ib. n. on l. 12. Add 'Zahn (*Forsch.* III. p. 111) thinks the scheme laid down in *Str.* IV. 1 may be regarded as a promise.'

p. 366 (Appendix). On Λα add 'For exx. from papyri cf. Deissmann, p. 201.'

p. 374. n. 1. Add 'Cf. also Bigg, p. 102 foll., p. 219 foll., Harn. *Dogmeng.* I.³ p. 200 foll.'

p. 375. n. 1. Add (on πάζω) 'See Herwerden, *Lex. Gr. s.v.* ἀμπάζονται.'

p. 379. Add at the end of the 1st paragraph, '*Exc. Theod.* 13 (ὁ υἱός) ἐστιν ἄρτος ἐπουράνιος καὶ πνευματικὴ τροφή...τὸ φῶς τῶν ἀνθρώπων, τῆς ἐκκλησίας δηλονότι. οἱ μὲν οὖν τὸν οὐράνιον ἄρτον φαγόντες ἀπέθανον, ὁ δὲ τὸν ἀληθινὸν ἄρτον τοῦ πνεύματος ἐσθίων οὐ τεθνήξεται...ὁ δὲ ἄρτος ὃν ἐγὼ δώσω, φησίν, ἡ σάρξ μού ἐστιν, ἥτοι ᾧ τρέφεται ἡ σὰρξ διὰ τῆς εὐχαριστίας ἤ, ὅπερ καὶ μᾶλλον, ἡ σὰρξ τὸ σῶμα αὐτοῦ ἐστιν ἡ ἐκκλησία...συναγωγὴ ὑλογημένη.'

p. 381. On the mystical meaning of the Passover, cf. Philo I. 450 μηδ' ὅτι ἡ ἑορτὴ σύμβολον ψυχικῆς εὐφροσύνης ἐστὶ καὶ τῆς πρὸς εὐχαριστίας, ἀποταξώμεθα ταῖς κατὰ τὰς ἐτησίους ὥρας πανηγύρεσι.

p. 383. 11. Add the reference *Paed.* II. 7 for πανδήμου τροφῆς.

p. 387. Add on ἀγάπη, 'Deissmann, p. 198 f.'

p. 388. Add on ἀθανασία, 'Deissmann, p. 293.'

p. 391. Insert 'ἀνάλογος: 867, see ἀνὰ λόγον *s.v.* λόγος.'

p. 392. Add on ἀναπέμπω 'Deissmann, p. 229,' after ἀναστρέφομαι 'Deissmann, p. 194.'

p. 394. After ἀξίωσις add 'see exx. of ἀξίωμα in Deissmann, p. 92.'

p. 396. On ἀπόστολος add 'Harn. *H. of D.* II. p. 58.'

p. 398. On ἀφεκτέος (before 'Themist.') add '170 *bis.*'

p. 400. On γινώσκω, add (at end) '658': on γραφή (last l. after '*ind.*') Harn. *H. of D.* II. 57 f.

p. 405. On ἐκκλησία add 'Harn. II. p. 80 foll.'

p. 407. On ἐμφυσιόω, after τέκνα insert '*bis.*'

ADDENDA.

p. 415. On θαυμάζω, 883 should be *ordinary type*.

p. 416. On θεώρημα, add Hatch *Gr. Ideas*, p. 118 n.

p. 417. On καθολικός, add 'Harn. II. p. 75 n.'

p. 418. On κανών, add 'Harn. II. p. 85 n.'

p. 421. On κυριακός (2nd l.), for *ib.* read 865 and 887, and *dele* 887 after διδασκαλία.

p. 425. On μυστήριον add 'Hatch, *Bibl. Gr.* p. 57 f.'

p. 426. On ὁμολογία, om. (l. 1) 'τὴν περὶ—*ib.*' Add at the end 'Harn. II. p. 86 n.'

p. 429. On παρεπίδημος add 'Deissmann, p. 149.'

p. 440. On ταμεῖον add 'On the form ταμεῖον see ὑγεία and Deissmann, p. 182.'

ΚΛΗΜΕΝΤΟΣ

ΣΤΡΩΜΑΤΕΩΝ Ζ´

M. C.

ΣΤΡΩΜΑΤΕΩΝ Ζ΄

ΚΕΦ. Α.

1. ἬΔΗ δὲ καιρὸς ἡμᾶς παραστῆσαι τοῖς Ἕλλησι μόνον ὄντως εἶναι θεοσεβῆ τὸν γνωστικόν, ὡς ἀναμαθόντας τοὺς φιλοσόφους, υἱός τίς ἐστιν ὁ τῷ ὄντι Χριστιανός, τῆς ἑαυτῶν ἀμαθίας καταγνῶναι εἰκῆ μὲν
5 καὶ ὡς ἔτυχεν διώκοντας τοὔνομα, μάτην δὲ ἀθέους ἀποκαλοῦντας ⟨τοὺς⟩ τὸν τῷ ὄντι θεὸν ἐγνωκότας. ἐναργεστέροις δ', οἶμαι, πρὸς τοὺς φιλοσόφους χρῆσθαι προσήκει τοῖς λόγοις, ὡς ἐπαΐειν ἐκ τῆς παρ' αὐτοῖς παιδείας ἤδη γεγυμνασμένους δύνασθαι, καὶ εἰ μηδέπω
10 ἀξίους ἑαυτοὺς μεταλαβεῖν τῆς τοῦ πιστεῦσαι δυνάμεως παρεσχήκασι. τῶν δὲ λέξεων τῶν προφητικῶν ἐπὶ τοῦ παρόντος οὐκ ἐπιμνησθησόμεθα, κατὰ τοὺς ἐπικαίρους τόπους ὕστερον ταῖς γραφαῖς συγχρησόμενοι· τὰ δ' ἐξ αὐτῶν δηλούμενα σημανοῦμεν κεφαλαιωδῶς τὸν
15 χριστιανισμὸν ὑπογράφοντες, ἵνα μὴ διακόπτωμεν τὸ συνεχὲς τοῦ λόγου συμπαραλαμβάνοντες τὰς γραφάς, καὶ ταῦτα τοῖς μηδέπω συνιεῖσιν τὰς λέξεις αὐτῶν· ἐπὰν δὲ τὰ σημαινόμενα ἐνδειξώμεθα, τότε αὐτοῖς ἐκ περιουσίας πιστεύσασι καὶ τὰ μαρτύρια φανερωθήσεται.
20 κἂν ἑτεροῖά τισι τῶν πολλῶν καταφαίνηται τὰ ὑφ' ἡμῶν λεγόμενα τῶν κυριακῶν γραφῶν, ἰστέον ὅτι ἐκεῖθεν

---

8. οἷός τίς H. οἷός τέ L.   6. τοὺς τὸν S. τοὺς om. L.   16. συμπαραλαμβάνοντες SD. συμπεριλαμβάνοντες LH.

MISCELLANIES, BOOK VII.

CHAPTER I.

§ 1. It is now time for us to prove to the Greeks that the gnostic alone is truly devout, so that the philosophers, learning what sort of person the true Christian is, may condemn their own folly for their careless and indiscriminate persecution of the name of Christian, while they irrationally abuse as atheists those who have the knowledge of the true God. And in addressing philosophers I think one should employ ratiocination as more convincing, since they are better trained to understand it from their previous course of instruction, even if they have not yet shown themselves worthy to participate in the power to believe. Of the sayings of the prophets we will make no mention at present, intending hereafter to avail ourselves of the Scriptures on the fitting occasions. For the present we will only give a summary indication of what is declared by them, in the form of a sketch of the Christian religion, in order that we may not break the thread of the discourse by constant references to the Scriptures, especially when addressing those who do not yet understand their phraseology. When we have shown their general purport, the exhibition of the testimonies shall be superadded afterwards on their believing. And if our words seem to some of the uninstructed to be different from the Lord's Scriptures, let them know that it is from the Scriptures that

ἀναπνεῖ τε καὶ ζῇ, καὶ τὰς ἀφορμὰς ἀπ' αὐτῶν ἔχοντα τὸν νοῦν μόνον, οὐ τὴν λέξιν, παριστᾶν ἐπαγγέλλεται. ἥ τε γὰρ ἐπὶ πλέον ἐπεξεργασία μὴ κατὰ καιρὸν γινομένη περισσὴ δόξειεν ἂν εἰκότως, τό τε μηδ' ὅλως ἐπεσκέφθαι τὸ κατεπεῖγον ῥᾴθυμον κομιδῇ καὶ ἐνδεές. μακάριοι δὲ ὡς ἀληθῶς οἱ ἐξερευνῶντες τὰ μαρτύρια Κυρίου, ἐν ὅλῃ καρδίᾳ ἐκζητήσουσιν αὐτόν· μαρτυροῦσιν δὲ περὶ Κυρίου ὁ νόμος καὶ οἱ προφῆται.

2. Πρόκειται τοίνυν παραστῆσαι ἡμῖν μόνον τὸν γνωστικὸν ὅσιόν τε καὶ εὐσεβῆ, θεοπρεπῶς τὸν τῷ ὄντι θεὸν θρησκεύοντα· τῷ θεοπρεπεῖ δὲ τὸ θεοφιλὲς ἕπεται καὶ φιλόθεον. τίμιον μὲν οὖν ἅπαν τὸ ὑπερέχον ἡγεῖται κατὰ τὴν ἀξίαν· καὶ τιμητέον ἐν μὲν τοῖς αἰσθητοῖς τοὺς ἄρχοντας καὶ τοὺς γονεῖς καὶ πάντα τὸν πρεσβύτερον, ἐν δὲ τοῖς διδακτοῖς τὴν ἀρχαιοτάτην φιλοσοφίαν καὶ τὴν πρεσβίστην προφητείαν, ἐν δὲ τοῖς νοητοῖς τὸ πρεσβύτερον ἐν γενέσει, τὴν ἄχρονον <καὶ> ἄναρχον ἀρχήν τε καὶ ἀπαρχὴν τῶν ὄντων, τὸν υἱόν, παρ' οὗ ἐκμανθάνειν τὸ ἐπέκεινα αἴτιον, τὸν πατέρα τῶν ὅλων, τὸ πρέσβιστον καὶ πάντων εὐεργετικώτατον, οὐκέτι φωνῇ παραδιδόμενον, σεβάσματι δὲ καὶ σιγῇ μετὰ ἐκπλήξεως ἁγίας σεβαστὸν καὶ σεπτὸν κυριώτατα, λεγόμενον μὲν πρὸς τοῦ κυρίου ὡς οἷόν τε ἦν ἐπαΐειν τοῖς μανθάνουσι, νοούμενον δὲ πρός γε τῶν ἐξειλεγμένων εἰς γνῶσιν παρὰ κυρίου, τῶν τὰ αἰσθητήρια, φησὶν ὁ ἀπόστολος, συγγεγυμνασμένων.

3. Θεραπεία τοίνυν τοῦ θεοῦ ἡ συνεχὴς ἐπιμέλεια τῆς ψυχῆς τῷ γνωστικῷ καὶ ἡ περὶ τὸ θεῖον αὐτοῦ κατὰ τὴν ἀδιάλειπτον ἀγάπην ἀσχολία. τῆς γὰρ περὶ τοὺς ἀνθρώπους θεραπείας ἡ μὲν βελτιωτική, ἡ δὲ

5. ἐνδεές, D.   7. αὐτόν, D.   9. τὸ L pr. m. erasum post ἡμῖν.   17. ἄχρονον καὶ PM. ἄχρονον LVD. om. Jackson.   19. ἐκμανθάνειν] fort. ἐκμανθάνει M. τὸν πατέρα] τῶν π. LV.   22. post κυριώτατα distinguit P, post σεπτόν H.

they draw their life and breath, and that it is their object, taking these as their starting-point, to set forth, not their phraseology, but their meaning only. For further elaboration being unseasonable would with good reason seem superfluous, while on the other hand it would be a very careless and unsatisfactory way of treating the subject if we were to omit all consideration of that which is of pressing importance. And *blessed* indeed *are they who search out the testimonies of the Lord: with their whole heart they will seek him*[1]. Now *they which testify of the Lord are the law and the prophets*[2].

§ 2. It is our business then to prove that the gnostic alone is holy and pious, worshipping the true God as beseems Him; and the worship which beseems God includes both loving God and being loved by Him. To the gnostic every kind of preeminence seems honourable in proportion to its worth. In the world of sense rulers and parents and elders generally are to be honoured; in matters of teaching, the most ancient philosophy and the earliest prophecy; in the spiritual world, that which is elder in origin, the Son, the beginning and first-fruit of all existing things, Himself timeless and without beginning; from whom the gnostic believes that he receives the knowledge of the ultimate cause, the Father of the universe, the earliest and most beneficent of all existences, no longer reported by word of mouth, but worshipped and adored, as is His due, with silent worship and holy awe; who was manifested indeed by the Lord so far as it was possible for the learners to understand, but apprehended by those whom the Lord has elected for knowledge, *those*, says the apostle, *who have their senses exercised*[3].

§ 3. The gnostic therefore pays service to God by his constant self-discipline and by cherishing that which is divine in himself in the way of unremitting charity. For as regards the service of men, part may be classed as meliorative treatment and part as ministrative service. Thus the medicinal

---

[1] Psalm cxix. 2, 1 Pet. i. 10.   [2] Jo. v. 39, Rom. iii. 21 (cf. Act. x. 43).
[3] Heb. v. 14.

ὑπηρετική· ἰατρικὴ μὲν σώματος, φιλοσοφία δὲ ψυχῆς βελτιωτική· γονεῦσι δὲ ἐκ παίδων καὶ ἡγεμόσιν ἐκ τῶν ὑποτεταγμένων ὑπηρετικὴ ὠφέλεια προσγίνεται. ὁμοίως δὲ καὶ κατὰ τὴν ἐκκλησίαν τὴν μὲν βελτιωτικὴν οἱ πρεσβύτεροι σώζουσιν εἰκόνα, τὴν ὑπηρετικὴν δὲ οἱ διάκονοι. ταύτας ἄμφω τὰς διακονίας ἄγγελοί τε ὑπηρετοῦνται τῷ θεῷ κατὰ τὴν τῶν περιγείων οἰκονομίαν, καὶ αὐτὸς ὁ γνωστικός, θεῷ μὲν διακονούμενος, ἀνθρώποις δὲ τὴν βελτιωτικὴν ἐνδεικνύμενος θεωρίαν, ὅπως ἂν καὶ παιδεύειν ᾖ τεταγμένος εἰς τὴν τῶν ἀνθρώπων ἐπανόρθωσιν. θεοσεβὴς γὰρ μόνος ὁ καλῶς καὶ ἀνεπιλήπτως περὶ τὰ ἀνθρώπεια ἐξυπηρετῶν τῷ θεῷ. ὥσπερ γὰρ θεραπεία φυτῶν ἀρίστη καθ' ἣν γίνονται οἱ καρποὶ καὶ συγκομίζονται ἐπιστήμῃ καὶ ἐμπειρίᾳ γεωργικῇ, τὴν ὠφέλειαν τὴν ἐξ αὐτῶν παρεχομένη τοῖς ἀνθρώποις, οὕτως ἡ θεοσέβεια τοῦ γνωστικοῦ τοὺς καρποὺς τῶν δι' αὐτοῦ πιστευσάντων ἀνθρώπων εἰς ἑαυτὴν ἀναδεχομένη, ἐν ἐπιγνώσει πλειόνων γινομένων καὶ ταύτῃ σωζομένων, συγκομιδὴν ἀρίστην δι' ἐμπειρίας ἐργάζεται. εἰ δ' ἡ θεοπρέπεια ἕξις ἐστὶ τὸ πρέπον τῷ θεῷ σώζουσα, θεοφιλὴς ὁ θεοπρεπὴς μόνος· οὗτος δ' ἂν εἴη ὁ εἰδὼς τὸ πρέπον καὶ κατὰ τὴν ἐπιστήμην καὶ κατὰ τὸν βίον, ὅπως βιωτέον ἐσομένῳ καὶ δὴ ἐξομοιουμένῳ ἤδη θεῷ.

4. Ταύτῃ ἄρα φιλόθεος τὸ πρῶτον. ὡς γὰρ ὁ τιμῶν τὸν πατέρα φιλοπάτωρ, οὕτως ὁ τιμῶν τὸν θεὸν φιλόθεος. ᾗ καί μοι καταφαίνεται τρία εἶναι τῆς γνωστικῆς δυνάμεως ἀποτελέσματα, <πρῶτον> τὸ γινώ-

---

2. γονεῦσι δὲ M. γ. μὴν Jackson. γονεῦσι μὲν L. γονεῦσιν μὲν edd. 6. διακονίας L, fort. θεραπείας M. 13. γίνονται] γίγνονται L. 14. συγκομίζονται L². -ζωνται L¹. 15. παρεχομένῃ Kl. D. παρεχομένη LP. 18. γινομένων] γιγνομένων L. 20. εἰ δ' M. εἰ δ' (η m. sec. superscr.) L. ἠδ' V. ᾖ δ' SD. 23. ὅπως H. ὅτῳ L. 25. φιλόθεος S. φιλόθεός τε L. 27. ᾗ S. ἢ L. 28. πρῶτον addidit D.

art is meliorative of the body and philosophy of the soul; but that which parents receive from children and rulers from subjects is ministrative aid. Similarly in the Church the meliorative service is imaged in the presbyters, the ministrative in the deacons. As both these services are performed by the ministering angels for God in their administration of earthly things, so they are also performed by the gnostic himself, while on the one hand he serves God, and on the other hand sets forth his meliorative philosophy to men, in whatsoever way he may be appointed to instruct them with a view to their improvement. For he alone is truly devout who ministers to God rightly and unblameably in respect to human affairs. For, as the best treatment of plants is that whereby the fruits grow and are gathered in by the science and art of husbandry, supplying to men the benefit derived from the fruits; so the best ingathering which the devoutness of the gnostic can accomplish by means of his art is the appropriation of the fruits of all who have come to believe through him, as one after another becomes possessed of knowledge and is thus brought into the way of salvation. And if by godliness we understand the habit of mind which preserves the fitting attitude towards God, then the godly alone is dear to God. And such would be he who knows what is fitting both in theory and in life, as to how one should live who will one day become god, aye and is even now being made like to God.

§ 4. Thus he is before all things a lover of God. For as he who honours his father is a lover of his father, so he who honours God is a lover of God. Hence too the gnostic faculty seems to me to reveal itself in three achievements: (1) in the knowledge of the facts <of the Christian religion>, (2) in the

σκειν τὰ πράγματα, δεύτερον τὸ ἐπιτελεῖν ὅ τι ἂν ὁ λόγος ὑπαγορεύῃ, καὶ τρίτον τὸ παραδιδόναι δύνασθαι θεοπρεπῶς τὰ παρὰ τῇ ἀληθείᾳ ἐπικεκρυμμένα. ὁ τοίνυν θεὸν πεπεισμένος εἶναι παντοκράτορα καὶ τὰ θεῖα μυστήρια παρὰ τοῦ μονογενοῦς παιδὸς αὐτοῦ ἐκμαθών, πῶς οὗτος ἄθεος; ἄθεος μὲν γὰρ ὁ μὴ νομίζων εἶναι θεόν, δεισιδαίμων δὲ ὁ δεδιὼς τὰ δαιμόνια, ὁ πάντα θειάζων καὶ ξύλον καὶ λίθον, καὶ πνεῦμα ἄνθρωπόν τε λογικῶς βιοῦντα καταδεδουλωμένος.

ΚΕΦ. Β.

5. Πίστις οὖν τὸ εἰδέναι θεὸν ἡ πρώτη, μετὰ <δὲ> τῆς τοῦ σωτῆρος διδασκαλίας τὴν πεποίθησιν τὸ κατὰ μηδένα τρόπον ἄδικα δρᾶν, τοῦτ' εἶναι πρέπον ἡγεῖσθαι τῇ ἐπιγνώσει τοῦ θεοῦ. ταύτῃ κράτιστον μὲν ἐν γῇ ἄνθρωπος ὁ θεοσεβέστατος, κράτιστον δὲ ἐν οὐρανῷ ἄγγελος, ὁ πλησιαίτερον κατὰ τόπον καὶ ἤδη καθαρώτερον τῆς αἰωνίου καὶ μακαρίας ζωῆς μεταλαγχάνων. τελειοτάτη δὲ καὶ ἁγιωτάτη καὶ κυριωτάτη καὶ ἡγεμονικωτάτη καὶ βασιλικωτάτη καὶ εὐεργετικωτάτη ἡ υἱοῦ φύσις ἡ τῷ μόνῳ παντοκράτορι προσεχεστάτη. αὕτη ἡ μεγίστη ὑπεροχή, ἣ τὰ πάντα διατάσσεται κατὰ τὸ θέλημα τοῦ πατρὸς καὶ τὸ πᾶν ἄριστα οἰακίζει, ἀκαμάτῳ καὶ ἀτρύτῳ δυνάμει πάντα ἐργαζομένη, δι' ὧν ἐνεργεῖ τὰς ἀποκρύφους ἐννοίας ἐπιβλέπουσα. οὐ γὰρ ἐξίσταταί ποτε τῆς αὑτοῦ περιωπῆς ὁ υἱὸς τοῦ θεοῦ, οὐ μεριζόμενος, οὐκ ἀποτεμνόμενος, οὐ μεταβαίνων ἐκ

---

8. ἄνθρωπον—βιοῦντα LPH. ἀνθρώπῳ—βιοῦντι SD.   9. καταδεδουλωμένος SPDH. καταδεδουλωμένον L.   10. εἰδέναι L, fort. εἶναι H.   ἐνεργεῖ post πεποίθησιν addit Lowth, fort. post εἰδέναι M.   δὲ post μετὰ addit M.
12. ἡγεῖσθαι] fort. ἡγούμενον M.   15. ὁ M. τὸ L.   17. τελειοτάτη] τελειωτάτη L.   δὲ M. δὴ L.   24. αὑτοῦ M. αὐτοῦ L.

accomplishment of whatever the Word enjoins, (3) in the capacity to impart to others after a godly manner the hidden things of truth. How then can he who is convinced that God is Almighty, and who has learnt the divine mysteries from His only-begotten Son,—how can such an one be an atheist? An atheist is one who does not believe in the existence of God, while we call by the name of superstitious him who fears the demons and who deifies everything down to stocks and stones, having brought into slavery the spirit and the <inner> man which lives in accordance with reason.

CHAPTER II.

§ 5. The effect of faith then in its early stage is the knowledge of God, and then (after a man has learnt to trust the Saviour's teaching) the conviction that the entire abstinence from wrong actions—this and this alone befits the knowledge of God. Thus the most excellent thing on earth is the most devout of men, and the most excellent in heaven is the angel, who is nearer in place <to the Deity> and already more purely participant of the eternal and blessed life. But most perfect and most holy of all, most sovereign, most lordly, most royal, and most beneficent, is the nature of the Son, which approaches most closely to the One Almighty Being. The Son is the highest Pre-eminence, which sets in order all things according to *the Father's will*[1], and steers the universe aright, performing all things with unwearying energy, beholding the Father's secret thoughts through His working. For the Son of God never moves from *His watch-tower*[2], being never divided, never disservered, never passing from place to place, but existing everywhere at all

---

[1] Mt. vii. 21, xii. 50, Joh. vi. 40. [2] Plato *Polit.* 272 E.

τόπου εἰς τόπον, πάντη δὲ ὢν πάντοτε καὶ μηδαμῆ περιεχόμενος, ὅλος νοῦς, ὅλος φῶς πατρῷον, ὅλος ὀφθαλμός, πάντα ὁρῶν, πάντα ἀκούων, εἰδὼς πάντα, δυνάμει τὰς δυνάμεις ἐρευνῶν. τούτῳ πᾶσα ὑποτέτακται στρατιὰ ἀγγέλων τε καὶ θεῶν, τῷ λόγῳ τῷ πατρικῷ τὴν ἁγίαν οἰκονομίαν ἀναδεδεγμένῳ διὰ τὸν ὑποτάξαντα, δι' ὃν καὶ πάντες αὐτοῦ οἱ ἄνθρωποι, ἀλλ' οἱ μὲν κατ' ἐπίγνωσιν, οἱ δὲ οὐδέπω, καὶ οἱ μὲν ὡς φίλοι, οἱ δὲ ὡς οἰκέται πιστοί, οἱ δὲ ὡς ἁπλῶς οἰκέται.

6. Ὁ διδάσκαλος οὗτος, ὁ παιδεύων μυστηρίοις μὲν τὸν γνωστικόν, ἐλπίσι δὲ ἀγαθαῖς τὸν πιστόν, καὶ παιδείᾳ τῇ ἐπανορθωτικῇ δι' αἰσθητικῆς ἐνεργείας τὸν σκληροκάρδιον. ἐντεῦθεν ἡ πρόνοια ἰδίᾳ καὶ δημοσίᾳ καὶ πανταχοῦ. υἱὸν δὲ εἶναι τοῦ θεοῦ, καὶ τοῦτον εἶναι τὸν σωτῆρα καὶ κύριον ὃν ἡμεῖς φαμέν, ἄντικρυς αἱ θεῖαι παριστᾶσι προφητεῖαι. ταύτῃ ὁ πάντων κύριος Ἑλλήνων τε καὶ βαρβάρων τοὺς ἐθέλοντας πείθει, οὐ γὰρ βιάζεται τὸν ἐξ αὐτοῦ τὴν σωτηρίαν λαβεῖν διὰ τοῦ ἑλέσθαι καὶ πάντα ἀποπληρῶσαι τὰ παρ' αὐτοῦ πρὸς τὸ λαβέσθαι τῆς ἐλπίδος, δυνάμενον. οὗτός ἐστιν ὁ διδοὺς καὶ τοῖς Ἕλλησι τὴν φιλοσοφίαν διὰ τῶν ὑποδεεστέρων ἀγγέλων. εἰσὶ γὰρ συνδιανενεμημένοι προστάξει θείᾳ τε καὶ ἀρχαίᾳ ἄγγελοι κατὰ ἔθνη· ἀλλ' ἡ μερὶς κυρίου ἡ δόξα τῶν πιστευόντων. ἤτοι γὰρ οὐ φροντίζει πάντων ἀνθρώπων ὁ κύριος,—καὶ τοῦτο ἢ τῷ μὴ δύνασθαι πάθοι ἄν (ὅπερ οὐ θεμιτόν, ἀσθενείας γὰρ σημεῖον) ἢ τῷ μὴ βούλεσθαι δυνάμενος (οὐκ ἀγαθοῦ δὲ τὸ πάθος· οὔκουν ὑπὸ τρυφῆς ῥάθυμος ὁ δι' ἡμᾶς τὴν παθητὴν ἀναλαβὼν σάρκα)·—ἢ κήδεται τῶν συμπάντων, ὅπερ καὶ καθήκει τῷ κυρίῳ πάντων γενομένῳ.

1. πάντη S. παντὶ L.   2. πατρῷον S. πατρῷος L.   4. πᾶσα] fort. ἡ πᾶσα M.   6. ἀναδεδεγμένος S. ἀναδεδειγμένῳ L.   7. ὃν H. ὢν L.   11. ἐλπίσι δὲ] ἐλπίσι τε L.   18. αὐτοῦ H. αὑτοῦ L.
19. αὐτοῦ H. αὑτοῦ L.

times and free from all limitations. He is *all reason, all eye, all light from the Father, seeing all things, hearing all things*[1], knowing all things, with power searching the powers. To Him is subjected the whole army of angels and of gods,—to Him, the Word of the Father, who has received the holy administration *by reason of Him who subjected it to Him*[2]; through whom also all men belong to Him, but some by way of knowledge, while others have not yet attained to this; *some as friends*[3], some as *faithful servants*[4], others as servants merely.

§ 6. This is the Teacher who educates the gnostic by means of mysteries, and the believer by means of good hopes, and him who is hard of heart with corrective discipline acting on the senses. He is the source of Providence both for the individual and the community and for the universe at large. And that there is a Son of God, and that this Son is the Saviour and Lord that we assert Him to be, is directly declared by the divine prophecies. Thus the Lord of all, whether Greek or barbarian, uses persuasion to those who are willing; for it is not His way to compel one who is able of himself to obtain salvation by the *exercise of free choice* and *by fulfilling* all that is required on *his part*[5] so as *to lay hold on the hope*[6]. This is He who bestows on the Greeks also their philosophy through the inferior angels. For by an ancient and divine ordinance *angels are assigned to the different nations*: but to be *the Lord's portion*[7] is the glory of the believers. Here we have the following alternatives: either the Lord cares not for all men,—which might arise from incapacity (but this it is forbidden to say, for incapacity is a mark of weakness), or from want of will on the part of one possessed with power (but such an affection is incompatible with goodness; in any case He who for our sake took upon Him our flesh with its capacity for suffering is not rendered indifferent to others' sorrow by self-indulgence),—or He has regard for us all, which also beseems Him who was made

---

[1] Xenophanes ap. Sext. Emp. IX. 144. [2] Rom. viii. 20. [3] Joh. xv. 14, 15.
[4] Heb. iii. 5. [5] Plat. *Rep.* x. 620 E. [6] Heb. vi. 18. [7] Deut. xxxii. 8, 9.

σωτὴρ γάρ ἐστιν, οὐχὶ τῶν μέν, τῶν δ' οὔ, πρὸς δὲ
ὅσον ἐπιτηδειότητος ἕκαστος εἶχεν, τὴν ἑαυτοῦ διένειμεν
εὐεργεσίαν Ἕλλησί τε καὶ βαρβάροις καὶ τοῖς ἐκ
τούτων προωρισμένοις μέν, κατὰ δὲ τὸν οἰκεῖον καιρὸν
κεκλημένοις, πιστοῖς τε καὶ ἐκλεκτοῖς. 7. Οὔτ' οὖν
φθονοίη ποτ' ἄν τισιν ὁ πάντας μὲν ἐπ' ἴσης κεκληκώς, ἐξαιρέτους δὲ τοῖς ἐξαιρέτως πεπιστευκόσιν
ἀπονείμας τιμάς, οὔθ' ὑφ' ἑτέρου κωλυθείη ποτ' ἂν
ὁ πάντων κύριος, καὶ μάλιστα ἐξυπηρετῶν τῷ τοῦ
ἀγαθοῦ καὶ παντοκράτορος θελήματι πατρός. ἀλλ' οὐδὲ
ἅπτεται τοῦ κυρίου ἀπαθοῦς ἀνάρχως γενομένου φθόνος, οὐδὲ μὴν τὰ ἀνθρώπων οὕτως ἔχει ὡς φθονητὰ
εἶναι πρὸς τοῦ κυρίου· ἄλλος δὲ ὁ φθονῶν, οὗ καὶ
πάθος ἥψατο. καὶ μὴν οὐδ' ὑπὸ ἀγνοίας ἔστιν εἰπεῖν
μὴ βούλεσθαι σῴζειν τὴν ἀνθρωπότητα τὸν κύριον διὰ
τὸ μὴ εἰδέναι ὅπως ἑκάστου ἐπιμελητέον· ἄγνοια γὰρ
οὐχ ἅπτεται τοῦ <υἱοῦ τοῦ> θεοῦ, τοῦ πρὸ καταβολῆς
κόσμου συμβούλου γενομένου τοῦ πατρός. αὕτη γὰρ ἦν
<ἡ> σοφία ᾗ προσέχαιρεν ὁ παντοκράτωρ θεός· δύναμις
γὰρ τοῦ θεοῦ ὁ υἱός, ἅτε πρὸ πάντων τῶν γενομένων
ἀρχικώτατος λόγος τοῦ πατρός, καὶ σοφία αὐτοῦ κυρίως
ἂν καὶ διδάσκαλος λεχθείη τῶν δι' αὐτοῦ πλασθέντων.
οὐδὲ μὴν ὑπό τινος ἡδονῆς περισπώμενος καταλείποι
ποτ' ἂν τὴν ἀνθρώπων κηδεμονίαν, ὅς γε καὶ τὴν
σάρκα τὴν ἐμπαθῆ φύσει γενομένην ἀναλαβὼν εἰς
ἕξιν ἀπαθείας ἐπαίδευσεν. πῶς δ' ἂν εἴη σωτὴρ καὶ
κύριος, εἰ μὴ πάντων σωτὴρ καὶ κύριος, ἀλλὰ τῶν μὲν
πεπιστευκότων σωτήρ, διὰ τὸ γνῶναι βεβουλῆσθαι,
τῶν δὲ ἀπειθησάντων κύριος, ἔστ' ἂν ἐξομολογήσασθαι
δυνηθέντες οἰκείας καὶ καταλλήλου τῆς δι' αὐτοῦ

1. οὔ, πρὸς δὲ M. οὔ. πρὸς δὴ LV edd. 12. οὐδὲ μὴν D. οὔτε μὴν L.
14. οὐδ' Kl. οὔθ' L. 17. τοῦ υἱοῦ τοῦ θεοῦ H. τοῦ θεοῦ L. 19. ἡ
σοφία H. σοφία L. 23. καταλείποι D. καταλείπει L. 26. εἴη D.
ἐστι L. 29. ἐξομολογήσασθαι S. ἐξομολογήσεσθαι L.

the Lord of all. For He is the Saviour not of one here and another there, but, to the extent of each man's fitness, He distributed His own bounty both to Greeks and to barbarians, and to the *faithful and elect*[1], who were *foreordained* out of them and were *called*[2] in their own season. § 7. Neither again could envy be the impelling principle with Him, who has called all alike, though He has assigned special honours to those who have shown special faith; nor could the Lord of all be hindered by opposition from without, especially when He is carrying out *the will of the* good and almighty *Father*[3]. No, as the Lord Himself is absolutely inaccessible to envy, being eternally free from passion, so neither is man's state such as to be envied by the Lord. It is another who envies, who is also acquainted with passion. Nor yet can it be said that the Lord from ignorance did not will to save mankind, because He knew not how to take care of each. For ignorance touches not <the Son of> God, who was *the Father's counsellor*[4] *before the foundation of the world*[5], *the Wisdom in which the Almighty God rejoiced*[6]. For *the Son is the power of God*[7], as being the original Word of the Father, prior to all created things: and He might justly be styled the *Wisdom of God*[7] and the Teacher of those who were made by Him. Neither indeed could He ever abandon His care for mankind through the distractions of any pleasure, seeing that, after He had taken upon Him our flesh, which is by nature subject to passion, He trained it to a habit of impassibility. And how could He be Saviour and Lord, if He were not Saviour and Lord of all, —Saviour of those who have believed, because they have determined to know, Lord of those who have been disobedient, until they have been enabled to confess their sins, and have received the grace which comes through Him, in the way adapted and

---

[1] Rev. xvii. 14. [2] Rom. viii. 30. [3] Mt. vii. 21, xii. 50, Joh. vi. 40.
[4] Job xv. 8, Isai. xl. 18, Rom. xi. 34. [5] Eph. i. 4.
[6] Prov. viii. 22—30. [7] 1 Cor. i. 24.

τύχωσιν εὐεργεσίας; πᾶσα δὲ ἡ τοῦ κυρίου ἐνέργεια ἐπὶ τὸν παντοκράτορα τὴν ἀναφορὰν ἔχει, καὶ ἔστιν ὡς εἰπεῖν πατρική τις ἐνέργεια ὁ υἱός.

8. Οὐκ ἂν οὖν ποτε ὁ σωτὴρ μισάνθρωπος, ὅς γε διὰ τὴν ὑπερβάλλουσαν φιλανθρωπίαν σαρκὸς ἀνθρωπίνης ἐμπάθειαν οὐχ ὑπεριδών, ἀλλ' ἐνδυσάμενος, ἐπὶ τὴν κοινὴν τῶν ἀνθρώπων ἐλήλυθεν σωτηρίαν· κοινὴ γὰρ ἡ πίστις τῶν ἑλομένων. ἀλλ' οὐδὲ τοῦ ἰδίου ποτ' ἂν ἀμελοίη ἔργου, τῷ μόνῳ τῶν ἄλλων ζῴων ἀνθρώπῳ ἔννοιαν κατὰ τὴν δημιουργίαν ἐνεστάχθαι θεοῦ. οὐδ' ἂν βελτίων τις ἄλλη καὶ ἁρμονιωτέρα διοίκησις ἀνθρώπων εἴη τῷ θεῷ τῆς τεταγμένης. προσήκει γοῦν ἀεὶ τῷ κρείττονι κατὰ φύσιν ἡγεῖσθαι τοῦ χείρονος, καὶ τῷ δυναμένῳ καλῶς τι διέπειν ἀποδεδόσθαι τὴν ἐκείνου διοίκησιν. ἔστιν δὲ τὸ ὡς ἀληθῶς ἄρχον τε καὶ ἡγεμονοῦν ὁ θεῖος λόγος καὶ ἡ τούτου πρόνοια, πάντα μὲν ἐφορῶσα, μηδενὸς δὲ τῶν οἰκείων ἑαυτῆς παρορῶσα τὴν ἐπιμέλειαν· οὗτοι δ' ἂν εἶεν οἱ ἑλόμενοι οἰκεῖοι εἶναι αὐτῷ, οἱ διὰ πίστεως τελειούμενοι. οὕτως ἁπάντων τῶν ἀγαθῶν θελήματι τοῦ παντοκράτορος πατρὸς αἴτιος ὁ υἱὸς καθίσταται, πρωτουργοῦ κινήσεως δύναμις ἄληπτος αἰσθήσει. οὐ γὰρ ὃ ἦν, τοῦτο ὤφθη τοῖς χωρῆσαι μὴ δυναμένοις διὰ τὴν ἀσθένειαν τῆς σαρκός, αἰσθητὴν δὲ ἀναλαβὼν σάρκα τὸ δυνατὸν ἀνθρώποις κατὰ τὴν ὑπακοὴν τῶν ἐντολῶν δείξων ἀφίκετο.

9. Δύναμις οὖν πατρικὴ ὑπάρχων ῥᾳδίως περιγίνεται ὧν ἂν ἐθέλῃ, οὐδὲ τὸ μικρότατον ἀπολείπων τῆς ἑαυτοῦ διοικήσεως ἀφρόντιστον· οὐδὲ γὰρ ἂν ἔτι ἦν αὐτῷ τὸ ὅλον εὖ εἰργασμένον. δυνάμεως δ', οἶμαι, τῆς

---

6. ἐμπάθειαν H. εὐπάθειαν L.   10. ἐνεστάχθαι S. ἐνεστάλθαι L.
11. βελτίων] βελτίω LV.   13. τῷ δυναμένῳ S. τοῦ δυναμένου L.
19. οὗτως H. οὗτοι L.   21. πρωτουργοῦ H. πρωτουργός L.
25. ἀφῖκται vel ἀφίκετο S (illud praefert D, hoc M), ἀφίκηται L.
27. ἀπολειπὼν L. ἀπολιπὼν D.

corresponding to their state? But all the activity of the Lord is referred to the Almighty, the Son being, so to speak, a certain activity of the Father.

§ 8. The Saviour then could never be a hater of men, seeing that it was owing to His abounding love for man that He scorned not the weakness of human flesh, but having clothed Himself with it, has come into the world for the common salvation of men. For faith is common to all who choose it. No, nor could He ever neglect man, His peculiar work, seeing that into man alone of all animals has an idea of God been instilled at his creation. Neither could there be any better government of men, or one more consonant to the divine nature, than that which has been ordained. At any rate it always belongs to him who is naturally superior to direct the inferior, and to him who is able to manage anything well, that he should have received the government of it as his due. But the true Ruler and Director is the Word of God and His Providence, superintending all things and neglecting the charge of none of her household. And such would be they who have chosen to attach themselves to the Word, viz. those who are being perfected through faith. Thus, by *the will of the* Almighty *Father*[1], the Son, who is the imperceptible *power of primaeval motion*[2], is made the cause of all good things. For He was not seen in His true nature, by those who could not apprehend it owing to the infirmity of the flesh, but having taken upon Him a body which could be seen and handled, He came into the world to reveal what was possible to man in the way of obedience to God's commandments.

§ 9. Being then the power of the Father, He easily prevails over whomsoever He will, not leaving even the smallest atom of His government uncared for: else the universe of His creation would have been no longer good. And methinks

---

[1] Mt. vii. 21, xii. 50, Joh. vi. 40.   [2] Plato *Leg.* x. 897 A.

μεγίστης ἡ πάντων τῶν μερῶν καὶ μέχρι τοῦ μικροτάτου προήκουσα δι' ἀκριβείας ἐξέτασις, πάντων εἰς τὸν πρῶτον διοικητὴν τῶν ὅλων ἐκ θελήματος πατρὸς κυβερνῶντα τὴν πάντων σωτηρίαν ἀφορώντων, ἑτέρων ὑφ' ἑτέρους ἡγουμένους τεταγμένων, ἔστ' ἄν τις ἐπὶ τὸν μέγαν ἀφίκηται ἀρχιερέα. ἀπὸ μιᾶς γὰρ ἄνωθεν ἀρχῆς τῆς κατὰ τὸ θέλημα ἐνεργούσης ἤρτηται τὰ πρῶτα καὶ δεύτερα καὶ τρίτα· εἶτα ἐπὶ τέλει τοῦ φαινομένου τῷ ἄκρῳ ἡ μακαρία ἀγγελοθεσία, καὶ δὴ μέχρις ἡμῶν αὐτῶν ἄλλοι ὑπ' ἄλλοις ἐξ ἑνὸς καὶ δι' ἑνὸς σωζόμενοί τε καὶ σώζοντες διαπετάχαται. ὡς οὖν συγκινεῖται καὶ μακροτάτη σιδήρου μοῖρα τῷ τῆς Ἡρακλείας λίθου πνεύματι διὰ πολλῶν τῶν σιδηρῶν ἐκτεινομένῳ δακτυλίων, οὕτω καὶ τῷ ἁγίῳ πνεύματι ἑλκόμενοι οἱ μὲν ἐνάρετοι οἰκειοῦνται τῇ πρώτῃ μονῇ, ἐφεξῆς δ' <οἱ> ἄλλοι μέχρι τῆς τελευταίας· οἱ δὲ ὑπὸ ἀσθενείας κακοί, δι' ἀπληστίαν ἄδικον καχεξίᾳ περιπεπτωκότες, οὔτε κρατοῦντες οὔτε κρατούμενοι περικαταρρέουσιν ἑλιχθέντες τοῖς πάθεσι καὶ ἀποπίπτουσι χαμαί. νόμος γὰρ ἄνωθεν οὗτος, αἱρεῖσθαι τὸν βουλόμενον ἀρετήν.

10. Διὸ καὶ αἱ ἐντολαὶ αἱ κατὰ νόμον τε καὶ πρὸ τοῦ νόμου οὐκ ἐννόμοις (δικαίῳ γὰρ νόμος οὐ κεῖται,) τὸν μὲν ἑλόμενον ζωὴν ἀΐδιον καὶ μακάριον γέρας λαμβάνειν ἔταξαν, τὸν δ' αὖ κακίᾳ ἡσθέντα συνεῖναι οἷς εἵλετο συνεχώρησαν· πάλιν τε αὖ τὴν βελτιουμένην ἑκάστοτε ψυχὴν εἰς ἀρετῆς ἐπίγνωσιν καὶ δικαιοσύνης αὔξησιν βελτίονα ἀπολαμβάνειν ἐν τῷ παντὶ τὴν τάξιν, κατὰ προκοπὴν ἑκάστην ἐπεκτεινομένην εἰς ἕξιν ἀπαθείας, ἄχρις ἂν καταντήσῃ εἰς ἄνδρα τέλειον, τῆς γνώσεώς τε ὁμοῦ καὶ κληρονομίας ὑπεροχήν. αὗται αἱ σωτήριοι περι-

2. προήκουσα SD. προσήκουσα LH. 4. ἀφορώντων H. ἐφορώντων L.
11. μακροτάτη M. μικροτάτη L. 13. ἐκτεινομένῳ Lowth. ἐκτεινομένη L.
15. οἱ ἄλλοι M. ἄλλοι L. 26. ἐπίγνωσιν M. ἐπίδοσιν (γνω m. pr. corr.) L³, unde ἐπίγησιν V. ἐπίκτησιν S. ἐπίδοσιν L¹. Canter. D.

the greatest power is shown where there is an inspection of all the parts, proceeding with minute accuracy even to the smallest, while all *gaze on*[1] the supreme Administrator of the universe, as He pilots all in safety according to *the Father's will*[2], rank being subordinated to rank under different leaders, till in the end *the great High Priest*[3] is reached. For on one original principle, which works in accordance with *the Father's will*[2], *depend the first and second and third gradations*[4]; and then at the extreme end of the visible world there is the blessed ordinance of angels; and so, even down to ourselves, ranks below ranks are appointed, all saving and being saved by the initiation and through the instrumentality of One. As then the remotest particle of iron is drawn by the influence of *the magnet extending through a long series of iron rings*[5], so also through the attraction of the Holy Spirit the virtuous are adapted to the highest *mansion*[6], and the others in their order even to the last mansion: but they that are wicked from weakness, having fallen into an evil habit owing to unrighteous greed, neither keep hold themselves nor are held by another, but collapse and fall to the ground, being entangled in their passions. For this is the law from the beginning, that he who would have virtue must choose it.

§ 10. Wherefore also both the commandments according to the law and the commandments previous to the law, given to those who were not yet *under law*[7],—*for law is not enacted for a just man*[8],—ordained that he who chose should obtain eternal life and a blessed reward, and on the other hand permitted him who delighted in wickedness to consort with what he chose. Again they ordained that the soul that at any time improved as regards the knowledge of virtue and increase in righteousness, should obtain an improved position in the universe, *pressing onwards*[9] at every step to a passionless state, until it *comes to a perfect man*[10], a preeminence at once of knowledge and of inheritance. These saving revolu-

---

[1] Heb. xii. 2. [2] See above p. 9. [3] Heb. iv. 14. [4] Plato *Epist.* II. 812 B.
[5] Plato *Ion* 533 D, E, 535 E, 536 A.   [6] Joh. xiv. 2.   [7] 1 Cor. ix. 21.
   [8] 1 Tim. i. 9.   [9] Phil. iii. 14.   [10] Eph. iv. 13.

τροπαὶ κατὰ τὴν τῆς μεταβολῆς τάξιν ἀπομερίζονται
καὶ χρόνοις καὶ τόποις καὶ τιμαῖς καὶ γνώσεσι καὶ
κληρονομίαις καὶ λειτουργίαις, καθ' ἑκάστην ἑκάστη
ἕως τῆς ἐπαναβεβηκυίας καὶ προσεχοῦς τοῦ κυρίου ἐν
ἀϊδιότητι θεωρίας. ἀγωγὸν δὲ τὸ ἐραστὸν πρὸς τὴν ἑαυτοῦ
θεωρίαν παντὸς τοῦ ὅλον ἑαυτὸν τῇ τῆς γνώσεως ἀγάπῃ
ἐπιβεβληκότος τῇ θεωρίᾳ.

11. Διὸ καὶ τὰς ἐντολὰς ἔδωκεν τάς τε προτέρας
τάς τε δευτέρας ἐκ μιᾶς ἀρυτόμενος πηγῆς ὁ κύριος,
οὔτε τοὺς πρὸ νόμου ἀνόμους εἶναι ὑπεριδὼν οὔτ' αὖ
τοὺς μὴ ἐπαΐοντας τῆς βαρβάρου φιλοσοφίας ἀφηνιάσαι
συγχωρήσας. τοῖς μὲν γὰρ ἐντολάς, τοῖς δὲ φιλοσοφίαν
παρασχὼν συνέκλεισεν τὴν ἀπιστίαν εἰς τὴν παρουσίαν,
ὅτε ἀναπολόγητός ἐστι πᾶς ὁ μὴ πιστεύσας. ἄγει γὰρ
ἐξ ἑτέρας <ἑτέρους> προκοπῆς Ἑλληνικῆς τε καὶ βαρβάρου ἐπὶ τὴν διὰ πίστεως τελείωσιν. εἰ δέ τις
Ἑλλήνων ὑπερβὰς τὸ προηγούμενον τῆς φιλοσοφίας
τῆς Ἑλληνικῆς εὐθέως ὥρμησεν ἐπὶ τὴν ἀληθῆ διδασκαλίαν, ὑπερεδίσκευσεν οὗτος, κἂν ἰδιώτης ᾖ, τὴν
ἐπίτομον τῆς σωτηρίας διὰ πίστεως εἰς τελείωσιν
ἑλόμενος.

12. Πάντ' οὖν ὅσα μηδὲν ἐκώλυεν ἑκούσιον εἶναι
τῷ ἀνθρώπῳ τὴν αἵρεσιν συνεργὰ πρὸς ἀρετὴν ἐποίησέν
τε καὶ ἔδειξεν, ὅπως ἀμηγέπη καὶ τοῖς ἀμυδρῶς διορᾶν
δυναμένοις ὁ τῷ ὄντι μόνος εἷς παντοκράτωρ ἀγαθὸς
ἀναφαίνηται θεός, ἐξ αἰῶνος εἰς αἰῶνα σῴζων διὰ υἱοῦ,
κακίας δ' αὖ πάντῃ πάντως ἀναίτιος. πρὸς γὰρ τὴν
τοῦ ὅλου σωτηρίαν τῷ τῶν ὅλων κυρίῳ πάντα ἐστὶ
διατεταγμένα καὶ καθόλου καὶ ἐπὶ μέρους. ἔργον οὖν

---

8. ἑκάστη H. ἑκάστης L.　6. τῇ τῆς γνώσεως] τοῦ τῆς γνώσεως LV.
8. ἐντολὰς H. ἐντολὰς ἃς L.　9. ἀρυτόμενος] ἀρυττόμενος L.　10. αὖ
τοὺς—τῆς βαρβάρου S. αὐτοὺς—τὰς βαρβάρους (pr. m. corr. ex ταῖς β.) L.
14. ὅτε] ὅθεν vel ὥστε S.　15. ἑτέρας ἑτέρους H. ἑτέρας L. ἑκατέρας
Barnard.　20. ἐπίτομον M. ἐπιτομήν L.　21. ἑλόμενος] ἁλάμενος S.

tions are each severally portioned off, according to the order of change, by variety of time and place and honour and knowledge and inheritance and service, up to the transcendent orbit which is next to the Lord, occupied in eternal contemplation. And *that which is lovely has power to draw to*[1] the contemplation of itself every one who through love of knowledge has applied himself wholly to contemplation.

§ 11. Therefore the commandments given by the Lord, both the former and the latter, all flow from one source, for neither did He negligently suffer those who lived before the law to be altogether *without law*[2], nor on the other hand did He permit those who were ignorant of the barbarian (*i.e.* Jewish) philosophy to run wild. For, by giving to the Jews commandments and to the Greeks philosophy, He *confined unbelief*[3] to the period of His own presence on earth, in which every one who believed not is *without excuse*[4]. For He leads <different> men by a different progress, whether Greek or barbarian, to the perfection which is through faith. But if any of the Greeks dispenses with the preliminary guidance of the Greek philosophy and hastens straight to the true teaching, he, even though he be unlearned, at once distances all competition, having chosen the short-cut to perfection, viz. that of *salvation through faith*[5].

§ 12. Accordingly He made all things to be helpful for virtue, in so far as might be without hindering the freedom of man's choice, and showed them to be so, in order that He who is indeed the One Alone Almighty might, even to those who can only see darkly, be in some way revealed as a good God, a Saviour from age to age through the instrumentality of His Son, and in all ways absolutely *guiltless of evil*[6]. For by the Lord of the universe all things are ordered both generally and particularly with a view to the safety of the whole. It is the work then of

---

[1] Plat. *Rep.* vii. 525, *Symp.* 204 c.
[2] 1 Cor. ix. 21.
[3] Rom. xi. 32. Gal. iii. 19—24.
[4] Rom. i. 20.
[5] Eph. ii. 8.
[6] Plato *Rep.* 617 e, *Tim.* 42 d.

τῆς δικαιοσύνης τῆς σωτηρίου ἐπὶ τὸ ἄμεινον ἀεὶ κατὰ
τὸ ἐνδεχόμενον ἕκαστον προάγειν. πρὸς γὰρ τὴν
σωτηρίαν τοῦ κρείττονος καὶ διαμονὴν ἀναλόγως τοῖς
ἑαυτῶν ἤθεσι διοικεῖται καὶ τὰ μικρότερα. αὐτίκα
5 μεταβάλλει πᾶν τὸ ἐνάρετον εἰς ἀμείνους οἰκήσεις, τῆς
μεταβολῆς αἰτίαν τὴν αἵρεσιν τῆς γνώσεως ἔχον, ἣν
αὐτοκρατορικὴν ἐκέκτητο ἡ ψυχή· παιδεύσεις δὲ αἱ
ἀναγκαῖαι ἀγαθότητι τοῦ ἐφορῶντος μεγάλου κριτοῦ
διά τε τῶν προσεχῶν ἀγγέλων διά τε προκρίσεων
10 ποικίλων καὶ διὰ τῆς κρίσεως τῆς παντελοῦς τοὺς ἐπὶ
πλέον ἀπηλγηκότας ἐκβιάζονται μετανοεῖν.

ΚΕΦ. Γ.

13. Τὰ δ' ἄλλα cιγῶ, δοξάζων τὸν κύριον. πλὴν
ἐκείνας φημὶ τὰς γνωστικὰς ψυχάς, τῇ μεγαλοπρεπείᾳ
τῆς θεωρίας ὑπερβαινούσας ἑκάστης ἁγίας τάξεως τὴν
15 πολιτείαν, καθ' ἃς αἱ μακάριαι θεῶν οἰκήσεις διωρισμέναι διακεκλήρωνται, ἁγίας ἐν ἁγίοις λογισθείσας καὶ
μετακομισθείσας ὅλας ἐξ ὅλων, εἰς ἀμείνους ἀμεινόνων
τόπων τόπους ἀφικομένας, οὐκ ἐν κατόπτροις ἢ διὰ
κατόπτρων ἔτι τὴν θεωρίαν ἀσπαζομένας τὴν θείαν,
20 ἐναργῆ δὲ ὡς ἔνι μάλιστα καὶ ἀκριβῶς εἰλικρινῆ τὴν
ἀκόρεστον ὑπερφυῶς ἀγαπώσαις ψυχαῖς ἑστιωμένας
θέαν ἀϊδίως ἀίδιον, εὐφροσύνην ἀκόρεστον καρπουμένας
εἰς τοὺς ἀτελευτήτους αἰῶνας, ταυτότητι τῆς ὑπεροχῆς
ἁπάσας τετιμημένας διαμένειν. αὕτη τῶν καθαρῶν τῇ
25 καρδίᾳ ἡ καταληπτικὴ θεωρία. αὕτη τοίνυν ἡ ἐνέργεια
τοῦ τελειωθέντος γνωστικοῦ, προσομιλεῖν τῷ θεῷ διὰ
τοῦ μεγάλου ἀρχιερέως ἐξομοιούμενον εἰς δύναμιν τῷ
κυρίῳ διὰ πάσης τῆς εἰς τὸν θεὸν θεραπείας, ἥτις εἰς

1. ἀεί] αἰεί L. 5. ἀμείνους D. ἀμείνω LV. 15. καθ' ἃς] fort.
καθ' ἣν M. 19. ἔτι P. ἐπὶ L. 24. ἁπάσας H. ἁπάσης L.
25. καταληπτικὴ P. καταληπτὴ L.

saving righteousness always to promote the improvement of each according to the possibilities of the case. For even the lesser things are managed with a view to the safety and continuance of the superior in accordance with their own characters. For instance, whatever is possessed of virtue changes to better habitations, the cause of the change being that independent choice of knowledge with which the soul was gifted to begin with; but those who are more *hardened*[1] are constrained to repent by necessary chastisements, inflicted either through the agency of the attendant angels or through various preliminary judgments or through the great and final judgment, by the goodness of the great Judge whose eye is ever upon us.

CHAPTER III.

§ 13. *As to the rest I keep silent*[2], giving glory to God: only I say that those gnostic souls are so carried away by the magnificence of the vision that they cannot confine themselves within the lines of the constitution by which each holy degree is assigned and in accordance with which the blessed abodes of the gods have been marked out and allotted; but being counted as *holy among the holy*[3], and translated absolutely and entirely to another sphere, they keep on always moving to higher and yet higher regions, until they no longer greet[4] the divine vision in or *by means of mirrors*[5], but with loving hearts feast for ever on the uncloying, never-ending sight, radiant in its transparent clearness, while throughout the endless ages they taste a never-wearying delight, and thus continue, all alike honoured with an identity of preeminence. This is the apprehensive *vision of the pure in heart*[6]. This, therefore, is the life-work of the perfected gnostic, viz. to hold communion with God through the *great High Priest*[7], being made like the Lord, as far as may be, by means of all his

---

[1] Eph. iv. 19. [2] Aesch. *Agam.* 36. [3] Isa. lvii. 15. [4] Heb. xi. 18.
[5] 1 Cor. xiii. 12. [6] Matt. v. 8. [7] Heb. iv. 14.

τὴν τῶν ἀνθρώπων διατείνει σωτηρίαν κατὰ κηδεμονίαν τῆς εἰς ἡμᾶς εὐεργεσίας κατά τε αὖ τὴν λειτουργίαν κατά τε τὴν διδασκαλίαν κατά τε τὴν δι' ἔργων εὐποιίαν. ναὶ μὴν ἑαυτὸν κτίζει καὶ δημιουργεῖ, πρὸς δὲ καὶ τοὺς ἐπαΐοντας αὐτοῦ κοσμεῖ, ἐξομοιούμενος θεῷ ὁ γνωστικός, τῷ φύσει τὸ ἀπαθὲς κεκτημένῳ τὸ ἐξ ἀσκήσεως εἰς ἀπάθειαν συνεσταλμένον ὡς ἔνι μάλιστα ἐξομοιῶν, καὶ ταῦτα ἀπερισπάστως προσομιλῶν τε καὶ συνὼν τῷ κυρίῳ. ἡμερότης δ', οἶμαι, καὶ φιλανθρωπία καὶ μεγαλοπρεπὴς θεοσέβεια γνωστικῆς ἐξομοιώσεως κανόνες.

14. Ταύτας φημὶ τὰς ἀρετὰς θυσίαν δεκτὴν εἶναι παρὰ θεῷ, τὴν ἄτυφον καρδίαν μετ' ἐπιστήμης ὀρθῆς ὁλοκάρπωμα τοῦ θεοῦ λεγούσης τῆς γραφῆς, ἐκφωτιζομένου εἰς ἕνωσιν ἀδιάκριτον παντὸς τοῦ ἀναληφθέντος εἰς ἁγιωσύνην ἀνθρώπου· σφᾶς γὰρ αὐτοὺς αἰχμαλωτίζειν καὶ ἑαυτοὺς ἀναιρεῖν, τὸν παλαιὸν ἄνθρωπον τὸν κατὰ τὰς ἐπιθυμίας φθειρόμενον ἀποκτιννύντας καὶ τὸν καινὸν ἀνιστάντας ἐκ τοῦ θανάτου τῆς παλαιᾶς διαστροφῆς, τό τε εὐαγγέλιον ὅ τε ἀπόστολος κελεύουσι, τὰ μὲν πάθη ἀποτιθεμένους, ἀναμαρτήτους δὲ γινομένους. τοῦτ' ἦν ἄρα ὃ ᾐνίσσετο καὶ ὁ νόμος τὸν ἁμαρτωλὸν ἀναιρεῖσθαι κελεύων, μετατίθεσθαι ἐκ θανάτου εἰς ζωήν, τὴν ἐκ πίστεως ἀπάθειαν· ὃ μὴ συνιέντες οἱ νομοδιδάσκαλοι, φιλόνεικον ἐκδεξάμενοι τὸν νόμον, ἀφορμὰς τοῖς μάτην διαβάλλειν ἐπιχειροῦσι παρεσχήκασι. Δι' ἣν αἰτίαν οὐ θύομεν εἰκότως ἀνενδεεῖ τῷ θεῷ τῷ τὰ πάντα τοῖς πᾶσι παρεσχημένῳ, τὸν δ' ὑπὲρ ἡμῶν ἱερευθέντα δοξάζομεν σφᾶς αὐτοὺς ἱερεύοντες εἴς τε τὸ ἀνενδεὲς ἐκ τοῦ ἀνενδεοῦς καὶ εἰς τὸ ἀπαθὲς

---

2. τὴν λειτουργίαν κατά τε τὴν διδασκαλίαν κατά τε τὴν—εὐποιίαν S. cum Herveto. τῇ λειτουργίᾳ, κατά τε τῇ διδασκαλίᾳ, κατά τε τῇ—εὐποιίᾳ L.
4. πρὸς δὲ S. πρὸς δὴ L. 20. γινομένους H. γενομένους L.
22. κελεύων M. κελεύων καὶ L. 23. ἀπάθειαν· H. ἀπάθειαν D.
25. παρεσχήκασι. H. παρεσχήκασι, D.

service towards God, a service which extends to the salvation of men by his solicitous goodness towards us and also by public worship and by teaching and active kindness. Aye, and in being thus *assimilated to God*[1], the gnostic is making and fashioning himself and also forming those who hear him, while, so far as may be, he assimilates to that which is by nature free from passion that which has been subdued by training to a passionless state: and this he effects by *undisturbed intercourse* and communion *with the Lord*[2]. Of this gnostic assimilation the canons, as it appears to me, are gentleness, kindness and a noble devoutness.

§ 14. These virtues I affirm to be *an acceptable sacrifice with God*[3], as the Scripture declares that *the unboastful heart* joined with a right understanding *is a perfect offering to God*[4], since every man who is won over for holiness is enlightened into an indissoluble unity. For both the Gospel and the Apostle command us to *bring ourselves into captivity*[5] and *put ourselves to death*[6], *slaying the old man which is being corrupted according to its lusts*[7] and raising up *the new man*[8] from the death of our old perversion, laying aside our passions and becoming free from sin. This it was which was signified also by the law when it commanded that *the sinner should be put to death*[9], viz. the change from death to life, that is, the 'apathy' which comes from faith. But the expounders of the law, not understanding this, took the law to be jealous, and have thus given a handle to those who without ground endeavour to discredit it.

It is for this reason, <because we are ourselves the sacrifice>, that we fitly refrain from making any <other> sacrifice to God, who has provided all things for all, being Himself in need of nothing; but we glorify Him who was consecrated for us, by consecrating ourselves also to ever higher degrees of freedom

---

[1] Plat. *Rep.* x. 613 B.   [2] 1 Cor. vii. 35.   [3] Phil. iv. 18.
[4] Ps. li. 16, 17.   [5] 2 Cor. x. 5.   [6] Matt. xvi. 25.
[7] Eph. iv. 22.   [8] Eph. iv. 24.   [9] Deut. xiii. 8, 9.

ἐκ τοῦ ἀπαθοῦς. μόνῃ γὰρ τῇ ἡμετέρᾳ σωτηρίᾳ ὁ θεὸς ἥδεται. εἰκότως ἄρα τῷ μὴ νικωμένῳ ἡδοναῖς θυσίαν οὐ προσάγομεν, κάτω που καὶ οὐδὲ μέχρι νεφῶν τῶν παχυτάτων, μακρὰν δὲ καὶ τούτων, τῆς διὰ τοῦ καπνοῦ ἀναθυμιάσεως φθανούσης εἰς οὓς καὶ φθάνει.

15. Οὔτ' οὖν ἐνδεὲς οὐδὲ μὴν φιλήδονον φιλοκερδές τε ἢ φιλοχρήματον τὸ θεῖον, πλῆρες ὂν καὶ πάντα παρέχον παντὶ τῷ γενητῷ καὶ ἐνδεεῖ, οὔτε θυσίαις οὐδὲ μὴν ἀναθήμασιν οὐδ' αὖ δόξῃ καὶ τιμῇ κηλεῖται τὸ θεῖον καὶ παράγεται τοιούτοις τισίν, ἀλλὰ μόνοις τοῖς καλοῖς κἀγαθοῖς ἀνδράσι φαίνεται, οἳ τὸ δίκαιον οὐκ ἄν ποτε προδῷεν ἢ φόβου ἕνεκεν ἀπειλουμένου ἢ δώρων ὑποσχέσει μειζόνων. ὅσοι δ' οὐ καθεοράκασι τὸ αὐθαίρετον τῆς ἀνθρωπίνης ψυχῆς καὶ ἀδούλωτον πρὸς ἐκλογὴν βίου, δυσχεραίνοντες τοῖς γινομένοις πρὸς τῆς ἀπαιδεύτου ἀδικίας, οὐ νομίζουσιν εἶναι θεόν. ἴσοι τούτοις κατὰ τὴν δόξαν οἵ, τῇ τῶν ἡδονῶν ἀκρασίᾳ καὶ ταῖς ἐξαισίοις λύπαις καὶ ταῖς ἀβουλήτοις τύχαις περιπίπτοντες καὶ πρὸς τὰς συμφορὰς ἀπαυδῶντες, οὔ φασιν εἶναι θεόν, ἢ ὄντα μὴ εἶναι πανεπίσκοπον. ἄλλοι δέ εἰσιν οἱ πεπεισμένοι παραιτητοὺς εἶναι θυσίαις καὶ δώροις τοὺς νομιζομένους θεούς, συναιρομένους ὡς εἰπεῖν αὐτῶν ταῖς ἀκολασίαις· καὶ οὐδ' ἐθέλουσι πιστεύειν μόνον εἶναι τὸν ὄντως θεὸν τὸν ἐν ταυτότητι τῆς δικαίας ἀγαθωσύνης ὄντα.

16. Εὐσεβὴς ἄρα ὁ γνωστικός, ὁ πρῶτον ἑαυτοῦ ἐπιμελόμενος, ἔπειτα τῶν πλησίον, ἵν' ὡς ἄριστοι γενώμεθα. καὶ γὰρ ὁ υἱὸς πατρὶ ἀγαθῷ χαρίζεται σπουδαῖον ἑαυτὸν καὶ ὅμοιον τῷ πατρὶ παρεχόμενος,

---

9. γενητῷ] γεννητῷ Arcerius.   10. κηλεῖται Lowth. καλεῖται L.
12. φαίνεται L. φαιδρύνεται H.   13. προδῷεν L. προδοῖεν D.   14. οὐ καθεοράκασι] (οὐκ ἀθεοράκασι LV.) οὐ καθεωράκασι S.   18. οἵ, M. οἱ LD.
24. αὐτῶν M. αὐτῶν LV.   οὐδ' ἐθέλουσι M. οὐδὲ θέλουσι L.

from want and from passion. For God takes pleasure only in our salvation. Fitly therefore do we abstain from offering sacrifice to Him who cannot be swayed by pleasures, bearing in mind also that the smoke of the sacrifice reaches those whom it does reach <i.e. the demons> in some low region far beneath the densest clouds.

§ 15. The Divine Nature then is neither wanting in anything nor is it fond of pleasure or gain or money, being of itself full and affording all things to every creature which is in need. Nor again is the Divine Nature propitiated by sacrifices or offerings or by glory and honour, nor is it allured by such things: it shows itself to the virtuous alone, who would never betray justice either on account of threatened terrors or from a promise of greater gifts. Those however who have not observed the freedom of man's spirit and its unfettered action in respect to choice of life, chafe at what is done by unchastened injustice, and disbelieve in the existence of God. Like to them in opinion are they who, from their incontinence in pleasure, being involved both in cross accidents and pains out of the common course, and losing heart at their calamities, say that there is no God, or that, if He exists, He is not the overseer of all. Another class consists of those who are persuaded that the gods of common belief are to be propitiated with sacrifices and gifts, being accomplices, so to speak, in men's own wickednesses, and who are even unwilling to believe that He alone is the true God who is unchangeably the same in His just beneficence.

§ 16. We are justified therefore in ascribing piety to the gnostic, whose care is first for himself and then for his neighbours with a view to our attaining the highest standard of excellence. For so the son tries to please a good father by showing himself virtuous and like his father, and likewise

καὶ ἄρχοντι ὁ ἀρχόμενος· ὅτι τὸ πιστεύειν τε καὶ
πείθεσθαι ἐφ' ἡμῖν· κακῶν δὲ αἰτίαν καὶ ὕλης ἄν τις
ἀσθένειαν ὑπολάβοι καὶ τὰς ἀβουλήτους τῆς ἀγνοίας
ὁρμὰς τάς τε ἀλόγους δι' ἀμαθίαν ἀνάγκας· ὑπεράνω
5 ‹ὧν›, καθάπερ θηρίων, διὰ μαθήσεως ὁ γνωστικὸς
γενόμενος· τὴν θείαν προαίρεσιν μιμούμενος, εὖ ποιεῖ
τοὺς ἐθέλοντας τῶν ἀνθρώπων κατὰ δύναμιν· κἂν εἰς
ἀρχὴν κατασταίη ποτέ, καθάπερ ὁ Μωυσῆς, ἐπὶ σωτηρίᾳ τῶν ἀρχομένων ἡγήσεται, καὶ τὸ ἄγριον καὶ
10 ἄπιστον ἐξημερώσεται τιμῇ μὲν τῶν ἀρίστων, κολάσει
δὲ τῶν μοχθηρῶν, τῇ κατὰ λόγον εἰς παιδείαν ἐγγραφομένῃ. μάλιστα γὰρ ἄγαλμα θεῖον καὶ θεῷ προσεμφερὲς
ἀνθρώπου δικαίου ψυχή, ἐν ᾗ διὰ τῆς τῶν παραγγελμάτων ὑπακοῆς τεμενίζεται καὶ ἐνιδρύεται ὁ πάντων
15 ἡγεμὼν θνητῶν τε καὶ ἀθανάτων, βασιλεύς τε καὶ
γεννήτωρ τῶν καλῶν, νόμος ὢν ὄντως καὶ θεσμὸς καὶ
λόγος αἰώνιος, ἰδίᾳ τε ἑκάστοις καὶ κοινῇ πᾶσιν εἷς ὢν
σωτήρ. οὗτος ὁ τῷ ὄντι μονογενής, ὁ τῆς τοῦ παμ-
βασιλέως καὶ παντοκράτορος πατρὸς δόξης χαρακτήρ,
20 ἐναποσφραγιζόμενος τῷ γνωστικῷ τὴν τελείαν θεωρίαν
κατ' εἰκόνα τὴν ἑαυτοῦ, ὡς εἶναι τρίτην ἤδη τὴν θείαν
εἰκόνα τὴν ὅση δύναμις ἐξομοιουμένην πρὸς τὸ δεύτερον
αἴτιον, πρὸς τὴν ὄντως ζωήν, δι' ἣν ζῶμεν τὴν ἀληθῆ
ζωήν, οἷον ὑπογράφοντες τὸν γνῶσιν γινόμενον ἡμῖν, περὶ
25 τὰ βέβαια καὶ παντελῶς ἀναλλοίωτα ἀναστρεφόμενοι.

17. Ἄρχων οὖν ἑαυτοῦ καὶ τῶν ἑαυτοῦ, βεβαίαν
κατάληψιν τῆς θείας ἐπιστήμης κεκτημένος, τῇ ἀληθείᾳ
γνησίως πρόσεισιν. ἡ γὰρ τῶν νοητῶν γνῶσις καὶ

---

2. ἐφ' ἡμῖν· M. ἐφ' ἡμῖν, D.   καὶ] fort. τὴν τῆς M.   4. ὑπεράνω ὧν H. ὑπεράνω L.   7. ἐθέλοντας L. θέλοντας V.   8. κατασταίη] fort. καταστῇ M. Μωυσῆς] μωσῆς L.   10. ἀρίστων] ἀπίστων L.   16. γεννήτωρ] γενήτωρ L.   24. ὑπογράφοντες H. ἀπογράφοντες L.   γνῶσιν M. γνωστικὸν L.   25. ἀναστρεφόμενοι H. ἀναστρεφόμενον L.

the subject to please a good ruler; since belief and obedience are in our own power. But the cause of evils one might find in the weakness of matter, and the random impulses of ignorance and the irrational forces to which we fall victims from our incapacity to learn; whereas the gnostic gets the better of these wild elements by his learning, and benefits all who are willing, to the best of his power, in imitation of the divine purpose for men. Should he be ever placed in authority, he will rule, like Moses, with a view to the salvation of his subjects, and will quell what is savage and faithless by showing honour to the best, and by punishing the bad, punishment that is rightly classed under the head of education. For above all things, the soul of the just man is an *Image divine, made like to God Himself*[1], seeing that in it is enshrined and consecrated, by means of obedience to His commands, the Ruler of all mortals and immortals, the King and Parent of all that is noble, who is indeed Law and Ordinance and Eternal Word, the one Saviour both for each individually and for all in common. He is in truth *the Only-begotten*[2], *the express image of the glory*[3] of the universal King and almighty Father, stamping on the mind of the gnostic the perfect vision after His own image; so that the divine image is now beheld in a third embodiment, assimilated as far as possible to the Second Cause, to Him, namely, who is *the Life indeed*[4], owing to whom we live the true life, copying the example of Him *who is made to us knowledge*[5], while we converse with the things which are stable and altogether unchangeable.

§ 17. Being ruler therefore of himself and of all that belongs to him the gnostic makes a genuine approach to truth, having a firm hold of divine science. For the name *science would fitly*

---

[1] Nauck *Fragm. Trag.* 688.   [2] Joh. i. 18.   [3] Heb. i. 3.
[4] 1 Tim. vi. 19.   [5] 1 Cor. i. 80; Col. ii. 2, 8.

κατάληψις βεβαία δεόντως ἂν λέγοιτο ἐπιστήμη, ἧς τὸ μὲν περὶ τὰ θεῖα ἔργον ἔχει σκοπεῖν τί μὲν τὸ πρῶτον αἴτιον, τί δὲ δι' οὗ τὰ πάντα ἐγένετο καὶ χωρὶς οὗ γέγονεν οὐδέν· τίνα τε αὖ τὰ μὲν ὡς διήκοντα, τὰ δὲ ὡς περιέχοντα, καὶ τινὰ μὲν συνημμένα, τινὰ δὲ διεζευγμένα, καὶ τίνα τούτων ἕκαστον ἔχει τὴν τάξιν καὶ ἣν δύναμιν καὶ ἣν λειτουργίαν εἰσφέρεται ἕκαστον· ἐν δὲ αὖ τοῖς ἀνθρωπίνοις τί τε αὐτός ἐστιν ὁ ἄνθρωπος καὶ τί αὐτῷ κατὰ φύσιν ἢ παρὰ φύσιν ἐστίν, πῶς τε αὖ ποιεῖν ἢ πάσχειν προσήκει, τίνες τε ἀρεταὶ τούτου καὶ κακίαι τίνες, περί τε ἀγαθῶν καὶ κακῶν καὶ τῶν μέσων, ὅσα τε περὶ ἀνδρείας καὶ φρονήσεως καὶ σωφροσύνης τῆς τε ἐπὶ πᾶσι παντελοῦς ἀρετῆς δικαιοσύνης. ἀλλὰ τῇ μὲν φρονήσει καὶ δικαιοσύνῃ εἰς τὴν τῆς σοφίας κατακέχρηται κτῆσιν, τῇ δὲ ἀνδρείᾳ οὐκ ἐν τῷ τὰ περιστατικὰ ὑπομένειν μόνον, ἀλλὰ κἂν τῷ ἡδονῆς τε καὶ ἐπιθυμίας, λύπης τε αὖ καὶ ὀργῆς <κρατεῖν>, καὶ καθόλου πρὸς πᾶν ἤτοι τὸ μετὰ βίας ἢ μετὰ ἀπάτης τινὸς ψυχαγωγοῦν ἡμᾶς ἀντιτάσσεσθαι. οὐ γὰρ ὑπομένειν δεῖ τὰς κακίας καὶ τὰ κακὰ ἀλλ' ἀποθέσθαι, καὶ τὰ φοβερὰ ὑπομένειν. χρήσιμος οὖν καὶ ἡ ἀλγηδὼν εὑρίσκεται κατά τε τὴν ἰατρικὴν καὶ παιδευτικὴν καὶ κολαστικήν, καὶ διὰ ταύτης ἤθη διορθοῦνται εἰς ὠφέλειαν ἀνθρώπων.

18. Εἴδη δὲ τῆς ἀνδρείας καρτερία, μεγαλοφροσύνη, μεγαλοψυχία, ἐλευθεριότης καὶ μεγαλοπρέπεια. δι' ἣν αἰτίαν οὔτε μέμψεως οὔτε κακοδοξίας τῆς ἐκ τῶν πολλῶν ἀντιλαμβάνεται ὁ γνωστικὸς οὔτε δόξαις οὔτε

2. ἔχει S. ἔχειν LD. 4. τὰ μὲν L. <τὰ συνέχοντα> τὰ μὲν M.
5. τινὰ μὲν...τινὰ δὲ M. τίνα μὲν...τίνα δὲ L. 7. ἐν δὲ Reinkens in Dissert. de γνώσει Clementis p. 853. ἔν τε L. 15. κατακέχρηται L. καταχρῆται H. κτῆσιν S. κτίσιν L. 16. κἂν τῷ DH. καὶ τῷ L.
17. ὀργῆς κρατεῖν P. ὀργῆς L. 19. ἀντιτάσσεσθαι P. ἀντιτάσσεται L.
20. κακὰ S. καλὰ L. ἀλλ' ἀποθέσθαι M. ἀλλ' ἀπωθεῖσθαι Jackson. ἀλλ' ἐπιθέσθαι H. ἀλλὰ πείθεσθαι L. 21. οὖν L. μὲν οὖν H. γοῦν M.
27. δι' ἣν H. καὶ δι' ἣν L.

be given to the knowledge and firm hold[1] of intellectual objects. Its function in regard to divine things is to investigate what is the First Cause and what that *through which all things were made and without which nothing has been made*[2]; what are the things <that hold the universe together> partly as pervading it and partly as encompassing it, some in combination and some apart, and what is the position of each of these, and the capacity and the service contributed by each: and again in things concerning man, to investigate what he himself is, and what is in accordance with, or is opposed to his nature; how it becomes him to act and be acted on, and what are his virtues and vices, and about things good and evil and the intermediates, and all that has to do with manhood and prudence and temperance, and the supreme all-perfect virtue, justice. Prudence and justice he employs for the acquisition of wisdom, and manhood not only in enduring misfortunes, but also in <controlling> pleasure and desire and pain and anger, and generally in withstanding all that sways the soul either by force or guile. For we must not endure vices and things that are evil, but must cast them off, and reserve endurance for things that cause fear. At any rate even suffering is found to be useful alike in medicine and in education and in punishment, and by means of it characters are improved for the benefit of mankind.

§ 18. Forms of manhood are fortitude, high-spirit, magnanimity, generosity, magnificence. It is owing to this that the gnostic takes no notice either of blame or of ill-repute from the world, nor is he in subjection to good opinions or flatteries of

---

[1] Sext. Emp. *Adv. Math.* vii. 151.   [2] Joh. i. 3.

κολακείαις ὑποβέβληται, ἔν τε τῷ ὑπομένειν πόνους, διαπραττόμενος ἅμα τι τῶν προσηκόντων καὶ ἀνδρείως ὑπεράνω πάντων τῶν περιστατικῶν γινόμενος, ἀνὴρ τῷ ὄντι ἐν τοῖς ἄλλοις ἀναφαίνεται ἀνθρώποις. σώζων τε αὖ τὴν φρόνησιν σωφρονεῖ ἐν ἡσυχιότητι τῆς ψυχῆς· παραδεκτικὸς τῶν ἐπαγγελλομένων ὡς οἰκείων, κατὰ τὴν ἀποστροφὴν τῶν αἰσχρῶν ὡς ἀλλοτρίων, γενόμενος. κόσμιος καὶ ὑπερκόσμιος, ἐν κόσμῳ καὶ τάξει <πάντα> πράσσων καὶ οὐδὲν οὐδαμῇ πλημμελῶν. πλουτῶν μὲν ὡς ὅτι μάλιστα ἐν τῷ μηδενὸς ἐπιθυμεῖν, ἅτε ὀλιγοδεὴς ὢν καὶ ἐν περιουσίᾳ παντὸς ἀγαθοῦ διὰ τὴν γνῶσιν τἀγαθοῦ. [δικαιοσύνης γὰρ αὐτοῦ πρῶτον ἔργον τὸ μετὰ τῶν ὁμοφύλων φιλεῖν διάγειν καὶ συνεῖναι τούτοις ἔν τε γῇ καὶ οὐρανῷ.]

19. Ταύτῃ καὶ μεταδοτικὸς ὧν ἂν ᾖ κεκτημένος· φιλάνθρωπός τε ὢν μισοπονηρότατος κατὰ τὴν τελείαν ἀποστροφὴν κακουργίας ἁπάσης, μαθὼν <ὡς> ἄρα δεῖ πιστὸν εἶναι καὶ ἑαυτῷ καὶ τοῖς πέλας, καὶ ταῖς ἐντολαῖς ὑπήκοον. οὗτος γάρ ἐστιν ὁ θεράπων τοῦ θεοῦ ὁ ἑκὼν ταῖς ἐντολαῖς ὑπαγόμενος· ὁ δὲ ἤδη μὴ διὰ τὰς ἐντολάς, δι᾽ αὐτὴν δὲ τὴν γνῶσιν καθαρὸς τῇ καρδίᾳ, φίλος οὗτος τοῦ θεοῦ. οὔτε γὰρ φύσει τὴν ἀρετὴν γεννώμεθα ἔχοντες, οὔτε γενομένοις, ὥσπερ ἄλλα τινὰ τῶν τοῦ σώματος μερῶν, φυσικῶς ὕστερον ἐπιγίνεται (ἐπεὶ οὐδ᾽ ἂν ἦν ἔθ᾽ ἑκούσιον οὐδὲ ἐπαινετόν)· οὐδὲ μὴν ἐκ τῆς τῶν συμβιούντων ἐπιγινομένη συνηθείας, ὃν τρόπον ἡ διάλεκτος, τελειοῦται ἡ ἀρετή (σχεδὸν γὰρ ἡ κακία τοῦτον ἐγγίνεται τὸν τρόπον)· οὐ μὴν οὐδὲ ἐκ τέχνης τινὸς ἤτοι τῶν ποριστικῶν ἢ τῶν περὶ τὸ σῶμα θερα-

---

2. ἅμα τι Arcerius. ἅλματι L.   4. ἀνθρώποις. M. ἀνθρώποις, D.
7. γενόμενος· M. γενόμενος D.   8. πάντα πράσσων H. πράσσων L.
15. ὧν S. ὧν L.   17. πάσης, μαθὼν ὡς H. ἀπάσης. μαθεῖν L. πάσης. μαθεῖν VPD.   25. τῆς τῶν συμβιούντων ἐπιγινομένῃ M. τ. τ. συμβάντων καὶ ἐπιγινομένης L. τῶν συμβάντων καὶ τῆς ἐπιγινομένης Barnard.   27. ἡ ἀρετή L¹, ἀρετή L².

others. In the endurance of labours he shows himself amongst other men as a man indeed, being always occupied in some good work at the same time that he is manfully surmounting difficulties of every kind. Again he is *temperate owing to his abiding good sense*[1] combined with tranquillity of soul; his readiness to take to himself the promises as his own being in proportion to his shrinking from base things as alien. He is a citizen of the world, and not of this world only, but of a higher order, doing <all things> in order and degree, and never misbehaving in any respect. [For the first effect of his justice is that he loves to be with those of kindred spirit, and to commune with them, both on earth and in heaven[2].] Rich he is in the highest degree because he covets nothing, having few wants and enjoying a superabundance of every good, owing to his knowledge of the absolute Good.

§ 19. For this reason also he is ready to impart to others of all that he possesses: and being a lover of men he has a profound hatred of the wicked through his abhorrence of every kind of evil doing, having learnt that one should be faithful both to oneself and to one's neighbours, as well as obedient to the commandments. For he who is willingly led on by the commandments may be called *God's servant*[3]; but he who is already *pure in heart*[4], not because of the commandments, but for the sake of knowledge by itself,—that man *is a friend of God*[5]. For neither are we born virtuous, nor is virtue a natural after-growth, as are some parts of the body (for then it would have been no longer voluntary or praiseworthy); nor yet is it acquired and perfected, as speech is, from the intercourse of those who live with us (for it is rather vice which originates in this way). Nor again is knowledge derived from any art connected with the supplies of life or the

---

[1] Ar. *Eth. N.* vi. 5.   [2] This sentence seems to be misplaced in the Greek.
[3] Heb. iii. 5.   [4] Matt. v. 8.   [5] Ja. ii. 23.

πευτικῶν ἡ γνῶσις περιγίνεται· ἀλλ' οὐδ' ἐκ παιδείας τῆς ἐγκυκλίου· ἀγαπητὸν γὰρ εἰ παρασκευάσαι μόνον τὴν ψυχὴν καὶ διακονῆσαι δύναιτο· οἱ νόμοι γὰρ οἱ πολιτικοὶ μοχθηρὰς ἴσως πράξεις ἐπισχεῖν οἷοί τε· 20. ἀλλ' οὐδὲ οἱ λόγοι οἱ πειστικοὶ ἐπιπόλαιοι ὄντες ἐπιστημονικὴν τῆς ἀληθείας διαμονὴν παράσχοιεν ἄν· φιλοσοφία δὲ ἡ Ἑλληνικὴ οἷον προκαθαίρει καὶ προεθίζει τὴν ψυχὴν εἰς παραδοχὴν πίστεως, ἐφ' ᾗ τὴν γνῶσιν ἐποικοδομεῖ ἡ ἀλήθεια.

οὗτός ἐστιν, οὗτος ὁ ἀθλητὴς ἀληθῶς, ὁ ἐν τῷ μεγάλῳ σταδίῳ, τῷ καλῷ κόσμῳ, τὴν ἀληθινὴν νίκην κατὰ πάντων στεφανούμενος τῶν παθῶν. ὅ τε γὰρ ἀγωνοθέτης ὁ παντοκράτωρ θεός, ὅ τε βραβευτὴς ὁ μονογενὴς υἱὸς τοῦ θεοῦ, θεαταὶ δὲ ἄγγελοι καὶ θεοί, καὶ τὸ παγκράτιον τὸ πάμμαχον ογ πρὸϲ αἷμα καὶ ϲάρκα, ἀλλὰ τὰς διὰ σαρκῶν ἐνεργούσας πνευματικὰϲ ἐξουϲίαϲ ἐμπαθῶν παθῶν. τούτων περιγενόμενος τῶν μεγάλων ἀνταγωνισμάτων, καὶ οἷον ἄθλους τινὰς τοῦ πειράζοντος ἐπαρτῶντος καταγωνισάμενος, ἐκράτησε τῆς ἀθανασίας· ἀπαραλόγιστος γὰρ ἡ τοῦ θεοῦ ψῆφος εἰς τὸ δικαιότατον κρίμα. κέκληται μὲν οὖν ἐπὶ τὸ ἀγώνισμα τὸ θέατρον, παγκρατιάζουσι δὲ εἰς τὸ στάδιον οἱ ἀθληταί· καὶ δὴ ἐκ τούτων περιγίνεται ὁ πειθήνιος τῷ ἀλείπτῃ γενόμενος. πᾶσι γὰρ πάντα ἴσα κεῖται παρὰ τοῦ θεοῦ καὶ ἔστιν αὐτὸς ἀμεμφής, ἑλεῖται δὲ ὁ δυνάμενος καὶ ὁ βουληθεὶς ἰσχύει. ταύτῃ καὶ τὸν νοῦν εἰλήφαμεν, ἵνα εἰδῶμεν ὃ ποιοῦμεν· καὶ τὸ ΓΝῶΘΙ ϹΑΥΤΟΝ ἐνταῦθα, εἰδέναι ἐφ' ᾧ γεγόναμεν· γεγόναμεν δὲ εἶναι πειθήνιοι ταῖς ἐντολαῖς, εἰ τὸ βούλεσθαι σώζεσθαι ἑλοίμεθα. αὕτη που ἡ Ἀδράστεια, καθ' ἣν οὐκ ἔστι διαδρᾶναι τὸν θεόν.

3. νόμοι γάρ] fort. νόμοι δὲ M.   5. πειστικοὶ M. πιστικοὶ L. edd.
6. διαμονὴν L. διανομὴν H.   17. περιγενόμενος H. περιγινόμενος L.
17. τῶν] fort. τις τῶν H.   23. ἐκ τούτων LH. καὶ τούτων S.
25. ἑλεῖται H post Bywater. ἔλεεῖται L. Cf. 846 ὁ λόγος καθάπερ τὸ κήρυγμα τ. Ὀλυμπίασι καλεῖ μὲν τ. βουλόμενον στεφανοῖ δὲ τὸν δυνάμενον.

service of the body, nor yet from the ordinary course of instruction: for we might be well satisfied if this could but prepare and sharpen the soul. The laws of the state, it is true, might perhaps be able to restrain evil practices. § 20. Again, mere persuasive arguments are too superficial in their nature to establish the truth on scientific grounds, but Greek philosophy does, as it were, provide for the soul the preliminary cleansing and training required for the reception of the faith, on which foundation the truth builds up the edifice of knowledge.

Here, here it is we find the true wrestler, who in the amphitheatre of this fair universe is crowned for the true victory over all his passions. For the president is God Almighty, and the umpire is the only-begotten Son of God, and the spectators are angels and gods, and our great contest of all arms is *not waged against flesh and blood, but against the spiritual powers*[1] of passionate affections working in the flesh. When he has come safe out of these mighty conflicts, and overthrown the tempter in the combats to which he has challenged us, the Christian soldier wins immortality. For the decision of God is unerring in regard to His most righteous award. The spectators then have been summoned to view the contest: the wrestlers are contending in the arena, and now the prize is won by him amongst them, who has been obedient to the orders of the trainer. For the conditions laid down by God are equal for all, and *no blame can attach to Him; but he who is able will choose*[2], and he who wills prevails. It is on this account also that we have received the gift of reason, in order that we may know what we do. And the maxim *Know thyself*[3] means in this case, to know for what purpose we are made. Now we are made to be obedient to the commandments, if our choice be such as to will salvation. This, methinks, is the real Adrasteia, owing to which we cannot escape from God.

[1] Eph. vi. 12. [2] Plato *Rep*. 617 E. [3] Chilon, *ap*. Stob. *Anth*. III. 79.

21. Τὸ ἄρα ἀνθρώπειον ἔργον εὐπείθεια θεῷ σωτηρίαν κατηγγελκότι ποικίλην δι' ἐντολῶν, εὐαρέστησις δὲ ὁμολογία. ὁ μὲν γὰρ εὐεργέτης προκατάρχει τῆς εὐποιίας, ὁ δὲ μετὰ τῶν δεόντων λογισμῶν παραδεξάμενος προθύμως καὶ φυλάξας τὰς ἐντολὰς πιστὸς οὗτος, ὁ δὲ καὶ εἰς δύναμιν ἀμειβόμενος δι' ἀγάπης τὴν εὐποιίαν ἤδη φίλος. μία δὲ ἀμοιβὴ κυριωτάτη παρὰ ἀνθρώπων, ταῦτα δρᾶν ἅπερ ἀρεστὰ τῷ θεῷ. καθάπερ οὖν ἰδίου γεννήματος καὶ κατά τι συγγενοῦς ἀποτελέσματος ὁ διδάσκαλος καὶ σωτὴρ ἀναδέχεται τὰς ὠφελείας τε καὶ ἐπανορθώσεις τῶν ἀνθρώπων, εἰς ἰδίαν χάριν τε καὶ τιμήν, καθάπερ καὶ τὰς εἰς τοὺς πεπιστευκότας αὐτῷ βλάβας, ἰδίας ἀχαριστίας τε καὶ ἀτιμίας ἡγούμενος. τίς γὰρ ἄλλη ἅπτοιτ' ἂν ἀτιμία θεοῦ; διόπερ ὅλην τοσοῦδε οὐδὲ ἔστιν ἀμοιβὴν κατ' ἀξίαν σωτηρίας ἀποδιδόναι πρὸς τὴν παρὰ τοῦ κυρίου ὠφέλειαν. ὡς δὲ οἱ τὰ κτήματα κακοῦντες τοὺς δεσπότας ὑβρίζουσι, καὶ ὡς οἱ τοὺς στρατιώτας τὸν τούτων ἡγούμενον, οὕτως τοῦ κυρίου ἐστὶν ἀνεπιστρεψία ἡ περὶ τοὺς καθωσιωμένους αὐτῷ κάκωσις. ὅνπερ γὰρ τρόπον ὁ ἥλιος οὐ μόνον τὸν οὐρανὸν καὶ τὸν ὅλον κόσμον φωτίζει γῆν τε καὶ θάλασσαν ἐπιλάμπων, ἀλλὰ καὶ διὰ θυρίδων καὶ μικρᾶς ὀπῆς πρὸς τοὺς μυχαιτάτους οἴκους ἀποστέλλει τὴν αὐγήν, οὕτως ὁ λόγος πάντη κεχυμένος καὶ τὰ σμικρότατα τῶν τοῦ βίου πράξεων ἐπιβλέπει.

ΚΕΦ. Δ.

22. Ἕλληνες δὲ ὥσπερ ἀνθρωπομόρφους οὕτως καὶ ἀνθρωποπαθεῖς τοὺς θεοὺς ὑποτίθενται, καὶ καθάπερ

---

8. ἀρεστὰ S. ἄριστα L.   9. οὖν M. ἂν L.   γὰρ D post Hervetum.
15. ὅλην LM. ὅλως D.   ἀμοιβὴν edd. post S. ἀμοιβῇ LD.   23. ὀπῆς fort. ὀπῆς πάσης M.   24. οἴκους] fort. οἰκίσκους M.

§ 21. Man's work then is submission to God, who has made known a manifold salvation by means of commandments, and man's acknowledgment thereof is God's good-pleasure. For the benefactor is the first to begin the kindness, and he who accepts it heartily, keeping due reckoning, and observes the commandments—such an one is *faithful*; but he who goes on to return the kindness to the best of his power by means of love, rises to the dignity of *friend*[1]. And the one most appropriate return from man is to do those things which are pleasing to God. Accordingly the Master and Saviour accepts as a favour and honour to Himself all that is done for the help and improvement of men, as being His own creation and in a certain respect an effect akin to its Cause; just as He accepts the wrongs done to those who have believed upon Him, regarding such wrongs as instances of ingratitude and dishonour to Himself. For what other dishonour could affect God? Wherefore it is impossible for so great a gift to make a return in full, corresponding to the benefit received from God, as measured by the worth of salvation. But, as they who injure the cattle put a slight on the owners, and those who injure the soldiers put a slight on their captain, so it shows disrespect for the Lord, when injury is done to those who are devoted to Him. For as the sun not only lights up the heaven and the whole world, shining on land and sea alike, but also darts his rays through windows and every little cranny into the innermost chambers; so the Word being shed abroad in all directions observes even the minutest details of our actions.

CHAPTER IV.

§ 22. But the Greeks assume their gods to be human in passions as they are human in shape; and, as each nation

---

[1] See above, § 5.

τὰς μορφὰς αὐτῶν ὁμοίας ἑαυτοῖς ἕκαστοι διαζωγραφοῦσιν, ὥς φησιν ὁ Ξενοφάνης Αἰθίοπές τε μέλανας σιμούς τε, Θρᾷκές τε πυρροὺς καὶ γλαυκούς, οὕτως καὶ τὰς ψυχὰς ὁμοίας ἕκαστοι ἑαυτοῖς ἀναπλάττουσιν. αὐτίκα βάρβαροι μὲν θηριώδεις καὶ ἀγρίους τὰ ἤθη, ἡμερωτέρους δὲ Ἕλληνες, πλὴν ἐμπαθεῖς. διὸ εὐλόγως τοῖς μὲν μοχθηροῖς φαύλας ἔχειν τὰς περὶ θεοῦ διανοήσεις ἀνάγκη, τοῖς δὲ σπουδαίοις ἀρίστας, καὶ διὰ τοῦτο ὁ τῷ ὄντι βασιλικὸς τὴν ψυχὴν καὶ γνωστικὸς οὗτος καὶ θεοσεβὴς καὶ ἀδεισιδαίμων, τίμιον, σεμνόν, μεγαλοπρεπῆ, εὐποιητικόν, εὐεργετικόν, ἁπάντων ἀρχηγὸν ἀγαθῶν, κακῶν δὲ ἀναίτιον μόνον εἶναι τὸν μόνον θεὸν πεπεισμένος. καὶ περὶ μὲν τῆς Ἑλληνικῆς δεισιδαιμονίας ἱκανῶς, οἶμαι, ἐν τῷ Προτρεπτικῷ ἐπιγραφομένῳ ἡμῖν λόγῳ παρεστήσαμεν, κατακόρως τῇ κατεπειγούσῃ συγκαταχρώμενοι ἱστορίᾳ.

23. Οὔκουν χρὴ αὖθις τὰ ἀριδήλως εἰρημένα μυθολογεῖν· ὅσον δὲ ἐπισημήνασθαι κατὰ τὸν τόπον γενομένους ὀλίγα ἐκ πολλῶν ἀπόχρη, καὶ τάδε εἰς ἔνδειξιν τοῦ ἀθέους παραστῆσαι τοὺς τοῖς κακίστοις ἀνθρώποις τὸ θεῖον ἀπεικάζοντας. ἤτοι γὰρ βλάπτονται πρὸς ἀνθρώπων αὐτοῖς οἱ θεοὶ καὶ χείρους τῶν ἀνθρώπων ὑφ' ἡμῶν βλαπτόμενοι δείκνυνται, ἢ εἰ μὴ τοῦτο, πῶς ἐφ' οἷς οὐ βλάπτονται, καθάπερ ὀξύχολον γραΐδιον εἰς ὀργὴν ἐρεθιζόμενον, ἐκπικραίνονται, ᾗ φασι τὴν Ἄρτεμιν δι' Οἰνέα Αἰτωλοῖς ὀργισθῆναι; πῶς γὰρ οὐκ ἐλογίσατο θεὸς οὖσα ὡς οὐ καταφρονήσας ὁ Οἰνεύς, ἀλλ' ἤτοι λαθόμενος ἢ ὡς τεθυκὼς ἠμέλησεν; εὖ δὲ καὶ ἡ Αὔγη

---

4. ὁμοίας ἕκαστοι ἑαυτοῖς H. ὁμοίας ἑαυτοῖς Karsten ad Xenoph. ὁμοιοῦσιν καὶ τοῖς αὐτοῖς L. ὁμοιοῦσιν. καὶ τοὺς αὐτοὺς Jackson. ἀναπλάττουσιν. L. ἀναπλάττουσιν Jackson. βάρβαροι H. βάρβαροι οἱ L. 10. ἀδεισιδαίμων H. ἀδεισιδαίμων ὢν L. μεγαλοπρεπῆ Jackson. μεγαλοπρεπές L. 21. ἀνθρώπων] ἀνῶν (ν pr. m. erasum) L. 25. ᾗ φασι Hervetus. ἢ φησι L. 28. ὡς τεθυκὼς] οὐ νενοηκὼς Valck. fort. ἐννενοηκὼς D. Αὔγη Grotius in Excerptis p. 375. αὐτὴ L.

paints their shape after its own likeness (according to the saying of Xenophanes, *the Ethiopians black with turned up nose, the Thracians with red hair and blue eyes*[1]), so each represents them as like itself in soul. For instance, the barbarians make them brutal and savage, the Greeks milder, but subject to passion. Hence the conceptions which the wicked form about God must naturally be bad, and those of the good must be excellent. And on this account he who is a gnostic and truly *royal in soul*[2] is both devout and free from superstition, persuaded that the only God is alone meet to be honoured and reverenced, alone glorious and beneficent, abounding in well-doing, the *author of all good and of nothing that is evil*[3]. As for the superstitions of the Greeks I think sufficient evidence has been adduced in my discourse entitled Protrepticus, where the necessary investigation is given at great length.

§ 23. What need is there then *the tale once clearly told to tell again*[4]? But as we are on this topic it will be enough just to give a small sample for proof, with a view to show that those are atheists who liken the Divinity to the worst of men. For either they make the gods injured by men, which would show them to be inferior to man as being capable of receiving injury from him; or, if this is not so, how is it that they are embittered at what is no injury, like an old shrew losing her temper, as they say Artemis was wroth with the Aetolians on account of Oeneus? Being a goddess, how did she fail to reflect that it was not from contempt for her, but *either from forgetfulness*[5], *or* because he had previously sacrificed, that he neglected her worship? Again, Augé, in pleading against Athena, because she

---

[1] Karsten, p. 40. [2] Plato *Phileb.* 30 D. [3] Plato *Rep.* 379 B.
[4] *Odyss.* XII. 453. [5] *Il.* IX. 533.

δικαιολογουμένη πρὸς τὴν Ἀθηνᾶν ἐπὶ τῷ χαλεπαίνειν
αὐτῇ τετοκυίᾳ ἐν τῷ ἱερῷ λέγει

σκῦλα μὲν βροτοφθόρα
χαίρεις ὁρῶσα καὶ νεκρῶν ἐρείπια,
κοὺ μιαρά σοι ταῦτ' ἔστιν, εἰ δ' ἐγὼ 'τεκον,
δεινὸν τόδ' ἡγεῖ—

καίτοι καὶ τὰ ἄλλα ζῷα ἐν τοῖς ἱεροῖς τίκτοντα οὐδὲν
ἀδικεῖ.

24. Εἰκότως τοίνυν δεισιδαίμονες περὶ τοὺς εὐοργήτους γινόμενοι πάντα σημεῖα ἡγοῦνται εἶναι τὰ συμβαίνοντα καὶ κακῶν αἴτια·

ἂν μῦς διορύξῃ βωμὸν ὄντα πήλινον,
κἂν μηδὲν ἄλλ' ἔχων διατράγῃ θύλακον,
ἀλεκτρυὼν τρεφόμενος ἂν ἀφ' ἑσπέρας
ᾄσῃ, τιθέμενοι τοῦτο σημεῖον τινός.

τοιοῦτόν τινα ἐν τῷ Δεισιδαίμονι ὁ Μένανδρος διακωμῳδεῖ·

ἀγαθόν τί μοι γένοιτο, ὦ πολυτίμητοι θεοί·
ὑποδούμενος τὸν ἱμάντα τῆς δεξιᾶς
ἐμβάδος διέρρηξ'. Εἰκότως, ὦ φλήναφε·
σαπρὸς γὰρ ἦν, σὺ δὲ μικρολόγος οὐκ ἐθέλων
καινὰς πρίασθαι.

χαρίεν τὸ τοῦ Ἀντιφῶντος· οἰωνισαμένου τινὸς ὅτι

---

1. τῷ S. τὸ L.   4. ὁρῶσα καὶ Jortin (*Remarks on Eccl. Hist.* ed. Troll. vol. 1, p. 284). ὀρόωσα ἀπὸ L.   5. κοὺ S. καὶ οὐ L.   6. ἡγεῖ] ἡγῆ L.   12. ἂν Meinekius. ἐὰν L. διορύξῃ L. διορίξῃ V.   13. ἀλλ'] ἄλλο L. θύλακον (ut infra) Porson. λυκήθιον L. ληκύθιον S.   14. ἂν ἀφ' Meinekius. ἐὰν ἀπὸ L.   15. τινός LP Kock. τινὲς SD.   16. Μένανδρος] Quae sequuntur, usque ad τῆς οἰκίας § 26, adducit etiam Theodoretus *Aff. Gr.* 6, p. 88.   18. ἀγαθόν—θεοί] Sic ap. Theod. quoque, ubi Gaisf. γένοιτ', ὦ πολύτιμοι. S. γένοιτο, πολύτιμοι, cui accedunt Mein. Kock (vol. III. p. 83).   19. γὰρ post ἱμάντα addit Meinekius *Com.* vol. IV. p. 101. ὑποδούμενος γὰρ ἐμβάδος τῆς δεξιᾶς τὸν ἱμάντα S. Gaisf.   20. διέρρηξ' (διέρρηξα L)] ἀπέρρηξ' Meinekius.   21. σαπρὸς] σαθρὸς Cobet. μικρολόγος] σμικρολόγος Theod.   οὐκ ἐθέλων καινὰς] οὐ θέλων καινὸν Grotius. ἆρ' οὐ θέλων καινὰς Meinekius.

was wroth with her for having given birth to a child in her temple, well says:

> Spoils of dead mortals thou delight'st to see
> And corpses strewn: these thou dost not abhor:
> But this new birth thou deem'st a sacrilege[1].

And yet no fault is found with other animals when they bring forth in the temples.

§ 24. In their dealings therefore with beings who are so quick to wrath men naturally become superstitious, and think that whatever happens is a sign and cause of evil. *If[2] a mouse digs through an altar of clay or gnaws through a sack for want of something better, or if a cock that is being fattened begins to crow in the evening, they take it as a portent of something.* Menander ridicules a fellow of this stamp in his play entitled 'The Superstitious Man[3]': *Heaven send me good luck! In putting on my right shoe I broke the thong. Of course you did, you noodle, because it was worn out, and you were too miserly to buy a new pair.* That was a pleasant saying of Antiphon's, when one made an omen of a sow's devouring her young:

---

[1] Eur. *Fr.* 268 Nauck.   [2] Kock, *Com. Att. Fr.* vol. III. p. 471.

[3] Kock, *Com. Att. Fr.* vol. III. p. 83.

κατέφαγεν ὗς τὰ δελφάκια, θεασάμενος αὐτὴν ὑπὸ λιμοῦ διὰ μικροψυχίαν τοῦ τρέφοντος κατισχναμένην, Χαῖρε εἶπεν ἐπὶ τῷ cημείῳ, ὅτι οὕτω πεινῶcα τὰ cὰ οὐκ ἔφαγεν τέκνα. Τί δὲ καὶ θαυμαcτὸν εἰ ὁ μῦc, *φησὶν ὁ Βίων*, τὸν θύλακον διέτραγεν, οὐχ εὑρὼν ὅ τι φάγῃ; τοῦτο γὰρ ἦν θαυμαcτὸν εἰ, ὥcπερ Ἀρκεcίλαοc παίζων ἐνεχείρει, τὸν μῦν ὁ θύλαξ κατέφαγεν.

25. Εὖ γ' οὖν καὶ Διογένης πρὸς τὸν θαυμάζοντα ὅτι ηὗρεν τὸν ὄφιν τῷ ὑπέρῳ περιειλημένον, Μὴ θαύμαζε, ἔφη· ἦν γὰρ παραδοξότερον ἐκεῖνο, εἰ τὸ ὕπερον περὶ ὀρθῷ τῷ ὄφει κατειλημένον ἐθεάcω. δεῖ γὰρ καὶ τὰ ἄλογα τῶν ζῴων τρέχειν καὶ ἐσθίειν καὶ μάχεσθαι καὶ τίκτειν καὶ ἀποθνήσκειν, ἃ δὴ ἐκείνοις ὄντα κατὰ φύσιν οὐκ ἄν ποτε ἡμῖν γένοιτο παρὰ φύσιν.

ὄρνιθες δέ τε πολλοὶ ὑπ' αὐγὰς ἠελίοιο
φοιτῶσιν.

ὁ κωμικὸς δὲ Φιλήμων καὶ τὰ τοιαῦτα κωμῳδεῖ·

ὅταν ἴδω (φησί) παρατηροῦντα τίς ἔπταρεν,
ἢ τίς ἐλάλησεν, ἢ τίς ἐστιν ὁ προϊὼν
σκοποῦντα, πωλῶ τοῦτον εὐθὺς ἐν ἀγορᾷ.
αὐτῷ βαδίζει καὶ λαλεῖ καὶ πτάρνυται
ἕκαστος ἡμῶν, οὐχὶ τοῖς ἐν τῇ πόλει.
τὰ πράγμαθ', ὡς πέφυκεν, οὕτως γίγνεται.

εἶτα νήφοντες μὲν ὑγείαν αἰτοῦνται, ὑπερεμπιπλάμενοι δὲ καὶ μέθαις ἐγκυλιόμενοι κατὰ τὰς ἑορτὰς νόσους ἐπισπῶνται. πολλοὶ δὲ καὶ τὰς γραφὰς δεδίασι τὰς

---

6. εἰ S. ἢ L.   θῦλαξ] θύλαξ L.   θύλακοc ap. Theod.   8. εὖ γ' οὖν M (cf. Klotz-Devar II. p. 349 seq.). εὖ γοῦν edd.   9. ηὗρεν] εὗρεν L.   ὄφιν H. ὄφιν ἐν L.   περιειλημένον S. περιειλημμένον L.   ὄφεως ὑπέρῳ ἑαυτὸν ἐνειλήσαντος Theod.   11. κατειλημένον S. κατειλιμμένον L. κατειλημμένον Theod.   12. ἐσθίειν Μ. θεῖν L. 13. δὴ L¹. δι' L².   18. ὅταν—γίγνεται] ap. Theod. p. 87. 50. 19. προϊών] προσιών ap. Theod.   20. πωλῶ S. πώλῳ L. ἀπολῶ ap. Theod.   21. αὐτῷ Theod. ἑαυτῷ L.   23. πράγμαθ'—γίγνεται Theod. πράγματα—γίνεσθαι L. οὕτως] οὕτω Theod.   24. ὑγείαν L. ὑγίειαν D.

seeing that the sow was a mere skeleton from her owner's niggardliness, *Well for you*, said he, *that the omen did not take the form of her devouring your own children in her hunger.* And, *What wonder is it*, says Bion, *if the mouse, finding nothing to eat, gnawed through the sack? The wonder would have been if, as Arcesilaus jestingly retorted, the sack had eaten the mouse.*

§ 25. Excellent too was the reply of Diogenes to him who marvelled because he found the snake coiled round the pestle. *Marvel not*, said he, *for it would have been far more surprising if you had seen the snake erect and the pestle coiled up round it.* For the irrational animals too have to run and eat and fight and breed and die; and these things being according to nature for them can never be portentous in relation to us. *Moreover many birds beneath the sunlight range*[1] <from which omens may be derived>. Follies of this sort are caricatured by the comic poet Philemon[2]. *When I behold*, says he, *a slave on the watch to see who sneezes, or who speaks, or who comes out of his house, I offer him at once to the first bidder. It is to himself that each of us walks and speaks and sneezes, and not to all the city. Things happen as 'tis their nature to.* And then we find them praying for health when sober, but bringing on diseases by cramming and drinking themselves drunk at the festivals. Many too have a superstitious fear of the mottoes that are written up.

---

[1] *Od.* II. 181. [2] Kock, *Com. Att. Fr.* vol. II. p. 510.

ἀνακειμένας. 26. Ἀστείως πάνυ ὁ Διογένης ἐπὶ οἰκίᾳ μοχθηροῦ τινος εὑρὼν ἐπιγεγραμμένον

ὁ καλλίνικος Ἡρακλῆς
ἐνθάδε κατοικεῖ· μηδὲν εἰσίτω κακόν·

καὶ πῶς ἔφη ὁ κύριος εἰϲελεύϲεται τῆϲ οἰκίαϲ; οἱ αὐτοὶ δ' οὗτοι πᾶν ξύλον καὶ πάντα λίθον, τὸ δὴ λεγόμενον, λιπαρὸν προσκυνοῦντες, ἔρια πυρρὰ καὶ ἁλῶν χόνδρους καὶ δᾷδας σκίλλαν τε καὶ θεῖον δεδίασι, πρὸς τῶν γοήτων καταγοητευθέντες κατά τινας ἀκαθάρτους καθαρμούς. θεὸς δέ, ὁ τῷ ὄντι θεός, ἅγιον μόνον οἶδεν τὸ τοῦ δικαίου ἦθος, ὥσπερ ἐναγὲς τὸ ἄδικον καὶ μοχθηρόν. ὁρᾶν γοῦν ἔστι τὰ ᾠὰ τὰ ἀπὸ τῶν περικαθαρθέντων, εἰ θαλφθείη, ζῳογονούμενα· οὐκ ἂν δὲ τοῦτο ἐγίνετο, εἰ ἀνελάμβανεν τὰ τοῦ περικαθαρθέντος κακά. χαριέντως γ' οὖν καὶ ὁ κωμικὸς Δίφιλος κωμῳδεῖ τοὺς γόητας διὰ τῶνδε

Προιτίδας ἁγνίζων κούρας, καὶ τὸν πατέρ' αὐτῶν
Προῖτον Ἀβαντιάδην, καὶ γραῦν πέμπτην ἐπὶ τοῖσδε,
δᾳδὶ μιᾷ σκίλλῃ τε μιᾷ, τόσα σώματα φωτῶν,
θείῳ τ' ἀσφάλτῳ τε πολυφλοίσβοιο θαλάσσης
ἐξ ἀκαλαρρείταο βαθυρρόου ὠκεανοῖο.
ἀλλὰ μάκαρ Ἀὴρ διὰ τῶν νεφέων διάπεμψον
Ἀντικύραν, ἵνα τόνδε κόριν κηφῆνα ποιήσω.

27. Εὖ γὰρ καὶ ὁ Μένανδρος

εἰ μέν τι κακὸν ἀληθὲς εἶχες, Φειδία,
ζητεῖν ἀληθὲς φάρμακον τούτου σ' ἔδει.

1. οἰκίᾳ V. οἰκείᾳ L.   7. χόνδρους] χρόνδους L.   12. ᾠὰ τὰ M. ᾠὰ Hervetus. ὦτα L.   15. γ' οὖν LVM. γοῦν edd.   17. πατέρ'] πρα L.   18. ἐπὶ (debebat ἐπὶ quod restituit Mein. Com. vol. IV. p. 416 D) τοῖσδε, δᾳδὶ μιᾷ S. ἐν τοῖσδε δασμίας L.   19. τόσα Grotius. πόσα L.   20. πολυφλοίσβοιο θαλάσσης] πολυφλοίσβοιοι θ. L. πολυφλοίσβῳ τε θαλάσσῃ S. Mein. Kock.   21. ἐξ ἀκαλαρρείταο ex Homero. ἐξακαλλαρίταο L.   23. Ἀντικύραν Kl. ἀντίκυραν L.   τόνδε—κηφῆνα S. τόν τε—κιφῆνα L.   25. Φειδία, ζητεῖν Grotius Exc. p. 751. φιλάζειν L.   26. τούτου σ' ἔδει Grotius. τούτους σε δεῖ (σεδεῖ conjunctim V) L.

§ 26. It was a witty remark of Diogenes, when he found the house of a man of bad character bearing the inscription *Here dwells the victorious Heracles: let no wickedness enter:* How then, said he, *is the master of the house to enter?* And the same people worship every stock and every shining stone, as the phrase is, and are in awe of red wool and grains of salt and torches and squills and brimstone, being bewitched by the sorcerers according to certain impure purifications. But the true God regards nothing as holy but the character of the just man, nothing as polluted but what is unjust and wicked. At any rate you may see the eggs, which have been removed from the body of those who have undergone purification, hatched by warmth, and this could not have happened, if they had contracted the ills of the person purified. And so the comic poet Diphilus[1] pleasantly satirizes the sorcerers in these words: *He purifies the daughters of Proetus with their father, the son of Abas, and an old crone besides to make up five—so many mortals with a single torch, a single squill, and brimstone and asphaltus of the boisterous surge, gathered from the deep pools of the soft-flowing ocean*[2]. *But, O blessed Air, send Anticyra from heaven that I may change this bug to a stingless drone.*

§ 27. Menander[3] too says well, *If you were suffering from any real evil, Pheidias, you ought to have sought a real remedy*

---

[1] Kock, *ib.* vol. II. p. 577.

[2] Hom. *Il.* VII. 422.

[3] Kock, *ib.* vol. III. p. 152 *seq.*

νῦν δ' οὐκ ἔχεις· κενὸν < οὖν > εὕρηκα τὸ φάρμακον
πρὸς τὸ κενόν· οἰήθητι δ' ὠφελεῖν τί σε.
περιμαξάτωσάν σ' αἱ γυναῖκες ἐν κύκλῳ
καὶ περιθεωσάτωσαν, ἀπὸ κρουνῶν τριῶν
ὕδατι περίρραν' ἐμβαλὼν ἅλας, φακούς.

πᾶς ἁγνός ἐστιν ὁ μηδὲν ἑαυτῷ κακὸν συνειδώς. αὐτίκα
ἡ τραγῳδία λέγει

Ὀρέστα, τίς σ' ἀπόλλυσιν νόσος;
Ἡ σύνεσις, ὅτι σύνοιδα δείν' εἰργασμένος.

τῷ γὰρ ὄντι ἡ ἁγνεία οὐκ ἄλλη τίς ἐστιν πλὴν ἡ τῶν
ἁμαρτημάτων ἀποχή. καλῶς ἄρα καὶ Ἐπίχαρμός φησι

καθαρὸν ἂν τὸν νοῦν ἔχῃς, ἅπαν τὸ σῶμα καθαρὸς εἶ.

αὐτίκα καὶ τὰς ψυχὰς προκαθαίρειν χρεών φαμεν ἀπὸ
τῶν φαύλων καὶ μοχθηρῶν δογμάτων διὰ τοῦ λόγου
τοῦ ὀρθοῦ, καὶ τότε οὕτως ἐπὶ τὴν τῶν προηγουμένων
κεφαλαίων ὑπόμνησιν τρέπεσθαι· ἐπεὶ καὶ πρὸ τῆς τῶν
μυστηρίων παραδόσεως καθαρμούς τινας προσάγειν
τοῖς μυεῖσθαι μέλλουσιν ἀξιοῦσιν, ὡς δέον τὴν ἄθεον
ἀποθεμένους δόξαν ἐπὶ τὴν ἀληθῆ τρέπεσθαι παράδοσιν.

ΚΕΦ. Ε.

28. Ἢ γὰρ οὐ καλῶς καὶ ἀληθῶς οὐκ ἐν τόπῳ τινὶ
περιγράφομεν τὸν ἀπερίληπτον οὐδ' ἐν ἱεροῖς καθείργνυμεν χειροποιήτοις τὸ πάντων περιεκτικόν; τί δ' ἂν καὶ
οἰκοδόμων καὶ λιθοξόων καὶ βαναύσου τέχνης ἅγιον
εἴη ἔργον; οὐχὶ ἀμείνους τούτων οἱ τὸν ἀέρα καὶ τὸ
περιέχον, μᾶλλον δὲ τὸν ὅλον κόσμον καὶ τὸ σύμπαν
ἄξιον ἡγησάμενοι τῆς τοῦ θεοῦ ὑπεροχῆς; γελοῖον

1. κενὸν οὖν εὕρηκα τὸ φάρμακον M. (εὕρηκας S.) οὖν om. L. κενὸν
ἄρα καὶ τὸ φάρμακον πρὸς τὸ κενόν· εἰ δ' οἴει τί σ' ὠφελεῖν τόδε Kock.
2, 3. δ'—σ' S. δὲ—σε L. 4. περιθεωσάτωσαν Mein. περι-
θειωσάτωσαν Bentleius. περιθέτωσαν L. 5. περίρραν' ἐμβαλὼν S. Mein.
Kock. περιρράναι ἐμβ. L. περιρράναι βαλὼν Lob. *Agl.* 632 n. h. 6. πᾶς...
συνειδώς] fort. sic a Menandro scriptum π. ἁ. ἐ. ὁ μηδὲν ἐξειργασμένος | κακὸν
συνειδώς M. συνειδώς Bentleius. συνιδών L. 8. σ' ἀπόλλυσιν—ἠ—
δείν'] σε ἀπόλλυσι—ἠ—δεινὰ L. 12. ἂν τὸν νοῦν Grotius. τὸν νοῦν
ἐὰν L. καθαρὸς ᾖ εἶ (pr. m. corr.) L. 18. ἀξιοῦσιν S. ἀξιοῦσθαι L.

for it. But as that is not so, I have devised a remedy as imaginary as the evil: simply imagine that it does you some good. Let the women rub you down and fumigate thoroughly: then sprinkle yourself with water from three springs, throwing in salt and beans. Every one is pure whose conscience is free from guilt. So in the tragedy[1] we read

> *Orestes, say, what canker saps thy life?*
> *Conscience, which tells me of a dark deed wrought.*

For indeed purity is no other than the abstaining from sin. Well therefore says Epicharmus, *If your mind is pure your whole body is pure too*[2]. Certainly it is our rule to begin by cleansing our souls from bad and wicked opinions by means of right reason, and then, after that, to turn to the mention of the more excellent principles; for so too, in the case of those who are about to be initiated, it is thought right to apply certain purifications before the communication of the mysteries, on the ground that the godless opinion must be got rid of before they are ready to have the truth communicated to them.

CHAPTER V.

§ 28. Surely it cannot be denied that we are following right and truth when we refuse to circumscribe in a given place Him who is incomprehensible, and to confine *in temples made with hands*[3] that which contains all things. And what work of builders and masons and of mechanic art could be called holy? Were not they more in the right who held that the air and the circumambient ether, or rather the whole world and the universe itself, were worthy of the divine dignity? It would indeed be

---

[1] Eur. *Orest.* 395.   [2] p. 256 Lorenz.   [3] Acts xvii. 24.

μεντἂν εἴη, ὡς αὐτοί φασιν οἱ φιλόσοφοι, ἄνθρωπον ὄντα παίγνιον θεοῦ θεὸν ἐργάζεσθαι καὶ γίνεσθαι παιδιαῖς τέχνης τὸν θεόν· ἐπεὶ τὸ γινόμενον ταὐτὸν καὶ ὅμοιον τῷ ἐξ οὗ γίνεται, ὡς τὸ ἐξ ἐλέφαντος ἐλεφάντινον καὶ τὸ ἐκ χρυσοῦ χρυσοῦν, τὰ δὲ πρὸς ἀνθρώπων βαναύσων κατασκευαζόμενα ἀγάλματά τε καὶ ἱερὰ ἐκ τῆς ὕλης τῆς ἀργῆς γίνεται, ὥστε καὶ αὐτὰ ἂν εἴη ἀργὰ καὶ ὑλικὰ καὶ βέβηλα· κἂν τὴν τέχνην ἐκτελέσῃς, τῆς βαναυσίας μετείληφεν. οὐκέτ᾽ οὖν ἱερὰ καὶ θεῖα τῆς τέχνης τὰ ἔργα. Τί δ᾽ ἂν καὶ ἱδρύοιτο μηδενὸς ἀνιδρύτου τυγχάνοντος, ἐπεὶ πάντα ἐν τόπῳ; ναὶ μὴν τὸ ἱδρυμένον ὑπό τινος ἵδρυται πρότερον ἀνίδρυτον ὄν. εἴπερ οὖν ὁ θεὸς ἵδρυται πρὸς ἀνθρώπων, ἀνίδρυτός ποτε ἦν καὶ οὐδ᾽ ὅλως ἦν. τοῦτο γὰρ ἦν ἀνίδρυτον, τὸ οὐκ ὄν, ἐπειδήπερ πᾶν τὸ μὴ ὂν ἱδρύεται. τὸ δὲ ὂν ὑπὸ τοῦ μὴ ὄντος οὐκ ἂν ἱδρυνθείη, ἀλλ᾽ οὐδ᾽ ὑπ᾽ ἄλλου ὄντος· ὂν γάρ ἐστι καὶ αὐτό. 29. Λείπεται δὴ ὑφ᾽ ἑαυτοῦ. καὶ πῶς αὐτὸ ἑαυτό τι γεννήσει; ἢ πῶς αὐτὸ τὸ ὂν ἑαυτὸ ἐνιδρύσει; πότερον ἀνίδρυτον ὂν πρότερον ἵδρυσεν ἑαυτό; ἀλλ᾽ οὐκ ἂν οὐδ᾽ ἦν, ἐπεὶ τὸ μὴ ὂν ἀνίδρυτον. καὶ τὸ ἱδρῦσθαι νομισθὲν πῶς <ἂν>, ὃ φθάσαν εἶχεν ὄν, τοῦθ᾽ ἑαυτὸ ὕστερον ποιοίη; οὗ δὲ τὰ ὄντα, πῶς οὖν τοῦτ᾽ ἂν δέοιτο τινός;

Ἀλλ᾽ εἰ καὶ ἀνθρωποειδὲς τὸ θεῖον, τῶν ἴσων δεήσεται τῷ ἀνθρώπῳ, τροφῆς τε καὶ σκέπης οἰκίας τε καὶ τῶν ἀκολούθων πάντων. οἱ ὁμοιοσχήμονες

---

1. αὐτοί φασιν S. αὐτοί φησίν L. 2. παιδιαῖς H. παιδιᾶς L. παιδιὰν S. παιδιᾷ Barnard. 3. ἐπεὶ τὸ γινόμενον—] In marg. L. m. rec. ση. ἀλλ᾽ ὁ Ὠριγένης οὐχ οὕτως φησίν, ἀλλ᾽ ἀνόμοιον τὸ ἐξ οὗ ἐστι ὁ τούτου μαθητής. 4. ἐλεφάντινον] ελεφαντίνου L. 8. ἐκτελέσῃς L. ἐξετάσῃς H. 12, 13. ἱδρύται bis M. ἱδρύεται L. 14. γὰρ ἦν Jackson, γὰρ ἂν ἦν L. 15. ἱδρύεται LH. οὐχ ἱδρ. edd. post Hervetum. ἱδρύεται. Jackson. ἱδρύεται, D. 16. ἱδρινθείη L. ἱδρινθείη D. ἄλλου ὄντος· ὂν P. ἄλλου· ὄντος ὂν L. ἄλλου· ὄντως ὂν S. 17. ὑφ᾽ Heinsius. ἐφ᾽ L. 19. ἐνιδρύσει M. εἶναι ἐνιδρύσει L. 20. ἀνίδρυτον M. ἀνίδρυτον, D. 21. πῶς ἂν M. πῶς L. 22. πῶς οὖν τοῦτ᾽ ἂν L. fort. πῶς ἂν τοῦτο M. 25. οἰκίας] οἰκείας L. 26. πάντων M. παθῶν L. ὁμοσχήμονες pr. m. corr. L.

ridiculous, as the philosophers themselves say, that *man being but a toy of God*[1] should make God, and that God should come into being through the *play*[1] of human art. For that which is produced resembles, and is indeed the same as, that from which it is produced: thus, what is made of ivory is ivory, and what is made of gold is golden; and in like manner statues and temples executed by the hands of mechanics, being composed of lifeless matter, must themselves also be lifeless and material and profane; and even though you should carry your art to perfection, they still retain something of the mechanical. This being so, we cannot regard works of art as sacred and divine.

<Again, among the heathen enshrinement is supposed to be essential to deity.> But what is it which could be localized in a shrine, if there is nothing unlocalized to start with (on the assumption that all things are in space)? And further, that which is enshrined has received enshrinement from something else, being itself previously unenshrined. If then God has received enshrinement from men, He was previously unenshrined and therefore non-existent. For <by the hypothesis> it is only the non-existent which was unenshrined, seeing that it is always the non-existent which undergoes the process of localization by enshrinement. And that which exists could not be localized by that which is non-existent, nor yet by anything else that exists: for it is itself also in existence <and therefore already localized in common with all other existing things>. § 29. It remains therefore that it must be enshrined by itself. But how is a thing to beget itself? Or how is the self-existent to localize itself in a shrine? Was it formerly unlocalized and did it afterwards localize itself? No, in that case it could not even have existed, since it is the non-existent which is unlocalized. And how could that which is supposed to have been localized make itself subsequently what it already was? Or that to which all existing things belong, <the self-existent Deity>, be itself in need of anything?

Again, if the Deity is in human shape, He will need the same things as man needs, food and covering and a house and all things belonging to them. For beings of like form and like

---

[1] Plato *Leg.* VII. 803 C.

γὰρ καὶ ὁμοιοπαθεῖς τῆς ἴσης δεήσονται διαίτης. εἰ δὲ τὸ ἱερὸν διχῶς ἐκλαμβάνεται, ὅ τε θεὸς αὐτὸς καὶ τὸ εἰς τιμὴν αὐτοῦ κατασκεύασμα, πῶς οὐ κυρίως τὴν εἰς τιμὴν τοῦ θεοῦ κατ' ἐπίγνωσιν ἁγίαν
5 γενομένην ἐκκλησίαν ἱερὸν ἂν εἴποιμεν θεοῦ, τὸ πολλοῦ ἄξιον καὶ οὐ βαναύσῳ κατεσκευασμένον τέχνῃ, ἀλλ' οὐδὲ ἀγγέλου χειρὶ δεδαιδαλμένον, βουλήσει δὲ τοῦ θεοῦ εἰς νεὼν πεποιημένον; οὐ γὰρ νῦν τὸν τόπον, ἀλλὰ τὸ ἄθροισμα τῶν ἐκλεκτῶν ἐκκλησίαν καλῶ.
10 ἀμείνων ὁ νεὼς οὗτος εἰς παραδοχὴν μεγέθους ἀξίας τοῦ θεοῦ. τὸ γὰρ περὶ πολλοῦ ἄξιον ζῷον τῷ τοῦ παντὸς ἀξίῳ, μᾶλλον δὲ οὐδενὸς ἀνταξίῳ, δι' ὑπερβολὴν ἁγιότητος καθιέρωται. εἴη δ' ἂν οὗτος ὁ γνωστικὸς ὁ πολλοῦ ἄξιος, ὁ τίμιος τῷ θεῷ, ἐν ᾧ ὁ θεὸς ἐνίδρυται,
15 τουτέστιν ἡ περὶ τοῦ θεοῦ γνῶσις καθιέρωται. ἐνταῦθα καὶ τὸ ἀπεικόνισμα εὕροιμεν ἄν, τὸ θεῖον καὶ ἅγιον ἄγαλμα, ἐν τῇ δικαίᾳ ψυχῇ, ὅταν μακαρία μὲν αὐτὴ τυγχάνῃ, ἅτε προκεκαθαρμένη μακάρια δὲ διαπραττομένη ἔργα. ἐνταῦθα καὶ τὸ ἐνίδρυτον καὶ τὸ ἐνιδρυό-
20 μενον, τὸ μὲν ἐπὶ τῶν ἤδη γνωστικῶν, τὸ δὲ ἐπὶ τῶν οἵων τε γενέσθαι, κἂν μηδέπω ὦσιν ἄξιοι ἀναδέξασθαι ἐπιστήμην θεοῦ. πᾶν γὰρ τὸ μέλλον πιστεύειν πιστὸν ἤδη τῷ θεῷ καὶ καθιδρυμένον εἰς τιμήν, ἄγαλμα ἐνάρετον ἀνακείμενον θεῷ.

ΚΕΦ. Ϛ.

25 30. Καθάπερ οὖν οὐ περιγράφεται τόπῳ θεὸς οὐδὲ ἀπεικονίζεταί ποτε ζῴου σχήματι, οὕτως οὐδὲ ὁμοιοπαθὴς οὐδὲ ἐνδεὴς καθάπερ τὰ γενητά, ὡς θυσιῶν, δίκην

7. ἀγγέλου M. ἀγύρτου L. Τυρίου Jackson.   δεδαιδαλμένον S. δεδαλμένον L.   8. πεποιημένον M. πεποιημένην L.   10. ἀξίας L. ἀξίαν SD.   18. διαπραττομένη] fort. διαπράττηται M.   19. ἐνίδρυτον H. Lowth. ἀνίδρυτον L.   ἐνιδρυόμενον H. ἐνιδρυμένον L.   23. τῷ θεῷ καὶ] καὶ τῷ θεῷ Herv.   27. θυσιῶν H. θυσίαν L.

passions will require the same kind of life. And if the word 'holy' is taken in two senses, as applied to God Himself and also to the building raised in His honour, surely we should be right in giving to the Church, which was instituted to the honour of God in accordance with sanctified wisdom, the name of a holy temple of God, that precious temple built by no mechanic art, nay, not embellished even by an angel's hand, but made into a shrine by the will of God Himself. I use the name Church now not of the place, but of the congregation of saints. This is the shrine which is best fitted for the reception of the greatness of the dignity of God. For to Him who is all-worthy, or rather in comparison with whom all else is worthless, there is consecrated that creature which is of great worth owing to its preeminent holiness. And such would be the gnostic, who is of great worth and precious in the sight of God, he in whom God is enshrined, *i.e.* in whom the knowledge of God is consecrated. Here too we should find the likeness, the divine and sanctified image,—here in the righteous soul, after it has been itself blessed, as having been already purified and now performing blessed deeds. Here we find both that which is enshrined and that which is in process of enshrinement, the former in the case of those who are already gnostics, the latter in those who are capable of becoming so, though they may not yet be worthy to receive the knowledge of God. For all that is destined to believe is already faithful in the eye of God and consecrated to honour, an image of virtue dedicated to God.

CHAPTER VI.

§ 30. As then God is not circumscribed in place, nor made like to the form of any creature, so neither is He of like passions, nor lacks He anything after the manner of created

τροφῆς, διὰ λιμὸν ἐπιθυμεῖν. ὧν ἅπτεται πάθος φθαρτὰ πάντα ἐστί, καὶ τῷ μὴ τρεφομένῳ προσάγειν βορὰν μάταιον. καὶ ὅ γε κωμικὸς ἐκεῖνος Φερεκράτης ἐν Αὐτομόλοις χαριέντως αὐτοὺς πεποίηκεν τοὺς θεοὺς
5 καταμεμφομένους τοῖς ἀνθρώποις τῶν ἱερῶν·

ὅτε τοῖσι θεοῖς θύετε, πρώτιστ' ἀποκρίνετε <τοῖς ἱερεῦσιν>
τὸ νομιζόμενον <πρώτοις> ὑμῶν, εἶτ' (αἰσχύνη τὸ κατειπεῖν)
οὐ τὼ μηρὼ περιλέψαντες μέχρι βουβώνων <κρέα πάντα>
καὶ τὴν ὀσφῦν κομιδῇ ψιλήν, λοιπὸν τὸν σπόνδυλον αὐτὸν
10 ὥσπερ <ῥίνῃ> ῥινήσαντες νέμεθ' ὥσπερ τοῖς κυσὶν ἡμῖν,
εἶτ' ἀλλήλους αἰσχυνόμενοι θυλήμασι κρύπτετε πολλοῖς;

Εὔβουλος δὲ ὁ καὶ αὐτὸς κωμικὸς ὧδέ πως περὶ τῶν θυσιῶν γράφει

αὐτοῖς δὲ τοῖς θεοῖσι τὴν κέρκον μόνην
15 καὶ μηρὸν ὥσπερ παιδερασταῖς θύετε.

καὶ παραγαγὼν τὸν Διόνυσον ἐν Σεμέλῃ διαστελλόμενον πεποίηκεν

πρῶτον μὲν ὅταν ἐμοί τι θύωσίν τινες,
<θύουσιν> αἷμα, κύστιν, †μὴ καρδίαν
20 μηδ' ἐπιπόλαιον· ἐγὼ γὰρ οὐκ ἐσθίω
γλυκεῖαν οὐδὲ μηρίαν†.

31. Μένανδρός τε τὴν ὀσφῦν ἄκραν πεποίηκεν, τὴν χολήν, ὀστέα τὰ ἄβρωτα, <ἃ,> φησί, τοῖς θεοῖς ἐπιτιθέντες

1. ὧν L. ὧν γὰρ Abbott. 2. πάντα] πάντως S. 3. μάταιον. M. μάταιον, D. 4. αὐτοὺς S. αὐτοῖς L. 5. τοῖς ἀνθρώποις] corr. pr. m. ex τοῖς ἀνοῖς L. 6. ὅτε—θεοῖς Grotius. ὅτι—θεοῖσι L. πρώτιστ' ἀποκρίνετε S. πρώτιστα ἀποκρίνεται L. τοῖς ἱερεῦσιν addit Herm. 7. πρώτοις ὑμῶν vel κάπειθ' ὑμῶν Herm. ὑμῶν L. εἶτ' αἰσχύνη τὸ κατειπεῖν vel αἰσχ. τοι τ. κ. Herm. αἰσχύνῃ τῷ κατ' εἰπεῖν L. 8. οὐ] εὖ Jackson. τὼ μηρὼ S. τῷ μηρῷ L. περιλέψαντες Herm. περιλάψαντες L. μέχρι βουβώνων κρέα πάντα Herm. κομιδῇ μέχρι β. L. 10. ῥίνῃ addit Herm. νέμεθ' Kl. ἐνέμεσθ' L. ὥσπερ Herm. ὥσπερ καὶ L. 11. θυλήμασι Ruhnken. οὐ λήμασι L. 18. θύωσιν S. θύωσι L. 19. θύουσιν addit S. μὴ L. fort. μὴ γὰρ M. 20. μηδ' S. μηδὲ L. ἐγὼ γὰρ οὐκ ἐσθίω κλυκείαν (γλυκεῖαν Herv. κοιλία substituit Arsenius Viol. p. 299) οὐδὲ μηρίαν (μηρία P. in not.) L. οὐκ ἐγὼ γὰρ ἐσθίω γλύκιον οὐδὲν μηρίων Herm. 22. Μένανδρος] Ipsa Menandri ex Δυσκόλῳ verba servavit Athenaeus 4. p. 146 e. οἱ δὲ τὴν ὀσφῦν ἄκραν | καὶ τὴν χολὴν ὀστᾶ τ' ἄβρωτα τοῖς θεοῖς | ἐπιθέντες αὐτοὶ τἆλλα κατατίνουσ' del. 23. τὰ ἄβρωτα LH. τ' ἄβρωτα D. ἃ addidit M.

things, so as from hunger to desire sacrifices for food. Things that are capable of suffering are all mortal; and it is useless to offer meat to that which is in no need of sustenance. The famous comic poet Pherecrates in his Deserters[1] wittily represents the gods themselves as finding fault with men for their offerings. *When you sacrifice to the gods, first of all you set apart what is customary for the priests first among you, and then —shame to say—do you not pick the thigh-bones clean to the groin and leave the hip-joint absolutely bare, assigning to us gods nothing but the dogs' portion, a back-bone polished as with a file, which you then cover with thick layers of sacrificial meal to save appearances?* And another comic poet, Eubulus, writes as follows about the sacrifices: *To the gods themselves you offer nothing but the tail and the thigh, as though they were enamoured of these*[2]. And, where he brings on Dionysus in his Semele[3], he represents him as distinguishing: *First of all, when any sacrifice to me, they sacrifice blood and bladder—don't mention heart or caul—the gall and thigh-bones are no food for me.* § 31. And Menander[4] has written of *the scrag end of the rump, the gall and dry bones,* <*which*>, says he, *they set before the gods, while they consume the*

---

[1] Cf. Kock *Com. Att.* i. p. 151.
[2] Kock *Com. Att.* ii. p. 210.
[3] *Ib.* p. 197.
[4] *Ib.* iii. p. 89.

αὐτοὶ τὰ ἄλλα ἀναλίσκουσιν. ἢ γὰρ οὐχ ἡ τῶν ὁλοκαυτωμάτων κνῖσα καὶ τοῖς θηρίοις ἀφεκτέα; εἰ δὲ τῷ ὄντι ἡ κνῖσα γέρας ἐστὶ θεῶν τῶν παρ᾽ Ἕλλησιν, οὐκ ἂν φθάνοιεν καὶ τοὺς μαγείρους θεοποιοῦντες, οἱ τῆς ἴσης εὐδαιμονίας ἀξιοῦνται, καὶ τὸν ἰπνὸν αὐτὸν προσκυνοῦντες, προσεχεστέραν <ἐσχάραν> γινομένην τῇ κνίσῃ τῇ πολυτιμήτῳ. καί που Ἡσίοδος κατά τινα μερισμὸν κρεῶν ἀπατηθέντα φησὶ πρὸς τοῦ Προμηθέως τὸν Δία λαβεῖν ὀcτέα λευκὰ βοὸc δολίῃ ἐπὶ τέχνῃ κεκαλυμμένα ἀργέτι δημῷ·

ἐκ τοῦ δ᾽ ἀθανάτοισιν ἐπὶ χθονὶ φῦλ᾽ ἀνθρώπων
καίουσ᾽ ὀστέα λευκὰ θυηέντων ἐπὶ βωμῶν.

ἀλλ᾽ οὐκ ἂν οὐδαμῶς φασὶ κατὰ τὴν ἐκ τῆς ἐνδείας ἐπιθυμίαν κακούμενον τρέφεσθαι τὸν θεόν. ὅμοιον οὖν αὐτὸν φυτῷ ποιήσουσιν ἀνορέκτως τρεφόμενον καὶ τοῖς φωλεύουσι θηρίοις. φασὶ γοῦν ταῦτα εἴτε ὑπὸ τῆς κατὰ τὸν ἀέρα παχύτητος εἴτ᾽ αὖ καὶ ἐξ αὐτῆς τῆς τοῦ οἰκείου σώματος ἀναθυμιάσεως τρεφόμενα ἀβλαβῶς αὔξειν. καίτοι εἰ ἀνενδεῶς τρέφεται αὐτοῖς τὸ θεῖον, τίς ἔτι χρεία τροφῆς τῷ ἀνενδεεῖ; Εἰ δὲ τιμώμενον χαίρει, φύσει ἀνενδεὲς ὑπάρχον, οὐκ ἀπεικότως ἡμεῖς δι᾽ εὐχῆς τιμῶμεν τὸν θεόν, καὶ ταύτην τὴν θυcίαν ἀρίστην καὶ ἁγιωτάτην μετὰ δικαιοcύνηc ἀναπέμπομεν τῷ δικαιοτάτῳ λόγῳ, γεραίροντεc δι᾽ οὗ παραλαμβάνομεν τὴν γνῶσιν, διὰ τούτου <δὲ> δοξάζοντες ὃν μεμαθήκαμεν. ἔστι γοῦν τὸ παρ᾽ ἡμῖν θυσιαστήριον ἐνταῦθα τὸ ἐπίγειον τὸ ἄθροισμα τῶν ταῖς εὐχαῖς ἀνακειμένων, μίαν ὥσπερ ἔχον φωνὴν τὴν κοινὴν καὶ μίαν γνώμην. Αἱ δὲ διὰ τῆς ὀσφρήσεως, εἰ καὶ θειότεραι τῶν διὰ

2, 3. κνῖσα Kl. κνίσσα L.   2. ἀφεκτέα] ἀφετέα H. fort. ἀπεχθής M.
5. τὸν ἰπνὸν αὐτὸν S post Hoeschelium. τ. ἰτμὸν αὐτὸν L. τὴν ἐσχάραν αὐτὴν D.
6. προσεχεστέραν ἐσχάραν M. προσεχεστέραν L.   9. Δία λαβεῖν S. δία λαβεῖν L. διαλαβεῖν V.   10. ἀργέτι ex Hesiodo. ἀργέτα L.   13. φασὶ S. φησὶ L.   25. τούτου δὲ δοξάζοντες ὃν H. τούτου δοξάζοντες ἃ L.

rest themselves. Why, the smoke of burnt sacrifices is intolerable even to the beasts. If however this smoke is really the meed of the gods of Greece, no time should be lost in deifying the cooks also (since they are deemed worthy of the same happiness) and in worshipping the stove itself, when it becomes an altar closely connected with the precious smoke. Hesiod[1] somewhere says that *Zeus, being outwitted in some division of the flesh of the sacrifice by Prometheus, chose the white bones of the ox craftily concealed in the glistening lard: and from that time the tribes of men on earth burn to the immortals white bones on fragrant altars.* Still they altogether deny that God's partaking of nourishment could be explained by the craving which grows out of want. Accordingly they must suppose Him nourished without appetite like plants or hibernating bears. At all events they say that these are not impeded in their growth, whether it be that they are nourished from the density of the air, or even from the exhalation arising from their own body. And yet, if they hold that the Deity is nourished without needing it, what is the use of nourishment to one who needs it not? But if the Deity, being by nature exempt from all need, rejoices to be honoured, we have good reason for honouring God by prayer, and for sending up to the most righteous Word this sacrifice, the best and holiest of *sacrifices* when joined with *righteousness*[2], *venerating*[3] Him through whom we receive our knowledge, <and> through Him glorifying Him (*i.e.* the Father) whom we have learnt to know. At any rate our altar here on earth is the congregation of those who are devoted to the prayers, having, as it were, one common voice and one mind.

As to the kinds of nutrition received through the sense of smell, though they may be less unworthy of the deity than

---

[1] *Theog.* 556.   [2] Ps. iv. 5.   [3] Plat. *Leg.* 799 A.

στόματος τροφαί, ἀλλὰ ἀναπνοῆς εἰσι δηλωτικαί. 32. Τί οὖν φασι περὶ τοῦ θεοῦ; πότερον διαπνεῖται ὡς τὸ τῶν δαιμόνων γένος; ἢ ἐμπνεῖται μόνον ὡς τὰ ἔνυδρα κατὰ τὴν τῶν βραγχίων διαστολήν; ἢ περιπνεῖται καθάπερ τὰ ἔντομα κατὰ τὴν διὰ τῶν πτερύγων ἐπίθλιψιν τῆς ἐντομῆς; ἀλλ' οὐκ ἄν τινι τούτων ἀπεικάσαιεν, εἴ γε εὖ φρονοῖεν, τὸν θεόν. ὅσα δὲ ἀναπνεῖ κατὰ τὴν τοῦ πνεύμονος πρὸς τὸν θώρακα ἀντιδιαστολὴν ῥυθμῷ ἕλκει τὸν ἀέρα. εἶτα εἰ σπλάγχνα δοῖεν καὶ ἀρτηρίας καὶ φλέβας καὶ νεῦρα καὶ μόρια τῷ θεῷ, οὐδὲν <ἀνθρώπου> διαφέροντα εἰσηγήσονται τοῦτον. Ἡ σύμπνοια δὲ ἐπὶ τῆς ἐκκλησίας λέγεται κυρίως. καὶ γάρ ἐστιν ἡ θυσία τῆς ἐκκλησίας λόγος ἀπὸ τῶν ἁγίων ψυχῶν ἀναθυμιώμενος, ἐκκαλυπτομένης ἅμα τῇ θυσίᾳ καὶ τῆς διανοίας ἁπάσης τῷ θεῷ. Ἀλλὰ τὸν μὲν ἀρχαιότατον βωμὸν ἐν Δήλῳ ἁγνὸν εἶναι τεθρυλήκασι, πρὸς ὃν δὴ μόνον καὶ Πυθαγόραν προσελθεῖν φασι φόνῳ καὶ θανάτῳ μὴ μιανθέντα· βωμὸν δὲ ἀληθῶς ἅγιον τὴν δικαίαν ψυχήν, καὶ τὸ ἀπ' αὐτῆς θυμίαμα τὴν ὁσίαν εὐχὴν λέγουσιν ἡμῖν ἀπιστήσουσιν; σαρκοφαγιῶν δ', οἶμαι, προφάσει αἱ θυσίαι τοῖς ἀνθρώποις ἐπινενόηνται. ἐξῆν δὲ καὶ ἄλλως ἄνευ τῆς τοιαύτης εἰδωλολατρίας μεταλαμβάνειν κρεῶν τὸν βουλόμενον. αἱ μὲν γὰρ κατὰ τὸν νόμον θυσίαι τὴν περὶ ἡμᾶς εὐσέβειαν ἀλληγοροῦσι, καθάπερ ἡ τρυγὼν καὶ ἡ περιστερὰ ὑπὲρ ἁμαρτιῶν προσφερόμεναι τὴν ἀποκάθαρσιν τοῦ ἀλόγου μέρους τῆς ψυχῆς προσδεκτὴν μηνύουσι τῷ θεῷ. εἰ δέ τις τῶν δικαίων οὐκ ἐπιφορτίζει τῇ τῶν κρεῶν βρώσει τὴν ψυχήν, λόγῳ τινὶ εὐλόγῳ χρῆται, οὐχ ᾧ Πυθαγόρας καὶ οἱ ἀπ' αὐτοῦ τὴν μετένδεσιν ὀνειροπολοῦντες τῆς ψυχῆς. δοκεῖ δὲ

---

9. ῥυθμῷ ἕλκει M. ῥυμουλκεῖ L. 11. οὐδὲν ἀνθρώπου (i.e. ἀνοῦ) M. οὐδὲν ἀνθρώπων vel ἡμῶν P. οὐδὲν L. 14. τῇ θυσίᾳ H. τῆς θυσίας L. 17. ὃν S. τὸν L. 23. εἰδωλολατρίας] Sic L, non εἰδωλολατρείας.

those received through the mouth, still they witness to respiration. § 32. What then is <the worshippers'> idea as to the breathing of God? Is it by means of transpiration as in the demons? or by inspiration only, as in fishes through the dilatation of their gills? or by circumspiration, as in insects through the pressure of the membranes on the waist? No, they would not liken God to any of these, if they were in their senses. But as for creatures that live by respiration, they draw in the air by rhythmic beats corresponding to the counter-dilatation of the lungs against the chest. Then if they assign viscera and arteries and veins and sinews and members to God, they will exhibit Him as in no respect differing from man. The word 'conspiration' is that which is properly used of the Church. For the Church's sacrifice is indeed speech rising, like incense, from holy souls, while every thought of the heart is laid open to God along with the sacrifice. They are fond of talking about the purity of the most ancient altar at Delos, that altar which, we are told, was the only one approached by Pythagoras, because it was unpolluted by slaughter and death: will they then refuse credence to us when we say that the truly hallowed altar is the righteous soul, and the incense which ascends from it, the prayer of holiness? Sacrifices, I believe, are an invention of mankind to excuse the eating of flesh, though, even apart from such idolatry, it was always possible for one who wished it to partake of flesh. The Mosaic sacrifices symbolize personal piety: for instance the dove and the pigeon offered for sins show that the purging away of the irrational part of the soul is acceptable to God. But if any of the righteous refuses to weigh down his soul by the eating of flesh, he does this on some reasonable ground, not as Pythagoras and his school from some dream as to the transmigration of souls. Xenocrates in a special treatise

Ξενοκράτης ἰδίᾳ πραγματευόμενος περὶ τῆς ἀπὸ τῶν ζῴων τροφῆς καὶ Πολέμων ἐν τοῖς περὶ τοῦ κατὰ φύσιν βίου συντάγμασι σαφῶς λέγειν ὡς ἀσύμφορόν ἐστιν ἡ διὰ τῶν σαρκῶν τροφὴ εἰργασμένη ἤδη καὶ ἐξομοιουμένη ταῖς τῶν ἀλόγων ψυχαῖς.

33. Ταύτῃ καὶ μάλιστα Ἰουδαῖοι χοιρείου ἀπέχονται, ὡς ἂν τοῦ θηρίου τούτου μιαροῦ ὄντος, ἐπεὶ μάλιστα τῶν ἄλλων τοὺς καρποὺς ἀνορύσσει καὶ φθείρει. ἐὰν δὲ λέγωσι τοῖς ἀνθρώποις δεδόσθαι τὰ ζῷα, καὶ ἡμεῖς συνομολογοῦμεν, πλὴν οὐ πάντως εἰς βρῶσιν, οὐδὲ μὴν πάντα, ἀλλ᾽ ὅσα ἀεργά. διόπερ οὐ κακῶς ὁ κωμικὸς Πλάτων ἐν ταῖς Ἑορταῖς τῷ δράματί φησιν

τῶν γὰρ τετραπόδων οὐδὲν ἀποκτείνειν ἔδει
ἡμᾶς τὸ λοιπόν, πλὴν ὑῶν· τὰ γὰρ κρέα
ἥδιστ᾽ ἔχουσι, κοὐδὲν ἀφ᾽ ὑὸς γίγνεται
πλὴν ὕστριχες καὶ πηλὸς ἡμῖν καὶ βοή.

ὅθεν καὶ ὁ Αἴσωπος οὐ κακῶς ἔφη τοὺς ὗς κεκραγέναι μέγιστον, ὅταν ἕλκωνται· συνειδέναι γὰρ αὑτοῖς εἰς οὐδὲν ἄλλο χρησίμοις πλὴν εἰς τὴν θυσίαν. διὸ καὶ Κλεάνθης φησὶν ἀνθ᾽ ἁλῶν αὐτοὺς ἔχειν τὴν ψυχήν, ἵνα μὴ σαπῇ τὰ κρέα. οἱ μὲν οὖν ὡς ἄχρηστον ἐσθίουσιν, οἱ δ᾽ ὡς λυμαντικὸν τῶν καρπῶν, καὶ ἄλλοι, διὰ τὸ κατωφερὲς εἰς συνουσίαν εἶναι τὸ ζῷον, οὐκ ἐσθίουσιν. ταύτῃ οὐδὲ τὸν τράγον ὁ νόμος θύει πλὴν ἐπὶ μόνῃ τῇ διοπομπήσει τῶν κακῶν, ἐπεὶ μητρόπολις κακίας ἡδονή. αὐτίκα καὶ συμβάλλεσθαι τὴν τῶν

4, 5. ἐξομοιουμένη] fort. ἐξωμοιωμένη M.   14, 15. ἔδει ἡμᾶς S.   ἐῶ ὑμᾶς Kock. ἡμᾶς ἔδει L. ἡμᾶς om. MS. Ottob.   15. ἡμᾶς] ὑμᾶς Cobet.   ὑῶν corr. ex υἱῶν L.   16. ἥδιστ᾽—κοὐδὲν S.   ἥδιστα—καὶ οὐδὲν L.   17. ὕστριχες LH. ὑστριχὶς D.   ἡμῖν hoc loco Heinsius (ὑμῖν Cobet.), post ὕστριχες L. 18. κακῶς] καλῶς L.   19. ὅταν ἕλκωνται post χρησίμοις L. Transposuit Rittershus.   αὑτοῖς] αὐτοῖς L.   20. πλὴν aut πλὴν ἢ Rittersh. ἢ πλὴν (ἢ pr. m. supra lineam) L.   23. λυμαντικὸν S. λοιμαντικὸν L.   26. διοπομπήσει LH. ἀποδιοπομπήσει D.

on animal food and Polemon in his book on Life according to Nature, seem to lay it down clearly that a flesh diet is inexpedient, as it has already passed through a process of digestion and been thus assimilated to the souls of irrational creatures.

§ 33. On this ground especially the Jews abstain from swine's flesh, considering that this animal is unclean because it roots up and destroys the fruits more than any other. But if it is argued that the animals are given to men, we too agree in this, only we say that they are not given entirely, nor indeed all, for the purpose of eating, but only those that do no work. Wherefore the comic poet Plato in his play of The Feasts[1] well says *Hereafter 'twere well to kill no beast but swine, for they are excellent eating, and we get nothing out of them but bristles and mire and squealing.* Hence it was well said by Aesop that *the reason why pigs make such an outcry when they are being dragged away is because they are conscious that they are good for nothing but to be sacrificed.* And so Cleanthes says that in them *the soul takes the place of salt to prevent the flesh from putrefying.* Some then eat it because it is useless, and others because it injures the fruits; while others again abstain from eating it because of its immoderate salacity. For the same reason the law never requires the sacrifice of a goat except with a view to banishing evils, since pleasure is the fountain-head of vice. Further, they tell us that the eating of goats'

---

[1] Kock, *Com. Fr.* I. p. 607.

τραγείων κρεῶν βρῶσιν πρὸς ἐπιληψίαν λέγουσι. φασὶ δὲ πλείστην ἀνάδοσιν ἐκ χοιρείων γίνεσθαι κρεῶν, διὸ τοῖς μὲν ἀσκοῦσι τὸ σῶμα χρησιμεύει, τοῖς δὲ αὐτὴν τὴν ψυχὴν αὔξειν ἐπιχειροῦσι διὰ τὴν νωθρίαν τὴν ἀπὸ τῆς κρεοφαγίας ἐγγινομένην οὐκέτι. τάχ᾽ ἄν τις τῶν γνωστικῶν καὶ ἀσκήσεως χάριν σαρκοφαγίας ἀπόσχοιτο καὶ τοῦ μὴ σφριγᾶν περὶ τὰ ἀφροδίσια τὴν σάρκα. οἶνος γάρ, φησὶν Ἀνδροκύδης, καὶ σαρκῶν ἐμφορήσεις σῶμα μὲν ῥωμαλέον ἀπεργάζονται, ψυχὴν δὲ νωχαλεστέραν. ἄθετος οὖν ἡ τοιαύτη τροφὴ πρὸς σύνεσιν ἀκριβῆ. διὸ καὶ Αἰγύπτιοι ἐν ταῖς κατ᾽ αὐτοὺς ἁγνείαις οὐκ ἐπιτρέπουσι τοῖς ἱερεῦσι σιτεῖσθαι σάρκας, ὀρνιθείοις τε ὡς κουφοτάτοις χρῶνται, καὶ ἰχθύων οὐχ ἅπτονται καὶ δι᾽ ἄλλους μέν τινας μύθους, μάλιστα δὲ ὡς πλαδαρὰν τὴν σάρκα τῆς τοιᾶσδε κατασκευαζούσης βρώσεως. 34. Ἤδη δὲ τὰ μὲν χερσαῖα καὶ τὰ πτηνὰ τὸν αὐτὸν ταῖς ἡμετέραις ψυχαῖς ἀναπνέοντα ἀέρα τρέφεται, συγγενῆ τῷ ἀέρι τὴν ψυχὴν κεκτημένα, τοὺς δὲ ἰχθῦς οὐδὲ ἀναπνεῖν φασι τοῦτον τὸν ἀέρα, ἀλλ᾽ ἐκεῖνον ὃς ἐγκέκραται τῷ ὕδατι εὐθέως κατὰ τὴν πρώτην γένεσιν, καθάπερ καὶ τοῖς λοιποῖς στοιχείοις, ὃ καὶ δεῖγμα τῆς ὑλικῆς διαμονῆς.

Δεῖ τοίνυν θυσίας προσφέρειν τῷ θεῷ μὴ πολυτελεῖς, ἀλλὰ θεοφιλεῖς, καὶ τὸ θυμίαμα ἐκεῖνο τὸ σύνθετον τὸ ἐν τῷ νόμῳ τὸ ἐκ πολλῶν γλωσσῶν τε καὶ φωνῶν κατὰ τὴν εὐχὴν συγκείμενον, μᾶλλον δὲ τὸ ἐκ διαφόρων ἐθνῶν τε καὶ φύσεων τῇ κατὰ τὰς διαθήκας δόσει σκευαζόμενον εἰς τὴν ἑνότητα τῆς πίστεως καὶ κατὰ τοὺς αἴνους συναγόμενον, καθαρῷ μὲν τῷ νῷ, δικαίᾳ δὲ καὶ ὀρθῇ τῇ πολιτείᾳ, ἐξ ὁσίων ἔργων εὐχῆς τε δικαίας· ἐπεὶ

4, 5. νωθρίαν LH. νωθρείαν Kl. D.   10. ἄθετος S. ἄθεος L.
18. συγγενῆ SPH. συγγενεῖ LD.   22. δεῖγμα] fort. δεσμὸς vel ἔρεισμα M.
30. συναγόμενον S. συναγόμενα L.

flesh conduces to epilepsy. And they say that the largest amount of nutriment is supplied from pork, for which reason it is of use to those who practise bodily training, but, owing to the sluggishness produced by eating flesh, it is of no use to those who try to encourage the growth of the soul. A gnostic might therefore abstain from flesh, both for the sake of discipline and to weaken the sexual appetite. For, as Androcydes says, *wine and fleshly gorging make the body strong, but the soul more sluggish*. Such a diet does not tend to precision of thought. Wherefore also the Egyptians in their purifications forbid their priests to eat flesh, and they themselves live on fowl as the lightest diet and abstain from fish for various fanciful reasons and especially from the idea that such food makes the flesh flabby. § 34. Besides this, the life of beasts and birds is supported by breathing the same air as our souls, their soul being akin to the air; but we are told that fishes do not even breathe our air, but that air which was infused into water, as into the other elements, on its first creation, which infusion is also the binding principle of the permanence of matter.

It is not then expensive sacrifices that we should offer to God, but such sacrifices as are dear to Him[1], viz. that *composite incense* of which the Law speaks[2], an incense compounded of many tongues and voices in the way of prayer, or rather which is being wrought into *the unity of the faith*[3] out of divers nations and dispositions by the divine bounty shown in the Covenants, and which is brought together in our songs of praise by purity of heart and righteous and upright living grounded in holy actions and righteous prayer. For (to add the charm of poetry)

---

[1] Theophr. *ap.* Porph. *Abst.* II. 19.   [2] Exod. xxx. 25.   [3] Eph. iv. 13.

τίς ὧδε μῶρος,

κατὰ τὴν ποιητικὴν χάριν,

καὶ λίαν ἀνειμένως
εὔπειστος ἀνδρῶν, ὅστις ἐλπίζει θεοὺς
ὀστῶν ἀσάρκων καὶ χολῆς πυρουμένης,
ἃ καὶ κυσὶν πεινῶσιν οὐχὶ βρώσιμα,
χαίρειν ἅπαντας καὶ γέρας λαχεῖν τόδε,

καὶ χάριν τούτων τοῖς δρῶσιν ἐκτίνειν, κἂν πειραταὶ κἂν λησταὶ κἂν τύραννοι τύχωσιν; φαμὲν δ' ἡμεῖς ἁγιάζειν τὸ πῦρ, οὐ τὰ κρέα, ἀλλὰ τὰς ἁμαρτωλοὺς ψυχάς, πῦρ οὐ τὸ παμφάγον καὶ βάναυσον, ἀλλὰ τὸ ϕρόνιμον λέγοντες, τὸ διϊκνούμενον διὰ ψυχῆς τῆς διερχομένης τὸ πῦρ.

ΚΕΦ. Ζ.

35. Σέβειν δὲ δεῖν ἐγκελευόμεθα καὶ τιμᾶν τὸν υἱὸν καὶ λόγον, σωτῆρά τε αὐτὸν καὶ ἡγεμόνα εἶναι πεισθέντες, καὶ δι' αὐτοῦ τὸν πατέρα, οὐκ ἐν ἐξαιρέτοις ἡμέραις, ὥσπερ ἄλλοι τινές, ἀλλὰ συνεχῶς τὸν ὅλον βίον τοῦτο πράττοντες καὶ κατὰ πάντα τρόπον   ἀμέλει τὸ γένος τὸ ἐκλεκτόν "ἑπτάκις τῆς ἡμέρας ἤνεσά ϲοι" φησί, κατ' ἐντολὴν δικαιούμενον. ὅθεν οὔτε ὡρισμένον τόπον οὔτε ἐξαίρετον ἱερὸν οὐδὲ μὴν ἑορτάς τινας καὶ ἡμέρας ἀποτεταγμένας, ἀλλὰ τὸν πάντα βίον ὁ γνωστικὸς ἐν παντὶ τόπῳ, κἂν καθ' ἑαυτὸν μόνος ὢν τυγχάνῃ, κἂν ὅπου τινὰς ἂν τῶν ὁμοίως πεπιστευκότων ἔχῃ, τιμᾷ

---

1. Hos versus citant Porphyr. περὶ ἀποχῆς ΙΙ. 58, et Cyril. adv. Jul. 9. p. 306.   μῶρος Porphyrius. μωρὸς L.   8. ἀνειμένως Grotius. ἀνειμένος L.   4. εὔπειστος Meinek. et S. in Ind. εὔπιστος L.   ἐλπίζει] ἐλπίζῃ Cyr.   6. κυσὶν] κυσὶ L.   7. ἅπαντας Porph. et Cyr. ἅπαντα L.   ἀπαρχῇ Grotius. ἀπαρχαῖς Porson. ad Eur. Hec. 41 et Kock.   8. ἐκτίνειν S. ἐκτείνειν L.   15. υἱὸν M. αὐτὸν L.   20. ὡρισμένον L. fort. καθ' ὡρισμένον vel ὡρ. οἶδε M.   21. οὔτε ἐξαίρετον] οὐδὲ ἐξαίρετον L.   23. κἂν ὅπου M. καὶ ὅπου L.   24. ὁμοίως S. ὁμοίων L.

what man is there so unwise and beyond measure credulous as to expect that, at the burning of bare bones and gall, which even hungry dogs would refuse, the gods would all rejoice, and accept this as their due meed[1]; aye, and would show their gratitude to the celebrants, though they might be pirates or robbers or tyrants? The Christian teaching is that the fire sanctifies, not flesh, but sinful souls, understanding by fire not the all-devouring flame of common life, but the *discerning flame*[2] which *pierces through*[3] *the soul that walks through fire*[4].

CHAPTER VII.

§ 35. Further, we are bidden to worship and honour the Son and Word, being persuaded that He is both Saviour and Ruler, and to honour the Father through Him, doing this not on special days, as some others do, but continuously all our life through, and in all possible ways; (though it is true *the chosen race*[5], being justified by obedience to the precept, say *Seven times a day did I praise Thee*[6]). Wherefore it is neither in a definite place or special shrine, nor yet on certain feasts and days set apart, that the gnostic honours God, returning thanks

---

[1] Kock, *Fragm.* III. p. 606.
[2] Clem. P. 995; Isa. iv. 4; 1 Cor. iii. 13.
[3] Heb. iv. 12. [4] Is. xliii. 2.
[5] 1 Pet. ii. 9. [6] Ps. cxix. 164.

τὸν θεόν, τουτέστιν χάριν ὁμολογεῖ τῆς γνώσεως καὶ τῆς πολιτείας. εἰ δὲ ἡ παρουσία τινὸς ἀνδρὸς ἀγαθοῦ διὰ τὴν ἐντροπὴν καὶ τὴν αἰδῶ πρὸς τὸ κρεῖττον ἀεὶ σχηματίζει τὸν ἐντυγχάνοντα, πῶς οὐ μᾶλλον ὁ συμπαρὼν ἀεὶ διὰ τῆς γνώσεως καὶ τοῦ βίου καὶ τῆς εὐχαριστίας ἀδιαλείπτως τῷ θεῷ οὐκ εὐλόγως ἂν ἑαυτοῦ παρ' ἕκαστα κρείττων εἴη εἰς πάντα καὶ τὰ ἔργα καὶ τοὺς λόγους καὶ τὴν διάθεσιν; τοιοῦτος ὁ πάντῃ παρεῖναι τὸν θεὸν πεπεισμένος, οὐχὶ δὲ ἐν τόποις τισὶν ὡρισμένοις κατακεκλεισμένον ὑπολαβών, ἵνα δὴ χωρὶς αὐτοῦ ποτε οἰηθεὶς εἶναι καὶ νύκτα καὶ μεθ' ἡμέραν ἀκολασταίνῃ. πάντα τοίνυν τὸν βίον ἑορτὴν ἄγοντες, πάντῃ πάντοθεν παρεῖναι τὸν θεὸν πεπεισμένοι, γεωργοῦμεν αἰνοῦντες, πλέομεν ὑμνοῦντες, κατὰ τὴν ἄλλην πολιτείαν ἐνθέως ἀναστρεφόμεθα. προσεχέστερον δὲ ὁ γνωστικὸς οἰκειοῦται θεῷ σεμνὸς ὢν ἅμα καὶ ἱλαρὸς ἐν πᾶσι, σεμνὸς μὲν διὰ τὴν ἐπὶ τὸ θεῖον ἐπιστροφήν, ἱλαρὸς δὲ διὰ τὸν ἐπιλογισμὸν τῶν ἀνθρωπείων ἀγαθῶν ὧν ἔδωκεν ἡμῖν ὁ θεός.

36. Φαίνεται δὲ τὸ ἔξοχον τῆς γνώσεως ὁ προφήτης ὧδε παριστάς, χρηϲτότητα καὶ παιδείαν καὶ γνῶϲιν δίδαξόν με· κατ' ἐπανάβασιν αὐξήσας τὸ ἡγεμονικὸν τῆς τελειότητος. οὗτος ἄρα ὄντως ὁ βασιλικὸς ἄνθρωπος, οὗτος ἱερεὺς ὅσιος τοῦ θεοῦ, ὅπερ ἔτι καὶ νῦν παρὰ τοῖς λογιωτάτοις τῶν βαρβάρων σῴζεται τὸ ἱερατικὸν γένος εἰς βασιλείαν προσαγόντων. οὗτος οὖν οὐδαμῇ μὲν ἑαυτὸν εἰς ὀχλοκρασίαν τὴν τῶν θεάτρων δεσπότιν ἐνδίδωσιν· τὰ λεγόμενα δὲ καὶ πραττόμενα καὶ ὁρώμενα ἡδονῆς ἀγωγοῦ χάριν οὐδὲ ὄναρ προσίεται· οὔτ' οὖν ταύτας τὰς ἡδονὰς τῆς θέας οὔτε τὰς διὰ τῶν ἄλλων ἀπολαυσμάτων ποικιλίας, οἷον θυμιαμάτων πολυτέλειαν

1, 2. καὶ (compendio expressum) τῆς πολιτείας L. καὶ om. V.
11. νύκτα L. fort. νύκτωρ M. 15. ἐνθέως H. ἐντέχνως L. δὲ M. δὴ L.

to Him for knowledge bestowed and the gift of the <heavenly> citizenship[1]; but he will do this all his life in every place, whether he be alone by himself or have with him some who share his belief. And if the presence of some good man always moulds for the better one who converses with him, owing to the respect and reverence which he inspires, with much more reason must he, who is always in the uninterrupted presence of God by means of his knowledge and his life and his thankful spirit, be raised above himself on every occasion, both in regard to his actions and his words and his temper. Such is he who believes that God is everywhere present, and does not suppose Him to be shut up in certain definite places, so as to be tempted to incontinence by the imagination, forsooth, that he could ever be apart from God whether by day or night. Accordingly all our life is a festival: being persuaded that God is everywhere present on all sides, we praise Him as we till the ground, we sing hymns as we sail the sea, we feel His inspiration in all that we do. And the gnostic enjoys a still closer intimacy with God, being at once serious and cheerful in everything, serious owing to his thoughts being turned towards heaven, and cheerful, as he reckons up the blessings with which God has enriched our human life.

§ 36. But the pre-eminence of knowledge is plainly set forth by the prophet in the words *Teach me goodness and instruction and knowledge*[2], where he presents in an ascending scale the guiding principle of perfection. Here then we truly have the royal man, the holy priest of God,—a combination which is still retained even at the present time among the most enlightened of the barbarians, who employ the priestly caste for government. Such an one is far from surrendering himself to the mob-government which tyrannizes over the theatres; and as for the things which are there said and done and seen with a view to the allurements of pleasure, he repudiates them even in a dream. He repudiates therefore both these spectacular pleasures and the other refinements of luxury, such as costly perfumes flattering the sense of smell, or

---

[1] Phil. iii. 20.
[2] Ps. cxix. 66 (LXX.).

τὴν ὄσφρησιν γοητεύουσαν, ἢ βρωμάτων συγκαττύσεις καὶ τὰς ἐξ οἴνων διαφόρων ἀπολαύσεις δελεαζούσας τὴν γεῦσιν, οὐδὲ τὰς πολυανθεῖς καὶ εὐώδεις πλοκὰς ἐκθηλυνούσας δι' αἰσθήσεως τὴν ψυχήν· πάντων δὲ τὴν σεμνὴν ἀπόλαυσιν ἐπὶ τὸν θεὸν ἀναγαγὼν ἀεί, καὶ τῆς βρώσεως καὶ τοῦ πόματος καὶ τοῦ χρίσματος, τῷ δοτῆρι τῶν ὅλων ἀπάρχεται, χάριν ὁμολογῶν καὶ τῆς δωρεᾶς καὶ τῆς χρήσεως διὰ λόγου τοῦ δοθέντος αὐτῷ· σπανίως εἰς τὰς ἑστιάσεις τὰς συμποτικὰς ἁπάντων, πλὴν εἰ μὴ τὸ φιλικὸν καὶ ὁμονοητικὸν ἐπαγγελλόμενον αὐτῷ τὸ συμπόσιον ἀφικέσθαι προτρέψαι. πέπεισται γὰρ εἰδέναι πάντα τὸν θεὸν καὶ ἐπαΐειν, οὐχ ὅτι τῆς φωνῆς μόνον, ἀλλὰ καὶ τῆς ἐννοίας, ἐπεὶ καὶ ἡ ἀκοὴ ἐν ἡμῖν, διὰ σωματικῶν πόρων ἐνεργουμένη, οὐ διὰ τῆς σωματικῆς δυνάμεως ἔχει τὴν ἀντίληψιν, ἀλλὰ διά τινος ψυχικῆς αἰσθήσεως καὶ τῆς διακριτικῆς τῶν σημαινουσῶν τι φωνῶν νοήσεως.

37. Οὔκουν ἀνθρωποειδὴς ὁ θεὸς τοῦδ' ἕνεκα ἵνα ἀκούσῃ, οὐδὲ αἰσθήσεων αὐτῷ δεῖ, καθάπερ ἤρεσεν τοῖς Στωικοῖς, μάλιστα ἀκοῆς καὶ ὄψεως κατὰ τὸ εὐπαθὲς τοῦ ἀέρος, μὴ γὰρ δύνασθαί ποτε ἑτέρως ἀντιλαβέσθαι· ἀλλὰ καὶ ἡ ὀξυτάτη συναίσθησις τῶν ἀγγέλων, ἥ τε τοῦ συνειδότος ἐπαφωμένη τῆς ψυχῆς δύναμις, δυνάμει τινὶ ἀρρήτῳ καὶ ἄνευ τῆς αἰσθητῆς ἀκοῆς ἅμα νοήματι πάντα γινώσκει. κἂν μὴ τὴν φωνήν τις ἐξικνεῖσθαι πρὸς τὸν θεὸν λέγῃ κάτω περὶ τὸν ἀέρα κυλινδουμένην, ἀλλὰ τὰ νοήματα τῶν ἁγίων τέμνει οὐ μόνον τὸν ἀέρα, ἀλλὰ καὶ τὸν ὅλον κόσμον. φθάνει δὲ ἡ θεία δύναμις, καθάπερ φῶς, ὅλην διιδεῖν τὴν ψυχήν.

1. συγκαττύσεις] συγκαταρτύσεις Jackson.   3. οὐδὲ] fort. οὔτε M.
8. τῆς δωρεᾶς H. διὰ τῆς δ. L.   χρήσεως S. χρίσεως L.   14. ἐν ἡμῖν Canter. μὲν ἡμῖν L.   18. τοῦδ' S. τοῦθ' L.   ἕνεκα ἵνα M. ἕνεκα καὶ ἵνα (per διττολογίαν) L.   20. Στωικοῖς] fort. hic legendum 'Επικουρείοις, verbis καθάπερ—Στωικοῖς post ἀντιλαβέσθαι (l. 22) repetitis M.   κατὰ τὸ εὐπαθὲς τοῦ ἀέρος hic M.   καὶ τὸ...ἀέρος post ἀλλὰ l. 22 L.   21, 22. ἀντιλαβέσθαι L. ἀντιλαμβάνεσθαι V.   24. τινὶ ἀρρήτῳ H. τῇ ἀρρ. L.

combinations of meats and the attractions of various wines enticing the palate, or fragrant wreaths of a variety of flowers which enfeeble the soul through the sense. Enjoying all things soberly, he refers his enjoyment in every case to God as its author, whether it be of food or drink or ointment, and offers to the Giver firstfruits of the whole, using the speech which He has bestowed, to thank Him both for the gift and for the use of it. But he seldom appears at convivial entertainments unless the banquet invites his attendance by promise of friendly intercourse with those of like mind. For he is persuaded that God knows all things, and hears not only the voice but the thought, since even in our own case the hearing, though set in action by means of the passages of the body, causes apprehension, not by the power of the body, but by a certain mental impression and by the intelligence which distinguishes between significant sounds.

§ 37. There is consequently no need for God to be in human shape in order that He may hear, nor does He need senses, as <the Epicureans> held, especially hearing and sight, dependent <as the Stoics held> on the sensitiveness of the air (as though He would otherwise be incapable of apprehension): but indeed the instantaneous perception of the angels, and the power of conscience touching the soul— these recognize all things with the quickness of thought by means of some indescribable faculty apart from sensible hearing. Even if one should say that it was impossible for the voice, rolling in this lower air, to reach to God, still the thoughts of the saints cleave, not the air alone, but the whole universe as well. And the divine power instantly penetrates

τί δ'; οὐχὶ καὶ αἱ προαιρέσεις φθάνουσι πρὸς τὸν θεὸν
προϊεῖσαι τὴν φωνὴν τὴν ἑαυτῶν; οὐχὶ δὲ καὶ ὑπὸ
τῆς συνειδήσεως πορθμεύονταί τινα; τίνα καὶ φωνὴν
ἀναμεῖναι ἂν ὁ κατὰ πρόθεcιν τὸν ἐκλεκτὸν καὶ πρὸ τῆc
5 γενέcεωc τὸ ἐσόμενον ὡς ἤδη ὑπάρχον ἐγνωκώc; ἢ οὐχὶ
πάντη εἰς τὸ βάθος τῆς ψυχῆς ἁπάσης τὸ φῶς τῆς
δυνάμεως ἐκλάμπει, τὰ ταμιεῖα ἐρεγνῶντοc, ᾗ φησιν ἡ
γραφή, τοῷ λύχνοῳ τῆς δυνάμεως; ὅλοc ἀκοὴ καὶ ὅλος
ὀφθαλμόc, ἵνα τις τούτοις χρήσηται τοῖς ὀνόμασιν,
10 ὁ θεός.

38. Καθόλου τοίνυν οὐδεμίαν σῴζει θεοσέβειαν
οὔτε ἐν ὕμνοις οὔτε ἐν λόγοις, ἀλλ' οὐδὲ ἐν γραφαῖς ἢ
δόγμασιν, ἡ μὴ πρέπουσα περὶ τοῦ θεοῦ ὑπόληψις,
ἀλλ' εἰς ταπεινὰς καὶ ἀσχήμονας ἐκτρεπομένη ἐννοίας
15 τε καὶ ὑπονοίας. ὅθεν ἡ τῶν πολλῶν εὐφημία δυσφημίας
οὐδὲν διαφέρει διὰ τὴν τῆς ἀληθείας ἄγνοιαν. Ὧν μὲν
οὖν αἱ ὀρέξεις εἰσὶ καὶ ἐπιθυμίαι καὶ ὅλως εἰπεῖν αἱ
ὁρμαί, τούτων εἰσὶ καὶ αἱ εὐχαί. [διόπερ οὐδεὶς ἐπιθυμεῖ
πόματος, ἀλλὰ τοῦ πιεῖν τὸ ποτόν, οὐδὲ μὴν κληρονομίας,
20 ἀλλὰ τοῦ κληρονομῆσαι, οὑτωσὶ δὲ οὐδὲ γνώσεως,
ἀλλὰ τοῦ γνῶναι· οὐδὲ γὰρ πολιτείας ὀρθῆς, ἀλλὰ τοῦ
πολιτεύεσθαι.] τούτων οὖν αἱ εὐχαὶ ὧν καὶ αἰτήσεις,
καὶ τούτων αἱ αἰτήσεις ὧν καὶ ἐπιθυμίαι. τὸ δὲ εὔχεσθαι
καὶ ὀρέγεσθαι καταλλήλως γίνεται εἰς τὸ ἔχειν τὰ
25 ἀγαθὰ καὶ τὰ παρακείμενα ὠφελήματα τῇ κτήσει.
ὁ τοίνυν γνωστικὸς τὴν εὐχὴν καὶ τὴν αἴτησιν τῶν
ὄντως ἀγαθῶν τῶν περὶ ψυχὴν ποιεῖται, καὶ εὔχεται
συνεργῶν ἅμα καὶ αὐτὸς εἰς ἕξιν ἀγαθότητος ἐλθεῖν,

---

3. συνειδήσεως] fort. συναισθήσεως M. πορθμεύονται; τίνα καὶ Heinsius. D. πορθ. τινα, καὶ L. fort. πορθμεύονταί τινα; τίνα καὶ M. 4. ἀναμεῖναι ἂν DH. ἀναμεῖναι S. ἀναμεῖναι L. 7. ᾗ] ἢ L. 23. ἐπιθυμίαι. M. ἐπιθυμίαι, D. 24. καταλλήλως Heinsius. κατ' ἀλλήλους L. καταλλήλους S. γίνεται P. γίνεσθαι L. 25. ὠφελήματα τῇ κτήσει. ὁ τοίνυν H. ὠφελήματα. τῇ κτήσει τοίνυν ὁ LD.

the whole soul, like light. Again do not our resolves also find their way to God, uttering a voice of their own? And are not some things also wafted heaven-ward by the conscience? Moreover can we conceive that He Who has *known* His elect *according to His eternal purpose*[1], and known *before its birth*[2] that which was to be, as already existing, must wait for the sound of a voice? Is it not true that the light of power shines forth in all directions even to the very bottom of the soul, since *the candle* of power, as the Scripture says, *searches the secret chambers*[3]? God is *all ear and all eye*[4], if one may make use of these expressions.

§ 38. Where then there is an unworthy conception of God, passing into base and unseemly thoughts and significations, it is impossible to preserve any sort of devoutness either in hymns or discourses or even in writings or doctrines. For which reason what most men call reverence is indistinguishable from irreverence, owing to their ignorance of the truth. Now the objects of the appetites and desires and of impulses generally are also the objects of our prayers. We pray therefore for the same things that we request, and we request the same things that we desire: and praying and longing are on the same footing as regards the possession of good things and the benefits attached to their acquisition. Accordingly the gnostic makes his prayer and request for the things that are really good, *i.e.* those pertaining to the soul, and he prays, and joins his own efforts as well, that he may attain to a habit of goodness; so that he may no longer have his good things attached to him like ornaments, but may be himself good. [Wherefore no one desires drink in the abstract but to drink, nor an inheritance, but to inherit; and in like manner no one desires knowledge,

---

[1] Rom. viii. 28, 29, ix. 11.   [2] Sus. 42.   [3] Prov. xx. 27.
[4] See above, § 5.

ὡς μηκέτι ἔχειν τὰ ἀγαθὰ καθάπερ ἀναθήματά τινα παρακείμενα, εἶναι δὲ ἀγαθόν.

39. Διὸ καὶ τούτοις μάλιστα προσήκει εὔχεσθαι τοῖς εἰδόσι τὸ θεῖον ὡς χρὴ καὶ τὴν πρόσφορον ἀρετὴν ἔχουσιν αὐτῷ, οἳ ἴσασι τίνα τὰ ὄντως ἀγαθὰ καὶ τίνα αἰτητέον καὶ πότε καὶ πῶς ἕκαστα. ἐσχάτη δὲ ἀμαθία παρὰ τῶν μὴ θεῶν ὡς θεῶν αἰτεῖσθαι, ᾗ τὰ μὴ συμφέροντα αἰτεῖσθαι, φαντασίᾳ ἀγαθῶν κακὰ αἰτουμένους σφίσιν. ὅθεν εἰκότως ἑνὸς ὄντος τοῦ ἀγαθοῦ θεοῦ παρ᾽ αὐτοῦ μόνου τῶν ἀγαθῶν τὰ μὲν δοθῆναι, τὰ δὲ παραμεῖναι εὐχόμεθα ἡμεῖς τε καὶ οἱ ἄγγελοι· ἀλλ᾽ οὐχ ὁμοίως, οὐ γάρ ἐστι ταὐτὸν αἰτεῖσθαι παραμεῖναι τὴν δόσιν ἢ τὴν ἀρχὴν σπουδάζειν λαβεῖν. καὶ ἡ ἀποτροπὴ δὲ τῶν κακῶν εἶδος εὐχῆς. ἀλλ᾽ οὐκ ἐπὶ τῇ τῶν ἀνθρώπων βλάβῃ τῇ τοιᾷδε συγχρηστέον εὐχῇ ποτε, πλὴν εἰ μὴ τὴν ἐπιστροφὴν τῆς δικαιοσύνης τεχναζόμενος τοῖς ἀπηλγηκόσιν ὁ γνωστικὸς οἰκονομοίη τὴν αἴτησιν. ἔστιν οὖν, ὡς εἰπεῖν τολμηρότερον, ὁμιλία πρὸς τὸν θεὸν ἡ εὐχή· κἂν ψιθυρίζοντες ἄρα μηδὲ τὰ χείλη ἀνοίγοντες μετὰ σιγῆς προσλαλῶμεν, ἔνδοθεν κεκράγαμεν· πᾶσαν γὰρ τὴν ἐνδιάθετον ὁμιλίαν ὁ θεὸς ἀδιαλείπτως ἐπαΐει.

40. Ταύτῃ καὶ προσανατείνομεν τὴν κεφαλὴν καὶ τὰς χεῖρας εἰς οὐρανὸν αἴρομεν τούς τε πόδας ἐπεγείρομεν κατὰ τὴν τελευταίαν τῆς εὐχῆς συνεκφώνησιν, ἐπακολουθοῦντες τῇ προθυμίᾳ τοῦ πνεύματος εἰς τὴν νοητὴν οὐσίαν, καὶ συναφιστάνειν τῷ λόγῳ τὸ σῶμα τῆς γῆς πειρώμενοι, μετάρσιον ποιησάμενοι, τὴν ψυχὴν ἐπτερωμένην τῷ πόθῳ τῶν κρειττόνων ἐπὶ τὰ ἅγια χωρεῖν βιαζόμεθα, τοῦ δεσμοῦ καταμεγαλοφρονοῦντες τοῦ σαρκικοῦ. ἴσμεν γὰρ εὖ μάλα τὸν γνωστικὸν τὴν

---

1. ἀναθήματα H. μαθήματα L.   4. πρόσφορον] Litteras op supra versum habet L.   5. τίνα ante τὰ in marg. pr. m. L.   ὄντος ex ὄντως corr. pr. m. L.   17. τοῖς D. τοῖς γ' S. τοῖς δ' L.

but to know; no, nor a right constitution, but to live under such a constitution[1].]

§ 39. Hence too prayer is most fitting for those who have a right knowledge of the Divinity and that excellence of character which is agreeable to Him, i.e. for those who know what are the things which are truly good, and what should be asked for, and when, and how, in each case. But it is the height of folly to ask of those who are not Gods as if they were Gods, or to ask what is inexpedient (*i.e.* what is evil for oneself), under the impression that it is good. Since then *the good God is One*[2], we and the angels are right in praying that we may receive from Him alone either the bestowal or continuance of good things. But we do not ask alike, for it is not the same thing to ask that the gift may be continued, and to strive to obtain it in the first instance. The warning of the bad is also a kind of prayer. But we must never employ a prayer of this kind for the injury of men, except where the gnostic might adapt his request so as to contrive for *those who were hardened*[3] their return to righteousness. Prayer, then, to speak somewhat boldly, is converse with God. Even if we address Him in a whisper, without opening our lips, or uttering a sound, still we cry to Him in our heart. For God never ceases to listen to the inward converse of the heart.

§ 40. For this reason also we raise the head and lift the hands towards heaven, and stand on tiptoe as we join in the closing outburst of prayer, following the eager flight of the spirit into the intelligible world: and while we thus endeavour to detach the body from the earth by lifting it upwards along with the uttered words, we spurn the fetters of the flesh and constrain *the soul, winged*[4] with desire of better things, to ascend into *the holy place*[5]. For we are well assured that of his own will the

---

[1] This sentence appears to be misplaced in the Greek.
[2] Matt. xix. 17. [3] See p. 21. [4] Plato, *Phaedr.* 246. [5] Heb. ix. 25.

ὑπέρβασιν παντὸς τοῦ κόσμου, ὥσπερ ἀμέλει τῆς Αἰγύπτου οἱ Ἰουδαῖοι, ἑκουσίως ποιούμενον, ἐνδεικνύμενον ἐναργῶς παντὸς μᾶλλον ὡς ὅτι μάλιστα σύνεγγυς ἔσοιτο τοῦ θεοῦ. εἰ δέ τινες καὶ ὥρας τακτὰς ἀπονέμουσιν εὐχῇ, ὡς τρίτην φέρε καὶ ἕκτην καὶ ἐνάτην, ἀλλ' οὖν γε ὁ γνωστικὸς παρὰ ὅλον εὔχεται τὸν βίον, δι' εὐχῆς συνεῖναι μὲν σπεύδων θεῷ, καταλελοιπέναι δέ, συνελόντι εἰπεῖν, πάντα ὅσα μὴ χρησιμεύει γενομένῳ ἐκεῖ, ὡς ἂν ἐνθένδε ἤδη τὴν τελείωσιν ἀπειληφὼς τοῦ κατὰ ἀγάπην δρωμένου. ἀλλὰ καὶ τὰς τῶν ὡρῶν διανομὰς τριχῇ διεσταμένας καὶ ταῖς ἴσαις εὐχαῖς τετιμημένας ἴσασιν οἱ γνωρίζοντες τὴν μακαρίαν τῶν ἁγίων τριάδα μονῶν.

41. Ἐνταῦθα γενόμενος ὑπεμνήσθην τῶν περὶ τοῦ μὴ δεῖν εὔχεσθαι πρός τινων ἑτεροδόξων, τουτέστιν τῶν ἀμφὶ τὴν Προδίκου αἵρεσιν, παρεισαγομένων δογμάτων. ἵνα οὖν μηδὲ ἐπὶ ταύτῃ αὐτῶν τῇ ἀθέῳ σοφίᾳ ὡς ξένῃ ὀγκύλλωνται αἱρέσει, μαθέτωσαν προειλῆφθαι μὲν ὑπὸ τῶν Κυρηναϊκῶν λεγομένων φιλοσόφων· ἀντιρρήσεως δ' ὅμως τεύξεται κατὰ καιρὸν ἡ τῶν ψευδωνύμων τούτων ἀνόσιος γνῶσις, ὡς μὴ νῦν παρεισδυομένη τὸ ὑπόμνημα οὐκ ὀλίγη οὖσα ἡ τούτων καταδρομὴ διακόπτῃ τὸν ἐν χερσὶ λόγον, δεικνύντων ἡμῶν μόνον ὄντως ὅσιον καὶ θεοσεβῆ τὸν τῷ ὄντι κατὰ τὸν ἐκκλησιαστικὸν κανόνα γνωστικόν, ᾧ μόνῳ ἡ αἴτησις κατὰ τὴν τοῦ θεοῦ βούλησιν ἀπονενεμημένη γίνεται καὶ αἰτήσαντι καὶ ἐννοηθέντι. ὥσπερ γὰρ πᾶν ὃ βούλεται δύναται ὁ θεός, οὕτως πᾶν ὃ ἂν αἰτήσῃ ὁ γνωστικὸς λαμβάνει. καθόλου γὰρ ὁ θεὸς οἶδεν τούς τε ἀξίους τῶν ἀγαθῶν καὶ μή· ὅθεν τὰ προσήκοντα ἑκάστοις δίδωσιν. διὸ πολλάκις μὲν αἰτήσασιν ἀναξίοις οὐκ ἂν δοίη, δοίη δὲ ἀξίοις δηλονότι ὑπάρχουσιν. οὐ

7. καταλελοιπέναι Jackson. καταλέλοιπεν L. 8. γενομένῳ H. γενόμενος L. 10. κατ' ἀγάπην Abbott. 26. ἀπονενεμημένη Heinsius. ἀπονενεμημένῳ L. 30, 31. μή· ὅθεν...δίδωσιν. M. μή· ὅθεν...δίδωσιν, D. 32. δοίη δέ] δοίη δὲ ἂν καὶ μὴ αἰτήσασιν Barnard.

gnostic leaves this world behind him, just as the Jews did Egypt, showing in the plainest way that he was destined to be as near as possible to God. And if there are any who assign fixed hours to prayer[1], such as the third and the sixth and the ninth, yet the gnostic at all events prays all his life through, striving to be united with God in prayer, and, in a word, to have done with everything that is useless for that higher life, as one who has already attained here below the perfection of loving action. However, the triple distribution of the hours and their observance by corresponding prayers is also familiar to those who are acquainted with the blessed triad of the holy *mansions*[2].

§ 41. At this point I am reminded of the opinions which are being secretly propagated by certain heterodox persons, belonging to the heresy of Prodicus, against the use of prayer. In order that they may not pride themselves on this their godless wisdom as though it were something novel, let these men learn that they are only following in the steps of the so-called Cyrenaic school. The refutation however of the impious knowledge of these *falsely called gnostics*[3] I reserve to its proper season, in order that the censure, which must be somewhat protracted, may not steal into my notes at this point and so interrupt the subject we have in hand; which is a demonstration that only he who is a gnostic according to the rule of the Church is really pious and devout, and that he alone has his petitions, whether oral or mental[4], granted according to the will of God. For as God is able to do every thing that He wills, so the gnostic *receives every thing that he may ask*[5]. For God knows generally those that are worthy to receive good things and those that are not; whence He gives to each what belongs to him. For this reason if request were made by unworthy persons He would often refuse to give it, but would give <unasked>

---

[1] See above, § 35. [2] See n. on § 9 and P. 797 on the Parable of the Sower.
[3] 1 Tim. vi. 20. [4] See below on § 73. [5] Mt. xxi. 22.

μὴν παρέλκει ἡ αἴτησις, κἂν χωρὶς ἀξιώσεως διδῶται τὰ ἀγαθά. αὐτίκα ἥ τε εὐχαριστία ἥ τε τῶν πέλας εἰς ἐπιστροφὴν αἴτησις ἔργον ἐστὶ τοῦ γνωστικοῦ. ᾗ καὶ ὁ κύριος ηὔχετο, εὐχαριστῶν μὲν ἐν οἷς ἐτελείωσεν τὴν διακονίαν, εὐχόμενος δὲ ὡς πλείστους ὅσους ἐν ἐπιγνώσει γενέσθαι, ἵν' ἐν τοῖς σωζομένοις διὰ τῆς κατ' ἐπίγνωσιν σωτηρίας ὁ θεός, ὁ μόνος ἀγαθὸς καὶ ὁ μόνος σωτήρ, δι' υἱοῦ δοξάζηται καὶ ἐξ αἰῶνος εἰς αἰῶνα ἐπιγινώσκηται. καίτοι καὶ ἡ πίστις τοῦ λήψεσθαι εἶδος εὐχῆς ἐναποκειμένης γνωστικῶς.

42. Ἀλλ' εἰ ἀφορμή τις ὁμιλίας τῆς πρὸς τὸν θεὸν γίνεται ἡ εὐχή, οὐδεμίαν ἀφορμὴν παραλειπτέον τῆς προσόδου τῆς πρὸς τὸν θεόν. ἀμέλει συμπλακεῖσα τῇ μακαρίᾳ προνοίᾳ ἡ τοῦ γνωστικοῦ ὁσιότης κατὰ τὴν ἑκούσιον ὁμολογίαν τελείαν τὴν εὐεργεσίαν ἐπιδείκνυσι τοῦ θεοῦ. οἱονεὶ γὰρ ἀντεπιστροφή τίς ἐστι τῆς προνοίας ἡ τοῦ γνωστικοῦ ὁσιότης καὶ ἀντίστροφος εὔνοια τοῦ φίλου τοῦ θεοῦ. οὔτε γὰρ ὁ θεὸς ἄκων ἀγαθὸς ὃν τρόπον τὸ πῦρ θερμαντικόν (ἑκούσιος δὲ ἡ τῶν ἀγαθῶν μετάδοσις αὐτῷ, κἂν προλαμβάνῃ τὴν αἴτησιν), οὔτε μὴν ἄκων σωθήσεται ὁ σωζόμενος, οὐ γάρ ἐστιν ἄψυχος, ἀλλὰ παντὸς μᾶλλον ἑκουσίως καὶ προαιρετικῶς σπεύσει πρὸς σωτηρίαν. διὸ καὶ τὰς ἐντολὰς ἔλαβεν ὁ ἄνθρωπος ὡς ἂν ἐξ αὐτοῦ ὁρμητικὸς πρὸς ὁπότερον οὖν καὶ βούλοιτο τῶν τε αἱρετῶν καὶ τῶν φευκτῶν. οὔκουν ὁ θεὸς ἀνάγκῃ ἀγαθοποιεῖ, κατὰ προαίρεσιν δὲ εὐποιεῖ τοὺς ἐξ αὐτῶν ἐπιστρέφοντας. οὐ γὰρ ὑπηρετική γέ ἐστιν ἡ εἰς ἡμᾶς θεόθεν ἥκουσα, οἷον ἐκ χειρόνων εἰς κρείττονας προϊοῦσα, ἡ πρόνοια. κατ' ἔλεον δὲ τῆς ἡμετέρας ἀσθενείας αἱ προσεχεῖς τῆς προνοίας ἐνεργοῦνται οἰκονομίαι, καθάπερ καὶ ἡ τῶν

---

1. διδῶται] δίδοται L. 7. κατ' ἐπίγνωσιν σωτηρίας M. σωτηρίας κατ ἐπίγνωσιν L. 8. δοξάζηται καὶ post υἱοῦ M. post θεός (l. 7) L. 9. ἐπιγινώσκηται. H. ἐπιγινώσκηται, D. ἐπιγινώσκεται L. 11. ἀφορμή] μορφή Barnard. 24. αὐτοῦ H. αὑτοῦ L. 25. οὖν M. ἂν L. 27. αὐτῶν P. αὑτῶν L.

provided they were worthy. Yet the petition is not superfluous, even though good things be granted without petition made. For instance, both thanksgiving and prayer for the conversion of his neighbours are the duty of the gnostic. Thus the Lord also prayed, returning thanks for the *accomplishment of his ministry*[1] and praying *that as many as possible might share in knowledge*[2], in order that God, *who alone is good*, alone is Saviour, *may be glorified through His Son*[3], in those who are being *saved through the salvation which is according to knowledge*[4], and that the knowledge of Him may grow from age to age. Howbeit the mere faith that one will receive is itself also a kind of prayer stored up in a gnostic spirit.

§ 42. But if prayer is thus an occasion for converse with God[5], no occasion for our approach to God must be neglected. Certainly the holiness of the gnostic, being bound up with the Divine Providence through a voluntary acknowledgment on his part, shows the beneficence of God in perfection. For the holiness of the gnostic is, as it were, a return back on itself of Providence and a responsive feeling of loyalty on the part of the friend of God. For neither is the goodness of God involuntary like the warmth of fire (but His imparting of good things is voluntary, even though He should wait to be asked); nor on the other hand will the man who is being saved be saved without his will, for he is no lifeless machine, but will most assuredly hasten to salvation with eager alacrity. It is on this account that the commandments were given to man as to a being who would be spontaneously impelled to whichever he might choose, whether of things eligible or ineligible. God therefore does not do good of necessity, but of His own free will He befriends those who turn to Him of their own accord. For the providence that comes to us from God is not ministrative[6], as though it proceeded from inferiors to superiors; but it is from pity of our weakness that the nearer dispensations

---

[1] Joh. xvii. 4. [2] Joh. xvii. 20, 23. [3] Matt. xix. 17, Joh. xvii. 1.
[4] Joh. xvii. 3. [5] See above, § 39. [6] See above, § 3.

ποιμένων εἰς τὰ πρόβατα καὶ ἡ τοῦ βασιλέως πρὸς τοὺς ἀρχομένους, καὶ ἡμῶν αὐτῶν πειθηνίως πρὸς τοὺς ἡγουμένους ἐχόντων, τοὺς τεταγμένως διέποντας καθ' ἣν ἐνεχειρίσθησαν τάξιν ἐκ θεοῦ. θεράποντες ἄρα καὶ θεραπευταὶ τοῦ θείου οἱ ἐλευθερικωτάτην καὶ βασιλικωτάτην θεραπείαν προσάγοντες, τὴν διὰ τῆς θεοσεβοῦς γνώμης τε καὶ γνώσεως.

43. Πᾶς οὖν καὶ τόπος ἱερὸς τῷ ὄντι ἐν ᾧ τὴν ἐπίνοιαν τοῦ θεοῦ λαμβάνομεν καὶ χρόνος· ὅταν δὲ ὁ εὐπροαίρετος ὁμοῦ καὶ εὐχάριστος δι' εὐχῆς αἰτῆται, ἀμηγέπη συνεργεῖ τι πρὸς τὴν λῆψιν, ἀσμένως δι' ὧν εὔχεται τὸ ποθούμενον λαμβάνων. ἐπὰν γὰρ τὸ παρ' ἡμῶν εὐεπίφορον ὁ τῶν ἀγαθῶν λάβῃ δοτήρ, ἀθρόα πάντα τῇ συλλήψει αὐτῇ ἕπεται τὰ ἀγαθά. ἀμέλει ἐξετάζεται διὰ τῆς εὐχῆς ὁ τρόπος πῶς ἔχει πρὸς τὸ προσῆκον. εἰ δὲ ἡ φωνὴ καὶ ἡ λέξις τῆς νοήσεως χάριν δέδοται ἡμῖν, πῶς οὐχὶ αὐτῆς τῆς ψυχῆς καὶ τοῦ νοῦ ἐπακούει ὁ θεός, ὅπου γε ἤδη ψυχὴ ψυχῆς καὶ νοῦς νοὸς ἐπαΐει; ὅθεν τὰς πολυφώνους γλώσσας οὐκ ἀναμένει ὁ θεὸς καθάπερ οἱ παρὰ ἀνθρώπων ἑρμηνεῖς, ἀλλ' ἀπαξαπλῶς ἁπάντων γνωρίζει τὰς νοήσεις, καὶ ὅπερ ἡμῖν ἡ φωνὴ σημαίνει, τοῦτο τῷ θεῷ ἡ ἔννοια ἡμῶν λαλεῖ, ἣν καὶ πρὸ τῆς δημιουργίας εἰς νόησιν ἥξουσαν ἠπίστατο. ἔξεστιν οὖν μηδὲ φωνῇ τὴν εὐχὴν παραπέμπειν, συντείνοντα μόνον ἔνδοθεν τὸ πνευματικὸν πᾶν εἰς φωνὴν τὴν νοητὴν κατὰ τὴν ἀπερίσπαστον πρὸς τὸν θεὸν ἐπιστροφήν.

Ἐπεὶ δὲ γενεθλίου ἡμέρας εἰκὼν ἡ ἀνατολή, κἀκεῖθεν τὸ φῶς αὔξεται ἐκ σκότους λάμψαν τὸ πρῶτον, ἀλλὰ καὶ τοῖς ἐν ἀγνοίᾳ καλινδουμένοις ἀνέτειλεν γνώσεως ἀληθείας

---

8. τεταγμένως P. τεταγμένους L. 10. αἰτῆται D. αἰτεῖται L. 13. λάβῃ L. λάβοι V. 14. αὐτῇ M. αὐτῆς L. 17. χάριν pr. m. corr. ex διὰ χάριν L. δέδοται pr. m. corr. ex δίδοται L. 24, 25. παραπέμπειν, συντείνοντα μόνον ἔνδοθεν Heinsius. παραπέμπειν συντείνοντα μόνον δ' ἔνδοθεν L. 30. ἀνέτειλεν L. ἀνέτειλε VD.

of Providence are set in motion, like the care of shepherds for their sheep and that of a king towards his subjects; while we ourselves also are submissive to our superiors, who govern us in an orderly manner according to the commission with which they were entrusted by God. They therefore are ministers and worshippers of the Divinity who offer the freest and most royal worship, viz. that which is rendered by devoutness both of purpose and of knowledge.

§ 43. Every place then and every time at which we entertain the thought of God is truly hallowed; but when he who is at once right-minded and thankful makes his request in prayer, he in a way contributes to the granting of his petition, receiving with joy the desired object through the instrumentality of his prayers. For when the Giver of all good meets with readiness on our part, all good things follow at once on the mere conception in the mind. Certainly prayer is a test of the attitude of the character towards what is fitting. And if voice and speech are given to us with a view to understanding, how can God help hearing the soul and the mind by itself, seeing that soul already apprehends soul, and mind apprehends mind? Wherefore God has no need to learn various tongues, as human interpreters have, but understands at once the minds of all men; and what the voice signifies to us, that our thought utters to God, since even before the Creation He knew that it would come into our mind. It is permitted to man therefore to speed his prayer even without a voice, if he only concentrates all his spiritual energy upon the inner voice of the mind by his undistracted turning to God.

And since the east symbolizes the day of birth, and it is from thence that the *light* spreads, after it has first *shone forth out of darkness*[1], aye, and from thence that the day of the knowledge of the truth *dawned* like the sun *upon those who were lying in*

---

[1] 2 Cor. iv. 6.

ἡμέρα κατὰ λόγον τοῦ ἡλίου, πρὸς τὴν ἑωθινὴν ἀνατολὴν
αἱ εὐχαί. ὅθεν καὶ τὰ παλαίτατα τῶν ἱερῶν πρὸς
δύσιν ἔβλεπεν, ἵνα οἱ ἀπαντιπρόσωποι τῶν ἀγαλμάτων
ἱστάμενοι πρὸς ἀνατολὴν τρέπεσθαι διδάσκωνται. κατεγ-
5 θγνθήτω ἡ προσεγχή μογ ὡς θγμίαμα ἐνώπιόν σογ, ἔπαρσις
τῶν χειρῶν μογ θγσία ἑσπερινή, οἱ ψαλμοὶ λέγουσιν.

44. Τοῖς μοχθηροῖς τοίνυν τῶν ἀνθρώπων ἡ εὐχὴ
οὐ μόνον εἰς τοὺς ἄλλους, ἀλλὰ καὶ εἰς σφᾶς αὐτοὺς
βλαβερωτάτη. εἰ γοῦν καὶ ἃ φασιν εὐτυχήματα
10 αἰτησάμενοι λάβοιεν, βλάπτει λαβόντας αὐτούς, ἀνεπι-
στήμονας τῆς χρήσεως αὐτῶν ὑπάρχοντας. οἱ μὲν γὰρ
ἃ οὐκ ἔχουσιν εὔχονται κτήσασθαι, καὶ τὰ δοκοῦντα
ἀγαθά, οὐ τὰ ὄντα, αἰτοῦνται. ὁ γνωστικὸς δὲ ὧν μὲν
κέκτηται παραμονήν, ἐπιτηδειότητα δὲ εἰς ἃ μέλλει
15 ἀποβαίνειν, καὶ ἀϊδιότητα ὧν οὐ λήψεται αἰτήσεται·
τὰ δὲ ὄντως ἀγαθὰ τὰ περὶ ψυχὴν εὔχεται εἶναί τε
αὐτῷ καὶ παραμεῖναι. ταύτῃ οὐδὲ ὀρέγεταί τινος τῶν
ἀπόντων ἀρκούμενος τοῖς παροῦσιν. οὐ γὰρ ἐλλιπὴς
τῶν οἰκείων ἀγαθῶν, ἱκανὸς ὢν ἤδη ἑαυτῷ ἐκ τῆς θείας
20 χάριτός τε καὶ γνώσεως· ἀλλὰ αὐτάρκης μὲν γενόμενος
ἀνενδεής τε τῶν ἄλλων, τὸ παντοκρατορικὸν δὲ βούλημα
ἐγνωκώς, καὶ ἔχων ἅμα καὶ εὐχόμενος, προσεχὴς τῇ
πανσθενεῖ δυνάμει γενόμενος, πνευματικὸς εἶναι σπου-
δάσας διὰ τῆς ἀορίστου ἀγάπης ἥνωται τῷ πνεύματι.
25 οὗτος ὁ μεγαλόφρων, ὁ τὸ πάντων τιμιώτατον, ὁ τὸ
πάντων ἀγαθώτατον κατὰ τὴν ἐπιστήμην κεκτημένος,
εὔϊκτος μὲν κατὰ τὴν προσβολὴν τῆς θεωρίας, ἔμμονον
δὲ τὴν τῶν θεωρητῶν δύναμιν ἐν τῇ ψυχῇ κεκτημένος,
τουτέστι τὴν διορατικὴν τῆς ἐπιστήμης δριμύτητα.
ταύτην δὲ ὡς ἔνι μάλιστα βιάζεται κτήσασθαι τὴν

---

3. ἀπαντιπρόσωποι H. ἅπαν τι πρόσωπον L. ἀντιπρόσωποι D post S in Ind. ἀπαντιπρόσωπον S. ἀπ' ἀντιπροσώπου Jackson. 9. γοῦν pr. m. corr. ex οὖν L. 15. ἀποβαίνειν Heinsius. ὑπερβαίνειν LH. ἀϊδιότητα] fort. ἀδιαφορότητα M. ἀνιδιότητα Abbott. ὧν οὐ λήψεται LH. ὧν λήψεται D post Heinsium. 18. ἐλλιπὴς S. ἐλλειπὴς L. 21. τε H. δὲ L. 25. οὗτος Barnard. οὕτως L.

ignorance[1], therefore our prayers are directed towards the rise of dawn. It was for this reason that the most ancient temples looked toward the west in order that they who stood facing the images might be taught to turn eastwards. *Let my prayer ascend up as incense before Thee, the lifting up my hands be an evening sacrifice*[2] is the language of the Psalms.

§ 44. In the case of the wicked then prayer is most hurtful, not only to others, but even to themselves. At any rate, if in answer to prayer they were to receive what they call pieces of good fortune, they are injured by receiving them, because they know not how to use them. For they pray to obtain what they have not got, and they ask for apparent, not real good. The gnostic, on the other hand, will ask for a continuance of the things he possesses and fitness for what is about to happen, and indifference as to what shall be denied: but as for the things that are really good, *i.e.* those pertaining to the soul, his prayer is that they may both be granted to him and may continue. Thus he does not even desire anything which he has not, being contented with his present lot. For he is not lacking in the good things that are proper to him, being already sufficient to himself through the Divine grace and knowledge. But, having his resources in himself and being independent of others, and having learnt to know the Omnipotent Will, so that he no sooner prays than he receives, he is brought close to the Almighty Power and, by his earnest striving after spirituality, is united to the Spirit through the love that knows no bounds. This is the man of lofty mind, who by the way of science has acquired the most precious and best of all possessions, being on the one hand quick to apply the faculty of contemplation, while on the other hand he retains permanently in his soul the power over the objects of contemplation, *i.e.* the keen clearness of science.

[1] Matt. iv. 16.   [2] Ps. cxli. 2.

δύναμιν ἐγκρατὴς γενόμενος τῶν ἀντιστρατεγομένων τῷ νῷ καὶ τῇ μὲν θεωρίᾳ ἀδιαλείπτως προσεδρεύων, τῇ ἐφεκτικῇ δὲ τῶν ἡδέων καὶ τῇ κατορθωτικῇ τῶν πρακτέων ἐγγυμνασάμενος ἀσκήσει· πρὸς τούτοις ἐμπειρίᾳ πολλῇ 5 χρησάμενος, τῇ κατὰ τὴν μάθησίν τε καὶ τὸν βίον, παρρησίαν ἔχει, οὐ τὴν ἁπλῶς οὕτως ἀθυρόγλωσσον δύναμιν, δύναμιν δὲ ἁπλῷ λόγῳ χρωμένην, μηδὲν τῶν λεχθῆναι δυναμένων κατὰ τὸν προσήκοντα καιρὸν ἐφ' ὧν μάλιστα χρὴ ἐπικρυπτομένην, μήτε διὰ χάριν μήτε 10 διὰ φόβον ἀξιολόγων.

45. Ὁ γοῦν τὰ περὶ θεοῦ διειληφὼς πρὸς αὐτῆς τῆς ἀληθείας χοροῦ μυστικοῦ λόγῳ τῷ προτρέποντι, τὸ μέγεθος τῆς ἀρετῆς κατ' ἀξίαν, αὐτήν τε καὶ τὰ ἀπ' αὐτῆς· ἐνδεικνυμένῳ, χρῆται, μετὰ διάρματος ἐνθέου τῆς 15 εὐχῆς τοῖς νοητοῖς καὶ πνευματικοῖς ὡς ἔνι μάλιστα γνωστικῶς οἰκειούμενος. ὅθεν ἥμερος καὶ πρᾶος ἀεί, εὐπρόσιτος, εὐαπάντητος, ἀνεξίκακος, εὐγνώμων, εὐσυνείδητος. αὐστηρὸς οὗτος ἡμῖν, αὐστηρὸς οὐκ εἰς τὸ ἀδιάφθορον μόνον, ἀλλὰ καὶ εἰς τὸ ἀπείραστον. οὐδαμῇ 20 γὰρ ἐνδόσιμον οὐδὲ ἁλώσιμον ἡδονῇ τε καὶ λύπῃ τὴν ψυχὴν παρίστησιν, δικαστής, ἐὰν ὁ λόγος καλῇ, ἀκλινὴς γενόμενος μηδ' ὁτιοῦν τοῖς πάθεσι χαριζόμενος, ἀμεταστάτως ᾗ πέφυκεν τὸ δίκαιον πορεύεσθαι βαδίζων, πεπεισμένος εὖ μάλα παγκάλως διοικεῖσθαι τὰ πάντα 25 καὶ εἰς τὸ ἄμεινον ἀεὶ τὴν προκοπὴν προϊέναι ταῖς ἀρετὴν ἑλομέναις ψυχαῖς, ἔστ' ἂν ἐπ' αὐτὸ ἀφίκωνται τὸ ἀγαθόν, ἐπὶ προθύροις ὡς εἰπεῖν τοῦ πατρὸς προσεχεῖς τῷ μεγάλῳ ἀρχιερεῖ γενόμεναι. οὗτος ἡμῖν ὁ γνωστικὸς ὁ πιστός, ὁ πεπεισμένος ἄριστα διοικεῖσθαι τὰ κατὰ

---

4. ἀσκήσει. M. ἀσκήσει, D. 7. χρωμένην S. χρωμένηι L. 9. ὧν] ᾧ S. 10. ἀξιολόγων H. ἀξιολόγως L. 12. προτρέποντι L. fort. προφέροντι H. 14. ἐνδεικνυμένῳ H. ἐνδεικνυμένων L. ἐνδεικνύμενος Heinsius in annot. 22. ἀμεταστάτως SH. ἀμεταστάτῳ L. 23. ᾗ] ᾗι L. 28. γενόμεναι V. γενόμεναι pr. m. corr. L.

This power he strives to the utmost to acquire by gaining the mastery *over all that wars against the reason*[1] and persisting in uninterrupted contemplation, while he exercises himself in the discipline which teaches the curbing of pleasures and the right direction of action. Besides this, from his wide experience, gathered both from study and from life, he has acquired freedom of speech, not the power of a mere random fluency, but the power of straightforward utterance, keeping back nothing that may be spoken in fitting time before a right audience, either from favour or fear of influential persons.

§ 45. At any rate he who has received a clear conception of the things concerning God from the mystical chorus of the truth itself, makes use of the word of exhortation, exhibiting the greatness of virtue according to its worth, both in itself and in its effects, being united as intimately as possible with things intellectual and spiritual in the way of knowledge along with an inspired exaltation of prayer. Hence he is always meek and gentle, affable, easy of access, forbearing, considerate, conscientious. In him we have a severity of virtue, such as is not only proof against corruption, but proof against temptation also. He presents a soul altogether unyielding and impregnable whether to the assaults of pleasure or of pain. If reason calls him to it, he is an unswerving judge, in no respect indulging his passions, but keeping inflexibly to the path in which it is the nature of justice to walk, being fully persuaded that all things are admirably ordered, and that, for the souls which have made choice of virtue, progress is always in the direction of what is better, until they arrive at the Absolute Goodness, being brought close to *the great High Priest*[2], *in the vestibule*[3], so to speak, of the Father. This is the faithful gnostic who is fully

---

[1] Rom. vii. 23. [2] Heb. iv. 14: above, pp. 17 and 21. [3] Plato, *Phileb.* 64 c.

τὸν κόσμον. ἀμέλει πᾶσιν εὐαρεστεῖται τοῖς συμβαίνουσιν.

46. Εὐλόγως οὖν οὐδὲν ἐπιζητεῖ τῶν κατὰ τὸν βίον εἰς τὴν ἀναγκαίαν χρῆσιν εὐθετούντων, πεπεισμένος ὡς ὁ τὰ πάντα εἰδὼς θεὸς ὅ τι ἂν συμφέρῃ καὶ οὐκ αἰτουμένοις τοῖς ἀγαθοῖς χορηγεῖ. καθάπερ γάρ, οἶμαι, τῷ τεχνικῷ τεχνικῶς καὶ τῷ ἐθνικῷ ἐθνικῶς, οὕτω καὶ τῷ γνωστικῷ <γνωστικῶς> ἕκαστα ἀποδίδοται. καὶ ὁ μὲν ἐξ ἐθνῶν ἐπιστρέφων τὴν πίστιν, ὁ δὲ εἰς γνῶσιν ἐπαναβαίνων τῆς ἀγάπης τὴν τελειότητα αἰτήσεται. κορυφαῖος δ' ἤδη ὁ γνωστικὸς θεωρίαν εὔχεται αὔξειν τε καὶ παραμένειν, καθάπερ ὁ κοινὸς ἄνθρωπος τὸ συνεχὲς ὑγιαίνειν. ναὶ μὴν μηδὲ ἀποπεσεῖν ποτε τῆς ἀρετῆς αἰτήσεται συνεργῶν μάλιστα πρὸς τὸ ἄπτωτος διαγενέσθαι. οἶδεν γὰρ καὶ τῶν ἀγγέλων τινὰς, ὑπὸ ῥᾳθυμίας ὀλισθήσαντας αὖθις χαμαί, μηδέπω τέλεον εἰς τὴν μίαν ἐκείνην ἕξιν ἐκ τῆς εἰς τὴν διπλόην ἐπιτηδειότητος ἐκθλίψαντας ἑαυτούς. τῷ δὲ ἐνθένδε εἰς γνώσεως ἀκρότητα καὶ τὸ ἐπαναβεβηκὸς ὕψος ἀνδρὸς ἐντελοῦς γεγυμνασμένῳ πρὸ ὁδοῦ τὰ κατὰ χρόνον καὶ τόπον ἅπαντα, ἀμεταπτώτως βιοῦν ἑλομένῳ καὶ ἀσκοῦντι διὰ τὴν τῆς γνώμης πάντοθεν μονότονον ἑδραιότητα· ὅσοις δὲ βρίθουσά τις ἔτι ὑπολείπεται γωνία κάτω ῥέπουσα, καὶ κατασπᾶται τὸ διὰ τῆς πίστεως ἀναγόμενον. τῷ ἄρα ἀναπόβλητον τὴν ἀρετὴν ἀσκήσει γνωστικῇ πεποιημένῳ φυσιοῦται ἡ ἕξις, καὶ καθάπερ τῷ λίθῳ τὸ βάρος, οὕτως τοῦδε ἡ ἐπιστήμη ἀναπόβλητος οὐκ ἀκουσίως, ἀλλ' ἑκουσίως, δυνάμει λογικῇ καὶ γνωστικῇ καὶ προνοητικῇ, καθίσταται.

4. εὐθετούντων H. εὐθετεῖν Jackson. οὐθότ' οὖν L. οὐθ' ὁτιοῦν S. οὐδ' ὁτιοῦν P. 8. γνωστικῶς addidit S. 20. πρὸ ὁδοῦ S. προόδου L. 23. γωνία L. fort. ἀτονία M. ἀγνωσία Jackson. 27. τοῦδε] fort. τῷδε M. ἀναπόβλητος Kl. H. ἀναπόβλητος· D post Heinsium. ἀκουσίως LH. ἀκ. γὰρ D post Heinsium.

persuaded that all things in the world are ordered for the best. Certainly he is well pleased with all that happens.

§ 46. He is right therefore in not seeking after any of the necessary conveniences of life, being persuaded that God, who knows all things, supplies whatever is expedient to the good, even without their asking. For as the artificer, I suppose, has each request granted to him in the way of his art, *qua* artificer, and the heathen *qua* heathen, so the gnostic has his <in the way of knowledge> *qua* gnostic. And he that turns to God from among the heathen will ask for faith, but he that aspires to knowledge will ask for *the perfection of love*[1]. And when he has now reached the summit, the gnostic prays that <the power of> contemplation may grow and abide with him, just as the common man prays for a continuance of health. Aye, and he will pray too that he may never fall away from virtue, cooperating to the best of his power that he may end his life without a fall. For he knows that even of the angels some, having slipped back to the ground from carelessness, have never yet succeeded in extricating themselves completely out of their tendency to duplicity into the former singleness <of heart>. But, to him who has been trained here below to the highest point of knowledge, and the supreme elevation of a perfect man, all incidents of time and space are favourable; for he is fixed to one unchanging course of life both by choice and practice, owing to his uniform stability of purpose. But in those who have still some remnant of *depressing* languor *that weighs them down*[2], the soaring impulse of faith also flags. In him, then, who has rendered his virtue indefectible by discipline based upon knowledge, habit is changed into nature; and in such an one his knowledge becomes an inseparable possession, like weight in a stone, not involuntarily, but of his own free will, by the power of reason and knowledge and forethought.

[1] 1 Joh. iv. 17.   [2] Plato, *Phaedr.* 247.

47. Ἐπεὶ δὲ τὸ μὴ ἀποβληθὲν δι' εὐλαβείας ἀναπόβλητον γίνεται, τῆς μὲν εὐλαβείας πρὸς τὸ μὴ ἁμαρτάνειν, τῆς δὲ εὐλογιστίας πρὸς τὸ ἀναπόβλητον τῆς ἀρετῆς ἀνθέξεται. ἡ γνῶσις δὲ ἔοικεν τὴν εὐλογιστίαν παρέχειν, διορᾶν διδάσκουσα τὰ βοηθεῖν πρὸς τὴν παραμονὴν τῆς ἀρετῆς δυνάμενα. μέγιστον <δ'> ἄρα ἡ γνῶσις τοῦ θεοῦ. διὸ καὶ ταύτῃ σῴζεται τὸ ἀναπόβλητον τῆς ἀρετῆς. ὁ δὲ ἐγνωκὼς τὸν θεὸν ὅσιος καὶ εὐσεβής. μόνος ἄρα ὁ γνωστικὸς εὐσεβὴς ἡμῖν εἶναι δέδεικται. οὗτος χαίρει μὲν ἐπὶ τοῖς παροῦσιν ἀγαθοῖς, γέγηθεν δὲ ἐπὶ τοῖς ἐπηγγελμένοις, ὡς ἤδη παροῦσιν—οὐ γὰρ λέληθεν αὐτὸν ὡς ἂν ἀπόντα ἔτι—δι' ὧν ἔγνω φθάσας οἷά ἐστιν. τῇ γνώσει οὖν πεπεισμένος ὡς ἔστιν ἕκαστον τῶν μελλόντων, καὶ κέκτηται τοῦτο. τὸ γὰρ ἐνδεὲς καὶ ἐπιδεὲς πρὸς τὸ ἐπιβάλλον μετρεῖται. εἰ γοῦν σοφίαν κέκτηται καὶ θεῖον ἡ σοφία, ὁ ἀνενδεοῦς μετέχων ἀνενδεὴς εἴη ἄν. οὐ γὰρ ἡ τῆς σοφίας μετάδοσις κινούντων καὶ ἰσχόντων ἀλλήλους τῆς τε ἐνεργείας καὶ τοῦ μετίσχοντος γίνεται, οὐδὲ ἀφαιρουμένου τινὸς οὐδὲ ἐνδεοῦς γινομένου· ἀμείωτος γοῦν ἡ ἐνέργεια δι' αὐτῆς τῆς μεταδόσεως δείκνυται. οὕτως οὖν πάντα ἔχει τὰ ἀγαθὰ ὁ γνωστικὸς ἡμῖν κατὰ τὴν δύναμιν, οὐδέπω δὲ καὶ κατὰ τὸν ἀριθμόν, ἐπεὶ κἂν ἀμετάθετος ἦν κατὰ τὰς ὀφειλομένας ἐνθέους προκοπάς τε καὶ διοικήσεις.

48. Τούτῳ συλλαμβάνει καὶ ὁ θεὸς προσεχεστέρᾳ τιμήσας ἐπισκοπῇ. ἢ γὰρ οὐχὶ τῶν ἀγαθῶν ἀνδρῶν χάριν καὶ εἰς τὴν τούτων χρῆσιν καὶ ὠφέλειαν, μᾶλλον

1. ἐπεὶ...ἀποβληθὲν H. ἐπὶ...ἀποβληθῆναι L. δι' εὐλαβείας] fort. omissum est καὶ εὐλογιστίας M. 6. δ' ἄρα M. ἄρα L. 9. ὁ γνωστικὸς L. casu om. ὁ D. 12. παροῦσιν—οὐ γὰρ...ἔτι—δι' ὧν M. παροῦσιν. οὐ γὰρ...ἔτι δι' ὧν L. 14. καὶ post μελλόντων M. post πεπεισμένος L. 15. Post τοῦτο fort. omissum est ἀνθρώπῳ δὲ ὄντι ἀγαπητὸν τὸ οὕτως κεκτῆσθαι vel tale aliquid M. ἐνδεὲς] ἀνενδεὲς M. 19. μετίσχοντος] fort. ex μετέχοντος propter vicinum ἰσχόντων corruptum M. 20. ἀφαιρουμένου] ἀφαιρομένου LV. 21. γοῦν M. δ' οὖν L. 27. τιμήσας] fort. τηρήσας M. 28. χρῆσιν ex κτῆσιν factum m. pr. L.

§ 47. And since that which has not been lost may be raised to a state of indefectibility by carefulness <and consideration>, the gnostic will hold fast to carefulness with a view to avoid sin, and to consideration with a view to the indefectibility of virtue. Now knowledge seems to be the parent of consideration, because it teaches us to discern the things which can help to the permanence of virtue. But it will be granted that the knowledge of God is the most important of all things. Wherefore in this way also the indefectibility of virtue is assured. And he who knows God is holy and pious. We have proved therefore that the gnostic alone is pious. He rejoices in his present blessings and delights himself in those that are promised, as though they were already present—for he has not lost sight of them as if they were still absent—because he already knows of what nature they are. Being therefore convinced by his knowledge that each of the things that shall be, really is, he <virtually> possesses each. <And this is enough for man>: for sufficient and insufficient are measured by that which is normal in each case. At any rate, if the gnostic is possessed of wisdom, and wisdom is divine, he who partakes of what has no defect must himself be without defect. For the communication of wisdom is not the resultant of energy on the part of the giver and inertia on the part of the recipient, nor is any abstraction or deficiency caused by it; at any rate the energy is shown to be undiminished by the very fact of the communication. Thus then our gnostic has all good in potentiality, though not yet in full tale; since he would otherwise have been incapable of change in reference to the inspired progresses and orderings which are still due to him by God's decree.

§ 48. God also assists him, honouring him with a closer oversight. For is it not the case that all things have been created for the sake of good men and for their use and benefit

δὲ σωτηρίαν, τὰ πάντα γέγονεν; οὔκουν ἀφέλοιτο ἂν τούτους τὰ δι' ἀρετήν, δι' οὓς τὰ γεγονότα. δῆλον γὰρ ὡς τὴν φύσιν αὐτῶν τὴν ἀγαθὴν καὶ τὴν προαίρεσιν τὴν ἁγίαν τιμῶν ἦν, ὅς γε καὶ τοῖς εὖ βιοῦν ἐπανῃρη-
5 μένοις ἰσχὺν πρὸς τὴν λοιπὴν σωτηρίαν ἐμπνεῖ, τοῖς μὲν προτρέπων μόνον, τοῖς δὲ ἀξίοις γενομένοις ἐξ ἑαυτῶν καὶ συλλαμβανόμενος. ἐπιγεννηματικὸν γὰρ ἅπαν τῷ γνωστικῷ τὸ ἀγαθόν, εἴ γε δὴ τὸ τέλος ἐστὶν αὐτῷ ἐπίστασθαι καὶ πράσσειν ἐπιστημόνως ἕκαστον.
10 ὡς δὲ ὁ ἰατρὸς ὑγείαν παρέχεται τοῖς συνεργοῦσι πρὸς ὑγείαν, οὕτως καὶ ὁ θεὸς τὴν ἀίδιον σωτηρίαν τοῖς συνεργοῦσι πρὸς γνῶσίν τε καὶ εὐπραγίαν· σὺν δὲ τῷ ποιεῖν ἓν τῶν ἐφ' ἡμῖν, ἃ προστάττουσιν αἱ ἐντολαί, καὶ ἡ ἐπαγγελία τελειοῦται. καί μοι δοκεῖ κἀκεῖνο
15 καλῶς παρὰ τοῖς Ἕλλησι λέγεσθαι· ἀθλητής τις οὐκ ἀγεννὴς ἐν τοῖς πάλαι, πολλῷ τῷ χρόνῳ τὸ σωμάτιον εὖ μάλα πρὸς ἀνδρείαν ἀσκήσας, εἰς Ὀλύμπι' ἀναβὰς εἰς τοῦ Πισαίου Διὸς τὸ ἄγαλμα ἀποβλέψας, εἰ πάντα εἶπεν ὦ Ζεῦ, δεόντωс μοι τὰ πρὸс τὸν ἀγῶνα παρεсκεύαсται,
20 ἀπόδοс φέρων δικαίωс τὴν νίκην ἐμοί. ὧδε γὰρ καὶ τῷ γνωστικῷ, ἀνεπιλήπτως καὶ εὐσυνειδήτως τὰ παρ' ἑαυτοῦ πάντα ἐκπεπληρωκότι εἴς τε τὴν μάθησιν εἴς τε τὴν συνάσκησιν εἴς τε τὴν εὐποίαν καὶ εἰς τὴν εὐαρέστησιν τῷ θεῷ, τὸ πᾶν συναιρεῖται πρὸς τὴν
25 τελειότητα τῆς σωτηρίας. ταῦτ' οὖν ἀπαιτεῖται παρ' ἡμῶν τὰ ἐφ' ἡμῖν, καὶ τῶν πρὸς ἡμᾶς ἀνηκόντων, παρόντων τε καὶ ἀπόντων, αἵρεσίς τε καὶ πόθος καὶ κτῆσις καὶ χρῆσις καὶ διανομή.

49. Διὸ καὶ ἄχραντον τὴν ψυχὴν ἔχειν χρὴ καὶ

1. ἂν addidit D. 4. τιμῶν ἦν ὅς γε Jackson. τιμώμενόs τε L.
7. ἐπιγεννηματικὸν D, post Routh ap. Steph. III. p. 1557. ἐπιγενηματικὸν L.
10, 11. ὑγείαν L. ὑγίειαν D. 13. ἕν τι τῶν vel ὁτιοῦν τῶν H. quem secutus ἓν τῶν Jackson. ὄντων L. 17. Ὀλύμπι' L. Ὀλυμπίαν D. 18. Πισαίου] πισσαίου L. 22. ἑαυτοῦ S. ἑαυτὸν L. 24. συναιρεῖται] fort. συναιρεται H. 25. τῆs σωτηρίαs M. τὴν σωτηρίαν L. 28. διανομή M. διαμονή L.

or, rather we should say, salvation? He would not therefore deprive of the rewards of virtue those for whom all things exist. For it is plain that He valued highly their good disposition and their holy choice, seeing that He breathes into those that have taken on themselves a good profession, strength for the completion of their salvation, in some cases by simple exhortation, but also by actual help in the case of those who have proved themselves worthy by their own efforts. For to the gnostic every kind of good comes as an accessory, seeing that his chief end is in each case knowledge and action in accordance with knowledge. And as the physician provides health for those who cooperate with him for health, so also God provides eternal salvation for those who cooperate with Him for knowledge and right action: and the moment that we do any one of the things in our power, which are enjoined by the commandments, the promise also receives its fulfilment. I like that story which is told among the Greeks of a famous athlete of former days, who had trained himself for feats of manhood by a long course of discipline. Having gone up to the Olympian games he turned to the image of Pisaean Zeus and uttered these words 'If I, O Zeus, have now done all that was fitting on my part in preparation for the contest, do thou make haste to bestow the victory I deserve.' For just so does the gnostic, when he has thoroughly and conscientiously performed his part with a view to learning and discipline and with a view to doing good and pleasing God, find the whole world contributing to perfect his salvation. The things then that are required of us are those which are in our own power, viz. choice and desire and acquisition and use and distribution of the things which concern us, according as they are present or absent.

§ 49. Wherefore also he who holds intercourse with God

ἀμίαντον εἰλικρινῶς τὸν προσομιλοῦντα τῷ θεῷ, μάλιστα μὲν ἀγαθὸν τελέως ἑαυτὸν ἐξειργασμένον, εἰ δὲ μή, καὶ προκόπτοντα ἐπὶ τὴν γνῶσιν καὶ ἐφιέμενον αὐτῆς, τῶν δὲ τῆς κακίας ἔργων τέλεον ἀπεσπασμένον. ἀλλὰ καὶ τὰς εὐχὰς ἁπάσας ἐπιεικῶς ἅμα καὶ μετ' ἐπιεικῶν ποιεῖσθαι πρέπον ἐστίν· σφαλερὸν γὰρ τοῖς ἑτέρων ἁμαρτήμασι συνεπιγράφεσθαι. περὶ τούτων ἄρα ὁ γνωστικὸς καὶ συνεύξεται τοῖς κοινότερον πεπιστευκόσι, περὶ ὧν καὶ συμπράττειν καθήκει. ἅπας δὲ ὁ βίος αὐτοῦ πανήγυρις ἁγία. αὐτίκα θυσίαι μὲν αὐτῷ εὐχαί τε καὶ αἶνοι καὶ αἱ πρὸ τῆς ἑστιάσεως ἐντεύξεις τῶν γραφῶν, ψαλμοὶ δὲ καὶ ὕμνοι παρὰ τὴν ἑστίασιν πρό τε τῆς κοίτης, ἀλλὰ καὶ νύκτωρ εὐχαὶ πάλιν. διὰ τούτων ἑαυτὸν ἑνοποιεῖ τῷ θείῳ χορῷ, ἐκ τῆς συνεχοῦς μνήμης εἰς ἀείμνηστον θεωρίαν ἐντεταγμένος. τί δ'; οὐ καὶ τὴν ἄλλην θυσίαν τὴν κατὰ τοὺς δεομένους ἐπίδοσιν καὶ δογμάτων καὶ χρημάτων γινώσκει; καὶ μάλα. ἀλλὰ τῇ διὰ στόματος εὐχῇ οὐ πολυλόγῳ χρῆται, παρὰ τοῦ κυρίου καὶ ἃ χρὴ αἰτεῖσθαι μαθών. ἐν παντὶ τοίνυν τόπῳ, οὐκ ἄντικρυς δὲ οὐδὲ ἐμφανῶς τοῖς πολλοῖς εὔξεται· ὁ δὲ καὶ περιπάτῳ χρώμενος καὶ ὁμιλίᾳ καὶ ἡσυχίᾳ καὶ ἀναγνώσει καὶ τοῖς ἔργοις τοῖς κατὰ λόγον κατὰ πάντα τρόπον εὔχεται· κἂν ἐν αὐτῷ τῷ ταμιείῳ τῆς ψυχῆς ἐννοηθῇ μόνον καὶ ἀλαλήτοις στεναγμοῖς ἐπικαλέσηται τὸν πατέρα, ὁ δὲ ἐγγὺς καὶ ἔτι λαλοῦντος πάρεστιν. τριῶν δ' ὄντων πάσης πράξεως τελῶν διὰ μὲν τὸ καλὸν καὶ τὸ συμφέρον πάντα ἐνεργεῖ, τὸ δὲ ἐπιτελεῖν <τι> διὰ τὸ ἡδὺ τοῖς τὸν κοινὸν βίον διώκουσιν καταλιμπάνει.

2. καὶ M. κἂν L. 8. κοινότερον M. καινότερον L. 12. πρό τε P. πρό γε LVD. 27. ἐπιτελεῖν τι M. ἐπιτελεῖν L. fort. ἔν τι τελεῖν H. 28. διὰ τὸ ἡδὺ τοῖς τὸν H. διὰ τὸν δύσοιστον L. ἡδέα τὸν δ. PD.

must have his soul undefiled and absolutely pure, having raised himself to a state of perfect goodness if possible, but at any rate both making progress towards knowledge and longing for it, and being entirely withdrawn from the works of wickedness. Moreover it is fitting that he should offer all his prayers in a good spirit and in concert with good men, for it is a dangerous thing to countenance the errors of others. The gnostic will therefore share the prayers of ordinary believers in those cases in which it is right for him to share their activity also. But all his life is a holy festival. For instance, his sacrifices consist of prayers and praises and the reading of the Scriptures before dining, and psalms and hymns during dinner and before going to bed, aye and of prayers again during the night. By these things he unites himself with the heavenly quire, being enlisted in it for ever-mindful contemplation in consequence of his uninterrupted thought <of heaven while on earth>. Again, is he not acquainted with that other sacrifice which consists in the free gift both of instruction and of money among those who are in need? Certainly he is. On the other hand he is *not wordy in his* uttered *prayers*[1], since he has been also taught by the Lord what to ask for. Accordingly he will pray in every place, not however publicly or for all to see; but in every sort of way his prayer ascends, whether he is walking or in company or at rest or reading or engaged in good works; and though *it be only a thought*[2] in *the secret chamber*[3] of the heart, while he *calls on the Father*[4] *in groanings which cannot be uttered*[5], yet *the Father is nigh at hand*[6], even *before he has done speaking*[7]. Of the three ends of action, the honourable, the expedient and the pleasant, he makes the two former his rule, and leaves it to those who follow the common life to be guided in any action by the third motive of pleasure.

---

[1] Matt. vi. 7.   [2] See the quotation in § 73 below, and *Str.* vi. p. 778.
[3] Matt. vi. 6.   [4] 1 Pet. i. 17.   [5] Rom. viii. 26.
[6] Ps. cxlv. 18.   [7] Isai. lxv. 24, Dan. ix. 21.

ΚΕΦ. Η.

50. Πολλοῦ γε δεῖ τὸν ἐν τοιαύτῃ εὐσεβείᾳ ἐξεταζόμενον πρόχειρον εἶναι περί τε τὸ ψεύσασθαι περί τε τὸ ὀμόσαι. ὅρκος μὲν γάρ ἐστιν ὁμολογία καθοριστικὴ μετὰ προσπαραλήψεως θείας. ὁ δὲ ἅπαξ πιστὸς πῶς ἂν ἑαυτὸν ἄπιστον παράσχοι, ὡς καὶ ὅρκου δεῖσθαι, οὐχὶ δὲ ἐμπέδως καὶ καθωρισμένως ὅρκον εἶναι τούτῳ τὸν βίον; ζῇ τε καὶ πολιτεύεται καὶ τὸ πιστὸν τῆς ὁμολογίας ἐν ἀμεταπτώτῳ καὶ ἑδραίῳ δείκνυσι βίῳ τε καὶ λόγῳ. εἰ δὲ ἐν τῇ κρίσει τοῦ δρῶντος καὶ λαλοῦντος τὸ ἀδικεῖν, οὐχὶ δὲ ἐν τῷ πάθει κεῖται τοῦ διαπονουμένου, οὔτε ψεύσεται οὔτε ἐπιορκήσει, <οὐχ> ὡς ἀδικῶν τὸ θεῖον, (τοῦτο φύσει ἀβλαβὲς ὑπάρχειν εἰδώς)· ἀλλ' οὐδὲ διὰ τὸν πλησίον ψεύσεται ἢ παραβήσεταί τι, ὅν γε ἀγαπᾶν μεμάθηκεν, κἂν μὴ συνήθης τυγχάνῃ· δι' ἑαυτὸν δὲ ἆρ' ἔτι μᾶλλον οὔτε ψεύσεται οὔτε ἐπιορκήσει, εἴ γε ἑκὼν οὐκ ἄν ποτε ἄδικος εἰς ἑαυτὸν εὑρεθείη. ἀλλ' οὐδὲ ὀμεῖται, ἐπὶ μὲν τῆς συγκαταθέσεως μόνον τὸ ναί, ἐπὶ δὲ τῆς ἀρνήσεως τὸ οὔ, προελόμενος τάσσειν ἐπίρρημα. ὀμνύναι γάρ ἐστι τὸ ὅρκον ἢ ὡς ἂν ὅρκον ἀπὸ διανοίας προσφέρεσθαι παραστατικῆς.

51. ἀρκεῖ τοίνυν αὐτῷ ἤτοι τῇ συγκαταθέσει ἢ τῇ ἀρνήσει προσθεῖναι τὸ "Ἀληθῶς λέγω" εἰς παράστασιν τῶν μὴ διορώντων αὐτοῦ τὸ βέβαιον τῆς ἀποκρίσεως. ἔχειν γάρ, οἶμαι, χρὴ πρὸς μὲν τοὺς ἔξω τὸν βίον ἀξιόπιστον, ὡς μηδὲ ὅρκον αἰτεῖσθαι, πρὸς ἑαυτὸν δὲ καὶ τοὺς συνιέντας εὐγνωμοσύνην, ἥτις ἐστὶν ἑκούσιος δικαιοσύνη. αὐτίκα εὔορκος μέν, οὐ μὴν εὐεπίφορος

---

10. διαπονουμένου M. διακονουμένου L. ἀδικουμένου Lowth. διωκομένου P.
11. οὐχ ὡς M. ὡς L.   17. ὀμεῖται H. οἴεται L. ὄμνυται P.
20. προσφέρεσθαι] προφέρεσθαι Hoeschel. παραστατικῆς H. παραστατικῶς L.   25. πρὸς ἑαυτὸν L, fort. πρὸς τοὺς ἑαυτοῦ M.   26. συνιέντας] συνόντας S.   εὐγνωμοσύνην LP. εὐγνωμωσύνην Kl. D.

CHAPTER VIII.

§ 50. He whose life is characterized by piety of this kind has little temptation to lying and swearing. For an oath is a definitive compact in which God is called to witness. And how could one who has once for all proved himself faithful, make himself unfaithful so as to stand in need of an oath, instead of allowing his life to carry with it the security and definiteness of an oath? Both in his life and in his intercourse with others he shows the faithfulness of his promise by unfailing steadfastness both of life and speech. And, if injustice consists in the determination of the doer and speaker, and not in the suffering of the aggrieved person, he will refrain both from lying and forswearing himself, <not> with an idea that he is doing injury to God (since he knows that God is naturally incapable of receiving injury); but also *for his neighbour's sake* he will refuse to lie or break any agreement, seeing that he has learnt to *love him*[1], even though he may not be a personal friend: and still more for his own sake he will refrain both from lying and from perjury, seeing that he would never, if he could help it, be found guilty of wronging himself. Nay, he will *not* even *swear* at all, preferring simply to use the particle '*yes*' in case of affirmation, and '*no*[2]' in case of denial. For to swear is to use an oath or its equivalent with intent to inspire confidence. § 51. It is enough for him therefore to add the words 'I speak the truth' either to his assent or denial, in order to give confidence to those who are too obtuse to see that his answer may be depended on. For, as regards those who are without, methinks his life should be worthy of trust, so that they should not even ask for an oath; but as regards his own family and *those who have a right understanding*[3] there should be confidence in his fairness, i.e. in his unforced desire to do right. In any case the gnostic is true to his oath, but slow to swear,

---

[1] Matt. xix. 19.   [2] Matt. v. 37.   [3] Prov. viii. 9.

ἐπὶ τὸ ὀμνύναι ὁ γνωστικός, ὅ γε σπανίως ἐπὶ τὸ
ὀμνύναι ἀφικνούμενος, οὕτως μέντοι ὡς ἔφαμεν. καίτοι
τὸ ἀληθεύειν κατὰ τὸν ὅρκον μετὰ συμφωνίας τῆς κατὰ
τὸ ἀληθὲς γίνεται· τὸ εὐορκεῖν οὖν συμβαίνει κατὰ τὴν
κατόρθωσιν τὴν ἐν τοῖς καθήκουσιν. ποῦ τοίνυν ἔτι
τοῦ ὅρκου χρεία τῷ κατὰ ἄκρον ἀληθείας βιοῦντι; ὁ
μὲν οὖν μηδὲ ὀμνὺς πολλοῦ γε δεῖ ἐπιορκήσει, ὁ δὲ
μηδὲν παραβαίνων τῶν κατὰ τὰς συνθήκας οὐδ' ἂν
ὀμόσαι πώποτε, ὅπου γε τῆς τε παραβάσεως καὶ τῆς
ἐπιτελέσεως ἐν τοῖς ἔργοις ἡ κύρωσις, ὥσπερ ἀμέλει
τοῦ ψεύδεσθαι καὶ τοῦ ψευδορκεῖν ἐν τῷ λέγειν καὶ τῷ
ὀμνύναι παρὰ τὸ καθῆκον. ὁ δὲ δικαίως βιοὺς μηδὲν
παραβαίνων τῶν καθηκόντων, ἔνθα ἡ κρίσις ἡ τῆς
ἀληθείας ἐξετάζεται, τοῖς ἔργοις εὐορκεῖ· παρέλκει
τοίνυν αὐτῷ τὸ κατὰ τὴν γλῶτταν μαρτύριον. πεπεισμένος οὖν πάντῃ τὸν θεὸν εἶναι πάντοτε, καὶ αἰδού-
μενος μὴ ἀληθεύειν, ἀνάξιόν τε αὑτοῦ καὶ ψεύδεσθαι
γινώσκων, τῇ συνειδήσει τῇ θείᾳ καὶ τῇ ἑαυτοῦ
ἀρκεῖται μόναις· καὶ ταύτῃ οὔτε ψεύδεται οὔτε παρὰ
τὰς συνθήκας ποιεῖ τι, ταύτῃ δὲ οὔτε ὄμνυσιν ὅρκον
ἀπαιτηθεὶς οὔτε ἔξαρνός ποτε γίνεται, ἵνα μὴ ψεύσηται
κἂν ἐναποθνήσκῃ ταῖς βασάνοις.

ΚΕΦ. Θ.

52. Πλέον δέ τι καὶ μᾶλλον ἐπιτείνει τὸ γνωστικὸν
ἀξίωμα ὁ τὴν προστασίαν τῆς τῶν ἑτέρων διδασκαλίας
ἀναλαβών, τοῦ μεγίστου ἐπὶ γῆς ἀγαθοῦ τὴν οἰκονομίαν
λόγῳ τε καὶ ἔργῳ ἀναδεξάμενος, δι' ἧς πρὸς τὸ θεῖον

4. εὐορκεῖν Heinsius. εὑρεῖν L. 7. δεῖ S. δὴ L. ἐπιορκήσει
LH. ἐπιορκήσειν D. 11. τοῦ ψεύδεσθαι M. τὸ ψ. L. τοῦ
ψευδορκεῖν M. τὸ ψ. L. τῷ ὀμνύναι P. τὸ ὀμνύναι L. 17. αὑτοῦ M.
αὐτοῦ L. 19. ταύτῃ] fort. ταύτῃ μὲν M. οὔτε ψεύδεται] οὐ ψεύδεται L.
20. ποιεῖ τι Jackson. τι ποιεῖται L. 20, 21. οὔτε...οὔτε M. οὐδὲ...οὐδὲ L.
23. πλέον D. πλεῖον L. 25. γῆς S. τῆς L.

since he rarely comes forward to take an oath, and that only as we have stated. Still to be true to one's oath is a part of the harmony of truth; so that the observance of an oath follows the rule for the performance of ordinary duties. Where then is there any further need for the oath to one who lives according to the highest standard of truth? He who does not even swear will be far indeed from perjuring himself, and he who observes every clause of his contracts would never swear at all, seeing that it is actions that decide whether contracts are broken or fulfilled; just as the question of falsehood and perjury is decided by speaking and swearing contrary to right. But he that lives justly, without violating any duty, is proved by his actions, wherein the judgment of the truth is sifted, to be true to his oath. The evidence of the tongue is therefore superfluous in his case. Being then persuaded that God is always present everywhere, and being ashamed not to tell the truth, and knowing that <not to speak of perjury> even a lie is unworthy of himself, he is satisfied with the witness of God and of his own conscience only. So, while on the one hand he neither lies nor does anything contrary to his agreements, on the other hand he neither takes an oath when it is demanded of him, nor denies < what he has done >, being resolute to be clear of lying, even though he should die under torture.

CHAPTER IX.

§ 52. But the dignity of the gnostic is carried even to a further pitch by him who has undertaken the direction of the teaching of others, assuming the management in word and deed of that which is the greatest blessing on earth, by virtue of which he becomes a mediator to bring about a close union

συνάφειάν τε καὶ κοινωνίαν ἐμμεσιτεύει. ὡς δὲ οἱ τὰ ἐπίγεια θρησκεύοντες τοῖς ἀγάλμασι καθάπερ ἐπαΐουσι προσεύχονται, βεβαίας ἐπὶ τούτων τιθέμενοι τὰς συνθήκας, οὕτως ἐπὶ τῶν ἐμψύχων ἀγαλμάτων, τῶν ἀνθρώπων, ἡ μεγαλοπρέπεια τοῦ λόγου ἡ ἀληθὴς πρὸς τοῦ ἀξιοπίστου παραλαμβάνεται διδασκάλου, καὶ ἡ εἰς τούτους εὐεργεσία εἰς αὐτὸν ἀναφέρεται τὸν κύριον, οὗ κατ' εἰκόνα παιδεύων ὁ τῷ ὄντι ἄνθρωπος δημιουργεῖ καὶ μεταρρυθμίζει καινίζων εἰς σωτηρίαν τὸν κατηχούμενον ἄνθρωπον. ὡς γὰρ τὸν σίδηρον Ἄρην προσαγορεύουσιν Ἕλληνες καὶ τὸν οἶνον Διόνυσον κατά τινα ἀναφοράν, οὕτως ὁ γνωστικός, ἰδίαν σωτηρίαν ἡγούμενος τὴν τῶν πέλας ὠφέλειαν, ἄγαλμα ἔμψυχον εἰκότως ἂν τοῦ κυρίου λέγοιτο, οὐ κατὰ τὴν τῆς μορφῆς ἰδιότητα, ἀλλὰ κατὰ τὸ τῆς δυνάμεως σύμβολον καὶ κατὰ τὸ τῆς κηρύξεως ὁμοίωμα.

53. Πᾶν ἄρα ὅτιπερ ἂν ἐν νῷ, τοῦτο καὶ ἐπὶ γλώσσης φέρει πρὸς τοὺς ἐπαΐειν ἀξίους ἐκ τῆς συγκαταθέσεως, καὶ ἀπὸ γνώμης λέγων ἅμα καὶ βιούς. ἀληθῆ τε γὰρ φρονεῖ ἅμα καὶ ἀληθεύει, πλὴν εἰ μή ποτε ἐν θεραπείας μέρει, καθάπερ ἰατρὸς πρὸς νοσοῦντας ἐπὶ σωτηρίᾳ τῶν καμνόντων, ψεύσεται ἢ ψεῦδος ἐρεῖ κατὰ τοὺς σοφιστάς. αὐτίκα Τιμόθεον ὁ γενναῖος περιέτεμεν ἀπόστολος, κεκραγὼς καὶ γράφων περιτομὴν τὴν χειροποίητον οὐδὲν ὠφελεῖν· ἀλλ' ἵνα μή, ἀθρόως ἀποσπῶν τοῦ νόμου πρὸς τὴν ἐκ πίστεως τῆς καρδίας περιτομήν, ἀφηνιάζοντας ἔτι τοὺς ἀκροωμένους τῶν Ἑβραίων ἀπορρῆξαι τῆς συναγωγῆς ἀναγκάσῃ, συμπεριφερόμενος Ἰουδαίοις Ἰουδαῖος ἐγένετο, ἵνα πάντας κερδήσῃ. ὁ τοίνυν μέχρι τῆς συμπεριφορᾶς διὰ τὴν τῶν πέλας σωτηρίαν συγκαταβαίνων ψιλήν, διὰ τὴν τῶν δι' οὓς συμπεριφέρεται σωτηρίαν, οὐδεμιᾶς ὑποκρίσεως διὰ

3. τούτων] τούτῳ S. τὰς ante συνθήκας M. ante βεβαίας L. 27. ἔτι S, pro ἐπί. 30. διὰ τὴν τῶν πέλας σωτηρίαν seclusit P. 31. ψιλήν M. ψιλῆς L.

and fellowship with God. And as they that worship earthly things pray to the images as though they heard them, confirming their covenants before them; so the true majesty of the word is received from the trustworthy teacher in the presence of men, the living images <of God>, and the benefit done to them is referred to the Lord Himself, after whose likeness the true man creates and moulds the character of the man under instruction, renewing him to salvation. For, as the Greeks call iron by the name of Ares and wine by that of Dionysus (according to the figure which carries back the effect to the cause), so the gnostic who regards good done to his neighbours as his own salvation, might well be called a living image of the Lord, not according to the particular outward form, but in so far as he symbolizes His power and resembles Him in preaching the Gospel.

§ 53. Whatever then he has in his mind, that he has also on his tongue, when addressing those who are worthy to hear it from their agreement with him, since both his word and his life are in harmony with his thought. For he not only thinks what is true, but he also speaks the truth, except it be medicinally, on occasion; just as a physician, with a view to the safety of his patients, will practise deception or use deceptive language to the sick, according to the sophists. For instance the great Apostle *circumcised Timothy*[1], though he proclaimed aloud and in writing that *circumcision made with hands profiteth not*[2]. But fearing that, if he were all at once to withdraw from the law to the *circumcision of the heart which is by faith*[3], he might drive the Hebrew disciples who were still restive to break off from the congregation; accommodating himself to the Jews, *he became a Jew that he might gain all*[4]. He then who stoops to accommodation merely for the salvation of his neighbours, i.e. for the salvation of those for whose sake he practises accommo-

---

[1] Acts xvi. 3. [2] Rom. ii. 25, Eph. ii. 11.
[3] Rom. ii. 29, iii. 30. [4] 1 Cor. ix. 19 f.

τὸν ἐπηρτημένον τοῖς δικαίοις ἀπὸ τῶν ζηλούντων κίνδυνον μετέχων, οὗτος οὐδαμῶς ἀναγκάζεται· ἐπὶ δὲ τῶν πλησίον ὠφελείᾳ μόνῃ ποιήσει τινά, ἃ οὐκ ἂν προηγουμένως αὐτῷ πραχθείη, εἰ μὴ δι' ἐκείνους ποιοίη. οὗτος ἑαυτὸν ἐπιδίδωσιν ὑπὲρ τῆς ἐκκλησίας, ὑπὲρ τῶν γνωρίμων οὓς αὐτὸς ἐγέννησεν ἐν πίστει, εἰς ὑπόδειγμα τοῖς διαδέξασθαι τὴν ἄκραν οἰκονομίαν τοῦ φιλανθρώπου καὶ φιλοθέου παιδευτοῦ δυναμένοις, εἰς παράστασιν τῆς ἀληθείας τῶν λόγων, εἰς ἐνέργειαν τῆς ἀγάπης τῆς πρὸς τὸν κύριον. ἀδούλωτος οὗτος ἐν φόβῳ, ἀληθὴς ἐν λόγῳ, καρτερικὸς ἐν πόνῳ, μηδὲ ἐν τῷ προφορικῷ λόγῳ ψεύσασθαι θέλων ποτέ, κἂν τούτῳ τὸ ἀναμάρτητον πάντοτε κατορθῶν, ἐπεὶ τὸ ψεῦδος αὐτῷ, ἅτε μετά τινος δόλου εἰρημένον, οὐκ ἀργός ἐστι λόγος, ἀλλ' εἰς κακίαν ἐνεργεῖ. 54. πάντοθεν ἄρα μαρτυρεῖ τῇ ἀληθείᾳ μόνος ὁ γνωστικὸς καὶ ἔργῳ καὶ λόγῳ· ἀεὶ γὰρ κατορθοῖ ἐν πᾶσι πάντως καὶ ἐν λόγῳ καὶ ἐν πράξει καὶ ἐν αὐτῇ τῇ ἐννοίᾳ.

Αὕτη μὲν οὖν, ὡς ἐν ἐπιδρομῇ φάναι, ἡ τοῦ Χριστιανοῦ θεοσέβεια. εἰ δὴ καθηκόντως ταῦτα ποιεῖ καὶ κατὰ λόγον τὸν ὀρθόν, εὐσεβῶς ποιεῖ καὶ δικαίως. εἰ δὲ ταῦτα οὕτως ἔχει, μόνος ἂν εἴη τῷ ὄντι εὐσεβής τε καὶ δίκαιος καὶ θεοσεβὴς ὁ γνωστικός. οὐκ ἄρα ἄθεος ὁ Χριστιανός, (τουτὶ γὰρ ἦν τὸ προκείμενον ἐπιδεῖξαι τοῖς φιλοσόφοις,) ὥστε οὐδὲν κακὸν ἢ αἰσχρόν, ὃ ἐστιν ἄδικον, κατὰ μηδένα τρόπον ἐνεργήσει ποτέ. ἀκολούθως τοίνυν οὐδὲ ἀσεβεῖ, ἀλλ' ἢ μόνος τῷ ὄντι θεοσεβεῖ, ὁσίως καὶ προσηκόντως τὸν ὄντως ὄντα θεὸν πανηγεμόνα καὶ βασιλέα παντοκράτορα κατὰ τὴν ἀληθῆ θεοσέβειαν προστρεπόμενος.

2. ἀναγκάζεται] ἀναχάζεται P.   4. ποιοίη. H. ποιοίη, Kl. D.
10. ἀληθὴς ἐν λόγῳ] melius post πόνῳ ponetur haec sententiola M.
18. αὐτῷ M. αὐτὸ V. αὐτὸ τε L, sed τε punctis notato.   29. βασιλέα M.
βασιλέα καὶ L.   30. προστρεπόμενος M. ὁσίως προστρεπόμενος F.
Morellus. ὁσίως προτρεπόμενος L.

dation, not dissembling under stress of the danger which threatens the righteous from those who are jealous of them,— such an one can by no means be said to act under compulsion; though, solely for the good of his neighbours, he will do some things, which would not be done by him in the first instance, were it not for them. He offers himself in behalf of the Church, in behalf of the disciples whom he has himself *begotten*[1] in the faith, for a pattern to those that are capable of succeeding to the exalted office of a teacher filled with love to God and love to man, for confirmation of the truth of his words, for the manifestation of his love to the Lord. He is not enslaved in fear, he is patient in toil, true in word, shrinking from falsehood even in the outward utterance, and herein always attaining strict accuracy, since a lie in his eyes is no idle word, but is active for wickedness, as being the expression of a kind of treachery. § 54. So then it is the gnostic alone that *witnesses to the truth*[2] in every way both by word and deed: for he is altogether right in all things, in word and act and even in thought itself.

Such then is a brief account of Christian devoutness. If now the Christian does these things fittingly and in accordance with right reason, he is acting piously and justly. And if this is so, the gnostic alone would be really pious and just and devout. The Christian therefore is no atheist—for this is what we proposed to prove to the philosophers—so that nothing bad or mean, i.e. nothing unjust, will ever be done by him in any wise. It follows from this that neither is he impious; rather it is he alone that is truly pious, fitly and piously worshipping after the rule of a true devotion Him who is in very deed the All-ruling God and Almighty King.

[1] 1 Cor. iv. 15.   [2] Joh. v. 18, xviii. 37.

ΚΕΦ. Ι.

55. Εστιν γάρ, ὡς ἔπος εἰπεῖν, ἡ γνῶσις τελείωσίς τις ἀνθρώπου, ὡς ἀνθρώπου, διὰ τῆς τῶν θείων ἐπιστήμης συμπληρουμένη κατά τε τὸν τρόπον καὶ τὸν βίον καὶ τὸν λόγον, σύμφωνος καὶ ὁμόλογος ἑαυτῇ τε καὶ τῷ θείῳ λόγῳ. διὰ ταύτης γὰρ τελειοῦται ἡ πίστις ὡς τελείου τοῦ πιστοῦ ταύτῃ μόνως γινομένου. πίστις μὲν οὖν ἐνδιάθετόν τί ἐστιν ἀγαθόν, καὶ ἄνευ τοῦ ζητεῖν τὸν θεὸν ὁμολογοῦσα εἶναι τοῦτον καὶ δοξάζουσα ὡς ὄντα. ὅθεν χρή, ἀπὸ ταύτης ἀναγόμενον τῆς πίστεως καὶ αὐξηθέντα ἐν αὐτῇ, χάριτι τοῦ θεοῦ, τὴν περὶ αὐτοῦ κομίσασθαι ὡς οἷόν τέ ἐστιν γνῶσιν. γνῶσιν δὲ σοφίας τῆς κατὰ διδασκαλίαν ἐγγινομένης διαφέρειν φαμέν. ᾗ μὲν γὰρ τί ἐστι γνῶσις, ταύτῃ πάντως καὶ σοφία τυγχάνει, ᾗ δέ τι σοφία οὐ πάντως γνῶσις. ἐν μονῇ γὰρ τῇ τοῦ προφορικοῦ λόγου τὸ τῆς σοφίας ὄνομα φαντάζεται. πλὴν ἀλλὰ τὸ μὴ διστάσαι περὶ θεοῦ, πιστεῦσαι δέ, θεμέλιος γνώσεως· ἄμφω δὲ ὁ Χριστός, ὅ τε θεμέλιος ἥ τε ἐποικοδομή, δι' οὗ καὶ ἡ ἀρχὴ καὶ τὰ τέλη. καὶ τὰ μὲν ἄκρα οὐ διδάσκεται ἥ τε ἀρχὴ καὶ τὸ τέλος, πίστις λέγω καὶ ἡ ἀγάπη, ἡ γνῶσις δὲ ἐκ παραδόσεως διαδιδομένη κατὰ χάριν θεοῦ τοῖς ἀξίους σφᾶς αὐτοὺς τῆς διδασκαλίας παρεχομένοις οἷον παρακαταθήκη ἐγχειρίζεται, ἀφ' ἧς τὸ τῆς ἀγάπης ἀξίωμα ἐκλάμπει ἐκ φωτὸς εἰς φῶς. εἴρηται γὰρ τῷ ἔχοντι προστεθήσεται, τῇ μὲν πίστει ἡ γνῶσις, τῇ δὲ γνώσει ἡ ἀγάπη, τῇ ἀγάπῃ δὲ ἡ κληρονομία.

56. Γίνεται δὲ τοῦτο, ὁπόταν τις ἐκκρεμασθῇ τοῦ

---

2. ἀνθρώπου P. ἀνθρώπῳ LVD. 13, 14. ᾗ μὲν...ᾗ δὲ] ἣ μὲν...ἣ δὲ L. ᾗ μὲν...ᾗ δὲ V. 13. ταύτῃ SH. τοῦτο LD. 15. μονῇ Jackson. μόνῃ L. 19. διδάσκεται] ται duplicatur L. 22. τοῖς—παρεχομένοις Herv. τοὺς—παρεχομένους L. 22. αὑτοὺς] ἑαυτοὺς L. 27. ἐκκρεμασθῇ M. κρεμασθῇ L.

CHAPTER X.

§ 55. For the knowledge of insight (γνῶσις) is, so to speak, a kind of perfection of man as man, harmonious and consistent with itself and with the divine word, being completed, both as to the disposition and the manner of life and of speech, by the science of divine things. For it is by insight that *faith is made perfect*[1], seeing that the man of faith only becomes perfect in this way. Now faith is a certain inward good: without making search for God, it both confesses His existence, and glorifies Him as existent. Hence a man must start with this faith, and having waxed strong in it by the grace of God, must thus attain to insight concerning Him, so far as is possible. We distinguish however between insight and the wisdom which is implanted by teaching. For in so far as anything deserves to be called insight, so far it is certainly wisdom also; but in so far as a thing is wisdom, it is not certainly insight. For the meaning of the term wisdom is shown in the continuance of the uttered word: while the foundation of insight, on the other hand, lies in having no doubt about God, but trusting Him implicitly: and Christ is both the foundation and the superstructure—Christ, through Whom are both the beginning and the ends. Now the extremes, i.e. the beginning and the end, I mean faith and love, are not matters of teaching; but knowledge (γνῶσις), being handed down by tradition according to the grace of God, is entrusted as a deposit to those who show themselves worthy of the teaching; and from this teaching the worth of love shines forth in ever-increasing light. For it is said, *to him that hath, shall be added*[2], knowledge added to faith, and love to knowledge, and to love, the heavenly inheritance.

§ 56. This takes place whenever any one hangs upon the

[1] James ii. 22.   [2] Luke xix. 26.

κυρίου διά τε πίστεως διά τε γνώσεως διά τε αγάπης,
και συναναβῇ αυτῷ ἔνθα εστίν ὁ τῆς πίστεως ἡμῶν
και αγάπης θεός και φρουρός· ὅθεν επί τέλει ἡ γνῶσις
παραδίδοται τοῖς εις τοῦτο επιτηδείοις και εγκρίτοις,
διά τό πλείονος παρασκευῆς και προγυμνασίας δεῖσθαι
και πρός τό ακούειν τῶν λεγομένων και εις καταστολήν
βίου και εις τό επί πλέον τῆς κατὰ νόμον δικαιοσύνης κατ'
επίστασιν προεληλυθέναι. αὕτη πρός τέλος ἄγει τό
ατελεύτητον και τέλειον, προδιδάσκουσα τήν εσομένην
ἡμῖν κατά θεόν μετά θεῶν δίαιταν, απολυθέντων ἡμῶν
κολάσεως και τιμωρίας απάσης, ᾶς εκ τῶν αμαρτη-
μάτων εις παιδείαν ὑπομένομεν σωτήριον· μεθ' ἥν
απολύτρωσιν τό γέρας και αἱ τιμαί τελειωθεῖσιν απο-
δίδονται, πεπαυμένοις μέν τῆς καθάρσεως, πεπαυμένοις
δέ και λειτουργίας τῆς ἄλλης, κἂν αγία ᾖ και εν
αγίοις· ἔπειτα καθαροῖς τῇ καρδίᾳ γενομένοις κατά τό
προσεχές τοῦ κυρίου προσμένει τῇ θεωρίᾳ τῇ ἀϊδίῳ
αποκατάστασις. και θεοί τήν προσηγορίαν κέκληνται
οἱ σύνθρονοι τῶν ἄλλων θεῶν, τῶν ὑπό τῷ σωτῆρι
πρώτων τεταγμένων, γενησόμενοι. ταχεῖα τοίνυν εις
κάθαρσιν ἡ γνῶσις και επιτήδειος εις τήν επί τό
κρεῖττον ευπρόσδεκτον μεταβολήν. 57. ὅθεν και
ραδίως εις τό συγγενές τῆς ψυχῆς θεῖον τε και ἅγιον
μετοικίζει και διά τινος οικείου φωτός διαβιβάζει τάς
προκοπάς τάς μυστικάς τόν ἄνθρωπον, ἄχρις ἂν εις
τόν κορυφαῖον αποκαταστήσῃ τῆς αναπαύσεως τόπον,
τόν καθαρόν τῇ καρδίᾳ πρόσωπον πρός πρόσωπον επιστη-
μονικῶς και καταληπτικῶς τόν θεόν εποπτεύειν διδάξασα.
ενταῦθα γάρ που τῆς γνωστικῆς ψυχῆς ἡ τελείωσις,
πάσας καθάρσεις τε και λειτουργίας ὑπερβᾶσαν σύν

---

5. διὰ τὸ H. διὰ τοῦ L.   10. θεὸν S. τῶν θεῶν L. θεῶν V.
18. κέκληνται] litera ν pr. m. addita L.   24. διαβιβάζει] μεταβιβάζει L,
sed μετα punctis notato et δια pr. m. in margine posito.   30. πάσας
καθάρσεις H. πάσης καθάρσεως L.

Lord by means of faith and knowledge and love, and ascends up with Him to the presence of the God and Guardian of our faith and love; who is the ultimate source from which knowledge is imparted to those who are fitted and approved for it, because they need further preparation and training both for the hearing of the words spoken, and with a view to soberness of life and to their careful advance to a point *beyond the righteousness of the law*[1]. This knowledge leads us on to that perfect end which knows no end, teaching us here the nature of the life we shall hereafter live with gods according to the will of God, when we have been delivered from all chastisement and punishment, which we have to *endure* as salutary *chastening*[2] in consequence of our sins. After this deliverance rank and honours are assigned to those who are perfected, who have done now with purification and all other ritual, though it be holy among the holy; until at last, when they have been made *pure in heart*[3] by their closeness to the Lord, the final restoration attends on their everlasting contemplation of God. And the name of gods is given to those that shall hereafter be enthroned with the other gods, who first had their station assigned to them beneath the Saviour. Knowledge therefore is swift to purify, and suitable for the welcome change to the higher state. § 57. Hence, too, it easily transplants a man to that divine and holy state which is akin to the soul, and by a light of its own carries him through the mystic stages, till it restores him to the crowning abode of rest, having taught *the pure in heart to look upon God*[3] *face to face*[4] with understanding and absolute certainty. For herein lies the perfection of the gnostic soul, that having transcended all

---

[1] Mt. v. 20, Rom. x. 5.
[2] Heb. xii. 7.
[3] Mt. v. 8.
[4] 1 Cor. xiii. 12.

τῷ κυρίῳ γίνεσθαι, ὅπου ἔστιν, προσεχῶς ὑποτεταγμένην.

Ἡ μὲν οὖν πίστις σύντομός ἐστιν, ὡς εἰπεῖν, τῶν κατεπειγόντων γνῶσις, ἡ γνῶσις δὲ ἀπόδειξις τῶν διὰ πίστεως παρειλημμένων ἰσχυρὰ καὶ βέβαιος, διὰ τῆς κυριακῆς διδασκαλίας ἐποικοδομουμένη τῇ πίστει εἰς τὸ ἀμετάπτωτον καὶ μετ᾽ ἐπιστήμης καταληπτὸν παραπέμπουσα. καί μοι δοκεῖ πρώτη τις εἶναι μεταβολὴ σωτήριος ἡ ἐξ ἐθνῶν εἰς πίστιν, ὡς προεῖπον, δευτέρα δὲ ἡ ἐκ πίστεως εἰς γνῶσιν· ἡ δέ, εἰς ἀγάπην περαιουμένη, ἐνθένδε ἤδη φίλον φίλῳ τὸ γινῶσκον τῷ γινωσκομένῳ παρίστησιν. καὶ τάχα ὁ τοιοῦτος ἐνθένδε ἤδη προλαβὼν ἔχει τὸ ἰσάγγελος εἶναι. Μετὰ γοῦν τὴν ἐν σαρκὶ τελευταίαν ὑπεροχὴν ἀεὶ κατὰ τὸ προσῆκον ἐπὶ τὸ κρεῖττον μεταβάλλων, εἰς τὴν πατρῴαν αὐλὴν ἐπὶ τὴν κυριακὴν ὄντως διὰ τῆς ἁγίας ἑβδομάδος ἐπείγεται μονήν, ἐσόμενος, ὡς εἰπεῖν, φῶς ἑστὸς καὶ μένον ἀϊδίως, πάντη πάντως ἄτρεπτον.

58. Ὁ πρῶτος τῆς κυριακῆς ἐνεργείας τρόπος τῆς εἰρημένης ἡμῖν κατὰ τὴν θεοσέβειαν ἀμοιβῆς δεῖγμα. πολλῶν ὅσων μαρτυρίων ὄντων παραστήσομαι ἓν κεφαλαιωδῶς πρὸς τοῦ προφήτου Δαβὶδ ὧδέ πως εἰρημένον, τίс ἀναβήсεται εἰс τὸ ὄροс τοῦ κυρίου; ἢ τίс сτήсεται ἐν τόπῳ ἁγίῳ αὐτοῦ; ἀθῷος χερсὶ καὶ καθαρὸс τῇ καρδίᾳ, ὃс οὐκ ἔλαβεν ἐπὶ ματαίῳ τὴν ψυχὴν αὐτοῦ οὐδὲ ὤμοсεν ἐπὶ δόλῳ τῷ πληсίον αὐτοῦ. οὗτος λήψεται εὐλογίαν παρὰ κυρίου καὶ ἐλεημοсύνην παρὰ θεοῦ сωτῆροс αὐτοῦ. αὕτη ἡ γενεὰ ζητούντων τὸν κύριον, ζητούντων τὸ πρόсωπον τοῦ θεοῦ Ἰακώβ. συντόμως, οἶμαι, τὸν γνωστικὸν ἐμήνυσεν ὁ προφήτης· κατὰ παραδρομήν, ὡς ἔοικεν, ἡμῖν θεὸν εἶναι τὸν σωτῆρα ἀπέδειξεν ὁ Δαβὶδ πρόсωπον αὐτὸν εἰπὼν τοῦ θεοῦ Ἰακώβ, τὸν εὐαγγελισάμενον καὶ διδάξαντα

---

1. ὑποτεταγμένην H. ὑποτεταγμένη L.   6. ἐπιστήμης S. ἐπιστήμης καὶ L.   καταληπτὸν LH. καταληπτικὸν PD.   10. περαιουμένη H. περαιουμένη. Kl D.   17. ἀϊδίως P. ἰδίως L.   20. πολλῶν L. πολλῶν δ᾽ D. μαρτυρίων S. μαρτυριῶν L.   29. κατά] fort. καὶ κατὰ M.

purifications and modes of ritual, *it should be with the Lord*[1] where He is, in immediate subordination to Him.

Faith then is a compendious knowledge of the essentials, but knowledge is a sure and firm demonstration of the things received through faith, being itself built up by the Lord's teaching on the foundation of the faith, and carrying us on to unshaken conviction and scientific certainty. As I mentioned before, there seems to me to be a first kind of saving change from heathenism to faith, a second from faith to knowledge; and this latter, as it passes on into love, begins at once to establish a mutual friendship between that which knows and that which is known. And perhaps he who has arrived at this stage has already *attained equality with the angels*[2]. At any rate, after he has reached the final ascent in the flesh, he still continues to advance, as is fit, and presses on through the holy Hebdomad into the Father's house, to that which is indeed the Lord's *abode*[3], being destined there to be, as it were, a light standing and abiding for ever, absolutely secure from all vicissitude.

§ 58. The first mode of the Lord's working gives evidence of the above-mentioned reward following on devoutness. Out of many testimonies I will adduce one, thus summarily stated by the prophet David: *Who shall ascend into the hill of the Lord? or who shall stand in his holy place? He that hath clean hands and a pure heart; who hath not lifted up his soul unto vanity nor sworn deceitfully to his neighbour. He shall receive a blessing from the Lord and mercy from God his Saviour. This is the generation of them that seek the Lord, that seek the face of the God of Jacob*[4]. The prophet is here briefly describing the gnostic, and in passing, as it seems, he shows that the Saviour is God, calling Him *the face of the God of Jacob*, i.e. one who preached and taught concerning the

---

[1] 1 Thes. iv. 17.
[2] Luke xx. 36.
[3] Job. xiv. 2.
[4] Ps. xxiv. 3—6.

περὶ τοῦ πατρός. διὸ καὶ ὁ ἀπόστολος χαρακτῆρα τῆς δόξης τοῦ πατρὸς τὸν υἱὸν προσεῖπεν, τὸν τὴν ἀλήθειαν περὶ τοῦ θεοῦ διδάξαντα καὶ χαρακτηρίσαντα ὅτι θεὸς καὶ πατὴρ εἷς καὶ μόνος ὁ παντοκράτωρ, ὃν οὐδεὶς ἔγνω εἰ μὴ ὁ υἱός, καὶ ᾧ ἐὰν ὁ υἱὸς ἀποκαλύψῃ. ἕνα δὲ εἶναι τὸν θεὸν διὰ τοῦ Ζητούντων τὸ πρόσωπον τοῦ θεοῦ Ἰακὼβ μεμήνυται, ὃν μόνον ὄντα θεὸν πατέρα ἀγαθὸν χαρακτηρίζει ὁ σωτὴρ ἡμῶν καὶ θεός. ἡ γενεὰ δὲ τῶν ζητούντων αὐτὸν τὸ γένος ἐστὶ τὸ ἐκλεκτόν, τὸ ζητητικὸν εἰς γνῶσιν.

59. Διὰ τοῦτο καὶ ὁ ἀπόστολός φησιν οὐδὲν ὑμᾶς ὠφελήσω, ἐὰν μὴ ὑμῖν λαλήσω ἢ ἐν ἀποκαλύψει ἢ ἐν γνώσει ἢ ἐν προφητείᾳ ἢ ἐν διδαχῇ. καίτοι πράσσεταί τινα καὶ πρὸς τῶν μὴ γνωστικῶν ὀρθῶς, ἀλλ' οὐ κατὰ λόγον, οἷον ἐπὶ ἀνδρείας. ἔνιοι γὰρ ἐκ φύσεως θυμοειδεῖς γενόμενοι εἶτα ἄνευ τοῦ λόγου τοῦτο θρέψαντες ἀλόγως ἐπὶ τὰ πολλὰ ὁρμῶσι καὶ ὅμοια τοῖς ἀνδρείοις δρῶσιν, ὥστε ἐνίοτε τὰ αὐτὰ κατορθοῦν οἷον βασάνους ὑπομένειν εὐκόλως, ἀλλ' οὔτε ἀπὸ τῆς αὐτῆς αἰτίας τῷ γνωστικῷ οὔτε καὶ τὸ αὐτὸ προθέμενοι, οὐδ' ἂν τὸ σῶμα ἅπαν ἐπιδιδῶσιν· ἀγάπην γὰρ οὐκ ἔχουσι κατὰ τὸν ἀπόστολον τὴν διὰ τῆς γνώσεως γεννωμένην. πᾶσα οὖν ἡ διὰ τοῦ ἐπιστήμονος πρᾶξις εὐπραγία, ἡ δὲ διὰ τοῦ ἀνεπιστήμονος κακοπραγία, κἂν ἔνστασιν σώζῃ, ἐπεὶ μὴ ἐκ λογισμοῦ ἀνδρίζεται μηδὲ ἐπί τι χρήσιμον τῶν ἐπὶ ἀρετῆς καταστρεφόντων τὴν πρᾶξιν κατευθύνει. ὁ δὲ αὐτὸς λόγος καὶ ἐπὶ τῶν ἄλλων ἀρετῶν, ὥστε καὶ ἐπὶ θεοσεβείας ἀνὰ λόγον. οὐ μόνον τοίνυν τοιοῦτος ἡμῖν κατὰ τὴν ὁσιότητα ὁ γνωστικός, ἀκόλουθα δὲ τῇ ἐπιστημονικῇ θεοσεβείᾳ καὶ τὰ περὶ τὴν ἄλλην πολιτείαν ἐπαγγέλματα. τὸν βίον γὰρ τοῦ γνωστικοῦ διαγράφειν ἡμῖν πρόκειται τανῦν, οὐχὶ τὴν τῶν δογ-

---

1. πατρὸς H. πνεύματος L. 6. τοῦ ζητούντων H. τῶν ζητούντων L. 17. βασάνους P. βασάνοις L. 20. ἐπιδιδῶσιν P. ἐπιδίδωσιν L. 25. ἐπὶ ἀρετῆς M. ἐπὶ ἀρετὴν καὶ ἀπὸ ἀρετῆς L. 27. ἀνὰ λόγον M. ἀνάλογον L. 31. τανῦν] τὰ νῦν L.

Father. Wherefore also the Apostle used the phrase, *impress of the Father's glory*[1] in reference to *the Son*, who taught the truth concerning God and gave this mark, that *One alone is God and Father*[2], viz. the Almighty, *whom no one knew but the Son, and he to whom the Son shall have revealed Him*[3]. That *God is one* is also declared by the phrase *seeking the face of the God of Jacob*, whom *alone*, being God the Father, our Saviour and God characterizes as *good*[4]. But *the generation of them that seek Him is the chosen race*[5] which seeks with a view to knowledge.

§ 59. For this reason also the Apostle says *I shall profit you nothing unless I speak unto you either in the way of revelation or of knowledge or of prophesying or of teaching*[6]. And yet some things are done rightly, though not on rational grounds, even by those who are not gnostics, as in the case of courage. For some men, being by nature full of spirit and having fostered this quality without the use of reason, act for the most part by irrational impulse and do the same sort of things as brave men, so as at times to exhibit the same height of virtue, as for instance to endure tortures calmly; but this is neither from the same cause nor even with the same purpose as the gnostic, even *though they should give up their whole body*[7]; for, as the Apostle says, they *have not the love* which proceeds from knowledge. All the action then of a man of understanding is of the nature of well-doing and all the action of him who is without understanding is ill-doing, even though he should be maintaining a principle, since his courage does not proceed from reason, nor does he direct his action for any useful purpose, such as has its end in virtue. The same thing may be said of the other virtues and therefore by analogy in the case of religion. Accordingly we shall find the gnostic to be such not in holiness only; but, in regard to the rest of his conduct also, his professions are in accordance with his enlightened piety. For it is the life of the gnostic which it is our purpose now to describe, and not to give a systematic view of his beliefs

---

[1] Heb. i. 3.   [2] Eph. iv. 6.   [3] Mt. xi. 27.   [4] Mt. xix. 17.
[5] 1 Pet. ii. 9.   [6] 1 Cor. xiv. 6.   [7] 1 Cor. xiii. 8.

μάτων θεωρίαν παρατίθεσθαι, ἣν ὕστερον κατὰ τὸν ἐπιβάλλοντα καιρὸν ἐκθησόμεθα, σώζοντες ἅμα καὶ τὴν ἀκολουθίαν.

ΚΕΦ. ΙΑ.

60. Περὶ μὲν οὖν τῶν ὅλων ἀληθῶς καὶ μεγαλοπρεπῶς διείληφεν, ὡς ἂν θείαν χωρήσας διδασκαλίαν. ἀρξάμενος γοῦν ἐκ τοῦ θαγμάζειν τὴν κτίσιν, δεῖγμα τοῦ δύνασθαι λαβεῖν τὴν γνῶσιν κομίζων οἴκοθεν, πρόθυμος μαθητὴς τοῦ κυρίου γίνεται, εὐθέως δὲ ἀκούσας θεόν τε καὶ πρόνοιαν ἐπίστευσεν ἐξ ὧν ἐθαύμασεν. ἐνθένδε οὖν ὁρμώμενος ἐκ παντὸς τρόπου συνεργεῖ πρὸς τὴν μάθησιν, πάντ' ἐκεῖνα ποιῶν δι' ὧν λαβεῖν δυνήσεται τὴν γνῶσιν ὧν ποθεῖ, (πόθος δὲ κατὰ προκοπὴν πίστεως ἅμα ζητήσει κραθεὶς συνίσταται,) τὸ δ' ἐστὶν ἄξιον γενέσθαι τῆς τοσαύτης καὶ τηλικαύτης θεωρίας. οὕτως γεύσεται τοῦ θελήματος τοῦ θεοῦ ὁ γνωστικός· οὐ γὰρ τὰς ἀκοάς, ἀλλὰ τὴν ψυχὴν παρίστησι τοῖς ὑπὸ τῶν λεγομένων δηλουμένοις πράγμασιν. οὐσίας τοίνυν καὶ τὰ πράγματα αὐτὰ παραλαβὼν διὰ τῶν λόγων εἰκότως καὶ τὴν ψυχὴν ἐπὶ τὰ δέοντα ἄγει, τὸ μὴ μοιχεύσῃς, μὴ φονεύσῃς ἰδίως ἐκλαμβάνων ὡς εἴρηται τῷ γνωστικῷ, οὐχ ὡς παρὰ τοῖς ἄλλοις ὑπείληπται.

61. Πρόεισιν οὖν ἐγγυμναζόμενος τῇ ἐπιστημονικῇ θεωρίᾳ εἰς τὸ ἐπαγωνίσασθαι τοῖς καθολικώτερον καὶ μεγαλοπρεπέστερον εἰρημένοις, εἰδὼς εὖ μάλα ὅτι ὁ διδάσκων ἄνθρωπον γνῶσιν, κατὰ τὸν προφήτην, κύριός ἐστιν, διὰ στόματος ἀνθρωπίνου κύριος ἐνεργῶν· ταύτῃ καὶ σάρκα ἀνείληφεν. εἰκότως οὖν οὐδέποτε τὸ ἡδὺ πρὸ τοῦ συμφέροντος αἱρεῖται, οὐδ' ἂν προκαλῆται

22. πρόεισιν Herv. πρόσεισιν L. 23. ἐπαγωνίσασθαι H. ἐναγωνίσασθαι L. 26. κύριος ἐνεργῶν] κυρίως ἐνεργῶν H.

CHAPTER XI.

§ 60. The gnostic then has a true and noble conception of the universe, as might be expected from one who has comprehended the divine teaching. *Starting with* that *admiration*[1] for the Creation which he brings with him as an evidence of his capacity to receive knowledge, he becomes an eager disciple of the Lord, and the moment he hears of God and Providence, his admiration prompts him to believe. Proceeding from this point he does his best to learn in every way, employing every means to obtain the knowledge of those things which he longs for (and longing joined with seeking arises as faith increases), that is, to be made worthy of such high and glorious contemplation. Thus the gnostic will taste of the will of God. For he lends, not his ears, but his soul, to the facts indicated by the spoken words. Since then what he receives through the words are realities and the facts themselves, he naturally brings his soul to his duties, understanding the commands *Do not commit adultery, do not kill*[2] in a special sense, as they are addressed to the gnostic and not as they are apprehended by the rest of the world.

§ 61. Training himself in scientific contemplation, he goes on to contend on the strength of these higher and more universal truths, being fully assured that *He who* (according to the prophet) *teaches man knowledge is the Lord*[3], the Lord using man's mouth as His organ. Hence also He has taken human flesh. With good reason therefore he never prefers what is pleasant to what is expedient, not even though he

---

[1] Pl. *Theaet.* 155 D.   [2] Exod. xx. 13, 15, Mt. v. 21, 27.   [3] Ps. xciii. 10, 11.

αὐτὸν κατά τινα περίστασιν προκαταληφθέντα ἑταιρικῶς ἐκβιαζομένῃ ὡραία γυνή, ἐπεὶ μηδὲ τὸν Ἰωσὴφ παράγειν τῆς ἐνστάσεως ἴσχυσεν ἡ τοῦ δεσπότου γυνή, ἀπεδύσατο δὲ αὐτῇ πρὸς βίαν κατεχούσῃ τὸν χιτῶνα, γυμνὸς μὲν τῆς ἁμαρτίας γενόμενος, τὸ κόσμιον δὲ τοῦ ἤθους περιβαλλόμενος. εἰ γὰρ καὶ οἱ τοῦ δεσπότου ὀφθαλμοὶ οὐχ ἑώρων, τοῦ Αἰγυπτίου λέγω, τὸν Ἰωσήφ, ἀλλ᾽ οἵ γε τοῦ παντοκράτορος ἐπεσκόπουν. ἡμεῖς μὲν γὰρ τῆς φωνῆς ἀκούομεν καὶ τὰ σώματα θεωροῦμεν, ὁ θεὸς δὲ τὸ πρᾶγμα, ἀφ᾽ οὗ φέρεται τὸ φωνεῖν καὶ βλέπειν, ἐξετάζει. ἀκολούθως ἄρα κἂν νόσος ἐπίῃ κἂν τι τῶν περιστατικῶν τῷ γνωστικῷ, καὶ δὴ μάλιστα ὁ φοβερώτατος θάνατος, ἄτρεπτος μένει κατὰ τὴν ψυχήν, πάντα εἰδὼς τὰ τοιαῦτα κτίσεως ἀνάγκην εἶναι, ἀλλὰ καὶ οὕτως δυνάμει τοῦ θεοῦ φάρμακον γίνεσθαι cωτηρίαc, διὰ παιδείας τοὺς ἀπηνέστερον μεταρρυθμιζομένους εὐεργετοῦντα, πρὸς τῆς ἀγαθῆς ὄντως κατ᾽ ἀξίαν μεριζόμενα προνοίας.

62. Χρώμενος τοίνυν τοῖς κτιστοῖς, ὁπόταν αἱρῇ λόγος, εἰς ὅσον αἱρεῖ, κατὰ τὴν ἐπὶ τὸν κτίσαντα εὐχαριστίαν, καὶ τῆς ἀπολαύσεως κύριος καθίσταται. οὐ μνησικακεῖ ποτέ, οὐ χαλεπαίνει οὐδενί, κἂν μίσους ἄξιος τυγχάνῃ, ἐφ᾽ οἷς διαπράττεται· σέβει μὲν γὰρ τὸν ποιητήν, ἀγαπᾷ δὲ τὸν κοινωνὸν τοῦ βίου, οἰκτείρων καὶ ὑπερευχόμενος αὐτοῦ διὰ τὴν ἄγνοιαν αὐτοῦ. καὶ δὴ καὶ συμπάσχει τῷ σώματι τῷ φύσει παθητῷ ἐνδεδεμένος, ἀλλ᾽ οὐ πρωτοπαθεῖ κατὰ τὸ πάθος. κατὰ γοῦν τὰς ἀκουσίους περιστάσεις ἀνάγων ἑαυτὸν ἀπὸ τῶν πόνων ἐπὶ τὰ οἰκεῖα οὐ συναποφέρεται τοῖς ἀλλοτρίοις αὐτοῦ, συμπεριφέρεται δὲ τοῖς ἀναγκαίοις αὐτοῦ μόνον εἰς ὅσον ἀβλαβὴς τηρεῖται ἡ ψυχή. οὐ γὰρ

---

10. πρᾶγμα] fort. πνεῦμα M.   11, 12. κἄν τι M. καὶ τι L.   19. αἱρῇ λόγοι...αἱρεῖ D. αἱρεῖ λ...αἱρεῖ Lowth. ἑρεῖ λ...ἑρεῖ L.   25. αὑτοῦ H. αὐτοῦ, Kl. D.

should be taken at a disadvantage and vehemently urged by the harlot arts of some fair wanton: for neither could Joseph be seduced from his firm purpose by his master's wife, but when she kept hold of his garment, he left it in her hands, being thus denuded of sin, but clothing himself in modesty. For, though the eyes of his master, I mean the Egyptian, did not see Joseph, yet the eyes of the Almighty were watching him. For we men hear the voice and see the bodily form, but *the Lord searcheth the spirit*[1], from which both speech and sight proceed. In like manner whether disease or accident befall the gnostic, aye, or even death the most terrible of all things, he continues unchanged in soul, knowing that all such things are a necessary result of creation, but that, even so, they are made by the power of God *a medicine of salvation*[2], benefiting by discipline those who are disposed to rebel against amendment, being distributed according to desert by a truly merciful Providence.

§ 62. The gnostic then uses God's creatures, when, and so far as, it is reasonable, in a spirit of thankfulness to the Creator, and so gains the mastery over his enjoyment of them. He never bears a grudge, is never angry with anyone, even though he should deserve hatred for his conduct: for he worships the Creator and loves his fellow man, pitying him and praying for him on account of his ignorance. Moreover, though he shares in the affections of the body, naturally sensitive as it is, in which he is imprisoned, yet he is not primarily affected by passion. At any rate, in the accidents which befall him against his will, he raises himself from his troubles to his native element, and is not carried away by things which have nothing to do with the true self, but accommodates himself to the necessities of the case, so far as it does not interfere with the welfare of the soul. For he does not wish to be faithful only in

---

[1] 1 Sam. xvi. 7, Jer. xvii. 10, &c.   [2] Eur. *Phoen.* 893.

που ἐν ὑπολήψει, ἀλλ' οὐδὲ ἐν τῷ δοκεῖν πιστὸς εἶναι βούλεται, γνώσει δὲ καὶ ἀληθείᾳ, ὅ ἐστιν ἔργῳ βεβαίῳ καὶ λόγῳ ἐνεργῷ. οὐκοῦν οὐ μόνον ἐπαινεῖ τὰ καλά, ἀλλὰ καὶ αὐτὸς βιάζεται εἶναι καλός, ἐκ τοῦ ἀγαθοῦ καὶ πιστοῦ δούλου μεταβαίνων δι' ἀγάπης εἰς φίλον διὰ τὸ τέλεον τῆς ἕξεως, ὃ ἐκ μαθήσεως τῆς ἀληθοῦς καὶ συνασκήσεως πολλῆς καθαρῶς ἐκτήσατο.

63. Ὡς ἂν οὖν ἐπ' ἄκρον γνώσεως ἥκειν βιαζόμενος, τῷ ἤθει κεκοσμημένος, τῷ σχήματι κατεσταλμένος, πάντα ἐκεῖνα ἔχων ὅσα πλεονεκτήματά ἐστιν τοῦ κατ' ἀλήθειαν γνωστικοῦ, εἰς τὰς εἰκόνας ἀφορῶν τὰς καλάς, πολλοὺς μὲν τοὺς κατωρθωκότας πρὸ αὐτοῦ πατριάρχας, παμπόλλους δὲ προφήτας, ἀπείρους δ' ὅσους ἡμῖν ἀριθμῷ λογιζομένοις ἀγγέλους, καὶ τὸν ἐπὶ πᾶσι κύριον τὸν διδάξαντα καὶ παραστήσαντα δυνατὸν εἶναι τὸν κορυφαῖον ἐκεῖνον κτήσασθαι βίον, διὰ τοῦτο τὰ πρόχειρα πάντα τοῦ κόσμου καλὰ οὐκ ἀγαπᾷ, ἵνα μὴ καταμείνῃ χαμαί, ἀλλὰ τὰ ἐλπιζόμενα, μᾶλλον δὲ τὰ ἐγνωσμένα ἤδη, εἰς κατάληψιν δὲ ἐλπιζόμενα. ταύτῃ ἄρα τοὺς πόνους καὶ τὰς βασάνους καὶ τὰς θλίψεις, οὐχ ὡς παρὰ τοῖς φιλοσόφοις οἱ ἀνδρεῖοι, ἐλπίδι τοῦ παύσασθαι μὲν τὰ ἐνεστῶτα ἀλγεινά, αὖθις δὲ τῶν ἡδέων μετασχεῖν, ὑπομένει, ἀλλ' ἡ γνῶσις αὐτῷ πεῖσμα βεβαιότερον ἐλπίδος ἐνεγέννησεν τῆς τῶν μελλόντων ἀπολήψεως. διόπερ οὐ μόνον τῶν ἐνταῦθα κολάσεων, ἀλλὰ καὶ τῶν ἡδέων ἁπάντων καταφρονεῖ. φασὶ γοῦν τὸν μακάριον Πέτρον θεασάμενον τὴν αὐτοῦ γυναῖκα

reputation or indeed in outward seeming, but in knowledge and in truth, that is to say, in consistent action and effectual speech. Wherefore he not only praises what is noble, but himself strives to be noble, passing from the condition of a *good and faithful servant*[1] to that of *a friend*[2] by means of love, owing to the perfection of the virtuous habit which he acquired in its purity by true instruction and long training.

§ 63. As one then who would force his way to the pinnacle of knowledge, orderly in character, sober in bearing, he possesses all the advantages which mark the true gnostic, fixing his eyes on noble images, on the many patriarchs who have fought their fight before him, on a still greater multitude of prophets, on angels beyond our power to number, on the Lord who is over all, who taught him, and made it possible for him to attain that crowning life. For this reason he loves none of the fair things that the world holds out to him, fearing lest they should tie him to the ground; but he loves the things which are hoped for, or rather are already known, but whose possession is hoped for. Thus he endures his labours and tortures and afflictions, not, like the brave men whom the philosophers talk of, from hope that the present evils will cease, and that he will again have a share of pleasures; no, knowledge has begotten in him a persuasion, surer than any hope, of the reaping of rewards to come. Wherefore he despises not only the persecutions, but also all the pleasures of this world. So we are told that the blessed Peter, when he beheld his wife on her way to execution,

[1] Mt. xxv. 23.   [2] Joh. xv. 15.

ἀγομένην τὴν ἐπὶ θάνατον ἡσθῆναι μὲν τῆς κλήσεως χάριν καὶ τῆς εἰς οἶκον ἀνακομιδῆς, ἐπιφωνῆσαι δὲ εὖ μάλα προτρεπτικῶς τε καὶ παρακλητικῶς ἐξ ὀνόματος προσειπόντα "μέμνησο, ὦ αὕτη, τοῦ κυρίου."

64. Τοιοῦτος ἦν ὁ τῶν μακαρίων γάμος καὶ ἡ μέχρι τῶν φιλτάτων τελεία διάθεσις. ταύτῃ καὶ ὁ ἀπόστολος ὁ γαμῶν φησὶν ὡς μὴ γαμῶν, ἀπροσπαθῆ τὸν γάμον ἀξιῶν εἶναι καὶ ἀπερίσπαστον τῆς πρὸς τὸν κύριον ἀγάπης, ἧς ἔχεσθαι ἀποδημούσῃ τοῦ βίου πρὸς τὸν κύριον τῇ γυναικὶ ὁ τῷ ὄντι ἀνὴρ παρῄνεσεν. ἆρ' οὐ πρόδηλος ἦν ἡ πίστις αὐτοῖς τῆς μετὰ θάνατον ἐλπίδος τοῖς καὶ ἐν αὐταῖς τῶν κολάσεων ταῖς ἀκμαῖς εὐχαριστοῦσι τῷ θεῷ; βεβαίαν γάρ, οἶμαι, τὴν πίστιν ἐκέκτηντο, ᾗ κατηκολούθουν πισταὶ καὶ ἐνέργειαι. ἔστιν οὖν ἐν πάσῃ περιστάσει ἐρρωμένη τοῦ γνωστικοῦ ἡ ψυχή, οἷον ἀθλητοῦ τὸ σῶμα ἐν ἄκρᾳ εὐεξίᾳ καὶ ῥώμῃ καθεστηκυῖα. εὔβουλος μὲν γὰρ ὑπάρχει περὶ τὰ ἀνθρώπων, τῷ δικαίῳ τὸ πρακτέον γνωματεύουσα, τὰς ἀρχὰς θεόθεν ἄνωθεν καὶ πρὸς τὴν θείαν ἐξομοίωσιν πραότητα ἡδονῶν καὶ λυπῶν σωματικῶν περιπεποιημένη· κατεξανίσταται δὲ τῶν φόβων εὐθαρσὴς καὶ πεποιθὼς τῷ θεῷ. ἀτεχνῶς οὖν ἐπίγειος εἰκὼν θείας δυνάμεως ἡ γνωστικὴ ψυχή, τελείᾳ ἀρετῇ κεκοσμημένη, ἐκ πάντων ἅμα τούτων, φύσεως, ἀσκήσεως, λόγου, συνηυξημένῃ. τοῦτο τὸ κάλλος τῆς ψυχῆς νεὼς γίνεται τοῦ ἁγίου πνεύματος, ὅταν διάθεσιν ὁμολογουμένην τῷ εὐαγγελίῳ κατὰ πάντα κτήσηται τὸν βίον.

65. Ὁ τοιοῦτος ἄρα κατεξανίσταται παντὸς φόβου, παντὸς δεινοῦ, οὐ μόνον θανάτου, ἀλλὰ καὶ πενίας καὶ

---

1. ἀγόμενον Cobet.   θάνατον] θανάτῳ Eus.   θανάτου Hoeschelius.
2. εἰς] Eusebii codices partim sic, partim ἐπ'.   3. τε om. Eus.
4. μέμνησο, ὦ αὕτη Eus.   μεμνῆσθω αὐτῇ L.   6. μέχρι om. Eus.
19. ἄνωθεν] fort. ἄνωθεν εἰληφυῖα M.   21. εὐθαρσῶς P. εὐθάρσως L.
εὐθαρσὴς L.   22. ἀτεχνῶς] ἀτέχνως L.   25. συνηυξημένῃ M.
συνηυξημένη Lowth.   συνηυξημένου L.

rejoiced on account of her call and her homeward journey, and addressed her by name with words of exhortation and good cheer, bidding her 'remember the Lord.'

§ 64. Such was the marriage of those blessed ones and such their perfect control over their feelings even in the dearest relations of life. So too the Apostle says *Let him that marrieth be as though he married not*[1], requiring that marriage should not be enslaved to passion *nor distracted from* the love to *the Lord*[2]; to which love the wife, when departing from this life to the Lord, was exhorted to cling by him who showed himself a husband indeed. Was not the faith in the hope after death clearly manifested by those who, even in the very height of persecution, could return thanks to God? The reason, I suppose, was the steadfastness of their faith, which was accompanied by acts of corresponding faithfulness. So in every difficulty the soul of the gnostic proves its strength, being in first-rate condition and vigour, like the body of the athlete. For it is well-advised in the affairs of men, measuring what has to be done by the rule of justice, <having received> its principles from God in the first instance, and having attained to moderation in the pleasures and pains of the body, in accordance with the divine likeness: thus he rises up against his fears with good courage, putting his trust in God. Accordingly the gnostic soul is just an earthly image of the divine Power, adorned with perfect virtue, built up by the combined action of nature, discipline, and reason. The soul thus beautified becomes *a temple of the Holy Spirit*[3], when it has acquired a temper of mind corresponding to the Gospel in every relation of life.

§ 65. Such an one rises up against every fear and all that is terrible, not death alone, but poverty and disease and dis-

---

[1] 1 Cor. vii. 29.   [2] 1 Cor. vii. 35.   [3] 1 Cor. vi. 19.

νόσου, ἀδοξίας τε καὶ τῶν ὅσα τούτοις συγγενῆ, ἀήττητος ἡδονῇ γενόμενος καὶ τῶν ἀλόγων ἐπιθυμιῶν κύριος. εὖ γὰρ οἶδεν τὰ ποιητέα καὶ μή, ἐγνωκὼς κατὰ κράτος τά τε τῷ ὄντι δεινὰ καὶ τὰ μή. ὅθεν ἐπιστημόνως ὑφίσταται ἃ δεῖν καὶ προσήκειν αὐτῷ ὁ λόγος ὑπαγορεύει, διακρίνων ἐπιστημόνως τὰ τῷ ὄντι θαρραλέα, τουτέστι τὰ ἀγαθά, ἀπὸ τῶν φαινομένων καὶ τὰ φοβερὰ ἀπὸ τῶν δοκούντων, οἷον θανάτου καὶ νόσου καὶ πενίας, ἅπερ δόξης μᾶλλον ἢ ἀληθείας ἔχεται. οὗτος ὁ τῷ ὄντι ἀγαθὸς ἀνὴρ ὁ ἔξω τῶν παθῶν, κατὰ τὴν ἕξιν ἢ διάθεσιν τῆς ἐναρέτου ψυχῆς ὑπερβὰς ὅλον τὸν ἐμπαθῆ βίον. τούτῳ πάντα εἰς ἑαυτὸν ἀνήρτηται πρὸς τὴν τοῦ τέλους κτῆσιν. τὰ μὲν γὰρ λεγόμενα τυχηρὰ δεινά, ταῦτα τῷ σπουδαίῳ οὐ φοβερά, ὅτι μὴ κακά, τὰ δὲ τῷ ὄντι δεινὰ ἀλλότρια Χριστιανοῦ τοῦ γνωστικοῦ, ἐκ διαμέτρου χωροῦντα τοῖς ἀγαθοῖς, ἐπειδὴ κακά· καὶ ἀμήχανον ἅμα τῷ αὐτῷ τὰ ἐναντία κατὰ ταὐτὸν καὶ πρὸς τὸν αὐτὸν ἀπαντᾶν χρόνον. ἀμεμφῶς τοίνυν ὑποκρινόμενος τὸ δρᾶμα τοῦ βίου, ὅπερ ἂν ὁ θεὸς ἀγωνίσασθαι παράσχῃ, τά τε πρακτέα τά τε ὑπομενετέα γνωρίζει.

66. Μή τι οὖν ἢ δι' ἄγνοιαν τῶν δεινῶν καὶ μὴ δεινῶν συνίσταται ἡ δειλία; μόνος ἄρα θαρραλέος ὁ γνωστικὸς τά τε ὄντα ἀγαθὰ καὶ τὰ ἐσόμενα γνωρίζων, συνεπιστάμενος δὲ τούτοις, ὥσπερ ἔφην, καὶ τὰ μὴ τῷ ὄντι δεινά, ἐπεὶ μόνην κακίαν ἐχθρὰν οὖσαν εἰδὼς καὶ καθαιρετικὴν τῶν ἐπὶ τὴν γνῶσιν προκοπτόντων, τοῖς ὅπλοις τοῦ κυρίου πεφραγμένος καταπολεμεῖ ταύτης. [οὐ γὰρ εἰ δι' ἀφροσύνην τι συνίσταται καὶ διαβόλου ἐνέργειαν, μᾶλλον δὲ συνέργειαν, τοῦτ' εὐθέως διάβολος

---

3. μή] τὰ μή Barnard.   5. δεῖν H et (litera ν pr. m. deleta) L. δεῖ edd. δὴ S.   6. τὰ τῷ ὄντι θαρραλέα M. τῷ ὄντι τὰ θ. L.   15. μὴ κακά, τὰ δὲ S. μὴ, κατὰ δὲ L.   17. κατὰ ταὐτὸν M. κατὰ τὸν αὐτὸν L.
18. ἀμεμφῶς P. ἀμέμφως L.   23. ἆρα θαρραλέος S. ἀθαρραλέος L.
25. καὶ τὰ μὴ τῷ ὄντι δεινά] fort. τά τε τῷ ὄντι δεινὰ καὶ τὰ μή M.

grace and whatever is akin to these, being invincible by pleasure and master of the irrational appetites. For he knows well what ought and what ought not to be done, having a thorough understanding of what is really formidable and what is not. Hence he undertakes with intelligence what reason dictates as right and fitting for him to do, distinguishing intelligently things that are really *encouraging*, i.e. *good things*[1], from those which only seem to be so, and that which is formidable from that which appears formidable, such as death and disease and poverty, which pertain rather to seeming than to truth. This is the truly good man who stands outside the passions, having risen above the whole life of passion by the habit or disposition of the virtuous soul. For him, all depends upon himself for the attainment of the end. For the so-called dangers of fortune are not formidable to the good man, because they are not really evil; but real dangers are foreign to the gnostic Christian, since, as evil, they are directly opposed to what is good; and it is *impossible that opposites can happen simultaneously to the same thing in the same respect and at the same time*[2]. Thus, playing irreproachably whatever part in life God may have assigned to him to act, he perceives both what he ought to do and what he ought to endure.

§ 66. Does cowardice then arise in any other way except through ignorance of what is, and what is not, to be feared? If not, the gnostic alone is of good courage, because he perceives what is good both in the present and in the future, and combines with this, as I said, the knowledge of the things which are not really to be feared. For, being convinced that vice alone is hostile and destructive to those who are on the road to knowledge, he wars against it, as such, being fortified with the armour of the Lord. [For it does not follow that, if an action has its rise in folly and the operation, or rather co-operation, of the devil, it is to be at once identified with folly or the devil;

---

[1] Plato, *Laches* 198 c.   [2] Plato, *Rep.* iv. 436 b.

ἢ ἀφροσύνη (ὅτι μηδεμία ἐνέργεια φρόνησις· ἕξις γὰρ ἡ φρόνησις, οὐδεμία δὲ ἐνέργεια ἕξις)· οὐ τοίνυν οὐδὲ ἡ δι' ἄγνοιαν συνισταμένη πρᾶξις ἤδη ἄγνοια, ἀλλὰ κακὴ μὲν δι' ἄγνοιαν, οὐ μὴν ἄγνοια· οὐδὲ γὰρ τὰ πάθη, οὐδὲ τὰ ἁμαρτήματα κακίαι, καίτοι ἀπὸ κακίας φερόμενα.] οὐδεὶς οὖν ἀλόγως ἀνδρεῖος γνωστικός· ἐπεὶ καὶ τοὺς παῖδας λεγέτω τις ἀνδρείους ἀγνοίᾳ τῶν δεινῶν ὑφισταμένους τὰ φοβερά (ἅπτονται γοῦν οὗτοι καὶ πυρός), καὶ τὰ θηρία τὰ ὁμόσε ταῖς λόγχαις πορευόμενα, ἀλόγως ὄντα ἀνδρεῖα, ἐνάρετα λεγόντων. τάχα δ' οὕτως καὶ τοὺς θαυματοποιοὺς ἀνδρείους φήσουσιν εἰς τὰς μαχαίρας κυβιστῶντας ἐξ ἐμπειρίας τινὸς κακοτεχνοῦντας ἐπὶ λυπρῷ τῷ μισθῷ. ὁ δὲ τῷ ὄντι ἀνδρεῖος, προφανῆ τὸν κίνδυνον διὰ τὸν τῶν πολλῶν ζῆλον ἔχων, εὐθαρσῶς πᾶν τὸ προσιὸν ἀναδέχεται, ταύτῃ τῶν ἄλλων λεγομένων μαρτύρων χωριζόμενος, ᾗ οἱ μὲν ἀφορμὰς παρέχουσιν σφίσιν αὐτοῖς, ἐπιρριπτοῦντες ἑαυτοὺς τοῖς κινδύνοις οὐκ οἶδ' ὅπως (εὐστομεῖν γὰρ δίκαιον), οἱ δὲ περιστελλόμενοι κατὰ λόγον τὸν ὀρθόν, ἔπειτα τῷ ὄντι καλέσαντος τοῦ θεοῦ προθύμως ἑαυτοὺς ἐπιδόντες, καὶ τὴν κλῆσιν ἐκ τοῦ μηδὲν αὐτοῖς προπετὲς συνεγνωκέναι βεβαιοῦσιν καὶ τὸν ἄνδρα ἐν τῇ κατὰ ἀλήθειαν λογικῇ ἀνδρείᾳ ἐξετάζεσθαι παρέχονται.

67. Οὔτ' οὖν φόβῳ τῶν μειζόνων δεινῶν τὰ ἐλάττω καθάπερ οἱ λοιποὶ ὑπομένοντες, οὔτ' αὖ ψόγον τὸν ἀπὸ τῶν ὁμοτίμων καὶ ὁμογνωμόνων ὑφορώμενοι τῇ τῆς κλήσεως ἐμμένουσιν ὁμολογίᾳ, ἀλλὰ διὰ τὴν πρὸς τὸν θεὸν ἀγάπην ἑκόντες πείθονται τῇ κλήσει, μηδένα ἕτερον σκοπὸν ἑλόμενοι ἢ τὴν πρὸς τὸν θεὸν εὐαρέστησιν, οὐχὶ δὲ διὰ τὰ ἆθλα τῶν πόνων. οἱ μὲν γὰρ φιλοδοξίᾳ, οἱ δὲ εὐλαβείᾳ κολάσεως ἄλλης δριμυτέρας,

4. κακὴ M. κακία L.   5. οὐδὲ τὰ] οὔτε τὰ L.   11. οὕτως L. οὗτοι S.
17. παρέχουσιν...ἐπιρριπτοῦντες H. παρέχοντες...ἐπιρριπτοῦντες L. παρέχοντες
...ἐπιρριπτοῦσιν D post Louthium.   ἑαυτοὺς Louth. αὐτοῖς L.   21. αὑτοῖς
P. αὐτοῖς L.

(because no operation is prudence; for prudence is a habit, and no operation is a habit): so neither is the action that originates in ignorance to be forthwith styled ignorance: it is a bad action caused by ignorance, not ignorance pure. For not even passions or sins are vices, though they proceed from vice[1].] No one, therefore, who is irrationally brave is a gnostic. Else we might be told that children are brave when they face dangers from ignorance of the grounds of fear—for instance they will even play with fire—and we may be told that wild beasts are virtuous when they rush upon the spears, being irrationally brave. On the same principle they will perhaps tell us that jugglers are brave when they have learnt the trick of tumbling among the swords, practising a base art for a miserable pittance. But he who is truly brave, though the peril arising from popular fury is plain before his eyes, awaits with confidence whatever comes. Herein is he distinguished from other so-called martyrs, in that they provide occasions for themselves by exposing themselves to dangers for whatever reason (for we must avoid harsh language); but the others, taking precautions in accordance with the dictates of reason, and then cheerfully offering themselves, when God really calls them, both *make their calling sure*[2], from the consciousness that they have not been guilty of any rash act, and give opportunity for testing their manhood by their truly rational courage.

§ 67. It is therefore neither through *enduring lesser terrors from fear of greater*[3] (as other people do), nor again through apprehension of fault-finding from people of their own station and way of thinking, that they abide by the confession of their calling: no, they willingly obey the divine call owing to their love to God, not for the sake of the prizes of the contests, since they prefer no other aim to the doing of that which is well-pleasing to God. For those that endure from love of glory, or from fear of

---

[1] This sentence seems to be out of place here.
[2] 2 Pet. i. 10.
[3] Plato, *Phaedo* 68 D.

οἱ δὲ διά τινας ἡδονὰς καὶ εὐφροσύνας τὰς μετὰ θάνατον ὑπομένοντες παῖδες ἐν πίστει, μακάριοι μέν, οὐδέπω δὲ ἄνδρες ἐν ἀγάπῃ τῇ πρὸς τὸν θεὸν καθάπερ ὁ γνωστικὸς γεγονότες) εἰσὶ γάρ, εἰσὶ καθάπερ ἐν τοῖς ἀγῶσι τοῖς γυμνικοῖς, οὕτως δὲ καὶ κατὰ τὴν ἐκκλησίαν στέφανοι ἀνδρῶν τε καὶ παίδων), ἡ δὲ ἀγάπη αὐτὴ δι' αὐτὴν αἱρετή, οὐ δι' ἄλλο τι. σχεδὸν οὖν τῷ γνωστικῷ μετὰ γνώσεως ἡ τελειότης τῆς ἀνδρείας ἐκ τῆς τοῦ βίου συνασκήσεως αὔξεται, μελετήσαντος ἀεὶ τῶν παθῶν κρατεῖν. ἄφοβον οὖν καὶ ἀδεᾶ καὶ πεποιθότα ἐπὶ κύριον ἡ ἀγάπη ἀλείφουσα καὶ γυμνάσασα κατασκευάζει τὸν ἴδιον ἀθλητήν, ὥσπερ δικαιοσύνη τὸ διὰ παντὸς ἀληθεύειν αὐτῷ τοῦ βίου περιποιεῖ. δικαιοσύνης γὰρ ἦν ἐπιτομὴ φάναι ἔσται ὑμῶν τὸ ναὶ ναὶ καὶ τὸ οὒ οὔ. ὁ δὲ αὐτὸς λόγος καὶ ἐπὶ τῆς σωφροσύνης. οὔτε γὰρ διὰ φιλοτιμίαν, καθάπερ οἱ ἀθληταὶ στεφάνων καὶ εὐδοξίας χάριν, οὔτ' αὖ διὰ φιλοχρηματίαν, ὥς τινες προσποιοῦνται σωφρονεῖν, πάθει δεινῷ τὸ ἀγαθὸν μεταδιώκοντες· οὐ μὴν οὐδὲ διὰ φιλοσωματίαν ὑγείας χάριν, ἀλλ' οὐδὲ δι' ἀγροικίαν ἐγκρατὴς καὶ ἄγευστος ἡδονῶν, οὐδεὶς κατ' ἀλήθειαν σώφρων. ἀμέλει γευσάμενοι τῶν ἡδονῶν οἱ τὸν ἐργάτην τρίβοντες βίον αὐτίκα μάλα καταγνύουσι τὸ ἀκαμπὲς τῆς ἐγκρατείας εἰς τὰς ἡδονάς. τοιοῦτοι δὲ καὶ οἱ νόμῳ καὶ φόβῳ κωλυόμενοι· καιρὸν γὰρ λαβόντες παρακλέπτουσι τὸν νόμον, ἀποδιδράσκοντες τὰ καλά. ἡ δὲ δι' αὐτὴν αἱρετὴ σωφροσύνη, κατὰ τὴν γνῶσιν τελειουμένη ἀεί τε παραμένουσα, κύριον καὶ αὐτοκράτορα τὸν ἄνδρα κατασκευάζει, ὡς εἶναι τὸν γνωστικὸν σώφρονα καὶ ἀπαθῆ,

---

7. αὐτὴν P. αὐτὴν L.   9. μελετήσαντος] fort. μελετήσαντι M.
10. ἀδεᾶ] Exspectes potius ἀδεῆ, ut ἐπιδεῆ p. 881, προσφυῆ p. 896, ὑγιῆ p. 647, nisi his quoque locis forma Attica restituenda D.   14. ἐπιτομὴ S. ἐπὶ τὸ μὴ L.   φάναι V. φᾶναι L.   τὸ οὒ L. τὸ om. V.   19. ὑγείας L. ὑγιείας D.   23. καταγνύουσι] fort. κατάγνυνται M.   25. καιρὸν M. καιροῦ L.   26. αὐτὴν] αὐτὴν L.

some severer punishment, or with a view to any joys or pleasures after death, these are mere children in faith, blessed indeed, but not yet having attained to manhood, like the gnostic, in their love to God,—for the Church too has its crowns both for men and for boys, just as the gymnasium has,—but love is to be chosen for its own sake, not for any other reason. It may be said therefore that the gnostic's perfection of courage grows with the growth of knowledge out of the discipline of life, because he has always studied how to control his passions. Love then, by her anointing and training, makes her own champion fearless and intrepid and full of trust in the Lord, just as righteousness wins for him the power of life-long truthfulness. For in the phrase *Your yea shall be yea and your nay nay*[1], there was given an abstract of righteousness. And the same may be said of temperance also. For a man is not made really temperate through ambition, as in the case of the athlete, for the sake of crowns and glory; nor again through covetousness, as some feign, pursuing a good end by means of a fatal passion; no, nor yet through the desire of bodily health, nor from boorish insensibility enabling him to abstain from pleasures for which he has no taste. Certainly those who live a life of toil, when they get a taste of pleasure, presently break down the rigour of their self-restraint in regard to pleasure. Such too are those who are kept in check only by law and by fear; for when they get a chance they evade the law, deserting the side of honour. But temperance that is chosen for her own sake, being perfected according to knowledge and taking up her abode in the heart, gives a man authority and makes him independent; so that the gnostic is

[1] James v. 12.

ταῖς ἡδοναῖς τε καὶ λύπαις ἄτεγκτον, ὥσπερ φασὶ τὸν ἀδάμαντα τῷ πυρί.

68. Τούτων οὖν αἰτία ἡ ἁγιωτάτη καὶ κυριωτάτη πάσης ἐπιστήμης ἀγάπη· διὰ γὰρ τὴν τοῦ ἀρίστου καὶ ἐξοχωτάτου θεραπείαν, ὃ δὴ τῷ ἑνὶ χαρακτηρίζεται, φίλον ὁμοῦ καὶ υἱὸν τὸν γνωστικὸν ἀπεργάζεται, τέλειον ὡς ἀληθῶς ἄνδρα εἰς μέτρον ἡλικίας αὐξήσαντα. ἀλλὰ καὶ ἡ ὁμόνοια ἡ περὶ ταὐτὸ πρᾶγμα συγκατάθεσίς ἐστι, τὸ δὲ ταὐτὸν ἕν ἐστιν, ἥ τε φιλία δι' ὁμοιότητος περαίνεται, τῆς κοινότητος ἐν τῷ ἑνὶ κειμένης. ὁ ἄρα γνωστικός, τοῦ ἑνὸς ὄντως θεοῦ ἀγαπητικὸς ὑπάρχων, τέλειος ὄντως ἀνὴρ καὶ φίλος τοῦ θεοῦ, ἐν υἱοῦ καταλεγεὶς τάξει. ταυτὶ γὰρ ὀνόματα εὐγενείας καὶ γνώσεως καὶ τελειότητος κατὰ τὴν τοῦ θεοῦ ἐποπτείαν, ἣν κορυφαιοτάτην προκοπὴν ἡ γνωστικὴ ψυχὴ λαμβάνει, καθαρὰ τέλεον γενομένη, πρόσωπον, φησί, πρὸς πρόσωπον ὁρᾶν ἀϊδίως καταξιουμένη τὸν παντοκράτορα θεόν. πνευματικὴ γὰρ ὅλη γενομένη πρὸς τὸ συγγενὲς χωρήσασα ἐν πνευματικῇ τῇ ἐκκλησίᾳ μένει εἰς τὴν ἀνάπαυσιν τοῦ θεοῦ.

ΚΕΦ. ΙΒ.

69. Ταῦτα μὲν οὖν ταύτῃ. οὕτω δὲ ἔχων ὁ γνωστικὸς πρὸς τὸ σῶμα καὶ τὴν ψυχήν, πρὸς τοὺς πέλας, κἂν οἰκέτης ᾖ κἂν πολέμιος νόμῳ γενόμενος κἂν ὅστις οὖν, ἴσος καὶ ὅμοιος εὑρίσκεται. οὐ γὰρ ὑπερορᾷ τὸν ἀδελφόν, κατὰ τὸν θεῖον νόμον ὁμοπάτριον ὄντα καὶ ὁμομήτριον· ἀμέλει θλιβόμενον ἐπικουφίζει παραμυθίαις, παρορμήσεσι, ταῖς βιωτικαῖς χρείαις ἐπικουρῶν,

---

5. θεραπείαν pr. m. corr. ex θεωρίαν L. 22. πρὸς τοὺς M. πρός τε τοὺς L. 27. παρορμήσεσι] fort. καὶ παρ. M.

temperate and passionless, proof against pleasures and pains, as, they say, the adamant is against fire.

§ 68. The cause of these things is love, love surpassing all knowledge in holiness and sovereignty. For by it the gnostic, owing to his worship of the Best and Highest, the stamp of which is unity, is made *friend*[1] and *son*[2] at once, *a perfect man* indeed, grown *to the full measure of stature*[3]. Aye, and concord also is defined to be agreement about the same thing, and by 'the same thing' we mean unity; and friendship is brought about by similarity, because fellowship lies in unity. The gnostic therefore, being naturally disposed to love God who is truly One, is himself a truly *perfect man* and a *friend of God*, being ranked and reckoned *as a son*. These are names expressive of nobility and knowledge and perfection in accordance with that vision of God, which is the crowning height attainable by the gnostic soul, when it has been perfectly purified, being now deemed worthy to behold for ever the Almighty, *face to face*[4]. For having been made entirely spiritual it departs to its kindred sphere and there, in the spiritual Church, abides in the rest of God.

CHAPTER XII.

§ 69. So much then for these things. But the gnostic, being such as we have described him in body and soul, is found to be fair alike towards all his neighbours, whatever their legal position, whether servant or foeman or whatever it be. For he does not despise him who, according to the divine law, stands to him in the relation of brother by the same parents: certainly, when he is in distress, he relieves him by consolations and encouragements and by making provision for

[1] Joh. xv. 15.   [2] Joh. i. 12.   [3] Eph. iv. 13.
[4] 1 Cor. xiii. 12.

διδοὺς τοῖς δεομένοις πᾶσιν, ἀλλ' οὐχ ὁμοίως, δικαίως δὲ καὶ κατὰ τὴν ἀξίαν, πρὸς δὲ καὶ τῷ καταδιώκοντι καὶ μισοῦντι, εἰ τούτου δέοιτο, ὀλίγα φροντίζων τῶν λεγόντων διὰ φόβον αὐτῷ δεδωκέναι, εἰ μὴ διὰ φόβον, δι' ἐπικουρίαν δὲ τοῦτο ποιοίη. οἱ γὰρ πρὸς ἐχθροὺς ἀφιλάργυροι καὶ ἀμνησιπόνηροι, πόσῳ μᾶλλον πρὸς τοὺς οἰκείους ἀγαπητικοί; ὁ τοιοῦτος ἐκ τούτου πρόεισιν ἐπὶ τὸ ἀκριβῶς εἰδέναι καὶ ὅτῳ ἄν τις μάλιστα καὶ ὁπόσον καὶ ὁπότε καὶ ὅπως ἐπιδῴη. τίς δ' ἂν καὶ ἐχθρὸς εὐλόγως γένοιτο ἀνδρὸς οὐδεμίαν οὐδαμῶς παρέχοντος αἰτίαν ἔχθρας; καὶ μή τι, καθάπερ ἐπὶ τοῦ θεοῦ οὐδενὶ μὲν ἀντικεῖσθαι λέγομεν τὸν θεὸν οὐδὲ ἐχθρὸν εἶναί τινος· (πάντων γὰρ κτίστης καὶ οὐδέν ἐστι τῶν ὑποστάντων ὃ μὴ θέλει, φαμὲν δ' αὐτῷ ἐχθροὺς εἶναι τοὺς ἀπειθεῖς καὶ μὴ κατὰ τὰς ἐντολὰς αὐτοῦ πορευομένους, οἷον τοὺς διεχθρεύοντας αὐτοῦ τῇ διαθήκῃ·) τὸν αὐτὸν τρόπον καὶ ἐπὶ τοῦ γνωστικοῦ εὕροιμεν ἄν. αὐτὸς μὲν γὰρ οὐδενὶ οὐδέποτε κατ' οὐδένα τρόπον ἐχθρὸς ἂν γένοιτο, ἐχθροὶ δὲ εἶναι νοοῖντο αὐτῷ οἱ τὴν ἐναντίαν ὁδὸν τρεπόμενοι. ἄλλως τε, κἂν ἡ ἕξις ἡ παρ' ἡμῖν μεταδοτικὴ δικαιοσύνη λέγηται, ἀλλὰ καὶ ἡ κατ' ἀξίαν διακριτικὴ πρὸς τὸ μᾶλλον καὶ ἧττον, ἐφ' ὧν καθήκει κατ' ἐπιστήμην γενέσθαι, ἀκροτάτης δικαιοσύνης εἶδος τυγχάνει. ἔστι μὲν οὖν ἃ καὶ κατὰ ἰδιωτισμὸν πρός τινων κατορθοῦνται, οἷον ἡδονῶν ἐγκράτεια. ὡς γὰρ ἐν τοῖς ἔθνεσιν, ἔκ τε τοῦ μὴ δύνασθαι τυχεῖν ὧν ἐρᾷ τις καὶ ἐκ τοῦ πρὸς ἀνθρώπων φόβου, εἰσὶ δ' οἳ διὰ τὰς μείζονας ἡδονὰς ἀπέχονται τῶν ἐν τοῖς ποσὶν ἡδέων, οὕτως κἂν τῇ πίστει ἢ δι' ἐπαγγελίαν ἢ διὰ φόβον θεοῦ ἐγκρατεύονταί τινες.

4. αὐτῷ] αὐτὸν H.   6. ἀμνησιπόνηροι Louth. μισοπόνηροι L. (Cf. P. 475, ubi μνησιπονηρεῖ pro μισοπονηρεῖ legendum monuit S.)
9. ἐπιδῴη M. ἐπιδῷ L.   16. τοὺς διεχθρεύοντας] om. τοὺς M.
18. εὕροιμεν] εὕτοιμεν Jackson.   21. λέγηται] λέγεται L.   25. κατορθοῦται] κατορθοῦνται L.   27. ἐρᾷ S. ὁρᾷ L.   29. οὕτως corr. pr. m. ex ὡς L.

the needs of daily life. While he gives to all who are in need, he does not do it to the same extent, but in accordance with justice and proportionately: moreover he gives even to one who persecutes and hates him, if he stands in need of it, caring little for those who insinuate that fear was his motive, provided that he was doing it not from fear, but only from a wish to help. For if a man is liberal and forgiving in dealing with enemies, how much more will he be loving to his friends? Such an one will proceed from this point to an exact understanding as regards the person, the amount, the time and the manner in which liberality would be best dispensed. And who could reasonably be the enemy of a man who affords no possible excuse for enmity? Perhaps, as, in speaking of God, we say that God is opposed to none and the enemy of none (for He is Creator of all things and there is no existing thing that He does not love, but we call those His enemies who are disobedient and do not walk according to His laws, as for instance those who hate His covenant); so we might find the same disposition in the case of the gnostic. For he himself could never be in any way hostile to any one, but they who take the contrary course might be thought hostile to him. Besides, even if our habit of freely sharing with others is called justice, still the habit which makes proportionate distinction of less or more in cases where distribution should be scientific, is a form of highest justice. There are indeed cases in which right is done, as in abstaining from pleasures, from vulgar motives. For, as among the heathen some practise abstinence from present pleasures, both through inability to obtain what they desire, and through fear of man; while there are others who abstain for the sake of greater pleasures; so also in the faith some are continent either on account of the promise or through fear of God.

70. Ἀλλ' ἔστι μὲν θεμέλιος γνώσεως ἡ τοιαύτη ἐγκράτεια καὶ προσαγωγή τις ἐπὶ τὸ βέλτιον καὶ ἐπὶ τὸ τέλειον ὁρμή. ἀρχὴ γὰρ σοφίας φησὶ φόβος κυρίου. ὁ τέλειος δὲ δι' ἀγάπην πάντα στέγει, πάντα ὑπομένει, οὐχ ὡς ἀνθρώπῳ ἀρέσκων, ἀλλὰ θεῷ. καίτοι καὶ ὁ ἔπαινος ἕπεται αὐτῷ κατ' ἐπακολούθημα, οὐκ εἰς τὴν ἑαυτοῦ ὠφέλειαν, ἀλλ' εἰς τὴν τῶν ἐπαινούντων μίμησίν τε καὶ χρῆσιν. λέγεται καὶ κατ' ἄλλο σημαινόμενον ἐγκρατὴς οὐχ ὁ τῶν παθῶν μόνον κρατῶν, ἀλλὰ καὶ ὁ τῶν ἀγαθῶν ἐγκρατὴς γενόμενος καὶ βεβαίως κτησάμενος τῆς ἐπιστήμης τὰ μεγαλεῖα, ἀφ' ὧν καρποφορεῖ τὰς κατ' ἀρετὴν ἐνεργείας. ταύτῃ οὐδέποτε περιστάσεως γενομένης τῆς ἰδίας ἕξεως ὁ γνωστικὸς ἐξίσταται. ἔμπεδος γὰρ καὶ ἀμετάβλητος ἡ τοῦ ἀγαθοῦ ἐπιστημονικὴ κτῆσις, ἐπιστήμη θείων καὶ ἀνθρωπείων πραγμάτων ὑπάρχουσα. οὔποτε οὖν ἄγνοια γίνεται ἡ γνῶσις οὐδὲ μεταβάλλει τὸ ἀγαθὸν εἰς κακόν· διὸ καὶ ἐσθίει καὶ πίνει καὶ γαμεῖ οὐ προηγουμένως, ἀλλὰ ἀναγκαίως. τὸ γαμεῖν δὲ ἐὰν ὁ λόγος αἱρῇ λέγω καὶ ὡς καθήκει· γενόμενος γὰρ τέλειος εἰκόνας ἔχει τοὺς ἀποστόλους. καὶ τῷ ὄντι ἀνὴρ οὐκ ἐν τῷ μονήρη ἐπανελέσθαι δείκνυται βίον, ἀλλ' ἐκεῖνος ἄνδρας νικᾷ ὁ γάμῳ καὶ παιδοποιίᾳ καὶ τῇ τοῦ οἴκου προνοίᾳ ἀνηδόνως τε καὶ ἀλυπήτως ἐγγυμνασάμενος, μετὰ τῆς τοῦ οἴκου κηδεμονίας ἀδιάστατος τῆς τοῦ θεοῦ γενόμενος ἀγάπης, καὶ πάσης κατεξανιστάμενος πείρας τῆς διὰ τέκνων καὶ γυναικὸς οἰκετῶν τε καὶ κτημάτων προσφερομένης. τῷ δὲ ἀοίκῳ τὰ πολλὰ εἶναι συμβέβηκεν ἀπειράστῳ. μόνου γοῦν ἑαυτοῦ κηδόμενος ἡττᾶται πρὸς τοῦ ἀπολειπομένου μὲν κατὰ τὴν ἑαυτοῦ σωτηρίαν, περιττεύοντος δὲ ἐν τῇ κατὰ τὸν βίον οἰκο-

---

7. μίμησιν pr. m. corr. ex μνήμην L.   19. αἱρῇ S. ἔρῃ L.
27. τέκνων] παίδων praemittit L, sed punctis notatum.

§ 70. Still even such continence as this serves as a foundation of knowledge and an introduction to what is better and a movement towards perfection. For *the fear of the Lord is* said to be *the beginning of wisdom*[1]. But he that is perfect *beareth all things and endureth all things*[2] for love's sake, *not as pleasing man, but God*[3]. Yet praise too attends him by way of natural consequence, not for his own benefit, but for the imitation and use of those who bestow the praise. The word ($ἐγκρατής$) is used in another sense also, not of him who only conquers his passions, but of him also who has become possessed of good and has a firm hold of the treasures of understanding, from which spring the fruits of virtuous activity. Thus the gnostic never departs from his own set habit in any emergency. For the scientific possession of good is fixed and unchangeable, being *the science of things divine and human*[4]. Knowledge therefore never becomes ignorance, nor does good change to evil. Hence with him eating and drinking and marrying are not the main objects of life, though they are its necessary conditions. I speak of marriage sanctioned by reason and in accordance with right: for being made perfect he has the Apostles as his patterns. And true manhood is shown not in the choice of a celibate life: on the contrary the prize in the contest of men is won by him who has trained himself by the discharge of the duties of husband and father and by the supervision of a household, regardless of pleasure and pain,—by him, I say, who in the midst of his solicitude for his family shows himself inseparable from the love of God and rises superior to every temptation which assails him through children and wife and servants and possessions. On the other hand he who has no family is in most respects untried. In any case, as he takes thought only for himself, he is inferior to one who falls short of him as regards his own salvation, but who has the advantage in

---

[1] Prov. ix. 10.   [2] 1 Cor. xiii. 7.   [3] 1 Thes. ii. 4.   [4] Stoic definition of wisdom.

νομία, εἰκόνα ἀτεχνῶς σώζοντος ὀλίγην τῆς τῇ ἀληθείᾳ προνοίας.

71. Ἀλλ' ἡμῖν γε ὡς ἔνι μάλιστα προγυμναστέον ποικίλως τὴν ψυχήν, ἵνα εὐεργὸς γένηται πρὸς τὴν τῆς γνώσεως παραδοχήν. οὐχ ὁρᾶτε πῶς μαλάσσεται κηρὸς καὶ καθαίρεται χαλκός, ἵνα τὸν ἐπιόντα χαρακτῆρα παραδέξηται; αὐτίκα ὡς ὁ θάνατος χωρισμὸς ψυχῆς ἀπὸ σώματος, οὕτως ἡ γνῶσις οἷον ὁ λογικὸς θάνατος, ἀπὸ τῶν παθῶν ἀπάγων καὶ χωρίζων τὴν ψυχὴν καὶ προάγων εἰς τὴν τῆς εὐποιίας ζωήν, ἵνα τότε εἴπῃ μετὰ παρρησίας πρὸς τὸν θεόν "ὡς θέλεις ζῶ." ὁ μὲν γὰρ ἀνθρώποις ἀρέσκειν προαιρούμενος θεῷ ἀρέσαι οὐ δύναται, ἐπεὶ μὴ τὰ συμφέροντα, ἀλλὰ τὰ τέρποντα αἱροῦνται οἱ πολλοί· ἀρέσκων δέ τις τῷ θεῷ τοῖς σπουδαίοις τῶν ἀνθρώπων εὐάρεστος κατ' ἐπακολούθημα γίνεται. τερπνὰ τοίνυν τούτῳ πῶς ἔτι ἂν εἴη τὰ περὶ τὴν βρῶσιν καὶ πόσιν καὶ ἀφροδίσιον ἡδονήν; ὅπου γε καὶ λόγον φέροντά τινα ἡδονὴν καὶ κίνημα διανοίας καὶ ἐνέργημα τερπνὸν ὑφορᾶται. οὐδεὶς γὰρ δύναται δυσὶ κυρίοις δουλεύειν, θεῷ καὶ μαμωνᾷ. οὐ τὸ ἀργύριον λέγων φησὶ ψιλῶς οὕτως, ἀλλὰ τὴν ἐκ τοῦ ἀργυρίου εἰς τὰς ποικίλας ἡδονὰς χορηγίαν· τῷ <γὰρ> ὄντι οὐχ οἷόν τε τὸν θεὸν ἐγνωκότα μεγαλοφρόνως καὶ ἀληθῶς ταῖς ἀντικειμέναις δουλεύειν ἡδοναῖς.

72. Εἷς μὲν οὖν μόνος ὁ ἀνεπιθύμητος ἐξ ἀρχῆς, ὁ κύριος ὁ φιλάνθρωπος ὁ καὶ δι' ἡμᾶς ἄνθρωπος· ὅσοι δὲ ἐξομοιοῦσθαι σπεύδουσι τῷ ὑπ' αὐτοῦ δεδομένῳ χαρακτῆρι ἀνεπιθύμητοι ἐξ ἀσκήσεως γενέσθαι βιάζονται. ὁ γὰρ ἐπιθυμήσας καὶ κατασχὼν ἑαυτοῦ καθάπερ καὶ ἡ χήρα διὰ σωφροσύνης αὖθις παρθένος.

---

1. ἀτεχνῶς] ἀτέχνως L. τῆς τῇ ἀληθείᾳ προνοίας M. τῇ τῆς ἀληθείας προνοίᾳ L. 9. ἀπάγων S. ἐπείγων L. 22. τῷ γὰρ M. τῷ L.
31. καθάπερ καὶ L. καθάπερ edd. post V.

the conduct of life, in as much as he actually preserves a faint image of the true Providence.

§ 71. In any case it is our duty to provide the most varied training for the soul so as to make it impressible for the reception of knowledge. Do you not see how wax is softened and copper refined that it may receive the stamp impressed upon it? Further as death is a separation of soul from body, so knowledge is, as it were, a rational death, leading off the soul from its passions and separating it from them, and leading it on to the life of virtuous activity, in order that it may then say with boldness to God, 'I live as thou wouldst have me.' For he who makes it his aim *to please men*[1], *cannot please God*[2], since the mass of men choose not the things that are expedient, but the things that are pleasant: but if one pleases God, he becomes as a natural consequence well pleasing to the good among men. How then could such an one any longer take delight in eating and drinking and sexual pleasure, when he is suspicious even of discourse that is productive of pleasure, and also of any movement of thought or exercise of will that causes delight? For *no man can serve two masters, God and mammon*[3]. This he says, not meaning money simply, but the provision that money supplies for the various kinds of pleasure. For indeed it is impossible for him who has a high and true knowledge of God to be a slave to the pleasures that are contrary to Him.

§ 72. There is then One alone who is free from desire to begin with, viz. the Lord, who is the lover of men, who for our sakes became man: but all that are eager to be assimilated to the stamp given by Him, strive to become free from desire by training. For he who has felt desire and has gained the mastery over himself, like the widow also, becomes virgin again through chastity. This is *the reward of knowledge*[4] to the

---
[1] Gal. i. 10.   [2] Rom. viii. 8.   [3] Luke xvi. 13.
[4] Joh. iv. 36, 1 Cor. ix. 18, cf. Is. liii. 11, Joh. xvii. 3, 15, 17.

οὗτος μισθὸς γνώσεως τῷ σωτῆρι καὶ διδασκάλῳ, ὃν
αὐτὸς ᾔτησεν, τὴν ἀποχὴν τῶν κακῶν καὶ τὴν ἐνέργειαν
τῆς εὐποιΐας, δι' ὧν ἡ σωτηρία περιγίνεται. ὥσπερ
οὖν οἱ τὰς τέχνας μεμαθηκότες δι' ὧν ἐπαιδεύθησαν
πορίζουσι τὰς τροφάς, οὕτως ὁ γνωστικὸς δι' ὧν ἐπίσταται πορίζων τὴν ζωὴν σῴζεται. ὁ γὰρ μὴ θελήσας
τὸ τῆς ψυχῆς ἐκκόψαι πάθος ἑαυτὸν ἀπέκτεινεν. ἀλλ'
ὡς ἔοικεν ἀτροφία μὲν ἡ ἄγνοια τῆς ψυχῆς, τροφὴ
δὲ ἡ γνῶσις. αὗται δέ εἰσιν αἱ γνωστικαὶ ψυχαί, ἃς
ἀπείκασεν τὸ εὐαγγέλιον ταῖς ἡγιασμέναις παρθένοις
ταῖς προσδεχομέναις τὸν κύριον. παρθένοι μὲν γὰρ ὡς
κακῶν ἀπεσχημέναι, προσδεχόμεναι δὲ διὰ τὴν ἀγάπην
τὸν κύριον, καὶ τὸ οἰκεῖον ἀνάπτουσαι φῶς εἰς τὴν τῶν
πραγμάτων θεωρίαν φρόνιμοι ψυχαί· "ποθοῦμέν σε
ὦ κύριε" λέγουσαι "ἤδη ποτὲ ἀπολαβεῖν· ἀκολούθως
οἷς ἐνετείλω ἐζήσαμεν, μηδὲν τῶν παρηγγελμένων
παραβεβηκυῖαι· διὸ καὶ τὰς ὑποσχέσεις ἀπαιτοῦμεν,
εὐχόμεθα δὲ τὰ συμφέροντα, οὐχ ὡς καθήκοντος τοῦ
αἰτεῖν τὰ κάλλιστα παρὰ σοῦ· καὶ πάντα ἐπὶ συμφόρῳ
δεξόμεθα, κἂν πονηρὰ εἶναι δοκῇ, τὰ προσιόντα γυμνάσια, ἅτινα ἡμῖν προσφέρει ἡ σὴ οἰκονομία εἰς
συνάσκησιν βεβαιότητος."

73. Ὁ μὲν οὖν γνωστικὸς δι' ὑπερβολὴν ὁσιότητος αἰτούμενος μᾶλλον ἀποτυχεῖν ἕτοιμος ἢ μὴ
αἰτούμενος τυχεῖν. εὐχὴ γὰρ αὐτῷ ὁ βίος ἅπας καὶ
ὁμιλία πρὸς θεόν, κἂν καθαρὸς ᾖ ἁμαρτημάτων, πάντως
οὗ βούλεται τεύξεται. λέγει γὰρ ὁ θεὸς τῷ δικαίῳ
αἴτησαι, καὶ δώσω σοί· ἐννοήθητι, καὶ ποιήσω. ἐὰν μὲν οὖν
συμφέροντα ᾖ, παραχρῆμα λήψεται· ἀσύμφορα δὲ
οὐδέποτε αἰτήσεται, διὸ οὐδὲ λήψεται· οὕτως ἔσται

2. αὐτὸς] fort. αὐτὸς τοῖς ἑαυτοῦ M.   7. post ἀπέκτεινεν omissum
videtur οὐ γὰρ ὁ θεὸς ἀπέκτεινεν vel tale aliquid. M.   10. ἡγιασμέναις]
—ποις L.   18. fort. post καὶ transponendum φρόνιμοι ψυχαί ex l. 14. M.
18. οὐχ ὡς] ὡς οὐ M.   καθήκοντος S. καθηκόντως L.   19. συμφόρῳ]
συμφέρῳ L.   25. γὰρ L. μὲν V.

Saviour and Teacher, which He Himself asked <for His own>, viz. abstinence from all evil and activity in well-doing, by which means salvation is procured. As, then, they that have learnt the arts get their livelihood by the training they underwent, so the gnostic gets spiritual life by his knowledge and is saved. For he who refuses to eradicate the passion of his soul causes his own death. But ignorance, as it seems, is the starvation of the soul and knowledge its sustenance. And the gnostic souls are those which the Gospel likened to *the* sanctified *virgins who wait for their Lord*[1]. For they are *virgins* as having abstained from evil and *awaiting their Lord* through love, and they are *wise* souls, since they kindle their own light to see the real facts, saying, 'We long to receive Thee, O Lord, at last: we have lived according to Thy commandments, we have transgressed none of Thy precepts: wherefore also we claim Thy promises; and we pray for what is expedient for us, feeling that it is unfitting for us to ask of Thee the highest rewards: even though they may seem to be evil, we will receive as expedient all the trials that meet us, whatever they may be, which Thy ordering employs for our training in steadfastness.'

§ 73. The gnostic indeed has risen to such a pitch of holiness that he is ready rather to pray and fail than to succeed without prayer. For all his life is prayer and communion with God, and if he is free from sins he will assuredly receive what he desires. For God says to the righteous *Ask and I will give to thee; think and I will do it*[2]. If then what he asks is expedient, he will receive it at once; but things inexpedient he will never ask for, and therefore will never receive: so he

---

[1] Matt. xxv. 1 ff. [2] The same quotation occurs P. 778, 790, cf. 855, 861.

ὃ βούλεται. κἄν τις ἡμῖν λέγῃ ἐπιτυγχάνειν τινὰς καὶ τῶν ἁμαρτωλῶν κατὰ τὰς αἰτήσεις, σπανίως μὲν τοῦτο διὰ τὴν τοῦ θεοῦ δικαίαν ἀγαθότητα, δίδοται δὲ τοῖς καὶ ἄλλους εὐεργετεῖν δυναμένοις. ὅθεν οὐ διὰ τὸν 5 αἰτήσαντα ἡ δόσις γίνεται, ἀλλ' ἡ οἰκονομία τὸν σώζεσθαι δι' αὐτοῦ μέλλοντα προορωμένη δικαίαν πάλιν ποιεῖται τὴν δωρεάν. τοῖς δ' ὅσοι ἄξιοι τὰ ὄντως ἀγαθὰ καὶ μὴ αἰτουμένοις δίδοται. ὅταν οὖν μὴ κατὰ ἀνάγκην ἢ φόβον ἢ ἐλπίδα δίκαιός τις ᾖ, ἀλλ' ἐκ 10 προαιρέσεως, αὕτη ἡ ὁδὸς λέγεται βασιλική, ἣν τὸ βασιλικὸν ὁδεύει γένος, ὀλισθηραὶ δὲ αἱ ἄλλαι παρεκτροπαὶ καὶ κρημνώδεις. εἰ γοῦν τις ἀφέλοι τὸν φόβον καὶ τὴν τιμήν, οὐκ οἶδ' εἰ ἔτι ὑποστήσονται τὰς θλίψεις οἱ γεννάδαι τῶν παρρησιαζομένων φιλοσόφων.

15 74. Ἐπιθυμίαι δὲ καὶ τὰ ἄλλα ἁμαρτήματα τρίβολοι καὶ σκόλοπες εἴρηνται. ἐργάζεται τοίνυν ὁ γνωστικὸς ἐν τῷ τοῦ κυρίου ἀμπελῶνι φυτεύων, κλαδεύων, ἀρδεύων, θεῖος ὄντως ὑπάρχων τῶν εἰς πίστιν καταπεφυτευμένων γεωργός. οἱ μὲν οὖν τὸ κακὸν μὴ 20 πράξαντες μισθὸν ἀξιοῦσιν ἀργίας λαμβάνειν, ὁ δὲ ἀγαθὰ πράξας ἐκ προαιρέσεως γυμνῆς ἀπαιτεῖ τὸν μισθὸν ὡς ἐργάτης ἀγαθός. ἀμέλει καὶ διπλοῦν λήψεται ὧν τε οὐκ ἐποίησεν καὶ ἀνθ' ὧν εὐηργέτησεν. ὁ γνωστικὸς οὗτος πειράζεται ὑπ' οὐδενός, πλὴν εἰ μὴ 25 ἐπιτρέψῃ ὁ θεὸς καὶ τοῦτο διὰ τὴν τῶν συνόντων ὠφέλειαν. ἐπιρρώννυνται γοῦν πρὸς τὴν πίστιν διὰ τῆς ἀνδρικῆς παρακαλούμενοι ὑπομονῆς. ἀμέλει καὶ διὰ τοῦτο οἱ μακάριοι ἀπόστολοι εἰς πῆξιν καὶ βεβαίωσιν τῶν ἐκκλησιῶν εἰς πεῖραν καὶ μαρτύριον τελειότητος 30 ἤχθησαν. ἔχων οὖν ὁ γνωστικὸς ἔναυλον τὴν φωνὴν τὴν λέγουσαν, ὃν ἐγὼ πατάξω, σὺ ἐλέησον, καὶ τοὺς

---

25. ἐπιτρέψῃ] ἐπιτρέψαι D. fort. ἐπιτρέψει M. 26, 27. ἐπιρρώννυνται... παρακαλούμενοι M. ἐπιρρώννυται...παρακαλούμενος L. 29. εἰς μάρ πεῖραν καὶ μ. pr. m. corr. L.

will always have what he desires. And if we should be told that sinners sometimes succeed in their prayers, on the one hand this occurs but rarely, because God's goodness is always just, and on the other hand it is to those who are able to benefit others that this favour is shown. Hence the gift is not bestowed for the sake of the petitioner, but the divine ordering has a foresight of the person who will be saved by his means, and thus reasserts the character of justice in the benefit imparted. But to such as are worthy, the things that are truly good are granted even without the asking. When then a man is righteous, not from compulsion or fear or hope, but of choice, this is called *the King's high-way*[1] traversed by the King's seed; but the others are all by-ways, slippery and precipitous. At any rate, if the motives of fear and honour were removed, I know not whether our brave outspoken philosophers would still be able to hold out against their troubles.

§ 74. Now lusts and other sins have been called *briars and thorns*[2]. The gnostic therefore toils in *the Lord's vineyard*[3], *planting*[4], pruning, *watering*, being indeed a divine husbandman for those who have been planted in the faith. They then who have not done evil expect to receive a reward for doing nothing, but he who has done good from choice alone claims the reward as a good labourer. Doubtless he will receive also a double reward, partly for what he has not done and partly in return for his good actions. Such a gnostic is tempted by none, except it be through divine permission, and that for the benefit of his associates. At any rate they are encouraged to believe, being cheered by his manly endurance. Doubtless it was for this cause also that the blessed Apostles were brought to give proof and witness of perfection with a view to establishing and confirming the churches. Since the gnostic then has ringing in his ears the voice which says Do thou show pity to him whom I shall smite, he prays for the repent-

---

[1] Num. xx. 17.   [2] Jer. iv. 3, Matt. xiii. 7, Heb. vi. 8.
[3] Is. v. 7, Matt. xxi. 33.   [4] 1 Cor. iii. 6.

μισοῦντας αἰτεῖται μετανοῆσαι. τὴν γὰρ τῶν κακούργων ἐν τοῖς σταδίοις ἐπιτελουμένην τιμωρίαν καὶ παίδων ἐστὶ μὴ θεάσασθαι. οὐ γὰρ ἔστιν ὅπως ὑπὸ τοιούτων παιδευθείη ποτ᾿ ἂν ὁ γνωστικὸς ἢ τερφθείη, ἐκ προαιρέσεως καλὸς καὶ ἀγαθὸς εἶναι συνασκήσας καὶ ταύτῃ ἄτεγκτος ἡδοναῖς γενόμενος. οὔποτε ὑποπίπτων ἁμαρτήμασιν ἀλλοτρίων κακῶν ὑποδείγμασιν οὐ παιδεύεται· πολλοῦ γε δεῖ ταῖς ἐπιγείοις ἡδοναῖς τε καὶ θεωρίαις εὐαρεστεῖσθαι τοῦτον, ὃς καὶ τῶν κοσμικῶν καίτοι θείων ὄντων ἐπαγγελιῶν κατεμεγαλοφρόνησεν. οὐ πᾶς ἄρα ὁ λέγων 'κύριε κύριε' εἰϲελεύϲεται εἰϲ τὴν βαϲιλείαν τοῦ θεοῦ, ἀλλ᾿ ὁ ποιῶν τὸ θέλημα τοῦ θεοῦ. οὗτος δ᾿ ἂν εἴη ὁ γνωστικὸς ἐργάτης, ὁ κρατῶν μὲν τῶν κοσμικῶν ἐπιθυμιῶν ἐν αὐτῇ ἔτι τῇ σαρκὶ ὤν, περὶ δὲ ὧν ἔγνω, τῶν μελλόντων καὶ ἔτι ἀοράτων, πεπεισμένος ἀκριβῶς ὡς μᾶλλον ἡγεῖσθαι τῶν ἐν ποσὶ παρεῖναι ταῦτα.

75. Οὗτος ἐργάτης εὔθετος, χαίρων μὲν ἐφ᾿ οἷς ἔγνω, συστελλόμενος δὲ ἐφ᾿ οἷς ἐπεγκυλίεται τῇ τοῦ βίου ἀνάγκῃ, μηδέπω καταξιούμενος τῆς ὧν ἔγνω ἐνεργούσης μεταλήψεως. ταύτῃ τῷ βίῳ τῷδε ὡς ἀλλοτρίῳ ὅσον ἐν ἀνάγκης συγχρῆται μοίρᾳ. οἶδεν αὐτὸς καὶ τῆς νηστείας τὰ αἰνίγματα τῶν ἡμερῶν τούτων, τῆς τετράδος καὶ τῆς παρασκευῆς λέγω. ἐπιφημίζονται γὰρ ἡ μὲν Ἑρμοῦ, ἡ δὲ Ἀφροδίτης. αὐτίκα νηστεύει κατὰ τὸν βίον φιλαργυρίας τε ὁμοῦ καὶ φιληδονίας, ἐξ ὧν αἱ πᾶσαι ἐκφύονται κακίαι· πορνείας γὰρ ἤδη πολλάκις τρεῖς τὰς ἀνωτάτω διαφορὰς παρεστήσαμεν κατὰ τὸν ἀπόστολον, φιληδονίαν, φιλαργυρίαν, εἰδωλολατρίαν.

76. Νηστεύει τοίνυν καὶ κατὰ τὸν νόμον ἀπὸ τῶν πράξεων τῶν φαύλων καὶ κατὰ τὴν τοῦ εὐαγγελίου

---

8. τοιούτων Heinsius. τῶν αὐτῶν L.   23. ἐπιφημίζονται] ἐπιφιμίζονται LV.   27. τρεῖς τὰς] τὰς τρεῖς S.

ance even of those that hate him. For the punishment of criminals, which is carried out in the amphitheatre, is a spectacle unsuited even for children. As for the gnostic it is impossible that he should be instructed or delighted with such shows, since he has trained himself of set purpose to be noble and good, and has thus become insensible to pleasure. As he never falls under the power of sins, he is not corrected by examples of other men's evils. Much less can *he* be satisfied with the pleasures and spectacles of earth, who thinks little even of the promises, divine though they be, of worldly blessings. *Not everyone* therefore *that saith Lord, Lord, shall enter into the kingdom of God, but he that doeth the will of God*[1]. And such would be the gnostic labourer, who has the mastery over his *worldly desires*[2] even while he is still in the flesh, and is so fully persuaded with regard to the unseen future which he knows, that he holds it to be more immediately present than the things which are actually before him.

§ 75. This is the capable labourer, who rejoices in his knowledge, but humbles himself for his entanglements in the necessities of life, being not yet held worthy of the active participation in those things which he knows. Thus he uses this life as something foreign to him, merely as an unavoidable necessity. He understands too the hidden meanings of the fasting of these days, I mean of Wednesday and Friday: for the one is dedicated to Hermes, the other to Aphrodite. At any rate he makes his life a fast both from love of money and love of pleasure, which are the springs of all the vices: for I have often ere now pointed out[3] that, according to the Apostle, the generic varieties of fornication are three, viz. love of pleasure, love of money and idolatry.

§ 76. Accordingly he fasts both from evil deeds according to the law and from wicked thoughts according to the per-

---

[1] Matt. vii. 21.   [2] Tit. ii. 12.   [3] Cf. p. 552, 816, Col. iii. 5.

τελειότητα ἀπὸ τῶν ἐννοιῶν τῶν πονηρῶν. τούτῳ καὶ οἱ πειρασμοὶ προσάγονται οὐκ εἰς τὴν ἀποκάθαρσιν, ἀλλ' εἰς τὴν τῶν πέλας, ὡς ἔφαμεν, ὠφέλειαν, εἰ πεῖραν λαβὼν πόνων καὶ ἀλγηδόνων κατεφρόνησεν καὶ παρεπέμψατο. ὁ δ' αὐτὸς καὶ περὶ ἡδονῆς λόγος. μέγιστον γὰρ ἐν πείρᾳ γενόμενον εἶτα ἀποσχέσθαι. τί γὰρ μέγα εἰ ἃ μὴ οἶδέν τις ἐγκρατεύοιτο; οὗτος ἐντολὴν τὴν κατὰ τὸ εὐαγγέλιον διαπραξάμενος κυριακὴν ἐκείνην τὴν ἡμέραν ποιεῖ, ὅταν ἀποβάλλῃ φαῦλον νόημα καὶ γνωστικὸν προσλάβῃ, τὴν ἐν αὑτῷ τοῦ κυρίου ἀνάστασιν δοξάζων. ἀλλὰ καὶ ὅταν ἐπιστημονικοῦ θεωρήματος κατάληψιν λάβῃ, τὸν κύριον ὁρᾶν νομίζει, τὰς ὄψεις αὐτοῦ πρὸς τὰ ἀόρατα χειραγωγῶν· κἂν βλέπειν δοκῇ ἃ μὴ βλέπειν ἐθέλῃ, κολάζων τὸ ὁρατικόν, ὅταν ἡδομένου ἑαυτοῦ κατὰ τὴν προσβολὴν τῆς ὄψεως συναίσθηται· ἐπεὶ τοῦτο μόνον ὁρᾶν βούλεται καὶ ἀκούειν ὃ προσῆκεν αὐτῷ. αὐτίκα τῶν ἀδελφῶν τὰς ψυχὰς θεωρῶν καὶ τῆς σαρκὸς τὸ κάλλος αὐτῇ βλέπει τῇ ψυχῇ, τῇ μόνον τὸ καλὸν ἄνευ τῆς σαρκικῆς ἡδονῆς ἐπισκοπεῖν εἰθισμένῃ.

77. Ἀδελφοὶ δ' εἰσὶ τῷ ὄντι κατὰ τὴν κτίσιν τὴν ἐξειλεγμένην καὶ κατὰ τὴν ὁμοήθειαν καὶ κατὰ τὴν τῶν ἔργων ὑπόστασιν, τὰ αὐτὰ ποιοῦντες καὶ νοοῦντες καὶ λαλοῦντες ἐνεργήματα ἅγια καὶ καλά, ἃ ὁ κύριος αὐτοὺς ἠθέλησεν ἐκλεκτοὺς ὄντας φρονεῖν. πίστις μὲν γὰρ ἐν τῷ τὰ αὐτὰ αἱρεῖσθαι, γνῶσις δὲ ἐν τῷ τὰ αὐτὰ μεμαθηκέναι καὶ φρονεῖν, ἐλπὶς δὲ ἐν τῷ τὰ αὐτὰ ποθεῖν. κἂν κατὰ τὸ ἀναγκαῖον τοῦ βίου ὀλίγον τι τῆς ὥρας περὶ τὴν τροφὴν ἀσχοληθῇ, χρεωκοπεῖσθαι οἴεται περισπώμενος ὑπὸ τοῦ πράγματος. ταύτῃ οὐδὲ ὄναρ ποτὲ μὴ ἁρμόζον ἐκλεκτῷ βλέπει. ἀτεχνῶς ξένος

2 ἀποκάθαρσιν] αὐτοῦ κάθαρσιν Jackson. 6. γενόμενον S. γενόμενος L. 7. μέγα] μεγάλα L, sed literis λα punctis notatis. 10. αὐτῷ M. αὑτῷ L edd. 11. δοξάζων. M. δοξάζων, D. 13. ἀόρατα Lowth. ὁρατά L. 14. κολάζων] fort. κολάζει M. 27. ποθεῖν Lowth. ποιεῖν L. 28. ὥρας M. ὥρας L. 30. βλέπει. ἀτεχνῶς P. βλέπει ἀτέχνως. L.

fection of the Gospel. He is also subjected to trials, not for his <own> purification, but, as we said, for the benefit of his neighbours, if, after experience of labours and troubles, he is seen to despise and disregard them. The same is to be said about pleasure: the great thing is to abstain from pleasure after having had experience of it. For what credit is it to practise self-control, where pleasure is unknown? The gnostic carries out the evangelical command and makes that the Lord's day on which he puts away an evil thought and assumes one suited for the gnostic, doing honour to the Lord's resurrection in himself. Moreover when he gets hold of a scientific principle, he believes that he sees the Lord, while he directs his eyes to the unseen: and if he fancies that he sees what he is unwilling to see, he chides the faculty of vision whenever he is conscious of a feeling of pleasure at the visual impression; since he desires to see and hear nothing but what beseems him. For instance, while contemplating the souls of his brethren, he sees also the beauty of the flesh with the soul itself, which has been trained to look on beauty alone apart from fleshly pleasure.

§ 77. And brethren indeed they are according to the elect creation and the similarity of disposition and the character of their actions, where thought and word and deed manifest that same holiness and beauty which the Lord willed them, as elect, to have in mind. For faith is shown in the choice of the same things, and knowledge in having learnt the same and keeping them in mind, and hope in desiring the same. And if, owing to the necessities of life, some slight portion of his care is occupied about food, he thinks he is defrauded by such distraction. Thus he never sees even a dream which is unsuited to an elect soul. For verily *a stranger and*

γὰρ καὶ παρεπίδημος ἐν τῷ βίῳ παντὶ πᾶς οὗτος, ὃς πόλιν οἰκῶν τῶν κατὰ τὴν πόλιν κατεφρόνησεν παρ' ἄλλοις θαυμαζομένων, καὶ καθάπερ ἐν ἐρημίᾳ τῇ πόλει βιοῖ, ἵνα μὴ ὁ τόπος αὐτὸν ἀναγκάζῃ, ἀλλ' ἡ προαίρεσις δεικνύῃ δίκαιον. ὁ γνωστικὸς οὗτος συνελόντι εἰπεῖν τὴν ἀποστολικὴν ἀπουσίαν ἀνταναπληροῖ βιοὺς ὀρθῶς, γινώσκων ἀκριβῶς, ὠφελῶν τοὺς ἐπιτηδείους, τὰ ὄρη μεθιστὰς τῶν πλησίον καὶ τὰς τῆς ψυχῆς αὐτῶν ἀνωμαλίας ἀποβάλλων· καίτοι ἕκαστος ἡμῶν αὐτοῦ τε ἀμπελὼν καὶ ἐργάτης. ὁ δὲ καὶ πράσσων τὰ ἄριστα λανθάνειν βούλεται τοὺς ἀνθρώπους, τὸν κύριον ἅμα καὶ ἑαυτὸν πείθων ὅτι κατὰ τὰς ἐντολὰς βιοῖ, προκρίνων ταῦτα ἐξ ὧν εἶναι πεπίστευκεν. ὅπου γὰρ ὁ νοῦς τινός, φησίν, ἐκεῖ καὶ ὁ θησαυρὸς αὐτοῦ. αὐτὸς ἑαυτὸν μειονεκτεῖ πρὸς τὸ μὴ ὑπεριδεῖν ποτε ἐν θλίψει γενόμενον ἀδελφὸν διὰ τὴν ἐν τῇ ἀγάπῃ τελείωσιν, ἐὰν ἐπίστηται μάλιστα ῥᾷον ἑαυτὸν τοῦ ἀδελφοῦ τὴν ἔνδειαν οἴσοντα.

78. Ἡγεῖται γοῦν τὴν ἀλγηδόνα ἐκείνου ἴδιον ἄλγημα· κἂν ἐκ τῆς ἑαυτοῦ ἐνδείας παρεχόμενος δι' εὐποιίαν πάθῃ τι δύσκολον, οὐ δυσχεραίνει ἐπὶ τούτῳ, προσαύξει δὲ ἔτι μᾶλλον τὴν εὐεργεσίαν. ἔχει γὰρ ἄκρατον πίστιν τὴν περὶ τῶν πραγμάτων, τὸ εὐαγγέλιον δι' ἔργων καὶ θεωρίας ἐπαινῶν. καὶ δὴ οὐ τὸν ἔπαινον παρὰ ἀνθρώπων, ἀλλὰ παρὰ τοῦ θεοῦ καρποῦται, ἃ ἐδίδαξεν ὁ κύριος, ταῦτα ἐπιτελῶν. οὗτος περισπώμενος ὑπὸ τῆς ἰδίας ἐλπίδος οὐ γεύεται τῶν ἐν κόσμῳ καλῶν, πάντων τῶν ἐνταῦθα καταμεγαλοφρονῶν· οἰκτείρων τοὺς μετὰ θάνατον παιδευομένους διὰ τῆς κολάσεως ἀκουσίως ἐξομολογουμένους, εὐσυνείδητος πρὸς τὴν ἔξοδον καὶ ἀεὶ ἕτοιμος ὤν, ὡς ἂν παρεπίδημος καὶ ξένος

---

9. ἀποβάλλων] fort. καταβάλλων. M.   αὐτοῦ Herv. αὐτοῦ L.   10. ἐργάτης. M. ἐργάτης, D.   14. αὐτοῦ. M. αὐτοῦ, D.   ἑαυτὸν] ἑαυτοῦ Jackson.   23. ἐπαινῶν. (or ἐπεξιών.) M. ἐπαινῶν, D.   25. περισπώμενος] fort. ἐπισπώμενος M.   26. ἰδίας] fort. ἀϊδίας M.

pilgrim[1] all his life through is every one who, dwelling in a city, despises the things that others admire in it, and lives in it as though it were in a desert, that he may not be constrained by locality, but that his own free will may show him to be just. To sum up, such a gnostic fills the vacant place of the apostles by his upright life, his exact knowledge, his assistance of the deserving, by *removing mountains*[2] from the hearts of his neighbours and casting down the inequalities of their souls; though indeed each one of us is his own vineyard and his own labourer. He however even in his best actions desires to escape the eyes of men, as long as he persuades the Lord and himself that he lives according to the commandments, preferring those things on which he believes that his life depends. For *where a man's heart is*, says one, *there is his treasure also*[3]. Through the perfection of his love he impoverishes himself that he may never overlook a brother in affliction, especially if he knows that he could himself bear want better than his brother.

§ 78. At any rate he esteems the other's grief as his own pain: and if he suffers any inconvenience through his kindness in making provision out of his own deficiency, he is not vexed at this, but only increases his bounty still further. For he has a faith unmixed with doubt, faith concerning the realities, while he commends the Gospel both in his actions and in his thoughts. And verily *the praise* he reaps *is not from men but from God*[4], as he fulfils the Lord's instructions. Being attracted by the eternal hope, he tastes not the fair things of this world, but disdains all that belongs to this life. He pities those who undergo discipline after death and are brought to repentance against their will by means of punishment, while he is himself of good conscience as regards his departure and is ever ready for it as being a *pilgrim and a stranger*[1]

---

[1] Heb. xi. 13.   [2] 1 Cor. xiii. 2.
[3] Matt. vi. 21, quoted with same variation in P. 944.
[4] Rom. ii. 29, Joh. v. 41—44.

τῶν τῇδε, κληρονομημάτων μόνων τῶν ἰδίων μεμνημένος, τὰ δὲ ἐνταῦθα πάντα ἀλλότρια ἡγούμενος· οὐ μόνον θαυμάζων τὰς τοῦ κυρίου ἐντολάς, ἀλλ' ὡς ἔπος εἰπεῖν δι' αὐτῆς τῆς γνώσεως μέτοχος ὢν τῆς θείας βουλήσεως, οἰκεῖος ὄντως τοῦ κυρίου καὶ τῶν ἐντολῶν, ἐξειλεγμένος ὡς δίκαιος, ἡγεμονικὸς δὲ καὶ βασιλικὸς ὡς γνωστικός, χρυσὸν μὲν πάντα τὸν ἐπὶ γῆς καὶ ὑπὸ γῆν, καὶ βασιλείαν τὴν ἀπὸ περάτων ἐπὶ πέρατα ὠκεανοῦ ὑπερορῶν, ὡς μόνης τῆς τοῦ κυρίου ἀντέχεσθαι θεραπείας. διὸ καὶ ἐσθίων καὶ πίνων καὶ γαμῶν, ἐὰν ὁ λόγος αἱρῇ, ἀλλὰ καὶ ὀνείρους βλέπων τὰ ἅγια ποιεῖ καὶ νοεῖ· ταύτῃ καθαρὸς εἰς εὐχὴν πάντοτε. ὁ δὲ καὶ μετ' ἀγγέλων εὔχεται, ὡς ἂν ἤδη καὶ ἰϲάγγελοϲ, οὐδὲ ἔξω ποτὲ τῆς ἁγίας φρουρᾶς γίνεται· κἂν μόνος εὔχηται, τὸν τῶν ἁγίων χορὸν συνιστάμενον ἔχει. διττὴν οὗτος οἶδε, καὶ τὴν μὲν τοῦ πιστεύοντος ἐνέργειαν, τὴν δὲ τοῦ πιστευομένου, τὴν κατ' ἀξίαν ὑπεροχήν, ἐπεὶ καὶ ἡ δικαιοσύνη διπλῆ, ἡ μὲν δι' ἀγάπην, ἡ δὲ διὰ φόβον.

79. Εἴρηται γοῦν ὁ φόβοϲ τοῦ κυρίου ἁγνὸϲ διαμένων εἰϲ αἰῶνα αἰῶνοϲ. οἱ γὰρ ἐκ φόβου εἰς πίστιν καὶ δικαιοσύνην ἐπιστρέφοντες εἰς αἰῶνα διαμένουσιν. αὐτίκα ἀποχὴν κακῶν ἐργάζεται ὁ φόβος, ἀγαθοποιεῖν δὲ προτρέπει ἐποικοδομοῦσα εἰς τὸ ἑκούσιον ἡ ἀγάπη, ἵνα τις ἀκούσῃ παρὰ τοῦ κυρίου, οὐκέτι ὑμᾶϲ δούλουϲ, ἀλλὰ φίλουϲ λέγω, καὶ πεποιθὼς ἤδη προσίῃ ταῖς εὐχαῖς. τὸ δὲ εἶδος αὐτῷ τῆς εὐχῆς εὐχαριστία ἐπί τε τοῖς προγεγονόσιν ἐπί τε τοῖς ἐνεστῶσιν ἐπί τε τοῖς μέλλουσιν, ὡς ἤδη διὰ τὴν πίστιν παροῦσιν· τούτου δὲ ἡγεῖται τὸ εἰληφέναι τὴν γνῶσιν. καὶ δὴ καὶ αἰτεῖται οὕτως ζῆσαι τὸν ὡρισμένον ἐν τῇ σαρκὶ βίον, ὡς γνωστικός, ὡς ἄσαρκος, καὶ τυχεῖν μὲν τῶν ἀρίστων,

6. γνωστικός M. ὁ γνωστικός L.   10. αἱρῇ S. ἔρῃ L.   15. οἶδε] πίστιν addit S.   16. om. καὶ M.   17. πιστευομένου] fort. ἐπισταμένου M.
22. φόβος S. φοβούμενος L.   26. αὐτῷ S. αὐτὸ L.   29. γνῶσιν. M. γνῶσιν, D.

to this present world, remembering only his own inheritance and regarding all things here as alien. And, as he not only admires the commandments of the Lord, but is made, so to speak, a partner of the Divine Will by actual knowledge, he is a true intimate of the Lord and of His commandments, elect as righteous, fitted as gnostic for rule and sovereignty, despising all the gold that is upon the earth and under the earth, and the sovereignty which extends from one ocean to the other, so as to hold fast to the one service of God. Wherefore also both in eating and drinking and in marrying, if reason so dictates, and even in his dreams, his actions and his thoughts are holy, so that he is always purified for prayer. He prays also with angels, as being already *equal to angels*[1], and never passes out of the holy keeping: even if he prays alone he has the chorus of saints banded with him. Such a man is aware of a twofold energy, the one that of him who believes, the other the deserved preeminence of him who knows, since righteousness also is twofold, the one caused by love, the other by fear.

§ 79. Certainly we are told that *the fear of the Lord is pure, enduring for ever*[2]. For they who turn to faith and righteousness from fear endure for ever. For instance fear brings about abstinence from evil, while love prompts us to do good, building us up to a willing mind, in order that one may hear from the Lord the words, *No longer do I call you servants, but friends*[3], and may thenceforward join with confidence in the prayers. And the form of his prayer is thanksgiving for what is past and what is present and what is future, as being already present through his faith: and this is preceded by the acquisition of knowledge. Moreover he prays that he may so live his appointed time in the flesh as a gnostic and as one free from the flesh, and that he may obtain the best things and

---

[1] Luke xx. 36. [2] Ps. xix. 9. [3] Joh. xv. 15.

φυγεῖν δὲ τὰ χείρονα· αἰτεῖται δὲ καὶ ἐπικουφισμὸν περὶ ὧν ἡμαρτήσαμεν ἡμεῖς καὶ ἐπιστροφὴν εἰς ἐπίγνωσιν· οὕτως ὀξέως ἑπόμενος τῷ καλοῦντι κατὰ τὴν ἔξοδον ὡς ἐκεῖνος καλεῖ, προάγων ὡς εἰπεῖν διὰ τὴν ἀγαθὴν συνείδησιν, σπεύδων ἐπὶ τὸ εὐχαριστῆσαι, κἀκεῖ σὺν Χριστῷ γενόμενος ἄξιον ἑαυτὸν παρασχεῖν διὰ καθαρότητα κατὰ ἀνάκρασιν ἔχειν τὴν δύναμιν τοῦ θεοῦ τὴν διὰ τοῦ Χριστοῦ χορηγουμένην. οὐ γὰρ μετουσίᾳ θερμότητος θερμὸς οὐδὲ πυρὸς φωτεινός, ἀλλ᾽ εἶναι ὅλος φῶς βούλεται. οὗτος οἶδεν ἀκριβῶς τὸ εἰρημένον ἐὰν μὴ μιϲήϲητε τὸν πατέρα καὶ τὴν μητέρα, πρὸϲ ἔτι δὲ καὶ τὴν ἰδίαν ψυχήν, καὶ ἐὰν μὴ τὸ ϲημεῖον βαϲτάϲητε. τάς τε γὰρ προσπαθείας τὰς σαρκικὰς πολὺ τῆς ἡδονῆς τὸ φίλτρον ἐχούσας μεμίσηκεν, καὶ καταμεγαλοφρονεῖ πάντων τῶν εἰς δημιουργίαν καὶ τροφὴν τῆς σαρκὸς οἰκείων, ἀλλὰ καὶ τῆς σωματικῆς ψυχῆς κατεξανίσταται, στόμιον ἐμβαλὼν ἀφηνιάζοντι τῷ ἀλόγῳ πνεύματι, ὅτι ἡ ϲὰρξ ἐπιθυμεῖ κατὰ τοῦ πνεύματοϲ. τὸ ϲημεῖον δὲ βαϲτάϲαι τὸν θάνατον ἐϲτιν περιφέρειν ἔτι ζῶντα πᾶϲιν ἀποταξάμενον, ἐπεὶ μὴ ἴση ἐστὶν ἀγάπη τοῦ σπείραντος τὴν σάρκα καὶ τοῦ τὴν ψυχὴν εἰς ἐπιστήμην κτίσαντος.

80. Οὗτος ἐν ἕξει γενόμενος εὐποιητικῇ θᾶττον τοῦ λέγειν καὶ ἄλλους εὐεργετεῖ, τὰ μὲν τῶν ἀδελφῶν ἁμαρτήματα μερίσασθαι εὐχόμενος εἰς ἐξομολόγησιν καὶ ἐπιστροφὴν τῶν ϲυγγενῶν, κοινωνεῖν δὲ τῶν ἰδίων ἀγαθῶν προθυμούμενος τοῖς φιλτάτοις. αὐτοὶ δὲ οὕτως αὐτῷ οἱ φίλοι. αὔξων οὖν τὰ παρ᾽ αὐτῷ κατατιθέμενα σπέρματα καθ᾽ ἣν ἐνετείλατο κύριος γεωργίαν, ἀναμάρτητος μὲν μένει, ἐγκρατὴς δὲ γίνεται, καὶ μετὰ τῶν ὁμοίων διάγει τῷ πνεύματι ἐν τοῖς χοροῖς τῶν ἁγίων, κἂν ἐπὶ γῆς ἔτι κατέχηται. οὗτος δι᾽ ὅλης ἡμέρας καὶ

6. παρασχεῖν Barnard. παρασχὼν L. 24. καὶ ἄλλους M. καλῶς L.
27. οὕτως] οὕτω L. 32. κατέχηται. M. κατέχηται, D.

escape the worse: aye, and he prays for us, that we may be comforted about our sins and may be converted to knowledge. No sooner does he hear the Master's call to depart, than he follows it; nay, owing to his good conscience even leads the way so to speak, hastening to offer his sacrifice of thanksgiving, and being joined with Christ there, to make himself worthy from his purity to receive by inward union the power of God which is supplied through Christ. For he does not desire to be warm through borrowed warmth or luminous through borrowed fire, but to be altogether light himself. Such an one knows accurately the word that is spoken, *Unless ye hate your father and mother, aye, and your own life also, and unless ye bear the sign*[1]. For he both hates the lusts of the flesh with their potent spell of pleasure, and disdains all that belongs to handicraft and the support of the flesh; nay he rises up against the corporeal soul, putting a bit in the mouth of the irrational spirit when it breaks loose, because *the flesh lusteth against the spirit*[2]. But *to bear the sign*[3] is *to carry about death*[4] whilst still alive, *having renounced all*[5], since higher love is due to Him who created the soul for knowledge than to him who begot the body.

§ 80. When he has once formed the habit of doing good, the gnostic loses no time in benefiting others also, praying that he may be reckoned *as sharing in the sins of his brethren*[6] with a view to the repentance and conversion of *his kinsfolk*, and eager to impart his own good things to those whom he holds dearest. And his friends for their part feel the same for him. Thus he helps the growth of the seeds deposited with him according to the husbandry enjoined by the Lord, and continues without sin and acquires self-control and lives in the spirit with those who are like him in the choirs of the saints, even though he be still detained on earth. Throughout the day

---

[1] Luke xiv. 26, 27.   [2] Gal. v. 17.   [3] Luke xiv. 27.
[4] 2 Cor. iv. 10.   [5] Luke xiv. 33.   [6] Cf. Exod. xxxii. 32, Rom. ix. 3.

νυκτὸς λέγων καὶ ποιῶν τὰ προστάγματα τοῦ κυρίου ὑπερευφραίνεται, οὐ πρωίας μόνον ἀναστὰς καὶ μέσον ἡμέρας, ἀλλὰ καὶ περιπατῶν καὶ κοιμώμενος, ἀμφιεννύμενός τε καὶ ἀποδυόμενος· καὶ διδάσκει τὸν υἱόν, ἐὰν υἱὸς ᾖ τὸ γένος, ἀχώριστος ὢν τῆς ἐντολῆς καὶ τῆς ἐλπίδος, εὐχαριστῶν ἀεὶ τῷ θεῷ καθάπερ τὰ ζῷα τὰ δοξολόγα τὰ διὰ Ἡσαΐου ἀλληγορούμενα. ὑπομονητικὸς πρὸς πᾶσαν πεῖραν, ὁ κύριος, φησίν, ἔδωκεν, ὁ κύριος ἀφείλετο. τοιοῦτος γὰρ καὶ ὁ Ἰώβ, ὃς καὶ τοῦ ἀφαιρεθῆναι τὰ ἐκτὸς σὺν καὶ τῇ τοῦ σώματος ὑγιείᾳ προσαπέθετο πάντα διὰ τὴν πρὸς τὸν κύριον ἀγάπην. ἦν γάρ, φησί, δίκαιος, ὅσιος, ἀπεχόμενος ἀπὸ πάσης πονηρίας. τὸ δὲ ὅσιον τὰ πρὸς τὸν θεὸν δικαίαν τὴν πᾶσαν οἰκονομίαν μηνύει, ἃ δὴ ἐπιστάμενος γνωστικὸς ἦν. χρὴ γὰρ μήτε, ἐὰν ἀγαθὰ ᾖ, προστετηκέναι τούτοις ἀνθρωπίνοις οὖσι, μήτε αὖ ἐὰν κακά, ἀπεχθάνεσθαι αὐτοῖς, ἀλλὰ ἐπάνω εἶναι ἀμφοῖν τὰ μὲν πατοῦντα, τὰ δὲ τοῖς δεομένοις παραπέμποντα. ἀσφαλὴς δὲ ἐν συμπεριφορᾷ ὁ γνωστικὸς μὴ λάθῃ ἢ ἡ συμπεριφορὰ διάθεσις γένηται.

ΚΕΦ. ΙΓ.

81. Οὐδέποτε τῶν εἰς αὐτὸν ἁμαρτησάντων μέμνηται, ἀλλὰ ἀφίησι· διὸ καὶ δικαίως εὔχεται ἄφες ἡμῖν λέγων, καὶ γὰρ ἡμεῖς ἀφίεμεν. ἓν γάρ ἐστι καὶ τοῦτο ὧν ὁ θεὸς βούλεται, μηδενὸς ἐπιθυμεῖν, μηδένα μισεῖν, ἑνὸς γὰρ θελήματος ἔργον οἱ πάντες ἄνθρωποι. καὶ μή τι τὸν γνωστικὸν τέλειον εἶναι βουλόμενος, ὁ σωτὴρ

---

7. ἀλληγορούμενα. M. ἀλληγορούμενα, D. 8. πεῖραν, M. πεῖραν. D.
9. καὶ τοῦ L. καὶ μέχρι τοῦ Heinsius, fort. καταμεγαλοφρονῶν τοῦ M. 11. τὴν —ἀγάπην Heinsius. τῆς—ἀγάπης L. 13. ὅσιον] ὅσιος Barnard. δικαίαν τὴν M. δίκαια καὶ τὴν L. 14. μηνύει, M. μηνύει. D. 18. ἀσφαλὴς δὲ...μὴ λάθῃ ἢ ἡ...γένηται] fort. ἀσφαλὴς δὲ ἔστω...μὴ λάθῃ ἡ...γινομένη M.

and night he is filled with joy uttering and doing the precepts of the Lord, not only at dawn on rising, and at midday, but also when *walking and lying down*, dressing and undressing; and he *teaches his son*[1], if his child be of that sex, never losing hold of the commandment and the hope, giving thanks always to God, like the creatures which give glory to God in Isaiah's allegory[2]. Patient under every trial he says *The Lord gave, the Lord hath taken away*[3]. For such also was Job, he who <despising> the loss of his outward prosperity, surrendered everything else along with his bodily soundness, owing to his love to the Lord. For it says *he was upright and holy and eschewed all evil*[4]. But the word 'holy' implies that his whole management of life was just in things pertaining to God; and his knowledge of these things made him a gnostic. For neither, if good things come, should a man be engrossed by them, seeing they are merely human, nor again should he quarrel with them, if evil, but should be superior to both, treading the one under his feet, and passing on the other to those who are in need. But let the gnostic be guarded in accommodating himself to others, lest accommodation should imperceptibly change into inclination.

CHAPTER XIII.

§ 81. He never remembers those who have sinned against him, but forgives them: wherefore also he has a right to pray *Forgive us, for we forgive*[5]. For this too is one of the things which God desires, that we should covet nothing and hate none, for all mankind are the work of one Will. And perhaps our Saviour, in desiring that the gnostic should be *perfect*

---

[1] Deut. vi. 7, xi. 19.   [2] Isai. ii. 3.   [3] Job i. 21.
[4] Job i. 1.   [5] Matt. vi. 12.

ἡμῶν, ὡς τὸν ογράνιον πατέρα, τουτέστιν ἑαυτόν, ὁ λέγων
δεῦτε τέκνα, ἀκούσατέ μου φόβον κυρίου, οὐ τῆς δι' ἀγγέλων
βοηθείας ἐπιδεῆ ἔτι εἶναι βούλεται τοῦτον, παρ' ἑαυτοῦ
δὲ ἄξιον γενόμενον λαμβάνειν, καὶ τὴν φρουρὰν ἔχειν
5 παρ' ἑαυτοῦ διὰ τῆς εὐπειθείας; ὁ τοιοῦτος ἀπαιτεῖ
παρὰ κυρίου, οὐχὶ δὲ καὶ αἰτεῖ. καὶ ἐπὶ τῶν πενομένων
ἀδελφῶν οὐκ αὐτὸς αἰτήσεται ὁ γνωστικὸς χρημάτων
περιουσίαν εἰς μετάδοσιν, ἐκείνοις δὲ ὧν δέονται χορηγίαν εὔξεται γενέσθαι. δίδωσι γὰρ οὕτως καὶ τὴν
10 εὐχὴν τοῖς δεομένοις ὁ γνωστικὸς καὶ τὸ διὰ τῆς εὐχῆς
ἀγνώστως ἅμα καὶ ἀτύφως παρέχεται. πενία μὲν οὖν
πολλάκις καὶ νόσος καὶ τοιαῦται πεῖραι ἐπὶ νουθεσίᾳ
προσφέρονται καὶ πρὸς διόρθωσιν τῶν παρεληλυθότων
καὶ πρὸς ἐπιστροφὴν τῶν μελλόντων. ὁ τοιοῦτος τὸν
15 ἐπικουφισμὸν τούτοις αἰτούμενος, ἅτε τὸ ἐξαίρετον τῆς
γνώσεως ἔχων, οὐ διὰ κενοδοξίας ἀλλὰ δι' αὐτὸ τὸ εἶναι
γνωστικός, αὐτὸς ἐργάζεται τὴν εὐποιΐαν, ὄργανον γενόμενος τῆς τοῦ θεοῦ ἀγαθότητος.

82. Λέγουσι δὲ ἐν ταῖς παραδόσεσι Ματθίαν τὸν
20 ἀπόστολον παρ' ἕκαστα εἰρηκέναι ὅτι "ἐὰν ἐκλεκτοῦ
γείτων ἁμαρτήσῃ, ἥμαρτεν ὁ ἐκλεκτός· εἰ γὰρ οὕτως
ἑαυτὸν ἦγεν ὡς ὁ λόγος ὑπαγορεύει, κατῃδέσθη ἂν
αὐτοῦ τὸν βίον καὶ ὁ γείτων εἰς τὸ μὴ ἁμαρτεῖν." τί
τοίνυν περὶ αὐτοῦ τοῦ γνωστικοῦ φήσαιμεν <ἂν>;
25 ἢ οὐκ οἴδατε, φησὶν ὁ ἀπόστολος, ὅτι ναός ἐστε τοῦ θεοῦ;
θεῖος ἄρα ὁ γνωστικὸς καὶ ἤδη ἅγιος, θεοφορῶν καὶ
θεοφορούμενος. αὐτίκα τὸ ἁμαρτῆσαι ἀλλότριον παρι-
στᾶσα ἡ γραφὴ τοὺς μὲν παραπεσόντας τοῖς ἀλλοφύλοις
πιπράσκει. μὴ ἐμβλέψῃς δὲ πρὸς ἐπιθυμίαν ἀλλοτρίᾳ γυναικὶ

---

1. ἑαυτόν] fort. ὡς ἑαυτόν M. 4. γενόμενον in marg. pr. m. L.
6. οὐχὶ δὲ καὶ αἰτεῖ] forsitan ex margine interpolata interrogatio M.
7. γνωστικὸς M. γνωστικὸς οὐ L. 10. τὸ M. τῷ L. 17. γνωστικός
M. γνωστικόν L. 24. ἂν addidit D. 27. τὸ ἁμαρτῆσαι M. τοῦ ἁμ. L.
29. ἐμβλέψῃς L. ἐμβλέψῃ edd. post V.

as the Father in heaven[1], that is, as Himself,—our Saviour, who says *Come ye children and I will teach you the fear of the Lord*[2],—desires that the gnostic should no longer need *the help given through the angels*[3], but being made worthy should receive it from himself, and have his protection from himself by means of his obedience. The prayer of such an one is the claiming of a promise from the Lord. And in the case of his brethren who are in need the gnostic will not ask a superfluity of wealth for himself to distribute, but will pray that there may be to them a supply of what they need. For so he not only gives his prayer to the needy, but he provides that which comes through prayer in a secret and unostentatious manner. Poverty indeed and disease and such-like trials are often used for admonition, with a view to produce both amendment of the past and care for the future. In virtue of the prerogative of knowledge, such an one becomes an instrument of the Divine Goodness by asking for relief for the sufferers, and himself does the kind action, not from vainglory, but simply because he is a gnostic.

§ 82. We are told in the Traditions that the Apostle Matthias was wont to say on occasion 'If the neighbour of an elect person sins, it is the fault of the elect; for if he had conducted himself as reason dictates, his neighbour's reverence for such a life would have prevented him from sinning.' What shall we say then about the gnostic himself? *Know ye not*, says the Apostle, *that ye are the temple of God*[4]? The gnostic therefore is already holy and divine, carrying God within him and being carried by God. Certainly the Scripture represents sin as something alien, where it sells to the strangers those that fall away[5]. And by the words *Look not with desire on another*

---

[1] Matt. v. 48.   [2] Ps. xxxiv. 11.   [3] Ps. xci. 11.
[4] 1 Cor. iii. 16.   [5] Cf. Jud. ii. 11—14 &c.

λέγουσα, ἄντικρυς ἀλλότριον καὶ παρὰ φύσιν τοῦ ναοῦ
τοῦ θεοῦ τὴν ἁμαρτίαν λέγει. ναὸς δέ ἐστιν ὁ μὲν
μέγας, ὡς ἡ ἐκκλησία, ὁ δὲ μικρός, ὡς ὁ ἄνθρωπος ὁ
τὸ σπέρμα σώζων τὸ Ἀβραάμ. οὐκ ἄρα ἐπιθυμήσει
τινὸς ἑτέρου ὁ ἔχων ἀναπαυόμενον τὸν θεόν. αὐτίκα
πάντα τὰ ἐμποδὼν καταλιπὼν καὶ πᾶσαν τὴν περισπῶσαν
αὐτὸν ὕλην ὑπερηφανήσας τέμνει διὰ τῆς
ἐπιστήμης τὸν οὐρανόν, καὶ διελθὼν τὰς πνευματικὰς
οὐσίας καὶ πᾶσαν ἀρχὴν καὶ ἐξουσίαν ἅπτεται τῶν θρόνων
τῶν ἄκρων, ἐπ' ἐκεῖνο μόνον ἱέμενος, ἐφ' ὃ ἔγνω μόνον.
μίξας οὖν τῇ περιστερᾷ τὸν ὄφιν τελείως ἅμα καὶ
εὐσυνειδήτως βιοῖ, πίστιν ἐλπίδι κεράσας πρὸς τὴν
τοῦ μέλλοντος ἀπεκδοχήν. αἰσθεται γὰρ τῆς δωρεᾶς
ἧς ἔλαβεν ἄξιος γενόμενος τοῦ τυχεῖν, καὶ μετατεθεὶς
ἐκ δουλείας εἰς υἱοθεσίαν ἀκόλουθα τῇ ἐπιστήμῃ, μήτε
μὴ γνοὺς τὸν θεόν, μᾶλλον δὲ γνωσθεὶς πρὸς αὐτοῦ, ἐπὶ τέλει
τε πρὸς ἀξίαν τῆς χάριτος ἐνδεικνύμενος τὰ ἐνεργήματα.
ἕπεται γὰρ τὰ ἔργα τῇ γνώσει ὡς τῷ σώματι ἡ σκιά.

83. Ἐπ' οὐδενὶ τοίνυν εἰκότως ταράσσεται τῶν
συμβαινόντων, οὐδὲ ὑποπτεύει τῶν κατὰ τὴν οἰκονομίαν
ἐπὶ τῷ συμφέροντι γινομένων <οὐδέν>, οὐδὲ αἰσχύνεται
ἀποθανών, εὐσυνείδητος ὤν, ταῖς ἐξουσίαις ὀφθῆναι,
πάντας ὡς ἔπος εἰπεῖν τοὺς τῆς ψυχῆς ἀποκεκαθαρμένος
σπίλους, ὅ γε εὖ μάλα ἐπιστάμενος ἄμεινον αὐτῷ μετὰ
τὴν ἔξοδον γενήσεσθαι. ὅθεν οὐδέποτε τὸ ἡδὺ καὶ τὸ
συμφέρον προκρίνει τῆς οἰκονομίας, γυμνάζων ἑαυτὸν
διὰ τῶν ἐντολῶν, ἵνα καὶ πρὸς τὸν κύριον εὐάρεστος ἐν
πᾶσι γένηται καὶ πρὸς τὸν κόσμον ἐπαινετός, ἐπεὶ τὰ
πάντα <ἐφ'> ἑνὸς τοῦ παντοκράτορος θεοῦ ἵσταται.
εἰς τὰ ἴδια, φησίν, ἦλθεν ὁ υἱὸς τοῦ θεοῦ καὶ οἱ ἴδιοι αὐτὸν οὐκ

---

4. τὸ Ἀβρ. L, τὸ Ἀβρ. D, fort. τοῦ Ἀβρ. M. 11. μίξας S. μείξας L.
15. ἀκόλουθα Barnard. ἀνακόλουθα L. μήτε seclusit D. 16. γνωσθείς...
ἐπὶ τέλει τε M. γνωσθείς τε...ἐπὶ τέλει L. 21. γινομένων οὐδὲν M. γινομένων L.
22. ἀποθανών Lowth. ἀποθανεῖν L. 25. γενήσεσθαι M.
γενέσθαι L. 29. ἐφ' ἑνὸς M. ἑνὸς L.

man's wife[1], it tells us in plain terms that sin is alien and contrary to the nature of the temple of God. Now the temple is either large like the Church or small like the individual who keeps safe *the seed of Abraham*[2]. He then who has God enthroned within him will not desire anything else. At any rate, leaving behind all hindrances and scorning all the distractions of matter, he cleaves the heaven by his wisdom, and having passed through the spiritual entities and *every rule and authority*[3], he lays hold of the throne on high, speeding to that alone, which alone he knows. So blending *the serpent with the dove*[4] he lives perfectly and with a good conscience, faith being mixed with hope as regards the expectation of that which is to come. For he feels that he has been made worthy to obtain the gift which he received, and that he has been *translated from servitude to sonship*[5] in accordance with his understanding, being on the one hand *not without a knowledge of God (or rather being known by Him*[6]), and on the other hand showing in the end the effects thereof in a manner worthy of the grace received. For works follow knowledge, as the shadow the body.

§ 83. Being then fully assured that it will be better for him after his decease, he has good reason for not being troubled at anything that happens, nor is he suspicious <of any> of those things which come to pass for good according to the divine order; and since his conscience is void of offence, he does not shrink from appearing before the unseen powers after his death, having been purged, so to speak, from every stain of the soul. Hence he never prefers the pleasant or the expedient to the divine order, but trains himself by means of the commandments that he may be both well-pleasing to the Lord in all things and praiseworthy as regards the world, since all things rest upon the one Almighty God. It was *to His own*, we read, *the Son of God came and His own children received Him not*[7].

---

[1] Cf. Matt. v. 28, Prov. vi. 24, 25.
[2] Joh. viii. 33 f., Gal. iii. 29 &c., 1 Joh. iii. 9.
[3] Eph. i. 21, vi. 12.   [4] Matt. x. 16.   [5] Rom. viii. 15.
[6] Gal. iv. 9.   [7] Joh. i. 11.

εδέξαντο. διὸ καὶ κατὰ τὴν τῶν κοσμικῶν χρῆσιν οὐ μόνον εὐχαριστεῖ καὶ θαυμάζει τὴν κτίσιν, ἀλλὰ καὶ χρώμενος ὡς προσῆκεν ἐπαινεῖται, ἐπεὶ τὸ τέλος αὐτῷ δι' ἐνεργείας γνωστικῆς τῆς κατὰ τὰς ἐντολὰς εἰς θεωρίαν περαιοῦται. ἐνθένδε ἤδη, δι' ἐπιστήμης τὰ ἐφόδια τῆς θεωρίας καρπούμενος μεγαλοφρόνως τε τὸ τῆς γνώσεως ἀναδεξάμενος μέγεθος, πρόεισιν ἐπὶ τὴν ἁγίαν τῆς μεταθέσεως ἀμοιβήν. ἀκήκοεν γὰρ τοῦ ψαλμοῦ λέγοντος κυκλώςατε Ϲιὼν καὶ περιλάβετε αὐτήν, διηγήςαςθε ἐν τοῖς πύργοις αὐτῆς. αἰνίσσεται γάρ, οἶμαι, τοὺς ὑψηλῶς προσδεξαμένους τὸν λόγον ὑψηλοὺς ὡς πύργους ἔσεσθαι καὶ βεβαίως ἔν τε τῇ πίστει καὶ τῇ γνώσει στήσεσθαι.

ΚΕΦ. ΙΔ.

84. Καὶ ταῦτα μὲν ὡς ἔνι μάλιστα διὰ βραχυτάτων περὶ τοῦ γνωστικοῦ τοῖς Ἕλλησι σπερματικῶς εἰρήσθω. ἰστέον δὲ ὅτι ἐὰν ἐν τούτων ὁ πιστὸς ᾖ καὶ δεύτερον κατορθώσῃ, ἀλλ' οὔ τί γε ἐν πᾶσιν, οὐδὲ μὴν μετ' ἐπιστήμης τῆς ἄκρας, καθάπερ ὁ γνωστικός. καὶ δὴ τῆς κατὰ τὸν γνωστικὸν ἡμῖν ὡς εἰπεῖν ἀπαθείας, καθ' ἣν ἡ τελείωσις τοῦ πιστοῦ δι' ἀγάπης εἰς ἄνδρα τέλειον εἰς μέτρον ἡλικίας προβαίνουσα ἀφικνεῖται, ἐξομοιουμένη θεῷ, ἰςάγγελος ἀληθῶς γενομένη, πολλὰ μὲν καὶ ἄλλα ἐκ γραφῆς μαρτύρια ἔπεισι παρατίθεσθαι, ἄμεινον δὲ οἶμαι ὑπερθέσθαι τὴν τοιαύτην φιλοτιμίαν διὰ τὸ μῆκος τοῦ λόγου, τοῖς πονεῖν ἐθέλουσι καὶ προσεκπονεῖν τὰ δόγματα κατ' ἐκλογὴν τῶν γραφῶν ἐπιτρέψας. μιᾶς δ' οὖν διὰ βραχυτάτων ἐπιμνησθήσομαι, ὡς μὴ ἀνεπισημείωτον παραλιπεῖν τὸν τόπον. λέγει γὰρ ἐν τῇ

---

15. εἰρήσθω. Μ. εἰρῆσθω, D.   17. οὐδὲ Μ. ἀλλ' οὐδὲ L.
18. γνωστικός. P. γνωστικός, D.   22. γενομένη, P. γενομένη. D.
26. ἐπιτρέψας Μ. ἐπιτρέψαντας S. ἐπιτρέψαντες L.

Wherefore also in his use of the things of the world he is not only full of thankfulness and of admiration for the creation, but he also receives praise himself for using it as he ought, since it is through intelligent action in obedience to the commands that the gnostic arrives at the goal of contemplation. From this point he advances, ever gathering from science new food for contemplation, and having embraced with enthusiasm the great idea of knowledge, till at last he receives the holy reward of his *translation*[1] hence. For he has heard the psalm which says *Walk about Sion and encompass it, declare in the towers thereof*[2]; the meaning of which is, I suppose, that those who receive the word in a lofty spirit will be lofty as towers, and will stand securely both in faith and in knowledge.

CHAPTER XIV.

§ 84. Let thus much be said in the briefest possible terms about the gnostic to the Greeks as seed for further thought. Though the simple believer may succeed in one or other of the points mentioned, yet it must be remembered that he cannot do so in all, nor with perfect science like the gnostic. And further, of our gnostic's apathy, if I may use the term, according to which the perfecting of the believer advances through love, till it arrives *at the perfect man, at the measure of the stature*[3], being made like to God and having become truly *equal to the angels*[4]—of this apathy many other evidences from Scripture occur to me, which I might adduce, but I think it better to defer so ambitious an attempt owing to the length of the discussion, leaving the task to those who are willing to take pains in elaborating the doctrines by extracts from Scripture. One Scripture however I will briefly refer to, so as not to leave the topic altogether unnoticed. The divine Apostle says, in his

[1] Heb. xi. 5.
[2] Ps. xlviii. 12.
[3] Eph. vi. 3.
[4] Luke xx. 36.

προτέρᾳ τῇ πρὸς Κορινθίους ἐπιστολῇ ὁ θεῖος ἀπόστολος τολμᾷ τισ ὑμῶν πρᾶγμα ἔχων πρὸσ τὸν ἕτερον κρίνεσθαι ἐπὶ τῶν ἀδίκων καὶ οὐχὶ ἐπὶ τῶν ἁγίων; ἢ οὐκ οἴδατε ὅτι ἅγιοι τὸν κόσμον κρινοῦσι; καὶ τὰ ἑξῆς. μεγίστης δ' οὔσης τῆς περικοπῆς, ταῖς ἐπικαίροις τῶν ἀποστολικῶν συγχρώμενοι λέξεσι, διὰ βραχυτάτων ἐξ ἐπιδρομῆς οἷον μεταφράζοντες τὴν ῥῆσιν, τὴν διάνοιαν τοῦ ῥητοῦ τοῦ ἀποστόλου παραστήσομεν, καθ' ἣν τοῦ γνωστικοῦ τὴν τελειότητα ὑπογράφει. οὐ γὰρ ἐπὶ τοῦ ἀδικεῖσθαι μᾶλλον ἢ ἀδικεῖν ἵστησι τὸν γνωστικὸν μόνον, ἀλλὰ καὶ ἀμνησίκακον εἶναι διδάσκει, μηδὲ εὔχεσθαι κατὰ τοῦ ἀδικήσαντος ἐπιτρέπων· οἶδεν γὰρ καὶ τὸν κύριον ἄντικρυς εὔχεσθαι ὑπὲρ τῶν ἐχθρῶν παραγγείλαντα. τὸ μὲν οὖν ἐπὶ τῶν ἀδίκων κρίνεσθαι τὸν ἠδικημένον φάσκειν οὐδὲν ἀλλ' ἢ ἀνταποδοῦναι βούλεσθαι δοκεῖν καὶ ἀνταδικῆσαι δεύτερον ἐθέλειν, ὅπερ ὁμοίως ἐστὶν ἀδικῆσαι καὶ αὐτόν. τὸ δὲ ἐπὶ τῶν ἁγίων κρίνεσθαι ἐθέλειν τινὰς λέγειν ἐμφαίνει τοὺς δι' εὐχῆς τοῖς ἀδικήσασιν ἀνταποδοθῆναι τὴν πλεονεξίαν αἰτουμένους, καὶ εἶναι μὲν τῶν προτέρων τοὺς δευτέρους ἀμείνους, οὐδέπω δὲ ἀπαθεῖς, ἢν μὴ ἀμνησίκακοι τέλεον γενόμενοι κατὰ τὴν τοῦ κυρίου διδασκαλίαν προσεύξωνται καὶ ὑπὲρ τῶν ἐχθρῶν.

85. Καλὸν οὖν καὶ φρένας καλὰς ἐκ μετανοίας αὐτοὺς τῆς εἰς τὴν πίστιν μεταλαβεῖν. εἰ γὰρ καὶ ἐχθροὺς ἡ ἀλήθεια τοὺς παραζηλοῦντας κεκτῆσθαι δοκεῖ, ἀλλ' οὔ τί γε αὐτὴ διεχθρεύεταί τινι. ὁ τε γὰρ θεὸσ ἐπὶ δικαίουσ καὶ ἀδίκουσ τὸν αὐτοῦ ἐπιλάμπει ἥλιον καὶ τὸν κύριόν γε αὐτὸν ἐπὶ δικαίους ἔπεμψεν καὶ ἀδίκους, ὅ τε ἐξομοιοῦσθαι βιαζόμενος θεῷ διὰ τῆς πολλῆς ἀμνησικακίας, ἀφεὶσ ἑβδομηκοντάκισ ἑπτά (οἷον κατὰ πάντα τὸν βίον καὶ καθ' ὅλην τὴν κοσμικὴν περιήλυσιν

---

1. τῇ πρὸς S. τῆς πρὸς L. 15. δοκεῖν] fort. δεικνύει M.
21. ἀπαθεῖς corr. ex ἀπειθεῖς sec. m. L. 27. αὐτὴ M. αὕτη L.

earlier epistle to the Corinthians, *Dare any of you, having a matter against another, go to law before the unjust, and not before the saints? Know ye not that the saints shall judge the world*[1] &c.? As the paragraph is very long, I will set forth the meaning of the Apostle's utterance by making use of such of the apostolic expressions as are most to the point, giving in the most concise language a rapid paraphrase of the passage where he describes the perfection of the gnostic. For he not only defines the gnostic's position as consisting in submitting to wrong rather than in inflicting wrong on another, but he also teaches him to forget injuries, not even allowing him to pray against him who has done the wrong: for he knows that the Lord also gave a plain command that we should *pray for our enemies*[2]. The assertion then that the injured party *goes to law before the unjust*[3], shows nothing else than a desire to retaliate and a willingness to commit a second wrong, that is, to be himself equally in fault. But the statement that some wish to go to law before the saints indicates those who ask in prayer that their oppressors may be requited for their extortion: it shows too that though the latter are better than the former, still they are not yet free from passion, unless they entirely forget their wrongs and pray even for their enemies, according to the teaching of the Lord.

§ 85. It is well then that they should also come to a better mind by repentance to faith. For if the truth seems to have enemies in those who *provoke her to jealousy*[4], still she is in no wise hostile to any herself. For as *God causes His sun to shine upon the just and the unjust*[5], aye, and sent the Lord Himself to just and unjust, so he who strives to be made like to God through the absence of all malice *forgives seventy times seven times*[6] (*i.e.* as one might say, throughout his whole life and the entire

---

[1] 1 Cor. vi. 1, 2.   [2] Matt. v. 44.   [3] 1 Cor. vi. 6.
[4] Deut. xxxii. 21, 1 Cor. x. 22.   [5] Matt. v. 45.   [6] Matt. xviii. 22.

150   ΣΤΡΩΜΑΤΕΩΝ Ζ΄   [p. 884, s. 319

ἑβδομάσιν ἀριθμουμέναις σημαινομένην) παντί τῳ
χρηστεύεται, εἰ καί τις τὸν πάντα τοῦτον ἐν σαρκὶ
βιοὺς χρόνον ἀδικεῖ τὸν γνωστικόν. οὐ γὰρ τὴν κρίσιν
μόνην ἄλλοις ἐπιτρέπειν ἀξιοῖ τὸν σπουδαῖον τῶν
5 ἠδικηκότων αὐτόν, ἀλλὰ καὶ παρ' ἐκείνων αἰτεῖσθαι
τῶν κριτῶν βούλεται τὸν δίκαιον τὴν ἄφεσιν τῶν
ἁμαρτιῶν τοῖς εἰς αὐτὸν πεπλημμεληκόσι, καὶ εἰκότως·
εἴ γε τὸ ἐκτὸς μόνον καὶ τὸ περὶ σῶμα, κἂν μέχρι
θανάτου προβαίνῃ, πλεονεκτοῦσιν οἱ ἀδικεῖν ἐπιχει-
10 ροῦντες, ὧν οὐδὲν οἰκεῖον τοῦ γνωστικοῦ. πῶς δ' ἂν
καὶ ἀγγέλους τις κρίναι τοὺς ἀποστάτας, αὐτὸς ἀποστάτης
ἐκείνης τῆς κατὰ τὸ εὐαγγέλιον ἀμνησικακίας γενόμενος; Διὰ τί οὐχὶ μᾶλλον ἀδικεῖσθε; φησί, διὰ τί οὐχὶ μᾶλλον
ἀποστερεῖσθε; ἀλλὰ ὑμεῖς ἀδικεῖτε (εὐχόμενοι κατὰ τούτων
15 δηλονότι τῶν κατ' ἄγνοιαν πλημμελούντων) καὶ ἀποστερεῖτε τῆς τοῦ θεοῦ φιλανθρωπίας τε καὶ ἀγαθότητος
τὸ ὅσον ἐφ' ὑμῖν τοὺς καθ' ὧν εὔχεσθε, καὶ τοῦτο ἀδελφούς,
οὐ τοὺς κατὰ πίστιν μόνον, ἀλλὰ καὶ τοὺς προσηλύτους
λέγων. 86. εἰ γὰρ καὶ ὁ νῦν διεχθρεύων ὕστερον
20 πιστεύσει οὐκ ἴσμεν οὐδέπω ἡμεῖς. ἐξ ὧν συνάγεται
σαφῶς εἰ καὶ μὴ πάντας εἶναι, ἡμῖν γε αὐτοὺς δοκεῖν
<δεῖν> εἶναι ἀδελφούς. ἤδη δὲ καὶ πάντας ἀνθρώπους
ἑνὸς ὄντας ἔργον θεοῦ καὶ μίαν εἰκόνα ἐπὶ μίαν οὐσίαν
885 p. περιβεβλημένους, κἂν τεθολωμένοι τύχωσιν ἄλλοι
25 ἄλλων μᾶλλον, μόνος ὁ ἐπιστήμων γνωρίζει, καὶ διὰ
τῶν κτισμάτων τὴν ἐνέργειαν, δι' ἧς αὖθις τὸ θέλημα
τοῦ θεοῦ προσκυνεῖ.

Ἢ οὐκ οἴδατε ὅτι ἄδικοι βασιλείαν θεοῦ οὐ κληρονομήσουσιν;
ἀδικεῖ οὖν ὁ ἀντιδικῶν εἴτ' οὖν ἔργῳ εἴτε καὶ λόγῳ εἴτε

8. κρίσιν M. κτῆσιν L.   11. κρίναι (vel κρίνοι) D. κρίνῃ L.   14. ἀδικεῖτε M. ἀδικεῖτε καὶ ἀποστερεῖτε L.   15. ἀποστερεῖτε P. ἀποστερεῖσθε L.   17. καὶ τοῦτο M. καὶ τούς L. καὶ ταῦτα P.   21. ἡμῖν γε L. fort. ἡμῖν δὲ vel ἀλλ' ἡμῖν γε M. αὐτοὺς δοκεῖν δεῖν M. αὐτοῖς δοκεῖν L.   27. προσκυνεῖ. P. προσκυνεῖ, D.   28. οὐ post θεοῦ casu om. D.   29. ἀντιδικῶν] fort. ἀνταδικῶν M.

cosmical revolution signified by the reckoning of sevens) and shows kindness to every one, even though some continue to ill-treat the gnostic all the time of their life here in the flesh. For it is not only the judgment of those who have wronged him that the Apostle requires the virtuous man to leave to others: he even desires that the just man should ask from those judges the forgiveness of their sins for those who have offended against him; and with good reason, seeing that they who attempt injustice damage only what is external and concerned with the body, even though it should go to the extent of death; but none of such things properly belongs to the gnostic. And how could one *judge* the apostate *angels*[1] if he is himself an apostate from the Gospel rule that we are to forget injuries? *Why do ye not rather take wrong?* he continues, *why do ye not rather suffer yourselves to be defrauded? Nay, ye do wrong* (namely, by praying against those who offend in ignorance) and, so far as in you lies, *ye defraud*[2] of the goodness and kindness of God those against whom ye pray, *and that your brethren*[3] (referring hereby, not only to those who are brethren by faith, but to those also who are strangers among you).

§ 86. For we know not yet whether even he who is at present hostile may not hereafter believe. From which we clearly gather, if not that all are brethren, yet that to us they should seem such. And further, that all men are the work of one God, invested with one likeness upon one nature (though in some the likeness may be more confused than in others),—the recognition of this is reserved for the man of understanding, who through the creation adores the Divine energy, through which again he adores the Divine Will.

Or know ye not that wrong-doers shall not inherit the kingdom of God[3]*?* He then is a wrong-doer who retaliates

---

[1] 1 Cor. vi. 3. [2] 1 Cor. vi. 7, 8. [3] 1 Cor. vi. 9.

καὶ τῇ τοῦ βούλεσθαι ἐννοίᾳ, ἣν μετὰ τὴν τοῦ νόμου παιδαγωγίαν τὸ εὐαγγέλιον περιγράφει. καὶ ταῦτά τινες ἦτε, τοιοῦτοι δῆλον ὁποῖοι ἔτι τυγχάνουσιν οἷς αὐτοὶ οὐ συγγινώσκετε· ἀλλὰ ἀπελούσασθε, οὐχ ἁπλῶς ὡς οἱ λοιποί, ἀλλὰ μετὰ γνώσεως τὰ πάθη τὰ ψυχικὰ ἀπερρίψασθε, εἰς τὸ ἐξομοιοῦσθαι ὅση δύναμις τῇ ἀγαθότητι τῆς τοῦ θεοῦ προνοίας διά τε τῆς ἀνεξικακίας διά τε τῆς ἀμνησικακίας, ἐπὶ δικαίους καὶ ἀδίκους τὸ εὐμενὲς τοῦ λόγου καὶ τῶν ἔργων καθάπερ ὁ ἥλιος ἐπιλάμποντες· εἴτ' οὖν μεγαλονοίᾳ τοῦτο περιποιήσεται ὁ γνωστικός, εἴτε μιμήσει τοῦ κρείττονος· τρίτη δ' αἰτία τὸ ἄφες καὶ ἀφεθήσεταί σοι, βιαζομένης ὥσπερ τῆς ἐντολῆς εἰς σωτηρίαν δι' ὑπερβολὴν ἀγαθότητος. ἀλλ' ἡγιάσθητε. τῷ γὰρ εἰς τοῦτο ἥκοντι ἕξεως ἁγίῳ εἶναι συμβαίνει, μηδενὶ τῶν παθῶν κατὰ μηδένα τρόπον περιπίπτοντι, ἀλλ' οἷον ἀσάρκῳ ἤδη καὶ ἄνω τῆσδε τῆς γῆς ἁγίῳ γεγονότι.

87. Διόπερ ἐδικαιώθητε φησὶ τῷ ὀνόματι τοῦ κυρίου· ἐποιήθητε ὡς εἰπεῖν ὑπ' αὐτοῦ δίκαιοι εἶναι ὡς αὐτός, καὶ τῷ πνεύματι τῷ ἁγίῳ ὡς ἔνι μάλιστα κατὰ δύναμιν ἀνεκράθητε. μὴ γὰρ οὐ πάντα μοι ἔξεστιν, ἀλλ' οὐκ ἐξουσιασθήσομαι, φησί, παρὰ τὸ εὐαγγέλιόν τι ποιῆσαι ἢ νοῆσαι ἢ λαλῆσαι; τὰ δὲ βρώματα τῇ κοιλίᾳ καὶ ἡ κοιλία τοῖς βρώμασιν, ἃ ὁ θεὸς καταργήσει, τουτέστιν τοὺς οὕτω λογιζομένους καὶ βιοῦντας ὡς διὰ τὸ ἐσθίειν γενομένους, μὴ οὐχὶ δὲ ἐσθίοντας ἵνα ζῶσι μὲν κατὰ τὸ ἀκόλουθον, κατὰ δὲ τὸ προηγούμενον τῇ γνώσει προσανέχοντας. καὶ μή τι οἷον σάρκας εἶναι τοῦ ἁγίου σώματος τούτους φησί; σῶμα δὲ ἀλληγορεῖται ἡ ἐκκλησία κυρίου, ὁ πνευματικὸς καὶ ἅγιος χορός, ἐξ ὧν οἱ τὸ ὄνομα ἐπικεκλημένοι μόνον, βιοῦντες δὲ οὐ κατὰ λόγον, σάρκες εἰσί. τὸ δὲ σῶμα τοῦτο πνευματικόν, τουτέστιν ἡ ἁγία ἐκκλησία,

13. τῷ] τὸ L.   16. ἄνω S. ἄνευ L.   26. προσανέχοντας L. fort. προσανέχωσιν M.   28. ἀλληγορεῖται] praecedit in L καλεῖται, sed punctis notatum. D.

either by deed or word or by the wish in the heart, which is excluded by the Gospel after *the schooling of the law*[1]. *And such were some of you*—such, manifestly, as those still are whom you refuse to pardon—*but ye washed yourselves*[2], not simply like the rest, but with knowledge you cast off the passions of the soul, so as to become assimilated to the goodness of the Divine Providence, to the best of your power, both by long-suffering and by forgiveness, *causing* the gentleness of your word and deeds to *shine like the sun upon just and unjust*[3] alike. The gnostic will attain this result either by his own greatness of mind, or by imitation of one who is better than himself; and there is a third cause denoted by the words *Forgive and it shall be forgiven you*[4], where the command seems to compel to salvation through its exceeding goodness. *But ye were sanctified*[2]. For he who has attained such a habit as this, must necessarily be holy, never falling into any passion in any way, but being, as it were, already freed from the flesh and having reached a holiness above this world.

§ 87. Wherefore, he says, *ye were justified by the name of the Lord*[2]; ye were, so to speak, made by Him to be just, as He is just, and ye were intimately joined with the Holy Spirit, so far as it is possible for man. For does he not say *All things are lawful for me, but I will not be brought under the power of any*[5], so as to do or think or speak anything contrary to the Gospel? And *meats are for the belly and the belly for meats, but the Lord shall destroy them*[6], that is, all who so reason and live as if they were born for eating, instead of eating to live as a subordinate aim, but devoting themselves to knowledge as their principal aim. And perhaps he means that these are, as it were, the fleshy parts of the Holy Body, *the Lord's Church* being figuratively described as *a body*[7], viz., that spiritual and holy quire, of whom those who are only called by the Name and do not live accordingly constitute the flesh. But this spiritual *body*,

---
[1] Gal. iii. 24.   [2] 1 Cor. vi. 11.   [3] Matt. v. 45.
[4] Matt. vi. 14, Polyc. *Phil.* 2, Clem. R. 1. 13.
[5] 1 Cor. vi. 12.   [6] 1 Cor. vi. 13.   [7] Eph. i. 23.

ΟΥ ΤΗ ΠΟΡΝΕΊΑ, οὐδὲ τῇ ἀπὸ τοῦ εὐαγγελίου ἀποστάσει πρὸς τὸν ἐθνικὸν βίον κατ' οὐδένα τρόπον οὐδ' ὁπωστιοῦν οἰκειωτέον.

88. Πορνεύει γὰρ εἰς τὴν ἐκκλησίαν καὶ τὸ ΑΥΤΟΥ ϲῶΜΑ ὁ ἐθνικῶς ἐν ἐκκλησίᾳ πολιτευόμενος, εἴτ' οὖν ἐν ἔργῳ, εἴτε καὶ ἐν λόγῳ, εἴτε καὶ ἐν αὐτῇ τῇ ἐννοίᾳ. ὁ ταύτῃ κολλώμενος τῇ πόρνῃ, τῇ παρὰ τὴν διαθήκην ἐνεργείᾳ, εἰϲ ϲάρκα Μίαν καὶ βίον ἐθνικὸν καὶ ἄλλην ἐλπίδα, ἄλλο σῶμα γίνεται, οὐχ ἅγιον· ὁ δὲ κολλώμενος τῷ κυρίῳ τὸ διάφορον τῆς συνόδου γένος ἐν πνεύματι, πνευματικὸν σῶμα. υἱὸς οὗτος ἅπας, ἄνθρωπος ἅγιος, ἀπαθής, γνωστικός, τέλειος, μορφούμενος τῇ τοῦ κυρίου διδασκαλίᾳ, ἵνα δὴ καὶ ἔργῳ καὶ λόγῳ καὶ αὐτῷ τῷ πνεύματι προσεχὴς γενόμενος τῷ κυρίῳ τὴν ΜΟΝΗΝ ἐκείνην τὴν ὀφειλομένην τῷ οὕτως ἀπηνδρωμένῳ ἀπολάβῃ.

Ἀπόχρη τὸ δεῖγμα τοῖς ὦτα ἔχουσιν. οὐ γὰρ ἐκκυκλεῖν χρὴ τὸ μυστήριον, ἐμφαίνειν δὲ ὅσον εἰς ἀνάμνησιν τοῖς μετεσχηκόσι τῆς γνώσεως, οἳ καὶ συνήσουσιν ὅπως εἴρηται πρὸς τοῦ κυρίου ΓΊΝΕϲΘΕ ὡϲ ὁ πατὴρ ὑμῶν τέλειοι, τελείως ἀφιέντες τὰς ἁμαρτίας καὶ ἀμνησικακοῦντες καὶ ἐν τῇ ἕξει τῆς ἀπαθείας καταβιοῦντες. ὡς γὰρ τέλειόν φαμεν ἰατρὸν καὶ τέλειον φιλόσοφον, οὕτως, οἶμαι, καὶ τέλειον γνωστικόν· ἀλλ' οὐδὲν τούτων, καίτοι μέγιστον ὄν, εἰς ὁμοιότητα θεοῦ παραλαμβάνεται. οὐ γάρ, καθάπερ οἱ Στωϊκοί, ἀθέως πάνυ τὴν αὐτὴν ἀρετὴν ἀνθρώπου λέγομεν καὶ θεοῦ. μή τι οὖν τέλειοι γίνεσθαι ὀφείλομεν ὡς ὁ πατὴρ βούλεται; ἀδύνατον γὰρ καὶ ἀμήχανον ὡς ὁ θεός ἐστι

---

1. ἀποστάσει πρὸς M. ἀποστάσει, ἅ πρὸς L.   2. ὁπωστιοῦν sic L, ὅπως τις οὖν V.   4. αὐτοῦ M. αὐτοῦ edd.   6. ἐννοίᾳ. P. ἐννοίᾳ, Kl. D.
8. ἔχει post βίον addidit Heinsius.   9. ἀλλὰ σῶμα γίνεται, οὐχ ἅγιον hic M. post ἐνεργείᾳ l. 8 L.   10. τὸ διάφορον τῆς συνόδου γένος hic M. ante υἱὸς L.
14. μονὴν L. μόνην D.   28. γίνεσθαι] γίνεσθε L.

i.e. the holy Church, *is not for fornication* nor must it be connected in any possible sort or way with the apostasy from the Gospel to the life of the heathen.

§ 88. For he who behaves like a heathen in the Church, whether in act or word or even merely in thought, commits fornication against the Church and *against his own body*[1]. *He that is joined to* this *harlot*[2] (viz. the activity which is contrary to the covenant), *for one flesh*[3] and for a heathenish life and another hope, becomes another body which is not holy: *but he that is joined to the Lord* after a different kind of union, in spirit, is a spiritual body. He is wholly a son, a holy man, passionless, gnostic, perfect, being formed by the Lord's teaching, in order that he may be brought close to Him in deed and word and in his very spirit, and may receive that *mansion*[4] which is due to one who has thus approved his manhood.

This may serve as a sample for those that have ears. For we must not divulge the mystery, but only indicate it so far as to recall it to those who have been partakers in knowledge, who will also understand what is the meaning of the Lord's saying *Be ye perfect as your Father is perfect*[5], perfectly forgiving sins and forgetting injuries, and being habitually free from passion. For as we speak of a perfect physician and a perfect philosopher, so, I suppose, we may speak of a perfect gnostic: but none of these perfections, to whatever height it may attain, is regarded as coming into comparison with God. For we do not agree in the impious opinion of the Stoics as to the identity of human and divine virtue. Perhaps then we ought to be as perfect as the Father wishes us to be: for it is impracticable and impossible that any one should be as perfect

---

[1] 1 Cor. vi. 18. [2] *v.* 16. [3] *v.* 17.
[4] Joh. xiv. 2. [5] Matt. v. 48.

γενέσθαι τινὰ τέλειον· βούλεται δὲ ὁ πατὴρ ζῶντας ἡμᾶς κατὰ τὴν τοῦ εὐαγγελίου ὑπακοὴν ἀνεπιλήπτως τελείους γίνεσθαι. ἢν οὖν, κατ' ἔλλειψιν λεγομένου τοῦ ῥητοῦ, προσυπακούσωμεν τὸ ἐνδέον, εἰς ἀναπλήρωσιν τῆς περικοπῆς τοῖς συνιέναι δυναμένοις ἀπολελειμμένον ἐκλαβεῖν, καὶ τὸ θέλημα τοῦ θεοῦ γνωριοῦμεν καὶ κατ' ἀξίαν τῆς ἐντολῆς εὐσεβῶς ἅμα καὶ μεγαλοφρόνως πολιτευσόμεθα.

ΚΕΦ. ΙΕ.

89. Ἐπειδὴ δὲ ἀκόλουθόν ἐστι πρὸς τὰ ὑπὸ Ἑλλήνων καὶ Ἰουδαίων ἐπιφερόμενα ἡμῖν ἐγκλήματα ἀπολογήσασθαι, συνεπιλαμβάνονται δὲ ἔν τισι τῶν ἀποριῶν ὁμοίως τοῖς προειρημένοις καὶ αἱ περὶ τὴν ἄλλην διδασκαλίαν αἱρέσεις, εὖ ἂν ἔχοι, πρότερον διακαθάραντας τὰ ἐμποδών, εὐτρεπεῖς ἐπὶ τὰς τῶν ἀποριῶν λύσεις εἰς τὸν ἑξῆς προϊέναι στρωματέα. πρῶτον μὲν οὖν αὐτὸ τοῦτο προσάγουσιν ἡμῖν, λέγοντες μὴ δεῖν πιστεύειν διὰ τὴν διαφωνίαν τῶν αἱρέσεων, παρατείνει γὰρ καὶ ἡ ἀλήθεια ἄλλων ἄλλα δογματιζόντων. πρὸς οὓς φαμεν ὅτι καὶ παρ' ὑμῖν τοῖς Ἰουδαίοις καὶ παρὰ τοῖς δοκιμωτάτοις τῶν παρ' Ἕλλησι φιλοσόφων πάμπολλαι γεγόνασιν αἱρέσεις, καὶ οὐ δήπου φατὲ δεῖν ὀκνεῖν ἤτοι φιλοσοφεῖν ἢ Ἰουδαΐζειν τῆς διαφωνίας ἕνεκα τῆς πρὸς ἀλλήλας τῶν παρ' ὑμῖν αἱρέσεων. ἔπειτα δὲ ἐπισπαρήσεσθαι τὰς αἱρέσεις τῇ ἀληθείᾳ, καθάπερ τῷ πυρῷ τὰ ΖΙΖΑΝΙΑ, πρὸς τοῦ κυρίου προφητικῶς εἴρητο, καὶ ἀδύνατον μὴ γενέσθαι τὸ προειρημένον ἔσεσθαι· καὶ τούτου ἡ αἰτία ὅτι παντὶ τῷ καλῷ μῶμος ἕπεται.

3. ἢν] ἦν L.   14. ἐμποδὼν S. ἐμποδῶν L.   18. παρατείνει] παραφθίνει Hoeschelius (non παραφαίνει ut D.).   22. ἢ Ἰουδαΐζειν M. καὶ Ἰουδ. L.   24. αἱρέσεων. M. αἱρέσεων, D.

as God *is*; but our Father wishes that we should arrive at an unimpeachable perfection by living according to the obedience of the Gospel. If then, since the saying is incomplete, we supply what is wanting for the completion of the passage, the explanation of which has been left to those who are capable of understanding, we shall both recognise the will of God and shall live a life of piety and aspiration, in a manner worthy of the commandment.

CHAPTER XV.

§ 89. The next thing is to reply to the charges brought against us by Greeks and Jews. And since the different schools in other departments of learning take their part in some of the difficulties raised, similarly to the above mentioned, it may be well to begin by clearing away obstacles and then to proceed to the next Miscellany fully prepared for the solution of the difficulties. The first charge they allege is this very point, that the diversity of sects shows belief to be wrong, for the voice of truth is drowned amid the din of conflicting assertions. To whom we reply that, both among you Jews and among the most approved of the Greek philosophers, there have been multitudes of sects, yet of course you do not say that one should hesitate to be a philosopher or a follower of the Jews on account of the internal discord of your sects. In the next place it was prophesied by the Lord that the seed of heresy would be sown upon the truth like *tares upon wheat*[1] (and what was prophesied cannot but come to pass), the cause of this being that the beautiful is always shadowed by its caricature.

[1] Matt. xiii. 25.

90. Μή τι οὖν, εἰ καὶ παραβαίη τις συνθήκας καὶ τὴν ὁμολογίαν παρέλθοι τὴν πρὸς ἡμᾶς, διὰ τὸν ψευσάμενον τὴν ὁμολογίαν ἀφεξόμεθα τῆς ἀληθείας καὶ ἡμεῖς; ἀλλ' ὡς ἀψευδεῖν χρὴ τὸν ἐπιεικῆ καὶ μηδὲν ὧν ὑπέσχηται ἀκυροῦν, κἂν ἄλλοι τινὲς παραβαίνωσι συνθήκας, οὕτως καὶ ἡμᾶς κατὰ μηδένα τρόπον τὸν ἐκκλησιαστικὸν παραβαίνειν προσήκει κανόνα· καὶ μάλιστα τὴν περὶ τῶν μεγίστων ὁμολογίαν ἡμεῖς μὲν φυλάττομεν, οἱ δὲ παραβαίνουσι. πιστευτέον οὖν τοῖς βεβαίως ἐχομένοις τῆς ἀληθείας. ἤδη δὲ καὶ ὡς ἐν πλάτει χρωμένοις τῇδε τῇ ἀπολογίᾳ ἔνεστι φάναι πρὸς αὐτοὺς ὅτι καὶ οἱ ἰατροὶ ἐναντίας δόξας κεκτημένοι κατὰ τὰς οἰκείας αἱρέσεις ἐπ' ἴσης ἔργῳ θεραπεύουσιν. μή τι οὖν κάμνων τις τὸ σῶμα καὶ θεραπείας δεόμενος οὐ προσίεται ἰατρὸν διὰ τὰς ἐν τῇ ἰατρικῇ αἱρέσεις; οὐκ ἄρα οὐδὲ ὁ τὴν ψυχὴν νοσῶν καὶ εἰδώλων ἔμπλεως, ἕνεκά γε τοῦ ὑγιᾶναι καὶ εἰς θεὸν ἐπιστρέψαι, προφασίσαιτο ⟨ἂν⟩ ποτε τὰς αἱρέσεις. ναὶ μὴν διὰ τοὺϲ δοκίμουϲ, φησίν, αἱ αἱρέϲειϲ· δοκίμους ἤτοι τοὺς εἰς πίστιν ἀφικνουμένους λέγει, ἐκλεκτικώτερον προσιόντας τῇ κυριακῇ διδασκαλίᾳ (καθάπερ τοὺϲ δοκίμουϲ τραπεζίταϲ τὸ κίβδηλον νόμισμα τοῦ κυρίου ἀπὸ τοῦ παραχαράγματος διακρίνοντας), ἢ τοὺς ἐν αὐτῇ τῇ πίστει δοκίμους ἤδη γενομένους κατά τε τὸν βίον κατά τε τὴν γνῶσιν.

91. Διὰ δὴ τοῦτο ἄρα πλείονος ἐπιμελείας καὶ προμηθείας δεόμεθα εἰς τὴν ἐξέτασιν τοῦ πῶς ἀκριβῶς βιωτέον καὶ τίς ἡ ὄντως οὖσα θεοσέβεια. δῆλον γὰρ ὅτι δυσκόλου καὶ δυσεργοῦ τῆς ἀληθείας τυγχανούσης διὰ τοῦτο γεγόνασιν αἱ ζητήσεις· ἀφ' ὧν αἱ φίλαυτοι καὶ φιλόδοξοι αἱρέσεις, μὴ μαθόντων μὲν μηδὲ παρειληφότων ἀληθῶς, οἴησιν δὲ γνώσεως εἰληφότων. διὰ

---

17. ἂν ποτε D. ποτε L.   21. κίβδηλον] ἀκίβδηλον Resch, Agr. p. 122. Cf. Str. vi. 780 διακρῖναι τὸ ἀκίβδηλον νόμισμα τοῦ παραχαράγματος.
25. πλείονος] πλέονος L.

§ 90. What then? If some one is guilty of breaking his engagements and neglecting his agreement with us, shall we let go the truth ourselves on account of him who has been false to his agreement? No, the good man must be true to his word and not belie any promise, however much others may break their engagements. And just so, we ought in no way to transgress the rule of the Church. Above all the confession which deals with the essential articles of the faith is observed by us, but disregarded by the heretics. Those then are to be believed who hold firmly to the truth. Using this defence broadly we are now entitled to reply to them, that physicians also, though holding different opinions in accordance with their particular schools, are still equally engaged in the practice of healing. Does then any one who is suffering in body and needs medical treatment refuse to call in a physician owing to the diversity of medical schools? So neither should he who is diseased in soul and full of idols plead the heresies as his excuse in regard to the recovery of health and conversion to God. Aye, and we are told that *heresies are for the sake of those who are approved*[1]; and by 'approved' is meant either those who are coming to the faith, if they show unusual discrimination in approaching the teaching of the Lord (like *the approved money-changers*[2] who distinguish the spurious from the legal coin by the false stamp), or those who are in the faith itself, and have already approved themselves therein, both by their life and their knowledge.

§ 91. It is for this reason therefore that we need more attention and consideration to determine how we should live with strictness, and what is true piety. For it is evident that the trouble and difficulty of ascertaining the truth have given rise to questionings, from whence spring vain and self-willed heresies, when men have not learnt or really received knowledge, but have merely got a conceit of it. We must therefore

---

[1] 1 Cor. xi. 19.   [2] Resch, *Agrapha*, pp. 116—127.

πλείονος τοίνυν φροντίδος ἐρευνητέον τὴν τῷ ὄντι ἀλήθειαν, ἣ μόνη περὶ τὸν ὄντως ὄντα θεὸν καταγίνεται. πόνῳ δὲ ἕπεται γλυκεῖα εὕρεσίς τε καὶ μνήμη. ἐπαποδυτέον ἄρα τῷ πόνῳ τῆς εὑρέσεως διὰ τὰς αἱρέσεις, ἀλλ' οὐ τέλεον ἀποστατέον. οὐδὲ γὰρ ὀπώρας παρακειμένης, τῆς μὲν ἀληθοῦς καὶ ὡρίμου τῆς δὲ ἐκ κηροῦ ὡς ὅτι μάλιστα ἐμφεροῦς πεποιημένης, διὰ τὴν ὁμοιότητα ἀμφοῖν ἀφεκτέον, διακριτέον δὲ ὁμοῦ τε τῇ καταληπτικῇ θεωρίᾳ καὶ τῷ κυρωτάτῳ λογισμῷ τὸ ἀληθὲς ἀπὸ τοῦ φαινομένου. καὶ ὥσπερ ὁδοῦ μιᾶς μὲν τῆς βασιλικῆς τυγχανούσης, πολλῶν δὲ καὶ ἄλλων τῶν μὲν ἐπί τινα κρημνόν, τῶν δὲ ἐπὶ ποταμὸν ῥοώδη ἢ θάλασσαν ἀγχιβαθῆ φερουσῶν, οὐκ ἄν τις ὀκνήσαι διὰ τὴν διαφωνίαν ὁδεῦσαι, χρήσαιτο δ' ἂν τῇ ἀκινδύνῳ καὶ βασιλικῇ καὶ λεωφόρῳ, οὕτως ἄλλα ἄλλων περὶ ἀληθείας λεγόντων οὐκ ἀποστατέον, ἐπιμελέστερον δὲ θηρατέον τὴν ἀκριβεστάτην περὶ αὐτῆς γνῶσιν· ἐπεὶ κἂν τοῖς κηπευομένοις λαχάνοις συναναφύονται καὶ πόαι· μή τι οὖν ἀπέχονται οἱ γεωργοὶ τῆς κηπευτικῆς ἐπιμελείας; ἔχοντες οὖν πολλὰς ἐκ φύσεως ἀφορμὰς πρὸς τὸ ἐξετάζειν τὰ λεγόμενα καὶ τῆς ἀληθείας τὴν ἀκολουθίαν ἐξευρίσκειν ὀφείλομεν. διὸ καὶ εἰκότως κρινόμεθα, οἷς δέον πείθεσθαι μὴ συγκατατιθέμενοι, μὴ διαστέλλοντες τὸ μαχόμενον καὶ ἀπρεπὲς καὶ παρὰ φύσιν καὶ ψεῦδος ἀπὸ τἀληθοῦς καὶ τοῦ ἀκολούθου καὶ τοῦ πρέποντος καὶ τοῦ κατὰ φύσιν, αἷς ἀφορμαῖς καταχρηστέον εἰς ἐπίγνωσιν τῆς ὄντως οὔσης ἀληθείας.

92. Ματαία τοίνυν τοῖς Ἕλλησιν ἡ πρόφασις αὕτη. τοῖς μὲν γὰρ βουλομένοις ἐξέσται καὶ τὸ εὑρεῖν τὴν ἀλήθειαν, τοῖς δὲ αἰτίας ἀλόγους προβαλλομένοις ἀναπολόγητος ἡ κρίσις. πότερον γὰρ ἀναιροῦσιν ἢ συγ-

---

5. ἀποστατέον. M. ἀποστατέον, D.
25. τἀληθοῦς M. τε τ' αληθες (ες in οὖν pr. m. correcto) L.

spend more thought in searching for the very truth, which alone has for its subject the very God. And sweet are the discovery and the remembrance which attend on toil. The effect of the heresies should therefore be to make one buckle to the toil of discovery and not to abandon it altogether. So too, if we have set before us on the one hand ripe natural fruit, and on the other fruit of wax made to resemble it as closely as possible, we ought not to abstain from both on account of their similarity, but to distinguish the real from the apparent both intuitively and by strict process of reasoning. And just as, if there were only one royal road, but many by-roads, some leading to a precipice, some to a rushing torrent, or deep sea, a man would not hesitate to travel because of this diversity, but would make use of the king's safe high-way; so we must not give up our search because there are different views as to the truth, but must hunt all the more earnestly for the most exact knowledge concerning it. For even among the herbs of the garden weeds spring up, but the husbandmen do not therefore desist from gardening. Since then nature supplies us with many helps for testing the things we are told, we ought also to discover the harmony of the truth. Hence we are rightly condemned if we withhold our assent to the things which we ought to believe, because we fail to distinguish what is incongruous and unseemly and unnatural and false from what is true and consistent and seemly and natural: and these helps we should make full use of in order to gain a knowledge of the real truth.

§ 92. This is therefore an idle excuse on the part of the Greeks: for those who desire it will be able also to discover the truth, while those who put forward irrational grounds *have no excuse for their judgment*[1]. For what is their view of

---

[1] Rom. ii. 1.

κατατίθενται εἶναι ἀπόδειξιν; οἶμαι πάντας ἂν ὁμολογήσειν ἄνευ τῶν τὰς αἰσθήσεις ἀναιρούντων. ἀποδείξεως δ' οὔσης ἀνάγκη συγκαταβαίνειν εἰς τὰς ζητήσεις καὶ δι' αὐτῶν τῶν γραφῶν ἐκμανθάνειν ἀποδεικτικῶς, ὅπως μὲν ἀπεσφάλησαν αἱ αἱρέσεις, ὅπως δὲ ἐν μόνῃ τῇ ἀληθεῖ καὶ τῇ ἀρχαίᾳ ἐκκλησίᾳ ἥ τε ἀκριβεστάτη γνῶσις καὶ ἡ τῷ ὄντι ἀρίστη αἵρεσις. τῶν δὲ ἀπὸ τῆς ἀληθείας ἐκτρεπομένων οἱ μὲν σφᾶς αὐτοὺς μόνους, οἱ δὲ καὶ τοὺς πέλας ἐξαπατᾶν ἐπιχειροῦσιν. οἱ μὲν οὖν δοξόσοφοι καλούμενοι, οἱ τὴν ἀλήθειαν ηὑρηκέναι νομίζοντες, οὐκ ἔχοντες ἀπόδειξιν οὐδεμίαν ἀληθῆ· ἑαυτοὺς οὗτοι ἀπατῶσιν ἀναπεπαῦσθαι νομίζοντες· ὧν πλῆθος οὐκ ὀλίγον τάς τε ζητήσεις ἐκτρεπομένων διὰ τοὺς ἐλέγχους, ἀποφευγόντων δὲ καὶ τὰς διδασκαλίας διὰ τὴν κατάγνωσιν. οἱ δὲ τοὺς προσιόντας ἐξαπατῶντες πανοῦργοι σφόδρα, οἳ καὶ παρακολουθοῦντες αὑτοῖς ὅτι μηδὲν ἐπίστανται πιθανοῖς ὅμως ἐπιχειρήμασι σκοτίζουσι τὴν ἀλήθειαν. ἑτέρα δ', οἶμαι, τῶν πιθανῶν ἐπιχειρημάτων καὶ ἑτέρα τῶν ἀληθῶν ἡ φύσις. καὶ ὅτι τῶν αἱρέσεων ἀνάγκη τὴν ὀνομασίαν πρὸς ἀντιδιαστολὴν τῆς ἀληθείας λέγεσθαι γινώσκομεν· ἀφ' ἧς τινὰ ἀποσπάσαντες ἐπὶ λύμῃ τῶν ἀνθρώπων οἱ σοφισταί, ταῖς ἐξηυρημέναις σφίσιν ἀνθρωπικαῖς τέχναις ἐγκατορύξαντες, αὐχοῦσι προΐστασθαι διατριβῆς μᾶλλον ἢ ἐκκλησίας.

ΚΕΦ. Ις΄.

93. Ἀλλ' οἱ πονεῖν ἕτοιμοι ἐπὶ τοῖς καλλίστοις οὐ πρότερον ἀποστήσονται ζητοῦντες τὴν ἀλήθειαν πρὶν ἂν τὴν ἀπόδειξιν ἀπ' αὐτῶν λάβωσι τῶν γραφῶν. ἔστι μὲν οὖν κοινά τινα τῶν ἀνθρώπων κριτήρια καθάπερ

---

1. ὁμολογήσειν] rectius ὁμολογῆσαι D.   6. ἀληθεῖ M. ἀληθείᾳ L.
7. αἵρεσις. P. αἵρεσις, Kl. D.   δὲ M. τε L.   10. ηὑρηκέναι] εὑρηκέναι L.   17. αὑτοῖς P. αὐτοῖς L.   23. ἐξηυρημέναις] ἐξευρημέναις L.

demonstration? Do they deny that there is such a thing or do they admit it? I suppose all would admit it except those who deny the evidence of the senses. But if there is such a thing as demonstration they must descend to investigation and be taught demonstratively from the Scriptures themselves how the heretical schools went astray, and how it is only in the true and the ancient Church that there is the most exact knowledge and the really best school of thought. But of those who turn aside from the truth some try to deceive themselves only; others to deceive their neighbours as well. They then who are termed 'wise in their own conceit,' those, I mean, who think they have discovered the truth without any true demonstration; these men deceive themselves, thinking to have attained rest: and of such persons there is no small number, men that avoid inquiry for fear of being refuted and also flee from instruction because it condemns themselves. But those who try to impose on their followers are utterly unscrupulous, who, being well aware that they are absolutely without knowledge, nevertheless darken the truth with plausible sophisms. But, in my opinion, the nature of such sophisms is entirely distinct from that of true arguments. Further we know that it is necessary to give the terminology of the heresies in order that the truth may be clearly distinguished from them. For the sophists steal certain fragments of the truth for the injury of mankind and bury them in the human systems they have themselves devised, and then glory in presiding over what is rather a school than a Church.

CHAPTER XVI.

§ 93. But they who are willing to work for the noblest prizes will not relinquish their search for truth, until they obtain the proof from the Scriptures themselves. Now there are certain criteria common to all men, such as the senses;

τὰ αἰσθητήρια, τὰ δ' ἄλλα τῶν βουληθέντων καὶ ἀσκησάντων τὰ ἀληθῆ, τὰ διὰ νοῦ καὶ λογισμοῦ τεχνικὰ λόγων ἀληθῶν τε καὶ ψευδῶν. μέγιστον δὲ τὸ καὶ τὴν οἴησιν ἀποθέσθαι, ἐν μέσῳ καταστάντας ἀκριβοῦς ἐπιστήμης καὶ προπετοῦς δοξοσοφίας, καὶ γνῶναι ὅτι ὁ τὴν αἰώνιον ἐλπίζων ἀνάπαυσιν γινώσκει καὶ τὴν εἴσοδον αὐτῆς ἐπίπονον οὖσαν καὶ τεθλιμμένην. ὁ δὲ ἅπαξ εὐαγγελισθεὶς καὶ τὸ σωτήριον, φησίν, ἐν ᾗ ὥρᾳ ἐπιγνῷ, μὴ ἐπιστρεφέσθω εἰς τὰ ὀπίσω καθάπερ ἡ Λὼτ γυνή, μηδὲ εἰς τὸν πρότερον βίον τὸν τοῖς αἰσθητοῖς προσανέχοντα, μηδὲ μὴν εἰς τὰς αἱρέσεις παλινδρομείτω· ἐθνίζουσι γὰρ ἀμηγέπη, τὸν ὄντα μὴ γινώσκουσαι θεόν. ὁ γὰρ φιλῶν πατέρα ἢ μητέρα ὑπὲρ ἐμέ, τὸν ὄντως πατέρα καὶ διδάσκαλον τῆς ἀληθείας, τὸν ἀναγεννῶντα καὶ ἀνακτίζοντα καὶ τιθηνούμενον τὴν ψυχὴν τὴν ἐξειλεγμένην, οὐκ ἔστι μου ἄξιος, λέγει, τοῦ εἶναι υἱὸς θεοῦ καὶ μαθητὴς θεοῦ ὁμοῦ καὶ φίλος καὶ συγγενής. οὐδεὶς γὰρ εἰς τὰ ὀπίσω βλέπων καὶ ἐπιβάλλων τὴν χεῖρα αὐτοῦ ἐπ' ἄροτρον εὔθετος τῇ βασιλείᾳ τοῦ θεοῦ.

Ἀλλ' ὡς ἔοικεν τοῖς πολλοῖς καὶ μέχρι νῦν δοκεῖ ἡ Μαριὰμ λεχὼ εἶναι διὰ τὴν τοῦ παιδίου γέννησιν, οὐκ οὖσα λεχώ (καὶ γὰρ μετὰ τὸ τεκεῖν αὐτὴν μαιωθεῖσάν φασί τινες παρθένον εὑρεθῆναι)· 94. τοιαῦται δ' ἡμῖν αἱ κυριακαὶ γραφαί, τὴν ἀλήθειαν ἀποτίκτουσαι καὶ μένουσαι παρθένοι μετὰ τῆς ἐπικρύψεως τῶν τῆς ἀληθείας μυστηρίων. τέτοκεν καὶ οὐ τέτοκεν φησὶν ἡ γραφή, ὡς ἂν ἐξ αὐτῆς, οὐκ ἐκ συνδυασμοῦ συλλαβοῦσα. διόπερ τοῖς γνωστικοῖς κεκυήκασιν αἱ γραφαί,

---

7. τεθλιμμένην. M. τεθλιμμένην Kl. D.   δὲ M.   τε L.   9. ἐπιγνῷ] fort. ἐπέγνω μετὰ χαρᾶς λαβών, vel tale quid M. ἐπιγνῶ L.   11. παλινδρομείτω S. παλινδρομήτω L.   12. ἐθνίζουσι M. ἐθίζουσι L.
17. συγγενῆς. M. συγγενής, Kl. D.   19. θεοῦ. M. θεοῦ, Kl. D.
20. ὡς ἔοικεν τοῖς πολλοῖς] ὡς τοῖς πολλοῖς ὡς ἔοικεν M.   23. εὑρεθῆναι)· τοιαῦται M. εὑρεθῆναι. Τοιαῦται LV edd.   27. αὐτῆς P. αὑτῆς L. συλλαβοῦσα. P. συλλαβοῦσα, Kl. D.   28. γραφαί, M. γραφαί. edd.

while the other technical criteria acquired by thought and reasoning, to distinguish between true and false arguments, are confined to those who have made truth their aim and practice. But the chief thing is to get rid of self-conceit, taking a position midway between exact science and rash opinionativeness, and to recognize that he who hopes for the eternal rest knows also that the entrance to it is toilsome and *strait*[1]. But let not him who has once received the Gospel and, as it says, <*embraced* salvation *with joy*[2]> in the hour when he became acquainted with it,—*let not him*, I say, *turn back like Lot's wife*[3], nor recur to his former life which was devoted to the things of sense, nor yet to the heresies, for they in a sort imitate the heathen, not knowing the true God. For *he that loveth father or mother more than Me*[4], *i.e.* than the true Father and Teacher of the truth, who regenerates and re-creates and nourishes the elect soul—*he*, saith He. *is not worthy of Me*, worthy, that is, to be a son of God and at once a disciple and friend and kin to God. For *no man who looks backward and puts his hand to the plough is fit for the kingdom of God*[5].

But, just as most people even now believe, as it seems, that Mary ceased to be a virgin through the birth of her child, though this was not really the case—for some say that she was found by the midwife to be a virgin after her delivery[6];—(§ 94) so we find it to be with the Lord's Scriptures, which bring forth the truth and yet remain virgins, hiding within them the mysteries of the truth. *She has brought forth and has not brought forth*[7], says the Scripture, speaking as of one who had conceived of herself and not from another. Wherefore the Scriptures are pregnant to the gnostics, but the heresies, not having examined

---

[1] Matt. vii. 14.   [2] Matt. xiii. 20.   [3] Luke xvii. 31, 32.
[4] Matt. x. 37.   [5] Luke ix. 62.   [6] Cf. Thilo, *Cod. Apocr.* p. 879.
[7] Cf. Tert. *De Carne Christi* 23 *legimus apud Ezechielem de vacca illa quae peperit et non peperit.*

αἱ δὲ αἱρέσεις οὐκ ἐκμαθοῦσαι ὡς μὴ κεκνηκυίας παραπέμπονται. πάντων δὲ ἀνθρώπων τὴν αὐτὴν κρίσιν ἐχόντων οἱ μὲν ἀκολουθοῦντες τῷ αἱροῦντι λόγῳ ποιοῦνται τὰς πίστεις, οἱ δὲ ἡδοναῖς σφᾶς αὐτοὺς ἐκδεδωκότες βιάζονται πρὸς τὰς ἐπιθυμίας τὴν γραφήν. δεῖ δ', οἶμαι, τῷ τῆς ἀληθείας ἐραστῇ ψυχικῆς εὐτονίας· σφάλλεσθαι γὰρ ἀνάγκη μέγιστα τοὺς μεγίστοις ἐγχειροῦντας πράγμασιν, ἢν μὴ τὸν κανόνα τῆς ἀληθείας παρ' αὐτῆς λαβόντες ἔχωσι τῆς ἀληθείας. οἱ τοιοῦτοι δέ, ἅτε ἀποπεσόντες τῆς ὀρθῆς ὁδοῦ, καὶ τοῖς πλείστοις τῶν κατὰ μέρος σφάλλονται εἰκότως, διὰ τὸ μὴ ἔχειν ἀληθῶν καὶ ψευδῶν κριτήριον συγγεγυμνασμένον ἀκριβῶς τὰ δέοντα αἱρεῖσθαι. εἰ γὰρ ἐκέκτηντο, ταῖς θείαις ἐπείθοντο ἂν γραφαῖς.

95. Καθάπερ οὖν εἴ τις ἐξ ἀνθρώπου θηρίον γένοιτο παραπλησίως τοῖς ὑπὸ τῆς Κίρκης φαρμαχθεῖσιν, οὕτως ἄνθρωπος εἶναι τοῦ θεοῦ καὶ πιστὸς τῷ κυρίῳ διαμένειν ἀπολώλεκεν ὁ ἀναλακτίσας τὴν ἐκκλησιαστικὴν παράδοσιν καὶ ἀποσκιρτήσας εἰς δόξας αἱρέσεων ἀνθρωπίνων. ὁ δὲ ἐκ τῆσδε τῆς ἀπάτης παλινδρομήσας, κατακούσας τῶν γραφῶν καὶ τὸν ἑαυτοῦ βίον ἐπιστρέψας τῇ ἀληθείᾳ, οἷον ἐξ ἀνθρώπου θεὸς ἀποτελεῖται. ἔχομεν γὰρ τὴν ἀρχὴν τῆς διδασκαλίας τὸν κύριον, διά τε τῶν προφητῶν διά τε τοῦ εὐαγγελίου καὶ διὰ τῶν μακαρίων ἀποστόλων πολυτρόπως καὶ πολυμερῶς ἐξ ἀρχῆς εἰς τέλος ἡγούμενον τῆς γνώσεως. τὴν ἀρχὴν δ' εἴ τις ἑτέρου δεῖσθαι ὑπολάβοι, οὐκέτ' ἂν ὄντως ἀρχὴ φυλαχθείη. ὁ μὲν οὖν ἐξ ἑαυτοῦ πιστὸς τῇ κυριακῇ γραφῇ τε καὶ φωνῇ ἀξιόπιστος, εἰκότως ἂν διὰ τοῦ κυρίου πρὸς τὴν τῶν ἀνθρώπων εὐεργεσίαν ἐνεργούμενος. ἀμέλει πρὸς τὴν

8. αἱροῦντι Lowth. ἐροῦντι L.
22. ἐπιστρέψας] ἐπιτρέψας Hervetus.
30. ἂν] scribendum videtur ἂν εἴη D.
15. ἀνθρώπου M. ἀνθρώπων L.
27. ἑτέρου Heinsius. ἕτερον L.
31. ἐνεργούμενος M. ἐνεργουμένη LD. ἐνεργουμένῃ P.

them, dismiss them as barren. And though all men have the same faculty of judgment, some find their grounds for belief in following the dictates of reason, while others surrender themselves to pleasures and wrest the Scripture to suit their desires. But, methinks, the lover of truth needs energy of soul; for they who set themselves to the greatest tasks must meet the greatest disasters, unless they have received the canon of the truth from the truth itself. And such persons, having fallen away from the right path, generally go wrong in particulars also, as might be expected, because they have no criterion of truth and falsehood accurately trained to make the right choice. Otherwise they would have believed the divine Scriptures.

§ 95. As if, then, one were to become a beast instead of a man, like those who were changed by Circe's drugs[1], so is it with him who has spurned the tradition of the Church and has suddenly taken up with the fancies of human sects: he has lost the character of a man of God, and of enduring trust in the Lord. But he who has returned from this deceit, after hearing the Scriptures, and has turned his life to the truth, such a one becomes in the end as it were a god instead of a man. For in the Lord we have the first principle of instruction, guiding us to knowledge from first to last *in divers ways and divers portions*[2] through the Prophets and the Gospel and the blessed Apostles. And, if any one were to suppose that the first principle stood in need of something else, it could no longer be really maintained as a first principle. He then who of himself believes the Lord's Scripture and His actual voice is worthy of belief, being one who would be naturally moved by the Lord to act for the benefit of men. Certainly we use it as a

---

[1] Hom. *Od.* x. 235 f.   [2] Heb. i. 1.

τῶν πραγμάτων εὕρεσιν αὐτῇ χρώμεθα κριτηρίῳ· τὸ κρινόμενον δὲ πᾶν ἔτι ἄπιστον πρὶν κριθῆναι, ὥστ' οὐδ' ἀρχὴ τὸ κρίσεως δεόμενον. εἰκότως τοίνυν πίστει περιλαβόντες ἀναπόδεικτον τὴν ἀρχήν, ἐκ περιουσίας καὶ τὰς ἀποδείξεις παρ' αὐτῆς τῆς ἀρχῆς περὶ τῆς ἀρχῆς λαβόντες, φωνῇ κυρίου παιδευόμεθα πρὸς τὴν ἐπίγνωσιν τῆς ἀληθείας. οὐ γὰρ ἁπλῶς ἀποφαινομένοις ἀνθρώποις προσέχομεν, οἷς καὶ ἀνταποφαίνεσθαι ἐπ' ἴσης ἔξεστιν. εἰ δ' οὐκ ἀρκεῖ μόνον ἁπλῶς εἰπεῖν τὸ δόξαν, ἀλλὰ πιστώσασθαι δεῖ τὸ λεχθέν, οὐ τὴν ἐξ ἀνθρώπων ἀναμένομεν μαρτυρίαν, ἀλλὰ τῇ τοῦ κυρίου φωνῇ πιστούμεθα τὸ ζητούμενον, ἣ πασῶν ἀποδείξεων ἐχεγγυωτέρα, μᾶλλον δὲ ἣ μόνη ἀπόδειξις οὖσα τυγχάνει· καθ' ἣν ἐπιστήμην οἱ μὲν ἀπογευσάμενοι μόνον τῶν γραφῶν πιστοί, οἱ δὲ καὶ προσωτέρω χωρήσαντες ἀκριβεῖς γνώμονες τῆς ἀληθείας ὑπάρχουσιν, οἱ γνωστικοί, ἐπεὶ κἂν τοῖς κατὰ τὸν βίον ἔχουσί τι πλέον οἱ τεχνῖται τῶν ἰδιωτῶν καὶ παρὰ τὰς κοινὰς ἐννοίας ἐκτυποῦσι τὸ βέλτιον.

96. Οὕτως οὖν καὶ ἡμεῖς, ἀπ' αὐτῶν περὶ αὐτῶν τῶν γραφῶν τελείως ἀποδεικνύντες, ἐκ πίστεως πειθόμεθα ἀποδεικτικῶς. κἂν τολμήσωσι προφητικαῖς χρήσασθαι γραφαῖς καὶ οἱ τὰς αἱρέσεις μετιόντες, πρῶτον μὲν οὐ πάσαις, ἔπειτα οὐ τελείαις, οὐδὲ ὡς τὸ σῶμα καὶ τὸ ὕφος τῆς προφητείας ὑπαγορεύει, ἀλλ' ἐκλεγόμενοι τὰ ἀμφιβόλως εἰρημένα εἰς τὰς ἰδίας μετάγουσι δόξας, ὀλίγας σποράδην ἀπανθιζόμενοι φωνάς, οὐ τὸ σημαινόμενον ἀπ' αὐτῶν σκοποῦντες, ἀλλ' αὐτῇ ψιλῇ ἀποχρώμενοι τῇ λέξει. σχεδὸν γὰρ ἐν πᾶσιν οἷς προσφέρονται ῥητοῖς εὕροις ἂν αὐτοὺς ὡς τοῖς ὀνόμασι

---

4. περιλαβόντες M. περιβαλόντες L.   8. προσέχομεν (vel προσέχοιμεν ἄν) D. προσέχοιμεν L.

criterion for the discovery of the real facts. But whatever comes into judgment is not to be believed before it is judged, so that what is in need of judgment cannot be a first principle. With good reason therefore having apprehended our first principle by faith without proof, we get our proofs about the first principle *ex abundanti* from the principle itself, and are thus trained by the voice of the Lord for the knowledge of the truth. For we pay no attention to the mere assertions of men, which may be met by equally valid assertions on the other side. If, however, it is not enough just simply to state one's opinion, but we are bound to prove what is said, then we do not wait for the witness of men, but we prove the point in question by the voice of the Lord, which is more to be relied on than any demonstration, or rather which is the only real demonstration. From this science it comes that, while they who have but tasted of the Scriptures are believers, the gnostics, who have made further progress, are accurate judges of the truth; since even in the ordinary concerns of life craftsmen have an advantage over laymen, and give shape to finer models far surpassing common ideas.

§ 96. So too we, obtaining from the Scriptures themselves a perfect demonstration concerning the Scriptures, derive from faith a conviction which has the force of demonstration. And though it be true that the heretics also have the audacity to make use of the prophetic Scriptures, yet in the first place they do not use them all, and in the second place they do not use them in their entirety, nor as the general frame and tissue of the prophecy suggest; but picking out ambiguous phrases, they turn them to their own opinions, plucking a few scattered utterances, without considering what is intended by them, but perverting the bare letter as it stands. For in almost all the passages they employ, you will find how

μόνοις προσανέχουσι τὰ σημαινόμενα ὑπαλλάττοντες, οὔθ' ὡς λέγονται γινώσκοντες, οὔθ' ὡς ἔχειν πεφύκασι χρώμενοι αἷς καὶ δὴ κομίζουσιν ἐκλογαῖς. ἡ ἀλήθεια δὲ οὐκ ἐν τῷ μετατιθέναι τὰ σημαινόμενα εὑρίσκεται (οὕτω μὲν γὰρ ἀνατρέψουσι πᾶσαν ἀληθῆ διδασκαλίαν), ἀλλ' ἐν τῷ διασκέψασθαι τί τῷ κυρίῳ καὶ τῷ παντοκράτορι θεῷ τελέως οἰκεῖόν τε καὶ πρέπον, κἂν τῷ βεβαιοῦν ἕκαστον τῶν ἀποδεικνυμένων κατὰ τὰς γραφὰς ἐξ αὐτῶν πάλιν τῶν ὁμοίων γραφῶν. οὔτ' οὖν ἐπιστρέφειν ἐπὶ τὴν ἀλήθειαν ἐθέλουσιν, αἰδούμενοι καταθέσθαι τὸ τῆς φιλαυτίας πλεονέκτημα, οὔτ' ἔχουσιν ὅπως διάθωνται τὰς αὑτῶν δόξας ⟨μὴ⟩ βιαζόμενοι τὰς γραφάς. φθάσαντες δὲ ἐξενεγκεῖν εἰς τοὺς ἀνθρώπους δόγματα ψευδῆ σχεδὸν ἁπάσαις ταῖς γραφαῖς ἐναργῶς μαχόμενα, καὶ ἀεὶ ὑφ' ἡμῶν τῶν ἀντιλεγόντων αὐτοῖς ἐλεγχόμενοι, τὸ λοιπὸν ἔτι καὶ νῦν ὑπομένουσι τὰ μὲν μὴ προσίεσθαι τῶν προφητικῶν, τὰ δὲ ἡμᾶς αὐτοὺς ὡς ἄλλης γεγονότας φύσεως μὴ οἵους τε εἶναι συνεῖναι τὰ οἰκεῖα ἐκείνοις διαβάλλουσιν, ἐνίοτε δὲ καὶ τὰ ἑαυτῶν διελεγχόμενοι ἀρνοῦνται δόγματα, ἄντικρυς ὁμολογεῖν αἰδούμενοι ἃ κατ' ἰδίαν αὐχοῦσι διδάσκοντες.

97. Οὕτω γὰρ κατὰ πάσας ἔστιν ἰδεῖν τὰς αἱρέσεις, ἐπιόντας αὐτῶν τὰς μοχθηρίας τῶν δογμάτων. ἐπειδὰν γὰρ ἀνατρέπωνται πρὸς ἡμῶν δεικνύντων αὐτοὺς σαφῶς ἐναντιουμένους ταῖς γραφαῖς, δυοῖν θάτερον ὑπὸ τῶν προεστώτων τοῦ δόγματος ἔστι θεάσασθαι γινόμενον· ἢ γὰρ τῆς ἀκολουθίας τῶν σφετέρων δογμάτων ἢ τῆς προφητείας αὐτῆς, μᾶλλον δὲ τῆς ἑαυτῶν ἐλπίδος καταφρονοῦσιν, αἱροῦνται δὲ ἑκάστοτε τὸ δόξαν αὐτοῖς ὑπάρχειν ἐναργέστερον ἢ τὸ πρὸς τοῦ κυρίου διὰ τῶν

---

18. μὴ βιαζόμενοι M. βιαζόμενοι L. γραφάς. M. γραφάς, Kl. D.
15. μαχόμενα M, μαχόμενοι L. 17. προσίεσθαι Heinsius. προίεσθαι L.
19. συνεῖναι] probabilius συνιέναι D. 22. διδάσκοντες M. διδάσκοντες οὕτως (per διττολογίαν) L.

they attend to the words alone, while they change the meaning, neither understanding them as they are spoken, nor even using in their natural sense such extracts as they adduce.

But the truth is discovered not by altering the meanings of words (for by so doing they will subvert all true teaching), but by considering what is perfectly fitting and appropriate to the Lord and the Almighty God, and by confirming each thing that is proved according to the Scriptures from similar passages of the Scriptures themselves. Hence they are neither ready to turn to the truth, being ashamed to derogate from their own importance, nor have they any way of setting forth their own opinions but by doing violence to the Scriptures. Having hastily published to the world their false doctrines, which are palpably at variance with almost all the Scriptures, and being always confuted by our opposing arguments, they still even now persist in their refusal to accept some of the prophetic writings; while on the other hand they accuse us of inability to understand what is peculiar to them, as though we were quite of another nature; and at other times they are driven to deny even their own doctrines, being ashamed to confess openly what in private they boast of teaching.

§ 97. For so we shall find it to be in all the heresies, when we examine the iniquities of their doctrines. When they are refuted by plain proof on our part that they are opposed to the Scriptures, you may see the upholders of the doctrine in question taking one or other of two courses: they either make light of the consistency of their own doctrines, or they make light of prophecy itself, in other words, of that which constitutes their own hope; preferring on each occasion that which seems to them to be more perspicuous, rather than that which was

προφητῶν εἰρημένον καὶ ὑπὸ τοῦ εὐαγγελίου, προσέτι
δὲ καὶ τῶν ἀποστόλων, συμμαρτυρούμενόν τε καὶ
βεβαιούμενον. ὁρῶντες οὖν τὸν κίνδυνον αὐτοῖς οὐ
περὶ ἑνὸς δόγματος, ἀλλὰ περὶ τοῦ τὰς αἱρέσεις διατη-
ρεῖν, οὐ τὴν ἀλήθειαν ἐξευρίσκειν (τοῖς μὲν γὰρ ἐν
μέσῳ καὶ προχείροις ἐντυχόντες παρ' ἡμῖν ὡς εὐτελῶν
κατεφρόνησαν) ὑπερβῆναι δὲ σπουδάσαντες τὸ κοινὸν
τῆς πίστεως, ἐξέβησαν τὴν ἀλήθειαν. μὴ γὰρ μαθόντες
τὰ τῆς γνώσεως τῆς ἐκκλησιαστικῆς μυστήρια, μηδὲ
χωρήσαντες τὸ μεγαλεῖον τῆς ἀληθείας, μέχρι τοῦ
βάθους τῶν πραγμάτων κατελθεῖν ἀπορραθυμήσαντες,
ἐξ ἐπιπολῆς ἀναγνόντες παρεπέμψαντο τὰς γραφάς.

98. Ὑπὸ δοξοσοφίας τοίνυν ἐπηρμένοι ἐρίζοντες
διατελοῦσι, δῆλοι γεγονότες ὡς τοῦ δοκεῖν μᾶλλον ἤπερ
τοῦ φιλοσοφεῖν προνοοῦνται. αὐτίκα οὐκ ἀναγκαίας
ἀρχὰς πραγμάτων καταβαλλόμενοι δόξαις δὲ ἀνθρωπίναις κεκινημένοι, ἔπειτα ἀναγκαίως τέλος ἀκολουθεῖν
αὑτοῖς ἐκποριζόμενοι, διαπληκτίζονται διὰ τοὺς ἐλέγχους
πρὸς τοὺς τὴν ἀληθῆ φιλοσοφίαν μεταχειριζομένους·
καὶ πάντα μᾶλλον ὑπὸ φιλοτιμίας ὑπομένουσι καὶ
πάντα, φασί, κάλων κινοῦσι, κἂν ἀσεβεῖν διὰ τὸ ἀπιστεῖν ταῖς γραφαῖς μέλλωσιν, ἤπερ μετατίθενται τῆς
αἱρέσεως καὶ τῆς πολυθρυλήτου κατὰ τὰς ἐκκλησίας
αὐτῶν πρωτοκαθεδρίας, δι' ἣν κἀκείνην τὴν συμποτικὴν
τῆς ψευδωνύμου ἀγάπης πρωτοκλισίαν ἀσπάζονται. ἡ παρ'
ἡμῖν δὲ τῆς ἀληθείας ἐπίγνωσις ἐκ τῶν ἤδη πιστῶν τοῖς
οὔπω πιστοῖς ἐκπορίζεται τὴν πίστιν, ἥτις οὐσία ὡς
εἰπεῖν ἀποδείξεως καθίσταται. ἀλλ' ὡς ἔοικεν πᾶσα

4. περὶ τοῦ M. περὶ τὸ L. 6. προχείροις M. προχείρως L.
11. ἀπορραθυμήσαντες] ἀποραθυμήσαντες L. 16. δὲ M. τε L.
18. αὑτοῖς] αὐτοῖς L. ἐκποριζόμενοι L. fort. ἐκπονούμενοι M.
20. ὑπὸ φιλοτιμίας post μᾶλλον M. post μετατίθενται (v. 22) L. 21. κάλων]
κάλον L. 22. μέλλωσιν] μέλλουσιν L. 24. συμποτικὴν M.
συμποτικὴν διὰ L. 25. πρωτοκλισίαν S. πρωτοκλησίαν L. 27. οὕπω
Herv. οὕτω L.

spoken by the Lord through the Prophets and is attested and confirmed by the Gospel as well as by the Apostles. Perceiving, then, that it was not merely a single doctrine which was at stake, but the keeping up of their heresies, and having no desire to discover the truth—for after reading the books we commonly use in public, they despised them as worthless—and aiming simply to exceed the common rule of the faith, they abandoned the truth. For being ignorant of the mysteries of the knowledge of the Church, and incapable of apprehending the grandeur of the truth, they were too sluggish to penetrate to the bottom of the matter, and so laid aside the Scriptures after a superficial reading.

§ 98. Being elated therefore by a conceit of wisdom they are constantly quarrelling, showing that they care *more to be thought* philosophers *than to be*[1] so in reality. For instance, though they lay no foundation of necessary principles, but are moved simply by the opinions of men, yet afterwards they labour to make the conclusion follow necessarily on their premises, and, for fear of being confuted, keep sparring with those who pursue the true philosophy: and their vanity impels them to endure everything, and stir every stone, as the phrase is, even going to the length of impiety through disbelieving the Scriptures, rather than surrender their heresy and the much-talked-of *precedence in their assemblies*, for the sake of which they so eagerly affect *the first couch*[2] in the drinking-bout of their mis-named Agapè. But the knowledge of truth, which is found among us Christians, supplies, from what is already believed, faith for what is not yet believed,—faith which is, so to speak, the substance of demonstration. On the other

---

[1] Aesch. *S. c. Th.* 577, cf. Plat. *Rep.* II. p. 861 B. [2] Mt. xxiii. 6.

αἵρεσις ἀρχὴν ὦτα ἀκούοντα οὐκ ἔχει τὸ σύμφορον, μόνον δὲ τοῖς πρὸς ἡδονὴν ἀνεῳγότα, ἐπεὶ κἂν ἰάθη τις αὐτῶν, εἰ πείθεσθαι τῇ ἀληθείᾳ μόνον ἠβουλήθη. τριττὴ δὲ θεραπεία οἰήσεως, καθάπερ καὶ παντὸς πάθους, μάθησίς τε τοῦ αἰτίου καὶ τοῦ πῶς ἂν ἐξαιρεθείη τοῦτο, καὶ τρίτον ἡ ἄσκησις τῆς ψυχῆς καὶ ὁ ἐθισμὸς πρὸς <τὸ> τοῖς κριθεῖσιν ὀρθῶς ἔχειν ἀκολουθεῖν δύνασθαι.

99. Ὡς γὰρ ὀφθαλμὸς τεταραγμένος, οὕτως καὶ ἡ ψυχὴ τοῖς παρὰ φύσιν θολωθεῖσα δόγμασιν οὐχ οἷά τε τὸ φῶς τῆς ἀληθείας διιδεῖν ἀκριβῶς, ἀλλὰ καὶ τὰ ἐν ποσὶ παρορᾷ. ἐν γοῦν θολερῷ ὕδατι καὶ τὰς ἐγχέλεις ἁλίσκεσθαί φασιν ἀποτυφλουμένας. καὶ καθάπερ τὰ πονηρὰ παιδία τὸν παιδαγωγὸν ἀποκλείει, οὕτως οὗτοι τὰς προφητείας εἴργουσιν ἑαυτῶν τῆς ἐκκλησίας, ὑφορώμενοι δι' ἔλεγχον καὶ νουθεσίαν. ἀμέλει πάμπολλα συγκαττύουσι ψεύσματα καὶ πλάσματα, ἵνα δὴ εὐλόγως δόξωσι μὴ προσίεσθαι τὰς γραφάς. ταύτῃ οὖν οὐκ εὐσεβεῖς, δυσαρεστούμενοι ταῖς θείαις ἐντολαῖς, τουτέστι τῷ ἁγίῳ πνεύματι. ὥσπερ δὲ αἱ ἀμυγδάλαι κεναὶ λέγονται οὐκ ἐν αἷς μηδέν ἐστιν, ἀλλ' ἐν αἷς ἄχρηστον τὸ ἐνόν, οὕτως τοὺς αἱρετικοὺς κενοὺς τῶν τοῦ θεοῦ βουλημάτων καὶ τῶν τοῦ Χριστοῦ παραδόσεων εἶναί φαμεν, πικριζόντων ὡς ἀληθῶς κατὰ τὴν ἀγρίαν ἀμυγδάλην ἐξάρχοντας δογμάτων, πλὴν ὅσα δι' ἐνάργειαν τῶν ἀληθῶν ἀποθέσθαι καὶ ἀποκρύψαι οὐκ ἴσχυσαν.

100. Καθάπερ τοίνυν ἐν πολέμῳ οὐ λειπτέον τὴν τάξιν ἣν ὁ στρατηγὸς ἔταξεν τῷ στρατιώτῃ, οὕτως οὐδὲ ἣν ἔδωκεν ὁ λόγος, ὃν ἄρχοντα εἰλήφαμεν γνώσεώς τε καὶ βίου, λειπτέον τάξιν. οἱ πολλοὶ δὲ οὐδὲ τοῦτο

5. τοῦ πῶς M. τὸ πῶς L. 6. πρὸς τὸ τοῖς M. πρὸς τοῖς L. 7. ἔχειν L. ἔχων V. 11. γοῦν M. οὖν L. 14. ante ἑαυτῶν trium fere litterarum rasura. 15. δι' ἔλεγχον] δὴ ἔλεγχον Cobet. 21. κενοὺς Hoeschel. τοὺς κενοὺς L. 23. πικριζόντων M. πικρίζοντας L. 24. ἐνάργειαν Hoeschel. cum Herveto. ἐνέργειαν L. 28. ἣν ἔδωκεν Herv. ὃν ἔδωκεν L. ὃν ἄρχοντα Herv. ὃν om. L. 29. λειπτέον] ληπτέον L.

hand it seems that heresy of every kind has absolutely no ear for what is expedient, but listens only to what is pleasurable; otherwise a heretic might have been healed, if he had only been willing to obey the truth. Now conceit, like every other ailment, requires a three-fold treatment: there must be a knowledge of the cause, and of the way in which this may be removed, and thirdly there must be discipline of the soul and the training which enables us to follow what is judged to be right.

§ 99. For, as a clouded eye, so too the soul that is confused by unnatural opinions is unable to discern accurately the light of truth, but sees amiss even what lies before it. Certainly we are told that eels also lose their sight and are easily caught in turbid water. And just as naughty children lock out their tutor, so the heretics shut out the prophecies from their church, holding them in suspicion because they convict and admonish them. I grant they patch up many lying inventions to give a sort of decent excuse for their neglect of the Scriptures: and herein they show their want of piety, quarrelling as they do with the divine commands, that is, with the Holy Spirit. And as we call almonds empty, not only when they have nothing in them, but when what is in them is worthless, so we say that the heretics are empty of the divine purposes and of the traditions of Christ, because they are the authors of dogmas which are in truth as bitter as the wild almond, except in so far as the clearness of the truth made it impossible for them to set aside or conceal it.

§ 100. As then in war the soldier must not leave the post assigned to him by the general, so neither must we leave the post to which we are appointed by the Word, whom we have received as our captain both of knowledge and of life. But the

ἐξητάκασιν, εἰ ἔστι τινὶ ἀκολουθητέον καὶ τίνι τούτῳ καὶ ὅπως. οἷος γὰρ ὁ λόγος, τοιόσδε καὶ ὁ βίος εἶναι τῷ πιστῷ προσήκει, ὡς ἕπεσθαι δύνασθαι τῷ θεῷ, ἐξ ἀρχῆς τὰ πάντα εὐθεῖαν περαίνοντι. ἐπὰν δὲ παραβῇ τις τὸν λόγον καὶ διὰ τούτου τὸν θεόν, εἰ μὲν διὰ τὸ αἰφνίδιον προσπεσεῖν τινα φαντασίαν ἠσθένησεν, προχείρους τὰς φαντασίας τὰς λογικὰς ποιητέον, εἰ δὲ τῷ ἔθει τῷ προκατεσχηκότι ἡττηθεὶς γέγονεν, ᾗ φησιν ἡ γραφή, χυδαῖος, ἀποπαυστέον τὸ ἔθος εἰς τὸ παντελὲς καὶ πρὸς τὸ ἀντιλέγειν αὐτῷ τὴν ψυχὴν γυμναστέον. εἰ δὲ καὶ μαχόμενα δόγματα ἐφέλκεσθαί τινας δοκεῖ, ὑπεξαιρετέον ταῦτα καὶ πρὸς τοὺς εἰρηνοποιοὺς τῶν δογμάτων πορευτέον, οἳ κατεπᾴδουσι ταῖς θείαις γραφαῖς τοὺς ψοφοδεεῖς τῶν ἀπείρων, τὴν ἀλήθειαν διὰ τῆς ἀκολουθίας τῶν διαθηκῶν σαφηνίζοντες. ἀλλ', ὡς ἔοικεν, ῥέπομεν ἐπὶ τὰ ἔνδοξα μᾶλλον, κἂν ἐναντία τυγχάνῃ, ἤπερ ἐπὶ τὴν ἀλήθειαν· αὐστηρὰ γάρ ἐστι καὶ σεμνή.

Καὶ δὴ τριῶν οὐσῶν διαθέσεων τῆς ψυχῆς, ἀγνοίας, οἰήσεως, ἐπιστήμης, οἱ μὲν ἐν τῇ ἀγνοίᾳ τὰ ἔθνη, οἱ δὲ ἐν τῇ ἐπιστήμῃ ἡ ἐκκλησία ἡ ἀληθής, οἱ δὲ ἐν οἰήσει οἱ κατὰ τὰς αἱρέσεις. 101. οὐδὲν γοῦν σαφέστερον ἰδεῖν ἔστι τοὺς ἐπισταμένους περὶ ὧν ἴσασι διαβεβαιουμένους ἢ <τούτους> περὶ ὧν οἴονται, ὅσον γε ἐπὶ τῷ διαβεβαιοῦσθαι ἄνευ τῆς ἀποδείξεως. καταφρονοῦσι γοῦν ἀλλήλων καὶ καταγελῶσιν, καὶ συμβαίνει τὸν αὐτὸν νοῦν παρ' οἷς μὲν ἐντιμότατον εἶναι, παρ' οἷς δὲ παρανοίας ἡλωκέναι. καὶ μέντοι μεμαθήκαμεν ἄλλο εἶναι ἡδονήν, ἣν τοῖς ἔθνεσιν ἀπονεμητέον, ἄλλο δέ τι ἔριν, ἣν ταῖς αἱρέσεσι προσκριτέον, ἄλλο χαράν, ἣν

---

7. τὰς φ. Herv. τοὺς τὰς φ. L.   14. τῶν duplicatur L.
24. ἢ τούτους περὶ Heinsius praeeunte Herveto. καὶ περὶ L.   28. καὶ μέντοι μεμαθήκαμεν ἄλλο M. καίτοι μεμ. ἄ. μέντοι L. καίτοι μ. ἄ. μέν τι D.
29. ἣν τοῖς M. ἣν ἐν τοῖς L.   30. ἣν ταῖς M. ἣν ἐν ταῖς L. αἱρέσεσι S. ἐρέσεσι L. προσκριτέον M. προκριτέον L.

greater part of men have not even inquired whether they ought to follow any guide, and, if so, whom, and how he should be followed. For *as is the word, such too should the life*[1] of the believer be, so as to be able *to follow God, as He holds His unswerving path*[2] in all things from the beginning. But when a man breaks his word and so sins against God, if his weakness was due to a sudden impression, he must take care to have reasonable impressions in readiness; but if he is mastered by a habit that has gained dominion over him, and has so become what the Scripture calls *gross*[3], he must put an absolute stop to the habit and train his soul to resist it. And if there are some who seem to be attracted by contradictory opinions, they must gradually get rid of them, and resort to those *who can introduce harmony*[4] of opinions, those who can charm the timid and inexperienced with the spell of the divine Scriptures, making the truth plain by means of the agreement of the Testaments. But, as it seems, we incline rather to the common opinion, though it may involve contradiction, than to the truth with its sternness and severity.

Again of the three different mental conditions, ignorance, conceit, knowledge, ignorance is the characteristic of the heathen, knowledge of the true Church, conceit of the heretics. § 101. Certainly one does not find scientific men making more positive and definite assertions about the objects of their knowledge, than these men about their opinions, so far as depends on unproved assertion. At any rate they despise and laugh at one another; and it sometimes happens that the same interpretation is held in the highest honour by one set and regarded as insane by another. And further we have learnt that there is a difference between voluptuousness, which must be assigned to the heathen, and strife which we must adjudge to the heresies, and on the other hand between joy which one

---

[1] Stoic maxim.   [2] Plato, *Legg.* IV. 716 A.   [3] Exod. i. 7.   [4] Matt. v. 9.

τῇ ἐκκλησίᾳ προσοικειωτέον, ἄλλο δὲ εὐφροσύνην, ἣν τῷ κατὰ ἀλήθειαν ἀποδοτέον γνωστικῷ. ὡς δὲ ἐὰν πρόσσχῃ τις Ἰσχομάχῳ, γεωργὸν αὐτὸν ποιήσει, καὶ Λάμπιδι ναύκληρον, καὶ Χαριδήμῳ στρατηγόν, καὶ Σίμωνι ἱππικόν, καὶ Πέρδικι κάπηλον, καὶ Κρωβύλῳ ὀψοποιόν, καὶ Ἀρχελάῳ ὀρχηστήν, καὶ Ὁμήρῳ ποιητήν, καὶ Πύρρωνι ἐριστικόν, καὶ Δημοσθένει ῥήτορα, καὶ Χρυσίππῳ διαλεκτικόν, καὶ Ἀριστοτέλει φυσικόν, καὶ φιλόσοφον Πλάτωνι, οὕτως ὁ τῷ κυρίῳ πειθόμενος καὶ τῇ δοθείσῃ δι' αὐτοῦ κατακολουθήσας προφητείᾳ τελέως ἐκτελεῖται κατ' εἰκόνα τοῦ διδασκάλου ἐν σαρκὶ περιπολῶν θεός. Ἀποπίπτουσιν ἄρα τοῦδε τοῦ ὕψους οἱ μὴ ἑπόμενοι θεῷ ᾗ ἂν ἡγῆται, ἡγεῖται δὲ κατὰ τὰς θεοπνεύστους γραφάς. μυρίων γοῦν ὄντων κατ' ἀριθμὸν ἃ πράσσουσιν ἄνθρωποι σχεδὸν δύο εἰσὶν ἀρχαὶ πάσης ἁμαρτίας, ἄγνοια καὶ ἀσθένεια, ἄμφω δὲ ἐφ' ἡμῖν, τῶν μήτε ἐθελόντων μανθάνειν μήτε αὖ τῆς ἐπιθυμίας κρατεῖν. τούτων δὲ δι' ἣν μὲν οὐ καλῶς κρίνουσι, δι' ἣν δὲ οὐκ ἰσχύουσι τοῖς ὀρθῶς κριθεῖσιν ⟨ἀκολουθεῖν⟩· οὔτε γὰρ ἀπατηθείς τις τὴν γνώμην δύναιτ' ἂν εὖ πράττειν, κἂν πάνυ δυνατὸς ᾖ τὰ γνωσθέντα ποιεῖν, οὔτε καὶ κρίνειν τὸ δέον ἰσχύων ἄμεμπτον ἑαυτὸν παράσχοιτ' ἂν ἐν τοῖς ἔργοις ἐξασθενῶν.

102. Ἀκολούθως τοίνυν δύο τῷ γένει καὶ παιδείαι παραδίδονται πρόσφοροι ἑκατέρᾳ τῶν ἁμαρτιῶν, τῇ μὲν ἡ γνῶσίς τε καὶ ἡ τῆς ἐκ τῶν γραφῶν μαρτυρίας ἐναργὴς ἀπόδειξις, τῇ δὲ ἡ κατὰ λόγον ἄσκησις ἐκ πίστεώς τε καὶ φόβου παιδαγωγουμένη· ἄμφω δ' εἰς τὴν τελείαν ἀγάπην συναύξουσιν. τέλος γὰρ οἶμαι τοῦ γνωστικοῦ τό γε ἐνταῦθα διττόν, ἐφ' ὧν μὲν ἡ θεωρία ἡ ἐπιστημονική, ἐφ' ὧν δὲ ἡ πρᾶξις.

8. πρόσσχῃ] πρόσχηι L.   8. Ἀριστοτέλει S. ἀριστοτέλη L.
13. ᾗ ἂν S. ἐὰν L.   16. ἄγνοια Herv. ἄνοια L.   20. ἀκολουθεῖν addidit S.   21. δύναιτ'] δύνατ' L.   27. ἐναργὴς S. ἐνεργὴς L.

must appropriate to the Church, and gladness which must be imputed to the true gnostic. And just as Ischomachus will make those who attend to his instructions husbandmen, and Lampis sea-captains, and Charidemus commanders, and Simon horsemen, and Perdix hucksters, and Crobylus cooks, and Archelaus dancers, and Homer poets, and Pyrrho wranglers, and Demosthenes orators, and Chrysippus logicians, and Aristotle men of science, and Plato philosophers, so he who obeys the Lord and follows the prophecy given through Him, is fully perfected after the likeness of his Teacher, and thus becomes a god while still moving about in the flesh.

It is from such a height then that they fall who do not follow God wherever He may lead them, and He leads them by way of *the inspired writings*[1]. Certainly, though the number of human actions is infinite, it may be said that there are only two causes of all failure, both of which are in our own power, viz. ignorance and weakness on the part of those who are neither willing to learn nor to gain the mastery over their desires. The former makes men judge wrongly, the latter prevents them from following out right judgments; for neither could any one act rightly if he were deceived in his judgment, even though he were perfectly able to carry out his determinations; nor on the other hand would he show himself blameless if he were a weakling in act, whatever might be his capacity to discern what was right.

§ 102. Corresponding to these there are also two kinds of discipline provided, suitable for either class of failings; for the one, knowledge and the plain proof derived from the witness of the Scriptures; for the other, training according to reason controlled by faith and fear: and both of these grow up into perfect love. For the end of the gnostic on earth is in my opinion twofold, in some cases scientific contemplation, in others action.

[1] 2 Tim. iii. 16.

Εἴη μὲν οὖν καὶ τούσδε τοὺς αἱρετικοὺς καταμαθόντας ἐκ τῶνδε τῶν ὑπομνημάτων σωφρονισθῆναί τε καὶ ἐπιστρέψαι ἐπὶ τὸν παντοκράτορα θεόν. εἰ δὲ καθάπερ οἱ κωφοὶ τῶν ὄφεων τοῦ καινῶς μὲν λεγομένου, ἀρχαιοτάτου δὲ μὴ ἐπαΐοιεν ᾄσματος, παιδευθεῖεν οὖν πρὸς τοῦ θεοῦ, τὰς πρὸ τῆς κρίσεως πατρῴας νουθεσίας ὑπομένοντες, ἔστ' ἂν καταισχυνθέντες μετανοήσωσιν, ἀλλὰ μὴ εἰς τὴν παντελῆ φέροντες ἑαυτοὺς διὰ τῆς ἀπηνοῦς ἀπειθείας ἐμβάλοιεν κρίσιν. γίνονται γὰρ καὶ μερικαί τινες παιδεῖαι, ἃς κολάσεις ὀνομάζουσιν, εἰς ἃς ἡμῶν οἱ πολλοὶ τῶν ἐν παραπτώματι γενομένων ἐκ τοῦ λαοῦ τοῦ κυριακοῦ κατολισθάνοντες περιπίπτουσιν. ἀλλ' ὡς πρὸς τοῦ διδασκάλου ἢ τοῦ πατρὸς οἱ παῖδες, οὕτως ἡμεῖς πρὸς τῆς προνοίας κολαζόμεθα. θεὸς δὲ οὐ τιμωρεῖται (ἔστι γὰρ ἡ τιμωρία κακοῦ ἀνταπόδοσις), κολάζει μέντοι πρὸς τὸ χρήσιμον καὶ κοινῇ καὶ ἰδίᾳ τοῖς κολαζομένοις. ταυτὶ μέν, ἀποτρέψαι βουλόμενος τῆς εἰς τὰς αἱρέσεις εὐεμπτωσίας τοὺς φιλομαθοῦντας, παρεθέμην· τοὺς δὲ τῆς ἐπιπολαζούσης, εἴτε ἀμαθίας εἴτε ἀβελτερίας εἴτε καχεξίας εἴθ' ὅ τι δή ποτε χρὴ καλεῖν αὐτήν, ἀποπαῦσαι γλιχόμενος, μεταπεῖσαι δὲ καὶ προσαγαγεῖν τῇ ἀληθείᾳ τούς γε μὴ παντάπασιν ἀνιάτους ἐπιχειρῶν, τοῖσδε συνεχρησάμην τοῖς λόγοις.

103. Εἰσὶ γὰρ οἳ οὐδὲ ἀνέχονται τὴν ἀρχὴν ἐπακοῦσαι τῶν πρὸς τὴν ἀλήθειαν προτρεπόντων· καὶ δὴ φλυαρεῖν ἐπιχειροῦσι βλασφήμους τῆς ἀληθείας καταχέοντες λόγους, σφίσιν αὐτοῖς τὰ μέγιστα τῶν ὄντων ἐγνωκέναι συγχωροῦντες, οὐ μαθόντες, οὐ ζητήσαντες, οὐ πονέσαντες, οὐχ εὑρόντες τὴν ἀκολουθίαν· οὓς ἐλεήσειεν ἄν τις ἢ μισήσειεν τῆς τοιαύτης διαστροφῆς.

---

1. εἴη μὲν L. εἴη μὲν ἂν D. 12. κατολισθάνοντες] κατολισθαίνοντες L. Vid. ad p. 260 D. 14. πρὸς] πρὸ L. κολαζόμεθα. P. κολαζόμεθα, D.
19. fortasse post τοὺς δὲ omissum est ἤδη αἱρετικοὺς vel eius modi aliquid. M.
20. ἀβελτερίας D. ἀβελτηρίας L.

Would that even these heretics would take a lesson from these suggestions and be reformed and turn to the Almighty God! But if, *like deaf adders, they refuse to listen to the charm*[1], new in form, but most ancient in substance, may they at any rate undergo the divine discipline, submitting to the corrections of their heavenly Father before the Judgment, until they become ashamed and repent, instead of rushing headlong into utter condemnation through their stubborn disobedience! For there are also partial forms of discipline, which are called chastisements, into which most of us, who have trespassed from among the Lord's people, slip and fall. But as children are chastened by their teacher or their father, so are we by Providence. For God does not take vengeance (for vengeance is a retaliation of evil), but he chastens with a view to the good, both public and private, of those who are chastened. These things I have set forth, desiring to turn aside from their proclivity to heresy those who are eager to learn: but as for others, I have used these arguments out of a longing desire to make them cease from the prevailing ignorance or stupidity or ill condition or whatever it is to be called, and endeavouring to persuade and bring over to the truth those who are not yet altogether incurable.

§ 103. For there are some who absolutely refuse to give ear to those who urge them to seek the truth: aye, and they aim at smartness, pouring out blasphemous words against the truth, while they credit themselves with the possession of the highest knowledge, though they have not learnt or sought or laboured or discovered the harmony of truth,—men who excite our pity rather than our hate for such perverseness. But if

---

[1] Ps. lviii. 4, 5.

εἰ δέ τις ἰάσιμος τυγχάνει, φέρειν δυνάμενος, ὡς πῦρ ἢ σίδηρον, τῆς ἀληθείας τὴν παρρησίαν, ἀποτέμνουσαν <καὶ> καίουσαν τὰς ψευδεῖς δόξας αὐτῶν, ὑπεχέτω τὰ ὦτα τῆς ψυχῆς. ἔσται δὲ τοῦτο, ἐὰν μὴ ῥᾳθυμεῖν ἐπειγόμενοι ἀποδιωθῶνται τὴν ἀλήθειαν ἢ δόξης ὀριγνώμενοι καινοτομεῖν βιάζωνται. ῥᾳθυμοῦσι μὲν γὰρ οἵ, παρὸν τὰς οἰκείας ταῖς θείαις γραφαῖς ἐξ αὐτῶν τῶν γραφῶν πορίζεσθαι ἀποδείξεις, τὸ παράπαν καὶ ταῖς ἡδοναῖς αὐτῶν συναιρούμενον ἐκλεγόμενοι· δόξης δὲ ἐπιθυμοῦσιν ὅσοι τὰ προσφυῆ τοῖς θεοπνεύστοις λόγοις ὑπὸ τῶν μακαρίων ἀποστόλων τε καὶ διδασκάλων παραδεδομένα ἑκόντες εἶναι σοφίζονται δι' ἑτέρων παρεγχειρήσεων, ἀνθρωπείαις διδασκαλίαις ἐνιστάμενοι θείᾳ παραδόσει ὑπὲρ τοῦ τὴν αἵρεσιν συστήσασθαι. τίς γὰρ ὡς ἀληθῶς ἐν τηλικούτοις ἀνδράσιν, κατὰ τὴν ἐκκλησιαστικὴν λέγω γνῶσιν, ὑπελείπετο λόγος Μαρκίωνος, φέρε εἰπεῖν, ἢ Προδίκου, καὶ τῶν ὁμοίων τὴν ὀρθὴν οὐ βαδισάντων ὁδόν; οὐ γὰρ ἂν ὑπερέβαλον σοφίᾳ τοὺς ἔμπροσθεν ἄνδρας, ὡς προσεξευρεῖν τι τοῖς ὑπ' ἐκείνων ἀληθῶς ῥηθεῖσιν, ἀλλ' ἀγαπητὸν ἦν αὐτοῖς, εἰ τὰ προπαραδεδομένα μαθεῖν ἠδυνήθησαν.

104. Ὁ γνωστικὸς ἄρα ἡμῖν μόνος, ἐν αὐταῖς καταγηράσας ταῖς γραφαῖς, τὴν ἀποστολικὴν καὶ ἐκκλησιαστικὴν σῴζων ὀρθοτομίαν τῶν δογμάτων, κατὰ τὸ εὐαγγέλιον ὀρθότατα βιοῖ, τὰς ἀποδείξεις ἃς ἂν ἐπιζητήσῃ ἀνευρίσκειν ἀναπεμπόμενος ὑπὸ τοῦ κυρίου ἀπό τε νόμου καὶ προφητῶν. ὁ βίος γάρ, οἶμαι, τοῦ γνωστικοῦ οὐδὲν ἄλλο ἐστὶν ἢ ἔργα καὶ λόγοι τῇ τοῦ κυρίου ἀκόλουθοι παραδόσει. ἀλλ' ογ πάντων ἡ γνῶcιc.

3. καὶ καίουσαν M. καίουσαν L.   ὑπεχέτω L. ἐπεχέτω D.
5—6. ὀριγνώμενοι—βιάζωνται] ὀριγνόμεναι—βιάζονται L.   8. aut omittendum καί, aut pro παράπαν legendum παραπέμπον ἅπαν, vel tale quid. M.
9. συναιρούμενον] συναιρόμενον H. supra p. 84. 24.   12. παραδεδομένα M. παραδιδόμενα L.   26. ἃς Lowth. ὡς L.   27. ἀναπεμπόμενος] fort. παραπεμπόμενος M. ὑπὸ] ἀπὸ S.

any one is still curable, able to endure the plain-speaking of the truth, when it burns and cuts away their false opinions, like the cautery or the knife, let him lend an attentive ear. And this will be so unless, in their slothfulness, they thrust away the truth, or through ambition press after novelties. For those are slothful who, having it in their power to provide the fitting proofs for the Divine Scriptures from the Scriptures themselves, nevertheless select what is exclusively favourable to their own pleasures; and those are ambitious who, of set purpose, explain away by other spurious arguments the beliefs which attach to the inspired words, beliefs handed down by the blessed Apostles and teachers, and thus oppose divine tradition with human doctrines in order to establish their heresy. For indeed what place was left among the great men of old—I mean, according to the judgment of the Church—for Marcion, say, or Prodicus or the like, who walked not along the straight road? For they could not have surpassed in wisdom the men that went before, so as to discover something beyond what had been truly spoken by them; but might have been well content if they had been able to understand what had been already handed down.

§ 104. We find then that the gnostic alone, having grown old in the study of the actual Scriptures, guards the orthodox doctrine of the Apostles and the Church and lives a life of perfect rectitude in accordance with the Gospel, being aided by the Lord to discover the proofs he is in search of both from the law and the prophets. For the life of the gnostic, as it seems to me, is nothing else than deeds and words agreeable to the tradition of the Lord. *But knowledge belongeth not to all*[1].

---

[1] 1 Cor. viii. 7.

ογ θέλω γὰρ ὑμᾶϲ ἀγνοεῖν ἀδελφοί, *φησὶν ὁ ἀπόστολος*,
ὅτι πάντεϲ ὑπὸ τὴν νεφέλην ἦϲαν καὶ πνευματικοῦ βρώματόϲ
τε καὶ πόματοϲ μετέλαβον· *κατασκευάζων σαφῶς μὴ
πάντας τοὺς ἀκούοντας τὸν λόγον κεχωρηκέναι τὸ
μέγεθος τῆς γνώσεως ἔργῳ τε καὶ λόγῳ. διὸ καὶ
ἐπήγαγεν* ἀλλ' ογκ ἐν πᾶϲιν αὐτοῖϲ ηὐδόκηϲεν. *τίς οὗτος;
ὁ εἰπὼν* τί με λέγετε, κύριε, καὶ ογ ποιεῖτε τὸ θέλημα τοῦ
πατρόϲ μου; *τουτέστι τὴν διδασκαλίαν τοῦ σωτῆρος,
ἥτις ἐστὶ* βρῶμα ἡμῶν πνευματικὸν *καὶ* πόμα δίψαν ογκ
ἐπιϲτάμενον, ὕδωρ ζωῆϲ *γνωστικῆς. ναί, φασίν,* ἡ γνῶϲιϲ
εἴρηται φυϲιοῦν. *πρὸς οὓς φαμεν, τάχα μὲν ἡ δοκοῦσα
γνῶσις φυσιοῦν λέγεται, εἴ τις τετυφῶσθαι τὴν λέξιν
ἑρμηνεύειν ὑπολάβοι. εἰ δέ, ὅπερ καὶ μᾶλλον, τὸ
μεγαλείως τε καὶ ἀληθῶς φρονεῖν μηνύει ἡ τοῦ ἀποστόλου φωνή, λέλυται μὲν τὸ ἠπορημένον. ἑπόμενοι
δ' οὖν ταῖς γραφαῖς κυρώσωμεν τὸ εἰρημένον.*

105. ἡ ϲοφία *φησὶν ὁ Σολομῶν* ἐνεφυϲίωϲεν τὰ
ἑαυτῆϲ τέκνα. *οὐ δήπου γὰρ τῦφον ἐνεποίησεν ὁ κύριος
ταῖς μερικαῖς κατὰ τὴν διδασκαλίαν· ἀλλὰ τὸ ἐπὶ τῇ
ἀληθείᾳ πεποιθέναι καὶ εἶναι μεγαλόφρονα ἐν γνώσει,
τῇ διὰ τῶν γραφῶν παραδιδομένῃ, ὑπεροπτικὸν τῶν εἰς
ἁμαρτίαν ὑποσυρόντων παρασκευάζει, ὃ σημαίνει ἡ*
ἐνεφυϲίωϲε *λέξις· μεγαλοπρέπειαν τῆς σοφίας τῆς κατὰ
τὴν μάθησιν τέκνοις ἐμφυτευθείσης διδάσκει. αὐτίκα
φησὶν ὁ ἀπόστολος καὶ* γνώϲομαι ογ τὸν λόγον τῶν πεφυϲιω-
μένων, ἀλλὰ τὴν δύναμιν, *εἰ μεγαλοφρόνως, ὅπερ ἐστὶν
ἀληθῶς (ἀληθείας δὲ μεῖζον οὐδέν),* τὰϲ γραφὰϲ ϲυνίετε.
ἐνταῦθα γὰρ ἡ δύναμις τῶν πεφυσιωμένων τέκνων τῆς

---

9. ἡμῶν L. ἡμῖν V. edd. 10. φασὶν Arcerius. φησὶν L. 12. εἴ τις
Herv. ἦτις L. 17. Σολομῶν] σαλομὼν L. 18. δήπου γὰρ L. fort.
δήπου M. 22. ὑποσυρόντων Herv. ὑποσυρέντων L. 23. τῆς (vel τῇ
τοῖς) κατὰ M. τοῖς κατὰ L. 24. ἐμφυτευθείσης Lowth. ἐμφυτευσάσης L.
διδάσκει] fort. διδάσκουσα M. 27. ἀληθείας δὲ] fort. ἀλ. γὰρ M.
τὰς γραφὰς συνίετε M. τὰς γ. συνιέναι pr. m. corr. ex τῆς γραφὰς συνιέναι L.
τῆς γραφῆς συνίετε SD.

For I would not have you ignorant, says the Apostle, *that all were under the cloud and partook of spiritual meat and drink*[1], evidently arguing that not all who hear the word have been capable of understanding the greatness of knowledge, both in deed and word. Wherefore also he added, *But He was not well pleased with all*[2]. Who is meant by 'He'? It is He who said, *Why call ye me 'Lord,' and do not the will of my Father*[3]? the teaching, that is, of the Saviour, which is our *spiritual food*[4] and *a drink that knows no thirst*[5], *the water of* gnostical *life*[6]. 'Aye,' say they, 'we are told that *Knowledge puffeth up*[7].' To whom we reply, perhaps seeming knowledge is said to puff up, if it is supposed that the interpretation of the word is self-conceit. But if, as is rather the case, the Apostle's language means to have lofty and true thoughts, then the objection vanishes. Let us however confirm what has been said by following the Scriptures.

§ 105. *Wisdom*, says Solomon, *inspirited her own children*[8]. Assuredly the Lord did not infuse conceit by means of the particular courses of instruction; but faith in truth and confidence in the knowledge handed down through the Scriptures, make a man disdain the seductions to sin; and it is this disdain that is signified by the term 'inspirited': it teaches the sublimity of the wisdom implanted in children by learning. At any rate the Apostle says, *And I will know not the speech of them that are 'inspirited,' but the power*[9], whether ye have a lofty, that is, a true *understanding of the Scriptures*[10] (for nothing is higher than truth); for herein lies the power of the 'inspirited' children of wisdom; meaning something of this

---

[1] 1 Cor. x. 1—4. [2] *Ib.* x. 5.
[3] Luke vi. 46, Mt. vii. 21. [4] 1 Cor. x. 3. [5] Joh. iv. 14.
[6] Rev. xxii. 17. [7] 1 Cor. viii. 1.
[8] Sir. iv. 11. [9] 1 Cor. iv. 19. [10] Lu. xxiv. 45.

σοφίας· οἷον, "εἴσομαι," φησίν, "εἰ δικαίως ἐπὶ τῇ γνώσει μέγα φρονεῖτε." Γνωστὸς γὰρ κατὰ τὸν Δαβὶδ ἐν τῇ Ἰουδαίᾳ ὁ θεός, τουτέστι τοῖς κατ' ἐπίγνωσιν Ἰσραηλίταις. Ἰουδαία γὰρ ἐξομολόγησις ἑρμηνεύεται. εἰκότως ἄρα εἴρηται πρὸς τοῦ ἀποστόλου, τὸ Οὐ μοιχεύσεις, Οὐ κλέψεις, Οὐκ ἐπιθυμήσεις, καὶ εἴ τις ἑτέρα ἐντολή, ἐν τούτῳ τῷ λόγῳ ἀνακεφαλαιοῦται, ἐν τῷ Ἀγαπήσεις τὸν πλησίον σου ὡς σεαυτόν. οὐ γὰρ χρή ποτε, καθάπερ οἱ τὰς αἱρέσεις μετιόντες ποιοῦσι, μοιχεύειν τὴν ἀλήθειαν οὐδὲ μὴν κλέπτειν τὸν κανόνα τῆς ἐκκλησίας, ταῖς ἰδίαις ἐπιθυμίαις καὶ φιλοδοξίαις χαριζομένους ἐπὶ τῇ τῶν πλησίον ἀπάτῃ, οὓς παντὸς μᾶλλον ἀγαπῶντας τῆς ἀληθείας αὐτῆς ἀντέχεσθαι διδάσκειν προσήκει. εἴρηται γοῦν ἄντικρυς ἀναγγείλατε ἐν τοῖς ἔθνεσι τὰ ἐπιτηδεύματα αὐτοῦ, ἵνα μὴ κριθῶσιν, ἀλλὰ ἐπιστραφῶσιν οἱ προακηκοότες. ὅσοι δὲ ταῖς γλώσσαις αὐτῶν δολιοῦσιν, ἔγγραφα ἔχουσι τὰ ἐπιτίμια.

ΚΕΦ. ΙΖ.

106. Οἱ τοίνυν τῶν ἀσεβῶν ἁπτόμενοι λόγων ἄλλοις τε ἐξάρχοντες, μηδὲ εὖ τοῖς λόγοις τοῖς θείοις ἀλλὰ ἐξημαρτημένως συγχρώμενοι, οὔτε αὐτοὶ εἰσίασιν εἰς τὴν βασιλείαν τῶν οὐρανῶν οὔτε οὓς ἐξηπάτησαν ἐῶσιν τυγχάνειν τῆς ἀληθείας. ἀλλ' οὐδὲ τὴν κλεῖν ἔχοντες αὐτοὶ τῆς εἰσόδου, ψευδῆ δέ τινα καί, ὥς φησιν ἡ συνήθεια, ἀντικλεῖδα, δι' ἧς οὐ τὴν αὐλείαν ἀναπετάσαντες, ὥσπερ ἡμεῖς διὰ τῆς τοῦ κυρίου παραδόσεως εἴσιμεν, παράθυρον δὲ ἀνατεμόντες καὶ διορύξαντες λάθρα τὸ τειχίον τῆς ἐκκλησίας, ὑπερβαίνοντες τὴν ἀλήθειαν, μυσταγωγοὶ τῆς τῶν ἀσεβῶν ψυχῆς καθίστανται. ὅτι γὰρ μεταγενεστέρας τῆς καθολικῆς ἐκ-

---

4. ἑρμηνεύεται] εὑρίσκεται L, sed ἑρμηνεύεται in margine, pr. m. corr.
7. σεαυτόν ex ἑαυτόν pr. m. corr. L, ἑαυτόν V edd.   22. ἀληθείας. Μ. ἀληθείας D.   24. αὐλείαν Μ. αὐλαίαν L.   26. εἴσιμεν S. εἴσειμεν L.

sort, 'I shall know whether ye take a just pride in knowledge.' For, as David says, *In Judah is God known*[1], i.e. to those who are Israelites according to knowledge. For Judah is by interpretation 'Confession.' With reason therefore has it been said by the Apostle *This, thou shalt not commit adultery, thou shalt not steal, thou shalt not covet, and if there be any other command, it is briefly comprehended in this saying, Thou shalt love thy neighbour as thyself.*[2] For we must never adulterate the truth, nor steal the rule of the Church, as those who follow the heresies, gratifying our own desires and ambitions with a view to the deception of our neighbours, whom we ought to love above every thing and teach to cling to the truth itself. At any rate it has been expressly said, *Tell among the heathen His doings*[3], in order that those who have been thus forewarned may not be judged, but may be converted. But as many as *flatter with their tongues*[4] have their punishments prescribed.

CHAPTER XVII.

§ 106. They then who engage in impious words and introduce them to others, and make no good use, but an utterly wrong use, of the divine words, such men *neither enter themselves into the kingdom of God, nor permit*[5] those whom they have deceived to attain to the truth. Nay, they have not even got the *key*[6] of the door themselves, but only a false or, as it is commonly called, a skeleton key, which does not enable them to throw open the main door[7], and enter, as we do, through the tradition of the Lord; but they cut a side door and break secretly through the wall of the Church; and so overstepping the bounds of truth, they initiate the soul of the impious into their mysteries. For it needs no long discourse to prove that the merely human assemblies which they have

---

[1] Ps. lxxvi. 1.   [2] Rom. xiii. 9.   [3] Ps. ix. 11.   [4] Ps. v. 9.
[5] Mt. xxiii. 14.   [6] Mt. xvi. 19, Lu. xi. 52.   [7] Joh. x. 1 ff.

κλησίας τὰς ἀνθρωπίνας συνηλύσεις πεποιήκασιν, οὐ πολλῶν δεῖ λόγων. ἡ μὲν γὰρ τοῦ κυρίου κατὰ τὴν παρουσίαν διδασκαλία ἀπὸ Αὐγούστου Καίσαρος ἀρξαμένη μεσούντων τῶν Τιβερίου χρόνων τελειοῦται, ἡ δὲ τῶν ἀποστόλων αὐτοῦ μέχρι γε τῆς Παύλου λειτουργίας ἐπὶ Νέρωνος τελειοῦται, κάτω δὲ περὶ τοὺς Ἀδριανοῦ τοῦ βασιλέως χρόνους οἱ τὰς αἱρέσεις ἐπινοήσαντες γεγόνασι, καὶ μέχρι γε τῆς Ἀντωνίνου τοῦ πρεσβυτέρου διέτειναν ἡλικίας, καθάπερ ὁ Βασιλείδης, κἂν Γλαυκίαν ἐπιγράφηται διδάσκαλον, ὡς αὐχοῦσιν αὐτοί, τὸν Πέτρου ἑρμηνέα. ὡσαύτως δὲ καὶ Οὐαλεντῖνον Θεοδᾶ διακηκοέναι φέρουσιν· γνώριμος δ' οὗτος γεγόνει Παύλου. 107. Μάρκος γὰρ κατὰ τὴν αὐτὴν αὐτοῖς ἡλικίαν γενόμενος ὡς πρεσβύτης νεωτέροις συνεγένετο, μεθ' ὃν Σίμων ἐπ' ὀλίγον κηρύσσοντος τοῦ Πέτρου ἐπήκουσεν.

Ὧν οὕτως ἐχόντων συμφανὲς ἐκ τῆς προγενεστάτης καὶ ἀληθεστάτης ἐκκλησίας τὰς μεταγενεστέρας ταύτας καὶ τὰς ἔτι τούτων ὑποβεβηκυίας τῷ χρόνῳ κεκαινοτομῆσθαι παραχαραχθείσας αἱρέσεις. ἐκ τῶν εἰρημένων ἄρα φανερὸν οἶμαι γεγενῆσθαι μίαν εἶναι τὴν ἀληθῆ ἐκκλησίαν τὴν τῷ ὄντι ἀρχαίαν, εἰς ἣν οἱ κατὰ πρόθεσιν δίκαιοι ἐγκαταλέγονται. ἑνὸς γὰρ ὄντος τοῦ θεοῦ καὶ ἑνὸς τοῦ κυρίου, διὰ τοῦτο καὶ τὸ ἄκρως τίμιον κατὰ τὴν μόνωσιν ἐπαινεῖται, μίμημα ὂν ἀρχῆς τῆς μιᾶς. τῇ γοῦν τοῦ ἑνὸς φύσει συγκληροῦται ἐκκλησία ἡ μία, ἣν εἰς πολλὰς κατατέμνειν βιάζονται αἱρέσεις. κατά τε οὖν ὑπόστασιν κατά τε ἐπίνοιαν κατά τε ἀρχὴν

---

3. Αὐγούστου Montacutius. αὐγούστου καὶ τιβερίου L. 4. τῶν Τιβερίου Montacutius cum Herveto. τῶν Αὐγούστου L. 7. οἱ] οἳ L. 8. μέχρι γε τῆς] γε pr. m. additum L. 12. Θεοδᾶ διακηκοέναι Bentleius. θεοδάδι ἀκηκοέναι L. 13. Μάρκος H. post Gieseler in A. L. Z. Halle, Apr. 1823 p. 826. Μαρκίων L. 15. μεθ' ὃν L. μεθ' οὗ Dodwell. 16. ἐπήκουσεν Dodwell. ὑπήκουσεν L. 24. κυρίου, M. κυρίου. D. qui etiam ἑνός γε pro ἑνὸς γὰρ scribendum censet.

instituted were later in time than the Catholic Church. For the teaching of our Lord, during His life upon earth, begins with Augustus, and is completed in the middle of the reign of Tiberius, and the preaching of His Apostles, at least up to the end of Paul's ministry, is completed under Nero; while the heresiarchs begin quite late about the time of the emperor Hadrian and lasted to the age of Antoninus the elder, as was the case with Basilides, in spite of his claiming to have been taught by Glaucias, whom they themselves boast to have been the interpreter of Peter. So too they report that Valentinus heard Theodas, who was a disciple of Paul. § 107. For Marcus, who lived about the same time, associated with them as an elder with his juniors, and after him Simon was for a short time a hearer of Peter.

Such being the case, it is evident that these later heresies and those which are still more recent are spurious innovations on the oldest and truest Church. From what has been said I think it has been made plain that unity is a characteristic of the true, the really ancient Church, into which those that are righteous according to the divine purpose are enrolled. For God being one and the Lord being one, that also which is supremely honoured is the object of praise, because it stands alone, being a copy of the one First Principle: at any rate the one Church, which they strive to break up into many sects, is bound up with the principle of Unity. We say then that the ancient and Catholic Church stands alone in essence and idea

κατά τε ἐξοχὴν μόνην εἶναί φαμεν τὴν ἀρχαίαν καὶ καθολικὴν ἐκκλησίαν, εἰς ἑνότητα πίστεως μιᾶς, τῆς κατὰ τὰς οἰκείας διαθήκας, μᾶλλον δὲ κατὰ τὴν διαθήκην τὴν μίαν διαφόροις τοῖς χρόνοις, ἑνὸς τοῦ θεοῦ τῷ βουλήματι δι' ἑνὸς τοῦ κυρίου συνάγουσαν τοὺς ἤδη κατατεταγμένους· οὓς προώρισεν ὁ θεός, δικαίους ἐσομένους πρὸ καταβολῆς κόσμου ἐγνωκώς. ἀλλὰ καὶ ἡ ἐξοχὴ τῆς ἐκκλησίας, καθάπερ ἡ ἀρχὴ τῆς συστάσεως, κατὰ τὴν μονάδα ἐστίν, πάντα τὰ ἄλλα ὑπερβάλλουσα καὶ μηδὲν ἔχουσα ὅμοιον ἢ ἴσον ἑαυτῇ.

108. Ταυτὶ μὲν οὖν καὶ εἰς ὕστερον. τῶν δ' αἱρέσεων αἱ μὲν ἀπὸ ὀνόματος προσαγορεύονται, ὡς ἡ ἀπὸ Οὐαλεντίνου καὶ Μαρκίωνος καὶ Βασιλείδου, κἂν τὴν Ματθίου αὐχῶσι προσάγεσθαι δόξαν,—μία γὰρ ἡ πάντων γέγονε τῶν ἀποστόλων, ὥσπερ διδασκαλία, οὕτως δὲ καὶ ἡ παράδοσις,—αἱ δὲ ἀπὸ τόπου, ὡς οἱ Περατικοί, αἱ δὲ ἀπὸ ἔθνους, ὡς ἡ τῶν Φρυγῶν, αἱ δὲ ἀπὸ ἐνεργείας, ὡς ἡ τῶν Ἐγκρατητῶν, αἱ δὲ ἀπὸ δογμάτων ἰδιαζόντων, ὡς ἡ τῶν Δοκιτῶν καὶ ἡ τῶν Αἱματιτῶν, αἱ δὲ ἀπὸ ὑποθέσεων ὧν τετιμήκασιν, ὡς Καϊανισταί τε καὶ οἱ Ὀφιανοὶ προσαγορευόμενοι, αἱ δὲ ἀφ' ὧν παρανόμως ἐπετήδευσάν τε καὶ ἐτόλμησαν, ὡς τῶν Σιμωνιανῶν οἱ Ἐντυχιταὶ καλούμενοι.

ΚΕΦ. ΙΗ.

109. Ὀπὴν οὖν τινα ὀλίγην ὑποδείξαντες τοῖς φιλοθεάμοσι τῆς ἐκκλησίας ἐκ τοῦ κατὰ τὰς θυσίας νόμου περὶ καθαρῶν καὶ ἀκαθάρτων ζῴων, περί τε Ἰουδαίων τῶν χυδαίων περί τε τῶν αἱρέσεων, μυστικῶς

---

1. τὴν S. ᾗ L. 4. ἑνὸς τοῦ θεοῦ S. ἐν οἷς τοῦ θεοῦ L. 12. ἡ L. fort. al M. 18. Ἐγκρατητῶν L. ἐγκρατιῶν VS. 19. Δοκιτῶν L. Δοκητῶν PD. 20. ὑποθέσεων] fort. ὑποστάσεων M. ὧν M. καὶ ὧν L. 23. Ἐντυχιταὶ L. Ἐντυχηταὶ ex Theodoreto D. 25. περὶ—ψύων hic Louth, post ἀπὸ τῆς (p. 192. 1) LPD. 26, 27. περί τε—περί τε] ὥς—καὶ Louth.

and principle and preeminence, gathering together, by the will of one God through the one Lord, into the unity of the one faith, built upon the fitting covenants (or rather the one covenant given at different times) all those who are already enlisted in it, whom God foreordained, having known before the foundation of the world that they would be righteous. And further the preeminence of the Church, like the principle of its constitution, is in accordance with the Monad, surpassing all other things and having nothing like or equal to itself.

§ 108. Of this we shall speak on a future occasion. But of the heresies some are called after the name of the founder, as that which is called after Valentinus and Marcion and Basilides; though they profess to cite the opinion of Matthias. I say 'profess,' for, as the teaching, so also the tradition of all the Apostles has been one and the same. Other heresies are called from the place where they arose, as the Peratici; others from their nationality, as the Phrygian heresy; others from their practice, like the Encratites; others from peculiar opinions, as the Docetae and Haematitae; others from the personages they admire, as the Cainites and those who are styled Ophites; others from their unblushing immoralities, as the so-called Entychitae among the Simonians.

CHAPTER XVIII.

§ 109. Before closing my discourse I should like, for the benefit of the more speculative members of the Church, to throw a little light from the sacrificial law, concerning clean and unclean beasts, in reference to the ordinary Jews and the

διακρινομένων, ὡς ἀκαθάρτων, ἀπὸ τῆς θείας ἐκκλησίας, καταπαύσομεν τὸν λόγον. τὰ μὲν γὰρ διχηλοῦντα καὶ μηρυκισμὸν ἀνάγοντα τῶν ἱερείων καθαρὰ καὶ δεκτὰ τῷ θεῷ παραδίδωσιν ἡ γραφή, ὡς ἂν εἰς πατέρα καὶ εἰς υἱὸν διὰ τῆς πίστεως τῶν δικαίων τὴν πορείαν ποιουμένων—αὕτη γὰρ ἡ τῶν διχηλούντων ἑδραιότης—τῶν τὰ λόγια τοῦ θεοῦ νύκτωρ καὶ μεθ᾽ ἡμέραν μελετώντων καὶ ἀναπεμπαζομένων ἐν τῷ τῆς ψυχῆς τῶν μαθημάτων δοχείῳ, ἣν καὶ συνάσκησιν γνωστικὴν ὑπάρχουσαν καθαροῦ ζῴου μηρυκισμὸν ὁ νόμος ἀλληγορεῖ. ὅσα δὲ μήτε ἑκάτερον μήτε τὸ ἕτερον τούτων ἔχει, ὡς ἀκάθαρτα ἀφορίζει. αὐτίκα τὰ ἀνάγοντα μηρυκισμόν, μὴ διχηλοῦντα δέ, τοὺς Ἰουδαίους αἰνίσσεται τοὺς πολλούς, οἳ τὰ μὲν λόγια τοῦ θεοῦ ἀνὰ στόμα ἔχουσιν, τὴν δὲ πίστιν καὶ τὴν βάσιν δι᾽ υἱοῦ πρὸς τὸν πατέρα παραπέμπουσαν οὐκ ἔχουσιν ἐπερειδομένην τῇ ἀληθείᾳ. ὅθεν καὶ ὀλισθηρὸν τὸ γένος τῶν τοιούτων θρεμμάτων, ὡς ἂν μὴ σχιδανοπόδων ὄντων μηδὲ τῇ διπλόῃ τῆς πίστεως ἐπερειδομένων· οὐδεὶς γὰρ φησὶ γινώσκει τὸν πατέρα εἰ μὴ ὁ υἱὸς καὶ ᾧ ἂν ὁ υἱὸς ἀποκαλύψῃ. ἔμπαλίν τε αὖ ἀκάθαρτα ὁμοίως κἀκεῖνα, ὅσα διχηλεῖ μέν, μηρυκισμὸν δὲ οὐκ ἀνάγει. ταυτὶ γὰρ τοὺς αἱρετικοὺς ἐνδείκνυται ὀνόματι μὲν πατρὸς καὶ υἱοῦ ἐπιβεβηκότας, τὴν δὲ τῶν λογίων ἀκριβῆ σαφήνειαν λεπτουργεῖν καὶ καταλεαίνειν ἐξασθενοῦντας, πρὸς δὲ καὶ τὰ ἔργα τῆς δικαιοσύνης ὁλοσχερέστερον, οὐχὶ δὲ ἀκριβέστερον μετερχομένους, εἴ γε καὶ μετέλθοιεν.

110. Τοιούτοις τισὶν ὁ κύριος λέγει τί με λέγετε κύριε κύριε, καὶ οὐ ποιεῖτε ἃ λέγω; ἀκάθαρτοι δὲ πάμπαν οἱ μὴ διχηλοῦντες μηδὲ ἀνάγοντες μηρυκισμόν.

2. καταπαύσομεν M. καταπαύσωμεν L. 3. ἱερείων ex ἱερῶν pr. m. corr. L. 6. ἑδραιότης τῶν] fort. ἑδρ. καὶ M. 11. μήτε τὸ] fort. μήτ᾽ οὖν τὸ M. 16. ἔχουσιν] ἔχουσαν L.

heresies which are mystically distinguished, as unclean, from the Church of God. We are taught by the Scriptures that the victims *which divide the hoof and chew the cud are clean*[1] and acceptable to God, implying that the righteous make their approach to the Father and the Son through their faith,—for in this consists the stability of those that divide the hoof,—and that they *study* and ruminate *the oracles of God*[2] *by night and day*[3] in the mental receptacle of knowledge, which being also a kind of gnostic discipline, is figuratively described in the law as the chewing of the cud by a clean animal. But those who are wanting in both or even in one of these qualifications are rejected. For instance, those which chew the cud without dividing the hoof signify the Jews generally, who have *the oracles of God*[2] in their mouth, but have not the firm footing of faith stayed upon truth, which carries them to the Father through the Son. Whence this class of creatures is liable to slip, as is natural where the foot is not parted and they are not stayed upon the doubleness of faith. For we read *No one knows the Father but the Son, and he to whom the Son may reveal Him*[4]. On the other hand, those too are unclean which divide the hoof without chewing the cud. For this phrase denotes the heretics who take their stand on the name of the Father and of the Son, but have no power to bring out the exact perspicuity of the oracles by subtle distinctions and by smoothing away of difficulties, while their prosecution of the works of righteousness, if they prosecute them at all, is rough and careless rather than exact.

§ 110. It is to some such persons that the Lord says *Why call ye me Lord, Lord, and do not the things which I say*[5]*?* But those who do not divide the hoof nor chew the cud are

---

[1] Lev. xi. 3 f.   [2] Rom. iii. 2; Num. xxiv. 16.   [3] Ps. i. 2.
[4] Lu. x. 22.   [5] Ib. vi. 46.

ὑμεῖς δ', ὦ Μεγαρεῖς,

φησὶν ὁ Θέογνις,

οὔτε τρίτοι οὔτε τέταρτοι
οὔτε δυωδέκατοι οὔτ' ἐν λόγῳ οὔτ' ἐν ἀριθμῷ,

ἀλλ' ἢ ὡς ὁ χνοῦς, ὃν ἐκρίπτει ὁ ἄνεμος ἀπὸ προσώπου τῆς γῆς,
καὶ ὡς σταγὼν ἀπὸ κάδου.

τούτων ἡμῖν προδιηνυσμένων καὶ τοῦ ἠθικοῦ τόπου ὡς ἐν κεφαλαίῳ ὑπογραφέντος, σποράδην, ὡς ὑπεσχήμεθα, καὶ διερριμμένως τὰ ζώπυρα τῶν τῆς ἀληθοῦς γνώσεως ἐγκατασπείραντες δογμάτων, ὡς μὴ ῥᾳδίαν εἶναι τῷ περιτυχόντι τῶν ἀμυήτων τὴν τῶν ἁγίων παραδόσεων εὕρεσιν, μετίωμεν ἐπὶ τὴν ὑπόσχεσιν.

III. Ἐοίκασι δέ πως οἱ στρωματεῖς οὐ παραδείσοις ἐξησκημένοις ἐκείνοις τοῖς ἐν στοίχῳ καταπεφυτευμένοις εἰς ἡδονὴν ὄψεως, ὄρει δὲ μᾶλλον συσκίῳ τινὶ καὶ δασεῖ κυπαρίσσοις καὶ πλατάνοις δάφνῃ τε καὶ κισσῷ, μηλέαις τε ὁμοῦ καὶ ἐλαίαις καὶ συκαῖς καταπεφυτευμένῳ, ἐξεπίτηδες ἀναμεμιγμένης τῆς φυτείας καρποφόρων τε ὁμοῦ καὶ ἀκάρπων δένδρων, διὰ τοὺς ὑφαιρεῖσθαι καὶ κλέπτειν τολμῶντας τὰ ὥρια ἐθελούσης λανθάνειν τῆς γραφῆς. ἐξ ὧν δὴ μεταμοσχεύσας καὶ μεταφυτεύσας ὁ γεωργὸς ὡραῖον κατακοσμήσει παράδεισον καὶ ἄλσος ἐπιτερπές. οὔτ' οὖν τῆς τάξεως οὔτε τῆς φράσεως στοχάζονται οἱ στρωματεῖς, ὅπου γε ἐπίτηδες καὶ τὴν λέξιν οὐχ <ἡδυσμένην> Ἕλληνες εἶναι βούλονται καὶ τὴν τῶν δογμάτων ἐγκατασπορὰν λεληθότως καὶ οὐ κατὰ τὴν ἀλήθειαν πεποίηνται, φιλο-

---

7—12 ap. Phot. Bibl. cxi. 7.   7. τόπου Hervet. τρόπου L. τύπου Phot.   8. κεφαλαίῳ ὑπογραφέντος] κεφαλαίοις ὑπογράφοντος Phot. σποράδην] σπορ. τέως Phot. σπ. τε ὡς Barnard.   9. τῶν L¹. τῶι L², om. Phot.   10. ἐγκατασπείραντες δογμάτων M. ἐγκατασπειράντων δόγματα L. ἐγκ. μαθήματα Phot.   12. παραδόσεων om. Phot. ὑπόσχεσιν] fort. ὑπόθεσιν M.   14. στοίχῳ S. στοιχείῳ L, vitio frequenti, de quo Bast. ad Greg. Cor. p. 840 D.   17. μηλέαις S. in Indice. μηλαίαις L.   25. οὐχ ἡδυσμένην vel οὐ κεκαλλωπισμένην M. οὐχ ὡραίαν Heinsius, οὐχ L.

utterly unclean. As Theognis says, *You Megarians are neither in the third class, nor the fourth, nor even the twelfth, nor in any number or account whatever;* but are *like the chaff which the wind scattereth from the face of the earth*[1], and *as a drop of a bucket*[2].

Having completed this introduction, and given a summary outline of ethical philosophy, wherein we have scattered the sparks of the doctrines of the true knowledge dispersedly here and there, as we promised, so that it should not be easy for the uninitiated who came across them to discover the holy traditions; let us pass on to our general argument. § 111. Now it seems that what are known as Miscellanies are not to be compared to ornamental parks with rows of ordered plantations to please the eye, but rather to some thickly wooded hill, overgrown with cypresses and planes and bay-tree and ivy, and at the same time planted with appletrees and olives and figs, the cultivation of fruit-bearing and of woodland trees being intentionally mingled together, since the Scripture desires to withdraw from observation on account of those who venture secretly to steal its fruits. It is by transplanting the suckers and trees from these preserves that the gardener will furnish a beautiful park and pleasure-ground. Our Miscellanies therefore make no pretence of order or of choice diction, seeing that in this kind of composition the Greeks purposely object to over-sweetness of style, and sow their doctrines secretly

---

[1] Ps. i. 4. [2] Is. xl. 15.

πόνους καὶ εὑρετικοὺς εἶναι τοὺς εἴ τινες ἐντύχοιεν 15
παρασκευάζοντες. πολλὰ γὰρ τὰ δελέατα καὶ ποικίλα
διὰ τὰς τῶν ἰχθύων διαφοράς.

καὶ δὴ μετὰ τὸν ἕβδομον τοῦτον ἡμῖν στρωματέα
τῶν ἑξῆς ἀπ' ἄλλης ἀρχῆς ποιησόμεθα τὸν λόγον.

1. ἐντύχοιεν S. τύχοιεν L. 8. Subscriptum in L, στρωματεὺς ἕβδομος ὁ καὶ ἦτα.

and not in a plain, unmistakeable manner, seeking to exercise the diligence and ingenuity of the readers, if there should be such. For we must provide a large variety of baits owing to the varieties of fish.

And now, having concluded our seventh Miscellany, we will make a new start in our discussion of what is to follow.

NOTES.

§ 1. p. 2, line 2 foll. Christians were reputed to be atheists, partly from their rejection of the popular gods, partly from the absence of outward signs associated with worship. H. At the beginning of the previous book Clement declares it to be his intention in Books VI. and VII. to describe the character of the gnostic, and to show to the philosophers that he is οὐδαμῶς ἄθεον, ὡς ὑπειλήφασιν, μόνον δὲ τῷ ὄντι θεοσεβῆ. So Polycarp retorted on the heathen the cry αἶρε τοὺς ἀθέους raised against the Christians (*Mart. Polyc.* 9). Cf. Lightfoot's note on Ignat. *Trall.* 3, where he cites Justin *Apol.* I. 6, 13, Athenag. 3, 4, 30, Tert. *Apol.* 10.

ὡς in sense of ὥστε. H. Cf. below P. 837 *ad fin.*, 846, 877, 879 and *passim*, also W. Schmid *Atticismus* IV. 87.

3. οἷος τίς for MS. οἷός τέ: τέ seems to have nothing answering to it. H.

5. διώκοντας τοὔνομα. Cf. James ii. 7; 1 Pet. iv. 14, 16; 3 Jo. 7; Acts iv. 17 foll., v. 28, 40, 41, ix. 21, xxvi. 9, &c. H. Justin *Apol.* 4 ἐφ' ἡμῶν τὸ ὄνομα εἰς ἔλεγχον λαμβάνετε, Tert. *Apol.* 2 oditur itaque in hominibus innocuis etiam nomen innoxium. Proinde Plinius ad Trajanum haesitare se refert, nomen ipsum, etiamsi flagitiis careat, an flagitia cohaerentia nomini puniantur, also P. 885 τὸ ὄνομα ἐπικεκλημένοι μόνον, and P. 511 *init.*

7—9. ἐναργεστέροις...τοῖς λόγοις. Clement often speaks of the use of philosophical training as a preparation for Christianity, as in *Str.* I. P. 331 χρησίμη πρὸς θεοσέβειαν (ἡ φιλοσοφία) γίνεται, προπαιδεία τις οὖσα τοῖς τὴν πίστιν δι' ἀποδείξεως καρπουμένοις, P. 341 *fin.*, P. 785 f., cf. Faye, Pt II. ch. 6. Here τοῖς λόγοις seems to mean 'reasoning,' as opposed to the 'witness of prophecy,' cf. P. 378 ταῖς τῶν λόγων ἀνάγκαις. Unfavourable examples of such reasoning may be found below in P. 845, and 852.

8. ἐπαΐειν: a favourite word with Plato and Clement, from ἀΐω, a Homeric term for any sense-perception (chiefly hearing, but also sight and feeling): used especially of acquaintance with any art or science, = *peritus esse*. H.

10. τῆς τοῦ πιστεῦσαι δυνάμεως. Cf. Plato *Rep.* I. 328 εἰ ἔτι ἐν δυνάμει ἦν τοῦ πορεύεσθαι πρὸς τὸ ἄστυ, and for meaning Joh. v. 44 πῶς δύνασθε πιστεύειν, vi. 65 οὐδεὶς δύναται ἐλθεῖν πρός με, ἐὰν μὴ ᾖ δεδομένον αὐτῷ ἐκ τοῦ πατρός, Heb. xii. 2, &c.

11. τῶν προφητικῶν. Why should the prophets alone be mentioned to the exclusion of all other testimony to Christ?

13. ὕστερον ταῖς γραφαῖς συγχρησόμενοι. See below on τὰ μαρτύρια l. 19.

15. χριστιανισμόν. The word is used more than once by Ignatius. See Lightfoot's n. on *Magn.* 10.

16. συμπαραλαμβάνοντες. H. prefers the MS. reading συμπεριλαμβάνοντες. The two are often confounded in MSS., and Sylburg's emendation seems to me more appropriate here. Cf. Arist. *de Anima* I. 2 *init.* τὰς τῶν προτέρων δόξας συμπαραλαμβάνειν, *Rhet.* I. 3. 5 with Cope's n.

17. λέξεις, 'modes of language': just below λέξις is opposed to νοῦς. H. But it is also used simply for 'saying' or 'speech,' as λέξεων προφητικῶν above, and in P. 856 ἡ λέξις τῆς νοήσεως χάριν δέδοται ἡμῖν, and P. 883 ταῖς ἐπικαίροις τῶν ἀποστολικῶν συγχρώμενοι λέξεσι.

18. ἐκ περιουσίας, *ex abundanti*, a flexible phrase arising from the general sense of easy superfluity. Aristotle, *Top.* 118 a. 6—15, contrasts τὰ ἐκ περιουσίας with τὰ ἀναγκαῖα, e.g. τὸ εὖ ζῆν with τὸ ζῆν, τὸ φιλοσοφεῖν with τὸ χρηματίζεσθαι. H. See Index, s.v. περιουσία.

19. τὰ μαρτύρια, 'the actual testimonies,' i.e. passages of Scripture. Probably a reference to the *Eclogae Propheticae* in the *Hypotyposes*, a book intended for advanced Christians. H. See below p. 4. 6, 100. 20, 146. 23, and (for the reference) the Introduction.

21. τῶν κυριακῶν γραφῶν. The same phrase occurs below P. 890.

p. 4, line 1. ἀνασπᾷ. Cf. P. 625 εἰ καὶ ὁ Παῦλος τοῖς χρόνοις νεάζει... ἀλλ' οὖν ἡ γραφὴ αὐτῷ ἐκ τῆς παλαιᾶς ἤρτηται διαθήκης, ἐκεῖθεν ἀναπνέουσα καὶ λαλοῦσα.

2. παριστᾶν. The form ἱστᾶν occurs in Plat. *Cratyl.* 437 B, συνιστᾶν in Eus. *Pr. Ev.* VI. 8. 3. Winer (p. 94, Moulton) cites ἀποκαθιστᾷ Mk ix. 12, ἀφιστᾷ *Test. Jud.* p. 610, συνιστᾶν Chariton, p. 140, where Dorville refers to Artemid. II. 42 for ἀνιστᾶν. Other exx. will be found in Graevius' n. on Lucian, *Soloec.* 7, where the form is condemned. See *Paed.* I. P. 131 οἱ βασιλεῖς Περσῶν παιδαγωγοὺς τοῖς σφῶν αὐτῶν ἐφίστων παισίν, W. Schmid *Attic.* IV. 605, Veitch *Gr. V.* ἱστάω.

3. ἐπεξεργασία, 'working out,' either in investigation or in exposition; usually with a sense of special minuteness. H.

5. τὸ κατεπεῖγον, 'what is specially pressing, urgent.' So the phrase οὐ κατεπείγει. Usage common from the orators onward. H.

§ 2. 9. πρόκειται. See Lightfoot, *Ign.* vol. II. p. 272 n.

10—12. θεοπρεπῶς...θεοφιλές...φιλόθεον. See below p. 6, ll. 20—27. H. Verbal adjectives in -ης have commonly a passive or neuter force, as θεομισής, θεομανής, but also an active force as in θεοσεβής. Those in -ος sometimes combine both meanings, distinguished by the accent, as θεοφόρος, 'bearing God,' θεόφορος, 'borne' or 'sent by God.' For the combination of θεοφιλής and φιλόθεος cf. Philo's description of Moses as φιλόθεός τε καὶ θεοφιλής (M. 2, p. 145), Eus. *Pr. Ev.* VII. 4, p. 303 b οὕτω δὴ φιλόθεοι ὁμοῦ καὶ θεοφιλεῖς ἀναφανέντες, θεραπευταί τινες ὄντως καὶ ἱερεῖς τοῦ ὑψίστου θεοῦ ἀπεφάνθησαν.

11. τῷ θεοπρεπεῖ. See Index, and Lightfoot on Ign. vol. II. p. 108.

12. ἄπαν τὸ ὑπερέχον, 'every class of pre-eminence.' For the art. with distributive πᾶς in the singular cf. Orig. *Joh.* tom. I. 12 (p. 14 R.) πᾶς ὁ τῶν μαθητῶν τοῦ Ἰησοῦ προδότης εἶναι λελόγισται τοῦ Ἰησοῦ προδότης. So just below we have πάντα τὸν πρεσβύτερον. Cf. Plato *Leg.* v. 731 c πᾶς ὁ ἄδικος οὐχ ἑκὼν ἄδικος, Arist. *Pol.* I. 4. 1 ὥσπερ ὄργανον πρὸ ὀργάνων πᾶς ὁ ὑπηρέτης. H. I suppose this is intended to meet the charge of irreverence. 'It is true the Christians do not honour the gods of the heathen, nor worship the emperor, nor bow down before popular opinion: still we do pay honour where it is due.'

13, 14. τιμητέον...πάντα τὸν πρεσβύτερον. Cf. the address of Pythagoras in Jambl. *V. Pyth.* VIII. 37 ἔν τε τῷ κόσμῳ καὶ τῷ βίῳ καὶ ταῖς πόλεσι καὶ τῇ φύσει μᾶλλον τιμώμενον τὸ προηγούμενον ἢ τὸ χρόνῳ ἑπόμενον κ.τ.λ.

15. διδακτοῖς, a Socratic and Platonic word as applied to Virtue. Here contrasted with νοητός, another Platonic word, to express what is directly perceived by the highest powers of the mind. H. See below on p. 68. 26.

τὴν ἀρχαιοτάτην φιλοσοφίαν. By this Cl. means the revelation given to Israel, which he often calls ἡ βάρβαρος φιλοσοφία. Compare his proof of the priority of Moses to the teachers of Greece, who stole from him their wisdom, *Str.* I. P. 350 f. Plato is said to have confessed as much in the words Ἕλληνες ἀεὶ παῖδές ἐστε...οὐδεμίαν ἔχετε δι᾽ ἀρχαίαν ἀκοὴν παλαιὰν δόξαν οὐδὲ μάθημα χρόνῳ πολιόν (*Tim.* 22), cf. *Str.* P. 355—7, 426. Hence Tertullian (*de Praescr. Haer.* 31) contrasts *principalitatem veritatis* and *posteritatem mendacii*, and Cl. speaks (below, P. 888) of the one true and ancient Church. See, on the claim to antiquity, Kaye p. 22.

17. ἄχρονον <καὶ> ἄναρχον. The word ἄχρονος is used with αἰτία, *Str.* P. 931. It also occurs in Ignat. *Polyc.* 3 (where see Lightfoot) and is common in Plotinus; but perhaps H. J. is right in suggesting that it may be a marginal explanation of ἄναρχος. If we omit it, the play of words (ἄναρχον ἀρχήν τε καὶ ἀπαρχήν) is brought out more distinctly. Cf. P. 638 ὁ θεὸς ἄναρχος ἀρχὴ τῶν ὅλων, and P. 733.

19. ἐκμανθάνειν. If we keep the inf. we must suppose it to depend on the *orat. obl.* implied in ἡγεῖται (l. 12), but the ind. is a far more natural construction.

τὸ ἐπέκεινα αἴτιον, 'the ulterior cause.' The Son is called τὸ δεύτερον αἴτιον below, § 16. H. There is a reminiscence here of Plato *Rep.* VI. 509 B, where it is said that τὸ ἀγαθόν is not the same as οὐσία, but ἐπέκεινα τῆς οὐσίας πρεσβείᾳ καὶ δυνάμει, and of *Tim.* 28 C τὸν ποιητὴν καὶ πατέρα τοῦδε τοῦ παντός. H. J. Cl. speaks of the Son as ἐπ. τοῦ νοητοῦ P. 669, and of God as ἐπ. τοῦ ἑνός P. 140.

20. εὐεργετικώτατον. See below, p. 8, l. 18.

21. οὐκέτι φωνῇ παραδιδόμενον. At first the gnostic received his knowledge of God by hearing from others, but now he knows by intimate union. Cf. Joh. iv. 42.

σιγῇ. Cf. Rom. viii. 26 στεναγμοῖς ἀλαλήτοις, Plotin. *Enn.* v. 1. 6, p. 906, and C.'s favourite quotation ἐννοήθητι καὶ ποιήσω, P. 876, &c. This seems to contradict Bigg's assertion (quoted with approval by Harnack[3] *Dogmengesch.* p. 559 n.) that 'the Silent Prayer of the Quietist' is not to be found in Cl.

26. συγγεγυμνασμένων. The original has γεγυμνασμένα ἐχόντων.

§ 3. 27—8. The ἐπιμέλεια τῆς ψυχῆς is illustrated by p. 16. 25; 26. 26. Cf. *Str.* IV. P. 633 θεὸν ὁ θεραπεύων ἑαυτὸν θεραπεύει· ἐν οὖν τῷ θεωρητικῷ βίῳ ἑαυτοῦ τις ἐπιμελεῖται, θρησκεύων τὸν θεόν. H.

28. This diligence applied to the divine part of the soul implies a contradiction unless there is an unceasing love of men. Cf. *Str.* II. 438 *med.* εἰκὼν τοῦ θεοῦ ἄνθρωπος εὐεργετῶν ἐν ᾧ καὶ αὐτὸς εὐεργετεῖται. H. On the divine part of the soul cf. *Exc. ex Th.* P. 981, *Str.* II. P. 703, *Protr.* P. 59. In this doctrine, as in so much besides, Cl. follows the guidance both of the Bible (Gen. ii. 7) and of Greek philosophy, esp. the Stoics.

p. 6, line 2. γονεῦσι &c. H. J.'s emendation μήν for the MS. μέν is supported by *Str.* II. P. 441 ἡ μὲν σοφία φρόνησις, οὐ μὴν πᾶσα φρόνησις σοφία, Pl. *Phaedrus* 268 E, *Epist.* VII. 326 E ἴσως μὲν κατὰ τύχην, ἔοικε μὴν κ.τ.λ. Orig. *Cels.* III. 9 νῦν μὲν οὖν τάχα...οὐ μὴν κατὰ τὴν ἀρχήν, where μήν is opposed to μέν. Cf. Klotz Devar. I. 132, II. 659.

5. πρεσβύτεροι...διάκονοι. Cf. *Str.* VI. P. 793 *passim*, H. (where, as in *Str.* I. P. 318, comparison is made between the orders of the ministry and the angels, a comparison probably suggested by Apoc. i. 20, &c.); also *Str.* IV. P. 593 εἰκὼν τῆς οὐρανίου ἐκκλησίας ἡ ἐπίγειος. The comparison is elaborated in the treatises on the Heavenly and on the Ecclesiastical Hierarchy by Dionysius Areop., on which see below, p. 16. 4 *n*. Lightfoot in his essay on the Christian Ministry (Philipp. pp. 98, 229) quotes this passage as showing that at the end of the second century the bishop of Alexandria was still not clearly distinguished from the presbytery. In fact we are told that till the middle of the third century both the election and the consecration of the bishop of Alexandria were in the hand of the presbyters. Before the episcopate of Demetrius (A.D. 190—233) there was only one bishop for the whole of Egypt (*ib.* pp. 231, 2). Elsewhere, however, Cl. recognizes the three orders, as in *Paed.* III. P. 309, *Str.* III. P. 552, *Str.* VI. P. 793. The last passage begins with the mention of presbyters and deacons only: 'the true gnostic is enrolled' εἰς τὴν ἐκλογὴν τῶν ἀποστόλων. οὗτος πρεσβύτερός ἐστι τῷ ὄντι τῆς ἐκκλησίας, καὶ διάκονος ἀληθὴς τῆς τοῦ θεοῦ βουλήσεως...οὐχ ὑπ' ἀνθρώπων χειροτονούμενος, οὐδ', ὅτι πρεσβύτερος, δίκαιος νομιζόμενος, ἀλλ', ὅτι δίκαιος, ἐν πρεσβυτερίῳ καταλεγόμενος, κἂν ἐνταῦθα ἐπὶ τῆς γῆς πρωτοκαθεδρίᾳ μὴ τιμηθῇ, ἐν τοῖς εἴκοσι καὶ τέσσαρσι καθεδεῖται θρόνοις, but just below he speaks of αἱ ἐνταῦθα κατὰ τὴν ἐκκλησίαν προκοπαί, ἐπισκόπων, πρεσβυτέρων, διακόνων κ.τ.λ. In *Q. D. S.* he uses the titles ἐπίσκοπος and πρεσβύτερος of the same person (P. 959).

6. διακονίας. As two kinds of θεραπεία (not of διακονία) have been spoken of, and the words διάκονοι and διακονούμενος are used, in the preceding and following sentences, distinctively of one kind of θεραπεία, I think the scribe carelessly wrote διακονίας for θεραπείας.

7. ὑπηρετοῦνται. The middle is only found in late Greek. Just below we find the active of the compound ἐξυπηρετῶ, but the middle in P. 562.

περιγείων: contrasted with οὐράνιος in Plut. *Mor.* 745 B, 887 B. Cf. P. 755 ψυχὰς (previously called ἀγγέλους) ἐξουσίαν λαβούσας διὰ καθαρότητα τοῦ βίου τῇ θείᾳ προνοίᾳ εἰς τὴν ἀνθρώπων λειτουργίαν τὸν περίγειον περιπολεῖν τόπον, 822 αἱ τῶν ἐναρέτων ἀνθρώπων ἐπίνοιαι κατὰ ἐπίπνοιαν θείαν γίνονται, διατιθεμένης πως τῆς ψυχῆς καὶ διαδιδομένου τοῦ θείου θελήματος εἰς τὰς ἀνθρωπίνας ψυχάς, τῶν ἐν μέρει θείων λειτουργῶν συλλαμβανομένων εἰς τὰς τοιαύτας διακονίας, κ.τ.λ.

9. βελτιωτικὴ θεωρία. So philosophy is said just above to be β. ψυχῆς. Cf. *Paed.* I. P. 98 *init.* τὸ τέλος τοῦ παιδαγωγοῦ βελτιῶσαι τὴν ψυχήν, οὐ διδάξαι, σώφρονός τε, οὐκ ἐπιστημονικοῦ, καθηγήσασθαι βίου. The word βελτιόω and its derivatives are found in Plutarch and are very common in Philo, see Wytt. on Plut. *Mor.* p. 75 A τὴν αὐτοῦ βελτιουμένου πρὸς ἀρετὴν συναίσθησιν.

12. ἐξυπηρετῶν occurs again below, p. 12. 9.

13. θεραπεία φυτῶν. See P. 319 and below p. 138. 28.

21. θεοφιλής. As Cl. here ascribes this quality to the gnostic, so Hierocles to the Wise Man, *in Carm. Aur.* I. μόνος ἱερεὺς ὁ σοφός, μόνος θεοφιλής, μόνος εἰδὼς εὔξασθαι.

23. ἰσομένῳ θεῷ. Cf. P. 865, also *Protr.* P. 88, where Potter gives many illustrations from Clement. See esp. *Paed.* III. P. 250 foll. H. Nothing in Clement is more startling to the reader of the present day than his repeated assertion of the deification of the gnostic, not merely in the future (as here), but in this present life, as in P. 894 ὁ τῷ κυρίῳ πειθόμενος καὶ τῇ δοθείσῃ δι' αὐτοῦ κατακολουθήσας προφητείᾳ τελέως ἐκτελεῖται κατ' εἰκόνα τοῦ διδασκάλου, ἐν σαρκὶ περιπολῶν θεός, 890 ἐξ ἀνθρώπου θεὸς ἀποτελεῖται, 632 τούτῳ δυνατὸν τῷ τρόπῳ τὸν γνωστικὸν ἤδη γενέσθαι θεόν. In proof of this doctrine he cites passages both from the Bible and from secular authors, e.g. Ps. lxxxii. 6 (quoted in P. 94, 113, 494, 632), Heraclitus ἄνθρωποι θεοί, θεοὶ ἄνθρωποι (P. 251), Plato *Soph.* p. 216 (P. 634), Empedocles (P. 632). He might also have referred to 2 Pet. i. 4 θείας κοινωνοὶ φύσεως, and to the Stoic claim of equality with God (cf. Cic. *Somn. Sc.* 24 deum te igitur scito esse, siquidem est deus qui viget, qui sentit,...qui tam regit et moderatur id corpus cui praepositus est, quam hunc mundum ille princeps deus, *N. D.* II. 154). Yet strangely enough Cl. denies the identity of divine and human virtue (see P. 886). The deification of man was also maintained by Theophilus *Aut.* II. 27 οὔτε οὖν ἀθάνατον αὐτὸν ἐποίησεν ἀλλὰ δεκτικὸν (ἀθανασίας) ἵνα...μισθὸν κομίσηται τὴν ἀθανασίαν καὶ γένηται θεός, *ib.* 24 ὅπως τέλειος γενόμενος, ἔτι δὲ καὶ θεὸς ἀναδειχθείς, εἰς τὸν οὐρανὸν ἀναβῇ: by Irenaeus IV. 38. 4 nos autem imputamus ei quoniam non ab initio di facti sumus, sed primo quidem homines, tunc demum di: by Hippolytus *Philos.* X. 33 (p. 540. 2) εἰ γὰρ θεόν σε ἠθέλησε ποιῆσαι, ἐδύνατο...ἄνθρωπον θέλων, ἄνθρωπόν σε ἐποίησεν· εἰ δὲ θέλεις καὶ θεὸς γενέσθαι ὑπάκουε τῷ πεποιηκότι, *ib.* 34 (p. 544. 37) ἴσῃ ὁμιλητὴς θεοῦ καὶ συγκληρονόμος Χριστοῦ...γέγονας γὰρ θεός: by Athanas. *de Incarn.* 54 αὐτὸς ἐνηνθρώπησεν ἵνα ἡμεῖς θεοποιηθῶμεν. See also quotations

in Suicer s.v. θεοποιέω, θεόω, θέωσις, Harnack *Dogmengesch.*, who goes so far as to say that the idea of deification is to be found 'in all the Fathers of the ancient Church after Origen' (vol. III. 164 n. tr.), cf. his Excursus on the use of the word θεός (vol. I. 119) and the references in the Index under the heading 'Deification.' Aquinas explains the appellation as follows: (*Summa* I. qu. 108) sancti homines participative dicuntur dei.

ἐξομοιουμένῳ. The idea of man's assimilation to God is connected by Cl., as by Philo (M. I. 16, 106), with the statement in Gen. i. 26 καὶ εἶπεν ὁ θεός, ποιήσωμεν ἄνθρωπον κατ' εἰκόνα ἡμετέραν καὶ καθ' ὁμοίωσιν (quoted in P. 156, 576, 642, 662, 703), and also with the famous passage in the *Theaetetus*, p. 176 πειρᾶσθαι χρὴ ἐνθένδε ἐκεῖσε φεύγειν ὅ,τι τάχιστα. φυγὴ δὲ ὁμοίωσις θεῷ κατὰ τὸ δυνατόν· ὁμοίωσις δὲ δίκαιον καὶ ὅσιον μετὰ φρονήσεως γενέσθαι (quoted P. 482, 499, 500, 502, 792). Cf. Faye, p. 263 foll.

θεῷ. The dative here has a double use; in its first use, as understood after ἐσομένῳ, it is governed by βιωτέον, in its second use by ἐξομοιουμένῳ.

§ 4. 27. ᾗ. The reference seems to be to lines 14—20 in the preceding paragraph.

28. ἀποτέλεσμα, a favourite word with Polybius and later writers. For the three gnostic ἀποτελέσματα cf. P. 453 τριῶν τούτων ἀντέχεται ὁ ἡμεδαπὸς φιλόσοφος, πρῶτον μὲν τῆς θεωρίας, δεύτερον δὲ τῆς τῶν ἐντολῶν ἐπιτελέσεως, τρίτον ἀνδρῶν ἀγαθῶν κατασκευῆς· ἃ δὴ συνελθόντα τὸν γνωστικὸν ἐπιτελεῖ.

πρῶτον. The omission of πρ. in the MS. is probably due to its being written as α', which would easily disappear after the preceding α.

p. 8, line 1. πράγματα. One would hardly expect to find this word used as equivalent to θεωρία in P. 453 (quoted on ἀποτέλεσμα just above), but it occurs elsewhere in Cl. with a pregnant force = 'reality.' Cf. P. 875 φρόνιμοι ψυχαὶ τὸ οἰκεῖον ἀνάπτουσαι φῶς εἰς τὴν τῶν πραγμάτων θεωρίαν, 867 fin. οὐσίας τοίνυν καὶ τὰ πράγματα αὐτὰ παραλαβὼν διὰ τῶν λόγων, εἰκότως καὶ τὴν ψυχὴν ἐπὶ τὰ δέοντα ἄγει, Iren. IV. 18. 5 ἀπὸ γῆς ἄρτος, προσλαμβανόμενος τὴν ἐπίκλησιν τοῦ θεοῦ, οὐκέτι κοινὸς ἄρτος ἐστίν, ἀλλ' εὐχαριστία, ἐκ δύο πραγμάτων συνεστηκυῖα, ἐπιγείου τε καὶ οὐρανίου.

3. τὰ παρὰ τῇ ἀληθείᾳ ἐπικεκρυμμένα. Cf. above, p. 2, l. 8 τῆς παρ' αὐτοῖς παιδείας.

5. μυστήρια. See Introduction.

6. ἄθεος. See above, § 1. 5.

7. δεισιδαίμων. Cf. P. 450 ἡ δεισιδαιμονία πάθος, φόβος δαιμόνων οὖσα ἐκπαθῶν τε καὶ ἐμπαθῶν. By δ. are meant the heathen gods. Cf. 1 Cor. x. 20. In *Protr.* P. 21 Cl. speaks of atheism and superstition as the two extremes of ἀμαθία. See Plutarch's interesting treatise *De Superstitione.*

8. ἄνθρωπον. For the pregnant sense cf. *Protr.* P. 89 τῆς γνώσεως αἱ ἀκτῖνες ἀνατειλάτωσαν τὸν ἐγκεκρυμμένον ἔνδον ἐκφαίνουσαι ἄνθρωπον, Theoph. *Aut.* I. 2 ἐὰν φῇς Δεῖξόν μοι τὸν θεόν σου, κἀγώ σοι εἴποιμι ἂν Δεῖξόν μοι τὸν ἄνθρωπόν σου (*internum hominem*).

§ 5. 10. On rudimentary and other faith see P. 644 foll. H. The reference to πίστις is probably suggested by θεὸν πεπεισμένος εἶναι above

(l. 4). Faith in the existence of God comes first, then the acceptance of Christ's teaching. The text presents many difficulties. How can it be said that a rudimentary faith *is* knowledge, and how does the rest of the sentence bear on this proposition? We may escape the first difficulty by inserting ἐνεργεῖ, which might easily be lost after εἰδέναι, and thus we also gain a construction for ἡγεῖσθαι, if we connect the two sentences by inserting δέ after μετά, as in *Str.* vi. P. 791 τὰ μὲν πρῶτα ἄφεσιν ἁμαρτιῶν αἰτήσεται, μετὰ δὲ τὸ μηκέτι ἁμαρτάνειν, ἔπειτα (MS. ἐπὶ τὸ) εὐποιεῖν δύνασθαι. I should prefer however to make τὸ δρᾶν dependent on ἐνεργεῖ, changing ἡγεῖσθαι into ἡγούμενον. The two stages of faith correspond to the 1st and 2nd stage of knowledge (l. 1). For πίστις see Introduction.

11. **πεποίθησιν.** Cf. *Str.* v. P. 697 πέποιθεν ἀληθῆ εἶναι τὴν διδασκαλίαν τοῦ Υἱοῦ. ὡς δὲ ἡ μάθησις τὰς φρένας αὔξει, οὕτως ἡ εἰς τὸν θεὸν πεποίθησις αὔξει τὴν πίστιν, P. 444, where πεπ. is defined as διάληψις βεβαία περί τινος· διὸ πιστεύομεν ᾧ ἂν πεποιθότες ὦμεν εἰς σωτηρίαν· πεποίθαμεν δὲ τῷ μόνῳ θεῷ, Sext. Emp. *P. H.* iii. p. 238 ἡ πεποίθησις τοῦ τάδε μὲν εἶναι φύσει ἀγαθά, τάδε δὲ κακά. See Wetst. on 2 Cor. i. 15. H. J., putting a colon after διδασκαλίας, and substituting τοῦ for τὸ after πεποίθησιν, would translate 'Faith in its first form is the knowledge of God and of the Saviour's injunction to regard the resolution to do no injustice in any way as proper to the knowledge of Him.'

15. **ἄγγελος ὁ πλησιαίτερον...μεταλαγχάνων.** In the MS. ὁ is changed into τό owing to a misunderstanding of the adverbial use of the neuter comparative. Probably the reference is to the archangel Michael.

17. On the Divinity of the Son, cf. Bull, vol. vi. p. 239 foll. **H.**

20. **ἡ μεγίστη ὑπεροχή.** Cf. above p. 4. 12 τίμιον ἅπαν τὸ ὑπερέχον ἡγεῖται κατὰ τὴν ἀξίαν, and below p. 136. 16 τὴν κατ' ἀξίαν ὑπεροχήν.

κατὰ τὸ θέλημα κ.τ.λ. Cf. below, p. 12. 8 foll. &c. **H.**

21. **οἰακίζει.** Cf. Diod. xviii. 59 ὁ κοινὸς βίος ὥσπερ ὑπὸ θεῶν τινος οἰακιζόμενος, Heracl. Byw. 28 πάντα οἰακίζει κεραυνός, Philo M. I. 419 ὁ κυβερνήτης θεὸς τῶν ὅλων, οἰκονομῶν καὶ πηδαλιουχῶν σωτηρίως τὰ σύμπαντα, ib. 437, below, p. 16. 4 κυβερνῶντα τὴν πάντων σωτηρίαν.

22. **δι' ὧν ἐνεργεῖ.** So Numenius (*ap.* Eus. *Pr. Ev.* xi. 18) compares the pilot steering by the stars with the δημιουργὸς τὴν ὕλην ταῖς ἰδέαις οἰακίζων, βλέπων ἀντὶ τοῦ οὐρανοῦ εἰς τὸν ἄνω θεόν, which Eus. illustrates by quoting Joh. v. 19 οὐδὲν δύναται ὁ υἱὸς ποιεῖν ἀφ' ἑαυτοῦ ἐὰν μή τι βλέπῃ τὸν πατέρα ποιοῦντα: cf. also Joh. viii. 28, 38, Philo M. I. 414 ὁ γεννηθείς, μιμούμενος τὰς τοῦ πατρὸς ὁδούς, πρὸς παραδείγματα ἀρχέτυπα ἐκείνου βλέπων ἐμόρφου τὰ εἴδη, *Strom.* P. 635 οἷον ἄγγελος ἤδη γενόμενος σὺν Χριστῷ ἔσται, ἀεὶ τὸ βούλημα τοῦ θεοῦ σκοπῶν, P. 323 ὁ σωτὴρ ἀεὶ ἐργάζεται ὡς βλέπει τὸν πατέρα.

23. **ἐπιβλέπουσα,** 'watching,' i.e. while acting; quoted in Theodoret *Aff. Gr.* p. 63. **H.**

24. **περιωπῆς,** 'look-out place,' apparently a reference to Plato, *Politicus,* 272 E τότε δὴ τοῦ παντὸς ὁ μὲν κυβερνήτης οἷον πηδαλίων οἴακος ἀφέμενος εἰς τὴν αὑτοῦ περιωπὴν ἀπέστη, where the pilot of the universe leaves the helm

and retires into the περιωπή. The true Divine pilot, he means to say, is at the περιωπή and at the helm all at once. Clement's application may have been suggested by Numenius, who, as quoted by Euseb. *Prep. Ev.* XI. 18, speaks (539 c, d) of the δεύτερος θεός as guiding the world &c. βλέπων εἰς τὸν ἄνω θεόν (cf. below, p. 16. 2—4) and of what ensues when he μεταστρέφει εἰς τὴν ἑαυτοῦ περιωπήν (537 d, cf. 538 b). Contrasted with these is the language of Greg. Naz. *Or.* 37. 3 εἰ ἐπὶ τῆς ἰδίας ἔμεινε περιωπῆς, εἰ μὴ συγκατέβη τῇ ἀσθενείᾳ,...ὀλίγον ἂν ἠκολούθησαν τυχόν. H. Cf. *Protr.* 59 (even the heathen acknowledge) τὸν θεὸν ἄνω που περὶ τὰ νῶτα τοῦ οὐρανοῦ ἐν τῇ ἰδίᾳ καὶ οἰκείᾳ περιωπῇ ὄντως ὄντα ἀεί, Orig. *Jo.* 22. 18 ὁ πατὴρ ἐν τῇ ἑαυτοῦ περιωπῇ ἐπὶ τῇ ἑαυτοῦ θεωρίᾳ εὐφραίνεται.

οὐ μεριζόμενος. Cf. 1 Cor. i. 13 μεμέρισται ὁ Χριστός; Aug. *Epist.* 187. 19 Deus totus adesse rebus omnibus potest et singulis totus. Cl. may have in mind the contrary doctrine of some gnostics and of Numenius (Eus. *Pr. Ev.* XI. 15) ὁ μὲν πρῶτος θεός ἐστιν ἁπλοῦς διὰ τὸ ἑαυτῷ συγγινώμενος διόλου μήποτε εἶναι διαιρετός, ὁ θεὸς μέντοι ὁ δεύτερος...συμφερόμενος τῇ ὕλῃ δυάδι οὔσῃ, ἑνοῖ μὲν αὐτήν, σχίζεται δὲ ὑπ' αὐτῆς. *Protr.* P. 87 ὁ Χριστὸς οὐ μερίζεται, *Str.* II. P. 431 οὐδ' ἐν μέρει καταγίνεταί ποτε (ὁ θεὸς) οὔτε περιέχων οὔτε περιεχόμενος ἢ κατὰ ὁρισμόν τινα ἢ κατὰ ἀποτομήν, *ib.* III. P. 542 μεθ' ὧν ἡ πανεπίσκοπος τοῦ θεοῦ δύναμις ἀμερῶς μεριστή, *ib.* IV. P. 635 ὁ λόγος οὐδαμοῦ διάστασιν λαβών, *Exc. Theod.* P. 967 οὐδὲ διεκέκοπτο ἢ ἄνωθεν μετέστη δεῦρο, τόπον ἐκ τόπου ἀμείβων, ὡς τὸν μὲν ἐπιλαβεῖν, τὸν δὲ ἀπολιπεῖν· ἀλλ' ἦν τὸ πάντῃ ὂν καὶ παρὰ τῷ πατρὶ κἀνταῦθα, P. 969 *init.* οὐδέποτε τοῦ μείναντος ὁ καταβὰς μερίζεται...ἀμέριστος εἷς θεός, *ib.* P. 978 ἐπεὶ δὲ ἡμεῖς ἦμεν οἱ μεμερισμένοι, διὰ τοῦτο ἐβαπτίσατο (ἢ ἐβιάσατο) ὁ Ἰησοῦς τὸ ἀμέριστον μερισθῆναι, Philo M. 1, p. 209 τέμνεται οὐδὲν τοῦ θείου κατ' ἀπάρτησιν, ἀλλὰ μόνον ἐκτείνεται, Justin M. *Dial.* c. 128 τὸν λόγον γεγεννῆσθαι ἀπὸ τοῦ πατρὸς δυνάμει καὶ βουλῇ αὐτοῦ ἀλλ' οὐ κατ' ἀποτομήν, ὡς ἀπομεριζομένης τῆς τοῦ πατρὸς οὐσίας, ὁποῖα τὰ ἄλλα μεριζόμενα οὐ τὰ αὐτά ἐστιν ἃ καὶ πρὶν τμηθῆναι, Orig. *Princip.* I. 2. 6. Dr Gifford supplies the following reff.: Athanas. *de Sent. Dionys.* § 16 μερίζει τὸν υἱόν, Euseb. Caes. ap. Athan. *Epist. de Decretis*, §§ 4, 7.

p. 10, line 2. **ὅλος νοῦς**, taken from Xenophanes (Karsten, p. 35) οὖλος ὁρᾷ, οὖλος δὲ νοεῖ, οὖλος δέ τ' ἀκούει. In his note, K. cites Plin. *H. N.* II. 5 Deus totus est sensus, totus visus, totus auditus, totus animae, totus animi, totus sui; Iren. ap. Epiphan. *Haer.* 33 ὅλος ἔννοια ὤν, ὅλος θέλημα, ὅλος νοῦς, ὅλος ὀφθαλμός, ὅλος ἀκοή, ὅλος πηγὴ πάντων ἀγαθῶν. See below § 37 and § 79, and Psellus (Boiss. p. 34) τὸ δαιμόνιον, πνεῦμα δι' ὅλου ὂν κατὰ φύσιν αἰσθητικήν, κατὰ πᾶν ἑαυτοῦ μέρος ἀμέσως ὁρᾷ τε καὶ ἀκούει, also Seneca *N. Q.* I. *prob.* 14.

4. **τὰς δυνάμεις ἐρευνῶν.** Cf. Apoc. ii. 23 ἐγώ εἰμι ὁ ἐρευνῶν νεφροὺς κ. καρδίας, 1 Cor. ii. 10 τὸ πνεῦμα πάντα ἐρευνᾷ καὶ τὰ βάθη τοῦ θεοῦ, Rom. viii. 38 οὔτε δυνάμεις,...οὔτε ὕψωμα, οὔτε βάθος, οὔτε τις κτίσις ἑτέρα δυνήσεται ἡμᾶς χωρίσαι ἀπὸ τῆς ἀγάπης τοῦ θεοῦ, Apoc. ii. 24 τὰ βάθη τοῦ Σατανᾶ, 1 Joh. iv. 1 δοκιμάζετε τὰ πνεύματα, Luke iv. 36 ἐν ἐξουσίᾳ καὶ δυνάμει

ἐπιτάσσει τοῖς ἀκαθάρτοις πνεύμασιν. Iren. II. 28. 7 spiritus Salvatoris qui in eo est scrutatur omnia et altitudines Dei. *Strom.* P. 425 ἡ ἀληθὴς διαλεκτικὴ τὰς δυνάμεις καὶ τὰς ἐξουσίας δοκιμάζουσα ὑπεξαναβαίνει περὶ τὴν πάντων κρατίστην οὐσίαν...ἐπιστήμην τῶν θείων καὶ οὐρανίων ἐπαγγελλομένη, foll., P. 635 κύκλος ὁ υἱὸς πασῶν τῶν δυνάμεων εἰς ἓν εἰλουμένων. *Strom.* P. 431 πάρεστιν ἀεὶ τῇ τε ἐποπτικῇ τῇ τε εὐεργετικῇ τῇ τε παιδευτικῇ ἁπτομένῃ ἡμῶν δυνάμει δύναμις τοῦ θεοῦ, *Exc. Theod.* P. 988 ὁ ἄρτος καὶ τὸ ἔλαιον ἁγιάζεται τῇ δυνάμει τοῦ ὀνόματος...δυνάμει εἰς δύναμιν πνευματικὴν μεταβέβληται, *Strom.* P. 366 ἔνιοι δυνάμεις τινὰς ὑποβεβηκυίας ἐμπνεῦσαι τὴν φιλοσοφίαν ὑπειλήφασιν. This power was shown by our Lord in the Temptation, and in His Passion, see Lightfoot on Col. ii. 15.

πᾶσα ὑποτέτακται στρατιά. For a similar anarthrous use of στρατιά see Plato, *Phaedr.* 246 τῷ δ' ἕπεται στρατιὰ θεῶν τε καὶ δαιμόνων, Lk. ii. 13 πλῆθος στρατιᾶς οὐρανίου. The absolute supremacy of the Son, as opposed to the gnostic worship of angels, is asserted by St Paul in Col. i. 15—19, ii. 18, 19. See below n. on p. 16. 4.

καὶ θεῶν. Cf. p. 20. 15 αἱ μακάριοι θεῶν οἰκήσεις, 32. 14 θεαταὶ ἄγγελοι καὶ θεοί. In Ephr. Syr. (quoted by Lightfoot on Col. i. 15) the first rank of the hierarchy consists of θεοί, θρόνοι, κυριότητες.

6. **διὰ τὸν ὑποτάξαντα.** 1 Cor. XV. 27 πάντα ὑπέταξεν ὑπὸ τοὺς πόδας αὐτοῦ. H.

8, 9. **ὡς φίλοι...ὡς οἰκέται.** Cf. P. 423 ἔξεστι δὲ μὴ εἶναι ἀπειθείας υἱόν, ἀλλὰ...δοῦλον μὲν τὰ πρῶτα, ἔπειτα δὲ πιστὸν γενέσθαι θεράποντα, φοβούμενον κύριον τὸν θεόν· εἰ δέ τις ἐπαναβαίη, τοῖς υἱοῖς ἐγκαταλέγεται, below p. 34. 5, 109. 5, 136. 23.

§ 6. 12. **παιδείᾳ.** Cf. below, p. 20. 7.

δι' αἰσθητικῆς ἐνεργείας. Cf. *Exc. Theod.* P. 972 πῶς δὲ καὶ αἱ κολαζόμεναι ψυχαὶ συναισθάνονται μὴ σώματα οὖσαι.

τὸν σκληροκάρδιον. See below n. on p. 20. 7 *f*.

13. **ἰδίᾳ καὶ δημοσίᾳ.** See my n. on Cic. *N. D.* II. 164 singulis provideri.

18. **τὸν ἐξ αὐτοῦ τὴν σωτηρίαν λαβεῖν...δυνάμενον.** Cf. *Paed.* P. 118 πεπιστεύκαμεν ἐκουσίῳ προαιρέσει σωζόμενοι, Str. P. 788 ἡμᾶς ἐξ ἡμῶν αὐτῶν βούλεται σώζεσθαι, *Q. D. S.* 940 P. δίδωσι βουλομένοις ἵνα οὕτως ἴδιον αὐτῶν ἡ σωτηρία γένηται· οὐ γὰρ ἀναγκάζει ὁ θεός, βία γὰρ ἐχθρὸν θεῷ, P. 947. See below n. on p. 16. 19. Orig. *de Orat.* 29 *fin.* οὐ γὰρ βούλεται ὁ θεός τινι τὸ ἀγαθὸν ὡς κατ' ἀνάγκην γενέσθαι, ἀλλ' ἑκουσίως, *Hom.* XIX. *in Jer.* ὁ θεὸς οὐ τυραννεῖ, ἀλλὰ βασιλεύει, καὶ βασιλεύων οὐ βιάζεται, ἀλλὰ πείθει.

19. **ἀποπληρῶσαι.** Plat. *Rep.* X. 620 E τὴν Λάχεσιν ἑκάστῳ ὃν εἵλετο δαίμονα τοῦτον φύλακα ξυμπέμπειν τοῦ βίου καὶ ἀποπληρωτὴν τῶν αἱρεθέντων. H.

21. **ὑποδεεστέρων** (has no positive), 'inferior' generally, as here; esp. poorer, or feebler, or more insignificant. Similarly applied to angels by Origen (*in Mt.* tom. 14. 21) 3. 644 R. (ἡ ψυχή) μετὰ τιμωρίας ὑπό τινα ὑποδεέστερον γίνεται παρὰ τὸν Μιχαήλ, ὑποδεέστερος γὰρ ἐκείνου ὁ τῆς μετανοίας. H. Cf. P. 366, quoted on l. 4 τὰς δυνάμεις, and see Potter's note there.

23. ἄγγελοι κατὰ ἔθνη. *Strom.* P. 822 κατὰ τὰ ἔθνη καὶ πόλεις νενέμηνται τῶν ἀγγέλων αἱ προστασίαι, Deut. xxxii. 8 ὅτε διεμέριζεν ὁ ὕψιστος ἔθνη... ἔστησεν ὅρια ἐθνῶν κατὰ ἀριθμὸν ἀγγέλων θεοῦ, *ib.* iv. 19; Daniel x. 13, 20, 21; cf. Sir. xvii. 14 ἑκάστῳ ἔθνει κατέστησεν ἡγούμενον, καὶ μερὶς κυρίου Ἰσραήλ ἐστιν.

24—29. ἤτοι γὰρ οὐ φροντίζει κ.τ.λ. Cf. Plato *Leg.* x. 901 D, where it is shown that God's Providence extends to individuals (1) because He is Omnipotent, (2) because He is perfect in goodness, whence it follows that He cannot be actuated by ῥαθυμίᾳ καὶ τρυφῇ (οὔκουν ὑπὸ τρυφῆς ῥᾴθυμος l. 28) in any of His dealings.

27. Cf. below p. 14. 4 foll. H., also *Paed.* I. P. 135.

p. 12, line 4. κατὰ τὸν οἰκεῖον καιρόν. Tit. i. 2, 3 ζωὴν...ἐπηγγείλατο πρὸ χρόνων αἰωνίων, ἐφανέρωσε δὲ καιροῖς ἰδίοις τὸν λόγον αὐτοῦ.

5, 6. οὔτ' οὖν φθονοίη. Cf. Theoph. *Aut.* II. 25 οὐχ ὡς φθονῶν ὁ θεός, ὥς οἴονταί τινες, ἐκέλευσεν μὴ ἐσθίειν ἀπὸ τῆς γνώσεως, in allusion to the Just and Jealous God of Marcion. See below p. 22. 24. In the translation the word 'envy' is employed both here and in ll. 11—13. Perhaps however the meaning *here* is rather that of 'bearing a grudge.' The case of Ishmael and of Esau may have been adduced as proving such φθόνος on the part of the Demiurge.

9. ἐξυπηρετῶν. Potter cites Bull II. 6, 7. H.

§ 7. 11. ἀνάρχως means that in the Lord ἀπάθεια was not the result of a struggle and process, as in man; see below, ll. 24—26. H.

13. ὁ φθονῶν. *Str.* P. 569, Iren. IV. 40. 3 ἐκ τότε ἀποστάτης ὁ ἄγγελος ἀφ' ὅτε ἐζήλωσε τὸ πλάσμα τοῦ θεοῦ, *ib.* v. 24. 4 invidens homini apostata a divina factus est lege: invidia enim aliena est a Deo; Theodoret, *Gr. Aff.* p. 54, 19 foll. Cf. Plato, *Phaedr.* 247 φθόνος ἔξω θείου χοροῦ ἵσταται, *Tim.* 29 E ἀγαθὸς ἦν (ὁ θεός), ἀγαθῷ δὲ οὐδεὶς περὶ οὐδενὸς οὐδέποτε γίγνεται φθόνος.

οὐ καὶ πάθος ἥψατο, e.g. the passion of hate, see Joh. viii. 44. Of the demons Clement says ἄγγελοί τινες ἀκρατεῖς γενόμενοι ἐπιθυμίᾳ ἁλόντες οὐρανόθεν δεῦρο καταπεπτώκασιν P. 538.

18. συμβούλου...σοφία. Cf. *Strom.* P. 769 (the Creator) σοφία εἴρηται πρὸς ἁπάντων τῶν προφητῶν. οὗτός ἐστιν...ὁ σύμβουλος τοῦ θεοῦ τοῦ τὰ πάντα προεγνωκότος, P. 101 *init.*

19—21. The verse Χριστὸν θεοῦ δύναμιν καὶ θεοῦ σοφίαν is also referred to in *Str.* I. P. 377, 421 and 424.

20. ἅτε...ἀρχικώτατος. ἀρχικός, being explained by πρὸ πάντων τῶν γενομένων, seems here to mean 'original.' We find it joined with λόγος in *Str.* 821 *init.* ἡ φρόνησις ἄνευ θεωρίας παραδεξαμένη τὸν ἀρχικὸν λόγον ...πίστις λέγεται, where Lowth's n. is 'Filium Dei'; also P. 604 ἀρχικὸς ὁ λόγος, 'the subject is of primary importance,' and 927 (of the causes of scepticism) τούτων αὐτῶν τῶν ἀρχικωτάτων τῆς ἐποχῆς τὸ μὲν ἀβέβαιον τῆς διανοίας γεννητικόν ἐστι διαφωνίας. For examples of ἅτε not followed by a participle see Plato, *Rep.* VIII. 551 E, 568 B αὐτούς...οὐ παραδεξόμεθα ἅτε τυραννίδος ὑμνητάς, *ib.* 619 D ἅτε πόνων ἀγυμνάστους.

26. ἀπαθείας. See below, P. 834, 836 and Introduction.

p. 14, line 3. πατρική τις ἐνέργεια. So, at the beginning of § 9, the Son is called δύναμις πατρική.

§ 8. 7, 8. κοινή γάρ justifies κοινήν. H. Besides this universal goodness the Saviour has a special inducement in His special relation to man (ἰδίου ἔργου): cf. P. 80 τὸ οἰκεῖον αὐτοῦ καὶ ἐξαίρετον καὶ ἰδιωματικὸν παρὰ τὰ ἄλλα ζῷα. For ἑλομένων cf. below, l. 18, also pp. 10. 19, 12. 28, and esp. p. 16. 19.

9. τῷ μόνῳ. The former dat. is causal, the latter governed by ἐνεστάχθαι. It would have been easy to avoid confusion by using διὰ τό, but Cl. is careless in such matters; see below, p. 24. 18, and 18. 6, 7. For ἐνεστάχθαι cf. *Protr.* P. 59 πᾶσιν ἐνέστακται ἀπόρροια θεϊκή, Herodian I. 4, 5 πόθον τῆς αὐτῶν χρηστότητος ταῖς τῶν ἀρχομένων ψυχαῖς ἐνέσταξαν.

11. ἁρμονιωτέρα goes with τῷ θεῷ. Cf. P. 447 τοῖς ἐκ περιπάτου... ἁρμόνιος ἥδε ἡ δόξα: =cl. ἁρμόδιος. H.

12. προσήκει τῷ κρείττονι ἡγεῖσθαι. Cf. Plat. *Leg.* III. 690 B τὸ μέγιστον ἀξίωμα...ἕπεσθαι μὲν τὸν ἀνεπιστήμονα, τὸν δὲ φρονοῦντα ἡγεῖσθαι, *Rep.* IX. 590 D (it is right that the worse should be subject to the better) οὐκ ἐπὶ βλάβῃ τῇ τοῦ δούλου οἰόμενοι δεῖν ἄρχεσθαι αὐτόν, ἀλλ' ὡς ἄμεινον ὂν παντὶ ὑπὸ θείου καὶ φρονίμου ἄρχεσθαι, μάλιστα μὲν οἰκεῖον ἔχοντος (ἢ ἔχοντι) ἐν αὐτῷ, εἰ δὲ μή, ἔξωθεν ἐφεστῶτος, Arist. *Pol.* I. c. 5, 6.

17. τῶν οἰκείων. Gal. vi. 10 τοὺς οἰκείους τῆς πίστεως, Eph. ii. 19 συμπολῖται τῶν ἁγίων καὶ οἰκεῖοι τοῦ θεοῦ, Heb. iii. 6.

19. διὰ πίστεως τελειούμενοι. Cf. below p. 18. 16 τὴν διὰ πίστεως τελείωσιν.

21. πρωτουργοῦ κινήσεως. Plato (*Leg.* x. 897 A, a passage which is also cited in *Str.* v. P. 701) speaks of the soul moving all things in heaven and earth with her own movements, such as wishing, thinking, loving, &c. These and such-like πρωτουργοὶ κινήσεις make use of τὰς δευτερουργοὺς κινήσεις of bodies, and cause physical change. H. Plato goes on to describe how the soul νοῦν μὲν προσλαβοῦσα ἀεὶ θεῖον ὀρθῶς, θεὸς ὡς, ὀρθὰ καὶ εὐδαίμονα παιδαγωγεῖ πάντα, which may have led Cl. to identify the δύναμις πρωτ. κιν. with the Son. The term πρωτουργός is also used by Proclus and Julian, and frequently by Dion. Areop.

§ 9. 26. δύναμις. See *Strom.* v. P. 647 *init.*

28. διοικήσεως. Often used by the Stoics of the divine government of the world.

29 f. 'It belongs to (it requires) the greatest Power (to make) the fitting' &c. (cf. 27 foll.). προήκουσα might do if μέχρι stood earlier, but it can hardly go with καὶ μέχρι τοῦ μικροτάτου alone; nor is there reason to disturb προσήκουσα. H. I have kept Sylburg's προήκουσα because (1) I think προσήκουσα superfluous with the following δι' ἀκριβείας, and (2) μέχρι seems to call for a word implying progress, to which it sets a limit. The order does not seem to me harsh for Clement. Perhaps it might be made clearer by putting the clause καὶ—προήκουσα in brackets.

p. 16, line 2 foll. refers back to p. 8. 20 foll., where see the reference to Numenius. H.

3. κυβερνῶντα τὴν πάντων σωτηρίαν, an unusual expression for κυβερνῶντα πάντα εἰς σωτηρίαν. For the metaphor, cf. Lightfoot on Ign. *Polyc.* 2 (vol. II. p. 339), *Q. D. S.* 950 P. εἰ βλέποιεν πρὸς τὸν κύριον ἀτενεῖ τῷ βλέμματι, καθάπερ εἰς ἀγαθοῦ κυβερνήτου νεῦμα δεδορκότες...τί σημαίνει, τί δίδωσι τοῖς αὑτοῦ ναύταις τὸ σύνθημα, above p. 8. 21.

4. ἑτέρων ὑφ' ἑτέρους. Cf. the answer of the centurion, Mt. viii. 9. The conception of the Celestial Hierarchy was elaborated by Dionysius (pseudo-Areopagita), probably in the fifth century, from whom it passed to Scotus Erigena, Aquinas, and Dante, and so to Spenser and Milton. According to this, three orders (διακοσμήσεις, or ἱεραρχίαι in the narrower sense) are divided into nine choirs. The first order consists of Seraphim (Isa. vi. 2, 3), Cherubim (Ps. lxxx. 1, Heb. ix. 5, &c.), and Thrones (Col. i. 16), receiving their glory immediately from God, and transmitting it to the second order; which consists of Dominations (κυριότητες), Virtues (δυνάμεις), Powers (ἐξουσίαι), all mentioned by St Paul in Col. i. 16, Eph. i. 21, cf. Rom. viii. 38. Again, the second triad pass on their light to the third, which consists of Principalities (ἀρχαί) mentioned both in Col. i. 16 and Eph. i. 21, and of archangels (1 Th. iv. 16, Jude 9) and angels. Bp Lightfoot in his excellent note on Col. i. 16 traces the gradual development of this theory in its earlier stages, citing the description of the seven heavens in *Test. Levi* 3, where the highest or seventh heaven is occupied by θρόνοι and ἐξουσίαι (the account of the other heavens seems to me confused); Orig. *Princ.* I. 5. 3 where the different dignities of *principatus, potestates, throni, dominationes, virtutes* are said to have been attained by desert, just as other angels were degraded by their own fault (of which an instance is found in Ezek. xxviii. 13, Isa. xiv. 12 f.). Ignatius seems to refer to some generally recognized hierarchy in *Trall.* 5, μὴ οὐ δύναμαι ὑμῖν τὰ ἐπουράνια γράψαι;...δύναμαι νοεῖν τὰ ἐπουράνια καὶ τὰς τοποθεσίας τὰς ἀγγελικὰς καὶ τὰς συστάσεις τὰς ἀρχοντικάς, where Lightfoot cites *Smyrn.* 6, Papias (Routh *Rel. Sacr.* I. 14) ἐνίοις δὲ αὐτῶν, δηλαδὴ τῶν πάλαι θείων ἀγγέλων, καὶ τῆς περὶ τὴν γῆν διακοσμήσεως ἔδωκεν ἄρχειν. See Appendix on Cl.'s Angelology, Lupton's art. on Dionysius *Dict. of Chr. Biog.* I. 841, *ib.* Plumptre *s.v.* 'Angels' p. 113, Mrs Jameson *Sacred and Legendary Art* vol. I. p. 41 foll.

5. μέγαν ἀρχιερέα. The phrase, taken from Heb. iv. 14, occurs frequently in Clem., see P. 93, 835 (with n.), 858.

7. ἤρτηται τὰ πρῶτα καὶ δεύτερα καὶ τρίτα, an allusion to the Platonic Epistle II. p. 312 E περὶ τὸν πάντων βασιλέα πάντ' ἐστί, καὶ ἐκείνου ἕνεκα πάντα, καὶ ἐκεῖνο αἴτιον ἁπάντων τῶν καλῶν· δεύτερον δὲ περὶ τὰ δεύτερα, καὶ τρίτον περὶ τὰ τρίτα[1]. Cf. Plot. I. 82 πρῶτα καὶ δεύτερα τἀγαθὰ καὶ τρίτα· περὶ τὸν πάντων βασιλέα πάντα ἐστί, καὶ ἐκεῖνο αἴτιον πάντων καλῶν, καὶ πάντα ἐστιν ἐκείνου· καὶ δεύτερον περὶ τὰ δεύτερα καὶ τρίτον περὶ τὰ τρίτα:

---

[1] This is the reading in all the editions, but, as I have stated below, I should prefer to read δεύτερον δὲ πέρι, καὶ τρίτον πέρι.

II. 9. 13, &c. H. The doctrine of the Platonic Trinity is built on the very enigmatic sentence in the pseudo-Platonic epistle. It formed an important part of the Neo-Platonic system and is discussed at length by Plotinus in his Fifth Ennead. His triad is made up of (1) τὸ ἓν or τἀγαθόν, (2) νοῦς, and (3) ψυχή, the latter being subdivided into the creative and the animating spirit of the world. The relation between the Christian Trinity and the Platonic in its various forms is fully treated of by Euseb. *Pr. Ev.* Bk XI. chapters 12 to 24, by Cudworth and Mosheim in the former's *Intellectual System*, vol. II. pp. 312—486 ; see too W. H. Thompson in A. Butler's *Lectures*, vol. II. p. 38, Caesar Morgan on the *Trinity of Plato*, ed. Holden.

The same quotation is referred to in *Protr.* P. 60, where ὁ βασιλεύς is explained by θεὸς τῆς τῶν ὄντων ἀληθείας τὸ μέτρον, also in *Str.* v. P. 710, where Cl. adds οὐκ ἄλλως ἔγωγε ἐξακούω ἢ τὴν ἁγίαν τριάδα μηνύεσθαι· τρίτον μὲν γὰρ εἶναι τὸ ἅγιον πνεῦμα, τὸν υἱὸν δὲ δεύτερον, δι' οὗ πάντα ἐγένετο κατὰ βούλησιν τοῦ πατρός. Here however it seems impossible that there should be any allusion either to the Christian or Platonic Trinity, as Cl. makes his three degrees depend on the Son (ἀρχῆς τῆς κατὰ τὸ θέλημα ἐνεργούσης). Though the expression is taken from Plato, the thought is probably taken from St Paul's words in 2 Cor. xii. 2 foll. οἶδα ἄνθρωπον ἐν Χριστῷ...ἁρπαγέντα...ἕως τρίτου οὐρανοῦ· καὶ οἶδα τὸν τοιοῦτον ἄνθρωπον...ὅτι ἡρπάγη εἰς τὸν παράδεισον, which Cl. paraphrases in *Strom.* v. P. 693 ἁρπαγέντα ἕως τρίτου οὐρανοῦ κἀκεῖθεν εἰς τὸν παράδεισον ; see the whole passage 690—694, *Exc. Theod.* P. 981 ἐν τῷ παραδείσῳ, τῷ τετάρτῳ οὐρανῷ, δημιουργεῖται (ἡ ψυχή), and compare Papias ap. Iren. v. 36 εἶναι δὲ τὴν διαστολὴν ταύτην τῆς οἰκήσεως τῶν τὰ ἑκατὸν καρποφορούντων καὶ τῶν τὰ ἑξήκοντα καὶ τῶν τὰ τριάκοντα· ὧν οἱ μὲν εἰς τοὺς οὐρανοὺς ἀναληφθήσονται, οἱ δὲ ἐν τῷ παραδείσῳ διατρίψουσιν, οἱ δὲ τὴν πόλιν κατοικήσουσιν[1]. καὶ διὰ τοῦτο εἰρηκέναι τὸν κύριον, ἐν τοῖς τοῦ πατρός μου μονὰς εἶναι πολλάς· τὰ πάντα γὰρ τοῦ θεοῦ. So in l. 5. 2 Paradise is said to be ὑπὲρ τρίτον οὐρανόν. Cf. below § 40 τὴν μακαρίαν τῶν ἁγίων τριάδα μονῶν. Since the angelic orders are replenished from among the saints, as they pass from this world (see P. 1004), we may perhaps understand the three heavens, the three mansions and the three degrees of fruitfulness, in reference to the three Orders of the Hierarchy, mentioned in the n. on l. 4 above. We may then take ἤρτηται κ.τ.λ. as answering to πρωτότοκος πάσης κτίσεως in Col. i. 15. The Platonic quotation is explained of the Christian Trinity in Justin, *Apol.* I. 60, p. 93 BC δευτέραν χώραν τῷ παρὰ θεοῦ λόγῳ... δίδωσι (Πλάτων), τὴν δὲ τρίτην τῷ λεχθέντι ἐπιφέρεσθαι τῷ ὕδατι πνεύματι, εἰπὼν "τὰ δὲ τρίτα περὶ τὸν τρίτον" (which suggests that we should read τρίτον περὶ in the Platonic Epistle, as indeed it is given in Eus. *Pr. Ev.* XIII. 13. 29), and Celsus declared that the Christians had stolen their doctrine from Plato (Orig. *c. Cels.* p. 287, Spencer), so Cyr. *c. Jul.* p. 34.

---

[1] Just before, the highest class are described as those who τὴν λαμπρότητα τῆς πόλεως καθέξουσι.

8. εἶτα ἐπὶ τέλει τοῦ φαινομένου. If we are right in interpreting τρίτα of the Third Hierarchy, consisting of ἀρχαί, ἀρχάγγελοι, and ἄγγελοι, the εἶτα is used a little carelessly, as the ἀγγελοθεσία is included in the τρίτα, and does not come afterwards as a separate order. Though unseen, the angels have their place on the verge of the visible world, κατὰ τὴν τῶν περιγείων οἰκονομίαν as we read above p. 6. 7: see too Papias cited on l. 4. There may also be a reference to the stars, which were identified with angels by the Jews, and the worship of which Cl. considers excusable among the heathen P. 795, cf. P. 817 τὰ ἄστρα, τουτέστιν αἱ δυνάμεις αἱ διοικητικαί, προσετάγησαν ἐκτελεῖν τὰ εἰς οἰκονομίαν ἐπιτήδεια καὶ αὐτά τε πείθεται ἄγεταί τε πρὸς τῶν ἐπιτεταγμένων αὐτοῖς, ᾗ ἂν ἡγῆται τὸ ῥῆμα κυρίου, 668, 1003.

9. ἀγγελοθεσία. Used again *Ecl. Pr.* 57, *s.f.* P. 1004, and apparently nowhere else. Cf. ἀστροθεσία *Exc. Theod.* 74, P. 986. **H.** See Lightfoot on τοποθεσίαι ἀγγελικαί, Ign. *Trall.* 5 (vol. II. p. 164).

11 foll. Founded on Plat. *Ion*, 533 DE, where the power of the Muse (θεία δύναμις) communicating itself from one to another is compared to that of the Magnet or Heraclean stone, communicated to a ὁρμαθός of rings (πᾶσι δὲ τούτοις ἐξ ἐκείνης τῆς λίθου ἡ δύναμις ἀνήρτηται)[1]. Cf. Lucr. VI. 906—916 (usque adeo permananter vis pervolat eius); Philo, M. I. 34, &c. for the rings. **H.**

μακροτάτη. As Cl. is here insisting on the far-reaching influence of the magnet, it seems necessary to change μικροτάτη (naturally suggested by μικρότατον in p. 14. 27) to μακροτάτη, esp. as the original has ὁρμαθὸς μακρὸς πάνυ σιδηρῶν δακτυλίων ἐξ ἀλλήλων ἤρτηται. For the meaning 'remote,' cf. Herod. II. 32 εἴ τι πλέον ἴδοιεν τῶν τὰ μακρότατα ἰδομένων.

12. πνεύματι. *Strom.* II. P. 443 ἡ λίθος ἡ θρυλουμένη ἕλκει τὸν σίδηρον διὰ συγγένειαν...πείθεται δὲ τὰ ἑλκόμενα ἀρρήτῳ ἑλκόμενα πνεύματι. The word was used by the Stoics to denote the element of aether which holds together all the parts of the world by its attractive force, shown particularly in the magnet, cf. Philo, M. I. 277 λίθων καὶ ξύλων δεσμὸν κραταιότατον ἕξιν εἰργάζετο· ἡ δέ ἐστι πνεῦμα ἀναστρέφον ἐφ' ἑαυτό, Alex. Aphr. *de Mixt.* 142 (ap. Zeller, IV. 119) ἡνῶσθαι ὑποτίθεται Χρύσιππος τὴν σύμπασαν οὐσίαν πνεύματός τινος διὰ πάσης αὐτῆς διήκοντος. Celsus (Orig. VI. 71) charged the Christians with borrowing from the Stoics their doctrine of an all-pervading Spirit, cf. Cic. *N. D.* II. 19, Plut. *Mor.* 1085 D.

15. μονῇ. Cf. *Str.* V. P. 667, where, in his explanation of the mystical meaning of the Tabernacle, he says, after speaking of the showbread, εἶεν δ' ἂν μοναί τινες εἰς ἓν σῶμα καὶ σύνοδον μίαν συμπνεουσῶν ἐκκλησιῶν, VI. P. 794 &c. where after quoting John x. 16, he continues πλης αὐλῆς καὶ μονῆς ἀναλόγως τῆς πίστεως κατηξιωμένα, and shortly after, ἀποθέσθαι τα πάθη ἀνάγκη τὸν πιστόν, ὡς εἰς τὴν μονὴν τὴν οἰκείαν χωρῆσαι δυνηθῆναι... ἀπεκδυσάμενος τὰ πάθη μέτεισιν ἐπὶ τὴν βελτίονα τῆς προτέρας μονήν, *Ecl. Pr.* 56 *fin.* (P. 1003) where he has ἐπαναβησόμενοι κατὰ προκοπὴν ἀφίξονται

---

[1] See the notes in the Variorum edition

ἐπὶ τὴν πρώτην μονήν, see the whole passage. H. See also n. on p. 70. 12, 13, below.

16. ὑπὸ ἀσθενείας κακοί. Cf. P. 894 fin. σχεδὸν δύο εἰσὶν ἀρχαὶ πάσης ἁμαρτίας ἄγνοια καὶ ἀσθένεια.

καχεξίᾳ περιπεπτωκότες. Both medical terms, as well as ἀπληστία. H.

17. περικαταρρέουσιν. So περικαταρρέω τῇ φθορᾷ, Protr. P. 89: 'collapse,' as of buildings (Lys. p. 185. 20). The simple verb is used in the same sense. H.

18. ἀποπίπτουσι. Esp. of any 'falling away' from a normal attachment, as of leaves from a tree, a soldier from the army, a wife from her husband. H.

19. αἱρεῖσθαι τὸν βουλόμενον ἀρετήν. The fact of man's free-will is much insisted on by Cl. in opposition to the doctrine of Basilides and other gnostics, who held that men were naturally predestined to belief or unbelief (Str. II. P. 433 φυσικὴν ἡγοῦνται τὴν πίστιν, IV. p. 600 f., v. p. 645), cf. above, p. 10. 18 f., below pp. 18. 22, 24. 14, and P. 434 ὁ θεμέλιος τῆς σωτηρίας ἡ ἑκούσιος πίστις...τὴν αἵρεσιν καὶ φυγὴν δεδόσθαι τοῖς ἀνθρώποις αὐτοκρατορικὴν παρὰ τοῦ κυρίου διὰ τῶν γραφῶν παρειλήφαμεν. The same doctrine was strongly held by the Stoics, see Seneca Ep. 80. 4 Quid tibi opus est ut sis bonus ? velle. [It forms the subject of the Sixth Book of Eus. Pr. Ev. Gifford.]

§ 10. 22. οὐκ ἐννόμοις seems to belong to πρὸ τοῦ νόμου only. H. Compare for the contrast between the state under the law and that prior to the law, Rom. v. 13, 14, and for the unwritten law of the prior state Rom. ii. 14, 15, 26, 27, also § 11 below, and P. 532 (Christ fulfilled the law) τῷ τὰς κατὰ νόμον προφητείας ἐπιτελεῖς γενέσθαι κατὰ τὴν αὐτοῦ παρουσίαν, ἐπεὶ τὰ τῆς ὀρθῆς πολιτείας καὶ τοῖς δικαίοις βεβιωκόσι πρὸ τοῦ νόμου διὰ τοῦ λόγου ἐκηρύσσετο, and P. 568 init. In P. 809 Clement speaks of the two tables of the law as embodying τὰς πρὸ τοῦ νόμου παραδεδομένας ἐντολάς. Instances of special ἐντολαί in the prior state are those to Adam and to Noah, see P. 1001, and Euseb. Pr. Ev. VII. 6 and 8.

δικαίῳ νόμος οὐ κεῖται. It is difficult to see the appropriateness of the quotation. The pre-Mosaic generations with few exceptions are described as the opposite of righteous. Is it a reference to Abraham, to whom the promise was made, and whose faith was counted for righteousness long before the law was given (Gal. iii. 17 foll.) ? Compare Str. II. P. 452 init. ὁ ποιμὴν δικαίους οἶδέ τινας ἐν ἔθνεσι καὶ ἐν Ἰουδαίοις, οὐ μόνον πρὸ τῆς τοῦ κυρίου παρουσίας, ἀλλὰ καὶ πρὸ νόμου, ὡς Ἄβελ, ὡς Νῶε.

23. τὸν ἐλόμενον—συνεχώρησαν. Deut. xxx. 19 'I have set before you life and death, blessing and cursing : therefore choose life.'

24. συνεῖναι οἷς εἵλετο. Cf. Str. VI. P. 789 ὁ μὲν κακὸς φύσει, ἁμαρτητικὸς διὰ κακίαν γενόμενος, φαῦλος καθίστηκεν, ἔχων ἣν ἑκὼν εἵλετο, Ps. cvi. 15 ' He gave them their request, but sent leanness into their soul.' Hos. iv. 17 ' Ephraim is joined to idols, let him alone.'

25. βελτιουμένην. See above n. on p. 6. 9.

26. The corruption of ἐπίγνωσις into ἐπίδοσις is as natural as the

reverse would be unnatural. We have also a reference to γνῶσις in l. 29. For the expression cf. Rom. iii. 20 ἐπιγν. ἀμαρτίας, Philemon 6 ἐπιγν. παντὸς ἀγαθοῦ, Plut. *Mor.* 1145 A ἐπιγν. μουσικῆς.

27. βελτίονα...τὴν τάξιν. Cf. ἀμείνους οἰκήσεις below, p. 20. 5.

28. προκοπήν. A term employed by the Stoics to denote a relaxation of their original uncompromising division of mankind into wise and fools, the former possessed of all perfection, the latter all alike vicious and miserable. The more reasonable Stoics allowed that among those who had not attained to wisdom there were some who were making advances towards it, προκόπτοντες, *proficientes*. Cf. Upton's Index to Epictetus.

30. γνώσεως καὶ κληρονομίας ὑπεροχήν. Cf. the semi-personal ὑπεροχή of p. 8. 20 above. H. See below, p. 96. 25, where we have the steps πίστις, γνῶσις, ἀγάπη, κληρονομία.

περιτροπαί, first 'revolutions,' then all 'turns,' *vices*. H. I think Cl. still has the original meaning in view. The salutary influence of the heavenly revolutions (governed, as we have seen on p. 16. 8, according to Cl. by the presiding angels) is often referred to by the Stoics, cf. Cleomedes *de Motu Circ. Corp. Caelest.* L. 3 ὁ οὐρανὸς κύκλῳ εἰλούμενος καὶ ταύτην τὴν κίνησιν προνοητικὴν οὖσαν ἐπὶ σωτηρίᾳ τῶν ὅλων ποιούμενος, Cic. *N. D.* II. 60 (of the stars) ita feruntur ut ad omnia conservanda et tuenda consensisse videantur, *ib.* 56 caelestium admirabilis ordo ex quo conservatio et salus omnium omnis oritur; also Plat. *Rep.* VIII. 546 ὅταν περιτροπαὶ ἑκάστοις κύκλων περιφορὰς ξυνάπτωσι, *Phaedr.* 246 foll. where the soul is represented as carried round with the gods in their circuit, from which the gnostic Carpocrates borrowed his description of the pre-existence of Jesus (Hippol. *Philos.* VII. 32 τὴν δὲ ψυχὴν αὐτοῦ εὔτονον γεγονυῖαν διαμνημονεῦσαι τὰ ὁρατὰ μὲν αὐτῇ ἐν τῇ μετὰ τοῦ ἀγεννήτου θεοῦ περιφορᾷ). Even in Dionysius, the account of the Heavenly Hierarchy contains allusions to the movements of the spheres; and Clement's idea of it is coloured by reminiscences of the procession of the gods in Plato's *Phaedrus* (P. 732) and of the Platonic vision of Er (P. 713); see also P. 636, and P. 986 διὰ τοῦτο ἀνέτειλεν ξένος ἀστὴρ καὶ καινὸς καταλύων τὴν παλαιὰν ἀστροθεσίαν, καινῷ φωτὶ οὐ κοσμικῷ λαμπόμενος, ὁ καινὰς ὁδοὺς καὶ σωτηρίους τρεπόμενος, αὐτὸς ὁ κύριος. Pachimeres on Dion. *Cael. Hier.* VII. says ἔστι καὶ ἐπὶ τῶν θείων καὶ οὐρανίων νόων ὁρμὴ καὶ κίνησις, ἡ πρὸς τὸ θεῖον ἔφεσις καὶ ἡ περὶ αὐτὸ ὡς περὶ κέντρον κυκλικὴ χορεία. Clem. speaks below (P. 866) of three μεταβολαὶ σωτήριοι (1) from heathenism to faith, (2) from faith to knowledge, (3) from knowledge to love.

p. 18, line 3. καθ' ἑκάστην, feminine to suit περιτροπαί, as in Plato *Tim.* 83 D πομφολύγων ξυστασῶν καθ' ἑκάστην μὲν ἀοράτων διὰ σμικρότητα, ξυναπασῶν δὲ τὸν ὄγκον παρεχομένων ὁρατόν.

ἑκάστη. Potter explains the genitive of the MS. as referring to μεταβολῆς (Lowth having proposed ἑκάστοις): but it is more likely a corruption of ἑκάστη, sc. περιτροπή. H.

4. ἐπαναβεβηκυίας, 'supreme,' so used of γένος, κριτήριον, τρόποι, μονάς in Sext. Empir. (*P. H.* 160). Stephanus cites 'Diosc. 7' ἐπαναβεβηκυῖα καὶ καθολικὴ αἰτία. Orig. *Mt.* tom. x. § 14 (III. 458 R.) ἐπαναβεβηκότως νοηθέν. Also Clem. *Str.* IV. P. 626 med. ἡ ἐπαναβεβηκυῖα τῆς πίστεως ἰδιότης. H. Below p. 80. 19.

5. θεωρίας. 'Contemplation of the Lord.' προσεχοῦς put where it is because it means closeness to the Lord, though expressed absolutely. Otherwise we should have τῷ κυρίῳ, as in the kindred passage 886 init. H. L. and S. quote exx. of the genitive from Dion. H. and Pausan., and another is given in the note on p. 20. 9 below. I prefer therefore to take θεωρίας after ἰδιότητι and understand περιτροπῆς with προσεχοῦς. [Cf. Eus. *Pr. Ev.* IV. 1 *pr.* τὸ ἱστορικόν, ὃ δὴ μυθικὸν ἀποκαλοῦσι, καὶ τὸ ἐπαναβεβηκὸς τοὺς μύθους, ὃ δὴ φυσικὸν ἢ θεωρητικόν. Gifford.]

ἀγωγόν may possibly come from Plat. *Rep.* VII. 525 B ταῦτα δέ γε φαίνεται ἀγωγὰ πρὸς ἀλήθειαν; and τὸ ἐραστόν more probably from *Symp.* 204 C καὶ γὰρ ἔστι τὸ ἐραστὸν τὸ τῷ ὄντι καλὸν καὶ ἁβρὸν καὶ τέλεον καὶ μακαριστόν. H. Cf. Arist. *Met.* XI. 7, p. 1072 b. 3 κινεῖ (τὸ ὂν καλὸν) ὡς ἐρώμενον, Strom. P. 630 ἀγάπη τοῦ ὄντως (L ὄντος) ἐραστοῦ ἑλκόμενος θεοσεβεῖ, Faye, p. 282.

6, 7. θεωρία here (unlike p. 6. 9) seems used not in its Aristotelian sense, but as 'contemplation,' already with something of the Neo-Platonic tinge (cf. Creuzer on Plot. III. 8 init.). In Plato himself there is no distinct trace of this use of the word, though his use of θεῶμαι paves the way for it. But two places in the *Republic* seem to have given rise to the later use: VI. 486 A, speaking of a soul μελλούσῃ τοῦ ὅλου καὶ παντὸς ἀεὶ ἐπορέξεσθαι θείου τε καὶ ἀνθρωπίνου, he refers to its μεγαλοπρέπεια καὶ θεωρία παντὸς μὲν χρόνου, πάσης δὲ οὐσίας: and in the same vein VII. 517 D to one coming ἀπὸ θείων θεωριῶν ἐπὶ τὰ ἀνθρώπεια. Very possibly there is a secondary reference to the beholding of solemn religious rites, this use of θεωρία being common in Plato. H. For the combination of different datives, τῇ ἀγάπῃ...τῇ θεωρίᾳ, see above on p. 14. 9.

§ 11. 8. ἐντολάς. It seems necessary to omit the following ἃς of the MS. and to take τάς τε προτέρας...πηγῆς as the predicate, what follows being epexegetic. H. In the translation τάς τε προτέρας, τάς τε δευτέρας are taken attributively. They are the two classes of ἐντολαί distinguished at the beginning of § 10, where see notes. The one source of both is the divine love.

10. ὑπεριδών does not seem to be used with the infin. elsewhere, as περιοράω often is.

11. τῆς βαρβάρου φιλοσοφίας, often used of the Christian religion as contained in the Jewish Scriptures; cf. P. 376 σχεδὸν οἱ πάντες ἄνευ τῆς ἐγκυκλίου παιδείας καὶ φιλοσοφίας τῆς Ἑλληνικῆς, οἱ δὲ καὶ ἄνευ γραμμάτων τῇ θείᾳ καὶ βαρβάρῳ κινηθέντες φιλοσοφίᾳ, τὸν περὶ θεοῦ διὰ πίστεως παρειλήφαμεν λόγον, αὐτουργῷ σοφίᾳ πεπαιδευμένοι, and the references in the Index *s.v.*, also Plato *Tim.* 22 cited on p. 4, l. 15.

ἀφηγήσει. See n. on p. 92. 27 below, and Index *s.v.*

13. **συνέκλεισεν τὴν ἀπιστίαν εἰς τὴν παρουσίαν.** C. has in his mind Rom. xi. 32 συνέκλεισεν ὁ θεὸς τοὺς πάντας εἰς ἀπείθειαν ἵνα τοὺς πάντας ἐλεήσῃ, and Gal. iii. 22 (cited in *Strom.* P. 421) συνέκλεισεν ἡ γραφὴ τὰ πάντα ὑπὸ ἁμαρτίαν, but how can it be said that unbelief is shut up to the time of our Lord's earthly life? The passage from Galatians continues ἵνα ἡ ἐπαγγελία ἐκ πίστεως Ἰησοῦ Χριστοῦ δοθῇ τοῖς πιστεύουσι. πρὸ τοῦ δὲ ἐλθεῖν τὴν πίστιν, ὑπὸ νόμον ἐφρουρούμεθα, συγκεκλεισμένοι εἰς τὴν μέλλουσαν πίστιν ἀποκαλυφθῆναι. C. appears to have argued that, if faith was impossible before the coming of Christ, unbelief also must have been impossible, the Jew being saved by obedience to the law, the Greek by his philosophy. We may compare *Str.* VI. P. 823 εἰκότως Ἰουδαίοις μὲν νόμος, Ἕλλησι δὲ φιλοσοφία μέχρι τῆς παρουσίας, ἐντεῦθεν δὲ ἡ κλῆσις ἡ καθολική (the call to believe only came with the founding of the Church), 762 τοῖς κατὰ νόμον δικαίοις ἔλειπεν ἡ πίστις, τοῖς δὲ κατὰ φιλοσοφίαν δικαίοις οὐχ ἡ πίστις μόνον ἡ εἰς τὸν κύριον, ἀλλὰ καὶ τὸ ἀποστῆναι τῆς εἰδωλολατρείας ἔδει.

14. **ὅτι ἀναπολόγητος.** Acts xvii. 30, 31 τοὺς μὲν οὖν χρόνους τῆς ἀγνοίας ὑπεριδὼν ὁ θεὸς τὰ νῦν παραγγέλλει τοῖς ἀνθρώποις πάντας πανταχοῦ μετανοεῖν, now that life and immortality have been brought to light through the Gospel (2 Tim. i. 10).

15. **ἐξ ἑτέρας <ἑτέρους> προκοπῆς.** P. 338 *fin.* αἱ μὲν εἰς δικαιοσύνην ὁδοί, πολυτρόπως σώζοντος τοῦ θεοῦ, πολλαί τε καὶ ποικίλαι.

16. **τὴν διὰ πίστεως τελείωσιν.** See above, p. 14. 19 διὰ πίστεως τελειούμενοι.

17. **προηγούμενον**: usually 'primary' in the sense of importance or independence, but here simply as antecedent in time: so *Str.* II. P. 434 *med.* where it is partly in its special sense of a prior *cause.* H. Cf. P. 331 ἡ φιλοσοφία προηγουμένως τοῖς Ἕλλησιν ἐδόθη πρὶν ἢ τὸν κύριον καλέσαι, 540 γένεσιν καὶ φθορὰν προηγουμένως γίνεσθαι ἀνάγκη μέχρι...ἀποκαταστάσεως.

19. **ὑπερεδίσκευσεν,** a very rare word, elsewhere with accus., but here absolute. H. The form ὑπερδισκέω occurs in the same metaphorical sense Bekker's *Anecd.* 62. 27 πάντας πονηρίᾳ ὑπ. L. and S. compare ὑπερακοντίζω.

20. **τὴν ἐπιτομήν** must be governed by ἑλόμενος and mean 'compendious substance.' His simple faith has enabled him to dispense with the preparation of Greek philosophy. H. For the reading ἐπίτομον given in the text, compare Luc. *Mort. Dial.* VII. 2, p. 357 οὐδὲ σὲ τὴν ἐπίτομον ἐχρῆν τραπέσθαι· ἧκε γὰρ ἄν σοι διὰ τῆς λεωφόρου ἀσφαλέστερον εἰ καὶ ὀλίγῳ βραδύτερον and other exx. in *Index.* σύντομος is similarly used in P. 66 σύντομοι σωτηρίας ὁδοὶ αἱ γραφαί, 103, 865 ἡ πίστις σύντομός ἐστι τῶν κατεπειγόντων γνῶσις. For the thought see P. 376 quoted above on l. 11.

§ 12. 25. **μόνος εἷς**: so Dion. Hal. *Ant.* III. 64 μόνος εἷς ὁ ἀγών.

27. **πρὸς τὴν τοῦ ὅλου σωτηρίαν.** The scope of Divine Providence was much discussed by the Stoics; see Epict. *Diss.* I. 12 and my note on Cic. *N. D.* II. 164.

θεὸς ἀναίτιος, a saying of Plato's, to which constant allusion is made by the Christian Fathers and esp. by Cl. See P. 138 (with Potter's n.), 318, 368, 468, 632, 731 (with P.'s n.), 841.

p. 20, lines 2, 3. Cf. Epict. *Diss.* II. 10. 5 εἰ προῄδει ὁ καλὸς καὶ ἀγαθὸς τὰ ἐσόμενα, συνήργει ἂν καὶ τῷ νοσεῖν καὶ τῷ ἀποθνήσκειν καὶ τῷ πηροῦσθαι, αἰσθανόμενός γε ὅτι ἀπὸ τῆς τῶν ὅλων διατάξεως τοῦτο ἀπονέμεται, κυριώτερον δὲ τὸ ὅλον τοῦ μέρους καὶ ἡ πόλις τοῦ πολίτου.

5. ἀμείνους οἰκήσεις, above, p. 16. 25 f.

7. αὐτοκρατορικήν. P. 434, quoted on p. 16. 19 above. H.

παιδεύσεις...ἀγαθότητι τοῦ...κριτοῦ. See above p. 10. 12, 12. 29 f., below p. 134. 28, 180. 5, also P. 422, 423, 580 τοῦ μετανοοῦντος τρόποι δύο, ὁ μὲν κοινότερος φόβος ἐπὶ τοῖς πραχθεῖσιν, ὁ δὲ ἰδιαίτερος ἡ δυσωπία ἡ πρὸς ἑαυτὴν τῆς ψυχῆς ἐκ συνειδήσεως, εἴτ᾽ οὖν ἐνταῦθα εἴτε καὶ ἀλλαχῇ, ἐπεὶ μηδεὶς τόπος ἀργὸς εὐποιίας θεοῦ, *Ecl. Proph.* P. 996 πῦρ ἦλθον βαλεῖν ἐπὶ τὴν γῆν, δηλονότι δύναμιν τῶν μὲν ἁγίων καθαρτικήν, τῶν δὲ ὑλικῶν, ὡς μὲν ἐκεῖνοί φασιν, ἀφανιστικήν, ὡς δὲ ἡμεῖς ἂν φαίημεν, παιδευτικήν, and compare the remarkable words of the prayer quoted from Chrysostom (*in Col.* 10. 3) by Neander (*Memorials of Chr. Life*, p. 259) εὐχαριστοῦμεν ὑπὲρ πασῶν τῶν εὐεργεσιῶν σου...ὑπὲρ τῶν φανερῶν, ὑπὲρ τῶν ἀφανῶν...τῶν ἑκοντί, τῶν ἀκοντί...ὑπὲρ θλίψεων, ὑπὲρ ἀνέσεων, ὑπὲρ τῆς γεέννης, ὑπὲρ τῆς κολάσεως, ὑπὲρ βασιλείας τῶν οὐρανῶν.

9. προσεχῶν might mean 'heedful,' 'watchful' (as in Hippol. *Prov.* p. 616 B, Migne, it is used of 'attentive' hearers, though προσεκτικός is more commonly found in this sense). But in *Ecl. Proph.* 51 (P. 1001) it is used of the angels next to the πρωτόκτιστοι, and of the next rank generally; also (if not corrupt) of those in immediate attendance on the prophets, τοὺς προσεχεῖς τοῖς προφήταις ἀγγέλους. So also Julian (*Cyr.* 96 B) uses the phrase τὸν προσεχῆ τοῦ κόσμου τούτου of the Creator, as being in close proximity to the creation, in contradistinction to the supreme God; and so Cyril. H. In *Ecl. Proph.* 56 (P. 1003) the πρωτόκτιστοι are said to be enjoying ἀνάπαυσις, relieved from all other service and engaged in μόνῃ τῇ θεωρίᾳ τοῦ θεοῦ, οἱ δὲ προσεχέστεροι τούτοις (those next below them) προκόψουσιν εἰς ἣν ἐκεῖνοι ἀπολελοίπασι τάξιν, καὶ οὕτως οἱ ὑποβεβηκότες ἀναλόγως. In the *Adumbr.* P. 1008 προσεχής is translated by *propinquus nobis angelus*, in 1009 by *vicinus et infimus*. See also P. 824 δι᾽ ἀγγέλων ἡ θεία δύναμις παρέχει τὰ ἀγαθά...πᾶσα ὠφέλεια βιωτικὴ κατὰ μὲν τὸν ἀνωτάτω λόγον ἀπὸ τοῦ παντοκράτορος θεοῦ...δι᾽ υἱοῦ ἐπιτελεῖται...κατὰ δὲ τὸ προσεχὲς ὑπὸ τῶν προσεχῶν ἑκάστοις κατὰ τὴν τοῦ προσεχοῦς τῷ πρώτῳ αἰτίῳ κυρίου ἐπίταξιν.

προκρίσεων. *Ecl. Proph.* 40, P. 999 *fin.* καλὴ ἡ κρίσις τοῦ θεοῦ, ἥ τε διάκρισις ἡ τῶν πιστῶν ἀπὸ τῶν ἀπίστων, ἥ τε πρόκρισις ὑπὲρ τοῦ μὴ μείζονι περιπεσεῖν κρίσει, ἥ τε κρίσις παίδευσις οὖσα. H. Cf. also P. 895, 1007 *praecedentia iudicia* (*bis*), and the parallel passage below, p. 180. 5 f. For the punitive action of angels see P. 700, where the ἄνδρες διάπυροι of Plato *Rep.* p. 615 are explained to be angels οἱ παραλαβόντες τοὺς ἀδίκους κολάζουσιν.

§ 13. 12. τὰ δ' ἄλλα σιγῶ, 'I will not dilate on the economy of punishment leading to universal salvation.' See below p. 154. 17 f., where there is the same breaking off (οὐ γὰρ ἐκκυκλεῖν χρὴ τὸ μυστήριον) in the midst of his description of future blessedness, also P. 324.

πλὴν κ.τ.λ. Resumption of the digression beginning § 5 *post init.* H. Or is it rather an exception to the statement τὰ δ' ἄλλα σιγῶ?

14. ὑπερβαινούσας τὴν πολιτείαν. It is strange to find this sort of πλεονεξία attributed to the gnostic souls. Is there any allusion to Mt. xi. 12, 'the violent take it by force,' or to the μανία of the *Phaedrus* 245? We may compare P. 696 τὸ ἐν ἡμῖν αὐτεξούσιον, εἰς γνῶσιν ἀφικόμενον τἀγαθοῦ, σκιρτᾷ τε καὶ πηδᾷ ὑπὲρ τὰ ἐσκαμμένα, ᾗ φασιν οἱ γυμνασταί, πλὴν οὐ χάριτος ἄνευ τῆς ἐξαιρέτου πτεροῦταί τε καὶ ἄνω τῶν ὑπερκειμένων αἴρεται ἡ ψυχή. This may be explained by P. 1004, where it is said that the perfected saints are admitted to the highest angelic orders. See above p. 16. 28, 18. 3 f.

15. αἱ μακάριαι θεῶν οἰκήσεις. Cf. Plat. *Phaedr.* 246 D ἄνω...ᾗ τὸ τῶν θεῶν γένος οἰκεῖ. What follows is evidently full of reminiscences of this part of the *Phaedrus* (245 foll.); e.g. ἑστιωμένας, θέαν, καρπουμένας (often in Plato with ἡδόνην). H. For θεῶν cf. below, p. 98. 10, 18 f. and P. 697.

16. ἁγίας ἐν ἁγίοις. The same phrase occurs below § 56 κἂν ἁγία ᾖ καὶ ἐν ἁγίοις ἡ λειτουργία, Isa. lvii. 15 ἅγιος ἐν ἁγίοις ὄνομα αὐτῷ; cf. the frequent ἅγιος ἁγίων Exod. xxx. 10, xxvi. 34.

17. ἀμείνους ἀμεινόνων τόπων τόπους. Cf. below p. 22. 29 εἰς τὸ ἀνενδεὲς ἐκ τοῦ ἀνενδεοῦς.

18. διὰ κατόπτρων. See Wetst. on 1 Cor. xiii. 12, Ps.-Cypr. *De duobus montibus* (ap. Resch *Agr.* p. 221), Christum in nobis tamquam in speculo videmus, ipso nos instruente et monente in epistola Johannis discipuli sui ad populum : 'ita me in vobis videte, quomodo quis vestrum se videt in aquam aut in speculum.' Plato illustrates the difference between opinion and knowledge, and between the mediate and immediate knowledge of Absolute Good, by contrasting the sight of the sun himself with the sight of his image in a mirror or in water (*Rep.* 510 A, 516 A); and so Dion. Ar. compares the different ranks of the heavenly hierarchy to mirrors receiving light from above and reflecting it in turn to the rank which follows (*Cael. Hier.* III. 2). Possibly Cl. may have some such idea in his mind, when he speaks of the gnostic souls moving to higher and yet higher regions until at last they come into the very presence of God, and are thus made equal to the Seraphim, whom Dion. affirms ἀμέσως ἡνῶσθαι with the Divinity (*ib.* VI. 2).

23. ταυτότητι τῆς ὑπεροχῆς. But how does this agree with the diversity of μοναί and the different degrees of moral progress? Do the gnostics all belong to one μονή? Perhaps ταυτότης should be rather taken as equivalent to πάντῃ πάντως ἄτρεπτον in p. 100. 17, cf. p. 24. 25 θεὸν τὸν ἐν ταυτότητι ὄντα. But elsewhere Cl. contemplates an eternity of progress.

25. The καταληπτικὴ φαντασία of the Stoics was an impression carrying with it a clear conception, the ἀκατάληπτος φ. being μὴ τρανὴς μηδὲ ἔκτυπος.

Clem. substitutes θεωρία. H. See below p. 160. 8, Zeller³ IV. 83 and Upton's Index to Epict. s.v. The vision of God, granted to the pure in heart, is no illusion, but carries conviction with it. 'Scribendum ἡ καταληπτική (pro καταληπτή) θεωρία. Sic μεθεκτοί pro μεθεκτικοὶ superius positum *Strom.* I. p. 348, ἐφεκτοί pro ἐφεκτικοί *Strom.* VIII. p. 924, διδακτικήν pro διδακτήν *Strom.* I. p. 334.' Potter.

27. ἀρχιερέως. Cf. above p. 16. 5, *Str.* P. 633 init., Philo M. I. p. 653 δύο ἱερά θεοῦ, ἐν μὲν ὅδε ὁ κόσμος, ἐν ᾧ καὶ ἀρχιερεὺς ὁ πρωτόγονος αὐτοῦ θεῖος λόγος (called in 654 ὁ μέγας ἀρχ.), ἕτερον δὲ λογικὴ ψυχή, ἧς ἱερεὺς ὁ πρὸς ἀλήθειαν ἄνθρωπος, and Lightfoot on Clem. R. I. 36, Ign. *Phil.* 9 (vol. II. 274 f.).

28. τῆς εἰς τὸν θεὸν θεραπείας. See above § 3.

p. 22, line 1. κηδεμονίαν implies unflinching care, as of a father, not mere indulgence: so *Paed.* I. P. 142 οὐδὲ ἀλλότριον τοῦ σωτηρίου λόγου κηδεμονικῶς λοιδορεῖσθαι: cf. P. 143 (§ 76 init.) νουθέτησίς ἐστι ψόγος κηδεμονικός, νοῦ ἐμποιητικός. H. Also P. 548 τὴν τοῦ οἴκου κηδεμονίαν.

2. τῆς εἰς ἡμᾶς εὐεργεσίας. Clement puts himself on a level with the ordinary believer both here and below p. 24. 29.

τὴν λειτουργίαν. See Lightfoot on Philipp. ii. 17. It is used of public worship, *Paed.* II. P. 193 τὴν λειτουργίαν τὴν θεϊκὴν διαχωρίζον ψάλλει τὸ πνεῦμα 'αἰνεῖτε αὐτῷ ἐν ἤχῳ σάλπιγγος,' of service in general P. 546 ἔχει καὶ ὁ γάμος ἰδίας λειτουργίας καὶ διακονίας τῷ κυρίῳ διαφερούσας, τέκνων λέγω κήδεσθαι, κ.τ.λ., P. 548 τῇ οἰκονομίᾳ πειθόμενος εὐαρέστως, καθ' ἣν ἀπερίσπαστος τῆς τοῦ κυρίου γέγονε λειτουργίας, P. 838 ἣν δύναμιν καὶ ἣν λειτουργίαν εἰσφέρεται; cf. P. 755 and 822 cited above on περιγείων p. 6. 7. On the particulars of this service, see P. 824 θεόθεν λαβὼν τὸ δύνασθαι ὠφελεῖν κ.τ.λ. As it is distinguished from διδασκαλία and εὐποιία, it seems best to take it of worship in this passage, and so probably in 865 τῆς γνωστικῆς ψυχῆς ἡ τελείωσις πάσας καθάρσεις καὶ λειτουργίας ὑπερβᾶσαν σὺν τῷ κυρίῳ γίνεσθαι.

4, 5. ἑαυτὸν κτίζει...ἐξομοιούμενος. Cf. P. 633 θεὸν ὁ θεραπεύων ἑαυτὸν θεραπεύει· ἐν οὖν τῷ θεωρητικῷ βίῳ ἑαυτοῦ τις ἐπιμελεῖται θρησκεύων τὸν θεόν κ.τ.λ. On ἐξομοιούμενος see above p. 6. 23, and cf. Plato *Tim.* 90 D, Faye p. 266.

6. τὸ ἐξ ἀσκήσεως εἰς ἀπάθειαν συνεσταλμένον. See above p. 12. 25 τὴν σάρκα τὴν ἐμπαθῆ φύσει γενομένην εἰς ἕξιν ἀπαθείας ἐπαίδευσεν, p. 16. 28, and below P. 859 τῷ ἀναπόβλητον τὴν ἀρετὴν ἀσκήσει γνωστικῇ πεποιημένῳ φυσιοῦται ἡ ἕξις, *Str.* VI. P. 777 f., also Cognat's *Clement* lib. IV. ch. 7. The Stoics made the same distinction between virtue, innate in God, acquired in man, see Cic. *N. D.* II. § 34 with my notes.

7. εἰς ἀπάθειαν συνεσταλμένον. Plut. *Vit.* 809 συστελλόμενοι ὑπ' ἀνάγκης εἰς τὴν Λακωνικὴν δίαιταν ('like a weaned child').

8. ἀπερισπάστως. 1 Cor. vii. 35 πρὸς τὸ εὔσχημον καὶ εὐπάρεδρον τῷ κυρίῳ ἀπερισπάστως.

9. ἡμερότης. P. 858 the gnostic is described as ἥμερος καὶ πρᾷος.

Plato speaks of this quality as necessary in the Guardians of his Ideal State (*Rep.* 410 D).

10. μεγαλοπρεπὴς θεοσέβεια. The same epithet is used with γνῶσις P. 646, with νόησις P. 798, with ἀρετή Xen. *Mem.* I. 2. 64. So we have μεγαλοπρέπεια τοῦ λόγου P. 862, μ. σοφίας P. 897.

§ 14. 12, 13. τὴν ἄτυφον καρδίαν...ὁλοκάρπωμα. Ps. li. 17 θυσία τῷ θεῷ πνεῦμα συντετριμμένον, καρδίαν...τεταπεινωμένην ὁ θεὸς οὐκ ἐξουδενώσει. ὁλοκάρπωμα and ὁλοκαύτωμα (Ps. li. 16) are used in the LXX for the same Hebrew word, see *Index*, and Lightfoot on *Mart. Pol.* 14 (Ign. vol. II. p. 970).

13, 14. ἐκφωτιζομένου εἰς ἕνωσιν. The word φωτισμὸς was commonly used for baptism, see P. 113 βαπτιζόμενοι φωτιζόμεθα, φωτιζόμενοι υἱοποιούμεθα, υἱοποιούμενοι τελειούμεθα, τελειούμενοι ἀπαθανατιζόμεθα, and just below καλεῖται δὲ τὸ ἔργον τοῦτο φώτισμα, δι' οὗ τὸ ἅγιον ἐκεῖνο φῶς τὸ σωτήριον ἐποπτεύεται, cf. Hebr. vi. 4, x. 32. The rare compound ἐκφ. is found in P. 663 πᾶσα ἡ νὺξ ἐκφωτίζεται τῷ τοῦ νοητοῦ φωτὸς ἡλίῳ. Dr Gifford supplies me with another example from Plut. *Mor.* 922 E φωτὸς ἂν ἐπιψαύσῃ μόνον...ὁ ἀὴρ διόλου τρεπόμενος ἐκφωτίζεται. 'Baptized into unity,' i.e. 'made a member of Christ.' Cf. P. 72 σπεύσωμεν εἰς σωτηρίαν, ἐπὶ τὴν παλιγγενεσίαν, εἰς μίαν ἀγάπην συναχθῆναι οἱ πολλοί, κατὰ τὴν τῆς μοναδικῆς οὐσίας ἕνωσιν σπεύσωμεν ἀγαθοεργούμενοι, ἀναλόγως ἑνότητα διώκωμεν, τὴν ἀγαθὴν ἐκζητοῦντες μονάδα. ἡ δὲ ἐκ πολλῶν ἕνωσις ἐκ πολυφωνίας καὶ διασπορᾶς ἁρμονίαν λαβοῦσα θεϊκὴν μία γίνεται συμφωνία, P. 792 φῶς ἡνωμένον ψυχῇ δι' ἀγάπης ἀδιαστάτου, Lightfoot on Ign. *Magn.* 1 (vol. II. p. 108) ἕνωσιν εὔχομαι σαρκὸς καὶ πνεύματος Ἰ. Χρ.

14. ἀδιάκριτον. In his excellent note on this word, Lightfoot (Ign. II. p. 39) quotes Arist. *de Somn.* 3 διὰ δὲ τὸ γίνεσθαι ἀδιακριτώτερον τὸ αἷμα μετὰ τὴν τῆς τροφῆς προσφορὰν ὁ ὕπνος γίνεται, ἕως ἂν διακριθῇ τοῦ αἵματος τὸ μὲν καθαρώτερον εἰς τὰ ἄνω, τὸ δὲ θολερώτερον εἰς τὰ κάτω, for the sense 'inseparable.'

18. τῆς παλαιᾶς διαστροφῆς. Cf. ἡ διαστροφή absolute in Orig. *Cels.* III. 40 ἡ διαστροφὴ δεδύνηται τοῖς πολλοῖς ἐμφυτεῦσαι τὸν περὶ ἀγαλμάτων λόγον ὡς θεῶν. H. Lk ix. 41 γενεὰ διεστραμμένη, Eph. iv. 22 ἀποθέσθαι κατὰ τὴν προτέραν ἀναστροφὴν τὸν παλαιὸν ἄνθρωπον, P. 896 *init.* οὓς ἐλεήσειεν ἄν τις τῆς τοιαύτης διαστροφῆς, Epict. *Diss.* III. 6. 8 οἱ μὴ διεστραμμένοι τῶν ἀνθρώπων. Dr Gifford compares Eus. *Pr. Ev.* IV. 21 *fin.* where Porphyry is cited as holding that the daemons were the ultimate causes τῆς τοῦ πλήθους διαστροφῆς.

19. τό τι εὐαγγέλιον ὅ τι ἀπόστολος. See Lightfoot, Ign. vol. II. p. 260 f., *Strom.* VI. P. 784, Westcott, *Bible in the Church*, p. 126.

20. ἀναμαρτήτους. Cf. P. 770 and 776, below p. 94. 12, 138. 29, and on the other hand *Paed.* III. P. 307 μόνος ἀναμάρτητος αὐτὸς ὁ λόγος· τὸ γὰρ ἐξαμαρτάνειν πᾶσιν ἔμφυτον καὶ κοινόν, *ib.* I. P. 99.

21. τοῦτ' ἦν ὃ ᾐνίσσετο ὁ νόμος. Ezek. xviii. 4, cf. *Strom.* II. P. 507 ὁ νόμος πρὸς ἀναστολὴν τῆς εὐεπιφορίας τῶν παθῶν ἀναιρεῖσθαι προστάττει τὴν

μοιχευθεῖσαν...οὐ δὴ μάχεται τῷ εὐαγγελίῳ ὁ νόμος...ἡ γάρ τοι πορνεύσασα ζῇ μὲν τῇ ἁμαρτίᾳ, ἀπέθανεν δὲ ταῖς ἐντολαῖς, ἡ δὲ μετανοήσασα οἷον ἀναγεννηθεῖσα...παλιγγενεσίαν ἔχει ζωῆς κ.τ.λ., also P. 100 init., Jos. Ap. II. 30 ζημία ἐστι τοῖς πλείστοις τῶν παραβαινόντων ὁ θάνατος.

23. ἀπάθειαν. See above, l. 7.

24. νομοδιδάσκαλοι. See 1 Tim. i. 6, 7, explained by Baur of Marcion, more probably to be understood of the rabbinical interpreters.

φιλόνεικον. Cf. Plat. *Lys.* 215 D, Plut. *Mor.* 91, 92, where φιλονεικία is joined with φθόνος and similar words. For a defence of the Law see *Strom.* I. 422 μὴ τοίνυν καταπρεχέτω τις τοῦ νόμου διὰ τὰς τιμωρίας ὡς οὐ καλοῦ κἀγαθοῦ, P. 445 f., 449 (against Marcion), 492, esp. 548 f. (against Tatian), 567 f., *Paed.* I. P. 135 foll., below p. 70. 22 n. on καταδρομή, also Epiphan. *Haer.* XXXIII. 10 (against the gnostic Ptolemaeus) ἑάλως συκοφαντῶν τὸν νόμον...διὰ τὸ εἰρηκέναι Ὀφθαλμὸν ἀντὶ ὀφθαλμοῦ, καὶ ἐπειδὴ φονεύει ὁ νόμος τὸν φονευτήν, Theoph. *Aut.* II. 25 οὐχ ὡς φθονῶν ὁ θεός, ὡς οἴονταί τινες, ἐκέλευσεν μὴ ἐσθίειν ἀπὸ τῆς γνώσεως.

25. τοῖς μάτην διαβάλλειν ἐπιχειροῦσι. The reference is to men like Marcion, who contrasted the *good* God of the N.T. with the *just* God of the O.T. Clement, like Philo, tries in vain to get rid of the opposition by applying the principle of allegory, used by the Stoics in their interpretation of the Greek mythology. The true explanation is to be found in the idea of development as exhibited, for instance, in J. B. Mozley's *Lectures*.

26. οὐ θύομεν. Cl. here returns to the subject of § 2. The absence of outward sacrifices is no proof of atheism. Cf. below § 34, Ps. l. 8—14.

28. ἱερευθέντα. Used by Origen in the sense 'to offer as a victim,' by Philo of simple slaughter (*de Abr.* 40, M. II. 34). Here distinguished from θύομεν, as by Plut. II. 729 c ἰχθύων δὲ θύσιμος οὐδεὶς οὐδὲ ἱερεύσιμός ἐστιν, so that it seems to be a rather weaker word. **H.**

29. ἐκ τοῦ (repeated) seems to mean the foundation made by Christ's sacrifice; **εἰς τὸ** (repeated) the resulting state of self-sacrifice on the part of the believer. **H.** In the translation it is taken, like ἐκ δυνάμεως εἰς δύναμιν Ps. lxxxiii. 7, ἀπὸ δόξης εἰς δόξαν 2 Cor. iii. 18, Rom. i. 17 ἐκ πίστεως εἰς πίστιν (explained by Cl. in *Str.* v. P. 644), of the transition from a lower to a higher stage, below § 55 (p. 96. 24) ἐκ φωτὸς εἰς φῶς.

p. 24, line 4. **μακράν.** With genit. 'distant from,' not common. **H.** L. and S. cite as instances of this use Eur. *Iph. T.* 629, Polyb. 3. 50. 8. Cl. has it in *Str.* I. P. 341, μακρὰν τῆς ἐκείνων διαθέσεως.

τῆς διὰ τοῦ καπνοῦ ἀναθυμιάσεως. If we distinguish between these, ἀν. would be the fumes arising from the sacrifice, κ. the smoke of the burning wood through which they ascend. ἀναθ. was divided into two kinds ἡ μὲν ὑγρά, ἀτμιώδης, ἡ δὲ ξηρά, καπνώδης, Arist. *Meteor.* II. 3 (357 b. 24).

5. εἰς οὓς καὶ φθάνει. An allusion to demons, and their supposed delight in the reek of burnt offerings. Cf. the brief reference to the devil above p. 12. 13. **H.** See also § 31 below, and Porphyry quoted there. This use of φθάνω is found in N.T.

12. τοις καλοίς κἀγαθοίς φαίνεται. Cf. Joh. xiv. 21 ἐγὼ ἀγαπήσω αὐτὸν καὶ ἐμφανίσω αὐτῷ ἐμαυτόν, and the appearances to the patriarchs in the O.T. So Orig. c. Cels. IV. 16 ἑκάστῳ τῶν εἰς ἐπιστήμην ἀγομένων φαίνεται ὁ λόγος ἀνάλογον τῇ ἕξει τοῦ εἰσαγομένου.

§ 15. 14—26. Copied from Plato, *Leg.* x. 885, where it is said that all impiety may be traced to one of three opinions about the divine nature, either the denial of the existence of the Gods, or τὸ δεύτερον, ὄντας οὐ φροντίζειν ἀνθρώπων· ἢ τρίτον, θυσίαις τε καὶ εὐχαῖς παραγομένους. (Potter.)

14. τὸ αὐθαίρετον. See above p. 16. 19 n. and 19. 22. Faith is defined as ψυχῆς αὐτεξουσίου λογικὴ συγκατάθεσις P. 645.

17. Contrast with l. 22. *Here* other cause of same opinion, *there* other opinion. H.

18. οἱ...περιπίπτοντες...οὔ φασιν. The following participle naturally led to the substitution of the article for the relative. Compare for a similar collocation P. 889 πανοῦργοι οἱ παρακολουθοῦντες...σκοτίζουσι τὴν ἀλήθειαν, 567 τέταται ἡ ψυχὴ πρὸς τὸν θεόν, ἥ γε, διὰ φιλοσοφίας παιδευομένη, πρὸς τοὺς ἄνω σπεύδει συγγενεῖς. Mr Barnard would prefer to keep the article and put a colon after περιπίπτοντες, thus making the sentence parallel to that which follows. I think however that it is more natural to regard λύπαις καὶ τύχαις περιπίπτοντες as the 1st step, and ἀπαυδῶντες as the 2nd step leading to atheism. He suggests that καὶ should be omitted after ἀκρασίᾳ (as caused by dittography of ιαι), and this certainly makes it easier to separate between ἀκρασίᾳ and the following datives.

τῇ τῶν ἡδονῶν ἀκρασίᾳ. One's first impulse is to regard this dative as governed by περιπίπτοντες, like those which follow; but it is not like Clement to treat incontinence as a misfortune into which we fall. I think therefore it is better to regard it as a causal dative. For the combination of dissimilar datives see Eus. *Pr. Ev.* VII. 2, p. 299 b μόνῃ τῇ τῶν σωμάτων προσανασχόντες αἰσθήσει τῷ μηδὲν περὶ τῆς ἐν αὐτοῖς ψυχῆς διειληφέναι '*because* they had formed no clear conception of the soul.' Cf. n. on p. 14. 9.

19. ἀβουλήτοις. Cf. v. 663 *fin.* ὀδύναις ἐπὶ τοῖς ἀβουλήτως συμβαίνουσιν. H. See Dion. H. *Ant. Rom.* v. 74 οὐ μόνον ἐν ταῖς ἀβουλήτοις συμφοραῖς ἀλλὰ κἂν ταῖς ὑπερβαλλούσαις εὐτυχίαις, Plut. *Mor.* 90 A πράγμασιν ἀβουλήτοις περιπεσόντες διδάσκονται τὸ χρήσιμον, where Wytt. translates 'ingratum, calamitas, quod nolumus et aversamur,' and gives many exx. from later Greek. It is used in a different sense below p. 26. 3.

20. πρὸς τὰς συμφορὰς ἀπαυδῶντες. ἀπαυδάω, 'to lose the power of speech,' and so all other power: said even of plants. H. Cf. Plut. *Mor.* 438 D ἀπαυδᾶν πρὸς τὸ ἀΐδιον, so ἀπαγορεύω Eus. *Pr. Ev.* VIII. 14. 23 πρὸς τὸ ὑπολειπόμενον ὕψος ἀπειρηκότες.

22. παραιτητοὺς εἶναι θυσίαις. Cf. Plato *Rep.* II. 365 foll. and *Legg.* x. 905 foll. τὸ δὲ παραιτητοὺς αὖ τοὺς θεοὺς εἶναι τοῖς ἀδικοῦσιν, δεχομένους δῶρα, οὔτε τινὶ συγχωρητέον κ.τ.λ.

23. συναιρομένους, 'becoming accomplices in,' used of all help to a person, but esp. in a conspiracy or a crime. H.

24. οὐδ' ἐθέλουσι, 'have even no desire.' H. As ἐθέλω is the usual form in Clement, it seems better to divide as above, rather than οὐδὲ θ. as in L.

25. ταυτότης opposed to fickleness involved in παραιτητούς. H. See above p. 20. 23 ταυτότητι τῆς ὑπεροχῆς, which perhaps would be better translated 'with an unchanging preeminence'; also P. 973 ὁ λόγος σὰρξ ἐγένετο...ἐν ἀρχῇ ὁ ἐν ταυτότητι λόγος κατὰ περιγραφὴν καὶ οὐ κατ' οὐσίαν γενόμενος.

τῆς δικαίας ἀγαθωσύνης. The combination of the two complementary virtues of justice and goodness. H. These had been opposed to one another by Marcion, see n. on p. 22. 24, and compare *Paed.* I. P. 150 ἀγαθὸς μὲν ὁ θεὸς δι' ἑαυτόν, δίκαιος δὲ ἤδη δι' ἡμᾶς, καὶ τοῦτο ὅτι ἀγαθός.

§ 16. 27, 28. πρῶτον ἑαυτοῦ...ἔπειτα τῶν πλησίον. See above p. 5. 27 f., and p. 22. 1. As in the latter passage, so here Cl. identifies himself with the objects of the gnostic's care (γενώμεθα l. 29).

p. 26, lines 2, 3. ὕλης ἀσθένειαν. *Str.* III. P. 515 οἱ ἀπὸ Μαρκίωνος κακὴν τὴν γένεσιν ὑπειλήφεσαν...φύσιν κακὴν ἔκ τε ὕλης κακῆς καὶ ἐκ δικαίου γενομένην δημιουργοῦ, Philo M. I. p. 495, ἐπῄνεσε δὲ ὁ θεὸς οὐ τὴν δημιουργηθεῖσαν ὕλην, τὴν ἄψυχον καὶ πλημμελῆ καὶ διαλυτόν...ἀλλὰ τὰ ἑαυτοῦ τεχνικὰ ἔργα. The derivation of evil from matter is ascribed by Aristotle (*Metaph.* I. 6) to Plato. It was the doctrine of most of the gnostic sects (Iren. I. p. 915 Stieren, of Valentinus). In man ὕλη is represented by the body, which may explain ἀσθένεια. The contrary doctrine was held by Cl. *Str.* IV. P. 639 οὔτε ἀγαθὸν ἡ ψυχὴ φύσει οὔτε αὖ κακὸν φύσει τὸ σῶμα, and Orig. *Cels.* IV. 66 τὴν ὕλην...τοῖς θνητοῖς ἐμπολιτευομένην αἰτίαν εἶναι τῶν κακῶν, καθ' ἡμᾶς οὐκ ἀληθές· τὸ γὰρ ἑκάστου ἡγεμονικὸν αἴτιον τῆς ὑποστάσης ἐν αὐτῷ κακίας ἐστίν, ἥτις ἐστὶ τὸ κακόν.

3. ἀβουλήτους, 'purposeless.' H. Cf. Joseph. *Ap.* II. 23 οὐκ ἂν ὑπέστη τι τῶν ὄντων ἀβουλήτως ἔχοντος τοῦ θεοῦ, εἰ δὲ βουλομένου, θεόθεν ἡ φιλοσοφία, and for a different use p. 24. 19 above.

4. ἀλόγους ἀνάγκας. Cf. Plato *Leg.* XII. 967 A (it is commonly thought that men of science are atheists) καθεορακότας γιγνόμενα ἀνάγκαις πράγματ' ἀλλ' οὐ διανοίαις βουλήσεως.

4, 5. ὑπεράνω ὤν. Cf. below, p. 30. 3 ὑπ. πάντων τῶν περιστατικῶν γενόμενος, Ael. *V. H.* IX. 7 Σωκράτης ἦν λύπης ὑπεράνω πάσης.

7, 8. κἄν...κατασταίη. For the use of the optative with κἄν or ἐάν in late Greek see Schmid *Atticismus* I. 244, II. 59, IV. 90, 620.

11. ἐγγραφομένῃ. Cf. *Str.* I. P. 320 fin. ἀλλ' οὐδὲ ἀντιμισθίας ἐφίεσθαι χρὴ τῷ εἰς ἄνδρας ἐγγραφομένῳ, Heb. xii. 23 πρωτοτόκων ἐν οὐρανοῖς ἀπογεγραμμένων. H. See Segaar, n. on *Q. D. S.* 947 P. (D. III. p. 399. 26) τοῖς ἐν οὐρανοῖς ἐγγραφησομένοις. Properly 'to register amongst,' then 'to class as, or under.' H. J. compares for the sentiment Plato *Prot.* 324 B ἀποτροπῆς ἕνεκα κολάζει and Arist. *N. Eth.* II. 3 § 4 αἱ κολάσεις ἰατρεῖαί εἰσιν.

12. ἄγαλμα. *Protr.* P. 78 fin. ὁ τῶν ὅλων δημιουργός, ὁ ἀριστοτέχνας πατήρ, τοιοῦτον ἄγαλμα ἔμψυχον τὸν ἄνθρωπον ἔπλασεν, *Ecl. Proph.* P. 999 ἄγαλμα θεῖον τὸν ἄνθρωπον παρασκευάζουσα ἡ ἀρετή, Hierocl. *in Carm. Aur.*

1. p. 421 Didot, ἄγ. θ. τεκταίνει τὴν ἑαυτοῦ ψυχήν, below p. 48. 16, 92. 4, 13.

14. ἐνιδρύεται, see n. on ἐνιδρύσει, below, p. 46. 19, § 28 f.

16. θεσμός, a Stoic name for God; cf. Cic. *N. D.* I. 36.

20. **ἐναποσφραγιζόμενος**. *Protr.* P. 84 καλὸς ὕμνος τοῦ θεοῦ ἀθάνατος ἄνθρωπος...ἐν ᾧ τὰ λόγια τῆς ἀληθείας ἐγκεχάρακται...ταύτας οἶμαι τὰς θείας γραφὰς ἐναποσφραγισαμένους χρὴ τῇ ψυχῇ κ.τ.λ., 'impressing the stamp.' H.

τὴν τελείαν θεωρίαν. Above, p. 20. 19, οὐκ ἐν κατόπτροις ἔτι τὴν θεωρίαν ἀσπαζόμεναι τὴν θείαν.

21. **κατ' εἰκόνα**. See *Protr.* P. 78 *fin.* εἰκὼν τοῦ θεοῦ ὁ λόγος αὐτοῦ ...εἰκὼν δὲ τοῦ λόγου ὁ ἄνθρωπος <ὁ> ἀληθινός, ὁ νοῦς ὁ ἐν ἀνθρώπῳ, ὁ κατ' εἰκόνα τοῦ θεοῦ καὶ καθ' ὁμοίωσιν διὰ τοῦτο γεγενῆσθαι λεγόμενος, with Potter's n., *Str.* v. P. 703 εἰκὼν θεοῦ λόγος θεῖος καὶ βασιλικός, ἄνθρωπος ἀπαθής, εἰκὼν δ' εἰκόνος ἀνθρώπινος νοῦς. Cl. distinguishes between the εἰκών, in which man is born, and the ὁμοίωσις, which is gradually formed within him as he grows in grace, see Kaye, p. 134 f.

22. **τὴν ὅση δύναμις ἐξομοιουμένην**. See Index *s.v.* ὅσος.

τὸ δεύτερον αἴτιον. See the fuller description from St John in p. 28. 3 (there opposed to τὸ πρῶτον αἴτιον). H. *Str.* P. 779 quoted below on ἔχει p. 28. 2, P. 824 quoted on προσεχῶν p. 20. 9, Euseb. *Pr. Ev.* XI. 18 (p. 140 Hein.) περὶ τοῦ πῶς ἀπὸ τοῦ πρώτου αἰτίου τὸ δεύτερον ὑπέστη, τοιάδε φησὶν (Νουμήνιος), κ.τ.λ., *ib.* VII. 12 περὶ τῆς τοῦ δευτέρου αἰτίου θεολογίας.

24. **ἀπογράφοντες** requires the sense 'copying,' which belongs only to the middle (Hein. on Eus. *H. E.* 112 § 4 defends the sense, but without examples, and his text requires only 'record'). It seems therefore necessary to write ὑπογράφοντες, 'depicting in outline Him who is made to us a Gnostic by ourselves (reading ἀναστρεφόμενοι) living, &c.' This is the idea suggested by p. 28, l. 3 foll. The use of ὑπογράφειν probably suggests that the image is for others to see: cf. p. 24. 28 foll. H. For the MS. γνωστικόν (which seems to me barely intelligible—how can it be said that 'Christ *is made to us* a gnostic'?) I read γνῶσιν, referring to 1 Cor. i. 30 ἐν Χριστῷ Ἰησοῦ ὃς ἐγενήθη ἡμῖν σοφία ἀπὸ θεοῦ. Cf. *Str.* P. 635 ὁ υἱὸς σοφία τέ ἐστι καὶ ἐπιστήμη καὶ ἀλήθεια, καὶ ὅσα ἄλλα τούτῳ συγγενῆ, P. 737 *fin.* ἡ γνῶσις δὲ ἡμῶν καὶ ὁ παράδεισος ὁ πνευματικὸς αὐτὸς ἡμῶν ὁ σωτὴρ ὑπάρχει foll., P. 771 *init.*, Ign. *Eph.* λαβόντες θεοῦ γνῶσιν, ὅ ἐστιν Ἰησοῦς Χριστός. For ὑπογράφοντες cf. 2 Cor. iii. 3 ἐστὲ ἐπιστολὴ Χριστοῦ...ἐγγεγραμμένη οὐ μέλανι ἀλλὰ πνεύματι θεοῦ ζῶντος, οὐκ ἐν πλαξὶ λιθίναις, ἀλλ' ἐν πλαξὶ καρδίας.

p. 28, § 17, line 1. The Stoics laid down three gradations: δόξα (=ἀσθενὴς καὶ ψευδὴς συγκατάθεσις, found only in the φαῦλοι), κατάληψις (=καταληπτικῆς φαντασίας συγκατάθεσις, which was κοινὴ ἀμφοτέρων), and ἐπιστήμη (=ἀσφαλὴς καὶ βεβαία καὶ ἀμετάθετος ἀπὸ λόγου κατάληψις, found in the wise alone), cf. Sext. *Log.* I. 150 foll. (*adv. Math.* VII. p. 404). H. In P. 768 σοφία is defined as κατάληψις βεβαία καὶ ἀμετάπτωτος, in P. 825

ἐπιστήμη is defined as κατάληψις βεβαία διὰ λόγων ἀληθῶν καὶ βεβαίων ἐπὶ τὴν τῆς αἰτίας γνῶσιν ἀνάγουσα, cf. *Str.* II. P. 433 τὴν ἐπιστήμην ὁρίζονται φιλοσόφων παῖδες ἕξιν ἀμετάπτωτον ὑπὸ λόγου.

2. ἔχει, 'he has': it is his ἔργον in one sense, that of the ἐπιστήμη in another; cf. below, p. 30. 12 δικαιοσύνης...πρῶτον ἔργον τὸ μετὰ τῶν ὁμοφύλων φιλεῖν διάγειν. H. I take τὸ μὲν περὶ τὰ θεῖα as the subject of ἔχει: 'that part of ἐπιστήμη which concerns divine things has for its function the investigation &c.' (so S. 'cuius ea pars, quae circa res divinas versatur, id negotii habet ut speculetur'). The quotation from p. 30 shows that an ἔργον may be predicated of abstractions: see too p. 19. 29 foll., where it is said to be the ἔργον of righteousness ἐπὶ τὸ ἄμεινον ἕκαστον προάγειν. The subject-matter of γνῶσις is also defined in *Str.* VI. P. 779 οὐ μόνον τὸ πρῶτον αἴτιον καὶ τὸ ὑπ' αὐτοῦ γεγεννημένον (MS. γεγενημένον) αἴτιον κατείληφεν...ἀλλὰ καὶ περὶ ἀγαθῶν καὶ περὶ κακῶν, περί τε γενέσεως ἁπάσης καὶ συλλήβδην εἰπεῖν περὶ ὧν ἐλάλησεν ὁ κύριος κ.τ.λ., *Str.* III. P. 531.

3. τί δὲ δι' οὗ κ.τ.λ., the second cause, spoken of in p. 26. 22.

4. τίνα τε αὖ τὰ μὲν ὡς διήκοντα, τὰ δὲ ὡς περιέχοντα. We need a subject here for τίνα, and a whole to embrace the two classes distinguished by τὰ μέν and τὰ δέ. The most natural supplement is, I think, τὰ συνέχοντα, which would easily be lost by the copyist's eye passing on from τά to τὰ μέν. Compare *Str.* P. 674 τάχα μὲν (ἡ Σφίγξ) ὁ διήκων πνευματικὸς τόνος καὶ συνέχων τὸν κόσμον εἴη ἄν, ἄμεινον δὲ ἐκδέχεσθαι τὸν αἰθέρα, πάντα συνέχοντα καὶ σφίγγοντα, Orig. *Cels.* VI. 71 (the Stoics say that) ὁ θεὸς πνεῦμά ἐστι διὰ πάντων διεληλυθὸς καὶ πάντ' ἐν ἑαυτῷ περιέχον, Diels *Doxogr.* p. 450 (a quotation from Stob. *Ecl.* I. 22. 1), where Aristotle is said to have held that the supreme Deity was τὸν πάσας (τὰς σφαίρας) περιέχοντα, ζῷον ὄντα λογικὸν καὶ...συνεκτικὸν καὶ προνοητικὸν τῶν οὐρανίων, *ib.* p. 571 (a quotation from Hippolytus) διὰ πάντων διήκειν τὴν πρόνοιαν.

διήκοντα, 'pervading'; a favourite Stoic term of the generative aether or air or fire in all things. H.

περιέχοντα, used either of the atmosphere or the heaven. H. See *s.v.* in Index to Ritter and Preller, ed. 8. H. J. Cf. also Theoph. *Aut.* 5 ἡ πᾶσα κτίσις περιέχεται ὑπὸ πνεύματος θεοῦ, Anaximenes ap. Stob. *Ecl.* I. 10. 12 ἡ ψυχὴ ἡ ἡμετέρα ἀὴρ οὖσα συγκρατεῖ ἡμᾶς, καὶ ὅλον τὸν κόσμον πνεῦμα καὶ ἀὴρ περιέχει.

5. τινὰ μέν...τινὰ δέ. The interrogative τίνα of the MS. makes no sense, as there were no physical principles thus distinguished, and it is of course impossible to suppose any allusion to the logical distinction made by the Stoics between συνημμένα, hypothetical, and διεζευγμένα, disjunctive propositions or judgements. Reading τινά, we get a discrimination (like that of τὰ μέν, τὰ δέ above) between the modes of action of the above-named physical principles. Could this division have reference to the Hierarchy, συνημμένα applying to the subordinate choirs, which make up each of the three great orders, διεζευγμένα to the demarcation between the orders themselves?

6 foll. τούτων follows ἕκαστον, τίνα goes with τάξιν, δύναμιν, and

λειτουργίαν: but in the two latter cases τήν is replaced by ήν εἰσφέρεται ἕκαστον. The δύναμις of each condition is λειτουργία. The τάξις is external and common, therefore not contributed by each. H.

7. εἰσφέρεται, 'contributes'; as it were, brings into the common stock: this verb could not be used of τάξιν. H.

ἐν δὲ αὖ answers to τὸ μὲν περὶ τὰ θεῖα in ll. 1, 2.

11. The Stoics held that some ἀγαθά are ἀρεταί, as φρόνησις, σωφροσύνη, ἀνδρεία: some not, as χαρά, εὐφροσύνη, θάρσος, βούλησις. So of κακά some are κακίαι, as ἀφροσύνη, ἀκολασία, ἀδικία, δειλία, μικροψυχία, ἀδυναμία: some not, as λύπη, φόβος. Cf. Stob. Ecl. II. p. 92. H.

12. The four virtues adopted from Plato by the Stoics. But they made the highest φρόνησις = ἐπιστήμη ἀγαθῶν καὶ κακῶν καὶ οὐδετέρων. Cf. Zeller IV. 220 foll. H. Cl. preposterously derives the classification of the cardinal virtues from the Book of Wisdom viii. 7, quoted in Str. P. 787 fin. ἤδη δὲ καὶ τὰς τέσσαρας ἀρετὰς ἡ παρ' ἡμῖν σοφία ὧδέ πως ἀνακηρύσσει, ὥστε καὶ τούτων τὰς πηγὰς τοῖς Ἕλλησιν παρὰ Ἐβραίων δεδόσθαι. μαθεῖν δ' ἐκ τῶνδ' ἔξεστιν " καὶ εἰ δικαιοσύνην ἀγαπᾷ τις, οἱ πόνοι ταύτης εἰσὶν ἀρεταί. σωφροσύνη γὰρ καὶ φρόνησις ἐκδιδάσκει δικαιοσύνην καὶ ἀνδρείαν," see also Str. P. 470.

13. παντελοῦς. So Plato says of justice that it is that which gives to the remaining virtues τὴν δύναμιν ὥστε ἐγγενέσθαι καὶ ἐγγενομένοις γε σωτηρίαν παρέχειν (Rep. 433 B) and in 444 D he appears to identify it with ἀρετή generally, characterizing it as ὑγίειά τις καὶ κάλλος καὶ εὐεξία ψυχῆς, and Arist. Eth. N. v. 1. 15 αὕτη μὲν οὖν ἡ δικαιοσύνη ἀρετή μέν ἐστι τελεία, ἀλλ' οὐχ ἁπλῶς ἀλλὰ πρὸς ἕτερον. καὶ διὰ τοῦτο πολλάκις κρατίστη τῶν ἀρετῶν εἶναι δοκεῖ...καὶ παροιμιαζόμενοί φαμεν

ἐν δὲ δικαιοσύνῃ συλλήβδην πᾶσ' ἀρετή 'στιν,

and αὕτη ἡ δικαιοσύνη οὐ μέρος ἀρετῆς ἀλλ' ὅλη ἀρετή ἐστιν.

13—15. The origin of wisdom is elsewhere stated to be 'the fear of the Lord,' but it is not a bad account of it to say that it results from the combination of prudence with righteousness. Who is responsible for this definition? It seems, however, scarcely consistent to make δικαιοσύνη 'all-perfect,' and yet to call in another virtue φρόνησις for the production of a third virtue, not included among the cardinal virtues. See quotation from Wisdom in n. on p. 28. 12.

15. κατακέχρηται. The perf. seems to be employed in the present sense, perhaps from the analogy of κέκτημαι, cf. P. 325 fin. πάντες ὅσοι ταῖς ὄψεσι κεχρήμεθα, 343 οἱ λόγῳ ἀγαθῷ κεχρημένοι, 417 ἐπὶ τὴν ἔρημον ἐτρέπετο καὶ νύκτωρ τὰ πολλὰ τῇ πορείᾳ ἐκέχρητο, 226 συνουσίᾳ κεχρῆσθαι ἑκάστοτε, 48 Ἑρμῆς προσηγορεύετο ὁ Νικαγόρας καὶ τῇ στολῇ τοῦ Ἑρμοῦ ἐκέχρητο, 193 τῷ λόγῳ ἡμεῖς κεχρήμεθα, 405 οὐ δήπου νεύματι ἀφανεῖ τῶν ἀλόγων ζῴων κεχρημένων οὐδὲ μὴν τῷ σχήματι μηνυόντων σφίσιν, 550 γάμῳ κεχρημένον σωφρόνως, Theodoret Gr. Aff. p. 163. 39 f. ὅτι μὲν οὖν ἀψευδὴς οὗτος ὁ λόγος καὶ τὰ πράγματα βοᾷ, μεγίστῃ κεχρημένα τῇ φωνῇ, ib. p. 164. 40, Heliod. Aeth. I. 16 κέχρησο ὅ τι βούλει, ib. II. 10.

ἀνδρεία was said to be concerned περὶ τὰς ὑπομονάς (Stoics ap. Stob. *Ecl.* II. 104). **H.** In P. 632 ἀνδρεία is said to be ἐν ὑπομονῇ καὶ καρτερίᾳ καὶ τοῖς ὁμοίοις· ἐπὶ δὲ τῇ ἐπιθυμίᾳ τάττεται καὶ ἡ σωφροσύνη καὶ ἡ σωτήριος φρόνησις. Cf. below, P. 870.

16. **περιστατικά.** Cf. Orig. *Cels.* I. 31 βίος περιστατικός. **H.** The word περίστασις is frequently used by the Stoics, not of circumstances generally, but of difficulties and dangers, see Epict. *Diss.* I. 24. 1 αἱ περιστάσεις εἰσὶν αἱ τοὺς ἄνδρας δεικνύουσαι and other passages in Upton's Index and Gataker's nn. on M. Anton. I. 12 τὰ περιεστῶτα πράγματα, IX. 13 ἐξῆλθον πάσης περιστάσεως. The derivative περιστατικός occurs in Plut. *Mor.* 169 (in reference to the Jews refusing to defend themselves if attacked on the sabbath) τοιαύτη ἐν τοῖς ἀβουλήτοις καὶ περιστατικοῖς λεγομένοις πράγμασι ἡ δεισιδαιμονία, where perhaps the phrase λεγομένοις implies that the word was unfamiliar in this sense. In Clem. it is common, see Index.

18. **ἤτοι τὸ μετὰ βίας ἢ μετὰ ἀπάτης.** The more correct order would be τὸ ἤτοι κ.τ.λ. H. J. compares for the thought *Str.* I. P. 341 βιάζεται πολλάκις ὀδύνη καὶ ἀληδών...καὶ ἐπὶ πᾶσι γοητεύονται οἱ ἤτοι ὑφ᾽ ἡδονῆς κηληθέντες ἢ ὑπὸ φόβου τι δείσαντες and the passage of Plato *Rep.* III. 412 E foll. from which both are derived, οὐκοῦν κλαπέντες ἢ γοητευθέντες ἢ βιασθέντες (ἀληθοῦς δόξης στερίσκονται);...τοὺς τοίνυν βιασθέντας λέγω οὓς ἂν ὀδύνη τις ἢ ἀληδὼν μεταδοξάσαι ποιήσῃ...τοὺς μὴν γοητευθέντας...κἂν σὺ φαίης εἶναι οἳ ἂν μεταδοξάσωσιν ἢ ὑφ᾽ ἡδονῆς κηληθέντες ἢ ὑπὸ φόβου τι δείσαντες. See his paper in *J. of Phil.* XXIV. p. 264 foll.

19. **ψυχαγωγοῦν.** Cf. *Str.* I. P. 340 λύκοι οὗτοι ἅρπαγες προβάτων κῳδίοις ἐγκεκρυμμένοι, ἀνδραποδισταί τε καὶ ψυχαγωγοὶ εὔγλωσσοι. Dr Gifford cites Numen. *ap.* Eus. *Pr. Ev.* XIV. 8 (speaking of the persuasive power of Carneades) λέγων ἐψυχαγώγει.

20. **τὰ περιστατικά** would come under the head of μέσα, therefore neither κακίαι nor even κακά. See above on l. 11. **H.**

For **ἀλλὰ πείθεσθαι** read ἀλλ᾽ ἐπιθέσθαι, 'assail,' either literally or as here and in Plut. III. 226 E ἐπιθέσθαι τῇ τρυφῇ (Lycurgus). **H.** Would not the dative αὐτοῖς be needed after ἐπιθέσθαι? I prefer ἀποθέσθαι as in P. 794 ἀποθέσθαι τὰ πάθη, below p. 44. 19 ἀποθ. τὴν ἄθεον δόξαν, and frequently both in Clem. and in the N.T.

21. True φοβερά are distinguished from false (death, poverty, &c.), see below, § 65, P. 870. The φοβερά here referred to are what are commonly regarded as such. The endurance of these may be a result of the opposition to κακίαι. **H.**

§ 18. 25. Each primary virtue has subordinate virtues: καρτερία, θαρραλεότης, μεγαλοψυχία, εὐψυχία, φιλοπονία are named as subordinate to ἀνδρεία by a Stoic writer ap. Stob. *Ecl.* II. 106. Again μεγαλοψυχία, ἐλευθεριότης, and μεγαλοπρέπεια come from Arist. *Eth. Nic.* II. 7, and μεγαλοφροσύνη is coupled with ἀνδρεία by Plat. *Symp.* 194 A. **H.** Cf. below p. 102. 14 f. 112—116.

28. **ἀντιλαμβάνεται.** Said by Lucian to be wrongly used for συνίημι (*Soloec.* 7), where Graevius quotes ἀντιλαβέσθαι κτύπου from Josephus.

p. 30, line 3. ὑπεράνω. See above, p. 26. 4.

5. σωφροσύνη δὲ σωτηρία, οὗ νῦν δὴ ἐσκέμμεθα, φρονήσεως Plat. *Crat.* 411 E; whence Arist. (Eudemus) *Eth. Nic.* VI. 5 ἔνθεν καὶ τὴν σωφροσύνην τούτῳ προσαγορεύομεν τῷ ὀνόματι, ὡς σῴζουσαν τὴν φρόνησιν. **H.**

5—7. ἡσύχιος, κόσμιος much used by Plato of σωφροσύνη. **H.** Cf. the saying attributed to Socrates in Plut. *Mor.* 600 F οὐκ Ἀθηναῖος οὐδὲ Ἕλλην ἀλλὰ κόσμιος, and the suggestion at the end of the 9th book of Plato's *Republic* that the Ideal Commonwealth may only exist in heaven. **H. J.** The saying is also given in Epict. *Diss.* I. 9. 1, Cic. *Tusc.* v. 108.

6. παραδεκτικός used also *Str.* II. P. 437. **H.**

τῶν ἐπαγγελλομένων. Used in passive sense, as in Gal. iii. 19, 2 Macc. iv. 27, *Str.* P. 812 *init.*

6, 7. οἰκείων...ἀλλοτρίων. Cf. below, § 78 ξένος τῶν τῇδε, κληρονομημάτων μόνων τῶν ἰδίων μεμνημένος, τὰ δὲ ἐνταῦθα πάντα ἀλλότρια ἡγούμενος, with Segaar's n. on *Q. D. S.* Dind. p. 397. 8 (P. 946).

ἀποστροφή, 'aversion to.' Very rare in this sense, and almost wholly of physical aversion to particular foods or smells. **H.** Cf. below, l. 17.

8. ὑπερκόσμιος. Basilides is cited (P. 639) as holding ξένην τὴν ἐκλογὴν τοῦ κόσμου, ὡς ἂν ὑπερκόσμιον φύσει οὖσαν: for other exx. see Index. The word is common in Dionysius and in the Neo-Platonists, where it is opposed to ἐγκόσμιος, see Sallust in Gale's *Mythogr.* c. 6, Proclus in Plat. *Alc.* I. p. 19 Creuzer. There is a similar play on the word κόσμιος in *Paed.* P. 243.

9. πλουτῶν. It was one of the Stoic paradoxes that the Wise Man was rich. In the translation I have interchanged this sentence with the following, as *that* has reference to the ὑπερκόσμιος of the preceding sentence, and has no connexion with § 19 which follows; whereas *this* is out of place where it stands, but explains the liberality recommended in § 19.

12. αὐτοῦ...ἔργον. Cf. p. 28. 2, 19. 29 f. **H.**

13. ὁμοφύλων, 'compatriots,')(ἀλλόφυλοι, used in the LXX. of the Philistines and others.

§ 19. 15. μεταδοτικός. See below p. 120. 21 ἡ ἕξις ἡ παρ' ἡμῖν μεταδοτική.

17. ἀποστροφή as above, l. 6. **H.**

19—21. θεράπων...φίλος. See above, p. 10. 8, 9.

20. ταῖς ἐντολαῖς ὑπαγόμενος. Apparently 'led along by the commandments.' Often used of deceptive leading: here rather 'gently.' Cf. the use in IV. 596 of heathens εἰς πίστιν ὑπαγόμενοι by wonder. **H.** 4 Macc. iv. 13 τούτοις ὑπαχθεὶς (al. ἐπαχθεὶς) τοῖς λόγοις, Eus. *Pr. Ev.* VIII. 10 *fin.* τὴν πληθὺν ταῖς τῶν νόμων ὑποθήκαις ὑπῆγε.

21. δι' αὐτὴν τὴν γνῶσιν καθαρός. Cf. P. 581 ἡ γνῶσις τοῦ ἡγεμονικοῦ τῆς ψυχῆς κάθαρσίς ἐστι κ.τ.λ. which suggests the translation 'owing to' for δι' αὐτήν, instead of that given in the text.

22 foll. The origin of virtue was a common subject of discussion in Plato's time, cf. the *Meno* throughout, *Protag.* 318 foll., *Rep.* VII. 518.

ούτε φύσει την άρετην γεννώμεθα έχοντες. P. 788 init. φύσει μὲν ἐπιτήδειοι γεγόναμεν πρὸς ἀρετήν, οὐ μὴν ὥστε ἔχειν αὐτὴν ἐκ γενετῆς, ἀλλὰ πρὸς τὸ κτήσασθαι ἐπιτήδειοι, ib. ἡ δὲ ἐπιτηδειότης φορὰ πρὸς ἀρετήν...ἀλλ' ὁ μὲν μᾶλλον, ὁ δ' ἧττον πρόσεισι τῇ τε μαθήσει τῇ τε ἀσκήσει.

25, 26. ἐκ τῆς τῶν συμβιούντων ἐπιγινομένη συνηθείας. Cf. Plato, *Protag.* 327 πάντες διδάσκαλοί εἰσιν ἀρετῆς...καὶ οὐδείς σοι φαίνεται. εἶθ' ὡς ἂν εἰ ζητοῖς τίς διδάσκαλος τοῦ 'Ελληνίζειν, οὐδ' ἂν εἰς φανείη. The MS. reading συμβάντων καὶ ἐπιγινομένης seems to me to give no sense. Probably ἐπιγινομένη was altered to agree with συνηθείας and καὶ inserted to make some construction.

29. ποριστικῶν. Cf. p. 138. 15 below καταμεγαλοφρονεῖ πάντων τῶν εἰς δημιουργίαν καὶ τροφὴν τῆς σαρκὸς οἰκείων, P. 573 ἡ πενία τῆς θεωρίας ἀπασχολεῖν βιάζεται τὴν ψυχὴν περὶ τοὺς πορισμοὺς διατρίβειν ἀναγκάζουσα, P. 509 τὴν περὶ τὸν πορισμὸν τῶν ἐπιτηδείων ἀσχολίαν. Sext. Emp. *P. H.* I. § 66 ὁ κύων...τέχνην ἔχει ποριστικὴν τῶν οἰκείων, τὴν θηρευτικήν, ib. 72.

p. 32, line 1. ἡ γνῶσις. Comes in unexpectedly here instead of ἀρετή, but γνῶσις was mentioned in p. 30. 21 as the ground of virtue; and in *Str.* VI. P. 779 it is described as originating in the same way as virtue οὐ συγγεννᾶται τοῖς ἀνθρώποις ἀλλ' ἐπίκτητός ἐστιν ἡ γνῶσις, καὶ προσοχῆς μὲν δεῖται κατὰ τὰς ἀρχὰς ἡ μάθησις αὐτῆς ἐκθρέψεώς τε καὶ αὐξήσεως, ἔπειτα δὲ ἐκ τῆς ἀδιαλείπτου μελέτης εἰς ἕξιν ἔρχεται.

1, 2. ἐκ παιδείας τῆς ἐγκυκλίου. Cf. *Str.* P. 332, 333 (on the importance of preparatory training) ὡς τὰ ἐγκύκλια μαθήματα συμβάλλεται πρὸς φιλοσοφίαν, οὕτω καὶ φιλοσοφία αὐτὴ πρὸς σοφίας κτῆσιν συμβάλλεται, 373 ἡ ἐγκ. παιδεία συνεργεῖ πρὸς τὸ διεγείρειν καὶ συγγυμνάζειν πρὸς τὰ νοητὰ τὴν ψυχήν, (shown in detail in P. 780), Quintil. I. 10. 1 haec de Grammatica...nunc de ceteris artibus quibus instituendos...pueros existimo,...ut efficiatur orbis ille doctrinae, quam Graeci ἐγκύκλιον παιδείαν vocant. Included in this training were music, geometry, astronomy, grammar, rhetoric, developed later into the seven liberal arts (constituting the Trivium and Quadrivium) as described by Martianus Capella in the 5th century. In his estimate of the παιδ. ἐγκ. Cl. follows Philo, see Zeller, v. p. 408, n. 1, and Potter on P. 333 *init.*

3. διακονῆσαι, 'sharpen.' The lexicons give the word without examples. ἀκονάω and παρακονάω are similarly used. H.

γάρ. If this is the true reading, it is probably to be explained by ellipsis occasioned by rapidity of expression. ('It is no good to think of law) *for* all that law could do is to control action,' see my nn. on the transitional use of *nam* in Cic. *N. D.* I. 27, II. 67.

§ 20. 5. οἱ λόγοι οἱ πιστικοί, 'doctrines of persuasion,' *i.e.* rhetoric. H. I prefer to take it more generally 'persuasive reasonings.' On the form πιστικός found in the MS. see Lobeck on *Aj.* 151.

6. For διαμονὴν read διανομήν, comparing the use of διανενεμημένως *Str.* VI. P. 800 med. and Plat. *Leg.* IV. 714 Α τὴν τοῦ νοῦ διανομὴν ἐπονομάζονται νόμον. H. The definition of ἐπιστήμη as κατάληψις βεβαία (above,

p. 28. 1) and ἕξις ἀμετάπτωτος ὑπὸ λόγου (P. 433) sufficiently support the MS. reading διαμονήν. H. J. cites Arist. *Top.* IV. 4. 125 b εἰ γὰρ ὁπωσοῦν ἐστιν ἡ μνήμη μονὴ ἐπιστήμης κ.τ.λ.

7. **φιλοσοφία.** On the use of philosophy see *Str.* VI. P. 780 f.

8. **ἐφ' ᾗ τὴν γνῶσιν ἐποικοδομεῖ.** Cf. Jude 20 τῇ πίστει ἐποικοδομοῦντες ἑαυτούς, 1 Cor. iii. 10—14, Col. iii. 7.

10. **ὁ ἀθλητής,** 2 Tim. ii. 5, 1 Cor. ix. 24—27 οὐκ οἴδατε ὅτι οἱ ἐν τῷ σταδίῳ τρέχοντες κ.τ.λ. Ignat. *Polyc.* 1 πάντων τὰς νόσους βάσταζε ὡς τέλειος ἀθλητής, *ib.* 3 with Lightfoot's nn. See also his note on Clem. Rom. 5 οἱ ἔγγιστα γενόμενοι ἀθληταί (of the martyrs). A favourite metaphor with the Stoics. Barnard cites *Q. D. S.* 937 P.

11. **τῷ καλῷ κόσμῳ.** Plato *Tim.* 29 A καλός ἐστιν οὗτος ὁ κόσμος καὶ ὁ δημιουργὸς ἀγαθός, *Plac. Phil.* I. 6 (Diels, p. 293), Cic. *N. D.* II. 15.

12. **ἀγωνοθέτης...βραβευτής.** *Protr.* P. 77 ἐν τῷ τῆς ἀληθείας σταδίῳ γνησίως ἀγωνιζώμεθα, βραβεύοντος μὲν τοῦ λόγου τοῦ ἁγίου, ἀγωνοθετοῦντος δὲ τοῦ δεσπότου τῶν ὅλων, *ib.* 3 λόγος οὐράνιος ὁ γνήσιος ἀγωνιστὴς ἐπὶ τῷ παντὸς κόσμου θεάτρῳ στεφανούμενος, *Q. D. S.* 937 P. αὐτὸν ὑποβαλέτω φέρων γυμναστῇ μὲν τῷ λόγῳ, ἀγωνοθέτῃ δὲ τῷ Χριστῷ. Tert. *ad Mart.* 3 bonum agonem subituri estis in quo agonothetes Deus, xystarchus Spiritus Sanctus, epistates Christus. H.

14. **θεαταί...θεοί.** Cf. 1 Cor. iv. 9, Heb. xii. 1, 2, 22 foll., and for θεοί, above n. on καὶ θεῶν p. 10. 5, and below § 57.

15. **παγκράτιον,** a combination of boxing and wrestling: cf. Philo II. 449 M, also Arist. *Rhet.* I. 14. H. The figure was taken from the Stoics, like so much in the early Christian writers, see the interesting quotation from Panaetius in Gell. XIII. 27 vita hominum, qui aetatem in medio rerum agunt ac sibi suisque esse usui volunt, negotia periculaque ex improviso assidua et prope quotidiana fert. Ad ea cavenda atque declinanda proinde esse oportet animo semper prompto atque intento, ut sunt athletarum, qui pancratiastae vocantur. Nam sicuti illi ad certandum vocati proiectis alte brachiis consistunt, caputque et os suum manibus oppositis quasi vallo praemuniunt; membraque eorum omnia, priusquam pugna mota est, aut ad vitandos ictus cauta sunt aut ad faciendos parata: ita animus atque mens viri prudentis, etc. Plato applies the phrase to the sophist Euthydemus (*Euth.* 271) coupling it with πάμμαχος, as here.

πάμμαχον. Cf. Plut. II. 804 B πρὸς οὐ φαῦλον, ἀλλὰ πάμμαχον ἀγῶνα, τὸν τῆς πολιτείας, ἠθληκότα. H.

οὐ πρὸς αἷμα καὶ σάρκα. The Apostle continues ἀλλὰ πρὸς τὰς ἀρχάς, πρὸς τὰς ἐξουσίας, πρὸς τοὺς κοσμοκράτορας τοῦ αἰῶνος τούτου, πρὸς τὰ πνευματικὰ τῆς πονηρίας ἐν τοῖς ἐπουρανίοις.

17. **ἀνταγωνισμάτων** seems to be abstract for concrete, denoting the antagonists themselves. So Heliod. *Aeth.* VII. 6, p. 263 K. τύχη τις καινὸν ἐπεισόδιον ἐπετραγῴδει τοῖς δρωμένοις, ὥσπερ εἰς ἀνταγώνισμα δράματος ἀρχὴν ἄλλου παρεισφέρουσα. H. In Didot's ed. the last sentence is translated 'quasi aemulatione quadam initium alterius fabulae afferens,'

which gives no support to H.'s view, and in the translation I have taken it literally.

18. ἐπαρτάω. Generally spoken of fears, but also used with words like δουλείαν and τιμωρίας. Cf. Ael. N. A. I. 19. 8 with Jacobs' n., where there is an allusion to the stone of Tantalus, which possibly suggested the use. H. See Str. II. P. 492 θείως ὁ νόμος τὸν φόβον ἐπαρτᾷ.

20. ἀπαραλόγιστος. Either 'not deceiving' or 'not deceived': here the latter, 'unmoved by the sophistry of advocates.' H.

ψῆφος, 'decision,' sc. as ἀγωνοθέτης. H.

21. κρίμα, 'a judgement': this sense is common in LXX. and N.T., but rare in classical writers. H.

22. παγκρατιάζουσι must mean 'are already engaged in the contest,' not preparing for it. H. See above, l. 15 παγκράτιον.

εἰς. For the confusion between εἰς and ἐν in later Greek, see below p. 118. 20 μένει εἰς τὴν ἀνάπαυσιν, Exc. Theod. P. 969 (ὁ λόγος) εἰς τὸν κόλπον τοῦ πατρὸς εἶναι λέγεται copied from Joh. i. 18, also Blass, Gr. N.T. § 39. 3, Jannaris § 1548; (unless we suppose Cl. to distinguish between three stages, the entrance of the spectators, the entrance of the wrestlers, the awarding of the prize.)

23. ἐκ of the ms. is right, for οἱ ἀθληταί cannot mean only the adverse wrestlers, but both sides. H.

πειθήνιος, 'obedient,' without reference to etymology: see below, l. 28 and Str. II. 467 βούλημά ἐστι τοῦ θεοῦ σώζεσθαι τὸν ταῖς ἐντολαῖς πειθήνιον, often in Plut. H.

ἀλείπτῃ. Cf. Paed. I. 132 passim. H. 'Qui certaturos ungebat aliptes dicebatur. Idem leges ac totam rationem certaminis docebat. Hinc... Greg. Naz. ap. Suid. ἀλείπται τῆς ἀρετῆς....Clemens metaphorice voce ἀλείπτου usus est, Paed. I. P. 132 ὁ λόγος ἦν ὁ ἀλείπτης ἅμα τῷ Ἰακὼβ καὶ παιδαγωγὸς τῆς ἀνθρωπότητος.' Potter. See Lightfoot on Ignat. vol. II. p. 38.

25, 26. ἐλεῖται...ἰσχύει. See the Olympian proclamation quoted in the critical note.

27. γνῶθι σαυτόν. Explained in Str. I. P. 351 as bidding us τὴν γνῶσιν μεταδιώκειν. οὐκ ἔστι γὰρ ἄνευ τῆς τῶν ὅλων οὐσίας εἰδέναι τὰ μέρη, δεῖ δὲ τὴν γένεσιν τοῦ κόσμου πολυπραγμονῆσαι, δι' ἧς καὶ τὴν τοῦ ἀνθρώπου φύσιν καταμαθεῖν ἐξέσται.

ἐνταῦθα. Used sometimes for 'here on earth,' as in P. 895 τέλος τοῦ γνωστικοῦ τό γε ἐνταῦθα διττόν, ἐφ' ὧν μὲν ἡ θεωρία, ἐφ' ὧν δὲ ἡ πρᾶξις: at other times with a logical force as in 897 γνώσομαι εἰ μεγαλοφρόνως τῆς γραφῆς συνίετε· ἐνταῦθα γὰρ ἡ δύναμις τῶν τέκνων τῆς σοφίας, 'for herein lies the power of the children of wisdom,' 865 ἐνταῦθα τῆς γνωστικῆς ψυχῆς ἡ τελείωσις, πάσας καθάρσεις ὑπερβᾶσαν σὺν τῷ κυρίῳ γίνεσθαι ὅπου ἐστὶν προσεχῶς ὑποτεταγμένην, where it seems to be explained by the following infinitive, 'herein, viz. in being brought into immediate contact with the Lord,' a perfection which seems to belong rather to heaven than to earth, and so to preclude the other meanings.

28, 29. γεγόναμεν εἶναι πειθήνιοι...εἰ ἑλοίμεθα. This form of conditional sentence is not uncommon in CL, see *Protr.* P. 71 οὐδὲ εἰ τὸν Πακτωλόν τις ...ἀπομετρήσαι, ἀντάξιον σωτηρίας μισθὸν ἀριθμήσει. In the present case however εἰ ἑλοίμεθα is the protasis of a sentence πειθήνιοι ἐσόμεθα εἰ αἱρησόμεθα, which is then subordinated to γεγόναμεν. For the thought cf. above, § 9 *ad fin.*

30. Ἀδράστεια. For this explanation of the name Potter cites Theodoret. *Serm.* VI. Ἀδράστειαν τὴν αὐτὴν (πρόνοιαν) ὅτι οὐδὲν αὐτὴν ἀποδιδράσκει. Cf. also Ps.-Arist. *de Mundo* 7 ἀναπόδραστος αἰτία, Plutarch quoted in Stob. *Ecl. Phys.* 186 ὅτι πέρας ταῖς αἰτίαις ἠναγκασμένον ἐπιτίθησιν, ἀνέκφευκτος οὖσα καὶ ἀναπόδραστος, Porphyr. *ad Marc.* 21 ἡ τῶν θεῶν ἀναπόδραστος ἐφόρασις. CL seems to mean that we cannot escape the divine Will, which ordains our obedience through our own choice. He is probably thinking of Plato *Phaedr.* 248 θεσμὸς Ἀδραστείας ὅδε, ἥτις ἂν ψυχὴ θεῷ ξυνοπαδὸς γιγνομένη κατίδῃ τι τῶν ἀληθῶν...εἶναι ἀπήμονα, where see Ast, also Creuzer's n. on Plotin. *Enn.* IV. 389 ἀναπόδραστος γὰρ ὁ θεῖος νόμος ὁμοῦ ἔχων ἐν ἑαυτῷ τὸ ποιῆσαι τὸ κριθὲν ἤδη.

§ 21. p. 34, line 2. ποικίλην, cf. *Protr.* 8 πολύφωνος ὁ σωτὴρ καὶ πολύτροπος εἰς ἀνθρώπων σωτηρίαν κ.τ.λ. See *Str.* I. P. 331 *init.* εἰκότως τοίνυν ὁ ἀπόστολος πολυποίκιλον εἴρηκεν τὴν σοφίαν τοῦ θεοῦ...διὰ τέχνης, διὰ ἐπιστήμης, διὰ πίστεως, διὰ προφητείας, τὴν ἑαυτῆς ἐνδεικνυμένην δύναμιν εἰς τὴν ἡμετέραν εὐεργεσίαν.

δι' ἐντολῶν. Not by way of wages, but of inward result. H.

εὐαρέστησις. Cf. P. 860 πάντα ἐκπεπληρωκέναι...εἴς τε τὴν εὐποιίαν καὶ εἰς τὴν εὐαρέστησιν τῷ θεῷ, 871 ἡ πρὸς τὸν θεὸν εὐαρέστησις, *Testam. Issach.* 4 εἶδον ἐν καρδίᾳ πᾶσαν εὐαρέστησιν Κυρίῳ, Clem. Rom. 58 εἰς εὐαρέστησιν τῷ ὀνόματι αὐτοῦ, *ib.* 49 δίχα ἀγάπης οὐδὲν εὐάρεστον τῷ θεῷ, Wisdom iv. 10, Phil. iv. 18, Rom. xii. 1, 1 Pet. ii. 5, Heb. xiii. 16, 'an act well-pleasing to God.' A favourite word with the Stoics, see Epict. *Diss.* I. 12.

3. ὁμολογία. Probably 'an acknowledgment,' sc. in return for His gracious purpose. Cf. ὁμολογεῖν χάριν *bis* in the similar passage *Paed.* I. 158. H.

ὁ μὲν...προκατάρχει τῆς εὐποιίας. Aristotle *Eth. N.* VIII. 6, 7, distinguishes between the friendship of equality and that of superiority (τὸ καθ' ὑπεροχὴν εἶδος). The latter is the case of rulers and parents: καὶ τὸ δίκαιον ἐν τούτοις οὐ ταὐτό, ἀλλὰ τὸ κατ' ἀξίαν· οὕτω γὰρ καὶ ἡ φιλία, *ib.* § 11 τοὺς ἴσους μὲν κατ' ἰσότητα δεῖ τῷ φιλεῖν καὶ τοῖς λοιποῖς ἰσάζειν, τοὺς δ' ἀνίσους τῷ ἀνάλογον ταῖς ὑπεροχαῖς ἀποδιδόναι, *ib.* § 13 οὕτω δὴ...τῷ εἰς χρήματα ὠφελουμένῳ ἢ εἰς ἀρετὴν τιμὴν ἀνταποδοτέον, ἀνταποδιδόντα τὸ ἐνδεχόμενον· τὸ δυνατὸν γὰρ ἡ φιλία ἐπιζητεῖ οὐ τὸ κατ' ἀξίαν· οὐδὲ γὰρ ἔστιν ἐν πᾶσι, καθάπερ ἐν ταῖς πρὸς τοὺς θεοὺς τιμαῖς,...εἰς δύναμιν δὲ ὁ θεραπεύων ἐπιεικὴς εἶναι δοκεῖ, *ib.* IX. 2 ἐνίοτε οὐδ' ἐστὶν ἴσον τὸ τὴν προϋπαρχὴν ἀμείψασθαι.

4. λογισμόν, i.e. taking into consideration both the relative positions of the benefactor and benefited, and the value of the benefit.

5. φυλάξας τὰς ἐντολάς. Joh. xiv. 15 ἐὰν ἀγαπᾶτέ με, τὰς ἐντολὰς τὰς ἐμὰς τηρήσατε.

5—7. πιστὸς φίλος. See above, p. 10. 8, 9.

9. ἰδίου γεννήματος &c. seems to be in apposition with τῶν ἀνθρώπων, which is itself an objective genitive after ὠφελείας. H. Cf. below, p. 164. 17, *Paed.* I. P. 101 *fin.* εἰκότως φίλος ὁ ἄνθρωπος τῷ θεῷ, ἐπεὶ καὶ πλάσμα αὐτοῦ ἐστί· καὶ τὰ μὲν ἄλλα κελεύων μόνον πεποίηκεν, τὸν δὲ ἄνθρωπον δι' αὐτοῦ ἐχειρούργησεν καί τι αὐτῷ ἴδιον ἐνεφύσησεν foll.

11. εἰς ἰδίαν χάριν. Mt. x. 40—42, xxv. 34—45, quoted in P. 467, where Cl. adds that God οὐδεμίαν ἔχει πρὸς ἡμᾶς φυσικὴν σχέσιν, but of His mercy κήδεται ἡμῶν μήτε μορίων ὄντων μήτε φύσει τέκνων.

15. ἀμοιβὴν κατ' ἀξίαν. See Arist. *Eth. N.* VIII. 14, p. 1163 quoted above on l. 3.

ὅλην, predicative use.

19. ἀνεπιστρεψία, 'regardlessness.' Apparently used only here and Epict. II. 1. 14: from ἐπιστρέφομαι, 'to care about, give heed to.' H. Cf. also ἀνεπιστρέπτως (*negligenter*) Epict. II. 9. 4, ἀνεπιστρεπτεῖν (*non curare*) *ib.* II. 59, ἀνεπίστρεπτος Synes. 145 C, and its synonyms ἀνεπιστρεφής, ἀνεπίστροφος.

24. οἴκους. A chamber connected with the Roman baths was called oecus, see Casaub. on Theophr. *Char.* IX. 120. I think however that we should read οἰκίσκους here.

25. ὁ λόγος πάντη κεχυμένος. A Stoic phrase, cf. Anton. V. 32 τὸν δι' ὅλης τῆς οὐσίας διήκοντα λόγον, Cic. *N. D.* I. 39 'Chrysippus ait vim divinam in ratione esse positam...ipsumque mundum deum dicit esse et *eius animi fusionem universam*,' Orig. *Cels.* VI. 71 κατὰ μὲν οὖν τοὺς ἀπὸ τῆς στοᾶς...καὶ ὁ λόγος τοῦ θεοῦ ὁ μέχρι ἀνθρώπων καὶ τῶν ἐλαχίστων καταβαίνων οὐδὲν ἄλλο ἐστὶν ἢ πνεῦμα σωματικόν, *Protr.* P. 58 οὐδὲ μὴν τοὺς ἀπὸ τῆς στοᾶς παρελεύσομαι, διὰ πάσης ὕλης καὶ διὰ τῆς ἀτιμοτάτης τὸ θεῖον διήκειν λέγοντας, Sirac. XXIII. 19.

§ 22. p. 36, line 2. **Αἰθίοπες,** κ.τ.λ. The verses may have run Αἰθίοπές τε θεοὺς μέλανας σιμούς τε γράφουσι, Θρᾷκες δ' αὖ πυρροὺς καὶ γλαυκούς. Cl. seems to quote from the same poem in P. 714 f. Potter cites Theodoret speaking of Xenophanes, τοὺς μὲν γὰρ Αἰθίοπας μέλανας καὶ σιμοὺς γράφειν ἔφησε τοὺς οἰκείους θεούς...τοὺς δέ γε Θρᾷκας γλαυκούς τε καὶ ἐρυθρούς· καὶ μέντοι καὶ Μήδους καὶ Πέρσας, σφίσιν αὐτοῖς ἐοικότας· καὶ Αἰγυπτίους ὡσαύτως.

4. ὁμοίας ἕκαστοι ἑαυτοῖς. This reading is easily obtained from the MS. ομοιουσ|ινκαιτοι|σαυτοις|, though less near to it than H. J.'s ὁμοιοῦσιν. καὶ τοὺς αὐτοὺς ἀναπλάττουσιν αὐτίκα βάρβαροι μὲν θηριώδεις κ.τ.λ. My objection to the latter is that there seems to be no special reason for the insertion of τοὺς αὐτούς: also αὐτίκα is more commonly found at the beginning of a sentence.

9. βασιλικὸς τὴν ψυχήν. Perhaps derived from Plato *Phileb.* 30 D. H. J. See reff. in Kaye p. 148 n. 7.

9, 10. οὗτος καὶ θεοσεβής. The predicate is introduced by οὗτος as above, p. 30. 20 f. ὁ καθαρὸς τῇ καρδίᾳ φίλος οὗτος τῷ θεῷ, p. 34. 5 ὁ φυλάξας τὰς ἐντολὰς πιστὸς οὗτος, below, p. 94. 2 οὗτος οὐδαμῶς ἀναγκάζεται taking up ὁ μέχρι τῆς συμπεριφορᾶς συγκαταβαίνων.

10. ἀδεισιδαίμων ὤν. ὤν must be omitted, as πεπεισμένος cannot be the predicate, and καὶ θεοσεβὴς καὶ ἀδεισιδαίμων makes a quite natural predicate: all from τίμιον to the end is probably a justification of ἀδεισιδαίμων. H.

11. μεγαλοπρεπῆ. This was naturally changed by the copyist to μεγαλοπρεπές, to suit the seeming neuter nominatives.

11, 12. ἁπάντων ἀρχηγὸν ἀγαθῶν—ἀναίτιον. See Plato *Rep.* II. 379 B οὐκ ἄρα πάντων γε αἴτιον τὸ ἀγαθόν, ἀλλὰ τῶν μὲν εὖ ἐχόντων αἴτιον, τῶν δὲ κακῶν ἀναίτιον, and n. on p. 18. 27 above.

14. ἐν τῷ Προτρεπτικῷ. See esp. ch. II. §§ 11—37.

15. κατακόρως, 'to the full': expresses saturation as well as satiation. H.

τῇ κατεπειγούσῃ. See n. on p. 4. 5.

16. συγκαταχρώμενοι, found also in IV. P. 615 *med.* H. (a corrupt passage).

§ 23. 17. μυθολογεῖν, simply 'tell the story of.' H. ἀριζήλως and μυθολογεύειν in the original.

20. τοῖς κακίστοις ἀνθρώποις τὸ θεῖον ἀπεικάζοντας. Having shown that the Christians are not ἄθεοι, Cl. goes on to show that the heathen are ἄθεοι, cf. above, § 1, also Plut. *de Superst.* 160 A ὁ μὴ νομίζων θεοὺς εἶναι ἀνόσιός ἐστιν· ὁ δὲ τοιούτους νομίζων οἵους οἱ δεισιδαίμονες, οὐ μακρῷ δόξαις ἀνοσιωτέραις σύνεστιν: ib. 170 ὁ δεισιδαίμων τῇ προαιρέσει ἄθεος ὤν, ἀσθενέστερός ἐστι τοῦ δοξάζειν περὶ θεῶν ἃ βούλεται.

22. αὐτοῖς, 'according to their view': as below, p. 52. 19. H.

27. ὁ Οἰνεύς. The story is given in *Il.* IX. 532: Artemis sent the Calydonian boar against the Aetolians because Oeneus neglected to offer sacrifice to her: ἢ λάθετ' ἢ οὐκ ἐνόησεν (l. 537). Hence Valckenaer's emend. οὐ νενοηκώς for ὡς τεθυκώς. D.'s ἐννενοηκώς was suggested by the *Schol.* ἤτοι ἐννοήσας θῦσαι ἐπελάθετο, ἢ οὐδ' ὅλως ἐνόησε.

28. Auge, daughter of the king of Tegea and priestess of Athena, laid the infant, which she had borne to Heracles, in the temple of the goddess, who in consequence sent a pestilence upon the land.

p. 38, line 3. Potter quotes from Eur. *I. T.* 380 τὰ τῆς θεοῦ δὲ μέμφομαι σοφίσματα, ἥτις, βροτῶν μὲν ἤν τις ἅψηται φόνου, ἢ καὶ λοχείας ἢ νεκροῦ θίγῃ χεροῖν, βωμῶν ἀπείργει, μυσαρὸν ὡς ἡγουμένη, αὐτὴ δὲ θυσίαις ἥδεται βροτοκτόνοις. H.

7. Chrysippus (*ap.* Plut. II. 1045 A) makes use of the same defence, maintaining that what is allowable in animals is so also in the case of men. H.

§ 24. 9. εὐοργήτους. Usually 'easy-tempered': here 'easily angered,' as Plut. II. 413 C εὐόργητος γάρ ἐστιν [ὁ θεὸς] καὶ οὐ πρᾶος. H.

12, 13. ἂν μῦς...διατράγῃ θύλακον. Cic. *de Div.* II. 59 nos ita inconsiderati sumus ut, si mures corroserint aliquid, monstrum putemus. ante vero Marsicum bellum quod clipeos Lanuvii mures rosissent, maximum id portentum haruspices esse dixerunt, foll., Casaubon on Theoph. *Char.* 16.

19. τὸν ἱμάντα διέρρηξα. Cf. Cic. *de Divin.* II. 84 quae si suscipiamus, pedis offensio nobis et abruptio corrigiae et sternutamenta erunt observanda.

23. Ἀντιφῶντος. See Diog. L. II. 46 and Hermogenes *de Form. Orat.* II. p. 497 quoted in the note in Hübner's ed. where it is said that there were two Antiphons, the orator, and ὁ καὶ τερατόσκοπος καὶ ὀνειροκρίτης λεγόμενος γενέσθαι, οὕπερ οἱ περὶ τῆς ἀληθείας λέγονται λόγοι κ.τ.λ.

p. 40, line 4. Βίων. The Scythian philosopher (fl. 250 B.C.) to whom Horace refers (*Epist.* II. 2. 60 *Bioneis sermonibus*), cf. Diog. L. IV. 46 f. A saying of his is quoted below on p. 56. 26, and in the n. on p. 42. 9.

6. ἐνεχείρει. Cf. Sext. Emp. p. 362 ὁ μὲν πρὸς τὰ ἐγκεχειρημένα λόγος ἐστὶ τοιοῦτος, Str. P. 376 μόνη ἡ κυρία ἀλήθεια ἀπαρεγχείρητος, Plut. *Mor.* 687 E ἐδόκει δή μοι ταῦτα πιθανῶς μὲν ἐγκεχειρῆσθαι, πρὸς δὲ τὸ μέγιστον ἐναντιοῦσθαι τῆς φύσεως τέλος, V. *Cic.* c. 21 αὐτός...ἐνεχείρησεν εἰς ἑκάτερον, τὰ μὲν τῇ προτέρᾳ τὰ δὲ τῇ γνώμῃ Καίσαρος συνειπών.

§ 25. 9. ἐν ὑπέρῳ. The preposition is supported by Theodoret 88 ὄφεως ὑπέρῳ ἑαυτὸν ἐνειλήσαντος, but seems to be an intrusion. H. Cf. Cic. *de Div.* II. 62 interpres portentorum non inscite respondisse dicitur ei qui ad eum rettulisset, quasi ostentum, quod anguis domi vectem circumiectus fuisset: *tum esset*, inquit, *ostentum, si anguem vectis circumplicavisset.*

12. ἐσθίειν. The reading of the MS. θεῖν is plainly impossible after τρέχειν, and the preceding quotations seem to require a word to express 'eating.'

13. ἐκείνοις ὄντα κατὰ φύσιν οὐκ ἂν ποτε ἡμῖν γένοιτο παρὰ φύσιν. Chrys. ap. Plut. *Mor.* 1045 A πρὸς τὰ θηρία, φησί, δεῖν ἀποβλέπειν καὶ τοῖς ὑπ' ἐκείνων γινομένοις τεκμαίρεσθαι τὸ μηδὲν ἄτοπον μηδὲ παρὰ φύσιν εἶναι τῶν τοιούτων.

15. ὄρνιθες δέ τε πολλοί. The answer of the scoffing Eurymachus to the forebodings of Halitherses. 'There are plenty of birds, but the omens drawn from them are not all true': οὐδέ τε πάντες ἐναίσιμοι.

18. τίς ἔπταρεν. See Cic. quoted above on p. 38. 19, Catull. XLV. 9 dextram sternuit approbationem, Arist. *Probl.* XXXIII. 11, Xen. *Anab.* III. 2. 9.

25. ἐγκυλιόμενοι, 'rolling,' or 'wallowing' in drunkenness, cf. Sirac XXIII. 17 εἰ ἁμαρτίαις οὐκ ἐγκυλισθήσονται, Prov. vii. 18 ἐγκυλισθῶμεν ἔρωτι. The form κυλινδέω or καλινδέω occurs in P. 856 τοῖς ἐν ἀγνοίᾳ καλινδουμένοις, *Protr.* P. 3 and 49.

ἑορτάς, of the gods: this makes the contradiction, as the αἰτήσεις are also addressed to the gods. H.

26. γραφάς, 'inscriptions,' perhaps including paintings.

§ 26. p. 42, line 1. ὁ Διογένης. Potter remarks that this is a combination of two stories given by Diog. L. VI. 39 εὐνούχου μοχθηροῦ ἐπιγράψαντος ἐπὶ τὴν οἰκίαν, Μηδὲν εἰσίτω κακόν· ὁ οὖν κύριος τῆς οἰκίας πῶς εἰσελεύσεται; ib. 50 νεογάμου ἐπιγράψαντος ἐπὶ τὴν οἰκίαν, Ὁ τοῦ Διὸς παῖς Ἡρακλῆς καλλίνικος ἐνθάδε κατοικεῖ, μηδὲν εἰσίτω κακόν· ἐπέγραψε, Μετὰ τὸν πόλεμον ἡ συμμαχία.

6, 7. λίθον...λιπαρόν. Theophr. Char. 16 (of superstition) καὶ τῶν λιπαρῶν λίθων τῶν ἐν ταῖς τριόδοις παριὼν ἐκ τῆς ληκύθου ἔλαιον καταχεῖν, καὶ ἐπὶ γόνατα πεσὼν καὶ προσκυνήσας ἀπαλλάττεσθαι, where see Casaubon: Arnob. I. 39 si quando conspexeram lubricatum lapidem et ex olivi unguine ordinatum, tanquam inesset vis praesens, adulabar, affabar (given with other quotations in Potter's ed.).

7. ἔρια πυρρά. Cf. Protr. P. 9 καθαρσίων μεταλάμβανε θεοπρεπῶν, οὐ δάφνης πετάλων καὶ ταινιῶν τινων ἐρίῳ καὶ πορφύρᾳ πεποικιλμένων, Heb. ix. 19, Theocr. Φαρμακ. 2 στέψον τὰν κελέβαν φοινικέῳ οἰὸς ἀώτῳ.

ἁλῶν χόνδρους. These are mentioned as used in the Mysteries, Protr. P. 13, 19. See below, p. 44, 5.

8. δᾷδας σκύλλαν τε καὶ θεῖον. Luc. Necyom. 7 ἐπὶ τὸν ποταμὸν ἀγαγὼν ἐκάθηρέ τέ με καὶ ἀπέμαξε καὶ περιήγνισε δᾳδὶ καὶ σκίλλῃ καὶ ἄλλοις πλείοσιν, Theophr. Char. 16 ἱερείας καλέσας σκίλλῃ ἢ σκύλακι κελεῦσαι αὐτὸν περικαθᾶραι.

9. ἀκαθάρτους καθαρμούς. Servius, commenting on Virg. Aen. VI. 740 f. (aliae panduntur inanes suspensae ad ventos: aliis sub gurgite vasto infectum eluitur scelus aut exuritur igni), says that 'in sacris Liberi omnibus tres sunt istae purgationes; nam aut taeda purgantur et sulphure (δᾷδας καὶ θεῖον, l. 8, 19, 20), aut aqua abluuntur (p. 42. 4 ἀπὸ κρουνῶν τριῶν ὕδατι περιρρᾶναι), aut aere ventilantur.' The fourth element was also used for purification by smearing the body with clay, to which reference is made by Demosthenes in his account of the bringing up of Aeschines, καθαίρων τοὺς τελουμένους καὶ ἀπομάττων τῷ πηλῷ καὶ τοῖς πιτύροις (de Cor. 313), on which Reiske notes 'Loti fricabantur creta ochra argilla et furfuribus, quae sunt res abstergendis sordibus perquam accommodatae.' Cf. Wytt. on Plut. de Superst. 166 τὴν περιμακτρίαν καλεῖ γραῦν, 'istius modi lustrationis pars erat ut corpus lustrandum circumlineretur in primis luto, tum abstergeretur: quorum illud est περιμάττειν, hoc ἀπομάττειν: sed utrumque promiscue de tota lustratione dicitur.' This purification was known as πήλωσις. He also cites ib. 168 D περιθυόμενος οἴκοι κάθηται περιματτόμενος, αἱ δὲ γρᾶες, καθάπερ παττάλῳ, φησὶν ὁ Βίων, ὅ τι ἂν τύχωσιν αὐτῷ περιάπτουσι. Allusion is made to the πήλωσις in p. 44. 3 below, and to the περιάμματα in p. 42. 12. Cf. Protr. P. 89 οἱ μὲν τοῖς γόησι πεπιστευκότες τὰ περίαπτα καὶ τὰς ἐπαοιδὰς ὡς σωτηρίους δῆθεν ἀποδέχονται.

10. ἅγιον οἶδεν τὸ ἦθος. For this use of οἶδα cf. Str. II. P. 452 init. ὁ ποιμήν (sc. Hermas) δικαίους οἶδέ τινας ἐν ἔθνεσιν, Schweigh. Lex. Herodot. s.v. εἰδέναι and ἐπίσταμαι, Schmid Att. IV. 415-7.

12. τὰ ἐκ τὰ ἀπὸ τῶν περικαθαρθέντων. Beside the ordinary modes of purification, the stain of sin might be removed by vicarious atonement, as

by the execution of the δημόσιοι or φαρμακοί at Athens, or by animals which were either slaughtered or driven into the wilderness bearing the curse in behalf of the people, like the scape-goat. The fastening of eggs to the person of the individual who needed purification, brought him into immediate contact with a form of animal life, which (as drawing to itself the punishment he had deserved) ought at least to become sterilized. The fact that this was not the case proves the inefficacy of the ceremony. On the use of eggs in purification see Luc. *Dial. Mort.* I. 1, where the impiety of the Cynic is shown by his eating the offerings to Hecate or ᾠὸν ἐκ καθαρσίου. Cognat cites Ov. *A. A.* II. 329 et veniat quae lustret anus lectumque locumque, praeferat et tremula sulphur et ova manu, Juv. VI. 516.

17. **Προιτίδας.** Abas, king of Argos, the son of Lynceus, had two twin sons, Acrisios and Proetos, who contended for the kingdom after his death. The latter being defeated took refuge in Lycia, where he married Sthenoboea the king's daughter, and by his aid established himself in Tiryns, while Acrisios ruled Argos. The three daughters of Proetos were stricken with madness as a punishment for pride and impiety, and Melampus was called in to restore them to their senses. The common legend says nothing of these incantations, but speaks only of sacred dances. In the scholia to *Od.* XV. 225 the cure is said to have been wrought by sacrifices and prayers to Hera. Others attributed the cure to Asclepius.

20. **πολυφλοίσβοιο θαλάσσης.** Probably this refers to the Dead Sea, *Lacus Asphaltites*, from which the ancients obtained most of their bitumen (Plin. *N. H.* XXXV. 15). Tacitus (*Hist.* V. 6) describes how it was collected, 'undantes bitumine moles pelli manuque trahi ad littus.' Some read πολυφλοίσβῳ τε θαλάσσῃ, understanding it of salt water. We read of the use of bitumen in incantations (Virg. *Ecl.* VIII. 82). Many of the ingredients mentioned by Diphilus are prescribed as a remedy for diseases of sheep by Virgil: 'et spumas miscent argenti et sulfura viva, Idaeasque pices et pingues unguine ceras, scillamque elleborosque graves nigrumque bitumen' (*Geo.* III. 449).

22. **Ἀήρ.** Identified with Zeus by Philemon (*Fab. Inc.* II. 3) Ἀήρ, ὃν ἄν τις ὀνομάσειε καὶ Δία.

23. **Ἀντικύραν.** Used for the hellebore which grew there, as in Hor. *Sat.* II. 3. 83 nescio an Anticyram ratio illis destinet omnem, *A. P.* 300 tribus Anticyris caput insanabile.

κόριν. Kock translates 'ut huic mordaci homini aculeum adimam.' Cf. Philostr. *V. Soph.* II. 3, p. 588 δήγματα κόρεων τὰς λοιδορίας καλῶν, Hor. *Sat.* I. 10. 78 Men moveat cimex ?

§ 27. p. 44, line 3. **περιμάξάτωσαν.** See n. on p. 42. 9, and Wytt. on Plut. *de Superstitione,* p. 166 A τὴν περιμακτρίαν κάλει γραῦν, Lobeck, *Agl.* 632 foll.

5. **φακούς.** See Lobeck *Agl.* p. 254 n.

6. ταῖς ἁγνός ἐστιν—συνειδός. The rhythm and the thought both suggest that this is a continuation of the quotation, and this is confirmed by the emphatic τῷ γὰρ ὄντι of l. 10.

13. αὐτίκα. See the Appendix.

χρεών = χρεὼν εἶναι. S.

14. διὰ τοῦ λόγου τοῦ ὀρθοῦ. See below p. 94. 21.

15. τῶν προηγουμένων. Barnard compares *Str.* VI. § 162 ὁ γνωστικὸς ἐν τοῖς κυριωτάτοις ἀεὶ διατρίβει, εἰ δέ που σχολὴ ἀπὸ τῶν προηγουμένων, ἀντὶ τῆς ἄλλης ῥᾳθυμίας, καὶ τῆς Ἑλληνικῆς ἅπτεται φιλοσοφίας.

17. μυστηρίων. See pp. 8. 5, 10. 10, and Appendix.

§ 28. **20. ἐν τόπῳ τινὶ περιγράφομεν.** See 1 Kings viii. 27, Isa. lxvi. 1, *Str.* v. P. 691.

22. περιεκτικόν. Often absolute 'comprehensive,' but also, as here, 'comprehending.' H.

23. βαναύσου τέχνης. Cf. the description of these arts in P. 45, where the ἄγαλμα is defined as ὕλη νεκρὰ τεχνίτου χερὶ μεμορφωμένη, also P. 50 and 78, where even Pheidias and Praxiteles are said to practise βαναύσους τέχνας, below pp. 46. 5, 48. 6.

24. οὐχὶ ἀμείνους κ.τ.λ. The allusion is to the Stoics; see the account of the theology of Cleanthes in Cic. *N. D.* I. 37 'tum ipsum mundum deum dicit esse, tum totius naturae menti atque animo tribuit hoc nomen, tum ultimum et altissimum atque undique circumfusum et extremum omnia cingentem atque complexum ardorem, qui aether nominetur certissimum deum iudicat.' It is impossible that Clement, who writes thus here, could have charged the Stoics with anthropomorphism, as he is made to do by the corrupt reading in § 37 (p. 64. 20).

p. 46, lines 1—3. Plat. *Legg.* VII. 803 C ἄνθρωπον δέ...θεοῦ τι παίγνιον εἶναι μεμηχανημένον: in the context παιδιά occurs often, especially in the same sentence, τούτῳ δὴ δεῖν τῷ τρόπῳ ξυνεπόμενον καὶ παίζοντα ὅτι καλλίστας παιδιὰς πάντ' ἄνδρα...διαβιῶναι, which explains παιδιαῖς τέχνης. H. See also *Legg.* X. 889, where it is said that the greatest things are produced by nature and chance, and only the smaller by art, τέχνην δὲ ὕστερον...αὐτὴν θνητὴν ἐκ θνητῶν γεγεννηκέναι παιδιάς τινας, ἀληθείας οὐ σφόδρα μετεχούσας ...οἷα ἡ γραφικὴ γεννᾷ καὶ μουσικὴ καὶ ὅσαι ταύταις εἰσὶ συνέριθοι τέχναι. 'It is to the play of such arts that we are indebted for our belief in the gods'; Cic. *N. D.* I. 81 Vulcanum, Apollinem, reliquosque deos ea facie novimus qua pictores fictoresque voluerunt; and the argument on enshrinement which follows below (l. 11—25).

10—23 resumes p. 44. 20 foll. Evidently taken from some other writer. H. The style of argument resembles that (taken probably from Carneades or some other Academic) which we find in Cic. *N. D.* III. and in Sext. Empiricus. Cl. is here answering the charge brought against the Christians, that the absence of images and temples proves them to be atheists. He met this, at the beginning of § 28, by an argument drawn from the nature of God. 'How can the Infinite Spirit be confined to one spot of earth?' But he is not content with this: he wishes to show that the enshrinement which the heathen think essential to the idea of divinity is really an evidence of the non-entity of their gods. 'Before enshrinement they were nothing: how can this action, this whim (παιδιά) on the part of man, give being and life and power to that which was previously non-existent?' Apparently there is a play on the two senses of ἱδρύω, 'to fix in place' and 'to consecrate,' i.e. to enshrine the God in a temple or image, the latter being one of the παιδιαὶ τέχνης referred to by Plato (l. 2). H. J. thus sums up the argument: 'Gods are spoken of as ἱδρυμένοι. (A) Now nothing can be ἱδρυμένον unless it has passed through a process of ἱδρύεσθαι, and this process implies a previous stage in which the thing was ἀνίδρυτον. (B) Hence if God ἱδρύεται, he was previously ἀνίδρυτος and non-existent: for by ἀνίδρυτον and μὴ ὄν we mean the same thing. (C) But the existent cannot be 'set up' either by a non-existent or by another existent, since it exists of itself. Can the existent then be set up by itself? No. It did not set up itself having been previously not-set-up: for then it would have been non-existent, since it is the non-existent (and not the existent) which is not-set-up. Finally that which is supposed to have been set up cannot make itself what it was already.'

10. ἀνιδρύτου. Usually 'unfixed,' 'unstable': but here it implies the negation of the religious sense of ἱδρύω and ἐνιδρύω, 'to set up' an altar, or god. Cf. Orig. *Cels.* III. 34. 36. **H.** Lobeck *Phryn.* p. 730 gives many exx. of the word, which is often written ἀίδρυτος. It is found with its usual meaning in Plut. *Mor.* 925 F, ὁ κόσμος ἀνέστιος καὶ ἀνίδρυτός ἐστιν ἐν ἀπείρῳ κενῷ φερόμενος, Dion. H. *Ant.* I. 15 ἡ νῆσος ἀνίδρυτός ἐστι, Philo M. 1. 272 ὁ μὲν φαῦλος ἄοικος καὶ ἄπολις καὶ ἀνίδρυτος καὶ ψυγάς, ib. 2. 112 τὸ τῆς ψυχῆς ἀνίδρυτον, 2. 268 ὁ φιλήδονος ἀνίδρυτος, 2. 382 (and 454) ἀνερμάτιστα καὶ ἀνίδρυτα ἤθη, 2. 413 τὸ ἀίδρυτον καὶ πεπλανημένον δόξης, 2. 361 (and 216) τύχη ἀβέβαιος καὶ ἀίδρυτος, 1. 650 ἀίδρυτοι μὲν οἱ λογισμοί...ἀνίδρυτον δὲ καὶ τὸ σῶμα...ἀνίδρυτα δὲ καὶ τὰ ἐκτός. In our passage the word occurs six times in the sense 'unenshrined.'

12. Two points: the setting up of a god implies a prior place to set him up in, and also a prior agent by whom he was set up. **H.**

§ 29. 18. αὐτὸ τὸ ὄν. The Being of beings, the localisation of which in an individual shrine is a special contradiction. **H.**

19. ἐνιδρύσει. The word occurs above p. 26. 14 (ἀνθρώπου δικαίου ψυχὴ ἐν ᾗ τεμενίζεται καὶ ἐνιδρύεται ὁ πάντων ἡγεμών, and below p. 48. 14 ὁ γνωστικὸς ἐν ᾧ ὁ θεὸς ἐνίδρυται and l. 19 τὸ ἐνίδρυτον καὶ τὸ ἐνιδρυόμενον, also in P. 755 οἱ ἔμπειροι τοῦ λόγου κατὰ τὰς ἱδρύσεις ἐν πολλοῖς τῶν ἱερῶν καὶ σχεδὸν πάσαις ταῖς θήκαις (MS. πάσας τὰς θήκας) τῶν κατοιχομένων ἐνιδρύσαντο <ψυχάς>, δαίμονας...καλοῦντες, Philo M. 2. 412 εἰσοισάμενος ἐκ πρώτης ἡλικίας ἄχρι γήρως ἐνιδρύεται (ταῖς ψυχαῖς ὁ τῦφος), Anton. III. 6 ὁ ἐνιδρύμενος ἐν σοὶ δαίμων, Plut. *Mor.* 924 D ἄνω τὴν σελήνην ἐνιδρύοντας, οὐχ ὅπου τὸ μέσον ἐστί. The MS. inserts εἶναι before ἐνιδρύσει, probably owing to dittography.

21. ὃ φθάσαν εἶχεν ὄν. 'Which was its condition already.'

22. οὐ δὲ τὰ ὄντα. i.e. all particular ὄντα belong to αὐτὸ τὸ ὄν. H.

24. ἀνθρωποειδές, the most usual classical term for human form, whether in beasts or deities, from Herod. (who also uses ἀνθρωποφυής) onward, including Aristot. (*Met.* 997 b 10; 1074 b 5). Probably includes both σχῆμα or μορφή and πάθη. H.

25. σκέπης, used of a coat in P. 325.

26. ἀκολούθων πάντων. The MS. reading, παθῶν, is unsuitable here, where (as we see from the following line) the argument is that those who are ὁμοιοσχήμονες and ὁμοιοπαθεῖς with man, must share the same kind of life. If the middle letters of πάντων had got rubbed, the copyist may have been led to write παθῶν from the following ὁμοιοπαθεῖς. Whether understood of human passions or of the conditions attaching to food, &c., it seems to me impossible that Cl. should have written it.

p. 48, line 2. On the spiritual temple see Hort, *Ecclesia*, p. 163 f. and Cl. *Protr.* P. 90 *fin.*

3. κατασκεύασμα, 'apparatus' generally, but especially applied to buildings and statues. H.

7. The MS. reading ἀγύρτου does not seem appropriate; but there may be a reference to Daedalus (who might be called an ἀγύρτης) in δεδαιδαλμένον. He was said to have introduced life-like statues: cf. Athenag. *Supp.* c. 17 and Diod. iv. 76 foll., also i. 61. 97, and Plato *Meno* 97 D. H. In these words Cl. meets the charge of atheism brought against the Christians from the absence of a material temple, as he does in § 30 that based on the absence of sacrifices. H.'s defence of ἀγύρτου seems to me too far-fetched. I had thought of οὐδὲ ἀγγέλου χειρὶ δεδαιδαλμένον, as we find the same contrast between the work of angels and of God in *Str.* P. 769 ἀνθρώπων μὲν οὐδεὶς ἀλλ' οὐδὲ ἄγγελός τις... (but God himself is the teacher of men): also in Heb. i., ii. Christ is contrasted with angels. Angels were believed by the Jews to have been concerned in the giving of the law, including of course the injunctions respecting the tabernacle, cf. Gal. iii. 19, Acts vii. 53, Heb. ii. 2. An angel is represented by Ezek. xl. 3 foll. as planning the new temple; cf. Rev. xxi. 9. Valentinus held that man was made by the angels, *Str.* P. 448 and 449 ὁ φόβος ἐπιβούλους τοῦ σφετέρου πλάσματος πεποίηκε τοὺς ἀγγέλους, ὡς ἐνιδρυμένου τῷ δημιουργήματι τοῦ σπέρματος τῆς ἄνωθεν αἰτίας. The same doctrine was held by Simon Magus, Saturninus, and Carpocrates (Iren. I. 24. 1, 25. 1); see *ib.* IV. 20. 1 'Non ergo angeli fecerunt nos neque plasmaverunt nos, neque angeli potuerunt imaginem facere Dei,—nec enim indigebat horum Deus, quasi ipse suas non haberet manus,' *ib.* I. 22. 1, IV. 7. 4. On the whole however I prefer H. J.'s emendation Τυρίου, referring to the Tyrian artist sent by Hiram to Solomon (1 Kings vii. 13, 14): ἀλλ' οὐδέ will then contrast the finer work of decoration (δεδαιδαλμένον) done by the artist, with the work of the common builder (βάναυσος). The corruption in the MS. is more easily explained from the somewhat obscure ΤΥΡΙΟΥ (ΑΓΥΡΤΟΥ) than from the familiar ΑΓΓΕΛΟΥ (ΑΓγεΤΟΥ); and we find Hiram referred to as ἀρχιτέκτων Τύριος in *Str.* I. P. 396 *fin.*

δεδαιδαλμένον. Before Clement apparently only poetic. He uses it in *Protr*. P. 43 Ὄσιριν δαιδαλθῆναι ἐκέλευσεν πολυτελῶς. H.

8. νῦν implies that the building was already called ἐκκλησία. H.

10. ἀξίας τοῦ θεοῦ. Cf. *Const. Apost*. VI. 27. 3 ἐγυμνώθη τῆς ἀξίας, ἀντὶ ἀρχαγγέλου διάβολος αἱρεσάμενος εἶναι.

12. οὐδενὸς ἀνταξίῳ. Cf. P. 71 ἀντάξιος σωτηρίας μισθός.

16. ἀπεικόνισμα, common in Philo and Greek Fathers. H.

17. ἄγαλμα is properly not the mere image, but the image considered as set up in honour of the god, from the old sense of ἀγάλλω, 'to venerate.' Cf. Plat. *Legg*. XI. 931 A. Hier. in *Aur. Carm*. 25. H. See above n. on p. 26. 12, and l. 23 below.

αὐτή = 'in itself,' as distinguished from διαπραττομένη ἔργα. On διαπρ. see above p. 30, l. 2. H. After μακαρία μὲν αὐτὴ τυγχάνῃ, we naturally expect μακάρια δὲ διαπράττηται ἔργα. The contractions used in verbal terminations are often confused.

19. The present ἐνιδρυόμενον is necessary in opposition to ἐνίδρυτον. H.

22. τὸ μέλλον πιστεύειν πιστὸν ἤδη τῷ θεῷ, 'faithful already in God's eyes': cf. "Lord, I believe; help thou mine unbelief." H. *Paed*. P. 113 τὸ μέλλον τοῦ χρόνου τῇ δυνάμει τοῦ θελήματος προλαμβάνεται.

23. ἐνάρετον. Cf. above p. 16. 14, 20. 5, below p. 112. 11, 114. 10, *Str*. I. 376 *med*. τὸν κεκοσμημένον τὴν ψυχὴν ἐναρέτως. H. See also Lob. *Phryn*. 328.

§ 30. 25. See above § 28.

27. θυσιῶν. It seems necessary to correct the MS. θυσίαν. There are instances of ἐπιθυμεῖν with the accusative as in LXX, Exod. XX. 17 and Deut. V. 21 οὐκ ἐπιθυμήσεις τὴν γυναῖκα τοῦ πλησίον σου κ.τ.λ., but not in such good writers as Clement (in *Str*. I. p. 412 τέκνον δὲ ἐπιθυμοῦσα, Dind. reads τέκνων from Philo), and the plural is more likely here. H. In *Str*. III. P. 513 *fin*. Cl. keeps the τὴν γυναῖκα of the LXX, but has τῆς γυναικός eight lines before and twelve lines after. H. J.

p. 50, line 1. ὧν ἅπτεται πάθος φθαρτὰ πάντα ἐστί. This is the argument of Carneades given in Cic. *N. D*. III. 29 cumque omne animal patibilem naturam habeat, nullum est eorum quod effugiat accipiendi aliquid extrinsecus, id est quasi ferendi et patiendi, necessitatem, et, si omne animal tale est, immortale nullum est...mortale igitur omne animal et dissolubile, cf. Sext. Emp. IX. 146 εἰ οὖν αἰσθάνεται ὁ θεός, καὶ ἑτεροῦται· εἰ δὲ ἑτεροῦται, ἑτερώσεως δεκτικός ἐστι καὶ μεταβολῆς κ.τ.λ. The phrase ἅπτεται πάθος is used in a different sense above p. 12. 14.

5. καταμεμφομένους τοῖς ἀνθρώποις τῶν ἱερῶν. The classical constr. is καταμ. τινά τι or τινί or ἐπί τινι. In later Gr. we find the dat. of the person, as in Longus *Past*. II. 21 ταῖς Νύμφαις ὡς προδούσαις κατεμέμφετο, and gen. of the thing, as in Plut. *Dion*. 8. μέμφομαι is used in classical writers with the acc., gen. or dat. of the person, and acc. or gen. of the thing: cf. Aesch. *Th*. 652 οὔποτ' ἀνδρὶ τῷδε κηρυκευμάτων μέμψει.

8. τὰ μηρὰ περιλέψαντες...κρέα πάντα. We have an example of the

double accusative after π. in Il. l. 236 περὶ γάρ ῥά ἑ χαλκὸς ἔλεψεν φύλλα τε καὶ φλοιόν.

9. **σφόνδυλον**, Att. σφόνδυλον, see Lob. *Phryn.* p. 110 foll., Moeris ed. Kock, p. 238 *s.v.* σχινδαλμός.

16. **διαστελλόμενον**, 'explaining.' H. Comparing the other passages in which the word is used by Cl., *e.g. Str.* P. 376 εἰ δὲ διαστέλλεσθαι διὰ τοὺς φιλεγκλήμονας δεήσει, 449 διαστέλλειν τὸ ἀγαθὸν τοῦ δικαίου, 888 διαστέλλειν τὸ ψεῦδος ἀπὸ τἀληθοῦς, also the use of διαστολή in P. 781 ἡ διαστολὴ τῶν τε ὀνομάτων καὶ τῶν πραγμάτων...μέγα φῶς ἐντίκτει ταῖς ψυχαῖς, I think it is better to translate 'distinguishing' or 'particularizing,' which seems to me to suit the passage better than 'explaining.' Or it might be taken in the sense of 'giving orders' as in the LXX and N. T.

20. **ἐπιπόλαιον** (Hesych. ap. Mein. v. 83)=ἐπίπλοον, *omentum*. H. Cf. Juv. XIII. 114 foll. Juppiter...cur in carbone tuo charta pia tura soluta ponimus et sectum vituli iecur albaque porci omenta?

21. **γλυκεῖαν**, 'gall,' as Meineke shows, IV. 613 foll. H.

§ 31. p. 52, line 1. **ἡ τῶν ὁλοκαυτωμάτων κνῖσα καὶ τοῖς θηρίοις ἀφεκτέα.** The neuter alone is recognized in L. and S., and certainly the commoner construction is the impersonal, τῆς κνίσης τοῖς θηρίοις ἀφεκτέον, 'beasts must abstain from the smoke of the sacrifice.' We have an example of the personal (gerundive) construction in Epiphan. *Haer.* XXXIII. 5 (the ten commandments are) εἴς τε ἀναίρεσιν τῶν ἀφεκτέων καὶ εἰς πρόσταξιν τῶν ποιητέων. Cf. below p. 60. 6 ἃ καὶ κυσὶν πεινῶσιν οὐχὶ βρώσιμα.

3. **γέρας**, 'meed' exactly: the special prize of the chieftain, set apart for him before the spoil is divided. H. Used here of the gods, as in the speech of Zeus (*Il.* IV. 48) οὐ γάρ μοί ποτε βωμὸς ἐδεύετο δαιτὸς ἐΐσης, λοιβῆς τε κνίσης τε· τὸ γὰρ λάχομεν γέρας ἡμεῖς, referred to in *Protr.* P. 15. Cf. below p. 60. 8, and Porph. *de Abst.* II. 42 (the evil daemons rejoice) λοιβῇ τε κνίσῃ τε δι' ὧν αὐτῶν τὸ πνευματικὸν καὶ σωματικὸν πιαίνεται. ζῇ γὰρ τοῦτο ἀτμοῖς καὶ ἀναθυμιάσεσι...καὶ δυναμοῦται ταῖς ἐκ τῶν αἱμάτων καὶ σαρκῶν κνίσαις, 'wherefore a wise man will refrain from participating in sacrifices which bring him near to such beings.' See above p. 24. 5, and passages quoted in Cudworth, vol. III. 350 f.

οὐκ ἂν φθάνοιεν καὶ τοὺς μαγείρους θεοποιοῦντες. So Aristaeus *ap.* Euseb. *Pr. Ev.* VIII. 9 § 371 C (referring to the deification of the discoverers of wheat and wine, &c.) ἔτι καὶ νῦν εὑρετικώτεροι...τῶν πρὶν εἰσι πολλοί, καὶ οὐκ ἂν φθάνοιεν αὐτοὺς προσκυνοῦντες, cf. W. Schmid *Att.* IV. p. 427.

5. **τὸν ἰπνὸν αὐτόν.** Possibly we should read τὴν κάπνην αὐτήν: κάπνη is the hole for the smoke, used Ar. *Vesp.* 143; Alex. in Mein. III. 464. Cf. Hesych. *s. v.* ὀργητός. καπνοδόχη has the same meaning, cf. Pherec. (Mein. II. 325):

κἄπειθ' ἵνα μὴ πρὸς τοῖσι βωμοῖς πανταχοῦ
ἀεὶ λοχῶντες βωμολόχοι καλώμεθα,
ἐποίησεν ὁ Ζεὺς καπνοδόχην μεγάλην πάνυ.

Or ὀπήν may be right, with the same sense. H. I think ἰπνόν must certainly be retained, cf. Arist. *Vesp.* 837 ὁ κύων παράξας ἐς τὸν ἰπνὸν ἀναρπάσας τροφαλίδα τυροῦ Σικελικὴν κατεδήδοκεν. The only difficulty is the following feminine, which may be easily explained by supposing that ἐσχάραν has been lost after προσεχεστέραν. For the last word see below p. 62. 15 προσεχέστερον ὁ γνωστικὸς οἰκειοῦται θεῷ, p. 82. 26 ὁ θεὸς προσεχεστέρᾳ τηρήσας ἐπισκοπῇ, P. 798 ὁ γνωστικὸς προσεχεστέραν ἀναμάσσεται σωτηρίαν.

13. **κατὰ τὴν ἐπιθυμίαν κακούμενον**, 'being distressed owing to the craving.' Cf. P. 530 ἐπιθυμία λύπη τις καὶ φροντὶς δι᾽ ἔνδειαν ὀρεγομένη τινός.

17, 18. **ἐξ αὐτῆς τῆς τοῦ οἰκείου σώματος ἀναθυμιάσεως**. A common explanation was that they lived by sucking their paws (Plin. *N. H.* VIII. 35). Heraclitus held τὴν μὲν τοῦ κόσμου ψυχὴν ἀναθυμίασιν ἐκ τῶν ἐν αὐτῷ ὑγρῶν, τὴν δὲ ἐν τοῖς ζῴοις ἀπὸ τῆς ἐκτὸς καὶ τῆς ἐν αὐτοῖς ἀναθυμιάσεως (*Plac. Phil.* IV. 3, 4); so the Stoics, αὐτὴν τὴν ψυχὴν ὁρίζονται πνεῦμα συμφυὲς καὶ ἀναθυμίασιν αἰσθητικὴν ἀναπτομένην ἀπὸ τῶν ἐν σώματι ὑγρῶν (Plut. *V. Hom.* § 127), τοιοῦτον δὴ καὶ αὐτὴ ἡ ζωὴ ἑκάστου οἷον ἡ ἀφ᾽ αἵματος ἀναθυμίασις καὶ ἡ ἐκ τοῦ ἀέρος διάπνευσις (Anton. VI. 15)

19. **αὐτοῖς**, 'in their view,' as above p. 36. 22. H.

22. Plat. *Legg.* VII. 799 A καὶ χορείαις ποίαισι γεραίρειν τὴν τότε θυσίαν. But it is hard to take γεραίροντες with θυσίαν here, as τῷ δικαιοτάτῳ λόγῳ cannot be instrumental. H.

23. When accompanied by righteousness (as in the 4th psalm) the prayer is best and holiest. H.

ἀναπέμπω, of hymns, and especially their close: doubtless with uplifted voice, expressing oblation. See Hein. on Eus. *H. E.* IV. 15. 34 (ἀναπέμψαντος αὐτοῦ τὸ Ἀμήν); Just. *Apol.* I. 65, 67; and the end of Clement's *Paed.* 310 foll. esp. 311 *fin.*, which well illustrates the whole passage. H.

τῷ δικαιοτάτῳ λόγῳ, superlative of the Platonic phrase ὁ δίκαιος λόγος; here used personally: cf. 1 John ii. 1 παράκλητον...δίκαιον. The offering is made to Him as in *Paed.* 311 (τῷ λόγῳ προσευξώμεθα), apparently as thereby made to the Father. Origen distinguishes the process of sending to the High Priest and Paraclete for Him to present to the Father. See *de Orat.* 15 foll. and Ashton's notes; also *in Celsum* iii. 34 *fin.* He uses ἀναπέμπω, προσάγω to the Father, προσφέρω to the Son. H. The same phrase is used instrumentally (='most justly') in Plut. *Mor.* 737 E τὰ φωνήεντα τῷ δικαιοτάτῳ λόγῳ πρωτεύει τῶν ἀφώνων, *ib.* 1072 D. Perhaps it would be better to take it thus with γεραίροντες, putting a comma after ἀναπέμπομεν instead of after λόγῳ.

24. The sense apparently is that we γεραίρομεν and δοξάζομεν the Father through Him (better so probably than 'thereby'). H.

25. **δοξάζοντες ὃν μεμαθήκαμεν**. The change of MS. ᾆ to ὅν is indispensable. Cf. *Paed.* 310 δι᾽ ἣν (οἰκονομίαν)...ὁ ἄνθρωπος...παιδαγωγούμενος πατέρα...ἐκεῖ (ἐν οὐρανοῖς) λαμβάνει, ὃν ἐπὶ γῆς μανθάνει. Either καὶ before διὰ or δὲ before δοξάζοντες is a gain, though perhaps not necessary. H. Cf. *Protr.* P. 89 μάθωμεν θεόν, 82 οὐ γὰρ πιστεύουσι τῷ θεῷ οὐδὲ ἐκμανθάνουσι τὴν δύναμιν αὐτοῦ, *Str.* P. 829 τὸν υἱὸν παρ᾽ οὗ ἐκμανθάνει τὸ ἐπέκεινα αἴτιον.

26, 27. τὸ ἐπίγειον, implying in contrast another altar, not among us or here or on earth: cf. Heb. xiii. 10. H.

27. ταῖς εὐχαῖς. Cf. Acts ii. 42 ἦσαν δὲ προσκαρτεροῦντες τῇ διδαχῇ τῶν ἀποστόλων καὶ τῇ κοινωνίᾳ, τῇ κλάσει τοῦ ἄρτου καὶ ταῖς προσευχαῖς, Ign. *Smyrn.* 6 εὐχαριστίας καὶ προσευχῆς ἀπέχονται with Lightfoot's n., below p. 136. 25.

§ 32. p. 54, line 2. διαπνεῖται. The word is used of external ventilation (as in the case of the rustling of leaves in the wind), and of internal, as in the arteries which were supposed to transmit air through the body (see my n. on Cic. *N. D.* II. 138 spiritus per arterias). To this latter was compared the imbibing of sacrificial fumes by the airy body of the demon. Cf. Arist. *Probl.* I. 21 ὅπερ ἐν θώρακι ἀναπνοή, τοῦτο ἐν τῷ σώματι διαπνοὴ διὰ τῶν ἀρτηριῶν and *Resp.* 4, 5, Galen (*Hippocr. de Diaeta* 15) ὀνομάζω ἀναπνοὴν μὲν τὴν διὰ στόματος ἔξω τε καὶ ἔσω φορὰν τοῦ πνεύματος, διαπνοὴν δὲ τὴν δι' ὅλου τοῦ σώματος ὁμοίως γιγνομένην, esp. Ὑγιεινά I. c. 12 quoted by Gataker on M. Ant. p. 81, also *ib.* pp. 228, 229, (VI. 16) τίμιον οὔτε τὸ διαπνεῖσθαι ὡς τὰ φυτά, οὔτε τὸ ἀναπνεῖν ὡς τὰ βοσκήματα, where Gat. quotes many parallels, and proposes to read δένδρων for δαιμόνων here. The correctness of the MS. reading is however proved by Psellus (Boiss. p. 13) quoting a certain Marcus, οἱ δαίμονες τρέφονται οἱ μὲν δι' εἰσπνοῆς, ὡς τὸ ἐν ἀρτηρίαις καὶ ἐν νεύροις πνεῦμα, οἱ δὲ δι' ὑγρότητος, ἀλλ' οὐ στόματι καθ' ἡμᾶς, ἀλλ' ὥσπερ σπόγγοι, σπῶντες τῆς παρακειμένης ὑγρότητος ἔξωθεν, Basil on Isa. cited by Cudworth, vol. III. p. 351, δαίμοσιν αἱ θυσίαι φέρουσί τινα ἡδονὴν καὶ χρείαν ἐκθυμιώμεναι, διὰ τῆς καύσεως ἐξατμιζομένου τοῦ αἵματος καὶ οὕτω διὰ τῆς τοιαύτης λεπτοποιήσεως εἰς τὴν σύστασιν αὐτῶν ἀναλαμβανομένου· ὅλοι γὰρ δι' ὅλων τρέφονται τοῖς ἀτμοῖς, οὐ διὰ μασήσεως καὶ κοιλίας. Mosheim in his n. on Cudworth says that this view was combated by Jamblichus *de Myst. Aegypt.* v. 10, p. 125.

3. ἐμπνεῖται. In classical writers the verb is commonly used in one of three senses, (1) 'to breathe upon,' (2) 'to breathe' or 'live,' (3) of divine inspiration. I do not know any example of the special sense it bears here: Aristotle however carefully distinguishes the breathing of fishes from that of animals (*Part. An.* IV. 13) ἀδύνατον ἅμα τὸ αὐτὸ ἀναπνεῖν καὶ βράγχια ἔχειν, (*de Resp.* 1) ὅσα μὴ ἔχει πλεύμονα οὐδὲν ἀναπνεῖ, (*ib.* 2) εἰ ἀνάγκη τὰ ἀναπνέοντα ἐκπνεῖν καὶ εἰσπνεῖν, ἐκπνεῖν δὲ μὴ ἐνδέχεται...φανερὸν ὡς οὐδ' ἀναπνεῖ, (*ib.* 10) ὅσα δὲ βράγχια ἔχει πάντα καταψύχεται δεχόμενα τὸ ὕδωρ... τὰ δὲ βράγχια πρὸς τὴν ἀπὸ τοῦ ὕδατος κατάψυξίν ἐστι, (*ib.* 21) αἰρομένου μὲν τοῦ θερμοῦ τοῦ ἐν τῷ αἵματι...αἴρονται καὶ τὰ βράγχια καὶ διιᾶσι τὸ ὕδωρ· κατιόντος δὲ πρὸς τὴν καρδίαν διὰ τῶν πόρων καὶ καταψυχομένου συνίζουσι καὶ ἀφιᾶσι τὸ ὕδωρ.

4. διαστολήν. The process is explained in the last quotation from Arist. *de Resp.* The word is more commonly used of the lungs.

4, 5. περιπνεῖται. The process is explained by Arist. (*de Resp.* 9) 'the longer-lived insects have a fissure below the waist, and the membrane which covers this fissure is thinner than elsewhere, so that refrigeration may take place through it. The sort of panting sound made by certain insects is produced by the innate spirit (τῷ ἐμφύτῳ πνεύματι) within the body, which by the rise and fall which it occasions causes friction (τρίψιν) against the membrane, for there is a motion of this part in insects corresponding to the motion of the lungs in animals and of the gills in fishes.' Cf. *Cambridge Nat. Hist.* vol. v. pp. 128—132 ' Placed along the sides of the body are little apertures for the admission of air to the respiratory system. They are called *spiracles* or *stigmata*, varying in number.' ' There are in insects no lungs, but air is carried to every part of the body by means of the spiracles attached to tracheae': also Ogle's ed. of Arist. *Part. An.* II. 16, p. 182. As in the case of ἐμπνέω, this seems to be a unique use of the verb.

8. ἀντιδιαστολήν, elsewhere 'distinction'; here means the dilatation of the lungs following on and corresponding to the dilatation of the thorax. Cf. Theoph. *Corp. Hum. Fabr.* III. 2 ὁ πνεύμων οὐ καθ' αὑτὸν κινεῖται, ἀλλὰ τῇ κινήσει τοῦ θώρακος συγκινεῖται κατὰ τὴν τοῦ κενοῦ ὑποχώρησιν, *ib.* 4 ἡ χρεία τῆς ἀναπνοῆς διὰ τὴν καρδίαν, δεομένης αὐτῆς τοῦ ἔξωθεν ἀέρος...ἀναψύχει γὰρ αὐτὴν ὁ ἔξωθεν ἀὴρ εἰσπνεόμενος ὑπὸ θερμότητος ζέουσαν. διπλῆς δὲ τῆς κινήσεως τῆς ἐν καρδίᾳ οὔσης κατὰ διαστολὴν καὶ συστολήν, ἐν μὲν τῷ διαστέλλεσθαι καταψύχεται, ἐν δὲ τῷ συστέλλεσθαι τὰ λιγνυώδη περιττώματα ἀπωθεῖται, *ib.* 11 ὁ θώραξ ὄργανόν ἐστι ψυχικὸν κινούμενον μὲν κατὰ προαίρεσιν ...κατὰ διαστολὴν καὶ συστολὴν ὑπὸ μυῶν καὶ νεύρων. διεστάλη τοιγαροῦν ὁ θώραξ...ἐπηκολούθησε δὲ καὶ ὁ πλεύμων...ἕλκεται οὖν ὁ ἔξωθεν ἀὴρ ὑπὸ τοῦ πνεύματος διασταλέντος, Galen *Resp.* vol. IV. p. 466 τοῦ πνεύμονος τὰς διαστολάς τε καὶ συστολὰς ὁ θώραξ οἰακίζει.

9. ῥυθμῷ ἕλκει. The MS. ῥυμουλκεῖ is only used of towing a ship. The word ἕλκει is regularly used of inhaling the breath and ῥυθμῷ has the sense of 'rhythmically' as in Arist. *Spirit.* 4. 7 ὁ σφυγμὸς ὁ αὐτὸς ὢν ῥυθμῷ, Plut. *V. Lyc.* 22 ῥυθμῷ πρὸς τὸν αὐλὸν ἐμβαίνειν.

9, 10. εἰ σπλάγχνα δοῖεν...καὶ μόρια τῷ θεῷ. Cf. Cic. *N. D.* I. 92 habebit igitur linguam deus et non loquetur, dentes, palatum, fauces nullum ad usum, quaeque procreationis causa natura corpori adfinxit, ea frustra habebit deus, &c., *ib.* 94, 99.

11. εἰσηγήσονται. Cf. Plat. *Symp.* 189 πειράσομαι εἰσηγήσασθαι τὴν δύναμιν τοῦ ἔρωτος. For constr. (ind. after opt.) cf. *Str.* II. 507 *init.* εἰ μὴ δέχοιτο, ἀνακάμψει, *ib.* IV. P. 599 *init.* εἰ εὖ φρονοῖμεν, χάριν εἰσόμεθα, below pp. 76. 9, 128. 12.

12. σύμπνοια, not another physiological mode of respiration, but ' taking breath together,' as horses do: Plat. *Legg.* IV. 708 D τὸ δὲ συμπνεῦσαι καί, καθάπερ ἵππων ζεῦγος, καθ' ἕνα εἰς ταυτόν, τὸ λεγόμενον, ξυμφυσῆσαι. Plut. II. 618 D applies the figure ἵνα ᾖ σύμπνους ἡ φάλαγξ δι' ὅλης ἔμψυχον ἔχουσα δεσμόν. Similarly Stoics and Platonists spoke of a σύμπνοια of the world. H. Cf. Cic. *N. D.* III. 28 naturam quasi cognatione continuatam conspirare, *Strom.* v. P. 667 συμπνεουσῶν ἐκκλησιῶν.

13. ἡ θυσία...λόγος...ἀναθυμιώμενος. See above p. 22. 11 foll., below l. 18 f., p. 58. 24 f., p. 86. 10 f., P. 469 *fin.*, P. 720 f. A metaphor borrowed from the sacrifices and incense of Pagan worship.

14. ἐκκαλυπτομένης, used rather widely for 'discover,' 'disclose'; but the force as applied to θυσία does not appear; so that it seems necessary to read τῇ θυσίᾳ instead of the MS. τῆς θυσίας. H. Perhaps ἐκκ. may have some reference to the *extispicium* of pagan sacrifices.

16 foll. ἀρχαιότατον. So Porph. *de Abst.* § 27 ἀπ' ἀρχῆς αἱ τῶν καρπῶν ἐγίνοντο τοῖς θεοῖς θυσίαι, Ov. *F.* I. 337 f.

βωμὸν ἐν Δήλῳ. Laert. in Pythag. VIII. 13 βωμὸν προσκυνῆσαι μόνον ἐν Δήλῳ τοῦ Ἀπόλλωνος τοῦ γενέτορος...διὰ τὸ πυροὺς καὶ κριθὰς καὶ τὰ πόπανα μόνα τίθεσθαι ἐπ' αὐτοῦ ἄνευ πυρός, ἱερεῖον δὲ μηδέν, ὥς φησιν Ἀριστοτέλης ἐν Δηλίων πολιτείᾳ. Potter. Cf. Iambl. *V. P.* v. 25, VII. 35, XXIV. 108. H. Porph. *de Abst.* II. 28.

ἁγνόν, 'unpolluted,' used of unbloody sacrifices. See Thucyd. I. 126 θύματα ἐπιχώρια cited by Pollux I. 26: also Plat. *Legg.* VI. 782 C ἁγνὰ θύματα, 759 C φόνου ἁγνόν, Porph. *de Abst.* II. 31 and Bernays 28. 155. H.

19. τὸ θυμίαμα τὴν ὁσίαν εὐχήν. See Lightfoot on Ign. II. p. 44.

20, 21. See Theophr. ap. Porph. II. 27 ὡς οὐκ ἄτιμα ποιούμενοι τὰ θεοῖς θύματα, γεύσασθαι τούτων προήχθησαν, καὶ διὰ τὴν ἀρχὴν τῆς πράξεως ταύτης προσθήκη ἡ ζῳοφαγία γέγονεν τῇ ἀπὸ τῶν καρπῶν τροφῇ κ.τ.λ., Bernays 118 foll. H.

προφάσει. So Thuc. III. 86 ἔπεμψαν οἱ Ἀθηναῖοι τῆς μὲν οἰκειότητος προφάσει, βουλόμενοι δὲ κ.τ.λ., V. 53. 1 πόλεμος ἐγένετο προφάσει μὲν περὶ τοῦ θύματος τοῦ Ἀπόλλωνος, VI. 76. 1 ἤκουσι...προφάσει μὲν ᾗ πυνθάνεσθε, διανοίᾳ δὲ ἣν πάντες ὑπονοοῦμεν, *Str.* P. 319 πλεονεξίας προφάσει.

24. αἱ μὲν γὰρ κατὰ τὸν νόμον θυσίαι. The use of γάρ here is elliptical, implying a limitation on what precedes. 'I speak of heathen sacrifices, for, &c.' For other instances of this use, see n. on p. 32. 3.

τὴν περὶ ἡμᾶς, *i.e.* that which is shown in the care and purification of ourselves. H. Or does it mean 'piety that has to do with us,' *i.e.* the piety of Christians, as opposed to that of the Jews under the law?

25. ἡ τρυγὼν καὶ ἡ περιστερά. Cf. Lev. xii. 8 λήψεται δύο τρυγόνας ἢ δύο νοσσοὺς περιστερῶν, μίαν εἰς ὁλοκαύτωμα καὶ μίαν περὶ ἁμαρτίας, *Paed.* I. P. 106 *init.* ὅταν φῇ ὡς μοσχάρια γαλαθηνά, ἡμᾶς πάλιν ἀλληγορεῖ, καὶ ὡς περιστερὰν ἄκακον καὶ ἄχολον, πάλιν ἡμᾶς. νεοττοὺς τε ἔτι δύο περιστερῶν...ὑπὲρ ἁμαρτίας κελεύει...προσφέρεσθαι, τὸ ἀναμάρτητον...τῶν νεοττῶν εὐπρόσδεκτον εἶναι λέγων τῷ θεῷ καὶ τὸ ὅμοιον τοῦ ὁμοίου καθάρσιον ἡγούμενος κ.τ.λ.

31. μετενδύσεσιν. Probably 'changing of prisons.' Not found elsewhere. μετενδεῖσθαι is joined with ἐνσωματοῦσθαι and μεταγγίζεσθαι in *Str.* III. 516 *med.* H. For the Pythagorean and Platonic notion of the soul's imprisonment in the body, see *Str.* III. P. 516—519 and Lightfoot's Essay on the Essenes (*Coloss.* p. 88). On Transmigration see Zeller[4] I. 418, Sext. Emp. *adv. Physicos* IX. 127 οἱ μὲν οὖν περὶ τὸν Πυθαγόραν...φασὶ μὴ μόνον ἡμῖν πρὸς ἀλλήλους καὶ πρὸς τοὺς θεοὺς εἶναί τινα κοινωνίαν, ἀλλὰ καὶ πρὸς τὰ ἄλογα τῶν ζῴων· ἓν γὰρ ὑπάρχειν πνεῦμα τὸ διὰ παντὸς τοῦ κόσμου διῆκον ψυχῆς τρόπον, τὸ καὶ ἐνοῦν ἡμᾶς πρὸς ἐκεῖνα. διὸ καὶ κτείνοντες αὐτὰ καὶ ταῖς σαρξὶν αὐτῶν τρεφόμενοι ἀδικήσομέν τε καὶ ἀσεβήσομεν, ὡς συγγενεῖς ἀναιροῦντες κ.τ.λ.

p. 56, line 1. **Ξενοκράτης**. Succeeded Speusippus as head of the Academy and was himself succeeded by his pupil Polemo. See *Str.* I. P. 353, II. 500, Zeller II.³ 862—883, 896.

ἰδίᾳ πραγματευόμενος περὶ... 'In a special treatise on the subject of...' Perhaps the same as περὶ ὁσιότητος (Diog. IV. 12), to which Bernays (31) refers three laws of Triptolemus mentioned by Xenocrates (*ap.* Porph. IV. 22) as still extant at Eleusis. **H.**

2. **περὶ τοῦ κατὰ φύσιν βίου**. There is no distinct notice of this book elsewhere (indeed we have but scanty knowledge of Polemo): but traces of this doctrine of Nature are characteristic of the earliest Academy, before it was taken up by the Stoics. Cf. Cic. *Fin.* IV. 14 cum superiores, e quibus planissime Polemo, secundum naturam vivere summum bonum esse dixissent, his verbis tria significari Stoici dicunt, Plut. *Comm. Not.* 1069 τίνας δὲ Πολέμων καὶ Ξενοκράτης λαμβάνουσιν ἀρχάς; οὐχὶ καὶ Ζήνων τούτοις ἠκολούθησεν, ὑποτιθέμενος στοιχεῖα τῆς εὐδαιμονίας τὴν φύσιν καὶ τὸ κατὰ φύσιν; (cited by Zeller II. 880). **H.**

4. **εἰργασμένη**. So Arist. *de Juvent.* 4. 4 ἐργάζεται καὶ πέττει τῷ φυσικῷ θερμῷ τὴν τροφὴν πάντα, cf. κατεργασία, *conficio*.

§ 33. 6. The same view is put into the mouth of Pythagoras by Ovid *Met.* XV. 112 foll., cf. *Fast.* I. 349 foll. See other classical instances in Bochart I. 982 foll. **H.**

11. **ἀεργά**, a poetic word, used *e.g.* of horses turned loose. Possibly these two words may be a quotation. **H.** Cf. Cic. *N. D.* II. 159 'tanta putabatur utilitas percipi e bubus ut eorum visceribus vesci scelus haberetur,' with my notes.

17. ὕστριξ and ὑστριχίς are equally well attested for a scourge of hogs' bristles. See passages in Steph. *Thes.* VIII. 524, where Dindorf quite arbitrarily gets rid of this sense of ὕστριξ. **H.**

18. Cf. Ael. *V. H.* X. v. where the fable is given at greater length: τὴν ὗν, ἐάν τις ἅψηται αὐτῆς, βοᾶν καὶ μάλα γε εἰκότως· οὔτε γὰρ ἔργα ἔχει, οὔτε ἄλλο τι· καὶ ὀνειροπολεῖ εὐθὺς τὸν θάνατον, εἰδυῖα εἰς ὅ τι τοῖς χρησομένοις λυσιτελεῖ: 'so it is with tyrants.'

20 foll. Cf. ii. 484, Plut. Fr. (iii. 57 Düb.) *ap.* Porph. iii. 20. Cf. Doehner *An. Plut.* i. 46 foll.; ii. 32 foll. **H.**

21. **Κλεάνθης**. The witticism is with more probability attributed to Chrysippus by Cic. *N. D.* II. 160, where see note.

25. **τὸν τράγον ὁ νόμος θύει**. Lev. XVI. 10 τὸν χίμαρον ἐφ' ὃν ἐπῆλθεν ὁ κλῆρος τοῦ ἀποπομπαίου, στήσει αὐτὸν ζῶντα ἔναντι κυρίου τοῦ ἐξιλάσασθαι ἐπ' αὐτοῦ, ὥστε ἀποστεῖλαι αὐτὸν εἰς τὴν ἀποπομπήν, Num. XXVIII. 15, 22, 30, XXIX. 5, 11, 16, 19, &c.

26. **διοπομπήσει**. Phrynichus, quoted by Ruhnken on Tim. *Lex. s. v.* ἀποδιοπομπεῖσθαι (ἀποπέμπεσθαι τὰ ἁμαρτήματα συμπράκτορι χρώμενος τῷ Διΐ), mentions the shorter form, but says that the form compounded with

ἀπό is Ἀττικώτατον. So also Eustath. and Lexx. have διοπομπεῖσθαι, though it is apparently not found elsewhere in literature. See passages cited by Ruhnken and also by Wytt. Plut. II. 73 D. **H.**

μητρόπολις. So Bion ap. Stob. *Flor.* x. 38 τὴν φιλαργυρίαν μητρόπολιν ἔλεγε πάσης κακίας, Phil. M. 1. 560 ἡ μὲν πρεσβυτάτη μητρόπολις ὁ θεῖός ἐστι λόγος.. αἱ δ' ἄλλαι πέντε, ὡς ἂν ἀποικίαι δυνάμεις εἰσὶ τοῦ λέγοντος, Porphyr. *de Abst.* I. 33 οἷον μητρόπολις ἡ αἴσθησις ἦν τῆς ἐν ἡμῖν ἐκφύλου τῶν παθῶν ἀποικίας, Plut. *Mor.* 718 E γεωμετρία ἀρχὴ καὶ μητρόπολις οὖσα τῶν ἄλλων τεχνῶν.

27. **αὐτίκα.** See Appendix.

p. 58, line 2. **ἀνάδοσιν**, used in Greek physiology for the distribution through the body of the results of digestion, and generally for the later processes of digestion. The corresponding verb is common in Plutarch. Cf. Porph. I. 45 foll. **H.** The word occurs *Paed.* II. P. 163 τῆς τροφῆς τὸ εὔκολον, εἴς τε τὰς ἀναδόσεις καὶ τοῦ σώματος τὴν κουφότητα χρησιμεῦον, *Str.* II. P. 489 αἱ τῶν σαρκικῶν ἐπιθυμιῶν ἀναδόσεις καχεξίαν προστρίβονται ψυχῇ κατασκεδαννύουσαι τὰ εἴδωλα τῆς ἡδονῆς ἐπίπροσθε τῆς ψυχῆς. Compare also Polyb. III. 57. 8 οἱ λίχνοι οὔτε κατὰ τὸ παρὸν ἀληθινῶς ἀπολαύουσι τῶν βρωμάτων, οὔτε εἰς τὸ μέλλον ὠφέλιμον ἐξ αὐτῶν τὴν ἀνάδοσιν καὶ τροφὴν κομίζονται, Orig. *de Orat.* 27 (Lomm. XVII. p. 214) ὁ σωματικὸς ἄρτος ἀναδιδόμενος εἰς τὸ τοῦ τρεφομένου σῶμα.

7. **σφριγᾶν.** The parallel passage *Str.* II. 484 ἢ ἕνεκα τοῦ τὰς σάρκας σφριγᾶν shows that nothing more than fulness of flesh is intended: the evil sense comes from περὶ τὰ ἀφροδίσια. **H.**

8. **Ἀνδροκύδης.** sc. ὁ Πυθαγορικός, of whom we read (*Str.* v. 672) τὰ Ἐφέσια καλούμενα γράμματα συμβόλων ἔχειν φησὶ τάξιν. Little is known of him. See Fabr. *B. Gr.* I. 481 (Harl. i. 830). **H.** The saying is quoted anonymously by Plut. *Mor.* 472 C and by Theopompus ap. Athen. IV. 157 D. Potter attributes it to the physician, of whom Pliny (*N. H.* XIV. 7) relates that he wrote to Alexander warning him against intemperance, 'vinum poturus memento te bibere sanguinem terrae,' see Fabr. XIII. p. 60. But why may we not identify the physician with the Pythagorean ?

10. **νωχαλής** or **νωχελής**, a poetic word, used (νωχελεύομαι at least) by Aquila and by late philosophers, nearly in the sense of νωθρός. **H.**

11. **Αἰγύπτιοι.** For the absence of the art. see P. 670 ὅθεν καὶ Αἰγ. and 757. So Ἰουδαῖοι above p. 56. 6.

13. **ὀρνιθείοις.** Arist. *Eth. Nic.* VI. 7. 7 εἰ γὰρ εἰδείη ὅτι τὰ κοῦφα εὔπεπτα κρέα καὶ ὑγιεινά, ποῖα δὲ κοῦφα ἀγνοοῖ, οὐ ποιήσει ὑγίειαν, ἀλλ' ὁ εἰδὼς ὅτι τὰ ὀρνίθεια κοῦφα καὶ ὑγιεινὰ ποιήσει μᾶλλον. **H. J.**

15. **πλαδαρός,** 'flabby' and watery. See *Paed.* II. 177 νοσηλευομένῳ καὶ πλαδῶντι σώματι (of Timothy wanting wine); *ib.* 184 *fin.* πλαδῶσα ὄρεξις, a depraved appetite for peculiar wines. **H.**

§ 34. 18. **συγγενῆ τῷ ἀέρι τὴν ψυχήν.** Cf. the Orphic belief (Arist. *Anim.* I. 5. 15) τὴν ψυχὴν ἐκ τοῦ ὅλου εἰσιέναι ἀναπνεόντων, φερομένην ὑπὸ τῶν ἀνέμων, also Democritus (Ar. *de Resp.* 4) ἐν τῷ ἀέρι πολὺν ἀριθμὸν εἶναι τῶν τοιούτων (minute spherical atoms) ἃ καλεῖ ἐκεῖνος νοῦν καὶ ψυχήν· ἀναπνέοντος οὖν, καὶ εἰσιόντος τοῦ ἀέρος, συνεισιόντα ταῦτα...κωλύειν τὴν ἐνοῦσαν ἐν τοῖς ζῴοις διιέναι ψυχήν (which would otherwise be squeezed out by the pressure of the external air), and the Stoics (Euseb. *Pr. Ev.* xv. 20. 2) εἶναι δὲ ψυχὴν ἐν τῷ ὅλῳ φασίν, ὃ καλοῦσιν αἰθέρα καὶ ἀέρα κύκλῳ περὶ γῆν καὶ θάλασσαν, καὶ ἐκ τούτων ἀναθυμιάσεις, τὰς δὲ λοιπὰς ψυχὰς προσπεφυκέναι ταύτῃ, ὅσαι τε ἐν ζῴοις εἰσὶ καὶ ὅσαι ἐν τῷ περιέχοντι.

οὐδὲ ἀναπνεῖν. That fishes inhale air from water was denied by Aristotle (*Resp.* 2, 3), affirmed by Anaxagoras and Diogenes and later by Pliny *H. N.* ix. 6 and Galen (*Us. Part.* ii. 9). See Ogle (*Aristotle on Youth*, &c. *Intr.* p. 9).

20, 21. ἐγκέκραται τῷ ὕδατι. Arist. *Gen. An.* iii. 11 γίγνεται δ᾽ ἐν γῇ καὶ ἐν ὑγρῷ τὰ ζῷα καὶ τὰ φυτὰ διὰ τὸ ἐν γῇ μὲν ὕδωρ ὑπάρχειν, ἐν δ᾽ ὕδατι πνεῦμα, ἐν δὲ τούτῳ παντὶ θερμότητα ψυχικήν, ὥστε τρόπον τινὰ πάντα ψυχῆς εἶναι πλήρη, cf. Cic. *N. D.* i. 40 with my n.

22, 23. τῆς ὑλικῆς διαμονῆς, probably 'the permanence of material things.' The exact phrase does not seem to occur: but Plut. *Mor.* 425 D and 1055 BD uses διαμονή in reference to the universe in arguing against Chrysippus (τί γάρ ἐστι κυριώτερον τῆς τοῦ κόσμου διαμονῆς καὶ τοῦ τὴν οὐσίαν ἡνωμένην τοῖς μέρεσι συνέχεσθαι πρὸς αὑτήν;). The idea seems Pythagorean: it occurs in a Doric fragment in Iambl. *V. P.* c. 28. 146 *fin.* speaking of number as θείων καὶ θεῶν καὶ δαιμόνων διαμονᾶς ῥίζαν, where Kuster refers to Philolaus *ap.* 'Iambl. *in Nicom. Arith.* p. 11' (ἀριθμὸν εἶναι) τῆς τῶν κοσμικῶν αἰωνίας διαμονῆς τὴν κρατιστεύουσαν καὶ αὐτογενῆ συνοχήν; and Philolaus (Stob. *Ecl.* i. 420) says that the world διαμένει τὸν ἄπειρον αἰῶνα (*init. bis*). H. Instead of the MS. δεῖγμα—how can the pervading air be an *evidence* of the mundane eternity?—I think we must read some word which would correspond to συνοχήν in the above quotation from Iambl. *in Nicom.* Either ἔρεισμα or δεσμός would do. Cf. *Protr.* P. 5 (τὸ ᾆσμα τὸ καινὸν) τὸ πᾶν ἐκόσμησεν ἐμμελῶς καὶ τῶν στοιχείων τὴν διαφωνίαν εἰς τάξιν ἐνέτεινε συμφωνίας...ἔρεισμα τῶν ὅλων καὶ ἁρμονία τῶν πάντων, ἀπὸ τῶν μέσων ἐπὶ τὰ πέρατα καὶ ἀπὸ τῶν ἄκρων ἐπὶ τὰ μέσα διαταθέν, Cic. *N. D.* ii. 115 'maxime autem corpora inter se iuncta permanent, cum quasi quodam *vinculo* circumdato colligantur; quod facit ea natura quae per omnem mundum omnia mente et ratione conficiens funditur et ad medium rapit et convertit extrema.' 'This binding principle,' he goes on to say, 'is found in air and aether.' (§ 117) 'Huic (aquae) continens aer fertur ille quidem levitate sublimis, sed tamen in omnes partes se ipse fundit.' (§ 101) 'restat ultimus...omnia cingens et coercens caeli complexus, qui idem aether vocatur.' Philo (*Deus Immutabilis*) M. 1. 277 *fin.* τῶν σωμάτων τὰ μὲν ἐνεδήσατο ἕξει, τὰ δὲ φύσει, τὰ δὲ ψυχῇ...λίθων μὲν οὖν καὶ ξύλων...δεσμὸν κραταιότατον ἕξιν εἰργάσατο· ἡ δέ ἐστι πνεῦμα ἀναστρέφον ἐφ᾽ ἑαυτό. ἄρχεται μὲν γὰρ ἀπὸ τῶν μέσων ἐπὶ τὰ πέρατα τείνεσθαι, ψαῦσαν δὲ ἄκρας ἐπιφανείας ἀνακάμπτει πάλιν...ἕξεως ὁ συνεχὴς οὗτος δίαυλος ἄφθαρτος, *ib.* 330 *fin.* νόμος (*al.* λόγος) ὁ ἀίδιος θεοῦ...τὸ βεβαιότατον ἔρεισμα τῶν ὅλων ἐστί. οὗτος ἀπὸ τῶν μέσων ἐπὶ τὰ πέρατα...ταθεὶς δολιχεύει τὸν τῆς φύσεως δρόμον...συνάγων τὰ μέρη καὶ σφίγγων· δεσμὸν γὰρ αὐτὸν ἄρρηκτον τοῦ παντὸς ὁ γεννήσας ἐποίει πατήρ, ib. p. 499 τὰ ἄλλα λόγῳ σφίγγεται θείῳ. κόλλα γὰρ καὶ δεσμὸς οὗτος, πάντα τὰ τῆς οὐσίας ἐκπεπληρωκώς, Plut. Mor. 1125 E (ἡ περὶ θεῶν δόξα) τὸ συνεκτικὸν ἁπάσης κοινωνίας... ἔρεισμα. See my n. on N. D. II. 115, Zeller³ IV. 118, 131, and Lightfoot on Col. iii. 14 σύνδεσμος τελειότητος.

24. δεῖ τοίνυν goes back to p. 54. 13. H.

μὴ πολυτελεῖς, taken from Theophrastus ap. Porph. de abst. II. 19 δεῖ τοίνυν καθηραμένους τὸ ἦθος ἰέναι θύσοντας, τοῖς θεοῖς θεοφιλεῖς τὰς θυσίας προσάγοντας, ἀλλὰ μὴ πολυτελεῖς. H. On true sacrifice cf. Str. VI. P. 686, and above p. 22. 26.

25. τὸ θυμίαμα τὸ σύνθετον. Exod. xxx. 34—36. (Verse 25 which is referred to in the translation describes the making of the holy oil.) For the spiritual significance see Ps. 141. 2 κατευθυνθήτω ἡ προσευχή μου ὡς θυμίαμα ἐνώπιόν σου· ἔπαρσις τῶν χειρῶν μου θυσία ἑσπερινή and Apoc. v. 8 φιάλας γεμούσας θυμιαμάτων, αἵ εἰσιν αἱ προσευχαὶ τῶν ἁγίων.

28. τὰς διαθήκας. 'Old and New Testament' certainly, perhaps different testaments under the old. See esp. P. 899 fin. εἰς ἑνότητα πίστεως μίας, τῆς κατὰ τὰς οἰκείας διαθήκας, μᾶλλον δὲ κατὰ τὴν διαθήκην τὴν μίαν διαφόροις τοῖς χρόνοις and the whole passage: also P. 894 init. τὴν ἀλήθειαν διὰ τῆς ἀκολουθίας τῶν διαθηκῶν σαφηνίζοντες. In Str. v. P. 666 init. he seems to speak of four 'ancient covenants.' H.

δόσις, 'a Divine bounty': it is possible, as διαθήκας occurs here, that there is some allusion to 'bequest' as distinguished from intestate succession by descent. H.

29. αἴνους. Apparently 'songs of praise': a biblical use. H. See below p. 86. 10 θυσίαι μὲν αὐτῷ εὐχαί τε καὶ αἶνοι, Paed. III. P. 311 καλῶς ἂν ἔχοι ἡμᾶς αἶνον ἀναπέμψαι κυρίῳ, Const. Apost. II. 59.

31. πολιτείᾳ. See below p. 62. 2.

p. 60, line 2. κατὰ τὴν ποιητικὴν χάριν. Cf. P. 663 where the same phrase follows a quotation. So we have χάρις Σωκρατική, Ἀττική.

6. Cf. above p. 52. 1.

8. δρῶσιν, 'perform the rites': see Wytt. on Plut. Mor. 352 c. H. Athen. 14. p. 660 A οἱ παλαιοὶ τὸ θύειν δρᾶν ὠνόμαζον. Cf. Plato Rep. II. 365 E ἀδικητέον καὶ θυτέον ἀπὸ τῶν ἀδικημάτων.

10. τὰ κρέα. The flesh of the sacrifice.

11. τὸ φρόνιμον πῦρ. So Ecl. Pr. P. 995 fin. διὸ καὶ φρόνιμον λέγεται παρὰ τοῖς προφήταις τοῦτο τὸ πῦρ (see the whole passage). Also Paed. iii. P. 280 med. and Protr. P. 47 init. τὸν ἐν Δελφοῖς Ἀπόλλωνος νεὼν ἠφάνισε πῦρ σωφρονοῦν. Again Hippol. in Dan. iii. 23 (p. 175 Lagarde). So the Latin fathers, sapiens ignis Minuc. Fel. 35; Tert. Scorp. 3; Hier. in Dan. iii. 92, p. 643 A; Paulin. Ep. ad Sever. fol. 62. H. Cf. Heb. xii. 29 ὁ θεὸς ἡμῶν πῦρ καταναλίσκον, 1 Cor. iii. 13 ἑκάστου τὸ ἔργον πῦρ δοκιμάσει, Matt. iii. 11 αὐτὸς ὑμᾶς βαπτίσει ἐν πνεύματι ἁγίῳ καὶ πυρί, Mk. ix. 49 πᾶς γὰρ πυρὶ ἁλισθήσεται, Isa. iv. 4 (cited in Paed. P. 282) τὸν τρόπον

τῆς καθάρσεως ἐπήγαγεν ὁ λόγος εἰπών, "ἐν πνεύματι κρίσεως καὶ ἐν πνεύματι καύσεως," Cl. *Protr.* P. 46 οἶδα ἐγὼ πῦρ ἐλεγκτικὸν καὶ δεισιδαιμονίας ἰατικόν· εἰ βούλει παύσασθαι τῆς ἀνοίας, φωταγωγήσει σε τὸ πῦρ. The distinction between two kinds of fire τὸ παμφάγον καὶ βάναυσον and τὸ φρόνιμον, here made by Clem., is borrowed from the Stoic distinction mentioned by Cic *N. D.* II. 41 'hic noster ignis, quem usus vitae requirit, confector est et consumptor omnium...quocunque invasit, cuncta disturbat et dissipat: contra ille corporeus vitalis et salutaris, omnia conservat, alit, auget.' This latter is identified with the aether, πνεῦμα νοερὸν καὶ φρόνιμον, the πῦρ τεχνικὸν ὁδῷ βαδίζον εἰς γένεσιν, to which they gave the name of Nature and God. Cf. Hippolyt. *Ref. Haer.* I. 4, Stob. *Ecl.* I. 1, I. 25 § 538, *Plac. Phil.* I. 6, Wisdom vii. 22, *Strom.* P. 708, *Exc. Theod.* P. 971 οἱ μὲν ἄγγελοι νοερὸν πῦρ καὶ πνεύματα νοερά...φῶς δὲ νοερὸν ἡ μεγίστη προκοπὴ (ἢ προβολὴ) ἀπὸ τοῦ νοεροῦ πυρός, *Ecl. Proph.* P. 995 *fin.* ἀγαθὴ δύναμις τὸ πῦρ νοεῖται... φθαρτικὴ τῶν χειρόνων καὶ σωστικὴ τῶν ἀμεινόνων, Orig. *de Orat.* 29 (L. vol. XVII. 262), and see art. on Purgatory in Schaff-Herzog's *Encyclopaedia*, Addis and Arnold's *Catholic Dictionary*.

12. Cf. Is. xliii. 2 ἐὰν διέλθῃς διὰ πυρός, οὐ μὴ κατακαυθῇς, φλὸξ οὐ κατακαύσει σε. H. This is quoted by Origen (*Hom. iii. in Ps. xxxvi*, vol. 12, p. 181 L.) in reference to the purgatorial fire: 'ut ego arbitror, omnes nos venire necesse est ad illum ignem. Etiamsi Paulus sit aliquis vel Petrus, venit tamen ad illum ignem. Sed illi tales audiunt "etiamsi per ignem transeas, flamma non aduret te." Si vero aliquis similis mei peccator sit...non sic transiet sicut Petrus et Paulus.'

§ 35. 15. Either something must be lost before καὶ λόγον, or αὐτὸν must be corrupt, as He has not been mentioned in the preceding context. On the sentence cf. p. 52. 20—25. H. Acting on this hint, I read υἱόν for αὐτόν.

16. ἐν ἐξαιρέτοις ἡμέραις. See below p. 70. 4, 130. 22.

20. κατ' ἐντολὴν δικαιούμενον. Ps. cxix. 172, 3 πᾶσαι αἱ ἐντολαί σου δικαιοσύνη· γενέσθω ἡ χείρ σου τοῦ σῶσαί με, ὅτι τὰς ἐντολάς σου ᾑρετισάμην, below p. 72. 24. H.

20. ὡρισμένον τόπον. There is no government for this acc. I have suggested the insertion of either κατά or οἶδε.

22. ἀποτεταγμένας, 'detached,' 'reserved,' 'set apart for special uses.' H.

23. κἂν μόνος ὢν τυγχάνῃ, κἂν ὅπου...ἂν...ἔχῃ. The sequence κἂν—κἂν is as common as ἐάντε—ἐάντε (see below § 89, p. 118. 23 κἂν οἰκέτης ᾖ, κἂν πολέμιος, κἂν ὁστισοῦν), but not κἂν—καί, as in the MS. Of course ἂν τυγχάνῃ must be supplied in thought before ὅπου. I think the potential ἔχοι is wanted instead of the indefinite ἔχῃ, which may have been assimilated to the preceding τυγχάνῃ.

p. 62, line 1. τῆς γνώσεως. Cf. p. 60. 24, 62. 1. H.

2. τῆς πολιτείας. P. 318 (the evangelist ministers to his hearers) ἀρχὴν πίστεως, πολιτείας προθυμίαν, ὁρμὴν τὴν ἐπὶ τὴν ἀλήθειαν, P. 321 μισθὸν ἀξιόλογον ἀπολαμβάνων τὴν πολιτείαν αὐτήν, above p. 58. 31.

ἡ παρουσία τινὸς ἀνδρὸς ἀγαθοῦ. Cf. Sen. *Epist.* 11 aliquis vir bonus nobis eligendus est ac semper ante oculos habendus, ut sic tanquam illo spectante vivamus et omnia tanquam illo vidente faciamus, *ib.* 41 sacer intra nos spiritus sedet, malorum bonorumque nostrorum observator et custos, Orig. *de Orat.* 8, and the Traditions of Matthias cited below, p. 142. 19 f.

4. σχηματίζα τὸν ἐντυγχάνοντα. Cf. P. 824 ὁ γνωστικὸς ὀνίνησι τοὺς μὲν τῇ παρακολουθήσει σχηματίζων, τοὺς δὲ κ.τ.λ.

7. παρ' ἕκαστα, 'time by time,' 'occasion by occasion.' H.

11. μεθ' ἡμέραν came early to mean simply 'in the day-time,' but originally was 'after day was begun,' according to a grammarian *ap.* Herm. *Emend. Gr. Gr.* 341 who says that it arose out of νύκτωρ καὶ μεθ' ἡμέραν, νύκτωρ καὶ being dropped. The formula here seems unique (Paus. IV. 21, cited by Lob. has μεθ' ἡμέραν ἀεὶ καὶ νύκτα *ordine inverso*), the usual forms being νυκτὸς καὶ μεθ' ἡμέραν, or *vice versa*, or μεθ' ἡμέραν καὶ νύκτωρ, or *vice versa.* See Lobeck *Paralip.* 62 foll. H. The explanation of the grammarian seems to me extremely doubtful. μεθ' ἡμέραν is usually associated with the phrase μετὰ χεῖρας ἔχειν. As Cl. uses the phrase νύκτωρ καὶ μεθ' ἡμέραν elsewhere (see P. 901, 471) I think νύκτωρ should be written here for νύκτα, unless it is a verse quotation.

13. πάντῃ, properly 'in every direction,' πάντοθεν, 'on every side,' 'from every quarter.' But here πάντῃ may vaguely intensify πάντοθεν, as it sometimes does πάντως. H. I think πάντῃ has the meaning 'everywhere,' as in l. 9 below, in P. 764 ἡ δύναμις ἡ ἐνεργητικὴ πάντῃ ἐστὶ καὶ ἀεὶ ἐργάζεται, and P. 862 (p. 90. 16) πεπεισμένος πάντῃ τὸν θεὸν εἶναι πάντοτε.

15. Read ἐνθέως, comparing p. 78. 14 μετὰ διάρματος ἐνθέου, *Paed.* II. 194 *ad fin.*, where a long passage about the various kinds of praise is followed by ἐπὶ πᾶσίν τε πρὶν ὕπνου λαχεῖν εὐχαριστεῖν ὅσιον τῷ θεῷ...ὡς καὶ ἐπὶ τὸν ὕπνον ἰέναι ἡμᾶς ἐνθέως, and Hierocles *in Carm. Aur.* p. 24 ἡ τῶν προσφερομένων πολυτέλεια τιμὴ εἰς θεὸν οὐ γίνεται, εἰ μὴ μετὰ τοῦ ἐνθέου φρονήματος προσάγοιτο...τὸ δὲ ἔνθεον φρόνημα...συνάπτει θεῷ. H.

17. ἐπιστροφήν seems to be used, not, as in the Old and New Testaments, of 'turning to the Lord,' but rather in the classical (? Pythagorean) sense of 'having regard to Him,' as opposed to ἀνεπιστρεψία (in p. 34. 19). So Hierocl. *in C. A.* II. 2 ἡ μὲν πρώτη καὶ ἀπόρρητος εὐορκία διὰ τῆς εἰς θεὸν ἐπιστροφῆς κ.τ.λ. H. I rather prefer the former meaning, which is, I think, more appropriate even in the passage from Hierocles, if we supply the actual words of the context (instead of κ.τ.λ.) αὖθις ἀναλαμβάνεσθαι πέφυκε τοῖς ταῖς καθαρτικαῖς ἀρεταῖς τὴν παρέκβασιν ἰωμένοις τοῦ θείου ὅρκου, the Latin translation being 'Prima vero illa et mystica iurisiurandi sanctitas per conversionem ad Deum rursus potest recuperari, &c.' In p. 72. 3 below, ἥ τε εὐχαριστία ἥ τε τῶν πέλας εἰς ἐπιστροφὴν αἴτησις ἔργον ἐστὶ τοῦ γνωστικοῦ, the meaning 'conversion' seems to me best suited to the context, and so in p. 138. 2 αἰτεῖται ἐπιστρ. εἰς ἐπίγνωσιν, and l. 26 εἰς ἐξομολόγησιν καὶ ἐπιστροφὴν τῶν συγγενῶν, cf. use of ἐπιστρέφω in p. 80. 9, p. 136. 20, and Index. μεταστροφή is used in the same sense P. 525 *fin.*

18. ἐπιλογισμόν, 'reckoning up'; or (commoner) 'consideration.' Cf. Wytt. on Plut. *Mor.* 40 B. Chrysippus (*ap.* Plut. 1045 B) has both words: (dogs, asses, children disregard sanctity of places), μηδεμίαν ἐπιστροφὴν μηδ' ἐπιλογισμὸν ἔχοντα περὶ τῶν τοιούτων. H.

§ 36. 22. κατ' ἐπανάβασιν. P. 457 αἱ ἡμέραι μόριον βίου τοῦ κατ' ἐπανάβασιν, 576 εὐεργεσίαν ἀγάπη ἐπαγγέλλεται ἡ κυριεύουσα τοῦ σαββάτου κατ' ἐπανάβασιν γνωστικήν, 'love is not content with mere rest from doing wrong, but rises to active benevolence.'

τὸ ἡγεμονικόν, not in the technical sense, but 'the ruling quality,' the faculty which gives power of government: see what follows. H. This would make τελειότητος a subjective genitive 'the sovereignty which belongs to the perfect man': is it not better taken as objective = ἡγεμονικὸν πρὸς τελειότητα? What follows would then refer to ἔξοχον rather than to ἡγεμονικόν.

23. ὁ βασιλικὸς ἄνθρωπος. See above p. 36. 9, and, for the combination of priest and king, Apoc. v. 10.

25. λογιωτάτοις, 'accomplished.' Hein. on Eus. *H. E.* III. 36. Apparently the Egyptians are meant. Potter quotes Plato *Politicus* p. 290 DE περὶ μὲν Αἴγυπτον οὐδ' ἔξεστι βασιλέα χωρὶς ἱερατικῆς ἄρχειν· ἀλλ' ἐὰν ἄρα καὶ τύχῃ πρότερον ἐξ ἄλλου γένους βιασάμενος, ὕστερον ἀναγκαῖον εἰς τοῦτο εἰστελεῖσθαι αὐτὸν τὸ γένος. H.

26. προσαγόντων may be either 'introduce,' or 'make use of.' H.

27. ὀχλοκρασία, a late form of ὀχλοκρατία, needlessly doubted by Lob. (*Phryn.* p. 526). The word is a favourite with Philo. H.

29. οὐδὲ ὄναρ προσίεται. Plat. *Theaet.* 173 D δεῖπνα καὶ σὺν αὐλητρίσι κῶμοι, οὐδ' ὄναρ πράττειν προσίσταται αὐτοῖς. Cf. below pp. 132. 30, 136. 11.

30. τὰς ἡδονάς. I have followed H. J. in removing the full stop after προσίεται, so as to allow of its governing ἡδονάς. For the evil influence of the theatres and spectacles, see P. 298 οὐδὲ ἐπὶ τὰς θέας ὁ παιδαγωγὸς ἄξει ἡμᾶς, οὐδὲ ἀπεικότως τὰ στάδια καὶ τὰ θέατρα καθέδραν λοιμῶν προσείποι τις ἄν, foll. and below p. 130. 1 foll.

31. ἀπολαυσμάτων, 'modes of enjoyment.' H.

θυμιαμάτων, any artificial odours made by burning: cf. *Paed.* III. 207 *fin.* H. Cf. above pp. 54. 19, 58. 25.

p. 64, line 1. συγκαττύσεις, 'stitchings together.' An odd figure, and therefore possibly meant literally. H. No other example of the noun is recorded. The verb is used metaphorically below, P. 893, of the heretics who πάμπολλα συγκαττύουσι ψεύσματα καὶ πλάσματα to excuse their rejection of the Scriptures; and P. 528 ἔκ τινων προφητικῶν περικοπῶν λέξεις ἀπανθισάμενοι καὶ συγκαττύσαντες κακῶς : literally by Lucian, *Conscr. Hist.* 23 θώραξ πάνυ γελοῖος ἐκ ῥακῶν ἢ ἐκ δερμάτων σαπρῶν συγκεκαττυμένος. συγκαταρτύσεις is suggested by H. J. Neither this nor the verb συγκαταρτύω is found, and κατάρτυσις is used in a quite different sense, of moral amendment, by Iambl. *V. P.*; but Lucian (*Hist. Conscr.* 44) compares an affected style to τοῖς κατηρτυμένοις τῶν ζωμῶν, and Artemidorus (I. c. 70), after speaking of the good fortune indicated by dreams of roast or boiled pork, continues τὰ δὲ κατηρτυμένα οὕτως ὑπὸ ὀψοποιῶν μετὰ κακουχίας τὰς ὠφελείας ἢ μετὰ προαναλωμάτων φέρει. Cl. declaims against luxurious eating in *Paed.* II. P. 163.

3. **πολυανθέσι καὶ εὐώδεσι πλοκαῖς**. Probably the wreaths of flowers worn at banquets, cf. *Paed.* II. P. 211 τὸ πλεκτὸν στέφανον ἐξ ἀκηράτου λειμῶνος κοσμήσαντας οἴκοι περιφέρειν οὐ σωφρόνων. There is no example of πλοκή in this sense, but it may be inferred from the song in the Anthologia quoted by Becker (*Charicles*, p. 95 tr.) πλέξω λευκοΐον, πλέξω δ' ἁπαλὴν ἅμα μύρτοις νάρκισσον, πλέξω καὶ τὰ γελῶντα κρίνα κ.τ.λ.

4. **πάντων**, explained in 6 foll. H.

8. **διὰ λόγου**, the instrument of speech, itself another gift of God. Cf. *Paed.* II. 193 *fin.* ἑνὶ...ὀργάνῳ, τῷ λόγῳ μόνῳ τῷ εἰρηνικῷ, ἡμεῖς κεχρήμεθα. H.

9, 10. **ἀπαντῶν εἰς**, 'being present at,' 'putting in an appearance at.' H.

10. **πλὴν εἰ μὴ τὸ φιλικὸν...προτρέψαι**, 'unless the entertainment by promising him the benefit of friendship and concord should urge him to come.' ἀφικέσθαι in the almost technical sense of going in answer to an invitation. H. Cf. Plato *Symp.* 217 C προκαλοῦμαι δὴ αὐτὸν πρὸς τὸ συνδειπνεῖν... ἐπειδὴ δὲ ἀφίκετο τὸ πρῶτον δειπνήσας ἀπιέναι ἐβούλετο. For the thought cf. *Paed.* II. P. 200 εἰ γὰρ δι' ἀγάπην αἱ ἐπὶ τὰς ἑστιάσεις συνελεύσεις, συμποσίου δὲ τὸ τέλος ἡ πρὸς τοὺς συνόντας φιλοφροσύνη...πῶς οὐ λογικῶς ἀναστρεπτέον; εἰ γὰρ ὡς ἐπιτείνοντες τὴν πρὸς ἀλλήλους εὔνοιαν σύνιμεν, πῶς ἔχθρας διὰ τοῦ σκώπτειν σκαλεύομεν; For the pleonastic use of πλήν with ἀλλά, εἰ μή, &c. in late Greek, see W. Schmid *Attic.* Index *s.v.*

14. **ἐνεργουμένη**, 'brought about'; passive, as always. H. See my note on St James v. 16. H. J. compares Arist. *Physic.* II. 3. 195 b, 28 τὰ ἐνεργοῦντα πρὸς τὰ ἐνεργούμενα, and he would translate here 'acted upon.' See also *de An.* III. 2. 4 ἔστι γὰρ ἀκοὴν ἔχοντα μὴ ἀκούειν· καὶ τὸ ἔχον ψόφον οὐκ ἀεὶ ψοφεῖ· ὅταν δ' ἐνεργῇ τὸ δυνάμενον ἀκούειν, καὶ ψοφῇ τὸ δυνάμενον ψοφεῖν, τότε ἡ κατ' ἐνέργειαν ἀκοὴ ἅμα γίνεται καὶ ὁ κατ' ἐνέργειαν ψόφος.

πόρων. Cf. Cic. *Tusc.* I. 46 foramina illa quae patent ad animum a corpore callidissimis artificiis natura fabricata est. For the sentiment H. J. compares Porph. *ad Marcellam* 8 λαμβάνομεν δὲ οὐ παρὰ τῶν ἔξωθεν τὰ εἰς τὰ παρ' αὐτῶν ἡμῖν ἐντεθειμένα. Add Epicharmus (p. 255 Lorenz) νοῦς ὁρᾷ καὶ νοῦς ἀκούει, τἆλλα κωφὰ καὶ τυφλά, cited by Cl. P. 442, and *Str.* VI. P. 825 τὰ σώματα...τῶν ψυχῶν ὄργανα, ὧν μὲν ἐνιζήματα, ὧν δὲ ὀχήματα, ἄλλων δὲ ἄλλον τρόπον κτήματα.

15. **ἔχει τὴν ἀντίληψιν**. See below ἀντιλαβέσθαι, l. 21, and above p. 28. 28. I am inclined to take ἔχει here in the sense of παρέχει (see exx. in Krüger's index to Thuc.), but H. J. takes it as a periphrasis = 'apprehends.' Strictly speaking ἡ ἀκοή does not apprehend, but Cl. is here dealing with a materialistic hypothesis.

§ 37. 18. Clement can hardly have meant to attribute anthropomorphism to the Stoics: cf. *Protr.* p. 58 *sub init.* τοὺς ἀπὸ τῆς Στοᾶς διὰ πάσης ὕλης καὶ διὰ τῆς ἀτιμοτάτης τὸ θεῖον διήκειν λέγοντας, Strom. I. 346 σῶμα ὄντα τὸν θεὸν διὰ τῆς ἀτιμοτάτης ὕλης πεφοιτηκέναι λέγουσιν, 699 σῶμα εἶναι τὸν θεὸν οἱ Στωϊκοὶ καὶ πνεῦμα κατ' οὐσίαν ὥσπερ ἀμέλει καὶ τὴν ψυχήν, 'misinterpreting the description of wisdom in the book so-called,' c. VII. 24 (διήκει καὶ χωρεῖ διὰ πάντων διὰ τὴν καθαριότητα). Zeller³ IV. 314 n. suggests a confusion arising from the *reductio ad absurdum* argument against the Stoics, such as we find in Sext. *Math.* IX. 139 f. **H.** If there is one thing in which it was impossible for Cl. to make a mistake, it is the distinction between Epicurean anthropomorphism and Stoic pantheism. The Epicurean criticism in Cic. *N. D.* turns just on the points here mentioned, cf. I. 23 qui vero mundum ipsum animantem sapientemque esse dixerunt nullo modo viderunt *animi natura intellegentis in quam figuram cadere posset*, ib. 36 (Zeno) aethera deum dicit, *si intellegi potest nihil sentiens deus*, ib. 37 (on Cleanthes), 39 (Chrysippus) vim divinam in ratione esse positam... ipsumque mundum deum dicit esse et eius animi fusionem universam, tum eius ipsius principatum qui in mente et ratione versetur...ignem praeterea et...aethera...solem, lunam, sidera, universitatemque rerum qua omnia continerentur: see too Philodemus (quoted in the n.) τὸν κόσμον ἔμψυχον εἶναι καὶ θεόν,...καὶ παιδαριωδῶς λέγεσθαι...θεοὺς ἀνθρωποειδεῖς (by the Epicureans). On the other hand the Epicurean insists that intelligence is impossible except as connected with the human organization '*numquam vidi animam rationis consiliique participem in ulla alia nisi humana figura*' (87). I have no doubt therefore that Cl. meant to write Ἐπικουρείοις here. Possibly, in a moment of absent-mindedness, his hand may have written Στωϊκοῖς, just as one might write 'addition' instead of 'subtraction'; but I think it far more probable that the clause καθάπερ ἤρεσεν τοῖς Στωϊκοῖς was a marginal gloss appended to the words κατὰ τὸ εὐπαθὲς τοῦ ἀέρος by a reader who was aware that this latter was a Stoic, and not an Epicurean doctrine (for which see below); and that this gloss was taken by a later copyist to be a correction of the earlier clause καθάπερ τοῖς Ἐπικουρείοις ἤρεσεν and inserted in its place.

20. **κατὰ τὸ εὐπαθὲς τοῦ ἀέρος.** In the MS. we have in l. 22 f. ἀλλὰ καὶ τὸ εὐπαθὲς τοῦ ἀέρος καὶ ἡ ὀξυτάτη αἴσθησις τῶν ἀγγέλων...ἅμα νοήματι πάντα γινώσκει. But it is surely nonsense to talk of the 'sensitiveness of the air' as 'knowing.' The slight change which I have made gives us a parallel to the Stoic doctrine stated in *N. D.* II. 83 (where see notes) ipse aer nobiscum videt, nobiscum audit, nobiscum sonat, ib. 66 Stoici effeminarunt (aerem) Junonique tribuerunt quod nihil est eo mollius (εὐπαθές), Theophr. *C. Pl.* v. 14. 1 εὐψυχότερος καὶ εὐπαθέστερος ὁ λεπτὸς ἀήρ, Plut. *Mor.* 589 C (on the manner in which the δαιμόνιον communicated with Socrates) ὁ ἀὴρ τρεπόμενος δι' εὐπάθειαν ἐνσημαίνεται τοῖς θείοις καὶ περιττοῖς ἀνδράσι τὸν τοῦ νοήσαντος λόγον, see the whole passage, Wisdom of Sol. i. 7 πνεῦμα κυρίου πεπλήρωκε τὴν οἰκουμένην, καὶ τὸ συνέχον τὰ πάντα γνῶσιν ἔχει φωνῆς with Grimm's n. Euseb. *Pr. Ev.* XV. 20 ἀναθυμίασιν τὴν ψυχὴν ἀποφαίνει Ζήνων, αἰσθητικὴν δὲ αὐτὴν εἶναι διὰ τοῦτο λέγει, ὅτι τυποῦσθαί τε δύναται τὸ μέρος τὸ ἡγούμενον αὐτῆς...διὰ τῶν αἰσθητηρίων καὶ παραδέχεσθαι

τὰς τυπώσεις· ταῦτα γὰρ ἴδια ψυχῆς ἐστιν. Epicurus held that we see by means of the images discharged from the surfaces of things, and hear by the audible atoms which strike on the ear, cf. Usener *Epicurea* pp. 219—224.

22. **συναίσθησις**, not necessarily more than 'apperception': but here probably σύν has its full force. H. On angels as the medium of divine communications see *Strom.* VI. P. 822 αἱ τῶν ἐναρέτων ἀνθρώπων ἐπίνοιαι κατὰ ἐπίπνοιαν θείαν γίνονται, διατιθεμένης πως τῆς ψυχῆς καὶ διαδιδομένου τοῦ θείου θελήματος εἰς τὰς ἀνθρωπίνας ψυχάς, τῶν ἐν μέρει θείων λειτουργῶν συλλαμβανομένων εἰς τὰς τοιαύτας διακονίας, 824 ἡ θεόθεν διατείνουσα εἰς ἀνθρώπους ὠφέλεια γνώριμος καθίσταται συμπαρακαλούντων ἀγγέλων· καὶ δι' ἀγγέλων γὰρ ἡ θεία δύναμις παρέχει τὰ ἀγαθά...ὅτε δὲ καὶ κατὰ τὰς ἐπινοίας τῶν ἀνθρώπων...ἐμπνεῖ τι καὶ ἡ θεία δύναμις καὶ ἐντίθησι ταῖς φρεσὶν ἰσχύν τε καὶ συναίσθησιν ἀκριβεστέραν, *Exc. Theod.* P. 976 τοὺς λειτουργοὺς τῶν ἀναφερομένων εὐχῶν ἀγγέλους, August. *de Gen. ad Litt.* XII. 30 sunt quaedam excellentia quae demonstrant angeli miris modis, utrum visa sua facili quadam et praepotenti iunctione vel commixtione etiam nostra esse facientes, an, &c. But in P. 769 Cl. argues that angels could not have taught men philosophy, on the ground that they are incapable of communicating with men, οὐδ' ὡς ἡμῖν τὰ ὦτα, οὕτως ἐκείνοις ἡ γλῶττα, οὐδ' ἂν ὄργανά τις δοίη φωνῆς ἀγγέλοις, χείλη λέγω καὶ τὰ τούτοις παρακείμενα...καὶ πνεῦμα καὶ πλησσόμενον ἀέρα...πολλοῦ γε δεῖ τὸν θεὸν ἐμβοᾶν.

23. **ἡ τοῦ συνειδότος ἐπαφωμένη τῆς ψυχῆς δύναμις**. 'The power of conscience touching the soul (*e.g.* as a lyre).' H. The difficulty of this interpretation is that it occurs in an attempt to explain how our prayers may be heard by God, though He is without any organ of hearing. This is illustrated first by the angels who are able to participate in our thoughts (an attempt to prove *ignotum per ignotius*); but how by our consciousness or conscience, which is identical with our very self? Probably we are to understand by it the conscience as judge, speaking in the name of God, cf. Chrys. (*in Ps.* 142) quoted by Suidas *s.v.* ὁ δικαστὴς ὁ ἔνδον, τὸ συνειδὸς λέγω τὸ ἡμῖν ἐγκαθήμενον, (*Hom.* III. *in Isa.* vi. 2) τοῦτο τὸ δικαστήριον οὐ χρήμασι διαφθείρεται, οὐ κολακείαις ἐνδίδωσι. θεῖον γάρ ἐστι καὶ παρὰ θεοῦ ταῖς ἡμετέραις ἐνιδρυμένον ψυχαῖς. One wonders why Cl. should have cared to add anything to Seneca's 'nihil prodest inclusam esse conscientiam; patemus Deo' (*Frag. Exhort.* 24), and 'illius divinitati omne praesens est' (*N. Q.* II. 36) or to his own remarks in P. 821 γυμνὴν ἔσωθεν τὴν ψυχὴν βλέπων καὶ τὴν ἐπίνοιαν τὴν ἑκάστου...ἔχει δι' αἰῶνος. See below, p. 74. 17 f., and compare a curious argument in P. 756, where Cl. tries to explain the miraculous voice on Sinai. There is the same confusion in Orig. *Cels.* II. 72 τοιαύτη ἐστὶν ἡ θεία φωνή, ἀκουομένη μόνοις ἐκείνοις, οὓς βούλεται ἀκούειν ὁ λέγων. οὐδέπω δὲ λέγω ὅτι οὐ πάντως ἐστὶν ἀὴρ πεπληγμένος ἢ πληγὴ ἀέρος, ἢ ὅ τί ποτε λέγεται ἐν τοῖς περὶ φωνῆς, ἡ ἀναγραφομένη φωνὴ τοῦ θεοῦ.

25—27. **τὴν φωνήν...κυλινδουμένην**, cf. 24. 4—6.

27, 28. **τέμνει...τὸν κόσμον**, cf. Sirac XXXV. 17 προσευχὴ ταπεινοῦ νεφέλας διῆλθε, below p. 144. 7 (the gnostic) τέμνει διὰ τῆς ἐπιστήμης τὸν οὐρανὸν καὶ...ἅπτεται τῶν θρόνων τῶν ἄκρων.

p. 66, line 1. προαιρέσεις. If this may be taken for granted, what need was there to argue the matter at all?

φθάνουσι. Cf. above p. 24. 14, Mt. xii. 28 ἔφθασεν ἐφ᾽ ὑμᾶς ἡ βασιλεία τοῦ θεοῦ, Phil. iii. 16, &c. The construction with the Inf. which we had in the preceding line is common in late Gr., see 1 Kings xii. 18 ὁ βασιλεὺς ἔφθασεν ἀναβῆναι 'made haste to go up,' quoted with other exx. in Jannaris *Gr.* 2121, also φθ. ἐξενεγκεῖν below p. 170. 14.

2. ὑπὸ τῆς συνειδήσεως πορθμευόνται. Cf. Eur. *Andr.* 1230 δαίμων ὅδε τις λευκὴν αἰθέρα πορθμευόμενος, Dion. Areop. *Cael. Hier.* 2 τῆς ἀγγελικῆς ἐπωνυμίας ἐκκρίτως ἠξίωνται διὰ τὸ πρώτως εἰς αὐτὰς ἐγγίνεσθαι τὴν θεαρχικὴν ἔλλαμψιν καὶ δι᾽ αὐτῶν εἰς ἡμᾶς διαπορθμεύεσθαι τὰς ὑπὲρ ἡμᾶς ἐκφαντορίας. Steph. cites Synes. *de Insomniis* τὰ παρὰ τοῦ θείου πορθμευόμενα. In p. 64. 23 we had the conscience apparently judging men, here it seems to act the part of a mediator transmitting prayers to heaven: at least this is suggested by the πρὸς θεόν of the preceding sentence. I have inserted τινα in the text to serve as a subject of the verb (the plural of the verb being often found with a neuter plural noun in late Greek). To understand προαιρέσεις would add a fresh complication: what distinction could we draw between 'resolves forwarded by conscience,' and 'resolves which speak with a voice of their own'? Supposing τινα to have been lost before τίνα, we may understand it of pious feeling of any kind.

4. ἀναμεῖναι. Cf. p. 74. 19, 168. 12, below P. 778 τούτου φωνὴν οὐκ ἀναμένει κύριος.

πρὸ τῆς γενέσεως. Cf. Susanna 42 ὁ τῶν κρυπτῶν γνώστης, ὁ εἰδὼς τὰ πάντα πρὶν γενέσεως αὐτῶν, below p. 74. 23.

7, 8. τῆς δυνάμεως *bis*, referring to p. 64. 29. **H.** Prov. xx. 27 is also quoted and explained in P. 611.

8. ὅλος ἀκοή. See n. on p. 10. 2.

§ 38. 12. λόγοις. Oratorical, but not metrical. **H.**

15. ὑπονοίας. Cf. *Strom.* v. 658 *fin.*, 659 *init.* οἱ ποιηταὶ δι᾽ ὑπονοίας πολλὰ φιλοσοφοῦσι...ὅπως εἰς τὴν τῶν αἰνιγμάτων ἔννοιαν ἡ ζήτησις παρεισδύουσα ἐπὶ τὴν εὕρεσιν τῆς ἀληθείας ἀναδράμῃ. **H.** Plato *Rep.* II. 378 D ὁ νέος οὐχ οἷός τε κρίνειν ὅ τι τε ὑπόνοια καὶ ὃ μή foll.

εὐφημία, 'devotion,' used of prayers: mostly found in poetry, but also in Plat. *Alcib.* II. 149 B (the god Ammon is said to have preferred τὴν Λακεδαιμονίων εὐφημίαν to all the worship of the other Greeks) τὴν γοῦν εὐφημίαν οὐκ ἄλλην τινά μοι δοκεῖ λέγειν ἢ τὴν εὐχὴν αὐτῶν, (the others try to bribe the gods to assent to their petitions whether bad or good) βλασφημούντων οὖν αὐτῶν ἀκούοντες οἱ θεοὶ οὐκ ἀποδέχονται τὰς πολυτελεῖς θυσίας. **H.**

δυσφημίας, 'profaneness,' a rare sense. So probably δύσφημος in 2 Macc. xiii. 11: τὸν ἄρτι ἀνεψυχότα λαὸν μὴ ἐᾶσαι τοῖς δυσφήμοις ἔθνεσιν ὑποχειρίους γενέσθαι, xv. 32. **H.**

16 foll. *i.e.* the prayers of those whose desires are base must themselves be base. From l. 11 to l. 18 the subject is worthlessness of prayers to misconceived deities: from here to p. 68. 6 worthlessness of prayers when desires are misdirected; from which point the two are combined. This very hard passage seems Stoic. Probably the idea is that, as in the case of all objects of desire, it is the personal use of them that is desired, so most of all is this the case with the highest good, which is only attained by *being* good. **H.** Cl. is still elaborating the idea that prayer is good or bad according to the character of the petitioner. This is so, because prayer is the religious vesture of desire, and therefore varies according to the nature of the desire. I take ὧν μὲν as gen. object. after ὀρέξεις, ὁρμαί, εὐχαί, as below, l. 26 τὴν εὐχὴν τῶν ὄντως ἀγαθῶν ποιεῖται. The Stoics distinguished between ὁρμή and ὄρεξις, see Epict. *Diss.* III. 2. 1 τρεῖς εἰσι τόποι περὶ οὕς ἀσκηθῆναι δεῖ...ὁ περὶ τὰς ὀρέξεις καὶ τὰς ἐκκλίσεις ἵνα μήτ' ὀρεγόμενος ἀποτυγχάνῃ μήτ' ἐκκλίνων περιπίπτῃ· ὁ περὶ τὰς ὁρμὰς καὶ ἀφορμὰς καὶ ἁπλῶς ὁ περὶ τὸ καθῆκον...τρίτος...ὁ περὶ τὰς συγκαταθέσεις. Chrysippus limited the ὁρμή to actions (Plut. *Stoic. Rep.* 11. 6, p. 1037) ἡ ὁρμὴ τοῦ ἀνθρώπου λόγος ἐστὶ προστακτικὸς αὐτῷ τοῦ ποιεῖν. In P. 617 *init.* Cl. quotes a distinction between ὄρεξις and ἐπιθυμία, the latter being related to ἡδοναῖς καὶ ἀκολασίᾳ, the former being a λογικὴ κίνησις ἐπὶ τῶν κατὰ φύσιν ἀναγκαίων.

18—22. διόπερ οὐδεὶς ἐπιθυμεῖ πόματος, ἀλλὰ τοῦ πιεῖν...πολιτεύεσθαι. This seems to be out of place here. It interrupts the connexion between the preceding and the following sentence (τούτων—ἐπιθυμίαι), and it is difficult to see how it can be a consequence of the preceding (διόπερ). If ὁρμαί alone were spoken of, we might make use of the distinction of Chrysippus, which limits these to action, but Cl. is speaking of ὀρέξεις and ἐπιθυμίαι as well, and he gives its widest sense to ὁρμαί by the phrase ὅλως εἰπεῖν. In the translation I have placed the sentence at the end of the section, but the force of διόπερ, in that or any other position, is far from clear. We should rather have expected ὅτι. Perhaps something has been lost. For the opposition of the verb to the substantive cf. *Str.* IV. P. 581 προσεχέστερον ἐν ἕξει γίνεται ταυτότητος ἀπαθοῦς, ὡς μηκέτι ἐπιστήμην ἔχειν καὶ γνῶσιν κεκτῆσθαι, ἐπιστήμην δὲ εἶναι καὶ γνῶσιν, Epict. *Diss.* III. 20. 4 ὑγεία ἀγαθόν, νόσος δὲ κακόν; οὔ, ἄνθρωπε. ἀλλὰ τί; τὸ καλῶς ὑγιαίνειν ἀγαθόν, τὸ κακῶς κακόν, *Paed.* I. 136 τὸ δὲ ἀγαθὸν [εἶναι] οὐ τῷ τὴν ἀρετὴν ἔχειν ἀγαθὸν εἶναι λέγεται...ἀρετὴ γάρ ἐστιν αὕτη, ἀλλὰ τῷ αὐτὴν καθ' αὑτὴν καὶ δι' αὑτὴν ἀγαθὴν εἶναι, below p. 138. 9 f. Zeller³ IV. 224, 225. This opposition seems to be connected with the Aristotelian doctrine that man's work and happiness consists in an ἐνέργεια, and also with the Stoic distinction between τὰ ἐφ' ἡμῖν and τὰ οὐκ ἐφ' ἡμῖν. Stobaeus' account of the Stoic philosophy seems to show that this was a subject of controversy among them (*Ecl.* II. 196 ἔχειν...ὀρεγόμεθα τἀγαθά,...τὴν γὰρ φρόνησιν αἱρούμεθα ἔχειν καὶ τὴν σωφροσύνην, οὐ μὰ Δία τὸ φρονεῖν καὶ σωφρονεῖν, ἀσώματα ὄντα καὶ κατηγορήματα).

24. καταλλήλως γίνεται εἰς, 'correspond in regard to,' cf. p. 12. 30

οἰκεία καὶ κατάλληλος εὐεργεσία, Epict. Diss. I. 22. 9 τὰς φυσικὰς προλήψεις ἐφαρμόζειν ταῖς ἐπὶ μέρους οὐσίαις καταλλήλως τῇ φύσει.

25. παρακείμενα, cf. below p. 68. 2, Plut. Mor. 36 B ἂν τὸ μὲν εἴρηκεν ἐναργῶς, τὸ δὲ τῷ εἰρημένῳ παρακείμενόν ἐστιν, Strom. P. 769 χείλη καὶ τὰ τούτοις παρακείμενα.

26. ὁ τοίνυν γνωστικός. Possibly the reading of the MS. (τοίνυν ὁ) may be correct, as τοίνυν often stands first in late Gr. (see Lob. Phryn. 342); but I do not know of any instance in Clem.

τῶν ὄντως ἀγαθῶν. Cf. below p. 76. 16.

28. συνεργῶν, cf. below p. 74. 11, 80. 14. H.

p. 68, line 1. μηκέτι ἔχειν...εἶναι δέ. Cf. below p. 138. 9, 10 οὐ μετουσίᾳ πυρὸς φωτεινός, ἀλλ᾽ εἶναι ὅλος φῶς. For the use of δέ = ἀλλά, see W. Schmid IV. p. 549 f.

§ 39. line 3. προσήκει: contrast with § 44. H.

8. φαντασίᾳ ἀγαθῶν, 'from an imagination of good.' The technical word for any mental 'impression,' Lat. visum or species, cf. Laert. VII. 45 f., Gat. on Ant. III. 16, Upton, Index to Epict. s.v., and such phrases as φ. μοι ἐγένετο ἐλαίου Ep. Diss. II. 20. 29, φ. ἡδονῆς τινος ib. Ench. 34. For the sentiment cf. Plat. Alc. II. p. 138 B οὐκοῦν δοκεῖ σοι πολλῆς προμηθείας γε προσδεῖσθαι ὅπως μὴ λήσει τις αὑτὸν εὐχόμενος μεγάλα κακά, δοκῶν δὲ ἀγαθά;

11. ἀλλ᾽ οὐχ ὁμοίως. The angels' prayer is solely for a continuance of what they have already. H. But elsewhere Cl. speaks of heaven as a state of progressive virtue and happiness, see p. 20. 5 μεταβάλλει πᾶν τὸ ἐνάρετον εἰς ἀμείνους οἰκήσεις, ib. ll. 17, 18 εἰς ἀμείνους ἀμεινόνων τόπων τόπους ἀφικομένας: and the angels, who have their station at the end of the visible world (p. 16. 8), have their ranks filled from among men (P. 1004), who are again promoted to the higher orders. Perhaps Cl. may have been thinking of the clause in the Lord's Prayer in which heaven is represented as the pattern and standard for earth.

13. ἀποτροπή, 'deprecation' of evils, by prayer or sacrifice: cf. ἀποτρόπαιος. This implies that the true conception of prayer goes beyond αἴτησις, cf. p. 66, l. 26 (for αἴτησις would equally include positive and negative), and involves positive communion with God, which means more than anything desired for ourselves. The deprecation of evil therefore is, in a sense, prayer, but only subordinately. H. It seems unnecessary to state that deprecation is a form of prayer. Can ἀποτροπή have the more literal sense of 'turning away' (transitive = 'deterrence') which it bears in Plat. Leg. IX. 853 O νομοθετεῖν ἀπειλοῦντα, ἐάν τις τοιοῦτος γίγνηται, καὶ τούτων ἀποτροπῆς τε ἕνεκα καὶ γενομένων κολάσεως τιθέναι ἐπ᾽ αὐτοῖς νόμους, 881 A τούτων δεῖ τινος ἀποτροπῆς ἐσχάτης, Alc. II. 148 D, or neuter (of repentance) which it has in Plut. Mor. 519 F χρήσιμον πρὸς τὴν ἀποτροπὴν ἡ τῶν προεγνωσμένων ἀνάμνησις, 520 D μέγιστον πρὸς τὴν τοῦ πάθους ἀποτροπὴν ὁ ἐθισμός, ἐὰν πόρρωθεν ἀρξάμενοι γυμνάζωμεν ἑαυτοὺς ἐπὶ ταύτην τὴν ἐγκράτειαν? Another εἶδος εὐχῆς is mentioned in p. 72. 10 below.

14 foll. **οὐκ ἐπὶ τῇ τῶν ἀνθρώπων βλάβῃ**. Deprecation of evil becomes wrong the moment it involves the diversion of the evil upon the heads of others: such a prayer is lawful only in contemplation of a higher good wrought out to them by God's Providence. H. Both this and the preceding sentence would be more intelligible if Cl. were speaking, not of deprecation, but of imprecation. In speaking of different kinds of prayer it was natural to consider whether the imprecatory prayers of the Psalms were allowable to Christians; and perhaps the rule laid down here may be supported by St Paul's language in 1 Cor. v. 3—5 on delivering over the offender to Satan, εἰς ὄλεθρον τῆς σαρκός, ἵνα τὸ πνεῦμα σωθῇ ἐν τῇ ἡμέρᾳ τοῦ κυρίου. In his note on the passage, Alford says this threat was held '*in terrorem* over the offender.' This may explain the word ἀποτροπή here used. Imprecation (such as the curses on Mount Ebal) is a species of 'deterrent.' Cf. below the prayer for heretics in p. 180, of which Cl. says ἀποτρέψαι βουλόμενος παρεθέμην (l. 17).

16. **ἐπιστροφή**, 'regard for,' as before. H. In the n. on p. 62. 17 I have given my reasons for preferring the sense 'conversion.' Compare also Str. VI. P. 763 ἵνα...τὰ ἔθνη εἰς ἐπιστροφὴν ἀγάγωσι, Sirac. xviii. 20, Psalm. Sol. xvi. 11. Perhaps here with the gen. the other meaning is easier, see below p. 142. 14 πρὸς ἐπιστροφὴν τῶν μελλόντων.

18. **ὁμιλία πρὸς τὸν θεόν**. See below p. 72. 11.

19 foll. Probably a reference to Hannah in 1 Sam. i. 13. (Sylb.)

21. **ἐνδιάθετον**, opposed to προφορικών in the Stoic distinction of λόγος, as thought and as speech (Zeller IV. 61). Applied further by Philo and by the Fathers. Various examples occur in Wytt. Plut. II. 44 D. H. See below p. 70. 27, 126. 28, and compare the Pythian oracle (referred to by Tert. *Orat*. 17) καὶ κωφοῦ συνίημι καὶ οὐ φωνεῦντος ἀκούω.

§ 40. 24. **τὰς χεῖρας εἰς οὐρανὸν αἴρομεν**. Cf. Tert. *Ap*. 30; *Orat*. 14; Orig. *Orat*. 31, &c., Augusti v. 378 foll., Bingh. 138. 3. 10. H. Origen defends the practice by referring to 1 Tim. ii. 8, Ps. cxli. 2. It was common with the heathen also, cf. Ps.-Arist. *de Mundo* 6 πάντες οἱ ἄνθρωποι ἀνατείνομεν τὰς χεῖρας εἰς τὸν οὐρανὸν εὐχὰς ποιούμενοι. It is rather strange that Cl. says nothing of kneeling or of the φίλημα.

24. **τοὺς πόδας ἐπεγείρομεν**. Cf. *Paed*. I. P. 107 οὐκ ἄρ' ἔτι κυλιόμεθα οἱ νήπιοι χαμαί...ἀνατεινόμενοι δὲ ἄνω τῇ ἐννοίᾳ, κόσμῳ καὶ ἁμαρτίαις ἀποτεταγμένοι, ὀλίγῳ ποδὶ ἐφαπτόμενοι τῆς γῆς, ὅσον ἐν κόσμῳ εἶναι δοκεῖν, σοφίαν μεταδιώκομεν ἁγίαν. We may compare the *tripudiatio* of the Romans, the dances of oriental worship (2 Sam. vi. 14) and the Jumpers and Shakers of modern times. Perhaps it is against such gesticulation that Chrysostom warns his hearers in *Hom*. XIX. *Matt*. p. 247, εἰσί τινες...ἀσχημονοῦντες ἐν εὐχῇ...καὶ τῷ σχήματι καὶ τῇ φωνῇ καταγελάστους ποιοῦντες ἑαυτούς.

25. **συνεκφώνησιν**, 'simultaneous utterance,' referring to the joint uplifting of the voice at the close. In a different application *Strom*. I. 374 *init*. ἂν γὰρ προεκφώνησίν τις εἴπῃ καὶ συνεκφώνησιν αἰτιάσηται, προφητείας εἴδη λέγει. H. Probably the final Amen is referred to, cf. 1 Cor. xiv. 16,

Justin *Apol.* I. 65 (τοῦ προεστῶτος) συντελέσαντος τὰς εὐχὰς καὶ τὴν εὐχαριστίαν, πᾶς ὁ παρὼν λαὸς ἐπευφημεῖ λέγων ἀμήν, Eus. *H. E.* II. 17 ἐνὸς μετὰ ῥυθμοῦ κοσμίως ἐπιψάλλοντος, οἱ λοιποὶ καθ' ἡσυχίαν ἀκροώμενοι τῶν ὕμνων τὰ ἀκροτελεύτια συνεξηχοῦσιν, quoting Philo (M. 2. p. 484) as describing customs still in vogue in the Christian Church.

26, 27. νοητὴν οὐσίαν. The adjective was used by Parmenides in opposition to δοξαστός, by Plato in opposition to ὁρατός (*Rep.* 509 D), or more generally to αἰσθητός (*Tim.* 92) ὁ κόσμος...εἰκὼν τοῦ νοητοῦ θεοῦ αἰσθητός, cf. Alcinus ap. Laert. III. 10 ὁ Πλάτων φησὶν αἰσθητὸν μὲν εἶναι... τὸ ἀεὶ ῥέον καὶ μεταβάλλον...ταῦτα δ' ἐστὶν ὧν ἀεὶ γένεσις, οὐσία δὲ μηδέποτε πέφυκε· νοητὸν δὲ ἐξ οὗ μηδὲν ἀπογίνεται μηδὲ προσγίνεται. See above p. 4. 13—17, p. 26. 28, below 74. 26, 78. 15, and compare *Str.* I. P. 425 ἡ ἀληθὴς διαλεκτικὴ ὑπεξαναβαίνει περὶ τὴν πάντων κρατίστην οὐσίαν, τολμᾷ τε ἐπέκεινα ἐπὶ τὸν τῶν ὅλων θεόν.

27. συναφιστάνειν, 'detach along with the uttered words.' H.

28. ἐπτερωμένην. *Str.* P. 318 ἐφόδια ζωῆς ἀϊδίου λαβόντες εἰς οὐρανὸν πτεροῦνται, P. 642 ἐγὼ δὲ ἂν εὐξαίμην τὸ πνεῦμα τοῦ Χριστοῦ πτερῶσαί με εἰς τὴν Ἱερουσαλὴμ τὴν ἐμήν.

30. τοῦ δεσμοῦ. See n. on p. 54. 31 above.

καταμεγαλοφρονοῦντες. Several times in Clement, not elsewhere. H. See Index.

p. 70, line 1. **ὑπέρβασιν,** 'passage through and beyond the world,' which is often compared to Egypt. Philo several times calls the Passover διάβασις (διαβατήρια); and says (I. 534 *med.*) ὅλον γὰρ ὑπερκύψας τὸ ἔργον ἐπόθει τὸν τεχνίτην...τοῦτ' ἔστι κυρίως εἰπεῖν τὸ ψυχικὸν πάσχα, ἡ παντὸς πάθους καὶ παντὸς αἰσθητοῦ διάβασις κ.τ.λ.: cf. Orig. *Cels.* VIII. 22, a passage rather like this (remembering that Christ is our Passover, he always keeps) τὸ πάσχα, ὅπερ ἑρμηνεύεται Διαβατήρια, διαβαίνων ἀεί...ἀπὸ τῶν τοῦ βίου πραγμάτων ἐπὶ τὸν θεὸν καὶ ἐπὶ τὴν πόλιν αὐτοῦ σπεύδων. Ὑπέρβασις was Aquila's rendering of Pesakh (see Field's note on Ex. ii. 11). So also Joseph. *Ant.* 2. 14. 6 τὴν ἑορτὴν πάσχα καλοῦντες, σημαίνει δὲ ὑπερβάσια (*al.* ὑπερβασίαν) διότι κατ' ἐκείνην τὴν ἡμέραν ὁ θεὸς αὐτῶν ὑπερβὰς Αἰγυπτίοις ἐναπέσκηψε τὴν νόσον. H. The word ὑπέρβασις is used, like διάβασις, of crossing over a sea or river (Strabo XVI. 2. 30), or of a mountain pass (*ib.* IV. 6. 12).

4. ἴσοιτο. Optative to express the Gnostic's own belief and expectation. See Jelf 807 B. H.

ὥρας τακτάς. On the Hours see Bingh. 139. 8. H. Also *D. of Chr. Ant.* s.v. 'Hours of Prayer,' Funk on Didachè VIII. 3. Cf. Acts iii. 1, x. 9, Ps. lv. 17, Dan. vi. 10, and n. in Potter's ed. Cl. writes here in the tone of St Paul (Gal. iv. 10, 11) on which see Orig. *Cels.* VIII. 21–23.

6. ἀλλ' οὖν γε. See Klotz-Devar I. 7, II. 16 f.

9, 10. τοῦ κατὰ ἀγάπην δρωμένου. The word δράω is frequently used of religious worship, like the Lat. *facere*, cf. above n. on p. 60. 8, Plut. *Mor.* 352 C τὰ δεικνύμενα καὶ δρώμενα περὶ τοὺς θεούς, where Wytt. cites *ib.* 280 B καθαρμός ἐστι τῆς πόλεως τὰ δρώμενα with other exx. So taken it might mean 'having received the perfection of that which is exhibited in the Agape,' cf. P. 166 ἀγάπη δὲ τῷ ὄντι ἐπουράνιός ἐστι τροφή. See App. on Ἀγάπη.

10. τὰς τῶν ὡρῶν διανομὰς τριχῇ διεσταμένας. Cyprian *de Orat. Dom.*, quoted in Potter's n., seems to speak of three Trinities (the three Hierarchies?) as symbolized by the Hours of Prayer: prima hora in tertiam veniens, consummatum numerum trinitatis ostendit: itemque ad sextam quarta procedens declarat alteram trinitatem: et quando a septima nona completur, per tertiam horam trinitas perfecta numeratur.

12, 13. τὴν μακαρίαν τῶν ἁγίων τριάδα μονῶν. The word τριάς is used of the three Christian graces in P. 588 ἡ ἁγία τριάς, πίστις, ἐλπίς, ἀγάπη, and in P. 542, where Cl., in a discussion on the meaning of the words 'where two or three are gathered together in my name, there am I in the midst of them,' mentions different explanations, *e.g.* that the three are θυμός, ἐπιθυμία, λογισμός, or σάρξ, ψυχή, πνεῦμα, and then continues, τάχα δὲ καὶ τὴν κλῆσιν, τήν τε ἐκλογὴν δευτέραν, καὶ τρίτον τὸ εἰς τὴν πρώτην τιμὴν κατατασσόμενον γένος αἰνίσσεται ἡ προειρημένη τριάς: cf. above n. on p. 16. 4 ἑτέρων ὑφ' ἑτέρους, l. 7 τὰ πρῶτα καὶ δεύτερα καὶ τρίτα, and l. 15 n. on μονῇ. See § 57 below, where it is said that knowledge carries a man through τὰς προκοπὰς τὰς μυστικάς, and shortly afterwards we have the three saving μεταβολαί, to faith, to knowledge, and to love, followed by the ascent ἐπὶ τὴν κυριακὴν ὄντως διὰ τῆς ἁγίας ἑβδομάδος μονήν: also P. 793 *init.*, where the three Orders of the Ministry are associated with the heavenly Hierarchy, αἱ ἐνταῦθα κατὰ τὴν ἐκκλησίαν προκοπαί, ἐπισκόπων πρεσβυτέρων διακόνων, μιμήματα ἀγγελικῆς δόξης κἀκείνης τῆς οἰκονομίας τυγχάνουσιν κ.τ.λ. In the present passage the triad connects the three stages of Christian progress with the three hours of prayer. Comparing these passages and P. 797 *fin.* ταύτας ἐκλεκτὰς οὔσας τὰς τρεῖς μονὰς οἱ ἐν τῷ εὐαγγελίῳ ἀριθμοὶ αἰνίσσονται, "ὁ τριάκοντα καὶ ὁ ἑξήκοντα καὶ ὁ ἑκατόν," I think it may be concluded that Cl. was glad to find an excuse for introducing the mystical number Three, as connected with the μοναί, into the parable of the Sower. Cf. his account of the number seven in *Str.* P. 813 foll.

§ 41. 16. Προδίκου. On the antinomian doctrines of Prodicus see *Strom.* III. 525. He is mentioned also I. 357 *fin.*, VII. 896 *med.* H. Origen controverts the opinion of Prodicus on Prayer in *De Orat.* 5 foll.

19. Κυρηναϊκῶν. See *Strom.* II. P. 495—498. Theodorus 'the Atheist' belonged to this school. In *Protr.* P. 20 *fin.* Cl. defends him from the charge of atheism. Origen (*Cels.* II. 13) speaks of the Peripatetics as denying the use of prayer.

20. κατὰ καιρόν. Probably alluding to the Διδάσκαλος, see Introduction.

21. ψευδωνύμων. Cf. *Strom.* III. 525 οἱ ἀπὸ Προδίκου ψευδωνύμως γνωστικοὺς σφᾶς αὐτοὺς ἀναγορεύοντες. The great book of Irenaeus is entitled Ἔλεγκος τῆς ψευδωνύμου γνώσεως (Potter).

22. καταδρομή. Cf. P. 429, 511 foll., 550 κατατρέχει τις γενέσεως, 561 τοῦ νόμου κατατρέχοντες, and see n. on φιλόνεικον, p. 23. 24. Cl. returns to this subject in § 106 f. (below p. 186).

24. τὸν ἐκκλησιαστικὸν κανόνα. Cf. vi. 803 *med.* κανὼν δὲ ἐκκλησιαστικὸς ἡ συνῳδία καὶ ἡ συμφωνία νόμου τε καὶ προφητῶν τῇ κατὰ τὴν τοῦ κυρίου παρουσίαν παραδιδομένῃ διαθήκῃ. **H.** Also p. 158. 6, 166. 8, 186. 10.

26. ἀπονενεμημένη. Cf. l. 30 foll. **H.**

27. καὶ αἰτήσαντι καὶ ἐννοηθέντι, *i.e.* the ἐννόησις by itself suffices: see on p. 74. 22. **H.** Cf. P. 790 *fin.* τῇ Ἅννῃ ἐννοηθείσῃ μόνον τοῦ παιδὸς ἐδόθη σύλληψις...αἴτησαι, φησὶν ἡ γραφή, καὶ ποιήσω, ἐννοήθητι καὶ δώσω, also P. 778 and below p. 127. 28. Resch does not refer to this saying in his *Agrapha*.

28, 29. How would Cl. explain the apparent denial of St Paul's petition 2 Cor. xii. 8 ?

32. δοίη δέ. ἄν is supplied in thought from the previous clause, cf. Jelf. § 432, *obs.* 2. However, some such insertion as that proposed by Mr Barnard seems to be required.

ὑπάρχουσιν, being such already, not needing any αἴτησις. **H.**

p. 72, line 3. **ἐπιστροφήν.** See n. on p. 62. 17 above.

4. εὐχαριστῶν ἐν οἷς ἐτελείωσεν = ἐν τῷ τελειῶσαι. Cl. is fond of the periphrastic use of the relative clause instead of the infinitive with article, cf. below p. 74. 11, 12 δι᾽ ὧν εὔχεται τὸ ποθούμενον λαμβάνειν = διὰ τοῦ εὔχεσθαι, p. 104. 9 ἐπίστευσεν ἐξ ὧν ἐθαύμασεν = ἐκ τοῦ θαυμάσαι, P. 765 τὴν κόλασιν δικαίαν εἶναι δι᾽ ὧν οὐκ ἐπίστευσαν ὁμολογοῦσιν = διὰ τοῦ μὴ πιστεῦσαι.

5. ὡς πλείστους ὅσους. A pleonastic expression for ὡς πλείστους or πλείστους ὅσους (probably at first employed to add force to the latter), cf. ὡς ὅτι τάχιστα.

9 foll. *i.e.* in any case the mere faith that he will receive is in itself a kind of prayer in gnostical quiescence. **H.**

10. ἐναποκειμένης, 'stored,' and so quiescent (Stoic), Plut. II. 961 C τὰς νοήσεις, ἃς ἐναποκειμένας μὲν ἐννοίας καλοῦσι, κινουμένας δὲ διανοήσεις. **H.** Cf. P. 9 αἱ πρόδρομοι τοῦ κυρίου φωναί...αἰνίττονταί μοι τὴν ἐναποκειμένην σωτηρίαν, P. 807 (on the symbolical meaning of the Table of the Law) θεοῦ...εἰδοποιία ἐναποκειμένη τῇ πλακὶ δημιουργίᾳ τοῦ κόσμου τυγχάνει, Philo M. 1. 277 ἔννοιαν καὶ διανόησιν, τὴν μὲν ἐναποκειμένην οὖσαν νόησιν, τὴν δὲ νοήσεως διέξοδον.

§ 42. **11. ἀφορμὴ ὁμιλίας.** See above p. 68. 18.

15. ὁμολογίαν, 'acceptance and consent.' **H.**

16. ἀντεπιστροφή seems to be found only in an account of the Pythagorean doctrine of vision, *ap.* Plut. *Plac.* 901 D: cf. ἀντεπιστρέφω (of repartee) Plut. II. 810 E. The point is that it is the πρόνοια itself returning back upon itself. **H.** Perhaps we may compare P. 822 τῇ τοῦ θεοῦ βουλήσει ἡ τῶν ἀγαθῶν ἀνδρῶν προαίρεσις ὑπακούει...συγκινεῖ τοὺς ἐπιτηδείους εἰς τὴν ὠφέλιμον ἐξεργασίαν, 160 ὁ βίος ὁ Χριστιανῶν...σύστημα λογικῶν πράξεων...ὑποθῆκαι πνευματικαί...πρός τε ἡμᾶς αὐτοὺς καὶ πρὸς τοὺς πέλας εὔθετοι· καὶ δὴ καὶ αὗται αὖθις πρὸς ἡμᾶς ἀνταναστρέφουσι, καθάπερ πρὸς τῶν βαλλόντων ἡ σφαῖρα διὰ τὴν ἀντιτυπίαν παλινδρομοῦσα. Apparently Cl. means that human goodness, though involving an effort of man's free will, figured by the repercussion of the tennis-ball, is yet due only to the will of God, as the return of the ball is due to the will of the player. There is a similar expression in Moule's *Secret of the Presence* p. 150 'Human love is the return, the repercussion, of a tenderness that has first gone freely out as the unselfish gift of the asker's heart.'

17. ἀντίστροφος, 'responsive' or 'corresponding,' considered only as a second movement answering to the first. H.

25. πρὸς ὁποτερονοῦν καὶ βούλοιτο. So I read for ὁπότερον ἂν καὶ β. of MS., the optative having merely the indefinite force, cf. P. 318 ἡ κηρυκικὴ ἐπιστήμη ἥδε πως ἀγγελική, ὁποτέρως ἂν ἐνεργῇ.

26. ἀγαθοποιεῖ, 'benefits,' neutral, as an unconscious power might do. H.

27. εὐποιεῖ, 'is beneficent to,' as a conscious agent. H. Cf. *Str.* I. P. 369 τῆς θείας σοφίας καὶ ἀρετῆς καὶ δυνάμεως ἔργον ἐστὶν οὐ μόνον τὸ ἀγαθοποιεῖν—φύσις γάρ, ὡς εἰπεῖν, αὕτη τοῦ θεοῦ, ὡς τοῦ πυρὸς τὸ θερμαίνειν καὶ τοῦ φωτὸς τὸ φωτίζειν,—ἀλλὰ κἀκεῖνο μάλιστα τὸ διὰ κακῶν...ἀγαθόν τι τέλος ἀποτελεῖν.

28. ὑπηρετική. See above p. 6. 1.

29. χειρόνων. If providence were the result of mere fate or impersonal law, the benefit received from unconscious agents by man would be received by a superior from inferiors, but as it is they come as a voluntary gift from the Ruler to his subjects.

30. προσεχεῖς, 'immediate': probably each designed in close fitness to the present circumstances. H. I understand the word in the sense 'proximate.' See above pp. 8. 19, 18. 4, 20. 9, n.

§ 43. p. 74, line 8 foll. The connexion seems to be this: sanctity of place or time adds nothing to a prayer, but the following combination of qualities does. H.

11. δι' ὧν εὔχεται. See above on p. 72. 4.

12, 13. τὸ παρ' ἡμῶν εὐεπίφορον. Cf. below p. 88. 28, and P. 551 εὐεπ. εἰς τὸν δεύτερον γάμον.

14. τῇ συλλήψει αὐτῇ, cf. n. on p. 70. 27.

18. ὅπου γε. See Index. The assertion of the principle which follows makes the argument of § 37 superfluous.

19. πολυφώνους, 'many-voiced,' P. 5 ὁ λόγος ψάλλει διὰ τοῦ πολυφώνου ὀργάνου (τοῦ ἀνθρώπου). The word is used of Christ, P. 8 *init.* πολύφωνός γε ὁ σωτὴρ καὶ πολύτροπος εἰς ἀνθρώπων σωτηρίαν. The Epicureans held that the gods spoke Greek, see Zeller IV. 436 n.

22. ἔννοια, the individual notion, νόησις (cf. VI. 820 *fin.*), the mental process of its formation. A probably apocryphal saying, αἴτησαι καὶ ποιήσω, ἐννοήθητι καὶ δώσω is quoted VI. 778 τούτου φωνὴν κατὰ τὴν εὐχὴν οὐκ ἀναμένει κύριος κ.τ.λ. below p. 126. 28. See pp. 70. 27, 86. 24. H.

23. τῆς δημιουργίας. Cf. VI. 791, where the same thought about God seeing the light as good beforehand is more fully worked out. H. See above p. 66. 5.

28. γενεθλίου ἡμέρας εἰκὼν ἡ ἀνατολή. Is there a reference here to Christmas or Epiphany? Originally the Birth and the Baptism were celebrated together on the festival of the Epiphany, from which Christmas seems to have been separated towards the end of the 4th century, see *D. of Chr. Ant.* under 'Christmas' and 'Epiphany,' and cf. *Constit. Ap.* v. 13 τὰς ἡμέρας τῶν ἑορτῶν φυλάσσετε ἀδελφοί, καὶ πρώτην γε τὴν γενέθλιον, ἥτις ὑμῖν ἐπιτελείσθω εἰκάδι πρώτῃ τοῦ ἐνάτου μηνός, Basil. *Orat.* 25, vol. I. p. 593 (*ap.* Suicer) ἑορτάσωμεν τὰ σωτήρια τοῦ κόσμου, τὴν γενέθλιον ἡμέραν τῆς ἀνθρωπότητος. It would seem from *Str.* P. 407 that the observance of the day was at all events not universal when Cl. wrote. He says there that there were some who fixed the day of our Saviour's birth (περιεργότερον τῇ γενέσει τοῦ σωτῆρος...καὶ τὴν ἡμέραν προστιθέντες), and (408) that the followers of Basilides kept the day of His baptism. P. 511 οἱ Κεφαλλῆνες γενέθλιον ἀποθέωσιν κατὰ νουμηνίαν θύουσιν Ἐπιφάνει. Possibly it may be better to understand the phrase generally of the day of birth, cf. Eus. *Pr. Ev.* III. 1 γένεσις ἡ εἰς ἥλιον καὶ φῶς ἐκ σκότους πορεία.

30. γνώσεως ἀληθείας ἡμέρα κατὰ λόγον τοῦ ἡλίου. Cf. Mal. iv. 2 ἀνατελεῖ ὑμῖν τοῖς φοβουμένοις τὸ ὄνομά μου ἥλιος δικαιοσύνης, Lk. ii. 78 ἐπεσκέψατο ἡμᾶς ἀνατολὴ ἐξ ὕψους, 2 Pet. i. 19 (τὸν προφητικὸν λόγον) ᾧ καλῶς ποιεῖτε προσέχοντες ὡς λύχνῳ φαίνοντι ἐν αὐχμηρῷ τόπῳ, ἕως οὗ ἡμέρα διαυγάσῃ καὶ φώσφορος ἀνατείλῃ ἐν ταῖς καρδίαις ὑμῶν. For the anarthrous nouns compare my Introduction to St James pp. cxci foll.

p. 76, line 1. **πρὸς τὴν ἑωθινὴν ἀνατολὴν αἱ εὐχαί.** See *Const. Apost.* VII. 44. 3, Bingham, Bk XIII. 8. 15, and XI. 7. 4. Various far-fetched reasons were assigned for this position, which originated no doubt in the worship of the sun, and is on that account reprobated by Ezekiel (viii. 16). Pious Jews looked towards Jerusalem in prayer (Dan. vi. 10, 1 K. viii. 44), as Mohammedans towards Mecca. See my n. on Cic. *N. D.* I. 79 constiteram exorientem Auroram forte salutans.

2. τὰ παλαίτατα τῶν ἱερῶν πρὸς δύσιν ἔβλεπεν. Vitruvius (IV. 5) asserts this generally, but Hyginus (*de Agr. Lim.* p. 153 Goes) agrees with Cl., 'antiqui architecti in occidentem templa spectare recte scripserunt: postea placuit omnem religionem eo convertere, ex qua parte caeli terra illuminatur'; and in the art. on 'Templum' in Smith's *Dict. of Ant.* it is said that most of the existing 'temples in Attica, Ionia, and Sicily have their entrance towards the east.' See arts. on 'Orientation' and 'East' in *D. of Chr. Ant.*

3. No need to change Sylburg's ἀπαντιπρόσωπον except as to termination, though it is ἅπαξ λεγόμενον. We have ἀπαντίον and ἀπαντικρύ. H. ἀπ' ἀντιπροσώπου is suggested by H. J.

4. The quotation is probably intended to show that prayer, being a kind of sacrifice, should be under the same rule as sacrifice in regard to the attitude of the worshipper: or can Cl. have taken ἑσπερινή in the sense of 'western'?

9. ἃ...λάβοιεν βλάπτει. For a similar form of the conditional sentence see P. 947 εἰ ἀποσταῖεν...συνεστάλη, P. 507 εἰ μὴ δέχοιτο...ἀνακάμψει, 599 εἰ εὖ φρονοῖμεν χάριν εἰσόμεθα, above pp. 54. 11, below 166. 15.

§ 44. 15. ἀποβαίνειν. The MS. ὑπερβαίνειν seems right, with a reference to the ὑπέρβασις of p. 70. 1. H. But would not these supermundane goods be included in the τὰ ὄντως ἀγαθά of the next sentence? It seems to me that Cl. is here contrasting the gnostic and the μοχθηρός, as to their feeling in regard to mundane good.

ἀϊδιότητα. The prayer of the gnostic has relation to present good and to the possibilities of the future. He asks that he may be fitted to meet what may be in store for him, and, if any thing which he desires is denied,—surely not that it may be eternal, but—that he may be resigned to the disappointment. Dr Abbott has suggested ἀνιδιότητα with the slightest possible change. The word is not found, but ἀνίδιος occurs, meaning 'without property.' If we can extend this so as to get the sense 'non-appropriation of a thing,' this would do very well. I had thought of ἀδιαφορότης in the sense of 'indifference to.' Compare Basil *in Ps.* xxvii., p. 246 (*ap.* Suicer, *s.v.*) λήθην ποιοῦνται τῶν προτέρων, ἀδιαφοροῦντες ἐπ' αὐτοῖς. The objection to it is that, though διαφορότης is found *Str.* P. 434 (If faith comes by nature, as the Gnostics say) πᾶσα ἡ τῆς πίστεως καὶ ἀπιστίας ἰδιότης καὶ διαφορότης οὔτε ἐπαίνῳ οὔτε μὴν ψόγῳ ὑποπέσοι ἄν (translated 'nulla fidei et incredulitatis proprietas aut differentia laudi vel vituperationi fuerit obnoxia'), Philo M. 2. 370, &c.; yet the privative is not ἀδιαφορότης but ἀδιαφορία. Lobeck however remarks on the rareness of some of these nouns in -της (*Phryn.* p. 350), and as διαφορία is found, though rarely, by the side of διαφορότης, so the converse might be the case with ἀδιαφορότης. The form ἀδιαφορία is used both of things (Sext. Emp. *P. H.* 152 παρὰ Μασσαγέταις τὸ μοιχεύειν ἀδιαφορίας ἔθει (? εἴδει) παραδεδόσθαι), and of persons (as in Epict. II. 5. 20, where it is opposed to ἐπιμέλεια).

16. τὰ δὲ ὄντως ἀγαθά. See above p. 66. 27.

19. ἱκανὸς ὢν ἑαυτῷ. Cf. below p. 112. 13 τούτῳ πάντα εἰς ἑαυτὸν ἀνήρτηται πρὸς τὴν τοῦ τέλους κτῆσιν, and *Ecl. Proph.* P. 993 *init.* ὁ μὲν πιστεύσας ἄφεσιν ἁμαρτημάτων ἔλαβεν παρὰ τοῦ κυρίου, ὁ δ' ἐν γνώσει γενόμενος ἅτε μηκέτι ἁμαρτάνων παρ' ἑαυτοῦ τὴν ἄφεσιν τῶν λοιπῶν κομίζεται, P. 788 (the Lord) ἡμᾶς ἐξ ἡμῶν αὐτῶν βούλεται σώζεσθαι, *Q. D. S.* 957 P. τῶν μὲν οὖν προγεγενημένων θεὸς δίδωσιν ἄφεσιν, τῶν δὲ ἐπιόντων αὐτὸς ἕκαστος ἑαυτῷ, and the ambiguous passage in p. 142. 3 below.

20. αὐτάρκης. Cl. here follows the Stoics, who maintained the selfsufficingness of the wise man.

24. ἥνωται τῷ πνεύματι. It seems best to take πνεῦμα here of the Holy Spirit, rather than to translate 'in his spirit.' Cf. below p. 78. 15 τοῖς νοητοῖς...οἰκειούμενος, *Str.* III. P. 559 τὸ ῥῆμα τοῦ κυρίου τὸ χρῖσαν τὴν ψυχὴν

καὶ ἐνῶσαν τῷ πνεύματι, ib. P. 553 ὅταν ἐκ μετανοίας καταισχυνθεὶς πνεῦμα καὶ ψυχὴν ἐνώσῃ (MS. ἐνώσει) κατὰ τὴν τοῦ λόγου ὑπακοήν, τότε οὐκ ἔνι ἐν ὑμῖν οὐκ ἄρρεν, οὐ θῆλυ, Paed. II. P. 178 (the Spirit is mingled with man by the Divine will) καὶ γὰρ ὡς ἀληθῶς τὸ πνεῦμα φκείωται τῇ ἀπ' αὐτοῦ φερομένῃ ψυχῇ, and n. ou ἕνωσις p. 22. 14.

26. ἀγαθώτατον. This form is found in Diod. XVI. 85 *fin.*, Hermas *Vis.* I. 2. 3, see Lob. *Phryn.* p. 93, Blass *Gr. N. T.* p. 34.

27. ὠκύτος, 'quick,' 'ready': usually with the tongue, but also with the eye or other faculty. H.

προσβολήν, 'glance' or look,' usually with τῶν ὀμμάτων or τῆς ὄψεως, but also alone, as VI. 821 *fin.* ἕκαστον ἐν μέρει μιᾷ προσβολῇ προσβλέπει. The two words are used together, of quick mental vision, by Philo (I. 286 *fin.*) εὐθυβόλῳ καὶ εὐθίκτῳ χρησάμενοι προσβολῇ, opposed to νωθίστεροι καὶ βραδεῖς τὰς ψυχάς, ὥσπερ οἱ τὰ ὄμματα πεπηρωμένοι. H. The verb προσβάλλω is used either of a person turning the eye upon some object, as in Eur. *Med.* 860 προσβαλοῦσα ὄμματα τέκνοις, cf. Orig. *de Orat.* 25 ὁ νοῦς προσβάλλει χωρὶς αἰσθήσεως τοῖς νοητοῖς; or more commonly of the object of sight or sound or smell affecting the organ, as in Plat. *Theaet.* 154 A ὃ δὴ ἕκαστον εἶναί φαμεν χρῶμα, οὔτε τὸ προσβάλλον (the object) οὔτε τὸ προσβαλλόμενον (the eye) ἀλλὰ μεταξύ τι. From the former use we get the meaning of προσβολή in the example quoted by H., and in *Theaet.* 153 E χρῶμα ἐκ τῆς προσβολῆς τῶν ὀμμάτων πρὸς τὴν προσήκουσαν φορὰν φανεῖται γεγενημένον; from the latter the meaning in Soph. *Fr.* 737 βραδεῖα μὲν γὰρ ἡ λόγοισι προσβολὴ μόλις δι' ὠτὸς ἔρχεται. In Plotin. *Enn.* VI. 2. 8 ἐν προσβολῇ τῆς τοῦ ὄντος φύσεως γεγενημένος (dum videlicet entis naturam inspicit) we have the tropical use. So in Lat. we find the expressions 'coniectus animorum' (Cic. *Sen.* 115), 'coniectus rationis, id est, directio quaedam ad veritatem' (Quintil. III. 6. 30), as well as 'coniectus oculorum' (Cic. *de Orat.* III. 222).

Is θεωρίας to be taken as a subjective or an objective genitive, and does it mean outward observation or inward contemplation? The parallel *coniectus rationis* suggests that it is subjective, and this seems to suit better with the high-flown language of ll. 25 and 26. For the same reason it seems better to understand it of contemplation. If we read οὗτος with Barnard in l. 25, the general drift of the sentence will be 'the true gnostic (described in ll. 13—24) is on the one hand quick to lay hold of spiritual realities by the faculty of contemplation, and at the same time the things contemplated do not pass away like a vision, leaving no trace behind; he retains them in his memory, and can use them for the purpose of science.' Compare St Paul's 'I will pray with the spirit and I will pray with the understanding also.'

28. τὴν τῶν θεωρητῶν δύναμιν. Here too it may be questioned whether the gen. is subjective or objective: is it the power which flows from the objects of contemplation, or the power which the gnostic has over them? The latter seems more suitable here. For θεωρητός cf. Diog. L. x. 139, where the Epicurean theology is explained, τοὺς θεοὺς λόγῳ θεωρητούς,

which Cic. translates 'eam esse naturam deorum ut primum non sensu sed mente cernatur' (*N. D.* I. 49), and Cl. *Str.* v. P. 653 ὁ ἐλπίζων τῷ νῷ ὁρᾷ τὰ νοητά...νῷ ἄρα θεωρητὸς ὁ λόγος.

29. **τὴν διορατικὴν...δριμύτητα.** Cf. P. 116 φωτισμὸς ἄρα ἡ γνῶσίς ἐστιν ὁ ἐξαφανίζων τὴν ἄγνοιαν καὶ τὸ διορατικὸν ἐντιθείς, Philo M. 1. 486 χάριν ἔδωκας ἐξαίρετον τῷ διορατικῷ γίνει, Plato *Rep.* VII. 535 B δριμύτης πρὸς τὰ μαθήματα.

30. **βιάζεται κτήσασθαι.** For this use of β. cf. Thuc. VII. 79. 1 ἐβιάσαντο ἐλθεῖν (which Poppo calls unique) and Lys. 115. 29 βιαζόμενοι βλάπτειν. It is common in Cl., cf. below p. 108, l. 4 βιάζεται εἶναι καλός, *ib.* l. 8 ἐπ' ἄκρον γνώσεως ἥκειν β., p. 124. 29 ἀνεπιθύμητοι γενέσθαι β. See Index, *s.v.*

p. 78. 2. **ἐφεκτικῇ,** 'exercising restraint.' H. A metaphor from holding in a horse, ἐπέχειν *inhibere*. In P. 924 we find the word in its technical sense, 'sceptic' as opposed to 'dogmatist.'

4. **ἐγγυμνασάμενος ἀσκήσει.** See Index.

6. **ἀθυρόγλωσσον.** Cf. P. 165 ἀθύρῳ γλώσσῃ χρῆσθαι. For other exx. see Index.

10. For ἀξιολόγως of MS. read **ἀξιολόγων,** 'of distinguished persons.' H.

§ 45. 11. **διειληφώς,** 'received a clear understanding of.' Cf. VI. 816½ τὴν ἐκκλησιαστικὴν καὶ ἀληθῆ γνῶσιν καὶ τὴν περὶ θεοῦ διάληψιν. H. Below p. 104. 5.

11—14. Sentences like this (which are far from uncommon in Cl.) remind one of Aristotle's criticism on ὁ σκοτεινός in *Rhet.* III. 5. 6 τὰ γὰρ Ἡρακλείτου διαστίξαι ἔργον, διὰ τὸ ἄδηλον εἶναι ποτέρῳ πρόσκειται, τῷ ὑστέρῳ ἢ τῷ προτέρῳ. Is ἀληθείας governed by πρός or by χοροῦ? is χοροῦ governed by πρός or by λόγῳ? is τὸ μέγεθος governed by προτρέποντι or by ἐνδεικνυμένῳ? Comparing p. 166. 8, 9 below, ἢν μὴ τὸν κανόνα τῆς ἐκκλησίας παρ' αὑτῆς λαβόντες ἔχωσι τῆς ἀληθείας, we should be inclined to take ἀληθείας here with πρός, but, before deciding, it is necessary to ascertain the meaning of χοροῦ. It occurs below p. 152. 28 ἡ ἐκκλησία κυρίου, ὁ πνευματικὸς καὶ ἅγιος χορός, 86. 14 διὰ τούτων (prayers, &c.) ἑαυτὸν ἐνοποιεῖ τῷ θείῳ χορῷ, 136. 13 κἂν μόνος εὔχηται τὸν τῶν ἁγίων χορὸν συνιστάμενον ἔχει, Ign. *Rom.* 2 ἵνα ἐν ἀγάπῃ χορὸς γενόμενοι ᾄσητε τῷ πατρὶ ἐν Ἰησοῦ Χριστῷ, where Lightfoot's n. is 'the Roman Christians are asked to form into a chorus and sing the sacrificial hymn round the altar...The metaphor is taken from a heathen sacrificial rite; see K. F. Hermann *Gottesd. Alt.* II. 29.' Here however the epithet μυστικός suggests an allusion to the dancing at the mysteries (of which Lucian, *de Saltat.* 15, says, τελετὴν ἀρχαίαν οὐδεμίαν ἐστὶν εὑρεῖν ἄνευ ὀρχήσεως, Ὀρφέως δηλαδὴ καὶ Μουσαίου...νομοθετησάντων σὺν ῥυθμῷ καὶ ὀρχήσει μυεῖσθαι· ὅτι δὲ οὕτως ἔχει...τοὺς ἐξαγορεύοντας τὰ μυστήρια ἐξορχεῖσθαι λέγουσιν) with the further connotation, that this chorus is to be spiritually interpreted. Cf. *Protr.* P. 92 ὄρος ἐστὶ τοῦτο θεῷ πεφιλημένον, οὐ τραγῳδίαις, ὡς Κιθαιρών, ὑποκείμενον, ἀλλὰ τοῖς τῆς ἀληθείας ἀνακείμενον δράμασιν,...Βακχεύουσι δὲ ἐν αὐτῷ...αἱ ἀμνάδες αἱ καλαὶ τὰ σεμνὰ τοῦ λόγου θεσπίζουσαι ὄργια, χορὸν ἐγείρουσαι σώφρονα, and a little below, ταῦτα τῶν ἐμῶν μυστηρίων τὰ βακχεύματα καὶ σὺ μυοῦ, καὶ χορεύσεις μετ' ἀγγέλων ἀμφὶ τὸν...μόνον ὄντως θεόν. Actual dancing was a part of the religious services of the Therapeutae described by Philo M. 2. 484, 485. There seems no reason why ἀληθείας should not be appended to χορός here as it is to δράμασιν in P. 92, cf. P. 100 δεισιδαιμονίας ἄθεοι χορευταί. The meaning will then be, that it is through and from the Church that the individual Christian is instructed in the things of God. If we prefer the other construction, governing χοροῦ by λόγῳ, we must translate (with H.) 'uses a language belonging to a mystic chorus.' In that case, it is difficult to explain προτρέποντι. Taking it as equivalent to προτρεπτικῷ, and governing τὸ μέγεθος by ἐνδεικνυμένῳ, as I have done in the translation, we may illustrate the sense from Cl.'s treatise of that name, where he enlarges (as in the later chapters) on the excellence of Christianity, cf. *Paed.* P. 98 *init.* προτρεπτικὴ ἡ πᾶσα θεοσέβεια, ζωῆς τῆς νῦν καὶ τῆς μελλούσης ὄρεξιν ἐγγενῶσα τῷ συγγενεῖ λογισμῷ.

14. **διάρματος.** Cf. Wytt. on Plut. *Mor.* 165 C τὸ γαῦρον ἐνίοις καὶ ὑψηλὸν καὶ διηρμένον ἔνεστιν ὑπὸ κουφότητος: 'sic supra p. 116 D διαιρεῖσθαι πρὸς ἀλαζονείαν. Et διαιρεῖσθαι se erigere Arist. *de Mund.* init. φιλοσοφία διαραμένη πρὸς τὴν τῶν ὄντων θέαν. Et διάρμα Plut. *Mor.* 853 C ὄγκος καὶ δίαρμα, Laert. ιχ. 5 διάρμα ψυχῆς.'

15. **τοῖς νοητοῖς...οἰκειούμενος.** Cf. p. 76. 24 ἥνωται τῷ πνεύματι, p. 152. 19 τῷ πνεύματι ἀνεκράθητε, Eph. ii. 6.

18. **αὐστηρός,** 'grave,' 'serious'; cf. *Strom.* ιι. 494 *init.* H. *Protr.* 85 τὸ αὐστηρὸν τῆς σωτηρίας ὑπομένειν οὐ καρτερεῖτε.

21. **δικαστής, ἐὰν ὁ λόγος καλῇ.** Above p. 26. 8.

26. **αὐτὸ τὸ ἀγαθόν.** See p. 30. 11, Plato *Rep.* vi. 505

27. **ἐπὶ προθύροις.** Cf. Plat. *Phileb.* 64 C ἐπὶ τοῖς τοῦ ἀγαθοῦ νῦν ἤδη προθύροις ἐφεστάναι. H. J.

p. 80. 1. **εὐαρεστεῖται.** Cf. Epict. *Diss.* ι. 12. 8 πῶς ἂν εὐαρεστοίην τῇ θείᾳ διοικήσει; *ib.* ιι. 23. 49, above n. on p. 34. 2.

§ 46. 3—6. Cf. Mt. vi. 25—34. **ἐπιζητεῖ** 'seeks in addition.'

4. **εὐθετούντων** (for MS. οὐθότ' οὖν, where the last syllable may have been lost through its resemblance to the penultimate), 'useful': often followed by εἰς. H. Cf. Diod. xix. 98 τῆς χρείας εἰς φάρμακα εὐθετούσης, Diosc. v. 136 τὸ εὐθετοῦν εἰς τοὺς πολέμους. Cl. has in mind Mt. vi. 31—33. H. J. suggests εὐθετεῖν with transitive force 'to arrange.' I am not sure that P.'s reading οὐδ' ὁτιοῦν may not be defended, as giving more reason for the clause εἰς τὴν ἀναγκαίαν χρῆσιν, 'the gnostic seeks none of the βιωτικά, nothing at all as absolutely necessary.' Or should we read εὐθετῶν 'being provided for all necessary use he seeks nothing further (ἐπιζητεῖ) of the things pertaining to this life'?

7. **ἐθνικῶς.** See below p. 154. 5 ὁ ἐθνικῶς ἐν ἐκκλησίᾳ πολιτευόμενος, *Str.* vi. P. 761 *init.* ἐδήλωσεν τὸν ἕνα καὶ μόνον θεὸν ὑπὸ μὲν Ἑλλήνων ἐθνικῶς, ὑπὸ δὲ Ἰουδαίων Ἰουδαϊκῶς, καινῶς δὲ ὑφ' ἡμῶν καὶ πνευματικῶς γινωσκόμενον. The general meaning seems to be that prayer cannot be

regarded as an abstract thing, apart from the mind and character of him who prays; and thus the answer to prayer is limited by the receptive power of the suppliant. The prayer for knowledge, *e.g.*, would be differently conceived and answered in the three cases supposed. See above, §§ 38 and 44.

9. ἐπιστρέφων, intransitive: the two stages of discipleship need different gifts. H. See *Str.* VI. P. 770 ὁ καθαρισμὸς τῆς ψυχῆς οὗτός ἐστιν, ἡ ἀποχὴ τῶν κακῶν...καὶ ἔστιν ἁπλῶς τοῦ κοινοῦ πιστοῦ ἡ τελείωσις αὕτη, τοῦ δὲ γνωστικοῦ μετὰ τὴν ἄλλοις νομιζομένην τελείωσιν ἡ δικαιοσύνη εἰς ἐνέργειαν εὐποιίας προβαίνει, καὶ ὅτῳ δὴ ἡ ἐπίτασις τῆς δικαιοσύνης εἰς ἀγαθοποιίαν ἐπιδέδωκεν, τούτῳ ἡ τελείωσις ἐν ἀμεταβόλῳ ἕξει εὐποιίας καθ᾽ ὁμοίωσιν τοῦ θεοῦ διαμένει, below p. 100. 7 f.

10. ἐπαναβαίνων. Cf. *Str.* V. P. 690 ἐὰν ἐπιχείρῃ τις ἐπ᾽ αὐτὸ ὅ ἐστιν ἕκαστον ὁρμᾶν καὶ μὴ ἀποστατεῖν τῶν ὄντων, πρὶν ἐπαναβαίνων ἐπὶ τὰ ὑπερκείμενα αὐτὸ (MS. αὐτῷ) ὅ ἐστιν ἀγαθὸν αὐτῇ νοήσει λάβῃ, above p. 62. 22 κατ᾽ ἐπανάβασιν αὐξήσας, below l. 19 ἐπαναβεβηκός.

12. συνεχῶς, adverbial, as often: 'uninterruptedly.' H. So Arist. *Eq.* 21, Luc. *Somn.* 4, Epict. *Diss.* II. 21. 8, cf τέλεον below p. 86. 4.

14. συνεργῶν, cf. p. 66. 28.

16. ὀλισθήσαντας αὖθις χαμαί. Does αὖθις imply that the angels originally belonged to a lower sphere (see *Ecl. Proph.* § 57)? or should we understand it in the sense it bears in Xen. *Mem.* I. 2. 23 σωφρονήσαντα πρῶτον αὖθις μὴ σωφρονεῖν, Eur. *Or.* 907 κἂν μὴ παραυτίκ᾽, αὖθίς εἰσι χρήσιμοι, of which Klotz (on Dev. II. 214) says 'reiecta alia re iam nova inducitur, quasi, antequam fuisset illa, haec fuisset.' On the fall of the Angels cf. *Paed.* III. P. 250 *fin.*, *ib.* P. 280. C.'s language here implies the possibility of the restoration of the fallen Angels, and even a certain progress towards this end (μηδέπω τέλεον). Similarly Origen *de Princ.* I. 6. 3, and elsewhere, cf. Huet *Originiana* II. 5 *de Angelis*, Hagenberg *Hist. of Doctr.* 1 § 52. 5.

τὴν μίαν ἐκείνην ἕξιν, 'that single habit.' Cf. *Str.* IV. P. 633 *init.* μυστικῶς οὖν ἐφ᾽ ἡμῶν καὶ τὸ Πυθαγόρειον ἐλέγετο ἕνα γενέσθαι καὶ τὸν ἄνθρωπον δεῖν, ἐπεὶ καὶ αὐτὸς ὁ ἀρχιερεὺς εἰς ἑνὸς ὄντος τοῦ θεοῦ κατὰ τὴν ἀμετάτρεπτον τοῦ ἀεὶ θεῖν τὰ ἀγαθὰ ἕξιν, *ib.* εἰς τὴν ἀπάθειαν θεούμενος ἄνθρωπος ἀχράντως μοναδικὸς γίνεται, where Potter cites P. 777 ἐν τῇ μιᾷ ἕξει μένει τῇ ἀμεταβόλῳ, and 635 τὸ εἰς αὐτὸν καὶ τὸ δι᾽ αὐτοῦ πιστεῦσαι μοναδικόν ἐστι γίνεσθαι, ἀπερισπάστως ἑνούμενον ἐν αὐτῷ· τὸ ἀπιστῆσαι διστάσαι ἐστὶ καὶ διαστῆναι καὶ μερισθῆναι. H. Cf. also below p. 190. 9 κατὰ τὴν μονάδα, and *Protr.* P. 72 there quoted, P. 1009 (*Adumbr. in Joh.* I. 5) una quippe via est secundum praecepta divina. Monas namque Dei opus est, dyas autem, et quicquid praeter monadem constat, ex vitae perversitate contingit. See Kaye *Clem.* p. 149 n. 6. μίαν ἕξιν seems here to be equivalent to ἑνότητος ἕξιν.

17. διπλόην. See Tim. *Lex. s.v.* διπλόον. ἐπὶ σιδήρου εἴρηται ὅταν ἀπό τινος ἑνώσεως ἀπόλυσίς τις ᾖ εἰς παράθεσιν μᾶλλον ἢ ἕνωσιν· ἐπὶ δὲ ἤθους τροπικῶς τὸ μὴ ὑγιὲς δηλοῖ, where Ruhnken cites many exx. It is used in a different sense below P. 901. Cf. δίψυχος and διψυχία St James i. 8.

The angels fell when other motives interfered with their single-hearted devotion to God.

ἐπιτηδειότητος, 'aptness': used in a neutral as well as a good sense. H.

18. ἐκθλίψαντας. Cp. Arist. *H. A.* IX. 40 'the bee leaves its sting in the wound and so perishes,' ἐὰν μὴ ὁ πληγεὶς τὸ κέντρον ἐκθλίψῃ, 'unless he squeezes out the sting,' *De Anima* I. 2. 3 'Democritus held that life is sustained by respiration, which supplies fresh atoms in place of those which are forced out' (ἐκθλίβοντος τοῦ περιέχοντος), *de Resp.* 4, *Meteor.* I. 4. 7 'when the air contracts from cold, the heat is squeezed out' (ἐκκρούεται καὶ ἐκθλίβεται), *ib.* 9 of falling stars, II. 9. 8 'lightning is caused by the expulsion (ἐκθλιβόμενον) of the air (πνεῦμα) inclosed in the cloud,' *ib.* IV. 6. 5, *de Audib.* I. 'the lungs by their contraction ἐκθλίβουσι the air,' Plut. *Mor.* 81 C.

19. ἐπαναβεβηκός. See on p. 18. 4.

20. πρὸ ὁδοῦ, 'advantageous,' 'appropriate': originally 'forward,' but later like προύργου. H.

22. μονότονον, 'bent one way.' H. Chiefly used of music, also metaphorically of obstinacy.

ἑδραιότητα. Cf. below p. 88, l. 9 ἐν ἀμεταπτώτῳ καὶ ἑδραίῳ βίῳ, p. 192. 6 ἡ τῶν διχηλούντων ἑδραιότης.

23. βρίθουσα. Cf. Plato *Phaedr.* 247 A βρίθει γὰρ ὁ τῆς κάκης ἵππος μετέχων, ἐπὶ τὴν γῆν ῥέπων, Wisdom ix. 15 φθαρτὸν γὰρ σῶμα βαρύνει ψυχήν, καὶ βρίθει τὸ γεῶδες σκῆνος νοῦν πολυφροντίδα, *Str.* V. P. 696 ἄνω τῶν ὑπερκειμένων αἴρεται ἡ ψυχὴ πᾶν τὸ βρῖθον ἀποτιθεμένη, Anton. x. 26 τὴν βρίθουσαν καὶ τὴν ἀνωφερῆ δύναμιν (centripetal ✕ centrifugal).

The γωνία of the Ms. making no sense, the emendation which naturally suggests itself is ἀγωνία. This may be thought to receive some support from *Il.* XXI. 385 θεοῖσιν ἔρις πέσε βεβριθυῖα, but it does not suit the context. ἀγνωσία is suggested by H. J. with a reference to γνώσεως ἀκρότητα in l. 18, and makes very good sense; but I am rather disposed to prefer ἀτονία, for which compare Plut. *Mor.* 535 D ἔοικεν ἡ τῆς ψυχῆς ἀτονία σώματος κράσει κακῶς πεφυκυίᾳ, below p. 166. 6 δεῖ τῷ τῆς ἀληθείας ἐραστῇ ψυχικῆς εὐτονίας· σφάλλεσθαι γὰρ ἀνάγκη μέγιστα τοὺς μεγίστοις ἐγχειροῦντας πράγμασιν ἢν μὴ τὸν κανόνα τῆς ἀληθείας παρ' αὐτῆς λαβόντες ἔχωσι τῆς ἀληθείας, Carpocrates ap. Hippol. *Haer.* VII. 32 τὴν ψυχὴν Ἰησοῦ εὔτονον καὶ καθαρὰν γεγονυῖαν διαμνημονεῦσαι τὰ ὁρατὰ μὲν αὐτῇ ἐν τῇ μετὰ τοῦ ἀγενήτου θεοῦ περιφορᾷ (Plato *Phaedr.* 246 f.).

24. 'In them even what is uplifted by their faith [the lower stage which they have reached] is dragged down.' H.

26. φυσιοῦται, 'becomes a nature.' H. Cf. Arist. *Cat.* 8 διαθέσεις λέγονται ἅ ἐστιν εὐκίνητα καὶ ταχὺ μεταβάλλοντα...εἰ μή τις καὶ αὐτῶν τούτων τυγχάνοι διὰ χρόνου πλῆθος ἤδη πεφυσιωμένη...ἣν ἄν τις ἴσως ἕξιν ἤδη προσαγορεύσαι. Used in a different sense below P. 896 *fin.*

καθάπερ τῷ λίθῳ τὸ βάρος. The same illustration is used in Arist. *Eth. N.* II. 1 οὐδεμία τῶν ἠθικῶν ἀρετῶν φύσει ἡμῖν ἐγγίνεται· οὐθὲν γὰρ τῶν φύσει ὄντων ἄλλως ἐθίζεται, οἷον ὁ λίθος φύσει κάτω φερόμενος οὐκ ἂν ἐθισθείη ἄνω φέρεσθαι. Cf. p. 72. 18 f., of the goodness of God.

§ 47. p. 82, line 1. ἐπεὶ τὸ μὴ ἀποβληθέν. The MS. has ἐπὶ for ἐπεὶ also in P. 684; ἀποβληθῆναι for ἀποβληθέν is explained by the following ΔΙ mistaken for ΑΙ, and by the constant confusion of long and short vowels. The following μέν and δέ make it probable that καὶ εὐλογιστίας has been lost after εὐλαβείας.

3. τῆς εὐλογιστίας. A branch of φρόνησις according to the Stoics, the others being εὐβουλία ἀγχίνοια νουνέχεια εὐμηχανία Stob. Ecl. II. p. 106. Cf. Philo M. 1. 130 ἐὰν γὰρ ἔλθῃ εἰς τὴν διάνοιαν ἔννοια θεοῦ, εὐλογιστεῖ εὐθύς.

6. μέγιστον δ' ἄρα. The particle is wanted to show that we have here not the conclusion, but the minor premiss, and Δ is easily lost before Α as in l. 1.

9. μόνος. This may be true, but does not follow from the argument. Why may not ὁ πιστεύων be εὐσεβής as well as ὁ γνωστικός? Perhaps we are to take γνῶσις here as including faith, see p. 136. 28 below.

13. δι' ὧν ἔγνω φθάσας οἷά ἐστιν. I think this is an instance of the use of the finite verb with the relative to express the infinitive with article = διὰ τοῦ φθάσας γνῶναι οἷά ἐστιν, cf. below n. on p. 104. 9 ἐπίστευσεν ἐξ ὧν ἐθαύμασεν, p. 130. 17 χαίρων μὲν ἐφ' οἷς ἔγνω, συστελλόμενος δὲ ἐφ' οἷς ἐγκυλίεται.

14. καὶ κέκτηται τοῦτο. The changed position of καὶ in the MS. is probably to be accounted for by its omission before κέ-. It would naturally be inserted in the margin by the corrector, and might then be misplaced by a subsequent copyist. For the thought cf. Mk. xi. 24 and Str. VI. P. 777 init. ὁ δὲ ἐν οἷς ἔσται δι' ἀγάπης ἤδη γενόμενος, τὴν ἐλπίδα προειληφὼς διὰ τῆς γνώσεως οὐδὲ ὀρέγεταί τινος, ἔχων ὡς οἷόν τε αὐτὸ τὸ ὀρεκτόν, P. 778 τὴν ἐν οἷς ἐστι κατάστασιν βεβαίαν τῶν μελλόντων κατάληψιν εἰδὼς δι' ἀγάπης προαπαντᾷ τῷ μέλλοντι, also p. 136. 26 below.

15. The connexion is hard to seize. Probably it means 'what he has is only inchoate and imperfect, but its true nature is seen by reference to the perfect standard,' 'is measured by what is fitting (normal).' See what follows. H. There seems no reason for drawing a fine distinction between τὸ ἐνδεὲς καὶ ἐπιδεές, while it is important to state that both sufficient and insufficient must be determined by reference to a standard. I propose therefore to read ἀνενδεές.

πρὸς τὸ ἐπιβάλλον. Cf. Luke xv. 12 τὸ ἐπιβάλλον μέρος, and Wytt. on Plut. Mor. 37 F, who cites Pl. 1036 A ἐπιβάλλει τοῦτο ποιεῖν (convenit facere), 1034 D ἐπιτελεῖν τὰ ἐπιβάλλοντα, Diogenianus ap. Eus. Pr. Ev. VI. 8 τὸ χρεὼν εἰρῆσθαι τὸ ἐπιβάλλον καὶ καθῆκον κατὰ τὴν εἱμαρμένην, also Anton. VII. 7 ἐνεργεῖν τὸ ἐπιβάλλον, where see Gataker's excellent n.

17. ὁ ἀνενδεοῦς μετέχων ἀνενδεὴς εἴη ἄν. Cf. Paed. I. P. 113 οὐκοῦν ἀτελὴς ὁ ἐγνωκὼς τὸ τέλειον.

18. κινούντων καὶ ἰσχόντων, 'moving and stopping' (correlatives). H.

19. ἐνεργείας. Probably 'inspiration': or at least 'Divine action.' H.

μετίσχοντος. Rare and chiefly Platonic. **H**. As we have the form μετέχων in l. 17, it is possible that this form is due to ἰσχόντων in l. 18: still Cl. often uses ἴσχω = ἔχω (as in *Paed*. P. 114) and we find ὑπίσχουσι τὴν τιμωρίαν P. 598.

20. ἀφαιρουμένου, 'being robbed.'

ἀμείωτος. See Index.

22. κατὰ τὴν δύναμιν...κατὰ τὸν ἀριθμόν. So we have δυνάμει opposed to ἀριθμῷ in Arist. *de Gen. et Corr.* I. 3 νόησις ἡ ἐνέργεια· ὥστε ἐξ ἐνεργείας ἡ δύναμις· καὶ διὰ τοῦτο ποιοῦντες γιγνώσκουσιν· ὕστερον γὰρ γενέσει ἡ ἐνέργεια ἡ κατ' ἀριθμόν (cited by Trend. on Ar. *de An*. p. 308). The more common opposition is that of κατ' εἶδος to κατ' ἀριθμόν, contrasting qualitative to quantitative (see my n. on *N. D.* I. 49 *ad numerum* and Waitz on *Cat.* 2, p. 276). As opposed to δυνάμει it is nearly equivalent to ἐνεργείᾳ 'in actual reality.'

24. ἐνθέους προκοπάς. Cf. p. 16. 5, 28 f., p. 20. 5, 15 f., p. 78. 25.

§ 48. 26. προσεχεστέρᾳ. See Index.

27. τιμήσας. One would rather expect τηρήσας, as in *Protr*. P. 10, where I am disposed to read γεράνδρυον δὲ ψάμμοις ἐρήμαις τετηρημένον for τετιμημένον.

p. 84, line 1. He will not take away whatever is for the sake of virtue from them, as it is for their sake that all things exist. **H**.

4. τιμῶν ἦν ὅς γε. **H. J.**'s excellent emendation of the MS. τιμώμενός τε: cf. for the periphrastic tense Mk. x. 22 ἦν γὰρ ἔχων χρήματα πολλά, Blass *N. T. Gr*. p. 202 f., Schmid *Att*. III. pp. 112—115.

7. καὶ συλλαμβανόμενος, middle here, as active in p. 82, l. 26, 'helping' as well as 'exhorting.' **H**.

ἐπιγεννηματικόν. A Stoical and medical word for what is accessory and accidental. Cf. Epictet. III. 7. 7 οὐδέ, τοῦ προηγουμένου μὴ ὄντος ἀγαθοῦ, [δύναται] τὸ ἐπιγέννημα ἀγαθὸν εἶναι. **H**. The adjective seems to be found only in Cic. *Fin*. III. 32 posterum quodam modo et consequens putandum est, quod illi ἐπιγεννηματικόν appellant, cf. Laert. VII. 94 where (after defining τὸ ἀγαθόν as τὸ τέλειον κατὰ φύσιν λογικοῦ ὡς λογικοῦ) Zeno continues τοιοῦτον δ' εἶναι τὴν ἀρετήν...ἐπιγεννήματα δὲ τήν τε χαρὰν καὶ τὴν εὐφροσύνην καὶ τὰ παραπλήσια. Similarly δυσθυμία and δυσφροσύνη are mentioned as ἐπιγεννήματα of vice, *ib*. 85 *fin*. ὃ δὲ λέγουσί τινες, πρὸς ἡδονὴν γίγνεσθαι τὴν πρώτην ὁρμὴν τοῖς ζῴοις, ψεῦδος ἀποφαίνουσιν· ἐπιγέννημα γάρ φασι, where see Menage, and Seneca *V. B*. c. 9 (quoted in his note) 'voluptas non est merces nec causa virtutis, sed accessio.' It is equivalent to Aristotle's ἐπιγινόμενόν τι τέλος in τελειοῖ τὴν ἐνέργειαν ἡ ἡδονή, οὐχ ὡς ἡ ἕξις ἐνυπάρχουσα, ἀλλ' ὡς ἐπιγινόμενόν τι τέλος (*Eth. N*. x. 4).

12. εὐπραγίαν, cf. below p. 102. 22, and P. 802 *init*. **H**.

13—14. God's Commandments and His Promise are indissolubly joined: the promise receives fulfilment simultaneously with the performance of a commandment. **H**.

16. πολλῷ τῷ χρόνῳ. The dative marking one cause of the result. **H**.

I rather doubt this. The dat. is often used of duration of time in late Greek. See Schmid *Att.* IV. 58, Blass *Gr. N. T.* § 38. 5, Jannaris § 1394, Winer, p. 273.

17. εἰς Ὀλύμπι' ἀναβάς. There is no reason to depart from the MS., cf. Cic. *Divin.* II. 144 ad Olympia proficisci.

20. φέρων, 'make haste and': the pass. φερόμενος (lit. 'being carried along') is similarly used. H. Possibly the act. may get its meaning from the use of the imperative φέρε, 'come now,' or = our 'took and gave.' For exx. see P. 569 τῷ τὸ σωμάτιον αἰτοῦντι φέρων προσδίδωσι, P. 535 Σαμουὴλ κωλεόν φ. ἔδωκε τῷ Σαοὺλ φαγεῖν, P. 44 *fin.* Ῥωμαῖοι φέροντες ἀνέθηκαν τὴν τύχην, Q. D. S. 937 P. αὐτὸν ὑποβαλέτω φέρων γυμναστῇ, where see Segaar's n., Luc. *Necyom.* 8 ἐμὲ δὲ φέρων ἐνεσκεύασε τῷ πίλῳ, *Dial. Mort.* VI. 3 τοῖς ἀτέκνοις τῶν γερόντων εἰσποιεῖτε φέροντες αὐτούς where many exx. are given by Hemst., also Plut. *V.* 159, 353, Plut. *Mor.* 4 with Wytt.'s n. The moral of the anecdote is scarcely in harmony with such texts as Lk. xvii. 10, but it agrees with p. 126. 15. Cf. Epict. *Diss.* IV. 10. 14—16 ἀρκεῖ μοι ἂν δύνωμαι πρὸς τὸν θεὸν ἀνατεῖναι τὰς χεῖρας καὶ εἰπεῖν ὅτι, Ἃς ἔλαβον ἀφορμὰς παρά σου πρὸς τὸ αἰσθέσθαι σου τῆς διοικήσεως καὶ ἀκολουθῆσαι αὐτῇ, τούτων οὐκ ἠμέλησα· οὐ κατῄσχυνά σε τὸ ἐμὸν μέρος. ἰδοὺ πῶς κέχρημαι ταῖς αἰσθήσεσιν, ἰδοὺ πῶς ταῖς προλήψεσιν. μή ποτέ σε ἐμεμψάμην, μή τι τῶν γινομένων τινὶ δυσηρέστησα; κ.τ.λ.

24. εὐαρέστησιν τῷ θεῷ. Cf. below p. 114. 29 τὴν πρὸς τὸν θεὸν εὐαρέστησιν, above n. on p. 34. 2, p. 80 l. 1.

No use of συναιροῦμαι (apparently never deponent) seems possible here. What is wanted is συναίρεται, 'is helpful,' cf. above p. 24. 23. Yet συναιρούμενον appears to be similarly used, P. 896½ τὸ παράπαν ταῖς ἡδοναῖς συναιρούμενον. H.

25. τὴν σωτηρίαν, in apposition with τὴν τελειότητα. H. The gen. read in the text seems to me far more natural.

26. καὶ τῶν πρὸς ἡμᾶς ἀνηκόντων, 'which concern us.' So with πρός often Polyb. Diod., with εἰς Demosth. Aristot., &c. H. I take καί here in the epexegetic sense, cf. Winer *Gr.* p. 545 n. 4, Hermann-Viger p. 525.

28. διανομή. So I read, instead of the διαμονή of MS., because I cannot see how the latter could be reckoned among τὰ ἐφ' ἡμῖν (l. 26). Compare Epict. *Ench.* I. 1 τῶν ὄντων τὰ μέν ἐστιν ἐφ' ἡμῖν, τὰ δὲ οὐκ ἐφ' ἡμῖν. ἐφ' ἡμῖν μὲν ὑπόληψις, ὁρμή, ὄρεξις, ἔκκλισις, καὶ ἑνὶ λόγῳ ὅσα ἡμέτερα ἔργα. It is true the same objection might be made to κτῆσις, as we read in *Diss.* III. 24. 68 κτῆσις οὐκ ἐμή, συγγενεῖς, οἰκεῖοι, φίλοι...σὸν οὖν τί; χρῆσις φαντασιῶν; but perhaps we may distinguish between two uses of the word. In Epict. κτῆσις evidently means 'possession,' in the text we may understand it of the act of acquiring.

§ 49. p. 86, line 5. τὰς εὐχὰς...ποιεῖσθαι. There is a rule against praying with heretics in *Const. Ap.* VII. 28 οὔτε μὴ προσεύξησθε τῷ ψευδοδιδασκάλῳ ἵνα μὴ συμμανθῆτε αὐτῷ.

ἐπιεικῶς καὶ μετ' ἐπιεικῶν. Here used in the wide sense given to it in Plato and Aristotle. See my note on the word in St James iii. 17.

7. συνεπιγράφεσθαι. The act. ἐπιγράφω ἐμαυτόν τινι is used of endorsement, and so the p. ἐπιγράφεσθαι ἀλλοτρίαις γνώμαις. Hence the compound means 'to give one's name to,' cf. Philo M. 1. p. 517 τῷ ψευδεῖ συνεπιγράφεται πᾶς ὁ τῶν ἀγελαίων ὄχλος.

8. τοῖς κοινότερον πεπιστευκόσι. So I read instead of καινότερον, cf. Str. v. P. 659 τὴν κοινὴν πίστιν πῇ μὲν θεμέλιον λέγει, πῇ δὲ γάλα, ib. P. 892 (p. 172. 7) ὑπερβῆναι σπουδάσαντες τὸ κοινὸν τῆς πίστεως, ἐξέβησαν τὴν ἀλήθειαν, P. 608 πίστεως τελειότης πρὸς τὴν κοινὴν διαστέλλεται πίστιν, Plut. Mor. 568 c εἰ δὲ κοινότερον ἐθέλοι τις ταῦτα συγγράψαι κ.τ.λ.

10. πανήγυρις, used esp. of a great religious gathering such as that of the Olympic games, cf. above p. 62. 12 πάντα τὸν βίον ἑορτὴν ἄγοντες, Jer. Ep. 151 nobis qui in Christum credimus resurgentem iugis et aeterna festivitas est, Justin Dial. 12 σαββατίζειν ὑμᾶς ὁ καινὸς νόμος διὰ παντὸς ἐθέλει, and, for what follows, Paed. II. P. 228 init. μεθ' ἡμέραν...εὐχῆς καὶ ἀναγνώσεως καὶ τῶν...εὐέργων ἔργων ὁ καιρός, ἑσπέρας δὲ ἀναπαύσασθαι καθήκει μετὰ τὴν ἑστίασιν καὶ μετὰ τὴν ἐπὶ ταῖς ἀπολαύσεσιν εὐχαριστίαν, above p. 58. 24 f., p. 22. 11, below p. 140. 3 f. and Str. II. P. 506.

11. ἐντεύξεις, 'private reading,' cf. Polyb. IX. 1. 3 οἱ μὲν γὰρ ἄλλοι συγγραφεῖς...πολλοὺς ἐφέλκονται πρὸς ἔντευξιν τῶν ὑπομνημάτων, and n. on ἐντυχόντες, below p. 172. 6. See Const. Ap. VI. 27. 3. H.

12. παρὰ τὴν ἑστίασιν. Paed. II. P. 194 ὡς ἁρμόδιόν ἐστι πρὶν ἡμᾶς μεταλαβεῖν τροφῆς τῶν συμπάντων εὐλογεῖν τὸν ποιητήν, οὕτως καὶ παρὰ πότον καθήκει ψάλλειν αὐτῷ τῶν αὐτοῦ μεταλαμβάνοντας κτισμάτων...ἐπὶ πᾶσί τε, πρὶν ὕπνου λαχεῖν, εὐχαριστεῖν ὅσιον τῷ θεῷ κ.τ.λ., Str. VI. P. 785 init.

13. νύκτωρ εὐχαί. Paed. II. P. 218 init. ἐπεγερτικῶς ἀπονυστακτέον ...διὸ πολλάκις καὶ τῆς νυκτὸς ἀνεγερτέον τῆς κοίτης καὶ τὸν θεὸν εὐλογητέον.

14. τῷ θείῳ χορῷ, cf. above p. 78. 12.

14, 15. ἐκ τῆς συνεχοῦς μνήμης. Potter cites Basil, p. 14 οὔτε γὰρ ἁμαρτίαις καιρόν τινα δώσομεν, οὔτε τῷ ἐχθρῷ τόπον ἐν ταῖς καρδίαις ἡμῶν καταλείψομεν, διὰ τῆς συνεχοῦς μνήμης ἔνοικον ἔχοντες ἑαυτῶν τὸν θεόν.

15. ἀείμνηστος is either active or passive: here probably active. Probably τῆς συνεχοῦς μνήμης is the present human state, ἀείμνηστον θεωρίαν the supernal or angelic state. H. So πολύμνηστος has both the active and passive meanings.

16. τὴν ἄλλην. Prayer and alms often associated. H. As in Acts x. 4.

18. Mt. vi. 7 προσευχόμενοι δὲ μὴ βαττολογήσητε ὥσπερ οἱ ἐθνικοί· δοκοῦσι γὰρ ὅτι ἐν τῇ πολυλογίᾳ αὐτῶν εἰσακουσθήσονται κ.τ.λ.

18, 19. εὐχῇ...μαθών. Matt. vi. 6—13.

20. ἄντικρυς, 'publicly,' cf. Ar. Plut. 134 καὶ νὴ Δί' εὔχονταί γε πλουτεῖν ἄντικρυς: often used of open warfare. H.

21. ὁ δὲ καὶ περιπάτῳ χρώμενος. Cf. above p. 62. 13 f. For the pleonastic ὁ δέ, continuing the subject of the preceding sentence, see Schweigh. Lex. Herod. s.v. ὁ, Krüg. Gr. 50. 1. 4, Jelf 655. 6. 2. It is also

often used to introduce the apodosis, as in *Paed.* I. P. 137 ὁ κύριος οὐ διὰ μῖσος τοὺς ἀνθρώποις λοιδορεῖται, οὓς ἐξὸν αὐτῷ ἀπολέσαι, ὁ δὲ ὑπὲρ ἡμῶν καὶ πέπονθεν, Q. D. S. 935 P. ἀσεβεῖς μὲν...ἐπίβουλοι δέ, ὅτι καὶ αὐτῆς τῆς περιουσίας καθ' αὑτὴν ἱκανῆς οὔσης χαυνῶσαι τὰς ψυχάς...οἱ δὲ προσεκπλήσσουσι, also P. 430 ...αἱ δὲ σκαλεύουσαι ἐκλέγονται, cf. Jacob's Aelian *N. A. praef.* XXVI. f.

24. **ἐννοηθῆ μόνον.** See above p. 70. 27.

26. **τριῶν δ' ὄντων...τελῶν.** The relations between the *honestum*, the *utile* and the *dulce* are discussed in Cic. *de Off.* and *de Fin.* The Stoics held that the second was a constant accompaniment of the first, see *de Off.* III. c. 3, *Str.* IV. 499.

§ 50. p. 88, line 1. **ἐξεταζόμενον.** Cf. Wyttenbach on Plut. II. 74 B μέτριοι ἐν τοῖς ἀνηκέστοις ἐξεταζόμενοι, who says of this use 'elegans usus verbi inserviens paraphrasi, pro ὄντες, sed ita ut notio *famae, cognitionis, et iudicii apud alios homines* subsit; *spectari, censeri in aliquo ordine, spectandum se praebere, ostendere*'; and quotes many exx. H. It is frequently followed by a participle, or by the gen. pl. or ἐν with dat. pl. or, more rarely, dat. sing. as here.

2. **πρόχειρον,** 'prompt,' 'readily disposed.' H.

3. **καθοριστική.** καθορίζω very rare, used by Cyr. Al. (Soph. *Lex.*) of God defining penalties for sin. The definition is evidently from another source, probably Stoic. H. On the prohibition against swearing see notes on St James v. 12.

4. **προσπαραλήψεως.** Very rare. Somewhat similarly Philo I. 285 *fin.* μόνῳ θεῷ χωρὶς ἑτέρου προσπαραλήψεως οὐ ῥᾴδιον πιστεῦσαι, 'without calling in the help of something else.' In *Strom.* VIII. P. 927½ we have προσπαραληπτέον used in a cognate sense. H. παραλαμβάνω μάρτυρα is the regular term for 'producing a witness.'

6. **καθωρισμένως,** 'definitively.' H. See on l. 3 above.

8. **ἐν ἀμεταπτώτῳ καὶ ἑδραίῳ βίῳ.** See above p. 80. 21 f. ἀμεταπτώτως βιοῦν ἑλομένῳ διὰ τὴν τῆς γνώμης ἑδραιότητα.

10. **τοῦ διαπονουμένου.** Cf. Acts iv. 2 οἱ Σαδδουκαῖοι διαπονούμενοι διὰ τὸ διδάσκειν αὐτοὺς τὸν λαόν, *ib.* xvi. 18, Eccles. x. 9 ἐξαίρων λίθους διαπονηθήσεται ἐν αὐτοῖς.

11. **<οὐχ> ὡς ἀδικῶν τὸ θεῖον.** The negative seems required not only by the protasis, which lays down the principle that guilt is determined by the intention of the agent, not by the suffering of the injured party; but also by the confirmatory clause, affirming that God can suffer no injury.

13 foll. Three grounds of abstinence from perjury: duty toward God, neighbour and self. H.

19. **ἐπίρρημα.** Schömann (*Die Lehre von den Redetheilen*, p. 164) quotes the definition of Dion. Hal. ἐπίρρημά ἐστι μέρος λόγου ἄκλιτον, κατὰ ῥήματος λεγόμενον ἢ ἐπιλεγόμενον ῥήματι. It included the particles of affirmation and negation (p. 153). For the order τὸ ναὶ ἐπίρρημα cf. ὁ Εὐφράτης ποταμός, Krüger *Gr.* 50. 7.

20. ὅρκον...προσφέρεσθαι, 'to employ an oath,' cf. below P. 891 (p. 168. 30) ἐν πᾶσιν οἷς προσφέρονται ῥητοῖς, Demosth. 284. 1 προσφέρεσθαι φιλοτιμίαν.

ἀπὸ διανοίας...παραστατικῆς. Cf. Euseb. *Pr. Ev.* VI. 6. 51 γένοιτο δ' ἂν καὶ ἄλλα τοῦ προβλήματος παραστατικὰ μυρία, Plut. *Mor.* 238 A κέντρον δ' εἶχε ταῦτα τὰ μέλη ἐγερτικὸν θυμοῦ καὶ φρονήματος καὶ παραστατικὸν ὁρμῆς ἐνθουσιώδους, and n. on παράστασιν, l. 22 below, Orig. *de Orat.* 24 ὄνομά ἐστι προσηγορία τῆς ἰδίας ποιότητος τοῦ ὀνομαζομένου παραστατική.

§ 51. 22. **εἰς παράστασιν.** Suidas *s.v.* (interpreting by ὁρμή, προθυμία) cites Diod. *Fr.* XXXIII. (vol. X. p. 88 W.) παράστασις ψυχῆς πρὸς ἐλευθερίαν ἐνέπεσε τοῖς πλήθεσι (*libertatis studium*): Schweig. *Lex. Polyb.* quotes exx., where the meaning is *impetus, studium, animi ardor*, as in Pol. V. 9. 6 παράστασις εἶχε τὸν βασιλέα *fiducia regem tenebat*, XVI. 13. 2 μετὰ παραστάσεως equivalent to τετολμηκότως. Cf. Diod. XIV. 52 τοιαύτης παραστάσεως ἐμπεσούσης εἰς τὰς τῶν πολιορκουμένων ψυχάς (*haec pertinacia cum animos incessisset*), Polyb. III. 63 λαμβάνειν ὁρμὴν καὶ παράστασιν, *ib.* VIII. 23 τοιοῦτος ἐνθουσιασμὸς ἐγένετο καὶ παράστασις τοῦ στρατοπέδου, *ib.* X. 5 περιχαρὴς οὖσα...μετὰ παραστάσεως ἠσπάζετο τοὺς νεανίσκους, similarly παράστημα in Cl. P. 589 τὴν χεῖρα ἐπὶ τοῦ πυρὸς θεὶς ἀτρέπτῳ πάνυ τῷ παραστήματι, Jos. *B. J.* XX. 7. 580 'Ρωμαῖοι δι' ἀλκὴν σώματος καὶ ψυχῆς παράστημα...κρατοῦσιν. Similarly the verb παραστῆσαι is used in the sense 'to rouse' or 'stimulate,' Polyb. VI. 53. 10 *fin.* τὸ γὰρ τὰς τῶν ἐπ' ἀρετῇ δεδοξασμένων ἀνδρῶν εἰκόνας ἰδεῖν...τίν' οὐκ ἂν παραστήσαι; and παραστῆναι in a neuter sense Diod. XVII. 43 τὸ δεινὸν ἔχοντες ἐν ὀφθαλμοῖς...ταῖς ψυχαῖς οὕτω παρέστησαν πρὸς τὸν κίνδυνον ὥστε τοῦ θανάτου καταφρονῆσαι, *ib.* c. 99 τούτῳ τῷ θυμῷ παραστάς. The metaphor seems to be taken from soldiers standing in battle array. More commonly the substantive is used in the sense of 'proof,' as in P. 864 (p. 94. 8) εἰς παράστασιν ἀληθείας.

25. **ὡς μηδὲ ὅρκον αἰτεῖσθαι.** As in the case of Xenocrates, Cic. *Ep. ad Att.* I. 16. 40.

πρὸς ἑαυτόν. How can it be said that the gnostic χρὴ ἔχειν εὐγνωμοσύνην *towards himself*? His life is to be a sufficient guarantee as regards outsiders: those who know him more intimately should have a further assurance from their experience of his fairness of mind. I think we must read τοὺς ἑαυτοῦ and possibly (as Sylburg) συνόντας. Probably ἀξιόπιστον ἔχειν should be understood with εὐγν.

26. **τοὺς συνιόντας,** 'those who have a right understanding,' seems justified by the quotation from Prov. viii. 9 in VI. P. 803½. **H.**

27. **αὐτίκα.** For its meaning here see Appendix.

p. 90, line 4 foll. Observance of the oath is exactly correspondent with observance of the simple rules of duty, and therefore needs no special rule. **H.**

5. **κατόρθωσιν...καθήκουσιν.** The Stoics distinguished between κατόρθωμα (or καθῆκον τέλειον, *officium perfectum*), and καθῆκον (or καθῆκον μέσον), see Cic. *Fin.* III. 58, *Off.* I. 8. Here the word κατόρθωσις (used by

Cic. *Fin.* III. 45 in its technical sense, *recta effectio,—κατόρθωσιν enim ita appello, quoniam recte factum* κατόρθωμα)—seems to be used in a more general sense.

7. **πολλοῦ γε δεῖ ἐπιορκῆσαι.** This, the MS. reading, is explained by the adverbial use of the phrase π. γ. δ. = οὐδαμῶς. It is followed by an ind. in Dem. 631. 5 πολλοῦ γε δεῖ διώρισεν, ὅς γε πάντα τἀναντία εἴρηκεν, where Reiske questions the reading; but Schaefer's *dictum* 'Vulgata est sanissima' is confirmed by its frequent use, without an infinitive, as an appendage to a sentence, cf. Arist. *Ach.* 543 καθῆσθ' ἂν ἐν δόμοισιν; ἢ πολλοῦ γε δεῖ, *Str.* II. P. 429 οὐκ ἀμυνομένων ἡμῶν τοὺς κατηγόρους, πολλοῦ γε καὶ δεῖ.

9. **πώποτε.** Used in later Greek as a strengthened form of ποτέ, see exx. in Lobeck *Phryn.* p. 458.

16. **πάντῃ τὸν θεὸν εἶναι πάντοτε.** For the meaning of πάντῃ see above p. 62. 9 and 13.

20. **ποιεῖ τι.** H. J.'s emendation for τι ποιεῖται. Probably, the true reading having been corrupted into ποιεῖται, the correction τι was made in the margin and wrongly inserted in the text.

22. **ἐναποθνήσκῃ ταῖς βασάνοις.** The same phrase is used in Athen. XIII 596 *fin.* Λέαινα ἡ ἑταίρα αἰκιζομένη ὑπὸ τῶν περὶ Ἱππίαν τὸν τύραννον, οὐδὲν ἐξειποῦσα ἐναπέθανε ταῖς βασάνοις.

§ 52. p. 92, line 1. **συνάφειαν,** 'combination'; close fellowship or coupling. **H.**

ἐμμεσιτεύει, 'brings about by his mediation': not used elsewhere, but μεσιτεύω in just this sense and transitive in the historians. **H.**

3. **ἐπί,** 'in the presence of,' common of judges or witnesses: so in the fourth line it seems to refer to the presence of a congregation at the κατήχησις. **H.**

4. On the force of ἀγαλμάτων see line 13 foll. **H.**

6. **παραλαμβάνεται.** Specially used of the reception of wisdom and learning by a disciple from a teacher. **H.**

8. **ὁ τῷ ὄντι ἄνθρωπος.** The teacher more than others is the true man, the true image of God as exercising specially a function like God's. **H.**

δημιουργεῖ. See above p. 22. 4 ἑαυτὸν κτίζει καὶ δημιουργεῖ...ἐξομοιούμενος θεῷ.

9. **μεταρρυθμίζει.** Below p. 106. 16.

10. **σίδηρον Ἄρην.** Cf. *Protr.* 56 πολλοὶ τὸ ξίφος μόνον πήξαντες ἐπιθύουσιν ὡς Ἄρει.

12. **ἀναφοράν.** Cf. p. 14. 2. **H.** See ἀναφέρεται just above, l. 7, and for exx. Cic. *N. D.* II. 60 with notes.

14. **οὐ κατὰ τὴν τῆς μορφῆς ἰδιότητα.** Cf. P. 798 ἡ δὲ ὁμοίωσις οὐχ, ὥς τινες, ἡ κατὰ τὸ σχῆμα τὸ ἀνθρώπειον, P. 809 κατ' εἰκόνα θεοῦ γεγονέναι ὁ ἄνθρωπος εἴρηται οὐ κατὰ τῆς κατασκευῆς τὸ σχῆμα, ἀλλ' ἐπεὶ ὁ μὲν θεὸς λόγῳ τὰ πάντα δημιουργεῖ, ὁ δὲ ἄνθρωπος ὁ γνωστικὸς γενόμενος τῷ λογικῷ τὰς καλὰς πράξεις ἐπιτελεῖ. See reff. in Kaye, pp. 134 f.

15. **κατὰ τὸ τῆς δυνάμεως σύμβολον.** Probably a reference to δημιουργεῖ

in l. 8: also *Paed.* P. 220 κατὰ τοῦτο εἰκὼν ὁ ἄνθρωπος γίνεται τοῦ θεοῦ καθὸ εἰς γένεσιν ἀνθρώπου ἄνθρωπος συνεργεῖ.

18. **ἐκ τῆς συγκαταθέσεως.** Cf. below p. 118. 8, 9 ἡ ὁμόνοια ἡ περὶ ταὐτὸ πρᾶγμα συγκατάθεσις.

§ 53. 19. **ἀπὸ γνώμης.** Cf. Wytt. Plut. II. 44 D, where exx. are given of two meanings, (1) *ratione et consilio*)(*temere et casu* p. 798 E, (2) *ex animi iudicio et sententia*. H. For the harmony of thought, word, and action see below p. 176. 2.

21. **ἐν θεραπείας μέρει.** See Plato *Rep.* II. 382 and III. 389 B with the nn. of Stallbaum and Ast, also Philo M. 1. p. 141, and Orig. *in Joh.* x. 4 σωζομένου πολλάκις τοῦ ἀληθοῦς πνευματικοῦ ἐν τῷ σωματικῷ ψευδεῖ (of allegorical interpretation), and in a fragment of *Strom.* VI. where he comments on Plato, cf. Gieseler *tr.* I. 235 n.

22. **ψεύσεται ἡ ψεῦδος ἐρεῖ.** Cf. *Str.* VI. P. 802 ψεῦσται τῷ ὄντι οὐχ οἱ συμπεριφερόμενοι δι' οἰκονομίαν σωτηρίας, οὐδ' οἱ περί τινα τῶν ἐν μέρει σφαλλόμενοι, ἀλλ' οἱ εἰς τὰ κυριώτατα παραπίπτοντες. Potter refers to Gell. II. 11, quoting Nigidius: 'inter mendacium dicere et mentiri distat. Qui mentitur ipse non fallitur, sed alterum fallere conatur: qui mendacium dicit ipse fallitur...vir bonus praestare debet ne mentiatur, prudens ne mendacium dicat.' H.

26. **ἀποσπῶν** might be taken in its usual transitive sense: but the position suggests the intransitive, found in Lucian and other writers. H. Cf. Luc. *Dial. Deorum* XX. 5 πολὺ προϊόντες ἀπεσπάσαμεν τῶν ἀστέρων, 'progressi longius processimus a stellis,' where Hemst. says that, in its later use, the verb, whether in the p. (as Lk. xxii. 41 ἀπεσπάσθη ἀπ' αὐτῶν), or intr., as here, 'simpliciter pro χωρισθῆναι *digredi* ponitur.' He cites 2 Macc. xii. 10 ἐκεῖθεν ἀποσπάσαντες σταδίους ἐννέα, Luc. *Dial. Mar.* XII. 1 ἐπειδὰν πολὺ ἀπὸ τῆς γῆς ἀποσπάσωσιν.

27. **ἀφηνιάζοντας.** Common in late writers. See Index, Schmid *Att.* III. 234, and Siegfried's *Philo* p. 62, *s.v.* ἀφηνιασμός and ἀφηνιαστής.

27, 28. **τοὺς ἀκροωμένους τῶν Ἑβραίων,** 'his disciples (cf. *Str.* I. 323 *med.*) among the Hebrews.' H.

28. **ἀπορρῆξαι,** intransitive, as rarely (Steph. p. 1646 c); once in Lucian *Abd.* 6 ὑποικουροῦν ἐν τῇ ψυχῇ κακὸν ἀπέρρηξε καὶ ἐς τοὐμφανὲς ἐξενίκησε. H.

συναγωγῆς, apparently not used by Clement for 'Judaism': probably 'the religious assembly,' Jewish or Christian: cf. *Paed.* III. § 80, P. 300 and Heb. x. 25 ἐπισυναγωγήν. H. Other instances in my n. on St James ii. 2.

συμπεριφερόμενος, 'consorting,' especially with assimilation to another's ways, or even blandishments. Often in Epictet., *e.g.* III. 147, and LXX. H. Cf. below, p. 106. 30 συμπεριφέρεται τοῖς ἀναγκαίοις, p. 140. 19 ἀσφαλὴς ἐν συμπεριφορᾷ, and P. 802 (quoted just above on l. 22), where the case of Timothy is discussed.

29. **πάντας.** This reading of DFG vg. occurs also in *Str.* VI. P. 802

and (with τούς) P. 656: but πάντως τινάς P. 332. **H.** The subjunctive κερδήσῃ is found also in the original after the past indicative.

30. **μέχρι τῆς συμπεριφορᾶς.** Cf. P. 802 κατὰ συμπεριφορὰν σώζων τὰ κύρια τῶν δογμάτων. No need to omit the words διὰ τὴν τῶν πέλας σωτηρίαν, which Dindorf brackets; they express the limitation in general terms, the sense being afterwards repeated, with a closer reference, to prevent misunderstanding. The double διά is like the double ὑπέρ in p. 94. 5 below. **H.**

31. **ψιλήν.** Emphatically at the end; cf. for the predicative use P. 737 κατὰ ψιλὴν τὴν τῆς ψυχῆς ἐνέργειαν, P. 891 αὐτῇ ψιλῇ ἀποχρώμενος τῇ λέξει, and often, as we have ἐπὶ τῶν πλησίον ὠφελείᾳ μόνῃ just below.

p. 94, line 2. **ἀναχάζεται.** Some word expressing falsehood or shirking seems required. ἀναχάζεται suggested by Potter seems too poetic, though Xenophon has it ('retreats'). **H.** Perhaps the ms. reading may be retained with Potter's explanation: '*is nequaquam cogitur*, metu scilicet, quem ad modum paulo post dicitur ἀδούλωτος οὗτος ἐν φόβῳ,' cf. below p. 134. 4 ἵνα μὴ ὁ τόπος ἀναγκάζῃ.

6. **γνωρίμων.** Often found in this special sense in later Greek. See below p. 188. 12, and W. Schmid *Att.* Index *s.v.*

8. **εἰς παράστασιν τῆς ἀληθείας.** See n. on p. 88, l. 22, and Index *s.v.* παρίστημι.

11. We have here the Stoic distinction between the spoken and unspoken word (λόγος προφορικός and λόγος ἐνδιάθετος), which was also used by Christian writers in regard to the Word. Cf. Zeller³, vol. IV. p. 65 f., Wytt. on Plut. *Mor.* 44 A, Philo M. 1. pp. 209, 215, 270, M. 2. p. 347.

12. **τὸ ἀναμάρτητον.** See nn. on p. 22. 20 above, and p. 138. 29 below.

13. **αὐτῷ.** For the dat. cf. above pp. 36. 22, 52. 19.

§ 54, line 21. **κατὰ λόγον τὸν ὀρθόν.** See p. 44. 14, Stein *Erkenntnistheorie d. Stoa* II. p. 254.

24. **τουτὶ γὰρ ἦν τὸ προκείμενον.** See above § 1, p. 2.

27. **οὐδὲ ἀσεβεῖ, ἀλλ' ἢ μόνος θεοσεβεῖ.** See below p. 194. 5 ἀλλ' ἢ ὡς ὁ χνοῦς. ἀλλ' ἢ in later Gr. is often used for ἀλλά, much as εἰ μή and πλήν; see below on p. 96. 16, and Index, also p. xvii of my Introd. to St James. Probably the use arose from comic phraseology, such as we find in Arist. *Pax* 474 οὐδ' οἶδε γ' εἷλκον οὐδὲν Ἀργεῖοι πάλαι, ἀλλ' ἢ κατεγέλων τῶν ταλαιπωρουμένων.

29. **βασιλέα παντοκράτορα.** The ms. inserts καί, probably because π. is often used as a substantive; but it is evident that β. needs an epithet to balance the preceding θεὸν πανηγεμόνα: cf. below P. 895 *med.* τὸν παντοκράτορα θεόν.

30. **προστρεπόμενος.** The ms. here repeats ὁσίως from l. 28.

§ 55. p. 96, line 1. Sharp opposition to the Pseudo-gnostics, who drew an impassable line between the γνωστικός and other men. Clement looks on Gnosis as what should be the aim of every man. See below 6 foll. **H.**

3, 4. κατά τε τὸν τρόπον καὶ τὸν βίον καὶ τὸν λόγον. Cf. below p. 176. 2 οἷος ὁ λόγος, τοιόσδε καὶ ὁ βίος.

5. τελειοῦται. See below p. 98. 30, and St James i. 4, ii. 22, iii. 2, Kaye p. 143 foll.

7. ἐνδιάθετον. Cf. above p. 68. 21 τὴν ἐνδιάθετον ὁμιλίαν ὁ θεὸς ἐπαίει. The contrasted word προφορικόν appears above p. 94. 11 and below l. 15, where it is used to characterize σοφία. As used to distinguish πίστις from γνῶσις, ἐνδ. probably implies that the former is inarticulate, cannot give an account of itself.

ἄνευ τοῦ ζητεῖν. The gnostic belongs to τὸ γένος τὸ ἐκλεκτόν, τὸ ζητητικὸν εἰς γνῶσιν, below p. 102, l. 9.

9. ἀναγόμενον, 'starting,' specially 'putting to sea.' H. Cf. *Str.* III. P. 511 οἱ ἀπὸ Καρποκράτους ἀναγόμενοι, Plut. *Mor.* 392 γ ἀπὸ τῶν αἰτῶν ἀναγόμενος, 'eadem institutus disciplina.'

12 foll. The distinction between γνῶσις and σοφία here given is very difficult to follow; indeed it seems to me to be an amalgamation of contradictory notions. In l. 12 the difference between them is said to lie in the fact that σοφία comes through teaching; but in l. 21 foll. we are told that γνῶσις is handed down by tradition and is intrusted as a deposit to those who show themselves worthy of being taught, and in l. 2 that it is completed by the science of divine things. Then in l. 13 we are told that γνῶσις is a species of σοφία, and in l. 15 that the name σοφία is somehow connected with the uttered word, while γνῶσις is founded in faith. In § 77 below (p. 132. 24 foll.) γνῶσις is said to be shown ἐν τῷ τὰ αὐτὰ μεμαθηκέναι καὶ φρονεῖν, while faith is shown ἐν τῷ τὰ αὐτὰ αἱρεῖσθαι: again in § 61 (p. 104. 25) it is said that knowledge is taught by the Lord through the mouth of man. Turning to Bk VI. P. 771, we read that if we call Christ our wisdom, σοφία εἴη ἂν ἡ γνῶσις, ἐπιστήμη οὖσα καὶ κατάληψις τῶν ὄντων τε καὶ ἐσομένων καὶ παρῳχηκότων βεβαία καὶ ἀσφαλής, ὡς ἂν παρὰ τοῦ υἱοῦ τοῦ θεοῦ παραδοθεῖσα...ἡ γνῶσις δὲ αὕτη (MS. αὐτή) ἡ κατὰ διαδοχὰς εἰς ὀλίγους ἐκ τῶν ἀποστόλων ἀγράφως παραδοθεῖσα κατελήλυθεν, ἐντεῦθεν δ' ἄρα γνῶσιν εἴτε σοφίαν συνασκηθῆναι χρὴ εἰς ἕξιν θεωρίας ἀίδιον. The last sentence seems to refer to the narrower meaning of γνῶσις as the knowledge of a secret tradition handed down by the initiated. In Barnabas γνῶσις is used of allegorical interpretation, cf. x. 10 and Harnack's n. on i. 5. The fundamental difference, however, between γιγνώσκω and γνῶσις on one side, and οἶδα and σοφία on the other, as they are generally used, is that the former implies direct cognizance of an object, the latter right judgment about it. This would agree fairly with the distinction in l. 12. If γνῶσις is the result of a direct inspiration it is in that respect distinguished from the knowledge which is the result of study and instruction. But I do not remember to have read of σοφία being limited to this latter. In P. 333 and elsewhere Cl. defines σοφία, with Philo and the Stoics, ἐπιστήμη θείων καὶ ἀνθρωπίνων καὶ τῶν τούτων αἰτιῶν (cf. Cic. *Off.* II. 5): in P. 331 γνῶσις is identified with ἡ ἐν θεοσεβείᾳ αἴσθησις, see P. 531 ὁ γὰρ ὀφθαλμὸς ἐν σώματι, τοῦτο ἐν τῷ νῷ ἡ γνῶσις, P. 454 ἡ ἐποπτικὴ θεωρία, ἡ τῷ ὄντι ἐπιστήμη...αὕτη

ἂν εἴη μόνη ἡ τῆς σοφίας γνῶσις and P. 775 init. γνῶσις δὲ αὐτὸ τοῦτο θέα τίς ἐστι τῆς ψυχῆς τῶν ὄντων, ἤτοι τινὸς ἢ τινῶν, cf. Kaye p. 140 foll.

13. ἡ μὲν γάρ τί ἐστι γνῶσις, ταύτῃ πάντως καὶ σοφία τυγχάνει. Cf. P. 441 ἡ μὲν σοφία φρόνησις, οὐ μὴν πᾶσα φρόνησις σοφία. Thus φρόνησις includes more, has a wider extension, than σοφία, and σοφία again has a wider extension than γνῶσις. See P. 820 fin. πολυμερὴς οὖσα ἡ φρόνησις δι' ὅλου τεταμένη τοῦ κόσμου...μεταβάλλει τὴν προσηγορίαν, καὶ ἐπειδὰν μὲν ἐπιβάλλῃ τοῖς πρώτοις αἰτίοις νόησις καλεῖται, ὅταν δὲ ταύτην ἀποδεικτικῷ λόγῳ βεβαιώσηται γνῶσίς τε καὶ σοφία καὶ ἐπιστήμη ὀνομάζεται...καὶ ἄνευ θεωρίας παραδεξαμένη τὸν ἀρχικὸν λόγον...πίστις λέγεται, κἂν τοῖς αἰσθητοῖς, πιστωσαμένη τό γε δοκοῦν...ἀληθέστατον, δόξα ὀρθή (and under other conditions is called τέχνη and ἐμπειρία).

15. ἐν μονῇ. So I read with H. J. instead of μόνῃ which would require the addition of a substantive. He compares Plato *Meno* 97, 98 where the difference between δόξα ὀρθή and ἐπιστήμη is made to depend on the *permanence* of the latter. See also Joh. xv. 7 ἐὰν τὰ ῥήματά μου ἐν ὑμῖν μένῃ.

τῇ τοῦ προφορικοῦ λόγου τὸ τῆς σοφίας ὄνομα φαντάζεται. H. J. translates 'For the meaning of the word σοφία is shown in the abiding of the uttered word,' and suggests that there is an allusion to the etymology of σοφία (from συθῆναι=φέρεσθαι, and ἐπαφή) given in Plat. *Cratyl.* 412 B (φορᾶς ἐπαφὴν σημαίνει ἡ σοφία, ὡς φερομένων τῶν ὄντων). This very ingenious explanation of a most difficult passage supplies a reason for the use of προφορικοῦ (being one of the φερόμενα as distinguished from the ἐνδιάθετος λόγος). Otherwise, it is strange to find Cl. defining wisdom by the memory of uttered words, say, of the Creed or Pater Noster; esp. as in P. 323 we read οὐχὶ τῇ ἐκφράσει ἡσθέντες, μόνῃ δὲ τῇ κατὰ τὴν ὑποσημείωσιν τηρήσει, and in P. 646 ὁ τοῦ πατρὸς τῶν ὅλων λόγος οὐχ οὗτός ἐστιν ὁ προφορικός, σοφία δὲ καὶ χρηστότης φανερωτάτη τοῦ θεοῦ, where wisdom is opposed to the προφορικὸς λόγος. In Theoph. *ad Aut.* II. 22 we have both terms used of the Divine λόγος. ὁ μὲν πατὴρ τῶν ὅλων ἀχώρητός ἐστιν...ὁ δὲ λόγος αὐτοῦ, δι' οὗ τὰ πάντα πεποίηκεν...οὗτος ὡμίλει τῷ Ἀδάμ. (For the voice which spoke to Adam signifies) τὸν λόγον τὸν ὄντα διὰ παντὸς ἐνδιάθετον ἐν καρδίᾳ θεοῦ. πρὸ γάρ τι γίνεσθαι τοῦτον εἶχε σύμβουλον, ἑαυτοῦ νοῦν καὶ φρόνησιν ὄντα. ὁπότε δὲ ἠθέλησεν ὁ θεὸς ποιῆσαι ὅσα ἐβουλεύσατο, τοῦτον τὸν λόγον ἐγέννησε προφορικόν, πρωτότοκον πάσης κτίσεως, οὐ κενωθεὶς αὐτὸς τοῦ λόγου.

16. πλὴν ἀλλά. This pleonastic expression is frequent in late Greek, see Index, and W. Schmid *Atticismus* I. 285, III. 343, IV. 559, πλήν being used by itself in the sense of ἀλλά or even δέ, as in *Str.* VI. P. 797 init. κομπώδους μὲν ψυχῆς καύχημα πλὴν εὐσυνειδήτου, Herodian III. 4. 1 πολλὴν στρατιὰν πλὴν ἄπειρον, cf. Jaunaris *Gr. SS.* 1734; πλὴν εἰ μή above p. 64. 10, and the use of ἀλλ' ἤ above p. 94. 27.

18. ὅ τε θεμέλιος ἤ τε ἐποικοδομή. Eph. ii. 20 ἐποικοδομηθέντες ἐπὶ τῷ θεμελίῳ τῶν ἀποστόλων καὶ προφητῶν, ὄντος ἀκρογωνιαίου αὐτοῦ Ἰησοῦ Χριστοῦ, ἐν ᾧ πᾶσα ἡ οἰκοδομὴ αὔξει εἰς ναὸν ἅγιον ἐν κυρίῳ. In 1 Cor. iii. 12

Paul speaks of himself as having laid the foundation, viz. Christ, on whom other teachers build.

19. τὰ τέλη. Cf. VI. 792 fin. ἐκλεγέντες πρὸς τοῦ καὶ τὰ τέλη προορωμένου. H. The one ἀρχή has many ends, but these may all be summed up in ἀγάπη.

20. πίστις καὶ ἡ ἀγάπη. Ign. Eph. 14 ἀρχὴ μὲν πίστις τέλος δὲ ἀγάπη with Lightfoot's n. (vol. II. p. 67). They begin and end the list of graces in 2 Peter i. 5—7, see below p. 100. 8—10.

23. οἷον παρακαταθήκη. Cf. Str. I. P. 322 fin. οἱ μὲν τὴν ἀληθῆ τῆς μακαρίας σῴζοντες διδασκαλίας παράδοσιν εὐθὺς ἀπὸ Πέτρου τε καὶ Ἰακώβου, Ἰωάννου τε καὶ Παύλου...παῖς παρὰ πατρὸς ἐκδεχόμενος...ἦκον δὴ καὶ εἰς ἡμᾶς τὰ...ἀποστολικὰ καταθησόμενοι σπέρματα.

24. ἐκ φωτὸς εἰς φῶς. Cf. above p. 22. 29 εἰς τὸ ἀνενδεὲς ἐκ τοῦ ἀνενδεοῦς.

25. προστεθήσεται. See Resch Agrapha, p. 231 foll.

26. ἡ κληρονομία. Col. iii. 24, Eph. i. 18, above p. 16. 29 γνώσεώς τε καὶ κληρονομίας ὑπεροχήν, p. 18. 3 κληρονομίαις, and Protr. P. 75 with the quotation from Isa. liv. 17.

§ 56. 27. ἐκκρεμασθῇ τοῦ κυρίου. Cf. P. 936 τῆς ἐνταῦθα ζωῆς ἐκκρεμασθέντες. The change from the MS. κρεμασθῇ is required by the genitive.

p. 98, line 3. ἐπὶ τέλει, probably 'ultimately,' as immediately from the Son: hence also παραδίδοται: the Son transmits what He has received. H. Cf. p. 144. 16 below.

4. ἐγκρίτοις. See Lobeck on Phryn. p. 385 where he explains the word ἐγκριτέον 'traductum a senatorum et athletarum probatione,' Stallb. on Plato Leg. VII. 802 B, XI. 936 A, where ἐγκρίνω is opposed to ἀποκρίνω, and ib. XII. 952 A. In Leg. 966 D Stallbaum reads τῶν πρὸς ἀρετὴν ἐγκρίτων γίγνεσθαι.

5. διὰ τό, κ.τ.λ. Apparently gnosis is given them as a means of perfecting life, because they need more preparation than without it they could receive: cf. l. 21 below. H.

6. καταστολὴν βίου. Cf. κ. παθῶν P. 137, 778, κ. ἤθους P. 785.

7. ἐπὶ πλέον τῆς κατὰ νόμον δικαιοσύνης. See Barnard Cl.'s Bibl. Text p. 6.

κατ' ἐπίστασιν. The word is often used by Polybius in cases where 'subsistimus ad rem et ei immoramur ad eam considerandam' (Schweigh.), as in II. 2. 2 μετ' ἐπιστάσεως)(παρέργως, and XXII. 17. 2 where it is contrasted with ἐκ παραδρομῆς. Similarly ἐξ ἐπιστάσεως is opposed to ἐκ παρέργου, ib. III. 58. 3. [See also Berlin Index to Aristotle s.vv. ἐπίστασις, ἐφιστάναι. H. J.]

8. τέλος ἀτελεύτητον. So P. 500 ἡμῖν εἰς τέλος ἀτελεύτητον ἀφικέσθαι πρόκειται.

9. προδιδάσκουσα, 'supplying in this life a preliminary teaching.' H.

10. μετὰ θεῶν. See above pp. 20. 15, 32. 12, and below l. 18 foll.

11. ἅς. κόλασις and τιμωρία are alike εἰς παιδείαν σωτήριον. H. Cf.

above pp. 20. 7 f., 28. 22. Elsewhere Cl. denies τιμωρία of God, below p. 180. 14 f. θεὸς δὲ οὐ τιμωρεῖται (ἔστι γὰρ ἡ τιμωρία κακοῦ ἀνταπόδοσις), κολάζει μέντοι, where see n., also P. 794 foll.

15. **λειτουργίας**. Cf. line 30: apparently 'ritual' in both places. H. See n. on p. 22. 2.

κἂν ἁγία ᾖ καὶ ἐν ἁγίοις. Even the holiest forms are now a thing of the past. Cf. for phrase p. 20. 16.

16. **τὸ προσεχές**, i.e. in the future life. H. On the word see Index, and above p. 18. 4 ἕως τῆς προσεχοῦς τοῦ κυρίου θεωρίας, and p. 20. 9 with n.

17. **προσμένει**. For the following dative cf. 1 Tim. v. 5 ἡ δὲ ὄντως χήρα προσμένει ταῖς δεήσεσι, Acts xiii. 43 ἔπειθον αὐτοὺς προσμένειν τῇ χάριτι τοῦ θεοῦ. The realization of the ideal of humanity depends upon the contemplation of the Divine, like the victory over Amalek on the uplifted arms of Moses.

τῇ θεωρίᾳ. The contemplation of God promised to the pure in heart; on which waits ἀποκατάστασις. H. I think this is a better construction than to make θεωρίᾳ depend on ἀποκατάστασις. Such a dative would be very harsh, and ἀποκατάστασις, so limited, would surely have required the definite article (ἡ τῇ θεωρίᾳ ἀποκ.), cf. *Str.* II. P. 500 ἡ πρὸς τὸν ὀρθὸν λόγον ὡς οἷόν τε ἐξομοίωσις τέλος ἐστὶ καὶ εἰς τὴν τελείαν υἱοθεσίαν διὰ τοῦ υἱοῦ ἀποκατάστασις. Moreover, the contemplation of the pure in heart seems to precede the restoration to bliss, ll. 26, 27 below. The word ἀποκ. (Acts iii. 21), like παλιγγενεσία (Mt. xix. 28), was borrowed from the Stoics, see Zeller IV. 155. If the reading here is correct, the absence of the article is to be explained by the word being treated as a proper name.

19. **οἱ σύνθρονοι**. Cf. *Ecl. Proph.* P. 1004 τὸ ὑπεράνω πάσης ἀρχῆς καὶ ἐξουσίας...οἱ τελειωθέντες εἰσὶν ἐξ ἀνθρώπων, ἄγγελοι, ἀρχάγγελοι, εἰς τὴν πρωτόκτιστον τῶν ἀγγέλων φύσιν κ.τ.λ.

20. **πρώτων**, probably both 'first' in time and 'highest' in place: cf. πρωτοτόκων in Heb. xii. 23. H. Comparing *Str.* VI. P. 813 ἑπτὰ μέν εἰσιν οἱ τὴν μεγίστην δύναμιν ἔχοντες πρωτόγονοι ἀγγέλων ἄρχοντες, and the seven πρωτόκτιστοι mentioned in *Exc. Theod.* P. 969 fin. foll., of whom it is said that ὁμοῦ τε ἐγένοντο καὶ τὸ ἐντελὲς ἀπειλήφασιν...οὐδὲ ὑπολείπεταί τις αὐτοῖς προκοπὴ ἐξ ἀρχῆς, and that (P. 971) τόν τε υἱὸν ὁρῶσι καὶ ἑαυτοὺς καὶ τὰ ὑποβεβηκότα, ὥσπερ καὶ οἱ ἀρχάγγελοι τοὺς πρωτοκτίστους, I think the reference is rather to Apoc. viii. 2, Tobit xii. 15. Cf. above p. 16. 4 f.

21. **εἰς κάθαρσιν**. Cf. P. 581 κἂν τῷ ὄντι τὸ ἀληθὲς σκοπῶμεν, ἡ γνῶσις τοῦ ἡγεμονικοῦ τῆς ψυχῆς κάθαρσίς ἐστι καὶ ἐνέργειά ἐστιν ἀγαθή (the converse of Mt. v. 8 cited below l. 27. Cf. above p. 30. 21).

22. **εὐπρόσδεκτον**, sc. to God, the question being whether Christian gnosis renders men dear to God (θεοφιλές § 2, &c.). But also see *Paed.* I. P. 106 init. on the offering of doves (τὸ ἀναμάρτητον...τῶν νεοττῶν εὐπρόσδεκτον εἶναι λέγων τῷ θεῷ, καὶ τὸ ὅμοιον τοῦ ὁμοίου καθάρσιον ὑφηγούμενος). H. I think it makes better sense to take εὐπρ. as in Plut. *Mor.* 801 c ὅπως εὐπρόσδεκτος γένηται τοῖς πολλοῖς. If it is to be taken εὐπρ. θεῷ, I

should understand it more generally as that which is in accordance with the divine Will, rather than with a reference to θεοφιλές, which seems to me far-fetched.

§ 57. 23. εἰς τὸ συγγενὲς τῆς ψυχῆς. Cf. P. 80 init. τὸν ἄνθρωπον ἐπὶ τὴν οὐρανοῦ γενόμενον θέαν, φυτὸν οὐράνιον ὡς ἀληθῶς, and above n. on p. 34. 9, below p. 118. 19.

24. διά τινος οἰκείου φωτός. This mystic light is referred to in *Str.* I. P. 323 μεταδιδόναι τῶν θείων μυστηρίων καὶ τοῦ φωτὸς ἐκείνου τοῦ ἁγίου τοῖς χωρεῖν δυναμένοις. *Protr.* P. 92 ὦ τῶν ἁγίων ὡς ἀληθῶς μυστηρίων, ὦ φωτὸς ἀκηράτου. δαδουχοῦμαι, τοὺς οὐρανοὺς καὶ τὸν θεὸν ἐποπτεύσας, ἅγιος γίνομαι μυούμενος, ἱεροφαντεῖ δ' ὁ κύριος καὶ τὸν μύστην σφραγίζεται φωταγωγῶν. *Paed.* I. P. 113 βαπτιζόμενοι φωτιζόμεθα, φωτιζόμενοι υἱοποιούμεθα...φώτισμα δὲ δι' οὖ τὸ ἅγιον ἐκεῖνο φῶς τὸ σωτήριον ἐποπτεύεται. Compare the description of the mysteries given by Themistius (*ap.* Stob. *Flor.* 120, § 28) πρὸ τοῦ τέλους αὐτοῦ τὰ δεινὰ πάντα...ἐκ δὲ τούτου φῶς τι θαυμάσιον ἀπήντησε καὶ τόποι καθαροὶ καὶ λειμῶνες ἐδέξαντο, and Apuleius (*Met.* XI. 23) accessi confinium mortis et calcato Proserpinae limine per omnia vectus elementa remeavi, nocte media vidi solem candido coruscantem lumine, &c.

τὰς προκοπάς. Cognate accusative [or is it not rather expressive of movement over, as in Polyb. II. 34 διαβ. αὐτοὺς τὸν Πάδον? M.]. Cf. κατὰ προκοπὴν ἑκάστην P. 834 *med.* (p. 16. 28): indeed all § 10 illustrates this passage. H. 'Alludit auctor ad varias illas lustrationes, quas certo ordine subibant qui Cereris Eleusiniae mysteria ἐποπτεύειν cupiebant.' Potter.

25. τὰς μυστικάς. See n. on p. 78. 12 above.

26. ἀναπαύσεως. Cf. *Str.* IV. P. 636 τῇ ἑβδόμῃ γὰρ ἡ ἀνάπαυσις θρησκεύεται, τῇ δὲ ὀγδόῃ ἱλασμὸν προσφέρει...εἴτ' οὖν ὁ χρόνος εἴη ὁ διὰ τῶν ἑπτὰ περιόδων τῶν ἀριθμουμένων εἰς τὴν ἀκροτάτην ἀνάπαυσιν ἀποκαθιστάς, εἴτε ἑπτὰ οὐρανοί...εἴτε καὶ ἡ ἀπλανὴς χώρα ἡ πλησιάζουσα τῷ νοητῷ κόσμῳ ὀγδοὰς λέγοιτο. H. Also P. 793 *fin.* οἱ τοιοῦτοι, κατὰ τὸν Δαβίδ, καταπαύσουσιν ἐν ὄρει ἁγίῳ θεοῦ, τῇ ἀνωτάτω ἐκκλησίᾳ...οἱ μὴ καταμείναντες ἐν ἑβδομάδι ἀναπαύσεως, ἀγαθοεργίᾳ δὲ θείας ἐξομοιώσεως εἰς ὀγδοαδικῆς εὐεργεσίας κληρονομίαν ὑπερκύψαντες foll., P. 667 τὰ ἐπὶ τῆς ἁγίας κιβωτοῦ ἱστορούμενα μηνύει τὰ τοῦ νοητοῦ κόσμου, *ib.* εἴτ' οὖν ὀγδοὰς καὶ ὁ νοητὸς κόσμος, εἴτε καὶ ὁ πέριξ πάντων περιεκτικός...δηλοῦται θεός, τὰ νῦν ὑπερκείσθω λέγειν· πλὴν ἀνάπαυσιν μηνύει τὴν μετὰ τῶν δοξολόγων πνευμάτων. See Index, Mt. xi. 29, Apoc. xiv. 13.

27. ἐπιστημονικῶς καὶ καταληπτικῶς τὸν θεὸν ἐποπτεύειν. Below p. 100. 6 μετ' ἐπιστήμης καταληπτόν, p. 104. 22 ἐγγυμναζόμενος τῇ ἐπιστημονικῇ θεωρίᾳ, p. 132. 11 ὅταν ἐπιστημονικοῦ θεωρήματος κατάληψιν λάβῃ, τὸν κύριον ὁρᾶν νομίζει, 178. 31, ἡ καταληπτικὴ θεωρία above p. 20. 25, below p. 160. 9.

29. ἐνταῦθα, 'in this life': the contrast comes below p. 100. 13. H. But can it be said that the Christian attains such perfection in this life? Has he now got beyond πάσας καθάρσεις καὶ λειτουργίας? Is he now σὺν τῷ κυρίῳ ὅπου ἐστὶν προσεχῶς ὑποτεταγμένος? I translate ἐνταῦθα 'herein,' see n. on p. 32. 27 above.

30. ὑπερβάσαν. Seems never to take the genitive: so that either this is an unique usage, or more probably we must read the plural accusative πάσας καθάρσεις, which may have been corrupted through ἡ τελείωσις. H. See above n. on l. 15.

p. 100, line 3. σύντομος. Cf. p. 18. 20 τὴν ἐπίτομον τῆς σωτηρίας διὰ πίστεως.
4. τῶν κατεπαγόντων. See n. on p. 4. 5 above.
ἡ γνῶσις δὲ ἀπόδειξις. Cf. Str. II. P. 454 ἡ γνῶσις ἂν εἴη ἐπιστημονικὴ ἀπόδειξις τῶν κατὰ τὴν ἀληθῆ φιλοσοφίαν παραδιδομένων.
6. ἐποικοδομουμένη τῇ πίστει. Cf. p. 32. 9 above, P. 646.
7. καταληπτόν. See above p. 20. 25 n., Exc. Theod. P. 975 ὅσον καταληπτὸν τοῦ πατρὸς δι' υἱοῦ δεδιδαγμένοι θεωροῦσι. Barnard.
9. μεταβολὴ σωτήριος. Cf. p. 16. 30 σωτήριοι περιτροπαί and P. 986 σωτηρίους ὁδούς quoted in the n., also Str. IV. P. 587 ὁ μὲν οὖν πρῶτος βαθμὸς τῆς σωτηρίας ἡ μετὰ φόβου διδασκαλία, δι' ἣν ἀπεχόμεθα τῆς ἀδικίας, δεύτερος δὲ ἡ ἐλπὶς δι' ἣν ἐφιέμεθα τῶν βελτίστων, τελειοῖ δὲ ἡ ἀγάπη, ὡς προσῆκόν ἐστι, γνωστικῶς ἤδη παιδεύουσα.
ὡς πρόσιτον. Above p. 80. 9.
11. περαιουμένη, 'passing over' (a sea or river). The stop in Dindorf's text is fatal. The point is that the second transition already makes the object and subject of gnosis dear to each other by its own approach to ἀγάπη. What follows is not so much a μετάβασις as a continuous process. H.
12. τὸ γινῶσκον τῷ γινωσκομένῳ. Cf. p. 136. 15, 16 τὴν μὲν τοῦ πιστεύοντος ἐνέργειαν, τὴν δὲ τοῦ πιστευομένου (if the text is right).
13. ἰσάγγελος. Cf. below p. 136. 11 ὁ δὲ καὶ μετ' ἀγγέλων εὔχεται ὡς ἂν ἤδη καὶ ἰσάγγελος, 146. 22 ἐξομοιουμένη θεῷ ἰσάγγελος ἀληθῶς γενομένη, P. 792 ὁ τοίνυν...εἰς ἀπάθειαν μελετήσας αὐξήσας τε εἰς εὐποιίαν γνωστικῆς τελειότητος ἰσάγγελος μὲν ἐνταῦθα, φωτεινὸς δὲ ἤδη καὶ ὡς ὁ ἥλιος λάμπων κατὰ τὴν εὐεργεσίαν, σπεύδει τῇ γνώσει τῇ δικαίᾳ δι' ἀγάπης θεοῦ ἐπὶ τὴν ἁγίαν μονήν. [The word also occurs in P. 120 and P. 974. Barnard.]
14. ὑπεροχήν. See above p. 16. 30. H.
16. κυριακήν, sc. 'the eighth': cf. Str. V. P. 712 fin. 713 τὴν τε κυριακὴν ἡμέραν ἐν τῷ δεκάτῳ τῆς Πολιτείας ὁ Πλάτων διὰ τούτων καταμαντεύεται, Ἐπειδὴ δὲ τοῖς ἐν τῷ λειμῶνι ἑκάστοις ἑπτὰ ἡμέραι γένοιντο, ἀναστάντας ἐντεῦθεν δεῖ τῇ ὀγδόῃ πορεύεσθαι, where C. explains the seven days to be ἑκάστην κίνησιν τῶν ἑπτὰ καὶ πᾶσαν τὴν ἐργαστικὴν τέχνην εἰς τέλος ἀναπαύσεως σπεύδουσαν, but the eighth day is the movement up to the unchanging heavens beyond the planetary spheres. H. See also the passages quoted on ἀναπαύσεως, p. 98. 26, and Exc. Theod. P. 984 fin. ἡ μὲν οὖν τῶν πνευματικῶν ἀνάπαυσις ...ἐν ὀγδοάδι, ἡ κυριακὴ ὀνομάζεται...αἱ δὲ ἄλλαι πισταὶ ψυχαὶ παρὰ τῷ δημιουργῷ, περὶ δὲ τὴν συντέλειαν ἀναχωροῦσι καὶ αὗται εἰς ὀγδοάδα, ib. P. 987 ὃν γεννᾷ ἡ μήτηρ, εἰς θάνατον ἄγεται καὶ εἰς κόσμον, ὃν δὲ ἀναγεννᾷ Χριστός, εἰς ζωὴν μετατίθεται <καὶ> εἰς ὀγδοάδα. Cl., according to his wont, is delighted to find in Plato a parallel or illustration for ideas

derived from another source. See Kaye p. 152 n. 'By the Hebdomas according to the Gnostic doctrine was meant the rest from evil-doing, with reference to the Jewish Sabbath: by the Ogdoas, the creation of man anew to a life of active well-doing, with reference to our Lord's resurrection on the 1st or 8th day.' He cites *Str.* IV. P. 612 εἶτα ἑβδομάδος καὶ ὀγδοάδος μυστήριον γνωστικὸν ἐπιφέρει...γνῶσιν γὰρ αἰνίττεται διὰ τούτων μετά τε ἀποχῆς κακῶν μετά τε ἐνεργείας ἀγαθῶν...τελειοῦσθαι διδάσκων, *Str.* VI. P. 810 ἡ ἑβδόμη τοίνυν ἡμέρα ἀνάπαυσις κηρύσσεται, ἀποχὴ κακῶν, ἑτοιμάζουσα τὴν ἀρχέγονον ἡμέραν τὴν τῷ ὄντι ἀνάπαυσιν ἡμῶν, τὴν δὴ τῷ ὄντι φωτὸς γένεσιν foll., P. 667. I don't think there is much ground for Dr Bigg's suggestion (*Christian Platonism* p. 54) that one reason why Cl. insists on the mystery of the Ogdoad is the Ebionite observance of the sabbath, which made it necessary to point out the higher sanctity of the Lord's day. The words ὀγδοάς and ἑβδομάς play an important part in the Gnostic systems. Basilides gives the former name to his Ethereal Creation, which was under the control of the Great Archon, reaching down to the sphere of the moon; and the latter name to the inferior creation of the Aerial World, which was under the rule of the Second Archon. See Hort's Art. on Basilides in *D. of Chr. Biog.*, Hippolyt. *Ref. Haer.* p. 368. 59, 370. 89, 379. 15 foll. Similarly Valentinus, according to Iren. I. 5. 2 'Εβδομάδα καλοῦσιν τὸν Δημιουργόν, τὴν δὲ μητέρα τὴν 'Αχαμώθ 'Ογδοάδα.

πατρῴαν αὐλήν. Probably a reference to Joh. XIV. 2 ἐν τῇ οἰκίᾳ τοῦ πατρός μου μοναὶ πολλαί εἰσιν. The same words occur *Paed.* III. P. 300 τοὺς καπηλεύοντας τὴν ἀλήθειαν τῆς πατρῴας ἐξέβαλεν αὐλῆς, cf. Joh. ii. 16.

17. **μονήν.** Cf. *Str.* VI. 792 *fin.* quoted under ἰσάγγελος l. 13. **H.**

φῶς, κ.τ.λ. So P. 418⅔, the pillar of fire δηλοῖ τὸ ἑστὸς καὶ μόνιμον τοῦ θεοῦ καὶ τὸ ἄτρεπτον αὐτοῦ φῶς καὶ ἀσχημάτιστον. **H.** Cf. p. 20. 23 ταυτότητι τῆς ὑπεροχῆς, and see Potter's n. on P. 456 in reference to the title ὁ ἑστώς used of Simon Magus by his followers.

§ 58. 19. **ὁ πρῶτος τρόπος,** i.e. the Old Dispensation, the method of law as opposed to the method of grace.

28. **τὸν κύριον.** The Ps. has αὐτόν. **H.**

30. **κατὰ παραδρομήν.** Cf. *Protr.* P. 55 τὴν φιλοσοφίαν...δαιμόνια ἄττα ἐκθειάζουσαν κ. π. παραστῆσαι, Arist. *Pol.* VII. 17. 12 νῦν μὲν οὖν τούτων ἐν παραδρομῇ πεποιήμεθα τὸν λόγον· ὕστερον ἐπιστήσαντας δεῖ διορίσαι μᾶλλον.

31. **πρόσωπον.** Similarly *Paed.* I. P. 132 *med.* πρόσωπον τοῦ θεοῦ ὁ λόγος, ᾧ φωτίζεται ὁ θεὸς καὶ γνωρίζεται (where see Potter), *Strom.* V. P. 665 *s.f.* Cf. Newman *Theological Tracts* 49 foll. The assumption comes from the parallelism of ζητούντων τὸν κύριον, ζητούντων τὸ πρόσωπον. **H.** See also *Exc. Theod.* P. 970 οἱ δὲ διὰ παντὸς τὸ πρόσωπον τοῦ θεοῦ βλέπουσιν, πρόσωπον δὲ πατρὸς ὁ υἱός, δι' οὗ γνωρίζεται ὁ πατήρ, P. 971 ὁ δὲ υἱὸς ἀρχὴ τῆς πατρικῆς ὑπάρχει θέας, πρόσωπον τοῦ πατρὸς λεγόμενος, *ib.* P. 975 τάχα δὲ τὸ πρόσωπόν ἐστι μὲν καὶ ὁ υἱός, ἔστι δὲ καὶ ὅσον καταληπτὸν τοῦ πατρὸς δι' υἱοῦ δεδιδαγμένοι θεωροῦσι, τὸ δὲ λοιπὸν ἄγνωστόν ἐστι τοῦ πατρός.

p. 102, line 4. **ὃν οὐδεὶς ἔγνω.** Our text of Mt. xi. 27 has οὐδὲ τὸν πατέρα τις ἐπιγινώσκει. In *Q. D. S.* 939 P. Clem. has ὃν οὐδεὶς ἐπιγινώσκει εἰ μὴ ὁ υἱός, and οὐδεὶς γινώσκει below p. 192. 19; but elsewhere ἔγνω, as here and *Protr.* P. 10, *Paed.* I. P. 109, P. 142, P. 150, *Str.* I. P. 425, v. P. 697. See Barnard *C.'s Bibl. Text* p. 16.

7. **μόνον ὄντα...ἀγαθόν.** Above p. 72. 7.

9. **ζητητικόν.** See below p. 104. 13. The addition εἰς γνῶσιν is probably intended to distinguish these Seekers from the sceptical school so named, see Diog. L. IX. 69 οὗτοι πάντες Πυρρώνειοι μὲν ἀπὸ τοῦ διδασκάλου, ἀπορητικοὶ δὲ καὶ σκεπτικοὶ καὶ ἔτι ἐφεκτικοὶ καὶ ζητητικοὶ ἀπὸ τοῦ οἷον δόγματος προσηγορεύοντο.

§ 59. 10. **οὐδέν.** The original has τί.

14. **θυμοειδεῖς.** On courage see above § 18, below §§ 63—67. 'Haud aliter Aristoteles (*Eth. ad Nic.* III. 8. 10) καὶ τὸν θυμὸν δὲ ἐπὶ τὴν ἀνδρείαν ἐπιφέρουσιν· ἀνδρεῖοι γὰρ εἶναι δοκοῦσιν οἱ διὰ θυμὸν ὥσπερ τὰ θηρία ἐπὶ τοὺς τρώσαντας φερόμενοι, *ib.* § 11 οἱ δὲ διὰ ταῦτα μάχιμοι μέν, οὐκ ἀνδρεῖοι δέ, οὐ γὰρ διὰ τὸ καλόν, οὐδ' ὡς ὁ λόγος, ἀλλὰ διὰ τὸ πάθος.' Potter.

17. **δρῶσι,** the most external of words. H. See quotation in Arist. *Nic. Eth.* VII. 8 1151 a 9 Μιλήσιοι ἀξύνετοι μὲν οὐκ εἰσίν, δρῶσιν δ' οἷά περ ἀξύνετοι. H. J.

βασάνους. See below §§ 63 and 64.

18. **οὔτε...οὔτε καί.** See below P. 895 *init.* οὔτε...οὔτε καὶ κρίνειν.

19. **οὐδ' ἂν τὸ σῶμα ὅταν ἐπιδιδῶσιν.** W.H. read in 1 Cor. xiii. 3 κἂν παραδῶ τὸ σῶμά μου ἵνα καυχήσωμαι with AB Sin. Most MSS. have ἵνα καυθήσωμαι. Clem. again omits the doubtful clause in *Str.* IV. P. 614 *init.* ἐὰν τὸ σῶμά μου ἐπιδῶ, φησίν, ἀγάπην δὲ μὴ ἔχω, but adds it a few lines afterwards, ἔστι καὶ ἄλλος παραδιδοὺς τὸ σῶμα ἵνα καυθήσεται.

21. **τὴν διὰ τῆς γνώσεως γεννωμένην.** See above p. 100. 9—11, and 96. 21—26.

21, 22. **πᾶσα ἡ διὰ τοῦ ἐπιστήμονος πρᾶξις εὐπραγία.** Action is good or bad as it is done through the instrumentality of a wise man or a fool. See P. 796 πᾶσα πρᾶξις γνωστικοῦ μὲν κατόρθωμα, in accordance with the Stoic doctrine ἐν πᾶσιν ἁμαρτωλὸν εἶναι τὸν ἀμαθῆ, περὶ πάντα δ' αὖ κατορθοῦν τὸν ἀστεῖον. Compare Mt. vii. 18 οὐ δύναται δένδρον ἀγαθὸν καρποὺς πονηροὺς ποιεῖν οὐδὲ δένδρον σαπρὸν καρποὺς καλοὺς ποιεῖν, and 1 Joh. v. 18, 19.

22. **εὐπραγία.** *Str.* V. P. 801 *fin.* ἡ σωτηρία διά τε εὐπραγίας διά τε γνώσεως παραγίνεται, ὧν ἀμφοῖν ὁ κύριος διδάσκαλος. H.

23. **ἔνστασις,** 'rule or fixed manner of life.' Seemingly Stoic, cf. Epictet. *Ench.* 23 ἐάν ποτέ σοι γένηται ἔξω στραφῆναι πρὸς τὸ βούλεσθαι ἀρέσαι τινί, ἴσθι ὅτι ἀπώλεσας τὴν ἔνστασιν, *Diss.* III. 22. 19, 14. 7 τῶν πραττομένων τὰ μὲν προηγουμένως πράττεται, τὰ δὲ κατὰ περίστασιν, τὰ δὲ κατ' οἰκονομίαν, τὰ δὲ κατὰ συμπεριφοράν, τὰ δὲ κατ' ἔνστασιν (Upton, n.). Also below p. 106. 3 παράγειν τῆς ἐνστάσεως, *Paed.* II. P. 190⅔ ἀκόλουθον εἶναι ταῖς ἐνστάσεσι τοῦ χριστιανοῦ δεῖ ('*Christiani hominis instituto conformem esse oportet.*' Potter). H. See also Index *s.v.* and Eus. *Pr. Ev.*

VI. 6. 49 ἀγαπητικῶς ὑπομεῖναι βασάνους δι' ἔνστασιν εὐσεβείας, Orig. Cels. II. 10 τοιαύτην ὑπομονὴν καὶ ἔνστασιν μέχρι θανάτου ἀνειληφέναι τοὺς Χριστοῦ μαθητὰς κ.τ.λ.

24. ἐπεὶ μή. The use of μή after ἐπεί and ὅτι is very common in late Greek. See Jannaris *Gr. Gr.* § 1818.

25. καταστρεφόντων. The v. means 'to turn sharp round,' 'to bring' (or 'come') 'to an end': with εἰς, or ἐπί followed by acc. or gen., 'to end in,' *e.g.* Polyb. III. 4. 1 καταστρέφειν τὴν διήγησιν ἐπὶ τὰς ῥηθείσας πράξεις, *ib.* III. 118. 10 ταύτην τὴν βίβλον ἐπὶ τούτων τῶν ἔργων καταστρέψομεν, and intransitive *ib.* IV. 2. 8 ἡ σύνταξις ἐπὶ τούτους καταστρέφει τοὺς καιρούς, Alciphron III. 70 αἱ τοιαῦται μεταβολαὶ εἰς ἀπώλειαν καταστρέφουσι. The reading of the MS. τῶν ἐπὶ ἀρετῆς καὶ ἀπὸ ἀρετῆς καταστρεφόντων probably originated in the text τῶν ἐπὶ ἀρετὴν καταστρεφόντων, corrected in margin to ἐπὶ ἀρετῆς, which would naturally be added to the text and corrected to ἀπὸ ἀρετῆς. I cannot see that the latter phrase has any meaning here.

27. οὐ μόνον, 'true not of ὁσιότης alone, but,' &c. According to the Christian conception (ἡμῖν, not the pseudo-Gnostics) the Gnostic is a Gnostic not only in this single region. H.

p. 104, line 1. παρατίθεσθαι. Plato *Leg.* v. 735 C τὰ μὲν παραδείγματος ἕνεκα μόνον ἄξια παραθέσθαι τῷ λόγῳ, *Tim.* 47 E δεῖ δὲ καὶ τὰ δι' ἀνάγκης γιγνόμενα τῷ λόγῳ παραθέσθαι.

ὕστερον ἐκθησόμεθα. The reference is to a doctrinal treatise to follow the Στρωματεῖς, which (according to Faye, p. 81) was to bear the name Διδάσκαλος. See Introduction. [In P. 516 and 520 mention is made of an intended treatise ἡ περὶ ἀρχῶν καὶ θεολογίας ἐξήγησις: in *Q.D.S.* § 26, P. 950 it is already written. Barnard.]

2. σώζοντες τὴν ἀκολουθίαν. *Str.* v. P. 550 τὴν ἀκολουθίαν σώζουσαι τοῦ νόμου πρὸς τὸ εὐαγγέλιον.

§ 60. 5. χωρῆσαι. Mt. xix. 11 οὐ πάντες χωροῦσι τοῦτον τὸν λόγον. See Index.

6. Plat. *Theaet.* 155 D μάλα γὰρ φιλόσοφον τοῦτο τὸ πάθος τὸ θαυμάζειν· οὐ γὰρ ἄλλη ἀρχὴ φιλοσοφίας ἢ αὕτη (referred to in *Strom.* II. P. 453). Hence Arist. *Met.* I. 2, § 9 (Bekk.) διὰ τὸ θαυμάζειν οἱ ἄνθρωποι καὶ τὸ νῦν καὶ τὸ πρῶτον ἤρξαντο φιλοσοφεῖν. H. Two sayings attributed to Christ are recorded in *Str.* II. P. 453, one taken from the *Gospel of the Hebrews* ὁ θαυμάσας βασιλεύσει καὶ ὁ βασιλεύσας ἀναπαήσεται, the other from the *Traditions of Matthias* θαύμασον τὰ παρόντα, cf. Resch *Agrapha* p. 378.

7. κομίζων οἴκοθεν, 'bringing from his own sources.' κομίζω seems to imply a person to whom a thing is offered, or a place to which it is brought. H. H. J. cites Plat. *Soph.* 252 C τὸ λεγόμενον οἴκοθεν τὸν πολέμιον...ἔχοντες, ἐντὸς ὑποφθεγγόμενον...περιφέροντες ἀεὶ πορεύονται.

8 foll. As wonder precedes faith, so faith knowledge. H.

9. ἐξ ὧν ἐθαύμασεν = ἐκ τοῦ θαυμάσαι. In later Greek a relative phrase is often substituted for an infinitival or participial or adverbial phrase, *e.g.* *Q.D.S.* 943 δυνάμενον καὶ καλῶς τούτοις χρῆσθαι καὶ κακῶς, ἀφ' ὧν ἂν πλῆται,

ib. 945 πτωχεύουσα ἐν ἄν τις ὑπὸ πλούτου διαφθαρῇ; above p. 72. 4 εὐχαριστῶν ἐν οἷς ἐτελεύτησεν τὴν διακονίαν, p. 130. 17 χαίρων ἐφ' οἷς ἔγνω, συστελλόμενος ἐφ' οἷς ἐπεγκυλίεται, Protr. P. 90 μιμεῖσθαί τις δυνήσεται τὸν θεὸν δι' ὧν ὁσίως θεραπεύσει, Str. IV. P. 616 δι' οὗ τεθαύμακεν κρίνεται, Herodian I. 4. 2 ἐκ γὰρ ὧν αὐτὸς διάκειμαι πρὸς ὑμᾶς, ἀμοιβαίαν εὔνοιαν εἰκότως ἤλπικα, ib. II. 10. 2 τὸ πιστὸν ὑμῶν δεδηλώκατε δι' ὧν ἀγανακτεῖτε ἐφ' οἷς οἱ κατὰ τὴν 'Ρώμην στρατιῶται ἐτόλμησαν, ib. 3 τὸ ἐλεούμενον ἐφ' οἷς ἐσφάλλετο, ib. VI. 1. 9 χάριν εἰδὼς ἐφ' οἷς ἐτιμᾶτο...αἰτιώμενον δὲ ἐφ' οἷς ὑβρίζετο, Const. Apost. VIII. 12. 17 εὐχαριστοῦντές σοι ἐφ' οἷς κατηξίωσας ἡμᾶς ἑστάναι ἐνώπιόν σου, Ign. Eph. 15 (we are the temple of God) ὅπερ φανήσεται ἐξ ὧν δικαίως ἀγαπῶμεν αὐτόν.

12. "As faith advances, a desire mingled with seeking arises." H. See above p. 102. 9 τὸ γένος τὸ ζητητικόν. Clem. held in opposition to Tertullian that the Christian must always be a seeker. Cf. Tert. de Praescr. 7 nobis curiositate opus non est post Christum Jesum; nec inquisitione post Evangelium. Cum credimus, nihil desideramus ultra credere, 14 cedat curiositas fidei; cedat gloria saluti, and the whole passage from § 7 to § 16. On the other hand Clem. says (Str. I. P. 346) τὴν ζήτησιν εἰς εὕρεσιν περαιοῖ, τὴν καινὴν ἐξελάσας φλυαρίαν, ἐγκρίνων δὲ τὴν ὀχυροῦσαν τὴν πίστιν ἡμῖν θεωρίαν: at the beginning of Bk IV. he mentions πίστις and ζήτησις as subjects of which he had yet to treat, and in Bk V. P. 646 says τὴν μὲν μετὰ πίστεως συνιοῦσαν ζήτησιν, ἐποικοδομοῦσαν τῷ θεμελίῳ τῆς πίστεως τὴν μεγαλοπρεπῆ τῆς ἀληθείας γνῶσιν, ἀρίστην ἴσμεν: see also P. 650 τὴν πίστιν τοίνυν οὐκ ἀργὴν καὶ μόνην ἀλλὰ σὺν ζητήσει δεῖν προφαίνειν φαμέν, 651 τὸ δὲ ἄρα ζητεῖν περὶ θεοῦ, ἂν μή τις εἰς ἔριν, ἀλλὰ εἰς εὕρεσιν τείνῃ, σωτήριόν ἐστι...οἱ γὰρ ζητοῦντες κατὰ τὴν ζήτησιν τὴν ἀληθῆ αἰνοῦντες κύριον ἐμπλησθήσονται...τῆς γνώσεως, P. 655 init., P. 914.

14. τοσαύτης καὶ τηλικαύτης, often combined as in Plato Symp. 177 D, Plut. Cic. 22, Pomp. 8, Isocr. V. 98, XV. 257 cited in Rost and Palm.

17. οὐσίας...καὶ τὰ πράγματα αὐτά. πράγματα as distinguished from the forms and sounds which convey them to the senses: "essences and things themselves," almost synonymous: cf. p. 106. 10 below. H. See above p. 8. 1, Exc. Theod. P. 970 οἱ πρωτόκτιστοι εἰ καὶ ἀριθμῷ διάφοροι... ἀλλ' ἡ ὁμοιότης τῶν πραγμάτων ἑνότητα ἐπιδείκνυται, P. 976 (ἡ ψυχὴ ἐκείνη) ἀξιοῦται πρόσωπον πρὸς πρόσωπον θεὸν ὁρᾶν...ἐπὶ τὴν γνῶσιν καὶ κατάληψιν τῶν πραγμάτων ἔρχεται κ.τ.λ., and Orig. in Joh. I. 9 τὰ πράγματα ὧν αἰνίγματα ἦσαν αἱ πράξεις.

19. τὰ δέοντα, 'duties.' The mental perception generates a simultaneous ethical aspiration. H.

20. ἐκλαμβάνων ὡς εἴρηται τῷ γνωστικῷ, i.e. in the spiritual sense as explained in Mt. V., perhaps also in the allegorical sense explained in Str. VI. P. 816, and below p. 186. 9 f.

§ 61. 22. There is perhaps no need for change, though πρόεισιν is better. Not two distinct stages, but the discipline and the action within the same. Cf. Strom. VIII. P. 928½ (ἐπιστήμη not of individual particulars, but resting on καθολικὰ and ὡρισμένα θεωρήματα). H.

ἐγγυμναζόμενος. Above p. 78. 4, below p. 122. 24.

23. Possibly ἐπαγωνίσασθαι, 'to contend by virtuous conduct on the base of —.' Cf. Jude 3 παρακαλῶν ἐπαγωνίζεσθαι τῇ ἅπαξ παραδοθείσῃ τοῖς ἁγίοις πίστει. H. It seems impossible to make sense of the MS. reading. The passage in Jude is usually rendered 'to contend for the faith,' as in Plut. *Mor.* 1075 D ἐπαγωνιζόμενος τῇ ἐκπυρώσει, and in Cl. P. 553 ἐπ. τῇ ἀθέῳ δόξῃ. In Plut. V. 65 C ἑτέροις ἐπαγωνίζεσθαι τεκμηρίοις, it has the same sense as in our passage.

25. κύριός ἐστιν...κύριος ἐνεργῶν. H. suggests that the second κύριος may be a corruption of κυρίως, but there seems no special reason for the latter. [Perhaps it might mean 'normally': 'though at times He may speak directly by miracle, He speaks usually by the mouth of a man.'] Or we may suppose that the second κύριος was carelessly added by the scribe from the line above. Cl. however uses similar repetition of the subject in *Paed.* I. P. 98 κεκλήσθω δ' ἡμῖν παιδαγωγός, πρακτικὸς οὐ μεθοδικὸς ὢν ὁ παιδαγωγός, ib. II. P. 166 ἡ δὲ ἐπίγειος εὐωχία δεῖπνον καλεῖται...δι' ἀγάπην μὲν γινόμενον τὸ δεῖπνον, ἀλλ' οὐκ ἀγάπη τὸ δεῖπνον. We may compare the resumptive use of ὁ δὲ in *Paed.* I. 137 ὁ κύριος οὐ διὰ μῖσος τοῖς ἀνθρώποις λοιδορεῖται οὓς ἐξὸν αὐτῷ ἀπολέσαι, ὁ δὲ ὑπὲρ ἡμῶν καὶ πέπονθεν, p. 86. 19 f. ἐν παντὶ τοίνυν τόπῳ... εὔξεται· ὁ δὲ καὶ περιπάτῳ χρώμενος...εὔχεται. The thought resembles that in Ps. xciv. 9 'He that formed the eye, shall not He see?'

28. τὸ ἡδὺ πρὸ τοῦ συμφέροντος. Above p. 86. 26, and below p. 144. 25.

p. 106, line 1. περίστασιν. Cf. below l. 28, and n. on περιστατικά p. 28. 16.

2. ἐπεὶ μηδέ. For μή following ἐπεί and ὅτι see nn. on p. 102. 24, and p. 112. 15.

3. ἐνστάσεως. See above p. 102. 23.

10. τὸ πρᾶγμα ἀφ' οὗ φέρεται τὸ φωνεῖν. If the reading is right, cf. for the use of πρᾶγμα p. 104. 17. But πνεῦμα would be more natural here, cf. *Plac. Phil.* IV. 19 Πλάτων τὴν φωνὴν ὁρίζεται πνεῦμα διὰ στόματος ἀπὸ διανοίας ἠγμένον, ib. IV. 21 οἱ Στωικοί φασιν εἶναι τῆς ψυχῆς ἀνώτατον μέρος τὸ ἡγεμονικόν...ἡ μὲν ὅρασις ἐστὶ πνεῦμα διατεῖνον ἀπὸ ἡγεμονικοῦ μέχρις ὀφθαλμῶν...τὸ δὲ 'φωνᾶεν' ὑπὸ τοῦ Ζήνωνος εἰρημένον...ἐστι πνεῦμα διατεῖνον ἀπὸ τοῦ ἡγεμονικοῦ μέχρι φάρυγγος καὶ γλώττης, Zeller[3] vol. IV. p. 198; with which agrees the language of Clem. in *Str.* VI. P. 808 διὰ τοῦ σωματικοῦ ἄρα πνεύματος αἰσθάνεται ὁ ἄνθρωπος, ἐπιθυμεῖ, ἥδεται, ὀργίζεται...καὶ δὴ πρὸς τὰς πράξεις διὰ τούτου πορεύεται τὰ κατ' ἔννοιάν τε καὶ διάνοιαν, P. 178 τὸ πνεῦμα ᾠκείωται τῇ ἀπ' αὐτοῦ φερομένῃ ψυχῇ.

12. τῶν περιστατικῶν. See n. on p. 28. 16 above.

14. κτίσεως ἀνάγκην. Cf. p. 130. 19—21 τῇ τοῦ βίου ἀνάγκῃ.

15. φάρμακον σωτηρίας. A phrase of Euripides, cf. Plato *Phaedr.* 274 σοφίας φάρμακον, Diod. I. 25 ἀθανασίας φ. of Isis; the same phrase is used of the Eucharist by Ignatius, *Eph.* XX. More frequently the gen. is used to express what is averted.

16. ἀπηνέστερον, 'reluctantly.' H. Cf. below p. 180. 9 ἀπείθεια ἀπηνής,

Odyss. XXIII. 230 νῦν δ' ἐπεὶ ἤδη σήματ' ἀριφραδέα κατέλεξας...πείθεις δή μευ θυμὸν ἀπηνέα περ μάλ' ἐόντα. The original meaning seems to be 'surly,' 'unaccommodating,' as opposed to προσηνής. It corresponds here to σκληροκάρδιος above p. 10. 13.

μεταρρυθμιζομένους. Cf. above p. 92. 9 μεταρρυθμίζει τὸν κατηχούμενον.

§ 62. 20. **τὴν ἐπὶ τὸν κτίσαντα εὐχαριστίαν.** This use of ἐπί instead of πρός is rare.

21 foll. His thanksgiving and reverence (σέβει) to the Creator leads him to a right treatment of God's creatures, his fellow man, his own body. H.

25. **ὑπερευχόμενος...διὰ τὴν ἄγνοιαν.** Cf. Lk. xxiii. 34.

27. **ἐνδεδεμένος.** Cf. above p. 68. 30 τοῦ δεσμοῦ τοῦ σαρκικοῦ, p. 54. 31 μετένδεσιν.

πρωτοπαθεῖ. Athenag. *Res.* 21. p. 64 A ἐν οἷς πρωτοπαθεῖ τὸ σῶμα καὶ τὴν ψυχὴν ἕλκει πρὸς συμπάθειαν καὶ κοινωνίαν τῶν ἐφ' ἃ δεῖται πράξεων. A medical word, denoting a primary affection, out of which a secondary arises by συμπάθεια. Cf. *Strom.* II. 498 *s.f.* Ἐπίκουρος πᾶσαν χαρὰν τῆς ψυχῆς οἴεται ἐπὶ πρωτοπαθούσῃ τῇ σαρκὶ γενέσθαι, also VI. 808½ τὸ πνεῦμα τὸ σαρκικόν...διὰ τοῦ λοιποῦ σώματος πορευόμενόν τε καὶ πρωτοπαθοῦν. H.

28. **περιστάσεις.** See above l. 1, *Q.D.S.* 957 P.

29. **τὰ οἰκεῖα...τοῖς ἀλλοτρίοις.** Cf. Epict. *Diss.* IV. 1. 77 ὃ οὐκ ἔστιν ἐπὶ σοὶ παρασκευάσαι ἢ τηρῆσαι ὅτε θέλεις, τοῦτο ἀλλότριον, *Enchir.* 14 ἐὰν θέλῃς τὰ τέκνα σου πάντοτε ζῆν, ἠλίθιος εἶ· τὰ γὰρ μὴ ἐπὶ σοὶ θέλεις ἐπὶ σοὶ εἶναι καὶ τὰ ἀλλότρια σὰ εἶναι, Lk. xvi. 12 εἰ ἐν τῷ ἀλλοτρίῳ πιστοὶ οὐκ ἐγένεσθε, τὸ ὑμέτερον τίς ὑμῖν δώσει; Cf. below p. 134. 31 μόνων τῶν ἰδίων μεμνημένος, τὰ δὲ ἐνταῦθα πάντα ἀλλότρια ἡγούμενος, where see n.

30. **συμπεριφέρεται.** Cf. above p. 92. 28—30.

p. 108, line 1. **ὑπολήψει.** Cf. Plut. *Mor.* 1121 E ὑπόληψιν ἐμποιεῖ ἀγραμμάτοις ἅτε δὴ πολυγράμματος ὤν, Herodian VII. 1. 14 εἶναι ἐν ὑπολήψει ἀγχινοίας, *ib.* VIII. 3. 5 καθεῖλον τοὺς ἐν ὑπολήψει ἀνδρείας, *ib.* 8. 4 ἔχειν ὑπολήψεις ἐμπειρίας, see Rost and Palm *s.v.*

2, 3. **ἔργῳ βεβαίῳ καὶ λόγῳ ἐνεργῷ.** The MS. has καὶ ἐνεργῷ, which suggests some such reading as βεβαίῳ κἂν λόγῳ καὶ ἐν ἔργῳ. Keeping the present reading, I suppose that ἔργῳ and ἐνεργῷ refer to ἀληθείᾳ, and βεβαίῳ and λόγῳ to γνώσει: ἐνεργῷ would then mean 'operant,' 'carried out in deed.'

4. **βιάζεται,** 'presses forward,' properly 'forces his way,' usually with εἰς, πρός, or ἐπί. Cf. Steph. 239 B. H. See below l. 8 and Index.

5. **ἐκ τοῦ δούλου εἰς φίλον,** above p. 10. 8.

7. **καθαρῶς ἐκτήσατο.** See W. Schmid *Atticismus*, vol. II. p. 119, where many exx. of its use = παντελῶς are given, as καθαρῶς ἡσυχάζουσι, Aristid. XIII. p. 261 D.

§ 63. 9. **κατεσταλμένος.** See καταστολή in Index.

15. **παραστήσαντα δυνατὸν εἶναι.** Usually π. means to 'show' in Clem., see above p. 2. 1 παραστῆσαι μόνον εἶναι θεοσεβῆ τὸν γνωστικόν, p. 4. 9, &c.,

but here and in p. 100. 11 it is perhaps better to take it as in Plut. *Mor.* 821 B ἄνθρωπον πρᾷον πίστις παρίστησιν, ib. 1057 B πρακτικὴν ὁρμὴν οὐ παρίστησι φαντασία δίχα συγκαταθέσεως.

16. τὸν κορυφαῖον βίον. Cf. above p. 98, 26.

17. τὰ τοῦ κόσμου καλὰ οὐκ ἀγαπᾷ. Cf. below p. 134, 26.

19. γνῶσις (γινώσκειν) of them has come, but not yet κατάληψις. H. Cf. 1 Cor. xiii. 12, contrast of δι' ἐσόπτρου and πρόσωπον πρὸς πρόσωπον.

21. ὡς παρὰ τοῖς φιλοσόφοις. See below p. 128. 12 f.

ἀνδρεῖοι ἐλπίδι. Arist. *Eth. Eud.* III. 1. 1229 a ᾗ λη δ' (ἀνδρεία) ἡ κατ' ἐλπίδα, ib. 1229 b ἔνιοι δὲ δι' ἄλλας ἡδονὰς ὑπομένουσιν· καὶ γὰρ ὁ θυμὸς ἡδονὴν φέρει, μετ' ἐλπίδος γάρ ἐστι τιμωρίας· ἀλλ' ὅμως οὔτ' εἰ διὰ ταύτην οὔτ' εἰ δι' ἄλλην ἡδονὴν ὑπομένει τις τὸν θάνατον ἢ φυγὴν μειζόνων λυπῶν, οὐδεὶς δικαίως ἀνδρεῖος λέγοιτ' <ἄν>, *Eth. N.* III. 7. 11 τὸ θαρρεῖν εὐέλπιδος. With this is contrasted the confidence which proceeds from knowledge. See Index under 'Courage.'

24. πεῖσμα βεβαιότατον...ἀπολήψεως. This is contrasted with the ἐλπίς of earthly pleasure. The MS. has ἐλπίδος, corrected to ἐλπίδων, before ἀπολήψεως. Dindorf omits this, possibly regarding it as a corruption of ἐλπίδα, which may have been a marginal gloss on πεῖσμα. On the other hand it would make good sense, if placed after βεβαιότατον to emphasize the superiority of knowledge to hope. In that case the superlative would seem to be used for the comparative, as often in late Greek: see Kühner *Gr. Gr.* II. p. 21 f., Hermann-Viger p. 718 f., Blass *N.T. Gr.* p. 34, W. Schmid *Att.* vol. IV. p. 62 and cf. Eus. *Pr. Ev.* VI. 6. 41 καὶ τίς ἂν τούτων γένοιτ' ἂν ἕτερος λόγος ἀσεβέστατος; below p. 118. 3 ἡ ἁγιωτάτη πάσης ἐπιστήμης ἀρετή. The lexicons give no example of the word ἀπόληψις in the sense answering to the verb ἀπολαμβάνω 'to receive one's due.' This looking forward to the future consequences of action does not seem quite consistent with p. 114. 30, and p. 116 f.

25. κολάσεων, 'persecutions,' as below p. 110. 12. H. Cf. *Polyc. Mart.* 2 fin. εἰς τὰ θηρία κριθέντες ὑπέμειναν δεινὰς κολάσεις.

27. We know that Peter was married from Matt. ix. 14 and 1 Cor. ix. 5. Cl. tells us that he and Philip had children (*Str.* III. P. 535). The story of his wife's martyrdom rests solely on the authority of this passage, and Cobet suggests that ἀγόμενον is the true reading in p. 110. 1. This would involve the transposition of ἀγόμ. τ. ἑ. θ. before θεασάμενον and indeed the recasting of the sentence. Eus. *H. E.* III. 30 quotes it, as our MS. has it.

p. 110, line 1. Cobet may have rightly divined what stood in Clement's authority. It makes good sense to suppose that the warning here addressed by Peter to his wife may have been that she should remember the Lord whenever the moment of her own death should come. H.

τὴν ἐπὶ θάνατον. See Bos, *Ellipses*, ed. Schäfer p. 188, on the omission of ὁδόν. The more common construction is with the dative which is read here in Eus, cf. Herodian p. 478 δήμιος ὁ ἀπάγων τὴν ἐπὶ θανάτῳ, Orig. *Philocal.* 1 τὴν ἐπὶ θανάτῳ κινδυνεύουσι, Eus. *H. E.* VI. 3 ἀπάγειν τὴν ἐπὶ θανάτῳ, but ib. § 4 we have τὴν ἐπὶ θάνατον ἀπάγειν, see many exx. in Heinichen's n. on H. E. VI. 5.

τῆς κλήσεως χάριν. See below p. 114. 21, and Epict. Diss. I. 29. 46—49.

2. ἐπιφωνῆσαι. Cf. Plut. V. 620 fin. ὁ δῆμος ἐπεφώνησε τὸ τοῖς γαμοῦσιν ἐπιφωνούμενον ἐξ ἔθους παλαιοῦ.

4. ὦ αὕτη. Heinichen on Eus. l.c. refers to Viger p. 448 for examples of αὕτη used in this sense without ὦ.

§ 64. 7. ἀπροσπαθῆ, a rare word: the adverb ἀπροσπαθῶς occurs in P. 570 ἀπρ. βιοῦν, P. 187 τοῖς παρατυχοῦσιν ἀπ. χρῆσθαι. The simple προσπάθεια is found in P. 880 (p. 138. 13 below) πρ. σαρκική, P. 320 μὴ προσπαθείᾳ νικᾶσθαι, P. 128 προσπ. is contrasted with ἀντιπάθεια: προσπαθῶς in P. 554 οὐ πρ. τῇ κτήσει χρώμενοι, P. 577 πρ. κεκτῆσθαι: προσπαθεῖν in Epict. Diss. II. 16. 31 ἂν τοιούτοις προσπαθῇς, ib. IV. 1. 130 ἄν τινι τούτων ὡς ἰδίων προσπαθῇς, δώσεις δίκην ὡς ἀλλοτρίων ἐφιέμενος: similarly προσπάσχω, Epict. II. 5. 9 μηδενὶ προσπάσχειν τῶν ἀλλοτρίων. Gataker on Anton. p. 421 distinguishes four degrees ἀπάθεια, προπάθεια, πάθος, προσπάθεια.

8. ἀπερίσπαστον τῆς ἀγάπης. For the gen. cf. P. 548 ἀπ. τῆς τοῦ κυρίου λειτουργίας.

12. ταῖς ἀκμαῖς. The plural is used by Hippocrates of the crisis of a disease. See L. and S.

15. περιστάσει. See above p. 106. 1.

18. γνωματεύουσα, 'measuring,' 'judging by the standard of.' So in various late writers: in Plat. Rep. VII. 516 E of discerning the shadows in the cave. H. See Ruhnken s.v. in Tim. Lex. Below p. 168. 17 the gnostic is said to be ἀκριβὴς γνώμων τῆς ἀληθείας.

19. τὰς ἀρχὰς θεόθεν ἄνωθεν. I think some such word as εἰληφυῖα has been lost. The word περιπεποιημένη is properly used of what man gains by his own effort, but hardly I think of the principles received θεόθεν ἄνωθεν.

20. πραότητα ἡδονῶν. Cf. Plut. Mor. 37 B μετὰ πολλῆς πραότητος ἅπτεσθαι τῶν περὶ τὸ σῶμα ἡδονῶν.

22. πεποιθώς. The gender shows a sudden change from the soul to the man. So again in l. 23 followed by 28. H.

25. συνηυξημένη. The dat. seems required as it is ἀρετή, not the soul, which grows up under the joint influence of φύσις (personified in Isaac), ἄσκησις (in Jacob), λόγος or μάθησις (in Abraham). See Gfrörer Philo p. 425 foll., Str. I. P. 334, and reff. to Plato in n. on p. 30. 22 above.

§ 65. p. 112, line 1. τῶν ὅσα. For the art. before relatives cf. below p. 128. 7 τοῖς ὅσοι ἄξιοι τὰ ἀγαθὰ δίδοται, p. 150. 15 f. ἀποστερεῖτε τὸ ὅσον ἐφ' ὑμῖν τοὺς καθ' ὧν εὔχεσθε, Protr. P. 60 νόμους τοὺς ὅσοι ἀληθεῖς: other exx. will be found in Jannaris Hist. Gr. § 1219. Similarly we find (below p. 196. 1) εὑρετικοὺς εἶναι τοὺς εἴ τινες ἐντύχοιεν παρασκευάζουσιν.

7, 8. τὰ θαρραλέα...τὰ φοβερά. Plato Laches 195 B οἱ δημιουργοὶ ἅπαντες τὰ ἐν ταῖς αὑτῶν τέχναις δεινά τε καὶ θαρραλέα ἴσασιν, ib. 198 δεινὰ μὲν εἶναι ἃ καὶ δέος παρέχει, θαρραλέα δὲ ἃ μὴ δέος παρέχει...δεινὰ μὲν τὰ μέλλοντα κακά φαμεν εἶναι, θαρραλέα δὲ τὰ μὴ κακὰ ἢ ἀγαθὰ μέλλοντα, Arist. *Eth. Eud.* III. 1. 22 τῷ θρασεῖ τὰ φοβερὰ θαρραλέα (δοκεῖ εἶναι).

9. **δόξης μᾶλλον ἢ ἀληθείας ἔχεται.** Cf. Plato *Rep.* II. 362 A φήσουσι τὸν ἄδικον, ἅτε ἐπιτηδεύοντα πρᾶγμα ἀληθείας ἐχόμενον καὶ οὐ πρὸς δόξαν ζῶντα, οὐ δοκεῖν ἄδικον ἀλλ' εἶναι ἐθέλειν.

11. **ἕξιν ἢ διάθεσιν.** They are distinguished also in *Str.* IV. P. 627 (the ἕξις never departs from itself) ἀποπεσοῦσα τοῦ ἕξις εἶναι· εἴτ' οὖν ἕξις ἡ γνῶσις εἴτε διάθεσις εἶναι λέγοιτο κ.τ.λ., *ib.* VI. P. 779 οἱ φιλόσοφοι τὰς ἀρετὰς ἕξεις καὶ διαθέσεις καὶ ἐπιστήμας οἴονται. The distinction is explained in Arist. *Categ.* 8. 86. 25 διαθέσεις λέγονται ἃ ἐστιν εὐκίνητα καὶ ταχὺ μεταβάλλοντα, οἷον...νόσος καὶ ὑγίεια...διαφέρει ἕξις διαθέσεως τῷ τὸ μὲν εὐκίνητον εἶναι, τὸ δὲ πολυχρονιώτερόν τε καὶ δυσκινητότερον, see Waitz's note.

ἐνάρετος, p. 16. 15, p. 114. 10.
ὑπερβάς, as before p. 98. 30. H.

12. **ἐμπαθῆ,** cf. p. 32. 16. H.

πάντα εἰς ἑαυτὸν ἀνήρτηται. Cf. Plato *Meno* 88 E τῷ ἀνθρώπῳ τὰ μὲν ἄλλα πάντα εἰς τὴν ψυχὴν ἀνηρτῆσθαι, τὰ δὲ τῆς ψυχῆς αὐτῆς εἰς φρόνησιν, *Menex.* 247 E ὅτῳ πάντα εἰς ἑαυτὸν ἀνήρτηται. For the thought see above p. 76. 19.

14. **τυχηρά.** Plut. *Mor.* 23 F τὰ τυχηρὰ τῶν ἀγαθῶν...πάντα ὅλως τὰ ἐκτός.

14, 15. **ὅτι μή.** See above p. 102. 24, p. 106. 2 ἐπεὶ μηδὲ τὸν Ἰωσὴφ παράγειν ἴσχυσεν, below p. 114. 1 ὅτι μηδεμία, *Str.* I. P. 324 ἐπεὶ μὴ ῥᾴδιος ἡ τοιάδε διακονία, P. 510 ἐπεὶ μηδὲ ταῦτα πράττειν συγχωροῦσι, P. 437 οὐ μὴν μαθήσεταί τις ἄνευ πίστεως, ἐπεὶ μηδὲ ἄνευ προλήψεως, P. 512 ἐπεὶ μὴ διακρίνει πλούσιον ἢ πένητα, P. 406 ἐπεὶ μὴ ἔστιν παῖς εὐδαίμων ποτέ, P. 551 ὅτι μή, P. 488, Jannaris *Hist. Gr.* § 1818, Winer p. 594 n., W. Schmid *Attic.* IV. p. 91. 623.

16. **ἐκ διαμέτρου.** Cf. Lucian *Cat.* 14 ἐκ διαμέτρου ἡμῖν οἱ βίοι.

17. **κατὰ ταὐτόν.** The MS. has κατὰ τὸν αὐτόν which would be merely pleonastic. Cl. evidently has in mind such passages as Plato *Rep.* IV. 436 B ταὐτὸν τἀναντία ποιεῖν ἢ πάσχειν κατὰ ταὐτόν γε καὶ πρὸς ταὐτὸν οὐκ ἐθελήσει ἅμα, where κατὰ ταὐτόν is illustrated by the top spinning round, which stands κατὰ τὸ εὐθύ but moves κατὰ τὸ περιφερές. The reasoning seems to be that as the Gnostic has all good things, he cannot have that which is diametrically opposed to them, viz. evil.

18. **ἀπαντᾶν**: used of things ('to happen'), for exx. see Schmid *Att.* II. 215, III. 232.

19. See Plato *Phileb.* 50 B ἐν τῇ τοῦ βίου ξυμπάσῃ τραγῳδίᾳ καὶ κωμῳδίᾳ λύπας ἡδοναῖς ἅμα κεράννυσθαι, Epict. *Ench.* 17 μέμνησο ὅτι ὑποκριτὴς εἶ δράματος οἵου ἂν θέλῃ ὁ διδάσκαλος...ἂν πτωχὸν ὑποκρίνασθαί σε θέλῃ, ἵνα καὶ τοῦτον εὐφυῶς ὑποκρίνῃ· ἂν χωλόν, ἂν ἄρχοντα, ἂν ἰδιώτην. σὸν γὰρ τοῦτ' ἔστι, τὸ δοθὲν ὑποκρίνασθαι πρόσωπον καλῶς· ἐκλέξασθαι δ' αὐτὸ ἄλλου. [Also *Q. D. S.* § 40 ἐπὶ τῇ καταστροφῇ τοῦ δράματος. Barnard.] Other references in Potter.

§ 66. 22. "Surely cowardice cannot arise in any way, can it, save from ignorance?, &c." A direct application of the Stoic theory that passions are nothing but wrong judgments respecting good and evil. Cf. Zeller IV. 208 foll. ἡ is sometimes found for ἄλλος (or ἄλλως) ἢ after negatives or interrogatives, specially in Xen., cf. Kühner II. 842 a. 4. H. One may compare Plato *Crito* 53 E τί ποιῶν ἢ εὐωχούμενος ἐν Θετταλίᾳ; *Protr.* P. 90 οὐ γὰρ μιμεῖσθαί τις δυνήσεται τὸν θεὸν ἢ δι' ὧν ὁσίως θεραπεύσει, and the ellipse of μᾶλλον below p. 180. 30 οὓς ἐλεήσειεν ἄν τις ἢ μισήσειεν, but the text seems to me very harsh. [Barnard would read καί for ἢ, but this hardly suits the context. It has been assumed throughout that knowledge is essential to true courage.]

25. συνεπισταμένος τούτοις. Usually this verb takes a dat. of the person, with whom knowledge is shared: here the dat. expresses things already known, to which fresh knowledge is added, the preposition having more the force of πρός. Compare the use of σύν in συγκλείω Isocr. 238 A, συγκεράννυμι Aesch. *Choeph.* 744, συγκρίνω Anthol. XII. 204. 3, συμβιβάζω Thuc. II. 29, συμπλέκω Plato *Soph.* 262 D.

28. The combination of πεφραγμένος with arms is curious: two other examples are given by Rost and Palm from Aelian and Heliodorus. H. Cf. also Soph. *Fr.* 376 ἀλλ' ἀσπιδίτην ὄντα καὶ πεφραγμένον, ὡς ἀσπιδοῦχος, ἡ Σκύθης τοξεύμασι and Plut. *Dem.* v. 12 ἄνδρα καὶ πλούτῳ...καὶ φίλοις εὖ πεφραγμένον, Herodian III. 4. 8 πανοπλίᾳ φράσσοντες αὑτούς, ib. II. 6. 13 ἀναλαβόντες τὰς πανοπλίας καὶ φράξαντες αὑτούς, ib. III. 4. 8, VII. 11. 7.

ταύτην. No other example known of καταπολεμεῖν with genitive: but the sense is probably different: with accusative 'to war down,' with genitive 'to war against.' H.

29.—p. 114, line 6. The sentence οὐ γὰρ εἰ...φερόμενα has nothing to do with this context; while that which follows (οὐδεὶς οὖν ἀλόγως κ.τ.λ.) is naturally connected with the sentence preceding.

p. 114, line 4. κακή. The MS. κακία contradicts the statement in l. 2 that no ἐνέργεια is a ἕξις, for πρᾶξις is an ἐνέργεια and κακία a ἕξις.

5. ἁμαρτήματα, opposed to κατορθώματα. The passage is probably chiefly Stoic. H.

ἀπὸ κακίας φερόμενα. See above p. 106. 10 and P. 178 quoted in the n.

6. ἀλόγως ἀνδρεῖος. See above § 59, p. 102. 16. Potter cites Plato *Laches* 197 A οὐ γάρ τι ἔγωγε ἀνδρεῖα καλῶ οὔτε θηρία οὔτε ἄλλο οὐδὲν τὸ τὰ δεινὰ ὑπὸ ἀνοίας μὴ φοβούμενον, ἀλλὰ ἄφοβον καὶ μωρόν· ἢ καὶ τὰ παιδία πάντα οἴει με ἀνδρεῖα καλεῖν, ἃ δι' ἄνοιαν οὐδὲν δέδοικεν;...ἐγὼ δὲ ἀνδρείας μὲν καὶ προμηθείας πάνυ τισὶν ὀλίγοις οἶμαι μετεῖναι· θρασύτητος δὲ καὶ τόλμης καὶ τοῦ ἀφόβου μετὰ ἀπρομηθείας πάνυ πολλοῖς καὶ ἀνδρῶν καὶ γυναικῶν καὶ παίδων καὶ θηρίων, Arist. *Eth. Eud.* III. 1. 10 ἡ γὰρ ἀνδρεία ἀκολούθησις τῷ λόγῳ ἐστίν, ὁ δὲ λόγος τὸ καλὸν αἱρεῖσθαι κελεύει and ib. 13 foll. on the spurious kinds of courage, μία μὲν πολιτική· αὕτη δ' ἐστὶν ἡ δι' αἰδῶ οὖσα. δευτέρα ἡ στρατιωτική· αὕτη δὲ δι' ἐμπειρίαν...τρίτη δ' ἡ δι' ἀπειρίαν καὶ ἄγνοιαν δι' ἣν

τὰ παιδία καὶ οἱ μαινόμενοι, οἱ μὲν ὑπομένουσι τὰ φερόμενα, οἱ δὲ λαμβάνουσι τὰς ὄψεις. ἄλλη δ' ἡ κατ' ἐλπίδα...ἄλλη δὲ διὰ πάθος ἀλόγιστον, also *Eth. N.* III. 8.

12. **εἰς τὰς μαχαίρας κυβιστῶντας.** Cf. Xen. *Mem.* I. 3. 9 οὐ σὺ Κριτόβουλον ἐνόμιζες εἶναι τῶν σωφρονικῶν ἀνθρώπων μᾶλλον ἢ τῶν θρασέων;... νῦν τοίνυν νόμιζε αὐτὸν θερμουργότατον εἶναι καὶ λεωργότατον· οὗτος κἂν εἰς μαχαίρας κυβιστήσειε, κἂν εἰς πῦρ ἅλοιτο, Xen. *Symp.* II. 11, Plato *Euthyd.* 294.

ἐξ ἐμπειρίας. *Eth. N.* III. 8. 6 δοκεῖ δὲ καὶ ἡ ἐμπειρία ἡ περὶ ἕκαστα ἀνδρεία τις εἶναι, ὅθεν καὶ Σωκράτης ᾠήθη ἐπιστήμην εἶναι τὴν ἀνδρείαν.

κακοτεχνοῦντες. The word is used of sculpture *Protr.* P. 41, 51, of music P. 195, of rhetoric P. 339, cf. Lightfoot's n. on Ign. *Polyc.* 5 τὰς κακοτεχνίας φεῦγε, where he explains it of heretics.

13. **λυπρῷ,** 'wretched' in both senses: used of unproductive regions, scanty food, &c. H. Cf. Diog. L. X. 4 γράμματα διδάσκειν λυπροῦ τινος μισθαρίου.

14. **διὰ ζῆλον.** So Clem. Rom. I. 5 makes ζῆλος ('envy') the cause of persecution generally, and of the deaths of St Peter and St Paul. It seems difficult to introduce the idea of envy here. Perhaps we should translate 'fury' (cf. ζέω), or possibly unpopularity (*invidia*).

16. **λεγομένων μαρτύρων.** Cf. *Str.* IV. P. 571 λέγομεν δὲ καὶ ἡμεῖς τοὺς ἐπιπηδήσαντας τῷ θανάτῳ (εἰσὶ γάρ τινες οὐχ ἡμέτεροι, μόνον τοῦ ὀνόματος κοινωνοί, οἱ δὴ αὑτοὺς παραδιδόντες σπεύδουσι, τῇ πρὸς τὸν δημιουργὸν ἀπεχθείᾳ, οἱ ἄθλιοι, θανατῶντες), τούτους ἐξάγειν ἑαυτοὺς ἀμαρτύρως λέγομεν, κἂν δημοσίᾳ κολάζωνται. οὐ γὰρ τὸν χαρακτῆρα σώζουσι τοῦ μαρτυρίου τοῦ πιστοῦ, τὸν ὄντως θεὸν μὴ γνωρίσαντες, θανάτῳ δὲ ἑαυτοὺς ἐπιδιδόασι κενῷ, and P. 597.

17. **παρέχουσιν...ἐπιρριπτοῦντες.** Possibly the two participles of the MS. are right, the second clause alone having a verb by inadvertence through its length. If not, it seems better to alter παρέχοντες. ἐπιρριπτεῖν is once used intransitively by Xen., but Clement has it transitive *Paed.* II. P. 171½. H.

18. **οὐκ οἶδ' ὅπως,** a polite way of avoiding an offensive term, such as θρασύτερον, see passages quoted above on l. 16, also Plat. *Rep.* III. 400 B οὐκ οἶδα ὅπως διακοσμοῦντος, *Phaedr.* 265 B οὐκ οἶδ' ὅπῃ τὸ ἐρωτικὸν πάθος ἀπεικάζοντες, Luc. *Timon* 20 πεμφθεὶς ὑπὸ Διὸς οὐκ οἶδ' ὅπως, βραδύς εἰμι, and compare Beier's n. on Cic. *Off.* I. § 146 where he explains *nescio quomodo* as expressing 'quae odiosa aut molesta sunt...ut vere id valeat quod *secius quam fieri debet, temere, inconsulto*.'

εὐστομέω, usually 'to utter pleasant sounds': but also = εὐφημέω (Hesych.). Cf. Aristid. XL. p. 754 τοὺς μὲν παῖδας κελεύομεν εὐστομεῖν, κἂν τοῖς διδασκαλείοις καὶ κατ' οἰκίαν προδιδάσκοντες ὡς ἃ ποιεῖν αἰσχρὸν οὐδὲ λέγειν καλόν. H. Arist. *Nub.* 833 εὐστόμει καὶ μηδὲν εἴπῃς φλαῦρον ἄνδρας δεξιούς.

19. **περιστελλόμενοι.** The same word is used of avoiding persecution in IV. 597 *fin.* where Bywater reads ὑποστελλόμενος. It is there followed by the acc. τὸν διωγμόν, meaning 'keep out of the way of,' 'conceal oneself

from.' Not noticed in lexica. H. I take it here of 'guarding oneself from danger,' cf. the construction of φυλάττομαι.

21. τὴν κλῆσιν...βεβαιοῦσιν. Cf. 2 Pet. i. 10 σπουδάσατε βεβαίαν ὑμῶν τὴν κλῆσιν...ποιεῖσθαι. Here κλ. seems to have the same force as in p. 110. 1 and below l. 28, but in l. 27 the more general sense seems required.

22. τὸν ἄνδρα, the man within them, shown in ἀνδρεία. On the passion for martyrdom see IV. 597 foll. H.

§ 67. 24. φόβῳ τῶν μειζόνων δεινῶν. Cf. Pl. Phaedo 68 D οὐκοῦν φόβῳ μειζόνων κακῶν ὑπομένουσιν αὐτῶν οἱ ἀνδρεῖοι τὸν θάνατον, ὅταν ὑπομένωσι; Ar. Eth. N. III. 8.

25. ψόγον—ὑφορώμενοι, cf. Eth. N. III. 8.

30. ἆθλα τῶν πόνων. So Pindar Nem. IV. 1 ἄριστος εὐφροσύνα πόνων κεκριμένων ἰατρός. The view here taken seems hardly consistent with p. 108. 22, above.

31. εὐλαβείᾳ κολάσεως. So Plato Legg. VII. 815 A εὐλ. πληγῶν. For the thought Lowth compares Str. IV. P. 629.

ἄλλης. Other than that inflicted by the heathen. H.

p. 116, line 1. διά τινας ἡδονάς. Cf. Str. IV. P. 625 fin.

3. ἄνδρες. Cf. ἀπηνδρωμένος p. 154. 15 below, Str. L. P. 320 οὐδὲ ἀντιμισθίας ἐφίεσθαι χρὴ τῷ εἰς ἄνδρας ἐγγραφομένῳ, and Eph. iv. 13, 14.

4. εἰσὶ γάρ, εἰσί. For examples of emphatic repetition (epanadiplosis) cf. Protr. P. 4 fin. ἦμεν γάρ, ἠμέν ποτε καὶ ἡμεῖς ἀνόητοι, P. 52 ἡμεῖς γάρ, ἡμεῖς ἐσμὲν οἱ τὴν εἰκόνα τοῦ θεοῦ περιφέροντες, P. 75 μὴ δῆτα οὖν, μὴ δῆτα ἐξανδραποδισθῶμεν, P. 88 ἀφέλωμεν οὖν, ἀφέλωμεν τὴν λήθην τῆς ἀληθείας, P. 91 φύγωμεν οὖν τὴν συνήθειαν, φύγωμεν...φεύγωμεν, ὦ συνναῦται, φεύγωμεν τὸ κῦμα τοῦτο, P. 93 ἐθέλω γάρ, ἐθέλω καὶ ταύτης ὑμῖν μεταδοῦναι τῆς χάριτος, ib. σπεύσωμεν, δράμωμεν, ὦ θεοφιλῆ τοῦ λόγου ἀγάλματα, σπεύσωμεν, δράμωμεν, P. 94 ἡμᾶς γάρ, ἡμᾶς εἰσπεποίηται.

4, 5. καθάπερ ἐν τοῖς ἀγῶσι...οὕτως δὲ καὶ κατὰ τὴν ἐκκλησίαν. For δὲ in apodosi after a comparative protasis cf. Xen. Cyr. VIII. 5. 12 ἐκάθευδον ὥσπερ οἱ ὁπλῖται οὕτω δὲ καὶ οἱ πελτασταί, cited by Jelf Gr. § 770, and n. below on p. 164. 21—23.

6. στέφανοι παίδων. Puerorum certamina ab Eleis olymp. 37 primum instituta fuisse refert Pausanias, v. 8. 9. (Potter.)

7—9. τῷ γνωστικῷ...ἡ τελειότης...αὔξεται μελετήσαντος. It would seem that we ought to read either τοῦ γνωστικοῦ or μελετήσαντι. Possibly the latter may have been changed to suit the preceding βίου. We meet however with curious specimens of anacoluthon in Clement in connexion with the use of the gen. abs. The Guardians in Plato's Republic are an instance of knowledge based on discipline.

10. πεποιθότα ἐπὶ κύριον. The dat. by itself is the classical construction after πέποιθα or πιστεύω, but we find πεποιθότας ἐφ' ἑαυτοῖς Luke xviii. 9, πιστεύειν ἐπὶ πᾶσιν Luke xxiv. 25, and again πιστ. ἐπ' αὐτόν Mt. xxvii. 42, Acts ix. 42. See Winer tr. p. 292 and Jannaris § 1583 for exx. of the tendency to substitute the acc. for dat. after ἐπί.

11. **ἀλείφουσα.** Cf. *Str.* II. P. 484 ὁ θεῖος νόμος ἀλείφει τὸν ἄνθρωπον ἐπὶ τὴν ἐγκράτειαν. See Index.

14. **ἔσται ὑμῶν τὸ ναὶ ναὶ καὶ τὸ οὒ οὔ.** This is nearer to James v. 12 ἤτω δὲ ὑμῶν τὸ ναὶ ναὶ κ.τ.λ. than to Mt. v. 37 ἔσται δὲ ὁ λόγος ὑμῶν ναὶ ναί, οὒ οὔ, see Barnard *C.'s Bibl. Text* p. 7.

16. **διὰ φιλοτιμίαν,** sc. σωφρονοῦσι, suggested by προσποιοῦνται σωφρονεῖν.

καθάπερ οἱ ἀθληταί. Cf. *Str.* III. P. 534.

17. **διὰ φιλοχρηματίαν.** Cf. Plato's picture of the Oligarchical Man, *Rep.* VIII. 553 f. and *Phaedo* 82 c.

20. **δι' ἀγροικίαν.** Arist. *Eth. N.* II. 2. 7 ὁ πάσας φεύγων τὰς ἡδονάς, ὥσπερ οἱ ἀγροῖκοι, ἀναίσθητός τις.

23. **καταγνύουσι τὸ ἀκαμπές.** Cf. Xen. *Oec.* VI. 5 αἱ βαναυσικαὶ τέχναι τὰς ψυχὰς καταγνύουσι. The passive seems more appropriate here, as in Plat. *Prot.* 342 B οἱ μὲν ὦτα κατάγνυνται.

25. **καιρὸν λαβόντες.** It seems necessary to correct the gen. of the MS., as there is no instance of such a construction after the Active voice, and the sense is opposed to the Middle here.

παρακλέπτουσι τὸν νόμον. Cf. below p. 186. 9 κλέπτειν τὸν κανόνα τῆς ἐκκλησίας.

p. 118, line 1. **ἄτεγκτον.** See below p. 130. 6 ἄτεγκτος ἡδοναῖς.

2. **τὸν ἀδάμαντα τῷ πυρί.** *Clemens* (*Str.* VIII. P. 931) *exemplo ostendens nullam causam nisi in idoneam materiam agere posse, ait, καθάπερ τὸ πῦρ τῷ ξύλῳ· τὸν ἀδάμαντα γὰρ οὐ καύσει. Plinius H. N.* XXXVII. 4 *de certis adamantium generibus scribit,* 'Incudibus hi deprehenduntur ita respuentes ictum, ut ferrum utrimque dissultet, incudesque ipsae dissiliant. Quippe duritia inenarrabilis est, simulque ignium victrix natura, et numquam incalescens.* (Potter.) Dr Gifford adds a reference to Theophr. *Fr.* II. 19.

§ 68. 3, 4. **κυριωτάτη ἐπιστήμης.** The reference is apparently to 1 Cor. xiii. 8—10, so that the superlative must be used with the comparative force. See Blass *N. T. Gr.* p. 33 'The absorption of the category of duality into that of plurality occasioned also the disappearance from the vulgar language of one of the two degrees of comparison,' usually the superlative as in *Protr.* P. 53 τὸ καινότερον, πρὸ τῆς συμπλοκῆς αἱ ὄψεις μεμοιχεύκασιν, but sometimes the comparative, as in πρῶτος for πρότερος as Joh. i. 15 πρῶτός μου, *Paed.* II. P. 166 οἱ ταῖς εὐτελεστάταις χρώμενοι τροφαῖς ἰσχυρότατοί εἰσι καὶ ὑγιεινότατοι καὶ γενναιότατοι, ὡς οἰκέται δεσποτῶν...καὶ οὐ μόνον ῥωμαλεώτεροι, cf. above n. on p. 108. 24 βεβαιότατον ἐλπίδος, Jacobs on Ael. *Anim.* I. c. 44, W. Schmid *Attic.* IV. 62. Or it might be possible to explain the genitive as depending on the meaning of the word κύριος, 'love which, beyond all other things, commands knowledge.'

5. **τῷ ἑνὶ χαρακτηρίζεται.** Cf. *Paed.* I. P. 136 τὰ τοῖς ἴσοις χαρακτηριζόμενα, and below p. 190 l. 8 f. ἡ ἐξοχὴ τῆς ἐκκλησίας κατὰ τὴν μονάδα ἐστίν. Love unites man to God and to his fellows and brings about an inner peace

and harmony in himself : cf. Plato's praise of Justice as that which gives unity to his Republic.

8. Apparently a Stoic definition of ὁμόνοια. Clement then translates the Stoic ταὐτό into his own τὸ ἕν. H. Cf. Epict. *Diss.* IV. 5. 35 ταῦτα τὰ δόγματα ἐν οἰκίᾳ φιλίαν ποιεῖ, ἐν πόλει ὁμόνοιαν, below p. 132. 21—27.

11. God's unity being His perfection (line 5), he who loves Him becomes perfect by that unity. H. Cf. below p. 188. 23 f.

15. κορυφαιοτάτην προκοπήν. Cf. p. 98. 24 f. διαβιβάζει τὰς προκοπὰς τὰς μυστικὰς τὸν ἄνθρωπον ἄχρις ἂν εἰς τὸν κορυφαῖον ἀποκαταστήσῃ τῆς ἀναπαύσεως τόπον.

19. πρὸς τὸ συγγενές. Cf. p. 98. 23 above, εἰς τὸ συγγενὲς τῆς ψυχῆς θεῖόν τε καὶ ἅγιον μετοικίζει.

20. μένει εἰς τὴν ἀνάπαυσιν. In P. 636 Clem. seems to identify the highest ἀνάπαυσις with the 7th heaven. In P. 866 (p. 98. 22 f.) he speaks of γνῶσις as transplanting man to that holy and divine state which is cognate to the soul, and restoring him at length to that highest ἀνάπαυσις where he sees God face to face. In P. 866 (above p. 100. 13 f.) the gnostic, after reaching the final ascent in the flesh, is said to press on through the Hebdomad into the Father's house, there to remain a light standing for ever. In P. 794 he speaks of those who shall rest in God's Holy Hill, the Church above, those who are not content to remain in the Hebdomad of ἀνάπαυσις but have attained εἰς ὀγδοαδικῆς εὐεργεσίας κληρονομίαν ὑπερκύψαντες, ἀκορέστου θεωρίας εἰλικρινεῖ ἐποπτείᾳ προσανέχοντες. Should εἰς here be taken as equal ἐν, as in p. 32. 22 παγκρατιάζουσιν εἰς τὸ στάδιον ? Naturally we should translate it 'abides until,' but that hardly seems the sense required. Is not the soul which is 'all spiritual' already in the ἀνάπαυσις ? Or if ἀνάπαυσις denotes a higher stage of glory, should we not rather have μένει τὴν ἀν. 'awaits the rest' ? See nn. on p. 98. 26, p. 100. 15, 16.

§ 69. 22. πρὸς τοὺς πέλας. The MS. has πρός τε τοὺς π. where τε was inserted under the idea that the phrase was subordinate to ἔχων like πρὸς τὸ σῶμα, whereas it depends on ἴσος καὶ ὅμοιος.

27. βιωτικαῖς χρείαις. Cf. 1 Cor. vi. 3, 4.

p. 120, line 2. πρὸς δέ. See Index *s.v.*

3. εἰ τούτου δέοιτο, sc. τοῦ δοῦναι.

4. Either αὐτόν or αὐτὸν αὐτῷ is indispensable. H. [Here H. ends.]

6. ἀφιλάργυροι. Seems to be only found elsewhere in 1 Tim. iii. 3 and Heb. xiii. 5.

ἀμνησιπόνηροι. This ἅπαξ λεγόμενον is an emendation by Lowth (in the incorrect form ἀμνησοπόνηροι, if we are to trust Potter's n.) for the MS. μισοπόνηροι. A similar emendation μνησιπονηρεῖ for μισοπονηρεῖ had been made by Sylburg in *Str.* II. P. 475 τοῖς γε κακῶς πεποιηκόσιν οὐ μνησιπονηρεῖ. Elsewhere Cl. uses the equivalent ἀμνησίκακος (below p. 148. 11), ἀμνησικακία (pp. 150. 12, 152. 8) and ἀμνησικακέω (p. 154. 22).

8, 9. ὅτῳ ἄν τις καὶ ὁπόσον καὶ ὁπότε καὶ ὅπως ἐπιδῴη. Cf. Arist. *Eth. N.* IV. 1. 12 ὁ ἐλευθέριος δώσει οἷς δεῖ καὶ ὅσα καὶ ὅτε καὶ τἆλλα ὅσα ἕπεται τῇ ὀρθῇ δόσει, καὶ ταῦτα ἡδέως ἢ ἀλύπως. The MS. has the subj. ἐπιδῷ for which I have written ἐπιδῴη (on this form see Veitch p. 167 f., Blass *N. T. Gr.* § 23. 4 and Jannaris § 996. 51), as the meaning requires ἄν with the opt.; or (omitting ἄν) we might take ἐπιδῷ as deliberative.

11. μή τι. See below n. on p. 152. 20.

13. πάντων γὰρ κτίστης. The fact of creation is alleged in proof of the Divine goodness in Wisdom xi. 25 f. ἀγαπᾷς γὰρ τὰ ὄντα πάντα καὶ οὐδὲν βδελύσσῃ ὧν ἐποίησας· οὐδὲ γὰρ ἂν μισῶν τι κατεσκεύασας· φείδῃ δὲ πάντων ὅτι σά ἐστι πάντα, δέσποτα φιλόψυχε, a passage referred to in *Paed.* I. P. 135 where Cl. continues οὐ γὰρ δήπου μισεῖ μέν τι, βούλεται δὲ αὐτὸ εἶναι ὃ μισεῖ, οὐδὲ βούλεται μέν τι μὴ εἶναι, αἴτιος δὲ γίνεται τοῦ εἶναι αὐτὸ ὃ βούλεται μὴ εἶναι, οὐδὲ μὴν οὐ βούλεται μέν τι [μὴ] εἶναι, τὸ δὲ ἔστιν. εἴ τι ἄρα μισεῖ ὁ λόγος, βούλεται αὐτὸ μὴ εἶναι· οὐδὲν δέ ἐστιν ᾧ (MS. οἱ) μὴ τὴν αἰτίαν τοῦ εἶναι ὁ θεὸς παρέχεται· οὐδὲν ἄρα μισεῖται ὑπὸ τοῦ θεοῦ·...εἰ δὲ οὐ μισεῖ τῶν ὑπ' αὐτοῦ γενομένων οὐδέν, λείπεται φιλεῖν αὐτά.

14. ὃ μὴ θέλει. One is tempted to read φιλεῖ, but in later Greek we find θέλω used transitively in the sense of 'desire' or 'love,' see Lightfoot on Ign. *Rom.* VIII. (p. 220) θελήσατε ἵνα καὶ θεληθῆτε, where he cites Athan. *c. Arian.* III. 66 ὁ υἱὸς τῇ θελήσει ᾗ θέλεται παρὰ τοῦ πατρὸς ταύτῃ καὶ αὐτὸς ἀγαπᾷ καὶ θέλει καὶ τιμᾷ τὸν πατέρα. It is common in the LXX, as in Ps. xviii. 19 ῥύσεταί με ὅτι ἠθέλησέ με, Ps. xxii. 8 ῥυσάσθω αὐτόν, ὅτι θέλει αὐτόν, Ps. xxxiv. 12 τίς ἐστιν ἄνθρωπος ὁ θέλων ζωήν; Ps. xli. 11 ἐν τούτῳ ἔγνων ὅτι τεθέληκάς με, see too Hos. vi. 7 ἔλεος θέλω ἢ θυσίαν, 1 Sam. xviii. 22 θέλει ἐν σοὶ ὁ βασιλεύς ('the king hath delight in thee'), 2 Sam. xv. 26, 1 Kings x. 9, Col. ii. 18 θέλων ἐν ταπεινοφροσύνῃ.

16. οἷον τοὺς διεχθρεύοντας αὐτοῦ τῇ διαθήκῃ. I am disposed to omit τούς. Without it, διεχθρ. will give a reason for speaking of τοὺς ἀπειθεῖς as ἐχθρούς, whereas it is difficult to think of a definite class who could be described as τοὺς δ. τ. δ. If there were a reference to the backsliding Israelites we should have expected the past participle. διεχθρεύομαι is used below (p. 148. 27) with the same force. See Index.

20. ἄλλως τε seems to be used in the sense of *atque etiam*, see Luc. *Dial. Mort.* xv. 3 ἄλλως τε ὁρᾷς ὅσοι ἐσμέν, Hermann-Viger p. 781, Klotz-Devar II. 83—91. Cl. here reverts to the subject of discrimination in giving. In l. 9 foll. it was maintained that such discrimination could give no ground for offence: here it is asserted to be a higher kind of justice than that simple readiness to share alike with others which Carpocrates called justice (see *Str.* III. P. 512 *init.* τὴν δικαιοσύνην τοῦ θεοῦ κοινωνίαν μετὰ ἰσότητος), carrying it to the extreme of communism. μεταδοτική agrees with what is said of the Gnostic above § 19. The distinguishing of less or more is shown in Aristotle's *distributive*, as compared with *corrective* justice.

22. ἀλλά introduces the apodosis after the conditional clause, as ἀτάρ does in *Protr.* P. 12 θηρεύουσι γάρ, εἰ καὶ ἄλλοι τινές, ἀτὰρ δὴ καὶ οἱ μῦθοι κ.τ.λ., cf. Rom. vi. 5 εἰ γὰρ σύμφυτοι γεγόναμεν τῷ ὁμοιώματι τοῦ θανάτου αὐτοῦ, ἀλλὰ καὶ τῆς ἀναστάσεως ἐσόμεθα, above p. 70. 6 εἰ δέ τινες καὶ ὥρας

τακτὰς ἀπονέμουσιν εὐχῇ, ἀλλ' οὖν γε ὁ γνωστικὸς παρὰ ὅλον εὔχεται τὸν βίον. See Klotz-Devar II. 93.

25. κατὰ ἰδιωτισμόν. Cf. Orig. *de Orat.* 23 διὰ τὸν ἰδιωτισμὸν μικρῷ καὶ βραχεῖ τόπῳ ἐμπεριλαμβάνουσι τὸν ἐπὶ πάντων θεόν, Epict. *Ench.* 33. 15 ἀπίστῳ δὲ τὸ γέλωτα κινεῖν· ὀλισθηρὸς γὰρ ὁ τρόπος εἰς ἰδιωτισμόν, *ib.* 6 (if you accept an invitation to dine) ἐντετάσθω σοι ἡ προσοχή, μήποτε ἄρα ὑπορρυῇς εἰς ἰδιωτισμόν. Potter also refers to *Ench.* 48. 1 ἰδιώτου στάσις καὶ χαρακτήρ· οὐδέποτε ἐξ ἑαυτοῦ προσδοκᾷ ὠφέλειαν ἢ βλάβην, ἀλλ' ἀπὸ τῶν ἔξω. φιλοσόφου στάσις καὶ χαρακτήρ· πᾶσαν ὠφέλειαν καὶ βλάβην ἐξ ἑαυτοῦ προσδοκᾷ.

26. ἐν τοῖς ἔθνεσιν. The question of right action springing from inferior motives is also treated of in pp. 108. 20 f., 114. 30, 116. 15 f., 128. 12 f. Cf. Plato *Phaedo* 68 D εἰ γὰρ ἐθέλεις ἐννοῆσαι τήν γε τῶν ἄλλων ἀνδρείαν τε καὶ σωφροσύνην, δόξει σοι εἶναι ἄτοπος...οὐκοῦν φόβῳ μειζόνων κακῶν ὑπομένουσιν αὐτῶν οἱ ἀνδρεῖοι τὸν θάνατον;...τῷ δεδιέναι ἄρα καὶ δέει ἀνδρεῖοί εἰσι πάντες πλὴν οἱ φιλόσοφοι...τί δέ; οἱ κόσμιοι αὐτῶν οὐ ταὐτὸν τοῦτο πεπόνθασιν; ἀκολασίᾳ τινὶ σώφρονές εἰσι;...φοβούμενοι γὰρ ἑτέρων ἡδονῶν στερηθῆναι...ἄλλων ἀπέχονται ὑπ' ἄλλων κρατούμενοι...μὴ γὰρ σκιαγραφία τις ᾖ ἡ τοιαύτη ἀρετὴ καὶ τῷ ὄντι ἀνδραποδώδης, *ib.* 82 c on the virtue of the φιλοχρήματοι and φιλότιμοι.

27. τυχεῖν ἂν ἐρᾷ τις. A quotation from Theognis 256 πρῆγμα δὲ τερπνότατον, τοῦ τις ἐρᾷ, τὸ τυχεῖν (Bergk). It appears in different forms in Arist. *Eth. N.* I. 8. 14 ἥδιστον δὲ πέφυχ' οὗ τις ἐρᾷ τὸ τυχεῖν and *Eth. Eud.* I. 1, p. 1214 a πάντων ἥδιστον κ.τ.λ.

29. κἂν τῇ πίστει = ἐν τοῖς πιστοῖς opposed to ἐν τοῖς ἔθνεσιν, l. 26. Cf. *Str.* II. P. 450 ἔδωκεν ἄλλην ἔτι τοῖς κἂν τῇ πίστει περιπίπτουσί τινι πλημμελήματι, Tit. iii. 15 ἄσπασαι τοὺς φιλοῦντας ἡμᾶς ἐν πίστει, Acts xiii. 8 διαστρέψαι τὸν ἀνθύπατον ἀπὸ τῆς πίστεως.

29, 30. ἢ δι' ἐπαγγελίαν ἢ διὰ φόβον. See above p. 114. 31 f. The difference of motive distinguishes the Gnostic from the ordinary Christian, cf. *Str.* IV. P. 625 ἔργον (τοῦ γνωστικοῦ) οὐχ ἡ ἀποχὴ τῶν κακῶν (ἐπιβάθρα γὰρ αὕτη προκοπῆς μεγίστης), οὐδὲ μὴν ποιεῖν τι ἀγαθὸν ἤτοι διὰ φόβον...ἀλλ' οὐδὲ δι' ἐλπίδα τιμῆς ἐπηγγελμένης...μόνη δ' ἡ δι' ἀγάπην εὐποιία, ἡ δι' αὐτὸ τὸ καλόν, αἱρετὴ τῷ γνωστικῷ, also *Str.* III. P. 537, 538.

§ 70. p. 122, line 6. **κατ' ἐπακολούθημα.** Cf. *Str.* I. P. 331 πάντων μὲν αἴτιος τῶν καλῶν ὁ θεός, ἀλλὰ τῶν μὲν κατὰ προηγούμενον, ὡς τῆς διαθήκης... τῶν δὲ κατ' ἐπακολούθημα, ὡς τῆς φιλοσοφίας, *Str.* VIII. P. 927 *fin.* τὰ ὀνόματα σύμβολά ἐστι τῶν νοημάτων κατὰ τὸ προηγούμενον, κατ' ἐπακολούθημα δὲ καὶ τῶν ὑποκειμένων 'primarily of concepts, incidentally of things,' below p. 124. 16, *Str.* VI. P. 789 τελειώτατον ἀγαθὸν ἡ γνῶσις δι' αὑτὴν οὖσα αἱρετή, κατ' ἐπακολούθημα δὲ καὶ τὰ διὰ ταύτης ἀκολουθοῦντα καλά, *Str.* II. P. 434 *init.* φασὶν ἐκλογὴν οἰκείαν εἶναι καθ' ἕκαστον διάστημα, κατ' ἐπακολούθημα δ' αὖ τῆς ἐκλογῆς τὴν κοσμικὴν συνέπεσθαι πίστιν, Sext. Emp. *Math.* VII. 34 πολλαχῶς λεγομένου τοῦ κριτηρίου πρόκειται τὸ σκέπτεσθαι προηγουμένως μὲν περὶ τοῦ λογικοῦ, κατ' ἐπακ. δὲ καὶ περὶ ἑκάστου τῶν κατὰ τὸν βίον, Anton.

III. 2 τὰ ἐπιγινόμενα τοῖς φύσει γινομένοις ἔχει τι εὔχαρι...ὥστε, εἴ τις ἔχει ἔννοιαν βαθυτέραν, σχεδὸν οὐδὲν οὐχὶ δόξει αὐτῷ καὶ τῶν κατ' ἐπακολούθησιν συμβαινόντων ἡδέως πως συνίστασθαι, ib. VI. 36 πάντα ἐκεῖθεν (ἐκ τοῦ κόσμου) ἔρχεται, ἀπ' ἐκείνου τοῦ κοινοῦ ἡγεμονικοῦ ὁρμήσαντα ἢ κατ' ἐπακολούθησιν, ib. 44 (if the gods) μὴ ἐβουλεύσαντο κατ' ἰδίαν περὶ ἐμοῦ, περί γε τῶν κοινῶν πάντως ἐβουλεύσαντο, οἷς κατ' ἐπακολούθησιν καὶ ταῦτα συμβαίνοντα στέργειν ὀφείλω, ib. VII. 76, ib. IX. 28 ἤτοι ἐφ' ἕκαστον ὁρμᾷ ἡ τοῦ ὅλου διάνοια...ἢ ἅπαξ ὥρμησε, τὰ δὲ λοιπὰ κατ' ἐπακολούθησιν. In his note on III. 2 Gataker quotes Max. Tyr. XXV. ἐν ταῖς τῶν τεχνῶν χειρουργίαις τὰ μὲν ἡ τέχνη προηγουμένως δρᾷ, στοχαζομένη τοῦ τέλους, τὰ δὲ ἕπεται τῇ χειρουργίᾳ, οὐ τέχνης ἔργα, ἀλλ' ὕλης πάθη, σπινθῆρες...καὶ ἄλλο τι ἀναγκαῖον μὲν τῇ ἐργασίᾳ, οὐ προηγούμενον δὲ τῷ τεχνίτῃ, Philo de Prov. (ap. Eus. Pr. Ev. VIII. 14) αἱ τῶν στοιχείων μεταβολαὶ ταῦτα γεννῶσιν (storms, &c.), οὐ προηγούμενα ἔργα φύσεως ἀλλ' ἑπόμενα τοῖς ἀναγκαίοις καὶ τοῖς προηγουμένοις ἐπακολουθοῦντα, ib. τὸ πῦρ φύσεως ἀναγκαιότατον ἔργον, ἐπακολούθημα δὲ τούτου καπνός, ib. (the rainbow, &c.) τῶν ἐγκρινομένων τοῖς νέφεσιν ἐπακολουθήματα, οὐκ ἔργα φύσεως προηγούμενα φυσικοῖς δὲ ἐπισυμβαίνοντα ἔργοις, Plut. Mor. 117 D οὐδὲν δεινὸν τῶν ἀναγκαίων βροτοῖς, οὔτε τῶν κατὰ προηγούμενον λόγον συμβαινόντων οὔτε τῶν κατ' ἐπακολούθησιν, where see Wytt. It is equivalent to ἐπιγεννηματικόν in p. 84. 7, and to Aristotle's ἐπιγινόμενόν τι τέλος in Eth. N. x. 4.

8. κατ' ἄλλο σημαινόμενον. Cf. Str. VIII. P. 921, 922, below p. 170. 1.

ἐγκρατής. I suppose this refers to such a use as that in Ar. Hist. An. IX. 536 b τὰ παιδία διαλέκτου οὐκ ἐγκρατῆ: for the words which follow (βεβαίως ...μεγαλεῖα) cf. Eth. N. VII. 1. 6 ὁ αὐτὸς ἐγκρατὴς καὶ ἐμμενετικὸς τῷ λογισμῷ... εἰδὼς ὅτι φαῦλαι αἱ ἐπιθυμίαι, οὐκ ἀκολουθεῖ διὰ τὸν λόγον.

12. περιστάσεως. See above p. 28. 16 n.

13. τῆς ἰδίας ἕξεως ὁ γνωστικὸς ἐξίσταται. See Arist. Eth. N. VII. 1. 6 (ὁ αὐτὸς) ἀκρατὴς καὶ ἐκστατικὸς τοῦ λογισμοῦ.

15. ἐπιστήμη θείων καὶ ἀνθρωπείων πραγμάτων. This definition of wisdom, due probably to Chrysippus, is also given in Paed. II. P. 181, Str. IV. P. 638, VI. P. 807 fin., P. 823, and more fully in Str. I. P. 333 init. ἡ σοφία ἐπιστήμη θείων καὶ ἀνθρωπίνων καὶ τῶν τούτων αἰτιῶν. Both definitions occur in Cicero, the shorter in Off. I. 153, the longer in Off. II. 5.

18. οὐ προηγουμένως ἀλλὰ ἀναγκαίως. For προηγουμένως see n. on l. 6 above, where exx. are given of its opposition to κατ' ἐπακολούθημα. For the contrast with ἀναγκαίως see Str. VI. P. 781 where the study of Greek learning is recommended οὐ κατὰ τὸν προηγούμενον λόγον, τὸν δὲ ἀναγκαῖον καὶ δεύτερον καὶ περιστατικόν, P. 779 fin., where simple diet is recommended, ἀλλὰ μηδὲ ταῦτα ὡς προηγούμενα, ἐκ δὲ τῆς κατὰ τὸν βίον κοινωνίας ὡς ἀναγκαῖα τῇ τῆς σαρκὸς ἐπιδημίᾳ εἰς ὅσον ἀνάγκη προσιέμενος· προηγουμένη γὰρ αὐτῷ ἡ γνῶσις. Other contrasted terms are κατὰ συμβεβηκός Plac. Phil. II. 3. 3 (Diels p. 330), παρακειμένως Sext. Emp. Math. VII. 182, ἀκολούθως ib. IX. 418, 419, κατὰ τὸ ἀκόλουθον below p. 152. 25, κατὰ περίστασιν Epict. Diss. III. 14. 7.

19. ἐὰν ὁ λόγος αἱρῇ. See below p. 136. 9.

20. **εἰκόνας τοὺς ἀποστόλους.** Peter was mentioned above (p. 106. 30 f.) as a pattern of married life. He and Philip are spoken of as having had children, and Paul as married in *Str.* III. P. 535 *fin.*, where see Potter. Below p. 134. 5 f. the Gnostic is said to fill the place of the Apostles.

22. **ἄνδρας νικᾷ.** See above p. 116. 4 f., *Str.* III. P. 546. For the cognate acc. after νικᾷ L. and S. cite Diog. Laert. VI. 33 Πύθια νικῶ ἄνδρας, Dem. 1342 *fin.* Ὀλυμπίασι παῖδας στάδιον νικᾷ, similarly ἅρμα ν., δίσκον ν.

25. **ἀδιάστατος.** Cf. *Str.* IV. P. 626 τὸ δὲ ἀεὶ νοεῖν οὐσία γινώσκοντος κατὰ ἀνάκρασιν ἀδιάστατον γενομένη, *Exc. Theod.* P. 969 ἀδιάστατος, ἀμέριστος, εἷς θεός. The lexx. give no example of this meaning, but it flows naturally from such a use as that in Arist. *Vesp.* 41 διιστάναι τινά τινος.

26. **κατεξανιστάμενος.** See above p. 110. 21, below p. 138. 17.

29. **ἀπειράστῳ.** See above p. 78. 19, and my n. on St James i. 13.

μόνου ἑαυτοῦ κηδόμενος. Cf. 1 Cor. vii. 32—34.

p. 124, line 1. **εἰκόνα σώζοντος τῆς τῇ ἀληθείᾳ προνοίας.** Cf. *Str.* III. P. 548 ἔχει γὰρ ὥσπερ ἡ εὐνουχία οὕτω καὶ ὁ γάμος ἰδίας λειτουργίας καὶ διακονίας τῷ κυρίῳ διαφερούσας, τέκνων λέγω κήδεσθαι καὶ γυναικός· πρόφασις γὰρ τῷ κατὰ γάμον τελείῳ ἡ τῆς συζυγίας οἰκειότης γίνεται, τὴν πρόνοιαν πάντων ἀναδεδεγμένῳ κατὰ τὸν οἶκον τὸν κοινόν κ.τ.λ., *ib.* VI. P. 779 ἀπ' ἐκείνων ἄνωθεν τῶν ἀρχετύπων τὴν περὶ τὰ ἀνθρώπεια αὐτὸς διοίκησιν ἀπογραφόμενος.

§ 71. 6. **καθαίρεται χαλκός.** Plat. *Polit.* 303 D χρυσὸν καθ.

7. **αὐτίκα.** See Appendix.

8. **ἡ γνῶσις οἷον ὁ λογικὸς θάνατος.** Cf. Plato *Phaedo* 66 E εἰ μέλλομέν ποτε καθαρῶς τι εἴσεσθαι ἀπαλλακτέον τοῦ σώματος καὶ αὐτῇ τῇ ψυχῇ θεατέον αὐτὰ τὰ πράγματα, 67 D οὐκοῦν τοῦτό γε θάνατος ὀνομάζεται, λύσις καὶ χωρισμὸς ψυχῆς ἀπὸ σώματος; λύειν δέ γε αὐτὴν προθυμοῦνται ἀεὶ μάλιστα οἱ φιλοσοφοῦντες ὀρθῶς. St Paul uses the same figure in regard to baptism, Rom. vi. 4 f., Col. ii. 20, 2 Tim. ii. 11. See above p. 22. 16, *Str.* V. P. 686 θυσία δὲ ἡ τῷ θεῷ δεκτὴ σώματός τε καὶ τῶν τούτου παθῶν ἀμετανόητος χωρισμός and P. 569.

9. **ἀπὸ τῶν παθῶν ἀπάγων...καὶ προάγων εἰς τὴν τῆς εὐποιίας ζωήν.** The two stages of Christian progress, abstinence from evil, produced by fear, active goodness produced by love, p. 136. 19 f., *Str.* IV. P. 576; compare the distinction between the Hebdomad and the Ogdoad, p. 100. 15 n., and p. 118. 20 n.

11. **ὡς θέλεις ζῶ.** There is the same self-complacent tone above, p. 84. 19 f.

12. **ἀνθρώποις ἀρέσκειν.** Gal. i. 10 ἢ ζητῶ ἀνθρώποις ἀρέσκειν, Col. iii. 22 μὴ ἐν ὀφθαλμοδουλίαις ὡς ἀνθρωπάρεσκοι.

13. **θεῷ ἀρέσαι οὐ δύναται.** Rom. viii. 8 οἱ δὲ ἐν σαρκὶ ὄντες θεῷ ἀρέσαι οὐ δύνανται. Probably Cl. may have had in his mind 1 Cor. vii. 32, 33 ὁ ἄγαμος μεριμνᾷ τὰ τοῦ κυρίου πῶς ἀρέσει τῷ κυρίῳ· ὁ δὲ γαμήσας μεριμνᾷ τὰ τοῦ κόσμου πῶς ἀρέσει τῇ γυναικί.

μὴ τὰ συμφέροντα ἀλλὰ τὰ τέρποντα. Cf. p. 86. 26.

15. κατ' ἐπακολούθημα. See n. on p. 122. 6 above.

§ 72. 26. ἀνεπιθύμητος. Cf. *Str.* IV. P. 632 θεὸς δὲ ἀπαθὴς ἄθυμός τε καὶ ἀνεπιθύμητος, Stob. *Ecl.* II. 304 σώφρονα μὲν γὰρ εἶναι οὔτε τὸν καθάπαξ ἀνεπιθύμητον οὔτε τὸν ἐπιθυμητικόν, τὸν μὲν γὰρ λίθου δίκην μηδὲ τῶν κατὰ φύσιν ὀρέγεσθαι κ.τ.λ.

27. φιλάνθρωπος. Cf. Wisdom i. 6 φιλάνθρωπον πνεῦμα σοφία, xi. 26 φείδῃ δὲ πάντων ὅτι σά ἐστι, δέσποτα φιλόψυχε.

28, 29. τῷ ὑπ' αὐτοῦ δεδομένῳ χαρακτῆρι. See above p. 118. 5.

30. κατασχὼν ἑαυτοῦ. For the gen. L. and S. quote Arist. *Cat.* 8. 4 τοὺς τῶν ἐπιστημῶν μὴ πάνυ κατέχοντας, Polyb. XIV. 1. 9, Diod. XII. 82, *al.*

31. ἡ χήρα. Cf. below, p. 132. 6. Potter refers to *Str.* III. P. 568 τῆς παρθένου τὴν χήραν εἰς ἐγκράτειαν προτείνουσι (? προτιμῶσι) καταμεγαλοφρονήσασαν ἧς πεπείραται ἡδονῆς.

p. 126, line 1. μισθὸς γνώσεως. It is stated here that both negative (ἀποχή) and positive virtue (εὐποιία) are the reward of γνῶσις. More commonly Cl. makes the former the mark of the lower religious stage (πίστις), the latter of γνῶσις: see *Str.* VI. P. 770 καθαρισμὸς τῆς ψυχῆς πρῶτος οὗτός ἐστιν, ἡ ἀποχὴ τῶν κακῶν, ἥν τινες τελείωσιν ἡγοῦνται, καὶ ἔστιν ἁπλῶς τοῦ κοινοῦ πιστοῦ ἡ τελείωσις αὕτη, τοῦ δὲ γνωστικοῦ μετὰ τὴν ἄλλοις νομιζομένην τελείωσιν ἡ δικαιοσύνη εἰς ἐνέργειαν εὐποιίας προβαίνει, also P. 791, 792. But it is further stated that these are the reward of knowledge to the Saviour, which He Himself asked for. In no passage of the N.T. is there any hint of our Lord making such a prayer for Himself, but Joh. xvii. is a prayer for His disciples, that they might be kept from sin, and might have that Eternal Life which consists in the knowledge of the Father and the Son. The nearest approach to our text is perhaps Is. liii. 11 'He shall see of the travail of his soul and be satisfied (μισθός): by his knowledge shall my righteous servant justify many,' where many take 'his knowledge' objectively='the knowledge of Him.' For μισθόν we may also compare Joh. iv. 36 καὶ ὁ θερίζων μισθὸν λαμβάνει καὶ συνάγει καρπὸν εἰς ζωὴν αἰώνιον, 1 Cor. ix. 18 f., *Str.* I. P. 319 ἐπεί. τοῦτον μόνον καρποῦται τὸν μισθόν, τὴν σωτηρίαν τῶν ἐπαϊόντων.

2. τὴν ἀποχήν. For this 'inverse attraction' of the noun into the case of the relative, see Jelf *Gr.* § 824, and cf. the Latin there cited, *haec est quam Scipio laudat temperationem rei publicae* (Cic. *Leg.* III. 12).

4, 5. δι' ὧν ἐπαιδεύθησαν...δι' ὧν ἐπίστανται. For the use of these relative clauses instead of the article with infinitive, see above p. 82. 13 δι' ὧν ἔγνω φθάσας, p. 104. 9 ἐπίστευσεν ἐξ ὧν ἐθαύμασεν, below p. 130. 17, 18 χαίρων ἐφ' οἷς ἔγνω, συστελλόμενος δὲ ἐφ' οἷς ἐπεγκυλίεται, Chrys. *Hom. in Matt.* VI. p. 79 F ὅρα τ. ἀρετὴν οὐκ ἀφ' ὧν ἦλθον, ἀλλ' ἀφ' ὧν παρρησιάζονται.

7. τὸ τῆς ψυχῆς ἐκκόψαι πάθος. Cf. Mt. v. 30 καὶ εἰ ἡ δεξιά σου χεὶρ σκανδαλίζει σε, ἔκκοψον αὐτήν. H. J. compares Plato *Rep.* 519 A, B τοῦτο τὸ τῆς τοιαύτης φύσεως εἰ ἐκ παιδὸς εὐθὺς κοπτόμενον περιεκόπη τὰ τῆς γενέσεως ξυγγενῆ ὥσπερ μολυβδίδας κ.τ.λ. and *Str.* IV. P. 570.

14. πραγμάτων θεωρίαν. Cf. p. 104. 17, 18.

16, 17. μηδὲν...παραβεβηκυίαι. The same tone as above, p. 124. 11, cf. Epict. *Diss.* III. 5. 8—11.

17. ἀπαιτοῦμεν. Below, p. 142. 5 ὁ τοιοῦτος ἀπαιτεῖ παρὰ τοῦ κυρίου.

18. οὐχ ὡς καθήκοντος. I have suggested ὡς οὐ κ., which gives a reason for asking τὰ συμφέροντα rather than τὰ κάλλιστα (like the sons of Zebedee, Mk x. 37). I can make nothing of the text.

19, 20. ἐπὶ συμφόρῳ δεόμεθα. Cf. such phrases as ἐπ' ἀγαθῷ ἐμνήσθη, Plut. *Mor.* 520 E.

§ 73. 23—25. Compare for a similar chivalrous sentiment *Str.* IV. P. 626 τολμήσας εἴποιμ' ἄν, οὐ διὰ τὸ σώζεσθαι βούλεσθαι τὴν γνῶσιν αἱρήσεται ὁ δι' αὐτὴν τὴν θείαν ἐπιστήμην μεθέπων τὴν γνῶσιν...εἰ γοῦν τις καθ' ὑπόθεσιν προθείη τῷ γνωστικῷ πότερον ἑλέσθαι βούλοιτο, τὴν γνῶσιν τοῦ θεοῦ ἢ τὴν σωτηρίαν τὴν αἰώνιον (εἴη δὲ ταῦτα κεχωρισμένα, παντὸς μᾶλλον ἐν ταυτότητι ὄντα), οὐδὲ καθ' ὁτιοῦν διστάσας ἕλοιτ' ἂν τὴν γνῶσιν τοῦ θεοῦ.

25. εὐχὴ ὁ βίος ἅπας. See above p. 60. 22 f., p. 68. 18 f., p. 70. 6.

28. ἐννοήθητι καὶ ποιήσω. See n. on p. 70. 27.

p. 128, line 3. **τὴν θεοῦ δικαίαν ἀγαθότητα.** Cl. combines the attributes which the Gnostics divided between their highest God and the Demiurgus, cf. above p. 24. 26, *Str.* VI. P. 795 ἀγαθὴ ἡ τοῦ θεοῦ δικαιοσύνη, καὶ δικαία ἡ ἀγαθότης.

5. ἡ οἰκονομία. See Kaye, p. 235 f.

7. τοῖς δ' ὅσοι ἄξιοι καὶ μὴ αἰτουμένοις δίδοται. Cf. above, p. 70. 31, 32, and Isa. lxv. 24, 1 Sam. i. 13, also Poet. ap. Plat. *Alc.* II. p. 143 Ζεῦ βασιλεῦ τὰ μὲν ἐσθλὰ καὶ εὐχομένοις καὶ ἀνεύκτοις ἄμμι δίδου, τὰ δὲ δεινὰ καὶ εὐχομένοις ἀπαλέξειν. For article with relative see Index *s.v.* ὅσος, and n. on p. 112. 1.

8—10. μὴ κατὰ ἀνάγκην...ἀλλ' ἐκ προαιρέσεως. See *Str.* IV. P. 126—131, and Frag. cited in Barnard's *Q. D. S.* § 42 *ad fin.* οὐ γὰρ τοὺς ἀνάγκῃ τῆς κακίας ἀπεχομένους, ἀλλὰ τοὺς προαιρέσει στεφανοῖ ὁ θεός. H. J. compares Arist. *Eth. N.* III. 8 §§ 3, 4, 5, 13, on the spurious ἀνδρεῖαι.

10. ὁδὸς βασιλική. The phrase is taken from Numb. xx. 17 ὁδῷ βασιλικῇ πορευσόμεθα· οὐκ ἐκκλινοῦμεν δεξιὰ οὐδὲ εὐώνυμα, on which Philo comments (M. I. 294 f. *Q. Deus est immutabilis*): he explains it as 'wisdom,' τὴν τοῦ αἰωνίου καὶ ἀφθάρτου τελείαν ὁδὸν τὴν πρὸς θεὸν ἄγουσαν...διὰ γὰρ ταύτης ὁ νοῦς ποδηγετούμενος εὐθείας καὶ λεωφόρου ὑπαρχούσης ἄχρι τῶν τερμάτων ἀφικνεῖται· τὸ δὲ τέρμα τῆς ὁδοῦ γνῶσίς ἐστι καὶ ἐπιστήμη θεοῦ, *ib.* 296 and M. 2, p. 364 quoted in my n. on St James ii. 8. Cf. below, p. 160. 10 f. ὥσπερ ὁδοῦ μιᾶς μὲν τῆς βασιλικῆς τυγχανούσης, πολλῶν δὲ καὶ ἄλλων τῶν μὲν ἐπί τινα κρημνόν...φερουσῶν κ.τ.λ., *Str.* VI. P. 825 ἐὰν μὴ πλεονάσῃ ὑμῶν ἡ δικαιοσύνη πλέον...τῶν κατὰ ἀποχὴν κακῶν δικαιουμένων... τῷ τὸν πλησίον ἀγαπᾶν...οὐκ ἔσεσθε βασιλικοί, *Str.* IV. P. 565 ζήτει καὶ εὑρήσεις, τῆς βασιλικῆς ὄντως ἐχόμενος ὁδοῦ.

11. τὸ βασιλικὸν γένος. Cf. 1 Pet. ii. 9 ὑμεῖς δὲ γένος ἐκλεκτόν, βασίλειον ἱεράτευμα, and below, p. 136. 5 βασιλικός ὡς γνωστικός.

παρεκτροπαί. The only example of this meaning.

12—14. Cf. above, p. 108. 20 f., and *Str.* VI. P. 827 where the endurance of the Christian martyr is contrasted with the timidity of the philosopher.

12. εἰ γοῦν τις ἄφιλοι—οὐκ οἶδ' εἰ ὑποστήσονται. Cf. above p. 54. 11.

14. γεννᾶσαι. Used with the same ironical force in *Str.* III. P. 527.

§ 74. 15, 16. τρίβολοι καὶ σκόλοπες. Cf. Heb. vi. 8 ἐκφέρουσα δὲ ἀκάνθας καὶ τριβόλους ἀδόκιμος καὶ κατάρας ἐγγύς, Ezek. xxviii. 24 οὐκ ἔσονται οὐκέτι ἐν τῷ οἴκῳ τοῦ Ἰσραὴλ σκόλοψ πικρίας καὶ ἄκανθα ὀδύνης. Mt. vii. 16 μήτι συλλέγουσιν ἀπὸ ἀκανθῶν σταφυλὴν ἢ ἀπὸ τριβόλων σῦκα;

17. κλαδεύων. See *Str.* I. P. 341 *fin.*, above p. 6. 13 f.

18. 19. τὸν εἰς πίστιν καταπεφυτευμένον. 2 Macc. i. 29 καταφύτευσον τὸν λαόν σου εἰς τὸν τόπον τὸν ἅγιόν σου, below p. 194. 14, 18.

20. μισθὸν ἀργίας. Cf. the parable of the Talents.

21. ἀπαιτεῖ τὸν μισθὸν ὡς ἐργάτης. Luke x. 7 ἄξιος γὰρ ἐργάτης τοῦ μισθοῦ.

22. διπλοῦν. 1 Tim. v. 17 οἱ καλῶς προεστῶτες πρεσβύτεροι διπλῆς τιμῆς ἀξιούσθωσαν.

24. πειράζεται ὑπ' οὐδενός. Cf. above, p. 78. 18, 19 αὐστηρὸς οὐκ εἰς τὸ ἀδιάφθορον μόνον ἀλλὰ καὶ εἰς τὸ ἀπείραστον.

25, 26. διὰ τὴν τῶν συνόντων ἀφέλειαν. See below p. 132. 3.

28. εἰς πῆξιν. We should rather have expected ἐπὶ πήξει.

30. ἔναυλον. See Ruhnken's n. on Tim. *Lex.* s.v.

31. ὃν ἐγὼ πατάξω, σὺ ἐλέησον. The nearest approach to this in the Bible seems to be Job xix. 21 Have pity on me, O my friends, for the hand of God hath touched me, or Ps. lxix. 26 They persecute him whom Thou hast smitten.

p. 130, line 1. τοὺς μισοῦντας αἰτεῖται μετανοῆσαι. The connexion is difficult. Cl. has been speaking of the persecution of Christians, which, in the following sentence, he contrasts with the punishment of criminals in the amphitheatre. He speaks of the beneficial effect of the former and the injurious effect of the latter upon spectators. It would seem as if the words ἔχων οὖν—μετανοῆσαι would come in best after μὴ θεάσασθαι. 'The gnostic cannot delight in seeing these wretches punished, for he remembers that he is bound to show mercy to those who are smitten of God and will therefore pray for their conversion.'

On the Spectacles cf. above § 36, *Protr.* P. 36 (the cruelty of the demons is shown by what is done at the Spectacles) ἀνθρωποκτονίας ἀπολαύοντες, νυνὶ μὲν τὰς ἐν σταδίοις ἐνόπλους φιλονεικίας...ἀφορμὰς σφίσιν ἡδονῆς ποριζόμενοι, *Paed.* III. P. 298 and 299 init. εἰ γὰρ καὶ ἐν παιδιᾶς μέρει παραλαμβάνεσθαι φήσουσι τὰς θέας εἰς θυμηδίαν, οὐ σωφρονεῖν φήσαιμ' ἂν τὰς πόλεις, αἷς καὶ τὸ παίζειν σπουδάζεται. οὐκέτι γὰρ παιδιαὶ αἱ φιλοδοξίαι <αἱ> ἀνηλεεῖς εἰς τοσοῦτον <ὥστε> θανατῶσαι κ.τ.λ., Tert. *Spect.* 19 Bonum est cum puniuntur nocentes...Et tamen innocens de supplicio alterius laetari non potest, cum magis competat innocenti dolere quod homo, par eius, tam nocens factus est ut tam crudeliter impendatur, *ib.* 21 Qui propter homicidae poenam probandam ad spectaculum veniat, idem gladiatorem ad homicidium flagellis compellat invitum, *ib.* 25 Poterit de misericordia moneri defixus in morsus ursorum? See a most interesting letter of Seneca (L 7, with Lipsius' notes) of which the drift is that 'nihil tam damnosum bonis moribus quam in aliquo spectaculo desidere': also Friedländer *Sitteng. Roms* vol. II. 2. 2 (Das Amphitheater), Martial *Spectac.* 7 (on the criminal who acts the part of Laureolus).

2, 3. καὶ παίδων ἐστὶ μὴ θεάσασθαι. 'Even neophytes (p. 116. 2 above) should have enough of Christian feeling to keep them from the amphitheatre.' Perhaps θέλειν may have been lost before θεάσασθαι. Compare *Protr.* P. 58 πολλοῦ γε δεῖ ἀνδράσιν ἐπιτρέπειν ἀκροᾶσθαι τοιούτων λόγων οἷς μηδὲ τοὺς παῖδας τοὺς ἑαυτῶν ἐθίζομεν παρηγορεῖσθαι μυθίζοντες. It is reported of the youthful Caracalla (Ael. Spart. I.) that si quando feris obiectos damnatos vidit, flevit aut oculos avertit. Dr Gifford notes 'a love for shows is more excusable in children, for whom also the sight of punishment might be supposed to be a useful deterrent.'

4. παιδευθείη. The cruelties of the circus were defended on the ground that they strengthened the character, see Plin. *Pan.* 33 visum est spectaculum non enerve...nec quod animos virorum molliret et frangeret, sed quod ad pulchra volnera contemptumque mortis accenderet, cum in servorum etiam noxiorumque corporibus amor laudis cerneretur.

6. ἄτεγκτος. Cf. p. 118. 1 above.

9. κοσμικῶν ἐπαγγελιῶν, *e.g.* the fancies of the Chiliasts, on which see Origen *de Princ.* II. 11 § 32 f.

10, 11. οὐ πᾶς...θεοῦ. This differs from St Matthew's text by omitting μου after λέγων, by reading βασιλείαν τοῦ θεοῦ instead of β. τῶν οὐρανῶν, and θέλημα τοῦ θεοῦ instead of θ. τοῦ πατρός μου τοῦ ἐν τοῖς οὐρανοῖς.

13. κοσμικῶν ἐπιθυμιῶν. Titus ii. 12 (ἀρνησάμενοι) τὰς κοσμικὰς ἐπιθυμίας.

15. On the gnostic's certain anticipation of the future, see above, p. 82. 11 f.

16. τῶν ἐν ποσί. Cf. above p. 121. 29 τῶν ἐν τοῖς ποσὶν ἡδέων.

§ 75. 17. εὔθετος. See Lk. ix. 62, quoted below p. 164. 19, *Str.* II. P. 503 εὔθετοι πρὸς γάμον, *Paed.* II. P. 189 εὔθ. εἰς πολλά.

χαίρων ἐφ' οἷς ἔγνω. For the use of the relative and finite verb instead of the art. and inf. see the next line, and above p. 104. 9 ἐπίστευσεν ἐξ ὧν ἐθαύμασεν.

18. συστελλόμενος. Above, p. 22. 7 εἰς ἀπάθειαν συνεσταλμένον.

ἐγκυλίεται. Apparently only used here: cf. ἐγκυλιώμενοι μέθαις, p. 40. 25.

22, 23. On the observance of days and hours, see above, p. 60. 16 f., p. 70. 4 f.

τῆς τετράδος καὶ τῆς παρασκευῆς. The earliest mention of the weekly 'stationes' is in the Didachè c. 8 αἱ δὲ νηστεῖαι ὑμῶν μὴ ἔστωσαν μετὰ τῶν ὑποκριτῶν· νηστεύουσι γὰρ δευτέρᾳ σαββάτων καὶ πέμπτῃ (Lk. xviii. 12), ὑμεῖς δὲ νηστεύσατε τετράδα καὶ παρασκευήν, cf. Hermas Sim. v. 1 νηστεύων...Βλέπω τὸν ποιμένα παρακαθήμενόν μοι καὶ λέγοντα· Τί ὄρθρινὸς ὧδε ἐλήλυθας; Ὅτι, φημί, στατίωνα ἔχω. Τί, φησίν, ἐστὶ στατίων; Νηστεύω, φημί, κύριε. Νηστεία δέ, φησί, τί ἐστιν αὕτη, ἣν νηστεύετε; Ὡς εἰώθειν, φημί, κύριε, οὕτω νηστεύω. Οὐκ οἴδατε, φησί, νηστεύειν τῷ κυρίῳ, οὐδέ ἐστιν νηστεία αὕτη ἡ ἀνωφελής...νήστευσον δὲ τῷ θεῷ νηστείαν τοιαύτην.—τήρησον τὰς ἐντολὰς αὐτοῦ κ.τ.λ., ib. 3, Tert. de Jejun. 14 cur stationibus quartam et sextam sabbati dicamus? See Bingham, Ant. xxI. 3.

23, 24. ἐπιφημίζονται ἡ μὲν Ἑρμοῦ, ἡ δὲ Ἀφροδίτης. Cf. Plut. Mor. 270 A τῶν ἡμερῶν τὰς μέν...ἱερὰς ἔθεντο, τὰς δὲ δαίμοσιν ἐπιφημίσαντες...ἀπράκτους ἐνόμισαν. The reason generally assigned for fasting on these days was that 'ipsa quarta sabbati...consilium reperiuntur ad occidendum Dominum fecisse Judaei; intermisso autem uno die passus est Dominus sexta sabbati' (Aug. ep. 86).

24, 25. νηστεύει φιλαργυρίας. Cf. below l. 30 v. ἀπὸ τῶν πράξεων τῶν φαύλων, Str. III. P. 558 μακάριοι οὗτοί εἰσιν οἱ τοῦ κόσμου νηστεύοντες, Str. VI. P. 791 νηστείαι δὲ ἀποχὰς κακῶν μηνύουσι, Ecl. Proph. P. 992 ἡ νηστεία ἀποχὴ τροφῆς ἐστι κατὰ τὸ σημαινόμενον...κατὰ δὲ τὸ μυστικὸν δηλοῖ ὅτι...τῶν κοσμικῶν νηστεύειν χρή, ἵνα τῷ κόσμῳ ἀποθάνωμεν...τροφὴ μὲν οὖν κοσμικὴ ὁ πρότερος βίος καὶ τὰ ἁμαρτήματα, τροφὴ δὲ θεϊκὴ πίστις ἐλπὶς ἀγάπη, Logia 2 λέγει Ἰησοῦς, ἐὰν μὴ νηστεύσητε τὸν κόσμον (ἢ τοῦ κόσμου) οὐ μὴ εὕρητε τὴν βασιλείαν τοῦ θεοῦ, Ptolemaeus (A.D. 160?) ad Floram (ap. Epiph. XXXIII. 5) νηστεύειν τὴν πνευματικὴν νηστείαν ἐν ᾗ ἐστιν ἀποχὴ πάντων τῶν φαύλων. For φιλ. see 1 Tim. vi. 10 ῥίζα γὰρ πάντων τῶν κακῶν ἐστιν ἡ φιλαργυρία.

26. ἐξ ὧν αἱ πᾶσαι κακίαι. See Lightfoot on Col. iii. 5, where he cites Bengel 'homo extra Deum quaerit pabulum in creatura materiali vel per voluptatem vel per avaritiam,' and Test. XII. Patr. Jud. 18 φυλάξασθε— ἀπὸ τῆς πορνείας καὶ τῆς φιλαργυρίας...ὅτι ταῦτα ἀφιστᾷ νόμου θεοῦ.

27. τὰς ἀνωτάτω διαφοράς. So Str. VI. P. 824 πᾶσα ὠφέλεια βιωτικὴ κατὰ μὲν τὸν ἀνωτάτω λόγον ἀπὸ τοῦ παντοκράτορος θεοῦ. Cf. Waitz (Arist. Cat. 1 b. 17) on διαφορά, Anal. Post. I. 20 (p. 82 a. 23) λέγω δ' ἄνω μὲν τὴν ἐπὶ τὸ καθόλου μᾶλλον, κάτω δὲ τὴν ἐπὶ τὸ κατὰ μέρος.

παρεστήσαμεν. Above, Str. III. P. 552 init. ὡς γὰρ ἡ πλεονεξία πορνεία λέγεται τῇ αὐταρκείᾳ ἐναντιουμένη, καὶ ὡς εἰδωλολατρία ἐκ τοῦ ἑνὸς εἰς τοὺς πολλοὺς ἐπινέμησίς ἐστι θεούς (MS. θεοῦ), οὕτως ἡ πορνεία ἐκ τοῦ ἑνὸς γάμου εἰς τοὺς πολλοὺς ἐστιν ἔκπτωσις· τριχῶς γάρ, ὡς εἴρηται, ἥ τε πορνεία ἥ τε μοιχεία παρὰ τῷ ἀποστόλῳ λαμβάνεται, Str. VI. P. 816 μοιχεία δ' ἐστὶν ἐάν τις καταλιπὼν τὴν ἐκκλησιαστικὴν καὶ ἀληθῆ γνῶσιν...ἐπὶ τὴν μὴ προσήκουσαν ἔρχηται ψευδῆ δόξαν...διόπερ ὁ γενναῖος ἀπόστολος ἕν τι τῶν τῆς πορνείας εἰδῶν τὴν εἰδωλολατρίαν καλεῖ.

28. κατὰ τὸν ἀπόστολον. St Paul only speaks of covetousness as idolatry. Cl. may be thinking of Eph. v. 5, where the three vices are named together (πᾶς πόρνος ἢ ἀκάθαρτος ἢ πλεονέκτης, ὅς ἐστιν εἰδωλολάτρης), but in the O.T. idolatry is often spoken of as adultery, and so in St James iv. 4.

§ 76. 30 f. See Mt. v. 21, 22, 27, 28. Potter cites Justin, *Dial.* 10 (p. 227) ὑμῶν δὲ καὶ τὰ ἐν τῷ λεγομένῳ εὐαγγελίῳ παραγγέλματα θαυμαστὰ οὕτως καὶ μεγάλα ἐπίσταμαι εἶναι, ὡς ὑπολαμβάνειν μηδένα δύνασθαι φυλάξαι αὐτά, and Joseph. *Ant.* XII. 9. 1 (§ 358), where Josephus expresses his surprise at Polybius ὃς ἀποθανεῖν λέγει τὸν Ἀντίοχον βουληθέντα τὸ...ἱερὸν συλῆσαι· τὸ γὰρ μηκέτι ποιῆσαι τὸ ἔργον βουλευσάμενον οὐκ ἔστι τιμωρίας ἄξιον, as showing the difference between the Jewish and the Christian conception of sin.

p. 132, line 2. ἀποκάθαρσιν. This word occurs above, p. 54. 26 τὴν ἀποκάθαρσιν τοῦ ἀλόγου, but probably H. J. is right in reading αὐτοῦ κάθαρσιν here.

3. εἰς τὴν τῶν ὅλων ὠφέλειαν. See above p. 128. 25.

6. ἐν πείρᾳ γενόμενον εἶτα ἀποσχέσθαι. Cf. above p. 124. 31, with n.

7, 8. ἐντολὴν τὴν κατὰ τὸ εὐαγγέλιον. Cf. above p. 130. 31, where the Gospel is distinguished from the Law as controlling thoughts.

8, 9. κυριακὴν τὴν ἡμέραν ποιεῖ. By rising out of our sins we commemorate the Resurrection of Christ; cf. Ign. *Magn.* 9 μηκέτι σαββατίζοντες ἀλλὰ κατὰ τὴν κυριακὴν ζῶντες, ἐν ᾗ καὶ ἡ ζωὴ ἡμῶν ἀνέτειλεν δι' αὐτοῦ, with Lightfoot's n. (vol. II. p. 129), Col. iii. 1, Eph. ii. 4—6, Ps. cxviii. 22—24.

11, 12. ὅταν ἐπιστημονικοῦ θεωρήματος κατάληψιν λάβῃ, τὸν κύριον ὁρᾶν νομίζει. We may compare Inge *Christian Mysticism* p. 249 "The peculiar happiness which accompanies every glimpse of insight into truth and reality, whether in the scientific, aesthetic, or emotional sphere, seems to me to have a greater apologetic value than has been generally recognized. It is the clearest possible indication that the true is for us the good, and forms the ground of a reasonable faith that all things...work together for good to those who love God."

12, 13. τὰς ὄψεις χειραγωγῶν. L. and S. quote Maximus Tyr. for the expression χειραγωγῶ τὴν ψυχήν.

15. κατὰ τὴν προσβολὴν τῆς ὄψεως. See n. on p. 76. 27 above.

16. προσῆκεν. For the imperfect cf. p. 146. 3 below, *Paed.* II. P. 212 *init.* τρυφᾶν προσῆκεν σωφρόνως, Plut. *Mor.* 7 B, 8 C, 11 D, F, 12 B, E, F.

18. τῆς σαρκὸς τὸ κάλλος αὐτῇ βλέπει τῇ ψυχῇ. Cf. *Str.* IV. P. 616 ἐὰν εἰς κάλλος σώματος βλέψῃ τις, καὶ αὐτῷ ἡ σὰρξ εἶναι κατ' ἐπιθυμίαν δόξῃ καλή, σαρκικῶς ἰδών...δι' οὗ τεθαύμακεν κρίνεται· ἔμπαλιν γὰρ ὁ δι' ἀγάπην τὴν ἁγνὴν προσβλέπων τὸ κάλλος οὐ τὴν σάρκα ἡγεῖται, ἀλλὰ τὴν ψυχὴν καλήν, τὸ σῶμα, οἶμαι, ὡς ἀνδριάντα θαυμάσας, δι' οὗ κάλλους ἐπὶ τὸν τεχνίτην καὶ τὸ ὄντως καλὸν αὐτὸς αἰτὸν παραπέμπει. [Cf. *Q. D. S.* § 35, P. 955 οὐ σαρκὸς τῆς σῆς ἅπτεσθαι δοκοῦσιν, ἀλλὰ τῆς ἑαυτοῦ ψυχῆς ἕκαστος, οὐκ ἀδελφῷ λαλεῖν, ἀλλὰ τῷ βασιλεῖ τῶν αἰώνων ἐν σοὶ κατοικοῦντι. Barnard.]

§ 77. 20, 21. τὴν κτίσιν τὴν ἐξειλεγμένην. Cf. γένος ἐκλεκτόν above, p. 60. 19, p. 102. 9, and ἐκλεκτός below, l. 30, p. 142. 20, 21. In *Str.* VI. P. 793 the elders of the Apocalypse (iv. 10) are called ἐκλεκτῶν ἐκλεκτότεροι. The actual word ἐξειλεγμένος is used above p. 4. 24 οἱ ἐξειλεγμένοι εἰς γνῶσιν, below p. 164. 15 ἡ ψυχὴ ἡ ἐξειλεγμένη. The phrase κτίσις ἐξειλ.

may perhaps be taken from 2 Cor. v. 17 εἴ τις ἐν Χριστῷ, καινὴ κτίσις, but more probably it was suggested by the Gnostic distinction of the πνευματικοί from the ψυχικοί, on which see below p. 170. 18 f. (the Gnostics accuse us) ὡς ἄλλης γεγονότας φύσεως μὴ οἴους τε εἶναι συνεῖναι τὰ οἰκεῖα ἐκείνοις, *Str.* III. P. 510 (the followers of Basilides claim immunity from guilt) διὰ τὴν ἔμφυτον ἐκλογήν, VI. P. 792 οὐχ ὅτι ἦσαν ἐκλεκτοὶ γενόμενοι ἀπόστολοι κατά τι φύσεως ἐξαίρετον ἰδίωμα, IV. P. 639 ξένην τὴν ἐκλογὴν τοῦ κόσμου ὁ Βασιλείδης εἴληφε λέγειν ὡς ἂν ὑπερκόσμιον φύσει οὖσαν κ.τ.λ., *ib.* P. 603 φύσει σωζόμενον γένος ὑποτίθεται Οὐαλεντῖνος ἐμφερῶς τῷ Βασιλείδῃ, ἄνωθεν δὲ ἡμῖν δεῦρο τοῦτο δὴ τὸ διάφορον γένος ἐπὶ τὴν τοῦ θανάτου καθαίρεσιν ἥκειν.

21. ὁμοήθειαν. See Index.

22. ἔργων ὑπόστασιν, 'groundwork,' 'foundation,' 'substance,' then 'existence,' 'essence,' 'character,' 'person.' Cf. p. 188. 28 f. below κατά τε οὖν ὑπόστασιν κατά τε ἐπίνοιαν...μόνην εἶναί φαμεν τὴν ἀρχαίαν ἐκκλησίαν, *Str.* V. P. 645 *init.* οὐσίαν καὶ φύσιν καὶ ὑπόστασιν, *Str.* IV. P. 626 τὸ δὲ ἀεὶ νοεῖν, οὐσία τοῦ γινώσκοντος...γενομένη καὶ ἀΐδιος θεωρία, ζῶσα ὑπόστασις μένει, *Paed.* I. P. 109 *init.* ὁ νήπιος...ἀνυπόκριτος, ἰθὺς τὴν γνώμην καὶ ὀρθός· τὸ δέ ἐστιν ἀπλάτητος καὶ ἀληθείας ὑπόστασις.

25. γνῶσις ἐν τῷ τὰ αὐτὰ μεμαθηκέναι. See above, p. 96. 21 f.

27, 28. ὀλίγον τι τῆς ὥρας. I do not see the force of the μή. ὥρας (though we find the expression εὔχεται πᾶσαν τὴν ὥραν in P. 791, perhaps with reference to Mt. xxvii. 40). Sometimes ὥρα seems to be used for ἡμέρα, as in Mt. xiv. 15 ἡ ὥρα ἤδη παρῆλθε, Polyb. XVII. 9. 2 ὁ Φίλιππος ἠξίου τὸν Τίτον ὑπερθέσθαι τὴν σύνοδον εἰς τὴν αὔριον διὰ τὸ τὴν ὥραν εἰς ὀψὲ συγκλείειν, *ib.* 7. 3 (which I think is wrongly translated in L. and S. 'as the season was now closing in, i.e. the days becoming shorter'). For ὥρας cf. Ael. *N. A.* I. 59 ὑπὲρ τούτων οὐδὲ ὀλίγην ἔθεντο ὥραν, *ib.* V. 50, VII. 17.

28. χρεωκοπεῖσθαι. Cf. Sext. Emp. *Math.* VI. 6 ὅθεν καὶ ἡμεῖς ὑπὲρ τοῦ μὴ δοκεῖν τι τῆς διδασκαλίας χρεωκοπεῖν τὸν ἑκατέρου δόγματος χαρακτῆρα ἐφοδεύσομεν, Plut. *Mor.* 829 c ὁ γὰρ οὐ γράφων ἔλαττον χρεωκοπεῖται.

30. ὄναρ μὴ ἁρμόζον ἐκλεκτῷ. See above, l. 13 f., and below, p. 137. 10. Plato contrasts the dreams of the bad and the good, *Rep.* IX. 572.

p. 134, lines 7, 8. τὰ ὄρη μεθιστᾶς. See *Str.* V. P. 644 ὁποῖοι ἦσαν οἱ ἀπόστολοι, ἐφ' ὧν τὴν πίστιν ὄρη μετατιθέναι καὶ δένδρα μεταφυτεύειν δύνασθαι εἴρηται. So here, the removing of mountains is regarded as a sign of a true Apostolical Succession (ἀπουσίαν ἀνταναπληροῖ l. 6). Cf. also p. 122. 20, 21.

8. τὰς τῆς ψυχῆς ἀνωμαλίας. The word is used by Plutarch both locally, as in *V.* 534 c χωρίων ἀνωμαλίαι, *ib.* 642 ἡ ἀνωμαλία καὶ τραχύτης τῶν ὄχθων, also 978, and metaphorically, as in *V.* 565 ἡ κακία ἀνωμαλία ἐστὶ τρόπου, *ib.* 1031.

9. αὐτοῦ τε ἀμπελῶν. The more correct order would be αὐτοῦ ἀμπελών τε.

13. ὅπου γὰρ ὁ νοῦς. As this reading occurs twice in Cl. we can hardly accept the transposition of Arcerius, approved of by Dindorf. See Barnard *Biblical Text of Cl.* p. 10. Is any support to be found for the reading in other Fathers?

14. ἑαυτὸν μειονεκτεῖ. If the text is correct, this is the only known example of the transitive use of the verb. The transitive force of πλεονεκτεῖν ('to defraud') is so different that it scarcely supplies a parallel. But we may compare its use in Maximus *Qu. ad Thalass.* 157 δευτέραν κοινωνίαν ὁ λόγος ἐκοίνησε τῇ φύσει...ὡς ἐξ ἀρχῆς καθαρὰν παραστήσῃ τὴν φύσιν, τῇ θεώσει πλεονεκτοῦσαν τὴν πρώτην διάπλασιν. H. J. suggests ἑαυτοῦ, 'gets less than his right.' Cf. for this use Xen. *Hiero* I. 18 οἱ τύραννοι τῇ εὐφροσύνῃ τῆς ἐλπίδος μειονεκτοῦσι τῶν ἰδιωτῶν, *ib.* § 19 and § 27.

16. μάλιστα would be more natural before ἐάν.

18. ἀλγηδόνα...ἄλγημα. The former seems to differ from the latter as being more subjective.

§ 78. 19. ἐκ τῆς ἑαυτοῦ ἐνδείας. Potter compares Mk xii. 44 αὕτη δὲ ἐκ τῆς ὑστερήσεως αὐτῆς πάντα ὅσα εἶχεν ἔβαλεν. See also 2 Cor. viii. 2—15.

22. πραγμάτων. For the pregnant force of the word cf. above p. 104. 18, and Index *s.v.*

23. ἐπαινῶν does not seem a very suitable word. Possibly it may have taken the place of ἐπεξιών, owing to the following ἔπαινον.

25. περισπώμενος ὑπὸ τῆς ἰδίας ἐλπίδος. The word περισπάω seems to be always used in a bad sense of that which distracts a man from his true aim. We want here an expression for the elevating influence of hope in leading a man to despise earthly honours, such as ἐπισπάω in Plut. V. 992 ἐπισπασθέντα τῷ ζήλῳ πρὸς τὸ καλὸν ὑπ' αὐτοῦ. Cf. however Orig. *Cels.* III. 2 οὐδένα τὸν ἐπαγγελλόμενον εἶχον προφητεύειν, καὶ δυνάμενον περισπᾶν τοὺς πόθῳ προγνώσεως αὐτομολεῖν <ἑτοίμους> πρὸς τοὺς παρ' ἄλλοις δαίμονας, unless we ought to read ἐπισπᾶν there also. For ἰδίας perhaps we should read ἀϊδίου[1], contrasted with the following τῶν ἐν κόσμῳ καλῶν and τῶν ἐνταῦθα. It is to be noted however that ἴδια and ἀλλότρια are contrasted just below (p. 136, l. 1), where see n.

25—p. 136. 9. Cl. is fond of using the participle instead of the finite verb. In this long series (καταμεγαλοφρονῶν—οἰκτείρων—ἕτοιμος ὤν—μεμνημένος—ἡγούμενος—θαυμάζων—μέτοχος ὤν—ὑπερορῶν) it seems best to supply ἐστιν with οἰκεῖος.

26. οὐ γεύεται τῶν ἐν κόσμῳ καλῶν. Cf. p. 108. 17 διὰ τοῦτο τὰ πρόχειρα πάντα τοῦ κόσμου καλὰ οὐκ ἀγαπᾷ...ἀλλὰ τὰ ἐλπιζόμενα, and § 74, p. 130.

27. τῶν ἐνταῦθα καταμεγαλοφρονῶν. See above p. 130. 10.

28. παιδευομένους διὰ τῆς κολάσεως. Cf. *Paed.* I. P. 140 κολάζειν μὲν αὐτὸν ὁμολογήσαιμι <ἄν> τοὺς ἀπίστους· ἡ γὰρ κόλασις ἐπ' ἀγαθῷ καὶ ἐπ' ὠφελείᾳ τοῦ κολαζομένου, ἔστι γὰρ ἐπανόρθωσις ἀντιτείνοντος...τιμωρία δέ ἐστιν ἀνταπόδοσις κακοῦ ἐπὶ τὸ τοῦ τιμωροῦντος συμφέρον ἀναπεμπομένη, *Str.* IV. P. 580 τοῦ μετανοοῦντος τρόποι δύο, ὁ μὲν κοινότερος φόβος ἐπὶ τοῖς πραχθεῖσιν, ὁ δὲ ἰδιαίτερος ἡ δυσωπία ἡ πρὸς ἑαυτὴν τῆς ψυχῆς ἐκ συνειδήσεως,

---

[1] When the initial α was lost, the termination -ου would naturally be changed to -ας. Cl. does not appear to have used the three terminations of ἀΐδιος, as was done by some later writers, cf. Lob. *Phryn.* pp. 105, 106, Schmid IV. 48.

εἶτ᾽ οὖν ἐνταῦθα εἴτε καὶ ἀλλαχῇ, ἐπεὶ μηδεὶς τόπος ἀργὸς εὐποιίας θεοῦ, Str. VI. P. 795 ἀγαθὴ ἡ τοῦ θεοῦ δικαιοσύνη καὶ δικαία ἐστὶν ἡ ἀγαθότης αὐτοῦ. κἂν παύσωνται ἄρα που αἱ τιμωρίαι κατὰ τὴν ἀποπλήρωσιν τῆς κτίσεως καὶ τῆς ἑκάστου ἀποκαθάρσεως μεγίστην ἔχουσι παραμένουσαν λύπην οἱ τῆς ἄλλης ἄξιοι εὑρεθέντες αὐλῆς ἐπὶ τῷ μὴ συνεῖναι τοῖς διὰ δικαιοσύνην δοξασθεῖσιν, below p. 180. 14, above p. 98. 11.

29. **εὐσυνείδητος πρὸς τὴν ἔξοδον.** See below p. 138. 3, p. 144. 22, Anton. VI. 30 ἵν᾽ οὕτως εὐσυνειδήτῳ σοι ἐπιστῇ ἡ τελευταία ὥρα ὡς ἐκείνῳ, Ign. *Mag.* 4 with Lightfoot's n. The word ἔξοδος is used of death in Luke ix. 31, 2 Pet. i. 15, cf. Wisdom vii. 6 μία δὲ πάντων εἴσοδος εἰς τὸν βίον ἔξοδός τε ἴση.

p. 136, line 1. **κληρονομημάτων τῶν ἰδίων.** See n. on p. 106. 29 above. Cl. adopts the Stoic distinction of ἴδια (= τὰ ἐφ᾽ ἡμῖν) and ἀλλότρια (= τὰ ἐκτός); cf. Epict. *Diss.* IV. 1. 130 τὸ σῶμα ἀλλότριον, τὰ μέρη αὐτοῦ ἀλλότρια, ἡ κτῆσις ἀλλοτρία. ἂν οὖν τινι τούτων ὡς ἰδίῳ προσπαθῇς, δώσεις δίκας ἃς ἄξιον τὸν τῶν ἀλλοτρίων ἐφιέμενον (other exx. in Schenkl's index s.v. ἀλλότριος), cf. the famous saying of Anaxarchus (*Str.* IV. 589) πτίσσε τὸν Ἀναξάρχου θύλακον· Ἀνάξαρχον γὰρ οὐ πτίσσεις. See too *Str.* IV. P. 605 ἀλλότρια ἡμεῖς φαμεν τὰ τοῦ κόσμου...ἐπειδὴ μὴ καταμένομεν ἐν αὐτοῖς τὸν πάντα αἰῶνα, κτήσει ὄντα ἀλλότρια καὶ τῶν κατὰ διαδοχὴν ὑπάρχοντα, *Q. D. S.* 946 P. *init.* (of two kinds of poverty) ὁ μὲν κατὰ πνεῦμα πτωχὸς τὸ ἴδιον, ὁ δὲ κατὰ κόσμον τὸ ἀλλότριον, where see Segaar. The word κληρονόμημα is very rare. In p. 96. 26 ἡ κληρονομία is mentioned as the goal of the Christian course. The usual punctuation is after κληρονομημάτων, in which case we should perhaps read μονῶν, but I think ξένοι reads best with τῶν τῇδε alone. In any case the plurals are a little difficult. Perhaps they are meant to imply that the κληρονομία is given in portions.

3. **θαυμάζων τὰς ἐντολάς.** Plato (*Theaet.* 155 D) and Aristotle (*Met.* I. 2) make wonder the beginning of philosophy. Cl. (above p. 104. 6, where see n., and below p. 146. 2) makes the admiration of the universe the starting point of faith and knowledge. In p. 108. 11 fol. the gnostic is described as keeping his eyes fastened on noble images: here it is the Divine Law which excites his wonder.

5. **οἰκεῖος τοῦ κυρίου καὶ τῶν ἐντολῶν.** Gal. vi. 10 οἰκείους τῆς πίστεως, Eph. iii. 19 οἰκεῖοι τοῦ θεοῦ, above p. 14. 17 οἱ οἰκεῖοι τῆς προνοίας.

ἐξειλεγμένος ὡς δίκαιος. Cf. p. 4. 24 ἐξειλ. εἰς γνῶσιν. Foreseen righteousness is the cause of their election, cf. *Str.* VI. P. 792 *fin.* οὐχ ὅτι ἦσαν ἐκλεκτοὶ γενόμενοι ἀπόστολοι κατά τι φύσεως ἐξαίρετον ἰδίωμα, ἐπεὶ καὶ ὁ Ἰούδας ἐξελέγη σὺν αὐτοῖς, ἀλλ᾽ οἷοί τε ἦσαν ἀπόστολοι γενέσθαι, ἐκλεγέντες πρὸς τοῦ καὶ τὰ τέλη προορωμένου, ib. P. 778 καθάπερ προῃρημένως κεῖται δι᾽ ὧν πράξει καὶ οὗ τεύξεται, οὕτως καὶ αὐτὸς προορίσας ἔχει δι᾽ ὧν (ms. ὃν) ἔγνω ὃν ἠγάπησεν. 'All the early Fathers agree that God predestines men to bliss or condemnation, as He foresees their good acts: the foreseeing of these acts is not the cause of them, but the acts are the cause of the foreknowledge.' Gieseler in Hagenberg, *Hist. Doctr.* I. p. 270.

6. βασιλικός. Cf. above p. 36. 9 ὁ τῷ ὄντι βασιλικὸς τὴν ψυχὴν καὶ γνωστικός, p. 62. 23 οὗτος ὁ β. ἄνθρωπος, οὗτος ἱερεὺς ὅσιος τοῦ θεοῦ.

ὡς γνωστικός. The omission of the MS. article seems required by the corresponding ὡς δίκαιος and by l. 30 below.

10. διὸ καὶ ἐσθίων, κ.τ.λ. Potter compares p. 122. 17 f. διὸ καὶ ἐσθίει κ.τ.λ. ἐὰν ὁ λόγος αἱρῇ. See Index s.v. αἱρέω.

11. ὀνείρους βλέπων. See above p. 62. 28, 132. 30. Potter compares *Str.* VI. P. 779 *fin.* ἄκαμπτος ἡδοναῖς ταῖς τε ὕπαρ ταῖς δὲ δι' ὀνειράτων· διαίτῃ γὰρ λιτῇ καὶ αὐταρκείᾳ συνειθισμένος, σωφρονικὸς ὑπάρχει.

11, 12. ἀλλὰ καὶ τὰ ἅγια ποιεῖ...καθαρὸς εἰς εὐχὴν πάντοτε. ὁ δὲ καὶ μετ' ἀγγέλων εὔχεται. Cf. for the use of ὁ δέ, referring to the subject of the preceding sentence, p. 86. 19 f. ἐν παντὶ τοίνυν τόπῳ...εὔξεται· ὁ δὲ καὶ περιπάτῳ χρώμενος...εὔχεται, Herodian III. 11. 4 οὗτος ὑπερβαλλόντως τὸν Πλαυτιανὸν ἐθεράπευε· καὶ πάντων τοῦτο ποιούντων, ἐκεῖνος δὲ πλείονι θρησκείᾳ ᾠκείωτο αὐτόν.

14. ἀγίας φρουρᾶς. Ps. xci. 11, 12.

τὸν τῶν ἁγίων χορὸν συνιστάμενον ἔχει. See above p. 86. 14 διὰ τούτων (εὐχῶν) ἑαυτὸν ἑνοποιεῖ τῷ θείῳ χορῷ, below p. 138. 31 μετὰ τῶν ὁμοίων διάγει τῷ πνεύματι ἐν τοῖς χοροῖς τῶν ἁγίων κἂν ἐπὶ γῆς ἔτι κατέχηται. Orig. *de Orat.* 11 οὐ μόνος ὁ ἀρχιερεὺς τοῖς γνησίως εὐχομένοις συνεύχεται, ἀλλὰ καὶ οἱ ἐν οὐρανῷ χαίροντες ἄγγελοι...αἵ τε τῶν προκεκοιμημένων ἁγίων ψυχαί.

15—18. The MS. reading is difficult here. As a makeshift I suggest the omission of καί after οἶδε (in which I find I am anticipated by D. in Potter's n. vol. IV. p. 439), the transposition of ἐνέργειαν after οἶδε, and the change of πιστευομένου into ἐπισταμένου on account of the words which follow. By itself, it makes good sense to speak of the joint energy of the believer and of Him in whom he believes (which is quite in accordance with l. 4 μέτοχος ὢν τῆς θείας βουλήσεως, and with p. 72. 16 f., where holiness is said to involve free choice on the part of God and man); but this does not seem to have any connexion with the subsequent distinction between the two kinds of righteousness, that of love, which belongs to the gnostic, that of fear, which belongs to the believer; cf. above p. 100. 7 f.

§ 79. **22. ἀποχὴν κακῶν ἐργάζεται ὁ φόβος.** For the contrast between the motives of fear and love, cf. *Str.* VI. P. 625 ἔργον τοῦ γνωστικοῦ οὐχ ἡ ἀποχὴ τῶν κακῶν (ἐπιβάθρα γὰρ αὕτη προκοπῆς μεγίστης), οὐδὲ μὴν ποιεῖν τι ἀγαθὸν διὰ φόβον...ἀλλ' οὐδὲ δι' ἐλπίδα τιμῆς...μόνη δ' ἡ δι' ἀγάπην εὐποιία, ἡ δι' αὐτὸ τὸ καλόν, αἱρετὴ τῷ γνωστικῷ, above p. 126. 1, n.

25. προσίῃ ταῖς εὐχαῖς. The plural with the article seems to imply the prayers of the Church, as in Acts ii. 42. Catechumens were not allowed to use the Lord's Prayer.

26. εὐχαριστία. Cf. above p. 72. 2 ἡ εὐχ. ἔργον τοῦ γνωστικοῦ, and Isidorus *ap.* Cl. *Str.* III. P. 510 *init.* ὅταν ἡ εὐχαριστία σου εἰς αἴτησιν ὑποπέσῃ, γάμησον.

27, 28. τοῖς μέλλουσιν ὡς ἤδη παροῦσιν. See above p. 82. 11 γέγηθεν ἐπὶ τοῖς ἐπηγγελμένοις ὡς ἤδη παροῦσιν, 130. 15 f.

28, 29. τούτου ἡγεῖται τὸ εἰληφέναι τὴν γνῶσιν. For this use of ἡγέομαι see below p. 166. 26 ἡγ. τῆς γνώσεως. Aristides I. p. 385 (*Orat*. 30) ὅτου γὰρ ἂν πράγματος μὴ τὸ δυνατὸν ἡγῆται, τό γε λοιπὸν ὕθλοι καὶ σκιαί.

31. ὡς ἄσαρκος. Below p. 152. 18.

τυχεῖν μὲν τῶν ἀρίστων. Called in p. 76. 16, and p. 68. 27, τὰ ὅπως ἀγαθὰ τὰ περὶ ψυχήν. We may pray for the ἄριστα, but not the κάλλιστα (above p. 126. 19).

p. 138, line 1. **ἐπικουφισμόν.** See p. 142. 15, and p. 118. 26 θλιβόμενον ἐπικουφίζει παραμυθίαις.

3—5. See above p. 134. 29 f., and below p. 144. 21—25, also *Str*. IV. P. 640 ἀπολιπὼν τὴν οἴκησιν καὶ τὴν κτῆσιν ἀπροσπαθῶς, προθύμως τῷ ἀπάγοντι τοῦ βίου συνεπόμενος, οὐδαμῶς ὀπίσω κατ' οὐδεμίαν ἀφορμὴν ἐπιστρεφόμενος...εὐλογῶν δὲ ἐπὶ τῇ ἐξόδῳ, τὴν μονὴν ἀσπαζόμενος τὴν ἐν οὐρανῷ, *ib*. P. 569 καλούμενος ὁ γνωστικὸς ὑπακούει ῥᾳδίως καὶ τῷ τὸ σωμάτιον αἰτοῦντι φέρων προσδίδωσι...εὐχαρίστως ἑνούμενος πρὸς τὸ συγγενές, οὐ μὴν ἀλλὰ καὶ τῷ τιμίῳ αἵματι τοὺς ἀπίστους δυσωπῶν.

4. προάγων. It seems better to take this of the gnostic rather than of ὁ καλῶν, in consequence of the following ὡς εἰπεῖν. That Christ goes before is literally true; that the martyr anticipates his call is only a hyperbolical expression to denote his willingness to obey the call.

εὐχαριστῆσαι is probably best understood as equivalent to εὐλογῶν in the passage quoted above from P. 640, but there seems to be some allusion to the blood of the martyr being offered as a eucharistic sacrifice; see *Str*. IV. P. 623 (the term 'perfect' cannot be used till the close of life) φθάσαντος ἤδη τοῦ γνωστικοῦ μάρτυρος τὸ τέλειον ἔργον ἐνδείξασθαι καὶ παραστῆσαι κυρίως, δι' ἀγάπης γνωστικῆς εὐχαριστηθέντος αἵματος. The following ἐκεῖ may then be understood of the martyrdom, or (as in Plato) of the other world.

7. κατὰ ἀνάκρασιν. Cf. below p. 152. 19 τῷ πνεύματι τῷ ἁγίῳ ἀνεκράθητε, Segaar's n. on *Q. D. S.* 956 P. ὁ θεὸς δι' ἀγάπην ἡμῖν ἀνεκράθη (al. ἐθεάθη), and Ign. *Eph*. 5 with Lightfoot's n. on ἀνακεκραμένους.

9. μετουσίᾳ θερμότητος θερμός. Cf. above p. 68. 1, and *Str*. IV. P. 581 ἀγαθὰ τὰ μὲν αὐτὰ καθ' ἑαυτά, τὰ δὲ μετέχοντα τῶν ἀγαθῶν, ὡς τὰς καλὰς πράξεις φαμέν...ὅταν τοίνυν ἐνδιατρίψῃ τῇ θεωρίᾳ...ὁ γνωστικῶς μετέχων τῆς ἁγίας ποιότητος προσεχέστερον ἐν ἕξει γίνεται ταυτότητος ἀπαθοῦς, ὡς μηκέτι ἐπιστήμην ἔχειν καὶ γνῶσιν κεκτῆσθαι, ἐπιστήμην δὲ εἶναι καὶ γνῶσιν. These somewhat hyperbolical expressions may perhaps be defended by such passages as Eph. iii. 19.

10. ὅλος φῶς. Cf. above p. 10. 2 (of the Son) ὅλος φῶς πατρῷον.

11. ἐὰν μὴ μισήσητε, κ.τ.λ. The original has εἴ τις...οὐ μισεῖ τὸν πατέρα αὐτοῦ καὶ τὴν μητέρα καὶ τὴν γυναῖκα καὶ τὰ τέκνα καὶ τοὺς ἀδελφοὺς καὶ τὰς ἀδελφάς, ἔτι τε καὶ τὴν ἑαυτοῦ ψυχήν, οὐ δύναταί μου (ἐμός *Q. D. S.* § 22) μαθητὴς εἶναι. καὶ ὅστις οὐ βαστάζει τὸν σταυρὸν ἑαυτοῦ καὶ ἔρχεται ὀπίσω μου, οὐ δύναταί μου εἶναι μαθητής.

12. **τὸ σημεῖον**. Potter compares *Str.* v. P. 666 fin. ἔχει δὲ καὶ ἄλλο αἴνιγμα ἡ λυχνία ἡ χρυσῆ τοῦ σημείου τοῦ χριστοῦ, οὐ τῷ σχήματι μόνῳ, *Str.* VI. P. 782 init. φασὶν οὖν εἶναι τοῦ μὲν κυριακοῦ σημείου τύπον κατὰ τὸ σχῆμα τὸ τριακοσιοστὸν στοιχεῖον, ib. P. 783 fin., *Exc. Theod.* P. 979 τὰ σπέρματα ὁ Ἰησοῦς, διὰ τοῦ σημείου ἐπὶ τῶν ὤμων βαστάσας, εἰσάγει εἰς τὸ πλήρωμα. See also Joh. iii. 14, xii. 32, *Q. D. S.* 939 P. fin. ὁ σωτὴρ ἀπὸ γενέσεως μέχρι τοῦ σημείου with Segaar's *Excursus* II., Tert. *Cor.* 3 fin. ad omnem aditum et exitum, ad calciatum, ad lavacra, ad mensas, ad lumina, ad cubilia, ad sedilia, quaecunque nos conversatio exerceat, frontem crucis signaculo terimus, Orig. *Sch. in Ezek.* c. 9 (a Christian writer regards the Egyptian Tau as symbolical of the cross) καὶ προφητεύεσθαι περὶ τοῦ γενομένου ἐν Χριστιανοῖς ἐπὶ τοῦ μετώπου σημείου· ὅπερ ποιοῦσιν οἱ πεπιστευκότες πάντες οὑτινοσοῦν προκαταρχόμενοι πράγματος καὶ μάλιστα ἡ εὐχῶν ἢ ἁγίων ἀναγνωσμάτων, Athan. *V. Ant.* 23 (apparitions sent by demons disappear) ἐὰν μάλιστα τῇ πίστει καὶ τῷ σημείῳ τοῦ σταυροῦ ἑαυτόν τις περιφράττῃ, and art. on 'Sign of the Cross' in *Dict. of Chr. Ant.* Probably this use of the word originated in the description of the Brazen Serpent (Num. xxi. 9), ἐποίησεν ὄφιν χαλκοῦν καὶ ἔστησεν αὐτὸν ἐπὶ σημείου, of which Justin says (c. *Tryph.* 94) ἐκήρυσσε σωτηρίαν τοῖς πιστεύουσιν ἐπὶ τὸν διὰ τοῦ σημείου τούτου, τουτέστι τοῦ σταυροῦ, θανατοῦσθαι μέλλοντα; cf. also Isa. xlix. 22 ἰδοὺ αἴρω εἰς τὰ ἔθνη τὴν χεῖρά μου καὶ εἰς τὰς νήσους ἀρῶ σύσσημόν μου, which is referred to the crucifixion by Ign. *Smyrn.* 1, and by Barnabas xii. 5. The word combines the ideas of a standard, a watchword, a token.

13. **προσπαθείας**. See n. on ἀπροσπαθής above p. 110. 7.

15. **τῶν εἰς δημιουργίαν οἰκείων**. See n. on ποριστικῶν, p. 30. 29 above.

16. **τῆς σωματικῆς ψυχῆς**. Cf. *Str.* VI. P. 808, quoted on p. 106. 27 above and the words which follow, διὰ τοῦ σωματικοῦ πνεύματος αἰσθάνεται ὁ ἄνθρωπος, ἐπιθυμεῖ, ἥδεται, ὀργίζεται, τρέφεται, αὔξεται· καὶ δὴ καὶ πρὸς τὰς πράξεις διὰ τούτου πορεύεται τὰ κατ' ἔννοιάν τε καὶ διάνοιαν, καὶ ἐπειδὰν κρατῇ τῶν ἐπιθυμιῶν, βασιλεύει τὸ ἡγεμονικόν, *Exc. Theod.* P. 981, where the οὐράνιος and θεία ψυχή is distinguished from the γεώδης and ὑλικὴ ψυχή, and Kaye, p. 138.

17. **ἀφηνιάζοντι**. See above p. 92. 27.

19. **τὸν θάνατον περιφέρειν**. 2 Cor. iv. 10 πάντοτε τὴν νέκρωσιν τοῦ κυρίου Ἰησοῦ ἐν τῷ σώματι περιφέροντες.

20. **πᾶσιν ἀποταξάμενον**. Luke xiv. 33 πᾶς ἐξ ὑμῶν ὃς οὐκ ἀποτάσσεται πᾶσι τοῖς ἑαυτοῦ ὑπάρχουσιν οὐ δύναταί μου εἶναι μαθητής.

§ 80. 23. **θᾶττον τοῦ λέγειν**. Cf. λόγου θᾶττον Heliod. IV. 7. 7, v. 9. 2, dicto citius Hor. *Sat.* II. 2. 80, θ. νοήματος Xen. *Mem.* IV. 3. 18.

24. **τὰ τῶν ἀδελφῶν ἁμαρτήματα μερίσασθαι εὐχόμενος**. Rom. ix. 3 ηὐχόμην γὰρ αὐτὸς ἐγὼ ἀνάθεμα εἶναι ὑπὲρ τῶν ἀδελφῶν μου, τῶν συγγενῶν μου κατὰ σάρκα.

25. **ἐξομολόγησιν**. Strictly used of the public confession of sin by the penitent, then for the whole course of penitential discipline; see art. s.v. in *Dict. of Chr. Ant.*

28. τὰ παρ' αὐτῷ κατατιθέμενα σπέρματα. Cf. Str. I. P. 323 (the successors of the Apostles) ἧκον καὶ εἰς ἡμᾶς τὰ προγονικὰ ἐκεῖνα καὶ ἀποστολικὰ καθησόμενοι σπέρματα, and (on the Lord's husbandry) above p. 6. 13 f., p. 129. 15 f.

29, 30. ἀναμάρτητος μέν, ἐγκρατὴς δὲ γίνεται. It is startling to find sinlessness spoken of as a state preceding self-control; but it is probably to be understood here of the lower stage, ἀποχὴ κακῶν, as opposed to the higher stage, ἐνέργεια εὐποιίας (above p. 126. 2), not yet a fixed habit of mind, like ἐγκράτεια. Cl. however seems in places to speak as if man could really attain to a sinless perfection here on earth; see above p. 22. 20 n., p. 94. 12, and Kaye, p. 146 n. 1.

30. μετὰ τῶν ὁμοίων. Above p. 86. 5.

31. ἐν τοῖς χοροῖς τῶν ἁγίων. Above p. 136. 13, p. 78. 12 n.

p. 140, line 2. οὐ πρωίας μόνον ἀναστὰς καὶ μέσον ἡμέρας. If we keep ἀναστάς (and it seems supported by διανιστάμενος in Deut. vi. 7), it will refer only to πρωίας. The word ἀναστάς had occurred to me as applicable at noon also; see p. 68. 28 τὴν ψυχὴν ἐπτερωμένην, with the passages quoted in the n., and Philo 2 M. p. 604 αἱ ψυχαὶ ὅθεν ὡρμήθησαν ἐκεῖσε πάλιν ἀνέπτησαν.

πρωίας occurs in LXX. and N.T. as in Matt. xxi. 18 πρωίας ἐπανάγων εἰς τὴν πόλιν. It had occurred to me that μεσημβρίας might be the true reading for μέσον ἡμέρας, as in Ps. lv. 17 ἑσπέρας καὶ πρωὶ καὶ μεσημβρίας διηγήσομαι; but the text is confirmed by Phil. ii. 15 τέκνα θεοῦ ἄμωμα μέσον γενεᾶς σκολιᾶς, Acts xxvii. 27 κατὰ μέσον τῆς νυκτός, Xen. Anab. I. 8. 8 ἤδη ἦν μέσον ἡμέρας, and especially Susanna 7 ἡνίκα ἀπέτρεχεν ὁ λαὸς μέσον ἡμέρας, εἰσεπορεύετο Σουσάννα, Theophr. Char. x. fin. τὸ μέσον τῆς ἡμέρας ὑπολυομένους, where Casaubon notes 'Atticum est pro κατὰ τὴν μεσημβρίαν.' See Lobeck, Phryn. pp. 53 and 465. For the thought cf. above p. 62. 12, 86. 10 f., and Deut. vi. 7 προβιβάσεις αὐτὰ τοὺς υἱούς σου καὶ λαλήσεις ἐν αὐτοῖς καθήμενος ἐν οἴκῳ καὶ πορευόμενος ἐν ὁδῷ καὶ κοιταζόμενος καὶ διανιστάμενος, ib. xi. 19.

5. ἐὰν υἱὸς ᾖ τὸ γένος. I understand this, not as excluding daughters, but as justifying the use of the term υἱός ('son,' assuming, that is, the child to be of the male sex; otherwise, 'daughter'). For τὸ γένος cf. Str. IV. P. 563 ὁμοίως φιλοσοφητέον κἂν ἀνὴρ ἢ γυνὴ τὸ γένος ὑπάρχῃ.

6, 7. τὰ ζῷα τὰ δοξολόγα. A similar phrase is used of the Cherubim in Str. v. 667 fin.

9. Job is taken as an example of the gnostic Christian in Str. IV. 572 (cf. St James v. 10, 11), where he is compared with the Stoic wise man.

12. ἦν γὰρ... πονηρίας. The words in Job i. 1 are καὶ ἦν ὁ ἄνθρωπος ἐκεῖνος ἀληθινός, ἄμεμπτος, δίκαιος, θεοσεβής, ἀπεχόμενος ἀπὸ παντὸς πονηροῦ πράγματος.

13. For the definition of holiness cf. Cic. N. D. I. 116 pietas justitia adversum deos, Sext. Emp. Math. IX. 123 ὁσιότης δικαιοσύνη τις πρὸς θεούς, and Str. VI. P. 803 ἡ δικαιοσύνη ἀνθρωπίνη οὖσα κοινὸν ὑποβέβηκε τῇ ὁσιότητι, θείᾳ δικαιοσύνῃ ὑπαρχούσῃ (MS. θείαν -ην -σαν).

15. προστετηκέναι, a favourite word in late Greek. The metaphorical sense is, I suppose, derived from the soldering of metals.

16. ἀπεχθάνεσθαι αὐτοῖς. Cf. Ael. V. H. II. 21 ἤρετο τί βουλόμενος οὕτω πυκνὰ ἀπεχθάνεται τῷ πάντων μάλιστα φιλοῦντι αὐτόν, ib. XII. 16 ἀπήχθετο Περδίκκᾳ Ἀλέξανδρος ὅτι ἦν πολεμικός, ib. XIV. 15 οὐκ ἠβούλετο ἀπεχθάνεσθαι τούτοις πρὸς οὓς διελέγετο. This meaning is not noticed in L. and S. Stephanus cites Jos. Ant. XIII. 9. 3 τῶν Σύρων πρὸς αὐτὸν ἀπεχθανομένων, πονηρὸς γὰρ ἦν, ib. 5. 3, and XL 4. 1.

18. ἀσφαλής. Heind. on Plato Soph. 231 explains 'hic, ut saepe, est cautius,' citing Xen. Mem. III. 1. 6 τὸν στρατηγὸν εἶναι δεῖ ἀσφαλῆ καὶ ἐπιθετικόν, Eur. Phoeniss. 599 ἀσφαλής γάρ ἐστ' ἀμείνων ἢ θρασὺς στρατηλάτης.

19. συμπεριφορᾷ. See above p. 92. 30 f.

μὴ λάθῃ ἡ συμπεριφορὰ διάθεσις γινομένη. I can make no sense of the MS. reading, which probably arose from dittography of η and the consequent alteration of the participle into the subjunctive. [Barnard suggests λάθρῃ for λάθῃ ἥ, but would Cl. have used the Ionic form?]

§ 81. 24. μηδενὸς ἐπιθυμεῖν. As this does not seem very appropriate to the context, it had occurred to me that ἐπιφθονεῖν should be read for ἐπιθυμεῖν, and μηδενί for μηδενός. It appears however to belong to a quotation, see Str. IV. P. 602 init. where Cl. quotes Basilides to the following effect, ἓν μέρος ἐκ τοῦ λεγομένου θελήματος τοῦ θεοῦ τὸ ἠγαπηκέναι ἅπαντα...ἕτερον δὲ τὸ μηδενὸς ἐπιθυμεῖν καὶ τρίτον μισεῖν μηδὲ ἕν.

26. μή τι. See p. 112. 22, 120. 11, 152. 20, 158. 1, 13.

τέλειον εἶναι βουλόμενος. The meaning of the text is again discussed in p. 154. 20 f.

p. 142, line 1. τουτέστιν ἑαυτόν. I think ὡς must have been lost before ἑαυτόν. Cl. could not have said that Christ *was* the Father in Heaven.

2. ἀκούσατέ μου. The original has διδάξω ὑμᾶς.

4, 5. τὴν φρουρὰν ἔχειν παρ' ἑαυτοῦ. This seems to contradict p. 136. 13 οὐδὲ ἔξω ποτὲ τῆς ἁγίας φρουρᾶς γίνεται. See however p. 112. 12 f., p. 76. 18 f., and the remarkable sentence in Q. D. S. 957 P. τῶν μὲν προγεγενημένων θεὸς δίδωσιν ἄφεσιν, τῶν δὲ ἐπιόντων αὐτὸς ἕκαστος ἑαυτῷ, and Ecl. Proph. P. 993 init. ὁ μὲν πιστεύσας ἄφεσιν ἁμαρτημάτων ἔλαβεν παρὰ τοῦ κυρίου· ὁ δὲ ἐν γνώσει γενόμενος ἅτε μηκέτι ἁμαρτάνων παρ' ἑαυτοῦ τὴν ἄφεσιν τῶν λοιπῶν κομίζεται.

6. οὐχὶ δὲ καὶ αἰτεῖ. The only way in which I can make sense of this is to suppose it a marginal query by a reader, who stumbled at the previous ἀπαιτεῖ. If it were a statement by Cl. himself, it must surely have run ἀλλ' οὐκέτι αἰτεῖ.

11. ἀτύφως παρέχεται. Cf. Matt. vi. 3, 4.

13, 14. διόρθωσιν...ἐπιστροφήν. Would not these be more appropriately interchanged, amendment being concerned with the future, repentance and conversion with the past? For ἐπιστρ. see p. 72. 3, and p. 68. 16.

15. ἐπικουφισμόν. See p. 138. 1.

§ 82. 19. The Traditions of Matthias are also cited in *Str*. II. P. 453 Ματθίας ἐν ταῖς παραδόσεσι παραινῶν (λέγει), θαύμησον τὰ παρόντα, βάθρον τοῦτο πρῶτον τῆς ἐπέκεινα γνώσεως ὑποτιθέμενος, *Str*. III. P. 523 λέγουσι γοῦν καὶ τὸν Μ. οὕτως διδάξαι, σαρκὶ μὲν μάχεσθαι καὶ παραχρῆσθαι, μηδὲν αὐτῇ πρὸς ἡδονὴν ἀκόλαστον ἐνδιδόντα, ψυχὴν δὲ αὔξειν διὰ πίστεως καὶ γνώσεως, below p. 190. 14, where Dindorf quotes Hippolyt. *Ref. Haer*. VII. 20 Βασιλείδης καὶ Ἰσίδωρος...φασὶν εἰρηκέναι Ματθίαν αὐτοῖς λόγους ἀποκρύφους, οὓς ἤκουσε παρὰ τοῦ Σωτῆρος κατ' ἰδίαν διδαχθείς. The name occurs in *Str*. IV. P. 579, but no doubt Ματθαίων should be read instead. The Traditions are probably the same as the Gospel mentioned by Origen (*Hom*. 1 *in Luc*.) where after stating that 'ecclesia quattuor habet evangelia, haereses plurima' he continues 'scio quoddam evangelium quod appellatur secundum Thomam et secundum Mathiam, et alia plura legimus, ne quid ignorare videremur propter eos qui se putant aliquid scire, si ista cognoverint.' It is also mentioned among spurious gospels by Euseb. *H. E*. III. 25. Dr Salmon thinks that it is referred to in a fragment of the Hypotyposes (*Adumbr. in Epist. Joh*. I. P. 1009) 'fertur in traditionibus [quoniam] Joannes ipsum corpus quod erat extrinsecus tangens, manum suam in profunda misisse, et ei duritiam carnis nullo modo reluctatam esse sed locum manui praebuisse discipuli.' See his art. on 'Matthias, Traditions of' in *D. of Christ. Biog*. vol. II. p. 863, and Resch *Agrapha* p. 447. For the thought cf. above p. 62. 2 f.

26. θεοφορῶν καὶ θεοφορούμενος. See Index *s.v*. and Lightfoot's n. on the double sense of θεοφόρος (Ign. vol. II. p. 21). He compares similar expressions of the Stoics, as of Epictetus (*Diss*. II. 8. 12 f.) οὐκ οἶδας ὅτι θεὸν περιφέρεις; ἐν σαυτῷ φέρεις αὐτόν, καὶ μολύνων οὐκ αἰσθάνῃ ἀκαθάρτοις μὲν διανοήμασι ῥυπαραῖς δὲ πράξεσι. καὶ ἀγάλματος μὲν τοῦ θεοῦ παρόντος οὐκ ἂν τολμήσαις τι τούτων ποιεῖν ὧν ποιεῖς· αὐτοῦ δὲ τοῦ θεοῦ παρόντος ἔσωθεν καὶ ἐφορῶντος πάντα καὶ ἐπακούοντος οὐκ αἰσχύνῃ; In our passage the ἐκλεκτός of Matthias is to others an ἄγαλμα θεῖον, but he himself, the gnostic, has a more prevailing witness in the God within him, who is also the moving and inspiring principle of his life. The passive is used by Lucian *Philops*. 38, and a play of Menander's bore the title ἡ θεοφορουμένη. Cf. 2 Pet. i. 21 ὑπὸ πνεύματος ἁγίου φερόμενοι ἐλάλησαν ἅγιοι τοῦ θεοῦ ἄνθρωποι, Justin M. *Apol*. I. 43 Ἠσαΐας θεοφορούμενος τῷ πνεύματι τῷ προφητικῷ. So Philo M. 1. 689 ὅταν ἐξ ἔρωτος θείου κατασχεθεὶς ὁ νοῦς ὁρμῇ καὶ σπουδῇ πάσῃ χρώμενος προέρχηται θεοφορούμενος, ἐπιλήσεται τῶν ἄλλων: he speaks also of a θεοφόρητος μανία M. 1. 229, 658, M. 2. 659. Cl. uses the phrase in relation to Plato (*Str*. I. P. 341).

28. ἡ γραφὴ τοὺς παραπεσόντας τοῖς ἀλλοφύλοις πιπράσκει. Cf. *Str*. II. P. 506 τὸ ὑποπεσεῖν τοῖς πάθεσιν ἐσχάτη δουλεία, ὥσπερ τὸ κρατεῖν τούτων ἐλευθερία μόνη. ἡ γοῦν θεία γραφὴ τοὺς παραβάντας τὰς ἐντολὰς πεπρᾶσθαι λέγει τοῖς ἀλλοφύλοις, τουτέστιν ἁμαρτίαις ἀνοικείοις τῇ φύσει, ἄχρις ἂν ἐπιστρέψαντες μετανοήσωσι, and *Str*. III. P. 552. The scripture reference is

to such passages as 1 Sam. xii. 9 ἐπελάθοντο Κυρίου τοῦ θεοῦ αὐτῶν καὶ ἀπέδοτο αὐτούς...εἰς χεῖρας ἀλλοφύλων, 2 Kings xvii. 17, and Isa. l. 1 ταῖς ἁμαρτίαις ὑμῶν ἐπράθητε. (I think Hervetus wrong in supposing the reference to be to the boastful Joseph, sold by his brothers to the Midianites.) πιπράσκει brachylogy for πιπράσκεσθαι λέγει.

29. μὴ ἐμβλέψῃς πρὸς ἐπιθυμίαν ἀλλοτρίᾳ γυναικί. Cf. Mt. v. 28 πᾶς ὁ βλέπων γυναῖκα πρὸς τὸ ἐπιθυμῆσαι [αὐτὴν] ἤδη ἐμοίχευσεν αὐτήν, with Barnard's n. on the reading in his *Biblical Text of Clement* (Texts and Studies, vol. v. no. 5, p. 6). ἀλλοτρία is added from Prov. vii. 5 &c. where it has the meaning 'strange,' not only in the sense of belonging to another man, but as belonging to a foreign nation, in which prostitution was not forbidden as in Israel.

p. 144, line 2. See above p. 48. 2—20.

4. τὸ σπέρμα σῴζων τὸ Ἀβραάμ. Gal. iii. 29 εἰ δὲ ὑμεῖς Χριστοῦ, ἄρα τοῦ Ἀβραὰμ σπέρμα ἐστί, κατ' ἐπαγγελίαν κληρονόμοι, Rom. iv. 16, 1 John iii. 9 πᾶς ὁ γεγεννημένος ἐκ τοῦ θεοῦ ἁμαρτίαν οὐ ποιεῖ, ὅτι σπέρμα αὐτοῦ μένει, above p. 138. 28 f. αὔξων τὰ παρ' αὐτῷ κατατιθέμενα σπέρματα ἀναμάρτητος μένει, Orig. *in Joh.* xix. 3 ὅσον γε σῴζομεν τὰ ἐνσπαρέντα ἡμῶν τῇ ψυχῇ τῆς ἀληθείας σπέρματα, οὐδέπω ἀπελήλυθεν ἀφ' ἡμῶν ὁ λόγος. In *Str.* vi. P. 770 *fin.* we find the σπέρμα Ἀβραάμ contrasted with the υἱοὶ Ἰακώβ as the κλητοί with the ἐκλεκτοί.

5. ἀναπαυόμενον τὸν θεόν. Cf. *Ecl. Proph.* P. 1003 θρόνοι ἂν εἶεν οἱ πρωτόκτιστοι διὰ τὸ ἀναπαύεσθαι ἐν αὐτοῖς τὸν θεόν, ὡς καὶ ἐν τοῖς πιστεύουσιν ...ἕκαστος ἔχει τὴν περὶ θεοῦ γνῶσιν, ἐφ' ᾗ γνώσει ἀναπαύεται ὁ θεός, *Str.* I. P. 329 μόνῳ τῷ πιστεύοντι ἐπαναπαύεται τὸ κεφάλαιον τῶν ὄντων, Orig. *de Orat.* 26 ὁ πρωτότοκος ᾧ ὁ πατὴρ ὡς θρόνῳ ἐπαναπαύεται, Isa. lvii. 15 τάδε λέγει ὁ ὕψιστος ἐν ὑψηλοῖς κατοικῶν τὸν αἰῶνα, ὕψιστος ἐν ἁγίοις ἀναπαυόμενος, 2 Sam. xxii. 10 ἐπεκάθισεν ἐπὶ τῷ χερουβὶμ καὶ ἐπετάσθη, Ezek. x. 18 δόξα κυρίου ἐπέβη ἐπὶ τὰ χερουβίμ, Ps. xcix. 1 ὁ καθήμενος ἐπὶ τῶν χερουβίμ.

7. ὑπερηφανήσας. For the transitive force see Index.

7, 8. τέμνει διὰ τῆς ἐπιστήμης τὸν οὐρανόν. Above p. 64. 27 τὰ νοήματα τῶν ἁγίων τέμνει τὸν ὅλον κόσμον. For διὰ τῆς ἐπιστήμης, cf. *Str.* I. P. 318 οἱ δὲ ἐντραφέντες γνησίως τοῖς τῆς ἀληθείας λόγοις ἐφόδια ζωῆς ἀιδίου λαβόντες εἰς οὐρανὸν πτεροῦνται, and above p. 98. 23 (ἡ γνῶσις) εἰς τὸ συγγενὲς τῆς ψυχῆς θεῖον μετοικίζει καὶ διαβιβάζει τὰς προκοπὰς τὰς μυστικὰς τὸν ἄνθρωπον, ἄχρις ἂν εἰς τὸν κορυφαῖον ἀποκαταστήσῃ τῆς ἀναπαύσεως τόπον.

8. διελθὼν τὰς πνευματικὰς οὐσίας. Cf. above p. 16. 14, 15, 25 f., p. 20. 17 f., p. 78. 26 f., p. 98. 23 f., p. 100. 13, p. 118. 11 f.

9. πᾶσαν ἀρχὴν καὶ ἐξουσίαν. On the celestial hierarchy see nn. on p. 16. 4, 7.

ἅπτεται τῶν θρόνων τῶν ἄκρων. This may refer to the thrones mentioned in Apoc. iv. 4 κυκλόθεν τοῦ θρόνου θρόνοι εἴκοσι καὶ τέσσαρες, καὶ ἐπὶ τοὺς θρόνους εἶδον τοὺς εἴκοσι καὶ τέσσαρας πρεσβυτέρους καθημένους, *ib.* xi. 16, xx. 4; or to the Thrones of the celestial hierarchy (see above p. 16. 4 n.)

which come immediately after the Seraphim and Cherubim and before the ἐξουσίαι and ἀρχαί; or (taking θρόνων as a plural of majesty) we may connect it with the promise in Apoc. iii. 21 δώσω αὐτῷ καθίσαι ἐπὶ τῷ θρόνῳ μου; or (which I think the most likely) Cl. combines them all into one vague idea.

10. **ἐπ' ἐκεῖνο ἱέμενος, ἐφ' ᾧ ἔγνω μόνον.** The simple construction ἐπ' ἐκεῖνο ἱέμ. ὃ ἔγνω goes through the stages, (1) ἐφ' ᾧ ἔγνω ἱέμ., (2) ἐφ' ᾧ ἐπ' ἐκεῖνο, (3) ἐπ' ἐκεῖνο ἐφ' ᾧ. For the repetition of the preposition with the relative, when it follows the demonstrative, see *Q. D. S.* 944 P. ἐν ἐκείνοις εὑρεθησόμενος ἐν οἷς εἵλετο, and Lyc. c. *Leocr.* 32 εἰς αὐτὸ τὴν τιμωρίαν τάξαντες, εἰς ὃ μάλιστα φοβούμενοι τυγχάνουσι, quoted by Jelf, *Gr.* § 822. The last clause is not easy. What is it which alone the gnostic knows? Does it mean that heaven alone is the true subject-matter of knowledge, all else being a matter of opinion only? This would agree with the description, given in the *Phaedrus* 247, of the ὑπερουράνιος τόπος, where alone the soul beholds absolute truth and righteousness, of which only shadows are to be found in this lower world. The aor. ἔγνω would then refer to the pre-existent state. The doctrine of pre-existence was certainly held by Origen.

11. **τῇ περιστερᾷ τὸν ὄφιν.** That is, knowledge (διὰ τῆς ἐπιστήμης, l. 7) with sinlessness (p. 142. 27).

12. **εὐσυνειδήτως.** See below l. 22, above p. 134. 29.

16. **ἐπὶ τέλει.** Used of the past cause in p. 98. 3, here of the future effect.

§ 83. 21. **γινομένων οὐδέν.** As ὑποπτεύω takes an acc. I have inserted οὐδέν which might easily be lost before οὐδέ.

21, 22. **οὐδὲ αἰσχύνεται ταῖς ἐξουσίαις ὀφθῆναι.** See above pp. 134. 29, 138. 3. Comparing Eph. vi. 12 οὐκ ἔστιν ἡμῖν ἡ πάλη πρὸς αἷμα καὶ σάρκα, ἀλλὰ πρὸς τὰς ἀρχάς, πρὸς τὰς ἐξουσίας κ.τ.λ. and also Apoc. xii. 10 ἐβλήθη ὁ κατήγωρ τῶν ἀδελφῶν κ.τ.λ., I think the ἐξουσίαι here are the accusing angels who oppose the admission of the dying Christian into Paradise. Cf. the quotation from the apocryphal Gospel of Philip in Epiphan. *Haer.* XXVI. 13 ἀπεκάλυψέ μοι ὁ κύριος, τί τὴν ψυχὴν δεῖ λέγειν ἐν τῷ ἀνιέναι εἰς τὸν οὐρανόν, καὶ πῶς ἑκάστῃ τῶν ἄνω δυνάμεων ἀποκρίνεσθαι. Origen (*Hom. v. in Ps.* vol. XII. 233 Lomm.) gives a description of this examination of the soul by the powers of darkness 'venit ad unamquamque animam de hoc mundo exeuntem princeps huius mundi et aereae potestates, et requirunt si inveniant in ea aliquid suum : si avaritiam invenerint, suae partis est : si iram, si luxuriam, si invidiam…suae partis est, et ad se eam trahunt.' This passage is quoted along with others of a similar nature in James' very interesting Introduction to the *Testament of Abraham*, p. 19. He considers that the original sources from which Origen drew were the *Assumption of Moses* (quoted in Jude 9) on which he gives the scholium, ἐβλασφήμει ὁ διάβολος κατὰ Μωσέως, φονέα τοῦτον καλῶν διὰ τὸ πατάξαι τὸν Αἰγύπτιον κ.τ.λ., and the *Testament*, in c. 12 of which the counting up and weighing of good and evil deeds is described. Such weighing would be familiar to one who was acquainted with the Egyptian Books of the Dead.

24. ἄμεινον αὐτῷ μετὰ τὴν ἔξοδον γενήσεσθαι. Cf. the words of Socrates (Plat. *Apol.* § 33) δῆλόν ἐστι τοῦτο ὅτι ἤδη τεθνάναι καὶ ἀπηλλάχθαι πραγμάτων βέλτιον ἦν μοι. The outlook of the gnostic here described resembles that of the philosopher in the *Phaedo* §§ 29, 32, 33.

25. τὸ ἡδὺ καὶ τὸ συμφέρον. See above p. 86. 26.

28. πρὸς τὸν κόσμον ἐπαινετός. As we read just below (p. 146. 2) θαυμάζει τὴν κτίσιν (on which see p. 104. 6) it might be thought that ἐπαινετικός was more suitable here; but in the following line we have ἐπαινεῖται. The gnostic deserves praise as regards the world's estimate, but to God he cannot be more than εὐάρεστος.

29. πάντα ἐφ' ἑνὸς ἵσταται. I have inserted ἐφ', giving the same construction as we have below p. 148. 9, 10 ἐπὶ τοῦ ἀδικεῖσθαι ἵστησι τὸν γνωστικόν. We may compare ἐν ταῖς ναυσὶ πάντα τὰ πράγματα ἕστηκε Aristid. vol. II. p. 279 D. Another way of mending the sentence would be to change ἵσταται into ἤρτηται.

30. εἰς τὰ ἴδια. I suppose this is cited in proof of the preceding. All depends upon Him, for all is His own.

p. 146, line 1. τὴν τῶν κοσμικῶν χρῆσιν. Cf. 1 Cor. vii. 31 οἱ χρώμενοι τῷ κόσμῳ, ὡς μὴ καταχρώμενοι.

3. προσῆκεν. For tense cf. p. 132. 16.

ἐπαινεῖται. Lowth translates *gloriatur*, referring to Ps. xxxiv. 2 ἐν τῷ κυρίῳ ἐπαινεθήσεται ἡ ψυχή μου, but this middle use seems to be only found with ἐν, and, as the phrase ἐπαινετὸς πρὸς τὸν κόσμον occurs a little before in p. 144. 28, it seems better to keep the ordinary passive force, as in p. 188. 25 τὸ ἄκρως τίμιον κατὰ τὴν μόνωσιν ἐπαινεῖται.

3–5. τὸ τέλος εἰς θεωρίαν περαιοῦται. There seems to be a mixture of two constructions: τὸ τέλος ἐστὶ θεωρία and ἡ ἐνέργεια ἡ κατὰ τὰς ἐντολὰς εἰς θεωρίαν περαιοῦται, cf. below l. 20 ἡ τελείωσις εἰς ἄνδρα τέλειον ἀφικνεῖται. In late Greek περαιόω is confounded with περαίνω, cf. *Str.* v. P. 734 *init.* ὧδε μὲν οὖν καὶ ὁ πέμπτος ἡμῖν στρωματεὺς περαιούσθω, *ib.* VI. P. 787 ὁ κυριακὸς λόγος εἰς ὃν περαιοῦται ὁ νόμος, 'in which the law finds its completion.'

5, 6. δι' ἐπιστήμης τὰ ἐφόδια τῆς θεωρίας καρπούμενος. Cf. *Str.* I. P. 318 cited in n. on p. 144. 7, 8 above.

10, 11. αἰνίσσεται τοὺς ὑψηλῶς προσδεξαμένους τὸν λόγον. For a similar allegorical interpretation see *Str.* VI. P. 802 ἐπὶ τῶν δωμάτων, φησί, κηρύξατε, μεγαλοφρόνως τε ἐκδεξάμενοι καὶ ὑψηγόρως παραδιδόντες.

§ 84. 15. σπερματικῶς. Cf. *Paed.* III. P. 308 *init.* σπερματικῶς τὰς ὑποθήκας ἐκθήσομαι.

16. ἐν...ἢ καὶ δεύτερον. Cf. Joseph. *Ant.* XVI. 10. 8 τῶν περὶ Ἡρώδην πεσόντος ἑνὸς καὶ δευτέρου, Schmid *Attic.* Index *s.v.*

19. τῆς κατὰ τὸν γνωστικὸν ἀπαθείας. This seems to be an instance of

the periphrastic use of κατά for the possessive genitive, as in p. 190. 24 τοῦ κατὰ τὰς θυσίας νόμου, see Blass § 42. 2, who quotes Acts xviii. 15 νόμου τοῦ καθ' ὑμᾶς, Eph. i. 15 τὴν καθ' ὑμᾶς πίστιν. For ἀπαθείας see Index s.v.

27. ἀνεπισημείωτον. Cf. *Str.* III. P. 544 *fin.* δοκῶ μοι μὴ παραλείψειν ἀνεπισημείωτον ὅτι τὸν αὐτὸν θεὸν ὁ ἀπόστολος κηρύσσει.

p. 148, line 3. The original has οὐκ οἴδατε ὅτι οἱ ἅγιοι.

5. **περικοπῆς.** Longinus (in Waltz's *Rhet.* IX. 566) defines the περικοπή as made up ἐκ δύο κώλων καὶ τριῶν. It is used more loosely by Christian writers of the portions of scripture, such as the Epistles and Gospels, appointed to be read in Church, see art. on Lectionary in *Dict. of Chr. Ant.* The word is used by Cl. below p. 156. 5, *Str.* III. P. 528 ἀναλέγονται δὲ καὶ οὗτοι ἔκ τινων προφητικῶν περικοπῶν λέξεις ἀπανθισάμενοι, *ib.* ὁ λαός, ἐφ' οὗ εἴρηται ἡ περικοπή,...διεγόγγυζον, P. 547 *init.* ἐπὶ τῆς προτέρας περικοπῆς "ἐθανατώθητε" φησὶ "τῷ νόμῳ," *ib.* ἡ δευτέρα δὲ περικοπὴ μονογαμίαν ἵστησιν, *Str.* IV. P. 596 τὰ μὲν ἄλλα φαίνεται ὁμοδοξεῖν ἡμῖν ὁ Ἡρακλέων κατὰ τὴν περικοπὴν ταύτην.

9, 10. **ἐπὶ τοῦ ἀδικεῖσθαι ἵστησι τὸν γνωστικόν.** See above p. 144. 29, and *Str.* II. P. 433 *fin.* ἐπὶ τῆς ἐκλογῆς τάττουσι τὴν πίστιν, IV. P. 575 *init.* ὁ σωτὴρ καὶ ἐπὶ τῶν πνευματικῶν καὶ ἐπὶ τῶν αἰσθητῶν τὴν πενίαν ἔταξεν.

15. **δοκεῖν.** Comparing the following sentence, we plainly want a principal verb, answering to ἐμφαίνει. Cl. probably wrote δεικνύει, for which the scribe carelessly put δοκεῖ: this latter would then be corrected by superposing the letters ει νυ, which might be taken as a correction of the last syllable.

16. **ἀνταδικῆσαι.** Potter cites Max. Tyr. *Diss.* XVIII. 5 εἰ τὸ ἀδικεῖν πονηρόν, καὶ τὸ ἀνταδικεῖν ὅμοιον· οὐ γὰρ τῷ ὑπάρξαι πλεονεκτεῖ κατὰ πονηρίαν ὁ ἀδικῶν, ἀλλὰ τῷ ἀμύνασθαι ἐξισοῦται κατὰ μοχθηρίαν ὁ ἀνταδικῶν. See Anton. VI. 6 ἄριστος τρόπος τοῦ ἀμύνεσθαι τὸ μὴ ἐξομοιοῦσθαι with Gataker's n.

§ 85. 24. **φρένας.** Cf. *Str.* VIII. P. 916 ἄνθρωπος ὁ μὲν ὄντως ἄνθρωπος ὁ τὰς κοινὰς φρένας κεκτημένος, ὁ δὲ ἄγριος καὶ θηριώδης, where κ. φρ. seems to mean *communis sensus.*

25 foll. See the parallel passage in p. 120. 11—18.

26. **τοὺς παραζηλοῦντας.** Deut. xxxii. 21, 1 Cor. x. 22.

27. **διεχθρεύεται.** This seems to be the only example of the middle. The active is used in the parallel passage, p. 120. 16, as well as below, p. 150. 19.

28. **θεὸς ἐπὶ δικαίους καὶ ἀδίκους τὸν αὐτοῦ ἐπιλάμπει ἥλιον.** The original has (ὁ πατὴρ ὑμῶν ὁ ἐν οὐρανοῖς) τὸν ἥλιον αὐτοῦ ἀνατέλλει ἐπὶ πονηροὺς καὶ ἀγαθούς, καὶ βρέχει ἐπὶ δικαίους καὶ ἀδίκους. For the different forms in which the quotation appears in Cl. see Barnard *Biblical Text of C.* p. 8. Another example of this rare causative use of ἐπιλ. occurs in p. 152. 9.

30. **βιαζόμενος.** On the construction see n. on p. 108. 4.

32. **καθ' ὅλην τὴν κοσμικὴν περιήλυσιν ἑβδομάσιν σημαινομένην.** So Chrys. *Hom.* LXI. 611 A quoted by Alf. on Mt. xviii. 22, οὐκ ἀριθμὸν τιθεὶς

ἐνταῦθα, ἀλλὰ τὸ ἄπειρον καὶ διηνεκὲς καὶ ἀεί. Does Cl. mean that the reduplication of the sacred number was regarded as the completion of the aeons, and that the jubilee was thus typical of the ἀποκατάστασις?

p. 150, line 1. **παντὶ τῷ.** Cf. *Protr.* P. 64 οἶμαι παντί τῷ δῆλον γεγονέναι (and the same phrase in Philo M. 2. 613), *Paed.* I. P. 153 συκοφαντοῦσι τὸ μακάριον ὡς πρᾶγμα οὐκ ἔχον αὐτό, οὔτε ἄλλῳ τῷ παρεχόμενον.

8, 9. τὸ περὶ σῶμα πλεονεκτοῦσιν. We should naturally translate this 'make their gains in what concerns the body,' were it not for the clause **κἂν μέχρι θανάτου προβαίνῃ** which seems to require the wider meaning of 'damage,' as in Dio C. XLI. c. 32 μηδὲν ἧττον πλεονεκτοῦντας ἐκείνων φανῆναι, explained in Index 'generalius *laedo*.' Compare the use in 2 Cor. vii. 2 οὐδένα ἠδικήσαμεν, οὐδένα ἐφθείραμεν, οὐδένα ἐπλεονεκτήσαμεν, *ib.* xii. 18 μήτι ἐπλεονέκτησεν ὑμᾶς Τίτος; *ib.* ii. 11 ἵνα μὴ πλεονεκτηθῶμεν ὑπὸ τοῦ Σατανᾶ, 1 Th. iv. 6 τὸ μὴ πλεονεκτεῖν ἐν τῷ πράγματι τὸν ἀδελφόν.

11. τοὺς ἀποστάτας. Most modern commentators extend the judgment to angels whether good or bad. Alford even limits it to the former on the mistaken supposition that the word ἄγγελος is used exclusively of the good.

14. ἀδικεῖτε. I have omitted the following καὶ ἀποστερεῖτε, which was probably a marginal correction of the MS. καὶ ἀποστερεῖσθε in l. 15, unless it was an unconscious continuance of the quotation on the part of the scribe.

17. τοὺς καθ' ὧν εὔχεσθε. For the combination of article and relative, see p. 128. 7.

καὶ τοῦτο. This is the reading of the best MSS. of the N.T., and is also nearer than Potter's καὶ ταῦτα to καὶ τούς the reading of the MS. here.

18. καὶ τοὺς προσηλύτους. As the stranger shared in the privileges of the Jewish sabbath (Exod. xx. 10, cf. Exod. xii. 49), so under the New Dispensation the stranger should benefit by the brotherly kindness of the Christian. See Index.

§ 86. **23. ἑνὸς ὄντος ἔργον θεοῦ.** So above p. 140. 25 ἑνὸς γὰρ θελήματος ἔργον οἱ πάντες ἄνθρωποι.

μίαν εἰκόνα ἐπὶ μίαν οὐσίαν περιβεβλημένους. We might have expected ἐπὶ μιᾷ οὐσίᾳ, but in later Gr. the accusative often takes the place of the dative in such constructions, cf. Philipp. ii. 27 ἵνα μὴ λύπην ἐπὶ λύπην σχῶ with Lightfoot's n., Blass *Gr.* § 43, Jannaris § 1583, who quotes Leont. Apoll. *V. J.* 100. 13 ἐπὶ τὴν κεφαλὴν στέφανον περιβεβλημένη.

24. τεθολωμένοι. See below p. 174. 9 f. ἡ ψυχὴ τοῖς παρὰ φύσιν θαλωθεῖσα δόγμασιν οὐκ οἷά τε τὸ φῶς διιδεῖν...ἐν οὖν θολερῷ ὕδατι αἱ ἐγχέλεις ἀποτυφλοῦνται. The noun θόλος is properly used of the juice of the cuttle-fish.

26 f. διὰ τῶν κτισμάτων τὴν ἐνέργειαν, δι' ἧς τὸ θέλημα προσκυνεῖ. Cf. p. 8. 22 δι' ὧν ἐνεργεῖ τὰς ἐννοίας ἐπιβλέπουσα.

29. ἀντιδικῶν. I hardly see the force of εἴτ' οὖν ἔργῳ εἴτε καὶ λόγῳ with this reading. Surely going to law can only be ἔργῳ. Should we read ἀνταδικῶν, comparing p. 148. 16?

p. 152, line 2. **περιγράφει**. The Gospel succeeds to the schooling of the law and draws the line round thought, as well as action. Cf. Aesch. p. 83 *fin*. περιγράψατέ με ἐκ τῆς πολιτείας, Plut. *Str*. 9 (*ap*. Diels p. 582. 1) τὴν ἄλλην φυσιολογίαν περιγράφει, μόνον ὠφέλιμον εἶναι λέγων τὸ ζητεῖν περὶ τοῦ κακοῦ καὶ ἀγαθοῦ.

3. **δῆλον ὁποῖοι**. H. J. conjectures with much probability δηλονότι οἶοι.

4. **ἀπελούσασθε**, i.e. in baptism.

6. **ὅση δύναμις** = εἰς or κατὰ δύναμιν, cf. p. 26. 22 τὴν θείαν εἰκόνα τὴν ὅση δύναμις ἐξομοιουμένην πρὸς τὸ δεύτερον αἴτιον.

8, 9. **ἐπὶ ἀδίκους τὸ εὐμενὲς ἐπιλάμποντες**. See above p. 148. 28.

11. **τρίτη δ' αἰτία** represents a third εἴτε.

ἄφες καὶ ἀφεθήσεταί σοι. Mt. vi. 14 ἐὰν γὰρ ἀφῆτε τοῖς ἀνθρώποις τὰ παραπτώματα αὐτῶν ἀφήσει καὶ ὑμῖν ὁ πατὴρ ὑμῶν ὁ οὐράνιος. The impersonal passive ἀφεθήσεται αὐτῷ is found in James v. 15, in Clem. Rom. I. 13 (where see Lightfoot's n.), Polyc. *Phil*. 2 ἀφίετε καὶ ἀφεθήσεται ὑμῖν, and in *Str*. II. P. 476 ἀφίετε ἵνα ἀφεθῇ ὑμῖν. See Barnard *C.'s Bibl. Text* p. 9.

12. **βιαζομένης ὥσπερ τῆς ἐντολῆς εἰς σωτηρίαν**. Cf. Plut. *V*. p. 738 D βιασάμενος εἰς τὴν οἰκίαν, Lk. xvi. 16 πᾶς εἰς τὴν βασιλείαν βιάζεται. The position of ὥσπερ is unusual.

16. **ἀσάρκῳ**. Cf. p. 136. 30.

ἄνω τῆς γῆς. A common construction in late Greek; cf. *Str*. v. P. 696 ἄνω τῶν ὑπερκειμένων αἴρεται, above p. 140. 17 ἐπάνω εἶναι ἀμφοῖν, p. 26, l. 4 ὑπεράνω ὢν καθάπερ θηρίων.

§ 87. 17. **τῷ ὀνόματι**. The original has ἐν τῷ ὀνόματι.

19, 20. **τῷ πνεύματι ἀνεκράθητε**. See note on p. 138. 7 κατ' ἀνάκρασιν ἔχειν τὴν δύναμιν τοῦ θεοῦ.

20. **μὴ γὰρ οὐ**. In late Greek we often find this phrase used as a modest or courteous ἆρ' οὐ, *e.g.* below p. 158. 13 f. μή τι οὖν κάμνων τις οὐ προσίεται ἰατρόν; Rom. x. 18 μὴ οὐκ ἤκουσαν; μενοῦν γε, 1 Cor. ix. 4 μὴ οὐκ ἔχομεν ἐξουσίαν φαγεῖν καὶ πιεῖν; Xen. *Mem*. IV. 2. 12 μὴ οὖν οὐ δύναμαι ἐγὼ τὰ τῆς δικαιοσύνης ἔργα ἐξηγήσασθαι; καὶ νὴ Δί' ἔγωγε τὰ τῆς ἀδικίας· ἐπεὶ οὐκ ὀλίγα ἐστὶ τοιαῦτα ὁρᾶν, see Blass *Gr*. p. 254. It is commonly said that the interrogative μή expects the answer 'no,' but this must not be taken too literally. In many cases it insinuates the answer 'yes,' as in 1 Cor. xi. 22 μὴ γὰρ οἰκίας ἔχετε εἰς τὸ ἐσθίειν; Joh. xxi. 5 μή τι προσφάγιον ἔχετε; Xen. *Mem*. IV. 2. 10 τί δὴ βουλόμενος ἀγαθὸς γενέσθαι συλλέγεις τὰ γράμματα; ἆρα μὴ ἰατρός; πολλὰ γὰρ καὶ ἰατρῶν ἐστι συγγράμματα. So too μῶν οὐ in Plato *Legg*. III. 676A μῶν οὐκ ἐνθένδε τις ἂν αὐτὴν ῥᾷστα κατίδοι; Πόθεν; Ὅθεν περ καὶ τὴν τῶν πύλεων ἐπίδοσιν θεατέον. Hence μή, μή τι and μήποτε are often used in the sense of 'perhaps,' as in Plato *Meno* 89c ἀλλὰ μὴ τοῦτο οὐ καλῶς ὡμολογήσαμεν; *Strom*. I. P. 317 μὴ γὰρ οὐ θεμιτὸν οὕτω φρονεῖν, *Str*. III. P. 518 *fin*. μή τι συνᾴδει τῷ θείῳ ἀποστόλῳ, above p. 140. 26 f. μή τι ὁ σωτὴρ οὐ τῆς δι' ἀγγέλων βοηθείας ἐπιδεῆ εἶναι βούλεται τοῦτον, below l. 27 μή τι οἶον σάρκας εἶναι τοῦ ἁγίου σώματος τούτους φησί; p. 154. 28 μή τι οὖν τέλειοι γίνεσθαι ὀφείλομεν;

21. **ἐξουσιασθήσομαι**. In the original ὑπό τινος is added. Cl. here makes the verb govern an infinitive, as in Eccl. v. 18 (and vi. 2) θεὸς ἐξουσίασεν αὐτῷ φαγεῖν ἀπ' αὐτοῦ. The passive is found also in Sir. xlvii. 19 ἐνεξουσιάσθης ἐν τῷ σώματί σου, where Grimm approves the translation 'in potestatem redactus es in corpore tuo,' i.e. 'victus libidine mulierum ut illae tibi dominatae fuerint.' In Eccles. the participle ὁ ἐξουσιάζων occurs often in the sense of 'ruler.' Cf. Achmet Οn. c. 31, p. 26 (in Steph. Thes.) εἰ μέν ἐστιν ὑπεξούσιος, ἀπολύσει τὸν ἐξουσιάζοντα αὐτόν. It would seem that we might translate either 'I will not be commanded' or 'I will not be empowered, or authorised, to act against the Gospel.'

23. **ἀ ὁ θεὸς καταργήσει**. The original has ὁ δὲ θεὸς καὶ ταύτην καὶ ταῦτα καταργήσει, on which Alf.'s n. is 'viz. at the appearing of the Lord, when we shall be changed from a σῶμα ψυχικόν to a σῶμα πνευματικόν.' The explanation of Euthym. Zig. seems to be more in accord with Cl., 'κοιλίαν' οὐ τὴν σωματικὴν γαστέρα ἀλλὰ τὴν γαστριμαργίαν.

24, 25. **μὴ οὐχὶ δὶ ἐσθίοντας**. Compare Kühner Gr. vol. II. p. 767, Dem. F. L. 379 αἱ πόλεις χαλεπαὶ λαβεῖν μὴ οὐ χρόνῳ καὶ πολιορκίᾳ, Plato Lysis 212 D οὐκ ἄρ' ἐστὶ φίλον τῷ φιλοῦντι οὐδέν, μὴ οὐκ ἀντιφιλοῦν, Isocr. x. 52, p. 216 τιμῆς τυχεῖν οὐχ οἷόν τε μὴ οὐ [τὸν] πολὺ τῇ γνώμῃ διαφέροντα, Strom. v. P. 730 οὐδὲ τὴν ἄλλην ἴσασιν οἰκονομίαν τῆς ἀληθείας, μὴ οὐ πρὸς αὐτῆς διδαχθέντες, Protr. P. 68 fin. οὐδὲ κεραία παρελεύσεται μία μὴ οὐχὶ ἐπιτελὴς γενομένη, ib. P. 71 init. (ἔμαθον) οὐκ ἂν ἄλλως σωθῆναι, μὴ οὐχὶ...πεπιστευκότας, Paed. I. P. 126 οὐ γὰρ τὸ αἷμά ποτε προήσεται φωνήν, μὴ οὐχὶ ὁ λόγος νοούμενος τὸ αἷμα, Q. D. S. 941 P. οὐ ζηλωτὸν τὸ τηνάλλως ἀπορεῖν χρημάτων μὴ οὐκ ἐπὶ λόγῳ ζωῆς, Eus. H. E. II. 2 μὴ ἄλλως τινὰ παρὰ Ῥωμαίοις θεοποιεῖσθαι μὴ οὐχὶ ψήφῳ καὶ δόγματι συγκλήτου, ib. IV. 7 πάντα δρᾶν χρῆναι διδάσκει...ὡς μὴ ἂν ἄλλως ἐκφευξομένους...μὴ οὐχὶ πᾶσιν ἀπονείμαντας χρέα. Cl.'s use in the present instance is contrary to the rule that μὴ οὐ is only found after a preceding negative, but even in classical writers it is sometimes hard to square the rule with the facts, as in the famous δυσάλγητος γὰρ ἂν εἴην τοιάνδε μὴ οὐ κατοικτείρων ἕδραν.

25, 26. **κατὰ τὸ ἀκόλουθον...κατὰ τὸ προηγούμενον**. See n. on p. 122. 6.

26. **προσανέχονται**. The contrasted ζῶσι μέν seems to require προσανέχωσιν, which may have been carelessly assimilated to the preceding participle.

27. **σάρκας**. For the pl. see n. on St James v. 3, and Orig. Str. x. (Lomm. vol. 17, p. 76) 'neque ergo spiritualis lacesset Christi carnes.'

28. **σῶμα δὲ ἀλληγορεῖται ἡ ἐκκλησία**. 1 Cor. xii. 12—27, Col. i. 24 ὑπὲρ τοῦ σώματος αὐτοῦ ὅ ἐστιν ἡ ἐκκλησία. The gen. κυρίου may be taken either with σῶμα or ἐκκλησία, perhaps better with the latter. For ἀλληγορεῖται see Index and Gal. iv. 24 with Lightfoot's n.

29. **χορός**. See n. above on p. 78. 11.

τὸ ὄνομα. See above on p. 2. 5.

p. 154, line 1. **πορνείᾳ**. See p. 130. 26.

ἀποστάσει πρὸς τὸν ἐθνικὸν βίον. Cf. Thuc. I. 75 αἱ ἀποστάσεις πρὸς ὑμᾶς ἐγίγνοντο, and for ἐθνικόν l. 5 below.

§ 88. 4. τὸ αὑτοῦ σῶμα. 1 Cor. vi. 18 ὁ πορνεύων εἰς τὸ ἴδιον σῶμα ἁμαρτάνει. The spiritual fornication, which consists in worshipping another God and transgressing the New Covenant (l. 7), naturally leads to the old Pagan indulgence in the lusts of the flesh (Eph. ii. 1—3).

7 f. ὁ ταύτῃ κολλώμενος τῇ πόρνῃ...εἰς σάρκα μίαν...ἄλλο σῶμα γίνεται. 1 Cor. vi. 16 ὁ κολλώμενος τῇ πόρνῃ ἐν σῶμά ἐστιν· ἔσονται γάρ, φησίν, οἱ δύο εἰς σάρκα μίαν. The MS. has (ll. 7—11) ὁ ταύτῃ κολλώμενος τῇ πόρνῃ, τῇ παρὰ τὴν διαθήκην ἐνεργείᾳ, [ἄλλο σῶμα γίνεται οὐχ ἅγιον] εἰς σάρκα μίαν καὶ βίον ἐθνικὸν καὶ ἄλλην ἐλπίδα· ὁ δὲ κολλώμενος τῷ κυρίῳ ἐν πνεύματι πνευματικὸν σῶμα [τὸ διάφορον τῆς συνόδου γένος][1]. If my reading is right, the clause εἰς σάρκα μίαν—ἐλπίδα was probably omitted from the text owing to the scribe's eagerness to complete the sentence, then supplied in the margin, and afterwards inserted in the wrong place.

9. ὁ δὲ κολλώμενος τῷ κυρίῳ...ἐν πνεύματι, πνευματικὸν σῶμα. The original (1 Cor. vi. 17) is ὁ δὲ κ. τ. κ. ἐν πνεῦμά ἐστι. Possibly ἐν πνεύματι is a corruption of the last three words.

10. τὸ διάφορον τῆς συνόδου γένος. I take this as a cognate accusative defining κολλώμενος, cf. *Str.* II. P. 502 γάμος ἐστὶ σύνοδος ἀνδρὸς καὶ γυναικὸς κατὰ νόμον, *ib.* P. 506 init. ἡ τῶν ἀλόγων ζώων σύνοδος. Kaye (p. 151 n.) thinks there may be some reference to the διάφορον σπέρμα of the Valentinians mentioned in *Exc. Theod.* § 41 and that the word μορφούμενος (l. 12) is to be explained by a reference to *Exc. Theod.* § 79 ἕως οὖν ἀμόρφωτον ἔτι τὸ σπέρμα, θηλείας ἐστὶ τέκνον· μορφωθὲν δὲ μετετίθη εἰς ἄνδρα. I should rather say that Cl. uses gnostic terms in a different sense, as St John in his Gospel. The loss of these words from their true place probably arose from the same cause as that in l. 7.

14. προσεχὴς γενόμενος τῷ κυρίῳ. Cf. above p. 76. 22 f., p. 78. 27 f. τὴν μονὴν τὴν ὀφειλομένην. Cf. p. 82. 24.

15. ἀπηνδρωμένῳ. Cf. *Str.* IV. P. 624 σπευστέον ἀπανδροῦσθαι γνωστικῶς, and Index s.v.

17, 18. οὐ γὰρ ἐκκυκλεῖν χρὴ τὸ μυστήριον. Cf. *Protr.* P. 11 τί δ' εἴ σοι καταλέγοιμι τὰ μυστήρια; οὐκ ἐξορχήσομαι μέν...ἀπογυμνώσω δὲ τὴν γοητείαν... καὶ αὐτοὺς τοὺς θεοὺς οἷον ἐπὶ σκηνῆς τοῖς τῆς ἀληθείας ἐκκυκλήσω θεαταῖς. The eccyclema was the stage machine for exhibiting an interior to the spectators. It is difficult to see why there is this affectation of mystery. Cl. breaks off in his description of the future blessedness of the gnostic, just as he did in p. 20. 12. What reason was there why this should not be divulged? Is it an imitation of the tone adopted by the initiated in speaking of the mysteries of Eleusis, or rather of St Paul's reticence in 2 Cor. xii. 4?

20, 21. γίνεσθε τέλειοι, quoted above p. 140. 26 f.

---

[1] The brackets mark the clauses which seem to me to have been misplaced. In my text I have inserted the former after ἐλπίδα, and the latter after κυρίῳ.

22. καταβιοῦντες, 'living out their life,' not necessarily 'bringing it to a close,' cf. Plut. *Mor.* 603 B ἡ Ἀκαδημία οἰκητήριον ἦν Πλάτωνος καὶ Ξενοκράτους αὐτόθι σχολαζόντων καὶ καταβιούντων τὸν ἅπαντα χρόνον.

25. οὐδὲν...εἰς ὁμοιότητα θεοῦ παραλαμβάνεται. 'None of these perfections is accepted as resembling the Divine.' One can scarcely believe that it is Clement who says this, when we remember his repeated references to the gnostic's assimilation to God (pp. 6. 23, 20. 27, 26. 22, 146. 21, 178. 11, 12, *Q. D. S.* 955 P. τοῦτ᾿ ἔστι τὸ σπέρμα εἰκὼν καὶ ὁμοίωσις θεοῦ) and even to his deification (see n. on ἐσομένῳ θεῷ, p. 6. 23).

26, 27. The Stoic doctrine of the identity of divine and human virtue is stated in Cic. *Leg.* I. 25 virtus eadem in homine ac deo est. Est autem virtus nihil aliud quam in se perfecta et ad summum perducta natura. This, which was the common Greek belief, was opposed by Aristotle (*Eth. N.* VII. 1) 'We can no more attribute virtue or vice to God than to a brute,' ἀλλ᾿ ἡ μὲν τιμιώτερον ἀρετῆς, ἡ δὲ ἕτερόν τι γένος κακίας. See also *ib.* x. 8 § 7 where it is argued that the divine activity must consist in θεωρία, as it would be absurd to ascribe to God practical virtues, such as courage or temperance or prudence. The later Academy followed Aristotle. Plotinus goes deeper 'If, as Plato says, we are made like to God by virtue, it would seem that we must ascribe virtue to God, but is it in accordance with reason to ascribe to Him the *political* virtues? God is the exemplar of all virtue, and man receives his virtues from Him, but the divine goodness is something beyond virtue. What we term virtues are merely purificatory habits, the object of which is to free the soul from the bondage of the flesh. With God virtue is nature, with man it is effort and discipline' (a brief abstract of *Enn.* I. 2). The Christian Fathers were divided on the subject. Clement, as we see, denying the identity both here and in *Str.* II. p. 501 Ἡσαΐας μὴ τὴν αὐτὴν εἶναι ἀρετὴν ἀνθρώπου καὶ θεοῦ παριστάς, ὧδέ φησι (quoting Is. lv. 8, 9 'my thoughts are not your thoughts, &c.'), and *Str.* VI. P. 798 init. ἡ δὲ ὁμοίωσις οὐχ...ἡ κατ᾿ ἀρετήν· ἀσεβὴς γὰρ καὶ ὅδε ἡ ἔκδοσις τὴν αὐτὴν ἀρετὴν εἶναι ἀνθρώπου καὶ τοῦ παντοκράτορος θεοῦ... ὑπείληθες. φησίν, ἀνομίαν, ὅτι ἔσομαί σοι ὅμοιος, while Origen affirms it, maintaining that καθ᾿ ἡμᾶς ἡ αὐτὴ ἀρετή ἐστι τῶν μακαρίων πάντων, ὥστε καὶ ἡ αὐτὴ ἀρετὴ ἀνθρώπου καὶ θεοῦ· διόπερ γενέσθαι τέλειοι, ὡς ὁ πατὴρ ἡμῶν ὁ οὐράνιος τέλειός ἐστι, διδασκόμεθα (*Cels.* IV. 29), though elsewhere he condemns the Stoic presumption in claiming for their wise man *equality* of virtue and happiness with God (*Cels.* VI. 48). There can be no doubt that the Christian Revelation proceeds throughout on the supposition of the real identity of goodness in God and man, and that this lies at the very heart of the doctrine of the Incarnation. Our idea of the goodness of God is simply goodness as we know it in man, but stripped of its association with human weakness. See further my n. on Cic. *N. D.* III. 38, and Bigg, *Christian Platonists*, p. 65.

29. ἀδύνατον...γενέσθαι τινὰ τέλειον. It is plain that we cannot accept Cl's explanation of the difficulty contained in these words; nor, I think, can we accept Alford's suggestion, that the verb is rather prophetic than imperative. It stands on the same footing as ἀγαπήσεις in Mt. v. 43 ('thou shalt love'), and οὐ φονεύσεις in v. 21 ('thou shalt not kill'). The point of the assertion is the same as that contained in two clauses of the Lord's Prayer, that the standard of heaven is the true standard of earth, that man is never to rest satisfied with any perfection lower than that of God. And how this is to be brought about is explained in Eph. iii. 19 and iv. 13, ἵνα πληρωθῆτε εἰς πᾶν τὸ πλήρωμα τοῦ θεοῦ, εἰς μέτρον ἡλικίας τοῦ πληρώματος τοῦ Χριστοῦ. Compare above p. 140. 26 f. where the same text is discussed.

p. 156, line 5. τῆς περικοπῆς. See above p. 148. 5.

6. ἐκλαβεῖν. See p. 48. 2 τὸ ἱερὸν διχῶς ἐκλαμβάνεται, p. 104. 20.

§ 89. 11—13. συνεπιλαμβάνονται—αἱρέσεις. The Sceptics and New Academy laid great stress on the variety of opinions, as proving that all were wrong, cf. Cic. *N. D.* i. 1 tam variae sunt doctissimorum hominum tamque discrepantes sententiae ut magno argumento esse debeat causam esse inscientiam, prudenterque Academicos a rebus incertis assensionem cohibuisse, where see n. The same argument was used by the Empiric school of medicine. See Sext. Emp. *P. H.* i. 14. 145, Orig. *Cels.* iii. 12.

12. αἱ περὶ τὴν ἄλλην διδασκαλίαν αἱρέσεις. Dr Abbott suggests that we have here an allusion to 2 Cor. xi. 4 εἰ μὲν γὰρ ὁ ἐρχόμενος ἄλλον Ἰησοῦν κηρύσσει ὃν οὐκ ἐκηρύξαμεν...ἢ εὐαγγέλιον ἕτερον ὃ οὐκ ἐδέξασθε κ.τ.λ. The phrase would thus mean 'heresies concerned with the other (*i.e.* the false) teaching.' For περί cf. above p. 54. 24 τὴν περὶ ἡμᾶς εὐσέβειαν. Two points in which the charges brought against the Church by the heretics resembled those brought by the heathen and the Jews were that both were founded in ignorance of facts and misinterpretation of the Scriptures, see below § 96.

15. τὸν ἑξῆς στρωματέα. This, then, was not intended to be the final Miscellany. See Introduction.

16. προσάγουσιν. Cf. Orig. *Cels.* iv. 4 ὅπερ ἡμῖν καὶ Ἰουδαίοις προσάγει ὁ Κέλσος, *Philoc.* ii. p. 24 λυέτωσαν τὰς προσαγομένας ὑφ' ἡμῶν αὐτοῖς ἀπορίας.

18. παρατείνει. This verb is used in the passive to denote exhaustion and prostration as in Xen. *Mem.* iii. 13. 6 παρετάθη μακρὰν ὁδὸν πορευθείς, Plat. *Symp.* p. 207 B ἕτοιμά ἐστιν ὑπὲρ τούτων καὶ διαμάχεσθαι τὰ ἀσθενέστατα τοῖς ἰσχυροτάτοις καὶ ὑπεραποθνῄσκειν, καὶ αὐτὰ τῷ λιμῷ παρατεινόμενα, ὥστ' ἐκεῖνα ἐκτρέφειν, quoted with many other exx. by Ruhnken *Tim. Lex.* We find also the reflexive use in the same sense in Philo *V. M.* 21 (M. 2, p. 100) οὐδεὶς προσενέγκασθαι τροφὰς ὑπέμεινεν, ἀλλ' ἡσυχίᾳ καὶ λιμῷ παρέτεινον αὑτούς. As παρατείνω is used intransitively, for the passive, in the sense 'to persist,' 'to extend,' 'to continue' (and similarly ἀνατείνω, ὑποτείνω, κατατείνω), it seems not impossible that it may be so also in the sense 'to faint.' I think therefore that it is unnecessary to adopt Hoeschel's παραφθίνει, of which no example is cited.

25. τῷ πυρῷ τὰ ζιζάνια. The original has ὁ ἐχθρὸς ἔσπειρε ζ. ἀνὰ μέσον τοῦ σίτου.

28. παντὶ τῷ καλῷ μῶμος ἕπεται. This reads like a quotation. Momus, the god of fault-finding and mockery, may naturally stand for criticism and caricature of any kind. I have not however found any exact parallel for the latter use, which seems the most appropriate here. The heretical sects are a caricature of the true Church, resembling it as tares resemble wheat, and intended by the enemy to bring it into discredit. Taking the word in the more common sense of 'blame,' we may understand it of jealous fault-finding aroused by the sight of superior excellence; as in the 59th fable of Babrius, where Zeus, Poseidon and Athene, striving τίς καλόν τι ποιήσει, appoint Momus to be umpire; but he has nothing but blame for their creations. So the heretics criticize the law of God, whether revealed in nature or in the Bible.

§ 90. p. 158, lines 1—3. εἰ παραβαίη...ἀφεξόμεθα. For this form of conditional sentence see Index s.v. 'Optative.'

6. τὸν ἐκκλησιαστικὸν κανόνα. See above p. 70. 24, 25 ὁ τῷ ὄντι κατὰ τὸν ἐκκλησιαστικὸν κανόνα γνωστικός, *Str.* VI. P. 803 κ. ἐκκ. ἡ συνῳδία καὶ ἡ συμφωνία νόμου τε καὶ προφητῶν τῇ κατὰ τὴν τοῦ κυρίου παρουσίαν παραδιδομένῃ διαθήκῃ, Kaye, p. 216, n. 4, and Westcott's excellent account of the word in App. A of his *Canon of the N.T.*

8. ὁμολογίαν, i.e. I suppose the baptismal confession, cf. 1 Tim. vi. 12 ὡμολόγησας τὴν καλὴν ὁμολογίαν.

10. ἐν πλάτει. Cf. Dion. H. *Comp. Verb.* XXI. ἔστι τῶν ἐν πλάτει θεωρουμένων, *ib.* XXIV. ὁρᾶται δὲ οὐ κατὰ ἀπαρτισμόν, ἀλλ' ἐν πλάτει ('non perfectionis absolutae ratione habita, sed in genere').

12. οἱ ἰατροὶ ἐναντίας δόξας κεκτημένοι. On the medical sects of antiquity see art. 'Medicina' in Smith's *D. of Ant.*, and cf. Galen VIII. 657 K. θᾶττον ἄν τις τοὺς ἀπὸ Μωϋσοῦ καὶ Χριστοῦ μεταδιδάξειεν ἢ τοὺς ταῖς αἱρέσεσι προστετηκότας ἰατρούς τε καὶ φιλοσόφους.

13, 14. μή τι οὖν οὐ προσίεται. See above on p. 152. 20.

16. εἰδώλων ἐμπλέως. Plato *Phaed.* 66 C ἄν τινες νόσοι προσπέσωσιν, ἐμποδίζουσιν τὴν τοῦ ὄντος θήραν· ἐρώτων δὲ καὶ ἐπιθυμιῶν καὶ φόβων καὶ εἰδώλων παντοδαπῶν καὶ φλυαρίας ἐμπίπλησιν ἡμᾶς πολλῆς.

18. διὰ τοὺς δοκίμους αἱ αἱρέσεις. The original has δεῖ γὰρ καὶ αἱρέσεις ἐν ὑμῖν εἶναι, ἵνα οἱ δόκιμοι φανεροὶ γένωνται ἐν ὑμῖν.

19. δοκίμους ἤτοι τοὺς ἐκλεκτικώτερον προσιόντας. Such as the Beroeans are described in the Acts.

20. τῇ κυριακῇ διδασκαλίᾳ. Cf. p. 148. 22 ἡ τοῦ κυρίου διδασκαλία. Below p. 190. 15 we read of ἡ τῶν ἀποστόλων διδασκαλία.

21—23. This remarkable saying of the Lord is referred to by Cl. in *Str.* I. P. 425 ἡ γραφὴ παραινεῖ "γίνεσθε δὲ δόκιμοι τραπεζῖται," τὰ μὲν ἀποδοκιμάζοντες, τὸ δὲ καλὸν κατέχοντες, *Str.* II. P. 436 ἔστι γὰρ δόκιμον νόμισμα καὶ ἄλλο κίβδηλον, ὅπερ οὐδὲν ἔλαττον ἀπατᾷ τοὺς ἰδιώτας, οὐ μὴν τοὺς ἀργυραμοιβούς, οἳ ἴσασι μαθόντες τό τε παρακεχαραγμένον καὶ τὸ δόκιμον χωρίζειν...οὕτως ὁ ἀργυραμοιβὸς τῷ ἰδιώτῃ τοῦτο μόνον, ὅτι κίβδηλόν ἐστι τὸ νόμισμα, φησί· τὸ δὲ πῶς, μόνος ὁ τραπεζίτου γνώριμος καὶ ὁ ἐπὶ τοῦτο ἀλειφόμενος μανθάνει, *Str.* vi. P. 780 τράπεζαν οὐκ ἔχει τὴν τῶν ἀργυραμοιβῶν, οὐδὲ μὴν τὸ κριτήριον τὸν λόγον. καὶ πῶς ἔτι τραπεζίτης οὗτος, δοκιμάσαι μὴ δυνάμενος καὶ διακρῖναι τὸ ἀκίβδηλον νόμισμα τοῦ παραχαράγματος; Comparing the last quotation, I think that Resch is right here in reading ἀκίβδηλον and contrasting it with παραχαράγματος. Otherwise the contrast will lie between τὸ κίβδηλον and τὸ κύριον, and ἀπὸ τοῦ παραχαράγματος would denote the flaw in the workmanship which betrays the forger. Origen (*in Joh. tom.* xix.) connects it with 1 Th. v. 21 as well as with a word of Christ's (probably Mt. xxv. 27). In *Constit. Apost.* ii. 36 it is limited to the judgment of the priests, to whom alone the commission was given γίνεσθε τραπεζῖται δόκιμοι. Apparently the earliest reference is found in the Clementine Homilies ii. 51, iii. 50, xviii. 20, or in Apelles (fl. c. 150 A.D.) *ap.* Epiphan. *Haer.* xliv. c. 2 οὕτως γάρ, φησίν, ἔφη ἐν τῷ εὐαγγελίῳ 'γ. δ. τρ.' χρῶ γάρ, φησίν, ἀπὸ πάσης γραφῆς ἀναλέγων τὰ χρήσιμα. Dionysius of Alexandria (a disciple of Origen's) makes use of it to justify his inquiry into the tenets of the heretics (Eus. *H. E.* vii. 7). He believed himself called to this work by a vision, which he obeyed, ὡς ἀποστολικῇ φωνῇ συντρέχον, τῇ λεγούσῃ πρὸς τοὺς δυνατωτέρους 'γ. δ. τρ.' Further information will be found in Fabricius *Cod. Apocr. N. T.* p. 330 ff., Suicer *Thes. s.v.* τραπεζίτης, Heinichen *Exc.* ix. ad Eus. *H. E.* vii. 7 (vol. iii. p. 389), Nicholson *Gospel acc. to the Hebrews,* p. 157 ff., Resch *Agrapha,* pp. 105, 116 ff., Ropes *die Sprüche Jesu* pp. 141 ff.

§ 91. p. 160, line 2. περὶ τὸν θεὸν καταγίνεται. Cf. *Protr.* P. 79 *init.* ὁ βίος τοσαύτῃ σπουδῇ περὶ τὴν ὕλην καταγίνεται, *Paed.* i. P. 101 περὶ τὸν ἄνθρωπον ἡ πᾶσα σπουδὴ καταγίνεται.

3, 4. ἐπαποδυτέον τῷ πόνῳ. Cf. *Paed.* i. P. 112 *fin.* ἔξεστι δ' ἡμῖν πρὸς τοὺς φιλεγκλήμονας ἐπαποδύσασθαι. The first instance of the metaphorical use seems to be Arist. *Lys.* 615 ἀλλ' ἐπαποδυώμεθ' ἄνδρες τουτῳὶ τῷ πράγματι. It is common in late Greek, esp. in Philo, see exx. in Siegfried p. 78.

8, 9. καταληπτικῇ θεωρίᾳ. See above p. 20. 25. The Stoics held that we could distinguish truth from falsehood intuitively by an infallible criterion, termed by Chrysippus καταληπτικὴ φαντασία, an impression in which the mind grasps reality, or, as it was also explained, which seizes the mind by a kind of irresistible shock[1]: this is followed by συγκατάθεσις, a declaration to ourselves that the impression is true. Cl. probably substitutes θεωρία for φαντασία in order to give prominence to the activity of the mind. In p. 20. 25 he uses θεωρία of the beatific vision of the pure in heart.

10, 11. ὁδοῦ μιᾶς τῆς βασιλικῆς. Cf. above p. 128. 10 f.

---

[1] On the history of the word and its ambiguous signification, see Stein *Erkenntnistheorie d. Stoa* ii. 154—186. καταλαμβάνω, as a rule, has for its subject the mind, and for its object that which is presented to the mind, as in Plato *Phaedr.* 250 D κατειλήφαμεν αὐτὸ διὰ τῆς ἐναργεστάτης αἰσθήσεως, Arist. *de Mundo* 391 a 15 ἡ ψυχὴ θείῳ ψυχῆς ὄμματι τὰ θεῖα καταλαβοῦσα, Epict. *Fragm.* 1 (p. 404 Sch.) ταῦτα χαίρεις ἐὰν ὁ τυχὸν μὲν ἀκατάληπτά ἐστι τῇ ἀνθρωπίνῃ γνώμῃ, εἰ δὲ καὶ τὰ μάλιστα θείη τις εἶναι καταληπτά, ἀλλ' οὖν τί ὄφελος καταληφθέντων;

17. θηρατόν. Zahn *Forsch.* III. p. 162 illustrates Cl.'s fondness for metaphors derived from the chase by instancing *Paed.* II. § 114 θήρατρον, *Str.* II. § 5 δυσθήρατον, VII. § 23 &c. It is of course borrowed from Plato, cf. *Rep.* IV. 432.

18, 19. συναναθέουσαι πόαι. Cf. *Str.* VI. P. 774 *init.* αἱ αἱρέσεις παρ' ἡμῖν συνανεφύησαν τῷ γονίμῳ πυρῴ. The word πόα, as defined by Theoph. *H. Pl.* I. 3. 1, includes corn (πόα τὸ ἀπὸ ῥίζης φυλλοφόρον προϊὸν ἀστελεχές, οὗ ὁ καυλὸς σπερμοφόρος, οἷον ὁ σῖτος καὶ τὰ λάχανα), and so it is used by Cl. *Paed.* II. P. 232 ἀγρὸς ὁ κόσμος, καὶ πόα ἡμεῖς οἱ τῇ χάριτι δροσιζόμενοι τοῦ θεοῦ...χόρτος δὲ ὁ χυδαῖος ἀλληγορεῖται ὄχλος...εἰς οὐδὲν ἀλλ' ἢ εἰς ὑπέκκαυμα εὔθετος. But elsewhere Cl. uses it of weeds, as in *Str.* II. P. 479 *fin.* τὰς συναναθαλλούσας τῷ γονίμῳ καρπῷ ματαίας τῆς ἐννοίας πόας and *Str.* I. P. 325 (the ground must be cleared) ἀπό τε τῶν ἀκανθῶν καὶ τῆς πόας ἁπάσης. These are also called ἄγριαι βοτάναι *Str.* VI. P. 770, and βοτάναι simply by Ign. *Eph.* x., where see Lightf.

21, 22. τῆς ἀληθείας τὴν ἀκολουθίαν. Cf. below p. 170. 28 τῆς ἀκολουθίας τῶν σφετέρων δογμάτων καταφρονοῦσιν, *Str.* I. P. 426 τὴν ἀκολουθίαν τῆς θείας διδασκαλίας θηρώμενοι, below p. 180. 29, Sext. Emp. *Math.* VIII. 288 (man differs from brutes) λόγῳ τε καὶ μεταβατικῇ φαντασίᾳ καὶ ἐν τῇ ἀκολουθίᾳ (i.e. *in facultate colligendi aliquid et consecutiones perspiciendi*) but this is limited to τὰ φαινόμενα, in regard to which he has τηρητικήν τινα ἀκολουθίαν καθ' ἣν μνημονεύων τίνα μετὰ τίνων τεθεώρηται, καὶ τίνα πρὸ τίνων, καὶ τίνα μετὰ τίνα, ἐκ τῆς τῶν προτέρων ὑποπτώσεως ἀνανεοῦται τὰ λοιπά.

23. διόν. The participle used for finite verb, as often in Cl.

24. τὸ μαχόμενον. Contrasted with τοῦ ἀκολούθου below, as in Epict. *Ench.* 52. 1 τί ἀκολουθία, τί μάχη, τί ἀληθές, τί ψεῦδος;

25. τἀληθοῦς. Like τἀγαθοῦ, τἀνδρός and even θάτερος for ὁ ἕτερος *Str.* I. P. 322, θάτερον for τὸν ἕτερον *Protr.* P. 24, θατέραν for τὴν ἑτέραν *Paed.* II. P. 236.

§ 92. 32. ἀναπολόγητος ἡ κρίσις. The original has ἀναπολόγητος εἶ... πᾶς ὁ κρίνων· ἐν ᾧ γὰρ κρίνεις τὸν ἕτερον σεαυτὸν κατακρίνεις.

πότερον ἀναιροῦσιν ἀπόδειξιν; This was done by the later Academics, esp. Arcesilaus and Carneades, who held that neither the reason nor the senses were to be trusted. For the arguments by which demonstration was overthrown see Cic. *Acad.* II. 91 foll. and Sext. Emp. *Math.* Bk VIII.

p. 162, line 4. **δι' αὐτῶν τῶν γραφῶν ἀποδεικτικῶς.** See below p. 168. 12 f. τῇ τοῦ κυρίου φωνῇ πιστούμεθα τὸ ζητούμενον, ἡ μόνη ἀπόδειξις οὖσα τυγχάνει.

5, 6. ἐν μόνῃ τῇ ἀληθεῖ καὶ τῇ ἀρχαίᾳ ἐκκλησίᾳ. It is a mere truism to say, with the MS., that ἐν μόνῃ τῇ ἀληθείᾳ is to be found the most exact knowledge. For the reading ἀληθεῖ cf. p. 188. 17 ἡ προγενεστάτη καὶ ἀληθεστάτη ἐκκλησία, and l. 21 μίαν εἶναι τὴν ἀληθῆ ἐκκλησίαν, τὴν τῷ ὄντι ἀρχαίαν, p. 176. 20 f. οἱ ἐν τῇ ἐπιστήμῃ ἡ ἐκκλησία ἡ ἀληθής, also above p. 4. 15 τὴν ἀρχαιοτάτην φιλοσοφίαν. The repetition of the article with the second epithet is not uncommon in Cl., cf. *Str.* I. P. 342 quoted in the n. on διδασκαλίας l. 14 below.

9, 10. οἱ δοξόσοφοι καλούμενοι. Cf. below p. 172. 13 ὑπὸ δοξοσοφίας ἐπηρμένοι, Prov. xxvi. 12, 1 Cor. iii. 18 εἴ τις δοκεῖ σοφὸς εἶναι ἐν ὑμῖν ἐν τῷ αἰῶνι τούτῳ, μωρὸς γενέσθω ἵνα γένηται σοφός. Clem. also uses the form δοκησίσοφος, as in *Protr.* P. 58 ἡ πρὸς τῶν δοκησισόφων τούτων καταγγελλομένη ἀθεότης, *Str.* I. P. 347 *fin.*, P. 370, and οἰησίσοφος *Str.* II. P. 454 and 456.

12. ἀναπεπαῦσθαι νομίζοντες. Cf. Plut. *Mor.* 694 D τὰ τῶν πρεσβυτέρων ἐπιχειρήματα (the arguments of the ancients) τοὺς μὲν ἀργοὺς οἷον ἀναπαύει.

14. διὰ τοὺς ἐλέγχους. See below p. 172. 18 διαπληκτίζονται διὰ τοὺς ἐλέγχους, p. 174. 14 τὰς προφητείας εἴργουσιν τῆς ἐκκλησίας ὑφορώμενοι δι' ἔλεγχον καὶ νουθεσίαν (=κατάγνωσιν here), *Protr.* P. 14 *init.* τὰ σύμβολα τῆς μυήσεως κινήσει γέλωτα καὶ μὴ γελασείουσιν ὑμῖν διὰ τοὺς ἐλέγχους.

διδασκαλίας. So *Str.* I. P. 342 *fin.* ὁ νοῦς τοῦ προφητικοῦ καὶ τοῦ διδασκαλικοῦ πνεύματος τὰς ἐντέχνους ἀπαιτεῖ πρὸς σαφήνειαν διδασκαλίας.

16, 17. παρακολουθοῦντες αὐτοῖς ὅτι. Cf. Epict. *Diss.* III. 5. 4 παρακολουθεὶς σεαυτῷ ὅτι ἀποβάλλεις τινὰ δόγματα.

17, 18. ἐπιχειρήμασι σκοτίζουσι τὴν ἀλήθειαν. Arist. *Top.* VIII. 11, p. 162. 15 ἔστι δὲ φιλοσόφημα συλλογισμὸς ἀποδεικτικός, ἐπιχείρημα δὲ συλλογισμὸς διαλεκτικός, σόφισμα δὲ συλλογισμὸς ἐριστικός, thus explained by Trendelenburg (*Log. Arist.* p. 100), *verum ratione et experiendo aggredi* (ἐπιχειρεῖν) *dialecticae est,* ἔστι δ' ἡ διαλεκτικὴ πειραστικὴ περὶ ὧν ἡ σοφία γνωριστική, ἡ δὲ σοφιστικὴ φαινομένη, οὖσα δ' οὔ (*Met.* III. 2. 20). Cf. also Schw. on Epict. *Diss.* I. 8. 1 ἐπιχείρημα est *quodlibet genus argumenti quo aggredimur adversarium*, Ernesti *Lex. Techn. Gr. s.v.*, Dion. H. p. 723. l. 10 ψυχρὰν καὶ ἀπίθανον ἐπιχείρησιν εἰσάγει, βιαζόμενος τὸ κακουργότατον τῶν ἐπιχειρημάτων ποιεῖν πιθανώτατον, where it seems to have the force of σόφισμα, as in the text. See Index and *Str.* II. P. 454 quoted below on p. 168. 5. For σκοτ. compare *Paed.* II. P. 214 οὐ πεφώτισται τὸν σκοτισμόν, οὐκ εἶδεν τὸν θεόν.

20. πρὸς ἀντιδιαστολήν. See Index *s.v.*

22. τινὰ ἀποσπάσαντες. Below p. 168. 24 f. ἐκλεγόμενοι...ὀλίγας σποράδην ἀπανθιζόμενοι φωνάς.

24. διατριβῆς. Cf. Gell. I. 26 'interrogavi in diatriba Taurum, an sapiens irasceretur,' XVII. 20 'recens in diatribam acceptus eram,' *Str.* I. P. 340 ἡ θρυλουμένη κατὰ τὰς διατριβὰς διαλεκτική.

§ 93. **26. πονεῖν ἐπὶ τοῖς καλλίστοις.** So in Plut. V. 913 διαγωνίσασθαι ἐπὶ τοῖς μεγίστοις ἄθλοις.

29. κοινά τινα κριτήρια. Cf. *Str.* II. P. 455 *init.* ἐν ἡμῖν γὰρ αὐτοῖς τρία κριτήρια μηνύεται, αἴσθησις μὲν αἰσθητῶν, λεγομένων δὲ ὀνομάτων καὶ ῥημάτων ὁ λόγος, νοητῶν δὲ νοῦς, below p. 166. 12 ἀληθῶν καὶ ψευδῶν κριτήριον, p. 168. 2 τῇ κυριακῇ γραφῇ χρώμεθα κριτηρίῳ. The Stoics were the first to give importance to the criterion as the foundation of their philosophy, see Zeller IV. p. 80 f. and esp. Stein *Erkenntnistheorie d. Stoa*, pp. 250—276.

p. 164, lines **3—5**. Comparing below p. 176. 19 f. τριῶν οὐσῶν διαθέσεων τῆς ψυχῆς, ἀγνοίας, οἰήσεως, ἐπιστήμης, of which οἴησις is said to be the mark of the heretics, and ἐπιστήμη of the true Church; it is strange that here Cl. is content to assign to the Christian a lower stage, intermediate to ἐπιστήμη and δοξοσοφία. Yet in *Str.* VI. P. 825 it is said that ἐπιστήμη belongs to the gnostic alone, ἡ τῷ ὄντι ἐπιστήμη, ἣν φαμεν μόνον ἔχειν τὸν γνωστικόν, κατάληψίς ἐστι βεβαία διὰ λόγων ἀληθῶν καὶ βεβαίων ἐπὶ τὴν τῆς αἰτίας γνῶσιν ἀνάγουσα, see above p. 26. 26 f., 100. 3 f., below p. 168. 12 f. We must suppose therefore, that, though Cl. here seems to speak as if Christians generally were only to aim at the mean between knowledge and conceit, he is really contemplating the case of an imperfect Christian, who has indeed received the Gospel, but is still in danger of turning back (ll. 8, 9), because he finds the entrance difficult. That the Stoics made a similar classification appears from Sextus Emp. *Math.* VII. 151 τρία γὰρ εἶναί φασιν ἐκεῖνοι τὰ συζυγοῦντα ἀλλήλοις, ἐπιστήμην καὶ δόξαν καὶ τὴν ἐν μεθορίῳ τούτων τεταγμένην κατάληψιν· ὧν ἐπιστήμην μὲν εἶναι τὴν ἀσφαλῆ καὶ βεβαίαν καὶ ἀμετάθετον ὑπὸ λόγου κατάληψιν, δόξαν δὲ τὴν ἀσθενῆ καὶ ψευδῆ συγκατάθεσιν, κατάληψιν δὲ τὴν μεταξὺ τούτων, ἥτις ἐστὶ καταληπτικῆς φαντασίας συγκατάθεσις...ὧν τὴν ἐπιστήμην ἐν μόνοις ὑφίστασθαι τοῖς σοφοῖς, τὴν δὲ δόξαν ἐν μόνοις τοῖς φαύλοις, τὴν δὲ κατάληψιν κοινὴν ἀμφοτέρων εἶναι. Probably Cl. makes πίστις (= ὀρθὴ δόξα) his mean between the extremes.

3, 4. μέγιστον τὸ τὴν οἴησιν ἀποθέσθαι. Above p. 158. 31 the heretics are said to have οἴησιν ἀληθείας. The aim of the Socratic method was to get rid of this οἴησις. It is condemned in two sayings ascribed to Heraclitus: οἴησις ἱερὰ νόσος, οἴησις προκοπῆς ἐγκοπὴ προκοπῆς[1], also by Epictetus *Diss.* II. 17. 1 τί πρῶτόν ἐστιν ἔργον φιλοσοφοῦντος; ἀποβαλεῖν οἴησιν· ἀμήχανον γὰρ ἅ τις εἰδέναι οἴεται ταῦτα ἄρξασθαι μανθάνειν.

6. ἀνάπαυσιν. Above p. 98. 26, *Paed.* I. P. 115 *fin.* τελείωσις ἐπαγγελίας, πέρας γνώσεως ἡ ἀνάπαυσις.

7. The original has στενὴ ἡ πύλη καὶ τεθλιμμένη ἡ ὁδός.

8. ἅπαξ εὐαγγελισθείς. Cf. Heb. vi. 4 τοὺς ἅπαξ φωτισθέντας, and iv. 6 οἱ πρότερον εὐαγγελισθέντες.

τὸ σωτήριον, φησίν, ἐν ᾗ ὥρᾳ ἐπιγνῷ. The sentence is evidently incomplete, there being no government for τὸ σωτήριον. From the word φησίν it would seem that it forms part of a quotation. I suggest that this may have been Mt. xiii. 20 οὗτός ἐστιν ὁ τὸν λόγον ἀκούων (= εὐαγγελισθείς), καὶ εὐθὺς (= ἐν ᾗ ὥρᾳ ἐπέγνω) μετὰ χαρᾶς λαμβάνων αὐτόν,...γενομένης δὲ θλίψεως ἢ διωγμοῦ εὐθὺς σκανδαλίζεται, and that Cl. wrote ἐν ᾗ ὥρᾳ ἐπέγνω μετὰ χαρᾶς λαβών, cf. Mt. xxiv. 44 ᾗ οὐ δοκεῖτε ὥρᾳ ὁ υἱὸς τοῦ ἀνθρώπου ἔρχεται, and 1 Tim. iv. 3 ἐπεγνωκόσι τὴν ἀλήθειαν. For τὸ σωτήριον see Lk. ii. 30, iii. 6.

9. μὴ ἐπιστρεφέσθω εἰς τὰ ὀπίσω. The original has ὁ ἐν τῷ ἀγρῷ ὁμοίως μὴ ἐπιστρεψάτω εἰς τὰ ὀπίσω. μνημονεύετε τῆς γυναικὸς Λώτ.

10. εἰς τὸν πρότερον βίον, i.e. before his conversion from heathenism, cf. Eph. iv. 22 ἀποθέσθαι ὑμᾶς κατὰ τὴν προτέραν ἀναστροφὴν τὸν παλαιὸν ἄνθρωπον, 1 Pet. i. 14.

---

[1] They are both classed as spurious in Bywater's ed. p. 51.

τοῖς αἰσθητοῖς προσανέχοντα. See above p. 152. 26, below p. 170. 1 τοῖς ὀνόμασι μόνοις προσανέχουσι. L. and S. lose the force of the word, which is rightly given in Rost and Palm 'seine Gedanken auf etwas richten.'

11. παλινδρομεῖτε. So in *Str.* vi. P. 777 ἐπὶ τὰ κοσμικὰ π. ἀγαθά, but below p. 166. 21 of a return from heresy to the Church.

12. ἐθνίζουσι γὰρ ἀμηγέπη. There is no authority for the word ἐθνίζω, which I venture to read here in place of the unmeaning ἐθίζουσι of the MS. There is a certain resemblance between heresy and paganism, cf. *Str.* iii. P. 538 where he compares the asceticism of some heretics with that of certain Gentiles, ἄλλως ἐγκρατευόμενοι καθάπερ τὰ πλεῖστα τῶν ἄλλων ἐθνῶν, and again, in reference to the Antinomian tenets of some of the followers of Basilides, P. 510 *fin.* μὴ τοίνυν, ὑποδυόμενοι τὸ ὄνομα τοῦ Χριστοῦ καὶ τῶν ἐν ἔθνεσιν ἀκρατεστάτων ἀκολαστότερον βιοῦντες, βλασφημίαν τῷ ὀνόματι προστριβέσθων, *Str.* 1. P. 375 ὁ παρεκτραπεὶς ἐκ τῆς κατ' ἀλήθειαν ἑδραιότητος, συνεκρυεὶς αὖθις εἰς τὰ ἐθνικά, also p. 154. 5 ὁ ἐθνικῶς ἐν ἐκκλησίᾳ πολιτευόμενος.

15. ἀνακτζονται. Cf. *Str.* iv. P. 631 *fin.* ἡ ἐκ τῆς διαθήκης ἀνάκτισίς τε καὶ ἀνανέωσις.

τιθηνούμενον, used with a middle force here, as well as in *Paed.* i. P. 123, ii. P. 174, but with passive force in P. 124 *fin.* τῷ γοῦν γάλακτι εὐθὺς μὲν ἀποκυηθέντες τιθηνούμεθα, and in Hippocrates.

ἐξαλεγμένην. Cf. p. 132. 21.

17—19. The original has οὐδεὶς ἐπιβαλὼν τὴν χεῖρα αὐτοῦ ἐπ' ἄροτρον καὶ βλέπων εἰς τὰ ὀπίσω εὐθετός ἐστιν εἰς τὴν βασιλείαν τοῦ θεοῦ, see Barnard *Biblical Text of C.* p. 42.

20—23. This sentence has no relation to what goes before, but merely prepares the way for the comparison between the Virgin Mother and the Scriptures. I think therefore we should read ἀλλ' ὡς τοῖς πολλοῖς, ὡς ἔοικεν, which would easily give rise to the MS. reading by the scribe's eye passing from the 1st to the 2nd ὡς, and the subsequent insertion of τοῖς πολλοῖς in the wrong place. The δὲ which follows τοιαῦται I take as marking the apodosis. This construction is very common in later Gr., cf. Jacobs Aelian *N. A. praef.* xxvi f., W. Schmid *Att.* vol. i. 183, 425, iii. 333 f., Klotz-Devar ii. 369 f., and see exx. fr. Cl. in n. on p. 86. 21, p. 116. 4, 5, also *Paed.* i. P. 137 ἐξὸν αὐτῷ ἀπολέσαι ἡμᾶς...ὁ δὲ ὑπὲρ ἡμῶν καὶ πέπονθεν.

20, 21. τοῖς πολλοῖς δοκεῖ λεχὼ εἶναι. On the belief in the miraculous birth, as well as the miraculous conception of our Lord (affirmed in the 79th canon of the Council *in Trullo* towards the end of the 7th century), see my *Introduction* to S. James p. xxxii foll. It is plain from Cl.'s words that it was due to an apocryphal Gospel, and was not generally accepted when he wrote. λεχώ lit. 'confined to her bed.' See *Paed.* i. P. 123 δὲ θαύματος μυστικοῦ...μία μόνη γίνεται μήτηρ παρθένος—ἐκκλησίαν ἐμοὶ φίλον αὐτὴν καλεῖν—γάλα οὐκ ἴσχεν...ὅτι μόνη μὴ γέγονεν γυνή, παρθένος δὲ ἅμα καὶ μήτηρ ἐστίν, and Tert. *de Virg. Vel.* 6, *de Carne Christi* c. 23 *si virgo concepit, in partu suo nupsit ipsa patefacti corporis lege...Apostolus non ex virgine, sed ex muliere editum Filium Dei pronuntiavit, agnovit adapertae vulvae nuptialem passionem.*

22. μαιωθεισάν φασί τινα παρθένον εύρεθήναι. This is stated in the *Protevangelium* xix. xx. (also in Pseudo-Matthew p. 379 Thilo), where Salome is introduced first as saying to the midwife ζῆ κύριος ὁ θεός, ἐὰν μὴ κατανοήσω, οὐ μὴ πιστεύσω ὅτι παρθένος ἐγέννησεν, and then as punished for her unbelief by the burning of her hand.

§ 94. 24. αἱ κυριακαὶ γραφαί. The same phrase is used p. 2. 21.

25. ἐπικρύψεις. Cf. *Str.* VI. P. 803 διὰ πολλὰς αἰτίας ἐπικρύπτονται τὸν νοῦν αἱ γραφαί, *ib.* P. 805 (in the case of Greek writings) αἱ καλούμεναι τῶν τρόπων ἐξαλλαγαὶ τὰς ἐπικρύψεις ποιοῦνται; and, for the comparison of the mysteries involved in Scripture and in the life of Christ (*ib.* P. 803 fin.), παραβολικὸς ὁ χαρακτὴρ ὑπάρχει τῶν γραφῶν, διότι καὶ ὁ κύριος οὐκ ἐν κοσμικὸς ὡς κοσμικὸς εἰς ἀνθρώπους ἦλθεν κ.τ.λ., and P. 804 (the economy of the Incarnation is like a parable to him who hears) τὸν υἱὸν τοῦ θεοῦ σάρκα ἀνειληφότα καὶ ἐν μήτρᾳ παρθένου κυοφορηθέντα.

26. τέτοκεν καὶ οὐ τέτοκεν. Cf. Tert. *de Carn. Chr.* c. 23 *agnoscimus signum contradicibile, conceptum et partum virginis Mariae; de quo Academici isti* (the followers of Marcion) '*Peperit et non peperit,*'...*legimus apud Ezechielem de vacca illa quae peperit et non peperit*. There is nothing like this in the canonical Ezekiel, and the reference is probably to some lost apocryphal work. See Zahn *Forsch.* vol. VI. p. 309. Allusion is made to it in Epiphan. *Haer.* XXX. c. 30 Ἰδοὺ γάρ, φησίν, ἡ παρθένος ἐν γαστρὶ ἕξει καὶ τέξεται υἱόν· οὐκ εἶπεν, Ἰδοὺ ἡ γυνή. καὶ πάλιν ἐν ἑτέρῳ τόπῳ λέγει, Καὶ τέξεται ἡ δάμαλις, καὶ ἐροῦσιν, Οὐ τέτοκεν κ.τ.λ.

27. ἐκ συνδυασμοῦ. Aristotle's usual phrase for sexual union.

p. 166, line 1. παραπέμπονται. See above p. 132. 4 f., below p. 172. 12 παρεπέμψυντο τὰς γραφάς, and Index *s.v.*

3. τῷ αἱροῦντι λόγῳ. See p. 106. 20, p. 122. 19, p. 136. 9.

4. πίστις. See Index to Cope's ed. of Arist. *Rhet.*

5. βιάζονται τὴν γραφήν. So p. 170. 13 below; cf. *Str.* III. P. 529 *init.* οἱ διαστρέφοντες τὰς γραφὰς πρὸς τὰς ἰδίας ἡδονάς, καί τινων προσῳδιῶν καὶ στιγμῶν μεταθέσει τὰ παραγγελθέντα σωφρόνως βιαζόμενοι πρὸς ἡδυπαθείας τὰς ἑαυτῶν, *ib.* P. 539 βιαζόμενοί τινας ὀλίγας γραφάς. Cf. 2 Pet. iii. 16.

6. ψυχικῆς εὐτονίας. Cf. Epict. *Diss.* II. 15. 2 θέλω γὰρ εἶναι τόνους ἐν σώματι, ἀλλ' ὡς ὑγιαίνοντι...ἂν δέ μοι φρενιτικοὺς τόνους ἔχων ἐνδεικνύῃ... τοῦτο οὐκ εἰσὶ τόνοι, ἀλλ' ἀτονία. ἕτερον τρόπον τοιοῦτόν τι καὶ ἐπὶ τῆς ψυχῆς πάσχουσιν...(8) οὐ θέλεις τὸ κρίμα σκέψασθαι πότερον ὑγιὲς ἢ οὐχ ὑγιές, καὶ οὕτω λοιπὸν ἐποικοδομεῖν αὐτῷ τὴν εὐτονίαν, see above n. on ἀτονία p. 80. 23. The beginning of § 93 shows why εὐτονία is needed.

8. τὸν κανόνα τῆς ἀληθείας. See on p. 70. 25, p. 158. 6.

9. παρ' αὐτῆς τῆς ἀληθείας, *i.e.* the Word, as stated below in ll. 29, 30 and p. 168. 7.

10, 11. καὶ τοῖς πλείστοις σφάλλονται. Should we read κἂν? The v. is sometimes followed by the simple dative, but only, I think, where this is instrumental, modal, or causal.

12. ἀληθῶν καὶ ψευδῶν κριτήριον συγγεγυμνασμένον. Potter compares Heb. v. 14 τὰ αἰσθητήρια γεγυμνασμένα ἐχόντων πρὸς διάκρισιν καλοῦ τε καὶ κακοῦ.

§ 95. 15. ἐξ ἀνθρώπου. The singular seems required, as we have just below (l. 22) ἐξ ἀνθρώπου θεὸς ἀποτελεῖται, and ἐξ ἀνθρώπων following τις could only mean 'one of mankind.'

18. ἀναλακτίσας τὴν ἐκκλησιαστικὴν παράδοσιν. Cf. below p. 174. 21 τοὺς αἱρετικοὺς κενοὺς τῶν τοῦ Χριστοῦ παραδόσεων εἶναί φαμεν, p. 186. 25 ἡμεῖς διὰ τῆς τοῦ κυρίου παραδόσεως ἐσμεν, p. 190. 14 f. μία γὰρ ἡ πάντων γέγονε τῶν ἀποστόλων, ὥσπερ διδασκαλία, οὕτως δὲ καὶ ἡ παράδοσις, p. 194. 11 τῶν ἁγίων παραδόσεων. The v. ἀναλ. is very rare: cf. λάξ in Aeschylus, and Deut. xxxii. 15 Ἰακὼβ ἀπελάκτισεν, Acts ix. 5 πρὸς κέντρα λακτίζειν, Protr. P. 143 εἰδὼς τὴν ἀναισχυντίαν τοῦ ἐκλακτίσαντος λαοῦ καὶ ἀποσκιρτήσαντος.

19. ἀποσκιρτήσας. See Str. II. P. 446 ἀποσκιρτήσας τῆς ἀληθείας, Luc. de Merc. Cond. 23 ἡ μνήμη τῆς ἐλευθερίας ἀποσκιρτᾶν σε ἐνίοτε ποιεῖ.

22. τὸν βίον ἐπιστρέψας τῇ ἀληθείᾳ. The common construction after ἐπιστρέφω is either εἰς or ἐπί (as in p. 170. 11), but the dative occurs in Jud. xix. 3 τοῦ ἐπιστρέψαι αὐτὴν αὐτῷ. I am inclined to prefer ἐπιτρέψας, the reading proposed by Hervetus, as it seems to denote a higher stage, and so to prepare us for the startling statement of the next line.

23. θεὸς ἀποτελεῖται. See above n. on p. 6. 23. It is contrasted here with the effect of Circe's bewitchment.

26. πολυτρόπως καὶ πολυμερῶς. In the inverse order in the original, where too it is God who speaks, first through the prophets and then through the Son.

ἡγούμενον τῆς γνώσεως. Cf. Str. VI. P. 736 ὁ πόνος ἡγεῖται τῆς γνώσεως, above p. 136. 28 f. τούτου δὲ ἡγεῖται τὸ εἰληφέναι τὴν γνῶσιν.

27, 28. τὴν ἀρχήν...φυλαχθείη. Potter quotes Arist. An. Post. I. 11 ἀρχὴ δ' ἐστὶν ἀποδείξεως πρότασις ἄμεσος· ἄμεσος δὲ ἧς μὴ ἄλλη προτέρα. There seems to be some confusion in the word ἀρχή, which is used first of Christ as our guide to knowledge and then of a logical first principle.

29. πιστὸς τῇ κυριακῇ γραφῇ. One would rather have expected πιστεύων, but cf. Plato Legg. VII. 824 B νυκτερευτὴν ἄρκυσι καὶ πλεκταῖς πιστόν. One who puts his faith in the divine teaching is contrasted with the heretics, as worthy to be trusted himself.

30. εἰκότως ἄν...ἐνεργούμενος. The reason for his being trusted is, because one who submits himself to the teaching of Christ is naturally moved to act in Christ's spirit for the good of men. The MS. ἐνεργουμένη is impossible, and Potter's correction ἐνεργουμένῃ, though grammatically admissible, spoils the meaning. For the force of the v. see above on p. 64. 14.

p. 168, line 1. τῶν πραγμάτων. Cf. above on p. 104. 18.

κριτηρίῳ. Above p. 166. 12. That which is still under examination is still undecided, and cannot therefore be used as a criterion or first principle.

3, 4. πίστα περιλαβόντες. Cf. Plut. Γ. 497 (Luc. 9) περιλαβὼν τῇ διανοίᾳ τὸ μέλλον, Polyb. Π. 52. 5 π. τὴν ἀρχὴν ταῖς ἐλπίσι. The word is constantly confused with the περιβαλόντες of the MS, which in the active has no such meaning as is here required. For faith as the ground of knowledge compare Str. II. P. 432 fin. πίστις πρόληψις ἑκούσιός ἐστι, θεοσεβείας συγκατάθεσις, "ἐλπιζομένων ὑπόστασις, πραγμάτων ἔλεγχος οὐ βλεπομένων," ib. P. 434 ὁ πιστεύσας ταῖς γραφαῖς, τὴν κρίσιν βεβαίαν ἔχων, ἀπόδειξιν ἀναντίρρητον τὴν τοῦ τὰς γραφὰς δεδωρημένου φωνὴν λαμβάνει θεοῦ. οὐκέτ' οὖν πίστις γίνεται δι' ἀποδείξεως ὠχυρωμένη, ib. P. 454 ἡ δοξαστικὴ ἀπόδειξις ἀνθρωπίνη τέ ἐστι καὶ πρὸς τῶν ῥητορικῶν γινομένη ἐπιχειρημάτων ἢ καὶ διαλεκτικῶν συλλογισμῶν. ἡ γὰρ ἀνωτάτη ἀπόδειξις ἐπιστημονικὴν πίστιν ἐντίθησι διὰ τῆς τῶν γραφῶν παραθέσεως κ.τ.λ.

ἐκ περιουσίας. See Index s.v.

5, 6. παρ' αὐτῆς τῆς ἀρχῆς περὶ τῆς ἀρχῆς. Thus, we must believe in the existence of God before we can believe in a revelation from Him; but from the revelation we get far stronger proofs for our original belief.

8. ἀνταποφαίνεσθαι. Cf. Str. VIII. P. 915 ἔξεστι καὶ τὸν ἀντικαθιστάμενον ἐπ' ἴσης ἀνταποφήνασθαι ὃ βούλεται, ἀλλὰ πιστώσασθαι χρὴ τὸ λεχθέν. The last clause is repeated below l. 11.

11, 12. τῇ τοῦ κυρίου φωνῇ. See above p. 166. 29, and P. 434 quoted above on ll. 3, 4.

14. ἀπογευσάμενοι μόνον. Paed. II. P. 179 init. ἄρτου μόνον ἀπογευσάμενοι ἀπεχέσθων πάμπαν τοῦ ποτοῦ.

16. γνώμονες τῆς ἀληθείας. See n. on γνωματεύουσα above p. 110. 18, Eun. Pr. Ev. XI. 18. 1 θεὸν ἑαυτοῦ γνώμονα γενόμενον τῷ λόγῳ.

19. ἐκτυποῦσι. Str. VIII. P. 927 fin. τρία ἐστὶ περὶ τὴν φωνήν, τά τε ὀνόματα σύμβολα ὄντα τῶν νοημάτων, δεύτερον δὲ τὰ νοήματα ὁμοιώματα καὶ ἐκτυπώματα τῶν ὑποκειμένων ὄντα· τρίτον δὲ τὰ ὑποκείμενα πράγματα, ἀφ' ὧν ἡμῖν τὰ νοήματα ἐκτυποῦται, Plut. Mor. 404 B κηρὸν μὲν ἐῶ καὶ χρυσὸν...ὅσα τε ἄλλα πλαττομένης οὐσίας εἴδη δέχεται μὲν ἰδέαν μίαν ἐκτυπουμένης ὁμοιότητος, ἄλλο δὲ ἄλλην ἀφ' ἑαυτοῦ τῷ μιμήματι διαφορὰν προστίθησι. For the thought cf. Diog. L. VII. 21 ἄλλως θεωρεῖται ὑπὸ τεχνίτου εἰκών, καὶ ἄλλως ὑπὸ ἀτέχνου with Menage's n.

20, 21. ἀπ' αὐτῶν περὶ αὐτῶν τῶν γραφῶν. Cf. below p. 182. 7.

§ 96. 23. οἱ τὰς αἱρέσεις μετιόντες. The same phrase occurs Str. I. P. 340, III. P. 547 and below p. 186. 8, cf. Str. I. P. 330 οἱ τὰς βαναύσους μετιόντες τέχνας, III. P. 536 οἱ τὴν ἀκόλαστον μετιόντες κοινωνίαν.

24, 25. τὸ σῶμα καὶ τὸ ὕφος. Aristotle (Rhet. I. 1. 3) uses σῶμα τῆς πίστεως for 'the substance of proof' as distinguished from appeals to feeling &c. It is used in an opposite sense in Str. VI. P. 289 init. οἱ μὲν τὸ σῶμα τῶν γραφῶν, τὰς λέξεις καὶ τὰ ὀνόματα, προσβλέπουσιν, οἱ δὲ τὰς διανοίας καὶ τὰ ὑπὸ τῶν ὀνομάτων δηλουμένα διορῶσι. For ὕφος cf. Longin. I. 4 τὴν τῶν πραγμάτων τάξιν οὐκ ἐξ ἑνὸς οὐδ' ἐκ δυοῖν, ἐκ δὲ τοῦ ὅλου τῶν λόγων ὕφους ἐκφαινομένην ὁρῶμεν.

27. ἀπανθισάμενοι. The same word is used of the heretics known as Antitactae in *Str.* III. P. 528 ἀναλέγονται δὲ καὶ οὗτοι ἔκ τινων προφητικῶν περικοπῶν λέξεις ἀπανθισάμενοι καὶ συγκαττύσαντες κακῶς, κατ' ἀλληγορίαν εἰρημένας ἐξ εὐθείας λαβόντες.

p. 170, line 1. **προσανέχουσι.** See above 164. 10.

6, 7. τί τῷ κυρίῳ πρέπον. This would be the principle followed in interpreting the anthropomorphic language of the O.T.

12. τὸ τῆς φιλαυτίας πλεονέκτημα. Cf. *Str.* II. P. 434 (Basilides held that) φύσεως πλεονέκτημα ἡ πίστις, *ib.* P. 433 (the Valentinians) τὴν μὲν πίστιν τοῖς ἁπλοῖς ἀπονείμαντες ἡμῖν, αὑτοῖς δὲ τὴν γνῶσιν, τοῖς φύσει σωζομένοις κατὰ τὴν τοῦ διαφέροντος πλεονεξίαν σπέρματος.

13. <μὴ> βιαζόμενοι τὰς γραφάς. See p. 166. 5. Cl. explains the way in which the heretics treat the Scriptures, (1) by their fear of losing their position, if they acknowledged that they were in the wrong, and (2) by the necessity of claiming the support of Scripture, which could only be done by forcing the sense.

14. φθάσαντες ἐνεγκεῖν. For φθ. c. inf. see above p. 64. 28, 1 Kings xii. 18 ὁ βασιλεὺς ἔφθασεν ἀναβῆναι, Jannaris *Gr.* § 2121.

17—20. ὑπομένουσι τὰ μὲν μὴ προσίεσθαι...τὰ δὲ ἡμᾶς αὐτοὺς...διαβάλλουσιν. The more regular construction would be τὰ μὲν μὴ προσιέμενοι, τὰ δὲ διαβάλλοντες.

18, 19. ὡς ἄλλης γεγονότας φύσεως. See quotations on l. 12 above, also *Str.* IV. 639 ξένην τὴν ἐκλογὴν τοῦ κόσμου ὁ Βασιλείδης λέγει ὡς ἂν ὑπερκόσμιον φύσει οὖσαν, and Kaye p. 154 f.

19. συνιέναι. There seems no reason to change this to συνιέναι. The aor. inf. is also found in *Str.* I. P. 336 συνεῖναι τὰ ἐν τῇ πίστει λεγόμενα (where D. reads συνιέναι after Hoeschel), II. P. 437 τὸ δὲ κατακοῦσαι συνεῖναί ἐστιν, *Str.* IV. P. 583 οὔτε κολάσεις συνεῖναι βούλονται, Plat. *Crat.* 414 D μηδ' ἕνα ἀνθρώπων συνεῖναι ὅ τί ποτε βούλεται τὸ ὄνομα, Anton. v. 6 *fin.* where Schultz would read συνιέναι. Cf. too *Str.* I. P. 337 χρὴ μετεῖναι τὸ ἐλεγκτικὸν εἶδος.

§ 97. **24. ἐπιόντας,** 'going over,' cf. Luc. *Herm.* 1 ἐπιὼν τῇ μνήμῃ ἅπαντα, *Str.* V. P. 733 εἰ τὰς λέξεις ἐπίοιμεν αὐτῶν, *Str.* VI. P. 737 τὰ περὶ ἀρχῶν τοῖς Ἕλλησιν εἰρημένα ἐπιόντες, Heliod. *Aeth.* II. 6 δέλτον ἀνελόμενος ἐπειρᾶτό τι τῶν ἐγγεγραμμένων ἐπιέναι.

28. τῆς ἀκολουθίας. See above p. 160. 22 and Index s.v.

29. προφητείας. On the importance attached to prophecy, see above l. 17 f. and p. 2. 11, below p. 174. 14.

30. αἱροῦνται ἑκάστοτε τὸ δόξαν...ἢ τὸ πρὸς τοῦ κυρίου εἰρημένον. For the omission of μᾶλλον with ἤ, cf. below p. 180. 30, above p. 112. 22. Potter cites Iren. III. 2 cum autem ad eam iterum traditionem, quae est ab apostolis, quae per successiones presbyterorum in ecclesiis custoditur, provocamus eos; adversantur traditioni, dicentes se non solum presbyteris, sed etiam apostolis existentes superiores, sinceram invenisse veritatem.

Apostolos enim admiscuisse ea quae sunt legalia Salvatoris verbis; et non solum apostolos, sed etiam ipsum Dominum modo quidem a Demiurgo, modo autem a Medietate, interdum autem a Summitate fecisse sermones; se vero indubitate et incontaminate et sincere absconditum scire mysterium.

31. ὑπάρχαν ἐναργέστερον. Perhaps 'to be *a-priori* the more probable.'

p. 172, lines 5, 6. τοῖς ἐν μέσῳ ἐντυχόντες. Cf. Schmid I. 141, 300, IV. 651, Polyb. Schw. Lex. s.v., n. on ἔντευξις above p. 86. 11.

8. ἐξέβησαν τὴν ἀλήθειαν. Cf. Arist. *Pol.* IV. 11. 16 οἱ τὸ μέσον ἐκβαίνοντες καθ' αὑτοὺς ἄγουσι τὴν πολιτείαν, Plato *Polit.* 295 D μὴ ἐκβαίνειν τὰ ἀρχαῖα.

12. παρεπέμψαντο τὰς γραφάς. See above p. 166. 1.

§ 98. 17. τέλος ἀκολουθὰν ἐκποριζόμενοι. I have suggested ἐκπονούμενοι (cf. *Str.* VI. P. 795 οὐκ ἐξεπόνησαν περιγενέσθαι πιστοί, Longus *Past. prooem.* τέτταρας βίβλους ἐξεπονησάμην) as I know no instance of an inf. following ἐκπορίζομαι, or of its being used of an unsuccessful attempt; for, I presume, we are not to suppose that the gnostics could really succeed in proving the connexion between their premisses and conclusions.

18. διαπληκτίζονται. See an excellent note of Holden's on Plut. *Timoleon* 14.

διὰ τοὺς ἐλέγχους. See above p. 162. 14.

20. ὑπὸ φιλοτιμίας ὑπομένουσι. I explain the transposition of the words ὑπὸ φιλοτιμίας in the MS. by the scribe's passing unconsciously from the first to the second ὑπό, and the insertion of the marginal correction in a wrong place.

21. πάντα κάλων κινοῦσι. The proverb is also used in the form π. κ. ἐξίασι, as in Arist. *Eq.* 756, and Eur. *Med.* 278.

24, 25. πρωτοκαθεδρίας...πρωτοκλισίαν. See Mt. xxiii. 6 φιλοῦσι τὴν πρωτοκλισίαν ἐν τοῖς δείπνοις καὶ τὰς πρωτοκαθεδρίας ἐν ταῖς συναγωγαῖς. The MS. has τὴν συμποτικὴν διὰ τῆς ψευδωνύμου. I have omitted διά as an unmeaning repetition of the διά before ἥν.

25. τῆς ψευδωνύμου ἀγάπης. Cf. *Paed.* II. 165 (τὰ βρώματα) ἐξ ὧν ὁ σαρκικὸς...ἀπήρτηται βίος, ὃν ἀγάπην τινὲς τολμῶσι καλεῖν...δειπνάριά τινα κνίσης καὶ ζωμῶν ἀποπνέοντα...τὴν ἀγάπην τὴν ἡγιασμένην κυθριδίοις καὶ ζωμοῦ ῥύσει καθυβρίζοντες, ποτῷ τε καὶ τρυφῇ καὶ καπνῷ βλασφημοῦντες τοὔνομα, σφάλλονται τῆς ὑπολήψεως, τὴν ἐπαγγελίαν τοῦ θεοῦ δειπναρίοις ἐξωνεῖσθαι προσδοκήσαντες...τὰς τοιαύτας δὲ ἑστιάσεις ὁ κύριος ἀγάπας οὐ κέκληκεν, ib. 166 ἀγάπη δὲ τῷ ὄντι ἐπουράνιός ἐστι τροφή, ἑστίασις λογική,... χαλεπώτατον δὲ πάντων πτωμάτων τὴν ἄπτωτον ἀγάπην ἄνωθεν ἐξ οὐρανοῦ ἐπὶ τοὺς ζωμοὺς ῥίπτεσθαι χαμαί,...οὐκ ἀγάπη τὸ δεῖπνον, δεῖγμα δὲ εὐνοίας κοινωνικῆς (directions for its use are given in P. 167), *Str.* III. P. 514 (of the followers of Carpocrates) τούτους φασὶν εἰς τὰ δεῖπνα ἀθροιζομένους (οὐ γὰρ ἀγάπην εἴποιμ' ἂν ἔγωγε τὴν συνέλευσιν αὐτῶν), where he goes on to impute to them the enormities which were falsely laid to the charge of Christians generally by the heathen. The name occurs in Jude 12, 2 Pet. ii. 13 ἐντρυφῶντες ἐν ταῖς ἀγάπαις αὐτῶν (where some MSS. have ἀπάταις). In both

of these passages, as well as in 1 Cor. xi. 20—34, reference is made to the abuses to which the Agape was liable. It is described by Tert. *Apol.* 39. See Lightf. on Ign. vol. I. p. 386, vol. II. p. 312 f., Suicer *Thes. s.v.*, Plumptre's art. in *Dict. of Chr. Ant.*, Bigg *Christian Platonists*, pp. 102—106.

§ 99. p. 174, line 8. τεταραγμένος. τάραξις is a technical term for a special inflammation of the eye.

9. θολωθείσα. See above p. 150. 24.

10. τά ἐν ποσί See above p. 120. 29.

11, 12. τὰς ἐγχέλυς ἁλίσκεσθαι. Cf. Arist. *Eq.* 864 ὅπερ γὰρ οἱ τὰς ἐγχέλεις θηρώμενοι πέπονθας. ὅταν μὲν ἡ λίμνη καταστῇ, λαμβάνουσιν οὐδέν· ἐὰν δ' ἄνω τε καὶ κάτω τὸν βόρβορον κυκῶσιν, αἱροῦσι, and the reference in *Nub.* 559.

15. δι' ἔλεγχον. Cf. above p. 162. 14 ζητήσεις ἐκτρεπόμενοι διὰ τοὺς ἐλέγχους, p. 172. 18 διαπληκτίζονται διὰ τοὺς ἐλέγχους, *Protr.* P. 14 *init.* κινήσει γέλωτα διὰ τοὺς ἐλέγχους.

16. συγκαττύουσι. Cf. *Str.* III. P. 528 (of the Antitactae) quoted in n. on p. 168. 27 above, and βρωμάτων συγκαττύσεις above p. 64. 1, where see n.

17. μὴ προσίεσθαι τὰς γραφάς. Above p. 170. 17.

22. τῶν τοῦ Χριστοῦ παραδόσεων. See above p. 166. 18 n.

23. πικριζόντων...δογμάτων. So I read in place of πικρίζοντας, as an epithet is wanted for δογμάτων. The verb is used of a species of honey by Strabo p. 498.

24. ἐξάρχοντας δογμάτων. Potter quotes ἐξάρχειν παντὸς δόγματος, 'auctorem fieri senatus-consultorum,' from Plut. *V.* 1056.

§ 100. p. 176, line 2. οἷος ὁ λόγος τοιόσδε καὶ ὁ βίος. Quoted also in *Str.* III. P. 531 τὰ γὰρ τῆς πολιτείας ἐλέγχει σαφῶς τοὺς ἐγνωκότας τὰς ἐντολάς, ἐπεὶ οἷος ὁ λόγος τοῖος ὁ βίος, and more fully in *Protr.* P. 95 *init.* ὧδέ πως ἔχει τὰ ἡμέτερα τῶν Χριστοῦ ὀπαδῶν· οἷαι μὲν αἱ βουλαί, τοῖοι καὶ οἱ λόγοι, ὁποῖοι δὲ οἱ λόγοι, τοιαίδε καὶ αἱ πράξεις, καὶ ὁποῖα τὰ ἔργα, τοιοῦτος ὁ βίος, where Potter cites Philo M. 2, p. 421 ἐὰν γὰρ οἷα τὰ βουλεύματα, τοιοῦτοι οἱ λόγοι, καὶ οἷα τὰ λεγόμενα, τοιαίδε αἱ πράξεις ὦσιν...εὐδαιμονία κρατεῖ. Seneca speaks of it as an old proverb (*Ep.* 114. 1) audire volgo soles quod apud Graecos in proverbium cessit 'talis hominibus fuit oratio, qualis vita.' See too Eus. *H. E.* VI. 3 (of Origen) τὰ κατὰ πρᾶξιν ἔργα αὐτῷ κατορθώματα εὖ μάλα θαυμαστὰ περιεῖχεν. οἷον γοῦν τὸν λόγον, τοιόνδε, φασί, τὸν τρόπον, καὶ οἷον τὸν τρόπον, τοιόνδε καὶ τὸν λόγον ἐπεδείκνυτο, Philo M. 2 p. 85 (of Moses) πράττων ἀκόλουθα τοῖς λεγομένοις, ἵν' οἷος ὁ λόγος, τοιοῦτος ὁ βίος, καὶ οἷος ὁ βίος, τοιοῦτος ὁ λόγος ἐξετάζωνται, καθάπερ ἐν ὀργάνῳ συνηχοῦντες. [Add Cic. *Tusc.* v. 47 (Socrates) sic disserebat: *qualis cuiusque animi adfectus esset, talem esse hominem; qualis autem homo ipse esset, talem eius esse orationem; orationi autem facta similia, factis vitam*, Diog. L. I. 58 (Σόλων) ἔλεγε τὸν μὲν λόγον εἴδωλον εἶναι τῶν ἔργων, Schol. in Hermog. (*ap.* Walz *Rhet.* vol. v. p. 534) Σωκράτης εἰώθεν λέγειν· οἷος ὁ βίος τοιοῦτος ὁ λόγος, καὶ οἷος ὁ λόγος τοιαῦται αἱ πράξεις, Publ. Syr. *Append.* 156

Ribbeck, ps.-Senec. *de Moribus* 72, Cowell, Art. on 'Thought, Word, and Deed' in *J. of Phil.* vol. III. p. 215, where this ethical division is traced back to the Brahmins and to the O. T. J. E. B. Mayor.] The same form is still used in the prayer, 'Grant, O Lord, that what we speak with our lips, we may believe in our hearts, and what we believe in our hearts, we may practise in our lives.' I am informed by Mr W. H. Frere that it is found in mediaeval pontificals for the ordination of a singer, and I have since read words to the same effect in the forms of Ordination for the Lector, Ostiarius, and Cantor contained in the *Pontificale Romanum.* Bingham (*Ant.* Bk III. ch. 7) cites the last as taken from Conc. Carth. IV. can. 10, 'vide ut quod ore cantas corde credas, et quod corde credis operibus comprobes'; and so *Dict. of Chr. Ant. s.v. cantor.*

3, 4. ἔπεσθαι τῷ θεῷ ἐξ ἀρχῆς τὰ πάντα εὐθείαν περαίνοντι. Plato *Legg.* IV. 714 E ὁ θεός, ὥσπερ καὶ ὁ παλαιὸς λόγος, ἀρχήν τε καὶ τελευτὴν καὶ μέσα τῶν ὄντων ἁπάντων ἔχων εὐθείᾳ (*al.* εὐθείαν) περαίνει κατὰ φύσιν περιπορευόμενος· τῷ δὲ ἀεὶ ξυνέπεται δίκη τῶν ἀπολειπομένων τοῦ θείου νόμου τιμωρός· ἧς ὁ μὲν εὐδαιμονήσειν μέλλων ἐχόμενος ξυνέπεται ταπεινὸς καὶ κεκοσμημένος, quoted again in *Protr.* P. 60, and *Str.* II. P. 499. See Stallb. *in loc.*, where a whole catena of quotations are given, including Anton. X. 11 οὐδὲν ἄλλο βούλεται ἡ εὐθείαν περαίνειν διὰ τοῦ νόμου, καὶ εὐθείαν περαίνοντι ἔπεσθαι τῷ θεῷ.

4, 5. ἐπὰν δὲ παραβῇ...τὸν θεόν. For ἐπάν see Klotz-Devar II. 546; for the acc. θεόν Dion. H. *Ant.* I. 23 μαντευόμενοι τίνα θεὸν παραβάντες τάδε πάσχουσι, and Herod. VI. 12.

7. προχείρους τὰς φαντασίας τὰς λογικὰς ποιητέον. Cf. Epict. *Diss.* II. 18. 23 f. ταῦτα ἀντιτιθεὶς νικήσεις τὴν φαντασίαν, οὐχ ἑλκυσθήσῃ ὑπ' αὐτῆς. τὸ πρῶτον δ' ὑπὸ τῆς ὀξύτητος μὴ συναρπασθῇς, ἀλλ' εἰπέ Ἔκδεξαί με μικρόν, φαντασία· ἄφες ἴδω τίς εἶ καὶ περὶ τίνος, ἄφες σε δοκιμάσω ...ἀλλὰ μᾶλλον ἄλλην τινὰ ἀντεπάγαγε καλὴν καὶ γενναίαν φαντασίαν καὶ ταύτην τὴν ῥυπαρὰν ἔκβαλε, *ib.* III. 10. 1 ἑκάστου δόγματος ὅταν ἡ χρεία παρῇ, πρόχειρον αὐτὸ ἔχειν δεῖ, *ib.* 18 δύο γὰρ ταῦτα πρόχειρα ἔχειν δεῖ· ὅτι ἔξω τῆς προαιρέσεως οὐδέν ἐστιν οὔτε ἀγαθὸν οὔτε κακόν, καὶ ὅτι οὐ δεῖ προηγεῖσθαι τῶν πραγμάτων, ἀλλ' ἐπακολουθεῖν, *ib.* 17. 6 πρόχειρον ἔχετε ὅτι νόμος οὗτος φυσικὸς τὸν κρείττονα τοῦ χείρονος πλέον ἔχειν, *ib.* 24. 115 ταῦτα (*e.g.* τὰ ἀγαθὰ ἔξω μὴ ζητεῖτε) ἔχων ἀεὶ ἐν χερσὶ καὶ τρίβων αὐτὸς παρὰ σεαυτῷ καὶ πρόχειρα ποιῶν, οὐδέποτε δεήσει τοῦ παραμυθουμένου, τοῦ ἐπιρρωνύντος, IV. 3. 1, 4. 39, 12. 15, Anton. III. 13 ὥσπερ οἱ ἰατροὶ ἀεὶ τὰ ὄργανα καὶ σιδήρια πρόχειρα ἔχουσιν πρὸς τὰ αἰφνίδια τῶν θεραπευμάτων· οὕτω τὰ δόγματα σὺ ἕτοιμα ἔχε, *ib.* V. 16 οἷα ἂν πολλάκις φαντασθῇς, τοιαύτη σοι ἔσται ἡ διάνοια· βάπτεται γὰρ ὑπὸ τῶν φαντασιῶν ἡ ψυχή. βάπτε οὖν αὐτὴν τῇ συνεχείᾳ τῶν τοιούτων φαντασιῶν, οἷον, ὅτι ὅπου ζῆν ἐστί, ἐκεῖ καὶ εὖ ζῆν. The definition of λογικὴ φαντασία given in Sext. Emp. *Math.* VIII. 70 is φαντασία καθ' ἣν τὸ φαντασθέν ἐστι λόγῳ παραστῆσαι.

8, 9. γέγονεν χυδαῖος. The passage referred to is Exod. i. 7 οἱ υἱοὶ Ἰσραὴλ χυδαῖοι ἐγένοντο 'increased abundantly.' Cl. applies the word in another sense, as in *Paed.* II. P. 232 πόα ἡμεῖς οἱ τῇ χάριτι δροσιζόμενοι τοῦ θεοῦ...χόρτος δὲ ὁ χυδαῖος ἀλληγορεῖται ὄχλος...ὁ φιλόκοσμος καὶ φιλόδοξος καὶ πάντα μᾶλλον ἡ φιλαλήθης, *Str.* VI. P. 761 fin. Ἑλλήνων τοὺς δοκιμωτάτους τῶν χυδαίων ἀνθρώπων διέκρινεν. We are told that this latter sense belongs to late Greek (see Eustath. χυδαῖοι πάλαι ἐλέγοντο οἱ πεπληθυσμένοι, νῦν δὲ οἱ οὐδαμινοί), but the word itself is unknown to classical writers.

11. μαχόμενα δόγματα. See above p. 170. 28 τῆς ἀκολουθίας τῶν σφετέρων δογμάτων καταφρονοῦσι, and below l. 16 κἂν ἐναντία τυγχάνῃ, and (for μαχόμενα) p. 170. 15.

12. εἰρηνοποιοὶ τῶν δογμάτων. The phrase is taken from Mt. v. 9 μακάριοι οἱ εἰρηνοποιοί, and modified with reference to the previous clause: cf. *Str.* IV. P. 581 μακ. οἱ εἰρ. τὸν ἀντιστρατηγοῦντα νόμον τῷ φρονήματι τοῦ νοῦ ἡμῶν...τιθασεύσαντες κ.τ.λ.

13. κατεπᾴδουσι τοὺς ψοφοδεεῖς. Cf. *Str.* VI. P. 785 ἐν τῷ παρὰ πότον ψάλλειν ἀλλήλοις προπίνομεν, κατεπᾴδοντες ἡμῶν τὸ ἐπιθυμητικὸν καὶ τὸν θεὸν δοξάζοντες. In speaking of those 'who are easily startled from their want of experience,' Cl. probably refers to novices who stumbled at the anthropomorphic language of the O.T.

14, 15. τὴν ἀλήθειαν διὰ τῆς ἀκολουθίας τῶν διαθηκῶν σαφηνίζοντες. See below p. 190. 1–5, *Str.* VI. P. 803 κανὼν δὲ ἐκκλησιαστικὸς ἡ συνῳδία νόμου τε καὶ προφητῶν τῇ κατὰ τὴν τοῦ κυρίου παρουσίαν παραδιδομένῃ διαθήκῃ. Many of the Gnostics opposed the Old Testament to the New.

17. αὐστηρὰ γάρ ἐστι. Cf. *Protr.* P. 85 τὸ αὐστηρὸν τῆς σωτηρίας ὑπομένειν οὐ καρτερεῖτε.

19. τριῶν οὐσῶν διαθέσεων τῆς ψυχῆς. See above p. 164. 3—5. Plato makes δόξα the mean between ἐπιστήμη and ἄγνοια (*Rep.* v. 477 foll.).

§ 101. 22—24. H. J. compares *Eth. Eud.* VII. 5, p. 1146 b. 29 ἔνιοι γὰρ πιστεύουσιν οὐδὲν ἧττον οἷς δοξάζουσιν ἢ ἕτεροι οἷς ἐπίστανται.

28. παρανοίας ἡλωκέναι. A metaphor from the law-courts, see *Dict. of Ant.* under *Paranoias Graphe.*

καὶ μέντοι μεμαθήκαμεν ἄλλο εἶναι ἡδονήν. I account for the MS. reading, καίτοι μεμ. ἄλλο μέντοι, by supposing that μέν had been carelessly omitted after καί by the copyist, and the correction μέντοι (for τοι) written in the margin, and wrongly inserted after ἄλλο. There is certainly no opposition between this sentence and what precedes, to justify καίτοι. The phrase καὶ μέντοι introduces a second set of characteristic differences between the heathen, the Church and the heretics. Dindorf keeps to the MS., only changing μέντοι into μέν τι. But there is no more reason for μέν τι after the first ἄλλο, than after the third in l. 30. On καὶ μέντοι see Klotz-Devar II. 649, Schmid *Atticismus* II. 307, III. 339.

29, 30. ἦν τοῖς ἔθνεσιν...ἦν ταῖς αἱρέσεσι. The ἐν inserted in the MS. after each ἦν is unmeaning, and seems to me to have been carelessly written for ἦν by the scribe in the first instance. I suppose the correction to have been made in the margin, and wrongly added in the text.

30. προσκριτέον. I see no sense in the MS. προκριτέον, which is

mistranslated 'quae in haeresibus praeponitur' in Potter's ed. For προσκριτέον compare Jos. B. J. prooem. 4 (let the reader) τὰ μὲν πράγματα τῇ ἱστορίᾳ προσκρινέτω, τὰς δ' ὀλοφύρσεις τῷ γράφοντι.

χαράν. This along with εὐφροσύνη was regarded by the Stoics as an ἐπιγέννημα of virtue (Laert. VII. 97), and, as such, contrasted with ἡδονή, cf. Sen. Epist. 59. 2 scio voluptatem rem infamem esse, et gaudium nisi sapienti non contingere. Est enim animi elatio suis bonis veraeque fidentis... Gaudio iunctum est non desinere nec in contrarium verti. Suidas s. v. ascribes to Prodicus and the Stoics the definitions χαρὰ εὔλογος ἔπαρσις. εὐφροσύνη ἡ διὰ λόγων ἡδονή. The N. T. use is marked by the same lofty character, cf. Joh. xv. 11 ταῦτα λελάληκα ὑμῖν ἵνα ἡ χαρὰ ἡ ἐμὴ ἐν ὑμῖν μείνῃ, Gal. v. 22, and for εὐφρ. Acts ii. 28 πληρώσεις με εὐφροσύνης μετὰ τοῦ προσώπου σου.

p. 178, line 1. προσοικιστέον. Cf. Strabo v. 244 τὸν τόπον τοῖς Κιμμερίοις προσοικειοῖ.

εὐφροσύνην. Above p. 20. 22, p. 116. 1.

2, 3. ἐὰν πρόσσχῃ τις, κ.τ.λ. I am indebted to H. J. for references (taken from Pape-Benseler's Eigennamen) on Crobylus and Archelaus in the following list. The former reference is to Ael. V. H. IV. 16, where we find a corresponding list: ἐὰν προσέχῃ τις Καλλίᾳ, φιλοπότην αὐτὸν ἐργάσεται ὁ Καλλίας· ἐὰν Ἰσμηνίᾳ, αὐλητήν· ἀλαζόνα, ἐὰν Ἀλκιβιάδῃ· ὀψοποιόν, ἐὰν Κρωβύλῳ κ.τ.λ. Aelian appears to have been a younger contemporary of Cl. Probably both copied from some earlier writer. Anyhow it is a queer list, combining the most obscure with the most famous names, and all to no purpose. The conclusion would have been just as indubitable, though no names had been mentioned. The same curious lapse from common sense is shown in the futile argumentation of § 37, p. 65 above.

3. Ἰσχομάχῳ. I suppose Cl. is thinking of the account which Ischomachus gives to Socrates of his work at his farm (Xen. Oec. XI.).

4. Λάμπιδι. Potter quotes Plut. (Mor. 787 A) Λ. ὁ ναύκληρος, ἐρωτηθεὶς πῶς ἐκτήσατο τὸν πλοῦτον, Οὐ χαλεπῶς, ἔφη, τὸν μέγαν, τὸν δὲ βραχὺν ἐπιπόνως καὶ βραδέως. See also ib. p. 234 F πρὸς τὸν μακαρίζοντα Λάμπιν τὸν Αἰγινήτην, διότι ἐδόκει πλουσιώτατος εἶναι ναυκλήρια πολλὰ ἔχων, Λάκων εἶπεν Οὐ προσέχω εὐδαιμονίᾳ ἐκ σχοινίων ἐπηρτημένῃ.

Χαριδήμῳ. The famous condottiere of whom we read in the speeches of Demosthenes.

5. Σίμωνι. Potter quotes Plin. H. N. XXXIV. 8 to the effect that S. was the first to write on the subject, and Xen. de re Eq. 1 συνέγραψε μὲν οὖν καὶ Σίμων περὶ ἱππικῆς, ὃς καὶ τὸν κατὰ τὸ Ἐλευσίνιον Ἀθήνησιν ἵππον χαλκοῦν ἀνέθηκε καὶ ἐν τῷ βάθρῳ τὰ ἑαυτοῦ ἔργα ἐτύπωσεν. Xen. adds that he has taken much from him for his own treatise.

Πέρδικι. Cf. Ps.-Plut. Prov. Alex. CXXIV. τὸ Πέρδικος σκέλος. ὁ Π. κάπηλος Ἀθήνησι χωλός, καὶ κωμῳδούμενος ἐπὶ χωλότητι.

Κρωβύλῳ. Nothing further seems to be known about him. It is very improbable that he was the comic poet. Perizonius, on Aelian quoted above, suggests that Cr. may be the informer, who, when Plato undertook the defence of Chabrias, threatened him with the fate of Socrates (D. Laert. III. 24).

6. **Ἀρχελάῳ.** Hegesander (ap. Athen. I. 34 c) says that he was highly esteemed by Antiochus the Great.

7. **Πύρρωνι ἐριστικόν.** P. died about 270 B.C., see Zeller IV. 480 foll. For ἐριστ. see Arist. *Rhet.* I. 11. 15 ἐπεὶ τὸ νικᾶν ἡδύ, ἀνάγκη καὶ τὰς παιδιὰς ἡδείας εἶναι τὰς μαχητικὰς καὶ ἐριστικάς...καὶ περὶ τὰς ἐσπουδασμένας δὲ παιδιὰς ὁμοίως...διὸ καὶ ἡ δικανικὴ καὶ ἡ ἐριστικὴ ἡδεῖα τοῖς εἰθισμένοις, where Cope quotes the definition from *Top.* VIII. 12, p. 162 b ἐριστικοὶ οἱ ἐκ τῶν φαινομένων ἐνδόξων, μὴ ὄντων δέ, συλλογιστικοὶ ἢ φαινόμενοι συλλογιστικοί: cf. *Strom.* I. P. 339 ἡ δὲ σοφιστικὴ τέχνη δύναμίς ἐστι φανταστικὴ διὰ λόγων, δοξῶν ἐμποιητικὴ ψευδῶν ὡς ἀληθῶν· παρέχει γὰρ πρὸς μὲν πειθὼ τὴν ῥητορικήν, πρὸς τὸ ἀγωνιστικὸν δὲ τὴν ἐριστικήν, ib. P. 340 τοιοῦτοι οἱ ἐριστικοὶ οὗτοι, εἴτε αἱρέσεις μετίοιεν εἴτε καὶ διαλεκτικὰ συνασκοῖεν τεχνύδρια, ib. P. 343 fin. τὴν δὲ ἐριστικὴν καὶ σοφιστικὴν τέχνην παραιτητέον παντελῶς.

8. **διαλεκτικόν.** Aristotle uses the word of one who reasons from probabilities, esp. in the way of question and answer, as contrasted with the continuous oration of the rhetorician. Hence the term ἐρώτημα, *interrogatio* used for argument generally. In *Str.* I. P. 424 fin. Cl. uses the term in its higher Platonic meaning, ἡ κατὰ Πλάτωνα διαλεκτικὴ τῆς τῶν ὄντων δηλώσεως εὑρετική τίς ἐστιν ἐπιστήμη, ib. P. 425 ἡ ἀληθὴς διαλεκτική... ὑπεξαναβαίνει περὶ τὴν πάντων κρατίστην οὐσίαν...ἐπιστήμην τῶν θείων καὶ οὐρανίων ἐπαγγελλομένη.

10. **τῇ δοθείσῃ δι' αὐτοῦ προφητείᾳ.** A remarkable phrase. We should rather have expected ὑπ' αὐτοῦ δι' ἄλλων. Probably it refers to the office of Christ as the Logos, through whom the Father manifests Himself. In that case προφητεία would probably have its original sense of 'telling forth,' not of 'telling beforehand.' We can hardly suppose that Cl. is here thinking of the life of Christ as typical of what man is to be.

11. **ἐν σαρκὶ περιπολῶν θεός.** See n. on p. 6. 23 above.

14. **θεοπνεύστους γραφάς.** See *Protr.* P. 71 where the words are given as a quotation from the Apostle.

15, 16. **ἀρχαὶ ἁμαρτίας, ἄγνοια καὶ ἀσθένεια.** Cf. above p. 16. 16 ὑπ' ἀσθενείας κακοί, p. 26. 2 κακῶν αἰτίαν καὶ ὕλης ἄν τις ἀσθένειαν ὑπολάβοι καὶ τὰς ἀβουλήτους τῆς ἀγνοίας ὁρμάς, also *Str.* II. P. 462 τὸ δὲ ἁμαρτάνειν ἐκ τοῦ ἀγνοεῖν κρίνειν ὅ τι χρὴ ποιεῖν συνίσταται, ἢ τῷ ἀδυνατεῖν ποιεῖν, ὥσπερ ἀμέλει καὶ βόθρῳ περιπίπτει τις, ἤτοι ἀγνοήσας ἢ ἀδυνατήσας ὑπερβῆναι δι' ἀσθένειαν σώματος. We find something like this in Plato, *Legg.* IX. 863 τρίτον μὴν ἄγνοιαν λέγων ἄν τις τῶν ἁμαρτημάτων αἰτίαν οὐκ ἂν ψεύδοιτο, where the two former causes are the incapacity to resist pleasure and anger. Cl. (after St James i. 14) substitutes ἐπιθυμία for these.

17. The gen. is a little awkward in consequence of the ἐφ' ἡμῖν, which

intervenes between it and what seems to be its governing nouns. Should we read ἐφ' ἡμῶν 'in our case'?

23. ἐξασθενῶν. See below p. 192. 25 καταλεαίνειν ἐξασθ.

§ 102. 24. τῷ γένει = γενικῶς, cf. Str. I. P. 349 ἀλλήλοις ἀνόμοια εἶναι δοκεῖ, τῷ γένει γε ὅλῃ τῇ ἀληθείᾳ ὁμολογοῦντα, Plut. Mor. 954 D πᾶσα γῆ τῷ γένει στύφειν καὶ ψύχειν πέφυκε. For the thought compare Str. II. P. 443 init. διπλοῦ τοίνυν ὄντος τοῦ τῆς κακίας εἴδους, τοῦ μὲν μετὰ ἀπάτης καὶ τοῦ λανθάνειν, τοῦ δὲ μετὰ βίας ἄγοντος, ὁ θεῖος λόγος κέκραγεν πάντας συλλήβδην καλῶν...ὅτι ἐφ' ἡμῖν τὸ πείθεσθαι καὶ μή, ὡς μὴ ἔχειν ἄγνοιαν προφασίσασθαί τινας...τοῖς μὲν γὰρ ὁμοῦ τῷ θέλειν καὶ τὸ δύνασθαι πάρεστιν, ἐκ συνασκήσεως ηὐξηκόσι τοῦτο καὶ κεκαθαρμένοις.

28, 29. ἐκ πίστεώς τε καὶ φόβου παιδαγωγουμένη· ἄμφω δ' εἰς ἀγάπην συνάξουσιν. Cf. Str. II. P. 458 προηγεῖται μὲν πίστις, φόβος δὲ οἰκοδομεῖ, τελειοῖ δὲ ἡ ἀγάπη. A gloss is quoted in Stephanus for the intransitive use of συναύξω, which seems more appropriate here, though usually Cl. makes it transitive. See however Str. VI. P. 736 ὁ παιδαγωγὸς ἡμῖν ἐν τρισὶ διαιρούμενος βίβλοις τὴν ἐκ παίδων ἀγωγήν τε καὶ τροφὴν παρέστησεν, τουτέστιν ἐκ κατηχήσεως συναύξουσαν τῇ πίστει πολιτείαν, translated in Potter's ed. *ostendit institutionem a pueritia, hoc est, vitae rationem quae ex catechesi per fidem incrementum accipit.* The simple verb is often intransitive in later Greek, as in p. 118. 7 (ἀγάπη) φίλον τὸν γνωστικὸν ἀπεργάζεται εἰς μέτρον ἡλικίας αὐξήσαντα, and so the compound ὑπεραυξάνω in 2 Th. i. 3.

29, 30. τέλος τό γε ἐνταῦθα διττόν. The distinction between the practical and contemplative life may be traced back to the βίος πολιτικός and θεωρητικός, and the ἠθικαί and διανοητικαὶ ἀρεταί of Aristotle (*Eth. N.* I. 5. 2, and 13. 20) and to the φύλακες and ἐπίκουροι of Plato's *Republic*.

p. 180, lines 4, 5. τοῦ καινῶς μὲν λεγομένου ἀρχαιοτάτου δὲ ᾄσματος. The original has θυμὸς αὐτοῖς...ὡσεὶ ἀσπίδος κωφῆς...ἥτις οὐκ εἰσακούσεται φωνὴν ἐπᾳδόντων. Cf. *Protr.* P. 6 τὸ ᾆσμα τὸ σωτήριον μὴ καινὸν οὕτως ὑπολάβῃς...πρὸ ἑωσφόρου γὰρ ἦν, where the Gospel is compared to the strain of Orpheus.

5. παιδευθεῖεν πρὸς τοῦ θεοῦ τὰς πρὸ τῆς κρίσεως νουθεσίας ὑπομένοντες. 1 Cor. xi. 32 κρινόμενοι δὲ ὑπὸ τοῦ κυρίου παιδευόμεθα ἵνα μὴ σὺν τῷ κόσμῳ κατακριθῶμεν.

10. μερικαί, as opposed to the παντελὴς κρίσις mentioned above, cf. below p. 184. 19.

12. καταλισθάνοντες. On the tendency in later Greek to change forms in -ανω into -αινω, see Jannaris § 900.

14. θεὸς δὲ οὐ τιμωρεῖται. H. J. compares Plato *Prot.* 324 οὐδεὶς κολάζει τοὺς ἀδικοῦντας, πρὸς τούτῳ τὸν νοῦν ἔχων καὶ τούτου ἕνεκα ὅτι ἠδίκησεν, ὅς τις μὴ ὥσπερ θηρίον ἀλόγιστον τιμωρεῖται· ὁ δὲ μετὰ λόγου ἐπιχειρῶν κολάζειν οὐ τοῦ παρεληλυθότος ἕνεκα ἀδικήματος τιμωρεῖται—οὐ γὰρ ἂν τό γε πραχθὲν ἀγένητον θείη—ἀλλὰ τοῦ μέλλοντος χάριν ἵνα μὴ αὖθις ἀδικήσῃ μήτε αὐτὸς οὗτος μήτε ἄλλος ὁ τοῦτον ἰδὼν κολασθέντα. For the distinction between κόλασις and τιμωρία see also *Paed.* I. 140 init. κολάζειν μὲν τὸν θεὸν

ἄν ὁμολογήσαιμι τοὺς ἀπίστους· ἡ γὰρ κόλασις ἐπ' ἀγαθῷ καὶ ἐπ' ὠφελείᾳ τοῦ κολαζομένου, ἔστι γὰρ ἐπανόρθωσις ἀντιτείνοντος· τιμωρεῖσθαι δὲ μὴ βούλεσθαι. τιμωρία δέ ἐστιν ἀνταπόδοσις κακοῦ ἐπὶ τὸ τιμωροῦντος συμφέρον ἀναπεμπομένη. οὐκ ἂν δὲ ἐπιθυμήσειε τιμωρεῖσθαι ὁ ὑπὲρ τῶν ἐπηρεαζόντων ἡμᾶς προσεύχεσθαι διδάσκων. This is in accordance with Cl.'s general teaching (see above on p. 20. 7 and Index *s.v.* 'Punishment'), but a contrary statement is quoted by Huber (*Philos. der Kirchenväter*, p. 149) from a fragment said to belong to the treatise Περὶ Ψυχῆς (P. 1020)[1], ἀθάνατοι πᾶσαι αἱ ψυχαὶ καὶ τῶν ἀσεβῶν, αἷς ἄμεινον ἦν μὴ ἀφθάρτους εἶναι. κολαζόμεναι γὰρ ὑπὸ τοῦ ἀσβέστου πυρὸς ἀπεράντῳ τιμωρίᾳ καὶ μὴ θνήσκουσαι ἐπὶ κακῷ τῷ (al. τὸ) ἑαυτῶν τέλος λαβεῖν οὐκ ἔχουσιν (preserved by Maximus *Loci Comm.* p. 656).

16. **κολάζει μέντοι.** See Klotz-Devar I. p. 125 and Arist. *Pol.* III. 4. 9 οὐχ ἡ αὐτὴ ἁπλῶς ἀρετὴ πολίτου καὶ ἀνδρός, τινὸς μέντοι πολίτου.

17. **ἀποτρέψαι βουλόμενος.** See Plat. *Protag.* 324 ἀποτροπῆς ἕνεκα κολάζει.

18. **τῆς εἰς τὰς αἱρέσεις εὐεμπτωσίας.** Cf. *Paed.* I. P. 99 ἡ κώλυσις τῆς εἰς τὴν συνήθειαν τῶν ἁμαρτημάτων εὐεμπτωσίας, Diog. L. VII. 115 ὡς ἐπὶ τοῦ σώματος εὐεμπτωσίαι τινές λέγονται, οἷον κατάρρους καὶ διάρροια, οὕτω κἀπὶ τῆς ψυχῆς εἰσιν εὐκαταφορίαι.

§ 103. 27. **φλυαρεῖν ἐπιχαίρουσι.** The common meaning of φλ. seems out of place here. Can it mean 'to be witty'? Cf. Plut. *Mor.* 873 E βατραχομαχίαν ἐν ἔπεσι παίζων καὶ φλυαρῶν ἔγραψε. In 3 Joh. 10 it has a transitive force, λόγοις πονηροῖς φλυαρῶν ἡμᾶς.

28, 29. **σφίσιν αὐτοῖς τὰ μέγιστα συγχωροῦντες.** Cf. Plato *Legg.* X. 906 συγκεχωρήκαμεν ἡμῖν αὐτοῖς τὸν οὐρανὸν πολλῶν εἶναι μεστὸν ἀγαθῶν (quoted by Cl. in *Str.* v. P. 702), Xen. *Hier.* I. 16 συγχωρῶ σοι τοὺς ἐπαίνους ἡδίστους εἶναι.

30. **πονέσαντες.** On this form see W. Schmid *Att.* IV. 693.

τὴν ἀκολουθίαν. Does this refer to the consistency of the truth, as in p. 160. 21, 22; or is it general, implying the absence of consistency in the heresies, as in p. 170. 28?

31. **ἢ μισήσειν.** For the omission of μᾶλλον, cf. Lk. XV. 7 χαρὰ ἔσται ἐπὶ ἑνὶ ἁμαρτωλῷ μετανοοῦντι ἢ ἐπὶ ἐννενηκονταεννέα δικαίοις, *ib.* XVII. 2 λυσιτελεῖ αὐτῷ εἰ ἔρριπται εἰς τὴν θάλασσαν ἢ ἵνα σκανδαλίσῃ ἕνα, Moulton-Winer pp. 301, 302, and above p. 112. 22 μή τι οὖν ἢ δι' ἄγνοιαν συνίσταται ἡ δειλία; p. 170. 30, *Str.* II. P. 434 *init.* τὴν γνῶσιν μακρῷ δὴ κεχωρισμένην τῆς πίστεως ἢ τὸ πνευματικὸν τοῦ λογικοῦ λέγουσιν.

p. 182, lines 2, 3. **ἀποτέμνουσαν <καὶ> καίουσαν.** Cf. *Paed.* I. P. 136 *fin.* ἔστι δὲ οἱονεὶ χειρουργία τῶν τῆς ψυχῆς παθῶν ὁ ἔλεγχος...ἃ χρὴ διελέγχειν

---

[1] Allusion is made to a future treatise with this title in *Str.* II. P. 488, *ib.* III. P. 516, *ib.* v. P. 699, but the fragment is entirely inconsistent with Clement's known views, and, in fact, as Zahn has shown (*Forsch.* vol. III. p. 63), it is taken from the Clementine Homilies, XI. 11.

διαιροῦντα τῆ τομῆ, where Potter cites Tert. adv. Marc. II. 16 Quid enim si medicum dicas esse debere, ferramenta vero eius accuses, quod secent et inurant et amputent et constrictent? See also Str. L. P. 422 τῆς μὲν τοῦ σώματος ὑγιείας ἕνεκα καὶ τομὰς καὶ καύσεις καὶ φαρμακοποσίας ὑφιστάμεθα, καὶ ὁ ταῦτα προσάγων σωτήρ τε καὶ ἰατρὸς καλεῖται,...τῆς δὲ ψυχῆς ἕνεκα οὐχ ὁμοίως ὑποστησόμεθα;

3. **ὑπεχέτω τὰ ὦτα τῆς ψυχῆς.** Cf. Aelian N. A. VIII. 17 ὅτῳ σχολὴ μανθάνειν, οὗτος ὑπέχων τὰ ὦτα ἀκουέτω, where Jacobs quotes ib. XII. 44 ὁ δὲ ὑπέχει τὰ ὦτα καὶ θέλγεται, Synes. de Prov. 90 A τῷ πατρὶ ὑπεῖχε τὰ ὦτα, Themist. Or. XV. p. 184 D. See also Dio Chr. L p. 661 λόγῳ τὰς ἀκοὰς ὑπέχουσι. There is therefore no reason for D.'s ἐπεχέτω.

4, 5. **ῥᾳθυμεῖν ἐπαγόμενοι** seems rather like a contradiction in terms. I suppose Cl. means 'from their love of ease.'

5. **ὀριγνώμενοι.** Cf. Plat. Axioch. 366 ἡ ψυχὴ τὸν οὐράνιον ποθεῖ καὶ σύμφυλον αἰθέρα, τῆς ἐκεῖσε διαίτης καὶ χορείας ὀριγνωμένη.

6. **καινοτομεῖν βιάζονται.** For inf. with β. see above p. 108. 4, below p. 188. 27.

7, 8. For the self-demonstration of Scripture see above p. 168. 6 and 21.

9. **συναιρούμενον.** Cf. p. 84. 24 τὸ πᾶν συναιρεῖται πρὸς τὴν τελειότητα τῆς σωτηρίας, where H. suggests συναίρεται. Perhaps we should read συναιρόμενον here: or was there a confusion between the two verbs in late Greek, as between περαίνω and περαιόω (on which see p. 146. 4)?

10. **τὰ προσφυῆ τοῖς θεοπνεύστοις λόγοις.** Cf. Plato Phileb. 67 c νοῦς ἡδονῆς προσφυέστερον πέφανται τῇ τοῦ νικῶντος ἰδέᾳ, Dion. H. p. 820 λέξιν τοῖς πράγμασι προσφυῆ.

12. **παραδεδομένα.** The pf. seems required instead of the present part. of the MS. See below l. 21 προπαραδεδομένα.

ἑκόντες εἶναι. It is usually said that this phrase is limited to negative sentences, but D. refers to Phryn. p. 274 f. where Lobeck gives many exx. of the neglect of the rule in later Greek. Cf. also Theodoret, Gr. Aff. p. 175. 22 ταῦτα ὁ Πορφύριος ἔφη καὶ ἀλλὰ ἅττα, ἃ ἑκὼν εἶναι παρέλιπον.

σοφίζονται. Cf. Str. III. P. 547 σοφίζεται τὴν ἀλήθειαν δι' ἀληθοῦς ψεῦδος κατασκευάζων.

13. **παρεγχειρήσεων,** 'cavillatio' gl. Philox.[1] Cf. Str. VI. P. 762 τὰ δυσβάστακτα φορτία αὐτοῖς (MS. αὐτοὺς) διὰ τῆς ἀνθρωπίνης παρεγχειρήσεως ἐπανατιθέμενοι, verb used by Plut. V. 276 εἰ μή τις βούλοιτο παρεγχειρεῖν ὅτι κ.τ.λ., Str. I. P. 376 ἡ κυρία αὕτη ἀλήθεια ἀπαρεγχείρητος, ἣν παρὰ τῷ υἱῷ τοῦ θεοῦ παιδευόμεθα. For the simple v. compare Plut. Mor. 687 D ἐδόκει ταῦτα πιθανῶς μὲν ἐγχειρῆσθαι, πρὸς δὲ τὸ μέγιστον ἐναντιοῦσθαι τῆς φύσεως τέλος. Philo M. 2, p. 677 (commenting on the word ἐγχειρίδιον in Exod. xx. 25) explains it to mean οἱ τὴν φύσιν παρεγχειρεῖν τολμῶντες καὶ τὰ ἔργα τῆς φύσεως ἐγχειρήμασιν ἰδίοις μεταμορφοῦντες.

13, 14. **ἐπιστάμενοι θείᾳ παραδόσει.** Arist. Top. VIII. p. 157 b 2 ἐνίστασθαι τῷ καθόλου.

---

[1] The word is wrongly explained in L. & S.

17. **Μαρκίωνος**. Also mentioned in *Str*. II. P. 449, III. P. 515, 519, 520, 522, IV. P. 584, 593.

Προδίκου. See above p. 70. 16 n.

§ 104. 25. **ὀρθοτομίαν τῶν δογμάτων**. Potter cites Eus. *H. E.* IV. 3 τῆς ἀποστολικῆς ὀρθοτομίας, where Valesius refers to 2 Tim. ii. 15 ὀρθοτομοῦντα τὸν λόγον τῆς ἀληθείας. Cf. Prov. iii. 6 ἵνα ὀρθοτομῇ τὰς ὁδούς σου.

27. **ἀναπεμπόμενος**. I can make no sense of this, and think it possible the true reading may be παραπεμπόμενος. The latter verb is a favourite with Cl. in the sense of 'to help along,' see below p. 192. 16 τὴν βάσιν δι' υἱοῦ πρὸς τὸν πατέρα παραπέμπουσαν οὐκ ἔχουσιν, *Protr.* P. 7 *init.* παρὰ τοῦ Χριστοῦ τὸ εὖ ζῆν ἐκδιδασκόμενοι εἰς ἀΐδιον ζωὴν παραπεμπόμεθα, also Anton. II. 17 τί οὖν τὸ παραπέμψαι δυνάμενον; φιλοσοφία.

30. **ἀλλ' οὐ πάντων**. In the original ἀλλ' οὐκ ἐν πᾶσιν.

p. 184, lines 1—6. The original has οὐ θέλω γὰρ ὑμᾶς ἀγνοεῖν, ἀδελφοί, ὅτι [οἱ πατέρες ἡμῶν] πάντες ὑπὸ τὴν νεφέλην ἦσαν καὶ [πάντες διὰ τῆς θαλάσσης διῆλθον, καὶ πάντες εἰς τὸν Μωυσῆν ἐβαπτίσαντο ἐν τῇ νεφέλῃ καὶ ἐν τῇ θαλάσσῃ, καὶ πάντες τὸ αὐτὸ] π ν ε υ μ α τ ι κ ὸ ν βρῶμα ἔφαγον, καὶ [πάντες τὸ αὐτὸ] π ν ε υ μ α τ ι κ ὸ ν ἔπιον πόμα, [ἔπινον γὰρ ἐκ πνευματικῆς ἀκολουθούσης πέτρας, ἡ πέτρα δὲ ἦν ὁ Χριστός]· ἀλλ' οὐκ ἐν τοῖς π λ ε ί ο σ ι ν α ὐ τ ῶ ν ηὐδόκησεν [ὁ θεός][1].

3. **κατασκευάζων**. Cf. Philo M. 2, p. 619 κατασκευάζει τὸ πρῶτον οὕτως, *ib*. πρὸς τὴν τοῦ τρίτου κατασκευὴν κεφαλαίου χρῶνται λόγῳ τοιῷδε, Epict. *Diss*. II. 20. 22 κατασκευάσω σοι ὅτι κ.τ.λ.

7. **τί με λέγετε, κύριε**. Quoted above p. 130. 10 f. The reading in Lk. vi. 46 is τί με καλεῖτε Κύριε [κύριε], καὶ οὐ ποιεῖτε ἃ λέγω; For ἃ λέγω Cl. substitutes words from Mt. vii. 21. See Barnard *Biblical Text of Cl.* p. 41.

9. **πόμα δίψαν οὐκ ἐπιστάμενον**. Cf. John iv. 14 ὃς δ' ἂν πίῃ ἐκ τοῦ ὕδατος οὗ ἐγὼ δώσω αὐτῷ, οὐ μὴ διψήσῃ εἰς τὸν αἰῶνα κ.τ.λ.

10. **ὕδωρ ζωῆς**. Rev. xxi. 6, xxii. 17, vii. 17.

ἡ γνῶσις εἴρηται φυσιοῦν. 1 Cor. viii. 1 ἡ γνῶσις φυσιοῖ, ἡ δὲ ἀγάπη οἰκοδομεῖ, where there can be no doubt of the meaning of the word, any more than in 1 Cor. iv. 6 ἵνα μὴ φυσιοῦσθε κατὰ τοῦ ἑτέρου, 18, 19 ἐφυσιώθησάν τινες...γνώσομαι οὐ τὸν λόγον τῶν πεφυσιωμένων, ἀλλὰ τὴν δύναμιν, *ib*. v. 2 ὑμεῖς πεφυσιωμένοι ἐστέ, *ib*. xiii. 4 ἡ ἀγάπη οὐ φυσιοῦται, Col. ii. 18 εἰκῇ φυσιούμενος ὑπὸ τοῦ νοὸς τῆς σαρκὸς αὐτοῦ. The sense is connected with φῦσα and φυσάω, of which we have exx. in Is. liv. 16 χαλκεὺς φυσῶν ἄνθρακας, Wisdom xi. 18 θῆρες πυρπνόον φυσῶντες ἆσθμα, and (metaphorically used) in Xen. *Mem.* I. 2. 25 ἐπηρμένω ἐπὶ πλούτῳ, πεφυσημένω δ' ἐπὶ δυνάμει. The form φυσιάω is similarly used in both senses. There is however another use of φυσιόω which is connected with φύσις, cf. above p. 80. 26, Arist. *Categ.* 8 (p. 9 a. 2) διάθεσις διὰ χρόνου πλῆθος ἤδη πεφυσιω-

---

[1] Words in square brackets are omitted by Cl., those in spaced type are altered.

μένη καὶ ἀνίατος, Simplic. *ad Epict.* p. 219 Schw. ὁ διὰ τῆς φαντασίας συνεθισμὸς φυσιοῖ πως ἡμᾶς οὕτως ἔχειν ('makes it natural to us to be so'). Elsewhere Cl. uses the word in the same sense as S. Paul, cf. *Paed.* I. P. 129 σφᾶς τελείους τινὲς τολμῶσι καλεῖν, ὑπὲρ τὸν ἀπόστολον φρονοῦντες, φυσιούμενοί τε καὶ φρυαττόμενοι, P. 108 *fin.* ἡμεῖς τοὺς παραφυσῶντας εἰς φυσίωσιν φυλαξάμενοι τῶν αἱρέσεων ἀνέμους, P. 112 *fin.* οἱ εἰς γνῶσιν πεφυσιωμένοι, *Str.* I. P. 347 *fin.* καὶ γνώσομαι, φησίν, οὐ τὸν λόγον τῶν πεφυσιωμένων, ἀλλὰ τὴν δύναμιν, τοὺς δοκησισόφους καὶ οἰομένους εἶναι, οὐκ ὄντας δέ, σοφοὺς ἐπιρραπίζων γράφει, so Ignat. *Magn.* 12, *Trall.* 4, 7, *Smyrn.* 6, *Polyc.* 4.

§ 105. 17. ἡ σοφία ἐνεφυσίωσεν τὰ ἑαυτῆς τέκνα. The LXX. of Sir. iv. 11 has ἡ σοφία υἱοὺς αὐτῆς ἀνύψωσε, where Itala has 'filiis suis vitam inspirat,' which Lansen thinks may represent an original ἐψύχωσεν (taken from n. in Potter's ed.). The word occurs in 1 Esdr. ix. 48 ἀνέγνωσκον τὸν νόμον ἐμφυσιοῦντες ἅμα τὴν ἀνάγνωσιν, which Ball translates '*breathing into them withal the reading*, *i.e.* inspiring the hearers therewith,' and also in v. 55 ἐνεφυσιώθησαν ἐν τοῖς ῥήμασιν οἷς ἐδιδάχθησαν. In classical writers the verb is used in the sense 'implant,' 'instil,' cf. Xen. *Lac.* III. 4 τὸ αἰδεῖσθαι ἐμφυσιῶσαι βουλόμενος αὐτοῖς. The cognate ἐμφυσάω is found in Ezek. xxi. 31 ἐν πυρὶ ὀργῆς μου ἐμφυσήσω ἐπί σε, Job iv. 21 ἐνεφύσησε γὰρ αὐτοῖς, καὶ ἐξηράνθησαν, 1 Kings xvii. 21 ἐνεφύσησε τῷ παιδαρίῳ τρίς. Clearchus (*ap.* Ath. 225 D) uses it in a metaphorical sense τῇ κολακείᾳ ἐμφυσώμενος, and Cl. has ἐμφύσημα of inspiration (*Str.* IV. P. 603 *fin.*) τοῦτ' ἔστι τὸ ἐμφ. τοῦ διαφέροντος πνεύματος καὶ καθόλου ὃ ἐμπνεῖται τῇ ψυχῇ.

19. ταῖς μερικαῖς. Above p. 180. 10 we have μερικαί τινες παιδεῖαι. If the reading in the text is correct, the phrase must have become so common as to admit of curtailing by the omission of the noun.

22. ὑποσυρόντων. Cf. *Paed.* II. P. 187 *init.* ταχὺ εἰς ἀταξίαν ὑποσύρεται γυνή.

27. τὰς γραφὰς συνιέτε. Lk. xxiv. 45 διήνοιξεν αὐτῶν τὸν νοῦν τοῦ συνιέναι τὰς γραφάς.

p. 186, line 4. 'Ιουδαία ἐξομολόγησις ἑρμηνεύεται. Cf. *Str.* I. P. 335 *init.* ὁ φιλομαθὴς 'Ιούδας—δυνατὸς δὲ ἑρμηνεύεται—πρὸς τὴν Θάμαρ ἐξέκλινεν, σώζων τὴν πρὸς τὸν θεὸν ὁμολογίαν, where Potter cites Philo M. 1, p. 349. 24 'Ιούδας, ὃς ἑρμηνεύεται κυρίῳ ἐξομολόγησις, *ib.* p. 59. 44 τοῦ μὲν ἐξομολογουμένου 'Ιούδας σύμβολον, *Constit. Ap.* II. 60, where Cotelerius notes 'passim auctores Judam de confessione et laude interpretantur.' The significance of the name appears in its use in Gen. xxix. 35 (Λεία) ἔτεκεν υἱόν, καὶ εἶπε, Νῦν ἔτι τοῦτο ἐξομολογήσομαι κυρίῳ· διὰ τοῦτο ἐκάλεσε τὸ ὄνομα αὐτοῦ 'Ιούδαν, cf. *ib.* xlix. 8.

5. οὐ μοιχεύσας—εἰς σεαυτόν. The original has οὐ φονεύσεις after μοιχεύσεις and οὐ ψευδομαρτυρήσεις after κλέψεις. The best MSS. have σεαυτὸν agreeing with the corrector in L.

8. οἱ τὰς αἱρέσεις μετιόντες. The same phrase occurs in p. 168. 24.

9. **μοιχεύαν τὴν ἀλήθειαν.** Cf. Str. III. P. 552 ὁ σωτὴρ τοὺς Ἰουδαίους, γενεὰν εἰπὼν μοιχαλίδα, διδάσκει μὴ ἐγνωκότας νόμον ὡς ὁ νόμος βούλεται... μοιχεύειν τὸν νόμον, ib. VI. P. 816 μοιχεία δ' ἐστίν, ἐάν τις καταλιπὼν τὴν ἐκκλησιαστικὴν καὶ ἀληθῆ γνῶσιν καὶ τὴν περὶ θεοῦ διάληψιν ἐπὶ τὴν μὴ προσήκουσαν ἔρχηται ψευδῆ δόξαν κ.τ.λ., and the corresponding use of πορνεύω above p. 154. 4 π. εἰς τὴν ἐκκλησίαν, p. 130. 26, also Protr. P. 53 ἡταίρηκεν ὑμῖν τὰ ὦτα, πεπορνεύκασιν οἱ ὀφθαλμοὶ καὶ τὸ καινότερον πρὸ τῆς συμπλοκῆς αἱ ὄψεις ὑμῖν μεμοιχεύκασιν, Jer. iii. 9 ἐμοίχευσε τὸ ξύλον καὶ τὸν λίθον.

κλέπταν τὸν κανόνα τῆς ἐκκλησίας. Cf. above p. 116. 25 παρακλέπτουσι τ. νόμον, Synes. Epist. 283 δεινὸν ἡ εὔνοια κλέψαι τὴν ἀλήθειαν, Aesch. p. 73 fin. τοῖς ὀνόμασι κλέπτων τὰ πράγματα. On κανών see above p. 70. 25.

16. **δολιοῦσιν.** The original has the irregular imperfect ἐδολιοῦσαν.

§ 106. 19. **ἐξάρχοντες.** See above p. 174. 24.

20. **οὔτε αὐτοὶ εἰσίασιν.** The original has κλείετε τὴν βασιλείαν τῶν οὐρανῶν ἔμπροσθεν τῶν ἀνθρώπων· ὑμεῖς γὰρ οὐκ εἰσέρχεσθε, οὐδὲ τοὺς εἰσερχομένους ἀφίετε εἰσελθεῖν.

22. **κλεῖν.** This, the Attic, form is found in Apoc. iii. 7 ὁ ἔχων τὴν κλεῖν Δαυείδ, ib. xx. 1; but in Lk. xi. 52 we have τὴν κλεῖδα τῆς γνώσεως and in Mt. xvi. 19 δώσω σοι τὰς κλεῖδας τῆς βασιλείας τῶν οὐρανῶν, like ἀντικλεῖδα l. 24 below.

24. **ἀντικλεῖδα,** 'a vice-key,' like ἀντιβασιλεύς, 'a vice-roy.' Cf. Pollux x. c. 4 παρὰ τοῖς νεωτέροις καὶ ἀντικλεῖδες εἴρηνται. It is used with a different force by Serap. Aegypt. (Migne Patr. Gr. vol. XL. p. 936 c) ὀφθαλμὸς ὁ πάλαι αἱρούμενος τῇ ἡδονῇ ἀντικλεῖδα τὴν σωφροσύνην εἶχεν.

τὴν αὔλειαν. The MS. αὐλαίαν means 'a curtain,' which is not opened by a key and is altogether out of place here: αὔλεια or αὔλειος (θύρα) is the regular word for the main entrance from the street into the courtyard (αὐλή) of the house, cf. Herodian II. 5. 3 ἕκαστος, ἣν ἐγκεχείριστο φρουρὰν λιπὼν ἢ ἐπὶ τῇ αὐλείῳ ἢ ἐπὶ ταῖς λοιπαῖς εἰσόδοις, ἔφευγον, ib. IV. 1. 5 παραφράττοντες πάσας εἰσόδους, εἴ τινες ἦσαν λανθάνουσαι, μόναις δὲ ταῖς δημοσίαις καὶ αὐλείοις χρώμενοι, Joh. x. 1 ὁ μὴ εἰσερχόμενος διὰ τῆς θύρας εἰς τὴν αὐλὴν τῶν προβάτων ἀλλὰ ἀναβαίνων ἀλλαχόθεν, ἐκεῖνος κλέπτης ἐστὶ καὶ λῃστής. Cl. refers to the same passage of S. John in Protr. P. 9 and continues ὅπως ἡμῖν ἀθρόας τῶν οὐρανῶν ἀναπετάσῃ πύλας· λογικαὶ γὰρ αἱ τοῦ λόγου πύλαι, πίστεως ἀνοιγνύμεναι κλειδί.

24—26. **δι' ἧς...ὥσπερ ἡμεῖς...εἴσιμεν.** The construction is attracted from εἰσίασι to εἴσιμεν by the intervening ὥσπερ ἡμεῖς. On this attraction, which is very common with οὐχ ὥσπερ, cf. Kühner Gr. Gr. vol. II. p. 1079.

26. **παράθυρον ἀνατεμόντες.** Cf. Philo M. 1, p. 16 ὁ μέγας ἡγεμὼν πολυσχιδεῖς ἀνατέμνων ὁδοὺς διὰ γῆς ἔρχεται, ib. 2, p. 362 ἐν ἀνοδίαις ἴσχυσεν λεωφόρους ὁδοὺς ἀνατεμεῖν, ib. 2, p. 2 ἐλπίδα οἷα λεωφόρον ὁδὸν ἡ φιλάρετος ἀνατέμνει καὶ ἀνοίγει ψυχῇ, Plut. Mor. 617 A δέδια μὴ δοκῶμεν τῇ αὐλείῳ τὸν τῦφον ἀποκλείοντες εἰσάγειν τῇ παραθύρῳ μετὰ πολλῆς ἀδιαφορίας.

27. ὑπερβαίνοντες τὴν ἀλήθειαν. See above p. 172. 7.

28. μυσταγωγοί. Cf. *Str.* IV. P. 637 *fin.* ἡμᾶς ὁ σωτὴρ μυσταγωγεῖ, *ib.* v. P. 693 ὡς θέμις τοῖς ἐκεῖ μυσταγωγεῖν τὰς ἐξειλεγμένας ψυχάς, *ib.* P. 727 (from Menander) ἅπαντι δαίμων ἀνδρὶ συμπαρίσταται εὐθὺς γενομένῳ μυσταγωγὸς τοῦ βίου ἀγαθός. On the Christian use of language belonging to the Mysteries see Lob. *Agl.* p. 32 f., Anrich *Das antike Mysterienwesen* pp. 154—162.

29. μεταγενεστέρας. See below p. 188. 18.

p. 188, line 1. **τὰς ἀνθρωπίνας συνηλύσεις.** The word σ. is also used in *Paed.* II. P. 175 and 167.

6. κάτω. Used in later Gr. of time, as ἄνω in earlier Gr., cf. Aristid. XIX. p. 453 πᾶς ὁ τῶν κάτω δυναστῶν κατάλογος, cited with other exx. by Schmid (*Att.* II. p. 220, III. p. 245). For the date of heresy cf. Euseb. *H. E.* III. 32 (commenting on Hegesippus) μέχρι τῶν τότε χρόνων (the martyrdom of Symeon under Trajan) παρθένος καθαρὰ καὶ ἀδιάφθορος ἔμεινεν ἡ ἐκκλησία... ὡς δὲ ὁ ἱερὸς τῶν ἀποστόλων χορὸς διάφορον εἰλήφει τοῦ βίου τέλος, παρεληλύθει τε ἡ γενεὰ ἐκείνη τῶν αὐταῖς ἀκοαῖς τῆς ἐνθέου σοφίας ἐπακοῦσαι κατηξιωμένων, τηνικαῦτα τῆς ἀθέου πλάνης τὴν ἀρχὴν ἐλάμβανεν ἡ σύστασις κ.τ.λ. The notices in the Epistles and the Apocalypse seem to show the existence of heresy at an earlier date, and Simon Magus and Cerinthus are certainly prior to Basilides, as indeed is admitted below ll. 10—16. For Basilides see Hort's art. in *D. of Chr. Biog.* I. p. 269.

10. Γλαυκίαν. Only mentioned here.

11. Πέτρου ἑρμηνέα. This office is generally ascribed to S. Mark, see Papias *ap.* Eus. *H. E.* III. 39 Μάρκος μέν, ἑρμηνευτὴς Πέτρου γενόμενος, ὅσα ἐμνημόνευσεν, ἀκριβῶς ἔγραψεν, but Jerome thinks that he employed more than one interpreter (*Ep. ad Hed.* CXX. 11) duae epistolae quae feruntur Petri stilo inter se et charactere discrepant structuraque verborum. Ex quo intellegimus pro necessitate rerum diversis eum usum interpretibus.

Οὐαλεντῖνον. See art. by Lipsius in *D. of Chr. Biog.* III. pp. 1076—1099.

12. Θεοδᾶ διακηκοέναι. For the use of the v. Potter compares Diog. L. II. 5. 3 Σωκράτης διήκουσεν Ἀρχελάου τοῦ φυσικοῦ (quoted in *Str.* I. P. 352 *fin.*), *ib.* II. 12. 1 (the sons of Crito) διήκουσαν Σωκράτους. Nothing is known of Theodas. Zahn (*Forsch.* III. 125) suggests that it may be another form of Theodotus, from whom Cl. has made excerpts, but Lipsius *l.c.* shows that this is improbable.

§ 107. **13. Μάρκος γάρ.** This is Gieseler's emendation adopted by Hort. The reading Μαρκίων followed by μεθ' ὅν (or even, as emended by Dodwell, μεθ' οὗ) Σίμων Πέτρου ἐπήκουσεν is in flagrant contradiction to the chronology, since Justin Martyr and Irenaeus both witness that Marcion flourished about 154. 'Mark the Evangelist was older than either Glaucias or Theodas, even though we should allow that these were disciples of the Apostles. He was older also than Simon, who undoubtedly heard S. Peter.' γάρ is here used like *nam* in passing on from one instance to another, see my note on Cic. *N. D.* i. 27 and above p. 32. 3. Gieseler supports his emendation by a reference to Greg. Naz. *Orat.* xxv. p. 441, where Μάρκου (the Gnostic) should be substituted for Μαρκίωνος.

16. **ἐπήκουσιν.** The same correction (ἐπ. for ὑπ.) is made by Zahn in *Str.* I. P. 324 τὸ πνεῦμα ἐκεῖνο τὸ κεχαριτωμένον οὖ κατηξιώθημεν ὑπακοῦσαι. I am not sure that it is required in either case.

19. **ὑποβεβηκυίας τῷ χρόνῳ.** I am not aware of any other instance in which ὑποβ. is used generally of posteriority in time: Cl. mostly uses it of subjects to be dealt with in later chapters, cf. *Str.* I. P. 366 *init.* ὡς ὀλίγον ὑποβάντες δείξομεν.

κεκαινοτομῆσθαι. Cf. above p. 182. 6.

20. **παραχαραχθείσας.** Cf. above παραχάραγμα p. 158. 22.

22. **οἱ κατὰ πρόθεσιν δίκαιοι.** Cf. Rom. viii. 28 τοῖς κατὰ πρόθεσιν κλητοῖς οὖσιν.

23. **ἐγκαταλέγονται.** Cf. *Protr.* P. 35 δαίμονες δευτέρᾳ ἐγκαταλεγόμενοι τάξει, *Str.* I. P. 350 *fin.* Ἀκουσίλαον ἐγκατέλεξαν τοῖς ἑπτὰ σοφοῖς, *ib.* P. 423 τοῖς υἱοῖς ἐγκαταλέγεται, Luc. *de Paras.* 3 παρασιτικὴν ταῖς ἄλλαις τέχναις ἐγκαταλέξομεν.

24, 25. **κατὰ τὴν μόνωσιν ἐπαινεῖται.** See n. on p. 190. 8—10 ἡ ἐξοχὴ τῆς ἐκκλησίας κατὰ τὴν μονάδα ἐστίν.

26. **τῇ τοῦ ἑνὸς φύσει συγκληροῦται ἐκκλησία ἡ μία.** Cf. Ael. *N. A.* xv. 28 σκῶπας ('owls') συγκεκληρῶσθαι σιωπῇ, where Jacobs quotes Max. Tyr. I. 4 συγκεκλήρωται ἡ ψυχὴ τοιούτῳ πάθει, *ib.* xvi. 9 ψυχὴ χρηστῷ δαίμονι συγκλ., other exx. in W. Schmid *Att.* II. 151, III. 152.

p. 190, line 2. **εἰς ἑνότητα πίστεως** κ.τ.λ. Cf. Eph. iv. 3–6, and Collect for Unity in the Accession Service.

3, 4. **κατὰ τὰς οἰκείας διαθήκας, μᾶλλον δὲ κατὰ τὴν διαθήκην τὴν μίαν.** Cf. *Str.* vi. P. 793 μία μὲν γὰρ τῷ ὄντι διαθήκη ἡ σωτήριος, ἀπὸ καταβολῆς κόσμου εἰς ἡμᾶς διήκουσα κατὰ διαφόρους γενεάς τε καὶ χρόνους, διάφορος εἶναι τὴν δόσιν ὑποληφθεῖσα, above p. 176. 14.

9. **κατὰ τὴν μονάδα ἐστίν.** Cf. above p. 80. 16 n. on τὴν μίαν ἐκείνην ἕξιν, p. 118. 4 f. διὰ τὴν τοῦ ἀρίστου θεραπείαν, ὃ δὴ τῷ ἑνὶ χαρακτηρίζεται, φίλον (ἡ ἀγάπη) τὸν γνωστικὸν ἀπεργάζεται, *Protr.* P. 72 σπεύσωμεν εἰς σωτηρίαν...εἰς μίαν ἀγάπην συναχθῆναι οἱ πολλοί, κατὰ τὴν τῆς μοναδικῆς οὐσίας ἕνωσιν σπεύσωμεν ἀγαθοεργούμενοι ἀναλόγως, ἑνότητα διώκωμεν τὴν ἀγαθὴν ἐκζητοῦντες μονάδα· ἡ δὲ ἐκ πολλῶν ἕνωσις ἐκ πολυφωνίας...ἁρμονίαν λαβοῦσα θεϊκὴν μία γίνεται συμφωνία, ἑνὶ χορευτῇ τῷ λόγῳ ἑπομένη, *Str.* v. P. 689. In *Str.* iii. P. 512 *init.* it is said that Epiphanes, the son of Carpocrates, καθηγήσατο τῆς μοναδικῆς γνώσεως. The term seems to have been borrowed from the Pythagoreans, see *Plac. Phil.* i. 7 (Diels p. 302) Πυθαγόρας τῶν ἀρχῶν τὴν μονάδα θεὸν καὶ τἀγαθόν, ἥτις ἐστὶν ἡ τοῦ ἑνὸς φύσις, αὐτὸς ὁ νοῦς· τὴν δ' ἀόριστον δυάδα δαίμονα καὶ τὸ κακόν, περὶ ἣν ἐστι τὸ ὑλικὸν πλῆθος.

§ 108. 12, 13. **ὡς ἡ ἀπὸ Οὐαλεντίνου.** One would rather expect *αἱ*, as three distinct schools are spoken of.

14. τὴν Ματθίου αὐχοῦσι προσάγεσθαι δόξαν. From a passage of Hippolytus cited in the n. on p. 142. 19 it would seem that this refers only to Basilides and his followers. For προσάγ. cf. Plut. Mor. 1049 B τὸν Εὐριπίδην μάρτυρα προσάγεται.

17. Περατικοί. The founders of the sect (a branch of the Ophites) are said to have been Εὐφράτης ὁ Περατικὸς καὶ Κέλβης ὁ Καρύστιος (Hippol. v. 13). The second name is also given as Ἀκέμβης (ib. IV. 2), and Ἀδέμης (ib. x. 10 and Theod. Haer. I. 17). For Euphrates see D. of Chr. Biog. II. p. 296, where it is said that the name may have taken its origin from the phrase Ἀβραμ ὁ περάτης (Gen. xiv. 13), which was understood to mean 'one who came from the other side of the Euphrates,' as explained by Jul. Africanus in Routh's Reliquiae II. 244 (Εβραῖοι γὰρ οἱ περᾶται ἑρμηνεύονται, διαπεράσαντος Εὐφράτην Ἀβραάμ). A mystical interpretation is given to this in Eus. Pr. Ev. VII. 8. 15 Περατικοί τινες ἑρμηνεύονται, τὴν ἀπὸ τῶν τῇδε ἐπὶ τὴν τοῦ τῶν ὅλων θεοῦ διάβασίν τε καὶ θεωρίαν στειλάμενοι...καὶ πέραν τῶν σαρκὸς ἡδονῶν ἐπὶ τὸν θεοσεβῆ βίον διαβεβηκότες ἀναγράφονται. Similarly Hippol. v. 16 Αἴγυπτον...τὸ σῶμα νομίζουσι, καὶ περᾶσαι τὴν θάλασσαν τὴν Ἐρυθράν, τουτέστι τῆς φθορᾶς τὸ ὕδωρ...καὶ γενέσθαι πέραν τῆς Ἐρυθρᾶς θαλάσσης...καὶ ἐλθεῖν εἰς τὴν ἔρημον, τουτέστιν ἔξω γενέσεως γενέσθαι. It would seem therefore that Cl. was unfortunate in taking this sect as an example of a geographical name. Perhaps he may have supposed them to belong to the Trans-Jordanic Peraea.

ἡ τῶν Φρυγῶν. Montanus was born in Phrygia; and Pepuza, the sacred city of his followers, was situated in the same province. See Salmon's art. in D. of Chr. Biog. III. 935, and Str. IV. P. 605 init., VI. P. 773 ὅπερ ἐπὶ τῶν προφητεύειν νῦν δὴ λεγομένων παρατηρητέον, and above p. 114. 18, where the allusion is probably to them.

18. Ἐγκρατητῶν. They were ascetics who boasted of their ἐγκράτεια. Cl. mentions them also in Paed. II. P. 186, Str. I. P. 359, and speaks of their leader Tatian in Str. III. P. 458, 550, 551 fin., Ecl. Proph. 999. They are called Ἐγκρατεῖς by Irenaeus, Ἐγκρατῖται by Hippolytus, see Salmon in D. of Chr. Biog. II. 118.

19. δογμάτων ἰδιαζόντων. Cf. Str. v. P. 675 fin. ἐν τῷ περὶ τῆς Ὀρφέως ποιήσεως τὰ ἰδιάζοντα (peculiar phrases) ἐκτιθέμενος.

Δοκιτῶν. 'Quia Christum δοκήσει, specie sola, humanam naturam induisse docebant' Potter. In Str. III. P. 552 Cl. quotes from ὁ τῆς δοκήσεως ἐξάρχων Ἰούλιος Κασσιανός, cf. P. 558 fin. Docetic doctrine was not confined to this particular sect, see Salmon's art. on 'Docetae' and 'Docetism' in D. of Chr. Biog. I. 865—870. Even Cl. himself comes very near it in Str. VI. P. 775, cf. Adumbr. in Joh. p. 1009. The form Δοκιτῶν is found in Hippolytus and others.

20. Αἱματιτῶν. This seems to be the only mention of them. The name may have referred to the substitution of blood for wine in the Eucharist, which was laid to the charge of some heretics, cf. Ps. xvi. 4 'their drink-offerings of blood will I not offer.'

ἀπὸ ὑποθέσεων [καὶ] ἃν τετιμήκασιν. I can make no sense of this, and propose to omit καί and read ὑποστάσεων. A similar substitution is suggested by Kiessling in Iambl. V. P. c. 8, p. 84 ἅμα τὴν τοῦ πατρὸς καὶ τῆς μητρὸς ὑπόθεσιν λαβεῖν. For the meaning of ὑπόστ. cf. Suidas s.v. φύσις λέγεται οἷον ἡ ἀγγελιότης· ὑποστάσεις δὲ αἱ ἰδικαὶ ἑκάστου προσηγορίαι, ἤγουν Μιχαὴλ καὶ Γαβριήλ. ὡσαύτως φύσις ἡ ἀνθρωπότης· ὑποστάσεις δὲ Πέτρος καὶ Παῦλος. The meaning of the passage will then agree with Epiphan. Pan. i. 3. 37 οἱ Ὀφῖται τὰς προφάσεις εἰλήφασιν ἀπὸ τῆς τοῦ Νικολάου αἱρέσεως· Ὀφῖται δὲ καλοῦνται δι' ὃν δοξάζουσιν ὄφιν. See art. 'Ophites' in *D. of Chr. Biog.* IV. 79—88.

21. **Καϊανισταί**. See Salmon in *D. of Chr. Biog.* I. 380, where they are said to have been a branch of the Ophites, who, regarding the Creator as evil, reversed all the moral judgments of the O.T. and held that the Serpent was the vehicle employed by Wisdom to free man from his bondage to the Demiurge, and that the death of Abel at the hands of Cain proved that the power from which the latter sprang was higher than that from which the former was derived.

23. **Σιμωνιανῶν**. Spoken of as οἱ ἀμφὶ τὸν Σίμωνα in *Str.* II. P. 456 fin., above p. 188. 15. See art. 'Simon Magus' in *D. of Chr. Biog.* IV. 681—688.

Ἐντυχῖται. The name embodies the common belief that promiscuous sexual intercourse was practised at the nightly meetings of the Carpocratians and other heretics, see *D. of Chr. Biog. s.v.*

§ 109. ὀπήν. See Index.

τοῖς φιλοθεάμοσι. Cf. Plato quoted in *Str.* I. P. 373, II. P. 442 init., v. P. 654 init. τοὺς δὲ ἀληθινοὺς φιλοσόφους τίνας λέγεις; τοὺς τῆς ἀληθείας, ἦν δ' ἐγώ, φιλοθεάμονας. Standing alone, the word is used by Plato for 'lovers of sight-seeing,' but frequently by Philo in the higher sense, e.g. M. 1, p. 376 τοῖς φιλοθεάμοσι καὶ τὰ ἀσώματα ὁρᾶν γλιχομένοις, ib. p. 566 ὁ θεὸς (τὴν σοφίαν) ταῖς εὐφυέσι καὶ φιλοθεάμοσιν ἄνωθεν ἐπιψεκάζει διανοίαις, other exx. in Siegfried p. 128.

24. **ὁ κατὰ τὰς θυσίας νόμος** = ὁ τῶν θυσιῶν ν., cf. above p. 146. 19 τῆς κατὰ τὸν γνωστικὸν ἀπαθείας, Diod. I. 65 τὴν δὲ τῆς εὐσεβείας ὑπερβολὴν συλλογίσαιτ' ἄν τις ἐκ τῆς κατὰ τὴν ἀρχὴν ἀποθέσεως, Aelian *V. H.* III. 36 αἰνιττόμενος τὸν καθ' αὑτὸν κίνδυνον ('ipsius periculum'), ib. II. 41 ἡ Πλάτωνος δόξα καὶ ὁ τῆς κατ' αὐτὸν ἀρετῆς λόγος εἰς Ἀρκάδας ἀφίκετο, Acts xvii. 28 οἱ καθ' ὑμᾶς ποιηταί, ib. xviii. 15 νόμος ὁ καθ' ὑμᾶς, ib. xxv. 14 τὰ κατὰ τὸν Παῦλον, Winer *Gr.* p. 241.

26. **χυδαίων**. Cf. above p. 176. 9.

p. 192, line 2 **καταπατήσομεν**. The future, stating the writer's intention, seems more appropriate here (as below p. 196. 5) than the subjunctive; and the long and short vowels are constantly confounded in the MS.

τὰ μὲν διχηλοῦντα κ.τ.λ. Cf. Lev. xi. 3 πᾶν κτῆνος διχηλοῦν ὁπλὴν καὶ ὀνυχιστῆρας ὀνυχίζον δύο χηλῶν καὶ ἀνάγον μηρυκισμόν...ταῦτα φάγεσθε, quoted by Barnabas x. 11 in the form φάγεσθε πᾶν διχηλοῦν καὶ μαρυκώμενον, and explained as follows, τί οὖν λέγει; κολλᾶσθε...μετὰ τῶν μελετώντων ὃ ἔλαβον διάσταλμα ῥήματος ἐν τῇ καρδίᾳ...μετὰ τῶν...ἀναμαρυκωμένων τὸν λόγον κυρίου. τί δὲ τὸ διχηλοῦν; ὅτι ὁ δίκαιος καὶ ἐν τούτῳ τῷ κόσμῳ περιπατεῖ καὶ τὸν ἅγιον αἰῶνα ἐκδέχεται. Reference is made to this passage of Barn. in *Str.* v. P. 677, *Paed.* III. P. 298 πᾶν γὰρ διχηλοῦν καὶ μαρυκώμενον καθαρόν ἐστιν, ὅτι τὸ διχηλοῦν δικαιοσύνην ἐμφαίνει τὴν ἰσοστάσιον, μηρυκάζουσαν τὴν οἰκείαν δικαιοσύνης τροφήν, τὸν λόγον, ἔκτοσθεν μὲν εἰσιόντα κατὰ ταὐτὰ τῇ τροφῇ διὰ κατηχήσεως, ἔνδοθεν δὲ ἀναπεμπόμενον ὥσπερ ἐκ κοιλίας τῆς διανοίας εἰς ἀνάμνησιν λογικήν κ.τ.λ. Philo gives a different account of διχηλοῦν (M. 1, p. 320) μηρυκάζει δὲ ὁ δίκαιος τὴν πνευματικὴν τροφὴν ἀνὰ στόμα ἔχων, τὸν λόγον. καὶ διχηλεῖ ἡ δικαιοσύνη, εἰκότως κἀνταῦθα ἁγιάζουσα καὶ εἰς τὸν μέλλοντα παραπέμπουσα αἰῶνα. ὥσπερ τὸ μηρυκώμενον τὴν προκαταβληθεῖσαν ὑπαναπλέουσαν αὖθις ἐπιλεαίνει τροφήν, οὕτως ἡ ψυχὴ τοῦ φιλομαθοῦς, ἐπειδάν τινα δι' ἀκοῆς δέξηται θεωρήματα, λήθῃ μὲν αὐτὰ οὐ παραδίδωσιν, ἠρεμήσασα δὲ καθ' ἑαυτὴν ἕκαστα μεθ' ἡσυχίας τῆς πάσης ἀναπολεῖ...μνήμη δ' οὐ πᾶσα ἀγαθόν, ἀλλ' ἡ ἐπὶ μόνοις τοῖς ἀγαθοῖς...οὗ ἕνεκα πρὸς τελειότητα χρεία τοῦ διχηλεῖν, ἵνα τοῦ μνημονικοῦ δίχα τμηθέντος ὁ λόγος διὰ στόματος ῥέων...διαστείλῃ τό τε ὠφέλιμον καὶ τὸ ἐπιζήμιον μνήμης γένους εἶδος κ.τ.λ., *ib.* p. 321 *fin.* διχηλήσει μέν, διαστέλλειν καὶ διακρίνειν ἕκαστα δυνάμενος. οὐ μηρυκηθήσεται δὲ ὡς ὠφελίμῳ χρῆσθαι τροφῇ κατὰ τὰς ὑπομνήσεις. Much the same account is found in Aristeas (at the end of Havercamp's Josephus vol. II. p. 117): μηρυκισμός signifies recollection, διχηλία signifies discrimination. Origen (*in Levit. hom.* VII. 6) gives a somewhat different explanation: 'revocat ruminationem qui ea, quae secundum literam legit, revocat ad sensum spiritualem...sed, si mediteris legem divinam...actus autem tui non sint tales ut habeas discretionem vitae praesentis et futuri ...non dividis...nec angustam viam a via spatiosa secernis.' Cl. here is in close agreement with Iren. v. 8. 3, as will be seen by the quotations which follow.

4, 5. ὡς ἂν εἰς πατέρα καὶ εἰς υἱὸν διὰ τῆς πίστεως τῶν δικαίων τὴν πορείαν ποιουμένων. Cf. Iren. *l.c.* 'qui sunt ergo mundi? qui in Patrem et Filium similiter iter firmiter faciunt.'

6. αὕτη γάρ ἡ τῶν διχηλούντων ἑδραιότης. Cf. Iren. *l.c.* 'haec est enim firmitas eorum qui duplicis sunt ungulae,' above p. 80 ἀμεταπτώτως βιοῦν ἀσκοῦντι διὰ τὴν τῆς γνώμης μονότονον ἑδραιότητα, p. 88. 9 ἑδραίῳ βίῳ καὶ λόγῳ.

7. τῶν τὰ λόγια τοῦ θεοῦ νύκτωρ καὶ μεθ' ἡμέραν μελετώντων. Cf. Ps. i. 2 ἐν τῷ νόμῳ αὐτοῦ μελετήσει ἡμέρας καὶ νυκτός, and Iren. *l.c.* 'et eloquia Dei meditantur die ac nocte.' The art. τῶν seems inappropriate here; comparing Iren., I am disposed to read καὶ in its place.

8. ἀναπεμπαζομένων. The verb is literally 'to reckon up on the fingers,' then to 'ponder over,' cf. Ruhnken Tim. *s.v.* where exx. of the middle are quoted from Plato and Max. Tyr (*Diss.* XVI. p. 187 ἀναπεμπάζεται τῇ μνήμῃ τὰ τοῦ νοῦ θεάματα), and of the active from later writers, *e.g.* Heliod. III. 137 ὥσπερ εἴ που γνωρίζοντες ἤ, ἰδόντες πρότερον, ταῖς μνήμαις ἀναπεμπάζοντες.

9. ἣν καὶ συνάσκησιν κ.τ.λ. If the reading is right, we must either

take πορείαν (l. 5) to be the antecedent to ἥν (which seems hardly possible), or we must suppose that ὅ (viz. τὸ μελετᾶν καὶ ἀναπεμπάζεσθαι) is attracted to the following συνάσκησιν. The attraction of the gender to the predicative noun is common enough (see Jelf § 821. 3); in this instance it would be to the noun in an appositional clause. There is also a difficulty in καί: 'what else is implied besides συνάσκησις? Perhaps τροφήν (which appears in Philo's explanation) may have been lost after ἥν.

10. **ἀλληγορεῖ.** For construction cf. above p. 152. 28 σῶμα ἀλληγορεῖται ἡ ἐκκλησία, Paed. II. P. 186 τὸν λόγον τὸν περὶ πολλῶν ἐκχεόμενον...ἅγιον ἀλληγορεῖ νᾶμα (ὁ κύριος).

11. **ὅσα μήτε ἑκάτερον μήτε τὸ ἕτερον τούτων ἔχει.** Apparently an awkward phrase for ὅσοις τὸ ἕτερον ἐπιλείπει. Or is ἑκάτερον used here for ἄμφω? see Plut. Mor. 1072 c φαίνεται πρὸ τῆς ἑτέρας ἀναγκαζόμενος ἀεὶ τὴν ἑτέραν διώκειν, ἀπολειπόμενος δὲ ἑκατέρας. But then we should have expected something to mark the climax, such as μήτ' οὖν τὸ ἕτερον. For the thought cf. Iren. l.c. 'immunda autem quae neque duplicem ungulam habent, neque ruminant.'

12. **ἀφορίζει.** Rare use, see Lk. vi. 22.

13. **τοὺς Ἰουδαίους αἰνίσσεται** κ.τ.λ. Cf. Iren. l.c. 'quae autem ruminant quidem, non habent autem ungulam duplicem, et ipsa immunda; haec Judaeorum est imaginalis descriptio, qui quidem eloquia Dei in ore habent, stabilitatem autem radicis suae non infigunt in Patre et in Filio.' Both here and above (ll. 4, 5) Irenaeus' interpretation seems to me to come nearer to the original figure, and therefore to be anterior to Cl.'s more guarded and reverent explanation.

17. **δῦον καὶ ὀλισθηρόν** κ.τ.λ. Cf. Iren. l.c. 'propter hoc autem et lubricum est genus ipsorum: etenim quae sunt unius ungulae animalia facile labuntur; firmiora autem sunt quae duplicem quidem ungulam habent, succedentibus invicem ungulis fissis secundum iter; et altera ungula subbaiulat aliam.'

18. **τῇ διπλόῃ.** Used in a different sense above p. 80. 17.

20—27. Cf. Iren. l.c. 'immunda autem similiter quae duplicem ungulam habent, non autem ruminant; haec est autem omnium videlicet haereticorum ostensio et eorum qui non meditantur eloquia Dei neque operibus iustitiae adornantur...Qui enim sunt tales in Patrem quidem et Filium dicunt se credere, nunquam autem meditantur eloquia Dei, quemadmodum oportet, neque iustitiae operibus sunt adornati.'

24. **λεπτουργεῖν.** Used properly of any fine or delicate work, cf. Plut. Mor. 997 where Lycurgus is said to have permitted the use of saws and axes, but forbidden that of chisels καὶ ὅσα λεπτουργεῖν πέφυκεν, Paed. II. P. 234 where Cl. allows women to use softer fabrics than men, μόνον τὰς μεμωραμένας λεπτουργίας καὶ τὰς ἐν ταῖς ὑφαῖς περιέργους πλοκὰς ἐκποδὼν μεθιστάντας. Plato uses it of minute logical division, Polit. 294 D λεπτουργεῖν οὐκ ἐγχωρεῖν ἡγοῦνται καθ' ἕνα ἕκαστον...ἀλλὰ παχύτερον οἴονται δεῖν ὡς ἐπὶ τὸ πολύ...ποιεῖσθαι τάξιν.

25. **καταλεαίνειν.** Used of the mastication of food in Paed. II. 179

ἐπεί. οὐδὲ γὰρ ὕδατος ἀνέδην ἐμφορεῖσθαι προσήκει, ὡς μὴ ἐκκλύζοιτο ἡ τροφή, καταλεαίνοιτο δὲ εἰς πέψιν, see quotation from Quintil. on l. 26. Stephanus cites Cyril. Al. *in Hagg.* II. p. 646 θεοῦ τὴν τῶν πρακτέων ἡμῖν οὐ καταλεαίνοντος ὁδόν ('making plain' or 'smooth').

ἐξασθενοῦντας. Above p. 178. 23 ἐν τοῖς ἔργοις ἐξασθενῶν.

τὰ ἔργα τῆς δικαιοσύνης. See Iren. cited in n. on 20—27.

28. **ὁλοσχερέστερον...μεταρχομένους.** See Anton. I. 7 τὸ ἀκριβῶς ἀναγινώσκειν καὶ μὴ ἀρκεῖσθαι περινοοῦντα ὁλοσχερῶς, where Gataker cites Quintil. X. 1. 19 'repetamus autem et retractemus et, ut cibos mansos ac prope liquefactos demittimus quo facilius digerantur, ita lectio non cruda sed multa iteratione mollita et velut confecta memoriae imitationique tradatur,' Sext. Emp. *P. H.* I. 13 ὡς ἂν ὁλοσχερίστερον εἴποι τις, Epicurus *ad Herod.* (Usener p. 3, l. 15 f.) τὸ κατὰ μέρος ἀκρίβωμα πᾶν ἐξευρεθήσεται, τῶν ὁλοσχερεστάτων τύπων εὖ περιειλημμένων.

§ 110. 28. **τί με λέγετε—λέγω.** Quoted by Iren. *l.c.*

p. 194, line 1. **ὑμεῖς δ', ὦ Μεγαρεῖς.** An oracle wrongly attributed to Theognis, which is given more at length in the schol. on Theocr. XIV. 48 ἄμμες δ' οὔτε λόγῳ τινὸς ἄξιοι, οὔτ' ἀριθμητοί, δύστηνοι Μεγαρῆες ἀτιμοτάτῃ ἐνὶ μοίρῃ, where the historian Deinias is cited as follows: οἱ Μεγαρεῖς φρονηματισθέντες ποτέ, ὅτι κράτιστοι τῶν Ἑλλήνων εἰσίν, ἐπύθοντο τοῦ θεοῦ τίνες κρείττονες τυγχάνοιεν. ὁ δὲ ἔφη· Γαίης μὲν πάσης τὸ Πελασγικὸν Ἄργος ἄμεινον, ἵπποι Θρηίκιαι, Λακεδαιμόνιαι δὲ γυναῖκες, ἄνδρες δ' οἱ πίνουσιν ὕδωρ καλῆς Ἀρεθούσης...ὑμεῖς δ' ὦ Μεγαρεῖς κ.τ.λ. Allusion is made to it in Callim. *Epigr.* 26 νῦν δ' ὁ μὲν ἄλλης δὴ θέρεται πυρί, τῆς δὲ ταλαίνης νύμφης, ὡς Μεγαρέων, οὐ λόγος οὔτ' ἀριθμός.

4. **οὔτ' ἐν λόγῳ οὔτ' ἐν ἀριθμῷ,** 'unworthy to be either mentioned or counted,' cf. Herod. I. 120 λόγου οὐδενὸς γινόμεθα πρὸς Περσέων, Eur. *fr.* δειλοὶ γὰρ ἄνδρες οὐκ ἔχουσιν ἐν μάχῃ ἀριθμόν. H. J. compares Plato *Phileb.* 17 E οὐκ ἐλλόγιμον οὐδ' ἐνάριθμον.

5. **ἀλλ' ἤ.** See above p. 94. 27, and cf. 2 Chron. XIX. 3, Dan. X. 7, 21.

7. **τοῦ ἠθικοῦ τόπου.** At the beginning of the Sixth Book Cl. sketches out what he has still to do ὁ δὲ δὴ ἕκτος ὁμοῦ καὶ ὁ ἕβδομος ἡμῖν...στρωματεὺς διαγράψας τὸν ἠθικὸν λόγον ἐν τούτοις περαιούμενον, καὶ παραστήσας ὅστις ἂν εἴη κατὰ τὸν βίον ὁ γνωστικός, πρόεισι δείξων κ.τ.λ. This does not seem quite consistent with the beginning of *Paed.* I. where he says τριῶν τούτων περὶ τὸν ἄνθρωπον ὄντων, ἠθῶν, πράξεων, παθῶν, ὁ προτρεπτικὸς εἴληχεν τὰ ἤθη αὐτοῦ. Again, at the beginning of the 4th *Strom.* he mentions various topics which he means to discuss ἵν' ὡς ἐν ἐπιδρομῇ τὸν ἠθικὸν συμπερανάμενοι λόγον, παραστήσωμεν τὴν εἰς Ἕλληνας ἐκ τῆς βαρβάρου φιλοσοφίας διαδοθεῖσαν ὠφέλειαν, ib. P. 564 *fin.* νυνὶ δὲ...τὸν ἠθικὸν ἀποπληρωτέον λόγον, *Str.* IV. P. 638 (ὁ θεὸς) ᾗ μέν ἐστιν οὐσία, ἀρχὴ τοῦ ποιητικοῦ (ἢ φυσικοῦ) τόπου· καθ' ὅσον ἐστὶ τἀγαθόν, τοῦ ἠθικοῦ· ᾗ δ' αὖ ἐστι νοῦς, τοῦ λογικοῦ καὶ κριτικοῦ τόπου. Cf. P. 469 Moses supplied to the Greeks ἀρχὴν παντὸς τοῦ ἠθικοῦ τόπου.

8. ὡς ὑπεσχήμεθα. See *Str.* I. P. 324, esp. 326 περιέξουσι δὲ οἱ στρωματεῖς ἀναμεμιγμένην τὴν ἀλήθειαν τοῖς φιλοσοφίας δόγμασι, μᾶλλον δὲ ἐγκεκαλυμμένην...ἁρμόζει γὰρ τῆς ἀληθείας τὰ σπέρματα μόνοις φυλάσσεσθαι τοῖς τῆς πίστεως γεωργοῖς.

9. τὰ ζώπυρα. First employed in this metaphorical sense by Plato *Legg.* III. 585 c. Many examples are given in Ruhnken on Tim. *Lex.*, cf. Julian *Ep.* 34, p. 406 D οἱονεὶ σπινθήρ τις ἱερὸς ἀληθοῦς καὶ γονίμου παιδεύσεως ὑπὸ σοὶ μόνῳ ζωπυρεῖται. Cl. has it also in *Str.* I. P. 321 *fin.* συνεξάπτει ἡ γραφὴ τὸ ζώπυρον τῆς ψυχῆς, and as an adjective *Str.* VI. P. 736 (οἱ στρωματεῖς) ἐμοὶ ὑπομνήματα εἶεν ἂν ζώπυρα.

11, 12. τῶν ἁγίων παραδόσεων. Cf. above p. 44. 19 ἡ ἀληθὴς παράδοσις, p. 182. 14 θεία παράδοσις, ib. l. 30 ἡ τοῦ κυρίου παράδοσις, p. 174. 22 αἱ τοῦ Χριστοῦ παραδόσεις, and Index *s.v.*

12. ἐπὶ τὴν ὑπόθεσιν. So I am inclined to read for ὑπόσχεσιν, which seems to have slipped in owing to the previous ὑπεσχήμεθα. The argument or theme of the Διδάσκαλος is laid down in the first chapter of *Str.* IV.

§ 111. 13. οἱ στρωματεῖς. See P. 565, and Introduction.

παράδεισος. Here the word is used of a formal garden, as shown by the description which follows; but in *Str.* VI. P. 736 of something like an English park, as it is joined with a meadow, ἐν μὲν οὖν τῷ λειμῶνι τὰ ἄνθη ποικίλως ἀνθοῦντα κἀν τῷ παραδείσῳ ἡ τῶν ἀκροδρύων φυτεία οὐ κατὰ εἶδος ἕκαστον κεχώρισται τῶν ἀλλογενῶν, cf. Becker's *Gallus*, exc. on 'Gardens,' Longus *Pastor.* IV. 2.

14. ἐξησκημένοις. Cf. Lycophr. *Cass.* 857 ὄρχατον φυτοῖσιν ἐξησκημένον.

καταπεφυτευμένοις. See above p. 128. 19, below l. 18.

16, 17. κυπαρίσσοις—συκαῖς. This agrees with the description in Longus *l.c.* εἶχε δὲ πάντα δένδρα, μηλέας, μυρρίνας, ὄχνας καὶ ῥοιὰς καὶ συκῆν καὶ ἐλαίας...τοσαῦτα ἥμερα· ἦσαν δὲ καὶ κυπάριττοι καὶ δάφναι καὶ πλάτανοι καὶ πίτυς...ἔνδον ἦν τὰ καρποφόρα φυτὰ καθάπερ φρουρούμενα, ἔξωθεν περιειστήκει τὰ ἄκαρπα.

21, 22. ἐξ ὧν δὴ μεταμοσχεύσας καὶ μεταφυτεύσας ὁ γεωργὸς ὡραῖον κατακοσμήσει παράδεισον. Cf. *Str.* VI. P. 736 *fin.* ὁ παράδεισος ὁ πνευματικὸς αὐτὸς ἡμῶν ὁ σωτὴρ ὑπάρχει, εἰς ὃν καταφυτευόμεθα μετατεθέντες καὶ μεταμοσχευθέντες εἰς τὴν γῆν τὴν ἀγαθὴν ἐκ βίου τοῦ παλαιοῦ.

23, 24. οὔτ' οὖν τῆς τάξεως—στοχάζονται. Cf. *Str.* II. P. 429 *fin.* ἔφαμεν δὲ πολλάκις ἤδη μήτε μεμελετηκέναι μήτε μὴν ἐπιτηδεύειν ἑλληνίζειν...δεῖ δ', οἶμαι, τὸν ἀληθείας κηδόμενον οὐκ ἐξ ἐπιβουλῆς καὶ φροντίδος τὴν φράσιν συντιθέναι, πειρᾶσθαι δὲ ὀνομάζειν μόνον ὡς δύναται ὃ βούλεται.

25. ἡδυσμένην. Cf. Plato *Rep.* x. 607 τὴν ἡδυσμένην μοῦσαν, Arist. *Poet.* 6. 3 λέγω δὲ ἡδυσμένον λόγον τὸν ἔχοντα ῥυθμὸν καὶ ἁρμονίαν καὶ μέλος, *Rhet.* III. 3. 3 τὰ Ἀλκιδάμαντος ψυχρὰ φαίνεται· οὐ γὰρ ἡδύσματι χρῆται ἀλλ' ὡς ἐδέσματι τοῖς ἐπιθέτοις, *Polit.* VIII. 5 *fin.* ἡ μουσικὴ φύσει τῶν ἡδυσμένων ἐστίν.

27. **λεληθότως καὶ οὐ κατὰ τὴν ἀλήθειαν.** For the same opposition H. J. compares Arist. *Eth. N.* VI. 5. 6 f. ἀνάγκη τὴν φρόνησιν ἕξιν εἶναι μετὰ λόγου ἀληθῆ...ἀλλὰ μὴν οὐδ' ἕξις μετὰ λόγου μόνον· σημεῖον δὲ ὅτι λήθη τῆς μὲν τοιαύτης ἕξεώς ἐστι, φρονήσεως δὲ οὐκ ἔστιν.

φιλοπόνους καὶ εὑρετικοὺς εἶναι τοὺς ἅ τινες ὑπέχουσιν παρασκευάζοντες. So in *Str.* VI. P. 736 τῷ εἰς γνῶσιν ἐπιτηδείῳ, εἴ πως περιτύχοι τοῖσδε (τοῖς ἐμοῖς ὑπομνήμασιν), πρὸς τὸ συμφέρον καὶ ὠφέλιμον μετὰ ἰδρῶτος ἡ ζήτησις γενήσεται. For the article see n. on p. 112. 1 τῶν ὅσα τούτοις συγγενῆ.

APPENDIX A.

Unrecorded Uses of αὐτίκα.

Beside the ordinary temporal uses of αὐτίκα, the Lexicons (Stephanus, Rost and Palm, L. and S.) only recognize the use, found not unfrequently in Plato and Aristophanes, by which a particular instance is introduced to confirm a preceding general statement. Many examples of this are given in Devarius, and in Ruhnken's note on Timaeus. There is however another use to be found in Clemens Alexandrinus, which approaches more nearly to γοῦν and justifies a previous statement, not necessarily by an example, but by reference to some generally recognized fact or principle, with which it is logically connected. Sylburg in his Index quotes two examples and translates it by *utique*. It is however very common, and it may be well here to put down the instances I have collected in order to ascertain its exact force. I will mention first one or two cases in which the rendering 'for instance' is admissible. *Str.* IV. 573 'Choice and rejection are in accordance with knowledge. Hence it is knowledge, not pleasure, which is the good, and owing to this we sometimes choose a particular kind of pain, *e.g.* (αὐτίκα) the martyr chooses the pleasure he hopes for by way of the immediate pain'; *Str.* VII. 841 'the heathen make their gods like men, not only in body, but in soul, *e.g.* (αὐτίκα) the barbarians make them savage in disposition, the Greeks gentler but passionate.' VII. 878 τοῦτο μόνον ὁρᾶν βούλεται ὃ προσῆκεν αὐτῷ. αὐτίκα τῶν ἀδελφῶν τὰς ψυχὰς θεωρῶν καὶ τῆς σαρκὸς τὸ κάλλος αὐτῇ βλέπει τῇ ψυχῇ, 'he desires to see that only which becomes him. *For instance*, while he contemplates the souls of his brethren, he beholds even the beauty of the flesh only with the eye of the mind.' So II. p. 570.

Now consider the following: (*a*) *Str.* I. 316 ψυχῆς ἔκγονοι οἱ λόγοι· αὐτίκα ('at any rate') πατέρας τοὺς κατηχήσαντάς φαμεν. The fact that we call our instructors by the name of father, is not an *instance* of the general statement that 'words are the offspring of the soul,' though it may be alleged in confirmation of it. *Ib.* 323 μεταδιδόναι τῶν θείων μυστηρίων τοῖς χωρεῖν δυναμένοις συγκεχώρηκεν. αὐτίκα οὐ πολλοῖς ἀπεκάλυψεν ἃ μὴ πολλῶν ἦν, 'he has permitted us to impart the divine mysteries to those who are capable of receiving them. *Certainly* he has not revealed to many what was beyond the capacity of many.' Here αὐτίκα introduces a clause to justify the limitation implied in τοῖς χωρεῖν δυναμένοις. *Ib.* 318 ἀμφω κηρύττουσι τὸν λόγον... τῇ δὲ αἰτίᾳ τοῦ μὴ τὸ βέλτιστον ἑλομένου θεὸς ἀναίτιος. αὐτίκα τῶν μὲν ἐκδανεῖσαι τὸν λόγον ἔργον ἐστίν, τῶν δὲ δοκιμάσαι καὶ ἤτοι ἑλέσθαι ἢ μή, 'God is not to be blamed; *at any rate* it is the duty of one set to communicate the word, of the others to test it.' *Ib.* 367 φασὶ γὰρ αἴτιον εἶναι κλοπῆς τὸν μὴ φυλάξαντα...ὡς τοῦ ἐμπρησμοῦ τὸν μὴ σβέσαντα... αὐτίκα κολάζονται πρὸς τοῦ νόμου οἱ τούτων αἴτιοι 'any *how* this is proved by the fact that such are punished by the law.' *Ib.* II. 447 ὁ νόμος οὐκ ἐποίησεν ἀλλ' ἔδειξεν τὴν ἁμαρτίαν...αὐτίκα ὁ ἀπόστολος γνῶσιν εἶπεν ἁμαρτίας διὰ νόμου πεφανερῶσθαι, 'the law did not cause, but revealed sin. *At any rate* the Apostle said that the knowledge of sin was brought to light by the law.' *Ib.* 462 τὸ ἑκούσιον ἢ τὸ κατ' ὄρεξίν ἐστιν ἢ τὸ κατὰ προαίρεσιν ἢ τὸ κατὰ διάνοιαν. αὐτίκα παράκειταί πως ταῦτα ἀλλήλοις, ἁμάρτημα ἀτύχημα ἀδίκημα, 'the voluntary is that which is done either in accordance with inclination, or with purpose, or with understanding: *at any rate* there is a close connexion between error, mishap, and wrong-doing.' (Or should this come under the following head *b*?) *Ib.* 472 κινδυνεύοντας ἀνεχαίτισε νουθετήσας φόβος· αὐτίκα οἱ περιλειφθέντες...κύριοι κατέστησαν τῶν πολεμίων, (speaking of the Israelites seduced by Midian) 'when they were in danger, fear rebuked them and pulled them up... *at any rate* the survivors defeated the enemy.' *Str.* III. 540 ('as woman is considered the cause of death owing to her child-bearing, so for the same reason she will be called the author of life') αὐτίκα...ζωὴ προσηγορεύθη διὰ τὴν τῆς διαδοχῆς αἰτίαν, τῶν τε γεννωμένων τῶν τε ἀποθνησκόντων (so Louth for ἁμαρτανόντων) γίνεται...μήτηρ, '*at any rate* Eve was called by a name meaning life, because she brought about the succession of birth and death.' *Ib.* 553 ('Cassianus thinks that the soul is of divine nature to begin with, but that it was rendered effeminate by desire, and descended here to birth and death') αὐτίκα βιάζεται τὸν Παῦλον ἐκ τῆς ἀπάτης τὴν γένεσιν συνεστάναι λέγειν, '*at any rate* he makes Paul say that generation is caused by deceit.' *Str.* IV. 570 (The martyr departs to the Lord with good courage and hears from Him the salutation 'Dear brother' because of the similarity of their life) αὐτίκα τελείωσιν τὸ μαρτύριον καλοῦσιν, '*at any rate* they call martyrdom perfection.' *Str.* IV. 574 ('Plutus makes men blind') αὐτίκα πρὸς τῶν ποιητῶν τυφλὸς ἐκ γενετῆς κηρύττεται, '*certainly* he is represented as blind from his birth.' *Ib.* 566 τὴν ἐπιγραφὴν κυρίαν ἔχουσιν οἱ τῶν ὑπομνημάτων στρωματεῖς κατὰ τὴν παλαιὰν ἐκείνην προσφοράν...αὐτίκα οἱ στρωματεῖς ἡμῶν...οὐκ' ἔλαιον ἰσχάδας μέλι προσοδεύουσι, '*at any rate.*' *Str.* V. 660 ἀποκεκαλυμμένως οὐχ οἷόν τε ἦν τὰ τοιαῦτα τῶν χαρισμάτων ἐπιστέλλειν. αὐτίκα τῆς βαρβάρου φιλοσοφίας πάνυ σφόδρα ἐπικεκρυμμένως ἤρτηται τὰ Πυθαγόρεια σύμβολα, 'it was not possible to set forth such graces without concealment. *At any rate* the allegorical precepts of Pythagoras which are derived from the Hebrew philosophy are most carefully shrouded.' *Str.* VII. 844 πᾶς ἁγνός ἐστιν ὁ μηδὲν ἑαυτῷ κακὸν συνειδώς. αὐτίκα ἡ τραγῳδία λέγει, 'Ὀρέστα, τίς σ' ἀπώλυσιν νόσος; ἡ σύνεσις, ὅτι σύνοιδα δεῖν' εἰργασμένος. τῷ γὰρ ὄντι ἡ ἁγνεία οὐκ ἄλλη τίς ἐστιν πλὴν ἡ τῶν ἁμαρτημάτων ἀποχή. καλῶς ἄρα καὶ Ἐπίχαρμός φησι, Καθαρὸν ἂν τὸν νοῦν ἔχης, ἄπαν τὸ σῶμα καθαρὸς εἶ. αὐτίκα καὶ τὰς ψυχὰς προκαθαίρειν χρεών φαμεν ἀπὸ τῶν φαύλων δογμάτων. 'Every one is pure whose conscience is clear. *At any rate* the tragic Orestes witnesses that to be conscious of guilt is a fatal disease. For purity consists in abstaining from sin. It is well said therefore that, if you have your mind pure, your whole body is pure. *Anyhow* we say that we must first cleanse our souls also from evil opinions.' *Ib.* 897 (discussing the meaning of the word φυσιοῦν, Clement says it does not imply vanity but a high-minded trust in God, and contempt for the world) αὐτίκα φησὶν ὁ ἀπόστολος 'καὶ γνώσομαι οὐ τὸν λόγον τῶν πεφυσιωμένων ἀλλὰ τὴν δύναμιν,' εἰ μεγαλοφρόνως τῆς γραφῆς συνίετε, '*at any rate* the Apostle says "I will know not their word, but their power," *i.e.* whether they have a lofty understanding of the Scripture.' *Protr.* p. 38 ('the demons are always plotting against men and are incapable of benefiting anyone) αὐτίκα γοῦν ἔχω σοι βελτίονα τῶν ὑμεδαπῶν θεῶν, τῶν δαιμόνων, ἐπιδείξαι τὸν ἄνθρωπον '*at any rate* I can show you that the man comes out much better than the gods in the story of Croesus.' The only example I have from other writers is Plut. *Mor.* p. 1137 D οὐ δι' ἄγνοιαν ἀπείχοντο ἐν τοῖς Δωρίοις τοῦ τετραχόρδου τούτου· αὐτίκα ἐπὶ τῶν λοιπῶν τόπων ἐχρῶντο, δηλονότι εἰδότες 'it was not owing to ignorance that they abstained from using this tetrachord in the Dorian mode; *at all events* they used it in the other modes, which shows their acquaintance with it.'

What is the origin of this peculiar use? The word αὐτίκα properly means 'on the instant' as αὐτοῦ means 'on the spot.' Hence it is employed like εὐθύς to introduce a sudden thought with the force of 'to go no further,' 'to take what first comes to hand,' and so is fitly joined with an example, implying that they are so abundant there is no need to spend time in looking for one. As the word γοῦν, which originally means 'at any rate,' is narrowed to mean 'for instance,' it is possible that αὐτίκα may have received a converse extension of meaning, especially as it is often united with γοῦν by Clement (cf. pp. 108, 113, 159). More probably however it is a parallel development from the root-meaning.

(b) Among the instances of the use of the word by Clement there are some which do not seem to come quite under either of the heads mentioned. Thus *Str.* I. 342, after speaking of the importance of regular training in husbandry, medicine and other pursuits, and showing that an athlete is thought little of without it, C. goes on αὐτίκα καὶ κυβερνήτην τὸν πολύπειρον ἐπαινοῦμεν. Here neither the interpretation 'for instance' nor 'at any rate' seems appropriate, as αὐτίκα merely continues the series of examples already commenced. Perhaps it may be equivalent to the Latin *jam* 'further.' *Str.* IV. 577 (What is the meaning of the parable of Lazarus, and of the saying no man can serve God and Mammon?) αὐτίκα εἰς τὴν κλῆσιν τοῦ δείπνου οἱ φιλοκτήμονες κληθέντες οὐκ ἀπαντῶσιν...διὰ τὸ προσπαθῶς κεκτῆσθαι. Here neither 'for instance' nor 'at any rate' will give a natural meaning to αὐτίκα, which, I think, must be translated 'further,' 'again.' *Str.* IV. 633 (God is passionless, without anger and without desire. This is the meaning of the Pythagorean precept that man should be one, as God is one) αὐτίκα ὁ σωτὴρ διὰ τῆς ἐπιθυμίας συνανῄρει καὶ τὸν θυμὸν τιμωρίας ὄντα ἐπιθυμίαν, 'further the Saviour did away with anger by forbidding desire, anger being a desire of vengeance.' *Ib.* 633 ἡ γὰρ σωφροσύνη ἑαυτὴν ἐπισκοποῦσα καὶ θεωροῦσα ἀδιαλείπτως ἐξομοιοῦται κατὰ δύναμιν θεῷ. αὐτίκα τὸ ἐφ' ἡμῖν ἐστιν οὗπερ ἐπ' ἴσης αὐτοῦ τε κύριοί ἐσμεν καὶ τοῦ ἀντικειμένου, 'self-control constantly surveying and observing itself is made like to God so far as is possible. *Now* that which is within our power is that in which we are masters alike of the thing and of its opposite.' *Str.* v. 659 (After a quotation from St Paul on the distinction between the spiritual and the psychical man) αὐτίκα ὁ ἀπόστολος πρὸς ἀντιδιαστολὴν γνωστικῆς τελειότητος τὴν κοινὴν πίστιν θεμέλιον λέγει, 'again the apostle calls ordinary faith the foundation in contrast to gnostic perfection.' *Ib.* 663 (After quoting sayings of Pythagoras which are taken from the Bible just as a candle is lighted from the sun, Clement proceeds) αὐτίκα ἐπιτομὴν τῶν περὶ δικαιοσύνης εἰρημένων Μωϋσεῖ ὁ Πυθαγόρας πεποίηται, λέγων ζυγὸν μὴ ὑπερβαίνειν, 'again P. has given an abstract of the words of Moses about justice in his phrase "not to exceed the balance."' *Ib.* 712 (Plato calls the light of this world night, and the descent of the soul into the body slumber and death; so David says of the Saviour, 'I laid me down and slept, I awaked for the Lord shall sustain me'), αὐτίκα ὁ αὐτὸς σωτὴρ παρεγγυᾷ γρηγορεῖτε, οἶον μελετᾶτε ζῆν καὶ χωρίζειν τὴν ψυχὴν τοῦ σώματος, 'again the same Saviour charges us to watch, *i.e.* to practise how to live and to separate the soul from the body.'

(c) There are some passages in which αὐτίκα is read, where the text seems to me corrupt. Such are *Str.* I. p. 426 (the Apostle used the phrase 'according to that ye are able' because he knew that some had only received milk) οὐδέπω δὲ καὶ βρῶμα, αὐτίκα οὐχ ἁπλῶς γάλα. Here I think we must read with Louth ἢ τάχα ('not yet allowed meat, perhaps not even milk unconditionally,' *i.e.* unless mixed with water): αὐτίκα makes no sense. *Str.* II. p. 460 πάθος δὲ...ὁρμὴ ἐκφερομένη καὶ ἀπειθὴς λόγῳ. παρὰ φύσιν οὖν κίνησις ψυχῆς κατὰ τὴν πρὸς λόγον ἀπείθειαν τὰ πάθη, ἡ δὲ ἀπόστασις καὶ ἔκστασις καὶ ἀπείθεια ἐφ' ἡμῖν...διὸ καὶ τὰ ἑκούσια κρίνεται. [αὐτίκα καθ' ἓν ἕκαστον τῶν παθῶν εἴ τις ἐπεξίοι, ἀλόγους ὀρέξεις εὕροι ἂν αὐτά]. τὸ γοῦν ἀκούσιον οὐ κρίνεται. I have elsewhere suggested that the sense requires us to transfer the sentence in brackets after ἀπειθὴς λόγῳ. This would give the force of 'at any rate' to αὐτίκα, which is meaningless as it stands, but would then justify the preceding words by reference to the fact that each particular passion is an ἄλογος ὄρεξις. *Str.* IV. 568 Ἐπίχαρμος μέμνασ' ἀπιστεῖν, φησιν, ἄρθρα ταῦτα τῶν φρενῶν. αὐτίκα τὸ μὲν ἀπιστεῖν τῇ ἀληθείᾳ θάνατον φέρει, ὡς τὸ πιστεύειν ζωήν, ἔμπαλιν δὲ τὸ πιστεύειν τῷ ψεύδει ἀπιστεῖν δὲ τῇ ἀληθείᾳ εἰς ἀπώλειαν ὑποσύρει. Here it seems to me that αὐτίκα has no meaning as it stands. If we exchange it with the following ἔμπαλιν δέ we should get the sense 'on the contrary to disbelieve the truth brings death...*at any rate* to believe a lie sweeps men to destruction.'

APPENDIX B[1].

On Clement's use of ἄν.

Abnormal uses of ἄν in late Greek.

Indefinite ἄν in connexion with relatives and particles:
   (a) *Joined with the indicative.*
   (b) *Joined with the optative.*

Potential ἄν:
   (a) *Omitted with optative or past indicative.*
   (b) *Inserted with subjunctive, or present, perfect, or future indicative.*

Indefinite ἄν in Clement.

   1. *Normal subjunctive with relatives.*
   Abnormal examples: indicative or optative for subjunctive.

   2. *Normal subjunctive with hypothetical particles.*
   Abnormal examples: optative for subjunctive.

   3. *Normal subjunctive with particles of time.*
   Abnormal examples: indicative or optative for subjunctive.

   4. *Normal subjunctive with particles of manner and place.*
   Abnormal examples: indicative or optative for subjunctive.

Potential ἄν in Clement.

   1. *Normal with optative in apodosi.*
   Abnormal use of ἄν in apodosi:
      with future optative,
      with present or future indicative,
      with subjunctive.
   Abnormal omission of ἄν in apodosi.
   Abnormal insertion of ἄν in protasi.

---

[1] On the subject of this Appendix compare the Grammars of Winer and Blass, and Viteau's *Étude sur le Grec du N.T.*, Vol. I. Chapters 15, 16, 17, Sophocles *Lex. s.v. ἄν*, Klotz-Devar *De Graecae Linguae Particulis*, Schmid *Atticismus*.

2. *With past indicative.*
Abnormal omission of ἄν in apodosi.
3. *Secondary uses of potential ἄν.*
   ἄν with infinitive.
   Abnormal use with future infinitive.
   ὡς ἄν with participle, with noun.

The spread of the Greek language through the world after the conquests of Alexander was naturally followed by the disappearance of many of the finer distinctions in the use of Cases, Moods, and Tenses, and also of particles, such as μή and ἄν. The most marked departure from classical use in regard to μή, which we meet with in the writings of Clement, is the substitution of μή for οὐ after ὅτι and ἐπειδή, of which examples will be found in the Index. Peculiarities in the use of ἄν are dealt with in this Appendix.

It may be well to begin by pointing out the exceptional uses to be found in the N. T. and in other post-classical writings.

A a. We will take first the use of ἄν in connexion with relatives and conjunctions, where according to the normal use of classical writers[1] it should depend on a principal tense, and be followed by the Subjunctive mood. In later Greek ἄν is not unfrequently omitted as in James ii. 10 ὅστις ὅλον τὸν νόμον τηρήσῃ, πταίσῃ δὲ ἐν ἑνί, and v. 7 μακροθυμῶν ἕως λάβῃ, Herm. *Sim.* VIII. 11. 3 ὅσοι καθαρίσωσιν ἑαυτούς. Sometimes we have the indicative instead of the subjunctive, (1) *e.g.* Luc. *Dial. Mort.* IX. 2 ὅντινα ἂν προσέβλεψα, Mk. xi. 19 ὅταν ἐγένετο, Apoc. iv. 9 ὅταν δώσουσιν, *ib.* ii. 22 ἐὰν μετανοήσουσιν, *ib.* viii. 1 ὅταν ἤνοιξεν, Luke xix. 40 ἐὰν σιωπήσουσιν, Acts ii. 45 διεμέριζον καθότι ἄν τις χρείαν εἶχεν, Lk. xvii. 33 ὃς ἐὰν ζητήσῃ τὴν ψυχήν...ἀπολέσει αὐτήν, ὃς δ᾽ ἂν ἀπολέσει ζωογονήσει αὐτήν, Clem. Rom. II. 12 (quot.) ὅταν ἔσται τὰ δύο ἕν: and even the present ind. as in Apoc. xiv. 4 ὅπου ἂν ὑπάγει, 1 John v. 15 ἐὰν οἴδαμεν, 1 Th. iii. 8 ἐὰν στήκετε, Mk. xi. 25 ὅταν στήκετε. In the following examples the frequentative ἄν with the past indicative is made subordinate, contrary to the ordinary classical use: Herm. *Sim.* IX. 4. 5 ὅταν ἐτέθησαν οἱ λίθοι ἐγένοντο λευκοί, Barn. 12. 2 ὁπόταν καθεῖλεν ἐθανατοῦντο, Mk. vi. 56 ὅπου ἐὰν εἰσεπορεύετο...ἐτίθεσαν, καὶ ὅσοι ἂν ἥψαντο...ἐσώζοντο, Mk. iii. 11 ὅταν ἐθεώρουν, προσέπιπτον, Gen. vi. 4 ὡς ἂν εἰσεπορεύοντο πρὸς τὰς θυγατέρας τῶν ἀνθρώπων...ἐκεῖνοι ἦσαν οἱ γίγαντες, Gen. xxxviii. 7 ὅταν εἰσήρχετο...ἐξέχεεν, Exod. xvii. 11 ὅταν ἐπῆρεν τὰς χεῖρας κατίσχυεν, Num. xi. 9 ὅταν κατέβη ἡ δρόσος κατέβαινε τὸ μάννα, Jud. vi. 3 ἐὰν ἔσπειραν κατέβαινον, Ez. i. 12, x. 11, Philo M. II. 112 ὅταν εἰς ἔννοιαν ἦλθε...συνεγίνωσκεν. (2) Sometimes the Optative is used after ἐάν or similar particles (see Klotz-Devar II. 457 f., 689, Jelf § 844 c *obs.*, Kuehner vol. II. p. 1054 f.) as by Socrates *H. E.* I. 8

---

[1] Exceptional uses are found in verse and (very rarely) in prose, in which ἄν is omitted.

APPENDIX B. 367

ου πρότερον καθίζειν ήρείτο, πριν άν επινεύσειαν, ib. I. 40 όπως άν άπολιμπάνοιντο, III. 1 ευδαιμονήσειν έλεγεν ήν κρατήσειεν, by Herodian (after ως άν) I. 1 ως άν μή λάθοιεν, I. 5 έδοξεν προαγαγείν τό μειράκιον ως άν διαλεχθείη, ib. I. 8, 9, II. 1, 6, 11, 13.

A b. There are also irregularities connected with the potential use of άν in apodosi, where it properly accompanies the optative or past indicative. It is often omitted with the latter, even by classical writers (especially if the verb implies necessity, possibility, &c), rarely with the former: cf. Joh. xv. 24 εί τά έργα μή εποίησα εν αυτοίς...άμαρτίαν ουκ είχοσαν, and Schmid I. 89 f., IV. 90, Jelf §§ 426, 858, 859, Kuehner II. 191.

A c. A more flagrant irregularity is the use of the potential άν with the future indicative, as in Artem. II. 70 ου γάρ εκατόν ζήσεται άν τις έτη, Sext. Emp. Math. VIII. 296 πώς άν ούτος χρήσεται τω σημείω; ib. X. 12 κάν άπαντα άνέλωμεν, ό τόπος ουκ άν αναιρεθήσεται, Socr. H. E. II. 40 άπαντήσει δ' άν τις προς τούτον, ib. III. 16 τούτο δ' ουκ άν πεισόμεθα ει μή...κτησαίμεθα καί φρονώμεν : or the subjunctive, as in Polyb. XI. 6. 6 κυριεύσαντες πόλεως ούτ' άν υβρίζειν υπομείνητε τους ελευθέρους ούτε εμπιμπράναι τ. πόλεις, Epict. I. 2. 17 τί ούν σε έδει φροντίζειν πώς άν όμοιος ής τοις άλλοις; ib. III. 13, 8 πώς άν θεραπευθή, πώς εξαιρεθή; IV. 6. 31 ζητεί τίν' άν ασπάσηται, τίνι δώρον πέμψη, cf. Kuehner II. 169, 170.

I proceed now to consider how far these and similar irregularities are to be found in Clement : and I will take first the use of indefinite άν.

B a. *After relatives (normal construction).* In Str. VII. we have the following exx.: § 4, p. 8. 1 επιτελείν ό τι άν ό λόγος υπαγορεύη; § 9, p. 14. 27 περιγίνεται άν άν εθέλη; § 19, p. 30. 15 μεταδοτικός ών άν ή κεκτημένος ; § 41, p. 70. 28 πάν δ άν αιτήση λαμβάνει ; § 46, p. 80. 5 ό θεός ό τι άν συμφέρη χορηγεί; § 65, p. 112. 19 όπερ άν ό θεός παράσχη ; § 101, p. 178. 13 επόμενοι θεώ ή άν ηγήται ; § 104, p. 182. 26 τάς αποδείξεις άς άν επιζητήση ανευρίσκει ; § 53, p. 92. 17 (subj. understood) ό τι περ άν εν νώ (φέρη), τούτο καί επί γλώσσης φέρει.

B b. *After hypothetical particles*: εάν, άν, ήν, κάν (= καί εάν). § 33, p. 56. 9 εάν λέγωσι δεδόσθαι τά ζώα, καί ημείς συνομολογούμεν ; § 45, p. 78. 21 εάν ό λόγος καλή ; § 70, p. 122. 19 (also in § 78, p. 136. 10) εάν ό λόγος αίρη ; § 73, p. 126. 28 εάν συμφέροντα ή ; § 77, p. 134. 16 εάν επίστηται ; § 80, p. 140. 4 εάν υιός ή ; ib. 15 εάν αγαθά ή...εάν κακά ; § 82, p. 142. 20 εάν αμαρτήση, ήμαρτεν ό εκλεκτός ; § 84, p. 148. 21 ήν μή προσεύξωνται ; § 88, p. 156. 3 ήν προσυπακούσωμεν ; § 94, p. 166. 8 ήν μή τόν κανόνα έχωσι ; § 101, p. 178. 2 εάν πρόσσχη ; § 103, p. 182. 4 εάν μή αποδιδώνται ; § 59, p. 102. 19 ουδ' άν τό σώμα επιδιδώσιν ; § 61, p. 104. 28 ουδ' άν προκαλήται.

κάν stands both for καί εάν and καί άν (potential): of the former (which alone comes for consideration under this head) we have examples in § 1, p. 1. 20 κάν ετεροία φαίνηται ; § 11, p. 18. 19 κάν ιδιώτης ή ; § 28, p. 46. 8 κάν τήν τέχνην εκτελέσης ; § 29, p. 48. 21 κάν μηδέπω έσμεν άξιοι ; § 34, p. 60. 8 κάν πειραταί κάν τύραννοι τύχωσιν ; ib. 24 κάν μόνος ών τυγχάνη ; § 37, p. 64. 25 κάν μή λέγη ; § 39, p. 68. 19 κάν ψιθυρίζοντες προσλαλώμεν ; § 42,

p. 72. 20 κἂν προλαμβάνῃ; § 49, p. 86. 23 κἂν ἐννοηθῇ; § 50, p. 88. 14 κἂν μὴ συνήθης τυγχάνῃ; § 51, p. 90. 22 κἂν ἐναποθνήσκῃ; § 56, p. 98. 15 κἂν ἁγία ᾖ; § 59, p. 102. 23 κἂν ἔνστασιν σώζῃ; § 61, p. 106. 11 κἂν νόσος ἐπίῃ κἄν τι; ib. 22 κἂν ἄξιος τυγχάνῃ; § 69, p. 118. 23 κἂν οἰκέτης ᾖ κἂν πολέμιος; § 69, p. 126. 20 κἂν λέγηται; § 72, p. 128. 20 κἂν πονηρὰ εἶναι δοκῇ; ib. 26 κἂν καθαρὸς ᾖ; § 73, p. 128. 1 κἄν τις λέγῃ; § 76, p. 132. 13 κἂν βλέπειν δοκῇ; ib. 27 κἂν ἀσχοληθῇ; § 78, p. 134. 19 κἂν πάθῃ τι; § 78, p. 136. 14 κἂν μόνος εὔχηται; § 80, p. 138. 32 κἂν κατέχηται; § 85, p. 150. 8 κἂν προβαίνῃ; ib. 24 κἂν τύχωσιν; § 90, p. 158. 5 κἂν παραβαίνωσι; § 96, p. 168. 22 κἂν τολμήσωσι; § 98, p. 172. 21 κἂν ἀσεβεῖν μέλλωσιν; § 100, p. 176. 16 κἂν ἐναντία τυγχάνῃ; § 108, p. 190. 13 κἂν αὐχῶσι.

b*. *Abnormal constructions* under this head are § 16, p. 26. 7 κἂν εἰς ἀρχὴν κατασταίη ποτὲ ἐπὶ σωτηρίᾳ ἡγήσεται, where I have suggested that we should read κατάστῃ; § 101, p. 178. 20 οὔτε ἀπατηθείς τις δύναιτ' ἂν εὖ πράττειν, κἂν πάνυ δυνατὸς ᾖ τὰ γνωσθέντα ποιεῖν, οὔτε κ.τ.λ. (here the more regular construction would have been εἰ καὶ δυνατὸς εἴη in the protasis, or else δυνήσεται in the apodosis; but such irregularity is not uncommon); § 69, p. 120. 8 εἰδέναι ὅτῳ ἄν τις μάλιστα καὶ ὁπόσον ἐπιδῷ (here there seems no place for the indefinite ἄν: we want either the deliberate subjunctive or the potential optative; I have accordingly changed ἐπιδῷ to ἐπιδοίη). § 41, p. 72. 1 παρέλκει ἡ αἴτησις κἂν χωρὶς ἀξιώσεως δίδοται τὰ ἀγαθά (here the editors have rightly substituted the subjunctive for the indicative of the MS, the long and short o being constantly interchanged). *Paed.* II. P. 201 *fin.* κἂν ἐκάθισας πρότερος μὴ ἐκτείνῃς χεῖρα (original has εἰ ἐκάθ.).

B *c*. ὅταν, ὁπόταν, ἐπάν, ἐπειδάν, ἔστ' ἄν, πρὶν ἄν, ἄχρις ἄν. § 1, p. 1. 18 ἐπὰν ἐνδειξώμεθα; § 33, p. 56. 19 ὅταν ἕλκωνται; § 43, p. 74. 12 ἐπὰν λάβῃ; § 56, p. 96. 27 ὁπόταν τις ἐκκρεμασθῇ; § 62, p. 106. 19 ὁπόταν αἱρῇ λόγος; § 73, p. 128. 8 ὅταν δίκαιός τις ᾖ; § 76, p. 132. 11 ὅταν κατάληψιν λάβῃ; ib. 14 ὅταν ἡδομένου ἑαυτοῦ συναίσθηται; § 97, p. 170. 24 ἐπειδὰν ἀνατρέπωνται; § 100, p. 176. 4 ἐπὰν παραβῇ; § 7, p. 12. 29 ἔστ' ἂν τύχωσι; § 9, p. 16. 5 ἔστ' ἄν τις ἀφίκηται; § 10, p. 16. 29 ἄχρις ἂν καταντήσῃ; § 45, p. 78. 26 ἔστ' ἂν ἀφίκωνται; § 57, p. 98. 25 ἄχρις ἂν ἀποστήσῃ; § 93, p. 162. 27 πρὶν ἂν λάβωσι; § 102, p. 180. 7 ἔστ' ἂν μετανοήσωσιν.

c*. *Abnormal construction* (indic. for subj.): § 43, p. 74. 9 ὅταν αἰτεῖται (MS), where D. reads αἰτῆται; cf. *Str.* III. § 93, p. 553 ὅταν οὖν μήτε τις θυμῷ μήτ' ἐπιθυμίᾳ χαρισάμενος...ἀλλ' ἀποδυσάμενος τὴν ἐκ τούτων ἀχλὺν...πνεῦμα καὶ ψυχὴν ἑνώσει...τότε οὐκ ἔνι ἐν ὑμῖν οὐκ ἄρρεν οὐ θῆλυ. Here it would be easy to correct ἑνώσῃ, but the length of the sentence may perhaps excuse the anacoluthon.

B *d*. ὡς ἄν, ὅπως ἄν, ὅπου ἄν. § 3, p. 6. 9 τὴν βελτιωτικὴν ἐνδεικνύμενος θεωρίαν ὅπως ἂν ᾖ τεταγμένος 'in whatever way he may be appointed.'

d*. *Abnormal* (opt. for subj.). After a historic tense the subjunctive with indefinite ἄν regularly changes to the simple optative. But in *Str.* VII. § 42, p. 72 we read τὰς ἐντολὰς ἔλαβεν ὁ ἄνθρωπος ὡς ἂν ἐξ αὑτοῦ ὁρμητικὸς πρὸς ὁπότερον ἂν καὶ βούλοιτο τῶν τε αἱρετῶν καὶ τῶν φευκτῶν. For the use of ὡς ἄν see E *b* below. The general construction of the sentence should either be λαμβάνει—πρὸς ὁπότερον ἂν βούληται, or ἔλαβεν πρὸς ὁπότερον βούλοιτο. Possibly the second ἂν represents an original οὖν, this particle being regularly used like the Lat. *cunque* with an indefinite force. Similarly *Str.* I. § 56, p. 348 ἐγκατεσπαρμένην ἔχουσι τὴν ἀλήθειαν ὅπως ἂν λάθοι τοὺς σπερμολόγους, unless we should here make ἂν potential, 'in a way in which it would elude the curious.' *Paed.* III. § 41, p. 279 πατρίδα ἐπὶ γῆς οὐκ ἔχομεν ὡς ἂν καταφρονοῖμεν τῶν ἐπιγείων; cf. Eus. *Pr. Ev.* I. 5. 12 θήσω δ' οὐκ ἐμὰς φωνὰς ἀλλ' αὐτῶν δὴ τῶν μάλιστα τὴν εὐσέβειαν περισπούδαστον πεποιηκότων, ὡς ἂν ὁ λόγος ἁπάσης[1] ἐκτὸς ὑπονοίας κατασταίη (perhaps we should read κατάστῃ as in *Str.* VII. 16), also exx. from Herodian given above under A a (2).

(Subj. for opt.) the ἂν being potential, *Str.* VII. § 35, p. 60. 22 ὁ γνωστικὸς ἐν παντὶ τόπῳ, κἂν καθ' ἑαυτὸν μόνος ὢν τυγχάνῃ, κἂν (MS. καὶ) ὅπου τινὰς ἂν τῶν ὁμοίως πεπιστευκότων ἔχῃ, τιμᾷ τὸν θεόν. Here I propose to read ἔχοι 'where he would have believers of like mind.' The indefinite force of ὅπου ἂν ἔχῃ is inappropriate, while the misreading is naturally accounted for.

C a. *Potential* ἂν *with opt. in apodosi following optative in protasi, expressed or understood.* *Str.* VII. § 1, p. 4. 2 ἡ ἐπὶ πλέον ἐπεξεργασία περισσὴ δόξειεν ἄν; § 3, p. 6. 22 οὕτως ἂν εἴη ὁ εἰδώς; § 6, p. 10. 25 τοῦτο πάθοι ἄν; § 6, p. 12. 5 οὔτ' οὖν φθονοίη ποτ' ἂν οὔτε κωλυθείη ποτ' ἄν; *ib.* 22 σοφία κυρίως ἂν λεχθείη; § 8, p. 14. 8 οὐδὲ τοῦ ἰδίου ποτ' ἂν ἀμελοίη ἔργου; *ib.* 11 οὐδ' ἂν βελτίων τις διοίκησις εἴη; *ib.* 18 οὗτοι δ' ἂν εἶεν οἱ ἑλόμενοι; § 15, p. 24. 13 τὸ δίκαιον οὐκ ἄν ποτε προδῷεν (D. unnecessarily προδοῖεν); § 16, p. 26. 2 κακῶν αἰτίαν ὕλης ἄν τις ἀσθένειαν ὑπολάβοι; § 17, p. 28. 1 κατάληψις βεβαία δεόντως ἂν λέγοιτο ἐπιστήμη; § 20, p. 32. 5 οὐδὲ οἱ λόγοι οἱ πειστικοὶ τῆς ἀληθείας διαμονὴν παράσχοιεν ἄν; § 21, p. 34. 14 τίς ἅπτοιτ' ἂν ἀτιμίᾳ θεοῦ; § 25, p. 40. 13 οὐκ ἄν ποτε γένοιτο παρὰ φύσιν; § 28, p. 44. 22 τί ἂν ἅγιον εἴη ἔργον; *ib.* p. 46. 1 γελοίων μεντἂν εἴη; *ib.* 7 τὰ ἀγάλματα αὐτὰ ἂν εἴη ἀργά; *ib.* 10 τί ἂν καὶ ἱδρύοιτο; *ib.* 16 τὸ ὂν οὐκ ἂν ἱδρυνθείη; § 29, p. 48. 13 εἴη δ' ἂν οὗτος ὁ γνωστικός; *ib.* 16 εὕροιμεν ἄν; § 31, p. 52. 3 οὐκ ἂν φθάνοιεν; § 33, p. 58. 6 ταχ' ἄν τις ἀπόσχοιτο; § 35, p. 62. 6 εὐλόγως ἂν ἑαυτοῦ κρείττων εἴη; § 47, p. 82. 17 ἀνενδεὴς εἴη ἄν; § 50, p. 88. 4 πῶς ἂν παράσχοι; *ib.* 16 οὐκ ἂν ἄδικος εὑρεθείη; § 51, p. 90. 8 οὐδ' ἂν ὀμόσαι πώποτε; § 53, p. 92. 13 εἰκότως ἂν λέγοιτο; *ib.* p. 94. 3 οὐκ ἂν πραχθείη εἰ μὴ ποιοίη; § 54, p. 94. 22 μόνος ἂν εἴη εὐσεβής; § 69, p. 120. 9 τίς ἂν ἐχθρὸς γένοιτο; *ib.* 18 τὸν αὐτὸν τρόπον εὕροιμεν ἄν; § 71, p. 124. 16 πῶς ἔτι ἂν εἴη τερπνά; § 74,

---

[1] Dr Gifford writes: 'This construction is however not uncommon in Eus. cf. *P. E.* IX. 1 ἄρξεται ὁ λόγος ἀπὸ τοῦ βίου ὡς ἂν μάθοις, *ib.* VI. 6. 8 τὸ δαιμόνιον σκήπτεται ἰδ', ἐν οἷς ἂν τῆς προρρήσεως ἀποτίπτοι, καταφυγὴ αὐτῷ πορίζοιτο, *ib.* I. 6. 6 μνημονεύσομαι τῆς ἱστορίας ὡς ἂν φανερὸν γένοιτο, *ib.* πιστωσόμεθα ὡς ἂν μὴ δοκοῖμεν, also II. 5. 1 and 17.' He also refers to *Str.* I. § 42, where Plato's words (Crito 46 B) ἐγώ...τοιοῦτος οἷος...μηδενὶ ἄλλῳ πείθεσθαι ἢ τῷ λόγῳ ὃς ἄν μοι λογιζομένῳ βέλτιστος φαίνηται, are altered to ὁποῖος οὐδενὶ ἄλλῳ ἢ τῷ λόγῳ πείθεσθαι ὃς ἄν μοι σκοπουμένῳ βέλτιστος φαίνοιτο. Here, I think, Cl. means us to understand ἂν φαίνοιτο as potential.

p. 130. 3 οὐκ ἔστιν ὅπως ὑπὸ τοιούτων παιδευθείη ποτ' ἂν ὁ γνωστικός; *ib.* 12 οὗτος ἂν εἴη ὁ γνωστικός; § 89, p. 156. 13 εὖ ἂν ἔχοι προιέναι; § 91, p. 160. 13 οὐκ ἄν τις ὀκνήσαι, χρήσαιτο δ' ἄν; § 95, p. 166. 27 εἴ τις ὑπολάβοι εἰκότως ἂν φυλαχθείη; § 96, p. 168. 30 εὕροις ἄν; § 103, p. 180. 31 οὖς ἐλεήσειεν ἄν τις.

a*. *Abnormal use of ἄν in apodosi with fut. opt.* In classical writers the future optative is only used for the purpose of representing the future indicative in *oratio obliqua* after a historical tense, cf. Madvig *Gr. Gr.* § 134, *rem.* 2. I am indebted to Dr Gifford for the following exx. from Eus. *Pr. Ev.*: πῶς προσίξοι ἄν (VI. 6. 8), εἰκότως πᾶν ἄθυρον ἀποφράξοι ἂν στόμα (L. 3. 8) where he would read ἀποφράξαι ἄν. Compare also Dion. H. *Ant. Rom.* III. 15 εἰ οὖν εἰσὶν οἵους ἀκούομεν προθυμότατα ἂν δέξοιντο, Philo M. I. 469 χειροηθεὶς εἰ γένοιτο ἥκιστα ἂν βλάψοι (where however Wendland corrects βλέψαι).

a**. *Abnormal use of ἄν in apodosi with fut. or pres. indicative.* Of this abnormal construction D. gives the following exx. in the Index. *Protr.* § 41, P. 36 *init.* τίνα δ' ἂν φωνήν, εἰ φωνὴν λάβοιεν Αἰγυπτίων θεοί...προήσονται. ἢ τὴν Ὁμηρικήν; This, I think, is a case of anacoluthon excused by the length of the sentence. *Paed.* I. § 47, P. 126 οὐ γὰρ τὸ αἷμα ἄν ποτε προήσεται φωνήν. Perhaps for ἂν ποτε we should read οὔ ποτε. *Paed.* I § 17, P. 108 εἰ δὲ εἷς διδάσκαλος ἐν οὐρανοῖς,...οἱ ἐπὶ γῆς εἰκότως ἂν πάντες κεκλήσονται μαθηταί, read perhaps ἄρα. *Str.* L § 143, P. 405 εἴ τις ἰχθῦς ἀνασπώμενος... ἀποδράσει, οὐκέτ' ἂν ἐν τῷ αὐτῷ τόπῳ τοῦ αὐτοῦ εἴδους ἰχθὺς αὐτῆς ἐκείνης εὑρεθήσεται τῆς ἡμέρας. The insertion of ἄν is easily explained by dittographia of ἐν, but the length of the sentence makes anacoluthon possible. *Str.* VI. § 4, P. 738 *init.* οἱ (? οἳ, Eus. has εἰ) γὰρ μηδὲ ἑαυτῶν, σχολῇ γε ἂν τῶν ἡμετέρων ἀφέξονται. Here D. would omit ἄν: possibly it stands for οὖν, or it may be that, in the phrase σχολῇ γ' ἄν, the ἄν has lost its force as sometimes in κἄν, and τάχ' ἄν (see exx. in Ast's *Lex. Plat.* and *Str.* III. § 86, P. 550 τάχα δ' ἄν...προφητεύει φθοράν). Of the pres. ind. D. cites two instances from *Str.* VII. § 7, p. 12 καταλείπει ποτ' ἂν τὴν ἀνθρώπων κηδεμονίαν and *ib.* l. 26 πῶς δ' ἄν ἐστι σωτήρ, εἰ μὴ πάντων σωτήρ, in both of which I have followed him in restoring the optative. He also cites *Str.* VI. § 159, P. 823 ἡ χρῆσις τῆς φιλοσοφίας οὐκ ἔστιν ἂν κακῶν, where I should read αὖ, referring to the preceding sentence, in which it is argued that philosophy must be good as the gift of God: further it is shown to be good from the character of the philosophers themselves.

a***. *Abnormal use of ἄν in apodosi with subjunctive.* *Str.* VII. § 85, p. 150. 10 πῶς δ' ἂν καὶ ἀγγέλους τις κρίνῃ. D. suggests either κρίνοι or κρίναι, but has the former in his text. I think the corruption is more easily explained by assuming that the latter was the reading of the archetype. *Protr.* § 55 πῶς ἂν ἐνδίκως οἱ ἄνθρωποι παρὰ τοῦ Διὸς αἰτήσωνται (Cobet *ap.* D. I. p. xxviii. *init.* αἰτήσονται) τὴν εὐτεχνίαν, ἣν οὐδ' αὐτῷ παρασχεῖν ἴσχυσεν; If we accept Cobet's emendation, I should be disposed to read γάρ for ἄν.

a†. Abnormal omission of ἄν in apodosi (a). § 29, p. 46, 21 f. πῶς, ὃ φθάσαν είχεν άν, τούθ' έαυτό ύστερον ποιοίη; ού δέ τά όντα πώς ούν τοΰτ' άν διοιτό τίνος; I see no excuse for the omission of ήν after the first πώς, or for the insertion of ούν after the second πώς, and am disposed to think that ούν represents an original marginal correction, inserting άν in the former place. § 37, p. 66. 3 τίνα καί φωνήν αναμείναι ό κατά πρόθεσιν τόν εκλεκτόν εγνωκώς; I think D. and H. are right in inserting άν after άναμείναι, the word άν being easily lost after -αι. § 48, p. 84. 1 ούκουν άφέλοιτο τούτους τά δι' άρετήν. D. inserts άν after άφέλοιτο: perhaps the loss would be more easily explained, if the original were ούκ άν ούν. § 69, p. 120. 18 αύτός μέν ούδενί εχθρός άν γένοιτο, εχθροί δ' είναι νοοίντο αύτώ οί τήν εναντίαν οδόν τρεπόμενοι. Here άν might be understood with νοοίντο from the former clause, as in § 41, p. 70. 31 αίτήσασιν άναξίοις ούκ άν δοίη, δοίη δέ άξίοις, where however Barnard conjectures δοίη δέ < άν καί μή αίτήσασιν > άξίοις. So, here, I am inclined to think that άν may have been lost before αύτώ. § 82, p. 142. 24 τί περί τού γνωστικού φήσαιμεν; I have followed D. in adding άν after φήσαιμεν. § 90, p. 158. 17 ούκ άρα ό τήν ψυχήν νοσών προφασίσαιτο τάς αίρέσεις. Here too I have followed D. in inserting άν. § 95, p. 168. 8 ούχ άπλώς άποφαινομένοις άνθρώποις προσέχομεν. Here D. suggests either προσέχομεν or προσέχοιμεν άν. I prefer the former, as it makes the appeal to actual fact. *Str.* I. § 57, P. 349 όσοι ταληθούς ώρέχθησαν, οί μέν ούκ ολίγα, οί δέ μέρος τι, είπερ άρα, τού τής αληθείας λόγου έχοντες άναδειχθείεν. It would be easy for άν to be lost after άναδειχθείεν. *Str.* III. § 8, P. 513 καί πώς έτι ούτος έν τώ καθ' ήμάς έξετασθείη λόγω; 'deest άν' D. *Str.* II. § 129, P. 497 τί δή σοι 'Αρίστωνα καταλέγοιμι; where D. inserts άν, but perhaps it might be understood from below, as Cl. continues (τέλος ούτος είναι τήν άδιαφορίαν έφη), ή τά Ήρίλλου είς μέσον παράγοιμ' άν; III. § 28, P. 534, συμμέτοχοι είεν < άν > (added by D.) αύτοίς οί σύες, είεν δ' άν έν ταίς μείζοσιν έλπίσιν αί πόρναι. A similar case is *Str.* III. § 72 P. 543 ού δείξειας εγκύμονι πλησιάσαντα, άλλ' ύστερον εύροις άν γινωσκομένας τάς γυναίκας, where, however, D. does not insert άν[1].

αττ. *Abnormal insertion of* άν *in protasi. Str.* III. § 91, P. 372 ζητείν τό θείον εί άρα ψηλαφήσειαν ή εύροιεν άν. The original (Acts XVII. 27) has καί εύροιεν; the insertion of άν is probably due to dittography of the preceding syllable. I cannot believe that Clement wrote it[2].

D a. άν *with past indicative in apodosi.* § 9, p. 14. 28 ούδέ γάρ άν έτι ήν τό όλον εύ ειργασμένον; 19, p. 30. 25 ούδ' άν ήν ίθ' εκούσιον; § 26, p. 42. 13 ούκ άν τούτο εγίνετο εί άνελάμβανεν; § 29, p. 46. 20 ούκ άν ούδέ ήν; § 82,

---

[1] Dr Gifford furnishes the following exx. from Eus. *Pr. Ev.* VI. 8. 18 πάλιν ούν κάνταύθα θαυμάσειέ τις, I. 5. 9 πώς ούν άλλως δόξαιμεν εύ πεποιηκέναι; where Hein. inserts άν after ούν. He adds that the interrogative use of the opt. without άν is common in Eus. Compare also Justin M. *Dial.* 7 τίνι ούν έτι τις χρήσαιτο διδασκάλω ή πόθεν ώφεληθείη τις εί μηδέ έν τούτοις τό άληθές εστιν;

[2] Dr Gifford suggests that Cl.'s reading may be due to one of the vv. ll. (εύροιαν or εύροισαν) in the original.

p. 142. 21 εἰ οὕτως ἑαυτὸν ἦγεν, κατηδέσθη ἂν τὸν βίον ὁ γείτων; § 98. p. 174. 2 κἂν (= καὶ ἂν potent.) λάθη, εἰ πείθεσθαι ἠβουλήθη; § 103 οὐκ ἂν ὑπερίβαλον σοφίᾳ τοὺς ἔμπροσθεν ἄνδρας; § 47, p. 82. 23 κἂν ἀμετάθετος ἦν.

a*. *Abnormal omission of ἄν.* § 24, 40. 5 τοῦτο γὰρ ἦν θαυμαστὸν εἰ τὸν μῦν ὁ θύλαξ κατέφαγεν. Str. III. § 29, P. 525 *init.* εἰ γὰρ οὗτοι πνευματικὰς ἐτίθεντο κοινωνίας, ἴσως τις αὐτῶν τὴν ὑπόληψιν ἐπεδέξατο <ἄν>. *Ib.* § 103, P. 559 πῶς δ' <ἂν> ἄνευ τοῦ σώματος ἡ κατὰ τὴν ἐκκλησίαν οἰκονομία τέλος ἐλάμβανεν; The first example is of a type in which ἂν is liable to omission in classical writers: in the 2nd and 3rd, I think ἂν should be inserted.

E. *Secondary uses of potential ἄν.*

a. With infinitive. Str. VII. § 31, p. 52. 13 οὐκ ἂν οὐδαμῶς φασὶ κατὰ τὴν τῆς ἐνδείας ἐπιθυμίαν κακούμενον τρέφεσθαι τὸν θεόν, where the ἂν with infinitive has its usual force as the *oratio obliqua* of ἂν τρέφοιτο. Str. I. § 18, P. 326 οἱ δὲ καὶ πρὸς κακοῦ ἂν τὴν φιλοσοφίαν εἰσδεδυκέναι τὸν βίον νομίζουσιν. Here the *oratio recta* would probably be ἡ φιλοσοφία ἂν εἰσεδεδύκει. Str. IV. § 1, P. 563 ἀκόλουθον δ' ἂν οἶμαι περὶ μαρτυρίου διαλαβεῖν. Here I think we should read εἴη for οἶμαι, as there seems no room for the ordinary force of ἂν with inf.

a*. *Abnormal use of future infinitive with ἄν.* Str. VII. § 92, p. 162. 1 οἶμαι πάντας ἂν ὁμολογήσειν, where D. notes 'rectius ὁμολογῆσαι.' Dr Gifford supplies an example from Eus. *Pr. Ev.* VI. 8. 21 καθείμαρται μὴ ἂν ἔσεσθαί τι τούτων.

b. With participle. Str. VII. § 95, p. 166. 30 ὁ πιστὸς ἀξιόπιστος, εἰκότως ἂν διὰ τοῦ κυρίου ἐνεργούμενος (= ὃς εἰκότως ἂν ἐνεργοῖτο). Str. VII. § 33, p. 56. 6 ταύτῃ Ἰουδαῖοι χοιρείου ἀπέχονται ὡς ἂν τοῦ θηρίου τούτου μιαροῦ ὄντος (*sc.* ἀπέχοιντο). *Ib.* § 40, p. 70. 9 (ὁ γνωστικὸς καταλέλοιπεν) πάντα ὅσα μὴ χρησιμεύει γενομένῳ ἐκεῖ (*sc.* ἐν οὐρανῷ), ὡς ἂν ἐνθένδε ἤδη τὴν τελείωσιν ἀπειληφώς (*sc.* καταλείποι). *Ib.* § 47, p. 82. 12 οὐ γὰρ λέληθεν αὐτὸν (τὰ ἐπηγγελμένα) ὡς ἂν ἀπόντα ἔτι (*sc.* λάθοι). § 60, p. 104. 5 περὶ τῶν ὅλων ἀληθῶς διείληφεν ὡς ἂν θείαν χωρήσας διδασκαλίαν (*sc.* διαλαμβάνοι). § 63, p. 108. 8 ὡς ἂν ἐπ' ἄκρον γνώσεως ἥκειν βιαζόμενος (*sc.* ποιοῖ), τῷ ἤθει κεκοσμημένος...τὰ πρόχειρα πάντα τοῦ κόσμου καλὰ οὐκ ἀγαπᾷ. § 94, p. 164. 27 τέτοκεν καὶ οὐ τέτοκεν ὡς ἂν ἐξ αὑτῆς οὐκ ἐκ συνδυασμοῦ συλλαβοῦσα (*sc.* τέκοι). § 109, p. 192. 18 ὀλισθηρὸν τὸ γένος τῶν τοιούτων ὡς ἂν (*sc.* εἴη) μὴ σχιδανοπόδων ὄντων.

From this usage ὡς ἄν (often written as one word) comes to be used simply like *quasi* without thought of a verb to be supplied, as in § 109, p. 192. 4 τὰ διχηλοῦντα καθαρὰ παραδίδωσιν ἡ γραφὴ ὡς ἂν εἰς πατέρα καὶ υἱὸν διὰ τῆς πίστεως τῶν δικαίων τὴν πορείαν ποιουμένων. Hence the participle disappears, as in § 42, p. 72. 24 τὰς ἐντολὰς ἔλαβεν ὁ ἄνθρωπος ὡς ἂν ἐξ αὑτοῦ ὁρμητικὸς πρὸς ὁπότερον οὖν καὶ βούλοιτο; § 78, p. 134 ἀεὶ ἕτοιμος ὢν ὡς ἂν παρεπίδημος καὶ ξένος; *ib.* p. 136. 13 ὁ δὲ καὶ μετ' ἀγγέλων εὔχεται ὡς ἂν ἤδη καὶ ἰσάγγελος; § 50, p. 88. 19 ὀμνύναι γάρ ἐστι τὸ ὅρκον ἢ ὡς ἂν ὅρκον προσφέρεσθαι.

APPENDIX B. 373

F. I subjoin a few other cases in which ἄν has found its way into the MS. without justification, as far as I can see. § 21, p. 34. 8 καθάπερ ἂν ἰδίου γεννήματος ὁ σωτὴρ ἀναδέχεται τὰς ὠφελείας τῶν ἀνθρώπων εἰς ἰδίαν χάριν, where D. after Herv. reads γάρ, but οὖν seems to me both an easier and a more suitable correction. *Str.* I. § 90, P. 371 *fin.* ἀγαθοῦ δ' ἂν ἀνάγκη θεοῦ ἀγαθὸν τὸν λόγον, where for ἂν I propose to read εἶναι. *Str.* IV. § 124, P. 620 τὰ μὲν οὖν ἄλλα εἴργειν δύναταί τις προσπολεμῶν, τὸ δ' ἐφ' ἡμῖν οὐδαμῶς, οὐδ' ἂν μάλιστα ἐνίσταιτο, where εἰ, or possibly ἂν (*sc.* δύναιτο) εἰ, should be read for ἄν.

The general conclusion which I should draw from the occurrence of these impossible readings, as well as from the prevalence of the normal usage, is that instances of the abnormal usage of ἄν should generally be set down to the credit of the copyist, and not to Clement himself.

APPENDIX C.

ON THE RELATION OF THE AGAPE TO THE EUCHARIST IN CLEMENT'S WRITINGS[1].

The order of the κυριακὸν δεῖπνον (1 Cor. xi. 20), which took the place of the Jewish feast of the Passover (Luke xxii. 15, 1 Cor. v. 7), was strictly observed by the Christians of the apostolic age. It was commemorated by an evening meal, and the eucharistic bread and wine were administered during the course, or at the close of the meal (Mk xiv. 22, Acts xx. 7—11, 1 Cor. xi. 24). At Corinth this common meal, expressive of the union of Christians in their Head, seems to have been regarded by some as merely on a level with the συσσίτια or ἔρανοι of their heathen countrymen, and St Paul, who condemns in the Corinthians much the same faults—selfishness and greediness—as Socrates is said to have done in the case of the partakers in an ἔρανος (Xen. *Mem.* III. 14), finds it necessary to remind them earnestly of the spiritual meaning of their feast of love, and of the punishment which might be expected to follow a careless or irreverent participation in the Communion of the Body of Christ. St Paul does not himself use the term Agape, but it occurs in Jude 12 οὗτοί εἰσιν οἱ ἐν ταῖς ἀγάπαις ὑμῶν σπιλάδες, συνευωχούμενοι ἀφόβως, ἑαυτοὺς ποιμαίνοντες, where the word οὗτοι is explained by v. 4, παρεισέδυσαν γάρ τινες ἄνθρωποι οἱ πάλαι προγεγραμμένοι εἰς τοῦτο τὸ κρίμα, ἀσεβεῖς, τὴν τοῦ θεοῦ ἡμῶν χάριτα μετατιθέντες εἰς ἀσέλγειαν, καὶ τὸν μόνον δεσπότην καὶ κύριον ἡμῶν Ἰησοῦν Χριστὸν ἀρνούμενοι. From these words and from the rest of the passage it would seem that the men who disgraced the Christian love-feasts by their greediness and licentiousness were antinomian heretics of a more advanced type than the disorderly members of the Corinthian Church, though the words of St Paul (1 Cor. xi. 19) seem to imply that the latter also entertained heretical views.

In the parallel passage, 2 Pet. ii. 13, the colours are even darker, ἡδονὴν ἡγούμενοι τὴν ἐν ἡμέρᾳ τρυφήν, σπίλοι καὶ μῶμοι ἐντρυφῶντες ἐν ταῖς ἀπάταις[2]

---

[1] The most recent works on the Agape are Keating's *Agape and Eucharist* and Achelis *Canones Hippolyti*.

[2] Bp Lightfoot on Ign. *Smyrn.* 8, vol. II. p. 313, speaks of this reading as an obvious error for ἀγάπαις, but in that case it is difficult to explain αὐτῶν. How could the heretics be 'feasting with you' if they were in their own agape? Reading ἀπάταις, we get the excellent sense 'taking part in (*i.e.* being admitted to) your feasts through their deceitful wiles.' I think these ἀπάται are alluded to

αὐτῶν συνευωχούμενοι ὑμῖν, ὀφθαλμοὺς ἔχοντες μεστοὺς μοιχαλίδος καὶ ἀκαταπαύστους[1] ἁμαρτίας, δελεάζοντες ψυχὰς ἀστηρίκτους. These men are further described (ib. ii. 1) as ψευδοδιδάσκαλοι, οἵτινες παρεισάξουσιν αἱρέσεις ἀπωλείας, καὶ τὸν ἀγοράσαντα αὐτοὺς δεσπότην ἀρνούμενοι, and we read that many ἐξακολουθήσουσιν αὐτῶν ταῖς ἀσελγείαις, δι' οὓς ἡ ὁδὸς τῆς ἀληθείας βλασφημηθήσεται.

Of the charges of immorality alleged against the Christian love-feasts we shall presently hear more; but there is no reference to them in Ignatius, the next writer to mention the agape by name. Compare *Smyrn.* § 8 ἐκείνη βεβαία εὐχαριστία ἡγείσθω, ἡ ὑπὸ τὸν ἐπίσκοπον οὖσα ἢ ᾧ ἂν αὐτὸς ἐπιτρέψῃ, *ib.* οὐκ ἐξόν ἐστιν χωρὶς τοῦ ἐπισκόπου οὔτε βαπτίζειν οὔτε ἀγάπην ποιεῖν, where εὐχαριστία and ἀγάπη seem to be identical, both standing for the complete eucharistic feast. In the longer recension 'the interpolator, living more than two centuries after the εὐχαριστία had been separated from the ἀγάπη, inserts the words οὔτε προσφέρειν οὔτε θυσίαν προσκομίζειν οὔτε δοχὴν ἐπιτελεῖν' (Lightfoot). For the use of δοχή in the sense of ἀγάπη, L. refers to *Apost. Const.* II. 28 τοῖς εἰς ἀγάπην ἤτοι δοχήν, ὡς ὁ κύριος ὠνόμασε (Lk. xiv. 13), προαιρουμένοις καλεῖν. Compare also Ign. *Eph.* 20 ἀπερισπάστῳ διανοίᾳ ἕνα ἄρτον κλῶντες, ὅ ἐστιν φάρμακον ἀθανασίας, ἀντίδοτον τοῦ μὴ ἀποθανεῖν, ἀλλὰ ζῆν ἐν Ἰησοῦ Χριστῷ διὰ παντός, where L. notes 'the reference will be to the agape, but more especially to the eucharistic bread, in which the agape culminated, and which was the chief bond of Christian union.... For κλᾶν ἄρτον comp. Acts ii. 42, 46, xx. 7, 11, 1 Cor. x. 16, where it occurs as a synonym for celebrating the eucharistic feast, apparently in all cases in conjunction with the agape.' On Ign. *Rom.* 7 ἄρτον θεοῦ θέλω, ὅ ἐστιν σὰρξ τοῦ Χριστοῦ...καὶ πόμα θέλω τὸ αἷμα αὐτοῦ, ὅ ἐστιν ἀγάπη ἄφθαρτος, L. says 'the reference here is not to the eucharist itself, but to the union with Christ which is symbolized and pledged in the eucharist...As the flesh of Christ represents the solid substance of the Christian life, so the blood of Christ represents the element of love, which circulates through all its pores and ducts, animating and invigorating the whole.' For similar allegorical and mystical interpretations, see *Trall.* 8 ἀνακτήσασθε ἑαυτοὺς ἐν πίστει, ὅ ἐστιν σὰρξ τοῦ κυρίου, καὶ ἐν ἀγάπῃ, ὅ ἐστιν αἷμα Ἰησοῦ Χριστοῦ, and quotations from Clem. Al. below. But elsewhere Ignatius uses far more definite language than we find in Clement, cf. *Smyrn.* § 6 (the Docetae) εὐχαριστίας καὶ προσευχῆς ἀπέχονται διὰ τὸ μὴ ὁμολογεῖν εὐχαριστίαν σάρκα εἶναι τοῦ σωτῆρος ἡμῶν Ἰ. Χ. τὴν ὑπὲρ ἁμαρτιῶν ἡμῶν παθοῦσαν, ἣν τῇ χρηστότητι ὁ πατὴρ ἤγειρεν.

in v. 14 δελεάζοντες ψυχὰς ἀστηρίκτους, and in v. 8 πλαστοῖς λόγοις ὑμᾶς ἐμπορεύσονται. Moreover it is only what might have been expected, when we find that, in some mss. ἀπάταις has been altered to suit the ἀγάπαις of Jude.

[1] W. H. read ἀκαταπαύστους (said to be from πάω a Doric form of παύω), but, as the line in Cod. B ends with -πα, it seems to me easier to suppose that the υ was accidentally omitted in the same way as the last syllable of ἔσχατα in the same ms. has been lost at the end of the line in v. 20.

Pliny's letter to Trajan has been much discussed in regard to the relation of the eucharist to the agape. He states that the Christians confessed 'quod essent soliti stato die ante lucem convenire carmenque Christo quasi deo dicere secum invicem, seque sacramento non in scelus aliquod obstringere sed ne furta, ne latrocinia, ne adulteria committerent, ne depositum appellati abnegarent quibus peractis morem sibi discedendi fuisse rursusque coeundi ad capiendum cibum, promiscuum tamen et innoxium, quod ipsum facere desisse post edictum meum, quo secundum mandata tua hetaerias esse vetueram' Lightfoot's comment (*Ign.* I. 50 f.) is 'The account here supposes two meetings in the course of the day, (1) before daylight, when a religious service was held; (2) later in the day, probably in the evening, when the agape was celebrated...The later meeting however was suppressed after the issue of Trajan's edict forbidding clubs.' He concludes that the eucharist had been already separated from the agape, and was celebrated before dawn; but notes that 'in some parts of Asia Minor, and probably at Antioch, the two were still connected when Ignatius wrote.' From the language of Tertullian and Clement it is plain that either the abolition of the agape was merely temporary, or that it was at any rate not universal. We learn from Origen *c. Cels.* I. 1 that Celsus, writing, say, 50 years after Pliny, spoke of the agape as forbidden by law, and Origen does not deny it. See, however, on the changes in the legal position of the agape, Keating *App.* B.

In the *Didachè*, chapters 9 and 10, we have an account of the eucharist as administered shortly before the time of Ignatius. It begins with thanksgiving for the vine of David and the life and knowledge revealed through Christ, followed by a prayer that the members of the Church may be united in one body, as the grains of wheat are united in the loaf which is broken. Then come the words μετὰ τὸ ἐμπλησθῆναι οὕτως εὐχαριστήσατε, implying that what precedes refers to the agape. This is followed by a form of prayer and thanksgiving for earthly and heavenly blessings, especially because ἐχαρίσω πνευματικὴν τροφὴν καὶ ποτὸν καὶ ζωὴν αἰώνιον διὰ τοῦ παιδός σου. It is added that prophets are to be allowed to utter thanksgiving in their own words, εὐχαριστεῖν ὅσα θέλουσιν. In c. 14 it is ordered that the eucharist should be regularly administered on Sunday after confession to those who are at peace with all, ἵνα μὴ κοινωθῇ ἡ θυσία ὑμῶν.

Justin Martyr goes further into details in regard to the eucharist, but without any allusion to the agape. After baptism, he says (*Apol.* I. 65), the newly baptized Christian joins in the prayers of the Church, and receives the kiss of peace; ἔπειτα προσφέρεται τῷ προεστῶτι τῶν ἀδελφῶν ἄρτος καὶ ποτήριον ὕδατος καὶ κράματος, καὶ οὗτος λαβὼν αἶνον καὶ δόξαν τῷ πατρὶ τῶν ὅλων διὰ τοῦ ὀνόματος τοῦ υἱοῦ καὶ τοῦ πνεύματος τοῦ ἁγίου ἀναπέμπει, καὶ εὐχαριστίαν ὑπὲρ τοῦ κατηξιῶσθαι τούτων παρ' αὐτοῦ ἐπὶ πολὺ ποιεῖται· οὗ συντελέσαντος τὰς εὐχὰς καὶ τὴν εὐχαριστίαν, πᾶς ὁ παρὼν λαὸς ἐπευφημεῖ λέγων Ἀμήν. After this, οἱ καλούμενοι παρ' ἡμῖν διάκονοι διδόασιν ἑκάστῳ τῶν παρόντων μεταλαβεῖν ἀπὸ τοῦ εὐχαριστηθέντος ἄρτου καὶ οἴνου καὶ ὕδατος.

καὶ τοῖς οὐ παροῦσιν ἀποφέρουσι. καὶ ἡ τροφὴ αὕτη καλεῖται παρ' ἡμῖν εὐχαριστία, ἧς οὐδενὶ ἄλλῳ μετασχεῖν ἐξόν ἐστιν ἢ τῷ πιστεύοντι ἀληθῆ εἶναι τὰ δεδιδαγμένα ὑφ' ἡμῶν, καὶ λουσαμένῳ τὸ ὑπὲρ ἀφέσεως ἁμαρτιῶν καὶ εἰς ἀναγέννησιν λουτρόν, καὶ οὕτως βιοῦντι ὡς ὁ Χριστὸς παρέδωκεν. οὐ γὰρ ὡς κοινὸν ἄρτον οὐδὲ κοινὸν πόμα ταῦτα λαμβάνομεν. In c. 67 he continues οἱ ἔχοντες τοῖς λειπομένοις πᾶσιν ἐπικουροῦμεν καὶ σύνεσμεν ἀλλήλοις ἀεί· ἐπὶ πᾶσί τε οἷς προσφερόμεθα εὐλογοῦμεν τὸν ποιητὴν τῶν πάντων. He then describes what takes place on Sunday, τῇ τοῦ ἡλίου λεγομένῃ ἡμέρᾳ πάντων κατὰ πόλεις ἢ ἀγροὺς μενόντων ἐπὶ τὸ αὐτὸ συνέλευσις γίνεται, καὶ τὰ ἀπομνημονεύματα τῶν ἀποστόλων ἢ τὰ συγγράμματα τῶν προφητῶν ἀναγινώσκεται μέχρις ἐγχωρεῖ. εἶτα παυσαμένου τοῦ ἀναγινώσκοντος ὁ προεστὼς διὰ λόγου τὴν νουθεσίαν...ποιεῖται. ἔπειτα ἀνιστάμεθα κοινῇ πάντες καὶ τὰς εὐχὰς πέμπομεν. καί, ὡς προέφημεν, παυσαμένων ἡμῶν τῆς εὐχῆς ἄρτος προσφέρεται καὶ οἶνος καὶ ὕδωρ, καὶ ὁ προεστὼς εὐχὰς ὁμοίως καὶ εὐχαριστίας, ὅση δύναμις αὐτῷ, ἀναπέμπει...οἱ εὐποροῦντες δὲ...κατὰ προαίρεσιν ἕκαστος τὴν ἑαυτοῦ ὃ βούλεται δίδωσιν, καὶ τὸ συλλεγόμενον παρὰ τῷ προεστῶτι ἀποτίθεται, καὶ αὐτὸς ἐπικουρεῖ ὀρφανοῖς τε καὶ χήραις...καὶ ἁπλῶς τοῖς ἐν χρείᾳ οὖσι κηδεμὼν γίνεται. Justin challenges unbelievers to find any fault with such a meeting as this. He allows however that abominable and utterly baseless charges were brought against the Christians (*Apol.* I. 10, 23, 27), charges circulated by Jews (*Dial.* 17) and supported by evidence extracted from slaves by torture (*Apol.* II. 12), and that he himself had once believed them (*Apol.* II. 12), till he was convinced of their falsehood by seeing how fearlessly the Christians faced death. Possibly such charges may be truly alleged against some of the heretics, though he will not affirm it (*Apol.* I. 26).

Clement of Alexandria and Tertullian have a good deal to tell us about the Love-Feast. Tertullian especially gives two remarkable sketches of the Agape, one written before, and the other after he became a Montanist. The former is contained in *Apol.* 39, cena nostra de nomine rationem sui ostendit; id vocatur quod dilectio penes Graecos est. Quantiscumque sumptibus constet, lucrum est pietatis nomine facere sumptum, siquidem inopes quosque refrigerio isto juvamus...Si honesta causa est convivii, reliquum ordinem disciplinae aestimate, qui sit de religionis officio. Nihil vilitatis, nihil immodestiae admittit: non prius discumbitur, quam oratio ad Deum praegustetur: editur quantum esurientes capiunt; bibitur quantum pudicis est utile. Ita saturantur, ut qui meminerint etiam per noctem adorandum Deum sibi esse[1]; ita fabulantur, ut qui sciant Dominum audire. Post aquam manualem et lumina, ut quisque de scripturis sanctis vel de proprio ingenio potest, provocatur in medium Deo canere: hinc probatur quo modo biberit. Aeque oratio convivium dirimit. Inde disceditur...ad eandem curam modestiae et pudicitiae, ut qui non tam cenam cenaverint quam disciplinam.

---

[1] See *D. of Chr. Ant.* under 'Vigils.'

Tertullian notices the charges made against the Christians, adding that they arose from a misunderstanding of the eucharistic feast (*Apol.* 7): dicimur sceleratissimi de sacramento infanticidii et pabulo inde, et post convivium incesto, quod eversores luminum canes, lenones scilicet, tenebrarum et libidinum impiarum inverecundia procurent (cf. also *ib.* 8, 9). Compare with this the account given of the catholic agape in his later Montanist treatise *De Jejuniis* 17: apud te (the 'homo psychicus') agape in cacabis fervet, fides in culina calet, spes in ferculis jacet. 'Sed major his est agape[1],' quia per hanc adolescentes tui cum sororibus dormiunt. Appendices scilicet gulae, lascivia atque luxuria.

It is plain from the language used in *Apol.* § 39 (*cena, per noctem, lumina*), that the agape, as described by Tertullian, takes place in the evening; but the eucharist is said by him to be celebrated in the early morning; cf. *De Corona* 3, where, among other examples of changes made from primitive use, it is said: Eucharistiae sacramentum et in tempore victus et omnibus mandatum a domino, etiam antelucanis coetibus, nec de aliorum manu quam praesidentium sumimus. Here it may be questioned whether *etiam* means 'as well as at the time of the evening meal,' or 'even before day-break,' enhancing the contrast to the primitive communion administered at nightfall. Perhaps it is better to suppose a complete change in the time, as there is in the mode of administration from the λάβετε τοῦτο καὶ διαμερίσατε εἰς ἑαυτούς (Lk. xxii. 17) to the distribution by the presiding minister. The passage quoted by Keating in support of this (*ad Uxorem* II. 5)—non sciet maritus quid secreto ante omnem cibum gustes ?—seems to be an allusion to the 'eulogia,' the portion of the 'panis ἐξορκισμοῦ,' which was distributed by the president at the beginning of the Agape and taken home by those present (Achelis p. 208), or else to the reservation mentioned in Basil's 93rd epistle (below p. 382).

Clement is much less definite than Tertullian. It is often difficult to know whether he is speaking of an ordinary feast, or of the agape, heretical or catholic, or of the eucharist, or simply of pious meditation. I will take first some passages in which he appears to be speaking of the eucharist. *Paed.* II. 29 μυστικὸν σύμβολον ἡ γραφὴ αἵματος ἁγίου οἶνον ὠνόμασεν. *Str.* I. p. 318 *fin.* § 5 τὴν εὐχαριστίαν τινὲς διανείμαντες, ὡς ἔθος, αὐτὸν δὴ ἕκαστον τοῦ λαοῦ λαβεῖν τὴν μοῖραν ἐπιτρέπουσιν. ἀρίστη γὰρ πρὸς τὴν ἀκριβῆ αἵρεσίν τε καὶ φυγὴν συνείδησις, *Str.* IV. § 161 P. 637 Μελχισεδὲκ ὁ τὸν οἶνον καὶ τὸν ἄρτον, τὴν ἡγιασμένην διδοὺς τροφήν, εἰς τύπον εὐχαριστίας, *Str.* VI. § 113 P. 797 δύναμιν λαβοῦσα κυριακὴν ἡ ψυχὴ μελετᾷ εἶναι θεός... ἀεὶ εὐχαριστοῦσα ἐπὶ πᾶσι τῷ θεῷ δι' ἀκοῆς δικαίας καὶ ἀναγνώσεως θείας, διὰ ζητήσεως ἀληθοῦς, διὰ προσφορᾶς ἁγίας, δι' εὐχῆς μακαρίας, αἰνοῦσα, ὑμνοῦσα, εὐλογοῦσα, ψάλλουσα.

In this and the following quotations the phraseology is eucharistic, but

---

[1] Tertullian applies 1 Cor. xiii. 13 in a different sense, 'There is a feast surpassing these luxurious meats,' viz. the following *lascivia*.

the feeding spoken of, the realization of the union of the Body with the Head, seems not to be limited to the actual reception of the eucharist. *Paed.* I. § 42 *fin.* φάγετέ μου, φησί, τὴν σάρκα καὶ πίετέ μου τὸ αἷμα, § 43 δ τοῦ παραδόξου μυστηρίου...σάρκα ἡμῖν τὸ πνεῦμα τὸ ἅγιον ἀλληγορεῖ ('ho uses the figure of flesh to describe the Holy Spirit') καὶ γὰρ ὑπ' αὐτοῦ δεδημιούργηται ἡ σάρξ, αἷμα ἡμῖν τὸν λόγον αἰνίττεται, καὶ γὰρ ὡς αἷμα πλούσιον ἐπικέχυται τῷ βίῳ· ἡ κρᾶσις δὲ ἡ ἀμφοῖν ὁ Κύριος, ἡ τροφὴ τῶν νηπίων. *Ib.* § 47 οὕτως πολλαχῶς ἀλληγορεῖται ὁ λόγος, καὶ βρῶμα καὶ σὰρξ καὶ τροφὴ καὶ ἄρτος καὶ αἷμα καὶ γάλα, ἅπαντα ὁ Κύριος εἰς ἀπόλαυσιν τῶν εἰς αὐτὸν πεπιστευκότων. *Q. D. S.* § 23 (Christ is speaking) ἐγώ σου τροφεύς, ἄρτον ἐμαυτὸν διδούς, οὗ γευσάμενος οὐδεὶς ἔτι πεῖραν θανάτου λαμβάνει, καὶ πόμα καθ' ἡμέραν ἐνδιδοὺς ἀθανασίας, *Paed.* I. § 38 (P. 121 *init.*) Cl. explains Joh. vi. 53 f. as follows: δι' ὧν (sc. τῆς πίστεως καὶ τῆς ἐπαγγελίας) ἡ ἐκκλησία ἐκ πολλῶν συνεστηκυῖα μελῶν ἄρδεται καὶ αὔξεται, συγκροτεῖταί τε καὶ συμπήγνυται ἐξ ἀμφοῖν, σώματος μὲν τῆς πίστεως, ψυχῆς δὲ τῆς ἐλπίδος, ὥσπερ καὶ ὁ κύριος ἐκ σαρκὸς καὶ αἵματος. τῷ γὰρ ὄντι αἷμα τῆς πίστεως ἡ ἐλπὶς ὑφ' ἧς (MS. ἐφ' ἧς) συνέχεται, καθάπερ ὑπὸ ψυχῆς, ἡ πίστις.

In contrast with these passages we may take the description of certain heretical agapae in *Str.* III. § 10, where Cl. relates what is reported of the Carpocratians and others, εἰς τὰ δεῖπνα ἀθροιζομένους (οὐ γὰρ ἀγάπην εἴποιμ' ἂν ἔγωγε τὴν συνέλευσιν αὐτῶν) ἄνδρας ὁμοῦ καὶ γυναῖκας μετὰ δὴ τὸ κορεσθῆναι, τὸ καταισχῦνον αὐτῶν τὴν πορνικὴν ταύτην δικαιοσύνην[1] ἐκποδὼν ποιησαμένους φῶς τῇ τοῦ λύχνου περιτροπῇ, μίγνυσθαι αἷς βούλοιντο, μελετήσαντας δὲ ἐν τοιαύτῃ ἀγάπῃ τὴν κοινωνίαν, μεθ' ἡμέραν ἤδη παρ' ὧν ἂν ἐθελήσωσι γυναικῶν ἀπαιτεῖν τὴν τοῦ Καρποκρατείου...νόμου ὑπακοήν. In *Str.* VII. P. 892 Cl. speaks of heretics who will endure anything rather than give up their heresy, καὶ τῆς πολυθρυλήτου κατὰ τὰς ἐκκλησίας αὐτῶν πρωτοκαθεδρίας, δι' ἣν καὶ ἐκείνην τὴν συμποτικὴν τῆς ψευδωνύμου ἀγάπης πρωτοκλισίαν ἀσπάζονται. In *Str.* I. 96 he applies Prov. ix. 17 (Stolen waters are sweet and bread eaten in secret is pleasant) to heretical sacraments. 'The phrase bread and water is here used': οὐκ ἐπ' ἄλλων τινῶν ἀλλ' ἢ ἐπὶ τῶν ἄρτῳ καὶ ὕδατι κατὰ τὴν προσφοράν, μὴ κατὰ τὸν κανόνα τῆς ἐκκλησίας, χρωμένων αἱρέσεων.

In the passages which follow Clement appears to be speaking of abuses to be found in the agapae of Catholics, to which he attributes the ill-repute of Christianity among the heathen, and at the same time to be setting forth a higher view of the meaning and use of the feast of love. *Paed.* III. § 81, P. 301 ἀξίως τῆς βασιλείας πολιτευώμεθα (MS. -όμεθα) θεὸν ἀγαπῶντες καὶ τὸν πλησίον. ἀγάπη δὲ οὐκ ἐν φιλήματι, ἀλλ' ἐν εὐνοίᾳ κρίνεται. οἱ δὲ οὐδὲν ἀλλ' ἢ φιλήματι καταψοφοῦσι τὰς ἐκκλησίας, τὸ φιλοῦν ἔνδον οὐκ ἔχοντες αὐτό. καὶ γὰρ δὴ καὶ τοῦτο ἐκπέπληκεν ὑπονοίας αἰσχρᾶς καὶ βλασφημίας, τὸ ἀνέδην χρῆσθαι τῷ φιλήματι, ὅπερ ἐχρῆν εἶναι

---

[1] The δικαιοσύνη of Carpocrates was communism, κοινωνία μετ' ἰσότητος *Str.* III. § 6.

APPENDIX C.

μυστικόν. *Paed.* II. § 4, P. 165, speaking of excess in eating, Cl. says that some have ventured to give to the fleshly life the title of ἀγάπη, τὸ καλὸν καὶ σωτήριον ἔργον τοῦ λόγου, τὴν ἀγάπην τὴν ἡγιασμένην, κυθριδίοις καὶ ζωμοῦ ῥύσει καθυβρίζοντες...τὴν ἐπαγγελίαν τοῦ θεοῦ δειπναρίοις ἐξωνεῖσθαι προσδοκήσαντες. τὰς μὲν γὰρ ἐπὶ τῆς εὐφροσύνης (ἴτῇ εὐφροσύνῃ) συναγωγὰς...δειπνάριά τε καὶ ἄριστα καὶ δοχὰς εἰκότως ἂν καλοῖμεν...τὰς τοιαύτας δὲ ἑστιάσεις[1] ὁ κύριος ἀγάπας οὐ κέκληκεν. § 14 πόρρω τῶν πασχητιώντων ἐδεσμάτων ἡ τράπεζα τῆς ἀληθείας, contrasted with τῶν δαιμονίων τὰς τραπέζας in § 10 *fin.* § 5 ἀγάπη δὲ τῷ ὄντι ἐπουράνιός ἐστι τροφή, ἐστίασις λογική· πάντα στέγει, πάντα ὑπομένει...μακάριος ὃς φάγεται ἄρτον ἐν τῇ βασιλείᾳ τοῦ θεοῦ· χαλεπώτατον δὲ πάντων πτωμάτων τὴν ἄπτωτον ἀγάπην ἄνωθεν ἐξ οὐρανῶν ἐπὶ τοὺς ζωμοὺς ῥίπτεσθαι χαμαί. § 6 ταύτης ὅλης ἀπήρτηται ἀγάπης ὁ νόμος καὶ ὁ λόγος, κἂν ἀγαπήσῃς τὸν θεόν σου καὶ τὸν πλησίον σου, ἐν οὐρανοῖς ἐστιν αὕτη ἡ ἐπουράνιος εὐωχία, ἡ δὲ ἐπίγειος δεῖπνον κέκληται...δι' ἀγάπην μὲν γινόμενον τὸ δεῖπνον, ἀλλ' οὐκ ἀγάπη τὸ δεῖπνον, δεῖγμα δὲ εὐνοίας κοινωνικῆς...οὐ γάρ ἐστιν ἡ βασιλεία τοῦ θεοῦ βρῶσις καὶ πόσις...ἀλλὰ δικαιοσύνη καὶ εἰρήνη...τούτου ὁ φαγὼν τοῦ ἀρίστου τὸ ἄριστον τῶν ὄντων τὴν βασιλείαν τοῦ θεοῦ κτήσεται, μελετήσας ἐνθένδε ἁγίαν συνήλυσιν ἀγάπης, οὐράνιον ἐκκλησίαν. § 7 ἀγάπη μὲν οὖν χρῆμα...τοῦ θεοῦ ἄξιον, ἔργον δὲ αὐτῆς ἡ μετάδοσις...αἱ δὲ εὐφροσύναι αὗται ἔναυσμά τι ἀγάπης ἔχουσιν ἐκ τῆς πανδήμου τροφῆς συνεθιζόμενον εἰς ἀΐδιον τροφήν. ἀγάπη μὲν οὖν δεῖπνον οὐκ ἔστιν, ἡ δὲ ἑστίασις ἀγάπης ἠρτήσθω... ἀλλὰ γὰρ τὸ δεῖπνον ἔστω λιτὸν ἡμῖν καὶ εὔζωνον...ἀγαθὴ γὰρ κουροτρόφος εἰς κοινωνίαν ἀγάπη, ἐφόδιον ἔχουσα πλούσιον τὴν αὐτάρκειαν, § 9 ἀγαστὸν μὲν οὖν ...τῆς ἄνω τροφῆς ἐξέχεσθαι καὶ τῆς τοῦ ὄντως ὄντος ἀπληρώτου ἐμπίμπλασθαι θέας...ταύτην γὰρ τὴν ἀγάπην ἐκδέχεσθαι δεῖν ἐμφαίνει ἡ βρῶσις ἡ Χριστοῦ... § 10 ὁ ἐσθίων κυρίῳ ἐσθίει καὶ εὐχαριστεῖ τῷ θεῷ...ὡς εἶναι τὴν δικαίαν τροφὴν εὐχαριστίαν, καὶ ὅ γε ἀεὶ εὐχαριστῶν οὐκ ἀσχολεῖται περὶ ἡδονάς. § 11 ἀνοήτου γὰρ σφόδρα θαυμάζειν...τὰ παρατιθέμενα ταῖς δημώδεσιν ἑστιάσεσιν μετὰ τὴν ἐν λόγῳ τρυφήν. By δημώδεσιν ἑστιάσεσιν we are probably to understand public as opposed to private agapae[2], preceded by readings from Scripture[3]. *Paed.* II. 53 εἰ γὰρ δι' ἀγάπην αἱ ἐπὶ τὰς ἑστιάσεις συνελεύσεις, συμποσίου δὲ τὸ τέλος ἡ πρὸς τοὺς συνόντας φιλοφροσύνη, παρεπόμενα δὲ τῇ ἀγάπῃ ἡ βρῶσις καὶ ἡ πόσις, πῶς οὐ λογικῶς ἀναστρεπτέον;

In the above passages there seems to be an attempt to sanctify not

---

[1] I agree with Dr Keating that ἑστίασις is perfectly general, not limited to the eucharist. See Index.

[2] Compare Keating pp. 86, 128.

[3] Dr Keating translates 'after the rich fare which is the Word' (written with a capital): a phrase which could only be used of the eucharist itself. It seems to me more natural to understand it of the reading of Scripture which formed the first part of the agape. Compare 2 Pet. ii. 13 ἡδονὴν ἡγούμενοι τὴν ἐν ἡμέρᾳ τρυφήν, which Dr Bigg translates 'counting our sober daylight joy a mere vulgar pleasure.' This may be illustrated by 1 Th. v. 5—8.

merely the agape, but ordinary entertainments, by connecting them with the thought of the eucharist, and of the brotherly kindness which every meal of Christians should symbolize. In what follows the original meaning of the Lord's Supper seems to be lost in mystical allegorization. § 19 ἡ ἄμπελος ἡ ἁγία τὸν βότρυν ἐβλάστησεν τὸν προφητικόν. τοῦτο σημεῖον...ὁ μέγας βότρυς, ὁ λόγος ὁ ὑπὲρ ἡμῶν θλιβείς[1], τοῦ αἵματος τῆς σταφυλῆς ὕδατι κίρνασθαι ἐθελήσαντος, τοῦ λόγου, ὡς καὶ τὸ αἷμα αὐτοῦ σωτηρίᾳ κίρναται. διττὸν δὲ τὸ αἷμα τοῦ κυρίου· τὸ μὲν γάρ ἐστιν αὐτοῦ σαρκικόν, ᾧ τῆς φθορᾶς λελυτρώμεθα, τὸ δὲ πνευματικόν, τουτέστιν ᾧ κεχρίσμεθα. καὶ τοῦτ' ἐστι πιεῖν τὸ αἷμα τοῦ Ἰησοῦ τῆς κυριακῆς μεταλαβεῖν ἀφθαρσίας· ἰσχὺς δὲ τοῦ λόγου τὸ πνεῦμα, ὡς αἷμα σαρκός. ('The meaning is that what the blood is for the flesh, its life and power, that the Spirit is for the Logos' Bähr ap. Hagenbach *H. of Doct.*) § 20 ἀναλόγως τοίνυν κίρναται ὁ μὲν οἶνος τῷ ὕδατι, τῷ δὲ ἀνθρώπῳ τὸ πνεῦμα· καὶ τὸ μὲν εἰς πίστιν εὐωχεῖ τὸ κρᾶμα, τὸ δὲ εἰς ἀφθαρσίαν ὁδηγεῖ τὸ πνεῦμα· ἡ δὲ ἀμφοῖν αὖθις κρᾶσις, ποτοῦ τε καὶ λόγου (Potter compares Iren. v. 2 ὁπότε οὖν καὶ τὸ κεκραμένον ποτήριον καὶ ὁ γεγονὼς ἄρτος ἐπιδέχεται τὸν λόγον τοῦ θεοῦ καὶ γίνεται ἡ εὐχαριστία σῶμα Χριστοῦ) εὐχαριστία κέκληται...ἧς οἱ κατὰ πίστιν μεταλαμβάνοντες ἁγιάζονται καὶ σῶμα καὶ ψυχήν, τὸ θεῖον κρᾶμα τὸν ἄνθρωπον τοῦ πατρικοῦ βουλεύματος πνεύματι καὶ λόγῳ συγκρινάντος μυστικῶς. *Str.* V. § 66, P. 685 fin. γάλα μὲν ἡ κατήχησις...βρῶμα δὲ ἡ ἐποπτικὴ θεωρία. σάρκες αὗται καὶ αἷμα τοῦ λόγου, τουτέστι κατάληψις τῆς θείας δυνάμεως καὶ οὐσίας... οὕτως γὰρ ἑαυτοῦ μεταδίδωσιν τοῖς πνευματικώτερον τῆς τοιαύτης μεταλαμβάνουσι βρώσεως...βρῶσις γὰρ καὶ πόσις τοῦ θείου λόγου ἡ γνῶσις ἐστὶ τῆς θείας οὐσίας. *Str.* 1. § 46 init. διὰ τοῦτο ὁ σωτὴρ ἄρτον λαβὼν πρῶτον ἐλάλησεν καὶ εὐχαρίστησεν· εἶτα κλάσας τὸν ἄρτον προέθηκεν, ἵνα δὴ φάγωμεν λογικῶς, καὶ τὰς γραφὰς ἐπιγνόντες (ἐπαναγνόντες) πολιτευσώμεθα καθ' ὑπακοήν. *Paed.* I. § 15, P. 103 fin. τὸν πῶλον, φησί, προσέδησεν ἀμπέλῳ· ἁπλοῦν τοῦτον καὶ νήπιον λαὸν τῷ λόγῳ προσδήσας, ὃν ἄμπελον ἀλληγορεῖ. φέρει γὰρ οἶνον ἡ ἄμπελος, ὡς αἷμα ὁ λόγος, ἄμφω δὲ ἀνθρώποις ποτὸν εἰς σωτηρίαν, ὁ μὲν οἶνος τῷ σώματι, τὸ δὲ αἷμα τῷ πνεύματι.

---

[1] The holy vine with the prophetic cluster of grapes is a reference to Num. xiii. 23, to be interpreted by Joh. xv. Lowth thinks the nom. ὁ νόμος ὁ θλιβείς should be in the gen. as it depends on σημεῖον, but perhaps we may keep the nom. if we translate 'This is a sign, the great cluster is the Word.' Herv. translates τοῦ αἵματος—κίρναται 'cum sanguis uvae, Verbum scilicet, aqua temperari voluerit, ut etiam sanguis ejus salute temperatur,' but the sense is very obscure. We might read τὸ αἷμα (acc. instead of gen.) and translate 'The Word having willed that the blood of the grape should be mingled with water,' a reference to the two sacraments, and to the blood and water which flowed from the side of the Saviour; or perhaps better, retaining τοῦ αἵματος, but transferring τοῦ λόγου to the next clause, we might read ὡς καὶ αὐτοῦ τοῦ λόγου τὸ αἷμα σωτηρίᾳ κίρναται: 'the blood of the grape craves to be mingled with water, as the Word is mingled with salvation' (the Water of Life).

I will conclude with a quotation from the *Exc. Theod.* § 82, which Harnack cites as an example of Gnostic tenets subsequently borrowed by the Catholic Church (*Dogmengesch.* I. 252 ed. 3): ὁ ἄρτος καὶ τὸ ἔλαιον (the eucharist bread and the chrism) ἁγιάζεται τῇ δυνάμει τοῦ ὀνόματος, οὐ[1] τὰ αὐτὰ ὄντα κατὰ τὸ φαινόμενον οἷα ἐλήφθη, ἀλλὰ δυνάμει εἰς δύναμιν πνευματικὴν μεταβέβληται.

Considering all these passages, it does not seem to me that we are able to assert positively either that the eucharist in Clement's circle was celebrated in the morning apart from the agape, as Dr Keating seems inclined to do, or (with Dr Bigg) that it was always joined with the evening agape. There is a sentence in *Str.* VII. § 40 which should perhaps be understood as implying that it did sometimes form a part of the agape. 'The gnostic is not limited to fixed hours of prayer, but prays all his life through, striving to be united with God in prayer, and to have done with all that is useless for the higher life (ἐκεῖ γενομένῳ), ὡς ἂν ἐνθένδε ἤδη τὴν τελείωσιν ἀπειληφὼς τοῦ κατὰ ἀγάπην δρωμένου. I have translated the last clause 'as one who has already obtained the perfection of loving action'; but I do not see why, if this was his meaning, Cl. might not have written simply ἀγάπης or ἐνεργείας ἀγαπητικῆς, and in the note I have suggested that it may mean 'having received the perfection of that which is exhibited (or represented) in the agape,' viz. the union with Christ and with the brethren[2].

We learn from Sozomen VII. 19, some 200 years after Clement, that it was still the custom in some parts of Egypt to administer the eucharist in the evening after the agape. After mentioning that Rome and Alexandria were exceptions to the general rule of holding religious services on Saturday as on Sunday, he continues παρὰ δὲ Αἰγυπτίοις ἐν πολλαῖς πόλεσι καὶ κώμαις, παρὰ τὸ κοινῇ πᾶσι νενομισμένον, πρὸς ἑσπέραν τῷ σαββάτῳ συνιόντες, ἠριστηκότες ἤδη, μυστηρίων μετέχουσι, or as it is more strongly put in Socr. v. 22, μετὰ τὸ εὐωχθῆναι καὶ παντοίων ἐδεσμάτων ἐμφορηθῆναι περὶ ἑσπέραν προσφέροντες τῶν μυστηρίων μεταλαμβάνουσι. Another peculiarity of the Egyptian Church is noticed by Basil (*Ep.* 93) where he justifies his advice to a layman to administer the sacrament to himself in time of persecution, by the example of the hermits and by the Egyptian usage: ἕκαστος τῶν ἐν λαῷ τελούντων ὡς ἐπὶ τὸ πλεῖστον ἔχει κοινωνίαν ἐν τῷ οἴκῳ αὐτοῦ καὶ ὅτε βούλεται λαμβάνει δι' ἑαυτοῦ. Apparently the bread had been already blest by the priest; for he goes on to say that the recipient in church receives the bread in his hand and applies it to his mouth himself, and that sometimes the priest gave several portions, which the recipient was at liberty to carry away.

All Clement's references to the eucharist seem to me to be characterized by the principle laid down in our Lord's teaching on the subject, τὸ πνεῦμά

---

[1] Dr Abbott would omit οὐ.
[2] For the liturgical sense of δράω see my note on the passage.

ἔστι τὸ ζωοποιοῦν, ἡ σὰρξ οὐκ ὠφελεῖ οὐδέν, and also to resemble in many points Plato's teaching in the *Symposium* (p. 211 C to E) where he traces the upward development of ἔρως from its beginning in the natural admiration for a beautiful person, to the unselfish delight in all objects of beauty, until it rises at last to the contemplation of αὐτὸ τὸ θεῖον καλόν, the Divine source of all beauty, whether in earth or heaven: ἀρχόμενον ἀπὸ τῶνδε τῶν καλῶν ἐκείνου ἕνεκα τοῦ καλοῦ ἀεὶ ἐπανιέναι ὥσπερ ἐπαναβαθμοῖς χρώμενον...τί δῆτα οἰόμεθα εἴ τῳ γένοιτο αὐτὸ τὸ καλὸν ἰδεῖν εἰλικρινές, καθαρόν, ἄμικτον; ἆρ' οἴει φαῦλον βίον γίγνεσθαι ἐκεῖσε βλέποντος ἀνθρώπου κἀκεῖνο δὴ θεωμένου καὶ ξυνόντος αὐτῷ: So Clement passes from the good fellowship of ordinary hospitality (ἐκ τῆς πανδήμου τροφῆς) to the more ideal fellowship of the love-feast; but there too the δεῖπνον is nothing, except so far as it is an ἐπουράνιος τροφή, ἑστίασις λογική, the manifestation of that inner feeling of love described by St Paul in his ep. to the Corinthians. In the eucharist itself, the actual bread and wine are nothing; the Body and Blood of Christ are no material body and blood, liable to accidents, such as were anxiously deprecated by some of his contemporaries[1]; but the Body is faith, the Blood hope (*Paed.* I § 38); the Flesh and Blood of the Logos are the apprehension of the Divine Power and Essence; the eating and drinking of the Logos is knowledge of the Divine Essence (*Str.* v. 66); the Flesh is the Spirit, the Blood is the Logos, the union of the two is the Lord who is the food of His people (*Paed.* I. § 43).

Indeed, as far as I am able to judge, Clement would not have dissented from Barclay's language (*Apology* p. 453): 'The Supper of the Lord and the supping with the Lord (Rev. iii. 20) and partaking of His Bread and Wine, is no way limited to the ceremony of breaking bread and drinking wine at particular times; but it is truly and really enjoyed as often as the soul retires into the Light of the Lord and feels and partakes of that Heavenly Life by which the inward man is nourished; which may be and is often witnessed by the faithful at all times, though more particularly when they are assembled together to wait upon the Lord.' This seems also to have been the view of Clement's pupil Origen, if we may judge from his language in the *Answer to Celsus* VIII. 22 ὁ νοήσας ὅτι τὸ πάσχα ἡμῶν ὑπὲρ ἡμῶν ἐτύθη Χριστός, καὶ χρὴ ἑορτάζειν ἐσθίοντα τῆς σαρκὸς τοῦ λόγου· οὐκ ἔστιν ὅτε οὐ ποιεῖ τὸ πάσχα, ὅπερ ἑρμηνεύεται Διαβατήρια, διαβαίνων ἀεὶ τῷ λογισμῷ καὶ παντὶ λόγῳ καὶ πάσῃ πράξει ἀπὸ τῶν τοῦ βίου πραγμάτων ἐπὶ τὸν θεὸν καὶ ἐπὶ τὴν πόλιν αὐτοῦ σπεύδων. Compare also *Comm. in Joh.* t. XXXII. § 16 νοείσθω δὲ ὁ ἄρτος καὶ τὸ ποτήριον τοῖς μὲν ἁπλουστέροις κατὰ τὴν κοινοτέραν περὶ τῆς εὐχαριστίας ἐξοχήν· τοῖς δὲ βαθύτερον ἀκούειν μεμαθηκόσι κατὰ τὴν θειοτέραν καὶ περὶ τοῦ τροφίμου τῆς ἀληθείας λόγου ἐπαγγελίαν: and *Comm. in Matt.* t. XL. § 14 where he applies the words οὐ τὸ εἰσερχόμενον εἰς τὸ στόμα κοινοῖ τὸν ἄνθρωπον to the eucharist, οὔτε ἐκ τοῦ μὴ φαγεῖν,

---

[1] Calicis aut panis etiam nostri aliquid decuti in terram anxie patimur. Tert. *De Coron.* 3.

παρ' αὐτὸ τὸ μὴ φαγεῖν, ἀπὸ τοῦ ἁγιασθέντος λόγῳ θεοῦ καὶ ἐντεύξει ἄρτου, ὑστερούμεθα ἀγαθοῦ τινος, οὔτε ἐκ τοῦ φαγεῖν περισσεύομεν ἀγαθῷ τινι· τὸ γὰρ αἴτιον τῆς ὑστερήσεως ἡ κακία ἐστί...καὶ τὸ αἴτιον τῆς περισσεύσεως ἡ δικαιοσύνη ἐστί...καὶ οὐχ ἡ ὕλη τοῦ ἄρτου, ἀλλ' ὁ ἐπ' αὐτῷ εἰρημένος λόγος ἐστὶν ὁ ὠφελῶν τὸν μὴ ἀναξίως τοῦ κυρίου ἐσθίοντα αὐτόν. καὶ ταῦτα μὲν περὶ τοῦ τυπικοῦ καὶ συμβολικοῦ σώματος.

For the rules laid down as to the management of the agape in the Apostolic Constitutions and elsewhere, and for the later history of the agape, see Keating pp. 107—165, Achelis *Canones Hippolyti*, and the articles on Agape in the *Dict. of Christ. Ant.* and on *Love-Feast* in Hastings' *Dict. of the Bible*.

INDEX TO QUOTATIONS AND ALLUSIONS.

BIBLE.

Gen. i. 26, § 3 (n. on ἐξομοιουμένῳ); xxix. 35, § 105 (n. on Ἰουδαία)
Exod. i. 7, § 100; xx. 13, 15, § 60; xxx. 34–36, § 34 (n. on θυμίαμα); xxxii. 32, § 80
Levit. xi. 3, § 109; xii. 8, § 32 (n. on ἡ τρυγών); xvi. 10, § 33 (n. on τράγον)
Num. xx. 17, § 73; xxi. 9, § 79 (n. on σημεῖον)
Deut. vi. 7, § 80 (n. on πρωΐας); xiii. 8, 9, § 14; xxxii. 8, § 6
Jud. ii. 11, § 82
1 Sam. i. 13, § 39 (n. on l. 19); xii. 9, § 82 (n. on πιπράσκει); xvi. 7, § 61
1 Kings vii. 13, § 29 (n. on ἀγύρτου)
Job i. 1, § 80, ib. 21, § 80
Psalms i. 4, § 110; iv. 5, § 81; v. 9, § 105; ix. 11, § 105; xix. 9, § 79; xxiv. 3–6, § 58; xxxiv. 11, § 81; xlviii. 12, § 83; li. 16, 17, § 14; lviii. 4, 5, § 102; lxxvi. 1, § 105; xci. 11, § 81; xciv. 10, 11, § 61; cxix. 2, § 1; cxix. 66, § 36; cxix. 164, § 35; cxli. 2, § 43; cxlv. 15, § 49
Prov. i. 7, § 70; viii. 9, § 51; viii. 22 f., § 7; ix. 10, § 70; xx. 27, § 37
Isa. iv. 4, § 84; v. 7, § 74; vi. 3, § 80; xl. 13, § 7; xl. 15, § 110; xliii. 2, § 34; lvii. 15, § 13; lxv. 24, § 49
Jer. iv. 3, § 74; xvii. 10, § 61
Ezek. xviii. 4, § 14
Dan. ix. 21, § 49
Matt. iv. 16, § 43; v. 8, §§ 13, 19, 56, 57; v. 9, § 100; v. 20, § 56; v. 28, § 82; v. 30, § 72 (n. on ἐκκόψαι); v. 37, §§ 50, 67; v. 44, § 84; v. 45, §§ 84, 86; v. 48, §§ 81, 88; vi. 6, § 49; vi. 7, § 49; vi. 12, § 81; vi. 14, § 86; vi. 21, § 77; vii. 14, § 93; vii. 21, §§ 5, 7, 8, 9, 104; x. 16, § 82; x. 37, § 93; xi. 27, § 58; xii. 50, § 5; xiii. 7, § 74; xiii. 20, § 93; xiii. 25, § 89; xvi. 19, § 106; xvi. 25, § 14; xvii. 20, § 77; xviii. 22, § 85; xix. 17, §§ 39, 41, 58; xix. 19, § 50; xxi. 22, § 41; xxi. 33, § 74; xxiii. 6, § 98; xxiii. 14, § 106; xxv. 1 f., § 72; xxv. 23, § 62; xxv. 34–45, § 21 (n. on εἰς ἰδίαν χάριν).

Luke vi. 46, §§ 104, 110; ix. 62, § 93; x. 22, § 109; xi. 52, § 106; xiv. 26, 27, § 79 bis; xiv. 33, § 79; xvi. 13, § 71; xvii. 31, § 93; xix. 26, § 55; xx. 36, §§ 57, 78, 84; xxiv. 45, § 105
John i. 3, § 17; i. 11, § 83; i. 12, § 68; i. 18, § 16; iv. 14, § 104; v. 13, § 54; v. 39, § 1; vi. 36–40, §§ 5, 7, 8, 9; viii. 33, § 82; x. 1 f., § 106; xiv. 2, §§ 9, 40, 57; xiv. 15, § 21; xv. 14, 15, §§ 5, 19, 21, 62, 68, 79; xvii. 3, § 41; xvii. 4, § 41; xvii. 20 f., § 41; xviii. 37, § 54
Acts vii. 48, § 28; x. 43, § 1; xvi. 8, § 53; xvii. 24, § 28
Rom. i. 20, and ii. 1, §§ 11, 92; ii. 25, § 53; ii. 29, §§ 53, 78; iii. 21, § 1; iii. 30, § 53; vii. 14, § 82; vii. 23, § 44; viii. 15, § 82; viii. 20, § 5; viii. 26, § 49; viii. 28, § 37; viii. 30, § 6; ix. 8, § 80; ix. 11, § 87; x. 5, 6, § 56; xi. 32, § 11; xi. 34, § 7; xiii. 9, § 105
1 Cor. i. 24, § 7; i. 30, § 16; ii. 7, § 107; iii. 6, § 74; iii. 13, § 84; iii. 16, §§ 64, 82; iv. 15, § 53; iv. 19, § 105; vi. 1–17, §§ 84–88; vi. 19, §§ 64, 82; vii. 29, § 64; vii. 32, § 71 (n. on θεῷ ἀρέσαι); vii. 35, §§ 13, 64; viii. 1, § 104; viii. 6, § 9; viii. 7, § 104; ix. 19, § 53; ix. 21, §§ 10, 11; x. 1–5, § 104; xi. 9, § 90; xiii. 2, § 77; xiii. 3, § 50; xiii. 7, § 70; xiii. 12, §§ 18, 57, 68; xiv. 6, § 59; xv. 27, § 5 (n. on ὑποτάξαντα)
2 Cor. iv. 2, § 43; iv. 10, § 80; x. 5, § 14
Gal. iii. 22, 23, § 11; iii. 24, § 86; iii. 29, § 82; iv. 9, § 82; v. 17, § 79
Eph. i. 4, § 7; i. 21, § 82; i. 23, § 87; ii. 8, § 11; ii. 11, § 53; ii. 20, § 55 (n. on θεμέλιος); iv. 6, § 58; iv. 13, §§ 10, 34, 68, 84; iv. 19, §§ 12, 39; iv. 22, § 14; iv. 24, § 14; v. 5, § 75; vi. 12, § 20
Phil. iii. 14, § 10; iii. 20, § 85; iv. 18, § 14
Col. ii. 3, § 16; iii. 5, § 75
1 Th. ii. 4, § 70; iv. 17, § 57
1 Tim. i. 6, 7, § 14; i. 9, § 10; iii. 8,

§ 69 (n. on ἀφιλάργυρον); vi. 19, § 16; vi. 20, § 41
Heb. i. 1, § 95; i. 3, §§ 16, 58; iii. 5, §§ 5, 19; iv. 12, § 84; iv. 14, §§ 9, 13, 45; v. 14, §§ 2, 94; vi. 18, § 6; ix. 25, § 40; xi. 13, §§ 13, 77, 78; xii. 2, § 9; xii. 7, § 56

James ii. 22, § 55; ii. 23, § 19; v. 12, § 67; v. 15, § 86
1 Pet. i. 10, § 1; i. 17, § 49; i. 20, § 107; ii. 9, § 35
2 Pet. i. 10, § 66
1 Joh. iv. 17, § 46
Rev. xvii. 14, § 6; xxii. 17, § 104

APOCRYPHAL WRITINGS.

Sirac iv. 11, § 105; xvii. 14, § 6 (n. on ἄγγελοι); xxxv. 17, § 87 (n. on τέμνει)
Susanna 42, § 37
Wisdom ii. 24, § 7 (ὁ φθονῶν); xi. 25, § 69 (n. on κτίστης)
Pseudepigrapha Vet. (Ezek.), § 94

Pseudepigrapha Nov. (Protevang. xix), § 98; (Trad. Matthiae), § 82
Agrapha (ἐννοήθητι καὶ ποιήσω), § 73; (ὃν ἐγὼ πατάξω σὺ ἐλέησον), § 74; (δόκιμοι τραπεζῖται), § 90

OTHER GREEK AUTHORS.

Æschylus, *Agam.* 36, § 18; *Theb.* 577, § 98
Æsop, *Fab.*, § 83
Androcydes, § 33
Antiphon, § 24
Aristophanes, *Eq.* 864, § 99
Aristoteles, *Eth. N.* II. 1, § 46 (n. on καθάπερ τῷ λίθῳ); II. 2, § 67 (n. on ἀγροικία); III. 8, §§ 59 (n. on θυμοειδεῖς), 66 (n. on ἀλόγως ἀνδρεῖος); v. 1, § 17 (n. on ταντελοῦτ); vi. 5, § 18; VIII. 6, § 21 (n. on προκατάρχει)
Basilides, § 81 (n. on μηδενὸς ἐπιθυμεῖν), § 96 (n. on ἄλλη φύσις)
Bion, § 24; § 33 (n. on μητρόπολις)
Chilon (γνῶθι σεαυτόν), § 20
Chrysippus (definition of wisdom), § 70; what is allowable in brutes right in man, §§ 23, 24
Cleanthes, § 33
Diogenes, § 26
Diphilus, § 26
Epicharmus, § 27
Eubulus, § 51 *bis*
Euripides, *Augè*, § 23; *Orestes*, 395, § 27; *Phœn.* 893, § 61
Frag. Com. §§ 24, 34
Frag. Trag. § 16
Hesiod, *Theog.* 556, § 31
Homer, *Il.* iv. 48, § 31 (n. on γέρας); vii. 422, § 26; ix. 533, § 23; *Od.* II. 181, § 25; x. 235, § 95; xii. 453, § 23
Irenæus, v. 8. 3, § 109 notes

Menander, *Deisidaimon*, § 24; *ib.* § 27; *ib.* § 31
Numenius, § 5 (n. on περιωπή and μεριζόμενος); § 16 (n. on δεύτερον αἴτιον)
Pherecrates, *Deserters*, § 30
Philemon, § 25
Plato, *Crat.* 412, § 55; *Epist.* II. 312, § 9; *Ion* 533–536, § 9; *Laches*, 195, § 65; *ib.* 197, § 66; *Legg.* III. 690, § 8 (n. on προσήκει τῷ κρείττονι); IV. 716, § 100; IV. 799, § 31; VII. 803, § 28; *ib.* x. 885, § 15 (n. on παραιτητούς); *ib.* x. 897, § 8; *ib.* 901, § 6; *Phædr.* 246, §§ 13, 40; *ib.* 247, §§ 7 (n. on φθονῶν), 46; *Phileb.* 30, § 22; *ib.* 64, § 45; *Polit.* 272, § 5; *Prot.* 313, § 19; *Rep.* II. 361, § 98; *ib.* 365, § 15 n.; *ib.* II. 382, § 53 n.; *ib.* 379, § 22; *ib.* III. 412, § 17; *ib.* IV. 436, § 65; VI. 509, § 2; VII. 525, § 10; x. 613, § 13; x. 617, §§ 12, 20; x. 620, § 6; *Symp.* 204, § 10; *Theæt.* 155, § 60; *ib.* 176, § 3; *Tim.* 29, § 7 (on ὁ φθονῶν); *ib.* 42, § 12; *ib.* 90, §§ 3, 13
Plato Com. § 33
Polemon (ὁ κατὰ φύσιν βίος), § 32
Sextus Empiricus, *Math.* VII. 121, § 17
Socrates (?), § 100 (n. on οἷος ὁ λόγος)
Theognis, § 110
Theophrastus, § 34
Xenocrates, § 32
Xenophanes, §§ 5, 22, 37
Xenophon, *Œcon.* XI., § 101

INDEX OF GREEK WORDS[1].

The list is meant to be complete for all the less common words and usages occurring in *Strom.* VII.

The figures in thick type denote that the word is commented on in the note on the passage. The references are ordinarily to Potter's pages, but a small 'p.' prefixed denotes a reference to the pages of this ed.

ἀβελτερία: 895 εἴτε ἀμαθίας εἴτε ἀβ. εἴτε καχεξίας
ἀβλαβής: p. 868 ἀβ. τηρεῖται ἡ ψυχή, 861 τὸ θεῖον φύσει ἀβλαβές
ἀβλαβῶς: 848 ἀβλαβῶς αὔξει
ἀβούλητος: 837 τύχαις ἀβ. περιπίπτοντες, ib. ἀβουλήτους ἀγνοίας ὁρμάς, see Schmid *Att.* II. 213
ἄβρωτος: (quot.) 847
ἀγαθοποιέω: 855 οὔκουν ὁ θεὸς ἀνάγκῃ ἀγαθοποιεῖ, 879 ἀγαθοποιεῖν προτρέπει ἡ ἀγάπη
ἀγαθός: 855 οὐκ ἄκων ἀγ. ὁ θεός
ἀγαθότης: 835 ἀγ. τοῦ κριτοῦ, 853 ἕξις ἀγαθότητος, 876 ἡ δικαία ἀγ. τοῦ θεοῦ, 882 init., 884, 885 ἀγ. προνοίας bis
ἀγαθωσύνη: 837 ὁ θεὸς ἐν ταυτότητι τῆς δικαίας ἀγαθωσύνης ἐστί
ἀγαθώτατος: 857
ἄγαλμα: 837 ἀγ. θεῖον δικαίου ψυχή, 846, 862 ἔμψυχα ἀγ. οἱ ἄνθρωποι, 863 ἀγ. ψυχικὸν τοῦ κυρίου ὁ γνωστικός, 52
ἀγαπάω: 835 ἀγαπώσαις ψυχαῖς ἑστιῶνται τ. ἀκόρεστον θέαν
ἀγάπη: (love-feast) 514, 854 τὸ κατὰ ἀγάπην δρώμενον, 892 ἡ συμποτικὴ διὰ τῆς ψευδωνύμου ἀγάπης πρωτοκλισία, cf. App. C and Elmenhorst on Minuc. Fel. pp. 308—310 ed. Ouzel: 865 προστεθήσεται τῇ γνώσει ἡ ἀγ., τῇ ἀγ. δὲ ἡ κληρονομία, see under 'Love'
ἀγαπητικός: 872 c. gen. ὁ γνωστικὸς θεοῦ ἀγαπητικός, 873 ἀγ. πρὸς τοὺς οἰκείους
ἀγαπητόν: 896 ἀγ. ἦν αὐτοῖς εἰ κ.τ.λ., 839 ἀγ. εἰ παρασκευάσαι δύναιτο
ἀγγελοθεσία: 833 fin. ἐπὶ τ. ἄκρῳ τέλει τ. φαινομένου ἡ ἀγγ. (only in Cl.)
ἄγγελος: 831 κράτιστον ἐν οὐρανῷ ἄγγ., 832 ὁ κύριος δίδωσι τ. Ἕλλησι τ. φιλοσοφίαν διὰ τ. ὑποδεεστέρων ἀγγέλων, ib. ἄγγελοι κατὰ ἔθνη, 839 θεαταὶ ἄγγελοι κ. θεοί, 835 οἱ προσεχεῖς ἄγγελοι, 852 ἡ συναίσθησις τῶν ἀγγ., 865 ἄπειροι ὅσοι ἀγγ., 879 μετ᾽ ἀγγ. εὔχεται, 881 ἡ δι᾽ ἀγγ. βοήθεια: (fallen) 859 τ. ἀγγέλων τινὰς ὀλισθήσαντας, 884 πῶς ἂν ἀγγέλους τις κρίναι τοὺς ἀποστάτας;
ἀγεννής: 860 ἀθλητὴς οὐκ ἀγεννής
ἄγευστος: c. gen. 872 ἀγ. ἡδονῶν, 945 ἀγ. δικαιοσύνης θεοῦ, see Schmid I. 238, III. 55
ἁγιάζω: 851 ἀγ. πῦρ ψυχάς, 875 ἡγιασμέναι παρθένοι
ἅγιος ἐν ἁγίοις: 835 ψυχαὶ ἀγ. ἐν ἀγ. λογισθεῖσαι, 865 κἂν ἁγία ᾖ καὶ ἐν ἁγίοις ἡ λειτουργία: 854 ἐπὶ τὰ ἅγια ('heaven') χωρεῖν: 879 τὸν τῶν ἁγίων χορὸν συνισταμένον ἔχει, ib. οὐδὲ ἔξω ποτε τῆς ἀγ. φρουρᾶς γίνεται
ἁγιότης: 846 δι᾽ ὑπερβολὴν ἁγιότητος
ἁγιωσύνη: 836 ἀναληφθεὶς εἰς ἁγιωσύνην
ἁγνεία: 844 ἡ ἁγνεία ἡ τῶν ἁμαρτημάτων ἀποχή: pl. 850 Αἰγύπτιοι ἐν τ. ἁγνείαις οὐκ ἐπιτρέπουσι σιτεῖσθαι σάρκας
ἁγνίζω: (quot.) 844
ἄγνοια: 837 κακῶν αἰτία αἱ ἀβούλητοι ἀγνοίας ὁρμαί, 868, 871 οὐδὲ ἡ δι᾽ ἄγνοιαν συνισταμένη πρᾶξις ἤδη ἄγνοια, ἀλλὰ κακή (MS. κακία) μὲν δι᾽ ἄγνοιαν, ib. οἱ παῖδες ἀγνοίᾳ τ. δεινῶν ὑφίστανται τὰ φοβερά: 870 δι᾽ ἄγνοιαν συνίσταται ἡ δειλία, 874 οὔποτε ἄγν. γίνεται ἡ γνῶσις, 875 ἀτροφία ἡ ἄγν. τ. ψυχῆς, 894 ἐν ἀγνοίᾳ τὰ ἔθνη
ἁγνός: 844 ἁγνὸς ὁ μηδὲν αὐτῷ συνειδώς: 845 βωμὸς ἀγν.
ἀγνώστως: 881 ἀγν. παρέχεται, 'secretly'

---
[1] *Note.* I am indebted to my brother, the Professor of Latin at Cambridge, for many of the illustrations from other authors.

ἄγριος : 898 ἀγ. ἀμυγδάλη, 837 τὸ ἄγριον ἐξημερώσεται, 841 θεοὶ ἄγρ. τὰ ἤθη

ἀγροικία : 872 δι' ἀγροικίαν ἐγκρατής

ἀγυρτής (?) : 846 see Τύριοι, 269 ἀγυρταί κ. μητραγύρται

ἀγχιβαθής : 888 θάλασσα ἀγχ.

ἄγω : 882 ἑαυτὸν ἄγει ὡς ὁ λόγος ὑπαγορεύει

ἀγωγός : 852 τὰ ὁρώμενα ἡδονῆς ἀγωγοῦ χάριν οὐ προσίεται, 834 ἀγ. τὸ ἐραστὸν παντός, Plut. Lyc. v. 5 δύναμις ἀνθρώπων ἀγωγός

ἀγών : 871 fin. ἀγ. γυμνικός

ἀγωνίζομαι : 870 ἀγ. δράμα

ἀγώνισμα : 840 init. κέκληται ἐπὶ τὸ ἀγ. τὸ θέατρον

ἀγωνοθέτης : 839 ὁ ἀγων. ὁ παντοκράτωρ θεός, cf. 77 ἀγωνοθετοῦντος τ. δεσπότου τ. ὅλων, but in 937 Christ is called the ἀγωνοθέτης, see βραβεύς

ἀδάμας : 872 ὁ ἀδ. ἀτεγκτος τῷ πυρί

ἀδεής : 872 ἄφοβον κ. ἀδεᾶ ἡ ἀγάπη κατασκευάζει τ. ἀθλητήν

ἀδεισιδαίμων : 841 ἀδ. ὁ τῷ ὄντι βασιλικός

ἀδελφός : 878 ἀδ. εἰσὶν τῷ ὄντι τὰ αὐτὰ ποιοῦντες κ. νοοῦντες κ. λαλοῦντες, 880 τὰ τῶν ἀδ. ἁμαρτήματα μερίσασθαι εὐχόμενος, 878 ἀδ. ὁμοπάτριος κ. ὁμομήτριος, 884 ἀδ. κατὰ πίστιν

ἀδιάκριτος : 836 ἕνωσις ἀδιάκριτος, 190 πίστις ἀδ., 474 ἀγάπη ἀδ., cf. ἀδιακρίτως 115

ἀδιάλειπτος : 829 fin. ἡ περὶ τὸ θεῖον κατὰ τ. ἀδιάλειπτον ἀγάπην ἀσχολία

ἀδιαλείπτως : 851 συμπαρῶν ἀδιαλείπτως τ. θεῷ, 854 ὁ θεὸς ἀδ. ἐπαΐει, 858 τῇ θεωρίᾳ ἀδ. προσεδρεύων

ἀδιάστατος : 874 ἀδ. τῆς τ. θεοῦ ἀγάπης, 792 φῶς ἡνωμένον ψυχῇ δι' ἀγάπης ἀδιαστάτου, see exx. in Siegfried's Philo p. 48

ἀδιάφθορος : 858 οὐκ εἰς τὸ ἀδιάφθορον μόνον, ἀλλὰ καὶ εἰς τ. ἀπείραστον

ἀδιαφορότης (?) : 857 ἀδιαφορότητα (MS. ἀϊδιότητα) ὧν λήψεται αἰτήσεται

ἄδικος : 861 ἀδ. εἰς ἑαυτόν

ἀδοξία : 870 κατεξανίσταται ἀδοξίας

ἀδούλωτος : 837 τὸ ἀδούλωτον τ. ψυχῆς πρὸς ἐκλογὴν βίου, 864 ἀδούλωτος ἐν φόβῳ

Ἀδράστεια : 840 αὕτη ἡ Ἀδρ. καθ' ἣν οὐκ ἔστι διαδρᾶναι τ. θεόν

Ἀδριανός : 898 περὶ τοὺς Ἀδρ. χρόνους

ᾄδω : (quot.) 842 ἀλεκτρυὼν ἄσῃ

ἀείμνηστος : 861 init. θεωρία ἀείμνηστος

ἄεργος : 849 ἄεργα ζῷα εἰς βρῶσιν

ἀήρ : 845 τ. ἀέρα κ. τὸ περιέχον ἄξιον ἡγησάμενοι τῆς τ. θεοῦ ὑπεροχῆς, 852 τὸ εὐπαθὲς τοῦ ἀ. : 850 συγγενὴς τῷ ἀέρι ἡ ψυχή, ib. ἀὴρ ἐγκέκραται τῷ ὕδατι, 844 Ἀήρ

ἀήττητος : c. dat. 870 ἀ. ἡδονῇ

ἀθανασία : 840 init. κρατεῖν τῆς ἀθ.

ἄθεος : 831 ἀθ. ὁ μὴ νομίζων εἶναι θεόν, 841 ἀθ. ὁ τοῖς κακίστοις τ. θεὸν ἀπεικάζων, cf. 19, 21, 864 οὐκ ἀθ. ὁ χριστιανός, 854 ἵνα μὴ ἐπὶ τῇ ἀθέῳ σοφίᾳ ὀγκύλλωνται

ἄθεσμος : 850 ἀθ. ἡ τοιαύτη σοφία πρὸς σύνεσιν

ἀθέως : 886 ἀθ. τ. αὐτὴν ἀρετὴν λέγουσιν ἀνθρώπων κ. θεοῦ

ἀθλητής : 839 ὁ τ. ἀληθῆ νίκην στεφανούμενος ἀθλ., 840 παγκρατιάζουσιν οἱ ἀθλ., 872 ἡ ἀγάπη γυμνάζει τὸν ἴδιον ἀθλητήν, 860 ἀθλ. τις εἰς Ὀλύμπι' ἀναβάς

ἆθλον : 871 ἑκόντες πείθονται οὐχὶ δὲ διὰ τὰ ἆθλα τῶν πόνων

ἆθλος : 839 fin. ἄθλους ἐπαρτᾷ ὁ πειράζων

ἄθροισμα : 846 τὸ ἀθρ. τ. ἐκλεκτῶν ἐκκλησίαν καλῶ, 848 τὸ ἀθρ. τῶν ταῖς εὐχαῖς ἀνακειμένων

ἀθρόος : 856 ἀθρ. ἕπεται τὰ ἀγαθά

ἀθρόως : 863 'all at once,' 958

ἀθυρόγλωσσος : 858 παρρησίαν ἔχει, οὐ τὴν ἁπλῶς οὕτως ἀθ. δύναμιν, 870 ὄχλος ἀθ., Eur. Or. 903

ἄθυρος : (quot) 866 ἀθ. χερσί

αἰδέομαι : 862 αἰδ. μὴ ἀληθεύειν, 891 αἰδ. καταθέσθαι τὸ πλεονέκτημα, 892

ἀΐδιος : see ἴδιος 879, and ἀϊδίως 835

ἀϊδιότης : 857 see ἀδιαφορότης

ἀϊδίως : 866 φῶς μένον ἀϊδίως, 835 ἔστιώνται θέαν ἀϊδίως ἀΐδιον, 873

Αἰθίοψ : (quot.) 841

αἰνέω : 851 γεωργοῦμεν αἰνοῦντες

αἴνιγμα : 877 τῆς νηστείας τὰ αἰν.

αἰνίσσομαι : 836, 883, 901 τὰ ἀπάγοντα μηρυκισμὸν τ. Ἰουδαίους αἰνίσσεται, 124 init. αἷμα ἡμῖν τὸν λόγον αἰνίττεται

αἶνος : 851 τὸ κατὰ τοὺς αἴνους συναγόμενον θυμίαμα, 860 θυσίαι αὐτῷ εὐχαί τε καὶ αἶνοι

αἵρεσις : (1) 'choice' 835 ἑκούσιος ἀνθρώπῳ ἡ αἵρεσις; (2) 'sect,' 'school' 854 ἡ Προδίκου, 886 αἱ περὶ τὴν ἄλλην διδασκαλίαν αἱρέσεις, 888 ἐν μόνῃ τῇ ἐκκλησίᾳ ἡ ἀρίστη αἵρ., ib. ἀπεσφάλησαν αἱ αἱρ., 887 init. μὴ δεῖν πιστεύειν διὰ τὴν διαφωνίαν τ. αἱρέσεων, ib. αἱ ἐν τῇ ἰατρικῇ αἱρ., ib. παρ' Ἕλλησι φιλοσόφων πάμπολλαι γεγόνασιν αἱρ., 889 ἡ ὀνομασία τῶν αἱρ., 890 αἱ αἱρέσεις παραπέμπονται τὰς γραφάς, 891, 892, 894 ἐν οἰήσει οἱ κατὰ τ. αἱρέσεις, 897 οἱ τὰς αἱρ. μετιόντες, 898 περὶ τοὺς Ἀδριανοῦ χρόνους οἱ τὰς αἱρ. ἐπινοήσαντες γεγόνασι, (list of) 900

αἱρετικός : 893 τοὺς αἱρ. κενοὺς τῶν τ. θεοῦ βουλευμάτων, 895

OF GREEK WORDS. 389

αἱρετός: 855 αἱρετὰ καὶ φευκτά, 872 ἡ ἀγάπη αὐτὴ δι' αὑτὴν αἱρετή
αἱρέω: 868 διὰ λόγοι αἱρεῖ (MB. ἐρεῖ), 874, 879 ἐὰν ὁ λ. αἱρῇ (MB. ἴρῃ), 890 ἀκολουθοῦντες τῷ αἱροῦντι λόγῳ (MB. ἐροῦντι), cf. 94 οὐ δὴ ἀμφιβάλλει ἐρεῖ (D. αἱρεῖ) ὁ λόγος: m., 893 αἱροῦνται τὸ δόξαν αὑτοῖς ἐναργέστερον ἢ τὸ πρὸς τοῦ κυρίου εἰρημένον, 884 αἱρεῖσθαι τὸν βουλόμενον ἀρετήν, 833 κοινὴ ἡ πίστις τ. ἑλομένων, ib. οἱ ἐλ. οἰκεῖοι εἶναι τῷ θείῳ λόγῳ, 840 ἐλεῖται ὁ δυνάμενος, ib. εἰ ἑλοίμεθα τὸ βούλεσθαι, 858 ἀρετὴν ἑλόμεναι ψυχαί
αἴσθησις: 852 ἡ ἀκοὴ διά τινος ψυχικῆς αἰσθήσεως ἔχει τ. ἀντίληψιν, ib. αἰσθήσεων οὐ δεῖ θεῷ, ib. ἐκθηλύνουσι δι' αἰσθήσεως τ. ψυχήν, 888 οἱ τὰς αἰσθήσεις ἀναιροῦντες
αἰσθητήριον: 889 κριτήρια τὰ αἰσθητήρια, 829 οἱ τ. αἰσθητήρια γεγυμνασμένοι (quot.), Sext. Emp. Math. VII. 350
αἰσθητικός: 831 fin. παιδεία δι' αἰσθητικῆς ἐνεργείας
αἰσθητός: 829 τὰ αἰσθητὰ ⋈ τὰ διδακτὰ and τὰ νοητά, 833 αἰσθητὴν ἀναλαβὼν σάρκα ὁ υἱός, 852 ἄνευ τ. αἰσθητῇ ἀκοῇ πάντα γινώσκει, 889 ὁ τοῖς αἰσθητοῖς προσανέχων βίος, 922 παρόντων τῶν αἰσθητῶν
αἴσθομαι: 882 c. part. αἰσθέται ἄξιοι γενόμενοι, 519 c. gen. αἰσθ. τῆς διακινήσεως καλῶς ἐχούσης, 4 ἀρετῆς αἰσθ., Ael. N. A. III. 2, Becker Anecd. Gr. 359. 6
αἰσχρός: 864 αἰσχρὸν ὅ ἐστιν ἀδικον
αἰσχύνη: (quot.) 847 αἰσχ. τὸ κατειπεῖν
αἰσχύνομαι: 882 οὐδ' αἰσχ. ταῖς ἐξουσίαις ὀφθῆναι
αἰτέω: 881 αἰτ.)(ἀπαιτέω, m. 881, 884, 876 τὰ ἀγαθὰ ἀξίοις κ. μὴ αἰτουμένοις δίδοται, cf. 855
αἴτησις: 853 τούτων αἱ εὐχαὶ ὧν αἰτήσεις κ. τούτων αἱ αἰτ. ὧν ἐπιθυμίαι, ib. αἴτησιν ποιεῖσθαι, 855 οὐ παρέλκει ἡ αἰτ., 876 ἐπιτυγχάνει κατὰ τὰς αἰτ.
αἰτητέον: 853
αἴτιον: 838 τὸ πρῶτον αἰτ., ib. τὸ δεύτερον αἰτ.
αἰφνίδιος: 898 αἰφνίδιον προσπεσεῖν τινα φαντασίαν
αἰχμαλωτίζω: 836 (quot.), c. 5
αἰών: 885 ἐξ αἰῶνος εἰς αἰῶνα, ib. ἀτελεύτητοι αἰῶνες, 879 εἰς αἰῶνα αἰώνοι
ἀκάθαρτος: 900 ἀκ. ζῷα, 844 init. ἀκ. καθαρμοί
ἀκαλαρρείτης: (quot.) 844
ἀκάματος: 831 ἀκ. καὶ ἄτρυτον δυνάμει
ἀκαμπής: 872 τὸ ἀκαμπὲς τῆς ἐγκρατείας εἰς τ. ἡδονάς, Theophr.

ἄκαρπος: 902 ἀκ. δένδρα
ἀκίβδηλος: 887 ἀκ. νόμισμα ἀπὸ τ. παραχαράγματος διακρίνειν (MB. κιβδήλου), 780
ἀκίνδυνος: 888 χρήσαιτο ἂν τῇ ἀκ. κ. βασιλικῇ κ. λεωφόρῳ (ὁδῷ)
ἀκλινής: 858 δικαστὴς ἀκλ.
ἀκμή: 869 ἐν ταῖς ἀκμαῖς τ. κολάσεων εὐχαριστεῖν
ἀκοή: 852 διὰ σωματικῶν πόρων ἐνεργεῖται ἡ ἀκοή, pl. 867 οὐ τὰς ἀκοὰς ἀλλὰ τ. ψυχὴν παρίστησι τοῖς πράγμασιν, Arist. Pol. III. 16. 12 δυοῖν ὄμμασιν κ. δυσὶν ἀκοαῖς κρίνων
ἀκολασία: pl. 837
ἀκολασταίνω: 851 μεθ' ἡμέραν ἀκ.
ἀκολουθέω: 892 ἀναγκαίως τέλος ἀκολουθεῖ, 890 ἀκ. τῷ αἱροῦντι λόγῳ, 893 ἄσκησις πρὸς τὸ ἀκολουθεῖν δύνασθαι
ἀκολουθητέον: 893 ἀκ. τινι
ἀκολουθία: 867 ἀκολουθίαν σώζειν, 550, 888 τ. ἀληθείας τ. ἀκολουθίαν ἐξευρίσκειν, 892 τῆς ἀκολουθίας τ. σφετέρων δογμάτων καταφρονοῦσι, 894 τ. ἀλήθειαν διὰ τῆς ἀκολουθίας τ. διαθηκῶν σαφηνίζων, 895, 896 init. οὐχ εὑρόντες τὴν ἀκ., Philo 2 p. 141 ἀκολουθία φύσεως, Clem. Hom. II. 8 ἀκ ὑποθέσεων
ἀκόλουθος: 846 οἰκεῖα τε κ. τὰ ἀκ. πάντα, 867 ἀκ. τῇ θεοσεβείᾳ, 896 λόγοι τῇ τ. κυρίου ἀκόλουθοι παραδόσει, 885 κατὰ τὸ ἀκόλουθον)(κατὰ τὸ προηγούμενον, 886 ἀκόλουθόν ἐστι πρὸς τὰ ἐγκλήματα ἀπολογήσασθαι, 888 διαστέλλειν τὸ μαχόμενον ἀπὸ τοῦ ἀκολούθου: (adv.) 882 ἀκόλουθα τῇ ἐπιστήμῃ (MB. ἀνακ.)
ἀκολούθως: 864 ἀκ. οὐδὲ ἀσεβεῖ, 875 ἀκ. οἷς ἐνετείλω ἐζήσαμεν, 868 ἀκολούθως ἄρα ἄτρεπτοι μένει, 895, 71 fin.
ἀκόρεστος: 835 ἀκ. θέα, ἀκ. εὐφροσύνη
ἀκούσιος: 868 ἀκ. περίστασις
ἀκουσίως: 859 τοῦδε ἡ ἐπιστήμη ἀναπόβλητος οὐκ ἀκ. ἀλλ' ἑκουσίως, 879 οἱ μετὰ τ. θάνατον ἀκ. ἐξομολογούμενοι
ἀκρασία: 837 ἀκρασίᾳ ἡδονῶν περιπίπτειν (?)
ἄκρατος: 879 ἀκ. πίστις
ἀκριβής: 850 σύνεσις ἀκρ., 888 ἡ ἀκριβεστάτη γνῶσις (bis)
ἀκριβῶς: 885 ἀκρ. εἰλικρινὴς θέα, 877 ἀκρ. πεπεισμένος, 887 ἀκρ. βιωτέον
ἀκροάομαι: 843 ὁ ἀκροώμενος = 'disciple'
ἄκρος: 814 διαδέξασθαι τ. ἄκραν οἰκονομίαν τ. παιδευτοῦ, 869 ἄκρας εὐεξίᾳ, 873 ἀκροτάτη δικαιοσύνη, 882 ἅπτεται τ. θρέψεων τ. ἄκρων, 888 ἐπιστήμη ἡ ἄκρα, 862 κατ' ἄκρον ἀληθείας βιοῦν, 869 ἐπ' ἄκρον γνώσεως ἥκειν, 864 τὰ ἄκρα οὐ διδάσκεται ἥ τε ἀρχὴ κ. τὸ τέλος, 847 (quot.) ἄκραν τὴν ὀφὺν

ἐναντία ἀπαντᾶν. 886 ἀμήχανον γενέσθαι τινα τέλεον ὡς θεός
ἀμίαντος: 860 ψυχὴ ἀμ.
ἀμνησικακέω: 886 ἀφιέντες κ. ἀμνησικακοῦντες, see μνησικακέω and n. on ἀμνησιπόνηροι 873
ἀμνησικακία: 884 ἐξομοιοῦσθαι θεῷ διὰ τ. ἀμνησικακίας, ib. ἡ κατὰ τὸ εὐαγγέλιον ἀμν., 885 ὁμοιοῦσθαι τ. ἀγαθότητι τ. θεοῦ διὰ τῆς ἀμν., cf. 474 fin.
ἀμνησίκακος: 883, 884
ἀμνησιπόνηρος: 873 (MS. μισοπόνηροι), ἅπ. λεγ.
ἀμοιβή: 840 ἀμ. κυριωτάτη παρὰ ἀνθρώπων, ib. ὅλην ἀποδιδόναι ἀμοιβὴν 'reward,' opp. to κόλασις 802, 866 ἡ κατὰ τ. θεοσέβειαν ἀμ., 883 τ. γνῶσιν ἀναδεξάμενος πρόεισιν ἐπὶ τ. ἁγίαν τῆς μεταθέσεως ἀμοιβήν
ἀμπελών: 876 ὁ τ. κυρίου ἀμπελών, 878 ἕκαστος αὐτοῦ τε ἀμπ. κ. ἐργάτης
ἀμυγδάλη: 893 ἀμυγδάλαι κεναί, ib. τοὺς αἱρετικοὺς πικρίζονται κατὰ τὴν ἀγρίαν ἀμυγδάλην
ἀμυδρός: 885 ἀμ. διορᾶν
ἀμύητος: 901 μὴ ῥᾴδιον εἶναι τὴν τ. παραδόσεων εὕρεσιν τ. ἀμυήτοις, 936 ἀμ. τῆς ἀληθείας, Philo
ἀμφί: 854 οἱ ἀμφὶ τὴν τ. Προδίκου αἵρεσιν
ἀμφιβόλως: 891 τὰ ἀμφ. εἰρημένα
ἀμφιέννυμι: 880 ἀμφιεννύμενοι κ. ἀποδυόμενοι
ἄν see Appendix B
ἀναγεννάω: 889 τ. πατέρα τ. ἀναγεννῶντα καὶ ἀνακτίζοντα, 948
ἀναγκαῖος: 892 ἀν. ἀρχαὶ πραγμάτων καταβάλλεσθαι, 868 (necessariis) συμπεριφέρεται τ. ἀναγκαίοις αὐτοῦ, 878 κατὰ τὸ ἀναγκαῖον τ. βίον, 858 οὐδὲν ἐπιζητεῖ εἰς τ. ἀναγκαίαν χρῆσιν, 885 αἱ ἀναγκ. παιδεύσεις
ἀναγκαίως: 892 ἀν. τέλος ἀκολουθεῖν ἐκπορισθόμενοι, 876 ἐσθίει οὐ προηγουμένως, ἀλλ' ἀναγκαίως
ἀνάγκη: 837 κακῶν αἰτία αἱ ἄλογοι δι' ἀμαθίαν ἀνάγκαι, 868 εἰδὼς τὰ τοιαῦτα (disease, &c.) κτίσεως ἀνάγκην εἶναι, 877 ἐπεγκυλίεται τῇ τοῦ βίου ἀνάγκῃ, ib. τῷδε τ. βίῳ ὅσον ἐν ἀνάγκῃ συγχρῆται μοίρᾳ
ἀνάγνωσις: 861 ἀναγνώσει χρώμενοι
ἀνάγω: 'exalt,' 859 τὸ διὰ τ. πίστεως ἀναγόμενον, 864 ἀπὸ τ. πίστεως ἀναγόμενον, 868 ἀνάγων ἑαυτὸν ἐπὶ τὰ οἰκεῖα, 85 εἰς οὐρανὸν ἀνάγει ἡ ἀλήθεια, 431 ἀνάγει ἡ τούτων μάθησις ἐπὶ τ. ἡγεμόνα, 239 ἀνάγονται οἱ πορφυρευταὶ κ. αὐτὰ τ. κογχύλια · 'to refer,' 862 τὴν ἀπόλαυσιν ἐπὶ τ. θεὸν ἀνάγειν. 901 ἀνάγειν μηρυκισμὸν bis
ἀναδέχομαι: 830 τ. καρποὺς τῶν πιστευ-

σάντων εἰς ἑαυτὴν ἀναδέχεται, 831, 862 τὴν οἰκονομίαν ἀναδ., 871 εὐφαρῶς τὰς ἀναδέχεται, 846 ἀναδ. ἐπιστήμην, 840 ὁ σωτὴρ ἀναδ. τὰς ὠφελείας ὡς ἰδίας χάριν, 863 τὸ τ. γνώσεως μέγεθος ἀναδ.
ἀνάδοσις: 'nutrition,' 850 πλείστη ἀνάδοσις ἐκ χοιρείων κρεῶν, 163 εἰς τὰς ἀναδόσεις χρησιμεύει, Cleanthes Fr. 55 Pearson
ἀνάθημα: 886 οὐδὲ ἀναθήμασι κηλεῖται τ. θεῖον, 858 καθάπερ ἀναθήματα (MS. μαθήματα) τινα παρακείμενα
ἀναθυμίασις: 836 ἡ διὰ τ. καπνοῦ ἀναθ. 846 τὰ φωλεύοντα θηρία ἐξ αὐτῆς τῆς τ. οἰκείου σώματος ἀναθυμιάσεως τρέφομεν, 184 αἱ ἐκ τ. οἴνου ἀναθ.
ἀναθυμιάω: m. 846 ἡ θυσία ἐστὶ λόγος ἀπὸ τ. ἁγίων ψυχῶν ἀναθυμιώμενος
ἀναιρέω: 836 ἑαυτοὺς ἀναιρεῖν τ. παλαιὸν ἄνθρωπον ἀποκτιννύντες, ib. τὸν ἁμαρτωλὸν ἀναιρεῖσθαι κελεύει ὁ νόμος, 883 ἀναιροῦσιν ἀπόδειξιν αἰσθήσεις
ἀναίτιος: (quot.) 835 κακίας ἂν ὁ θεός, 731 αἴτια ἑλομένου, θεὸς ἀν., Eus. Praep. Ev. vii 22 §§ 21, 37
ἀνάκειμαι: 843 τ. γραφαὶ δεδόασι τ. ἀνακειμέναι, 846 ἄγαλμα ἀνακείμενον θεῷ, 848 θυσιαστήριον ἐνταῦθα τὸ ἄθροισμα τῶν τ. εὐχαῖς ἀνακειμένων
ἀνακεράννυμι: 835 τῷ πνεύματι τῷ ἁγίῳ ἀνεκράθητε
ἀνακεφαλαιόω: 897 (quot.)
ἀνακόλουθος: 882 adv. μετατεθεὶς ἀνακόλουθα τῇ ἐπιστήμῃ, see ἀκόλουθος
ἀνακομιδή: 869 ἡ εἰς οἶκον ἀνακ., Polyb.
ἀνάκρασις: 830 διὰ καθαρότητα κατὰ ἀνάκρασιν ἔχει τ. δύναμιν τ. θεοῦ, 626 τὸ ἀεὶ νοεῖν οὐσία τ. γινώσκοντος κατ' ἀνακρ. ἀδιάστατον γενόμενα, see ἀνακεράννυμι
ἀνακτίζω: 889 ὁ ἀνακτίζων πατήρ
ἀναλαμπίζω: 890 ἀν. τ. παραδόσεις
ἀναλαμβάνω: 832 ἀναλαβὼν τὴν ἐμπαθῆ σάρκα bis, 833, 868, 836 ἀναληφθεὶς εἰς ἁγιωσύνην, 844 τὰ τ. περικαθαρθέντος κακὰ ἀν., 862 τ. προστασίαν ἀναλαβών, Eus. Pr. Ev. vii. 8. 312 b ἐν τοῖς θεοφιλέσι ἀνείληπται
ἀναλίσκω: 847 αὐτοὶ τὰ ἄλλα ἀναλ.
ἀναλλοίωτος: 838 τὰ βέβαια κ. ἀναλλοίωτα
ἀναλόγως: 835 ἀν. τοῖς ἑαυτῶν ἤθεσι διοικεῖται τὰ μικρότερα
ἀναμανθάνω: 828 ἀναμ. οἷός ἐστι ὁ Χριστιανὸς (elsewhere only in Herod.)
ἀναμάρτητος: 836 ἀν. γινόμενος, 864 τὸ ἀναμάρτητον κατορθῶν, 880 ἀναμ. μένει, ἐγκρατὴς δὲ γίνεται, see Potter on Paed. 1. § 4
ἀναμένω: 853 φωνὴν ἀναμεῖναι, 856

τὰς πολυφώνους γλώσσας οὐκ ἀναμένει ὁ θεός, 891 οὐ τὴν ἐξ ἀνθρώπων ἀναμένομεν μαρτυρίαν
ἀναμίγνυμι: 902 ἀναμεμιγμένη φυτεία καρποφόρων κ. ἀκάρπων δένδρων
ἀνάμνησις: 886 τὸ μυστήριον ἐμφαίνειν ὅσον εἰς ἀνάμνησιν
ἀνάξιος: 855 ἀναξίους οὐκ ἂν δοίη, 862 ἀνάξιον τὸ ψεύδεσθαι
ἀνάπαυσις: 845 ὁ κορυφαῖος τῆς ἀναπαύσεως τόπος, 115 τελείωσις ἐπαγγελίας ἡ ἀναπ., πέρας γνώσεως, 873 ἐν πνευματικῇ τῇ ἐκκλησίᾳ μένει [εἰς] τὴν ἀνάπαυσιν τ. θεοῦ, 839 ἡ αἰώνιος ἀν.
ἀναπαύω: p. 883 οὐκ ἐπιθυμήσει ἑτέρου ὁ ἔχων ἀναπαυόμενον τ. θεόν, 883 ἀναπεπαῦσθαι νομίζοντες
ἀναπεμπάζομαι: 901 τὰ λόγια τ. θεοῦ ἀναπεμπάζονται
ἀναπέμπω: 848 θυσίαν ἀρίστην ἀναπέμπομεν, 311 αἶνον ἀναπέμψαι κυρίῳ, 896 τὰς ἀποδείξεις ἀνευρίσκειν ἀναπεμπόμενοι (? παραπ.) ὑπὸ τ. κυρίου ἀπό τε νόμου κ. προφητῶν, 140 τιμωρία ἐστὶν ἀνταπόδοσις κακοῦ ἐπὶ τὸ τοῦ τιμωροῦντος συμφέρον ἀναπεμπομένη
ἀναπετάννυμι: 897 τὴν αὔλειαν ἀναπετάσαντες
ἀναπλάττω: 841 τὰς ψυχὰς τ. θεῶν ὁμοίας ἑκάσταις ἑαυτοῖς (MB. ὁμοιοῦσιν καὶ τοῖς αὑτοῖς) ἀναπλάττουσι
ἀναπλήρωσις: 886 εἰς ἀναπλ. τῆς περικοπῆς
ἀναπνέω: 848 ὅσα ἀναπνεῖ κατὰ τὴν τ. πνεύμονος ἀντιδιαστολήν, 850 τὰ πτηνὰ ἀναπνεῖ τὸν αὐτὸν ἀέρα τ. ἡμετέραις ψυχαῖς, ib. τοὺς ἰχθῦς οὐδὲ ἀναπνεῖν τοῦτον κ. ἀέρα, trop. 829 τὰ λεγόμενα ἐκεῖθεν ἀναπνεῖ κ. ζῇ, 950 θεὸν ἀναπνεῖ
ἀναπνοή: defined 848
ἀναπόβλητος: 859 ἀναπ. τὴν ἀρετὴν ἀσκήσει πεποιημένος quinquies
ἀναπόδεικτος: 891 πίστει περιλαβόντες ἀναπόδεικτον τ. ἀρχήν
ἀναπολόγητος: 888 ἀναπ. ἡ κρίσις, 834 ἀναπολόγητός ἐστι πᾶς ὁ μὴ πιστεύσας
ἀνάπτω: 875 τὸ οἰκεῖον ἀν. φῶς
ἀναρτάω: 870 πάντα εἰς ἑαυτὸν ἀνῆρτηται
ἄναρχος: 829 ἄναρχος ἀρχή τε κ. ἀπαρχὴ ὁ υἱός, 733, 638, 791 ἄναρχος πρόθεσις
ἀνάρχως: 832 ἀπαθὴς ἀνάρχως γενόμενος ὁ κύριος
ἀνάστασις: 877 τὴν ἐν αὐτῷ τ. κυρίου ἀνάστασιν δοξάζων
ἀναστρέφομαι: 838 περὶ τὰ βέβαια ἀναστρ., 852 ἐνθέως (MB. ἐντέχνως) ἀναστρεφόμεθα
ἀνατέλλω: 856 ἀνέτειλεν γνώσεως ἀληθείας ἡμέρα

ἀνατέμνω: 897 παράθυρον ἀνατεμών
ἀνατολή: 886 γενεθλίου ἡμέρας εἰσὶν ἡ ἀν., ib. πρὸς τ. ἑωθινὴν ἀνατολὴν αἱ εὐχαί
ἀνατρέπω: 891 ἀνατρέψουσι πᾶσαν ἀληθῆ διδασκαλίαν, 892 ἀνατρέπονται πρὸς ἡμῶν δεικνύντων αὐτοὺς ἐναντιουμένους
ἀναφαίνομαι: 838 ἀνὴρ τῷ ὄντι ἀναφ., 835 ὅταν ὁ παντοκράτωρ ἀγαθὸς ἀναφαίνηται
ἀναφέρω: 862 ἡ εὐεργεσία εἰς τὸν κύριον ἀναφέρεται
ἀναφορά: 833 ἡ τ. κυρίου ἐνέργεια ἐπὶ τ. παντοκράτορα τ. ἀναφορὰν ἔχει, 863 τ. σίδηρον Ἄρῳ προσαγορεύουσι κατά τινα ἀναφοράν
ἀναχάζομαι: 863 (so P. for MB. ἀναπάζεται), Numen. ap. Eus. Pr. Ev. XIV. 8. 3 οἱ ἀναχάζοντες θῆρες βιαιότερον ἑαυτοὺς ἱεῖσιν εἰς τὰς αἰχμάς
ἀνδρεία: forms of, 838, 867, 871
ἀνδρίζομαι: 867 μὴ ἐκ λογισμοῦ ἀνδρίζεται, 264 γυναῖκες ἀνδρίζονται
ἀνδρικός: 876 ἀνδρ. ὑπομονή
ἀνειμένος: (quot.) 851 ἀν. εὐπειστος
ἀνενδεής: 836 ὁ θεὸς ἀνενδ., ib. σφᾶς αὐτοὺς ἱερεύοντες εἰς τὸ ἀνενδεὲς ἐκ τοῦ ἀνενδεοῦς, 848 εἰ ἀνενδεῶς τρέφεται ὁ θεός, τίς χρεία τροφῆς τῷ ἀνενδεεῖ; 857 αὐτάρκης κ. ἀνενδεής, 859 τὸ ἀνενδεὲς (MB. ἐνδεές) κ. ἐπιδεές, ib. ὁ ἀνενδεοῦς μετέχων ἀνενδεὴς ἄν ᾖν, Philo
ἀνενδεῶς: 848 see ἀνενδεής
ἀνεξικακία: 885 ὁμοιοῦται (τῷ θεῷ) διά τε τ. ἀνεξικακίας διά τε τ. ἀμνησικακίας
ἀνεξίκακος: 858
ἀνεπιθύμητος: 875 εἷς ὁ ἀν. ἐξ ἀρχῆς, ὁ κύριος)(ἀνεπιθύμητος ἐξ ἀσκήσεως
ἀνεπιλήπτως: 830 θεοσεβὴς ὁ ἀνεπιλήπτως ἐξυπηρετῶν τῷ θεῷ, 860 ὁ γνωστικὸς πάντα ἀνεπ. ἐκπεπληρωκώς, 886 βούλεται ὁ θεὸς ἡμᾶς ἀν. τελείους γίνεσθαι, Philo
ἀνεπισημειώτος: 883 ὡς μὴ ἀνεπισημείωτον παραλιπεῖν τ. τόπον
ἀνεπιστήμων: 857 ἀν. τῆς χρήσεως, 867 πᾶσα ἡ διὰ τοῦ ἀνεπιστήμονος πρᾶξις κακοπραγία
ἀνεπιστροφία: 840 κυρίου ἐστὶν ἀν. ἡ περὶ τοὺς καθωσιωμένους αὐτῷ κάκωσις, only found elsewhere in Epict.
ἄνευ: 885 οἷον ἀσάρκῳ ἤδη κ. ἄνευ (S. ἄνω) τῆσδε γῆς ἁγίῳ γεγονότι, 888 πάντες ἄνευ τῶν τ. αἰσθήσεις ἀναιρούντων, 849
ἀντυρίσκω: 896 ἀν. ἀποδείξεις
ἀνέχομαι: 895 οὐδὲ ἀκοῦσαι ἀνέχονται τῶν προτρεπόντων
ἀνηδόνως: 874 see ἀλυπήτως

ἀνήκω: 860 τῶν πρὸς ἡμᾶς ἀνηκόντων αἱρέσεις, Ign.

ἀνήρ: (emphatic) 838 ἀνὴρ τῷ ὅτι ἐν τοῖς ἄλλοις ἀνθρώποις, 871 τ. ἄνδρα ἐν τ. λογικῇ ἀνδρείᾳ ἐξετάζεσθαι, 874 ἀνὴρ δείκνυται (cf. W. Headlam in C R. for 1901, pp. 898 foll.), ib. οὐδέπω ἄνδρες γεγονότες, 874 ἀνδρας νικᾷ 'wins in the contest of men'

ἀνθρώπινος: 852 τὰ ἀνθρ. ἀγαθά

ἀνθρωπικός: 889 τέχναι ἀνθρ.

ἀνθρώπινος: 890 αἱρέσεις ἀνθρ., 898 ἀνθρ. συνηλύσεις)(ἡ καθολικὴ ἐκκλησία

ἀνθρωποειδής: 846 init. εἰ ἀνθρ. τὸ θεῖον, τῶν ἴσων δεήσεται τ. ἀνθρώπῳ, 852 οὔκουν ἀνθρ. ὁ θεός

ἀνθρωπόμορφος: 841 θεοὶ ἀνθρ. κ. ἀνθρωποπαθεῖς

ἀνθρωποπαθής: 841, Orig. c. Cels. 1. 16 fin., Eus. Pr. Ev. III. 3 fin.

ἄνθρωπος: (emphatic) 830, 843 init. ὁ τῷ ὄντι ἀνθρ. δημιουργεῖ κατ' εἰκόνα τ. κυρίου, 836 (quot.) ἀνθρ. παλαιός, 890 ἀνθρ. θεοῦ, ib. ἐξ ἀνθρώπου θηρίον, ἐξ ἀνθρώπου θεός

ἀνθρωπότης: 882 σώζειν βούλεται τὴν ἀνθρωπότητα ὁ κύριος, 101 bis

ἀνίατος: 895 μεταπεῖσαι τοὺς μὴ πανταπασιν ἀνιάτους

ἀνιδιότης: 857 suggested for αἰδιότης

ἀνίδρυτος: 845 τὸ ἱδρυμένον ὑπό τινος ἵδρυται πρότερον ἀνίδρυτον ὄν, εἴπερ οὖν ὁ θεὸς ἱδρύεται πῶς ἀνθρώπων, ἀνίδρυτός ποτε ἦν καὶ οὐδ' ὅλως ἦν, &c.

ἀνίστημι: tr. 836 τ. καινὸν ἄνθρωπον ἀν.; intr. 880 πρωίας ἀναστάς

ἀνοίγω: 854 μηδὲ τ. χείλη ἀν., 899 fin. πᾶσα αἵρεσις ὦτα ἔχει μόνον τοῖς πρὸς ἡδονὴν ἀνεῳγότα

ἄνομος: ἀν.)(ἔννομος 884

ἀνορέκτως: 848 ὅμοιος φυτῷ, ἀνορέκτως τρεφόμενος

ἀνορύσσω: 849 χοῖροι ἀν. καρπούς

ἀνόσιος: 854 ἀν. γνῶσις

ἀνταγώνισμα: 839 περιγινόμενοι τ. μεγάλων ἀνταγωνισμάτων (rare)

ἀνταδικέω: 883 ἀνταδικῆσαι ἐθέλειν, see ἀντιδικέω

ἀνταναπληρόω: 878 ὁ γνωστικὸς τ. ἀποστολικὴν ἀπουσίαν ἀνταναπληροῖ

ἀντάξιος: 848 τὸ περὶ πολλοῦ ἄξιον ζῴον τῷ τ. παντὸς ἀξίῳ, μᾶλλον δὲ οὐδενὸς ἀντάξιος, καθίδρυται, 958 ὑπὲρ ἡμῶν κατέθηκε τ. ψυχὴν τ. ἀντάξιαν τῶν ὅλων

ἀνταποδίδωμι: 888 ἀνταποδοῦναι βούλεται, 884

ἀνταπόδοσις: 895 ἡ τιμωρία κακοῦ ἀνταπόδοσίς ἐστι

ἀνταποφαίνω: 891 ἀποφαινομένοις ἀνθρώποις οὐ προσέχομεν ἄν, οἷς κ. ἀνταποφαίνεσθαι ἐπ' ἴσης ἔξεστιν

ἀντεπιστροφή: 855 ἀντ. τίς ἐστι τ. προνοίας ἡ τ. γνωστικοῦ ὁσιότης κ. ἀντίστροφος εὔνοια

ἀντέχομαι: 879 μόνης τῆς τ. κυρίου ἀντέχεσθαι θεραπείας, 859 τ. εὐλογιστίας ἀντ., 897 τ. ἀληθείας ἀντ.

ἀντιδιαστολή: 843 ἡ τοῦ πνεύματος πρὸς τὸν θώρακα ἀντ., 889 τῶν αἱρέσεων ἡ ὀνομασία λέγεται πρὸς ἀντιδιαστολὴν τῆς ἀληθείας, 109 ὁ λαὸς ὁ καινὸς πρὸς ἀντιδ. τοῦ πρεσβυτέρου λαοῦ, 331, 545, 551

ἀντιδικέω: 885 ἀδικεῖ ὁ ἀντιδικῶν (? ἀνταδικῶν)

ἀντίκειμαι: 875 αἱ ἀντικείμεναι ἡδοναί, 873 θεὸς οὐδενὶ ἀντίκειται

ἀντικαλέω: 897 ἀντικλ. ψευδής τις κλῆσις (rare)

ἄντικρυς 832 ἀντ. παριστᾶσι, 841 ἐν παντὶ τόπῳ, οὐκ ἄντικρυς δὲ οὐδὲ ἐν φανῷ τοῖς πολλοῖς εὔξεται, 892 ἄντικρυς ὁμολογεῖν αἰδούμενοι, 882 ἀντ. ἀλλότριον τ. ἁμαρτίαν λέγει, 883, 897 Philo i. 688 ἀντ. θεοῦ = coram

Ἄντικυρα: 844 (quot.)

ἀντιλαμβάνω: 838 κακοδοξίας τῆς ἐκ τ. πολλῶν οὐκ ἀντιλαμβάνεται ὁ γνωστικός, 852 μὴ δύνασθαι ἑτέρως ἀντιλαβέσθαι (ἢ διὰ τ. αἰσθήσεων)

ἀντιλέγω: 894 πρὸς τὸ ἀντιλέγειν τῷ ἤθει τ. ψυχὴν γυμναστέον, 891 ὑπὸ τ. ἀντιλεγόντων ἐλεγχόμενοι

ἀντίληψις: 852 ἡ ἀκοὴ οὐ διὰ τ. σώματος δυνάμεως ἔχει τ. ἀντίληψιν

ἀντιπρόσωπος: see ἀπαντιπρόσωπος

ἀντίρρησις: 854 ἀντιρρήσεως τεύξεται ἡ ἀνόσιος γνῶσις

ἀντιστρατεύομαι: 858 ἐγκρατὴς τῶν ἀντιστρατευομένων τῷ νῷ

ἀντίστροφος: 855 ἀντ. εὔνοια τοῦ φίλου τ. θεοῦ

ἀντιτάσσω: m. 838 ἀντ. πρὸς τὰς τὸ ψυχαγωγοῦν

Ἀντωνῖνος: 898 μέχρι Ἀντ. διέτειναν αἱ αἱρέσεις

ἄνω: 877 πορείας τρεῖς τὰς ἀνωτάτω διαφορὰς παρεστήσαμεν: c. gen., 883 ἄνω (MS. ἄνευ) τῆς γῆς

ἄνωθεν 888 ἀπὸ μιᾶς ἀν. ἀρχῆς, 834 νόμος ἀν. οὗτος, 869 θεόθεν ἄνωθεν, 459 ἀν. ἀρχῆθεν προσιέναι

ἀνωμαλία: 878 αἱ τ. ψυχῆς ἀνωμαλίαι

ἀξία: 846 εἰς παραδοχὴν μεγέθους ἀξίας (S. ἀξίαν) τ. θεοῦ, cf. Chrys. Hom. in Matt. VII. p. 89 F. οὐδαμοῦ περὶ τῆς ἀξίας αὐτοῦ διαλέγονται οἱ προφῆται τοσοῦτον ὅσον περὶ τῆς εὐεργεσίας: 858 τὸ μέγεθος τ. ἀρετῆς κατ' ἀξίαν ἐνδεικνύμενος, 879 ἡ κατ' ἀξίαν ὑπεροχή, 829, 840, 882 πρὸς ἀξίαν τ. χάριτος ἐνδεικνύμενος τ. ἐνεργήματα, 886 κατ' ἀξίαν τ. ἐντολῆς πολιτευσόμεθα, 878 κατ' ἀξίαν διακριτική

ἀξιόλογος: μήτε διὰ χάριν μήτε διὰ φόβον ἀξιολόγων (MS. ἀξιολόγωι)
ἀξιόπιστος: 862 ἀξ. βίος, ib. ἀξ. διδάσκαλος, 890 ὁ πιστὸς τ. κυριακῇ φωνῇ ἀξιόπιστος
ἄξιος: 846 τὸ περὶ πολλοῦ ἀξ. τῷ τοῦ παντὸς ἀξίῳ καθιέρωται
ἀξιόω: 847 p. τῆς ἴσης εὐδαιμονίας ἀξιοῦνται
ἀξίωμα: 862 τὸ γνωστικὸν ἀξ., 865 τὸ τ. ἀγάπης ἀξ.
ἀξίωσις: 855 οὐ παρέλκει ἡ αἴτησις κἂν χωρὶς ἀξιώσεως διδῶται τὰ ἀγαθά
ἄοικος: 874 τῷ ἀοίκῳ τὰ πολλὰ εἶναι συμβέβηκεν ἀπειράστῳ
ἀόρατος: 877 τὰ μέλλοντα κ. ἀόρατα
ἀόριστος: ('unlimited') 857 διὰ τ. ἀορίστου ἀγάπης ἥνωται τ. πνεύματι
ἀπάγω: 875 init. ἀπὸ τῶν παθῶν ἀπ. (MS. ἐπείγων) τ. ψυχήν, see ἐπείγω
ἀπάθεια: 832 τ. σάρκα τ. ἐμπαθῆ φύσει ἀναλαβὼν εἰς ἕξιν ἀπαθείας ἐπαίδευσεν, 834, 886, 836 τὸ ἐξ ἀσκήσεως εἰς ἀπ. συνεσταλμένον, ib. ἡ ἐκ πίστεως ἀπάθεια, 883 ἡ κατὰ τ. γνωστικὸν ἀπάθεια
ἀπαθής: 832 ὁ κύριος ἀπ. ἀνάρχως γενόμενος, 836 ὁ φύσει τὸ ἀπαθὲς κεκτημένος, ib. σφᾶς αὐτοὺς ἱερεύοντες εἰς τὸ ἀπαθὲς ἐκ τοῦ ἀπαθοῦς, 872 ἀπ. ταῖς ἡδοναῖς τε κ. λύπαις ἀτεγκτος bis, 884, 886, see Potter on Paed. 1. § 4
ἀπαίδευτος: 837 ἀπ. ἀδικία
ἀπαιτέω: p. 860 ταῦτα ἀπαιτεῖται παρ' ἡμῶν τὰ ἐφ' ἡμῖν, 862 οὐδὲ ὄμνυσιν ὅρκον ἀπαιτηθείς: act. 875 τὰς ὑποσχέσεις ἀπ., 876 ἀπαιτεῖ τ. μισθὸν ὡς ἐργάτης ἀγαθός, 881 ὁ τοιοῦτος ἀπαιτεῖ παρὰ κυρίου [οὐχὶ δὲ καὶ αἰτεῖ]
ἀπαλγέω: 835 διὰ τ. κρίσεως τοὺς ἀπηλγηκότας ἐκβιάζονται μετανοεῖν, 854 τ. ἐπιστροφὴν τ. δικαιοσύνης τεχναζόμενος τοῖς ἀπηλγηκόσιν, 142 τ. ἀπηλγηκυῖαν ψυχήν
ἀπανδρόω: 886 ἡ μονὴ ἡ ὀφειλομένη τῷ οὕτως ἀπηνδρωμένῳ, 974 τὰ θηλυκὰ ἀπανδρωθέντα ἑνοῦται τοῖς ἀγγέλοις, 347 νήπιοι καὶ οἱ φιλόσοφοι ἐὰν μὴ ὑπὸ τ. Χριστοῦ ἀπανδρωθῶσιν, 118
ἀπανθίζομαι: 891 ὀλίγας ἀπανθ. φωνάς, 528 λέξεις ἀπ.
ἀπαντάω: 852 σπανίως εἰς τ. ἑστιάσεις τ. συμποτικὰς ἀπαντῶν, 870 ἀμήχανον ἅμα τῷ αὐτῷ τὰ ἐναντία ἀπαντᾶν (occurrere)
ἀπαντιπρόσωπος: 857 ἀπαντιπρόσωποι (MS. ἄπαν τι πρόσωπον) τῶν ἀγαλμάτων ἱστάμενοι (ἅπ. λεγ.), H. J. reads ἀπ' ἀντιπροσώπου
ἀπαξαπλῶς: 856 ἀπ. ἁπάντων γνωρίζει τ. νοήσεις
ἀπαραλόγιστος: 840 ἀπ. ἡ τ. θεοῦ ψῆφος

ἀπαρχή: 829 ἡ ἄχρονος ἀρχή τε κ. ἀπαρχὴ ὁ υἱός, 851 (quot.) θεοὺς χαίρειν ἀπαρχαῖς (MS. ἀπάντας)
ἀπάρχω: 852 m. τῷ δοτῆρι τ. ὅλων ἀπάρχεται
ἅπας: 829 ἅπαν τὸ ὑπερέχον
ἀπατάω: 888 ἑαυτοὺς ἀπατῶσιν, 895 οὔτε ἀπατηθεὶς τ. γνώμην δύναιτ' ἂν εὖ πράττειν
ἀπάτη: 838 τὸ μετὰ βίας ἢ μετὰ ἀπάτης ψυχαγωγοῦν, 890 ἐκ τ. ἀπάτης παλινδρομεῖν
ἀπαυδάω: 837 πρὸς τὰς συμφορὰς ἀπ. ('to lose heart at'), 594 init. οὐδ' ἀπαυδήσει ἡ γυνὴ κακῷ συνοικοῦσα ἀνδρί
ἀπείθεια: 895 ἡ ἀπηνὴς ἀπείθεια
ἀπειθέω: 833 τῶν ἀπειθησάντων κύριος
ἀπειθής: 873 θεῷ ἐχθροὶ οἱ ἀπ.
ἀπεικάζω: 841 τοῖς κακίστοις ἀνθρώποις τ. θεῖον ἀπ., 848
ἀπεικονίζω: 846 θεὸς οὐκ ἀπεικονίζεται ζῴου σχήματι, 41, Plato, Philo
ἀπεικόνισμα: 846 τ. θεῖον ἀπεικόνισμα ἐν δικαίᾳ ψυχῇ, Philo
ἀπεικότως: 848 οὐκ ἀπ. τιμῶμεν τ. θεόν
ἀπειλέω: pass. 837 φόβος ἀπ.: m. 142 fin. ὁ λόγος ἐλέγχων, ἀπειλούμενος
ἄπειμι: 857, 859
ἀπείραστος: 858 αὐστηρὸς οὐκ εἰς τὸ ἀδιάφθορον μόνον ἀλλὰ κ. εἰς τ. ἀπείραστον, 874 ὁ ἄοικος ἀπ.
ἄπειρος: 'infinite' 869 ἀπ. ὅσοι ἡμῖν λογιζομένοις ἄγγελοι: 'inexperienced' 894 κατεπᾴδουσι τ. ψοφοδεεῖς τῶν ἀπείρων
ἀπεκδοχή: 882 πίστιν ἐλπίδι κερώνας πρὸς τὴν τ. μέλλοντος ἀπεκδ. (rare)
ἀπεργάζομαι: 850 σῶμα ῥωμαλέον ἀπεργάζονται
ἀπερίληπτος: 845 ἐν τόπῳ περιγράφειν τὸν ἀπερίληπτον
ἀπερίσπαστος: 856 ἡ ἀπ. πρὸς τ. θεὸν ἐπιστροφή, 869 ἀπ. τῆς πρὸς τ. κύριον ἀγάπης, Epict. Diss. 3. 22. 69
ἀπερισπάστως: 836 ἀπ. συνὼν τῷ κυρίῳ
ἀπεχθάνομαι: 881 ἀπεχθάνεσθαι αὐτοῖς
ἀπέχω: m. 875 παρθένοι κακῶν ἀπεσχημέναι, 877 μέγιστον ἐν πείρᾳ γενόμενον εἶτα ἀποσχέσθαι, 887 ἀφεξόμεθα τῆς ἀληθείας, 888. 850 ἀσκήσεως χάριν ἀπόσχωνται ὦ, 874 init., 881 ἀπ. ἀπὸ πάσης πονηρίας
ἀπηνής: 895 ἀπείθεια ἀπ., 868 ἀπηνέστερον μεταρρυθμιζόμενοι
ἀπιστέω: 849 init. ἀπ. ἡμῖν, 892 ἀπ. ταῖς γραφαῖς, 87 ἀπ. ἡμᾶς μαθητὰς γενομένους
ἀπιστία: 834 τὴν ἀπ. συνέκλεισεν εἰς τ. παρουσίαν
ἄπιστος: 837 τὸ ἄγριον κ. ἄπιστον, 861 ὁ ἅπαξ πιστὸς πῶς ἂν ἑαυτὸν ἀπ. παρέχοι;

OF GREEK WORDS. 395

ἀπληστία: 834 ἀπλ. ἄδικος
ἁπλῶς: 858 ἁ. οὕτως
ἀποβάλλω: 877 ἀποβ. φαῦλον νόημα, 859 τὸ μὴ ἀποβληθέν (ΜΒ. ἀποβληθῆναι) δι' εὐλαβείας ἀναπόβλητον γίνεται. 878 τὰς τ. ψυχῆς ἀνωμαλίας ἀποβάλλων
ἀπογεύω: m. 891 ἀπογευσάμενοι μόνον τ. γραφῶν
ἀπογράφω: m. 779 ἀπὸ τῶν ἀρχετύπων τὴν διοίκησιν ἀπογρ., act. 838 οἷον ἀπογράφοντες (Η. ὑπογρ.) τ. γνωστικόν, p. 954 θεοῦ ἀπογεγραμμένος μαθητής, 157 ὁ ἀπογεγραμμένος Χριστῷ αὐτάρκη ἐπαναιρεῖται βίον
ἀποδείκνυμι: 891 ἀπ' αὐτῶν περὶ αὐτῶν τ. γραφῶν ἀποδείκνυμεν
ἀποδεικτικός: 888 διὰ τ. γραφῶν ἐκμανθάνειν ἀπ., 891 ἐκ πίστεως πειθόμεθα ἀπ.
ἀπόδειξις: 865 ἡ γνῶσις ἀπόδ. ἰσχυρὰ ἐποικοδομουμένη τ. πίστει, 888 πότερον ἀναιροῦσιν ἢ συγκατατίθενται εἶναι ἀπόδ. his, 889 ἡ ἀπ. ἀπ' αὐτῶν τῶν γραφῶν. 895 ἡ τῆς ἐκ τ. γραφῶν μαρτυρίας ἀπ., 896 τὰς ἀπ. ἀνευρίσκειν ἀπό τε νόμου κ. προφητῶν, ib. τὰς οἰκείας τ. γραφαῖς ἀπ' αὐτῶν τ. γραφῶν πορίζεσθαι ἀποδείξεις, 892 ἡ πίστις οὐσία ἀποδείξεως, 454 ἀπόδ. ἐπιστημονική, 891 ἡ φωνὴ τ. κυρίου πασῶν ἀποδείξεων ἐχεγγυωτέρα, μᾶλλον δὲ ἡ μόνη ἀπ., ib. τὰς ἀπ. παρ' αὐτῆς τ. ἀρχῆς περὶ τῆς ἀρχῆς λαβών, 894 ἄνευ ἀποδείξεως διαβεβαιοῦνται, cf. 1 Cor. ii. 4 ἐν ἀποδείξει πνεύματος
ἀποδημέω: 869 ἀποδημοῦσα τ. βίου πρὸς τ. κύριον γυνή
ἀποδιδράσκω: tr. 872 ἀποδιδράσκοντες τὰ καλά
ἀποδίδωμι: 838 'to assign as due,' 865
ἀποδιοπόμπησις: 850 (διοπόμπησις Η. with MS.)
ἀποδιωθέω: 896 ἀποδιωθοῦσθαι τ. ἀλήθειαν (rare)
ἀποδοτέον: 804 εὐφροσύνην ἀποδ. τῷ γνωστικῷ
ἀποδύω: m. 868 ἀπ. αὐτῇ τ. χιτῶνα, 880 ἀμφιεννύμενος κ. ἀπ.
ἀποκαθαίρω: 882 τοὺς τῆς ψυχῆς ἀποκεκαθαρμένος σπίλους
ἀποκάθαρσις: 877 πειρασμοὶ εἰς τὴν ἀποκ., 849 ἡ ἀποκ. τ. ἀλόγου μέρους τ. ψυχῆς
ἀποκαθίστημι: 865 εἰς τὸν κορυφαῖον ἀποκαταστήσει τ. ἀναπαύσεως τόπον
ἀποκαλέω: 828 ἀθέους ἀποκ. τοὺς τ. θεὸν ἐγνωκότας
ἀποκάλυψις: (quot.) 867
ἀποκατάστασις: 865 καθαροῖς τ. καρδίᾳ προσμένει τῇ θεωρίᾳ ἀποκατάστασις

ἀποκλείω: 893 πονηρὰ παιδία τ. παιδαγωγὸν ἀπ.
ἀποκρίνω: 'set apart' (quot.) 847
ἀποκρύπτω: 895 ὅσα ἀποκρύψαι οὐκ ἴσχυσαν
ἀπόκρυφος: 831 ἡ μεγίστη ὑπεροχὴ τὰς ἀποκρύφους ἐννοίας ἐπιβλέπει
ἀποκτείνω: 878 ὁ μὴ θέλων ἐκκόψαι πάθος ἑαυτὸν ἀποκτείνει
ἀποκτίννυμι: 836
ἀπολαμβάνω: 875 ποθούμεν σε ἀπολαβεῖν, 854 ἀπ. τὴν τελείωσιν, 886
ἀπόλαυσις: 852 τὰς ἐξ οἴνων ἀπολαύσεις, ib πάντων τ. σεμνὴν ἀπόλαυσιν ἐπὶ τ. θεὸν ἀνάγειν, 868 ἀπολαύσεως κύριος (ὁ γνωστικός)
ἀπόλαυσμα: 852 αἱ διὰ τ. ἄλλων ἀπολαυσμάτων ποικιλίαι
ἀπολείπω: p. 874 ἀπολ.)(περιττεύει, 886 ἀπολ. ἐκλαβεῖν
ἀπόληψις: 869 ἡ γνῶσις πεῖσμα ἐνεργέστερον τῆς τ. μελλόντων ἀπολήψεως
ἀπόλλυμι: 890 ἄνθρωπος εἶναι τ. θεοῦ ἀπολώλεκε
ἀπολογέομαι: 886 ἀπ. πρὸς ἐγκλήματα
ἀπολογία: 887 χρώμενος ἀπολογίᾳ
ἀπολούω: m. (quot.) 885
ἀπολύτρωσις: 865 ἀπολυθέντων ἡμῶν κολάσεως, μεθ' ἣν ἀπολύτρωσιν αἱ τιμαὶ ἀποδίδονται
ἀπολύω: 865 πάσης κολάσεως ἀπολυθείς
ἀπομερίζω: p. 834, αἱ περιτροπαὶ κατὰ τὴν τ. μεταβολῆς τάξιν ἀπ., Plato
ἀπονεμητέον: 894 ἡδονῆς [ἐν] τοῖς ἔθνεσιν ἀπονεμητέον
ἀπονέμω: 854 ὥρας τακτὰς ἀπονέμουσιν εὐχῇ, 855 ἡ αἴτησις ἀπονέμεται κατὰ τὴν τ. θεοῦ βούλησιν
ἀποπαυστέον: 894 ἀποπαυστέον τὸ ἔθος
ἀποπαύω: 895 τοὺς δὲ τῆς ἀμαθίας ἀποπαῦσαι γλιχόμενος
ἀποπίπτω: 834 οἱ κακοὶ ἀπ. χαμαί, 859 μὴ ἀποπεσεῖν τ. ἀρετῆς αἰτήσεται, 890 ἀποπ. τῆς ὀρθῆς ὁδοῦ, 894 ἀποπ. τοῦδε τοῦ ὕψους
ἀποπληρόω: 882 πάντα ἀπ. τὰ παρ' αὐτοῦ
ἀπορέω: 897 λέλυται τὸ ἠπορημένον ('problem')
ἀπορία: 886 αἱ τῶν ἀποριῶν λύσεις
ἀπορραθυμέω: 892 μέχρι τ. βάθους κατελθεῖν ἀπορραθυμήσαντες
ἀπορρήγνυμι: intr. 843 ἀπορρῆξαι τ. συναγωγῆς
ἀπορρίπτω: 885 τ. πάθη τ. ψυχικὰ ἀπερρίψασθε
ἀποσκιρτάω: 890 ἀποσκιρτήσας εἰς δόξας αἱρέσεων, 143 ἐκλακτίσαντος λαοῦ καὶ ἀποσκιρτήσαντος, Themist. 87[b]
ἀποσπάω: 860 τῶν τ. κακίας ἔργων ἀπεσπασμένος, 889 ἀποσπάσαντές τινα ἀπὸ τ. ἀληθείας, 843 intr. ἀπ. τοῦ νόμου

ἀπόστασις: **845** ἡ ἀπὸ τ. εὐαγγελίου ἀπ. πρὸς τὸν ἐθνικὸν βίον
ἀποστατέον: 888 οὐκ ἀποστ. (τοῦ πόνου) bis, Diod. Sic. 16. 1
ἀποστάτης: **884** πῶς ἂν ἀγγέλους τις κρίναι τοὺς ἀποστάτας, αὐτὸς ἀποστάτης γενόμενος (τ. εὐαγγελίου)
ἀποστέλλω: 840 fin. ἥλιος ἀπ. τ. αὐγὴν
ἀποστερέω: **884** (quot.) ἀποστερεῖσθε—ἀποστερεῖτε
ἀποστολικός: 883 αἱ ἐπίκαιροι τῶν ἀποστολικῶν λέξεις, 878 τ. ἀποστ. ἀπουσίαν ἀνταναπληροῖ ὁ γνωστικός, 896 ἡ ἀπ. κ. ἐκκλησιαστικὴ ὀρθοτομία τ. δογμάτων
ἀπόστολος: 898 ἡ τῶν ἀπ. διδασκαλία ἐπὶ Νέρωνος τελειοῦται, 883 ὁ θεῖος ἀπ., 876 οἱ μακάριοι ἀπ., 866, 867, 869, 877, 882, 900 διά τε τ. προφητῶν κ. τοῦ εὐαγγελίου κ. τῶν ἀποστόλων, 874 εἰκόνας ἔχει τοὺς ἀπ., 900 μία ἡ πάντων τ. ἀποστόλων παράδοσις καὶ διδασκαλία
ἀποστροφή: **838** fin. κατὰ τὴν ἀπ. τῶν αἰσχρῶν ὡς ἀλλοτρίων, 839 μισοπονηρότατος κατὰ τὴν τελείαν ἀποστροφὴν κακουργίας πάσης, 509 ἀπ. πρὸς γυναῖκα
ἀποσφάλλω: 888 ἀπεσφάλησαν αἱ αἱρέσεις
ἀποτάσσω: 851 ἡμέραι ἀποτεταγμέναι, **880** πᾶσιν ἀποταξάμενος
ἀποτέλεσμα: **830** τρία ἐστὶ τ. γνωστικῆς δυνάμεως ἀποτελέσματα, 840 καθάπερ ἰδίου γεννήματος κ. κατά τι συγγενοῦς ἀποτελέσματος ὁ σωτὴρ ἀναδέχεται τὰς ὠφελείας τ. ἀνθρώπων. Philo
ἀποτελέω: p. 890 ἐξ ἀνθρώπου θεὸς ἀποτελεῖται
ἀποτέμνω: 896 ἡ παρρησία ἀποτέμνουσα <καὶ> καίουσα τ. ψευδεῖς δόξας, 831 οὐκ ἀποτέμνεται ὁ υἱὸς τ. θεοῦ
ἀποτίθημι: 836 τὰ πάθη ἀποτιθεμένους, 838 οὐ γὰρ ὑπομένειν δεῖ τ. κακίας ἀλλ' ἀποθέσθαι (MB. ἀλλὰ πείθεσθαι), 845 τ. ἄθεον ἀποθέμενοι δόξαν, 889 οἴησιν ἀποθ.
ἀποτίκτω: 890 αἱ γραφαὶ τὴν ἀλήθειαν ἀποτίκτουσαι
ἀποτρέπω: 895 ἀποτρ. τ. φιλομαθοῦντας
ἀποτροπή: 853 ἡ ἀποτροπὴ τ. κακῶν εἶδος εὐχῆς, 221 init. παιδεραστίας ἐμφαίνει ἀποτροπὴν
ἀποτυγχάνω: 875 fin. αἰτούμενος μᾶλλον ἀποτυχεῖν ἕτοιμος ἢ μὴ αἰτούμενος τυχεῖν
ἀποτυφλόω: 893 τ. ἐγχέλεις ἁλίσκεσθαί φασιν ἀποτυφλουμένας
ἀπουσία: 878 ὁ γνωστικὸς τ. ἀποστολικὴν ἀπουσίαν ἀνταναπληροῖ
ἀποφαίνομαι: 891 οὐ γὰρ ἁπλῶς ἀποφαινομένοις ἀνθρώποις προσέχοιμεν ἄν

ἀποφεύγω: 880 fin. ἀπ. τὰς διδασκαλίας διά τ. καταγνῶσιν
ἀποχή: 844 ἡ ἁγνεία οὐκ ἄλλη ἐστί πλὴν ἡ τ. ἁμαρτημάτων ἀποχή, 875, 879 κακῶν ἀπ.
ἀποχράομαι: 891 ψιλῇ ἀποχρώμενοι τ. λέξει
ἀπόχρη: 841 ὀλίγα ἐκ πολλῶν ἀπόχρη, 886 ἀπόχρη τὸ δεῖγμα τοῖς ὦτα ἔχουσιν
ἁπρεπής: τὸ ἀπρ.)(τὸ πρέπον
ἀπροσπαθής: **869** γάμοι ἀπ., (-ῶς 640 init.)
ἅπτω: 832 πάθος ἅπτεταί τινος, 840 ἀτιμία ἅπτ. θεοῦ, **846** ὧν ἅπτ. πάθος, 882 διελθὼν τ. πνευματικὰς οὐσίας ἅπτεται τ. θρόνων τ. ἄκρων, 871 πυρὸς ἅπτονται, 897 ἅπτονται λόγων
ἄπτωτος: 859 συνεργῶν πρὸς τὸ ἄπτωτος διαγενέσθαι, Clem. Hom. II. 37 ἀπτώτως ἀκροατήν, III. 62 ἅπτ. εἰρήνη, Vita Polycarpi 31, Longin. (usual form ἀπτώς)
ἄρα: 887 διὰ δὴ τοῦτο ἄρα, cf. Xen. Oec. 18 § 9 σὺ μὲν δὴ ἄρα
ἀργής: (quot.) 848
ἀργία: 876 μισθὸς ἀργίας
ἀργός: 864 τὸ ψεῦδος οὐκ ἀργός ἐστι λόγος, 845 ἐξ ἀργῆς τ. ὕλης ἀργὰ γίνεται, cf. ἀεργός
ἀργύριον: 875 οὐ τὸ ἀργ. λέγων Μαμωνᾶ ἀλλὰ τὴν ἐξ ἀργ. χορηγίαν
ἀρδεύω: 876 ἐργάζεται ὁ γνωστικὸς ἀρδεύων
ἀρέσκω: 852 ἤρεσε τ. Στωικοῖς, 874, 875 (quot.) ἀρέσκειν τῷ θεῷ
ἀρεστός: 840 ἀρ. θεῷ
ἀρετή: **888** οὐχ ἡ αὐτὴ ἀρ. ἀνθρώπου κ. θεοῦ, 860 τὰ δι' ἀρετήν, 870 ἀρ. ἐκ φύσεως, ἀσκήσεως, λόγου
Ἄρης: 863 τ. σίδηρον Ἄρην προσαγορεύουσι
ἀριδήλως: (quot.) 841 τὰ ἀρ. εἰρημένα
ἀριθμός: 860 πάντα ἔχει τὰ ἀγαθὰ ὁ γνωστικὸς κατὰ τ. δύναμιν, οὐδέπω δὲ κατὰ τ. ἀριθμόν, 869 ἄπειροι ὅσοι ἀριθμῷ, **901** (quot.) οὔτ' ἐν λόγῳ οὔτ' ἐν ἀριθμῷ, 894 μυρίων ὄντων κατ' ἀριθμὸν ἃ πράττουσιν ἄνθρωποι
ἀρκέω: 857 ἀρκεῖται τοῖς παροῦσιν, 862 ἀρκεῖται τῇ συνειδήσει
ἁρμόνιος: 833 οὐκ ἂν ἁρμονιωτέρα διοίκησις ἀνθρώπων εἴη, Wisdom xvi. 20 ἁρμ. γεῦσις
ἀρνέομαι: 892 τὰ ἑαυτῶν ἀρν. δόγματα
ἄρνησις: 861 ἐπὶ τ. ἀρνήσεως τὸ 'οὐ' τάσσει ἐπίρρημα
ἄρρητος: 852 δυνάμει τινὶ (MB. τῇ) ἀρρήτῳ πάντα γινώσκει
ἀρτάω: 833 ἀπὸ μιᾶς ἀρχῆς ἤρτηται
ἀρτηρίον: 848 ἀρτ. κ. φλέβες
ἀρύτομαι: 834 τὰς ἐντολὰς ἐκ μιᾶς ἀρυτόμενος πηγῆς ὁ κύριος

ἀρχαῖος: 888 ἡ ἀρχ. ἐκκλησία, 895 ἄσμα ἀρχαιότατον, 829 φιλοσοφία ἀρχ., 848 βωμὸς ἀρχ.

ἀρχή: 894 δύο εἰσὶν ἀρχαὶ πάσης ἁμαρτίας, 869 τ. ἀρχὰς θεόθεν περιπεποιημένη, 882 διελθὼν πᾶσαν ἀρχὴν καὶ ἐξουσίαν, 890 τ. ἀρχὴν εἴ τις ἑτέρου δεῖσθαι ὑπολάβοι οὐκέτ' ἂν ἀρχὴ φυλαχθείη, 864 διὰ Χριστοῦ ἡ ἀρχὴ κ. τὰ τέλη, 891 πίστει περιλαβὼν ἀναπόδεικτον τ. ἀρχήν, 893 ἀναγκαῖαι ἀρχαὶ καταβαλλόμενοι, 135 αἱ ἀρχαὶ ἀναπόδεικται: (adv.) 893 πᾶσα αἵρεσις ἀρχὴν ὦτα ἀκούοντα οὐκ ἔχει τὸ σύμφορον, 895 οὐδὲ αὐτχωσται τ. ἀρχὴν ἐπακοῦσαι

ἀρχηγός: 841 ἀπάντων ἀρχ. ἀγαθῶν ὁ θεός

ἀρχιερεύς: 885 (quot.) προσομιλεῖν τ. θεῷ διὰ τ. μεγάλου ἀρχιερέως, 833, 858, 500

ἀρχικός: 832 ὁ υἱὸς πρὸ πάντων τῶν γενομένων ἀρχικώτατος λόγος τ. πατρός

ἄρχων: 893 ὁ λόγος ὃν ἄρχοντα εἰλήφαμεν γνώσεώς τε κ. βίου

ἄσαρκος: 880 εὕτως ζῆσαι τ. ὡρισμένον ἐν σαρκὶ βίον ὡς ἄσαρκος, 885 οἷον ἀσάρκῳ ᾔδη καὶ ἄνω τῆσδε τ. γῆς ἁγίῳ γεγονότι, 851 (quot.) ὀστᾶ ἄσ.

ἀσεβέω: 864 ἀκολούθως οὐδὲ ἀσεβεῖ, 894 ἀσεβεῖ διὰ τὸ ἀπιστεῖν

ἀσεβής: 897 τ. ἀσεβῶν ἁπτόμενοι λόγων

ἀσθένεια: 894 ἀρχαὶ πάσης ἁμαρτίας ἄγνοια κ. ἀσθένεια, 884 ὑπ' ἀσθενείας κακά, 837 ὅλης ἀσθ., 855 ἡ ἡμετέρα ἀσθ.

ἀσκέω: 860 τὸ σωμάτιον πρὸς ἀνδρείαν ἀσκήσας, 889 ἀσκ. τὰ ἀληθῆ, 859, 850 τοῖς ἀσκοῦσι τ. σῶμα χρησιμεύει τ. χορεία

ἄσκησις: 836 τὸ ἐξ ἀσκήσεως εἰς ἀπάθειαν συνεσταλμένον, 858 ἡ κατορθωτικὴ τῶν πρακτέων ἀσκ., 850 ἀσκήσεως χάριν, 875 ἀνεπιθύμητοι ἐξ ἀσκήσεως γενέσθαι, 893 ἡ ἀσκ. τ. ψυχῆι, 859 ἀσκ. γνωστικῆ, 895 ἡ κατὰ λόγον ἀσκ. ἐκ πίστεως κ. φόβου παιδαγωγουμένη, 870 ἀρετὴ ἐκ φύσεως, ἀσκήσεως, λόγου συνηυξημένη

ἆσμα: 895 ἀρχαιοτάτου ἑταίσιν ἄσματος

ἀσμένως: 856

ἀσπάζομαι: 835 τ. θεωρίαν ἀσπ. τ. θείαν, 892 τ. συμποτικὴν προτοκλισίαν ἀσπάζονται

ἀστεῖος: 848

ἀσύμφορος: 876 ἀσύμφορα οὐδέποτε αἰτήσεται

ἀσφαλής: 881 ἀσφ. <ὅστω> ἐν συμπεριφορᾷ ὁ γνωστικός

ἄσφαλτος: (quot.) 844

ἀσχήμων: 853 ἀσχ. ἔννοια

ἀσχολέω: 878 ὀλίγον τι τ. ὥρας περὶ τ. τροφῆς ἀσχολεῖται

ἀσχολία: 829 ἀπ. ἀσχ. περὶ τὸ θεῖον

ἄτε: not followed by participle 882

ἄτεγκτος: 872 ἄτ. ἡδοναῖς κ. λυπαῖς, 876

ἀτελεύτητος: 865 ἄτ. καὶ τέλειον τέλος, 500, 885 αἰὼν ἄτ.

ἀτεχνῶς: 874 εἰκόνα ἀτ. σώζων τῆς προνοίας, 878 ἄτ. ξένος

ἀτιμία: 840 τὰς βλάβας ἰδίας ἀτιμίας ἡγεῖται, ib. τίς γὰρ ἄλλη ἅπτοιτ' ἂν ἀτ. θεοῦ;

ἀτονία: 859 ὅσας βρίθουσά τις ἔτι ὑπολείπεται ἀτονία (MS. γωνία) κάτω ῥέπουσα: cf. 198 τ. ἀτόνοις κ. ἀσθενικοῖς τὸ μέτριον ὑπέρτονον δοκεῖ, 890 εὐτονία ψυχῆς

ἄτρεπτος: 865 φῶς ἐστὸς πάντη πάντων ἀτρ., 868 ἄτρ. μένει κατὰ τ. ψυχήν, Ign. L. vol. ii. p. 24

ἀτροφία: 875 ἀτρ. ἡ ἄγνοια τ. ψυχῆς

ἄτρυτος: 831 ἀκαμάτῳ κ. ἀτρύτῳ δυνάμει πάντα ἐργάζεται

ἄτυφος: 836 θυσία δεκτὴ παρὰ θεῷ ἡ ἄτυφος καρδία

ἀτύφως: 881 τὸ (MS. τῷ) διὰ τ. εὐχῆς ἀγνώστως κ. ἀτύφως παρέχεται

αὐγή: 840 fin. ἡλίου ἀποστέλλει τ. αὐγήν, (quot.) 848 ὑπ' αὐγὰς φοιτώσιν

Αὔγουστος: 898 ἡ διδασκαλία ἀπὸ Αὐγ. ἀρξαμένη

αὐθαίρετος: 837 τὸ αὐθ. τῆς ψυχῆς κ. ἀδούλωτον

αὖθις: 859 'backwards,' τῶν ἀγγέλων τινὰς ὀλισθήσαντες αὖθις χαμαί

αὐλαία: 'curtain' 269 ἀναπεπταμένης τῆς αὐλαίας, 665 ἡ ἔξωθεν περικειμένη αὐλαία (? αὐλή) ἡ πᾶσιν ἀνειμένη. see αὐλεία

αὐλεία: 'chief door' (MS. αὐλαία), 897 τ. αὐλείαν ἀναπετάσαντες)(παράθυρον

αὐλή: 866 μετὰ τ. ἐν σαρκὶ τελευταίαν ὑπεροχὴν μεταβάλλων εἰς τ. πατρῴαν αὐλήν, 794

αὔξησις: 834 δικαιοσύνης αὐξ.

αὔξω: intr. 848 ταῦτα ἐκ τῆς ἀναθυμιάσεως ἀβλαβῶν αὔξει, 859 θεωρίαν εὔχεται αὔξειν κ. παραμένειν, 872 ἀνὴρ εἰς μέτρον αὐξῆσαι: tr. 850 τὴν ψυχὴν αὔξειν ἐπιχειροῦσι, 852 αὔξεται τὸ ἡγεμονικόν: p. 856 τὸ φῶς αὔξεται, 864 αὐξηθεὶς ἐν πίστει, 872 ἡ τελειότης αὔξεται

αὐστηρός: 858 αὐστ. οὐκ εἰς τ. ἀδιάφθορον μόνον, ἀλλὰ κ. εἰς τ. ἀπείραστον, 894 αὐστ. κ. σεμνὴ ἡ ἀλήθεια

αὐτάρκης: 857 αὐτάρκης ἐνενδεὴς δὲ τῶν ἄλλων

αὐτίκα: see Appendix A

αὐτοκρατορικός: 835 τ. αἵρεσιν τ. γνώσεων αὐτοκρατορικὴν ἐκέκτητο ἡ ψυχή,

Philo II. 594, Galen XIV. 4 K., Dio. 57. 23. 5, 61. 5. 1. 63. 25. 3.

αὐτοκράτωρ: 872 σωφροσύνη κύρων κ. αὐτοκράτορα τ. ἔνδρα κατασκευάζει

αὐτός: 878 'alone' τὸ κάλλος αὐτῇ βλάπει τῇ ψυχῇ: 870 ἅμα τῷ αὐτῷ τὰ ἐναντία κατὰ ταὐτὸν (ms. τὸν αὐτὸν) καὶ πρὸς τὸν αὐτὸν ἐναντῶν χρόνον, 878 τὰ αὐτὰ αἱρεῖσθαι πίστις, φρονεῖν γνῶσις, ποθεῖν ἐλπίς

αὐτοῦ: only found once in the ms. of *Str.* VII. in P. 892 (p. 172. 18), where edd. read αὐτοῖς, but perhaps the aspirate should be retained, as we should otherwise expect αὐταῖς to suit the preceding feminines. Elsewhere the printed αὐτοῦ stands for ms. αὐτοῦ except in 843 (p. 40. 21), where the ms. has ἑαυτῷ for original αὐτῷ in a quotation. The other exx. are 831 (p. 8. 24), 832 *bis* (p. 10. 18, 19) 837 (p. 24. 24), 855 (p. 72. 24), 862 (p. 90. 17), 869 (p. 108. 27), 871 (p. 114. 21), 872 *bis* (p. 116. 7, 26), 877 (p. 132. 10), 878 (p. 134. 9), 885 (p. 154. 4), 889 (p. 162. 17), 890 (p. 164. 27). The aspirated form is found in the ms. of *Q. D. S.* p. 1. 10 (Barn.) καθ' αὑτήν, p. 4. 2 ἀλλ' αὑτόν, p. 16. 12 καθ' αὑτόν. Cf. on the question whether αὑτοῦ can be used for αὐτοῦ, Hort *N. T. App.* p. 144 f., and Winer *Gr.* p. 188 f.

αὐχέω: 892 αὐχοῦσι διδάσκοντες, 889 αὐχ. προΐστασθαι διατριβῆς, 898, 900

ἀφεκτός: 847 ἡ τ. ὁλοκαυμάτων κνῖσα τοῖς θηρίοις ἀφεκτέα (H. ὠφελέα), 888 οὐ διὰ τ. ὁμοιότητα ἀμφοῖν ἀφεκτέον, διακριτέον δέ, 785 init. οὐκ ἀφεκτέον τ. φιλομαθίας, Themist. 199°

ἄφεσις: 884 ἀφ. ἁμαρτιῶν

ἀφηνιάζω (trop.): 834 τοὺς μὴ ἐπαΐοντας τ. βαρβάρου φιλοσοφίας ἀφηνιάσαι οὐ συγχωρῆσαι, 863, 880 στόμιον ἐμβαλὼν ἀφηνιάζοντι τ. ἀλόγῳ πνεύματι, 73, 137 παρὰ τὸν νόμον ἀφηνιάζοντες, Orig. c. *Cels.* III. 55

ἀφίημι: 881 οὐδέποτε μέμνηται ἀλλὰ ἀφίησι, ib. (quot.), 886 ἀφιέντες τ. ἁμαρτίας, (quot.) 885 ἀφεθήσεταί σοι

ἀφικνέομαι: 852 (of accepting an invitation), 862 ἐπὶ τὸ ὀμνύναι ἀφ., 883 ἀφ. εἰς ἄνδρα τέλειον, 951 πῶς ἂν τὸ ἐλπισθὲν εἰς κτῆσιν ἀφίκοιτο;

ἀφιλάργυρος: 873 πρὸς ἐχθροὺς ἀφιλάργυρος κ. ἀμνησιπόνηρος

ἀφίστημι: pi. 889 οὐκ ἀποστήσονται ζητοῦντες

ἄφοβος: 872 ἀφ. κ. ἀδεής

ἀφοράω: 869 εἰς τὰς εἰκόνας ἀφορᾷ τ. καλάς, 833 πάντων εἰς τ. διοικητὴν ἀφορώντων (ms. ἐφορ.)

ἀφορίζω: 901 ὡς ἀκάθαρτα ἀφορίζα ('rejects'), Lk. vi. 22 ὅταν ἀφορίσωσιν ὑμᾶς

ἀφορμή: 855 ἀφ. τις ὁμιλίας πρὸς τ. θεὸν ἡ εὐχή, bis, 836, 871 ἀφορμὰς σφίσιν αὐτοῖς παρέχοντες ἐπιρρέπτουσιν ἑαυτούς τ. κινδύνοις, 888 ἔχομεν ἐκ φύσεως ἀφορμὰς πρὸς τὸ ἐξετάζειν, ib. ἀφορμαῖς καταχρηστέον, 829 ἀπὸ τῶν γραφῶν τὰς ἀφορμὰς ἔχει τὰ λεγόμενα

ἀφροδίσιος: 850 σφριγᾶν περὶ τὰ ἀφρ., 875 ἀφρ. ἡδονή

Ἀφροδίτη: 877 ἡ παρασκευὴ ἐπιφημίζεται Ἀφροδίτῃ

ἀφρόντιστος: 833 οὐδὲ τὸ μικρότατον ἀπολείπει τῆς ἑαυτοῦ διοικήσεως ἀφρόντιστον ὁ θεός

ἀφροσύνη: 871 οὐ γάρ, εἰ δι' ἀφροσύνην τι συνίσταται, τοῦτ' εὐθέως ἀφροσύνη

ἀχαριστία: 840

ἄχραντος: 860 ἀχρ. ψυχή

ἄχρηστος: 893 κεναὶ ἀμυγδάλαι λέγονται ἐν αἷς ἄχρηστον τὸ ἐνόν

ἄχρονος: 829 ἀχρ. ἀρχὴ τ. πάντων ὁ υἱός, cf. Plotinus *Enn.* IV. 4. 1

ἀχώριστος: 880 ἀχ. ὢν τῆς ἐντολῆς

ἀψευδέω: 887 ἀψευδεῖν χρὴ τ. ἐπιεικῆ

ἄψυχος: 855 οὐκ ἔστιν ἄψ. ὁ σωζόμενος

βαδίζω: 843 αὐτῷ β. ἕκαστος, 896 β. τ. ὀρθὴν ὁδόν

βάθος: 892 μέχρι τ. βάθους τ. πραγμάτων κατελθεῖν, 853 τὸ β. τῆς ψυχῆς

βαθύρροος: (quot.) 844

βαναυσία: 845 τὰ πρὸς ἀνθρώπων βαναύσων κατασκευαζόμενα τῆς βαναυσίας μετείληφεν

βάναυσος: 845 β. τέχνη, ib. β. ἄνθρωποι, 846 ἱερὸν οὐ βαναύσῳ κατεσκευασμένον τέχνῃ, 851 πῦρ οὐ τὸ παμφάγον κ. β. ἀλλὰ τὸ φρόνιμον

βάρβαρος: 834 ἡ β. φιλοσοφία, i.e. Jewish)(Greek, 364, 349 ἡ τε β. κ. ἡ Ἑλληνικὴ φιλοσοφία, cf. 355, 356, 359, 371, 700, 701, 702, 703, 693, 679, 680, 733, Eus. *H. E.* VI. 19

βάρος: 859 τῷ λίθῳ τὸ β. ἀναπόβλητον

βάσανος: 'tortures' 862 οὐ ψεύδεται κἂν ἐναποθνήσκῃ τ. βασάνοις, 867 β. ὑπομένειν εὐκόλως, 869 τ. βασάνους κ. τ. θλίψεις ὑπομένει

βασιλεύς: 898 Ἀδριανὸς ὁ β.

βασιλικός: 831 βασιλικωτάτη ἡ τ. υἱοῦ φύσις, 366 βασιλικωτάτη διδασκαλία, 841 ὁ τῷ ὄντι βασιλικὸς τ. ψυχὴν κ. γνωστικός, 852 οὗτος ὁ βασιλικὸς ἄνθρωπος ἱερεὺς ὅσιος τ. θεοῦ, 856 ἐλευθερικωτάτη κ. βασιλικωτάτη θεραπεία, 876 ὁδὸς βασ. ἦν τὸ βασιλικὸν ὁδεύει γένος, 888

OF GREEK WORDS.

βάσις: 901 β. δι' υἱοῦ πρὸς τ. πατέρα παραπέμπουσα
βαστάζω: 880 β. τὸ σημεῖον
βέβαιος: 838 βεβ. κατάληψις, 869 πεῖσμα βεβαιότερον ἐλπίδος
βεβαιότης: 875 γυμνάσια ἡμῖν προσφέρει ἡ σὴ οἰκονομία εἰς συνάσκησιν βεβαιότητος
βεβαιόω: 891 ἡ ἀλήθεια ἐν τῷ βεβαιοῦν ἕκαστον τῶν ἀποδεικνυμένων ἐξ αὐτῶν τ γραφῶν, 892 τὸ ὑπὸ τοῦ εὐαγγελίου βεβαιούμενον
βεβαίως: 874 β. κτησάμενος τῆς ἐπιστήμης τὰ μεγαλεῖα, 887 β. ἔχονται τῆς ἀληθείας, see Schm. iv. 717
βελτιόω: 834 ἡ βελτιουμένη ψυχὴ εἰς ἀρετῆς ἐπίγνωσιν βελτίονα ἀπολαμβάνει τάξιν, Orig. c. Cels. i. 9 fin.
βελτιωτικός: 830 τῆς θεραπείας ἡ μὲν βελτιωτικὴ ἡ δὲ ὑπηρετικὴ κ.τ.λ. bis
βία 838 μετὰ βίας ψυχαγωγεῖ
βιάζομαι: (c. inf.) 868 οὐ μόνον ἐπαινεῖ τ καλὰ ἀλλὰ αὐτὸς βιάζεται εἶναι καλός, 854 τ. ψυχὴν ἐπὶ τὰ ἅγια χωρεῖν β., 896 β. καινοτομεῖν, 869 ἐπ' ἄκρον γνώσεως ἥκειν β., 858 β. κτήσασθαι, 875 ἀνεπιθύμητοι ἐξ ἀσκήσεως γενέσθαι βιάζονται, 884 β. ἐξομοιοῦσθαι θεῷ, 899 β. καταπέμπειν τ. ἐκκλησίαν, cf 64 β. βαδίζειν, 328 β. ἐξευρίσκειν: 885 ἡ ἐντολὴ βιάζεται εἰς σωτηρίαν ('to strain a meaning') 890 βιάζονται πρὸς τ. ἐπιθυμίας τ. γραφήν, 891 bis
βίος: 840 fin. αἱ τοῦ β. πράξεις, 861 ὁ καιρὸς β., ib. ὁ β. ὅρος τῷ πιστῷ, 864 κατὰ τρόπον κ. β. κ. λόγον, 878 τὸ ἀναγκαῖον τ. βίου, 882, 891 ἐν τοῖς κατὰ τὸν βίον ἔχουσί τι πλέον οἱ τεχνῖται
βιόω: 868 ἀπὸ γνώμης λέγων ἅμα κ. βιούς, 831 λογικῶς βιοῦντα, 860 εὖ β., 862 κατ' ἄκρον ἀληθείας β.
βιωτέον: 887 πῶς ἀκριβῶς β., 830 ὅπως β. ἰσομέτρῳ θεῷ, 280 οὐ θνητῶς β ἁγιαζομένοις θεῷ, 104 ἄνευ ποιμένοι πρόβατα οὐ β.
βιωτικός: 873 αἱ β. χρεῖαι
βλαβερός: 857 τοῖς μοχθηροῖς ἡ εὐχὴ καὶ εἰς σφᾶς αὐτοὺς βλ.
βλάβη: 840 τὰς εἰς τ. πεπιστευκότας βλάβας ἰδίας ἡγεῖται, 853
βλάπτω: 841 χείρους τ. ἀνθρώπων βλαπτόμενοι δείκνυνται οἱ θεοί
βλάσφημος: 895 λόγοι βλ.
βοήθεια: 881 ἡ δι' ἀγγέλων β.
βοηθέω: 860 τὰ βοηθεῖν δυνάμενα
βορά: 846 προσάγειν β. τινι
βουβῶν: (quot.) 847
βούλημα: 857 τὸ παντοκρατορικὸν β.
βούλησις: 879 μέτοχος τ. θείας βουλήσεως
βραβευτής: 839 ἀγωνοθέτης ὁ θεὸς, βραβ. ὁ υἱός, θεαταὶ ἄγγελοι, cf. 77

βράγχιον: 848 ἡ τῶν βρ. διαστολή
βραχύς: 883 διὰ βραχυτάτων ter
βρίθω: 859 ὅσοις βρίθουσά τις ὑπαλείπεται ἀπονία (κβ. γωνία) κάτω μέπουσα, καταπατεῖται τὸ διὰ τῆς πίστεως ἀναγόμενον
βροτοφθόρος: (quot.) 841 σκῦλα βρ.
βρῶμα: 896 ἡ διδασκαλία τ. σωτῆρος βρ. ἐστι πνευματικόν, (quot.) 885 βρώματα τῇ κοιλίᾳ, 852 βρωμάτων συγκαττύσεις
βρῶσις: 850 ἡ τοιάδε β. πλαδαρὰν τ σάρκα παρασκευάζει, 849 βρ. τῶν κρεῶν, 850, 852 βρώσεως κ. πόματος ἀπόλαυσις, 875 βρ. κ. πόσις
βρώσιμος: (quot.) 851
βωμός: 842 (quot.) β. πήλινος, 848 β. ἅγιος ἡ δικαία ψυχή, 848 β. ἐν Δήλῳ

γαμέω: 874 γ. οὐ προηγουμένως ἀλλ' ἐὰν ὁ λόγος αἱρῇ, 879
γάμος: 869 ὁ τῶν μακαρίων γ., ib. γ. ἀπροσπαθής, 874 ὁ γάμῳ ἐγγυμνασάμενος
γάρ: (in 3rd place) 878 ἀτεχνῶς ξένοι γαρ: (elliptical) 839 οἱ νόμοι γάρ, 849 αἱ μὲν γὰρ κατὰ τ. νόμον θυσίαι
γε: 882 ἐκλεκτοῦ γ.
γελοῖος: 845 γελοῖον ἂν εἴη ἄνθρωπον θεὸν ἐργάζεσθαι
γενέθλιος: 858 γ. ἡμέρα
γένεσις: 850 ἡ πρώτη γ. 'creation, 829 πρεσβύτερον ἐν γενέσει, 853 πρὸ τῆς γ. τὸ ἐσόμενον ὡς ὑπάρχον ἐγνωκώς
γεννητός: 836 τὸ γ. κ. ἐνδεές, 846
γεννάδης: (iron.) 876 ὁ γενν. τ. παρρησιαζομένων φιλοσόφων
γενναῖος: 863 ὁ γ. ἀπόστολος
γεννάω: 864 init. οὓς ἐγέννησεν ἐν πίστει, 869 ἀγάπη διὰ τ. γνώσεως γεννωμένη
γέννημα: 840 γ. ἴδιον θεοῦ ὁ ἄνθρωπος
γέννησις: 889 fin. λεχὼ διὰ τὴν τ. παιδίου γέννησιν
γεννήτωρ: 837 τῶν καλῶν γ. ὁ θεός
γένος: 898 δύο τ. γένει παιδεία, πρόσφοροι ἑκατέρᾳ τ. ἁμαρτιῶν, 880 (= 'sex'), 563 fin. 851 γ ἐκλεκτόν
γεραίρω: 848 θυσίαν ἁγιωτάτην ἀνανέμομεν γεραίροντες (n. on δικαιοτάτῳ λόγῳ)
γέρας: 847 ἡ κνῖσα γέρας θεῶν τ. παρ' Ἕλλησιν, 851 (quot.), γ λαχεῖν τόδε, 866 μετὰ τ. ἀπολύτρωσιν τὸ γέρας κ αἱ τιμαί, 884 τὸν ἑλόμενον γ'. λαμβάνειν ἔταξεν
γεύομαι: 867 γεύεται τ. θελήματος θεοῦ ὁ γνωστικός, 879 οὐ γ. τῶν ἐν κόσμῳ καλῶν
γεῦσις: 852 αἱ ἀπολαύσεις δελεάζουσι τ. γεῦσιν
γεωργέω: 851 γεωργοῦσιν ἀπιόντες

400 INDEX

γεωργία: 880 (spiritual husbandry)
γεωργικός: 830 ἐμπειρία γ.
γεωργός: 876 ὁ γνωστικὸς θεῖος γεωργός, 888 μή τι ἀπέχονται οἱ γ. τ. κηπευτικῆς ἐπιμελείας; 894 Ἰσχόμαχος γεωργὸν ποιεῖ
γηθέω: 859 γέγηθεν ἐπὶ τοῖς ἐπηγγελμένοις
γίνομαι: 840 c. inf. γεγόναμεν εἶναι πειθήνιοι τ. ἐντολαῖς, 845 τὸ γινόμενον ταύτον τῷ ἐξ οὗ γίνεται
γινώσκω: 866 φίλον φίλῳ τὸ γινώσκον τῷ γινωσκομένῳ, 877 περὶ ὧν ἐγὼ (things revealed) τῶν μελλόντων κ. ἔτι ἀοράτων πεπεισμένος ἀκριβῶς, ib. μηδέπω καταξιούμενος τῆς ὧν ἐγὼ μεταλήψεως, ib. χαίρων ἐφ' οἷς ἔγνω, 882 ἱέμενος ἐφ' ὃ ἔγνω, 840 (quot) γνῶθι σαυτόν, 466 bis
γλαυκός: (quot.) 841
γλίχομαι: 895 c. inf. cf. Clem. Hom. index s.v.
γλυκεῖα: 'gall,' 847 (quot.)
γλυκύς: 888 init. γλ. εὕρεσις
γλῶσσα: 850 τὸ θυμίαμα τὸ ἐκ πολλῶν γλωσσῶν τε κ. φωνῶν κατὰ τ. εὐχὴν συγκείμενον, 856 τ. πολυφώνους γλώσσας οὐκ ἀναμένει ὁ θεός, 862 τὸ κατὰ τὴν γλ. μαρτύριον, 863 πᾶν ὅτιπερ ἐν νῷ τοῦτο κ. ἐπὶ γλώσσης φέρει
γνησίως: 838 τ. ἀληθείᾳ γν. πρόσεισιν
γνωματεύω: 869 τῷ δικαίῳ τὸ πρακτέον γνωματεύει ὁ γνωστικός, Themist. 36ᵇ πήχει κ. μέτρῳ γνωμ. τὴν ἀρετήν, 188ᵈ ὁπόθεν οἴεται γνωματεύειν τ. θεοειδῆ βασιλέα, 235ᵃ γνωματεύων τ. ἐπαξίους ἐγύμνους αὐτοῖς τὰ ἀγάλματα, 253ᵃ οὐ ταύτῃ τ. πλούσιον γνωματεύομεν εἰ δακτύλιον ὑπόχρυσον περιθέμενος κ.τ.λ.
γνώμη: 863 ἀπὸ γνώμης λέγειν
γνώμων: 891 ἀκριβεῖς γνώμονες τ. ἀληθείας οἱ γνωστικοί
γνωρίζω: 886 γν. τὸ θέλημα τ. θεοῦ, 854 γν. τὴν μακαρίαν τριάδα, 870 γν. τὰ πρακτέα
γνώριμος: 863 ἑαυτὸν ἐπιδιδωσιν ὑπὲρ τ. γνωρίμων οὓς αὐτὸς ἐγέννησεν ἐν πίστει, 898 Θεοδᾶς γν. Παύλου
γνῶσις: 838 ὁ γνῶσις (ms. γνωστικός) γινόμενος ἡμῖν, 839 ὁ μὴ διὰ τ. ἐντολάς, δι' αὑτὴν δὲ τὴν γν. καθαρὸς φίλος τ. θεοῦ, 853 οὐδεὶς ἐπιθυμεῖ γνῶσεως ἀλλὰ τοῦ γνῶναι, 864 ἡ γν. τελείωσίς τις ἀνθρώπου ὡς ἀνθρώπου, ib. γν. distinguished from σοφία, 865 ἡ γν. ἀπόδειξις τῶν διὰ πίστεως παρειλημμένων ἰσχυρά, ib. κυριακῆς διδασκαλίας ἐποικοδομουμένη τῇ πίστει, 775 γνῶσις θέα τίς ἐστι τῆς ψυχῆς, 897 γν. ἐκκλησιαστική
γνωστικός: 836 γν. ἐξομοίωσις, 830 τ. γνωστικῆς δυνάμεως τρία ἀποτελέσματα,
855 ὁ κατὰ τ. ἐκκλησιαστικὸν κανόνα γνωστικός, 885 ὁ τελειωθεὶς γν., 896 ζωὴ γν., 901 συνάσκησις γν., 858 τ. γνωστικῷ γνωστικῶς ἕκαστα ἀποδίδοται, 875 αἱ γν. ψυχαί, see under 'Gnostic'
γνωστικῆς: 858 ταῖς νοητοῖς γν. οἰκειούμενος, 855 εὐχὴ ἐναποκειμένη γν.
γνωστός: (quot.) 897 γν. ἐν Ἰουδαίᾳ ὁ θεός
γόης: 848 πρὸς τ. γοήτων κατεγοητευθέντες κατά τινας ἀκαθάρτους καθαρμούς, 844
γοητεύω: 852 θυμιαμάτων πολυτέλεια τὴν ὄσφρησιν γοητεύει
γραΐδιον: 841 ὀξύχολον γρ.
γραφή: (of Scripture) sing. 836 λέγα ἡ γρ., 892 ᾗ φησιν ἡ γρ., 883 πολλὰ ἐκ γραφῆς μαρτύρια παρατίθεσθαι, pl. 829 ταῖς γρ. συγχρησόμενοι ter, 883 κατ' ἐκλογὴν τῶν γρ., 895 ἡ ἐκ τῶν γρ. μαρτυρία, 896 ἐν αὑταῖς καταγηράσαι ταῖς γρ., 888 δι' αὑτῶν τ. γραφῶν ἐκμανθάνειν ἀποδεικτικῶς, 890 (cf. 829) αἱ κυριακαὶ γρ. τ. ἀληθείας ἀποτίκτουσαι, 891 γρ. προφητικαί, 894 θεὸς ἡγεῖται κατὰ τ. θεοπνεύστους γραφάς: (general) 843 τὰς γραφὰς δεδίασι τὰς ἀνακειμένας, 853 οὐδὲ ἐν γραφαῖς σώζει θεοσέβειαν ἢ μὴ πρέπουσα περὶ τ. θεοῦ ὑπόληψις, cf. Clem. Hom. ind., and see 'Scripture'
γυμνάζω: 859 ὁ εἰς ἀκρότητα γεγυμνασμένος, 872 ἡ ἀγάπη ἀλείφουσα κ. γυμνάσασα κατασκευάζει τ. ἴδιον ἀθλητήν, 882 γυμνάζει ἑαυτὸν διὰ τ. ἐντολῶν
γυμναστέον: 894 γ. τὴν ψυχὴν εἰς τὸ ἀντιλέγειν
γυμναστίον: 875 τὰ προσιόντα γ.
γυμνικός: 871 ἐν ἀγῶσι τ. γυμνικοῖς
γυμνός: 868 γ. τῆς ἁμαρτίας, 876 γ. προαίρεσις
γυνή: 869 ἡ Πέτρου γ., 889 ἡ Λὼτ γ.
γωνία: see ἀτονία

δαιδάλλω: 846 ἱερὸν οὗ χειρὶ δεδαιδαλμένον
δαιμόνιον: 881 δεισιδαίμων ὁ δεδιὼς τὰ δαιμόνια
δαίμων: 843 διαπνεῖται τὸ τ. δαιμόνων γένος
δακτύλιος: 834 πνεῦμα διὰ πολλῶν ἐκτεινόμενον δακτυλίων
δᾷς: 843 (quot.) 844
δασύς: 901 ὄρος δ. κυπαρίσσοις κ. πλατάνοις δάφνῃ τε
δάφνη: 901
δέ: = ἀλλὰ 888 οὐδὲ γὰρ ἀφεκτέον, διακριτέον δέ, ib. οὐκ ἀποστατέον, ἐπιμελέστερον δὲ θηρατέον, passim; in apodosi 871 fin., 890 init.

OF GREEK WORDS. 401

δεῖγμα: 'evidence' 866 ὁ πρῶτοι τ. κυριακῆς ἐνεργείας τρόποι τ. εἰρημένης ἀμοιβῆς δεῖγμα, 867 δ. τοῦ δύνασθαι λαβεῖν τ. γνῶσιν κομίζων (τὸ θαυμάζειν), 836 ἀποχρῆ τὸ δ. τοῖς ὦτα ἔχουσιν, 850 ἀὴρ ἐγκέκραται τοῖς στοιχείοις. ὁ κ. δεῖγμα τ. ὑλικῆς διαμονῆς (? see ἔρεισμα and δεσμός)
δέδω: 843 γραφὰς διδάσι
δειλία: 870 δι' ἄγνοιαν τ. δεινῶν κ. μὴ δεινῶν συνίσταται ἡ δειλία
δεῖν: (pleonastic) 851 σέβειν δεῖν ἐγκελευόμεθα, see πολύς
δεισιδαιμονία: 841 ἡ Ἑλληνικὴ δ.
δεισιδαίμων: 831 δ. ὁ πάντα θειάζων, 843 δεισιδαίμονες περὶ τοὺς εὐοργήτους, 842 ὁ Δεισιδαίμων, see δαιμόνιον
δεκτός: (quot.) 836 θυσία δ.
δελεάζω: 852 αἱ ἐξ οἴνων ἀπολαύσεις δελεάζουσι τ. γεῦσιν
δέλεαρ: 902 πολλὰ τ. δελέατα κ. ποικίλα
δελφάκιον: 842 κατέφαγεν ὅτι τὰ δ.
δένδρον: 902 καρποφόρα κ. ἄκαρπα δ.
δέον: (= δεῖ) 888 οἷς δέον πείθεσθαι μὴ πειθόμενοι κρινόμεθα
δεόντως: 888 ἡ τῶν νοητῶν κατάληψις δεόντως ἂν λέγοιτο ἐπιστήμη, 860 δεόντως μοι τὰ πρὸς τ. ἀγῶνα παρεσκεύασται
δεσμός: 854 τ. δεσμοῦ καταμεγαλοφρονεῖν τ. σαρκικοῦ, 850 (air mingled with the other elements is) δεσμός (нв. δεῖγμα) τ. ὑλικῆς διαμονῆς, see ἔρεισμα, and cf. Lightfoot on Col. i. 17 συνέστηκεν
δεσπότης: 852 δ. θεάτρων ὀχλοκρασία
δεῦτε: 881 (quot.)
δεύτερος: 833 ʄπ. τὰ πρῶτα κ. δεύτερα κ. τρίτα, 838 τὸ δεύτερον αἴτιον, 882 ἐὰν ἐν τούτῳ ἡ κ. δεύτερον κατορθώσῃ, 888 ἀνταδικῆσαι δεύτερον
δή ἄρα: see ἄρα
δηλονότι: 855, 884, 885 τοιοῦτοι δηλονότι οἷοι (нв. δῆλον ὁποῖοι)
δῆλος: 892 δῆλοι γεγονότες ὡς προσποιοῦνται = φανεροὶ προσποιούμενοι
δηλωτικός: 848 ἀσαφοῦς δ.
δημιουργέω: 836 ἑαυτὸν κτίζει κ. δημιουργεῖ ὁ γνωστικός, 863 ὁ τῷ ὄντι ἄνθρωπος δημιουργεῖ κ. μεταρρυθμίζει τ. κατηχούμενον
δημιουργία: 838 μόνῳ ἀνθρώπῳ κατὰ τ. δημιουργίαν ἔννοια ἐνέστακται θεοῦ, 856 πρὸ τ. δημιουργίας ὁ θεὸς ἠπίστατο, 880 τὰ εἰς δ. καὶ τροφὴν τ. σαρκὸς οἰκεία
δῆμος: (quot.) 848 init.
δημοσίᾳ: 832 init. ἰδίᾳ καὶ δ.
διά c. gen. = ὑπό: 890 διὰ τ. κυρίου ἐνεργούμενοι, 832 σοφία αὐτοῦ λεχθείη ἂν κ. διδάσκαλος τῶν δι' αὐτοῦ πλασθέ-

των (unless we read αὐτοῦ in accordance with Joh. i. 3), 867 ἡ διὰ τοῦ ἐπιστήμονος πρᾶξις, 880 τὰ διὰ Ἡσαΐου ἀλληγορούμενα ζῷα
διαβάλλω: 836 τ. νόμον διαβ., c. inf. 892 διαβάλλουσιν ἡμᾶς μὴ ἄνους τε εἶναι σινεῖσαι
διαβεβαιόομαι: 894 οἱ ἐπιστάμενοι περὶ ὧν ἴσασι διαβεβαιοῦνται
διαβιβάζω: 865 ἡ γνῶσις διαβιβάζει τὰς προκοπὰς τ. μυστικὰς τ. ἀνθρώπων
διάβολος: 871 οὐ γάρ, εἰ διὰ διαβόλου ἐνέργειαν τι συνίσταται, τοῦτ' εὐθέως διάβολον
διαγίνομαι: 859 συνεργῶν πρὸς τὸ ἀπτώτος διαγίνεσθαι
διαγράφω: 867 τ. βίον τ. γνωστικοῦ διαγράφειν ἡμῖν πρόκειται
διάγω. 840 init. μετὰ τῶν ὁμοίων δ τῷ πνεύματι, 839 μετὰ τῶν ὁμοφύλων φιλεῖν διάγειν
διαδέχομαι: 864 οἱ διαδέξασθαι τ. οἰκονομίαν τ. παιδευτοῦ δυνάμενοι
διαδίδωμι: 864 ἡ γνῶσις ἐκ παραδόσεως διαδίδοται
διαδιδράσκω: 840 αὕτη ἡ Ἀδράστεια καθ' ἣν οὐκ ἔστι διαδρᾶναι τ. θεόν (δ. τινὰ also in Herod.)
διαζεύγνυμι: 838 συντμημένα)(διεζευγμένα, cf. συνάπτω
διαζωγραφέω: 841 τὰς μορφὰς ὁμοίας ἑαυτοῖς διαζωγραφοῦσιν, Plato
διάθεσις: 851 τ. ἔργα κ. ἡ διάθ., 869 ἡ μέχρι τ. φιλτάτων διάθ., 870 διαθ. ὁμολογουμένη τῷ εὐαγγελίῳ, 881 μὴ ἡ συμπεριφορὰ δ. γένηται, 894 τρεῖς διαθέσεις τ. ψυχῆς ἄγνοια οἴησις ἐπιστήμη, 870 ἕξις ἡ διάθεσις
διαθήκη: 850 ἡ κατὰ τ. διαθήκας δόσις, 885 πορεύει τῇ παρὰ τ. διαθήκην ἐνεργείᾳ, 894 τ. ἀλήθειαν διὰ τ. ἀκολουθίας τ. διαθηκῶν σαφηνίζων, 899 fin. ἡ πίστις ἡ κατὰ τ. οἰκείας διαθήκας μᾶλλον δὲ κατὰ τ. μίαν διαφόροις τοῖς χρόνοις. 873 διεχθρεύων τῇ διαθήκῃ
δίαιτα: 846 αἱ ὁμοιοπαθεῖς τ. ἴσης δέονται διαίτης, 865 ἡ ἐσομένη ἡμῖν μετὰ θεῶν δίαιτα
διακαθαίρω: 886 διακαθάραντες τὰ ἐμπόδων εὐπρεπεῖς προϊέναι
διακληρόω: 835 αἱ μακάριαι θεῶν οἰκήσεις διακεκλήρωνται
διακονέω: 839 διακονῆσαι τ. ψυχὴν (ἅπ. λεγ.), cf. ἄκανδον 90
διακονέω: act. 190 init. ὁ λύχνος διακονήσει τὸ φῶς, p. 530 τρέφεται διακονούμενος εἰς ἀπόλαυσιν ἐπιθυμίᾳ, π. 880 ὁ γνωστικὸς θεῷ διακονεῖται, see διαπονέω
διακονία: 855 ὁ κύριος ἐτελείωσεν τ. διακονίαν, 830 ἄμφω τὰς δ. ἄγγελοι ὑπηρετοῦνται

M. C. 26

διάκονος: 830 τὴν μὲν βελτιωτικὴν οἱ πρεσβύτεροι σώζουσιν εἰκόνα, τὴν ὑπηρετικὴν δὲ οἱ διάκονοι, cf. 793 in n.

διακόπτω: 829 ἵνα μὴ διακόπτωμεν τὸ συνεχὲς τ. λόγου, 854 δ. τὸν ἐν χερσὶ λόγον

διακούω: 898 Οὐαλεντῖνον Θεοδᾶ διακηκοέναι φέρουσιν

διακρίνω: 870 διακ. τὰ θαρραλέα τῶν φαινομένων, 887 κίβδηλον κυρίου δ., 900

διακριτέον: 888 δ. τὸ ἀληθὲς ἀπὸ τ. φαινομένου

διακριτικός: 852 ἡ ἀκοὴ ἔχει τ. ἀντίληψιν διὰ τ. διακριτικῆς τῶν σημαινουσῶν τι φωνῶν νοήσεως, 873 ἕξις διακρ. πρὸς τὸ μᾶλλον κ. ἧττον, 448 init. (quot. fr. Basilides) σοφία φυλοκρινητικὴ κ. διακριτικὴ

διακωμῳδέω: 842

διαλαμβάνω: 858 τὰ περὶ τ. θεοῦ διειληφὼς πρὸς αὐτῆς τ. ἀληθείας χοροῦ μυστικοῦ, 867 περὶ τ. ὅλων ἀληθῶς διείληφεν

διαλεκτικός: 894 ἐὰν πρόσσχῃ τις Χρυσίππῳ δ. αὐτὸν ποιήσει

διάλεκτος: 839 ἐκ τῆς τ. συμβιούντων ἐπιγινομένη (MS. συμβάντων καὶ ἐπιγινομένης) συνηθείας ἡ διάλεκτος τελειοῦται

διαμένω: 835, 879

διάμετρος sc. γραμμή: 870 τὰ τῷ ὄντι δεινὰ ἐκ διαμέτρου χωρεῖ τ. ἀγαθοῖς

διαμονή: 835 πρὸς τὴν τ. κρείττονος διαμονὴν διοικεῖται τὰ μικρότερα, 839 ἐπιστημονικὴ τῆς ἀληθείας δ., 850 ἡ ὑλικὴ δ., 860 ἡ (? διανομὴ) τῶν πρὸς ἡμᾶς ἀνηκόντων

διανόησις: 841 αἱ περὶ τ. θεοῦ διανοήσεις

διάνοια: 862 ὅρκον προσφέρεσθαι ἀπὸ διανοίας παραστατικῆς, 883 τὴν δ. τοῦ ῥητοῦ, 848 ἡ δ. ἐκκαλύπτεται τ. θεῷ, 875 κίνημα διανοίας

διανομή: 854 αἱ τ. ὡρῶν διανομαὶ τριχῇ διεστάμεναι, 860 (for MS. διαμονή)

διαπέμπω: (quot.) 844

διαπληκτίζομαι: 892 διαπληκτίζονται πρὸς τοὺς τ. ἀληθῆ φιλοσοφίαν μεταχειριζομένους, Chrys. XI. 768 c

διαπνέω: p. 848 διαπνεῖται τὸ τ. δαιμόνων γένος, act. 221, cf. 124 αἱ φλέβες διαπνοῆς οὐ τυγχάνουσαι σφύζουσι

διαπονέω: 861 τὸ ἀδικεῖν οὐκ ἐν τῷ πάθει κεῖται τ. διαπονουμένου (MS. διακονουμένου, Lowth ἀδικουμένου), cf. Hesych. διαπονηθείς, λυπηθείς

διαπράττω: m. 868 μίσους ἄξιος ἐφ' οἷς διαπράττεται, 838 δ. τι τῶν προσηκόντων, 846 ψυχὴ μακάρια δ. ἔργα, 877 ἐντολὴν δ.

διάρμα: 858 δ. ἔνθεον ἡ εὐχή

διαστέλλω: m. 847 τ. Διόνυσον διαστελλόμενον πεποίηκε, act. 888 δ. τὸ ψευδὲς ἀπὸ τἀληθοῦς

διαστολή: 848 ἡ τ. βραγχίων δ.

διαστροφή: 836 ὁ θάνατος τῆς παλαιᾶς διαστροφῆς, 896 ἐλεῆσαι τ. τοιαύτῃ διαστροφῇ, cf. Eus. Pr. Ev. VIII. bis διαστροφὰς λαμβάνειν

διατάσσομαι: m. 831 ἡ μεγίστη ὑπεροχὴ τὰ πάντα δ., p. 834 ἄλλοι ὑπ' ἄλλοις διατετάχαται, 835 πρὸς τὴν τ. ὅλων σωτηρίαν πάντα ἐστὶ διατεταγμένα

διατείνω: 835 εἰς τὴν τ. ἀνθρώπων διατείνει σωτηρίαν, 898 μέχρι τῆς Ἀντωνίνου ἡλικίας δ.

διατελέω: 892 ἐρίζοντες διατελοῦσι

διατηρέω: 892 αἵρεσιν διατηρεῖ

διατίθημι: 891 οὐκ ἔχουσιν ὅπως διάθωνται τὰς αὐτῶν δόξας

διατριβή: 889 προΐστασθαι διατριβῆς μᾶλλον ἢ ἐκκλησίας, cf. Athen. 350 A, Clem. Hom. I. 3, II. 24

διατρώγω: 842 (quot.) bis

διαφέρω: 449 μαθόντες τὸ διαφέρον τὸ ἐν πληρώματι, 603 τὸ ἐμφύσημα τὸ διαφέρον τ. διαφέροντος πνεύματος, 604 τ. διαφέρον γένος, cf. διάφοροι

διαφορά: 877 τρεῖς αἱ ἀνωτάτω διαφοραί

διάφορος: 850 τὸ ἐκ διαφόρων ἐθνῶν κ. φύσεων σκευαζόμενον θυμίαμα, 856 τὸ διάφορον τ. συνόδου γένος κολλώμενον, 899 διαφόροις τοῖς χρόνοις, 603 ἄνωθεν τὸ δ. γένος, a phrase of Valentinus, see διαφέρω

διαφωνία: 887 μὴ δεῖν πιστεύειν διὰ τ. διαφωνίαν τ. αἱρέσεων bis, 888 δ. ὁδῶν

διδακτός: 829 διδ.)(νοητός

διδασκαλία: 831, 896 ἡ τ. σωτῆρος δ., 834 ἡ ἀληθὴς δ., 835, 862 προστασία τῆς δ., 864 σοφία κατὰ δ. ἐγγίνεται, 867 δ. θεία, 890 ἀρχὴ διδασκαλίας ὁ κύριος, 891, 896 διδασκαλίαι ἀνθρώπειαι, 900 μία ἡ πάντων τ. ἀποστόλων διδασκαλία, 884 ἡ τ. κυρίου δ., 886 αἱ περὶ τ. ἄλλην διδασκαλίαν αἱρέσεις, 887 ἡ κυριακὴ δ., 888 ἀποφεύγειν τὰς διδ.

διδάσκαλος: 831 ὁ δ. ὁ υἱός, 832, 840 ὁ δ. κ. σωτήρ, 862 ὁ ἀξιόπιστος δ. 889

διδάσκω: 864 fin. τὰ μὲν ἄκρα οὐ διδάσκεται, πίστις λέγω καὶ ἡ ἀγάπη

διελέγχω: 891 τὰ ἑαυτῶν διελεγχόμενα ἀρνοῦνται δόγματα

διέπω: 833 καλῶς τι δ., 855 τεταγμένως δ. Plut. aud poet.

διερριμμένως: 901 δ. τὰ ζώπυρα τ. γνώσεως ἐγκατασπεῖραι

διέρχομαι: (quot.) 851 ἡ διερχομένη τ. πῦρ ψυχὴ

διχθρεύω: act. 873 οἱ ἀπειθεῖς διεχ-

θρύουσι τῇ διαθήκῃ, 139 οἱ μὴ διεχθρεύοντες τῇ ἀληθείᾳ, 884 ὁ νῦν διεχθρεύων ὕστερον πιστεύσει, m. 884 ἡ ἀλήθεια οὔ τι διεχθρεύεταί τινι
διηγέομαι: (quot.) 883 δ. ἐν τοῖς πύργοις
διήκω: 838 τὰ μὲν ὡς διήκοντα τὰ δὲ ὡς περιέχοντα, 699 οἱ μὲν διήκειν διὰ πάσης τ. οὐσίας τ. θεόν φασιν, ἡμεῖς δὲ ποιητὴν μόνον αὐτὸν καλοῦμεν, Sap. vii. 24 διήκει διὰ πάντων ἡ σοφία, Clem. Hom. ind.
διικνέομαι: 851 τ. φρόνιμον πῦρ διὰ ψυχῆς δ.
διίστημι: 854 διανομὰς ὡρῶν τριχῇ διεσταμένας
δικαιολογέω: m. 841 εὖ δ. πρὸς τ. Ἀθηνᾶν
δίκαιος: 848 τῷ δικαιοτάτῳ λόγῳ, 876 δ. μὴ κατὰ ἀνάγκην ἢ φόβον ἢ ἐλπίδα, ἀλλ' ἐκ προαιρέσεως
δικαιοσύνη: 835 δ. σωτήριος, 872 δικαιοσύνη τὸ ἀληθεύειν περιποιεῖ, ib. δικαιοσύνης ἐπιτομή, 873 δ. μεταδοτική
δικαιόω: p. 851 κατ' ἐντολὴν δικαιούμενοι
δικαίως: 897 γνώσομαι εἰ δ. μέγα φρονεῖτε
δικαστής: 858 δ. ἀκλινής
διοικέω: p. 835 πρὸς τ. σωτηρίαν τ. κρείττονος δ. καὶ τ. μικρότερα, 858 εὖ μάλα παγκάλως δ. τὰ πάντα, ib. πεπεισμένοι ἄριστα διοικεῖσθαι τὰ κατὰ τ. κόσμον, act. 231 ὁ κύριος δ. τὸ σῶμα τ. ψυχῇ
διοίκησις: 833 δ. ἀνθρώπων, ib. τῷ δυναμένῳ καλῶς τι διέπειν ἀποδέδοται ἡ ἐκείνου δ., ib. οὐδὲ τὸ μικρότατον ἀπολιπὼν τῆς ἑαυτοῦ διοικήσεως ἀφρόντιστον, 860 ἀμετάθετος κατὰ τ. ἐνθέους διοικήσεις
διοικητής: 833 ὁ πρῶτος δ. τῶν ὅλων
Διόνυσος: 863 'wine'
διοπομπήσις: 850 τράγον θύει ἐπὶ διοπομπήσει τ. κακῶν (D. ἀποδιοπομπήσει)
διορατικός: 857 ἡ δ. τῆς ἐπιστήμης ὀξύτης, 785 ψυχὴ τοῦ ἀληθοῦς δ., 116 φωτισμὸς τὸ δ. ἐντιθείς, Orig. Cels. vii. 4, Philo
διοράω: 835 ἀμυδρῶς δ., 858 init. φθάνει ἡ θεία δύναμις διιδεῖν τ. ψυχῷ, 859 δ. τὰ βοηθεῖν δυνάμενα, 862 δ. τὸ βέβαιον τ. ἀποκρίσεως, 893 ἡ θολωθεῖσα ψυχὴ οὐχ οἷά τε τὸ φῶς διιδεῖν
διορθόω: p. 838 δ. εἰς ὠφέλειαν δι' ἀληθοῦς νόου
διόρθωσις: 881 δ. τῶν παρεληλυθότων
διορίζω: 885 αἱ μακάριαι οἰκήσεις διωρισμέναι διακεκλήρωνται
διορύσσω: 842 (quot.), 897 δ. τὸ τειχίον τ. ἐκκλησίας

διπλόη: 859 μηδέπω εἰς τ. μίαν ἕξιν ἐκ τῆς εἰς τ. διπλόην ἐπιτηδειότητος ἐκθλίψαντες ἑαυτούς, 901 τ. διπλόῃ τ. πίστεως ἐπερειδόμενοι, Philo
διπλοῦς: 879 ἡ δικαιοσύνη διπλῆ, 876 μισθὸς δ. ὧν τε οὐκ ἐποίησεν κ. ἀνθ' ὧν εὐηργέτησεν
διστάζω: 864 τὸ μὴ διστάσαι περὶ θεοῦ θεμέλιος γνώσεως
διττός: 879 δ. ἐνέργεια
διχηλέω: 900 τὰ διχηλοῦντα, 901 ἡ τ. διχηλούντων ἑδραιότης, ib. ἀνάγοντα μηρυκισμὸν μὴ διχηλοῦντα δέ, ib. διχηλεῖ μέν, μηρυκισμὸν δὲ οὐκ ἀνάγει
διχῶς: 846 δ. ἐκλαμβάνεται
δίψα: 896 πόμα δίψαν οὐκ ἐπιστάμενον
διώκω: 828 εἰκῇ διώκ. τοὔνομα
δόγμα: 844 φαῦλα κ. μοχθηρὰ δ., 858 οὐδεμίαν ἐν δόγμασιν σῴζει θεοσέβειαν, 891 δόγματα τ. γραφαῖς μαχόμενα, 892 αἱ μοχθηρίαι τῶν δ., ib. προεστῶτες τοῦ δ., 893 τὰ παρὰ φύσιν δ., ib. ἐξάρχοντες δογμάτων, 896 ὀρθοτομία δογμάτων, 900 ἀπὸ δ. προσαγορεύονται, 854 τὰ περὶ τοῦ μὴ δεῖν εὔχεσθαι παρεισαγόμενα δ., 867 τ. βίον τ. γνωστικοῦ διαγράφειν, οὐ τὴν τ. δογμάτων θεωρίαν παρατίθεσθαι, 883 προσεπινοεῖν τ. δόγματα κατ' ἐκλογὴν τ. γραφῶν, 894 μαχόμενα δόγματα, 892
δογματίζω: 887 παρατείνει ἡ ἀλήθεια ἄλλων ἄλλα δογματιζόντων, Philo
δοκέω: 857 init. δ.)(εἶναι, 868, 870, 891 οὐκ ἀρκεῖ εἰπεῖν τὸ δόξαν, ἀλλὰ πιστώσασθαι, 892 τοῦ δοκεῖν μᾶλλον ἢ τοῦ φιλοσοφεῖν προσοῦνται
δόκιμος: 887 οἱ δ. τραπεζῖται τ. κίβδηλον νόμισμα τ. κυρίου διακρίνουσι, ib. init. οἱ δοκιμώτατοι τ. φιλοσόφων, ib. δόκιμοι ἦτοι οἱ εἰς πίστιν ἀφικνούμενοι ἢ οἱ ἐν αὐτῇ τῇ πίστει
δόλιος: (quot.) 848
δολιόω: 897 (quot.) ταῖς γλώσσαις δ.
δόλος: 864 τ. ψεῦδος μετὰ δόλου εἴρηται, 866 (quot.) οὐδὲ ὤμοσεν ἐπὶ δόλῳ
δόξα: 838 ὁ γνωστικὸς οὐ δόξαις ὑποβέβληται, 845 δ. ἄθεοι, 870 δόξῃ μᾶλλον ἢ ἀληθείᾳ ἔχεται, 890 δόξαι αἱρέσεων, 892 δόξαις ἀνθρωπίναις κεκινημένοι
δοξάζω: 877 τὴν ἐν αὐτῷ τ. κυρίου ἀνάστασιν δ., 835 τ. κύριον δ., 864
δοξολόγος: 880 τ. ῥῆμα τ. δοξ. τὰ διὰ Ἡσαΐου ἀλληγορούμενα
δοξοσοφία: 889 ἐν μέσῳ καταστάντες ἀκριβοῦς ἐπιστήμης κ. προπετοῦς δ., 892 ὑπὸ δ. ἐπηρμένοι
δοξόσοφος: 888 οἱ δ. καλούμενοι ἑαυτοὺς ἀπατῶσι
δόσις: 876 οὐ διὰ τ. αἰτήσαντα ἡ δ. γίνεται ἀλλ' ἡ οἰκονομία δικαίαν ποιεῖται τ. δωρεάν

δοτήρ: 852 τοῦ πόματος τῷ δοτῆρι τ. ὅλων ἀπάρχεται
δουλεύω: 875 δ. ἡδοναῖς
δοῦλος: 868 ἐκ τ. πιστοῦ δούλου μεταβαίνων δι' ἀγάπης εἰς φίλον
δοχεῖον: 901 τὸ τ. ψυχῆς τῶν μαθημάτων δοχεῖον, Lucian
δρᾶμα: 870 ἀμεμφῶς ὑποκρινόμενος τὸ δρ. τ. βίου, 849 ὁ κωμικὸς ἐν τῷ δρ.
δράω: 851 (μωρὸς ἐλπίζει θεοὺς τῶν θυσιῶν) χάριν τοῖς δρῶσιν ('to the worshippers') ἐκτίνειν, 854 τ. τελείωσιν ἀπειληφὼς τοῦ κατ' ἀγάπην δρωμένου
δριμύς: 871 κόλασις ἄλλη δριμυτέρα
δριμύτης: 857 ἡ διορατικὴ τ. ἐπιστήμης δρ.
δύναμις: 839 ἡ τοῦ πιστεύσαι δ., 831 ὁ υἱὸς δυνάμει τ. δυνάμεις (the celestial powers) ἐρευνῶν, 833 πρωτούργου κινήσεως δύναμις ὁ υἱός, ib. δ. πατρικὴ ὑπάρχων, 853 φῶς τῆς δ., λύχνος τῆς δ., 857 ἔμμονον τὴν τ. θεωρητῶν δ. κεκτῆσθαι, 859 δ. λογική: δέη δύναμις (ἐστί), 884 τὴν εἰκόνα τὴν ὅσῃ δ. ἐξομοιουμένην: εἰς δύναμιν 840, 835: κατὰ δ.)(κατ' ἀριθμόν, 860 init.
δυσαρεστέομαι: 893 δ. τ. θείαις ἐντολαῖς, Polyb., Schäfer on Dionys. Hal. Comp. p. 124
δύσεργος: 887 δ. καὶ δύσκολος ἀλήθεια, Polyb.
δύσις: 857 init. τ. παλαίτατα τ. ἱερῶν πρὸς δ. ἔβλεπε
δύσκολος: 878 πάσχειν τι δύσκ., 887 δ. καὶ δύσεργος ἡ ἀλήθεια
δύσοιστος(?): 861 τὸ ἐπιτελεῖν διὰ τὸν δύσοιστον κοινὸν βίον διώκουσι καταλιμπάνει (H. τὸ ἔν τι τελεῖν διὰ τὸ ἡδὺ τοῖς τὸν κοινὸν κ.τ.λ.)
δυσφημία: 853 ἡ τ. πολλῶν εὐφημία δυσφημίας οὐδὲν διαφέρει
δυσχεραίνω: 887 δ. τοῖς γινομένοις πρὸς τῆς ἀδικίας, 878 fin.
δυσδίκατος: (quot) 901
δωρεά: 876, see δόσις

ἑβδομάς: 866 ἐπὶ τ. κυριακὴν ὄντως διὰ τ. ἁγίας ἑβδομάδος ἐπείγεται μονήν (cf. ἀνάπαυσις 873), 884 ἡ κοσμικὴ περιήλυσις ἑβδομάσιν ἀριθμουμέναις σημαίνεται
ἑβδομηκοντάκις: (quot.) 884
ἕβδομος: 902 ὁ ἑβδ. στρωματεύς
ἐγγεννάω: 869 ἡ γνῶσις πεῖσμα ἐνεγέννησεν
ἐγγίνομαι: 839 ἡ κακία ἐκ συνηθείας ἐγγίνεται, 850 ἡ ἀπὸ τ. κρεοφαγίας ἐγγινομένη νωθρία, 864 κατὰ διδασκαλίαν ἐγγ. ἡ σοφία
ἔγγραφος: 897 ἔγγραφα ἔχουσι τὰ ἐπίτιμα, 806 ἔγγραφος)(ἄγραφος παράδοσις
ἐγγράφω: p. 837 κόλασις ἡ κατὰ λόγον εἰς παιδείαν ἐγγραφομένη, 736 οἱ εἰς ἄνδρας ἐγγρ., 53 bis
ἐγγυμνάζω: m. 858 τ. κατορθωτικῇ τ. πρακτέων ἐγγυμνασάμενοι ἀσκήσει, 868 ἐγγ. τ. ἐπιστημονικῇ θεωρίᾳ, 874 ἐκεῖνος ἄνδρας νικᾷ ὁ γάμῳ ἐγγ., cf. Plut. Caes. 28
ἐγκαταλέγω: p. 899 οἱ δίκαιοι ἐγκαταλέγονται εἰς τ. ἐκκλησίαν
ἐγκατασπείρω: 901 τ. ζώπυρα ἐγκ., Plut., Philo
ἐγκατασπορά: 902 ἡ τ. δογμάτων ἐγκ.
ἐγκατορύσσω: 889 οἱ σοφισταὶ ταῖς τέχναις ἐγκ. τινά, Dion. H.
ἐγκελεύω: 851 p. σέβειν [δεῖν] ἐγκ.
ἔγκλημα: 886 πρὸς τὰ ἐγκ. ἀπολογήσασθαι
ἐγκράτεια: 874 θεμέλιος γνώσεως ἡ τοιαύτη ἐγκ.
ἐγκρατεύομαι: 877 τί γὰρ εἴ τις ἃ μὴ οἶδεν ἐγκρατεύοιτο, 874 ἐγκ. ἢ δι' ἐπαγγελίαν ἢ διὰ φόβον
ἐγκρατής: 858 ἐγκ. γενόμενος τ. ἀντιστρατευομένων τῷ νῷ, 872 δι' ἀγροικίαν ἐγκ., 874 ἐγκ. οὐχ ὁ τ. παθῶν μόνον κρατῶν ἀλλὰ καὶ ὁ τῶν ἀγαθῶν ἐγκ. γενόμενος, 880 ἀναμάρτητος μόνει ἐγκρ. δὲ γίνεται, 471 τὸ θεῖον οὐκ ἐγκ.
ἔγκριτος: 865 ἡ γνῶσις παραδίδοται τοῖς εἰς τοῦτο ἐγκ.
ἐγκύκλιος: 839 ἐγκ. παιδεία
ἐγκυλίομαι: 843 ἐγκ. μεθαῖς, see ἐπεγκ.
ἐγχειρέω: 842 'Ἀρκεσίλαος παίζων ἐνεχείρει, see ἐπιχείρημα below, 890 μεγίστοις πράγμασιν ἐγχειρεῖν
ἐγχειρίζω: 856 τάξιν ἐπεχειρίσθησαν ἐκ θεοῦ, 865 ἡ γνῶσις τοῖς ἀξίοις ἐγχειρίζεται
ἐγχέω: 893 ἐν θολερῷ ὕδατι τὰς ἐγχ. ἁλίσκεσθαι
ἑδραῖος: 861 ἀμετάπτωτος κ. ἑδρ. βίος
ἑδραιότης: 859 ἀμεταπτώτως βιοῦν κ. ἀσκεῖν μονότονον ἑδραιότητα, 901 ἡ τῶν διχηλούντων ἑδρ.
ἐθίζω: 878 μόνον τὸ καλὸν ἐπισκοπεῖν εἰθισμένη, see ἐθνίζω
ἐθισμός: 893 ὁ ἐθ. πρὸς <τὸ> τοῖς κριθεῖσιν ὀρθῶς ἔχειν ἀκολουθεῖν, cf. ἐθίζεσθαι πρός τι Arist.
ἐθνίζω: 839 αἱ αἱρέσεις ἐθνίζουσιν ἀμηγέπη (ms. ἐθίζουσι)
ἐθνικός: 858 τῷ ἐθνικῷ ἐθνικῶς ἕκαστα ἀποδίδοται, 885 ἡ ἀπὸ τ. εὐαγγελίου ἀπόστασις [ἃ] πρὸς τὸν ἐθν. βίον, 886
ἐθνικῶς: 858, 885, 761
ἔθνος: 859 ὁ ἐξ ἐθνῶν ἐπιστρέφων, 878 fin. ἐν τοῖς ἔθν. διὰ μείζονας ἡδονὰς ἀπέχονται τῶν ἡδέων, 900 ἀπὸ ἔθνους προσαγορεύονται, 866 μεταβολὴ σωτή-

OF GREEK WORDS. 405

ριος ἐξ ἐθνῶν εἰς πίστιν, 894 ἡδονὴν τοῖς ἐθν. ἀπονεμητέον

ἔθος: 894 init. τῷ προκατεσχηκότι ἔθει ἡττηθείς

εἰδωλολατρία: 849 ἑξῆς ἄνευ τῆς εἰδ. μεταλαμβάνειν κρεῶν, 877 πορνείας τρεῖς διαφοραί φιληδονία φιλαργυρία εἰδωλολατρία

εἴδωλον: 887 εἰδώλων ἔμπλεως τ. ψυχὴν

εἰκῆ: 828 εἰκῆ διώκουσι τοὔνομα

εἰκών: 838 init. τρίτην τὴν θείαν εἰκ., 862 τ. κυρίου κατ' εἰκόνα παιδεύων δημιουργεῖ τ. κατηχούμενον, 869 εἰς τὰς εἰκ. ἀφορῶν τ. καλάς, 894 τ. κυρίῳ πειθόμενοι ἐκτελεῖται κατ' εἰκόνα τοῦ διδασκάλου, 830 τ. βελτιωτικήν οἱ πρεσβύτεροι σώζουσιν εἰκόνα, 870 ἐπίγειος εἰκὼν θείας δυνάμεως, 874 εἰκόνας ἔχει τ. ἀποστόλους, ib. εἰκόνα σώζει τ. προνοίας, 884 μίαν εἰκόνα ἐπὶ μίαν οὐσίαν περιβεβλημένοι, cf. Stählin Clem Al. u. d. LXX. p. 12 foll.

εἰλικρινής: 835 ἐναργὴς κ. ἀκριβῶς εἰλ. θέα

εἰλικρινῶς: 860 ψυχὴ ἄμικτος εἰλ.

εἰμι 895 (opt. c. inf.) εἴη μὲν οὖν (< ἄν > D.) τοῦσδε τ. αἱρετικοὺς σωφρονεῖσθαι

εἰρηνοποιός: 894 πρὸς τοὺς εἰρ. τῶν δογμάτων πορευτέον, Xen.

εἰς = ἐν: 840 παγκρατιάζουσιν εἰς τὸ στάδιον, 873 μένει εἰς τ. ἀνάπαυσιν, frequent in N. T.; repeated with different sense 876 ἐν τῆξιν. εἰς πεῖραν

εἷς: 859 ἡ μία ἕξις)(ἡ διπλῆ, 899 ἑνὸς ὄντος τ. θεοῦ π. ἑνὸς τ. κυρίου τὸ ἄκρως τίμιον κατὰ τ. μόνωσιν ἐπαιρεῖται, ib. τῇ τ. ἑνὸς φύσει συγκληροῦται ἡ μία ἐκκλησία, 633 (from Pythag.) τ. ἀνθρωπον δεῖν ἕνα γενέσθαι, 696 καλοῦντες ἤτοι ἐν ἢ τἀγαθὸν ἢ θεὸν: 883 ἐν ἢ δεύτερον

εἴσειμι: 897 διὰ τῆς τ. κυρίου παραδόσεως εἴσιμεν

εἰσηγέομαι: 848 οὐδὲν διαφέροντα ἀνθρώπου εἰσηγ. θεόν

εἴσοδος: 889 ἡ εἰσ. τ. ἀναπαύσεως τεθλιμμένη, 897 ἡ κλεὶς τ. εἰσόδου

εἰσφέρω: 838 λειτουργίαν εἰσφέρεται ἕκαστος (late use of m. for classical act.)

εἴτ' οὖν .. εἴτε .. εἴτε: 885 bis without verb

ἐκ .. εἰς: 836 (of an ascending scale) ἐκ τοῦ ἀνενδεοῦς εἰς τὸ ἐνδεές, 865 ἐκ φωτὸς εἰς φῶς: ἐκ .. διὰ: 834 ἐξ ἑνὸς κ. δι' ἑνὸς σωζόμενοι, cf. 1 Cor. viii. 6

ἑκάτερος: 901 ὅσα μήτε ἑκάτερον μήτε τὸ ἕτερον τούτων ἔχει

ἐκβαίνω: 892 ἐκβ. τ. ἀλήθειαν

ἐκβιάζομαι: 835 διὰ τ. κρίσεως τοὺς ἀπηλγηκότας ἐκβ. μετανοεῖν, 858 ἐται-

ρικῶς ἐκβ. ὡραία γυνή: pass. in 84, 86 τῇ χρήσει τ. ἀληθείας ἐκβιαζόμενον φυγαδεύεται

ἐκδέχομαι: 835 φιλόνεικος ἐκδ. τ. νόμον, Arist.

ἐκδίδωμι: 890 σφᾶς αὐτοὺς ἡδοναῖς ἐκδ.

ἐκεῖ: 'in heaven' 884)(ἐνθένδε.

ἐκζητέω: (quot.) 829

ἐκκαλύπτω: 852 ἐνδυθεῖς πλοκαὶ ἐκθ. τ. ψυχήν, 164 Ατ. ἐκθ. τὴν εὐκολον βρῶσιν, Philo

ἐκθλίβω: 850 εἰς τ. μίαν ἕξιν ἐκ τῆς εἰς διπλόην ἐπιτηδειότητος ἐκθλ. ταυτάας, Plut. Mor. 878 τὰ μικρὰ κ. λεῖα σώματα ἐξεθλίβετο εἴς τε τὸ μετέωρον ἀνεφέρετο

ἐκκαλύπτω: 848 ἐκκαλύπτεται ἅμα τ. θυσίᾳ ἡ διάνοια τ. θεῷ

ἐκκλησία: 830 κατὰ τὴν ἐκκ. οἱ πρεσβύτεροι .. οἱ διάκονοι, 846 ἐκκ. ἱερὸν θεοῦ, ib. τὸ ἄθροισμα τ. ἐκλεκτῶν ἐκκ., 848 ἡ θυσία τῆς ἐκκ. λόγοι ἀπὸ τ. ἁγίου ψυχῆς ἀναθυμιώμενοι, 863 ἑαυτὸν ἐπιδίδωσιν ὑπὲρ τῆς ἐκκ., 871 εἰσὶ κατὰ τὴν ἐκκ. στέφανοι ἀνδρῶν τε κ. παίδων, 873 ἡ γνωστικὴ ψυχὴ ἐν πνευματικῇ τῇ ἐκκ. μένει [εἰς] τ. ἀνάπαυσιν, 882 ὁ μέγας ναὸς ἡ ἐκκ., 885 σῶμα ἀλληγορεῖται ἡ ἐκκ., 898 τ. προφητείας ἐργοῦσιν ἑαυτοὺς τῆς ἐκκλησίας, 888 ἐν μόνῃ τ. ἀληθεῖ (MS. ἀληθείᾳ) κ. τ. ἀρχαίᾳ ἐκκ. ἡ ἀκριβεστάτη γνῶσις, 894 χαρὰν τῇ ἐκκ. προσοικειωτέον, 892 ἡ πολυθρύλητος κατὰ τὰς ἐκκ. αὐτῶν πρωτοκαθεδρία, 899 ἡ προγενεστάτη κ. ἀληθεστάτη ἐκκλ. ib. μίαν εἶναι τὴν ἀληθῆ ἐκκ. τὴν τῷ ὄντι ἀρχαίαν, ib. ἀρχαία κ. καθολικὴ ἐκκλ. see εἷς and ἐξοχή

ἐκκλησιαστικός: 833, 826, 887 ὁ ἐκκ κανών, 890 ἡ ἐκκ. παράδοσις, 892, 896 ἡ ἐκκ. γνῶσις, ib. ἡ ἀποστολικὴ κ. ἐκκ. ὀρθοτομία δογμάτων

ἐκκόπτω: 875 ψυχῆς ἐκκόψαι πάθος

ἐκκρέμαμαι: 865 ὁπόταν τις ἐκκρεμασθῇ (MS. κρεμασθῇ) τ. κυρίου διὰ πίστεως, cf. 936

ἐκκυκλέω: 886 οὐκ ἐκκυκλεῖν χρὴ τὸ μυστήριον

ἐκλαμβάνω: 846 τὸ ἱερὸν διχῶς ἐκλαμβάνεται, 868 (τὸ ῥηθέν) ἰδίως ἐκλαμβάνον, 886 ἀπολέλειπται ἐκλαβεῖν τοῖς συνιέναι δυναμένοις, 111 Αr. ἔστιν ἑτέρως ἐκλαβεῖν, cf. Plut. Pericl. 6, Hein on Eus. H. E. vi. 8

ἐκλάμπω: 865 τὸ τ. ἀγάπης ἀξίωμα ἐκλ. ἐκ φωτὸς εἰς φῶς, 853 εἰς τὸ βάθος τ. ψυχῆς τὸ φῶς ἐκλ.

ἐκλέγω: p. 829 οἱ ἐξειλεγμένοι εἰς γνῶσιν. 878 ἐξειλεγμένη κτίσις, 879 ἐξειλ. ὁι δίκαιοι, 889 ἡ ψυχὴ ἡ ἔξειλ., 812 οἱ ὄρῳ ἐκλεγόντες, 792 ἐκλεγέντες πρὸτοῦ τ. τέλη προορωμένου, m. 891 ἐκλέγονται τὰ ἀμφιβόλως εἰρημένα, 896 τὸ τ. ἡδοναῖς συναιρούμενον ἐκλέγονται

ἐκλεκτικός: 887 δόκιμοι οἱ ἐκλεκτικώτερον προσιόντες τ. κυριακῇ διδασκαλίᾳ

ἐκλεκτός: 846 τὸ ἄθροισμα τ. ἐκλεκτῶν, 853 κατὰ πρόθεσιν τὸν ἐκλ. ἐγνωκώς, 851 and 866 τ. γένος τ. ἐκλεκτῶν, 793 and 955 ἐκλεκτῶν ἐκλεκτότεροι, 832 (quot.), 882 (saying of the Apostle Matthias) ἐὰν ἐκλεκτοῦ γείτων ἁμαρτήσῃ, ἥμαρτεν ὁ ἐκλ., 878

ἐκλογή: 837 τὸ ἀδούλωτον τ. ψυχῆς πρὸς ἐκλ. βίου, 883 προσεκπονεῖν τ. δόγματα κατ' ἐκλ. τῶν γραφῶν, 891 ἐκλογὰς κομίζουσι

ἐκμανθάνω: 829 παρὰ τ. υἱοῦ ἐκμ. τὸ ἐπέκεινα αἴτιον, 831 τ. θεῖα μυστήρια παρὰ τ. μονογενοῦς ἐκμ., 888 διὰ τ. γραφῶν ἐκμ. ἀποδεικτικῶς, 890 αἱ αἱρέσεις οὐκ ἐκμαθοῦσαι παραπέμπονται τ. γραφάς

ἐκούσιος: 879 ἐποικοδομεῖ ἐπὶ τὸ ἐκ. ἡ ἀγάπη

ἐκουσίως: 855 ἐκ. σπεύσει πρὸς σωτηρίαν

ἐκπικραίνω: 841 εἰς ὀργὴν ἐκπικραίνονται

ἔκπληξις: 830 ἔκπ. ἁγία

ἐκπληρόω: 860 εὐσυνειδήτως τὰ παρ' ἑαυτοῦ ἐκπ. εἰς τ. μάθησιν

ἐκπονέω: (c. inf.) m. 892 τέλος ἀκολουθεῖν ἐκπονούμενοι (MS. ἐκπορίζομενοι), cf. Eur. Med. 241 κἂν μὲν τάδ' ἡμῖν ἐκπονουμέναισιν εὖ πόσις ξυνοικῇ κ.τ.λ.; act. 795 οὐκ ἐξεπόνησαν γενέσθαι πιστοί

ἐκπορίζω: m. 892 ἡ τῆς ἀληθείας ἐπίγνωσις ἐκπ. τὴν πίστιν, act. 942, see ἐκπονέω

ἐκτείνω: 834 τ. πνεῦμα διὰ πολλῶν τ. σιδηρῶν ἐκτείνεται δακτυλίων

ἐκτελέω: 845 κἂν τ. τέχνην ἐκτελέσῃς, 894 p. ὁ τ. κυρίῳ πειθόμενος τελέως ἐκτελεῖται

ἐκτίθημι: 867 τὴν τ. δογμάτων θεωρίαν ὑστερον ἐκθησόμεθα

ἐκτίνω: 851 χάριν τούτων ἐκτίνειν

ἐκτός: 884 τὸ ἑ. μόνον πλεονεκτοῦσιν οἱ ἀδικεῖν ἐπιχειροῦντες: for τὰ ἐκτός see 881 init. ἀφῃρέθη τῶν ἐκτός, n. on p. 136, l. 1 and 943 fin. τὰ ἐκτός οὐ βλέπει

ἐκτρέπω: m. 853 εἰς ταπεινὰς ἐκτρ. ὑπονοίας, 888 οἱ ἀπὸ τ. ἀληθείας ἐκτρεπόμενοι, ib. c. acc. τὰς ζητήσεις ἐκτρέπονται

ἐκτυπόω: 891 οἱ τεχνῖται παρὰ τ. κοινὰς ἐννοίας ἐκτ. τὸ βέλτιον

ἐκφέρω: 891 ἐκφ. δόγματα

ἐκφύω: 877 ἐκ φιλαργυρίας κ. φιληδονίας αἱ πᾶσαι ἐκφύονται κακίαι

ἐκφωτίζω: 836 ἐκφωτιζομένου παντὸς εἰς ἕνωσιν, 663 ἡ νὺξ ἐκφωτίζεται τῷ ἡλίῳ, Constantine in Socr. H. E. i. 9

ἑκὼν εἶναι (affirmative): 896 δόξης ἐπιθυμοῦσιν ὅσοι ἑκόντες εἶναι σοφίζονται

ἔλεγχος: 888 τ. ζητήσεις ἐκτρέπονται διὰ τοὺς ἐλ., 892 διαπληκτίζονται διὰ τοὺς ἐλ., 893 ὑφορώμενα τ. προφητείας δι' ἔλεγχον

ἐλέγχω: p. 891 ὑπὸ τῶν ἀντιλεγόντων ἐλ.

ἐλεέω: 876 ὃν ἐγὼ πατάξω σὺ ἐλέησον, c. gen. 896 τούτους ἐλεήσειεν ἄν τις τῆς τοιαύτης διαστροφῆς, cf. 7 ᾠκτειρεν ἡμᾶς τῆς πλάνης

ἐλεημοσύνη: 866 (quot.)

ἔλεος: 855 κατ' ἔλεον

ἐλευθερικός: 856 init. ἐλευθερικωτάτη θεραπεία

ἐλευθεριότης: 838 a form of ἀνδρεία

ἔλεφας: 845 τὸ ἐξ ἐλέφαντος ἐλεφάντινον

ἑλίσσω: 834 ἑλιχθέντες τ. πάθεσι

ἕλκω: 834 τῷ ἁγίῳ πνεύματι ἑλκόμενοι

ἔλλειψις: 886 κατ' ἔλλ. λεγομένου τ. ῥητοῦ προσυπακούσωμεν τὸ ἐνθέον

ἐλλιπής: 857 ἐλλ. τ. οἰκείων ἀγαθῶν

ἐλπίζω: 851, 896 ἐλπιζόμενα εἰς κατάληψιν

ἐλπίς: 869 πεῖσμα βεβαιότερον ἐλπίδος ter, 892 τῆς ἑαυτῶν ἐλπίδος καταφρονοῦσι

ἐμβάλλω: 895 εἰς τ. κρίσιν ἑαυτοὺς ἐμβ.

ἐμβάς: 841 (quot.) ἱμάντα ἐμβάδος

ἐμβλέπω: 882 μὴ ἐμβ. πρὸς ἐπιθυμίαν ἀλλοτρίᾳ γυναικί

ἐμμ...: 871 τῇ τῆς κλήσεως ἐμμ. ὁμολογίᾳ

ἐμμεσιτεύω: (ἅπ. λεγ.) 862 κοινωνίας ἐμμ. πρὸς τ. θεόν

ἔμμονος: 857 ἔμμονος τ. θεωρητῶν δύναμις ἐν τ. ψυχῇ

ἐμπάθεια: 833 σαρκὸς ἀνθρωπίνης ἐμπ. (MS. εὐπ.)

ἐμπαθής: 832 τ. σάρκα τ. ἐμπ. φύσει εἰς ἕξιν ἀπαθείας ἐπαίδευσε, 839 πνευματικὰς ἐξουσίας ἐμπαθῶν παθῶν, 841 βάρβαροι ἄγριοι, Ἕλληνες ἐμπ., 870 ὁ ἐμπ. βίος

ἔμπαλιν: 901 ἐμπ. αὖ ἀκάθαρτα κἀκεῖνα

ἔμπεδος: 874 ἐμπ. ἡ τ. ἀγαθοῦ ἐπιστημονικὴ κτῆσις

ἐμπέδως: 861 τῷ γνωστικῷ ἐμπ. ὅρκος ἐστὶν ὁ βίος

ἐμπειρία: 871 ἐξ ἐμπ. κακοτεχνεῖν, 858 ἐμπειρίᾳ πολλῇ χρησάμενος κατά τε μάθησιν κ. βίον

ἐμπλέως: 887 ὁ τ. ψυχὴν νοσῶν κ. εἰδώλων ἐμπ.

ἐμπνέω: 860 ἰσχὺν ἐμπνεῖ, 848 ἐμπνεῖται τ. ἔνυδρα κατὰ τὴν τ. βραγχίων διαστολήν

ἐμποδών: 882 τὰ ἐμπ. καταλιπὼν τέμνει τ. οὐρανόν, 886

OF GREEK WORDS. 407

ἐμποιέω : 897 τύφον ἐπεποίησεν
ἔμπροσθεν: 896 οὐ γὰρ ὑπερέλαβον σοφίᾳ τ. ἐμπρ. ἄνδρας
ἐμφαίνω: 884 τὸ λέγειν ἐμφαίνει τοὺς αἰτουμένους, καὶ εἶναι τούτους ἀμείνους
ἐμφανής: 861 ἐμφ. τοῖς πολλοῖς, 886
ἐμφερής: 888 ἡ ἐκ κηροῦ ἐμφ. πεποιημένη τῇ ἀληθεῖ ὀπώρᾳ
ἐμφόρησις: (quot.) 850 σαρκῶν ἐμφορήσεις σῶμα ῥωμαλέον ἀπεργάζονται
ἐμφυσιόω (quot.) 897 ἡ σοφία ἐνεφυσίωσε τ. αὑτῆς τέκνα, see φυσιόω
ἐμφυτεύω: 897 ἡ σοφία τοῖς κατὰ τ. μάθησιν τέκνοις ἐμφυτευθεῖσα (MS. ἐμφυτεύσασα)
ἔμψυχος: 862, 863 ἐμψ. ἄγαλμα
ἐναγής: 844 θεὸς ἐναγὲς οἶδεν τ. ἄκκον ἦθος
ἐναγωνίζομαι: 868 ἐναγωνίσασθαι (Η. ἐναγ.) τοῖς καθολικώτερον εἰρημένοις
ἐναντιόομαι : 892 ἐν. ταῖς γραφαῖς
ἐναποθνήσκω: 862 ἐναπ. τοῖς βασάνοις, Philo
ἐναπόκειμαι : 855 εἶδος εὐχῆς ἐναποκειμένης γνωστικῶς, Plut., Philo
ἐναποσφραγίζομαι: 837 ὁ μονογενὴς ἐναποσφρ. τ. γνωστικῷ τ. τελείαν θεωρίαν κατ' εἰκόνα τὴν ἑαυτοῦ, 840 τὸ ἑταιρικὸν ἐναπ., 84 ταύτας τ. θείας γραφὰς ἐναποσφραγίσασθαι τῇ ψυχῇ, cf. 487 τὰ πάθη ἐναποσφραγίσματα τ. πνευματικῶν δυνάμεων, Sext. Math. vii 248
ἐνάργεια: 893 ἐν. τῶν ἀληθῶν
ἐναργής: 828 ἐναργεστέροις χρῆσθαι τ. λόγοις, 835 ἡ θέα ἐν. κ. εἰλικρινής, 892 τὸ δόξαν αὐτοῖς ὑπάρχειν ἐναργέστερον, 895 ἡ τ. μαρτυρίας ἐν. ἀπόδειξις
ἐναργῶς : 891 δόγματα ἐν. μαχόμενα, 854 ἐν. παντὸς μᾶλλον
ἐνάρετος: 834 οἱ ἐν. οἰκειοῦνται τ. πρώτῃ μονῇ, 835 μεταβάλλει πᾶν τὸ ἐν. εἰς ἀμείνους οἰκήσεις, 846 ἄγαλμα ἐν., 870 ἕξις τῆς ἐν. ψυχῆς, 871 τὰ θηρία ἐνάρετα λεγόντων, Lob. Phryn. 328
ἔναυλος: 875 ἔχει ὁ γνωστικὸς ἔναυλον τ. φωνὴν
ἐνδεής: 859 τὸ ἐνδ. (? ἀνενδ.) πρὸς τ. ἐπιβάλλον μετρεῖται, ib. ἐνδεοῦς γινομένου, 829 τὸ μὴ ἐπεσκέφθαι ῥᾴθυμον καὶ ἐνδεές, 886 οὐκ ἐνδ. τὸ θεῖον, ib. τὸ γεννητὸν κ. ἐνδ., 846 θεὸς οὐκ ἐνδ.
ἐνδεῖ: 886 προσυπακούσαι τὸ ἐνδέον
ἔνδεια: 848 κατὰ τὴν ἐκ τ. ἐνδείας ἐπιθυμίαν κακοῦται, 878 ῥᾶον τοῦ ἀδελφοῦ τ. ἐνδείαν οἴσεων bis
ἐνδείκνυμι: m. 901 ταυτὶ τ. αἱρετικοὺς ἐνδ. ὀφθαμὶ μὲν πατρὸς ἐπιβεβηκότας, 854 ἐνδ. ὅτι, 830 τ. θεωρίαν ἀνθρώποις ἐνδ., 829, 858, 882
ἔνδειξις : 841 ὀλίγα ἀπόχρη πρὸς ἐνδ.
ἐνδέχομαι: 835 κατὰ τὸ ἐνδεχόμενον

ἐνδέω: 868 τῷ σώματι ἐνδεδεμένος, see ἐνδεῖ
ἐνδιάθετος: 864 πίστις ἐνδιάθετόν τί ἐστιν ἀγαθόν, 854 τ. ἐνδ. ὁμιλίαν ὁ θεὸς ἐπαίει, cf. Clem. Hom. III 19 ἡ τῶν τέκνων πρὸς τ. πατέρα ἐνδ. τιμή, ib. xiii. 16 ἡ σώφρων τ. ἄνδρα ἐνδιαθέτως φιλεῖ, Prantl l. 420, 507, Walz Rhett. Gr. vii. 5, Galen t. 1, Philo De Abr. 18 (II. 13 M.)
ἐνδίδωμι: 853 εἰς ὀχλοκρασίαν ἑαυτὸν ἐνδ
ἔνδοθεν: 854 ἐνδ. κεκράγαμεν, 856
ἔνδοξος: 894 μέτομεν εἰς τὰ ἐνδ. μᾶλλον ἢ ἐπὶ τ. ἀλήθειαν
ἐνδόσιμος: 858 τ. ψυχὴν ἐνδ. ἡδονῇ παρίστησι, cf. Schmid iv. p. 354 [Stephanus cites from Greg. ἀποκλίνει ἐκ τοῦ ἀποτόμου πρὸς τὸ ἐνδόσιμον, Max. Tyr. i. 2 πρὸς τὰς τ. χειμώνος ἐμβολὰς ἀσθενεστάτη κ. ἐνδόσιμος ναῦς]
ἐνδύω: 883 σάρκα ἐνδυσάμενος ὁ σωτήρ
ἔνειμι: 837 ἔνεστι φάναι, 893 κεναὶ λέγονται ἐν αἷς ἄχρηστον τὸ ἐνόν
ἐνέργεια: 831 δι' αἰσθητικῆς ἐνεργ. παιδεύει τ. σκληροκάρδιον, 833 πατρικὴ τις ἐνέργεια ὁ υἱός, 859 κινούντων κ. ἰσχόντων ἀλλήλους τῆς τε ἐνεργείας κ. τοῦ μετίσχοντος, 864 οὗτ ἐγένυησεν εἰς ἐνέργειαν ἀγάπης, 866 κυριακὴ ἐν., 869 βεβαία πίστις ἡ ἀκολουθοῦσα πιστὴ ἐνέργ., 870 οὐδεμία ἐνέργ. ἕξις, ib διαβόλου ἐν. μᾶλλον δὲ συνέργεια, 875 ἐν εὐπιστίαις, 883 γνωστικὴ ἐνέργεια
ἐνεργέω p. 852 ἡ ἀκοὴ διὰ σωματικῶν πόρων ἐνεργουμένη ἔχει τ. ἀντίληψιν, 855 αἱ οἰκονομίαι ἐνεργοῦνται, 890 διὰ τ. κυρίου πρὸς τὴν τ. ἀνθρώπων εὐεργεσίαν ἐνεργούμενος (MS. -ουμένη); act 864 τὸ ψεῦδος οὐκ ἀργός ἐστι λόγος ἀλλ' εἰς κακίαν ἐνεργεῖ, 868 διὰ στόματος ἀνθρωπίνου κύριος ἐν., 877 ἡ ἐνεργοῦσα μετάληψις, 839 αἱ διὰ σαρκῶν ἐνεργοῦσαι ἐξουσίαι
ἐνέργημα: 855 ἐνέργ. τερπνὸν ὑφορᾶται, 878 ἐνεργήματα ἅγια ἃ ὁ κύριος αὐτοὺς ἠθέλησεν φρονεῖν, 809 διὰ τ. θείων ἐνεργημάτων τ. δύναμιν αὐτοῦ καταλαμβάνουσι, 882 ἐνδεικνύμενος τὰ ἐν.
ἐνεργός: 868 ἔργῳ βεβαίῳ κ. λόγῳ ἐνεργῷ πιστός
ἔνθεν : 859, 866 ἐνθ. ἤδη bis, 883
ἔνθεος: 858 δίαρμα ἐνθ. ἡ εὐχή, 860 ἐνθ. προσοπαί, Philo
ἐνθέως: 852 ἐνθ. (MS. ἐντέχνως) ἀναστρεφόμεθα
ἔνι: 883 ὡς ἔνι μάλιστα βραχύτατον, 836
ἐνίδρυτος: 846 τὸ ἐν. κ. τὸ ἐνιδρυόμενον (MS. ἀνίδρυτον...ἐνιδρυμένον)
ἐνιδρύω : 837 ἐν δικαίου ψυχῇ ἐνιδρύεται

ὁ πάντων ἡγεμών, 845 πῶς αὐτὸ τὸ ἐν ἑαυτὸ ἐπιδρύσει; 846 ὁ θεὸς ἐνίδρυται ἐν τ. γνωστικῷ, ib. see ἐνίδρυτος, m. 755 ἐν πολλοῖς τ. ἱερῶν τὰς θήκας ἐπιδρύσαντο

ἐνίστημι: 896 ἐνίστανται θείᾳ παραδόσει ('resist'): 869 τ. ἐνεστῶτα ἀλγεινά, 879 τ. ἐνεστῶτα)(τ. προγεγονότα and τ. μέλλοντα

ἐννοέω: m. 855 ἡ αἴτησις γίνεται κ. αἰτήσαντι κ. ἐννοηθέντι, 876 ἐννοήθητι κ. ποίησω

ἔννοια: 831 τ. ἀποκρύφους ἐνν. ἐπιβλέπειν, 833 ἔνν. θεοῦ, 852 ὁ θεὸς ἐπαίει τῆς ἐνν., 853 εἰς ἀσχήμονας ἐκτρέπεται ἐννοίας, 856 ὅπερ ἡμῖν ἡ φωνὴ σημαίνει, τοῦτο τ. θεῷ ἡ ἔννοια, 876 νηστεύει ἀπὸ τῶν ἐννοιῶν τ. πονηρῶν, 885 ἡ τοῦ βούλεσθαι ἔννοια, ib. εἴτε ἐν ἔργῳ εἴτε ἐν λόγῳ εἴτε ἐν τῇ ἐννοίᾳ, 891 παρὰ τὰς κοινὰς ἐνν. ἐκτυποῦσι τὸ βέλτιον

ἔννομος: (quot.) 834 αἱ ἐντολαὶ οὐκ ἐννόμοις

ἐνοποιέω: 861 ἑαυτὸν ἐνοπ. τ. θείῳ χορῷ, Arist.

ἑνότης: (quot.) 850 ἡ ἑν. τ. πίστεως, 899, 793, 776

ἐνός: 857 ὁ γνωστικὸς διὰ τ. ἀγάπης ἥνωται τ. πνεύματι, Philo, Clem. Hom. ind.

ἐνστάζω: 833 μόνῳ ἀνθρώπῳ ἔννοιαν ἐνεστάχθαι θεοῦ (ἐνεστάλθαι ms.), 59 πᾶσιν ἐνέστακται ἀπόρροια θεϊκή

ἐνστασις: 867 σώζειν ἐνστ., 868 τὸν Ἰωσὴφ παράγειν τῆς ἐνστ. οὐκ ἴσχυσεν, 190 ἐνστ. Χριστιανοῦ, 469 ἵνα ὦσιν οἱ λόγοι κ. ὁ βίος ἀκόλουθοι τῇ ἐνστάσει, 536 τ. Ἰωάννου τὴν ἔνστασιν τ. βίου, Clem. Hom. XIII. 14 τῇ πρὸς τὸ σωφρονεῖν ἐνστάσει σεμνῇ μείνασα σωθῆναι ἔχει, cf. Wytt. on Plut. Mor. 62 B, Schw. Index in Epict. s.v., ('principle,' 'obstinacy,' 'obstacle')

ἐντάσσω: 861 ἐντεταγμένος εἰς θεωρίαν

ἐνταῦθα: 854 ἐντ. γενόμενος 'at this point,' 615: 865 ἐνταῦθα ἡ τελείωσις 'herein,' explained by infin. following, as in 840, 897 ἐντ. ἡ δύναμις: 895 'in this world' τέλος τ. γνωστικοῦ ἐντ. διττόν

ἐντελής: 859 ἀνὴρ ἐντ.

ἐντέλλω: m. 875 ἀκολούθως οἷς ἐνετείλω ἐξήσαμεν, 880

ἔντευξις: 860 fin. αἱ πρὸ τ. ἑστιάσεως ἐντ. τ. γραφῶν

ἔντιμος: 894 ὁ αὐτὸς νοῦς παρ' οἷς μὲν ἐντιμότατος παρ' οἷς δὲ παρανοίας ἤλωκε

ἐντολή: 834 αἱ κατὰ νομον τε κ. πρὸ τ. νόμου ἐντ., ib. πρότεραι κ. δεύτεραι ἐντ., 877 ἐντολὰς διαπραξάμενος, 893 δυσαρεστούμενοι ταῖς θείαις ἐντολαῖς, τουτέστι τῷ θείῳ πνεύματι

ἐντομή: 848 see ἔντομος

ἔντομος: 845 περιπείται τὰ ἔ. κατὰ τὴν διὰ τ. πτερύγων ἐπιθλίψιν τ. ἐντομῆς

ἐντροπή: 851 ἡ ἐντρ. κ. ἡ αἰδώς

ἐντυγχάνω: 892 τοῖς ἐν μέσῳ ἐντυχόντες (sc. βιβλίοις), 851 ἡ παρουσία ἀνδρὸς ἀγαθοῦ σχηματίζει τὸν ἐντ.

ἔνυδρος: 845 τὰ ἐν. ἐμπνεῖται κατὰ τὴν τ. βραγχίων διαστολήν, cf. Theophr. H. P. I. 14. 8 μεγίστη διάστασις ἐπὶ τῶν ζώων ὅτι τὰ μὲν ἔνυδρα, τὰ δὲ χερσαῖα, Plat. Tim. L. 104 κούφων ψυχαὶ ἐς πτηνῶν μορφὰς μετενδύονται, ἀργῶν δὲ καὶ ἀμαθῶν ἐς τὴν τῶν ἐνύδρων ἰδέαν

ἕνωσις: 836 ἐκφωτίζεσθαι εἰς ἕν. ἀδιάκριτον

ἐξαίρετος: 882 ἐξαιρέτους τοῖς ἐξαιρέτως πεπιστευκόσιν ἀπονείμας τιμάς, 851 οὐκ ἐν ἐξ. ἡμέραις σέβειν τ. πατέρα, ib. ἐξ. ἱερόν, 881 τὸ ἐξ. τ. γνώσεως

ἐξαιρέτως: 832 see ἐξαίρετος, Lightf. Ign. p. 308

ἐξαίσιος: 837 ἐξ. λύπαις κ. ἀβουλήτοις τύχαις περιπίπτειν

ἐξαπατάω: 888 ἐξαπατῶν σφᾶς αὐτοὺς ἐπιχειροῦσιν, ib. οἱ τοὺς προσιόντας ἐξαπατῶντες πονηροί

ἔξαρνος: 862 ὁ δικαίως βιοὺς οὐδὲ ἔξαρνός ποτε γίνεται, Isaeus 40. 9 ἐξ. γίγνεται τ. μαρτυρίαν, Iren. I. 21. 1 ἐξάρνησις τοῦ βαπτίσματος

ἔξαρχω: 893 ἔξαρχ. δογμάτων, 897 τ. ἀσεβῶν λόγων ἐξ., 552 τῆς δοκήσεως ἐξ.

ἐξασθενέω: 805 ἐν τοῖς ἔργοις ἐξασθ., 901 τὴν τ. λογίων σαφήνειαν λεπτουργεῖν ἐξασθ., Arist., Philo, Ign. Phil. 6

ἐξασκέω: 901 παρέδεισοι ἐξησκημένοι

ἐξεπίτηδες: 901 ἐξ. ἀναμέμικται ἡ φυτεία

ἐξεργάζομαι: 860 ἀγαθὸν ἑαυτὸν ἐξεργάζεται

ἐξερευνάω: (quot) 829

ἐξετάζω: p. 856 διὰ τῆς εὐχῆς ἐξετάζεται ὁ τρόπος, 861 ὁ ἐν εὐσεβείᾳ ἐξεταζόμενος, 862 ἡ κρίσις τ. ἀληθείας ἐξετάζεται, 871 ἐν τ. λογικῇ ἀνδρείᾳ ἐξετάζεται: act. 868 ὁ θεὸς ἐξετάζει τὸ πνεῦμα (ms. πρᾶγμα), 888 ἀφορμὰς ἔχων πρὸς τὸ ἐξετ. τὰ λεγόμενα, 893 οὐδὲ τοῦτο ἐξητάκασιν εἰ ἔστι τινὶ ἀκολουθητέον

ἐξέτασις: 833, ἡ πάντων τ. μερῶν δι' ἀκριβείας ἐξ. 887 ἐξ. τοῦ πῶς βιωτέον

ἐξευρίσκω: 888 ἐξ. τὴν ἀκολουθίαν τ. ἀληθείας, 892, 889 αἱ ἐξηυρημέναι τ. σοφιστῶν τέχναι

ἐξημαρτημένως: 897 τ. λόγοις ἐξ. συγχρώμενοι

ἐξημερόω: m. 837 τὸ ἄγριον ἐξημερώσεται κολάσει τ. μοχθηρῶν

ἐξικνέομαι: 852 ἡ φωνὴ ἐξικν. πρὸς τ. θεόν

OF GREEK WORDS. 409

ἕξις: 880 θεοπρεπεια ἕξις ἐστὶ τὸ πρέπον τῷ θεῷ σώζουσα, 884 ἕξ. ἀπαθείας, 858 ὁ γνωστικὸς εὔχεται εἰς ἕξ. ἀγαθότητος ἐλθεῖν, 859 ἡ μία ἐκείνη ἕξ., ib. φυσιοῦται ἡ ἕξ., 869 τὸ τέλεον τ. ἕξ., 870 ἕξ. ἡ διάθεσις τ. ἀναρπάστου ψυχῆς, ib. οὐδεμία ἐνέργεια ἕξις, 885 τῷ εἰς τοῦτο ἥκοντι ἕξεως ἁγίῳ εἶναι συμβαίνει, 874 οὐδέποτε τ. ἰδίας ἕξ. ὁ γνωστικὸς ἐξίσταται, 873 ἡ ἕξις ἡ παρ᾽ ἡμῖν, 880 ἐν ἕξει γενόμενος εὐποιητικῇ, 886

ἐξίστημι: 831 οὐκ ἐξίσταται ποτε τῆς αὐτοῦ περιωπῆς ὁ υἱός, 874 see ἕξις

ἔξοδος: 879 εὐσυνείδητος πρὸς τὴν ἐξ., 886 ἑξέως ἐπόμενοι τ. καλοῦντι κατὰ τ. ἐξ., 832 ἐπιστάμενος ἀμείνων ἑαυτῷ μετὰ τ. ἔξοδον γενήσεσθαι (ΜS. γενήσεται). 961 ἐπ᾽ αὐτῆς τ. ἐξόδου τ. ἐπίδειξιν τ. δογμάτων ὄψεται

ἐξομοιόω: act. 836 τῷ φύσει (ἀπαθεῖ) τὸ ἐξ ἀσκήσεως ἀπαθὲς ἐξομοιῶν, p 830, 835, 836, 884, 885 ἐξομ. θεῷ, 888 ἡ θεία εἰκὼν ἡ ἐξομοιουμένη πρὸς τὸ δεύτερον αἴτιον, 849 τροφὴ ἐξ. ταῖς τ᾽ ἀλόγων ψυχαῖς, 875 ἐξ. χαρακτῆρι, 883 τελειώσει ἐξ. θεῷ

ἐξομοίωσις: 869 ἡ ψυχὴ πρὸς τ. θείαν ἐξ. πραότητα περιπεπυκνωμένη, 885 γνωστικῆς ἐξ. κανόνες

ἐξομολογέομαι: 888 ἔστ᾽ ἂν ἐξομολογήσασθαι δυνηθέντες τῆς εὐεργεσίας τύχωσιν, 879 διὰ τ. κολάσεως ἀκουσίως ἐξ.

ἐξομολόγησις: 880 εἰς ἐξ. κ. ἐπιστροφὴν τ. συγγενῶν, 897 Ἰουδαία ἐξ ἑρμηνεύεται

ἐξουσία: 832 πᾶσα ἀρχὴ κ. ἐξ., ib. οὐδὲ αἰσχύνεται τ. ἐξουσίαις ὀφθῆναι, 889 (quot.) πνευματικαὶ ἐξ.

ἐξουσιάζω: p. 885 (quot.)

ἐξοχή: 899 μόνη κατὰ ἐξ. ἡ ἀρχαία ἐκκλησία, 900 ἡ ἐξ. τ. ἐκκλησίας κατὰ τ. μονάδα ἐστί

ἔξοχος: 852 τὸ ἐξ. τῆς γνώσεως, 872 ἡ τ. ἐξοχωτάτου θεραπεία

ἐξυπηρετέω: act. 880 θεοσεβὴς ὁ ἐξυπηρετῶν τ. θεῷ, 882 θελήματι πατρὸς ἐξ. 537, 581, m. 582

ἔξω: 870 ὁ ἔ. τ. παθῶν, 862 οἱ ἔξω 'those outside the Church,' cf. 1 Cor. v. 12

ἑορτή: 848 κατὰ τὰς ἑορτάς, 851 bis

ἐπαγγελία: 860 ἡ ἐπ. τελειοῦται, 874 init. δι᾽ ἐπαγγελίας ἐγκρατεύονται, 877 init. κοσμικῶν ἐπ. καταφρονεῖ

ἐπαγγέλλω: m. 829 οὗ τ. λέξιν ταμιευτὴν ἐπαγγέλλεται, 852 τὸ συμπόσιον ἐπαγγέλλεται τὸ φιλικόν· p. 838 παραδεκτέοι τῶν ἐπαγγελλομένων, 859 γέγηθεν ἐπὶ τοῖς ἐπηγγελμένοις

ἐπάγγελμα: 867 τὰ περὶ τ. ἄλλην πολιτείαν ἐπαγγ.

ἐπάγω: 'to add,' 896 διὸ κ. ἐπήγαγε

ἐπαγωνίζομαι: 886 ἐπ. τοῖς εἰρημένοις (ΜS. ἐπάγων.)

ἐπαινετός: 883 πρὸς τ. κύριον εὐάρεστος πρὸς τ. κόσμον ἐπ., 889 ἐπαινετὸν ἡ ἀρετή

ἐπαινέω: act. 879 ἐπῄξ. τὸ εὐαγγέλιον δι᾽ ἔργων ἐπαινῶν (? ἐπεξιών), 868 fin. ἐπαινῶν τὰ καλά, p. 883 (τῇ κτίσει) χρώμενοι ὡς προσήκεν ἐπαινεῖται, 899 τὸ ἄκρον τίμιον ἐπ., see ἔπαινος

ἔπαινος: 874 ἐπ. ἔπεται κατ᾽ ἐπακολούθημα εἰς τὴν τ. ἐπαινουμένου μίμησιν

ἐπαίρω: 892 ὑπὸ δοξοσοφίας ἐπηρμένος

ἔπαιω: 839 ἐπαίειν γεγυμνασμένοι, 850, 863 οἱ ἐπαίειν ἄξιοι, c. gen. 852 θεοὶ ἐπ. τῆς ἐννοίας, 884 ἐπ. τῆς βαρβάρου φιλοσοφίας, 836 κοσμεῖ τ. ἐπαίοντας αὐτοῦ, 856 νοῦς νοὸς ἐπ., 862, 895 ἐπ. ἀρχαιοτάτου ᾄσματος, c. acc. 854 πᾶσαν τ. ὁμιλίαν ἐπαίει

ἐπακολουθέω: 854 ἐπ. τῇ προθυμίᾳ τ. πνεύματος

ἐπακολούθημα: 874 ὁ ἔπαινος ἔπεται κατ᾽ ἔπακ. οὐκ εἰς τ. αὐτοῦ ὠφέλειαν, 875 ἀρέσκων τ. θεῷ τ. σπουδαίοις εὐάρεστος κατ᾽ ἐπ. γίνεται, 927 κατ᾽ ἔπακ.)(κατὰ τὸ προηγούμενον, 429, 823, 331 πάντων αἴτιος τ. καλῶν ὁ θεός, τῶν μὲν κατὰ προηγούμενον, τῶν δὲ κατ᾽ ἐπακ., 789)(δι᾽ αὐτήν, Philo

ἐπακούω: 856 τ. ψυχῆς ἐπ. ὁ θεός, 895 ἐπ. τ. προτρεπόντων, 899 τοῦ Πέτρου ἐπ. (ΜS. ὑπήκουσεν)

ἐπάν: 893 fin., 856, 820

ἐπαναβαίνω: 889 ὁ εἰς ἐπίγνωσιν ἐπαναβαίνων αἰτήσεται τ. τελειότητα τ. ἀγάπης, ib. τ. ἀναβεβηκὸς ὕψος ἀνδρὸς ἐντελοῦς, 834 ἡ ἐπαναβεβηκυῖα κ. προσεχὴς τ. κυρίου περιτροπή, Sext. Emp.

ἐπανάβασις: 852 κατ᾽ ἐπαν. αὐξῆσαι τὸ ἡγεμονικόν, Synes. Ep. 11 and 95

ἐπαναιρέομαι: 860 οἱ εὖ βιοῦν ἐπανῃρημένοι, 874 οὐκ ἐν τῷ μοχθηρῷ ἐπαναιρεῖσθαι βίον δείκνυται ἀνήρ, 87

ἐπανόρθωσις: 830 ἡ τ. ἀνθρώπων ἐπαν., 841 ὁ σωτὴρ ἀναδέχεται τὰς ἐπαν. τ. ἀνθρώπων εἰς ἰδίαν χάριν, Philo

ἐπανορθωτικός: 881 ἡ ἐπ. παιδεία

ἐπάνω: 881 ἐπ. εἶναι ἀμφοῖν

ἐπαποδυτέον: 888 ἐπ. τ. πόνῳ τ. εὑρέσεως

ἐπαρσις: (quot.) 857 ἐπ. τ. χειρῶν μου θυσία

ἐπαρτάω: 839 fin. ἄθλους τινὰς ὁ σπειράζων ἐπαρτᾷ, 868 ὁ ἐπηρτημένος τοῖς δικαίοις κίνδυνος

ἐπαφάω: m. 852 ἡ τ. συνειδότος ἐπαφωμένη τ. ψυχῆς δύναμις, 59 εὖ ἐπαφᾶσαι τ. ἀληθείας, Themist. 144ᵃ

ἐπεγείρω: 854 τ. πόδας ἐπεγ. κατὰ τ. τελευταίαν τ. εὐχὴν συνεκφώνησιν

ἐπεγκυλίομαι (ἅπ. λεγ.): 877 συστελλό-

μενος ἐφ' οἷς ἐπεγκυλίεται τῇ τ. βίου ἀνάγκῃ, see ἐγκυλίομαι
ἐπεί: 'else' 871, see μή
ἐπείγω: 866 ἐπί τ. κυριακὴν μονὴν ἐπείγεται, 896 ῥαθυμεῖν ἐπειγόμενος, 90 σωθῆναί σε ἐπείγομαι, see ἀπάγω
ἔπειμι: 874 ὁ κηρὸς τ. ἐπιόντα χαρακτῆρα παραδέχεται, 883 πολλὰ ἐκ γραφῆς μαρτύρια ἔπεισι παρατίθεσθαι, 892 ἐπιόντες τ. μοχθηρίας τ. δογμάτων
ἐπέκεινα: 829 τὸ ἐπ. αἴτιον, 774 ἡ τελεία ἐπιστήμη ἐπ. κόσμου ἀναστρέφεται
ἐπεκτείνω: 834 ἡ ψυχὴ κατὰ προκοπὴν ἑκάστην ἐπεκτείνεται εἰς ἕξιν ἀπαθείας
ἐπεξεργασία: 829 ἡ ἐπὶ πλέον ἐπεξ. περισσή
ἐπερείδω: 901 πίστις ἐπερειδομένη τ. ἀληθείᾳ. ib. τῇ διπλόῃ τ. πίστεως ἐπερείδονται
ἐπέχω: 839 οἱ νόμοι ἐπ. πράξεις
ἐπί: c. gen. 'in presence of' 858 ἐφ' ὧν χρή, 862 ἐπὶ τῶν ἀγαλμάτων: 837 ἐφ' ἡμῖν τὸ πιστεύειν (for τὰ ἐφ' ἡμῖν see n. on p. 136. 1): **832** ἐπ' ἐκεῖνο μόνον ἵεται ἐφ' ὃ ἔγνω μόνον
ἐπιβαίνω: 901 οἱ αἱρετικοὶ ὀνόματι μὲν πατρὸς κ. υἱοῦ ἐπιβεβηκότες
ἐπιβάλλω: 834 ἑαυτὸν ἐπιβεβληκὼς τ. θεωρίᾳ, 859 τὸ ἐνδεὲς πρὸς τὸ ἐπιβάλλον μετρεῖται, 867 κατὰ τὸν ἐπιβάλλοντα καιρὸν ἐκθησόμεθα
ἐπιβλέπω: 831 τ. ἀποκρύφους ἐννοίας ἐπιβλ., 840 fin. ὁ λόγος τὰ μικρότατα ἐπιβλέπει
ἐπιβολή: 690 τὰς ἀκραιφνεῖς τῆς διανοίας ἐπιβολάς
ἐπίγειος: 848 τ. ἐπιγ. θυσιαστήριον τ. ἄθροισμα τῶν τ. εὐχαῖς ἀνακειμένων, 862 οἱ τὰ ἐπ. θρησκεύοντες τ. ἀγάλμασι προσεύχονται, 870 ἐπ. εἰκὼν θείας δυνάμεως, 876 αἱ ἐπ. ἡδοναί
ἐπιγεννηματικός: 860 ἐπ. ἅπαν τ. γνωστικῷ τὸ ἀγαθόν
ἐπιγίνομαι: 839 οὐ φυσικῶς ἐπιγ. ἡ ἀρετή bis
ἐπιγινώσκω: 855 ἵνα ὁ θεὸς δι' υἱοῦ ἐπιγινώσκηται, 889 ἐν ᾗ ὥρᾳ ἐπέγνω (ms. ἐπιγνῷ)
ἐπίγνωσις: 830, 855 ἐν ἐπίγν. πλείονες γίνονται, 831 ἐπ. θεοῦ, **834** ἀρετῆς ἐπίγν. (ms. 1st hand corr. fr. ἐπιδόσεις), 846 ἐπ. ἁγία, 897 οἱ κατ' ἐπ. Ἰσραηλῖται, 880 ἐπιστροφὴ εἰς ἐπ., 888
ἐπιγράφω: p. 841 ὁ Προτρεπτικὸς ἐπιγραφόμενος ἡμῖν λόγος, 843 ἐπὶ οἰκίᾳ εὑρὼν ἐπιγεγραμμένον: m. 898 Βασιλείδης Γλαυκίαν ἐπιγράφεται διδάσκαλον
ἐπιδεής: 859 τὸ ἐνδεὲς κ. ἐπιδ., 881 τῆς δι' ἀγγέλων βοηθείας ἐπιδ.

ἐπιδείκνυμι: act. 855
ἐπιδίδωμι: 863 ἑαυτὸν ἐπ. ὑπὲρ τ. ἐκκλησίας, 871, 878, 867 τ. σῶμα ἅπαν ἐπ.
ἐπίδοσις: 861 ἡ κατὰ τ. δεομένους ἐπ. κ. δογμάτων κ. χρημάτων, 834 see ἐπίγνωσις
ἐπιδρομή: 864 ὡς ἐν ἐπιδ. φάναι, 883 διὰ βραχυτάτων ἐξ ἐπιδρομῆς, Plut. V. 953 ἀνήρ, εἰπεῖν μὲν ἐξ ἐπιδρ., τῶν πώποτε ἱκανώτατος
ἐπιεικής: 860 τὰς εὐχὰς ἐπιεικῶς ἅμα κ. μετ' ἐπιεικῶν ποιεῖσθαι, 887
ἐπιεικῶς: see ἐπιεικής
ἐπιζητέω: 896 ἐπιζητεῖ ἀνευρίσκειν, 858 οὐδὲν ἐπιζ., 896 ἀποδείξεις ἐπιζητεῖ
ἐπίθλιψις: 848 ἡ διὰ τῶν πτερύγων ἐπ. τῆς ἐντομῆς
ἐπιθυμεῖν: 881 μηδενὸς ἐπ., 853 οὐδεὶς ἐπιθ. πόματος ἀλλὰ τοῦ πιεῖν
ἐπιθυμία: 853 ὧν αἱ ἐπιθ. τούτων αἱ εὐχαί, 882 ἐμβλέπειν πρὸς ἐπιθυμίαν
ἐπίκαιρος: 829 κατὰ τοὺς ἐπ. τόπους, 883 ἐπ. λέξεις
ἐπικαλέω: 885 p. οἱ τὸ ὄνομα ἐπικεκλημένοι μόνον
ἐπικουρία: 873 μὴ διὰ φόβον, δι' ἐπικουρίαν δέ
ἐπικουφίζω: 873 θλιβόμενον ἐπ. παραμυθίαις
ἐπικουφισμός: 880 αἰτεῖται ἐπ. περὶ ὧν ἡμάρτομεν, 881 τὸν ἐπικ. τούτοις αἰτούμενος
ἐπικρύπτω: 858 m. μηδὲν τῶν λεχθῆναι δυναμένων ἐπικρυπτόμενος, 831 p. τὰ παρὰ τ. ἀληθείᾳ ἐπικεκρυμμένα
ἐπίκρυψις: 890 ἡ ἐπ. τῶν τ. ἀληθείας μυστηρίων, Plut.
ἐπιλάμπω: tr. 884 ὁ θεὸς ἐπὶ δικαίους ἐπ. ἥλιον, 885 ἐπὶ δικαίους τὸ εὐμενὲς ἐπιλάμποντες, 840 θεὸς γῆν ἐπ., 781, 85, intr. 92, 86
ἐπίληψις: 850 τὰ τράγεια κρέα πρὸς ἐπ. συμβάλλεται
ἐπιλογισμός: 852 ἱλαρὸς διὰ τὸν ἐπ. τῶν ἀγαθῶν
ἐπιμέλεια: 829 ἡ συνεχὴς ἐπιμέλεια τῆς ψυχῆς θεραπεία ἐστὶ τ. θεοῦ, 833 μηδενὸς παρορᾷ τὴν ἐπ., 887 ἐπιμελείας δεόμεθα, 888 ἡ κηπευτικὴ ἐπιμ.
ἐπιμελέστερον: 888 ἐπιμ. θηρατέον τ. γνῶσιν
ἐπιμιμνήσκω: 829 τῶν λέξεων οὐκ ἐπιμνησόμεθα, 883 μιᾶς γραφῆς ἐπιμνησθήσομαι
ἐπινοέω: 849 p. σαρκοφαγιῶν προφάσει αἱ θυσίαι ἐπινενόηνται: act. 898 οἱ τ. αἱρέσεις ἐπινοήσαντες
ἐπίνοια: 899 κατὰ ἐπίνοιαν μόνην εἶναί φαμεν τ. ἀρχαίαν ἐκκλησίαν, 856 τὴν ἐπ. θεοῦ λαμβάνομεν
ἐπιορκέω: 861 bis, 862

ἐπισπολάζω : 895 ἡ ἐπιπολάζουσα ἀμαθία
ἐπιπόλαιον : subst. 847 (quot.)
ἐπιπόλαιος : 830 οἱ λόγοι οἱ τοιοῦτοι ἐπιπ.
ἐπιπολή : 892 ἐξ ἐπ. ἀναγνῶναι τ. γραφάς, Chrys. xi. 630 A, 719 D
ἐπίπονος : 889 ἡ εἴσοδος τ. ἀνατάσεως ἐπ.
ἐπίρρημα : 862 ἐπὶ τ. ἀρνήσεως τὸ οὐ τάσσει ἐπ.
ἐπιρριπτέω : 871 ἐπ. ἑαυτοὺς τοῖς κινδύνοις
ἐπιρρώννυμι : 876 ἐπιρρώννυνται πρὸς τ. πίστιν διὰ τ. ὑπομονῆς
ἐπισημαίνω : m. 841 ὅσον ἐπισημψασθαι
ἐπισκοπέω : 829 τὸ μηδ' ὅλως ἐπεσκέφθαι τὸ κατεπεῖγον, 868 οἱ τοῦ παντοκράτορος ὀφθαλμοὶ ἐπεσκόπουν, 878 μόνον τὸ καλὸν ἐπισκοπεῖ ἡ ψυχή
ἐπισκοπή : 860 ὁ θεὸς προσεχέστερα τιμήσας ἐπισκοπῇ
ἐπισπάω : m. 843 νόσους ἐπισπῶνται, 156 ἑαυτῶν αἰτίῳ τ. κριτὴν ἐπισπώμενος, pass. 879 ὑπὸ τ. ἰδίας ἐλπίδος ἐπ. (NB. περισπώμενος)
ἐπισπείρω : 887 τὰς αἱρέσεις ἐπισπαρήσεσθαι τῇ ἀληθείᾳ καθάπερ τῷ πυρῷ τ. ζιζάνια
ἐπίσταμαι : 895 πόμα δίψαν οὐκ ἐπιστάμενον, 875 ὁ γνωστικὸς δι' ὧν ἐπίσταται πορίζει τ. ζωήν
ἐπίστασις : 865 κατ' ἐπ. προέρχεσθαι, Polyb.
ἐπιστήμη : defined 838, 864 ἡ τ. θείων ἐπ., 874 ἐπ. θείων κ. ἀνθρωπείων πραγμάτων, 894 διαθέσεις τ. ψυχῆς ἄγνοια, οἴησις, ἐπιστήμη
ἐπιστημονικός : 867 ἐπ. θεοσέβεια, 868, 895 ἐπ. θεωρία, 874 ἡ τ. ἀγαθοῦ ἐπ. κτῆσις, 877 ἐπ. θεώρημα, 839 ἐπ. τῆς ἀληθείας διαμονή, 454 ἐπ.)(δοξαστικός, 98
ἐπιστημονικῶς : 865 ἐπ. κ. καταληπτικῶς τ. θεὸν ἐποπτεύειν
ἐπιστημόνως : 860 πράσσειν ἐπ., 870 ἐπιστημόνως ὑφίσταται ἃ δεῖ, ib. διακρίνων ἐπ.
ἐπιστήμων : 867 ἡ διὰ τοῦ ἐπ. πρᾶξις εὐπραγία
ἐπιστολή : 883 ἡ προτέρα πρὸς Κορινθίους ἐπ.
ἐπιστρέφω : intr. 855, 859 ὁ ἐξ ἐθνῶν ἐπ., 879 ἐκ φόβου εἰς πίστιν ἐπ., 891 ἐπὶ τ. ἀλήθειαν ἐπ., 895 ἐπὶ τ. θεὸν ἐπ., 887 εἰς θεὸν ἐπ., m. 889 ἐπιστρεφέσθω εἰς τὰ ὀπίσω, 890 trans. τὸν ἑαυτοῦ βίον ἐπ. τ. ἀληθείᾳ, 897 p. ἵνα ἐπιστραφῶσι
ἐπιστροφή : 855 ἡ τῶν πέλας εἰς ἐπ. αἴτησις, 880 ἐπ. εἰς ἐπίγνωσιν, ib. εἰς ἐπιστ. τ. συγγενῶν, 881 ἐπ. τ. μελλόντων, 882 ἡ ἐπὶ τ. θεῖον ἐπ., 856 ἡ

πρὸς τ. θεὸν ἐπ., 854 ἐπ. τ. δικαιοσύνης
ἐπιτείνω : 862 μᾶλλον ἐπ. τ. γνωστικὸν ἀξίωμα ὁ τ. προστασίαν τῆς διδασκαλίας ἀναλαβὼν
ἐπιτέλεσις : 862 ἡ ἐπ. τοῦ ὅρκου
ἐπιτελέω : 830 fin. ἐπιτ. ὅ τι ἂν ὁ λόγος ὑπαγορεύῃ, 861 ἐπιτ. τι διὰ τὸ ἠθό, 876 ἐν σταδίοις ἐπιτελεῖται ἡ τιμωρία, 879
ἐπιτερπής : 902 ἅλσοι ἐπ.
ἐπιτήδειος : 878 ὠφελεῖ τοὺς ἐπιτ.
ἐπιτηδειότης : 857 ἐπ. εἰς ἃ μέλλει, 859 ἐπ. εἰς τ. ἀπλόην, 833 ὅσον ἐπιτηδειότητος εἶχεν
ἐπιτηδές : 902 ἐπ. τὴν λέξιν οὐχ <ἢ δυναμένην> εἶναι βούλονται
ἐπιτήδευμα : 897 ἀπαγγείλατε τὰ ἐπιτ. αὐτοῦ
ἐπιτίθημι : m. 847 ἐπ. τοῖς θεοῖς ὀστᾶ
ἐπιτίμιον : 897 ἔγγραφα ἔχουσι τ. ἐπιτίμια, 954 οὐ τὸ ἐπιτίμιον κόλασις αἰώνιος
ἐπιτομή : 872 δικαιοσύνης ἦν ἐπιτομὴ φάναι, ἔσται ὑμῶν τὸ ναὶ ναί, καὶ τὸ οὒ οὔ, see ἐπίτομος
ἐπίτομος sc. ὁδός : 834 (NB. ἐπιτομή) 'short cut' ἐπ. τ. σωτηρίας διὰ πίστεως, cf. 66 init. σύντομος σωτηρίας ὁδοί, 79 ἡ συντομία τοῦ κηρύγματος, and Lucian vol. i. Scyth. 866, Harmon. 853, Hermot. 797
ἐπιτρέπω : 876 ἐπ. ὁ θεός, 883 τοῖς ποιεῖν ἐθέλουσι προσεκποιεῖν ἐπιτρέψας, ib. μηδὲ εὔχεσθαι κατὰ τοῦ ἀδικήσαντος ἐπιτρέπει
ἐπιτυγχάνω : 876 abs. ἐπιτ. κατὰ τὰς αἰτήσεις
ἐπιφέρω : 886 τὰ ὑπὸ Ἑλλήνων ἐπιφερόμενα ἡμῖν ἐγκλήματα
ἐπιφημίζω : c. gen. 877 ἐπιφημίζονται ἡ μὲν (ἡμέρα) Ἑρμοῦ, ἡ δὲ Ἀφροδίτης (cf. Strabo p. 250 Ἄρεως ἐπεφήμισαν), c. dat. 37, 46 οἷς τὰ ἀγάλματα ἐπιπεφήμισται
ἐπιφορτίζω : 849 οὐκ ἐπιφ. κρειῶν βρῶσιν τ. ψυχήν, Heliod. ii. 25 πάθοι ἐρωτικὸν ἐπιφορτισάμενος, ib. viii. 9 ξύλα ἐπιφ.
ἐπιφωνέω : 869 ἐπ. εὖ μάλα προτρεπτικῶς
ἐπιχειρέω : 884 οἱ ἀδικεῖν ἐπιχειροῦντες, 895 φλυαρεῖν ἐπιχ., ib. μεταπείσει ἐπιχ.
ἐπιχείρημα : 889 (bis) πιθανοῖς ἐπ. σκοτίζουσι τ. ἀλήθειαν, 890 λόγων τέχναι κ. ἐπιχειρημάτων δυνάμεις, 454 ἡ δοξαστικὴ ἀπόδειξις πρὸς τῶν ῥητορικῶν γίνεται ἐπιχειρημάτων, 889 τ. ῥητορικῆς ἔργον τὸ ἐπ., cf. παρεγχείρησις
ἐποικοδομέω : 879 ἐπ. εἰς τὸ ἀκούσιον ἡ ἀγάπη, 839 ἐπὶ τ. πίστει τὴν γνῶσιν ἐπ. ἡ ἀλήθεια, 865 ἡ γνῶσις ἀπόδειξις

ἐποικοδομουμένη τῇ πίστει, 646 ἡ μετὰ πίστεως ζήτησις ἐποικοδομεῖ τ. θεμελίῳ τὴν γνῶσιν

ἐποικοδομή : 864 ἄμφω ὁ Χριστὸς ὅ τε θεμέλιος ἥ τε ἐπ. Cf. 660 ταῦτα γνωστικὰ ἐποικοδομήματα τῇ κρηπῖδι τ. πίστεως

ἕπομαι : 856 ἅπαντα τ. συλλήψει ἕπ. τ. ἀγαθά, 893 ἕπ. τῷ θεῷ, 894, 897 ἕπ. ταῖς γραφαῖς

ἐποπτεία : 873 ἡ τ. θεοῦ ἐπ., 424 (the summit of the Mosaic philosophy is) ἡ ἐποπτεία τ. μεγάλων ὄντως μυστηρίων, 130 ἡ κατὰ θεὸν παιδαγωγία κατευθυσμός ἐστιν ἀληθείας εἰς ἐπ. θεοῦ, cf. 325 init. ἡ κατὰ τὴν ἐποπτικὴν θεωρίαν γνῶσις, 794 θεωρίας ἐπ.

ἐποπτεύω : 865 τ. θεὸν ἐπ., 114 τῷ τ. πνεύματος ὄμματι τὸ θεῖον ἐπ., 633 διὰ τ. ἰδίας καθάρσεως ἐπ. τ. θεόν, 686 τῷ νῷ τ. θεὸν ἐπ.

ἑπτάκις : (quot.) 851

ἐράω : 873 fin. τυχεῖν ὧν ἐρᾶ τις

ἐραστής : 890 ὁ τῆς ἀληθείας ἐραστής

ἐραστός : 834 ἀγαθὸν τὸ ἐραστόν, 776 συνὼν δι' ἀγάπης τῷ ἐραστῷ, 778

ἐργάζομαι : 849 p. ἡ διὰ τ. σαρκῶν τροφὴ εἰργασμένη ἤδη, m. 881 ἐργ. τὴν εὐπαιδαν

ἐργάτης : 872 ἐργάτην τρίβοντες βίον, 876 ἐργ. ἀγαθός, 877 ἐργ. εὔθετος, ib. ὁ γνωστικὸς ἐργ.

ἔργον : 838 ἔ. ἔχει σκοπεῖν, 882 ἕπεται ἔργα τ. γνώσει, 884 πάντες ἐνός εἰσιν ἔ. θεοῦ, 885 ἐν ἔργῳ, λόγῳ, ἐννοίᾳ (see λαλέω), 886 ἔργα κ. λόγοι ἀκόλουθοι τῇ τ. κυρίου παραδόσει

ἐρεθίζω : p. 841 εἰς ὀργὴν ἐρ.

ἐρείπια : (quot.) 841

ἔρεισμα : 850 ἐρ. (ms. δεῖγμα) τῆς ὑλικῆς διαμονῆς, Philo 2. 604 νόμος θεοῦ βεβαιότατον ἐρ. τῶν ὅλων ἐστὶν κ.τ.λ.

ἐρευνάω : 831 δυνάμει τ. δυνάμεις ἐρ., 853 τ. ταμεῖα ἐρ.

ἐρευνητέον : 887 ἐρ. τὴν τ. ὄντι ἀλήθειαν

ἐρημία : 878 καθάπερ ἐν ἐρημίᾳ βιοῖ

ἐρίζω : 892 ἐρίζοντες διατελοῦσι

ἔριον : 843 ἐρ. πυρρά

ἔρις : 894 ἔριδα ταῖς αἱρέσεσι προσκριτέον

ἐριστικός : 894 ἐὰν πρόσσχῃ τις Πύρρωνι ἐριστικὸν αὐτὸν ποιήσει

ἑρμηνεύς : 898 Γλαυκίας ὁ Πέτρου ἑρμ., 856 οἱ παρ' ἀνθρώπων ἑρμ.

ἑρμηνεύω : 896 τετυφῶσθαι τὴν λέξιν (sc. φυσιοῦν) ἑρμηνεύει : p. 897 Ἰουδαία ἐξομολόγησις ἑρμηνεύεται, cf. Schmid IV. 171

Ἑρμῆς : 877 see ἐπιφημίζω

ἐσθίω : 843 τρέχειν κ. ἐσθίειν (ms. θεῖν), 874, 879 ἐσθίει κ. πίνει κ. γαμεῖ

ἑσπέρα : (quot.) 842 ἀφ' ἑσπέρας

ἑσπερινός : (quot.) 857 θυσία ἑσπ.

ἑστιάομαι : 835 ἀκόρεστον θέαν ἑστιῶνται

ἑστίασις : 852 ἑστ. συμποτική, 860 αἱ πρὸ τῆς ἑστ. ἐντεύξεις, 841 ὅμοιοι παρὰ τὴν ἑστ.

ἐσχάρα : 847 τ. ἱππον αὐτὸν προσκυνοῦντες προσεχεστέραν <ἐσχάραν> γινομένην τ. κνίσῃ

ἑταιρικός : 868 ἐτ. ἐκβιαζομένη

ἑτερόδοξος : 854 πρὸς ἑτεροδόξων παρεισαγόμενα δόγματα

ἕτεροῖος : c. gen. 829 ἐτ. τῶν γραφῶν, Plat. Parm. 161

ἕτερος κ. ἕτερος : 833 ἕτεροι ὑφ' ἑτέρων τεταγμένοι, 889 ἑτέρα τῶν πιθανῶν ἐπιχειρημάτων καὶ ἑτέρα τῶν ἀληθῶν ἡ φύσις

εὖ : 858 εὖ μάλα παγκαλῶς διοικεῖται, 843 init. εὖ γ' οὖν

εὐαγγελίζομαι : m. 866 ὁ σωτὴρ ὁ εὐαγγελισάμενος, p. 889 (quot.) ὁ ἅπαξ εὐαγγελισθείς

εὐαγγέλιον : 836 τό τε εὐαγγέλιον ὅ τε ἀπόστολος, 890 διά τε τ. προφητῶν διά τε τ. εὐαγγελίου, κ. διὰ τῶν ἀποστόλων, 877 κατά τε τ. νόμον κ. κατὰ τὴν τ. εὐαγγελίου τελειότητα, ib. ἡ κατὰ τὸ εὐαγγέλιον ἐντολή, 879 τὸ εὐαγ. δι' ἔργων κ. θεωρίας ἑταιρῶν (? ἐπεξιῶν), 885 τ. ἔννοιαν περιγράφει τὸ εὐαγ., ib. παρὰ τὸ εὐαγ. ποιεῖν τι, 875 τὸ εὐαγ. ἀπείκασεν παρθένοις τ. γνωστικούς, 884 ἡ κατὰ τὸ εὐαγ. ἀμωμικακία, 889 ἡ τοῦ εὐαγ. ὑπακοή, 896 κατὰ τὸ εὐαγ. ὀρθύνται βίοι, 870 διάθεσις ὁμολογουμένη τῷ εὐαγ.

εὐαπάντητος : 858 εὐαπ. ὁ γνωστικός (rare)

εὐαρεστέομαι : 858 πᾶσιν εὐαρ. τ. συμβαίνουσι, 876 fin. ἐπιγείοις θεωρίαις εὐαρ., 508 εὐαρ. γάμῳ : act. in Diod., Epict., Clem. Hom. ind.

εὐαρέστησις : 840 εὐαρ. (ἐστιν) ὁμολογία, 860 πάντα ἐκπεπλήρωκεν εἰς τὴν εὐαρ. τῷ θεῷ, 871 ἡ πρὸς τ. θεὸν εὐαρ., 497 Ἡράκλειτος τὸ τέλος εὐαρ. εἶπεν

εὐάρεστος : 882 εὐάρ. πρὸς τ. κύριον, c. dat. 875 ἀρέσκων τ. θεῷ εὐ. τοῖς σπουδαίοις γίνεται, 481 εὐάρ. τῷ πατρὶ γενόμενος, 801 fin. τὸ σώζεσθαι ἡμᾶς εὐ. κυρίῳ

εὐβουλία : 869 εὐβ. περὶ τὰ ἀνθρώπων

εὐγένεια : 872 fin. εὐγ. κ. τελειότης

εὐγνωμοσύνη : 862 ἑκούσιος δικαιοσύνη ἡ εὐγν., cf. Chrys. III. 139 c, VII 39 c bis, XI. 230 c, 231 B, 246 c, Iambl. V. Pyth. 232: Plut. Mor. 116 A οὐδὲ οἱ τραπεζίται ἀπαιτούμενοι τὰ θέματα δυσχεραίνουσιν ἐπὶ τῇ ἀποδόσει ἐάνπερ εὐγνωμῶσι, Clem. Hom. ep. Cl. 10 πρὸς τ. παρακαταθήκας εὐγνωμονεῖτε,

εὐφημία: 853 ἡ τ. πολλῶν εὐφ. δυσφημίας οὐδὲν διαφέρει
εὐφροσύνη: 835 εὐφρ. ἀκόρεστον καρποῦνται, 894 εὐφρ. τῷ γνωστικῷ ἀποδοτέον, 871 οἱ διὰ εὐφροσύνας τὰς μετὰ θάνατον ὑπομένοντες
εὐχαριστέω: 855 εὐχ. ἐν οἷς ἐτελείωσεν τ. διακονίαν, 880 σπεύδων ἐπὶ τὸ εὐχ., ib. εὐχ. ἀεὶ τῷ θεῷ, 883 κατὰ τὴν τ. κοσμικῶν χρῆσιν εὐχ.
εὐχαριστία: 851 συμπαρὼν διὰ τῆς εὐχ. ἀδιαλείπτως τ. θεῷ, 855 ἡ εὐχ. ἔργον τ. γνωστικοῦ, 879 εἶδος τ. εὐχῆς εὐχαρ., 868 ἡ ἐπὶ τ. κτίσαντα εὐχ.: ('eucharist') 318 διανείμαι τ. εὐχ.
εὐχάριστος: 856 ὅταν ὁ εὐχ. αἰτῆται συνεργεῖ τι πρὸς τ. λῆψιν
εὐχή: 849 θυμίαμα ἡ ὁσία εὐχή, 851 init. ἐξ ὁσίων ἔργων εὐχῆς τε δικαίας, 854 ὁμιλία πρὸς τ. θεὸν ἡ εὐχή, 855 ἡ πίστις εἶδος εὐχῆς, 876 init. εὐχὴ ὁ βίος ἅπας, 881 δίδωσι τὴν εὐχὴν κ. τὸ διὰ τῆς εὐχῆς παρέχεται: 853 ὧν μέν αἱ ὁρμαὶ εἰσιν τούτων εἰσὶ κ. αἱ εὐχαί, 848 οἱ ταῖς εὐχαῖς ἀνακείμενοι, 879 ἵνα πεποιθὼς προσίῃ ταῖς εὐχαῖς, 856 πρὸς τ. ἀνατολὴν αἱ εὐχαί
εὐώδης: 852 ευ. πλοκαὶ ἐκθηλύνουσι τ. ψυχήν
ἐφεκτικός: 858 ἡ ἐφ. τ. ἡδέων (? ἡδονῶν) ἄσκησις
ἐφέλκω: m. 894 μαχόμενα δόγματα ἐφ. τινάς
ἔφεξῆς: 834
ἐφίημι: m. 860 ἐφ. γνώσεως
ἐφόδια: 883 δι' ἐπιστήμης τὰ ἐφ. τ. θεωρίας καρποῦται
ἐφοράω: 835 ὁ ἐφορῶν κριτής, see ἀφοράω
ἐχέγγυος: 891 ἡ τ. κυρίου φωνὴ πασῶν ἀποδείξεων ἐχεγγυωτέρα
ἔχθρα: 873 αἰτίαν ἔχθρας παρέχει
ἐχθρός: 870 μόνη κακία ἐχθρά, 873
ἔχω: (= παρέχω) 852 ἔχει τ. ἀντίληψιν, 853 τ. πρόσφορον ἀρετὴν ἔχουσι τῷ θεῷ: (intr. c. part.) 890 τ. κανόνα τ. ἀληθείας παρ' αὐτῆς λαβόντες ἔχουσι τ. ἀληθείας: m. 870 πενία δόξης μᾶλλον ἢ ἀληθείας ἔχεται: 887 βεβαίως ἐχ. τ. ἀληθείας
ἑωθινός: 856 πρὸς τ. ἑωθινὴν ἀνατολὴν αἱ εὐχαί

ζῆλος: 871 προφανὴς ὁ κίνδυνος διὰ τὸν τ. πολλῶν ζῆλον
ζηλόω: 863 ὁ ἐκκρημάμενος τ. δικαίοις ἀπὸ τ. ζηλούντων κίνδυνος
ζητέω: 864 πίστις ἄνευ τοῦ ζητεῖν ὁμολογεῖ θεόν, 866 (quot.) γενεὰ ζητούντων ter, 895 οἱ ζητήσας οὐ πονέσας, 889 ἀποστήσονται ζητοῦντες, 891 πιστούμεθα τὸ ζητούμενον
ζήτησις: 867 πόθος ζητήσει κραθείς,

887 τῆς ἀληθείας δυσκόλου οὔσης γεγόνασιν αἱ ζητήσεις, 888 bis
ζητητικός: 866 τὸ ζ. γένος, cf. 867 πόθος ἅμα ζητήσει κραθείς
ζιζάνια: (quot.) 887
ζωή: 838 ἡ ὄντως ζωὴ δι' ἣν ζῶμεν τ. ἀληθῆ ζωήν, 847 ζ. εὐποιίας, 896 ὕδωρ ζ. γνωστικῆς
ζωογονέω: 844 τ. ᾠδὰ ζωογονούμενα
ζῷον: τὸ πολλοῦ ἄξιον ζ., 849 ἀνθρώποις δέδοται τὰ ζ., 900 ζῷα καθαρὰ κ. ἀκάθαρτα
ζώπυρον: 901 τὰ ζ. τ. δογμάτων ἐγκατασπείραντες, 21 εἰς ἀλήθειαν φρονήσεως ζ. ἀναφύεται

ἤ: (= ἄλλως ἤ) 870: (= μᾶλλον ἤ) 896 οὓς ἐλεήσειεν ἄν τις ἢ μισήσειεν, 892 αἱροῦνται τὸ δόξαν ἢ τὸ εἰρημένον
ἦ γὰρ οὐχί: 860 and passim
ἡγεμονικός: 879 ἡγ. κ. βασιλικὸς ὡς γνωστικός, 852 τὸ ἡγεμ. τῆς τελειότητος, 822 οἱ ἡγεμ. κ. παιδευτικοί, 831 ἡγεμονικωτάτη ἡ υἱοῦ φύσις
ἡγεμών: 837 ὁ πάντων ἡγ., 851
ἡγέομαι: ('precedes') 880 τούτον ἡγ. τὸ εἰλῆφθαι τ. γνῶσιν, 890 ἡγεῖται τῆς γνώσεως
ἥδομαι: 869 ἡσθῆναι τῆς κλήσεως χάριν, 878 ὅταν ἡδομένου ἑαυτοῦ συναισθηταί
ἡδύνω: 902 λέξις < ἡδυσμένη >
ἡδύς: 868, 869 τῶν ἡδέων μετασχεῖν, ib. τῶν ἡδ. καταφρονεῖ, 873 τὰ ἐν ποσὶ ἡδέα, 882 τὸ ἡδύ)(τὸ συμφέρον, 861 τὸ δέ ἐν τι τελεῖν διὰ τὸ ἡδὺ τοῖς τὸν (so H., Ms. ἐπιτελεῖν διὰ τὸν δύσοιστον) κοινὸν βίον διώκουσιν καταλιμπάνει
ἠθικός: 901 ὁ ἠθ. τόπος
ἦθος: 835 ἀναλόγως τοῖς ἑαυτῶν ἤθεσι διοικεῖται τὰ μικρότερα, 844 init. ἅγιον μόνον τὸ δικαίου ἦθος, 868 τὸ κόσμον τ. ἤθους, 869 ἤθει κεκοσμημένος
ἥκω: 869 ἐπ' ἄκρον γνώσεως ἥκειν βιάζεται, 92 ἧκέ μοι ὦ παραπλήξ, ἧκέ μοι ὦ πρέσβυ
ἡλικία: 899 init. κατὰ τ. αὐτὴν ἡλ. αὐτοῖς γενόμενος, 898 ἡ Ἀντωνίνου ἡλ.
ἡμέρα: 851 νύκτα (?) καὶ μεθ' ἡμέραν, 901 τ. λόγια τ. θεοῦ νύκτωρ καὶ μεθ' ἡμέραν μελετῶντες, 880 πρωίας ἀναστὰς κ. μέσον ἡμέρας, 856 trop. ἡμ. γνώσεως
ἥμερος: 858 ἡμ. κ. πρᾷος ἀεί, 841 ἡμερωτέρους θεοὺς ἀναπλάττουσιν Ἕλληνες
ἡμερότης: 836 ἡμερότης κανὼν γνωστικῆς ἐξομοιώσεως
Ἡρακλεία λίθος: 834
ἡσυχία: 861 ἡσυχίᾳ χρώμενος εὔχεται
ἡσυχιότης: 838 fin. ἐν ἡσυχιότητι τ. ψυχῆς
ἡττάομαι: 874 μόνου ἑαυτοῦ κηδόμενος

ηττάται πρὸς τοῦ ἀπολειπομένου κατὰ τὴν ἑαυτοῦ σωτηρίαν, 894 init. ἔθει ἡττηθεὶς

θάλπω: 844 ὁρᾶν ἔστι τὰ ᾠά, εἰ θάλφθείη, ζωογονούμενα

θάνατος: 858 ὁ φοβερώτατος θ., 879 οἱ μετὰ θάνατον παιδευόμενοι, 880 (quot.) τὸν θ. περιφέρειν, 874 ὡς ὁ θάνατος χωρισμὸς ψυχῆς ἀπὸ τ. σώματος, οὕτως ὁ λογικὸς θ. ἀπὸ τ. παθῶν χωρίζει τ. ψυχήν, 862 ἡ γνῶη ἄγεται τὴν ἐπὶ θάνατον

θαρραλέος: 870 μόνος θ. ὁ γνωστικός, (of things) 870 τὰ τῷ ὄντι θαρραλέα τουτέστι τὰ ἀγαθά

θατέραν = τὴν ἑτέραν, 236: θάτερον = ὁ ἕτερος 322, θάτερον = τὸν ἕτερον 24, see Moeris 432, Clem. vol. I. p. 307 n. Dind.

θᾶττον: 880 θ. τοῦ λέγειν καλῶς (? καὶ ἄλλους) εὐεργετεῖ

θαυμάζω: 867 ἀρξάμενος ἐκ τοῦ θ. τ. κτίσιν μαθητὴς τ. κυρίου γίνεται, ib ἐπίστευσεν ἐξ ὧν ἐθαύμασε, 878 τὰ ὑπὸ τῶν ἄλλων θαυμαζόμενα, 879 θ. τὰς ἐντολάς, 883 θ. τὴν κτίσιν

θαυματοποιός: 871 αἱ θ. εἰς τ. μαχαίρας κυβιστῶντες

θέα. 852 αἱ ἡδοναὶ τῆς θέας

θεάομαι. 876 τὴν τ. κακούργων τιμωρίαν θεώμενος, 892 δυοῖν θάτερον ἔστι θεάσασθαι γινόμενον

θεατής: 839 θεαταὶ ἄγγελοι κ. θεοί

θέατρον: 840 (= θεαταί) κέκληται ἐπὶ τὸ ἀγώνισμα τὸ θ., 852 θεάτρων δεσπότις ὀχλοκρασία

θειάζω: 831 δεισιδαίμων ὁ πάντα θειάζων

θεῖον: 843 fin. θ. δεδίασι, 844 (quot.)

θεῖος: 883 ὁ θ. λόγος, 833 ὁ θ. ἀπόστολος, 853 ἡ θ. δύναμις ὅλην διορᾷ τ. ψυχήν, 829 ἡ περὶ τὸ θεῖον ἀσχολία, 836 οὐ φιλοχρήματος τὸ θ. bis, 841 τὸ θ. ἀπεικάζειν ἀνθρώπῳ, 831 τὰ θ. μυστήρια, 832 θ. προφητεία, θ πρόσταξις, 835 θ. θεωρία, 837 θ· προαίρεσις, ib. θ. ἄγαλμα, θ. ψυχή, θ. εἰκών, 981 θ. ψυχή)(ὑλικὴ ψ. 848 αἱ διὰ τ. ὀσφρήσεως θειότεραι τῶν διὰ στόματος τροφῶν

θέλημα: 833 ἡ ἀρχὴ ἡ κατὰ τ. θέλημα ἐνεργοῦσα, 832 (quot.) θ. πατρός, 833, 867 τοῦ θ. τ. θεοῦ γεύσεται ὁ γνωστικός. 885, 881 ἑνὸς θελήματος ἔργον οἱ πάντες, see 601 and cf. Ign L. π. 85, 290, 318, 357

θέλω: 873 οὐδέν ἐστι τῶν θεοστόντων ὃ μὴ θέλει ὁ κτίστης, cf. Ign. Rom. 6 ἐκεῖνον ζητῶ, ἐκ. θέλω, Magn. 3, Clem. Hom. ind.

θεμέλιος: 864 τὸ πιστεῦσαι θ. γνώσεως, ib. ἄμφω ὁ Χριστός ὁ τε θεμ. ἥ τε ἐποικοδομή, 874 θ. γνώσεως ἡ τοιαύτη ἐγκράτεια, 646 τῷ θεμ. τῆς πίστεως ἐποικοδομεῖ τ. γνῶσιν

θεμιτός: 833 ὅπερ οὐ θ., 792 εἰς ὅσον ἀνθρωπίνῃ θ. φύσει

θεόθεν: 855 ἡ εἰς ἡμᾶς θ. ἥκουσα πρόνοια, 869 τ. ἀρχὰς θ. ἄνωθεν <εἴλη φυῖα>, 821 θ. τὴν ἔπαυσιν εἰληφότα, 774 ἡ θ. δωρηθεῖσα γεωργία

θεόπνευστος: 894 αἱ θ. γραφαί, 896 θ λόγοι

θεοποιέω: 847 οὐκ ἂν φθάνοιεν τ. μαγείρους θεοποιοῦντες

θεοπρέπεια: 830 ἡ θ. ἕξις ἐστὶ τὸ πρέπον τ. θεῷ σῴζουσα

θεοπρεπής: 830 ὁ θ. μόνος θεοφιλής. 829 τῷ θ. τὸ θεοφιλὲς ἕπεται κ. φιλόθεον, 9 θ. καθάρσια, 955 πάντες οἱ πιστοὶ θεοπρεπεῖς, cf. Ign. Magn 1, Mart Polyc. 7, Luc. Alex. 15

θεοπρεπῶς: 829 θ. τ. θεὸν θρησκεύων, 831 θ παραδιδόναι τὰ παρὰ τ. ἀληθείᾳ ἐπικεκρυμμένα

θεός: (spoken of men or angels) 839 θεαταὶ ἄγγελοι καὶ θεοί, 831, 835 θεῶν οἰκήσεις, 865 θεοὶ κέκληνται οἱ σύνθρονοι τ. ἄλλων θεῶν τῶν ὑπὸ τ σωτῆρι πρῶτον τεταγμένων, 894 ὁ τ θεῷ πειθόμενος τελέων ἐκτελεῖται ἐν σαρκὶ περιπολῶν θεός, 830 ὅπως βιωτέον θεῷ ἰσομένῳ. see under 'God'

θεοσέβεια: 831 ἡ θ. συγκομιδὴν ἀρίστην ἐργάζεται, 836 μεγαλοπρεπὴς θεοσέβεια κανὼν ἐξομοιώσεως, 853 οὐδεμίαν σώζει θ. ἡ μὴ πρέπουσα περὶ τ. θεοῦ ὑπόληψις, 864, 866, 867 bis, 887 ὡς ἡ ὄντως οὖσα θ.

θεοσεβέω: 864 ὁ Χριστιανὸς μόνος θ

θεοσεβής: 830 θ. μόνος ὁ καλῶς ἐξυπηρετῶν τ. θεῷ, 841, 854 fin. 856 ἡ διὰ τῆς θεοσεβοῦς γνώμης κ. γνώσεως θεραπεία, 864, 831 κράτιστον ἐν γῇ ἄνθρωπος ὁ θεοσεβέστατος

θεοφιλής: 829, 830 see θεοπρεπής, 850 θυσία θεοφιλής

θεοφορία: 882 ὁ γνωστικὸς ἤδη ἅγιος θεοφορῶν κ. θεοφορούμενος, 841 Πλάτων οἷον θεοφορούμενός φησιν. 792 ἀγάπη θεοφοροῦσα κ. θεοφορουμένη, cf 976 θεοφόρος γίνεται ὁ ἄνθρωπος προσεχῶς ἐνεργούμενος ὑπὸ τ. κυρίου

θεραπεία: 829 θ. τοῦ θεοῦ ἡ συνεχὴς ἐπιμέλεια τ. ψυχῆς, 830 τῆς θ ἡ μὲν βελτιωτικὴ ἡ δ' ὑπηρετική, 835 ἡ εἰς θεὸν θ. διατείνει εἰς τὴν τ. ἀνθρώπων σωτηρίαν, 856 init. θ. ἐλευθεριωτάτη κ. βασιλικωτάτη, 872 ἡ τοῦ ἐξοχωτάτου θ., 879 ἡ τοῦ κυρίου θ., 887 θεραπείαι δεόμενος, 893 τριττὴ θ. τῆς αἰθέσεως κ. παντὸς πάθους, 863 ἐν θεραπείαις μέρει

θεραπευτής: 856 θ. τοῦ θείου

INDEX

Θεραπευτικός: 889 τὰ περὶ τ. σῶμα θεραπευτικά
Θεραπεύω: 887 ἐπ' ἴσης θεραπεύει
Θεράπων: 839 θ. τ. θεοῦ ὁ ἑκὼν τ. ἐντολαῖς ὑπαγόμενος, 856 θ. κ. θεράπευται τ. θείου οἱ βασιλικωτάτην θεραπείαν προσάγοντες
Θερμαντικός: 855 θ. τὸ πῦρ
Θερμότης: 880 οὐ μετουσίᾳ θερμότητος θερμός
Θεσμός: 837 (θεὸς) νόμος κ. θεσμὸς κ. λόγος αἰώνιος
Θεωρέω: 'see' 868 θ. τ. σώματα, 873 θ. τ. ψυχάς
Θεώρημα: 877 ἐπιστημονικοῦ θ. κατάληψις
Θεωρητός: 857 τὴν τ. θεωρητῶν δύναμιν ἔμμονον κεκτημένος
Θεωρία: 830 ἡ βελτιωτικὴ θ. (θεραπεία?), 834 ἀγωγὸν τὸ ἐραστὸν πρὸς τὴν ἑαυτοῦ θ., ib. ἐν διίδιότητι θεωρίας, 835 ἡ μεγαλοπρέπεια τῆς θ., ib. οὐκέτι ἐν κατόπτροις τὴν θ. ἀσπαζόμεναι τ. θείαν, ib. ἡ καταληπτικὴ θ. τ. καθαρῶν, 888, 837 ἡ τελεία θ., 868 and 895 ἡ ἐπιστημονικὴ θ., 857 εὔθικτος κατὰ τὴν προσβολὴν τῆς θ., 859, 861, 865 θ. ἀΐδιος, 867 θ. δογμάτων, ib. ἄξιον γενέσθαι τ. τοιαύτης θ., 875 θ. πραγμάτων, 879 τὸ εὐαγγέλιον διὰ θεωρίας ἐπαινῶν, 883 τὰ ἐφόδια τῆς θ. καρποῦται, ib. θ.)(ἐνέργεια, 794 ἀκορέστου θεωρίας ἐποπτείᾳ προσανέχοντες, 876 fin. 'spectacles' ἐπίγειοι θ.
Θηρατόν: 888 θ. τ. ἀκριβεστάτην γνῶσιν
Θηρίον: 871 θ. ὁμόσε λόγχαις πορεύεται, 890 θ. ἐξ ἀνθρώπου
Θηριώδης: 841 θεοὺς θ. τὰ ἤθη ἀναπλάττουσιν
Θησαυρός: (quot.) 878 ὅπου ὁ νοῦς ἐκεῖ ὁ θ.
Θλίβω: (quot.) 889 τεθλιμμένη ἡ εἴσοδος, 873 θλιβόμενον ἐπικουφίζει
Θλῖψις: 869 πόνοι κ. βάσανοι κ. θλ. 876, 878
Θολερός: 893 θ. ὕδωρ
Θολόω: 893 θολωθεῖσα δόγμασι ψυχῇ, 885 τεθολωμένοι ἄλλοι ἄλλων μᾶλλον
Θρᾷξ: (quot.) 841
Θρέμμα: 901 τῶν τοιούτων θ. ὀλισθηρὸν τὸ γένος, 956 θρ. τ. διαβόλου
Θρησκεύω: act. 829 μόνος ὁ γνωστικὸς τὸν τῷ ὄντι θεὸν θ., 862 τὰ ἐπίγεια θρ., 633, 778 θρ. τὸ θεῖον διὰ δικαιοσύνης: m. 19 θρησκεύεσθαι τὰς μυήσεις: pass. 636 ἡ ἀνάπαυσις θρησκεύεται
Θρόνος: 882 τῶν θρόνων τ. ἄκρων ἅπτεται
Θρυλέω: 848 τ. ἀρχαιότατον βωμὸν ἐν Δήλῳ ἁγνὸν εἶναι τεθρυλήκασιν
Θυηείς: (quot.) 848
Θύλακος: (quot.) 842 τί θαυμαστὸν εἰ ὁ μῦς τὸν θ. διέτραγεν;

Θύλαξ: (quot.) 842 τ. μῦν ὁ θ. κατέφαγεν
Θόλημα: Pherecrates ap. Cl. 847 init. (ms. has οὐ λήμασι)
Θυμίαμα: 849 τὸ ἀπὸ τ. δικαίας ψυχῆς θ. ἡ ὁσία εὐχή, 850 τὸ θ. τὸ σύνθετον, 852 θυμιαμάτων πολυτέλεια, 856 ἡ προσευχὴ ὡς θ., cf. Constit. Apost. 7. 33
Θυμοειδής: 867 ἐκ φύσεως θ. γενόμενοι ὅμοια τ. ἀνδρείοις δρῶσιν
Θυρίς: 840 διὰ θυρίδος ἥλιος ἀποστέλλει τ. αὐγήν
Θυσία: 837 θυσίαις παραιτητοί, 890 αἱ θ. σαρκοφαγιῶν προφάσει ἐπιπενόηνται, 861 θ. ἡ κατὰ τοὺς δεομένους ἐπίδοσις, 900 ὁ κατὰ τὰς θ. νόμος, 848 ἡ θ. τ. ἐκκλησίας λόγος ἀπὸ τ. ἁγίων ἀναθυμιώμενος, ib. θ. εὐχή, 856 θυσίαν προσάγειν, ib. θ. δεκτὴ ἀρεταί, ib. οὐ θυσίαις κηλεῖται τὸ θεῖον, 850 (quot.) θυσίας προσφέρειν μὴ πολυτελεῖς ἀλλὰ θεοφιλεῖς, 860
Θυσιαστήριον: 848 τ. ἐπίγειον θ. ἐστὶ τ. ἄθροισμα τῶν τ. εὐχαῖς ἀνακειμένων, cf. Lightfoot Ign. II. p. 44, 258, 913
Θώραξ: 848 ἡ τ. πνεύμονος πρὸς τὸν θ. ἀντιδιαστολή

Ἰάομαι: 893 p. κἂν λάθῃ τις, εἰ πέπεισθαι ἠβουλήθη
Ἰάσιμος: 896 εἴ τις ἰάσιμος, ὑπεχέτω τ. ὦτα τ. ψυχῆς
Ἰατρικός: 830 l. θεραπεία, 887 αἱ ἐν τῇ ἰατρικῇ αἱρέσεις
Ἰατρός: 863 l. ἐπὶ σωτηρίᾳ τ. καμνόντων ψεύσεται, 887 οἱ l. ἐναντίας δόξας κεκτημένοι ἐπ' ἴσης ἔργῳ θεραπεύουσιν, ib. ἰατρὸν οὐ προσίεται
Ἰδιάζω: 900 τ. αἱρέσεων αἱ μὲν ἀπὸ δογμάτων ἰδιαζόντων προσαγορεύονται, Heliod. VII. 12, Socr. H. E. v. 22, Philo
Ἴδιος: 833 ἴδιον ἔργον θεοῦ ἄνθρωπος, cf. 101 fin. τ. ἄνθρωπον δι' αὑτοῦ ἐχειρούργησεν καί τι αὑτῷ ἴδιον ἐνεφύσησεν, 879 ὁ γνωστικὸς ὑπὸ τ. ἰδίας ἐλπίδος περισπώμενος οὐ γεύεται τῶν ἐν κόσμῳ καλῶν, ib. κληρονομημάτων μόνων τ. ἰδίων μεμνημένος, τὰ δὲ ἐνταῦθα ἀλλότρια ἡγούμενος, 892 κατ' ἰδίαν
Ἰδιότης: 863 ἄγαλμα ἔμψυχον οὐ κατὰ τὴν τ. μορφῆς ἰδ., Philo
Ἰδίως: 868 ἰδ. ἐκλαμβάνει ὡς εἴρηται τ. γνωστικῷ
Ἰδιώτης: 891 ἔχουσί τι πλέον τεχνῖται ἰδιωτῶν
Ἰδιωτισμός: 873 κατὰ ἰδ. πρός τινων κατορθοῦται ἐγκράτεια, Diog. Laert. VII. 59
Ἰδρύω: 845 τί ἂν ἱδρύοιτο μηδενὸς ἐφιδρύτου τυγχάνοντος, ib. τὸ ἱδρυμένον

ὑπό τινος ἵδρυνται, ib. τὸ ὂν ὑπὸ τοῦ μὴ ὄντος οὐκ ἂν ἰδρυνθείη, 90 ἐν ἀνθρώποις ἱδρύειν τ. θεόν
ἱερατικός: 852 τὸ l. γένος εἰς βασιλείαν προσάγουσιν
ἱερεύς: 852 ὁ βασιλικὸς ἄνθρωπος l. τ. θεοῦ
ἱερεύω: 836 τὸν ὑπὲρ ἡμῶν ἱερευθέντα δοξάζομεν σφᾶς αὐτοὺς ἱερεύοντες
ἵημι: 882 ἐπ' ἐκεῖνο μόνον ἱέμενος ἐφ' ὃ ἔγνω μόνον
ἱκανός: 857 ἰκ. ἑαυτῷ
ἱλαρός: 852 σεμνὸς κ. ἱλαρὸς ὁ γνωστικός
ἱμάς: 842 τὸν ἱμ. διέρρηξα
ἵνα: 853 ὅλος ὀφθαλμός, ἵνα τις τούτοις χρήσηται τοῖς ὀνόμασιν (ut ita dicam), cf. Schmid *Att.* III. 81
Ἰουδαία: 897 = ἐξομολόγησις
Ἰουδαΐζω: 887 οὐ δεῖ ὀκνεῖν ιουδ. τῆς διαφωνίας ἕνεκα τ. αἱρέσεων
ἱπνός: 847 τ. ἱπνὸν (MS. ἱτμὸν) αὐτὸν προσκυνοῦντες
ἱππικός: 894 ἐὰν προσσχῇ τις Σίμωνι ἱππικὸν αὐτὸν ποιήσει
ἰσάγγελος: 879 μετ' ἀγγέλων εὔχεται ὡς ἂν ἤδη καὶ ἰσ., 883, 866, 792 ὁ ἀπαθὴς ἰσ., 120 τὸ πρόσωπον ἰσάγγελον ἔχει
ἴσος: 840 πᾶσι πάντα ἴσα κεῖται, 878 ἴσος κ. ὅμοιος, 900 ὅμοιος ἢ ἴσος, 887 ἐναντίας δόξας κεκτημένοι ἐπ' ἴσης θεραπεύουσιν, 832 πάντας ἐπ' ἴσης κεκληκώς
ἰστέον: 829, 883
ἵστημι: 883 οὐκ ἐπὶ τοῦ ἀδικεῖσθαι μᾶλλον ἢ ἀδικεῖν ἵστησι τ. γνωστικόν, 882 τὰ πάντα <ἐφ'> ἑνὸς τ. θεοῦ ἵσταται, 866 φῶς ἐστός, cf. Clem. Hom. ind. s.v.
ἱστορία: 841 συγκαταχρώμενοι ἱστορίᾳ
ἰσχύω: 840 ὁ βουληθεὶς ἰσχύει, 868 παράγειν αὐτὸν τῆς ἐνστάσεως οὐκ ἴσχυσεν
ἴσχω: 859 ἡ τ. σοφίας μετάδοσις οὐ κινούντων κ. ἰσχόντων ἀλλήλους τῆς τε ἐνεργείας κ. τοῦ μετέχοντος γίνεται: = ἔχω 114 fin., 590
ἰχθύς: 850 Αἰγύπτιοι ἰχθύων οὐχ ἅπτονται, 902 πολλὰ τ. δελέατα διὰ τὰς τ. ἰχθύων διαφοράς, 850 τοὺς l. οὐδὲ ἀναπνεῖν τούτον τ. ἀέρα ἀλλ' ἐκεῖνον ὃς ἐγκέκραται τ. ὕδατι

κάδος: 901 (quot) σταγὼν ἀπὸ κ.
καθαιρετικός: 870 καθ. τῶν ἐπὶ τ. γνῶσιν προκοπτόντων ἡ κακία, cf. Corn. (p. 184 Osann) Διόνυσος καθαιρετικὸς παντὸς οὑτινοσοῦν ὑπάρχων ἔδοξε καὶ πολεμιστὴς εἶναι, Orig. Cels. I. p. 25 τινας ὑπὲρ τοῦ κοινοῦ τεθνηκέναι καθαιρετικούς (al. -κῶς) τῶν προκαταλαβόντων τ. πόλεις κακῶν

καθαίρω: 874 καθαίρεται χαλκός
καθαρμός: 844 fin. κατά τινας ἀκαθάρτους καθαρμούς (cf. Plut. Mor. 172 B), 845 πρὸ τῆς τ. μυστηρίων παραδόσεως καθαρμούς τινας προσάγουσιν
καθαρός: 835 ἡ καταληπτικὴ θεωρία τῶν κ. τῇ καρδίᾳ, 844 (quot.) νοῦς καθαρός, 831 (adv.) ἄγγελος ὁ καθαρώτερον ζωῆς μεταλαγχάνων
καθαρότης: 880 ἄξιος διὰ καθαρότητα ἔχειν τ. δύναμιν τ. θεοῦ
κάθαρσις: 865 πάσας καθάρσεις (MS. πάσης καθάρσεως) καὶ λειτουργίας ὑπερβᾶσα τελείωσις, ib. ταχεῖα εἰς κ. ἡ γνῶσις, ib. πεπαυμένοι καθάρσεως
καθαρῶς: 869 τὸ τέλεον τ. ἕξεως ἐκ συνασκήσεως πολλῆς καθαρῶς ἐκτήσατο, 831 καθαρώτερον μεταλαγχάνων
καθείργνυμι: 845 οὐδ' ἐν ἱεροῖς καθείργνυμεν τὸ πάντων περιεκτικόν
καθήκει: 832 τὸ κήδεσθαι πάντων κ. τῷ κυρίῳ, 860 συμπράττειν κ., 878 ἐφ' ὧν κ.
καθηκόντως: 864 κ. ταῦτα ποιεῖ καὶ κατὰ λόγον
καθήκων: 862 ἡ ἐν τοῖς καθήκουσιν κατόρθωσις, ib. παρὰ τὸ καθῆκον, ib. μηδὲν παραβαίνων τ. καθηκόντων, 875
καθιδρύω: 846 ἄγαλμα καθιδρυμένον εἰς τιμήν
καθιερόω: 846 τῷ τοῦ παντὸς ἀξίῳ καθιέρωται
καθίστημι: 869 ἐν εὐεξίᾳ καθεστηκυῖα ψυχή
καθολικός: 868 τὰ καθολικώτερον εἰρημένα, 899 ἡ ἀρχαία καὶ καθ. ἐκκλησία, cf. Lightfoot on Ign. Smyrn. 8, p. 310
καθόλου: 835 κ. καὶ ἐπὶ μέρους
καθοράω: 837 οὐ καθεόρακασι τὸ αὐθαίρετον τ. ἀνθρωπίνης ψυχῆς
καθοριστικός: 861 ὁμολογία καθοριστικὴ ὅρκος (ἅπ. λεγ.)
καθοσιόω: 840 οἱ καθωσιωμένοι τ. κυρίῳ, Philo
καθωρισμένως: 861 ἐμπέδως κ. καθ. ὅρκος ἐστὶ τούτῳ ὁ βίος (ἅπ. λεγ.)
καινίζω: 863 κ. εἰς σωτηρίαν τὸν κατηχούμενον
καινός: 836 (quot) κ. ἄνθρωπος, see κοινός
καινοτομέω: 896 δόξης ὀριγνώμενοι καινοτομεῖν βιάζονται, 899 τ. αἱρέσεις κεκαινοτομῆσθαι, Philo
καινῶς: 895 καινῶς μὲν λεγόμενον ἀρχαιότατον δὲ ᾆσμα
καιρός: 872 καιρόν (MS. καιροῦ) λαβών
καίτοι = καίπερ: 871 καίτοι ἀπὸ κακίας φερόμενα, 73 καίτοι ἐπίζημα οὖσαι, 877 τ. κοσμικῶν καίτοι θεῖον ὄντων ἐπαγγελιῶν κατεμεγαλοφρόνησεν

Hom. II. 20 εύγνωμονοῦσα πρὸς τ. συνθήκας, IX. 4 πρὸς τ. ὅρκον εὐγνωμονεῖν. ib. εὐγνωμοσύνην πρὸς θεὸν ἀποσώζειν

εὐγνώμων 858, characteristic of the Christian

εὐδαιμονία 847 τῆς ἴσης εὐδαιμονίας ἀξιοῦνται

εὐδοκέω: (quot.) 896 ἐν πᾶσιν πόδδρησεν

εὐδοξία 872 εὐδοξίας χάριν σωφρονοῦσιν οἱ ἀθληταί

εὐεμπτωσία: 896 ἡ εἰς τ. αἱρέσεις εὐεμπτ.

εὐεξία 869 ἐν ἄκρᾳ εὐ. καθεστηκυῖα ψυχή

εὐεπίφορος: 856 ὅταν τὸ παρ' ἡμῶν εὐ. ὁ τῶν ἀγαθῶν λάβῃ δοτήρ, 862 οὐκ εὐεπ. ἐπὶ τὸ ὀμνύναι ὁ γνωστικός, 745 τὸ εὐεπ. εἰς κλοπήν, 551 εὐεπ. εἰς δεύτερον γάμον, 986 ἄνθρωποι ζωον εὐεπ. εἰς τὸ χεῖρον, 270 εὐεπ. οἱ ἀκόλαστοι πρὸς τ. ἀσέλγειαν, cf. 507 ἡ εὐεπιφορία τ. παθῶν, rare

εὐεργεσία: 833 κατάλληλος εὐεργ., 835 joined with εὐνοια, 855 ἡ εὐ. τ. θεοῦ 862 fin., 879 init., 890 ἐνεργούμενοι εἰς εὐεργ., 862

εὐεργετέω: 880 καὶ ἄλλους (MS. καλῶς) εὐεργετεῖ

εὐεργέτης: 840 ὁ εὐ. προκατάρχει τ. εὐποίίας

εὐεργετικός: 831 εὐεργετικωτάτη ἡ υἱοῦ φύσις, 829 τὸ πρεσβύτατον κ. εὐεργετικώτατον

εὐεργός 874 εὐ. πρὸς τὴν τ. γνώσεως παραδοχήν

εὐθαρσής: 870 κατεξανίσταται τ. φόβων εὐθ (MS. εὐθάρσων)

εὐθαρσῶς: 871 εὐθ. πᾶν τὸ προσιὸν δια δέχεται

εὐθετέω: 858 οὐδὲν ἐπιζητεῖ τῶν κατὰ τ. βίον εἰς τ. ἀναγκαίαν χρῆσιν εὐθετούντων (H. for MS. οὐθ' ὅτ' οὖν, H. J εὐθετεῖν, M. εὐθετῶν)

εὔθετος 889 (quot.) εὐθ. τῇ βασιλείᾳ 877 ἐργάτης εὐθ., Aristot., Polyb.

εὔθικτος: 857 εὐθ. κατὰ τ. προσβολὴν τ. θεωρίας, Philo II. 570, Plut. De Fato fin., Clem. Rom. 1. 64, Test. XII Patr. Is 4

εὐθύς 893 (subaud. ὁδός) ἐξ ἀρχῆς εὐθείαν περαίνει, Eus. Pr. Ev. VI. 8 p. 250 τ. εὐθεῖαν βαδίζει, P. 22 init ἔννοιαι παρηγμέναι τῆς εὐθείας

εὐκόλως: 867 βαρέως ὑπομένει εὐκ

εὐλάβεια: 869 δι' εὐλαβείας ἀναπόβλητον, 871 εὐλαβείᾳ κολάσεως ὑπομένουσιν

εὐλογία: (quot.) 866 εὐλογίαν λήψεται

εὐλογιστία: 859 τ. εὐλογιστίας ἀνθέξεται... ἡ γνῶσις τ. εὐλογιστίαν παρέχει Philo

εὔλογος 849 εὐλόγῳ λόγῳ χρῆται

εὐλόγως 841, 851, 858 εὐλ. οὐδὲν ἐπιζητεῖ, 898

εὐμενής: 885 ἐπὶ δικαίους τὸ εὐμ. τ. ἔργων ἐπιλάμπουσι

εὐνοια: 855 ἡ ἀντίστροφος εὐν. τ. φίλου τ. θεοῦ

εὐόργητος 862 ('irascible') δεισιδαίμων περὶ τοὺς εὐοργ.

εὐορκέω: 862 τὸ εὐ. συμβαίνει κατὰ τ. κατόρθωσιν, ib. τ. ἔργοις εὐορκεῖν

εὔορκος 862 εὐ. ὁ γνωστικός

εὐπαθής: 852 τὸ εὐπ. τοῦ ἀέρος, cf. εὐπάθεια 89

εὐπείθεια 840 ἀνθρώπειον ἔργον εὐπ. θεῷ, 881 τ. φρουρὰν ἔχει παρ' ἑαυτοῦ διὰ τῆς εὐπ.

εὐπίαστος (quot.) 851 ἀνείμενοι εὐπ.

εὐποιέω)(ἀγαθοποιέω 855 κατὰ προαίρεσιν εὐπ. τοὺς ἐπιστρέφοντας

εὐποιητικός: 841 εὐπ. ὁ θεός, 880 ἕξις εὐπ.

εὐποιία 836 τὴν δι' ἔργων εὐπ., 840 ὁ εὐεργέτης προκατάρχει τῆς εὐπ., 875 ἡ τῆς εὐπ. ζωή, ib. ἐνέργεια τῆς εὐπ., 878 fin., 881 ἐργάζεται τὴν εὐπ., 490 σπείρειν τὰς τ. θεοῦ εὐποιίας

εὐπραγία 860 συνεργεῖν πρὸς εὐπρ., 867 ἡ διὰ τ. ἐπιστήμονος πρᾶξις εὐπρ.

εὐπροαίρετος 856 εὐπρ. κ. εὐχάριστοι (rare)

εὐπρόσδεκτος: 865 εὐπ. μεταβολὴ ἐπὶ τὸ κρεῖττον

εὐπρόσιτος 858 characteristic of the Christian, 85 εὐνοια εὐπρ.

εὕρεσις: 888 πόνῳ ἕπεται γλυκεῖα εὑρ., 890 εἰς τὴν τ. πραγμάτων εὕρεσιν χρώμεθα τεκμηρίῳ, 901 ὡς μὴ ῥᾳδίαν εἶναι τὴν τ. παραδόσεων εὑρ.

εὑρετικός: 902 φιλόσοφοι κ. εὑρ.

εὐσέβεια: 849 αἱ θυσίαι τὴν περὶ ἡμᾶς εὐσ. ἀλληγοροῦσι

εὐσεβής: 829 εὐσ. κ. ὅσιος, 837, 859 μόνος εὐσ. ὁ γνωστικός, 864, 893

εὐσεβῶς 864

εὐστομέω = εὐφημέω: 871 οὐκ οἶδ' ὅπως, εὐστομεῖν γὰρ δίκαιον

εὐσυνείδητος: 797 ψυχῆς καύχημα εὐσυνειδήτου, 858 Christian characteristic, 879 εὐσ. πρὸς τ. ἔξοδον, 882 οὐδὲ αἰσχύνεται εὐσ. ὢν τ. ἐξουσίας ὀφθῆναι, Auton. VI. 30, Ign. Phil. 6

εὐσυνείδητως 860 εὐσ. τὰ παρ' ἑαυτοῦ πάντα ἐκπεπλήρωκε, 882 εὐσ. βιοῖ, 510 εὐσ. προσεύχου (cf. εὐσυνείδησία 797), Orig. Philocal. 48, 24, ed. Robinson

εὐτελής 892 ὡς εὐτελῶν καταφρονῆσαι

εὐτονία: 890 εὐτ. ψυχική, Plut., Epict.

εὔτρεπής: 886 εὐτρ. ἐπὶ τὰς τ. ἀπορίων λύσεις

εὐτύχημα 857 εὐτ. βλάπτει λαβόντας

κατακοσμέω: 902 ὡραῖον κ. παράδεισον
κατακούω: 890 κ. τῶν γραφῶν
καταλεαίνω: 901 τὴν τ. λογίων σαφήνειαν κ. (trop.)
καταλέγω: 872 ἐν υἱοῦ καταλεγεὶς τάξει
καταλείπω: 854 σπούδων καταλελοιπέναι πάντα, 882 τὰ ἐμποδὼν καταλιπών
καταληπτικός: 835 κ. θεωρία τ. καθαρῶν τ. καρδίᾳ, 888
καταληπτικῶς: 865 κ. τὸν θεὸν ἐποπτεύειν
καταληπτός: 866 init. τὸ ἀμετάπτωτον καὶ μετ' ἐπιστήμης κ. (P. καταληπτικόν)
κατάληψις: 838 βεβαία κ. δεόντως ἂν λέγοιτο ἐπιστήμη, 869 τὰ ἐγνωσμένα ἤδη, εἰς κατάληψιν δὲ ἐλπιζόμενα, 877 ἐπιστημονικοῦ θεωρήματος κατάληψιν λαβεῖν
καταλιμπάνω: 861, 956
κατάλληλος: 833 οἰκεία καὶ κατ. εὐεργεσία, 53, 177
καταλλήλως: 853 τὸ εὔχεσθαι καὶ ὀρέγεσθαι κ. γίνεται
καταμανθάνω: 895 καταμαθόντας ἐκ τῶνδε τ. ὑπομνημάτων σωφρονισθῆναι, 938
καταμεγαλοφρονέω: 854 κ. τοῦ σαρκικοῦ δεσμοῦ, 877 τῶν κοσμικῶν ἐπαγγελιῶν κ., 879 πάντων τῶν ἐνταῦθα κ., 880 τῶν εἰς τροφὴν οἰκείων κ., 274, 538, 558, 575 (only in Clem.)
καταμέμφομαι: (c. dat. pers. gen. rei) 846 κ. τοῖς ἀνθρώποις τῶν ἱερῶν
καταμένω: 869 τὰ τ. κόσμου καλὰ οὐκ ἀγαπᾷ ἵνα μὴ καταμείνῃ χαμαί
καταντάω: (quot.) 834 κατ. εἰς ἄνδρα τέλειον
καταξιόω: 873 ὁρᾶν καταξιούμενος τ. θεόν, 877 καταξιούμενοι τῆς ἐνεργούσης μεταλήψεως
καταπαύω: 900 κ. τὸν λόγον, Polyb. π. 8. 8, ιx. 31. 7 &c.
καταπολεμέω: (c. gen.) 870 τ. ὅπλοις τ. κυρίου καταπολεμεῖ κακίας
καταργέω: (quot.) 885
κατασκευάζω: 850 πλαδαρὰν τὴν σάρκα κατ. ἡ βρῶσις, 872 ἄφοβον ἡ ἀγάπη κ. τὸν ἀθλητήν, 896 ('proves') κ. μὴ πάντας τ. λόγον κεχωρηκέναι
κατασκεύασμα: 846 'building'
κατασπάω: 859 κατασπᾶται τὸ διὰ τ. πίστεως ἀναγόμενον
καταστέλλω: 869 τ. σχήματι κατεσταλμένος
καταστολή: 865 εἰς κ. βίον
καταστρέφω: 847 οἱ ἐπὶ ἀρετὴν κ. ἀπὸ ἀρετῆς καταστρέφοντες (?)
κατατάσσω: 899 ἡ ἐκκλησία συνάγει τοὺς ἤδη κατατεταγμένους
κατατέμνω: 899 τ. ἐκκλησίαν εἰς πολλὰς κ. αἱρέσεις
κατατίθημι: 891 αἰδούμενοι καταθέσθαι

τὸ πλεονέκτημα, 880 τὰ παρ' αὐτῷ κατατιθέμενα σπέρματα
καταφαίνομαι: 829 ἑτεροῖα καταφαίνεται τ. κυριακῶν γραφῶν, 880 τρία μοι κ. εἶναι τῆς γνωστικῆς δυνάμεως ἀποτελέσματα
καταφρονέω: 841, 878, 892 τῆς προφητείας κ., 894 κ. ἀλλήλων, 70 joined with περιφρονέω
καταφυτεύω: 876 θεῖοι γεωργοὶ τῶν εἰς πίστιν καταπεφυτευμένων, 901 bis
καταχέω: 895 βλασφημοῦς τ. ἀληθείας κ. λόγους
καταχράομαι: pf. in pres. sense 833, see χράομαι
καταχρηστέον: 888 ἀφορμαῖς κ. εἰς ἐπίγνωσιν
κατειλέω: (quot.) 842 παραδοξότερον ἦν εἰ τὸ ὕπερον περὶ τῷ ὄφει κατειλημένον ἑλέσω
κατεξανίσταμαι: 870 κ. τῶν φόβων, ib. κ. παντὸς φόβου, 874 κ. πάσης πείρας, 880 κ. τῆς σωματικῆς ψυχῆς, 776, Synes. Enc. Calv. 2 n. 31 Krab.
κατεπᾴδω: 894 κ. ταῖς θείαις γραφαῖς τ. ψοφοδεεῖς, 27 αἱ Μοῦσαι κατεπ. τὸν Μάκαρα, 960, 83 τὰ ὦτα πρὸς τ. κατεπᾴδοντας ἀποκέκλεισται, Orig. c. Cels. I. 6 init.
κατεπείγω: 829 τὸ μὴ ἐπεσκέφθαι τὸ κατεπεῖγον ῥᾳθύμου κομιδῇ, 841 ἡ κατεπείγουσα ἱστορία, 865 ἡ πίστις σύντομός ἐστι τ. κατεπειγόντων γνῶσις, 564 ἡ κατ. χρεία, cf. 99 οὐδὲν τοσοῦτον κ. 'is so pressing'
κατέρχομαι: 892 μέχρι τ. βάθους τ. πραγμάτων κ.
κατεσθίω: 842 ὃς κ. τὰ δελφάκια bis
κατευθύνω: 867 κ. τὴν πρᾶξιν, 856 (quot.) κατευθυνθήτω ἡ προσευχή
κατέχω: 868 κ. τὸν χιτῶνα, 880 κἂν ἐπὶ γῆς κατέχηται, c. gen. 875 ὁ κατασχὼν ἑαυτοῦ
κατηχέω: 863 καινίζων τ. κατηχούμενον εἰς σωτηρίαν
κατισχναίνω: 842 ὃς ὑπὸ λιμοῦ κατισχναμένη
κατολισθάνω: 895 εἰς κολάσεις οἱ πολλοὶ κατολισθάνοντες περιπίπτουσι, cf. 289 τρίχες εἰς πλοκάμους κατολισθάνουσαι γυναικείους, 56 εἰς ἑτέραν κ. ἀπάτην [ΜΒ. κατολισθαίνω]
κάτοπτρον: 835 οὐκ ἐν κατόπτροις ἢ διὰ κατόπτρων ἔτι ἀσπαζόμενοι τ. θείαν θεωρίαν
κατορθόω: 864 (the gnostic) τὸ ἀναμάρτητον πάντοτε κατορθοῖ, ib. κατορθοῖ ἐν πᾶσι πάντων, 867 ἐνίοτε τὰ αὐτὰ κ., 869 οἱ κατωρθωκότες πατριάρχαι, 883 ἐν ᾗ δεύτερον κατορθῶσαι: p. 878 ἔστιν δ πρὸς τινων κατορθοῦται, 958 μετὰ θεοῦ πᾶσῃ κατορθοῦται

27—2

κατόρθωσις: 862 ἡ ἐν τοῖς καθήκουσιν κ.
κατορθωτικός: 858 ἡ κ. τῶν πρακτέων ἄσκησις, Arist.
κάτω: 852 fin. κάτω περὶ τ. ἀέρα κυλινδουμένη φωνή: (of time) 896 κ. περὶ τοὺς Ἀδριανοῦ χρόνους
κατωφερής: 850 κ. εἰς συνουσίαν, Lobeck Phryn. 439
καχεξία: 834 καχεξίᾳ περιπίπτειν, 895 εἴτε ἀβελτερίας εἴτε καχεξίας
κεῖμαι: 840 πᾶσι πάντα ἴσα κεῖται παρὰ τ. θεοῦ
κενοδοξία: 881 οὐ διὰ κ. ἐργάζεται τ. εὔποιαν, 941 φήμης κενῆς κ. κενοδοξίας ἕνεκεν
κενός: 844 (quot.) κ. εὕρηκα φάρμακον πρὸς τὰ κ., 893 ἀμυγδάλαι κεναί, αἱρετικοὶ κ.
κεράννυμι: 867 πόθος ζητήσει κραθείς, 882 πίστιν ἐλπίδι κεράσας, cf. Heb. iv. 2
κέρκος: (quot.) 847
κεφάλαιον: 845 τὰ προηγούμενα κεφ., 901 ὡς ἐν κεφαλαίῳ ὑπογράφειν
κεφαλαιωδῶς: 829 κ. τὸν χριστιανισμὸν ὑπογράφοντες, 866 παραστήσομαι ἐν μαρτύριον κ.
κηδεμονία: 832 (obj. gen.) ἡ ἀνθρώπων κ., 874 ἡ τ. οἴκου κ.: (subj. gen.) 835 κατὰ κ. τῆς εἰς ἡμᾶς εὐεργεσίας: 143 ἡ κηδ. δείκνυσι τ. σωτηρίαν
κήδομαι: 832 κ. συμπάντων ὁ κύριος, 874 μόνου κ. ἑαυτοῦ
κηλέω: 836 οὐδὲ ἀναθήμασι κηλεῖται τὸ θεῖον
κηπευτικός: 888 ἡ κ. ἐπιμέλεια
κηπεύω: p. 888 ἐν τοῖς κηπευομένοις λαχάνοις συναναφύονται καὶ πόαι
κηρός: 874 κ. μαλάσσεται ἵνα τ. ἐπιόντα χαρακτῆρα παραδέξηται, 888 ἡ ἐκ κ. ὀπώρα
κήρυξις: 863 ἄγαλμα τ. κυρίου κατὰ τὸ τ. κηρύξεως ὁμοίωμα
κηρύσσω: 899 κηρύσσοντος Πέτρου ἐπήκουσεν
κηφήν: (quot.) 844
κίβδηλος: 887 κ. νόμισμα τ. κυρίου διακρίνειν (ἀκίβδηλον Resch)
κίνδυνος: 892 ὁ κ. οὐ περὶ ἑνὸς δόγματος
κινέω: 854 κινούντων καὶ ἰσχυόντων ἀλλήλους
κίνημα: 875 κ. διανοίας ὑφορᾶται
κίνησις: (quot.) 833 κ. πρωτουργός
Κίρκη: 890
κισσός: 901 ὄρος δασὺ κισσῷ
κλαδεύω: 876 ἐργάζεται ἐν τ. ἀμπελῶνι κλαδεύων
κλείς: 897 τὴν κλεῖν ἔχουσι τ. εἰσόδου
κλέπτω: 897 οὐ χρὴ κλέπτειν τ. κανόνα τ. ἐκκλησίας
κληρονόμημα: 879 κλ. τῶν ἰδίων μεμνημένος (only other ex. in Luc. Tyr. 6)

κληρονομία: 853 οὐδεὶς ἐπιθυμεῖ κληρονομίας ἀλλὰ τοῦ κληρονομεῖν, 894 (quot.), 865 προστεθήσεται τῇ γνώσει ἡ ἀγάπη, τῇ ἀγάπῃ δὲ ἡ κλ., 834 γνώσεως καὶ κληρονομίας ὑπεροχή, ib. κληρονομίαις ἀπομερίζονται
κλῆσις: (the call to die), 869 ἠσθῆναι τ. κλήσεως χάριν, 871 τὴν κ. ἐκ τοῦ μηδὲν αὐτοῖς συνεγνωκέναι βεβαιοῦσιν, ib. πείθονται τῇ κλήσει: (the Christian calling) 871 ἡ τ. κλήσεως ὁμολογία
κνῖσα: 847 ἡ τ. ὁλοκαυτωμάτων κν. γέρας ἐστὶ θεῶν tet
κοιμάομαι: 880 περιπατῶν κ. κοιμώμενος
κοινός: 859 ὁ κ. ἄνθρωπος, 892 ὑπερβῆναι τὸ κ. τῆς πίστεως, 891 κοιναὶ ἔννοιαι, 889 κ. κριτήρια, 895 κοινῇ καὶ ἰδίᾳ, 860 συνεύξεται τοῖς κοινότερον πεπιστευκόσι (for MS. καινότερον)
κοινότης: 872 ἡ κ. ἐν τῷ ἑνὶ κεῖται
κοινωνέω: 880 κ. τῶν ἰδίων τοῖς φιλτάτοις
κοινωνία: 862 πρὸς τ. θεῖον κοινωνίαν ἐμμεσιτεύει
κοινωνός: 868 ἀγαπᾷ τὸν κ. τοῦ βίου
κοίτη: 861 ψαλμοὶ πρὸ τῆς κ.
κολάζω: 878 κ. τὸ ὁρατικόν, 895 θεὸς οὐ τιμωρεῖται, κολάζει μέντοι πρὸς τὸ χρήσιμον, ib. πρὸς τ. προνοίας κολαζόμεθα
κολακεία: 838 ὁ γνωστικὸς οὐχ ὑποβέβληται κολακείαις
κόλασις: 837 κ. εἰς παιδείαν ἐγγράφεται, 871 κολάσεως εὐλαβείᾳ, 865 ἀπολυθεὶς κολάσεως, 869 αἱ ἐνταῦθα κ., ib. ἐν αὐταῖς τῶν κ. ταῖς ἀκμαῖς, 879 παιδευομένους διὰ τῆς κ., 895 μερικαί τινες παιδεῖαι ἃς κ. ὀνομάζουσι
κολαστική: 838 παιδευτικὴ καὶ κολ.
κολλάω: p. 885 κ. τῇ πόρνῃ (quot.), 886 κ. τῷ κυρίῳ
κομιδῇ: 829 see κατεπείγω, 847 (quot.)
κομίζω: 864 τὴν περὶ θεοῦ κομίσασθαι γνῶσιν, 867 τ. γνῶσιν κομίζων οἴκοθεν, 891 ('adduce') χρώμενοι αἷς κομίζουσιν ἐκλογαῖς, 551 ἐκεῖνο κομίζουσι τὸ ῥητόν, 511 οὗ τὰ συγγράμματα κομίζεται
κόρις: (quot.) 844
κορυφαῖος: adj. 859 κ. ἤδη ὁ γνωστικός, 865 ὁ κ. τόπος τ. ἀναπαύσεως, 869 ὁ κ. ἐκεῖνος βίος, 873 κορυφαιοτάτην προκοπὴν τὴν τ. θεοῦ ἐποπτείαν ἡ γνωστικὴ ψυχὴ λαμβάνει, 939 τὸ κορυφαιότατον μάθημα
κοσμέω: 836 ὁ γνωστικὸς τ. ἐπαΐοντας αὐτοῦ κ., 869 τ. ἤθει κεκοσμημένος, 870 τελείᾳ ἀρετῇ κεκοσμημένος
κοσμικός: 877 κ. ἐπαγγελίαι, ib. τῶν κ. ἐπιθυμιῶν κρατεῖ, 884 ἡ κ. περιήλυσις, 883 init. ἡ τῶν κ. χρῆσις
κόσμιος: 839 κ. καὶ ὑπερκόσμιος ἐν κόσμῳ

< πάντα > πράσσων, 868 τὸ κόσμιον τ. ἤθους περιβαλλόμενος
κόσμος: 839 ὁ καλὸς κ., see κόσμιος, 845 τὸν κ. ἄξιον ἡγησάμενοι τῆς τ. θεοῦ ὑπεροχῆς, 879 τὰ ἐν κόσμῳ καλά
κοῦφος: 850 τὰ ὀρνίθεια κ.
κράζω: 854 ἔνδοθεν κεκράγαμεν, 863
κρατέω: 834 'to hold' οὔτε κρατοῦντες οὔτε κρατούμενοι, cf. Mt. ix. 25: 840 κρ. τῆς ἀθανασίας
κράτος: 870 ἐγνωκὼς κατὰ κρ. ('thoroughly') τὰ δεινὰ καὶ τὰ μή, cf. Plut. V. 440 εἰ δὲ ἀληθὴς ὁ λόγος, ἐξελέγχει κατὰ κράτος τοὺς φάσκοντας κ.τ.λ.
κρέας: 849 κρεῶν βρώσεις, 850 χοίρεια κρ.
κρείττων: 833 προσήκει τῷ κρείττονι ἡγεῖσθαι τ. χείρονος, 835 πρὸς τ. σωτηρίαν τ. κρείττονος διοικεῖται τὰ μικρότερα, 851 ἑαυτοῦ κρ. ἂν εἴη, 855 ἐκ χειρόνων εἰς κρείττονας προϊοῦσα πρόνοια, 865 μεταβολὴ ἐπὶ τὸ κρ., 886
κρέμαμαι: 865 ὁπόταν τις κρεμασθῇ (? ἐκκρεμασθῇ) τ. κυρίου, 705 ἐν ταύταις τ. ἐντολαῖς τὸν νόμον κρέμασθαι
κρεοφαγία: 850 ἡ νωθρία ἡ ἀπὸ τῆς κρ., cf. σαρκοφαγία
κρημνός: 888 ὁδοὶ ἐπὶ κ. φέρουσαι
κρημνώδης: 876 ὀλισθηραὶ καὶ κρημνώδεις παρεκτροπαί
κρίμα: 840 init. ἀπαραλόγιστος ἡ τ. θεοῦ ψῆφος εἰς τὸ δικαιότατον κρ.
κρίνω: 883 (quot.) κρίνεσθαι ἐπὶ τῶν ἀδίκων, ib. (quot.) ἄγιος τ. κόσμιον κρ., 890 fin. τὸ κρινόμενον κάλλιστον πρὶν κριθῆναι, 893 τὰ κριθέντα ὀρθῶς ἔχειν, 895 κρίνειν τὸ δέον ἰσχύει
κρίσις: 835 κρ. ἡ παντελής, 884 ἄλλοις ἐπιτρέπει τὴν κρ., 895 τὰς πρὸ τ. κρίσεως πατρῴας νουθεσίας, 891 οὐδ' ἀρχὴ τὸ κρίσεως δεόμενον, 861 ἐν τ. κρίσει τὸ δοκεῖν οὐκ ἐν τῷ παθεῖν, 890 τ. αὐτὴν κρ. ἔχουσι πάντες
κριτήριον: 889 κοινά τινα κρ. τὰ αἰσθητήρια, 890 πρὸς τὴν τ. πραγμάτων εὕρεσιν τ. γραφῇ χρώμεθα κριτηρίῳ, ib. ἀληθῶν κ. ψευδῶν κριτήριον
κριτής: 835 ὁ ἐφορῶν κρ., 884 παρὰ τῶν κριτῶν αἰτεῖσθαι ἄφεσιν
κρουνός: (quot.) 844
κτῆμα: 840 οἱ τὰ κτ. κακοῦντες τ. δεσπότας ὑβρίζουσι
κτῆσις: 853, 870 ἡ τ. τέλους κτ.
κτίζω: 880 ὁ τ. ψυχὴν εἰς ἐπιστήμην κτίσας, 836 ἑαυτὸν κτίζει κ. δημιουργεῖ
κτίσις: 867 θαυμάζει τὴν κτ., 868 θάνατος κτίσεως ἀνάγνη, 878 ἀδελφοὶ κατὰ τ. κτίσιν τ. ἐξειλεγμένην
κτίσμα: 885 διὰ τῶν κτισμάτων τ. ἐνέργειαν τ. θεοῦ προσκυνεῖ, 776 μηδὲν τ. κτισμάτων τ. θεοῦ μισεῖν, James i. 18
κτίστης: 873 πάντων κτ. ὁ θεός

κτιστός: 868 χρώμενοι τοῖς κτ. ὁπόταν αἱρῇ λόγος
κυβερνάω: 833 κ. τὴν πάντων σωτηρίαν
κυβιστάω: 871 οἱ θαυματοποιοὶ εἰς τ. μαχαίρας κ., Ael. Ep. 16 σύ μοι δοκεῖς κἂν ἐς πῦρ ἅλασθαι κἂν ἐς μαχαίρας κυβιστῆσαι
κυέω: 890 τοῖς γνωστικοῖς κεκυήκασιν αἱ γραφαί, αἱ δὲ αἱρέσεις ὡς μὴ κεκυηκυίας παραπέμπονται
κυκλόω: (quot.) 883
κυλινδέω (καλινδέω): 852 φωνὴν περὶ τὸν ἀέρα κυλινδουμένην, 856 τοῖς ἐν ἀγνοίᾳ καλινδουμένοις, 3 οἱ ἐν σκότει κ., 49 πνεύματα περὶ τ. τάφους κ.
κυπάρισσος: 901 ὅρος δασὺ κυπαρίσσοις
κυριακός: 829 κ. γραφαί, 890, 866 κ. ἐνέργεια, ib. κ. διδασκαλία, 887, 866 ἐπὶ τὴν κ. μονὴν ἐπείγεται, 877 κ. ἐκείνην τ. ἡμέραν ποιεῖ ὅταν ἀποβάλλῃ φαῦλον νόημα, 895 κ. λαός
κύριος adj.: 872 ἡ κυριωτάτη πάσης ἐπιστήμης ἀγάπη, 888 διακριτέον τῷ κυριωτάτῳ λογισμῷ τ. ἀληθὲς ἀπὸ τ. φαινομένου: subst. 833 κ.)(σωτήρ, 843 ὁ κ. τῆς οἰκίας, see κυρίως
κυρίως: 829 σεπτὸν κυριώτατα, 832 σοφία κυρίως ἂν λεχθείη, 868 κ. ἐνεργῶν Η. (MS. κύριος), 888 κ. λέγεται
κυρόω: 877 ἑπόμενοι τ. γραφαῖς κ. τὸ εἰρημένον
κύρωσις: 862 ἐν τοῖς ἔργοις ἡ κύρ.
κύστις: (quot.) 847
κωλύω: 872 οἱ νόμῳ κ. φόβῳ κωλυόμενοι
κωμικός: 843 ὁ κ. Φιλήμων, 844, 846, 847
κωμῳδέω: 843, 844
κωφός: (quot.) 895 οἱ κ. τῶν ὄφεων
λάθρα: 897 διορύξας λ. τὸ τειχίον
λαλέω: 856 ἡ ἔννοια λ. τ. θεῷ, 861, 878, 885 ποιεῖν κ. λαλεῖν κ. νοεῖν
λαμβάνω: 872 καιροῦ (? καιρὸν) λαβόντες παρακλέπτουσι τ. νόμον, cf. however Clem. Hom. Contest. tit. περὶ τῶν τοῦ βιβλίου λαμβανόντων
λάμπω: (quot.) 856 φῶς ἐκ σκότους λ.
λανθάνω: 841 λαθόμενος ἡμέλησεν, 859 οὐ λέληθεν αὐτὸν ὡς ἂν ἀπόντα, 902 λανθάνειν ἐθέλει ἡ γραφή, 881
λαός: 895 λ. κυριακός
λάχανος: 888 οἱ κηπευόμενοι λ.
λεπτόν: 893 λ. τάξιν bis
λείπω: 845 λείπεται δὴ ὑφ' ἑαυτοῦ ἱδρῦσθαι
λειτουργία: 834 αἱ περιτροπαὶ λειτουργίαις ἀπομεμίζονται, 836 init. κατὰ τε τὴν λ. κατὰ τε τ. διδασκαλίαν, 838 λειτουργίαν εἰσφέρεται ἕκαστον, 865 πεπαῦσθαι τ. ἄλλης λ., ib. τελείωσις πάσας λ. ὑπερβάσα, 898 ἡ Παύλου λ.
λεληθότως: 902 τὴν τ. δογμάτων ἐγκα-

ταστοράν λ. ποιοῦνται, Cic. Fam. II.
2. 3, Att. VI. 5. 3, Orig. c. Cels.
I. 19 init.
λέξις: 902 ὅπου καὶ τὴν λ. οὐχ <ἡδυσμένην> εἶναι βούλονται, 829 αἱ προφητικαὶ λ., ib. μηδέπω συνιέντες τὰς λέξεις, ib. τ. νοῦν οὐ τὴν λέξιν, 856 ἡ φωνὴ κ. ἡ λέξις τ. νοήσεως χάριν δέδοται, 883 αἱ ἐπίκαιροι τ. ἀποστολικῶν λ., 898 ἡ τῶν ἀποστόλων λ., 897 ἡ "ἐνὶ φυσίωσε" λέξις
λεπτουργέω: 901 τὴν τ. λογίων σαφήνειαν λεπτ., Themist. 14ᵈ
λεχώ: 889 ἡ Μαριὰμ δοκεῖ λεχὼ εἶναι οὐκ οὖσα λεχώ
λεωφόρος: 888 ὁδὸς βασιλικὴ καὶ λ., 664 Πυθαγόρας ἀπαγορεύει τ. λεωφόρους ὁδοὺς βαδίζειν, Philo
λιθοξόος: 845 λιθοξόων ἔργον
λίθος: 859 τῷ λίθῳ τὸ βάρος ἀπαπόβλητον, 834 ἡ Ἡράκλεια λ., see λιπαρός
λιπαρός: 843 πάντα λίθον λ. προσκυνεῖν
λογίζομαι: m. 869 ἀπείρους ὅσους ἡμῖν λογιζομένοις (H. for -ους) ἀγγέλους, p. 835 ἁγίας ἐν ἁγίοις λογισθείσας ψυχάς
λογικός: 859 δύναμις λ. κ. προνοητική, 871 λ. ἀνδρεία, 874 ἡ γνῶσις οἷον ὁ λ. θάνατος
λογικῶς: 831 ἄνθρωπον λογικῶς βιοῦντα
λόγιον: 901 τὰ λ. τ. θεοῦ ter
λόγιος: 852 παρὰ τ. λογιωτάτοις τ. βαρβάρων σώζεται
λογισμός: 840 μετὰ τ. δεόντων λογισμῶν παραδεξάμενος τ. εὐποιίαν, 889 κριτήρια διὰ νοῦ κ. λογισμοῦ τεχνικά, 867 ἐκ λ. ἀνδρίζομαι, 888 ὁ κυριώτατος λ.
λόγος: 837 λόγος αἰώνιος ὁ υἱός, 858 δυνάμει ἁπλῷ λόγῳ χρώμενος, ib. ἐὰν ὁ λ. καλῇ, 893 ὁ λ. ἄρχων γνώσεώς τε καὶ βίου, ib. οἷος ὁ λόγος τοιόσδε καὶ ὁ βίος, 864 ἐν λόγῳ κ. ἐν πράξει κ. ἐν αὐτῇ τῇ ἐννοίᾳ, 867 ὁ αὐτὸς λόγος καὶ ἐπὶ τ. ἄλλων, 872, 877, 896 τίς λόγος ὑπελείπετο Μαρκίωνος; 901 ὑμεῖς οὔτ' ἐν λόγῳ οὔτ' ἐν ἀριθμῷ, 844, 864 ὁ ὀρθὸς λ., ib. λ. προφορικός, 848 θυσίαν ἀναπέμπομεν τ. δικαιοτάτῳ λόγῳ, 829 ἐναργεστέροις χρῆσθαι τ. λόγοις, 839 οἱ λόγοι οἱ πειστικοί, 837 κατὰ λόγον 'reasonably,' 861 τὰ κατὰ λόγον ἔργα, 856 κατὰ λ. τοῦ ἡλίου, 867, 885, 867 ἀνὰ λόγον, see αἱρέω
λόγχη: 871 ὁμόσε λόγχαις πορεύεσθαι
λοιπός: adv. τὸ λ. 891, 847 (quot.)
λυμαντικός: 830 λ. τῶν καρπῶν
λύμη: 889 ἀποσπάσαντές τινα ἐπὶ λύμῃ τ. ἀνθρώπων
λυπρός: 871 κακοτεχνῶν ἐπὶ λυπρῷ τῷ μισθῷ
λύσις: 886 αἱ τ. ἀποριῶν λύσεις

λύχνος: 853 λ. τ. δυνάμεων
λύω: 897 init. λέλυται τὸ ἀπορημένον

μάγειρος: 847 fin.
μάθημα: 901 τὸ τ. ψυχῆς τῶν μ. δοχεῖον
μάθησις: 869 τ. τέλεον τ. ἕξεων ἐκ μ. καὶ συνασκήσεως ἐκτήσατο, 893 μ. τοῦ πῶς ἂν ἐξαιρεθείη τὸ αἴτιον
μαιόομαι: p. 890 μαιωθεῖσάν φασί τινες παρθένον εὑρεθῆναι
μάκαρ: (quot.), 844 μ. Ἀήρ
μακάριος: 846 μ. μὲν αὐτὴ μ. δὲ διαπραττομένη ἔργα, 854 μ. τριάς, 869 τὸν μ. Πέτρον, 871 μακάριοι μέν, οὐδέπω δὲ ἄνδρες ἐν ἀγάπῃ, 896 μ. ἀπόστολοι
μακράν: c. gen. 836 μ. τῶν νεφῶν, Polyb.
μακρός: 834 συγκινεῖται μακροτάτη (ηε. μικρ., cf. 26 where the same corruption occurs) σιδήρου μοῖρα
μαλάσσω: 874 κηρὸς μαλάσσεται
μᾶλλον: 873 πρὸς τὸ μ. κ. ἧττον
μαμωνᾶς: (quot.) 875
μανθάνω: 848 δοξάζοντες ἃ (H. ὃν) μεμαθήκαμεν, cf. ἐκμανθάνω
μάρτυρ: 871 ὁ τῷ ὄντι ἀνδρεῖος τ. ἄλλων λεγομένων μαρτύρων χωρίζεται
μαρτυρέω: 864 ὁ γνωστικὸς μαρτυρεῖ τῇ ἀληθείᾳ
μαρτυρία: 895 ἡ ἐκ τῶν γραφῶν μ., 891 ἡ ἐξ ἀνθρώπων μ.
μαρτύριον: 862 τὸ κατὰ τ. γλῶτταν μ., 883 πολλὰ ἐκ γραφῆς μ. ἔπεισι παρατίθεσθαι, 876 οἱ ἀπόστολοι τὸ πεῖραν καὶ μ. τελειότητος ἤχθησαν, 866 πολλὰ μ., 829 (quot.) μ. κυρίου
μάταιος: 846 προσάγειν βορὰν τῷ μὴ τρεφομένῳ μάταιον
Ματθᾶς: 882 (a saying of) ἐὰν ἐκλεκτοῦ γείτων ἁμαρτήσῃ, ἥμαρτεν ὁ ἐκλεκτός, 900 Valentinus and Basilides τὴν Μ. αὐχῶσι προσάγεσθαι δόξαν
μάχαιρα: 871 εἰς μ. κυβιστᾶν
μάχομαι: 888 διαστέλλων τὸ μαχόμενον ἀπὸ τ. ἀκολούθου, 891 δόγματα μαχόμενα τ. γραφαῖς, 894 μ. δόγματα
μεγαλεῖον: 644 τὸ μ. τῆς δυνάμεως, 874 βεβαίως κτησάμενος τ. ἐπιστήμης τὰ μ., 892 μὴ χωρήσαντες τὸ μ. τῆς ἀληθείας, 937 τὸ μ. τῆς τ. κυρίου φιλανθρωπίας, Philo
μεγαλείως: 897 init. τὸ μ. φρονεῖν
μεγαλόνοια: 885 εἴτ' οὖν μεγαλονοίᾳ τοῦτο περιποιήσεται εἴτε μιμήσει τ. κρείττονος
μεγαλοπρέπεια: 835 ἡ μ. τῆς θεωρίας, 838 a form of ἀνδρεία, 862 ἡ μ. τοῦ λόγου, 897 μ. τῆς σοφίας
μεγαλοπρεπής: 836 μ. θεοσέβεια, 841 μ. ὁ θεός, 868 τὰ μεγαλοπρεπέστερον εἰρημένα

μεγαλοπρεπῶς: 867 περί τ. ὅλων μεγαλοπρεπῶν διέληφεν, 868 ἐταγωνίσασθαι τοῖς μεγαλοπρεπέστερον εἰρημένοις
μεγαλόφρονες: 875 τ. θεὸν ἔγνωκεν μ., 888 μ. τὸ τ. γνώσεως ἀναδεξάμενοι μέγεθος, 886 εὐσεβῶς καὶ μ. πολιτεύεσθαι, 897 μ. τῆι γραφῆι συνίετε
μεγαλοφροσύνη: 838 a form of ἀνδρεία
μεγαλόφρων: 897 μ. ἐν γνώσει, 857 ὁ μ. ἐθθιτοι κατὰ τ. προσβολὴν τ. θεωρίας
μεγαλοψυχία: 838 a form of ἀνδρεία
μέγεθος: 846 μ. ἀξίας τ. θεοῦ
μέθη: 848 pl. μέθαις ἐγκυλιόμενοι
μεθίστημι: 878 (quot.) ὅρη μ.
μειονεκτέω: 878 αὐτὸς ἑαυτὸν (H. J. ἑαυτοῦ) μ. πρὸς τὸ μὴ ὑπεριδεῖν ἐν θλίψει γενόμενον ἀδελφόν, Heliod. viii. 9 fin. νενικῆσθαι ὑπὸ θατέρου κ. μειονεκτεῖν τῶν ἐρωτικῶν οἰόμενος, Aristaen. i. 10 fin., Chion Ep. 6. 1, Philo
μελετάω: 872 μ. τῶν παθῶν κρατεῖν, 901 μελετᾷ τὰ λόγια τ. θεοῦ
μέλλω: 859 πεπεισμένος ὡς ἔστιν ἕκαστον τῶν μελλόντων, 869 ἡ τ. μελλόντων ἀπόληψις, 877 τὰ μέλλοντα μᾶλλον ἡγεῖται τῶν ἐν ποσὶ παρεῖναι, 879 fin. τὰ μέλλοντα)(τὰ προγεγονότα κ. τὰ ἐνεστῶτα
μέμψις: 838
μέντοι: 895 (= δέ) ἔστιν ἡ τιμωρία κακοῦ ἀνταπόδοσις, κολάζει μέντοι πρὸς τὸ χρήσιμον, cf. Schmid iv. 716: καὶ μέντοι 894
μένω: 873 μένει εἰς τ. ἀνάπαυσιν τ. θεοῦ
μερίζω: p. 868 πρὸς τῆς προνοίας κατ' ἀξίαν μεριζόμενα, 831 ὁ υἱὸς τ. θεοῦ οὐ μερίζεται: m. 880 τὰ τ. ἀδελφῶν ἁμαρτήματα μερίσασθαι
μερικός: 895 μ. τινες παιδεῖαι, 897 οὐ τύφον ἐνεποίησεν ταῖς μερικαῖς (sc. παιδείαις) κατὰ τ. διδασκαλίαν, 774 ἡ μερικὴ φιλοσοφία (sc. τῶν Ἑλλήνων), cf. 87
μερίς: (quot.) 832 ἡ τοῦ κυρίου
μερισμός: 848 μ. κρεῶν
μέρος: 890 τὰ κατὰ μέρος, 835 καθόλου κ. ἐπὶ μέρους, 863 ἐν θεραπείας μέρει
μέσος: 838 τὰ μέσα 'things indifferent.' 880 οὐ πρωίας μόνον καὶ μέσον ἡμέρας, 892 τὰ ἐν μέσῳ
μεσοῦν: 898 μεσούντων τῶν Τιβερίου χρόνων
μεταβαίνω: 868 fin. ἐκ τ. δούλου μ. εἰς φίλον
μεταβάλλω: 874 οὔποτε μεταβάλλει τὸ ἀγαθὸν εἰς κακόν
μεταβολή: 834 κατὰ τὴν τ. μεταβολῆς τάξιν, 835 τῆς μεταβολῆς αἰτία ἡ αἵρεσις τ. γνώσεως, 865 εὐπρόσδεκτοι μ. ἐπὶ τὸ κρεῖττον, 866 init. μ. σωτήριος πρώτη κ. δευτέρα

μεταγενέστερος: 898 μ. αἱ ἀνθρώπιναι συνηλόσαις τῆς καθολικῆς ἐκκλησίας, 899 ἐκ τ. προγενεστάτης ἐκκλησίας αἱ μ. αἱρέσεις κεκαινοτόμηνται, Diod.
μετάγω: 891 τὰ εἰρημένα εἰς τὰς ἰδίας μετάγουσι δόξας
μεταδιώκω: 872 τὸ ἀγαθὸν μ.
μετάδοσις: 855 ἑκούσιοι ἡ τ. ἀγαθῶν μ. τῷ θεῷ, 859 ἡ τ. σοφίας μ., 860 ἡ ἐνέργεια διὰ τ. μεταδόσεως δείκνυται, 881 χρημάτων περιουσία εἰς μετάδοσιν, 859 see μετέχω
μεταδοτικός: 839 μ. ὧν ἂν ᾖ κεκτημένος, 873 ἡ ἕξις ἡ παρ' ἡμῖν μεταδοτικὴ δικαιοσύνη
μετάθεσις: 888 πρόεσιν ἐπὶ τ. ἁγίαν τῆς μ. ἀμοιβήν
μετακομίζω: 835 ψυχὰς μετακομισθείσας ὅλας ἐξ ὅλων
μεταλαγχάνω: 831 τῆς αἰωνίου ζωῆς μ.
μεταλαμβάνω: 884 φρένας μ.
μετάληψις: 877 ἡ ἐνεργοῦσα μ. ὧν ἔγνω
μεταμοσχεύω: 902 μεταμοσχεύσας κ. μεταφυτεύσας ὡραῖον κατακοσμήσει παράδεισον
μετανοέω: 835 αἱ παιδεύσεις τοὺς ἀπηλγηκότας ἐκβιάζονται μετανοεῖν, 876, 895 νουθεσίας ὑπομένοντες ἔστ' ἂν μετανοήσω
μετάνοια: 884
μεταπείθω: 895 μεταπείσαι τοὺς μὴ παντάπασιν ἀνιάτους
μεταρρυθμίζω: 862 μ. τὸν κατηχούμενον, 868 οἱ ὑπηκέστερον μεταρρυθμιζόμενοι
μετάρσιος: 854 τὸ σῶμα μ. ποιησάμενοι
μετατίθημι: 882 μετατεθεὶς ἐκ δουλείας εἰς υἱοθεσίαν, 836 μετατίθεσθαι ἐκ θανάτου εἰς ζωήν, 891 ἡ ἀλήθεια οὐκ ἐν τῷ μετατίθεναι τ. σημαινόμενα εὑρίσκεται, 892 πάντα μᾶλλον ὑπομένουσιν ἤπερ μετατίθενται τ. αἱρέσεις
μεταφράζω: 883 οἷον μεταφράζων τ. ῥῆσιν
μεταφυτεύω: 902, 2, 88, see μεταμοσχεύω
μεταχειρίζομαι: 892 τ. ἀληθῆ φιλοσοφίαν μ., cf. μεταχείρισις 943
μέτειμι: 891 οἱ τ. αἱρέσεις μετιόντες, 897, 901 μετίωμεν ἐπὶ τὴν ὑπόθεσιν (NB. ὑπόσχεσιν)
μετένδεσις: 849 οἱ ἀπὸ Πυθαγόρου τὴν μ. ὀνειροπολοῦντες τ. ψυχῆς (ἅπ. λεγ.)
μετέρχομαι: 901 πρὸς τὰ ἔργα τ. δικαιοσύνης ὁλοσχερέστερον μετ. εἴ γε καὶ μετέλθοιεν
μετέχω: 859 ὁ ἀνενδεοῦς μετέχων ἀνενδεὴς εἴη ἄν, ib. οὐ γὰρ ἡ μετάδοσις κινούντων κ. ἰσχόντων ἀλλήλους τῆς ἐνεργείας κ. τοῦ μετίσχοντος γίνεται, 886 μ. γνώσεως
μετοικίζω: 865 ἡ γνῶσις εἰς τ. συγγενὲς θεῖον μ. τὸν ἄνθρωπον

μετουσία: 880 μετουσίᾳ θερμότητος θερμός
μέτοχος: 879 μ. τῆς θείας βουλήσεως
μετρέω: 859 τὸ ἐπιδεὲς πρὸς τὸ ἐπιβάλλον μετρεῖται
μέχρι: 869 ἡ μ. τῶν φιλτάτων τελεία διάθεσις, Clem. Hom. II. 22 μ. αὐτοῦ τ. θεοῦ ἀσεβεῖν
μή: after ἐπεί and ὅτι 870, 868, 867, cf. Jannaris § 1818
μὴ οὐ (with indic. in questions): 885 μὴ γὰρ οὐ πάντα μοι ἔξεστιν; 178 fin. μὴ γὰρ οὐκ ἔνεστιν καὶ ἐν εὐτελείᾳ σώφροσι πολυειδία ἐδεσμάτων ὑγιεινή;
μὴ οὐχί: (with part.) 885 βιοῦντας ὡς διὰ τὸ ἐσθίειν γενομένους, μὴ οὐχὶ δὲ ἐσθίοντας ἵνα ζῶσιν; (with inf.) 122 τίς ἡ ἀποκλήρωσις μὴ οὐχὶ καὶ τὸ αἷμα ἐπὶ τὸ λευκότατον τρέπεσθαι ὁμολογεῖν;
μή τι (with indic. in questions): 870 μή τι οὖν δι' ἄγνοιαν συνίσταται ἡ δειλία; 873 μή τι...τὸν αὐτὸν τρόπον ἐπὶ τοῦ γνωστικοῦ εὕροιμεν ἄν; 885 μή τι οἷον σάρκας εἶναι τοῦ ἁγίου σώματος τούτους φησίν; 886 μή τι οὖν τέλειοι γίνεσθαι ὀφείλομεν; 887 μή τι οὖν ἀφεξόμεθα τῆς ἀληθείας; 888 μή τι οὖν ἀπέχονται οἱ γεωργοὶ τῆς ἐπιμελείας; 519 μή τι συνᾴδει τῷ ἀποστόλῳ; 119
μή τι οὐ: 881 μή τι τ. γνωστικὸν οὐ τῆς δι' ἀγγέλων βοηθείας ἐπιδεῆ εἶναι βούλεται; 887 μή τι οὖν κάμνων τις οὐ προσίεται ἰατρόν;
μῆκος: 883 μ. τ. λόγου
μηλέα: 901 μ. καὶ ἐλαίαις καταπεφυτευμένον ὄρος
μήν (answering μέν like δέ): 830 init. (so H. J. for MS. μέν)
μηνύω: 849, 881, 897
μηρία: (quot.) 847
μηρός: (quot.) 847 bis
μηρυκισμός: 900 μ. ἀνάγειν, 901 bis
μήτε μή: 882 μήτε μὴ γνούς
μητρόπολις: 850 μ. κακίας ἡδονή, Diog. Laert. vi. 50 n., Isid. Pelus. Ep. II. 151
μιαίνω: 848 βωμὸς φόνῳ μὴ μιανθείς
μιαρός: (quot.) 842, 849
μίγνυμι: 882 μίξας τ. περιστερᾷ τ. ὄφιν
μικρολόγος: (quot.) 842
μικροψυχία: 842 η μ. τοῦ τρέφοντος
μιμέομαι: 837 μ. τὴν θείαν προαίρεσιν
μίμημα: 899 μ. ἀρχῆς τῆς μιᾶς
μίμησις: 874 ὁ ἔπαινος ἔπεται εἰς τὴν τ. ἐπαινούντων μ.
μιμνήσκω: 881 οὔποτε μέμνηται τῶν ἁμαρτησάντων
μισάνθρωπος: 833 οὔποτε ὁ σωτὴρ μ.
μισέω c. gen.: 896 οὓς ἐλεήσειεν ἄν τις ἢ μισήσειεν τ. τοιαύτης διαστροφῆς
μισθός: 875 μ. γνώσεως τῷ σωτῆρι, 871 ἐπὶ λυτρῷ τῷ μισθῷ, 876 μισθὸν ἀργίας λαμβάνω

μισοπόνηρος: 839 μισοπονηρότατος κατὰ τ. τελείαν ἀποστροφὴν κακουργίας, Philo, cf. Ps. cxxxix. 21, 22
μῖσος: 868 μίσους ἄξιος
μνήμη: 888 init. πόνῳ ἕπεται γλυκεῖα μ.
μνησικακέω: 868 οὐ μν. ποτὲ ὁ γνωστικός, see ἀμνησικακέω
μοῖρα: 877 ἐν ἀνάγκης μ., 834 μακροτάτη σιδήρου μ.
μοιχεύω: 868 init. μὴ μοιχεύσῃς μὴ φονεύσῃς (for the order see 816, Stählin Clem. u. LXX. p. 15, and my n. on James ii. 11): trop. 897 οὐ χρὴ μ. τὴν ἀλήθειαν (cf. πορνεύω)
μονάς: 900 ἡ ἐξοχὴ τ. ἐκκλησίας κατὰ τὴν μ. ἐστιν
μονή: 834 οἱ μὲν ἐνάρετοι οἰκειοῦνται τ. πρώτῃ μ., 854 γνωρίζοντες τὴν μακαρίαν τῶν ἁγίων τριάδα μονῶν, 864 ἐν μονῇ τ. προφορικοῦ λόγου (ἡ σοφία), 866 ἐπὶ τ. κυριακὴν διὰ τ. ἁγίας ἑβδομάδος ἐπείγεται μονήν, 886 ἡ ὀφειλομένη μ.
μονήρης: 874 βίος μ. (= μοναχικός Hesych.)
μονογενής: 831 ὁ μ. παῖς τ. θεοῦ, 837 ὁ τῷ ὄντι μ., 839
μόνος: 835 τῷ ὄντι μόνος εἷς παντοκράτωρ
μονότονος: 859 ἡ τ. γνώμης μ. ἑδραιότης (rare exc. of music)
μόνως: 899 τὸ ἀκρῶς τίμιον κατὰ τὴν μ. ἐπαινεῖται
μόριον: 848 μόρια δοῦναι τ. θεῷ
μορφή: 841 θεῶν μ. διαζωγραφοῦσιν, 863 κατὰ τὴν τ. μορφῆς ἰδιότητα
μορφόω: 886 μορφούμενος τῇ τ. κυρίου διδασκαλίᾳ
μοχθηρία: 892 αἱ μοχθηρίαι τ. δογμάτων
μοχθηρός: 839 μ. πρᾶξις, 841, 843, 844, 856
μυέω: p. 845 πρὸ τῆς τ. μυστηρίων παραδόσεως καθαρμούς τινας προσάγουσι τοῖς μυεῖσθαι μέλλουσιν
μυθολογέω: 841 οὐ χρὴ τὰ ἀριδήλως εἰρημένα μ.
μῦθος: 850 δι' ἄλλους τινὰς μύθους
μύριοι: 894 fin. μύρια ἐστιν ἃ πράσσουσιν ἄνθρωποι
μῦς: (quot.) 842 ter
μυσταγωγός: 897 μ. τῆς τ. ἀσεβῶν ψυχῆς
μυστήριον: 845 ἡ τ. μυστηρίων παράδοσις, 890 τὰ τῆς ἀληθείας μυστ., 892 τὰ τ. γνώσεως τ. ἐκκλησιαστικῆς μ., 886 οὐκ ἐκκυκλεῖν δεῖ τὸ μ., 831 τ. θεῖα μ. παρὰ τ. μονογενοῦς παιδὸς ἐκμαθών, 832 παιδεύων μυστηρίοις τ. γνωστικὸν ἐλπίσι δὲ τ. πιστόν, 956 init. θεῷ τὰ

τ. ἀγάπης μυστήρια κ. τότε ἐποπτεύσεις τ. κόλπον τ. πατρός, 120, see μνέω, Kaye, p. 150

μυστικός: 858 χορὸς μ. τῆς ἀληθείας, 865 αἱ μυστικαὶ προκοπαί

μυστικῶς: 900 μ. διακρινόμενοι ἀπὸ τ. ἐκκλησίας

μυχαίτατος: 840 ὁ ἥλιος πρὸς τοὺς μ. οἴκους (? οἰκίσκους) ἀποστέλλει τ. αὐγήν

μῶμος: 887 παντὶ τῷ καλῷ μ. ἕπεται

μωρός: (quot.) 851

ναὶ μήν (in asseveration): 859, 864, 865; ναὶ ναί 872; ναί, **φησίν** (introducing an objection): 896, 366, 446, 551, 598

ναύκληρος: 894 ἐὰν προσσχῇ τις Λάμπιδι ναύκληρον αὐτὸν ποιήσει

Νέρων: 898 ἡ Παύλου λειτουργία ἐπὶ Νέρωνος τελειοῦται

νεῦρον: 848 φλέβας κ. ν. δοῦναι τ. θεῷ

νέφος: 836 οὐδὲ μέχρι τῶν νεφῶν ἡ ἀναθυμίασις φθάνει

νεώς or **ναός**: 846 ἐκκλησία βουλήσει τ. θεοῦ εἰς νεὼν πεποίηται, 870 τ. κάλλος τ. ψυχῆ ν. γίνεται τ. ἁγίου πνεύματος, 882 ναοί ἐστε τ. θεοῦ, ib. ναός ἐστιν ὁ μὲν μέγας ἡ ἐκκλησία, ὁ δὲ μικρὸς ὁ ἄνθρωπος

νεώτερος: 899 ὡς πρεσβύτης νεωτέροις συνεγένετο Μάρκος (ΜΒ. Μαρκίων)

νηστεία: 877 τῆς ν. τὰ αἰνίγματα οἶδεν

νηστεύω: 877 ν. ἀπὸ τ. πράξεων τ. φαύλων, ib. ν. φιλαργυρίας

νήφω: 843 νήφοντες ὑγείας αἰτοῦνται

νικάω (with cogn. acc.): 874

νοέω: 829 νοούμενος πρὸς τῶν ἐξειλεγμένων εἰς γνῶσιν, 871 ἐχθροὶ ἂν νοοῦντο οἱ τ. ἐναντίαν ὁδὸν τρεπόμενοι

νόημα: 877 ἀποβάλλει φαῦλον ν. καὶ γνωστικὸν προσλαμβάνει, 852 fin. ἅμα νοήματι πάντα γινώσκει, ib. τὰ νοήματα τ. ἁγίων τέμνει τ. κόσμον

νόησις: 852 ἡ διακριτικὴ τ. σημαινουσῶν τι φωνῶν ν., 856 ἡ λέξις τῆς ν. χάριν δέδοται, ib. ὁ θεὸς γνωρίζει τὰς ν.

νοητός: 829 ν.)(αἰσθητός and διδακτός, 838 ἡ τῶν ν. γνῶσις δεόντως ἂν λέγοιτο ἐπιστήμη, 854 ν. οὐσία, 856 φωνὴ ν., 858 ν. καὶ πνευματικά

νομίζω: 837 οὐ ν. εἶναι θεόν, ib. οἱ νομιζόμενοι θεοί, 847 τὰ νομιζόμενα ἀποκρίνετε, 888 εὑρηκέναι ν.

νομοδιδάσκαλος: 836 οἱ ν. φιλόνεικον ἐκδεξάμενοι τ. νόμον

νόμος: 829 ὁ ν. κ. οἱ προφῆται, 896, 836 τοῦτο αἰνίσσεται ὁ ν., ib. φιλόνεικον ἐκδεξάμενοι τ. νόμον, 837 ν. καὶ θεσμὸς ὁ υἱός, 849 αἱ κατὰ τὸν ν. θυσίαι, 865 ἡ κατὰ ν. δικαιοσύνη, 878 πολέμιος νόμῳ, 885 ἡ τοῦ ν. παιδαγωγία

νόος: 850 νοῦς καθαρός, 889 κριτήρια διὰ νοῦ τεχνικά: 'interpretation' 894, for inflexions see Lob. Phryn. 458, Blass § 9. 3, Schm. Att. IV. 586

νοσέω: 887 ν. τ. ψυχήν

νουθεσία: 893 τ. προφητείας ὑφορῶνται διὰ νουθεσίαν, 895 τὰς πρὸ τ. κρίσεως πατρῴας ν. ὑπομένων, 881 πεῖραι ἐπὶ νουθεσίᾳ προσφέρονται

νύκτωρ: 861 ν. εὐχαὶ πάλιν, 901 τ. λόγια τ. θεοῦ ν. καὶ μεθ' ἡμέραν μελετᾶν, see νύξ, 471

νύξ: 851 νύκτα (? νύκτωρ) κ. μεθ' ἡμέραν ἀκολασταίνει

νωθρία: 830 ἡ ν. ἡ ἀπὸ τ. κρεοφαγίας

νωχαλέστερος: 850 σῶμα ῥωμαλέον ὑπεργάζονται, ψυχὴν ν.

ξένος: (quot.), 878, 879
ξύλον: 843 πᾶν ξ. προσκυνεῖ

ὁ δέ (pleonastic, continuing previous subject): 861 ὁ δὲ καὶ περιπάτῳ χρώμενος

ὀγκύλλομαι: 854 ἐπὶ τ. ἀθέῳ σοφίᾳ ὀγκ.

ὁδεύω: 876 see ὁδός, 888

ὁδός: 876 ὁ. βασιλική, ἣν τὸ βασιλικὸν ὁδεύει γένος, 888, 859 τῷ γεγυμνασμένῳ ἅπαντα πρὸ ὁδοῦ, see λεωφόρος

ὅθεν: 882 'wherefore'

οἰακίζω: 831 ἡ μεγίστη ὑπεροχὴ τὸ πᾶν ἄριστα οἰακίζει

οἶδα: 871 οὐκ οἶδ' ὅπως, 300, 452: ('regard as') 844 θεὸς ἅγιον οἶδεν τὸ τοῦ δικαίου ἦθος

οἴησις: 887 αἱ φιλόδοξοι αἱρέσεις οἴησιν γνώσεως εἰλήφασι, 889 μέγιστον τὸ τ. οἴησιν ἀποθέσθαι, 893 θεραπεία οἰήσεως μάθησις τ. αἰτίου, 894 οἱ ἐν οἰήσει οἱ κατὰ τ. αἱρέσεις

οἰκεῖος: 838, 868 οἰκ.)(ἀλλότρια, 838 οἰκ. εὐεργεσία, ib. οἱ οἰκεῖοι τῆς προνοίας, 879 οἰκ. τ. κυρίου κ. τῶν ἐντολῶν, 899 αἱ οἰκ. διαθῆκαι, 884 οἰκεῖον τοῦ γνωστικοῦ, 891 τί θεῷ οἰκεῖον;

οἰκειόω: 'to adapt,' 834, οἱ ἐνάρετοι οἰκειοῦνται τ. πρώτῃ μονῇ, 852 προσεχέστερον οἰκειοῦται θεῷ, 858 τοῖς νοητοῖς οἰκειούμενος, Polyb.

οἰκειωτός: 885 τ. σῶμα τοῦτο <τὸ> πνευματικὸν οὐ τ. πορνείᾳ οἰκ.

οἰκέτης: 831 contrasted with φίλος

οἴκησις: 885 μεταβάλλει πᾶν τ. ἐνάρετον εἰς ἀμείνους οἰκ., ib. αἱ μακάριαι θεῶν οἰκ.

οἰκίσκος (?): 840 ὁ ἥλιος πρὸς τ. μυχαιτάτους οἰκίσκους (ΜΒ. οἴκους) ἀποστέλλει τ. αὐγήν

οἰκοδόμος: 845 οἰκοδόμων ἔργον

οἴκοθεν: 867 κομίζων οἰκ. ('from himself')

οἰκονομέω: act. 854 ὁ γνωστικὸς οἰκ. τ. αἴτησιν: m. 146 μεμψιμοιρία σωτηρίαν οἰκονομεῖται: p. 943 fin. τὰ μετὰ φρονήσεως οἰκονομούμενα

οἰκονομία: 830 κατὰ τὴν τῶν περιγείων οἰκονομίαν, 882 οὐδέποτε τὸ ἡδὺ κ. τὸ συμφέρον προκρίνει τῆς οἰκονομίας, 881 δικαίαν τ. οἰκονομίαν μηνύει, 875 ἡ σὴ οἰκ. προσφέρει γυμνάσια, 831 ὁ λόγος ὁ πατρικὸς τ. ἁγίαν οἰκ. ἀναδέδεκται, 855 αἱ προσεχεῖς τ. προνοίας ἐνεργοῦνται οἰκ., 862 τ. μεγίστου ἀγαθοῦ τὴν οἰκ. ἀναδεξάμενος, 864 διαδέξασθαι τ. ἄκραν οἰκ. τοῦ παιδευτοῦ, 874 ἡ κατὰ τ. βίον οἰκ., 882 τὰ κατὰ τὴν οἰκ. ἐπὶ τ. συμφέροντι γινόμενα, 876 ἡ οἰκ. προορωμένη ποιεῖται τ. δωρεάν, Kaye p. 235

οἶκος: 'heaven' 869 ἡ εἰς οἶκον ἀνακομιδὴ

οἷον: 885 ('quasi') οἷον ἄσαρκος ἤδη γενόμενος, 890 οἷον ἐξ ἀνθρώπου θεός, 897 οἷον "εἴσομαι εἰ δικαίως φρονεῖτε"

οἱονεί: 855

οἷος: 893 οἷος ὁ λόγος τοιόσδε ὁ βίος εἶναι προσήκει

οἰωνίζομαι: 842 οἰωνισαμένου τινὸς ὅτι κατέφαγεν ὗς τ. δελφάκια

ὀκνέω: 887 ὀκν. φιλοσοφεῖν, 888 ὀκν. ὁδεῦσαι

ὀλιγοδεής: 839 πλουτεῖ ἐν τῷ μηδενὸς ἐπιθυμεῖν ἅτε ὀλ. ὤν, 83, Philo ap. Eus. Pr. Ev. viii. 14. 53 οἱ ὀλιγοδεεῖς σωφρονέστεροι, Polyb.

ὀλίγος: 899 Σίμων ἐπ' ὀλίγον τ. Πέτρου ἐπήκουσεν

ὀλισθάνω: 859 οἶδεν τ. ἀγγέλων τινὰς ὀλισθήσαντας χαμαί, 187 ἀνακόπτειν ὀλισθανούσας ὀρέξεις, Lob. Phr. p. 742, Philo M. i. 327, cf. κατολισθάνω

ὀλισθηρός: 876 ὀλ. κ. κρημνώδης παρεκτροπή, 901 ὀλ. τὸ γένος, 273, 23 ὀλ. παρεκβάσεις τ. ἀληθείας, cf. 66 ὁ βιωτικὸς ὄλισθος

ὁλοκάρπωμα: 836 ἡ ἄτυφος καρδία ὁλοκάρπωμα τ. θεοῦ, 609 ὡς ὀλ. θυσίας προσεδέξατο αὐτούς (quotation from Wisd. iii. 6), 688 ὀλ. ὑπὲρ ἡμῶν ὁ Χριστός

ὁλοκαύτωμα: 847 ἡ τῶν ὀλ. κνῖσα, cf. ὁλοκαυτεῖν 37. See Lightfoot on Ign. p. 470, vol. ii.

ὅλος: 831 ὅλ. νοῦς, ὅλ. φῶς, ὅλ. ὀφθαλμός, ὁ υἱός, 853 ὅλ. ἀκοὴ κ. ὅλ. ὀφθαλμὸς ὁ θεός, 833 ἦν αὐτῷ τὸ ὅλον εὖ εἰργασμένον, 835 πρὸς τὴν τ. ὅλου σωτηρίαν τῷ τ. ὅλων κυρίῳ πάντα ἐστὶ διατεταγμένα, ib. τ. γνωστικὰς ψυχὰς μετακομισθείσας ὅλας ἐξ ὅλων, 867 περὶ τ. ὅλων ἀληθῶς διείληφεν

ὁλοσχερής: 901 πρὸς τ. ἔργα τ. δικαιοσύνης ὁλοσχερέστερον μετερχόμενοι

Ὀλύμπια: 860

ὁμιλία: 854 ὁμ. πρὸς τ. θεὸν ἡ εὐχή, ib. ἡ ἐνδιάθετος ὁμ., 861 ὁμ. χρώμενος εὔχεται, 876

ὄμνυμι: 861 bis, 862

ὁμογνώμων: 871 ψόγον ἀπὸ τῶν ὁμοτίμων κ. ὁμογνωμόνων ὑφορῶνται, cf. ὁμογνωμοσύνη 451

ὁμήθεια: 878 ἀδελφοί εἰσι κατὰ τὴν ὁμ., cf. Ign. Polyc. 1, Magn. 6, Philostr. V. A. ii. 11

ὁμοιοπαθής: 846 θεὸς οὐχ ὁμ., cf. ὁμοιοσχήμων, [Ign.] Phil. 9, Trall. 10

ὁμοιοσχήμων: 846 οἱ ὁμοιοσχήμονες κ. ὁμοιοπαθεῖς τ. ἴσης δεήσονται διαίτης, Synes. Enc. Calv. 11, init.

ὁμοιότης: 872 ἡ φιλία δι' ὁμοιότητος περαίνεται, 886 οὐδὲν εἰς ὁμ. θεοῦ παραλαμβάνεται

ὁμοίως: 851 οἱ ὁμ. πεπιστευκότες

ὁμολογέω: 870 διάθεσιν ὁμολογουμένην τ. εὐαγγελίῳ κτήσασθαι, 851 χάριν ὁμ. τῆς γνώσεως, 852, 864 πίστις ἄνευ τοῦ ζητεῖν ὁμ. θεὸν εἶναι

ὁμολογία: 887 τὴν περὶ τῶν μεγίστων ὁμ. φυλάττομεν, ib. ὁμολογίαν παρελθεῖν, ὁμ. ψεύσασθαι, 855 ἡ ὁσιότης συμπλακεῖσα τ. προνοίᾳ κατὰ τὴν ἑκούσιον ὁμ., 871 τῇ τ. κλήσεως ἐμμένειν ὁμολογίᾳ, 840, 861 τὸ πιστὸν τῆς ὁμ., 887 ἡ περὶ τῶν μεγίστων ὁμ.

ὁμόλογος: 864 ἡ γνῶσις ὁμ. ἑαυτῇ τε κ. τ. θείῳ λόγῳ

ὁμομήτριος: 873, see ὁμοπάτριος

ὁμονοητικός: 852 τὸ φιλικὸν καὶ ὁμ. ἐπαγγέλλεται τὸ συμπόσιον

ὁμόνοια: 872 ἡ ὁμ. ἡ περὶ ταὐτὸ συγκατάθεσίς ἐστι

ὁμοπάτριος: 873 οὐχ ὑπερορᾷ τ. ἀδελφὸν ὁμ. ὄντα κ. ὁμομήτριον

ὁμόσε: 871 τ. θηρία ὁμ. τ. λόγχαις πορεύεται

ὁμότιμος: 871, see ὁμογνώμων

ὁμόφυλος: trop. 839

ὄναρ: 852 ἡδονὴν οὐδὲ ὄναρ προσίεται, 878 οὐδὲ ὄναρ ποτὲ μὴ ἁρμόζον ἐκλεκτῷ βλέπει

ὀνειροπολέω: 849 τ. μετένδεσιν ὀν. τῆς ψυχῆς, Philo

ὄνειρος: 879 ὄν. βλέπων τὰ ἅγια ποιεῖ

ὄνομα: 869 παρακλητικῶς ἐξ ὀνόματος προσεῖπεν τ. γυναῖκα, 891 ὀνόμασι μόνοις προσανέχουσι, 900 ἀπὸ ὀνόματος προσαγορεύονται αἱ αἱρέσεις: (pregnant) 828 εἰκῇ διώκουσι τοὔνομα, 885 οἱ τὸ ὄν. ἐπικεκλημένοι μόνον

ὀνομασία: 889 ἡ ὀν. τῶν αἱρέσεων

ὄντως: 887 ἡ ὄντως οὖσα θεοσέβεια, 888 ἡ ὄντως οὖσα ἀλήθεια, ib. ἡ τῷ ὄντι ἀλήθεια περὶ τ. ὄντως ὄντα θεὸν καταγίνεται

ὀξέως: 880 ὀξ. ἑπόμενος τῷ καλοῦντι

ὀξύς: 852 ἡ ὀξυτάτη συναίσθησις τ. ἀγγέλων
ὀξύχολος: 841 ὀξ. γραΐδιον
ὀπή: 840 ὁ ἥλιος διὰ μικρᾶς ὀπῆς ἀποστέλλει τ. αὐγήν, 900 ὀπὴν ὑποδεῖξαι 'window,' cf. Plut. *Mor.* 972A, Orig. *Philoc.* § 10 ὡς δι' ὀπῆς μεγίστων νοημάτων ἀφορμὴν παρέχει
ὀπίσω: 889 (quot.)
ὅπλον: 870 τ. ὅπλοις τ. κυρίου πεφραγμένοι
ὁποτεροσοῦν: 855 ὁ ἄνθρωπος ἐξ αὑτοῦ ὁρμητικὸς πρὸς ὁπότερον οὖν (MB. ἂν) βούλοιτο
ὅπου γε: 856 πῶς οὐχὶ αὐτῆς τ. ψυχῆς ἐπακούει ὁ θεός, ὅπου γε ψυχὴ ψυχῆς ἐπαΐει; 875 τερπνὰ τούτῳ πῶς ἂν εἴη τὰ περὶ τ. βρῶσιν, ὅπου γε κ. λόγον φέροντά τινα ἡδονὴν ὑφορᾶται; 862, 16
ὀπώρα: 888 ὀπ. ἡ μὲν ἀληθὴς ἡ δὲ ἐκ κηροῦ πεποιημένη
ὁρατικός: 878 κολάζων τὸ ὁρ.
ὄργανον: 881 ὀργ. γίνεται τῆς τ. θεοῦ ἀγαθότητος
ὀρέγω: m. 853 εὔχεσθαι κ. ὀρέγ. καταλλήλως γίνεται, 857 ὀρ. τῶν ἀπόντων
ὄρεξις: 853 ὧν αἱ ὀρέξεις κ. αἱ ὁρμαί, τούτων αἱ εὐχαί
ὀρθός: 843 περὶ ὀρθῷ τῷ ὄφει, 844 *fin.* τὰς ψυχὰς προκαθαίρει διὰ τ. λόγου τ. ὀρθοῦ, 864 κατὰ λόγον τὸν ὀ., 871, 500 ἡ πρὸς τ. ὀρθὸν λόγον ἐξομοίωσις, 846 ὀρθύτατα βιοῖ
ὀρθοτομία: 896 ἡ ἐκκλησιαστικὴ ὀρθ. τ. δογμάτων
ὀριγνάομαι: 896 δόξης ὀριγνώμενοι, 220, 526 τροφῆς ὀρ., cf. Cobet *Collectan.* p. 154
ὁρίζω: 851 ὡρισμένος τόπος bis, 880 τ. ὡρισμένον ἐν τῇ σαρκὶ βίον
ὅρκος: 861 ὅρκ. ἐστὶν ὁμολογία καθοριστικὴ μετὰ προσπαραλήψεως θείας, 862 bis
ὁρμάω: 867 ἔνιοι θυμοειδεῖς ἀλόγως ἐπὶ τ. πολλὰ ὁρμῶσι, ib. m. ἐνθένδε ὁρμώμενος συνεργεῖ πρὸς τ. μάθησιν
ὁρμή: 853 see ὄρεξις, 837 ἀβούλητοι ἄγνοιαι ὁρμαί
ὁρμητικός: 855 ὁ ἄνθρωπος ἐξ αὑτοῦ ὁρμ.
ὀρνίθειος: 850 ὀρνιθείοις ὡς κουφοτάτοις χρῶνται
ὄρνις: (quot.) 843
ὄρος: 878 ὀρ. μεθιστάς, 901 οἱ στρωματεῖς ὄρει συσκίῳ ἐοίκασι
ὀρχηστής: 894 ἐὰν πρόσσχῃ τις Ἀρχελάῳ ὀρχ. αὐτὸν ποιήσει
ὅς: (indirect interrogation) 838 see Winer *tr.* 207 f.: ὃς μὲν—ὃς δέ 895
ὅσιος: 881 Ἰὼβ ἦν ὅσιος, τὸ δὲ ὅσιον μηνύει δικαίαν οἰκονομίαν

ὁσιότης: 855, 867, its def. 881
ὅσος: 870 τὰ ὅσα τούτοις συγγενῆ, 876 τοῖς δ' ὅσοι ἄξιοι, τὰ ἀγαθὰ δίδοται, p. 60 νόμους τοὺς ὅσοι ἀληθεῖς, 884 ἀποστερεῖτε τῆς τ. θεοῦ ἀγαθότητος, τὸ ὅσον ἐφ' ὑμῖν, τοὺς καθ' ὧν εὔχεσθε, 838, 885 ἐξομοιοῦσθαι ὅσῃ δύναμις τῇ τ. θεοῦ ἀγαθότητι, cf. 99, ἐμφαίνειν τ. μυστήριον ὅσον εἰς ἀνάμνησιν, 841 ὅσων ἐπισημήνασθαι, 894 διαβεβαιοῦνται ὅσον γε ἐπὶ τῷ διαβεβαιοῦσθαι ἄνευ ἀποδείξεως: 855 ὡς πλεῖστοι ὅσοι, 866 πολλῶν ὅσων μαρτυρίων ὄντων, 869 ἀπείρους ὅσους λογιζόμενος ἀγγέλους, 175 μυρίων ὅσων (cf. Jannaris p. 321 § 1219)
ὅσπερ: 897 εἰ δέ, ὅπερ καὶ μᾶλλον, τὸ ἀληθῶς φρονεῖν μηνύει
ὀστέον: (quot.) 847 ὁ. τὰ ἄβρωτα
ὁστισπερ: 863 ὅτιπερ ἂν ἐν νῷ, τοῦτο κ. ἐπὶ γλώσσης φέρει
ὄσφρησις: 848 αἱ διὰ τῆς ὀσφ. τῶν διὰ στόματος τροφαὶ θειότεραι, 852 θυμιαμάτων πολυτέλεια τ. ὄσφρησιν γοητεύει
ὀσφύς: (quot.) 847 bis
οὐκέτι: logical 850
οὖν: (in apodosi) 895 εἰ δὲ μὴ ἐπαΐοιεν ...παιδευθεῖεν οὖν
οὐράνιος: 881 ὁ οὐρ. πατήρ
οὐρανός: 882 τέμνει τ. οὐρανόν
οὖς: 886 οἱ ὦτα ἔχοντες, 893 οὐκ ἔχει ὦτα ἀκούοντα τ. σύμφορον, 896 τὰ ὦτα τ. ψυχῆς
οὐσία: 854 οὐσία νοητή, 867 οὐσίας κ. τὰ πράγματα αὐτὰ παραλαβὼν διὰ τ. λόγων, 892 ἡ πίστις οὐσία ἀποδείξεως, 882 διελθὼν τὰς πνευματικὰς οὐσίας, 884
οὔτε...οὐδέ: 836 οὔτ' οὖν ἐνδεὲς οὐδὲ μὴν φιλοκερδὲς τ. θεῖον, ib. οὔτε θυσίαις οὐδὲ μὴν ἀναθήμασιν οὐδ' αὖ δόξῃ
οὔτε...οὔτε καί: 867
οὗτος: 869 μέμνησο ὦ αὕτη τ. κυρίου: 836 καὶ ταῦτα: διὰ τοῦτο: (introducing result of a gen. abs.) 899 ἑνὸς ὄντος τ. θεοῦ διὰ τοῦτο τὸ ἄκρως τίμιον ἐπαινεῖται, 887 δυσκόλου τ. ἀληθείας τυγχανούσης διὰ τοῦτο γεγόνασι ζητήσεις
οὐχὶ δέ: 901 πρὸς τ. ἔργα τ. δικαιοσύνης ὁλοσχερέστερον, οὐχὶ δὲ ἀκριβέστερον μετερχόμενοι, 881 οὐχὶ δὲ καὶ αἰτεῖ (?)
ὀφείλω: 860 αἱ ὀφειλόμεναι προκοπαί, 886 ἡ μονὴ ἡ ὀφειλομένη, ib. τέλειοι γίνεσθαι ὀφείλομεν, 888
ὀφθαλμός: 893 ὡς ὀφθ. τεταραγμένος οὕτως κ. ἡ ψυχή, 881, 853 ὅλον ὀφθ.
ὄφις: 843 ὀφ. ὑπέρῳ περιειλημένος bis, 895 (quot.), 882 μίξας τῇ περιστερᾷ τ. ὄφιν
ὀχλοκρασία: 852 ὀχλ. ἡ τ. θεάτρων δεσπότις, Philo *de Paenit.* 2

ὄψις: 877 τ. ὄψεις αὐτοῦ πρὸς τ. ἀόρατα χειραγωγεῖ, 878 init. ἡ προσβολὴ τῆς ὄψεως, 852 οὐ δεῖ θεῷ ὄψεως, 901 ὄψεως εἰς ἡδονὴν
ὀψοποιός: 894

παγκάλως: 858 εὖ μάλα π. διοικεῖται τ. πάντα
παγκρατιάζω: 840 π. εἰς τ. στάδιον οἱ ἀθληταί
παγκράτιον: 839 τὸ π. τὸ πάμμαχον οὐ πρὸς αἷμα
παθητός: 832 ὁ κύριος δι᾽ ἡμᾶς τ. παθητὴν ἀνέλαβεν σάρκα, 868 παθ. σώματι ἐνδεδεμένος
πάθος: 846 fin. ὧν ἅπτεται π. φθαρτὰ πάντα ἐστί, 872 δεινῷ πάθει τὸ ἀγαθὸν μεταδιώκει, 893 πάθους τριττὴ θεραπεία, 871 οὐδὲ τὰ π. οὐδὲ τ. ἁμαρτήματα κακίαι
παίγνιον: (quot.) 845 ἄνθρωπος π. θεοῦ
παιδαγωγέω: 895 ἡ κατὰ λόγον ἄσκησις ἐκ πίστεως παιδαγωγουμένη
παιδαγωγία: 885 ἡ τ. νόμου π.
παιδαγωγός: 898 τ. πονηρὰ παιδία τὸν παιδ. ἀποκλείει
παιδεία: 839 ἡ ἐγκύκλιος π., 869 διὰ παιδείας εὐεργετεῖ, 895 δύο π. παραδίδονται πρόσφοροι ἑκατέρᾳ τ. ἁμαρτιῶν, ib. μερικαί τινες π.
παιδεραστής: (quot.) 847
παίδευσις: 835 π. αἱ ἀναγκαῖαι
παιδευτής: 864 ὁ φιλάνθρωπος κ. φιλόθεος π.
παιδευτική: 838 χρήσιμος ἡ ἀλγηδὼν κατὰ τὴν π.
παιδεύω: 862 παιδεύων δημιουργεῖ τ. ἄνθρωπον, 876 ὑπὸ τοιούτων οὐ παιδεύται ὁ γνωστικὸς bis, 879 οἱ μετὰ θάνατον παιδευόμενοι
παιδιά: 845 γελοῖον γίνεσθαι παιδιαῖς (ms. παιδιᾶς) τέχνης τ. θεόν
παιδοποιία: 874 γάμῳ κ. παιδοποιίᾳ ἐγγυμνασάμενος
παίζω: 842 fin. παίζων ἐνεχείρει
παῖς: 871 π. ἐν πίστει, 876 'neophyte'
παλαιός: (quot.) 836 π. ἄνθρωπος, 856 τὰ παλαίτατα τ. ἱερῶν
πάλιν αὖ: 834
παλινδρομέω: 889 μηδὲ εἰς τ. αἱρέσεις π., 890 ἐκ τ. ἀπάτης π., 777 ἐπὶ τὰ κοσμικὰ ἀγαθὰ π., 23, Philo
παμβασιλεύς: 837 ὁ π. καὶ παντοκράτωρ πατήρ, Eus. Pr. Ev. 1. 1. 3 bis, ib. 4 § 9, π.)(βασιλεύς spoken of the Son, Barnab.
πάμμαχος: 839 see παγκράτιον
πάμπολυς: 893 πάμπολλα συγκαττύουσι ψεύσματα, 887 π. γεγόνασιν αἱρέσεις
παμφάγος: 851 πῦρ τὸ π. καὶ βάναυσον
πανεπίσκοπος: 837 οὐ φασιν εἶναι θεὸν ἢ ὄντα μὴ εἶναι π., 311 ὁ π. λόγος, Orac. Sibyll. 1. 152
πανηγεμών: 864 θεὸς π., Philo
πανήγυρις: 860 ἅπας ὁ βίος π. ἁγία, 953, cf. Const. Ap. 11. 62, Schm. IV. 718
πανοῦργος: 889 οἱ τ. προσιόντας ἐξαπατῶντες π.
πανσθενής: 857 προσεχὴς τῇ π. δυνάμει γενόμενος
παντάπασιν: 895 π. ἀνίατος
παντελής: 894 ἀποπαυστέον τ. ἔθος εἰς τὸ παντελές, 835 κρίσις ἡ π., 895 μὴ εἰς τὴν π. κρίσιν ἑαυτοὺς ἐμβάλοιεν, 838 ἡ π. ἀρετὴ δικαιοσύνη
παντελῶς: 838 π. ἀναλλοίωτα
πάντῃ: 835 π. πάντως ἀναίτιος, 866 π. πάντως ἄτρεπτον: 'everywhere' 862 πάντῃ πάντοτε εἶναι τ. θεόν, 764 πάντῃ ἐστὶ καὶ ἀεὶ ἐργάζεται, 831, 851 π. πάντοθεν πάρεστιν ὁ θεὸς bis
παντοκρατορικός: 857 τὸ π. βούλημα, 611 τὸ π. θέλημα, 564 αὐθεντία π., Clem. Rom. I. 8 fin. Lightfoot
παντοκράτωρ: subst. 833, 835, adj. 831 θεὸν πεπεισμένος εἶναι π., 839, 864 (where ms. wrongly inserts καί), and passim, 864 βασιλεὺς π. 833, 834 πατὴρ π.
παραβαίνω: 861 π. τι, 887 π. συνθήκας quinquies, 862 μηδὲν π. τῶν κατὰ τ. συνθήκας, 893 ἐὰν παραβῇ τις τ. θεόν, see παραγγέλλω
παράβασις: 862 τῆς π. καὶ τ. ἐπιτελέσεως ἐν τ. ἔργοις ἡ κύρωσις
παραγγέλλω: 875 μηδὲν τῶν παρηγγελμένων παραβέβηκα, 830 ὁ κύριος ἄντικρυς παραγγέλλει
παράγγελμα: 837 παραγγελμάτων ὑπακοή
παράγω: act. 847 τ. Διόνυσον παράγει, 868 παράγειν οὐκ ἴσχυσεν ἡ γυνή: p. 836 τὸ θεῖον οὐ παράγεται τοιούτοις
παράδεισος: 901 ἐν στοίχῳ καταπεφυτευμένοι π., ib. ὡραῖος π. 736
παραδεκτικός: 838 τ. τῶν ἐπαγγελλομένων, 437 πρόληψις τῶν λεγομένων παρ., cf. παραδοχή and παραδέχομαι
παραδέχομαι: 840 π. ἐντολάς, 874 κηρὸς χαρακτῆρα π.
παραδίδωμι: act. 831 τὸ παραδιδόναι τὰ παρὰ τῇ ἀληθείᾳ ἐπικεκρυμμένα, 900 τὰ διχηλοῦντα καθαρὰ π. ἡ γραφή, p. 895 δύο παιδεῖαι παραδίδονται ἑκατέρᾳ τ. ἁμαρτιῶν, 865 ἡ γνῶσις παραδίδοται τ. ἐπιτηδείοις, 897 ἡ διὰ τ. γραφῶν παραδιδομένη γνῶσις
παράδοξος: 843 ἦν γὰρ παραδοξότερον
παράδοσις: 845 ἡ τ. μυστηρίων παράδοσις, ib. ἐπὶ τὴν ἀληθῆ τρέπεσθαι π., 864 ἡ γνῶσις ἐκ π. διαδιδομένη οἷον παρακαταθήκη, 865, 890 ἡ ἐκκλησιαστικὴ παράδ., 896 θεῖα π.)(αἵρεσις,

OF GREEK WORDS. 429

ib. κυρίου π., 900 μία ή πάντων τ. ἀποστόλων π., 807, 897: pl. 882 λέγουσιν ἐν ταῖς π., 893 al τ. Χριστοῦ π., 901 π. ἅγι᾽

παραδοχή: 839 π. πίστεως, 846 ἀμείνων ὁ νεὼς εἰς π. τοῦ θεοῦ, 874 ἡ τ. γνώσεως π.

παραδρομή: 866 κατά π. ἀνέδειξεν, 65 κατά π. παραστῆσαι, Arist., Polyb., ἐν -ῇ Basil Ep. 258, 2 (III. 393 d)

παραζηλόω: 884 ἐχθροὶ οἱ π.

παράθυρος: 897 παράθυρον ἀνατεμόντες κ. διορύξαντες τ. τεῖχίον

παραινέω: 869 ὁ ἀνὴρ τῇ γυναικὶ ἀγάπης ἔχεσθαι παρήνεσεν

παραιτητός: 837 θυσίαις π. τοὺς θεούς

παρακαλέω: 876 διὰ τ. ἀνδρικῆς παρακαλούμενοι ὑπομονῆς

παρακαταθήκη: 865 init. οἷον π. ἐγχειρίζεται ἡ γνῶσις

παράκειμαι: 853 τ. παρακείμενα ὠφελήματα τ. κτήσει, ib. καθάπερ ἀναθήματα παρακείμενα, 838 ὅπωρα π.

παρακλήτωρ: 872 π. τὸν νόμον

παρακλητικός: 869 προτρεπτικός κ. τ. ἐπιφωνῆσαι

παρακολουθέω: 839 παρακολουθοῦντες αὐτοῖς ὅτι μηδὲν ἐπίστανται

παραλαμβάνω: act. 848 π. τ. γνῶσιν: p. 862 ἡ μεγαλοπρέπεια τ. λόγου πρὸς τ. διδασκάλου παραλαμβάνεται, 865 ἀποδείξει τῶν διὰ πίστεως παρειλημμένων, 887, 886 οὐδὲν τούτων εἰς ὁμοιότητα θεοῦ παραλαμβάνεται, Philo

παραληπτέον: 855 οὐδεμίαν ἀφορμὴν τῆς προσόδου πρὸς τ. θεόν π.

παραλείπω: 883 ἀνεπισημείωτον π. τ. τόπον

παραμένω: 853, 857 τὰ ὄντως ἀγαθά εὔχεται παραμεῖναι, 872

παραμονή: 857 ὁ γνωστικὸς ὧν κέκτηται π. αἰτήσεται, 859 τὰ βοηθεῖν εἰς τὴν π. τῆς ἀρετῆς δυνάμενα

παραμυθία: 873 ἐπικουφίζει τ. ἀδελφὸν παραμυθίαις

παράνοια: 894 ὁ αὐτὸς νοῦς παρ᾽ οἷς μὲν ἐντιμότατος παρ᾽ οἷς δὲ παρανοίας ἥλωκε

παραπέμπω: act. 856 ἔξεστιν μηδὲ φωνῇ τ. εὐχὴν παραπέμπειν, 866 ἡ γνῶσις εἰς τὸ ἀμετάπτωτον π., 881 τ. ἀγαθὰ τ. δεομένοις παραπέμπει, 901 ἡ πίστις δι᾽ υἱοῦ πρὸς τ. πατέρα π.: p. 898 τ. ἀποδείξεις ἀνευρίσκειν παραπεμπόμενος (MS. ἀναπ.) ὑπό τ. κυρίου, 7 παρ᾽ οὗ τὸ εὖ ζῆν ἐκδιδασκόμενοι εἰς ἀΐδιον ζωὴν παραπεμπόμεθα, 572 εἰς ἕξιν διδόστατος παραπέμπεται ὁ μελετήσας εὐχωλάν, Philo M. 1, 12 ὑπὸ φωτὸς ἄνω παραπεμφθεῖσα ἡ ὅρασις: m. 877 πόνους παρετέμψατο, 890 αἱ αἱρέσεις παραπέμπονται τ. γραφάς, 892, 86, cf.

Clem. Hom. π. 31 παραπέμπεται τ. ὅρκους, Plut. Mor. 1039 B προσήκει τὰ μὲν (ἁμαρτήματα) ὅλως παραπέμπεσθαι τὰ δὲ μικρὰ ἐπιστροφῆς τυγχάνειν

παραπίπτω: 863 τοὺς παραπεσόντας τοῖς ἀλλοφύλοις πιπράσκει, cf. Heb. vi. 6

παραπλησίως: 890

παράπτωμα: 895 αἱ ἐν παραπτώματι γενόμεναι εἰς κολάσεις περιπίπτουσιν

παρασκευάζω: 839 παιδεία π. τ. ψυχήν, 897 τὸ ἐπὶ τ. ἀληθείᾳ πεποιθέναι ὑπεροπτικὸν π. (᾽makes a man highminded᾽)

παρασκευή: 877 ᾽Friday᾽: 865 παρασκευῆς δεῖται

παράστασις: 862 ἀρκεῖ προσθεῖναι τὸ ἀληθῶς λέγω εἰς π. τῶν μὴ διορώντων, ᾽confirmation,᾽ 864 εἰς π. τῆς ἀληθείας, cf. Eus. H. E. vi. 19, Epict.

παραστατικός: 862 ὀμνύναι ἐστὶ τὸ ὅρκον ἀπὸ διανοίας προσφέρεσθαι παραστατικῆς (MS. -τικῶς)

παρατείνω: 887 τ. ἡ ἀλήθεια ἄλλων ἄλλα δογματιζόντων

παρατηρέω: (quot.) 843 π. τίς ἔπαρεν

παρατίθημι: 867 τ. βίον διαγράφειν οὐχὶ τ. θεωρίαν παρατίθεσθαι, 895 ταῦτα παρεθέμην, 883

παραχάραγμα: 887 τ. κίβδηλον νόμισμα τ. κυρίου ἀπὸ τοῦ π. διακρίνουσιν, [Ignat.] Magn. 5 bis δύο λέγω χαρακτῆρας ἐν ἀνθρώποις εὑρίσκεσθαι, τὸν μὲν νομίσματος, τὸν δὲ παραχαράγματος, ib. ὁ ἀσεβὴς κίβδηλον νόμισμα, παραχάραγμα, Basil Ep. 214, 3 init., Chrys xi. 551 c

παραχαράσσω: 899 αἱρέσεις παραχαραχθείσαι, Philo II. 568, Tatian 40, Lobeck Aglaoph. 603 n.

παρεγχείρησις: 896 σοφίζονται δι᾽ ἑτέρων π., cf. ἐπιχείρημα, ἐγχειρέω

πάρειμι: 898 παρὸν τὰς οἰκείας τ. θείαις γραφαῖς πορίζεσθαι ἀποδείξεις, 879 εὐχαριστία ἐπὶ τ. μέλλουσιν ὡς ἤδη διὰ πίστιν παροῦσι

παρεισάγω: 854 πρὸς τινων ἑτεροδόξων παρεισαγόμενα δόγματα, 2 Pet. ii. 1

παρεισδύομαι: 854 π. τὸ ὑπόμνημα ἡ τούτων καταδρομή, cf. παρεισδύω 870, 659, 666 Λn., Jude 4

παρεκτροπή: 876 ὀλίσθηραὶ κ. κρημνώδεις π.

παρέλκω: 855 οὐ π. ἡ αἴτησις κἂν χωρὶς ἀξιώσεως διδῶται, 862 π. αὐτῷ τὸ κατά τ. γλῶτταν μαρτύριον, cf. 645 π. αἱ ἐντολαί

παρεπίδημος: (quot.) 879 π. καὶ ξένοι τῶν τῇδε, 878

παρέρχομαι: 887 π. τὴν ὁμολογίαν, 881 παρεληλυθότα)(μέλλοντα

παρέχω: m. 836 τῷ θεῷ τῷ τὰ πάντα παρεσχημένῳ, 860 ὁ ἰατρὸς ὑγίειαν

παρέχεται, 871 τ. ἄνδρα ἐν τ. ἀνδρείᾳ ἐξετάζεσθαι παρέχονται, 881 τ. δεομένοις τὸ (MS. τῷ) διὰ τ. εὐχῆς ἀτύφως π., 895 ἄμεμπτον ἑαυτὸν π., act. 839 ἐπιστημονικὴν διαμονὴν παρέχουσιν, 836 ἀφορμὰς παρεσχήκασι
παρθένος: 875 ἡ χήρα διὰ σωφροσύνης αὖθις π., ib. ἡγιασμέναι π., ib. π. ὡς κακῶν ἀπεσχημέναι, 890 π. ὡς Μαριάμ, ib. αἱ γραφαὶ π. μένουσι
παρίστημι: 828 καιρὸς παραστῆσαι τ. Ἕλλησι μόνον εἶναι θεοσεβῆ τ. γνωστικόν, 829 τὰ ὑφ' ἡμῶν λεγόμενα τ. νοῦν τ. γραφῶν παριστᾶν ἐπαγγέλλεται, (cf. Clem. Hom. xv. 5 ἐκ στοχασμῶν δοκεῖ παριστᾶν τ. ἀποδείξεις), ib. πρόκειται παραστῆσαι ὑμῖν τ. γνωστικὸν ὅσιον, 832 τοῦτον εἶναι τ. σωτῆρα αἱ θεῖαι παριστᾶσι προφητεῖαι, 841 ἀθέους παραστῆσαι τοὺς τοῖς κακίστοις τὸ θεῖον ἀπεικάζοντας, ib. ἱκανῶς παρέστησα περὶ δεισιδαιμονίας, 852 φαίνεται τὸ ἔξοχον τ. γνώσεως ὧδε παριστάς, 858 οὐδαμῇ ἐνδόσιμον τ. ψυχὴν παρίστησιν, 866 φίλον τὸ γινῶσκον τ. γινωσκομένῳ π. bis, 867 τ. ψυχὴν παρίστησιν τοῖς πράγμασιν, 869 ὁ παραστήσας δυνατὸν εἶναι τ. κορυφαῖον κτήσασθαι βίον, 877, 882 τὸ ἁμαρτῆσαι ἀλλότριον π. ἡ γραφή, 883
παροράω: 833 ἡ πρόνοια μηδενὸς παρορῶσα τ. ἐπιμέλειαν, 893 οὐχ οἷά τε τὸ φῶς τ. ἀληθείας διιδεῖν ἀλλὰ τὰ ἐν ποσὶ παρορᾷ
παρόρμησις: 873 τ. ἀδελφὸν ἐπικουφίζει παρορμήσεσι
παρουσία: 851 ἡ π. ἀνδρὸς ἀγαθοῦ πρὸς τ. κρεῖττον σχηματίζει τ. ἐντυγχάνοντα: 834 συνέκλεισεν τ. ἀπιστίαν εἰς τὴν π. (the First Coming), 898 ἡ π. κυρίου κατὰ τὴν π. διδασκαλία, Lightf. Ign. II. 275 f.
παρρησία: 858 ἐμπειρίᾳ πολλῇ χρησάμενος π. ἔχει, 875 εἰπεῖν μετὰ π. πρὸς τ. θεόν, 896 ἡ π. τῆς ἀληθείας
παρρησιάζομαι: 876 οἱ γεννάδαι τ. παρρησιαζομένων φιλοσόφων
πᾶς: 878 πᾶς οὗτος ξένος: 829 πᾶς ὁ πρεσβύτερος, 835 πᾶν τὸ ἐνάρετον, 836 πᾶς ὁ ἀναληφθείς, 854 παντὸς μᾶλλον ἐναργῶς, 855, 897: πᾶς τις 884 παντὶ τῷ χρηστεύεται: 884 τὸ πᾶν 'the universe'
πατάσσω: 876 ὃν ἐγὼ πατάξω ἐλέησον
πατέω: 881 π. τὰ ἀνθρώπινα κακά
πατριάρχης: 869 οἱ κατωρθωκότες π.
πατρικός: 831, 68 ὁ λόγος ὁ π., 833 π. ἐνέργεια ὁ υἱός, ib. δύναμις π.
πατρῷος: 866 ἡ π. αὐλή, 895 νουθεσίαι π.
Παῦλος: 894 ἡ Π. λειτουργία
παύω: 865 πεπαῦσθαι καθάρσεως

παχύς: 836 οὐδὲ μέχρι νεφῶν τ. παχυτάτων
παχύτης: 848 ἡ κατὰ τ. ἀέρα π.
πειθήνιος: 840 π. τῷ ἀλείπτῃ, ib. γεγόναμεν εἶναι π. ταῖς ἐντολαῖς
παθηνίως: 856 π. ἔχειν πρὸς τ. ἡγουμένους
πεῖρα: 874 ἡ διὰ τέκνων προσφερομένη π., 876 εἰς πεῖραν τελειότητος ἤχθησαν, 877 πεῖραν λαβὼν πόνων κατεφρόνησε, ib. ἐν πείρᾳ γενόμενον ἀποσχέσθαι ἡδονῆς, 880 fin. ὑπομονητικὸς πρὸς πᾶσαν πεῖραν, 881 πενία κ. νόσος κ. τοιαῦται πεῖραι
πειράζω: 839 ἄθλους ἐπαρτᾷ ὁ πειράζων, 877 ὁ γνωστικὸς πειράζεται ὑπ' οὐδενὸς
πειρασμός: 877 οἱ π. προσάγονται τούτῳ εἰς τὴν τῶν πέλας ὠφέλειαν
πειρατής: 851 κἂν π. κἂν λῃσταὶ τύχωσιν
πεῖσμα: 869 π. βεβαιότατον τῆς τ. μελλόντων ἀπολήψεως (see critical n.), 785 πεῖσμα τ. ψυχῇ βέβαιον, 327 βέβαιον λαμβάνομεν πεῖσμα τ. ἀληθοῦς καταλήψεως, 488 π. δοῦναι ὅτι
πειστικός: 839 οἱ λόγοι οἱ π. (wrongly written πιστικός, cf. Lobeck Aj. p. 139, Plato Legg. 723 a)
πενία: 881
πέτομαι: 881 οἱ πετόμενοι ἀδελφοί
πέποιθα: 872 π. ἐπὶ κύριον, ἵνα πεποιθὼς προσίῃ τ. εὐχαῖς, 897 τὸ ἐπὶ τῇ ἀληθείᾳ πεποιθέναι
πεποίθησις: 831 τῆς τ. σωτῆρος διδασκαλίας ἡ πεποίθησις, cf. Eph. iii. 12
περαίνω: 872 ἡ φιλία δι' ὁμοιότητος περαίνεται, (quot.) 893 ἕπεσθαι τ. θεῷ ἐξ ἀρχῆς τὰ πάντα εὐθεῖαν περαίνοντι
περαιόω: p. 866 ἡ εἰς ἀγάπην περαιουμένη μεταβολή, 883 (pleonastic) τὸ τέλος δι' ἐνεργείας εἰς θεωρίαν περαιοῦται, 787
πέρας: 879 ἡ ἀπὸ τῶν περάτων ἐπὶ π. ὠκεανοῦ βασιλεία
περάτης: see n. on περατικοί 900, cf. Harnack Gesch. d. altchr. Litt. I. p. 168
περί: 849 αἱ θυσίαι τὴν π. ἡμᾶς εὐσέβειαν ἀλληγοροῦσι, cf. Xen. Hell. v. 4. 2 ἡ π. Φίλιππον τυραννίς, Plat. Phaedr. 279 A οἱ π. Λυσίαν λόγοι
περιβάλλω: act. 891 πίστει π. (? περιλαβόντες) ἀναπόδεικτον τ. ἀρχήν, π. 868 τὸ κόσμιον τοῦ ἤθους περιβαλλόμενος, 884 μίαν εἰκόνα ἐπὶ μίαν οὐσίαν περιβεβλημένοι, p. 954 σχῆμα ἔξωθεν ἡμῖν περιβεβλημένον
περίγειος: 830 ἡ τῶν π. οἰκονομία, Philo I. 416 M., Stob. Ecl. I. 488 Heeren, Heliod. x. 6 fin.
περιγίνομαι: 833 'prevail' π. ὧν ἂν ἐθέλῃ, 840 'survive,' 839 π. ἀνταγω-

νισμάτων: ib. 'result from' οὐδὲ ἐκ τέχνης π. ἡ γνῶσις, 875 δι' ὧν ἡ σωτηρία π.
περιγράφω: 845 οὐκ ἐν τόπῳ π. τὸν ἀπερίληπτον, 846 οὐ περιγράφεται τόπῳ θεός: 885 ἀδικεῖ ὁ ἀντιδικῶν καὶ τ. ἐννοίᾳ, ἦν τὸ εὐαγγέλιον π. ('excludes'), 273 ἔθει πονηρῷ περιγράφοντες (MS. παραγρ.) τὸν φόβον, 309 ἐκκόπτεται κακία κ. περιγράφεται ἀδικία, Heliod. III. 16 fin., IV. 21, v. 29, x. 20. 39 fin.
περιειλέω: 842 ὄφιν [ἐν] τ. ὑπέρῳ περιειλημένον
περιεκτικός: 845 οὐκ ἐν ἱεροῖς καθειργνυμεν τὸ πάντων π., Sext. Emp.
περιέχω: 831 ὁ υἱὸς μηδαμῇ περιεχόμενος, 838 τὰ μὲν ὡς διήκοντα, τὰ δὲ ὡς περιέχοντα, 845 τ. ἀέρα καὶ τὸ π. ἄξιον ἡγησάμενοι τῆς τ. θεοῦ ὑπεροχῆς
περιήλυσις: 884 ἡ κοσμικὴ π.
περιθειόω: (quot.) 844
περικαθαίρω: 844 γ. ᾠὰ ἀπὸ τ. περικαθαρθέντων ζῳογονούμενα bis, Philo
περικαταρρέω: 834 π. ἐλιχθέντες τ. πάθεσι, 89 π. τῇ φθορᾷ
περικοπή: 883 μεγίστης οὔσης τῆς π. διὰ βραχυτάτων τ. διάνοιαν παραστήσομεν, 886 εἰς ἀναπλήρωσιν τῆς π.
περιλαμβάνω: (quot.) 883, 891 see περιβάλλω
περιλέπω: (quot.) 847 τῷ μηρῷ περιλέψαντες (al. περιλαψ.)
περιμάσσω: (quot.) 844
περιουσία: 829 ἐκ περιουσίας τ. μαρτύρια φανερωθήσεται, 889 ἐν περιουσίᾳ ἀγαθῶν, 881 χρημάτων π., 891 ἐκ π. τὰς ἀποδείξεις λαβόντες, 13 ἐκ π. παρατεθέντα 112, 102
περιπατέω: 880 περιπατῶν κ. κοιμώμενος
περίπατος: 861 περιπάτῳ χρώμενος
περιπίπτω: 884 οἱ κακοὶ καχεξίᾳ π., 837 λύπαις π., 895 εἰς κολάσεις π., 885 μηδενὶ τ. παθῶν π.
περιπνέω: 848 περιπνεῖται καθάπερ τὰ ἔντομα
περιποιέω: m. 870 πραότητα περιπεποιημένη, 885 μεγαλονοίᾳ τοῦτο π., act. 872 δικαιοσύνη τὸ ἀληθεύειν π.
περιπολέω: 894 ὁ τ. κυρίῳ πειθόμενος ἐν σαρκὶ περιπολεῖ θεός
περιρραίνω: (quot.) 844
περισπάω: 832 ὑπὸ ἡδονῆς περισπώμενος, 878 π. ὑπὸ τ. πράγματος, 879 ὑπὸ τ. ἰδίας ἐλπίδος περισπώμενος (? ἐπισπ.), 882 τ. περιπώσαν αὐτὸν ὕλην ὑπερηφανήσας
περισσός: 829 ἡ ἐπὶ πλέον ἐπεξεργασία π. δόξειεν ἄν
περίστασις: 868 προκαταληφθεὶς κατά τινα π., ib. π. ἀκούσιος (cf. 957), 874 οὐδέποτε περιστάσεως γενομένης τ. ἰδίας

ἕξεως ἐξίσταται, 869 ἔστιν ἐν πάσῃ π. ἐρρωμένη τ. γνωστικοῦ ἡ ψυχή, 575, Polyb., Epict.
περιστατικός: 838 τὰ π. ὑπομένειν, ib. ὑπεράνω πάντων τῶν π. γινόμενος, 868 κἄν τι τ. περιστατικῶν ἐπίῃ τ. γνωστικῷ ἄτρεπτος μένει, 598 τοῖς περιστατικοῖς περιπίπτειν, Orig. De Orat. 30
περιστέλλω: 871 περιστελλόμενοι κατὰ λόγον τ. ὀρθόν
περιστερά: 849 ἡ τρυγὼν κ. ἡ π., 882 μίξας τῇ π. τ. ὄφιν
περιτέμνω: 863 Τιμόθεον ὁ γενναῖος περιέτεμεν ἀπόστολος
περιτομή: 863 γράφων π. τὴν χειροποίητον οὐδὲν ὠφελεῖν, ib. π. καρδίας
περιτροπή: 834 αἱ σωτήριαι π. ἀπομερίζονται χρόνοις
περιττεύω: 874 π. ἐν τῇ κατὰ τ. βίον οἰκονομίᾳ
περιτυγχάνω: 901 ὁ περιτυχὼν τ. ἀμυήτων
περιφέρω: 880 π. τὸν θάνατον
περιωπή: 831 οὐκ ἐξίσταταί ποτε τῆς ἑαυτοῦ π. ὁ υἱὸς τ. θεοῦ, 59 θεὸς ἐν τ. ἰδίᾳ π. ὢν ἀεί, Heliod. v. 14
πηγή: 834 ἐκ μιᾶς ἀρυτόμενος πηγῆς ὁ κύριος τ. ἐντολὰς ἔδωκεν
πήλινος: (quot.) 842 βωμὸς π.
πηλός: (quot.) 849
πῆξις: 876 οἱ ἀπόστολοι εἰς πῆξιν τ. ἐκκλησιῶν εἰς πεῖραν ἤχθησαν, 778 ἐν τῷ τρεπομένῳ ἀδύνατον λαβεῖν πῆξιν, Philo, Chrysippus
πιθανός: 889 π. ἐπιχειρήματα
πικρίζω: 893 οἱ αἱρετικοὶ π. κατὰ τ. ἀγρίαν ἀμυγδάλην
πίνω: 853 οὐδεὶς ἐπιθυμεῖ πόματος ἀλλὰ τοῦ πιεῖν τ. ποτόν
πιπράσκω: 882 (trop.) τ. παραπεσόντας τοῖς ἀλλοφύλοις π.
πιστευτέον: 887
πιστεύω: 879 ὁ πιστεύων...ὁ πιστευόμενος
πιστικός (see πειστικός): 839 οἱ λόγοι οἱ π. ἐπιστημονικὴν τ. ἀληθείας διαμονὴν παράσχοιεν ἄν, cf. ἡ π. τέχνη, Plato Polit. 304 D
πίστις: 864)(γνῶσις, 890 'proof' ἀκολοθοῦντες τ. αἱροῦντι λόγῳ ποιοῦνται τὰς π., 901 init. πίστει περιλαβὼν τ. ἀρχήν: (= Christians) 874, see 'Faith'
πιστός: 831 πιστὸς οἰκέτης, 846 πᾶν τὸ μέλλον πιστεύειν πιστὸν ἤδη τῷ θεῷ, 883 ἐὰν ἕν ὁ π. ἢ καὶ δεύτερον κατορθώσῃ, ἀλλ' οὗ τί γε ἐν πᾶσιν καθάπερ ὁ γνωστικός, 890 ὁ ἐξ ἑαυτοῦ πιστὸς τ. κυριακῇ γραφῇ ἀξιόπιστος, ib. π. τῷ κυρίῳ διαμένει, 892 ἡ ἐπίγνωσις ἐκ τῶν ἤδη π. τοῖς οὔπω π. ἐκπορίζεται τ. πίστιν, 861 τὸ πιστὸν τ. ὁμολογίας

πιστόω: π. 891 πιστώσασθαι δεῖ τὸ λεχθέν, ib. τῇ τ. κυρίου φωνῇ πιστούμεθα τ. ζητούμενον
πλαδαρός: 850 πλ. τὴν σάρκα ἡ τοιάδε κατασκευάζει βρῶσις
πλάσμα: 898 πάμπολλα συγκαττύουσι πλ.: 74 ὁ θεὸς ζητεῖ τὸ πλ....πλ. ὑμεῖς τ. θεοῦ, 53 τὸ ἔνθεον τ. πλάσματος, 101 ὁ λόγος ὁ δημιουργήσας τὸν ἄνθρωπον ὅλου κήδεται τ. πλάσματος
πλάσσω: 832 οἱ δι' αὑτοῦ πλασθέντες
πλάτανος: 901 ὄρος δασὺ πλατάνοις
πλάτος: 887 ὡς ἐν πλάτει χρώμενοι τ. ἀπολογίᾳ
πλέον: 862 πλ. τι καὶ μᾶλλον ἐπιτείνει τὸ γνωστικὸν ἀξίωμα ὁ τ. προστασίαν ἀναλαβών
πλεονεκτέω: 854 τὸ ἐκτὸς μόνον πλ. οἱ ἀδικεῖν ἐπιχειροῦντες, see μειονεκτέω
πλεονέκτημα: 869 τὰ πλ. τοῦ κατ' ἀλήθειαν γνωστικοῦ, 891 πλ. τῆς φιλαυτίας
πλέω: 852 init. πλέουεν ὑμνοῦντες
πλημμελέω: 839 οὐδὲν πλ., 884 πλημ. εἰς αὑτόν, ib. κατ' ἄγνοιαν πλ.
πλὴν ἀλλά: 864 π. ἀ. τὸ μὴ διστάσαι θεμέλιον γνώσεως, cf. 54, 108, 122, 132; πλὴν εἰ μὴ 852, Plut.; πλὴν = δὲ 115
πλήρης: 836 πλ.)(ἐνδεής
πλησιαίτερον: 831 ὁ πλ. κατὰ τόπον ἄγγελος, Heliod. x. 18 init.
πλησίον: 861 διὰ τὸν πλ.
πλοκή: 852 πολυανθεῖς κ. εὐωδεῖς πλ. ('wreaths')
πλουτέω: 839 πλ. ἐν τῷ μηδενὸς ἐπιθυμεῖν, cf. 438
πνεῦμα: 834 τὸ τ. Ἡρακλείας λίθου πνεῦμα διὰ πολλῶν τ. σιδηρῶν ἐκτείνεται δακτυλίων, 857 διὰ τ. ἀορίστου ἀγάπης ἤνωται τ. πνεύματι, 90 τὸ τ. ψυχῆς πνεῦμα, 880 στόμιον ἐμβαλὼν τῷ ἀλόγῳ πνεύματι (see πρᾶγμα 868)
πνευματικός: 856 συντείνων τ. πν. τὰν εἰς φωνὴν νοητήν, 857 πνευματικός εἶναι σπουδάζει, 873 πν. ὅλη γενομένη ἡ ψυχὴ ἐν πν. τῇ ἐκκλησίᾳ μένει, 882 διελθὼν τὰς πν. οὐσίας ἅπτεται τ. θρόνων τ. ἄκρων, 885 ἡ ἐκκλησία ὁ πν. καὶ ἅγιος χορός, 886 πν. σῶμα: (quot.) 839 πν. ἐξουσίαι, 896 πν. βρῶμα
πνεύμων: 848 ἡ τοῦ πν. πρὸς τ. θώρακα ἀντιδιαστολή
πόα: 888 ἐν τοῖς κηπευομένοις λαχάνοις συναναφύονται κ. πόαι ('weeds')
ποθέω: 856 ἀσμένως δι' ὧν εὔχεται τὸ ποθούμενον λαμβάνειν, 875 ποθοῦμέν σε ἀπολαβεῖν, 878 ἐλπὶς ἐν τῷ τὰ αὐτὰ ποθεῖν
πόθος: 854 ἡ ψυχὴ ἐπτερωμένη τῷ π. τῶν κρειττόνων, 860 ἀπαιτεῖται παρ'

ἡμῶν αἵρεσίς τε κ. πόθος, 867 π. κατὰ προκοπὴν πίστεως συνίσταται
ποιέω: 885 ἐποιήθητε δίκαιοι εἶναι, 847 ('represent') τ. Διόνυσον διαστελλόμενον π., ib. Μένανδρος τ. χολὴν πεποίηκεν, 846 fin. τ. θεοὺς καταμεμφομένους π.
ποιητός: 870 τὰ π. καὶ μή
ποιητής: 868 'the Creator,' 894 'poet'
ποιητικός: 851 κατὰ τ. ποιητικὴν χάριν
ποικιλία: 862 ἀπολαυσμάτων ποικιλίαι
ποίκιλος: 902 πολλὰ τ. δελέατα καὶ π., 840 ποικίλη σωτηρία, 835 π. προκρίσεις, 875 π. ἡδοναί
ποικίλως: 874 προγυμναστέον π. τὴν ψυχήν
ποιμήν: 855 ἡ τ. ποιμένος πρόνοια εἰς τὰ πρόβατα
πόλις: 878 πόλιν οἰκῶν τῶν κατὰ τὴν π. καταφρονεῖ
πολιτεία: 835 αἱ γνωστικαὶ ψυχαὶ ὑπερβαίνουσαι ἑκάστης ἁγίας τάξεως π. πολιτείαν, 851 χάριν ὁμολογεῖ τ. γνώσεως καὶ τ. πολιτείας, ib. π. δικαία κ. ὀρθή, 852 κατὰ τὴν π. ἐνθέως ἀναστρεφόμεθα, 867 τὰ περὶ τὴν ἄλλην π. ἐπαγγέλματα, 853 οὐδεὶς ἐπιθυμεῖ πολιτείας ὀρθῆς ἀλλὰ τοῦ πολιτεύεσθαι, Clem. Hom. ind.
πολιτεύομαι: 853, 863, 886
πολιτικός: 839 οἱ νόμοι οἱ π. πράξεις ἐπισχεῖν οἷοί τε
πολυανθής: 852 αἱ π. πλοκαὶ ἐκθηλύνουσι τ. ψυχήν
πολυθρύλητος: 892 ἡ π. κατὰ τ. ἐκκλησίας αὐτῶν πρωτοκαθεδρία, 58 fin., Heliod. ix. 20 init.
πολύλογος: 861 τῇ διὰ στόματος εὐχῇ οὐ πολυλόγῳ χρῆται
πολυμερῶς: (quot.) 890
πολύς: 866 πολλῶν ὅσων μαρτυρίων ὄντων, see ὅσος: πολλοῦ γε δεῖ (initial), 861, 876, 862 c. ind. ἐπιορκήσει
πολυτέλεια: 852 π. θυμιαμάτων
πολυτελής: 850 θυσίαι μὴ π.
πολυτίμητος: 841 (quot.) π. θεοί, 847 ἡ κνῖσα ἡ π.
πολύτροπος: (quot.) π. καὶ πολυμερῶς 890
πολύφλοισβος: (quot.) 844
πολύφωνος: 856 τὰς π. γλώσσας οὐκ ἀναμένει ὁ θεός, 58, Luc. Hist. Conscr. 4
πόμα: 896 π. δίψαν οὐκ ἐπιστάμενον, ib. (quot.) πνευματικὸν π., 853 οὐδεὶς ἐπιθυμεῖ πόματος ἀλλὰ τοῦ πιεῖν, 852 πόματος ἀπόλαυσις
πονέω: 895 οὐ ζητήσαντες οὐ πονέσαντες, 889 π. ἐπὶ τοῖς καλλίστοις
πόνος: 888 πόνῳ ἕπεται εὕρεσις, 864 καρτερικὸς ἐν π., 871 τὰ ἆθλα τ. πόνων,

OF GREEK WORDS. 433

868 ἀνάγων ἑαυτὸν ἀπὸ τῶν π. ἐπὶ τὰ οἰκεῖα

πορεία: 900 εἰς πατέρα διὰ τ. πίστεως οἱ δίκαιοι τ. πορείαν ποιοῦνται

πορεύομαι: 858 ᾗ πέφυκεν τὸ δίκαιον πορεύεσθαι βαδίζων, 873 κατὰ τ. ἐντολὰς π.

πορευτέον: 894 πρὸς τ. εἰρηνοποιοῦς π., al. πορευτέα Heliod. IX. 8 fin.

πορθμεύω: 853 αἱ προαιρέσεις ὑπὸ τ. συνειδήσεων πορθμεύονται

πορίζω: act. 875 δι' ὧν ἐπαιδεύθησαν πορίζουσι τὰς τροφάς...π. τὴν ζωήν, m. 896 οἰκείας πορίζεσθαι ἀποδείξεις

ποριστικός: 839 τέχνη τις ἤτοι τ. ποριστικῶν ἢ τ. θεραπευτικῶν, Chrys. XI. 254*, cf. EUS. Pr. Ev. VIII. 14. 17 (philosophers) μηδὲν πώποτε τῶν εἰς πορισμὸν ἐπιτηδεύσαντες

πορνεία: trop. 877, 885

πορνεύω: intr. 885 π. εἰς τ. ἐκκλησίαν ὁ ἐθνικῶς πολιτευόμενος, 52 πορνεύει τὰ ὦτα, 53 πορνεύουσι οἱ ὀφθαλμοί, cf. 163 ἐκπορνεύει ἡ γεῦσις

πόρος: 852 ἡ ἀκοὴ διὰ σωματικῶν πόρων ἐνεργεῖται

ποταμός: 888 π. ῥοώδης

ποτόν: 853 πιεῖν τὸ π.

πούς: 854 τ. πόδας ἐνεγείρομεν κατὰ τ. τελευταίαν τ. εὐχῆς συνεκφώνησιν, 878 τὰ ἐν τοῖς ποσὶν ᾔδεα, 893 οὐχ οἷα τε τ. φῶς ἰδεῖν, ἀλλὰ καὶ τὰ ἐν ποσὶ παρορᾷ

πρᾶγμα: 830 fin. (pregnant force), 867 fin. (' reality ') οὐσίας κ. τὰ πρ. ωπ̓ὰ παραλαβὼν διὰ τ. λόγων τ. ψυχὴν ἐπὶ τ. ὄντα ἄγει, 868 ἡμεῖς τ. φωνῆς ἀκούομεν κ. τ. σώματα θεωροῦμεν, ὁ θεὸς δὲ τ. πρᾶγμα (πνεῦμα?) ἀφ' οὗ φέρεται τ. βλέπειν ἐξετάζει, 878 περισπώμενος ὑπὸ τ. πράγματος (sc. τῆς τροφῆς), 879 ἡ περὶ τῶν πρ. πίστις, 892 ἀρχὰς πραγμάτων, 425 ἡ ἀληθὴς διαλεκτικὴ ἐπισκοπεῖ τὰ πράγματα, 875 ἡ πραγμάτων θεωρία, 976, 883 (quot.) πρ. ἔχων πρός τινα

πραγματεύομαι: 849 πρ. περὶ τῆς ἀπὸ τῶν ζώων τροφῆς

πρακτέος: 858 ἡ κατορθωτικὴ τ. πρακτέων ἄσκησις, 869 τ. δικαίῳ τὸ πρ. γνωματεύουσα, 870 τὰ πρ. καὶ ὑπομενετέα

πραότης: 869 πραότητα ἡδονῶν σωματικῶν περιπεποιημένη

πρέπω: 858 ἡ μὴ πρέπουσα περὶ τ. θεοῦ ὑπόληψις, 860 πρέπον ἐστὶ ποιεῖσθαι, 891 τί θεῷ πρ.

πρέσβιστος: 829 τιμητέον τ. ἀρχαιοτάτην φιλοσοφίαν κ. τ. πρεσβίστην προφητείαν, ib. τὸ πρέσβ.

πρεσβύτερος: 829 πᾶς ὁ πρ., ib. τὸ πρ. ἐν γενέσει, 830 τ. βελτιωτικὴν οἱ πρ.

σώζουσιν εἰκόνα, τ. ὑπηρετικὴν δὲ οἱ διάκονοι

πρεσβύτης: 899 ὡς πρ. νεωτέροις συνεγένετο

πρόαγω: tr. 885 ἔργον τ. δικαιοσύνη ἐπὶ τὸ ἄμεινον ἕκαστον προάγειν, 875 init. πρ. τ. ψυχὴν εἰς τ. ζωήν; instr. 830 προάγων διὰ τ. ἀγαθὴν συνείδησιν

προαίρεσις: 837 ἡ θεία πρ., 858 αἱ πρ. φθάσουσι πρὸς τ. θεόν, 855 ὁ θεὸς οὐκ ἀνάγκῃ ἀγαθοποιεῖ, κατὰ πρ. δὲ εὐποιεῖ, 860 τὴν ἁγίαν πρ. τιμᾷ ὁ θεός, 876 μὴ κατ' ἀνάγκην ἀλλ' ἐκ προαιρέσεως ler, 878

προαιρετικῶς: 855 ἑκουσίως καὶ πρ. σπεύδει πρὸς σωτηρίαν

προαιρέω: m. 875 init. ἀνθρώποις ἀρέσκειν πρ.

προακούω: 897 ἵνα ἐπιστραφῶσιν οἱ προακηκοότες, Aeschin. Tim. § 145, Heliod. VI. 9

προβαίνω: 883 εἰς μέτρον ἡλικίας πρ., 884 μέχρι θανάτου πρ.

προβάλλω: m. 888 προβ. ἀλόγους αἰτίας

προγενέστατος: 899 ἡ πρ. καὶ ἀληθεστάτη ἐκκλησία

προγίνομαι: 879 fin. τὰ προγεγονότα

προγυμνασία: 865 πλείονος πρ. δεῖται

προγυμναστέον: 874 πρ. τὴν ψυχήν

πρόδηλος: 869 πρ. ἦν ἡ πίστις

προδιανύω: 901 τούτων ἡμῖν προδιηνυσμένων, 645 ἀνόητοι οἱ ἄπιστοι ἐκ τῶν προδιηνυσμένων φαίνονται, 156, 65

προδιδάσκω: 865 πρ. ἐσομένην ἡμῖν μετὰ θεῶν δίαιταν

προδοκέω: 856 fin. προδ. τὸ δίκαιον

προσείζω: 839 πρ. τὴν ψυχήν

πρόειμι: 855, 858 ἡ προκοπὴ δεῖ εἰς τὸ ἄμεινον πρ., 873 πρ. ἐπὶ τὸ ἀκριβῶς εἰδέναι

προέρχομαι: 865 εἰς τὸ ἐπὶ πλέον πρ., 883, 886

προηγούμενος: 834 (' preliminary ') ὑπερβὰς τ. προηγούμενον τ. φιλοσοφίας, cf. 434: 845 (' leading ') τὰ πρ. κεφάλαια: 835 ἐσθίοντες ἵνα ζῶσι μὲν κατὰ τ. ἀκόλουθον κατὰ δὲ τ. προηγούμενον τῇ γνώσει προσανέχωσιν (MS. -έχοντας), 927 τὰ ὀνόματα σύμβολά ἐστι τ. νοημάτων κατὰ τὸ προηγ. κατ' ἐπακολούθημα δὲ καὶ τῶν ὑποκειμένων, 831, 887, Kaye p. 67

προηγουμένως: 868 fin. οὐκ ἂν προηγουμένως πραχθείη εἰ μὴ δι' ἐκείνους, 874 γαμεῖ οὐ πρ. ἀλλὰ ἀναγκαίως, 773 τ. δρέπανον ἕνεκεν τοῦ κλαδεύειν προηγ. γέγονεν ἀλλὰ καὶ...ἀκάνθας κόπτομεν, ib. ἄνθρωπος πρ. γέγονεν εἰς ἐπίγνωσιν θεοῦ ἀλλὰ καὶ γεωμετρεῖ: (' by way of preliminary ') 831 ἡ φιλοσοφία πρ. τοῖς Ἕλλησιν ἐδόθη

M. C. 28

πρὶν ἢ τ. κύριον καλέσαι, 540, Orig. c. Cels. iii. 47, 48, Philo ii. 22 M.
προήκω: 833 (mss. προσ.) μέχρι τοῦ μικροτάτου προήκουσα ἐξέτασις
πρόθεσις: 853 κατὰ πρ. τὸν ἐκλεκτὸν ἐγνωκώς, 869 οἱ κατὰ πρ. δίκαιοι
προθυμέομαι: 880 πρ. κοινωνεῖν
προθυμία: 854 ἡ πρ. τ. πνεύματος (cf. Mt. xxvii. 41)
πρόθυμος: 867 πρ. μαθητὴς τ. κυρίου γίνεται
πρόθυρον: 858 ἐπὶ προθύροις τ. πατρὸς
προίημι: 853 αἱ προαιρέσεις φθάνουσι προϊέσαι τ. φωτὴρ τ. ἑαυτῶν
προΐστημι: 892 οἱ προεστῶτες τ. δόγματος, 889 προΐστασθαι διατριβῆς μᾶλλον ἢ ἐκκλησίας
προκαθαίρω: 839 προκαθαίρει τ. ψυχήν, 844 τ ψυχὰς πρ. ἀπὸ τ. φαύλων δογμάτων, 846 προκεκαθαρμένη ψυχή, Themist. 52*
προκαλέω: 868 οὐδ᾽ ἂν προκαλῆται αὐτὸν κατά τινα περίστασιν προκαταληφθέντα ὡραία γυνή
προκαταλαμβάνω: 868, see προκαλέω
προκατάρχω: 840 ὁ εὐεργέτης πρ. τῆς εὐποιΐας. Polyb., Plut.
προκατέχω: 894 τ. ἔθει τ. προκατεσχηκότι ἡττηθείς
πρόκειμαι: 829 πρόκειται παραστῆσαι τ. γνωστικὸν ὅσιον, 867, 864 τουτὶ ἦν τὸ προκείμενον
προκοπή: 834 ψυχὴ κατὰ πρ. ἑκάστην ἐπεκτεινομένη εἰς ἕξιν ἀπαθείας, ib. ἄγει ἐξ ἑτέρας <ἑτέρους> προκοπὴ ἐπὶ τελείωσιν, 858 πεπεισμένοι εἰς τ᾽ ἄμεινον τὴν πρ. προϊέναι ταῖς ἀρετὴν ἑλομέναις ψυχαῖς, 860 ἐνθεοι πρ., 865 μυστικαὶ πρ., 867 προκοπὴ πίστεως, 873 κορυφαιοτάτη πρ.
προκόπτω: 860 πρ. ἐπὶ τ. γνῶσιν, 870 οἱ ἐπὶ τ. γνῶσιν προκόπτοντες
προκρίνω: 882 οὐδέποτε τ. ἡδὺ πρ. τῆς οἰκονομίας, 878 προκρ. ταῦτα ἐξ ὧν εἶναι πεπίστευκεν
πρόκρισις: 835 διὰ προκρίσεων ποικίλων τ ἀπηλγηκότας ἐκβιάζονται μετανοεῖν (this sense peculiar to Cl.)
προκριτέον: 894 ἐν τ. αἱρέσεσι πρ. ἔριν, cf. 236 τῆς ἐσθῆτος τὸ χρειῶδες προκρ. See προσκριτέον
προλαμβάνω: 854 μαθέτωσαν προειλῆφθαι, 855 προλ. τ. αἴτησιν, 866 προλαβὼν ἔχει τὸ ἰσάγγελος εἶναι
προμήθεια: 887 πλείονος πρ. δεόμεθα εἰς τ. ἐξέτασιν
προνοέω: 892 τοῦ φιλοσοφεῖν προνοοῦνται.
προνοητικός: 859 δυνάμει λογικῇ κ. γνωστικῇ κ. πρ. καθίσταται ἡ ἐπιστήμη
πρόνοια: 874 ἡ τοῦ οἴκου πρόνοια

(divine) 833 ἐντεῦθεν ἡ πρ. ἴδια κ. δημοσίᾳ κ. πανταχοῦ, 855 ἡ μακαρία πρ., ib. ἡ πρ. θεόθεν ἥκει, ib. αἱ προσεχεῖς τῆς πρ. οἰκονομίαι, 868 πρὸς τῆς ἀγαθῆς πρ. μερίζεται, 867 εὐθέως ἀκούσει τρόπους ἐπιστεύσαν, 874 ἀκόνα σώζων τῆς τ. ἀληθείας προνοίας (ms. τῇ τῆς ἀληθείας προνοίᾳ), 896 πρὸς τῆς πρ. κολαζόμεθα
προοράω: 876 ἡ οἰκονομία τὸν σώζεσθαι μέλλοντα προορωμένη
προορίζω: act. 900 πρ. ὁ θεὸς (cf. 1 Cor. ii. 7, 1 Pet. i. 20): p. 832 (quot.) τοῖς προωρισμένοις: m. 951 οὐ προωρίσατο τὸν πρὸ αἵματος
προσπαραδίδωμι: 896 τὰ προσπαραδεδόμενα μαθεῖν ἠδυνήθησαν
προσπέτης: 871 μηδὲν αὐτοῖς προσπετὲς συνεγνωκέναι, 889 δοξοσοφία πρ.
πρὸς δέ adv. 836 π. δ. καὶ τ. ἑταιότητας κοσμεῖ, 4, 24 πρὸς δέ γε καὶ, 26, 38, and passim
προσαγορεύω: 900 ἀπὸ ὑποθέσεων (? ὑποστάσεων) προσαγορεύονται, 862 σίδηρον Ἄρην πρ.
προσάγω act. 836 πρ. θυσίαν, 845 init. πρ. καθαρμούς, 852 οἱ βάρβαροι τ. ἱερατικὸν γένος εἰς βασιλείαν πρ., 856 βασιλικωτάτην θεραπείαν πρ., 886 πρῶτον τοῦτο πρ. ἡμῖν, 895 πρ. τῇ ἀληθείᾳ τοὺς μὴ ἀνιάτους: p. 877 οἱ πειρασμοί προσάγονται: m. 900 τὴν Ματθίου αὐχῶσι προσάγεσθαι δόξαν
προσαγωγή: 874 πρ. τις ἐπὶ τ. βέλτιον
προσανατείνω: 854 πρ. τ. κεφαλήν
προσανέχω: c. dat. 885 τῇ γνώσει πρ. 889 αἰσθητοῖς πρ., 891 ὀνόμασι μόνοις πρ. 22 γηΐνοις προσανέχειν πλάσμασι, 51 fin. ἀγαλματίοις προσανέχοντες Chrys. xi 624 c, d. 628 e, cf. Plac Phil. i. 6
προσαποτίθημι: 881 τὰ ἐκτὸς σὺν τῇ τ. σώματος ὑγιείᾳ Ἰὼβ προσαπέθετο πάντα
προσαύξω: 878 πρ. τὴν εὐεργεσίαν
προσβολή: 857 εὔθικτος κατὰ τὴν πρ. τ. θεωρίας, 878 ἡδόμενος κατὰ τὴν πρ. τῆς ὄψιος. see ἐπιβολή
προσδεκτός: 849 ἡ ἀποκάθαρσις τ ἀλόγου μέρους τ. ψυχῆς πρ. τ. θεῷ
προσδέχομαι: 875 (quot.) παρθένοι προσδέχονται τ. κύριον, 883 οἱ προσδεξάμενοι ὑψηλῶς τ. λόγον
προσεδρεύω: 858 τ. θεωρίᾳ ἀδιαλείπτως πρ., 63 (quot.) Aristot.
πρόσειμι: 838 ἄρχων ἑαυτοῦ τῇ ἀληθείᾳ προσεισιν, 871 πᾶν τὸ πρ., 887 προσιόντες τῇ διδασκαλίᾳ, 848 fin. τοῖς προσιόντας ἐξαπατῶσιν, 875 δεξόμεθα τὰ προσιόντα γυμνάσια εἰς συνάσκησιν, 879 ἵνα τις πεπαιθὼς προσίῃ τ. εὐχαῖς
προσεκπονέω: 883 ποιεῖν ἐθέλουσι κ

προσεκπονεῖν τ. δόγματα, 871 προσεκ. ζητοῦντα τ. ἀλήθειαν, 565 δεῖ τούτοις προσεκ. ἕτερα
προσεμφερής: (quot.) 837 πρ. θεῷ
προσεξευρίσκω: 896 πρ. τι τοῖς ὑπ' ἐκείνων ἀληθῶς ῥηθεῖσιν, Diog. Laert. x. 63, Philo
προσεχής: c. gen. 834 ἡ πρ. τοῦ κυρίου περιτροπή, 865 καθαροὶ γενόμενοι κατὰ τὸ πρ. τοῦ κυρίου, Sext. Emp. P. H. II. 240: c. dat. 881 προσεχεστάτη τῷ παντοκράτορι, 824 (πᾶσα ὠφέλεια ἐπιτελεῖται) κατὰ τ. προσεχὲς ὑπὸ τ. προσεχοῦς τ. πρώτῳ αἰτίῳ κυρίου ἐπίταξιν, 847 προσεχεστέρα <ἐσχάρα> γινομένη τῇ κνίσῃ, 852 προσεχέστερον οἰκειοῦται τ. θεῷ, 886 πρ. γενόμενος τῷ κυρίῳ, 857 πρ. τῇ πανσθενεῖ δυνάμει γενόμενος, 858 πρ. τῷ μεγάλῳ ἀρχιερεῖ γινόμενοι: abs. 835 οἱ πρ. ἄγγελοι, 855 αἱ πρ. τῆς προνοίας ἐνεργοῦνται οἰκονομίαι, 860 ὁ θεὸς προσεχεστέρᾳ τιμήσας ἐπισκοπῇ, 679 ἡ πρ. τ. σωτῆρος ἐνέργεια, 822 προσεχεστέρα ἐπισκοπή, 798 ὁ γνωστικὸς τ. προσεχεστέραν ἀναμάσσεται ὁμοιότητα
προσέχω: 891 οὐχ ἁπλῶς ἀποφαινομένοις προσέχομεν, 894 ἐὰν προσσχῇ τις Ἰσχομάχῳ
προσεχῶς: 865 πρ. ὑποτεταγμένη, 852 προσεχέστερον οἰκειοῦται θεῷ ὁ γνωστικός
προσηγορία: 865 θεοὶ τὴν πρ. κέκληνται οἱ σύνθρονοι τ. ἄλλων θεῶν
προσηκόντως: 864 ὁσίως κ. πρ. τὸν θεὸν προστρεπόμενος
προσήκω: imp. 878 τοῦτο μόνον ὁρᾶν βούλεται ὃ προσῆκεν αὐτῷ, 883 χρώμενος ὡς προσῆκεν, cf. 211: 866 δεῖ κατὰ τὸ προσῆκον ἐπὶ τ. κρεῖττον μεταβάλλει: 893 (debet personal) τοιόσδε ὁ βίος εἶναι τῷ πιστῷ προσήκει: 838 τὰ προσήκοντα, 855
προσήλυτος: 884 οὐ τοὺς κατὰ πίστιν μόνον ἀλλὰ κ. τοὺς πρ. λέγει, cf. 951 οὐ τὸν πρὸς αἵματος οὐδὲ τ. πολίτην οὐδὲ τ. προσήλυτον
προσίημι: m. 852 τὰ λεγόμενα ἡδονῆς χάριν οὐδὲ ὄναρ προσίεται, 887 μή τι οὖν κάμνων τις οὐ πρ. ἰατρόν; 891 τὰ μὲν μὴ προσίεσθαι τ. προφητικῶν, 893 ἵνα εὐλόγως δόξωσι μὴ προσίεσθαι τ. γραφάς
προσκριτέον: 894 ἔριν [ἐν] τ. αἱρέσεσι προσκριτέον (MS. προκρ.)
προσκυνέω: 843 πᾶν ξύλον πρ., 847 τὸν ἵππον πρ., 885 τὸ θέλημα θεοῦ πρ.
προσλαλέω: 854 μετὰ σιγῆς πρ. τῷ θεῷ
προσλαμβάνω: 877 πρ. γνωστικὸν νόημα
προσμένω: c. dat. 865 προσμένει τῇ θεωρίᾳ ἀποκατάστασις

πρόσοδος: 855 ἡ πρὸς τ. θεὸν πρ.
προσοικειωτέον: 894 χαρᾷν τ. ἐκκλησίᾳ πρ.
προσομιλέω: 885 αὕτη ἡ ἐνέργεια τ. γνωστικοῦ προσομιλεῖν τ. θεῷ, 886 ἀπερισπάστως πρ. τῷ κυρίῳ, 860 πρ. τῷ θεῷ
προσπάθεια: 880 τὰς πρ. τὰς σαρκικὰς μεμίσηκεν, 1000, Porphyr. Ad Marcell. 32, Vita Polycarpi 7, Isid. Pelus. Ep. I. 810, cf. ἀπροσπαθής
προσπαράληψις: 861 ὅρκος ἐστὶν ὁμολογία μετὰ πρ. θείας, Philo
προσπίπτω: 893 fin. φαντασία τις πρ.
προσποιέω: m. 872 πρ. σωφρονεῖν
πρόσταγμα: 880 ποιῶν τὰ πρ. τ. κυρίου ὑπερευφραίνεται
πρόσταξις: 832 εἰσὶ συνδιανενεμημένοι προστάξει θείᾳ ἄγγελοι κατὰ ἔθνη
προστασία: 862 ἡ πρ. τῆς τ. ἑτέρων διδασκαλίας, 822 αἱ πρ. τῶν ἀγγέλων
προστήκομαι: c. dat. 881 προστετηκὼς ἀνθρωπίνοις ἀγαθοῖς, 79 προστετηκὼς ἡδοναῖς, Galen VIII. 657, Themist. 251ᵇ, Ael. V. H. III. 81, Chrys. XI. 207ᵃ, 297ᵈ, 891ᵃ, Cobet Var. Lect. ed. 2, 519
προστρέπω: 864 τ. θεὸν προστρέπεται
προσυπακούω: 886 πρ. τὸ ἐνθέον
προσφέρω: act. 850 θυσίας δεῖ προσφέρειν τ. θεῷ: m. 862 ὀμνύναι ἐστὶ τὸ ὅρκον προσφέρεσθαι, 891 ἐν πᾶσιν οἷς προσφέρονται ῥητοῖς: pass. 849 ὑπὲρ ἁμαρτιῶν προσφέρονται αἱ θυσίαι, 874 ἡ διὰ τέκνων προσφερομένη πεῖρα, 881 πενία κ. νόσος ἐπὶ νουθεσίᾳ προσφέρονται
πρόσφορος: 853 τὴν πρ. ἀρετὴν ἔχουσιν αὐτῷ, 895 δύο παιδείαι πρόσφοροι ἑκατέρα τ. ἁμαρτιῶν
προσφυής: 896 τὰ πρ. τοῖς θεοπνεύστοις λόγοις ὑπὸ τ. ἀποστόλων παραδιδόμενα
πρόσωπον: 865 (quot.) πρ. πρὸς πρόσωπον τ. θεὸν ἐποπτεύειν, 873 (quot.) πρ. πρὸς πρόσωπον τ. θεὸν ὁρᾶν, 866 πρ. θεοῦ ὁ σωτήρ
προσωτέρω: 891 πρ. χωρεῖν
προτίθημι: m. 867 τὸ αὐτὸ πρ.
προτρεπτικός: 841 ὁ πρ. λόγος, Paed. I. § 1 ter, Stob. Flor. XCV. 21; title of books of Demetr. Phaler. (Diog. Laert. V. 81), and Cleanthes (VII. 175)
προτρεπτικῶς: 869 ἐπιφωνῆσαι εὖ μάλα πρ.
προτρέπω: act. 852 τὸ συμπόσιον ἀφικέσθαι πρ., 860 σωτηρίαν ἐμπνεῖ τοῖς μὲν προτρέπων μόνον, 858 ὁ προτρέπων λόγος: m. 941 προτρεψάμενον αὐτὸν πρὸς φυγήν
προφανής: 871 πρ. τὸν κίνδυνον ἔχει ὁ ἀνδρεῖος
πρόφασις: 888 ματαία ἡ πρ., adv. dat.

σαρκοφαγιῶν προφάσει αἱ θυσίαι ἐπινενόηνται, cf. Philipp. i. 18 εἴτε προφάσει εἴτε ἀληθείᾳ, Clem. Hom. ind.

προφασίζομαι: 887 οὐδὲ ὁ τ. ψυχὴν νοσῶν προφασίσαιτο ἂν τ. αἱρέσεις

προφητεία: 829 τ. πρεσβίστην προφητείαν, 892 τῆς προφητείας καταφρονοῦσι, 894 ἡ δοθεῖσα διὰ τ. κυρίου προφ., 891 τὸ σῶμα κ. τὸ ὕφος τῆς πρ., 832 αἱ θεῖαι πρ., 898 τὰς πρ. εἴργουσιν ἑαυτῶν τῆς ἐκκλησίας

προφήτης: 829 (quot.) ὁ νόμος κ. οἱ πρ., 852, 866, 868 ὁ πρ., 869 πατριάρχας, πρ., ἀγγέλους, 890 προφῆται οἱ ἅγιοι κ. τὸ εὐαγγέλιον κ. οἱ ἀπόστολοι, 892

προφητικός: 891 προφ. γραφαί, ib. τὰ μὲν μὴ προσίεσθαι τῶν προφητικῶν, 829 αἱ προφ. λέξεις

προφητικῶς: 887 πρὸς τ. κυρίου πρ. ἄρπτο, Martyr. Polycarpi 12 fin.

προφορικός: 864 ἐν μονῇ τῇ τ. προφ. λόγου τὸ τ. σοφίας ὄνομα φαντάζεται, ib. μηδὲ ἐν τῷ πρ. λόγῳ ψεύσασθαι, Philo π. 13 M.

πρόχαρος: 861 πρ. περὶ τὸ ψεύσασθαι, 892 τοῖς ἐν μέσῳ κ. προχείροις (MB. -ρως) ἐντυχόντες, 445 πρόχειρον τ. πίστιν, 869 τὰ πρ. πάντα τ. κόσμου καλὰ οὐκ ἀγαπᾷ, 893 fin. προχείρους τ. φαντασίας ποιητέον

πρωία: 880 πρωίας ἀναστάς

πρωτοκαθεδρία: 892 ἡ πολυθρύλητος πρ., Hermas Mand. xi. 12

πρωτοκλισία: 892 τ. συμποτικὴν πρ. ἀσπάζονται

πρωτοπαθέω: 868 συμπάσχει τ. σώματι ἀλλ' οὐ πρ. κατὰ τ. πάθος

πρωτουργός: 833 πρωτουργοῦ (MB. -γὸς) κινήσεως δύναμις ὁ υἱός

πταίρω: 843 (quot.)

πτάρνυμαι: 843 (quot.)

πτερόω: 854 ἡ ψυχὴ ἐπτερωμένη τ. πόθῳ

πτέρυξ: 848 περιπνεῖται κατὰ τὴν τ. πτερύγων ἐπιθλιψιν τ. ἐντομῆς

πτηνός: 850 τὰ πτηνὰ τὸν αὐτὸν τ. ἡμετέραις ψυχαῖς ἀναπνεῖ ἀέρα

πῦρ: 880 οὐ πυρὸς μετουσίᾳ φωτεινός, 896 φέρειν ὡς πῦρ ἢ σίδηρον, 851 π. οὐ τὸ παμφάγον κ. βάναυσον ἀλλὰ τ. φρόνιμον, cf. Heracl. B. 26 πάντα τὸ πῦρ κρινέει καὶ καταλήψεται

πύργος: 883 (quot.) διηγήσασθε ἐν τοῖς πύργοις, ib. ὑψηλοὺς ὡς π. ἔσεσθαι

πυρός: 887 ἐπισπαρήσεσθαι τῷ πυρῷ τ. ζιζάνια

πυρόω: (quot.) 851 χολῆς πυρουμένης

πυρρός: (quot.) 841 Θρᾷκες π. τοὺς θεοὺς διαζωγραφοῦσιν, 843 ἔρια πυρρά

πωλέω: (quot.) 843

πώποτε: = ποτε 862

ῥᾳθυμέω: 896 ῥᾳθυμεῖν ἐπειγόμενοι, ib. ῥᾳθυμοῦσιν οἱ τὸ ταῖς ἡδοναῖς αὐτῶν συναιρούμενον ἐκλεγόμενοι, 89

ῥᾳθυμία: 859 τ. ἀγγέλων τινὲς ὑπὸ ῥᾳθυμίας ὀλισθήσαντες χαμαί

ῥᾴθυμος: 832 ὑπὸ τρυφῆς ῥᾴθυμος, 829 ῥᾴθυμον τὸ μὴ ἐπεσκέφθαι τὸ κατεπεῖγον

ῥέπω: 859 βρίθουσά τις ἀπονία (MB. γωνία). κάτω ῥέπουσα, 894 ῥ. ἐπὶ τὰ ἐνδόξα

ῥῆσις: 883 μεταφράζοντες τ. ῥῆσιν

ῥητός: 883 τ. διάνοιαν τοῦ ῥ. παραστήσομεν, 886 κατ' ἔλλειψιν λέγεται τὸ ῥ., 891 ῥητὰ προσφέρονται

ῥήτωρ: 894

ῥινάω: (quot.) 847

ῥοώδης: 888 ἐπὶ ποταμὸν ῥ. φέρει

ῥυθμός: 848 ῥυθμῷ ἕλκει (MB. ῥυμουλκεῖ)

ῥυμουλκέω: 848 ὅσα ἀναπνεῖ ῥυμουλκεῖ (?) τ. ἀέρα

ῥυπάλεος: (quot.) 850 σῶμα ῥ.

ῥύμη: 869 ψυχὴ ἐν ῥώμῃ καθεστηκυῖα

ῥώννυμι: 869 ἐν πάσῃ περιστάσει ἐρρωμένη ἡ ψυχή

σαρκικός: 854 ὁ δεσμὸς ὁ σ., 876 σ. ἡδονή, 880 προσπάθειαι σ.

σαρκοφαγία: 849 σαρκοφαγιῶν προφάσει αἱ θυσίαι ἐπινενόηνται, 850 τάχ' ἄν τις τ. γνωστικῶν ἀσκήσεως χάριν σαρκοφαγίας ἀπόσχοιτο

σάρξ: 850 σφριγῇ ἡ σ., 878 σαρκὸς κάλλος βλέπει τῇ ψυχῇ, 894 ἐν σαρκὶ περιπολῶν θεός: pl. 839 διὰ σαρκῶν ἐνεργοῦσιν ἐξουσίαι, 885 οἷον σάρκας εἶναι τ. ἁγίου σώματος τούτους καλεῖ bis, 850 σαρκῶν ἐμφορήσεις

σαφήνεια: 901 ἡ τ. λογίων ἀκριβὴς σ., Philo

σαφηνίζω: 894 τ. ἀλήθειαν διὰ τ. ἀκολουθίας τ. διαθηκῶν σαφηνίζουσι

σέβασμα: 829 τὸ πρέσβιστον σεβάσματι κ. σιγῇ σεβαστὸν κ. σεπτὸν κυριώτατα

σεβαστός: 829, see σέβασμα

σέβω: 868 σ. τ. ποιητήν

σεμνός: 841 σ. ὁ θεός, 852 ὁ γνωστικὸς σ. διὰ τὴν ἐπὶ τὸ θεῖον ἐπιστροφήν, ib. πάντων σ. ἀπόλαυσις, 894 ἡ ἀλήθεια αὐστηρὰ καὶ σ.

σεπτός: 829, see σέβασμα

σημαίνω: 829 ἐπὰν τὰ σημαινόμενα ἐνδειξώμεθα, 874 κατ' ἄλλο σημαινόμενον λέγεται, 891 οὐ τὸ σημαινόμενον σκοποῦντες, ib. τὰ σημαινόμενα ὑπαλλάττοντες, μετατιθέμενοι, 852 τῶν σημαινουσῶν τι φωνῶν νόησις, 897 ὃ σημαίνει ἡ λέξις

σημεῖον: 'cross,' 880 τὸ σ. βαστάσαι τ. θάνατόν ἐστι περιφέρειν, 939 fin. ὁ σωτὴρ πάσχει ἀπὸ γενέσεως μέχρι τ. σημείου

σήπω: 849 ἀπ. ὑς ἔχει τ. ψυχὴν ἵνα μὴ σαπῇ τὰ κρέα
σιγή: 829 ἀπ. σιγῇ σεβαστόν, 854
σιδήρεος: 834 σ. δακτύλιοι
σίδηρος: 854, 863, 896
σιμός: (quot.) 841
σιτέομαι: 850 σ. σάρκας
σκέπη: 848 σκέπη δεήσεται
σκευάζω: 851 p. θυμίαμα ἐκ διαφόρων φύσεων σκ.
σκιά: 882 ἕπεται τ. ἔργα τ. γνώσει ὡς τ. σώματι ἡ σκιά
σκάλλη: 843, (quot.) 844
σκληροκάρδιος: 831 ἀπ., LXX., cf. Mk. xvi. 14 ὠνείδισεν τὴν σκληροκαρδίαν, Rom. ii. 5 κατὰ τ. σκληρότητα κ. ἀμετανόητον καρδίαν θησαυρίζεις σεαυτῷ ὀργὴν ἐν ἡμέρᾳ ὀργῆς
σκόλοψ: 876 ἐπιθυμίαι τρίβολοι κ. σκόλοπες εἴρηνται
σκοπός: 871 σκ. αἱρεῖσθαι
σκοτίζω: 889 πιθανοῖς ἐπιχειρήμασι σκοτίζουσι τ. ἀλήθειαν, cf. σκοτισμός 214
σκύλα: 841 (quot.) σκ. βροτοφθόρα
σοφία: σ.)(γνῶσις 844 ἐν μονῇ τῇ τ. προφορικοῦ λόγου τὸ τ. σοφίας ὄνομα φαντάζεται, def. 874, 832 σ. σύμβουλος θεοῦ ὁ υἱός, 897 ἡ σ. ἡ κατὰ τ. μάθησιν ἐμφυτευθεῖσα
σοφίζομαι: mid. tr. 896 τὰ ὑπὸ τ. ἀποστόλων παραδιδόμενα σοφίζονται δι' ἑτέρων ἐγχειρήσεων, 446 σ. τὰ ὀνόματα: pass. 67 Ἑβραῖοι σεσοφισμένοι
σοφιστής: 863 ἐπὶ σωτηρίᾳ ψεύσεται κατὰ τοὺς σ., 889 ἀπὸ τ. ἀληθείας ἀποσπῶνται τινα οἱ σ.
σπανίως: 852, 862, 876
σπείρω: 880 ὁ σπείρας τ. σάρκα
σπέρμα: 880 τὰ παρ' αὐτῷ κατατιθέμενα στ., 882 στ. σώζων τὸ Ἀβραάμ
σπερματικός: 883 ταῦτα στ. εἴρησθω, Clem. Hom. xvii. 18 ἐν τῇ ἐκ θεοῦ τεθείσῃ <νοήσει> σπερματικῶν πᾶσα ἔνεστιν ἡ ἀλήθεια
σπίλος: 882 τοὺς τ. ψυχῆς στ. ἀποκεκαθαρμένοι
σπλάγχνα: 848 σπλ. δοῦναι τ. θεῷ
σπόνδυλος: (quot.) 847
σποράδην: 891 ὀλίγας στ. ἀπανθιζόμενοι φωνάς, 901 σποράδην κ. διερριμμένως ἐγκατασπείραντες
σπουδάζω: 853 στ. λαβεῖν, 857
σπουδαῖος: 837, 841, 870
σταγών: (quot.) 901 ὡς σ. ἀπὸ κάδου
στάδιον: 839 τὸ μέγα στάδιον ὁ καλὸς κόσμος, 840 παγκρατιάζουσι εἰς τὸ στάδιον οἱ ἀθληταί, 87 τὸ τῆς ἀληθείας στ., 876 ἡ κακόφρων ἐν τοῖς στ. ἐπιτελουμένη τιμωρία
στέγω: (quot.) 874 πάντα στ.
στεναγμός: (quot.) 861 στ. ἀλάλητος
στέφανος: 871 εἰσὶ στ. ἀνδρῶν τε κ. παίδων, 872 στεφάνων χάριν σωφρονοῦσι
στεφανόω: 889 τ. ἀληθινὴν νίκην κατὰ πάντων στεφανούμενος τ. παθῶν
στοιχεῖον: 850 ἀὴρ ἐγκέκραται τ. λοιποῖς στ.
στοῖχος: 901 ἐν στοίχῳ καταπεφυτευμένοι παράδεισοι
στόμα: 901 ἀπὸ στ. ἔχων, 861 ἡ διὰ στόματος εὐχή, 868 διὰ στ. ἀνθρωπίνου κύριος ἐνεργεῖ
στόμιον: 890 στ. ἐμβαλὼν τ. ἀλόγῳ πνεύματι
στοχάζομαι: 902 οὔτε τ. φράσεως στοχάζονται οἱ στρωματεῖς
στρατηγός: 893 τάξιν ἔταξεν ὁ στρ. τ. στρατιώτῃ, 894
στρατιά: 831 πᾶσα ἀγγέλων στρ.
στρωματεύς: 886 εὖ ἂν ἔχοι εἰς τὸν ἑξῆς προϊέναι στρ., 901 ἐοίκασιν οἱ στρ. οὐ παραδείσοις, ὄρει δὲ συσκίῳ, 902 οὔτε τ. τάξεως οὔτε τ. φράσεως στοχάζονται οἱ στρ.
συγγενής: 840 σ. ἀποτέλεσμα τ. θεοῦ ὁ ἄνθρωπος, 850 τὰ πτηνὰ τ. ψυχὴν συγγενῆ (NB. συγγενεῖ) τῷ ἀέρι κεκτημένα, 865 τὸ σ. τῆς ψυχῆς θεῖον, 873 ἡ ψυχὴ πρὸς τὸ συγγενὲς χωρεῖ, 889 ἀπ. μαθητὴς κ. σ. θεοῦ
συγγινώσκω: 871 μηδὲν αὑτοῖς προπετὲς συνεγνωκέναι, 885
συγγυμνάζω: 829 (quot.) οἱ τ. αἰσθητήρια συγγεγυμνασμένοι, 890 κριτήριον συγγεγυμνασμένον τὰ δέοντα αἱρεῖσθαι
συγκαταβαίνω: 863 σ. μέχρι τῆς συμπεριφορᾶς, 888 σ. εἰς ζητήσεις
συγκατάθεσις: 861 ἐπὶ τῆς σ. μόνον τὸ ναὶ τάσσει ἐπίρρημα, 862, 863, 872 ἡ περὶ ταὐτὸ ὁμόνοια σ. ἐστι
συγκατατίθεμαι: 888 μὴ συγκαταθέμενοι οἷς δέον πείθεσθαι, ib. συγκατατίθενται εἶναι ἀπόδειξιν
συγκαταχράομαι: 841 τ. κατεπειγούσῃ σ. ἱστορίᾳ, 615
συγκάττυσις: 852 βρωμάτων σ. (H. J. συγκατάρτυσις)
συγκαττύω: (κατα-σύω, cf. καμμύω) 893 σ. ψεύσματα
σύγκειμαι: 850 τ. θυμίαμα, τὸ ἐκ πολλῶν γλωσσῶν συγκείμενον
συγκινέω: p. σ. μακροτάτη σιδήρου μοῖρα τῷ πνεύματι
συγκλείω: 834 τὴν ἀπιστίαν εἰς τ. παρουσίαν σ.
συγκληρόω: 899 τῇ τοῦ ἑνὸς φύσει συγκληροῦται ἐκκλησία ἡ μία
συγκομιδή: 830 σ. ἀρίστῳ ἐργάζεται, Herodian i. 1. 1
συγκομίζω: 830 p. οἱ καρποὶ σ.
συγχράομαι: 829 ὕστερον τ. γραφαῖς σ., 877 τ. βίῳ ὡς ἀλλοτρίῳ σ., 883 λέξεσι σ., 895

συγχρηστέον: 853 τῇ τοιᾷδε σ. εὐχῇ
συγχωρέω: 834 τὸν κακίᾳ ἡσθέντα συνεῖναι οἷς εἴλετο σ., ib. τοὺς μὴ ἐπαίοντας ἀφηπιᾶσαι σ., 886 fin. σφίσιν αὐτοῖς τὰ μέγιστα ἐγνωκέναι συγχωροῦντες, cf. Philostr. V. Ap. I. 21 οὐ συνεχώρει ἑαυτῷ ἀδεῶς ζῆν
συκῆ: 901 ὅροι συκαῖς καταπεφυτευμένων
συλλαμβάνω: 860 act. τούτῳ σ. ὁ θεός, ib. m. τοῖς ἀξίοις γενομένοις συλλαμβανόμενος, 890 ἐξ αὐτῆς κ. οὐκ ἐκ συδυασμοῦ συλλαβοῦσα
σύλληψις: 856 πάντα τ. συλλήψει αὐτῇ (MS. αὑτῆς) ἕπεται τὰ ἀγαθά
συμβαίνω: 882 ἐπ' οὐδενί τ. συμβαινόντων ταράσσεται, 885 ἁγίῳ εἶναι συμβαίνει, see συμβιόω
συμβάλλω: m. 850 συμβάλλεσθαι τὴν τ. τραγελίων κρεῶν βρῶσιν πρὸς ἐπιληψίαν
συμβιόω: 839 ἡ τῶν συμβιούντων (MS. συμβάντων) συνήθεια
σύμβολον: 863 ἄγαλμα κυρίου κατὰ τὸ τ. δυνάμεως σ.
σύμβουλος: (quot.) 832 σοφία σύμβ. θεοῦ
συμμαρτυρέω: 892 τὸ ὑπὸ τ. εὐαγγελίου συμμαρτυρούμενον
συμπαραλαμβάνω: 839 σ. τὰς γραφάς (read by S. for MS. συμπεριλαμβάνω)
συμπάρειμι: 851 ὁ συμπαρὼν ἀδιαλείπτως τ. θεῷ
συμπάσχω: 868 σ. τῷ σώματι τῷ φύσει παθητῷ
συμπεριφέρομαι: 863 συμπεριφερόμενος Ἰουδαίοις bis, 868 σ. τοῖς ἀναγκαίοις, Epict. Ench. 78, Stob. Flor. LXIV. 31
συμπεριφορά: 863 ὁ μέχρι τῆς σ. συγκαταβαίνων διὰ τὴν τῶν δι' οὓς συμπεριφέρεται σωτηρίαν, 881 ἀσφαλὴς ἐν συμπ., μὴ λάθῃ ἡ συμπ. διάθεσις γινομένη, see not. crit.
συμπλέκω: 855 συμπλακεῖσα τ. προνοίᾳ ἡ τ. γνωστικοῦ ὁσιότης
συμπληρόω: 864 ἡ γνῶσις συμπληροῦται διὰ τῆς τ. θείων ἐπιστήμης
σύμπνοια: 848 ἡ σ. ἐπὶ τ. ἐκκλησίας λέγεται κυρίως
συμπόσιον: 852 τὸ σ. ἐπαγγέλλεται τ. φιλικὸν κ. ὁμονοητικόν
συμποτικός: 852 σπανίως εἰς τ. ἑστιάσεις τὰς σ. ἀπαντῶν, 892 σ. πρωτοκλισίαν τ. ψευδωνύμου ἀγάπης
συμπράττω: 860 συνεύχεται περὶ ὧν συμπράττειν καθήκει
συμφανής: 899 συμφανὲς ἐκ τ. προγενεστάτης ἐκκλησίας τὰς μεταγενεστέρας αἱρέσεις κεκαινοτομῆσθαι
συμφέρων: 882 οὐδέποτε τὸ ἡδὺ κ. τὸ συμφέρον προκρίνει τῆς οἰκονομίας, ib. τὰ ἐπὶ τῷ συμφέροντι γινόμενα, 861 διὰ τὸ συμφέρον πάντα ἐνεργεῖ, 868 οὐδέποτε τὸ ἡδὺ πρὸ τ. συμφέροντος

αἱρεῖται, 875 μὴ τὰ συμφέροντα ἀλλὰ τὰ τέρποντα αἱροῦνται οἱ πολλοί, ib. τὰ σ. εὐχόμεθα
σύμφορος: 875 πάντα ἐπὶ συμφόρῳ δεξόμεθα τ. γυμνάσια ἃ προσφέρει ἡ σὴ οἰκονομία, 892 fin. ὅτα οὐκ ἀκούοντα τὸ σ., μόνον δὲ τοῖς πρὸς ἡδονὴν ἀνηγμένα
συμφωνία: 862 τὸ ἀληθεύειν μετὰ συμφωνίας γίνεται τῆς κατὰ τὸ ἀληθές
σύμφωνος: 864 ἡ γνῶσις σύμφωνος αὐτῇ τε κ. τῷ θείῳ λόγῳ
σὺν καί: 881 ἀφαιρεθῆναι τὰ ἐκτὸς σὺν καὶ τῇ τ. σώματος ὑγιείᾳ, 3 τ. ποιητὰς σὺν κ. τῷ ἄλλῳ χορῷ, 47 σὺν κ. τῇ ἱερείᾳ
συνάγω: 884 ἐξ ὧν συνάγεται σαφῶς ('is inferred'), 851 τ. θυμίαμα τὸ κατὰ τ. αἴνους συναγόμενον, 899 fin. ἡ ἐκκλησία σ. εἰς ἑνότητα πίστεως τοὺς ἤδη καταταγμένους
συναγωγή: 'congregation' 863
συναιρέω: (?) 860 τὸ πᾶν συναιρεῖται πρὸς τ. τελειότητα, 886 τὸ πάρπαν ταῖς ἡδοναῖς αὐτῶν συναιρούμενον ἐκλέγουσι
συναίρομαι: 837 οἱ θεοὶ συναίρονται τ. ἀκολασίαις, H. would read instead of συναιρέομαι in 860 and 896
συναισθάνομαι: 878 ὅταν ἡδομένου ἑαυτοῦ συναίσθηται, 147 σ. τῆς ἑαυτοῦ παρρησίας
συναίσθησις: 852 ἡ ὀξυτάτη σ. τῶν ἀγγέλων, 978 ἔχοντες σ. τοῦ πυρός, 831 εὑρετικὸν κ. ἐπινοητικὸν ἡ σ., 971 σ. κολάσεως, Oenom. ap. Eus. Pr. Ev. VI. 7. 10
συναναβαίνω: 865 συναναβαίνει τῷ κυρίῳ, ἔνθα ἐστίν
συναναφύομαι: 888 ἐν τ. κηπευομένοις λαχάνοις σ. πόαι (rare)
συναποφέρω: 868 οὐ συναποφέρεται τοῖς ἀλλοτρίοις συμπεριφέρεται δὲ τοῖς ἀναγκαίοις, 487 διακρίνειν τ. φαντασίας κ. μὴ συναποφέρεσθαι αὐταῖς
συνάπτω: 838 τινὰ μὲν συνημμένα τινὰ δὲ διεζευγμένα, cf. Clem. Hom. VI. 24 τὰ στοιχεῖα εἴτε ἀλλήλων διεστάλκει... εἴτε ἀεὶ ἀλλήλοις συνῆπτε, ὑπὸ τεχνίτου νοῦ πρὸς τὸ οἰκεῖον συναρμόζεται, ib. 25 ἀνάγκη τινὰ εἶναι ἀγέννητον τεχνίτην, ὃς τὰ στοιχεῖα ἢ διεστῶτα συνήγαγεν ἢ συνόντα ἀλλήλοις πρὸς ζῴου γένεσιν τεχνικῶς ἐκέρασε
συνασκέω: 876 καλὸς κ. ἀγαθὸς εἶναι σ., Iambl. Vit. Pyth. 68, 188, 225
συνάσκησις: 860 πάντα ἐκπεπλήρωκεν ὁ γνωστικὸς εἰς τὴν σ., 869 ἐκ μαθήσεως καὶ σ., 872 ἡ τ. βίου σ., 875 εἰς σ. βεβαιότητος, 901 σ. γνωστική, 317 τ. δύναμιν ἐκ συνασκήσεως αὔξειν, 443 ἐκ σ. ηὐξηκὼς τὸ δύνασθαι, 734 init.
συναύξω: tr. 870 ἀρετὴ ἐκ φύσεως, ἀσκήσεως, λόγου συνηυξημένη, 331 συναύξει

τ. ἐπιβολὴν ἡ συνάσκησις: init. 895 ἄμφω εἰς τ. τελείαν ἀγάπην συναύξουσιν

συνάφεια: 862 σ. καὶ κοινωνία πρὸς τ. θεῖον, Plut.

συναφιστάνω: 854 συναφιστάνειν τ. λόγῳ τ. σῶμα τῆς γῆς πειρώμενοι

συνδιανέμω: 832 εἰσὶ συνδιανενεμημένοι ἄγγελοι κατὰ ἔθνη

συνδυασμός: 890 ἐξ αὐτῆς οὐκ ἐκ συνδυασμοῦ συλλαβοῦσα, Philo

σύνεγγυς: 854 c. gen. ὡς σύνεγγυς ἔσοιτο τ. θεοῦ

συνείδησις: 853 αἱ προαιρέσεις ὑπὸ τῆς σ. πορθμεύονται, 862 τῇ σ. τῇ θείᾳ κ. τῇ ἑαυτοῦ ἀρκεῖται, 880 ἀγαθῇ σ., 318 ἀρίστῃ πρὸς τ. αἵρεσιν ἢ σὺν., 445 θεόθεν ἥκει ἡ σ.

σύνειμι: 839 σύνεστι τ. ὁμοφύλοις ἔν τε γῇ κ. οὐρανῷ, 854 συνεῖναι σπεύδων τ. θεῷ, see συνίημι

συνεκφώνησις: 854 ἡ τελευταία τ. εὐχῆς σ. (rare)

συνελόντι: 854, 878 ὁ γνωστικὸς συνελόντι εἰπεῖν τ. ἀποστολικὴν ἀπουσίαν ἀναπληροῖ

συνεπιγράφω: 860 p. σφαλερὸν τοῖς ἑτέρων ἁμαρτήμασι συνεπιγράφεσθαι, Philo

συνεπιλαμβάνω: m. 886 συνεπιλαμβάνονται τ. ἀποριῶν αἱ περὶ τ. ἄλλην διδασκαλίαν αἱρέσεις, Luc. Prom. 18 Hemst.

συνεπίσταμαι: (c. dat. rei) 870 σ. τούτοις τὰ μὴ δεινά

συνέργεια: 871 διὰ ἀφροσύνην κ. διαβόλου συνέργειαν συνίσταται

συνεργέω: 858 εὔχεται συνεργῶν ἅμα, 856 ὁ εὐπροαίρετος σ. πρὸς τ. λῆψιν, 859 σ. πρὸς τὸ διαγενέσθαι, 860 ὁ ἰατρὸς ὑγείαν παρέχεται τοῖς συνεργοῦσι πρὸς ὑγείαν bis, 867 σ. πρὸς τ. μάθησιν

συνεργός: 835 σ. πρὸς ἀρετήν

σύνεσις: 850 ἄθετος ἡ τοιαύτη τροφὴ πρὸς σύνεσιν: (=conscience) 844 (quot.), cf. Tobit iii. 8 οὐ συνιεῖς ἀποπνίγουσα τ. ἄνδρας;

συνεύχομαι: 860 ὁ γνωστικὸς σ. τοῖς κοινότερον (MB. καιν·) πεπιστευκόσι

συνεχής: 861 μνήμη σ., 829 τὸ συνεχὲς τ. λόγου, ib. ἐπιμέλεια σ., 859 (adv.) συνεχὲς ὑγιαίνειν εὔχεται

συνέχω: 838 τὰ συνέχοντα (n. on p. 28, l. 4)

συνεχῶς: 851 σ. τὸν ὅλον βίον τοῦτο πράττει

συνήθεια: 897 ἀντικλεῖς, ὥς φησιν ἡ σ., 889 ἡ τῶν συμβάντων (? συμβιούντων) συνήθεια

συνήθης: 861 of persons, see Clem. Hom. ind.

συνήλυσις: 893 μεταγενέστεραι τῆς ἐκκλησίας αἱ ἀνθρώπιναι σ. 165

σύνθετος: 850 τ. θυμίαμα τὸ σ.

συνθήκη: 862 μηδὲν παραβαίνων τῶν κατὰ τ. συνθήκας bis, 887 bis

σύνθρονος: 865 σ. τῶν θεῶν, Orig. c. Cels. III. 50 σύνθρονοι ταύτῃ ἀρεταί, Chrys. XI. 358* σ. τοῦ θεοῦ, Philo

συνίημι: 829 τοῖς μηδέπω συνιεῖσιν τὰς λέξεις, 886 συνήσουσιν ὅπως εἴρηται, 897 μεγαλοφρόνως τὰς γραφὰς συνίετε, 892 μὴ οἵους τε εἶναι συνεῖναι τ. οἰκεῖα, 862 πρὸς τ. συνιέντας (? συνιόντας) εὐγνωμοσύνην ἔχειν χρή

συνίστημι: p. 867 πόθος κατὰ προκοπὴν πίστεως συνίσταται, 870 δι' ἄγνοιαν τ. δεινῶν συνίσταται ἡ δειλία, 871 διὰ διαβόλου συνέργειαν σ., ib. ἡ δι' ἄγνοιαν συνισταμένη πρᾶξις οὐκ ἤδη ἄγνοια, 879 τὸν τ. ἁγίων χορὸν συνιστάμενον ἔχει, m. 896 ἐνιστάμενοι θείᾳ παραδόσει ὑπὲρ τοῦ τ. αἵρεσιν συστήσασθαι

σύνοδος: 886 ὁ κολλώμενος τ. κυρίῳ τὸ διάφορον τῆς σ. γένος

σύνοιδα: 844 πᾶς ἁγνὸς ὁ μηδὲν ἑαυτῷ κακὸν συνειδώς (MB. συνιδών), 849 τ. ὃς συνειδέναι αὐτοῖς εἰς οὐδὲν χρησίμοις, 852 ἡ τοῦ συνειδότος ἐπαφωμένη τ. ψυχῆς δύναμις

συνομολογέω: 849

σύνταγμα: 849

συντείνω: 856 σ. τὸ πνευματικὸν πᾶν εἰς φωνὴν τ. νοητήν

σύντομος: 865 ἡ πίστις σ. τῶν κατεπειγόντων γνῶσις, 108 ὁδὸς σ.

συντόμως: 866 σ. τὸν γνωστικὸν ἐμήνυσεν

σύσκιος: 901 ὄρος σ. καὶ δασύ, 92 ὄρος ἀγναῖς ὕλαις σ.

σύστασις: 900 ἡ ἀρχὴ τ. συστάσεως κατὰ τ. μονάδα ἐστίν

συστέλλω: ('to brace') 886 τὸ ἐξ ἀσκήσεως εἰς ἀπάθειαν συνεσταλμένον, 877 συστελλόμενος ἐφ' αἷς ἐπεγκυλίεται τῇ τ. βίου ἀνάγκῃ, cf. 128

σφαλερός: 860 σφαλερὸν τοῖς ἑτέρων ἁμαρτήμασι συνεπιγράφεσθαι

σφάλλω: m. 890 σφ. μέγιστα, ib. <ἐν> τοῖς πλείστοις τῶν κατὰ μέρος σφάλλονται

σφόδρα: 889 init. πανοῦργος σφ.

σφριγάω: 850 σφρ. περὶ τὰ ἀφροδίσια

σχεδόν: (of courtesy) 839, 872, 894

σχῆμα: 846 θεὸς οὐκ ἀπεικονίζεται ζῴου σχήματι, 869 σχήματι κατεσταλμένος

σχηματίζω: 851 ἡ παρουσία ἀνδρὸς ἀγαθοῦ σχ. τὸν ἐντυγχάνοντα, 824, Dio C.

σχιδανόπους: 901 ὡς σχιδανοπόδων τῇ διπλόῃ τ. πίστεως ἐπερειδομένων, Arist.

σάζω: 855 οἱ σωζόμενοι, ib. ὁ σωζόμενος οὐκ ἄκων σωθήσεται, 867 σ. τὴν ἀκολουθίαν, 853 ἡ μὴ πρέπουσα ὑπόληψις οὐδεμίαν σώζει θεοσέβειαν

σῶμα: 891 τό σ. καὶ τὸ ὕψος, 886 σ. πνευματικόν, 885 σ. ἀλληγορεῖται

σωματικός: 852 σ. πόροι, σ. δύναμις, 870 λύται σ., 860 τῆς σ. ψυχῆς κατεξανίσταται

σωμάτιον: 860 ἀθλητὴς τὸ σ. εὖ μάλα ἀσκήσας

σωτήρ: contrasted with κύριος 833, 837 ἰδίᾳ τε ἑκάστοις κ. κοινῇ πᾶσιν εἶς ὢν σωτήρ

σωτηρία: 835 ἡ τοῦ ὅλου σ., ib. ἡ τῶν κρειττόνων σ., 855 ἡ κατ' ἐπίγνωσιν σ.

σωτήριος: 834 αὗται αἱ σ. περιτροπαὶ ἀπομερίζονται κ. χρόνοις κ. τόποις (cf. 130 σωτ. δίαιτα), 866 μεταβολὴ σ., 865 παιδεία σ., 835 δικαιοσύνη σ., 889 τ. σωτήριον ἐν ᾗ ὥρᾳ ἐπιγνῷ (?)

σωφρονίζω: 895 τ. αἱρετικοὺς καταμαθόντας σωφρονισθῆναι

σωφροσύνη: 872 ἡ δι' αὑτὴν αἱρετὴ σ. αὐτοκράτορα τ. ἄνδρα κατασκευάζει, 838 etym., 875 ἡ χήρα διὰ σωφροσύνης αὖθις παρθένος

τακτός: 854 ὥρας τ. ἀπονέμουσιν εὐχῇ

τἀληθοῦς: 888, see θατέραν, and τἀδελφοῦ 960

ταμιεῖον: 861 τὸ τ. τῆς ψυχῆς, cf. 157, 858 (quot.) ἐρευνᾶν τὰ τ.

τάξις: 834 βελτίων τ. ἐν τῷ παντί, 835 ἑκάστης ἁγίας τάξεως ὑπερβαίνουσι τ. πολιτείαν, 838 τίνα ἕκαστον ἔχει τ. τάξιν, 839 ἐν τάξει πάντα πράττων, 855 ἣν τάξιν ἐνεχειρίσθησαν, 902 τ. τάξεως οὐ στοχάζονται οἱ στρωματεῖς, 872 ἐν υἱοῦ καταλεγεὶς τάξει, cf. 136 βοηθήματος ἔχει τ.

ταπεινός: 853 εἰς ταπεινὰς ὑπονοίας ἐκτρέπεται

ταράσσω: 882 ἐπ' οὐδενὶ ταράσσεται, 893 ὀφθαλμοὶ τεταραγμένοι

τάσσω: 833 οὐκ ἂν βελτίων διοίκησις ἀνθρώπων εἴη τ. θεῷ τῆς τεταγμένης

ταύτῃ: (initial) 850, 830, 831, 832 and passim

ταὐτόν: 845 τ. καὶ ὅμοιον, 870 ἀμήχανον ἅμα τῷ αὐτῷ τ. ἐναντία κατὰ ταὐτὸν (MS. τὸν αὐτόν) κ. πρὸς τὸν αὐτὸν ἀπαντᾶν χρόνον, 872 τὸ ταὐτὸν ἕν ἐστι

ταὐτότης: 835 ταυτότητι τῆς ὑπεροχῆς τετιμημέναι, 837 μόνος θεὸς ὁ ἐν ταυτότητί τ. δικαίας ἀγαθωσύνης ὤν, 973, Basil Ep. 129. 4 (III. 220 c), 189. 6 fin., 7 fin., Philo

τε δέ: 888 τάς τε ζητήσεις ἐκτρεπομένων ἀποφευγόντων δὲ τ. διδασκαλίας

τέκνον: 897 ἡ τέκνοις ἐμφυτευθεῖσα σοφία

τέλειος: 881, 886 τ. ὡς ὁ πατήρ, 886 τ. ἰατρός, 869 τὸ τέλειον τῆς ἕξεως, cf. Lightfoot on Phil. iii. 15

τελειότης: 852 τὸ ἡγεμονικὸν τῆς τελειότητος, 859 ἀγάπης τ. τελειότητα αἰτήσεται, 872 τελ. ἀνδρείας, 876 εἰς μαρτύριον τελειότητος, 877 νηστεύει κατὰ τὴν τ. εὐαγγελίου τελειότητα

τελειόω: 833 οἱ διὰ πίστεως τελειούμενοι, 864 διὰ γνώσεως τελειοῦται ἡ πίστις

τέλειος: 886 γίνεσθε τέλειοι τελείως ἀφέντες τ. ἁμαρτίας, 882 τ. βιοῖ

τελείωσις: 854 τελ. τοῦ κατ' ἀγάπην δρωμένου, 834 τὴν διὰ πίστεως τελείωσιν, 864 ἡ γνῶσίς τ. τις ἀνθρώπου, 865 ἡ τ. τῆς ψυχῆς, 883 ἡ τ. τοῦ πιστοῦ δι' ἀγάπης

τέλεον: adv. 859 μηδέπω τ. ἐκ τῆς εἰς τὴν διπλόην ἐπιτηδειότητος ἐκθλίψαντες ἑαυτούς, 860 τ. ἀπεσπασμένοι τῶν τ κακίας ἔργων, 873 τ. καθαρὰ γενομένῃ, 45, 884, 888, 40, 69, 98 f.

τελέως: 860 ἀγαθὸς τ.

τέλος: 861 τρία ἐστὶ πάσης πράξεως τέλη, τ. καλόν, τ. συμφέρον, τ. ἡδύ, 865 ἐπὶ τέλει παραδίδοται, 882 ἐπὶ τέλει ἐνδείκνυται τ. ἐνεργήματα, 883 τὸ τέλος εἰς θεωρίαν περαιοῦται, 895 τέλη τ. γνωστικοῦ ἐνταῦθα διττόν, pl. 864

τεμενίζω: 837 ἐν δικαίου ψυχῇ τεμενίζεται κ. ἐνιδρύεται ὁ πάντων ἡγεμών

τέμνω: 882 τ. τὸν οὐρανὸν καὶ ἅπτεται τῶν θρόνων τῶν ἄκρων, 852 fin.

τερπνός: 875 ἐνέργημα τ. ὑφορᾶται, ib. πῶς ἂν εἴη τ. τὰ περὶ τὴν βρῶσιν;

τέρπω: 874 τὰ τέρποντα αἱροῦνται οἱ πολλοί, 876 fin. οὐ τέρπεται τ. σταδίοις

τεταγμένως: 856 τ. διέποντες καθ' ἣν ἐνεχειρίσθησαν τάξιν ἐκ θεοῦ

τετράς: 877 ('Wednesday'), 744, Lobeck Aglaoph. 430—434, Constit. Apost. v. 15. 20, VII. 23, Socrates H. E. v. 22 ἐν Ἀλεξανδρείᾳ τῇ τετράδι κ. τῇ λεγομένῃ παρασκευῇ πάντα τὰ συνάξεως γίνεται δίχα τῆς τ. μυστηρίων τελετῆς

τεχνάζομαι: 854 init. τὴν ἐπιστροφὴν τεχναζόμενος

τέχνη: 839 τ. τις τῶν ποριστικῶν, 845 παιδιαῖς τέχνης γίνεται θεός, 875 τ. τέχνας μανθάνειν, ('system') 889

τεχνικός: 858 τῷ τεχνικῷ τεχνικῶς ἕκαστα ἀποδίδοται. 889 τὰ διὰ τοῦ κ λογισμοῦ τεχνικὰ λόγων

τεχνικῶς: 858, see τεχνικός

τεχνίτης: 891 ἔχουσί τι πλέον οἱ τ. τῶν ἰδιωτῶν

τηλικοῦτος: 896 τ. ἄνδρες, 867 ἡ τοσαύτη κ. τηλικαύτη θεωρία

Τιβέριος: 898 οἱ Τιβερίου χρόνοι

τίθημι: m. 842 (quot.) τ. τοῦτο σημεῖον, 862 βεβαίας τ. τὰς συνθήκας

OF GREEK WORDS.

τιθηνέω: m. 889 ὁ ἀναγεννῶν κ. τιθηνούμενος τὴν ψυχὴν τὴν ἐξειλεγμένην, cf. 123, 174, Themist. 225 B : p. Paed. i. 45 init.
τίκτω: 841 τ. ἐν τῷ ἱερῷ, 890 τέτοκεν κ. οὐ τέτοκεν φησίν (quot.)
τιμάω: act. 860 θεὸς προσεχεστέρᾳ τιμᾷ ἐπισκοπῇ, m. 860 τὴν προαίρεσιν τὴν ἁγίαν τιμώμενος (where H. J. reads τιμῶν ἢν δι), p. 848 τιμώμενον χαίρει τὸ θεῖον, 854 ὥραι εὐχαῖς τετιμημέναι
τίμιος: 829 τίμιον ἅπαν τὸ ὑπερέχον ἡγεῖται, 841 τ. ὁ θεός, 846 ὁ τίμιος τ. θεῷ, 857 τὸ πάντων τιμιώτατον, 899 τὸ ἄκρως τίμιον κατὰ τὴν μόρφωσιν ἐπαινεῖται
τιμωρέω: m. 895 οὐ τιμωρεῖται θεός, κολάζει μέντοι
τιμωρία: 865 κόλασις κ. τ., 895 τ.)(κόλασις, κακοῦ ἀνταπόδοσις ἡ τιμωρία, 876 τ. κακούργων, cf. Arist. Rhet. i. 10. 17 ἡ μὲν κόλασις τ. πάσχοντος ἕνεκα, ἡ δὲ τιμωρία τ. ποιοῦντος ἵνα ἀποπληρωθῇ with Cope's n.
τοίνυν (initial): 853 τοίνυν ὁ γνωστικὸς τὴν εὐχὴν ποιεῖται (?), in apod. 91 ἀνάγκη τοίνυν
τολμάω: 891
τολμηρότερον: (adv.) 854 τ. εἰπεῖν
τόπος: 835 εἰς ἀμείνους ἀμεινόνων τόπων τόπους ἀφικνοῦνται, 845 ἐν τόπῳ περιγράφειν, ib. πάντα ἐν τόπῳ, 856 τ. ἱερός, 878 ἵνα μὴ ὁ τ. ἀναγκάζῃ, 900 ἀπὸ τόπου προσαγορεύεται: 841 κατὰ τ. τόπου γενόμενος, 901 τ. ὁ ἠθικός, 469 (the Mosaic law gave to the Greeks) ἀρχὴν παντὸς τ. ἠθικοῦ τόπου
τράγειος: 850 τὰ τρ. κρέα
τράγος: 850 τὸν τρ. ἐπὶ διοτομπήσαι τ. κακῶν ὁ νόμος θύει
τραγῳδία: 844 ἡ τρ. λέγει
τραπεζίτης: 887 (quot.) οἱ δόκιμοι τρ. τὸ κίβδηλον νόμισμα διακρίνουσιν
τρέφω: 842 (quot.) ἀλεκτρυὼν τρεφόμενος, ib. διὰ μικροψυχίαν τοῦ τρέφοντος, 848 τ. θεὸν ἀνορέκτως τρεφόμενον ποιοῦσιν, ib. τ. θηρία ἐκ τῆς τ. οἰκείου σώματος ἀναθυμιάσεως τρέφεται, 867 τὸ θυμοειδὲς ἀλόγως τρ.
τριάς: 854 οἱ γνωρίζοντες τὴν μακαρίαν τῶν ἁγίων τριάδα μονῶν, 710, 588, 542
τρίβολος: 876 ἐπιθυμίαι τρίβολοι εἰρήνται
τρίβω: 872 οἱ τὸν ἐργάτην τρίβοντες βίον
τρίτος: 833 τὰ πρῶτα κ. δεύτερα κ. τρίτα
τριττός: 893 τριττὴ θεραπεία οἴησεως
τριχῇ: 854 διανομαὶ τρ. διεσταμέναι
τρόπος: 'character' 856 ἐξετάζεται διὰ τῆς εὐχῆς ὁ τρόπος, 864 τελείωσις κατὰ τὸν τρόπον, 873 τ. αὐτὸν τρ. ἐπὶ τ. γνωστικοῦ εὖρος: 840 ὥσπερ τρόπον ὁ ἥλιος φωτίζει, 855, 887 ἐκ παντὸς τρόπου: 886 ὁ πρῶτος τ. κυριακῆς ἐνεργείας τρ. ('dispensation')
τροφή: 846 init. σκέψις κ. τροφῆς τὸ θεῖον δεήσεται, 848 fin. θεὸς οὐκ ἐνδεὴς τροφῆς, 848 al διὰ τ. ὀσφρήσεως, al διὰ τ. στόματος τροφαί, 849 τρ. ἀπὸ ζῴων, ib. ἡ διὰ τῶν σαρκῶν τρ., 850 τρ. ἄθετοι πρὸς σύνεσιν, 875 πορίζουσι τὰς τρ., ib. ἀτροφία τ. ψυχῆς ἡ ἄγνοια, τρ. δὲ ἡ γνῶσις, 880 τῶν εἰς τροφὴν οἰκείων καταμεγαλοφροσύνη
τρυγών: 849 ἡ τρ. καὶ ἡ περιστερά
τρυφή: 882 ὑπὸ τρυφῆς ῥέθυμοι
Τύριος: 846 Τυρίου χειρὶ δεδαιδαλμένων (MB. ἀγύρτου)
τῦφος: 897 οὐ τῦφος ἐνεποίησεν ὁ κύριος
τυφόω: 896 εἴ τις (MB. ἦτις) τετυφῶσθαι τὴν λέξιν (sc. φυσιοῦν) ἐρμηνεύειν ὑπολάβοι
τυχηρός: 870 τὰ λεγόμενα τυχηρὰ δεινὰ ταῦτα τῷ σπουδαίῳ οὐ φοβερά

ὑβρίζω: 840
ὑγεία: 860 ὑγείαν παρέχεται ὁ ἰατρὸς τοῖς συνεργοῦσι πρὸς ὑγ., 872 ὑγείας χάριν σωφρονεῖν, 881, see Jannaris p. 85, § 148[b]
ὑγιαίνω: 859 συνεχὲς ὑγ.
ὕδωρ: 896 (quot.) ἡ διδασκαλία τ. σωτῆρος ὕδωρ ζωῆς γνωστικῆς, 850 ἀὴρ ἐγκέκραται τῷ ὕδατι
υἱοθεσία: (quot.) 882
υἱός: 851 ὁ υἱὸς κ. λόγος, see under 'God'
ὕλη: 837 κακῶν αἰτία ὕλης ἀσθένεια, 845, 882 ἡ περισσῶσα ὕ.
ὑλικός: 845 ἀγάλματα ἐκ τ. ὕλης τ. ἀργῆς ἀργὰ καὶ ὑλικά, 850 ἔρεισμα (MB. δείγμα) ὑλικῆς διαμονῆς
ὑμνέω: 852 init. πλέομεν ὑμνοῦντες
ὕμνος: 861 ψαλμοὶ κ. ὕμνοι παρὰ τ. ἑστίασιν
ὑπαγορεύω: 830, 870 and 882 ὁ λόγος ὑπ., 891 ὑπ τ. ὄψος τ. προφητείας ὑπ.
ὑπάγω: p. 839 ὑπαγόμενος ταῖς ἐντολαῖς, 596 εἰς πίστιν ὑπ., 532 ἐκ τῆς ἀδικίας εἰς δικαιοσύνην ὑπ.
ὑπακοή: 833 ὑπ. τ. ἐντολῶν, 806 ὑπ. τ. εὐαγγελίου
ὑπακούω: 899 τοῦ Πέτρου ὑπήκουσεν (al. ἐπήκ.)
ὑπαλλάττω: 891 τὰ σημαινόμενα ὑπαλλάττοντες
ὑπεξαιρετέον: 894 εἰ μαχόμενα δόγματα ὀφείλεσθαί τινας δοκεῖ, ὑπ. ταῦτα
ὑπεράνω: 837 ὑπ. <ὧν> καθάπερ θηρίων ὁ γνωστικὸς γενόμενος, 838 ὑπεράνω πάντων τῶν περιστατικῶν γενόμενοι

φιλικός: 852 τ. φιλικὸν κ. ὁμονοητικὸν ἐπαγγέλλεται τ. συμπόσιον
φιλοδοξία: 871 οἱ μὲν φιλοδοξίᾳ ὑπομένοντες παῖδες ἐν πίστει, 897 τ. ἰδίαις φιλοδοξίαις χαριζόμενοι, Philo
φιλόδοξος: 38, 887, see φίλαυτος
φιλοθεάμων: 895 ὁτῳ ὑποδεῖξαι τ. φιλοθεάμοσι, 654 (from Plato) the true philosopher is τῆς ἀληθείας φιλοθεάμων, 442, 873, 656 φιλοθεάμονος ψυχῆς ὄψις ἀθαμβής κ. ὀξυδερκής, Philo I. 38 M., ib. 566
φιλόθεος: 829, 830 φ. κ. θεοφιλὴς ὁ θεοπρεπής, 864 ὁ φιλάνθρωπος κ. φιλόθεος παιδευτής
φιλοκερδής: 836, see φιλήδονος
φιλομαθία: 895 ἀποτρέψαι τῆς εἰς τ. αἱρέσεις εὐεμπτωσίας τοὺς φιλομαθοῦντας
φιλόνεικος: 836 φ. ἐκδεξάμενοι τ. νόμον, cf. Cobet *Collectan.* 359, 364-5
φιλοπάτωρ: 830 φ. ὁ τιμῶν τ. πατέρα, Jos. *Bell. Iud.* I. 21. 9
φιλόπονος: 902 φ. καὶ εὑρετικοί
φίλος: 855 φ. τ. θεοῦ, 869 ἡ μέχρι τῶν φιλτάτων τελεία διάθεσις
φιλοσοφέω: 887 οὐ δεῖ ὀκνεῖν ἤτοι φιλοσοφεῖν ἢ Ἰουδαΐζειν, 892 τοῦ φιλοσοφεῖν προνοοῦνται
φιλοσοφία: 839 φ. ἡ Ἑλληνικὴ προκαθαίρει τ. ψυχήν, 892, see 'philosophy'
φιλόσοφος: 887 οἱ ἀνδρεῖοι παρὰ τοῖς φιλοσόφοις, 894
φιλοσωματία: 872, see φιλοτιμία
φιλοτιμία: 872 οὔτε διὰ φιλοτιμίαν οὔτ' αὖ διὰ φιλοχρηματίαν οὐδὲ διὰ φιλοσωματίαν οὐδεὶς σώφρων, 883 ἄμεινον ὑπερθέσθαι τ. τοιαύτην φ., 892 πάντα ὑπὸ φ. ὑπομένουσι
φιλοχρηματία: 872, see φιλοτιμια
φιλοχρήματος: 836, see φιλήδονος
φίλτρον: 880 αἱ προσπάθειαι αἱ σαρκικαὶ πολὺ τ. ἡδονῆς τὸ φ. ἔχουσι, 228 φίλτρα ἔρωτος
φλέψ: 848 φλέβες κ. νεῦρα
φλήναφος: (quot.) 842
φλυαρέω: 895 φλυαρεῖν ἐπιχειροῦσι
φοβερός: 870 τὰ δοκοῦντα φ., 838
φόβος: 895 ἄσκησις ἐκ φ. παιδαγωγουμένη
φοιτάω: (quot.) 843
φονεύω: 868 init., see μοιχεύω
φράσις: 902 τῆς φράσεως οὐ στοχάζονται οἱ στρωματεῖς
φράσσω: 870 τ. ὅπλοις τ. κυρίου πεφραγμένος
φρήν: 884 φρένας καλὰς ἐκ μετανοίας μεταλαβεῖν, 916 κοινὰς φρένας κεκτημένος
φρονέω: 848 εὖ φρ., 863 ἀληθῆ φρ., 878
φρόνησις: 871 ἕξις ἡ φρ., 838

φρόνιμος: 851 πῦρ οὐ τ. βάσανον ἀλλὰ τὸ φρ., 875 φρ. ψυχαί
φροντίζω: 832 φρ. πάντων, 873 ὀλίγα φρ. τινός
φροντίς: 887 διὰ πλείονος φρ. ἐρευνητέον τ. ἀλήθειαν
φρουρά: 879 οὐδὲ ἔξω ποτὲ τῆς ἁγίας φρ. γίνεται, 861 τ. φρουρὰν ἔχειν παρ' ἑαυτοῦ
φρουρός: 865 ὁ τ. πίστεως κ. ἀγαπῆς θεὸς κ. φρ.
φυσικός: 894 ἐὰν προσέχῃ τις Ἀριστοτέλει φ. αὐτὸν ποιήσει
φυσικῶς: 839 φ. ὕστερον ἐπιγίνεται μέρη τινὰ τ. σώματος
φυσιόω: 859 τῷ ἀναπόβλητον τ. ἀρετὴν πεποιημένῳ φυσιοῦται ἡ ἕξις ('becomes his nature'), 896 ἡ δοκοῦσα γνῶσις φυσιοῦν λέγεται εἴ τις (ΚΒ. ἥτις) τετυφῶσθαι τ. λέξιν ἑρμηνεύειν ὑπολάβοι, 897 ὁ λόγος τῶν πεφυσιωμένων (quot.), ib. τ. πεφυσιωμένα τέκνα τῆς σοφίας
φύσις: 870 φ., ἄσκησις, λόγος, 860 ἡ φ. αὐτῶν ἡ ἀγαθή, 831 ἡ υἱοῦ φ., 867 init. ἐκ φ. θυμοειδής, 838 τί κατὰ φ. ἢ παρὰ φ., 843, 849 περὶ τοῦ κατὰ φ. βίου, 882 ἁμαρτία παρὰ φ., 831 ἡμᾶς ὡς ἄλλης γεγονότας φύσεως μὴ οἷον τε εἶναι συνεῖναι διαβάλλουσιν
φυτεία: 902 ἀναμέμικται ἡ φ. καρποφόρων κ. ἀκάρπων δένδρων
φυτεύω: 876
φυτόν: 848 ὅμοιον φυτῷ ποιήσουσι θεόν
φωλεός: 848 τὰ φωλεύοντα θηρία, Philo II. 553 M., Eus. *H. E.* III. 32
φωνέω: 868, see φέρω
φωνή: 848 μία φ. ἡ κοινή, 850 θυμίαμα ἐκ πολλῶν φωνῶν συγκείμενον, 853 ἡ φ. τῶν προαιρέσεων, 890 ἡ κυριακὴ φ., 891 φωνῇ κυρίου παιδευόμεθα, ib. φ. κυρίου πασῶν ἀποδείξεων ἐχεγγυωτέρα, ib. ἀπανθιζόμενοι φωνᾶς, 852 αἱ σημαίνουσαί τι φωναί
φῶς: 831 ὅλος φ. πατρῷον, 880 εἶναι ὅλος φ. βούλεται, 865 ἀπὸ τ. γνώσεως τὸ τ. ἀγάπης ἀξίωμα ἐκλάμπει ἐκ φωτὸς εἰς φῶς, ib. φ. οἰκεῖον, 866 ἐσόμενος φῶς ἐστός. 893 τὸ φ. τῆς ἀληθείας
φῶς: 844 (quot.) τόσα σώματα φωτῶν
φωτεινός: 880 οὐ πυρὸς μετουσίᾳ φωτεινός
φωτίζω: 836 n. on ἐκφωτ., 840

χαίρω: 842 χαῖρε ἐπὶ τῷ σημείῳ
χαλεπαίνω: 841, 868
χαλκός: 874 χ. καθαλμένος
χαμαί: 834 οἱ κακοὶ ἀποπίπτουσι χ., 859 ὑπὸ ῥᾳθυμίας ὀλισθήσαντες χ., 869 τὰ τ. κόσμου καλὰ οὐκ ἀγαπᾷ, ἵνα μὴ καταμείνῃ χ.
χαρά: 894 χαρὰ τῇ ἐκκλησίᾳ προσοικειωτέα

χαρακτήρ: (quot.) 837 δόξης χ. ὁ μονογενής, 866 χαρακτῆρα τ. δόξης τ. υἱὸν προσεῖπεν, τ. χαρακτηρίσαντα ὅτι θεὸς μόνος ὁ παντοκράτωρ, 874 κηρὸς μαλάσσεται ἵνα τὸν ἐπιόντα χ. παραδέξηται, 875 ἐξομοιοῦσθαι τῷ δεδομένῳ χ.
χαρακτηρίζω: act. 866 ὃν ἀγαθῷ χ. ὁ σωτὴρ ἡμῶν, ib. see χαρακτήρ: p. 872 τὸ ἄριστον τῷ ἐπὶ χαρακτηρίζεται, 136: m. 156, Philo
χαρίεις: 842 χαρίεν τὸ τ. Ἀντιφῶντος
χαριέντως: 844 χ. ὁ κωμικὸς Δίφιλος κωμῳδεῖ τ. γόητας, 846 Φερεκράτης χ. πεποίηκε τ. θεοὺς καταμεμφομένους τ. ἀνθρώποις
χαρίζομαι: 837 ὁ υἱὸς πατρὶ ἀγαθῷ χ., 858 μηδ' ὁτιοῦν τ. πάθεσι χ.
χάρις: 851 κατὰ τ. ποιητικὴν χάριν, ib. χ. ὁμολογεῖ τ. γνώσεως, 852
χεῖλος: 854 μηδὲ τὰ χ. ἀνοίγοντες
χείρ: 854 τ. χεῖρας εἰς οὐρανὸν αἰρομεν
χειραγωγέω: 877 τ. ὄψεις πρὸς τὰ ἀόρατα χ., 92, 108 init.
χειροποίητος: (quot.) 845, 863
χείρων: 880 φυγεῖν τὰ χείρονα)(τυχεῖν τ. ἀρίστων, see κρείττων
χερσαῖος: 850 τ. χερσαῖα καὶ τ. πτηνὰ τὸν αὐτὸν τ. ἡμετέραις ψυχαῖς ἀναπνεῖ ἀέρα
χέω: 840 λόγοι πάντῃ κεχυμένοι
χήρα: 875 ἡ χ. διὰ σωφροσύνης αὖθις παρθένος
χιτών: 868 τὸν χ. ἀπεδύσατο
χνοῦς: (quot.) 901
χοίρειος: 850 φασὶ πλείστην ἀνάδοσιν ἐκ χοιρείων γίνεσθαι κρεῶν
χολή: (quot.) 847, 851
χόνδρος: 843 ἀλῶν χόνδρους κ. δᾷδας δεδίασι, 18, 19
χορηγέω: 858 ὁ θεὸς ὅ τι ἂν συμφέρῃ τ. ἀγαθοῖς χορηγεῖ, 880 δύναμις τ. θεοῦ διὰ τ. Χριστοῦ χορηγουμένη
χορηγία: 875 ἡ ἐκ τ. ἀργυρίου εἰς τ. ποικίλας ἡδονὰς χ., 881 χορηγίαν ὧν δέονται εὐξεται γενέσθαι
χορός: 858 τὰ περὶ θεοῦ διειληφὼς πρὸς αὐτῆς τ. ἀληθείας χοροῦ μυστικοῦ, 861 ὁ γνωστικὸς ἑαυτὸν ἐνοποίει τ. θείῳ χορῷ, 879 κἂν μόνος εὐξηται τὸν τ. ἁγίων χορὸν συνιστάμενον ἔχει, 880 ἐν τ. χοροῖς τ. ἁγίων, 885 ἡ ἐκκλησία ὁ πνευματικὸς κ. θεῖος χ. (cf. Lightfoot Ign. vol. II. p. 41), 6 χ. προφητικός, 656 τὸ ἄτακτον κ. ὑλικὸν ἔξω θείου χοροῦ ἵστασθαι δεῖ
χράομαι: κέχρημαι used in present sense, 838 n. on κατακέχρηται
χρεωκοπέω: 878 χρεωκοπεῖσθαι οἴεται περισπώμενος ὑπὸ τ. πράγματος
χρεών: (=χρῆναι) 844 τ. ψυχὰς προκαθαίρειν χρεών φαμεν ἀπὸ τ. φαύλων δογμάτων
χρησιμεύω: 850 χοίρειον κρέας χρ. τοῖς τὸ σῶμα ἀσκοῦσιν, 854
χρήσιμος: 838 χρ. ἡ ἀληθῶν, 895 κολάζει πρὸς τὸ χρ. τοῖς κολαζομένοις
χρῆσις: 852 χάριν ὁμολογεῖ τ. δωρεᾶς κ. τ. χρήσεως, 857 ἀνεπιστήμων τ. χρήσεως, 858 εἰς τ. ἀναγκαίαν χρ.
χρηστεύομαι: 884 ὁ ἐξομοιούμενος θεῷ παντὶ τῳ χρηστεύεται
χρηστότης: (quot.) 552
χρῖσμα: 852 χρίσματος ἀπόλαυσις
χριστιανισμός: 829 τ. χρ. ὑπογράφειν, Ignat. Magn. x. with L.'s n.
χριστιανός: 864 ἡ τ. χριστιανοῦ θεοσέβεια, ib. οὐκ ἄθεοι ὁ χρ., 870 τὰ τῷ ὄντι δεινὰ ἀλλότρια χριστιανοῦ τ. γνωστικοῦ
χρόνος: 880 πολλῷ τῷ χρόνῳ ἀσκῆσαι
χρυσός: 845 τὸ ἐκ χρ. χρυσοῦν, 879 χρυσὸν τὸν ἐπὶ γῆς κ. ὑπὸ γῆν ὑπεροπᾷ
χυδαῖος: 894 τῷ ἔθει ἡττηθεὶς γέγονεν χ., 900 Ἰουδαῖοι οἱ χ.
χωρέω: tr. 833 οὐκ ὤφθη τοῖς χωρῆσαι μὴ δυναμένοις, 809 τοῦτο ἐχώρουν μαθεῖν, 867 θείαν χωρῆσαι διδασκαλίαν, 892 μὴ χωρήσαντες τὸ μεγαλεῖον τ. ἀληθείας, 896 οὐ πάντες οἱ ἀκούοντες κεχωρήκασι τὸ μέγεθος τ. γνώσεως, cf. 214 γῇ βαστάζειν τοῦτο οὐ κεχώρηκεν, 88 χωρήσωμεν τ. φῶς ἵνα χ. τ. θεόν
χωρίζω: 875 init. θάνατος χ. τ. ψυχὴν ἀπὸ τῶν παθῶν
χωρισμός: 874 θάνατος χ. ψυχῆς ἀπὸ σώματος, 569, 568 ζωὴ ὁ χ. τῆς ἁμαρτίας

ψαλμός: 861 ψαλμοὶ κ. ὕμνοι παρὰ τὴν ἑστίασιν, 856 οἱ ψ. λέγουσιν, 888 ἀκήκοεν τοῦ ψ.
ψεύδομαι: 862 τοῦ (MB. τὸ) ψεύδεσθαι κ. τοῦ (MB. τὸ) ψευδορκεῖν ἡ κύρωσις ἐν τῷ λέγειν παρὰ τὸ καθῆκον, 863 ἰατρὸς πρὸς νοσοῦντας ψεύσεται ἢ ψεῦδος ἐρεῖ κατὰ τ. σοφιστάς, 887 ἐψεύσατο τ. ὁμολογίαν
ψευδορκέω: 862, see ψεύδομαι
ψευδώνυμος: 892 τ. συμπατικὴν διὰ τῆς ψ. ἀγάπης πρωτοκλισίαν ἀσπάζονται, 854 ἡ τῶν ψ. τούτων γνῶσις
ψεῦσμα: 893 πάμπολλα συγκαττύουσι ψεύσματα
ψῆφος: 840 ἡ τοῦ θεοῦ ψ.
ψιθυρίζω: 854 κἂν ψιθυρίζοντες προσλαλῶμεν ἔνδοθεν κεκράγαμεν
ψιλός: 863 διὰ τὴν τῶν πέλας σωτηρίαν συγκαταβαίνων ψιλήν (MB. ψιλῇς), 891 αὐτῇ ψιλῇ ἀποχρώμενοι τ. λέξει, 847 (quot.)

ψιλῶς: 875 οὐ τ. ἀργύριον λέγων φησί ψ. οὕτως

ψόγος: 871 ψόγον ὑφορώμενοι

ψοφοδεής: 894 κατεπᾴδουσι τ. θείαις γραφαῖς τοὺς ψ. τῶν ἀπείρων, 826, Dionys. Hal. *De Demosth.* 18, Plut. *Mor.* 529 *init.*

ψυχαγωγέω: 835 ἀντιτάσσεται πρὸς πᾶν τὸ ψυχαγωγοῦν ἡμᾶς

ψυχή: 858 τὰ ὄντως ἀγαθὰ τὰ περὶ τ. ψυχήν, 856 ψυχὴ ψυχῆς ἐπαίει, 896 τὰ ὦτα τῆς ψ.

ψυχικός: 852 αἴσθησίς τις ψ., 890 ψ. εὐτονία, 943, 885 μετὰ γνώσεως τ. πάθη τὰ ψ. ἀπερρίψασθε

ὠκεανός: 844 (quot.), 879 πέρατα ὠκεανοῦ

ᾠόν: 844 τὰ ἀπὸ τῶν περικαθαρθέντων ᾠά

ὥρα: 854 ὥρας τακτὰς ἀπονέμουσιν εὐχῇ, ib. αἱ τ. ὡρῶν διανομαὶ τριχῇ διέστανται, 873 ὀλίγον τι τ. ὥρας (ὥρας?) περὶ τ. τροφὴν ἀσχοληθεὶς (cf. Clem. Hom. XIX. 25 ὥρας οὐκ ὀλίγης οὔσης οἴκοι ἐκαθέσθη, ib. XII. 25 ἔτι ὥρας οὔσης ἔφην ἐγώ), 889 ἐν ᾗ ὥρᾳ ἐπιγνῷ (? ἐπέγνω)

ὡραῖος: 868 ὡρ. γυνή, 902 ὡρ. παράδεισον

ὥριμος: 888 ὀπώρα ἐληφθῆ κ. ὥριμος

ὥριος: 902 κλέπτειν τολμῶσι τὰ ὥ., 680

ὡς = ὥστε c. *inf.* 828, 837, 877, 879 and *passim*, cf. Jannaris § 1949, Rost and P. *s.v.* ὡς B. II.

ὡς ἄν: (with part. or adj.) 867 ὡς ἂν θείαν χωρήσας διδασκαλίαν, 879 ὡς ἂν παρεπίδημος, *ib.* ὡς ἂν ἰσάγγελοι, 890 ὡς ἂν ἐξ αὐτῆς συλλαβοῦσα, 900 ὡς ἂν ποιουμένων, &c. See App. B

ὡς ὅτι: 888 κηρὸς ὡς ὅτι μάλιστα ἐμφερής, 8 ὡς ὅτι μάλιστα τηλαυγὲς φῶς, 99, cf. Jannaris § 1754 and ὡς ἵνα *ib.* § 1767

ὡς πλείστους ὅσους: 855 εὐχόμενος ὡς πλείστους ὅσους ἐν ἐπιγνώσει γίνεσθαι

ὥσπερ: attracting the principal verb into subordinate clause, 897 οὐ τὴν αὔλειαν ἀναπετάσαντες ὥσπερ ἡμεῖς... εἴσιμεν, cf. Heind. on Plat. *Gorg.* 522

ὠφέλεια: 860 εἰς τὴν τ. ἀγαθῶν ὠφέλειαν πάντα γέγονεν, 863 ἰδία σωτηρία ἢ τῶν πέλας ὠφ. *bis*, 874 οὐκ εἰς τὴν αὐτοῦ ὠφ.

ὠφέλημα: 858 τὰ παρακείμενα ὠφ. τῇ κτήσει, Cic. *Fin.* III. 33 with Madvig's n.

INDEX OF SUBJECTS AND OF GRAMMAR.

Grammatical notes are distinguished by italics.

Abraham's seed preserved in the Christian § 82

abstinence from sin follows upon faith § 5; is the only true purity § 27; the negative side of goodness §§ 47, 49, 72, 74; flows from fear, as the positive side from love § 79; abstinence from tried pleasure is of more value than from untried § 76

accommodation (συμπεριφορά), danger attending § 80; practised by St Paul towards the Jews § 53

act distinguished from habit § 66

admiration leads on to faith and knowledge §§ 60, 83; also to endurance and hope § 63; admiration of the commandments unites us to God § 78

adultery, spiritual §§ 75, 88

Aesop, fable of § 83

agape, see App. C

air akin to the soul § 84; mixed with the other elements so as to bind them together § 84; the medium of hearing and speech § 36

allegorical interpretation, § 14 (Deut. xiii. 8, 9) death = conquest of passion; § 34 (Exod. xxx. 25) incense = prayers and praises; § 75 varieties of fornication, idolatry, love of pleasure and of money; § 82 (Jud. ii. 11—14) the selling of sinful Israel to strangers shows that sin is alien, and similarly Prov. vi. 24 'Lust not after another's wife'; § 83 (Ps. xlviii. 12) 'walk about Sion' explained of the gnostic; § 87 (1 Cor. vi. 13) 'meats for the belly' explained of the carnal members of the Church; § 88 (1 Cor. vi. 16) 'harlot' explained by unfaithfulness to the covenant; § 93 (apocryphal saying) τέτοκεν καὶ οὐ τέτοκεν explained of the pregnant force of Scripture; §§ 109, 110 (Lev. xi. 8) clean and unclean beasts explained of Christians, Jews and heretics

allusive reference to Satan § 7; to the demons § 14

altar, the Christian congregation § 81; the righteous soul § 32

Ambrose, his adaptation of the *De Officiis*, Introd. ch. II, p. xxvii

amphitheatre of the universe § 20; spectacles of the § 74

anacoluthon with gen. abs., see § 67 n.

angel, see nn. on § 9 and *s.v.* ἄγγελος

anthropomorphism of the heathen §§ 22 f., 30—32; of philosophers § 87

antiquity deserves honour § 2; a mark of truth §§ 92, 107

Antoninus Pius, heresies flourished under § 106

apathy is the natural attribute of the Lord § 7; acquired by the gnostic through discipline § 13; is the death of the Old Man, the life of the New § 14; man is consecrated to ever higher degrees of § 14; results from voluntary self-control §§ 67, 74; not yet attained by those who cannot forgive their enemies § 84; is a consequence of union with Christ § 88; by it the gnostic attains perfection §§ 84, 86; cf. Kaye p. 147, De Faye p. 274 foll.; see Introd. ch. II, p. xliii

apostles, their exemplary sufferings § 74; married § 63 n.

apostolic succession consists in following the apostles in their life and knowledge § 77 *Add.*

Archelaus the dancer § 101

arguments, weak, used by Clement on the practice of enshrinement § 27 f.; to prove that prayer is heard § 37; that the gnostic is perfect § 47; see Introd. p. xxxvi f.

Aristotle an instructor in science § 101

art leads to idolatry § 28

Artemis, her wrath against the Oetolians § 23

assimilation to God § 8; rules of gnostic assimilation § 18; by them the gnostic fashions himself and his hearers § 18; the divine likeness visible in the just man §§ 16, 29, 52, 64, 72, 84, 85, 86; the gnostic is a third embodiment of the divine image § 16

atheism, Christians accused of § 1; absurdity of the charge §§ 2, 4, 54; cause of atheism § 15; consists in having unworthy ideas of God § 23

Athena, see Augè

attraction, inverse of noun to relative § 72

Augè, her plea against Athena § 23

Augustus § 106

banquet seldom indulged in by Christians § 36, see App. on Agape pp. 378 foll.

Basilides fl. under Hadrian and Antoninus Pius §§ 106, 108

beatific vision (ἐποπτεία) the final perfection of the gnostic §§ 57, 68; (θεωρία) granted to the pure in heart § 13, see 'contemplation' and Introd. ch. III, pp. liv—lvi

beauty perceived with the spiritual eye § 76

believer knows God and knows that he is bound to do no wrong § 5; is educated by the divine Teacher by means of hope § 6; some are unworthy to receive power to believe § 1, is a faithful servant but not yet a friend of God § 21; acts from motives of hope and fear, while the gnostic is actuated by knowledge and by love §§ 67, 69; still he is on the way to perfection § 70; the inferiority of the believer to the gnostic § 84; he who believes the Scripture is himself worthy of trust § 95; the believer has but tasted of Scripture § 95, see 'faith'

bishops in Egypt § 3, n. on p. 6. 5, with *Add*

breathing of fish, of insects, of animals, of demons § 32

Cainites § 108

cause, the first, the Father §§ 2, 17; the second, the Son §§ 16 n., 17; who by the Father's will is the cause of all good § 8

celibacy inferior to marriage § 70, *Str.* II. 142

Charidemus § 101

choice, see 'freewill'

chorus, mystical, of the truth § 45, see Introd. ch. III, p. lii, n. 3

Christians attacked as atheists, see 'atheism'; on the ground of their divisions §§ 89—94; Christian childhood and manhood §§ 67, 68, 74

Chrysippus § 101

Church, the Lord's body § 87; one who behaves as a heathen in the Church is guilty of fornication against it § 88; the rule of the Church to be followed §§ 95, 105; knowledge and joy notes of the Church §§ 100, 101; intruders into § 106; the catholic §§ 106, 107; the most ancient is the true Church § 107; marked by unity § 107; ministrative and meliorative service in § 8

Circe § 95

citizenship, gnostic, not of this, but of a higher world § 18

clean and unclean meats § 83; meaning of law respecting §§ 109, 110

Clement, estimates of, Introd. ch. IV; his obligations to Greek philosophy, Introd. ch. II; to the Mysteries, ch. III; list of philosophical terms used by him in *Strom.* VII, Introd. pp. xlvii—xlix

collation, Stählin's of Laurentian MS., Introd. pp. lxxxv—xci

comment on Ps. xxiv. 3—6, § 58; on 1 Cor. VI, §§ 84—88

communication, spiritual, possible without speech §§ 37, 43, see 'worship,' 'silent'

communion with God through Christ § 13; by prayer §§ 39, 42, 44; requires purity of soul § 49; constitutes the life of the gnostic § 73

companionship, Christian, effect of § 35

comparison, degrees of (superl. for comp.) § 63, n. on βεβαιότατον, cf. *Paed.* II. 5 οἱ ταῖς εὐτελεστάταις χρώμενοι τροφαῖς ἰσχυρότατοί εἰσι ὡς οἰκέται δεσποτῶν

contemplation arises on the sight of what is lovely § 10; is the result of intelligent obedience § 83; a characteristic of the gnostic § 45; sought in prayer § 46; the occupation of the highest order of the blessed

§§ 10, 18, 56; the contemplative and the practical gnostic § 102; science supplies material for §§ 44, 83, see 'beatific vision'
cooperation on the part of man with God § 48
courage shown in endurance and resistance § 17; various forms of § 18; spurious, arising from mere impulse §§ 59, 66; from hope of pleasure § 63; from ignorance § 66; from training § 66; from fear § 67; courage of the gnostic free from rashness § 66; he distinguishes between true and false terrors §§ 65, 66; and endures hardships as incidental to life § 61; and as medicinal § 61; and leading to glory and blessedness § 63; his courage distinguished from that of the philosopher §§ 63, 78; and from that of the simple believer § 67; he has no fear of death §§ 78, 83
criterion, some common to all, as the senses § 93; others technical known only to few § 93; the heretics have no real criterion § 94; Scripture the true criterion § 95; faith is the criterion of knowledge Str. II. 15
Crobylus § 101
Cyrenaic school denied the efficacy of prayer § 41

dative, double use of § 8 fin.; combination of different datives §§ 8, 10, 15; of duration of time § 48
deacons, their service compared with that of the presbyters § 8
death signifies apathy §§ 14, 71; gnostic's readiness to die § 79
deification of the gnostic §§ 3 n., 95, 101
Deissmann on the secularization of religion, Introd. ch. II, p. xxiii n.
Delos, its unbloody altar § 82
deponent verbs used in passive signification Paed. II. 14 οὐδὲ ἡ τοῦ Χριστιανοῦ δίαιτα ἡδυπαθείᾳ περικτᾶται, Apost. Const. II. 58. 2 προσδεχέσθω ὑπὸ τῶν πρεσβυτέρων, ib. VIII. 32. 4, 6, Lightfoot on Ign. Smyrn. ἡγείσθω
Docetae § 108
dreams show the character §§ 77, 78

east symbolizes birth § 48; temples look to the east § 48
education, use of the ordinary curriculum § 19
Egyptian priests, their diet § 38
Encratites § 108
ends of action, the honourable, the expedient, the pleasant §§ 49, 61, 76, 88

enshrinement, pagan § 28
Entychitae § 108
envy alien from God, a characteristic of the devil § 7
Epicureans and Stoics confounded § 37
eucharist (of martyrdom), in it the Christian is united to Christ § 79, see App. on Agape
evil, origin of § 16

faith is open to all who choose § 8; but some have not the power to believe § 1; those who are being perfected through faith are included in the family of God §§ 8, 11; faith is a short cut to perfection § 11; a compendious knowledge of essentials § 57; leads on to 'apathy' § 14; philosophy prepares the soul to receive the faith § 20; faith is the desire of the heathen who turn to God §§ 46, 57; an inward good perfected by knowledge § 55; glorifies God instinctively § 55; is the first step in the ladder of virtue Str. II. 27 f., the lowest stage in the ascent through knowledge and love to the inheritance §§ 5, 55, 57; springs from admiration § 60; manifests itself in seeking and in knowledge § 60; witnessed in martyrdom § 64; the purest faith is that of the gnostic § 78; which makes what is future present § 79; may originate in fear § 79; first principles received by faith without proof § 95; faith has the force of demonstration § 96; that which is already believed supplies proof for what is not yet believed § 98; weakness is cured by rational training under the influence of faith and fear § 102; cf. De Faye ch. VII
falsehood is treachery § 58; when verbal falsehood is allowable, see 'reserve'
fasting customary on Wednesday and Friday § 75; spiritually understood of the mortification of the love of gain and of pleasure § 75; the gnostic fasts from evil thoughts as well as from evil deeds § 76; see Kaye p. 268 ff.
fear, use of §§ 79, 102; righteousness of fear compared with righteousness of love § 79
fire, the discerning, consecrates sinful souls § 84
fornication, three meanings of § 75
freewill essential to faith § 8; to virtue §§ 9, 10; to knowledge § 12; to

salvation § 42; not hindered by the divine ordering § 12; evils caused by § 15, cf. Bigg p. 77 foll.

friend, distinguished from servant, of God §§ 5, 19, 21, 62, 68, 79

friendship, reciprocation of § 21

Glaucias, teacher of Basilides, was one of Peter's interpreters § 106

gnosis, in what it consists § 17; how attained, does not come by nature or without conscious effort, nor from ordinary education, or rhetoric, or even philosophy §§ 19, 20; faith is made perfect by gnosis § 55; how distinguished from wisdom § 55; is the link between faith and love § 55; is a deposit handed down by tradition § 55; carries the soul on to the final perfection, which consists in the beatific vision § 56; is a demonstration of what has been intuitively received by faith § 57; is a rational death § 71; the food of the soul § 72; is it true that gnosis puffs up? § 105 f; see Kaye p. 140 f.

gnostic, alone pious §§ 2, 16, 47, 54; paying fitting worship to God § 2; elected for knowledge by the Lord § 2; how he serves God and man §§ 3, 18, is now being made like to God and will hereafter be deified §§ 3, 95; three stages of the gnostic § 4; is educated by the Divine Teacher through mysteries § 6, gnostic souls are always rising to higher grades of blessedness, till at last they attain to the beatific vision §§ 13, 68; the gnostic trains himself to apathy §§ 13, 14; holds communion with God through Christ § 13, by his learning conquers his lower nature § 16; gnostic as ruler § 16 as judge § 45; becomes the shrine of the Saviour §§ 16, 29; a third embodiment of the divine glory § 16; scope of his knowledge § 17; gnostic virtue §§ 18, 19, 59 f., 65 f.; precious in the sight of God § 29, honours God everywhere and at all times, enjoying His uninterrupted presence §§ 35, 43, 73, 80; combines cheerfulness with seriousness § 35; is truly rich § 18; a priest and king, despises all the pleasures of sense § 36; prays only for what is really good §§ 38, 44; strives to be united with God in prayer, rising above this lower world § 40; the true gnostic receives from God all his petitions §§ 41, 73; faith is a gnostic prayer § 41; the holiness of the gnostic involves the exercise of freewill on the part both of God and man § 42; having in himself all good things, the gnostic is self-sufficing through divine grace § 44; he possesses the faculty of contemplation joined to clearness of thought and speech § 44; qualities of the gnostic, his optimism § 45; he watches and prays that his virtue may be indefectible §§ 46, 47; as it is in some through discipline and knowledge § 46; he enjoys the future as already present to hope §§ 47, 74, 79; all works together for his good and nothing is required of him but what is in his own power § 48; the gnostic does not swear, but his word is as good as an oath §§ 50, 51; his highest work is teaching § 52; he is an image of the Lord §§ 52, 64; under what circumstances economy of truth is allowed him § 53; described by David § 58; his admiration for nature § 60; he understands the commandments in their spiritual sense § 60; he hears with his soul, not merely with his ears § 60; he knows that all trials are a medicine of salvation § 61; has his eye always fixed on noble images § 63; despises both the pleasures §§ 63, 74, 78, and the persecution of the world § 63, becomes a temple of the Holy Ghost § 64, gnostic courage §§ 65—67; gnostic temperance § 67; justice and liberality of the gnostic § 69; his continence § 70; gnostics compared to the wise virgins § 72; would prefer prayer without success to success without prayer § 73; how he works in the Lord's vineyard § 74; fasts from wrong acts and wrong thoughts §§ 75, 76; holds that to be the Lord's day on which he feels the power of the Resurrection in himself, believes that all truth is a revelation of the Lord Himself § 76; even his dreams are holy §§ 77, 78; he fills the place of the apostles § 77; is made a partner of the Divine Will, has angels and saints for his companions in prayer §§ 78, 79; the prayer of the gnostic §§ 79, 81 carries God within him and is carried by God § 82; has no fear of death § 83; contrasted with the simple believer § 84; to the gnostic the Bible is pregnant of truth §§ 94, 95, the gnostic guards the doctrine of the apostles by his knowledge of Scripture § 164; his life consists of deeds and words agreeable to the tradition of the Lord § 104; is already a god while on earth § 101; earnest in intercession §§ 79, 81; prays that he may bear the punishment of his brethren § 80; cf. Introd. p. xlii f., Kaye ch. v, pp. 134—153

gnostic, pseudo- § 41

God the Father, the ultimate *cause* (see *s.v.*), first and best of all beings § 2; manifested through the Son § 2; Almighty §§ 5, 12; all-sufficient § 15; proof that He loves all men §§ 6, 7; unchangingly good § 15; the universal king §§ 16, 54; presides over the amphitheatre of the world § 20; incomprehensible §§ 28, 30; beyond all worth § 29; to be honoured by us through the Son § 35; omnipresent §§ 35, 51; omniscient § 36; source of all good and of no evil §§ 12, 36, 43; knows, as present, all that shall be § 37; unity of §§ 39, 68; His goodness is voluntary § 42; He is absolute goodness §§ 18, 45; the cause of eternal salvation § 48; is near to all that call on Him § 49; insusceptible of injury § 50; the keeper of our faith and love § 56; known only to the Son and to those to whom the Son reveals Him §§ 58, 109; determines each man's life § 65; loves all that He has created § 69; His goodness and justice are inseparable §§ 15, 73; shines on all alike, and sent His Son both to just and unjust § 85; does not take vengeance, but chastens for good § 102; the knowledge of God possessed by Christians alone § 1, received from the Son § 2; see Introd. p. xxxviii f.

God the Son, testified to by the law and prophets § 1; the beginning and firstfruit of all things, Himself without beginning, manifests the Father § 2, and the divine mysteries § 4; the Word §§ 4, 5, 8, 21; only-begotten § 4; the highest Preeminence ordering all things according to the Father's will, undivided, all reason, all eye, all light § 5; the Teacher of man in various ways § 6; cares for all, using persuasion not compulsion § 6; free from envy and passion of every kind §§ 7, 72; is the Father's Counsellor, the Power and Wisdom of God, the Lord of the disobedient, the Saviour of believers § 7; the principle of all movement and the cause of all good things by the Father's will § 8; came into the world to reveal the possibilities of man's nature § 8; the great High Priest §§ 9, 13, 45; leaves no part of the universe uncared for § 9; is the cause of salvation drawing men upwards, as the magnet draws iron § 9; gave the law to Jews, philosophy to Greeks § 11; consecrated Himself for us § 14; the ruler of all mortals and immortals, Himself the Law and Ordinance and Eternal Word, being both Light and Life § 16; the Second Cause §§ 16, 17; the umpire in the amphitheatre of life § 20; feels, as done to Himself, the good or evil done to His followers § 21; Christ is the beginning and the ends, the foundation and superstructure of religion § 55; called 'the face of the God of Jacob,' 'impress of the Father's glory' § 58

God the Holy Ghost speaks in the commandments § 99; the gnostic by his earnest striving after spirituality is united to § 44

god, used of men (1), of other finite beings (2), of false gods (3)
(1) See 'deification,' *Protr.* 8 'The Word was made man that man might become god'; Clem. Hom. xvi. 16
(2) Coupled with angels § 20; inhabitants of heaven § 56; cf. Clem. Hom. xvi. 14
(3) Greek gods distinguished from barbarian § 22; exhibit a low ideal of divinity § 28 f.; live on the smoke of the sacrifice § 81

good things are such as pertain to the soul itself, not mere outward appendages § 38; the Christian prays for real, the wicked for seeming good § 44

Greek, Greeks make the diversity of sects a reason for disbelief § 89; their own philosophers might be condemned on the same ground §§ 89—92; see 'god'

habit a second nature § 46

Hadrian saw the rise of heresy § 106

Haematitae § 108

Harnack on Clement, Introd. p. xxxiii n.; on the secularization of Christianity *ib.* p. xxiii n.

Hatch on injurious effects of Hellenism, Introd. pp. xxii, xxvi—xxxi

hebdomad the stage of rest, preceding the ogdoad of loving activity § 57

Hellenism, its influence on Christianity, Introd. ch. ii

452 INDEX

Heracles § 26
heresy, existence of, urged against Christianity § 89; prophesied by the Lord § 89; not confined to Christianity § 89; permitted for the exercise of the judgment § 90; no excuse for refusing the aid of religion § 90; springs from hastiness and self-conceit § 91; to be cured by more earnest study § 91; the heretics build up their systems on fragmentary truths by means of sophistical arguments §§ 92, 103; they constitute a school rather than a church § 92; imitate the heathen § 93; find the Scriptures barren § 94; spurn the traditions of the Church § 95; misinterpret Scripture by neglecting the analogy of the faith, and forcing the meaning of words § 96; or even deny the authority of Scripture, and if pressed by argument, contradict themselves without shame § 97; their one aim is to gain applause and have the pre-eminence in their assemblies § 98; they are characterized by conceit and contentiousness § 101; to be cured by discipline and study § 102; some are incurable from their sloth and ambition § 103; the founders whom they extol cannot be compared with the Apostles § 104; they adulterate the truth and steal the canon of the Church § 105; do not enter the Church by the door § 106; date back only to the time of Hadrian § 106, thus their heresies are mere spurious innovations § 107; they have neither the unity nor the antiquity of the true Church § 107; names of different heresies § 108 they are like the unclean animals which do not chew the cud § 109, some denied the use of prayer § 41, their view of martyrdom § 66
hierarchy, celestial § 9 with notes
High Priest, Christ the great §§ 9, 13
honour, scale of gnostic § 2
hope is virtual possession §§ 47, 74
husbandry, spiritual § 3

ignorance and weakness the causes of evil § 16, and of error § 101, cf. Clem. Hom. x. 12, xi. 20; the soul is starved by ignorance § 72; ignorance contrasted with opinion and knowledge §§ 93, 100, 101
image, see 'assimilation'
incense the prayer of holiness § 82; the composite incense of the law denotes the joint prayer of many nations § 84

individual, the, and the whole § 12
inheritance ($κληρονομία = ἀθανασία, θεωρία, πατρῴα αὐλή, κυριακὴ μονή$) the reward of the Christian course with its three stages, faith, knowledge, love §§ 10, 55
involuntary action illustrated by the warmth of fire § 42, the weight of a stone § 46
Ischomachus § 101

Jewish law of clean and unclean § 109; Jews signified by animals that chew the cud without dividing the hoof §§ 109, 110
Job § 80
Joseph the patriarch § 61
Judah denotes confession § 105
judgment mercifully sent to lead men to repentance § 12; preliminary and final § 12
justice the all-perfect virtue § 17; the highest involves discrimination § 69

king's highway § 73
'know thyself,' meaning of § 20
knowledge contrasted with opinion §§ 93, 100; does it lead to self-conceit? §§ 104, 105

ladder of perfection, faith, knowledge, love, heaven § 55
Lampis § 101
Law of Moses testifies of Christ § 1, charged with inhumanity by heretics § 14; primaeval law that virtue involves choice § 9; Mosaic and prae-Mosaic § 10; not intended for the just § 10, Christ is law § 16; the law is a schoolmaster to bring us to the Gospel § 86
light used of the Word, whose light penetrates the universe §§ 5, 21
logical method employed by Clement, Introd. ch. ii. p. xxxvi f.
Lord's Day, the day on which we feel the power of the Resurrection § 76
love the highest stage of Christian progress, the two lower being faith and knowledge §§ 46, 53, 55—57, 68, 84; love to God the motive of the mature Christian §§ 64, 67, 68, 70, 93, anoints and trains the Christian athlete § 67, the gnostic loves all men §§ 3, 40, 69; even impoverishing himself to help them § 77; loves God and is loved by Him §§ 2, 4; loves that which is promised § 63; love of knowledge the way to contemplation § 10; love raises a man from the condition of servant to that of friend of God § 62; God

servant of God, how he becomes the friend §§ 5, 21, 62, 68, 79
service of God, in what it consists § 3; of man, meliorative and ministrative §§ 3, 13
sign used for cross § 79
silent worship §§ 2, 39, 43, 73
Simon, the equestrian § 101; the heretic §§ 107, 108
sin caused by ignorance and weakness §§ 9, 101
sinlessness, how possible for man § 14, cf. De Faye p. 281
smoke of burnt sacrifices the food of demons §§ 14, 31
soul akin to air § 34
speech, power of, a gnostic grace § 44; should be in harmony with thought and deed §§ 53, 100; see 'reserve'
Stoics identify divine and human virtue § 88; confused with Epicureans by a misreading § 87
Stromateus, meaning of, Introd. ch. I; why this form of composition was chosen by Clement ib. pp. xix—xxi; used by what other writers ib. pp. xiv, xv; text of Strom. vii, ch. v, classification of corruptions in ib. pp. lxvi—lxxix; various readings ib. pp. lxxx—lxxxv; Stählin's collation of ib. pp. lxxxv—xci
suffering, uses of § 17
superlative for comparative §§ 63, 68
superstition § 4; portents §§ 24—27
swine's flesh, why forbidden to Jews § 33; a favourite with Gentiles § 33

teaching the highest work of the gnostic § 52, Str. II. c. 19 *init.*; implies the training of character § 52
temperance § 18; genuine and spurious § 67
temple, Christian invisible § 28; the congregation of saints § 29
theatres shunned by Christians § 36
Theodas teacher of Valentinus and disciple of Paul § 106
thought, word, and deed, harmony of §§ 55 *init.*, 100
Tiberius § 106
Timothy, his circumcision an instance of accommodation § 53

tradition, the deposit of the faith § 55; contained in the Confession and Canon of the Church § 90; the heretics spurn the tradition of the Church § 95, which is also called the tradition of the Lord and of Christ §§ 99, 106, and of the Apostles § 108
triad of the holy mansions § 40; of the gradations which depend on the Word § 9
Trinity, the Platonic § 9, cf. Bigg p. 248 foll.
truth, a sight of is a sight of Christ § 76

unbelief limited to the period of Christ's presence on earth (?) § 11
unclean, see 'clean'
unity the mark of the true Church § 107

Valentinus a disciple of Theodas §§ 106, 108
vegetarianism advocated by Pythagoras, Xenocrates and Polemo §§ 32, 33
virgins, the wise symbolize the gnostic § 72
virtue is voluntary § 9; wrong views as to its origin § 19; cardinal virtues § 17, cf. Str. II. c. 18; height of gnostic virtue § 45; indefectibility of, how obtained §§ 46, 47; spurious forms of § 69 (see 'courage' &c.); better than innocence §§ 72, 76; identity of divine and human denied § 88; connexion of the different virtues Str. II. 45

weakness the cause of wickedness § 9
wisdom the result of prudence and justice § 17; distinguished from gnosis § 55
worship, true consists in love § 8; Christian not limited to special times or places §§ 85, 48; though it is customary to pray thrice in the day § 40; the gnostic's whole life is a festival § 40; see 'prayer'
wrestler, the Christian § 20

Zeus, the athlete's prayer to § 48

Lightning Source UK Ltd.
Milton Keynes UK
UKHW02f1648300818
328051UK00007B/842/P

For Product Safety Concerns and Information please contact our EU
representative GPSR@taylorandfrancis.com
Taylor & Francis Verlag GmbH, Kaufingerstraße 24, 80331 München, Germany

www.ingramcontent.com/pod-product-compliance
Lightning Source LLC
Chambersburg PA
CBHW071231300426
44116CB00008B/992